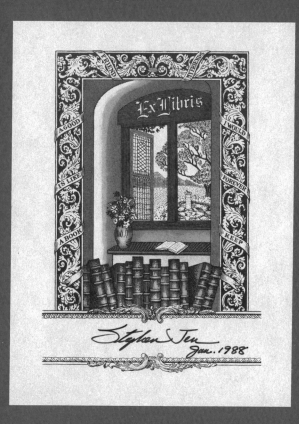

THE
LETTERS OF
Sean O'Casey
1942-54

Sean O'Casey in 1953 in London to watch a rehearsal of *Purple Dust*. Photo by Haywood Magee © Radio Times Hulton Picture Library.

THE
LETTERS OF
Sean O'Casey
1942-54

VOLUME II

Edited by

DAVID KRAUSE

Macmillan Publishing Co., Inc.
NEW YORK

Macmillan Publishing Co., Inc.
866 Third Avenue, New York, N.Y. 10022
Collier Macmillan Canada, Ltd.

Library of Congress Cataloging in Publication Data (Revised)

O'Casey, Sean, 1880–1964.
    The letters of Sean O'Casey.

    Includes bibliographical references.
    CONTENTS: v. 1. 1910–41.—v. 2. 1942–54.
    1. O'Casey, Sean, 1880–1964—Correspondence.
2. Dramatists, Irish—20th century—Correspondence.
I. Krause, David, 1917–   ed.   II. Title.
PR6029.C33Z53   1975   822'.9'12   74-11442
ISBN 0-02-566660-6 (v. 1)
ISBN 0-02-566670-3 (v. 2)

FIRST PRINTING 1980

Printed in the United States of America

CONTENTS

INTRODUCTION

I N this second volume of his letters, Sean O'Casey continues to project a formidable image of himself as an eloquent and prodigious word-fighter. Words were his abundant weapons of protest against all forms of injustice and an affirmation of his vision of the good life. Proud and compassionate, intemperate and courageous, he was always quick to aim his relentless anger and laughter at the enemies of progress. He had been exposed to a lifetime of deprivations which forced him to endure a constant struggle for survival, and his fighting instinct was therefore shaped by sheer necessity, as well as by artistic temperament and moral conscience. It was out of experience, then, and an unwavering sense of commitment to disadvantaged people, that he went on writing his irreverent plays, provocative volumes of autobiography, and thousands of vigorous letters, in all of which he consistently mocked those political and religious authorities, particularly in his native Ireland, who had by their indifference or fear of change condoned the conditions of grinding poverty and intellectual paralysis. He insisted he had been fighting for a charter of human rights for all people, and in one letter he said he had spent his whole life stressing the need for a "children's charter." Even a cursory reading of his work indicates how deeply he shared the views of Dickens on exploited children, and, particularly, the views of Blake on men, women, and children suffering unjustly everywhere:

> In every cry of every Man
> In every Infant's cry of fear
> In every voice, in every ban,
> The mind-forg'd manacles I hear.

That urgent voice of anguish in Blake's lines can be heard in many of O'Casey's letters. He was outraged when an Irish bishop cried "Communism" and helped defeat a plan that would have provided free meals for starving schoolchildren, and in a letter that was refused publication he stated, "It is a sad thing that today children should be kept tight and close to God by going about with empty bellies." When a woman in England asked him why he went on fighting and stirring up so much controversy, he replied: "I wish I could write more quietly—good for my health and good for my purse. Everything I write seems to raise up wrath somewhere." His chronically precarious health and purse were not improved by his private and public wrath, for the vigilant O'Casey could never be a quiet man. To a Russian friend with whom he carried on an argument about "Socialist realism" and propaganda literature, which O'Casey rejected as too didactic, at the same time defending the "bourgeois" work of T. S. Eliot and Picasso from what he considered unfair Soviet criticism, he confessed that writing letters was for him an essential yet burdensome task: "Again, letter-writing is a weariness of the flesh to me; but I write numerous letters all the same to people I know, and people I don't know in almost all countries in the world. I will withdraw from work and the world only when I am dead." In spite of this statement, there is seldom a sign of weariness in his letters—written in a state of near-blindness, and often just after he was recovering from recurring bouts of influenza due to a weak chest—mainly because the people he wrote to had become his own intimate audience and vital contact with the world at a time when his controverial plays were seldom performed. So for the exiled and isolated O'Casey, the exchange of letters might be called his ritualistic act of communion with friends and strangers.

When an American teacher wanted to print some of the letters in a university magazine and asked O'Casey if he wished to "censor" or modify any of his private views, he replied with characteristic candor: "I dont fear anything I've written, though I might laugh ruefully at a lot of it, for I'm not destitute of foolishness. However, the foolish things I've done, said, or written, are part of the living man, and should not be concealed so as to suggest infallibility—which God forbid! or make a mask to cause a man to look more like an angel—which God has already forbidden."

He was an unbeliever who liked to appeal to God and the Holy Ghost whenever he wanted to invoke the truth. He had no secrets to hide, no flattering mask to wear. Since he was such a forthright and open man, his fallibility and foolishness are usually the humanizing elements in his character that bring him down to earth when his anger makes him soar too high. He was a man of intense pride, of unguarded emotional excesses: he was capable of great love and great hatred; he was extreme in his impatience and imprudence; he was immoderate in his anger and condemnation. Nevertheless, he could often turn these belligerent excesses into virtues, particularly when he was fighting reluctant or reactionary dragons, though he obviously enjoyed the sport so much that he had a tendency to go on hurling words of fire after the enemy had expediently withdrawn from the field. For a man whose primary talent was literary, he could become too deeply immersed in complex religious and political arguments. He could be too uncompromising in some of his comments on Irish Catholicism, and too uncritical in some of his comments on Russian Communism, though he claimed it was his wish that the Irish would become more liberal and pragmatic in their Christianity, and his hope that the Russians would become less didactic and doctrinaire in their Marxism. For example, he protested that many Irish Catholics were victims of fear and superstition that had nothing to do with the heart of their faith; and in one letter he complained about the misguided advocates of Marxism, this time in Devon: "I've never met sillier or more actively stupid minds than the few local Communists here; all Marx and meddling, without sense or tact or understanding."

Although he described himself as a Communist, he often traced the source of his unique faith to the teachings of Christ as well as Marx, and in many letters added the names of other "great Communists" who had influenced him: "Of course, I am a Shelleyan Communist, and a Dickensian one, and a Miltonic one, and a Whitmanian one, & one like all those who thought big & beautifully, & who cared for others, as I am a Marxian one too." He liked to say that Communism was basically a natural application of common sense, and he could even turn to scripture to draw a special connection between Communism and St. Paul: " 'Whatsoever thy hand findeth to do, do it with all thy might'—good Communist doctrine, though it was said by St. Paul." And in another strange connection that might have startled most Christians and Marxists, he suggested his own version of the Second Coming: "I believe that He is here again in Communism." If there is an element of tragicomic Chekhovian idealism in this kind of all-embracing faith, it also indicates the depth of his intention to try to unite people all over the world in a common if unorthodox goal of brotherhood. He could be an anxious conciliator as well as a relentless fighter.

In his private letters he confided regularly with many intimate friends in many countries. In England, with his faithful publishers the Macmillans, whom he addressed with gracious deference as "Mr. Daniel" and "Mr. Harold"; with Bernard Shaw and Lady Astor; with dear friends like the Larkinite journalist Jack Carney and the loyal Frank MacCarthy and Peter Newmark. In Ireland, for a limited time now, with his old friend Gabriel Fallon; with the novelist Francis MacManus; the Moore Street Dubliner, Seumas Scully; and Eric Gorman of the Abbey Theatre. In America, with his most trusted friends, the critics George Jean Nathan, Brooks Atkinson, and Horace Reynolds. In Russia, with Mikhail Apletin of the Soviet Writers' Union. Most surprising, perhaps, was his unique correspondence with a Miss Sheila ———, which sometimes suggests the plot of an epistolary novel about a famous freethinking writer and an innocent young Irish Catholic girl who has suddenly been confronted by the alternatives of self-denial or experience, religion or rationalism in London. His relationship with her was always platonic, though it was obviously resonant with emotional sublimations for both of them. It was to be expected that her Jesuit mentor would caution her to avoid having any contact with the dangerous O'Casey, who was unmistakably "an agent of the devil." O'Casey replied to the girl and the Jesuit, sometimes in five-thousand-word letters, that he was really an agent of enlightenment and was opposed to the folly of a narrow-minded cleric who had frightened the poor girl with warnings of hell fire and convinced her to save herself from temptation by taking a lifelong vow of chastity. For his part, O'Casey tried to educate her about the honest virtue of a normal life free from fear of the palpable world, the natural flesh, and the metaphoric devil. Insisting that he had no intention of undermining the basic dogma of her Catholic faith, he wanted to convert the sheltered Sheila to common sense, not communism; to an active life of emotion and intellect, rather than a hidden life of blind obedience and mortification. Carefully and firmly he reasoned with Sheila about religious practice in relation to social justice, and he tried to convince her that it was not necessarily God's will that she must look forward to a lifetime of denial and accept her suffering in silence. The fact that she had on her own sought out the friendship and help of O'Casey indicated that she might be ready for a change of heart, not of religion, if it wasn't too late. The outcome of her conflict—the choice of following the advice of an austere Jesuit or a compassionate Communist—will have to wait for further revelations in Volume III of the letters.

O'Casey's choices were always determined by a code of personal honor and justice that called for immediate action. In his public letters to the press, he was therefore usually in a fighting mood because he felt he had to defend his work from unjust abuse. He was hypersensitive to all criticism, even when it was minor or frivolous, and couldn't resist the urge to put things right by counterattacking anyone who denigrated his unconventional writing and beliefs. He developed the habit of chastising critics and reviewers who had, he was convinced, through malice or carelessness, unfairly or inaccurately questioned his talent or his integrity; and though the editors of some papers and journals refused to print his letters of protest, or cut them drastically, many of these appear here now for the first time in their original form. For example, when George Orwell wrote a perverse review of *Drums Under the Windows* in 1945, sounding as if he were patriotically waving the Union Jack at an insignificant Irish rebel, the editor of *The Observer,* as he had done on several other occasions, refused to publish O'Casey's blistering reply, which Orwell too had read and ignored. Readers can now compare the unpublished letter with Orwell's review, which is also printed here, to see how effectively the aroused O'Casey could expose blatantly biased opinions and errors of fact. The comparison is also important for another reason, for when the suppressed O'Casey finally had an opportunity to have his formal rebuttal to Orwell published nine years later in *Sunset and Evening Star,* some reviewers of that book accused him of playing a coward's game by waiting until Orwell was dead and couldn't reply. It will be clear now, however, that O'Casey had immediately returned the ball with lightning speed to Orwell's court, and it was a then live Orwell's refusal or inability to counter with a defense of his jingoism that ended the game before it had properly begun.

With his apparent zest for a battle of words, together with his phenomenal memory and an overwhelming command of facts and sources, O'Casey was a fearless and powerful critic of his critics. In a letter to a friend, he once justified his combative ways in the following sly manner: "It is, of course, a Literary Canon here that a critic should never be criticised; but, then, I've always been careless about things canonical." When the Irish poet and playwright Patrick Galvin sounded as if he might be too canonical in attacking an O'Casey play, as the result of a misunderstanding which was later cleared up to the satisfaction of both men, O'Casey growled menacingly: "Indeed, if every Galvin were in six parts and every part a Galvin, and every Galvin shouted down with O'Casey, it wouldn't flutter me a bit." No one fluttered the bold O'Casey, who could sound like an educated version of his own Fluther Good whenever he suspected someone was making derogatory remarks about him. He went battling and scolding such critics as his old adversary James Agate on a matter of semantics; the poet Louis MacNeice, on the lack of hilarities in medieval drama; the dour St. John Ervine, on the relative merits of having been born in Belfast or Dublin; the imposing Bertrand Russell, on whether or not the Russian people were happy under Communism; Gerard Fay of the *Manchester Guardian,* on the distinctions between anticlericalism and anti-Catholicism; the Irish poets, Padraic Colum, on having made malicious and incorrect statements, and Austin Clarke, on having made careless errors of fact; and many more, including a bevy of Tories in Totnes, on having soldiered smugly onward with their nineteenth-century view of twentieth-century England. When his new friend Miss Sheila, who, surprisingly enough, seemed to have "connections" among the upper-class Catholics of England, told him that her wealthy and devout friends were saying terrible things about him and his writing, he replied proudly: "Never mind what they say about me. At any rate, you can tell them all neither I nor Eileen married for money; for neither of us had much more than what we stood up in. And we haven't a lot today; but we are not of them who see God's face on a coin, or see any message from Him on a pound note. We earn what we get—me by my writing; Eileen by her work for home and children. You can tell them who talk of me that O'Casey said they can go to hell."

He had the fierce pride of the underdog who had endured great hardships, and he carried the scars and memories around like battle wounds for the rest of his life. It would have been ludicrous for him to live his life to please people of considerable wealth and high position in state and church affairs, and he aggressively identified himself with the underprivileged all over the world, but mainly those people in Ireland who were still economically and culturally repressed. He confirms in many letters his belief that Irish capitalism, no less than British imperialism, had largely contributed to Ireland's "troubles," which were further aggravated by the Jansenism of the Irish clergy and the chauvinism of the Irish nationalists. As a direct outgrowth of the latter two forces, which he described as "holy church and holy nation," he associated the country's retrogression with Eamon de Valera's dream of a theocratic Ireland isolated from the world and resigned to a modest future of ample devotion and frugal comfort. O'Casey's solution to the whole problem was an immediate transfusion of Jim Larkin's democratic socialism for the people of Ireland, and he presented his mythic vision of this in a variety of dramatic symbols in such plays as *Purple Dust, Red Roses for Me, Cock-a-Doodle Dandy,* and *The Bishop's Bonfire,* where he also characterized the comic villains as British humbugs, Irish gombeen men, bigoted Orangemen, and book-burning clerics.

For too long the Irish had been fighting themselves as well as the British, and during the Civil War in 1922, when O'Casey's Juno Boyle was desperately praying for an intercession of divine love—"Sacred Heart o' Jesus, take away our hearts o' stone, and give us hearts o' flesh! Take away this murdherin' hate, an' give us Thine own eternal love"—at the same time Yeats was writing his parallel and prophetic lines about the brutalization of a nation that had lived too long on fantasies of freedom:

> We had fed the heart on fantasies,
> The heart's grown brutal from the fare;
> More substance in our enmities
> Than in our love. . . .

Twenty years after that tragic Civil War, when O'Casey's letters begin in this volume, neither he nor his countrymen could escape from the brutalization of those fantasies, and it is to be expected that his preoccupation with Ireland would still reflect the bitter harvest of those enmities. Nevertheless, there are also recurring signs of his deep love for the Irish people, for he was concerned only about their freedom and happiness, even in his most comic and satiric remarks about them. For example, highly skeptical as he was about the devout and otherworldly Irish, with their excessive fear of the sins of the world, the flesh, and the devil, he turned those terrible temptations into divine pleasures when he wrote to Father John O'Brien of Notre Dame University: "The Devil we know now isnt such a bad laddo, and, at worst, is but an illusion; and the world and the flesh are beautiful things, fashioned by God himself; so it seems to be a curious thing to renounce the works of His Hand." At this time, Ireland was dominated by such a repressive law of clerical-inspired and government-controlled censorship of publications, which spread fear and intimidation through all aspects of Irish life, that O'Casey was once moved to quip: "In Ireland they wear the fig-leaf on the mouth."

Irish reviewers, however, consistently refused to recognize themselves in the satiric mirror O'Casey held up in his plays and books. For example, the journalist and historian Aodh de Blacam hadn't forgiven O'Casey for his previous sins, and scornfully reminded readers of his popular column in 1944 that the insensitive Abbey Theatre was still reviving *The Plough and the Stars,* in which, he claimed, the great martyrs of the Easter Rising were desecrated by "abominable slander." Less predictable and more baffling, his once dear friend Gabriel Fallon, who had taken a job as drama critic of *The Standard,* the ultra-Catholic newspaper notorious for its yellow journalism, wrote a strange review of a production of *Red Roses For Me* in 1946 in which Fallon accused his friend O'Casey of "coldly calculated bigotry." The quarrel is recorded here, but for some definitive remarks in what O'Casey called "a short history" of his happy and unhappy times with Fallon, see his 27 October 1952 letter to Shaemas O'Sheel. Several years after Fallon's cruel attack, the influential drama critic of the *Irish Times,* Seamus Kelly, went to see the premiere of *Cock-a-Doodle Dandy* in England in 1949 and wrote a caustic review, which is reprinted here because it is so typical of the Irish reaction to O'Casey's later works, in which he described it as "a play to arouse anger and pity" because it was "a blindly and bitterly destructive blast against an Ireland that never existed outside the imagination of a lonely and homesick man in Devonshire." If one now reads the work of modern Irish historians on this subject, or the columns of the *Irish Times* throughout the enlightened 1970s, as recently, for example, as January 1979, one finds continual references to the "priest-ridden and book-burning" Ireland of the 1940s and 50s and to "the Irish God of fear, mindless religiosity, money and respectability." These and many similar comments confirm the images of repression reflected in O'Casey's work, references to the bland acceptance of the Irish version of McCarthyism, the direct and indirect victimization of writers who publicly questioned or tried to lift the green curtain of censorship and clerical authority.

In his reply to the *Irish Times* critic, O'Casey included George Jean Nathan's description of the review of *Cock* as "characteristic of almost all Irish reviews of your work; an explosion of patriotism at the expense of dramatic art." A careful study of criticism of O'Casey's plays in Ireland throughout his career would on the whole support Nathan's view, though one would have to add to the patriotic explosion an additional burst of religious fervor. If the plays were seldom produced in England and America, the reason for that neglect can directly be found in Yeats's rejection of *The Silver Tassie* in 1928, after which time O'Casey's name was usually associated with the noncommercial theatre, with experimental and visionary drama that was too literary and risky to survive the automatic box-office test of instant success or failure. Yeats's eccentric reasons for the rejection had nothing to do with Irish politics or religion, for he was then totally absorbed with his own experimental drama based on the Japanese Noh theatre and believed that plays should never deal with war or history. "The whole history of the world must be reduced to wallpaper in front of which the characters must pose and speak," he had lectured to the rejected O'Casey, even though earlier he had enthusiastically produced O'Casey's first three plays at the Abbey Theatre in the teeth of political and religious protest, plays that had no connection with a wallpaper world and dealt openly with recent Irish history and war. In retrospect now, it is ironic that both men have shared a common fate of neglect in the modern theatre repertoire, for the verse plays of Yeats, like the symbolic plays of O'Casey, have been ignored by the popular theatre and are seldom performed, except by university or art theatres. In some of his letters O'Casey had an opportunity to find sad comfort in the discovery that Lady Gregory had deeply regretted the rejection of *The Silver Tassie* and had recorded her disagreement with Yeats in her Journal, excerpts of which Lennox Robinson had edited and published in 1946. Furthermore, to his credit O'Casey was never vindictive about Yeats's crucial decision, and his letters invariably reveal his unqualified praise of Yeats as a great man and great poet. Yeats and Joyce and Shaw were his Irish literary giants.

Perhaps O'Casey never fully recovered from the reputation of being a rejected playwright, and that stigma of failure, together with the hardships he had endured, contributed to his instinctive trait of insecurity and aggression. Perhaps he had to compensate for his defeats and doubts, and in his bold attempt to stretch his artistic power while he struggled with uncertainty, he was a very vulnerable modern man; not a serene man for all seasons, but a gritty man for our season of disorder and discontent; a survivor who fought back to gain his unsung victories of the word and the spirit. It shows forth in his letters and autobiography, that courage to live with the climate of defeat and never forsake the vision of a better life somewhere in the future, the Chekhovian aspiration, for himself and all survivors everywhere in the world. In that determination to hammer out the words of promise, the spirit of O'Casey can be recognized in the ringing lines of Blake's "Jerusalem"—call it "Shelleyan Communism," substitute "Ireland" for "England," whatever, the apocalyptic vision of Blake and O'Casey is united there:

> And did the countenance divine
> Shine forth upon our clouded hills?
> And was Jerusalem building here
> Among these dark Satanic mills?

Bring me my bow of burning gold,
Bring me my arrows of desire,
Bring me my spear, O clouds, unfold!
Bring me my chariot of fire!

I will not cease from mental fight
Nor shall my sword sleep in my hand,
Till we have built Jerusalem
In England's green and pleasant land.

O'Casey had always been attracted to that Blakean and biblical imagery of the sword of the spirit, the sword of truth that he wielded in his battles against the equivalent of all those "dark Satanic mills" of the world. One of his friends in a letter accurately described him as "white-hot in the face of injustice." Characteristically he wrote to an actress who was featured in a play of his that had just failed: "The battle has gone against us, but we haven't lost our swords." Readers of Volume I of the letters may recall that when Charlotte Shaw ended one of her letters to him with the urgent plea: "And oh! dear Sean, don't be too belligerent!" he replied in a tone that owes a debt to Shakespeare as well as Blake: "God be my judge that I hate fighting. If I be damned for anything, I shall be damned for keeping the two-edged sword of thought tight in its scabbard when it should be searching the bowels of knaves and fools." Possibly it was the sharp edge of such powerful language that inspired Desmond MacCarthy to praise O'Casey as a superb rhetorician in his 1949 review of *Inishfallen, Fare Thee Well,* in which he wrote: "O'Casey is a tremendous rhetorician. Personally I love the superb but today despised Art of Rhetoric; and I can forgive O'Casey even when he continues intoxicated with his own, even after I have recovered my sobriety; I wait patiently for the phrase which will be final and quick as a blow—and I am seldom disappointed."

It should also be pointed out that O'Casey's prose style in the letters is compulsive but not quite so intoxicated as the formal writing in the autobiography. The cadence of the language in the letters is more colloquial and direct, delivered swiftly like conversation that demands an immediate response, and though the words can often flash out as sharply as a powerful blow, the natural sound of O'Casey's informal voice emerges freely without any self-conscious or affected mannerisms. In his 7 February 1949 letter of thanks to Desmond MacCarthy, taking exception only to the erroneous charge that he "loathed" the Catholic Church, O'Casey wrote his most moving defense of his appreciation of the divine mystery in the Catholic faith, while admitting that he could not personally partake in its "lovely" rituals. That revelation by a nonbeliever contains some of the finest language of our time. By contrast, the language of his plays is calculated to raise the level of normal speech to a higher power of artifice, to infuse the spoken word with the tension and rhythm of dramatic dialogue. The American playwright Paul Green admired O'Casey's plays, but like some critics he felt that the speeches were sometimes too elaborate and literary for dialogue; and in a letter to O'Casey he mentioned a disagreement he once had on that subject with Bernard Shaw:

> GREEN. Yes, his speeches get to be too long. They go on beyond the story point and are piled up for the sake of the language itself.

> SHAW. And why shouldn't they be? Let him talk, let the words pour out. Why be niggardly with speech? It's glorious. Yes, it's all a question of whether he has something to say—something important, something interesting, something—yes, beautiful. I think he has. Shakespeare did it now and then and rather well at that, and look at Dickens, how rich, profuse, what a gorgeous spilling of language.

Many readers will disagree with some of the things O'Casey says in his letters, but there too, as in his plays and autobiography, he is never niggardly with words—words that pour out richly and profusely, words that are often controversial and usually say something interesting and important and beautiful, words that demand our attention.

The first volume of these letters covered the years 1910 through 1941; this second volume deals with 1942 through 1954; and the third volume will conclude with the last years of his life, 1955 through 1964, up to the time of his death in his eighty-fourth year. During the twelve years of this second volume, from his sixty-second through his seventy-fourth year, the most productive decade of his life, he wrote four full-length plays: *Red Roses For Me, Cock-a-Doodle Dandy, Oak Leaves and Lavender, The Bishop's Bonfire;* three one-act plays: *Time to Go, Bedtime Story, Hall of Healing;* in addition to at least seventy articles and reviews, he finished the last five books of his six-volume autobiography: *Pictures in the Hallway, Drums Under the Windows, Inishfallen, Fare Thee Well, Rose and Crown, Sunset and Evening Star.*

When Daniel Macmillan suggested that the productive but struggling O'Casey might try to write a novel in order to find a wider audience of readers at a time when his plays were not being performed, and also earn some sorely needed money, O'Casey replied that he thought the novel had no future after Joyce and, further, he was certain he couldn't possibly write one himself. Perhaps he did the next best thing when he wrote his autobiography in a fictive form that allowed him to create the story of his life with the poetry and truth of an epic drama. Contrary to what some of his adversaries claimed, there is no fiction in the letters; nevertheless, in their natural and unpremeditated form, they are unified by the dynamism of a questing imagination that created the poetry and truth of an epic self-portrait for our time.

TEXT AND ACKNOWLEDGMENTS

ALL the letters in this edition are printed in their entirety, exactly as O'Casey wrote them, except for several instances where some pages have been lost or misplaced by the owners of the original copies. In a number of instances, mainly in his typed letters to newspapers and magazines, I have been able to restore cuts made by editors, which I have indicated by square brackets, since he often made carbon copies. Thanks to these carbon copies, which I found among O'Casey's private papers, I have also been able to preserve letters which some editors have refused to publish, letters which some private owners have refused to let me see or copy, letters which their owners have destroyed or lost, and letters to people I have been unable to locate.

Although O'Casey's handwriting and typing became very erratic in his final years when he was practically blind and wrote largely by instinct and determination, I have, with only a few exceptions, been able to transcribe his writing with what I trust is complete accuracy. His spelling was remarkably accurate, though in some instances I have corrected a misspelled word or name which he had previously spelled correctly. When in his near-blindness or haste he hit the wrong keys on the typewriter, I have made the logical corrections, in punctuation as well as spelling. All letters to newspapers and magazines would normally be addressed "To the Editor of *Irish Times*," but here this introduction has been shortened: "To *Irish Times*." For the translation of Irish phrases in the letters, I have relied upon Dinneen's *Irish-English Dictionary* and the valuable aid of Mr. Alfrid MacLochlainn.

A collection of letters which gives only one side of a natural dialogue can be frustrating to the reader. In the hope of alleviating some if not all of this frustration, I have tried to supply the other side of the dialogue in a variety of ways; in some instances by including several letters written to O'Casey (when they are available and pertinent), letters to newspapers and magazines written about him, and controversial reviews to which he responded. I have had to observe some measure of restraint in the introduction of this material, however, for otherwise this substantial edition would have overflowed into several more volumes.

I have also tried to tell some of the story behind the letters in a general introduction, in the brief introductions to each section, and in the footnotes, where the necessary background and context are provided. Because O'Casey was always vitally curious about playwrights and plays, I have tried to identify and date the plays he mentions; and because he was always deeply concerned about the actors who appeared in his plays, I have included the casts of his premieres as well as the leading players in some notable revivals.

My personal friendship with O'Casey during the last decade of his life, 1954 through 1964, when I was able to visit him at his home almost every summer, proved to be an invaluable help in clearing up many vague and puzzling references in the letters. Particularly during the final two and a half years of his life, I was able to ask him direct questions about complex situations and controversies. His replies were always straight and unequivocal. If he didn't know exactly when certain events took place—he was vague about dates—he had a phenomenal memory of what had happened and why it had happened. This edition of his letters could not have been completed in its present form without his great good help, as well as the very kind and generous assistance of his wife.

Over a period of seventeen years I have collected close to 2,400 letters, roughly 2,200 of which will appear in the three volumes of this edition. Volume I contained 653 letters; Volume II contains 807; Volume III will contain about 800. Since the publication of Volume I in 1975, I have collected several hundred more letters. Some of the new letters were finally released, after a ten-year delay, by the New York University Library, and I am especially grateful to the director for allowing me to make copies of the Jack Carney letters. I suspect that many hundreds of letters have been lost or destroyed; I know of many people who are withholding their letters, for various reasons; and I believe that many more letters will continue to turn up in the years ahead. In Volume III, I will indicate the final count of all the letters I have collected. All unprinted letters will be deposited in the National Library of Ireland in Dublin.

The letters are divided into three separate volumes, covering the following years: Volume I, 1910 through 1941; Volume II, 1942 through 1954; Volume III, 1955 through 1964.

Volume I contains 653 letters by O'Casey; 124 letters to or about O'Casey; 21 news reports and reviews by or about O'Casey's work; a total of 798 entries.

Volume II contains 807 letters by O'Casey; 15 letters by others to or about O'Casey; 5 reviews of O'Casey's work; 1 article by O'Casey; 1 statement to the press by O'Casey; a total of 829 entries.

*   *   *

I have used the following code to identify the nature of the original letter:

MS. Manuscript copy
TS. Typescript copy
TC. Typed carbon copy
PC. Printed copy

The location of each letter can be found in the following list of sources.

A. Institutions

British Museum, London
Colby College Library, Waterville, Maine
Cornell University Library, Ithaca, New York
League of Dramatists, London
Macmillan and Co. Ltd., London
Macmillan Publishing Co., Inc., New York
National Museum of Ireland, Dublin
New York University Library
Society of Authors, London
University of Texas Library, Austin

B. Periodicals

ACT, Leeds
The Author, London
The Bell, Dublin
Colby Literary Quarterly, Waterville, Maine
Daily Worker, London
Drama, London
English Churchman, London
Forward, Glasgow
International Literature, Moscow
Irish Democrat, London
Irish Freedom, London
Irish Independent, Dublin
Irish Press, Dublin
Irish Times, Dublin
Irish Writing, Cork
John O' London's Weekly, London
Manchester Guardian

Massachusetts Review, Amherst
New Statesman and Nation, London
New York Herald Tribune
New York Times
The Observer, London
Picture Post, London
Plebs, Tillicoultry, Scotland
Puck's Fare, Dublin
Randolph-Macon Bulletin, Ashland, Virginia
Reynolds News, London
Sean O'Casey Review, New York
The Spectator, London
The Standard, Dublin
Sunday Times, London
Time and Tide, London
Totnes Times, Devon
Tribune, London

C. *Private Owners*

Sir Bronson Albery, London
Mrs. Una Gwynn Albery, London
Nan Archer, Rush, Co. Dublin
Nancy Viscountess Astor Estate, London
Brooks Atkinson, New York
Oriana Atkinson, New York
Guy Boas, London
Marguerite Buller, Oxford
Patrick F. Byrne, Dublin
Cambridge University Hibernian Society
Curtis Canfield, New Haven, Connecticut
Barbara A. Cohen, New York
A. E. Copplestone, Totnes, Devon
D. L. E. Curran, Cambridge, England
Cyril Cusack, Dublin
Leslie Daiken, London
Jack Daly, Oxford
Edgar M. Deale, Dublin
Vincent de Baun, New Brunswick, New Jersey
Joseph Jay Deiss, Wellfleet, Massachusetts
R. L. De Wilton, New York
Barrows Dunham, Philadelphia
Elizabeth Freundlich, Vienna
John Gassner, New York
George Gilmore, Howth, Co. Dublin
Robert Emmett Ginna, New York

Lillian Gish, New York
Christine Gorman, Dublin
Eric Gorman, Dublin
Paul Green, Chapel Hill, North Carolina
Sheila May Greene, Dublin
Christopher Murray Grieve (Hugh MacDiarmid), Lanarkshire, Scotland
The Rev. Robert S. Griffin, Ballymore-Eustace, Co. Kildare
Roger Hayes, Dublin
G. W. Head, Dayton, Ohio
Robert Hogan, Newark, Delaware
Harold D. Jones, Brooklyn
Alfred Jordan, London
Jim Kavanagh, Dublin
Mrs. Elizabeth Kelly, Dublin
David Krause, Providence, Rhode Island
Mrs. Doris L. Leach, Hurley, Berkshire
Beatrix Lehmann, London
Oscar Lewenstein, London
Robert Lewis, Ridgefield, Connecticut
Mrs. Joy Lonergan, New York
Joan McAlevey, New York
Sir Desmond MacCarthy Estate, London
Frank McCarthy, London
Mrs. Grace McCormick, Gillingham, Suffolk
Roger McHugh, Dublin
Walter Macken, Galway
Francis MacManus, Dublin
Herbert Marshall, London
Sir Alec Martin, London
Frederick May, Dublin
Erna Meinel, London
Dr. Frank Morrell, New York
Mrs. Isabella Murphy, Dublin
Mary Frances Keating Newman, Dublin
Peter Newmark, Guildford, Surrey
Sean Nolan, Dublin
Rod Nordell, New York
Sylvia O'Brien, New York
Eileen O'Casey, Dun Laoghaire, Co. Dublin
Frank Hugh O'Donnell, Dublin
Brian O'Nolan, Dublin
Mrs. Kay O'Riordan, Dublin
Sean O'Rourke, Dublin
Mrs. Annette K. O'Sheel, New York
G. F. Parker, London

Joseph Prescott, Detroit
Horace Reynolds, Belmont, Massachusetts
Mrs. D. L. Robinson, Dublin
Gordon Rogoff, New York
Gilbert Ross, New York
Paul and Nan Ross, New York
Seumus Scully, Dublin
Miss Sheila ————, London
Ralph Thompson, New York
J. C. Trewin, London
Sam Wanamaker, London
Richard Watts, Jr., New York

For kind permission to publish copyrighted material, in letters written to or about O'Casey, and in reviews on O'Casey, I am grateful to the following: the James Agate review by permission of the Estate of James Agate; the Lady Astor letter by permission of the Honorable David Astor; the St. John Ervine letters by permission of the Society of Authors in behalf of the Estate of St. John Ervine; the Gabriel Fallon reviews by permission of Gabriel Fallon; the Eric Gorman letter by permission of Mrs. Christine Gorman; the Patrick Kavanagh letter by permission of Mrs. Kathleen Kavanagh; the Seamus Kelly review by permission of Seamus Kelly; the Robert Lewis letter by permission of Robert Lewis; the Peter Newmark letter by permission of Peter Newmark; the Eugene O'Neill letter by permission of Yale University as legatee under the will of Carlotta Monterey O'Neill; the George Orwell review by permission of A. M. Heath & Co. Ltd., for Mrs. Sonia Brownwell Orwell and Martin Secker and Warburg, Ltd.

While it would be impossible to list everyone who has helped me in my work, I must express a very deep debt of thanks to those who have given me valuable aid, counsel, and information—first singling out these heroic helpers: Mr. Alfrid MacLochlainn; Mr. Robert Lowery; Mr. John O'Riordan; Mr. Timothy O'Keeffe; Mr. Liam Miller; Mr. R. L. De Wilton; Mr. Jim Scully—and also the following: Mr. Ronald Ayling; Mrs. Mina Carney; Mr. and Mrs. Cyril Cusack; Mr. Michael Durkan; Mr. John Finegan; Mr. and Mrs. Eric Gorman; Mr. Martin Green; Mr. Patrick Henchy; Mr. Michael Hewson; Mrs. R. Kloegman; Mr. Emmet Larkin; Mr. Francis MacManus; Mr. Michael Martin; Mr. Francis Mins; Mr. Seumus Scully; Mr. Seán Stafford; Mr. James White. I must also acknowledge a special debt of gratitude and appreciation to Mr. Ray A. Roberts, whose sense of dedication and editorial wisdom brought the whole edition to life; to Mrs. Elisabeth Scharlatt, who, with the inspired help of John Jennings, edited the manuscript of the second volume; and to Miss Mary Donchez and Miss Anne Babatch, who guided it through the presses with loving care.

Finally, this second volume couldn't have been completed without the very valuable help of a fellowship from the John Simon Guggenheim Memorial Foundation.

Last and not least important, I have been fortified and blessed through many years of work by the love of my wife Anne, and the patient understanding of our four children who often wondered why I was so busy with O'Casey.

O'CASEY

CHRONOLOGY

1942	February 20	Publication of *Pictures in the Hallway,* second volume of his autobiography
	November 5	*The Plough and the Stars* is produced in an Irish translation at the Taibhdearc Theatre in Galway
	November 17	Publication of *Red Roses For Me*
	December 16	*Pictures in the Hallway* is banned in Ireland by the Censorship of Publications Board
1943	March 15	*Red Roses For Me* opens in Dublin at the Olympia Theatre, directed by Shelah Richards, the world premiere
	March 25	*Red Roses For Me* opens in Newcastle upon Tyne, produced by the People's Theatre, the English premiere by a nonprofessional company
	December 16	*Purple Dust* opens in Newcastle upon Tyne, produced by the People's Theatre, the world premiere by a nonprofessional company
1944	July	Finishes writing *Drums Under the Windows*

	October	Finishes writing *Oak Leaves and Lavender*
1945	January 17	Turns down an offer of up to $100,000 to write the scenario for a Hollywood film of Thomas Wolfe's *Look Homeward, Angel*
	October 16	Publication of *Drums Under the Windows*, third volume of his autobiography
	October 29	His reply to George Orwell's review of *Drums Under the Windows* is refused publication by the editor of *The Observer*
	October 31	*Purple Dust* opens in Liverpool at the Playhouse, presented by the Old Vic Company and directed by Eric Capon, the world premiere by a professional company
1946	February 26	*Red Roses For Me* opens in London at the Embassy Theatre, presented by Bronson Albery and directed by Ria Mooney, the London premiere
	April 9	*Purple Dust* is performed in Glasgow by the Glasgow Unity Theatre, directed by Robert Mitchell
	April 30	Publication of *Oak Leaves and Lavender*
	June 17	*Red Roses For Me* is performed in Dublin at the Gaiety Theatre, directed by Ria Mooney, accompanied by protests in the press against O'Casey and his play
	July 31	*The Star Turns Red* is performed in London at the Unity Theatre, directed by Ted Willis
	December	*The Plough and the Stars* is banned by the Cork Drama Festival
1947	January 11	His brother Michael Casey dies in Dublin at the age of 81
	January 30	His friend Jim Larkin, the Irish labor leader, dies in Dublin at the age of 71
	March	Finishes writing *Inishfallen, Fare Thee Well*
	May 13	*Oak Leaves and Lavender* opens in London at the Lyric Theatre, Hammersmith, presented by Bronson Albery and directed by Ronald Kerr, the world premiere

	May 26	*The Silver Tassie* is performed in Dublin at the Gaiety Theatre, directed by Ria Mooney
	August	Begins to write *Cock-a-Doodle Dandy*
	November 8	A protest demonstration is held in the Abbey Theatre by Valentine Iremonger and Roger Mc-Hugh to call attention to the poor quality of the current revival of *The Plough and the Stars*
	December	Finishes writing *Cock-a-Doodle Dandy*
	December 16	The Irish Censorship of Publications Board removes the ban against *I Knock at the Door* and *Pictures in the Hallway*
1948	February	His American agent, Richard J. Madden, is disturbed by the theme of *Cock-a-Doodle Dandy*
	March	Eddie Dowling, the American actor-director, decides not to produce *Cock-a-Doodle Dandy*
	August	The Macmillan Company of New York decides not to publish *Cock-a-Doodle Dandy* in America
1949	January 28	Publication of *Inishfallen, Fare Thee Well*, fourth volume of his autobiography
	April 8	Publication of *Cock-a-Doodle Dandy* by Macmillan of London
	September	Finishes writing *Hall of Healing*, a one-act play
	November 11	Publication of *Collected Plays*, Vols. I, II
	December	Finishes writing *Time to Go*, a one-act play
	December 10	*Cock-a-Doodle Dandy* opens in Newcastle upon Tyne, produced by the People's Theatre, directed by Peter Trower, the world premiere by a non-professional company
1950	January 30	*Cock-a-Doodle Dandy* opens in Dallas, Texas, at the Arena Theatre, directed by Margo Jones, the American premiere
	February	Finishes writing *Bedtime Story*, a one-act play
	November 2	His friend Bernard Shaw dies at the age of 94

1951	April	Finishes writing *Rose and Crown*
	April 25	*Red Roses For Me* opens in Houston, Texas, at the Playhouse, directed by John O'Shaughnessy, the American premiere, accompanied by protests against O'Casey and his play
	July 7	His American agent, Richard J. Madden, dies at the age of 71
	July 17	Publication of *Collected Plays,* Vols. III, IV
	July 18	The Abbey Theatre in Dublin is heavily damaged by fire several hours after a performance of *The Plough and the Stars*
	September 24	The Abbey Theatre reopens at its temporary quarters in the Queen's Theatre, an old music hall, with *The Silver Tassie*
1952	May	Plans for a production of *Cock-a-Doodle Dandy* in New York are abandoned
	May 7	*Bedtime Story, Hall of Healing,* and *Time to Go* open in New York at the Yugoslav-American Hall, directed by Joe Papirofsky (Papp), the world premiere
	July 4	Publication of *Rose and Crown,* fifth volume of his autobiography
	July 15	His reply to Louis MacNeice's review of *Rose and Crown* is refused publication by the editor of *The Observer*
	August	New plans are made for a production of *Cock-a-Doodle Dandy* in New York, but they are later abandoned
	September 23	Twenty-fifth anniversary of his marriage
	October	Plans for a production of *Purple Dust* in New York are abandoned
	November 12	Makes a recording of readings from his works for Caedmon, *Sean O'Casey Reading,* Vol. One
1953	April 27	*Purple Dust* opens in Glasgow at the Theatre

	Royal, directed by Sam Wanamaker, in preparation for a London premiere
May 23	*Purple Dust* closes in Brighton, after a tour of one-week engagements in Glasgow, Edinburgh, Blackpool, and Brighton, when, because of poor reviews and a lack of funds, the production is unable to make its scheduled opening in London
June 4	*Cock-a-Doodle Dandy* is performed by the students of Emerson College, Boston
June 20	*The Silver Tassie* is performed in West Berlin at the Schiller Theater in a German translation by Elizabeth· Freundlich and Gunther Anders, directed by Fritz Kortner, accompanied by protests in the theatre, partly an attack against O'Casey and his play, partly an anti-Semitic demonstration against Kortner's return to the Berlin theatre
September	Finishes writing *Sunset and Evening Star*
November 27	His friend Eugene O'Neill dies at the age of 65
December	Makes a second recording of readings from his works for Caedmon during the Christmas holiday, *Sean O'Casey Reading,* Vol. Two (This record was not released until September 1969)
1954 January	Starts writing *The Bishop's Bonfire*
February	The Chingford Unity Theatre, an amateur group in suburban London, is forced to withdraw *Bedtime Story* from a one-act play festival when the adjudicator calls it "blasphemous and unsavoury"
April	Finishes writing *The Bishop's Bonfire*
June 9	Moves from Totnes to 3 Villa Rosa Flats, 40 Trumlands Road, St. Marychurch, Torquay, Devon
July 26	*Life* magazine publishes an illustrated article, "The World of Sean O'Casey," with photographs of O'Casey and his Dublin by Gjon Mili
October	Begins negotiations with Cyril Cusack for the first production of *The Bishop's Bonfire,* which opens

	at the Gaiety Theatre in Dublin on 28 February 1955
October 29	Publication of *Sunset and Evening Star,* sixth and last volume of his autobiography
November	Signs a contract for a production of *Purple Dust* in New York, but the producer later changes his mind and withdraws
November	Agrees to allow Radio Eireann to make plans for a festival of O'Casey plays to be broadcast in May and June 1955

THE
LETTERS OF
Sean O'Casey
1942-54

I

IN THE WAKE
OF THE WAR,
1942

AND many thanks for the very graceful copy of Everyman. H. C. E. of poor Joyce; Humphrey, the Knight, and Humpty Dumpty, and Hump the publican, and a lot besides: all in one, and one in all—God help us. We're all at Finnegans Wake now.

And, lastly, I think, we can learn nothing if there is nothing in ourselves. Not in the Vedic Scriptures, nor the Hebrew sages, nor the Evangel of the New Testament. Nor in the Keltic Sagas, can we find comfort or safety. We must seek it in ourselves. The Kingdom of heaven is within us. Not yonder; but here. And, to me, Communism is the gateway. Believe me, there is loveliness in the hand of the craftsman hammering out sheet metal as there is in the hand of the craftsman hammering out gold.

A wide range of interests and activities absorbed the eternally curious and committed O'Casey during the war years in rural Totnes. In no way could dwellers for their worship of the statue of Our Lady of Eblana in *Red Roses For Me,* a play which O'Casey had already dedicated to the doctor. O'Casey's poignant defense of his sympathy for these poor Catholics is a moving statement of his absolute religious tolerance and compassion, and it affected Dr. Cummins so profoundly that he confessed he was shocked at his own earlier accusation, and in his reply he paid O'Casey the highest tribute, particularly since it came from an Irish Catholic: "I have never known a man so free from bias, so white-hot in the face of injustice as you." Several years later, however, Gabriel Fallon, who had initially praised the play, was to use that same incident of the statue to accuse O'Casey of "coldly calculated bigotry," provoking the end of their twenty-year friendship.

In his letter to the leaders of the Hedgerow Theatre in America, who had refused to serve in the war, O'Casey states that he favors the fight against Nazi tyranny but defends the sacred freedom of the theatre in war and peace, adding: "With conscientious objection I have naught to do, for I have been a fighter all my life." It might therefore be necessary to describe him as a conscious objector, a militant defender of all forms of freedom. The same impulse characterizes his protest against the wartime banning of the *Daily Worker* in his letter to Winston Churchill. He was always quick to use his name and his thundering words for the freedom of the theatre, the press, and the individual. Nevertheless, his militant way with words did not always help him earn enough of his daily bread. His new plays remained unproduced, and he was an important dramatist whose main source of income now came from his autobiography. His publisher, Daniel Macmillan, urged him to write a novel, assuming it was a more lucrative art form, but he felt he couldn't and shouldn't try to do it: "To me it is a dead art after Ulysses and Finnegans Wake." There are a number of significant personal revelations in that 12 October 1942 letter to Macmillan, not the least of which is his confession that he was paradoxically a rogue and a puritan: "Although I'm a damned rogue in many ways, in the way of Literature, like the noble Yeats, there is something of the damned Puritan in me." If he wanted to give the impression that he was an intemperate Dionysian in his life and a controlled Apollonian in his work, the truth is that he was often moved by both impulses in both areas; he was more Apollonian in his writing than many critics are willing to recognize, but his dominating impulse as an artist was the roguish or comic Dionysian.

He was reading the works of Joyce, Freud, Hemingway, Mayakovsky, and a Gaelic novel by Brian O'Nolan. He was continuing with his autobiography, writing articles on censorship and the war, and maintaining his steady flow of letters. In some of his letters to the *Totnes Times,* he was defending the call for a second front in the war effort; but on the home front things were going badly for him, for near the end of the year he had to appeal to his publisher for an advance of £100 in order to pay the overdue rent and a mounting pile of bills. It wouldn't have made him change his intemperate ways, but he might have recalled Juno Boyle's protest, when confronted by the noble sentiments of her children, that one can't pay the grocer with one's principles.

To Jack Carney [1]

MS. NYU LIBRARY

[TOTNES, DEVON]
18 JANUARY 1942

My dear Jack:

Thanks for papers, muffler, & kid gloves. It was a grand muffler, & they were grand gloves. Niall got hold of the muffler, & as he says he feels fine in it, & needs it more than I, he keeps it. Brian thinks the gloves will save his hands from frostbite, cycling to & from school; and as that is surely correct, I've let him have them for the winter.

Poor Miss Balantine! [2] Well, she's gone anyway. I was going to send a few stinging words; but the *Sunday Times* wrote suggesting an article for the next number of "Saturday Book"; so I've set out to do one about Lady Gregory [3]—one of 5,000 words, or more. So that's a very big job for me. John Burns,[4] with his wife, came here the other'day, about teatime, to

---

[1] Jack Carney (1888–1956), Irish journalist and union organizer; assistant to Jim Larkin in Dublin and helped him edit the *Irish Worker*. He left Dublin in 1936 and worked in London as a freelance journalist. From 1941 until the time of his death, he lived in a flat in Cliffords Inn, Fleet Street, with his wife Mina, a sculptor. In 1967 Mrs. Carney sold 126 O'Casey-to-Carney letters to the New York University Library, where they remained inaccessible for ten years. After a series of public appeals in the *Sean O'Casey Review* and the *New York Times* in 1977, the library finally relented and allowed me to obtain copies of the letters, most of which appear now for the first time in this volume. Letters written before 1942 will appear in an appendix in Vol. III. A carbon copy of one letter, 18 September 1931, was printed in Vol. I, pp. 434–35.

[2] In a letter to the *Irish Times*, 25 November 1941 (Vol. I, p. 910), O'Casey mentioned a Miss Ballantine who taught Sunday School classes at St. Barnabas Church in 1889 when he was a nine-year-old parishioner there, and he recalled that she unfairly favored some students over others. In a letter of reply in the *Irish Times*, 9 January 1942, Mrs. Lily Erwin (née Ballantyne), Drumcondra, Dublin, stated she was a teacher at St. Barnabas for over fifty years, and she protested that she never showed favoritism to any pupils, being "more inclined to caning than kissing."

[3] Sean O'Casey, "The Lady of Coole," *Saturday Book* (1942), ed. Leonard Russell. Much of the material in this article on Lady Gregory was later used in two chapters of *Inishfallen, Fare Thee Well* (1949), "Blessed Bridget of Coole" and "Where Wild Swans Nest."

[4] See O'Casey's letter to John Burns, 10 December 1941, Vol. I, pp. 914–15.

ask me to do something, or say something, or something. I didn't know they were in the kitchen, when I barged in; &, I fear, I was very rude to them. Anyway, I didn't wait to hear what they wanted me to do, but walked out of the kitchen, & waited till they went. Wanted me, I think, to propose some resolution or other. Propose a resolution! Jasus, an I fed on them all me life in Ireland! Anyway, he won't bother me for some time to come. Harry Pollitt [5] came here to tea, on his way to speak at Newton Abbot. Eileen went to the meeting & says it was fine: collection, £31. odd. Harry says the complaining every where is shocking. I'm afraid its usual. I can't see the Umpire [6] coming out of this. By the way, if you have any, or Jim [Larkin] has any, photos of himself, or one of Liberty Hall, I'd like to have a few for possible use in a future volume of biography. I understand *Pictures in the Hallway* will be out soon.

I am indeed glad that the few days you spent with us were happy ones. You & Mina fit in well, & that's the most that matters. I'm afraid I'm not courteous enough to stick, for a night & a day, a being that (as Jim might say) impinges on my easiness of mind & feeling. So, as long as we have a place, you & Mina will be welcome under the thatch.

The Red Army goes on well, still, though I will be pleased when the Hammer & Sickle flies once more over Rahov, Kharkov, Mosshaisk, & Taganrog—for a start.

> *My love to you & Mina.*
> *Ever yours,*
> *Sean*

PS. The Cake was a great cake. It shone at Niall's Birthday Party; & I et a lot of it; & (entre nous) et another slice when the curtains were drawn, everyone in bed, & all the house still.

[5] See O'Casey's letter to Harry Pollitt, 2 June 1948.
[6] British Empire.

To the Rev. Canon William Dudley Fletcher [1]

TC. O'CASEY

TOTNES, DEVON
30 JANUARY 1942

My dear Mr Dudley:

I was very pleased to get your letter which I am answering now, because various things kept me from attending to it before, principally an

[1] See O'Casey's letter to the *Irish Times,* 25 November 1941, note 2, Vol. I, p. 909.

attack of Influenza that laid us all out, one by one, myself, the wife, and our three children. We counter-attacked by shaking it off for the time being. We all live, right enough; but we dont all learn. If we did, it would be a different world. I daresay you read my second letter,[2] and poor Miss Ballantine's reminder of the Christian virtue of the cane rather than the kiss.[3] I was going to reply to her; but I remembered she must be an old woman, now, and, evidently, one of those who have learned nothing. So I left her alone. I met you once only—in Liberty Hall.[4] You were talking to Jim [Larkin], and I was by his side listening. If I remember right you werent so tall as your brother, Harry; sturdily built—rather a tough-looking nut, I'd say, meaning it as a compliment—and wore a beard. One of our Union Badges, a Red Hand, was in the lapel of your coat. Doesnt the "violence" of Jim look rather pitiful now, with the world at war. I must say I never cottoned on to the Evangelical side of the Irish Church; and, now, from the far distant hill—or hollow—of Communism, I dont think much of it, either. Devon is full of it—there are four or five different sects in Totnes—all out of touch with life, and the Anglican as far away from life and the slowest of the others. I do hope Mr Harry's little grandson will have a fine time in Killaloe—he should have, for your brother, when I knew him, had still a lot of the boy in him. I knew Bartholomew's well, as I did St John's, Sandymount, and All Saints, Grangegorman—they had a bad reputation with the Orangemen, a great many of whom, I knew well, too. All Saints' Preacher saying, "If Mr Fletcher put a notice on the board saying 'Porter given out free,' yous would be tearing the coats off your backs to get in," though, possibly true, has a touch of irony in it. He never asked himself the question, Why? Because they needed it, and hadnt the wherewithal to buy it. People will tear off their coats to get bread when it's scarce just as they would to get porter. Were it plentiful and within the power of all to get what they wanted, the need would slacken, and everything would be done, decently and in order. The porter is to the proletariat what cruises, wines, and fine meals are to the wealthier. But this is supply and demand argument; and I hope, when the war ends, we will all earn what we get, and get what we earn. My faith for many, many years has been that of Communism, and my hope for 25 years has been, and is, now, in the might of the Red Army; and, to me, Christian charity is the most hateful thing in the world—that is, alms giving. My book is a 2nd vol of biography; the first is called "I Knock at the Door"; the 2nd, "Pictures in the Hallway" was to come out in November, but the war put it back, and it is to appear shortly, I hope. I shouldnt advise you to get it—it is an outspoken book, full of turbulence and strife. There is, of course, the tribute to your brother, Harry, in the chapter called, "Death On The Doorstep." [5]

[2] See O'Casey's letter to the *Irish Times,* 15 December 1941, Vol. I, p. 916.

[3] See O'Casey's letter to Jack Carney, 18 January 1942, note 2.

[4] See O'Casey's letter to the *Irish Times,* 25 November 1941, note 8, Vol. I, p. 910.

[5] See "Death on the Doorstep," *Pictures in the Hallway* (1942).

Ever since the day I saw you in Liberty Hall, I have had an affectionate regard for you, strengthened by your many letters when you were Rector of Coolbanagher, especially the one that put the kybosh on that incomparable sham, Moran, Editor of "The Leader." [6]

You were always a man.

With all good wishes and affectionate regards—if you allow me to tender them,

Yours very sincerely,
[Sean O'Casey]

[6] D. P. Moran (1871–1936), influential Irish journalist; founder-editor of the *Leader,* from 1900 until his death. See O'Casey's letter in the *Leader,* 20 December 1924, Vol. I, p. 121.

To Jack Carney

MS. NYU LIBRARY

[TOTNES, DEVON]
6 FEBRUARY 1942

My dear Jack:

Thanks for papers and cuttings. [St. John] Ervine complains yearly about the people who want to produce plays for nothing.[1] It's of little use. They'll go on doing it. Today I got a letter from an Educational Group in Preston, Lancs, saying they were producing "Juno," & would I kindly say if a fee was payable. A week ago, a Scots lady said they were doing "End of the Beginning," but as the effort was for "Foreign Missions," they thought no fee should be charged. I wonder where were the "Foreign Missions"? Libya, maybe. Preaching the Gospel to the Indians fighting Rommel, maybe. Anyway, I said there was a fee, & mentioned it. I got a reply saying they wouldn't produce the play. They probably did. We can do little about it.

Evidently Joyce [2] is still a mystery to most people; though why Finnegan's Wake shouldn't suggest something to them, I don't know; & the world making a wake of itself, good & proper.

Sorry to hear about McIntosh. I met him once only—at a luncheon given by C. B. Cochran. I spoke to him only for five minutes. You should have taken the books.

[1] For an earlier comment on this point, by Ervine and O'Casey, see O'Casey's letter to Gabriel Fallon, 14 December 1927, note 6, Vol. I, p. 224.

[2] James Joyce (1882–1941), distinguished Irish writer; *A Portrait of the Artist as a Young Man* (1916); *Ulysses* (1922); *Finnegans Wake* (1939).

Thanks for the "Horizon." [3] It is very interesting. Curious how
O'Faolain & O'Connor always go together! I believe, they're out to make a
new Ireland of it. O'Connor wants a new theatre. He'll get it, too. They
want a helluva lot of things as well as a new theatre. Kavanagh has a
striking bit in the magazine. With a little luck, he'll outdo O'Connor &
O'Faolain. Who is Cyril Connolly? [4] Seems I heard the name before.

I have written, by request, a sketch of Lady Gregory for the next
number of "The Saturday Book." [5] Twenty-five quid, so I hope it goes—or
comes.

The "Plough" is on now in the Abbey [6]—2nd week—, & they expect it
to run for a third. That'll bring in a few badly needed pounds. I've missed
the Abbey now for a long time—it used to send me anything from £100 to
£150 a year, in comparison with the £3 or £5 or £9 I get here—not
counting requests to allow production for nix.

I see Lemass [7] says something like famine may come to Ireland! A
nice thing at the end of all the effort. And the country dedicated to the
Sacred Heart! They'll all be in the British Army soon. I hope to God the
Red Army may save them from that plight. I gave messages to Brian & to
Eileen. Eileen hasn't been well—a bad cold that looked damn like Influenza. I thought, for a few days, I was going down—or up—with it, too;
but I managed to frighten it off me. I don't want to live the life of a day
half up, & a week in bed. It has turned bitter cold down here. Some of your
snow coming along, I daresay.

Love to Mina & to you.
Yours ever
Sean

[3] *Horizon,* January 1942, Irish Number, ed. Cyril Connolly. This issue contains
three pieces to which O'Casey refers: Sean O'Faolain, "Yeats and the Younger
Generation"; Frank O'Connor, "The Future of Irish Literature"; Patrick Kavanagh,
"The Old Peasant," the first four parts of his epic poem *The Great Hunger* (1942).
[4] Cyril Connolly (1903–74), author and critic; founder-editor of *Horizon,*
1939–50.
[5] "The Lady of Coole," *The 1943 Saturday Book* (1942), ed. Leonard
Russell. Later O'Casey used parts of this essay for two chapters on Lady Gregory
in *Inishfallen, Fare Thee Well* (1949), "Blessed Bridget of Coole" and "Where
Wild Swans Nest."
[6] *The Plough and the Stars* was revived at the Abbey Theatre on 26 January
1942, directed by Frank Dermody, with Ria Mooney as Mrs. Gogan; F. J.
McCormick as Fluther Good; Eileen Crowe as Bessie Burgess; Joe Linnane as the
Young Covey; Phyllis Ryan as Nora Clitheroe; Denis O'Dea as Jack Clitheroe;
Joan Plunkett as Rosie Redmond; and Eric Gorman in his original role of Peter
Flynn.
[7] Sean Lemass (1899–1971), Irish politician and taoiseach (prime minister).
Served in de Valera's government as Minister for Industry and Commerce, 1941–45;
elected Taoiseach, 1959–66.

To Eric Gorman [1]

TS. CHRISTINE GORMAN

TOTNES, DEVON
6 FEBRUARY 1942

Dear Mr Gorman:

Ay, indeed, am I well pleased with the good reception given to THE PLOUGH AND THE STARS, and pleased, just as well, with the fine performance of the players. Please give them my warm thanks. I would indeed like to see the boul' F. J. [McCormick] playing the part of the "Captain." [2] I'm sure, too, Mrs F. J. [Eileen Crowe] did the part of Bessie Burgess in fine style, a rather hard part to play, I think. Many of the players are new to me, and you seem to have gathered together an entirely new company. Only yourself is left to play the old part of "Pether."

I see that Frank O'Connor, in HORIZON for the month of January, says, among other things, that "Two things must happen if Irish Literature is to survive the war. One is that somehow or other a theatre must be established, since the theatre is the only art form that can directly influence opinion."

Is he going to be another Yeats? "Establishing" a theatre is no easy job; and, anyway, no one can "establish" a theatre. Well, coming after Yeats, he has his work cut out for him.

I enclose receipt for royalties on first week of the Plough. By the way, I forwarded, a day or so after getting the cheque, a receipt for the Four Guineas advanced royalty. If it comes, or if youve got it, it can be cancelled. I always am prompt in acknowledging money. I'm certainly an expert in that respect.

With all good wishes to the Theatre, to yourself, personally, and to Mrs. Gorman.

Yours sincerely,
Sean O'Casey

Thanks for Programme. It looks well in its two colours.[3]

[1] Eric Gorman (1884–1971), secretary of the Abbey Theatre and actor in the company; married to the actress Christine Hayden.
[2] He must have meant Fluther. McCormick played the role of Clitheroe in the original production; see O'Casey's letter to Sara Allgood, 10 February 1926, note 1, Vol. I, p. 166.
[3] Added in longhand.

To Irish Times [1]

TC. O'CASEY

[? FEBRUARY 1942]

Meals for Schoolchildren

Dear Sir:

It's a queer thing that of the Bishop of Galway saying that the communal feeding of children means the thin edge of the wedge of Communism; and queerer still that he was backed up by Mr. McEntee. There is no clause in the Communist Manifesto, or in the writings of Marx, Engels, or Lenin laying down a law on the communal feeding of children. How can communal feeding be the thin edge of the wedge of Socialism any more than communal education? Even in Maynooth College, I myself have seen with my own two eyes great crowds of boys, separated from their families, eating away communally, as if to the manner born. Twenty-five or more years ago, I spoke on platforms, and gave out handbills in the streets, calling upon those in power to provide "meals for necessitous schoolchildren"; and it is a sad thing that today children should be kept tight and close to God by going about with empty bellies. It's a queer thing that Christian countries should find it necessary to have societies for the prevention of cruelty to children, while the one Socialist Nation in the world finds there's no need for one. As for the Socialistic scattering of families, here's two quotations that say strange things: One is taken from a little book called "Welsh Nationalism," and was bought by me eight years ago in Penmaenmawr, North Wales, so that what it says deals

---

[1] One can only assume that this undated typed carbon copy, written shortly after 6 February 1942—the date cited in the letter—was sent to the *Irish Times* and was refused publication by the editor. The plan to provide hot meals for disadvantaged schoolchildren was proposed to the Dublin Corporation in a leading article, "School Meals," in the *Irish Times,* 5 January 1942. Dr. Michael J. Browne, Bishop of Galway, in a speech reported in the *Irish Times,* 12 January, opposed the plan, warning people to "beware of creating panic, or allowing the present emergency to be used as propaganda material for a socialistic new order." A week later in a letter from Sean MacEntee, Minister for Local Government and Public Health, to the Corporation, reported in the *Irish Times,* 20 January, the plan was rejected; and a leading article in the same issue called the minister's statement "a masterpiece of unctuous folly and platitude." Meanwhile a series of letters in support of the plan appeared from prominent people like Dr. Owen Sheehy-Skeffington, Maud Gonne MacBride, and Dr. T. B. Rudmose-Brown, the latter stating on 21 January that it was nonsense to call the feeding of hot meals to poor children "the thin edge of the wedge of Communism." On the other side of the controversy, some people wrote stating there was no connection between the views of the bishop and the minister; but on 29 January a letter appeared from the playwright Paul Vincent Carroll in Glasgow, stating: "The source of Mr. MacEntee's well-fed unctuousness rather obviously lies in the Bishop of Galway's recent speech." By mid-February when O'Casey's letter arrived at the *Irish Times,* the editor may have rejected it because he did not want to prolong a fight for a cause that was now apparently lost.

with conditions existing long before the present war. The scene is the Ministry of Labour Court of Referees in Swansea.

Chairman: Why are you unwilling that your daughter should take work away from home?

The Mother (appearing for her daughter): One reason is that she isnt strong enough to leave home to work in a factory, and I dont want her to go far out of my sight.

Chairman: Indeed; You realise, of course, that it is on government money that you are living.

The Mother: Well, she has contributed towards that, too. You think you can do what you like with our children, and take them away from us.

So much for a Capitalist and Christian Board of Referees.

Here is a quotation from a leading Soviet paper, republished in "Soviet War News" Feb. 6th, 1942. It is from an article called, "Children First."

"In the various homes and kindergartens the children are assured of skilled care and normal food. They are given the opportunity of learning and resting, and are taught the habit of work. The children's homes, the boarding schools—these are excellent and essential. But they cannot take the place of the family, and many children who have been left without parents need a family. They miss the caress of their mother; their tiny hearts long for their homes, for their families. They must be helped."

That's Communism in action. Catholic Action, on the other hand, seem to be behindhand, and blame their laziness and indifference—for these are the kernel of their inactivity—on the dangers of Socialist Slums and hunger—the bucklers of Christianity. Christianity will find them a poor defence in time of trouble.

Yours sincerely,
Sean O'Casey

To Horace Reynolds [1]

TS. REYNOLDS

TOTNES, DEVON
[? FEBRUARY 1942]

My dear Horace:

I should have replied to you more'n a week ago, but we were, one after another, hauling ourselves out of an attack of Influenza. We're all on the right road again, so now I thank you most heartily for the tobacco,

[1] Horace Reynolds (1896–   ), writer and teacher; taught at Harvard and Brown universities. See O'Casey's many letters to Reynolds, Vol. I.

sweets, and tea from an t-oilean ur.[2] And now the trumpet of war is blowing in your own land, and the men of might are putting on their armour. Pearl Harbour was a very sad and unfortunate event for all of us. It beats me how we are so often surprised; and how we wait, like patience on a Bible for the other fellow to have a bang at us. "You fire first, gentlemen," is still our finest slogan. Oh, if theyd only opened their eyes a few years ago! If theyd given the Malayans better pay, the Nipponese wouldnt have had so many aides-de-camp. And, if theyd seen the value of China— as The Soviet Union did—, theyd have had a three-million well-armed Chinese force battering their way through the Japanese Hordes. They ought to move heaven and earth, after the Soviet Union, to give the Chinese what they need, for a victorious China would mean the end of Japan; just as a Soviet Union victory would mean the end of Hitler. Here they carry on the old curse-o-God snobbish divisions, with their D.F.C. for an officer, and a D.C.M. for one who isnt; getting Churchill to waste time and energy seeing the age old Duke of Connaught into his grave; giving places of power to those who have money and privilege; making a wild hillaballoo because a woman non-com, riding a motor bike, appeared at some ceremony in slacks instead of in a skirt. "There'll always be an England," yes, but what kind of an England? I learned from one who should know that there are more Irish in the B. Army than S. Africans and Aussies put together. I got a list of names in Merchant Ship casualties, and youd be surprised to see the Irish names that were among them. Kellys, Burkes, and Sheas—theyre everywhere now, as they figured years ago in the Maine.

"Purple Dust" has been abandoned by Eddie Dowling,[3] and I'm afraid it wont go on now. Well, it cant be helped. I've just written an article on Lady Gregory for the next issue of The Saturday Book. I hope it's good. And I'm working on another play to be called, I think, "At Sea in a Gold Canoe."[4] I hope that will be good too. It'll have some songs, "Rich Bunch of Red Roses," "The Scab," and "I Tucked up my Sleeves for to tie up Her Shoe."

I hope your Lad is doing well at Harvard. I wish mine was there. I've just begun to read him, Dickens' "Our Mutual Friend." I've read him all Dickens, a great deal of Twain's, Moby Dick, and a lot of others. I enjoy them myself again. I hope Peggy is well. She must be a blooming young lady now. And Kay, too. My love to you all.

Ever Yours, and thanks again.

Sean

[2] America, literally, the western island.

[3] Eddie Dowling, American actor, playwright, director, producer, made his Broadway debut in 1919 and remained active and successful in the theatre until the early 1960s. When he died in 1976, the obituary in the *New York Times,* 19 February 1976, said, "His age was somewhere between 80 and 86, but even his daughter did not know exactly." See O'Casey's letter to George Jean Nathan, 9 March 1948, note 1, with reference to Dowling's decision not to produce *Cock-a-Doodle Dandy.*

[4] *Red Roses For Me.*

To Jack Carney

MS. NYU LIBRARY

[TOTNES, DEVON]
13 FEBRUARY 1942

My dear Jack:
    Enclosed is a short thesis replying to Bill's remarks about me in
Plebs.[1] It grieves me to have to say a word to the wily old bugger, but it
mightn't be good to let it go by default. Perhaps, when you've read it,
you'd send it on to *Plebs.* In case you've no copy of the paper, I here put
down the address:

    N.C.L.C. Publishing Society, Ltd.
    Tillicoultry, Scotland

    Isn't it shocking about the Genesinau & Scharnhorst? Bombed to bits
hundreds of times, & now sailing up the English Channel, & the others
losing 46 planes trying to say hello. Honest to God, Tinkerbell must be
leading this country in this war, & Peter Pan G.O.C. of the combined
forces.
    The "Plough" has gone on in the Abbey for a third week.
    Love to you & Mina. If Jim [Larkin] comes, of course, if you can,
come along with him & Mina to have a chat & a cup o' tea.

Yours ever,
Sean

[1] See O'Casey's letter to *Plebs,* March 1942, note 1; and his unpublished letter,
6 March 1942. "Bill," William O'Brien (1881–1968), was a leading figure in the
Irish labor movement and a bitter rival of Jim Larkin. See O'Casey's letter to
O'Brien, ? November 1921, notes 1 and 3; 10 November 1921, Vol. I, pp. 97–98.

To Cornelius McElroy [1]

TC. O'CASEY

[TOTNES, DEVON]
16 FEBRUARY 1942

Dear Con:
    Well, we're still going weak; still handing things over on a gold plate;
still letting armies go off like the lost tribes of Israel. We'll have nothing

[1] Cornelius McElroy, son of William McElroy.

left soon, save a very thin smoke screen, with the Home Guard advancing at the treble with their pikes upon their shoulders at the risin of the moon. And Lord Croft, on a tin horse, leading them, St. George, Vict'ry, and England! I know now that the powerful Duke of York who marched an army up a hill and marched it down again, is no fairy tale; though the modern Duke marches them, and never marches them down again: they go over the top and—Gone! As AE says in his poems, when he gathers together a gorgeous vision, and then doesnt know what to do with it. If Percival could have got captured on his lone, all would have been well; but sixty thousand men—not counting material—is a big price to pay to get him out of the bloody way. How they couldnt see, when the Americans lost their fleet, and we lost the Repulse and Prince of Wales, that the Burma Road wasn't more important than a hundred Singapores, I dont know. If they'd only left Singapore to do the best for itself, and had concentrated their power before Rangoon, they would have been in the way of saving for themselves an army of 2 million of men. For if they lose this road, the Chinese Army is Harse de combat. And they look as though they may lose it. China and India, together, mean an Army of 5 millions of men, but theyre afraid to trust the Indians, and dont want China to become too strong either. And so, in fleets and armies, they hand over appetising hors-d'oeuvres to the greedy little golloping Nipponese.

And, again, the Scharnhorst and Gheneisau—how often have they been sent to the bottom? Hardly a day of the year passed that they hadnt their decks stove in, their bowels opened, and their arses blown to bits; and isnt the Atlantic Ocean covered with ships standing still, and smoke belching out of them? Dont be talking, man. What's to prevent them giving India a guarantee of Independence, within the B. Commonwealth, when the war ends, to get her united help? Nothing but the worn-out minds of Harrow and Eton.

What's the use of mentioning a "straight talk" with De Valera? Or anyone else? There's none of them capable of a straight talk. I had a talk with some of them at a lunch about this question of Partition; but the only one who had any idea of the problem was Malcolm MacDonald, and whaur's he th' noo? No Englishman knows anything about a country he governs. It's none of his business. It would be waste of time. Jasus, man, what dye want?

I want you, if you can, to get me a copy of THE CAPUCHIN ANNUAL, 1942, edited by Father Senan—a friend of mine, by the way— which might be very useful to me later on when writing a farther part of biography. Cant get it here. If you can lay a hand on it, I'll send you on the fee—10/6. Another thing: I've smashed my pipe again—no bomb this time, though one shook the house the other morning, just as I was waking out of a nice sleep. If you let me know the cost, I'll let you have cheque for both expenses.

And, now, farewell for the present. How's the Old Man?² Is he doing Falstaff—"What time o day is it, Hal?"

Ever yours,
[Sean]

² William "Billy" McElroy, best man at O'Casey's wedding on 23 September 1927, and backer of the first London production of *Juno and the Paycock*, which opened on 16 November 1925. See O'Casey's letter to Timmie McElroy, 26 May 1928, note 1; and Oliver St. John Gogarty's letter to O'Casey, 8 February 1929, note 1, Vol. I, pp. 253, 336.

*To Daniel Macmillan*¹

MS. MACMILLAN LONDON
TOTNES, DEVON
18 FEBRUARY 1942

Dear Mr. Daniel:

Thank you for your kind letter & cheque. I am very pleased with the format, inside & out, of "Pictures in the Hallway." I think the cover looks very dignified & graceful. I am downright glad that the book appealed to you so much. I think it better, on the whole, than "I Knock at the Door"; though that thought may be due to the illusion that the more you write, the better you get.

I enclose contract, signed as directed. I should be obliged, if you would let me have ten additional copies of the book, with two more to be sent to friends in Dublin,² whose addresses I will send to you later on. I'm glad that Mr. Harold has been promoted, though I wish he wasn't quite so diffident in the midst of his talents. Both of you, if I may say so as a friend, seem to pull back your intelligent desires. It's hard for an intelligent mind to plunge forward. The duffers do allright. Every poor duffer thinks himself the eldest son of one of the Wise Men who followed the Star, the time of the Epiphany. So they sit on plush in high places.

Every good wish to you & Mr. Harold.

Sean O'Casey

¹ Daniel Macmillan (1886–1965), publisher.
² Dr. J. D. Cummins and Gabriel Fallon.

To George Jean Nathan [1]

TS. CORNELL

TOTNES, DEVON
19 FEBRUARY 1942

My dear George:

I'm just writing a note to say that I haven't heard from you for years; that I got none of your new books—neither "Bachelor Born," [2] nor "Entertainment of a Nation." [3] However, hearing from Dick [Madden], I know you're well, and that's the main, the only thing to rejoice at. Dick is sending me another copy of Random House's Irish Plays,[4] copies of which were sent before, but never came.

I have heard from Dick how Eddie Dowling has given up all thought of producing "Purple Dust," which is a sad pity; but a thing that can't be helped. He is hopeful that John Tuerk [5] may take it up; but I don't like to think of the lovable John having more trouble with a play of mine. Or, indeed, you, either; but there's small use of talking to you.

Under another cover, I am sending a copy of PICTURES IN THE HALLWAY, and hope you'll get it allright. I'll post it tomorrow, along with one for Dick.

Between ourselves, I have written out the rough copy (four acts) of a proposed new play, to be called, I think, "At Sea in a Gold Canoe." But I'm not yet sure of the title.

The theatre here is as bad as it was, but worse. A play by Shakespeare, badly done; [6] and Coward's "Blithe Spirit," [7] and that's about all. For God's sake, send me a copy of your book on the theatre.

Things are getting tighter here; I and the wife have to do a lot about the house—she does the most; and it is a little upsetting; but I try to get on with a little work.

---

[1] George Jean Nathan (1882–1958), American drama critic, author, editor. For more information about Nathan, see O'Casey's first of many letters to him, 28 September 1932, note 1, Vol. I, p. 449.

[2] George Jean Nathan, *The Bachelor Life* (1941).

[3] George Jean Nathan, *The Entertainment of a Nation* (1942).

[4] *Five Great Modern Irish Plays* (1941), with a Foreword by George Jean Nathan. See O'Casey's letter to Nathan, 22 September 1941, note 1, Vol. I, p. 904.

[5] John Tuerk, one of the producers of *Within the Gates* in 1934. About the banning of the play in Boston, see O'Casey's letter to Nathan, 17 October 1934, note 1, Vol. I, p. 522; and Tuerk's letter to O'Casey, 5 March 1935, Vol. I, pp. 547–48.

[6] Shakespeare's *The Merry Wives of Windsor*, with Donald Wolfit as Falstaff, opened in London on 10 February 1942.

[7] Noel Coward's *Blithe Spirit* opened in London on 2 July 1941, and ran for 1,997 performances, until March 1946.

When you write to Eugene [O'Neill], send him my dear love, to him and Carlotta.

With love,
Ever yours,
Sean

To Gabriel Fallon [1]

TS. TEXAS

TOTNES, DEVON
20 FEBRUARY 1942

My dear Gaby:

Here at last is a note of fair greeting. Since I got your second last letter, many things had to be done; the children had to go through and get over the whooping cough, and I had to go through two bouts of Influenza. The war has, too, of course, upset the house as well as the country, and now Eileen has to do most of the housework, and all of the cooking. I give a hand as best I can, and the little I do, eats away a lot of time. But it's all in the day's work—it's in the regulations, and it must be done.

I was terribly sorry to hear of Frank MacManus's sore trouble; but what sympathy can one give in the circumstance of the loss of a child? Give him my love when you see him.

At last—due to difficulties of labour, it was long delayed—"Pictures in the Hallway" is coming out shortly; and soon I will send you a copy. I suppose, I'll have to soon start on the third volume! The jacket is my own designing; here, they seem to have little idea of how to set forth a book in pictures. I don't know myself, but I try; and, anyhow, it's not my business; though everything is everybody's business. I'm glad to hear that the old sycamore tree is still to the good. Many's the odd day and night I spent in that old house.

Poor Eire is going through tough times now. It is a sad state of life when death takes precedence of all things. And so much desire to do things, and so much to be done. With death shoving us all into a corner, and saying, Stay there till I call you. Hard on the chiselurs. If we can only manage to keep them going, it won't be so bad. But these are the last

---

[1] Gabriel J. Fallon (1898–   ), Abbey Theatre actor, drama critic, and a director of the Abbey, 1959–74. See O'Casey's first of many letters to him, 2 September 1924, note 1, Vol. I, p. 116.

things thought of. They don't matter a damn to me lord this and me lord
that, and Mr politician and the general with his knobs on: and all the riff
raff of life. However, I imagine this war will do away with a lot of things
that we can well spare; a lot of the straw and stubble will go, and the
people be saved so as by fire. Your eldest must be quite grown up. Ours
is thirteen, and a big fellow for his age.[2] We've just finished Ivanhoe, and
I've started Our Mutual Friend. Did you read Kavanagh's criticism, or review, of The Capuchin Annual in The Irish Times?[3] Kavanagh is a poet.
I met him—he came to see us—in London; and I seemed to gather that
London didn't suit him. I liked The Assembly at Drumceat, by O Farachain,[4] given over the wireless. He looks to be a poet, too. By the way,
isn't Roddy The Rover writing very stupidly in the Irish Press lately?
Why don't you have a shot at an article in the Saturday edition of the
Irish Times? Brinsley's The Three Thimbles[5] seems to have been a poor
one. He thinks, it seems to me, a little too much of a plot. Is this professional jealousy? I'll have to send the book straight from Macmillans, so
won't be able to add the usual greeting. Well, here it is, ould Dublin
buttie, in love to you, to Rose, and to all the children. And many thanks,
for the very graceful copy of Everyman. H. C. E. of poor Joyce;[6]
Humphrey, the Knight, and Humpty Dumpty, and Hump the publican,
and a lot besides: all in one, and one in all—God help us. We're all at
Finnegans Wake now. My love, again, to you all, and to Dublin.

Ever yours,
Sean

[2] Breon O'Casey.
[3] Patrick Kavanagh, "The Capuchin Annual for 1942," *Irish Times,* 10 January
1942.
[4] Roibeárd Ó Faracháin, *Assembly at Druim Ceat,* a verse play about St.
Colmcille, broadcast by Radio Eireann on 7 December 1941; later produced at the
Abbey Theatre on 21 March 1943.
[5] Brinsley Macnamara's *The Three Thimbles* opened at the Abbey Theatre on
24 November 1941.
[6] James Joyce, *Finnegans Wake* (1939).

To George Jean Nathan

MS. CORNELL

TOTNES, DEVON
21 FEBRUARY 1942

My very dear George:
Your book "Entertainment of a Nation," came today by the afternoon
post, a day after I had written you saying (complaining rather) that you

hadn't sent it. So I'm sending on this hasty note to say I have it safe. Thank you, old son. I was longing for it. I've just read your "Contribution of the Irish." [1] A hard wallop, George. And worse than that, it's terribly true. I'll have to watch my step. My new play [2] (if it ever be finished) has a clergyman (Protestant) in it, but he isn't a Canon, thank God. He's a character I drew, oh, 30 years ago, in a play called "The Harvest Festival" [3]—the only one in it; &, in a lazy way, I have remembered something of what was written, & have made him a part of the play. He's modelled on a dear dead friend [4] of mine—I have dedicated "Pictures in the Hallway" to him—, & stands up for the antagonistic element in his parish—as he did for me. I'll read that article of yours carefully again. There is a warning somewhere in it for me; & I must get it clearer. A thousand thanks for the book. I haven't read a book about the Theatre since your last one. And not many others either—Freud's "Moses," [5] & Hemingway's "For Whom the Bell Tolls," a good work; but somehow, I can't yell out grand over any of his books.

> *God be with you,*
> *& thanks again.*
> *Yours with my love*
> *Sean*

[1] George Jean Nathan, "The Contribution of the Irish," *The Entertainment of a Nation* (1942).

[2] *Red Roses For Me.*

[3] See the Abbey Theatre's rejection of this early play, "Reader's Opinion," 26 January 1920, Vol. I, pp. 91–92.

[4] The Rev. Edward Morgan Griffin (1852–1923), Rector of St. Barnabas Church, Dublin. Actually, the character in *Red Roses For Me,* the "Rev. E. Clinton, Rector of St. Burnupus Church," is a composite of the Rev. Harry Fletcher, who was Curate of St. Barnabas from 1896 to 1898, and Griffin, who became Rector in 1899.

[5] Sigmund Freud, *Moses and Monotheism* (1939).

To Jack Carney

MS. NYU LIBRARY

[TOTNES, DEVON]

2 MARCH 1942

My dear Jack:

Many thanks for the papers & the cake—the first one. It was gorgeous while it lasted; & the one that came today looks like its brother. Thanks again.

Myles na Coppalleen's article [1] dealt with the much argued question

[1] Myles na gCopaleen, "Cruiskeen Lawn," *Irish Times,* 24 February 1942.

of what is & what is not Irish Literature. It seems there's a paper published in Dublin—twice monthly, called an Glór—The Voice—, & an Editorial in it referred to things written by Yeats, Joyce, & all Irish who wrote in English, as Ersatz Literature. He may be right, though, in this case, the Ersatz Literature is much greater & better than the Real McCoy. Myles takes up the cudgels for Anglo-Irish writing, & slashes at what has been written in Gaedhilge; saying there isn't a line of literature in Canon O'Leary's Shendna, or in his Niamh; [2] & damn little in Padraic Conaire's work.[3] It's years since I read Shendna. It's an old legendary story, of the simple middle-age religious type of a man bargaining with the Devil; at the devil's effort to keep a grip on him; & of the man's cunning escape in the end by an act of helping an angel unawares. If I remember right, there was a fine description of the music of the union pipes—a picture that, in my opinion, if it wasn't literature, came very close to it. Myles defends Joyce; but his own stuff, I'm afraid, isn't very excellent. He's a kind of Gaelic Nathaniel Gubbins.[4] Anyhow, they can argue it out between them. It has been going on for years & years. Anyway, O'Leary's books are grand Irish, & that's a lot. Eire's fast moving toward an open (or shut) authoritarian Theocracy, & all the people will soon be going about like labouring gangs chained together by rosary beads. Isn't it a pity the Presbyterian North won't come in to bellow a protest against it? They're hanging themselves in their own orange sashes.

I do hope either (or both) the Russians or Chinese will save the world. Christ knows either civilization would be better than the one we have.

I'm always a little jealous of a fellow having a song I don't know. However, I've written a song "The Scab" to your air, & it will appear in the play I'm trying to write now. I enclose the words with this note.

Thanks for sending me Stonier's remarks on "Pictures in the Hall-way." [5]

And I shouldn't argue with Wynn. If she thinks Mina's below her intellectual level, well, let her. She won't go to heaven that way. People like Wynn, though they've been born, & move about, haven't caught up yet with the tail-end of life. They must be born again. I verily, verily say unto you, they must be born again.

[2] Canon Peter O'Leary (1839–1920), translated the Bible and *Aesop's Fables* into Irish, and wrote historical novels in Irish, notably *Seadhna* (1904) and *Niamh* (1907).

[3] Padraic O'Conaire (1883–1928), the well-known Gaelic storyteller. For one of his works in English translation, see *Field and Fair: Travels with a Donkey in Ireland,* translated by Cormac Breathnach, with "An Appreciation" by F. R. Higgins (1929).

[4] Nathaniel Gubbins, pseudonym of Edward Spencer, the popular comic columnist in the *Sunday Express,* who, in the words of L. W. Needham, former director of Beaverbrook Newspapers Ltd., "produced each joke as the laboured result of a journalistic Caesarian operation" (*50 Years of Fleet Street,* 1973).

[5] G. W. Stonier, *New Statesman and Nation,* 28 February 1942.

The Scab

by S. O'Casey

from Jack Carney's singing of the air

I

If we can't fire a gun, we can fire a hard stone,
Till the life of the scab shrivels into a moan;
    Let it sink in what I say,
    Let me say it again—
Tho' the good Lord made an odd scab, sure He also made men!

2

Th' one honor you'll get is a dusty black plume
On th' head of the nag takin' you to the tomb;
    Let it sink in what I say,
    Let it sink in what I tell—
The scab's curs'd be th' workers' book, candle, & bell!

3

There's room in th' world for Gentile an' Jew,
For the Bashi Bazook; but there's no room for you!
    Let it sink in what I say,
    Let it sink in what I tell—
You'll be lucky to find a spare place down in hell!

> *My love to Mina & to you.*
> *Ever yours*
> **Sean**

Glad to hear Jim's got a visa. Long live Larkin!

To Plebs

MARCH 1942

A Letter from Ireland

Dear Sir:

Permit me to say a word or two to the squeak that the still small voice of Bill O'Brien let out [of itself][1] against me in your February issue.[2]

---

[1] All passages in square brackets were omitted by the editor.

[2] William O'Brien, "A Letter from Ireland," *Plebs,* February 1942, a monthly labor journal published in Tillicoultry, Scotland. See O'Casey's letter to Jack Carney, 13 February 1942, note 1.

O'Brien says among other things that "the less said about O'Casey's association with the Irish Citizen Army the better. O'Casey severed his connection with it when Connolly took over in October 1914."

I don't very much wish for a controversy with Bill O'Brien, for he'd be small fry for me to tackle, even though he thinks himself an eminent fellow standing on the top of Jim Connolly's gravestone. Certainly, as far as I know, little more [or less] could be said of his connection with the Citizen Army, for he took delightful care to keep [well] away from it. But, perhaps, it is well, in such a Journal as *Plebs,* to refute what is an ignorant or a deliberately false statement. O'Casey resigned from the Citizen Army because of a difference with the Countess Marcievicz,[3] when Jim Larkin—not Jim Connolly—was in control of its organised members.

Had O'Brien valued the decency of his accuracy, he would have seen the facts set down in the little book, written by me twenty-four years ago, called "The Story of the Irish Citizen Army," published by Maunsel's, Dublin, in 1919.

Afterwards, Jim Larkin called a general meeting of the Army in the Concert Room of Liberty Hall, and tried hard to smooth things in his persuasive and eloquent way; but the Secretary (O'Casey) said "he was sorry he couldn't do what Jim suggested, and that his resignation was definite and final"—O'Brien can read it all in the little book—which of course he doesn't want to do. If, as O'Brien implies, Connolly wanted to make the Army more revolutionary, he went a curious way about it; for he never attended a single meeting of the Council till circumstances allowed him to become dictator, not of an army, but of a company of little more than a hundred men.

[As for O'Brien's "less said the better," he is, as far as I am concerned, free to say what he pleases about me, in *Plebs* or anywhere else, provided, always, that I am allowed to reply to whatever he may venture to say. Like everyone else (as an Irish proverb says), if my sins were written on my forehead, I'd pull my cap over my eyes; but Jesus help me, if I was timid about letting poor Bill O'Brien see the most of them.]

Yours,

Sean O'Casey

---

[3] Countess Constance Gore-Booth Markievicz (1868–1927), Irish nationalist leader; member of the Irish Volunteers and the Irish Citizen Army, 1914–16; sentenced to death for her role in the 1916 Easter Rising; commuted to life imprisonment, and released after the general amnesty of 1917. For the background of O'Casey's confrontation with the countess, see his letter to the *Voice of Labour,* 20 February 1926, note 3, Vol. I, p. 176; and his letter to Sean O'Faolain, 10 August 1932, note 2, Vol. I, p. 447.

To Plebs [1]

TC. O'CASEY

[TOTNES, DEVON]
6 MARCH 1942

Ireland

Dear Sir:

You added as a coda to the few remarks I made in your last issue the following: "This letter might have been less abusive." One of the "might have beens." Allright; but why, in all fairness, didnt you comment on the malicious and rat-like insinuation of O'Brien's "The less said about O'Casey's association with the Irish Citizen Army the better"? An assertion, too, that wasnt followed by even a single hint to justify it, except a statement by O'Brien proved to be false by a record published many years ago. Nor did you comment on statements made on the strength of documents that no one has ever seen, and that are snug in O'Brien's private museum, along with the twenty-five three feet high, illustrated volumes of Shakespeare that he loves so well. Surely a Journal like PLEBS should require something more substantial than mere malicious statements—proved to be false—about men who have done more for the Labour Movement than poor Bill has ever been able to do, and who have got a helluva lot less out of it.

Yours sincerely,
Sean O'Casey

[1] This letter was refused publication by the editor.

To Quidnunc [1]

PC. *Irish Times*

6 MARCH 1942

Dear Quidnunc,—

Recently, in a note of yours, you told us that the House of Coole was about to be torn down.[2] This is a sad fate for such a house, so different

[1] Quidnunc (Patrick Campbell) printed this letter in his column "An Irishman's Diary," *Irish Times,* 6 March 1942.

[2] In his column of 21 February 1942, Quidnunc announced that the demolition of Coole House would begin on 2 March. Lady Gregory had sold her home to

from the House of Usher. One would think they could have made it into a local Galway Art Gallery, preserving half the history of the places around it.

They have done more to embalm the deeds of others, not a tenth as good as Lady Gregory was to Ireland.

In your note, you mentioned that he who was to do the demolishing was to take pictures of the house, before and after its fall. I wonder if it would be possible for me to get a picture of the house before its destruction?

I should be very glad to have one.

Yours sincerely,
Sean O'Casey

---

the Land Commission before she died in 1932, and now a decade later the commission decided that since it had been unable to find a tenant and the rates were very high, it had to demolish the house.

To John Irwin [1]

TC. O'CASEY

TOTNES, DEVON
[10 MARCH 1942]

Dear Irwin:

1. If you send me your copy of "Pictures in the Hallway," with the return postage pre-paid, I will autograph it for you.

2. If you hitch-hike to Totnes for the sole purpose of seeing me, I will put up with ten minutes of your company.

3. Shut-up, and don't be a nuisance!

Yours sincerely,
Sean O'Casey

XXXXX Please *DELETE THAT WHICH DOESN'T APPLY*

[1] John Irwin, a 21-year-old British soldier stationed in Kent, had written a letter of great praise for O'Casey's work.

To George Jean Nathan

TS. CORNELL

TOTNES, DEVON
10 MARCH 1942

My very dear George:

I got your book allright, and have already sent you a letter saying so. I am reading it now, and enjoying it immensely. It is great reading. I wish you published one a week. I also got the Random House copy of Irish Plays, with your dear Inscription. And your delightful (to me) preface to the book. It is a very handsome volume, finely bound, and, altogether, a delightful addition to the bookshelf. Thanks a thousand.

Some time ago, I sent a copy of my new book, and I hope it arrived (after dodging the U Boats) safely in New York City, N.Y. I hope you may like it. I dread looking forward to writing the next volume. To get a rest, I'm trying to write a play—I think I mentioned this before, calling it "At Sea in a Gold Canoe"; but I've since changed the name to "Red Roses For Me," a strange change for a name to take. After reading your "Contribution of the Irish" several times, I find my new play will honour everything, almost, you condemn, or, rather, deprecate, and rightly so. There is the Clergyman—a Protestant one this time; and maybe that's a change; the Ingenue (I think), the Miracle; the Mysticism of a vision of Dublin in the third act; all, except the drinking sponger. Still, I think there is good in the play; or will be, rather, when it's finished. I'll send the first copy to you (if you don't mind), and, when you've read it, you could let Dick have it; or you could give it first to Dick, if you find the typing too bad to read comfortably, and wait for him to make a fair copy.

I agree with what you say about Maxwell Anderson. He isn't in the same town with Eugene [O'Neill]. Even in his Winterset—though I don't like to say it—, I find it hard to read, find it cold, like a marble Galatea that never comes to life. He often kicks a body, a cold kick, too; but never kisses a soul.

How did you know that "Tanyard Street" was first shown in the Abbey as "The Spanish Soldier"? [1] A fellow interested in its London production gave me here the synopsis of the play under the latter name; and I thought it good, and was nearly telling the Author to send it on to you— well, I didn't; and it was only when I read your book that I connected it with the "Tanyard Street" done in N.Y. However, I'm very chary of advising any playwright to send a play to G. J. Nathan, Esq, for so few of

---

[1] Louis D'Alton's *Tanyard Street,* which was produced in New York on 4 February 1941, had originally been produced at the Abbey Theatre under the title of *The Spanish Soldier* on 29 January 1940. See O'Casey's letter to Gabriel Fallon, 29 March 1941, note 10, Vol. I, p. 883.

them are able to stand up to a fair criticism; or fight an adverse one by trying to write a better play.

Things are, of course, getting stricter here in the way of living; but there is only the way to go on working as long as one is let. Good luck to MacArthur, a Gaelic name; and may he put it across the Nipponese. My deep love to you. All well here. *Yrs,*

Sean

To William Rust [1]

TC. O'CASEY

[TOTNES], DEVON

12 MARCH 1942

Dear Mr. Rust:

There's no possibility of my going to London on or near the 21 inst. Many circumstances keep me where I am. I do hope your gathering may be a big one, and very effective towards the campaign against the ban on the D.W.[2] Few stupidities on the part of the powers that be puzzle me, but this one does. The banning of the D.W. today is treason against our comrade-ally, the USSR; for if any Journal stood by the USSR, in bad report and good report, it was the D.W. While the rest of them stood in their corners—rich corners—and howled hatred, the D.W. stood out in the open, and cheered the Soviet effort and the power of her Red Army. I, for one, never thought the D.W. as good as it could be (nothing is, none of us are; if everything and everyone were as good as they could be, there'd be no Soviet Union, no British Commonwealth: we'd all be members of a world confederation of united Communistic nations); but the D.W. was good in its general policy, and splendid in its policy towards the USSR and India, a policy that the wise ones are now trying frantically to put into fruitful action. But the D.W. was critical—there was the rub! Stupidity didnt like to be challenged, especially when it had power to shut mouths, the one time when stupidity must be put into the pillory and mocked out of its power. Now, the House of Commons is deafened with cries of criticism. As far as I know, nothing more critical ever appeared in the D.W. as the shouted criticism of Admiral Keyes and Sir Murray Sueter heard in the H. of C. only yesterday: "The Swordfish, the only torpedo craft the Navy

---

[1] William Rust (1903–49), editor of the *Daily Worker,* London, 1941–49; fought with the International Brigade in the Spanish Civil War.

[2] See O'Casey's letter to Winston Churchill, 4 July 1942, on the British government's banning of the *Daily Worker.*

possessed is six years old, with a speed of about 90 miles an hour, quite outclassed by the sort of aircraft it is likely to encounter; they stood no chance against the opposition"; and Sueter's: "It was a disgrace and a scandal that the Admiralty appeared to have been let down in their technical people." The difference between this sort of thing and the criticism of the D.W. being that while the D.W. criticism came a little too early, apparently, for the wiseheads, this criticism of Keyes and Sueter seems to come along a little late. Had the early views of the D.W. been even half way met, we shouldnt be where we are now, plunging about in a wild effort to save ourselves. Above everything today, we need an inspiration among the workers; for they alone, in Army, Navy, field, factory, and workshop, can save the nation. No Journal that I know of is so likely to create this inspirational surge as the D.W. is. Today it is not so much a matter even of the freedom of the Press as it is a matter of life and death. The man or men who stand in the way of the lifting of the ban is, in my opinion, an enemy of the people; not of this part or that part of the people, but of all the peoples gathered together under one flag to fight against Fascism.

My best wishes.
[*Sean O'Casey*]

To John Irwin

TC. O'CASEY

TOTNES, DEVON
17 MARCH 1942
(ST. PATRICK'S DAY)

Dear Friend.

Dont think I am either a prophet or a philosopher, I'm not. But I am an intelligent man; and that's something. None of them you mention— Marx, Lenin, or Nietzsche—, or all jumbled together make the human race. There are others. All these were great, very great spirits, and have sent us marching forward. Of course, Socialism isnt enough. Who said it was? And I dont mean that Socialism that has Bevin, Wilkinson, Attlee, and the rest, as its banner-bearers. Such have shut themselves away from the vision of song and story, canvas or plain jewelled with colour, or cut stone of statue, or piled stone of mighty buildings. While I believe that Socialism (I'd rather say Communism) will inevitably come, I dont think it will come trotting up to us as readily as you seem to think. Wasnt it Lenin who said "Communism wont come to us as a scheduled train comes,

puffing up to time, into a first-class German Station." There will be a big
fight for it. And my ideal isnt quite so near as you say it is. My ideal lies
behind Communism. A jewelled land of jewelled labour. Communism, so
far from being the end, is but the beginning. I look for it, not that we may
rest from our labours, but that we may begin them. They have begun in the
USSR; we havent been able to start yet. No-one can determine now how we
can prevent things being mismanaged or abused under Socialism; that must
be evolved during the transition period, out of actual experience. Just as
no school can teach us actual battle experience; but only the battle itself.
(These, mind you, are not dogma, but opinions.) You say there's a
difference of perspective of 40 years between you and me. Is there? A
difference in what is called time, yes; but thought? An Irish saying says "A
cracked yellow skin round a shining heart," and I think I've still got a
shining heart. I've always been among the young. I've three of my own,
from 2½, to seven, up to 14; so I've a lot of actual experience. Two of
them are always asking questions; I answer the children, though I dont always answer the questions, for they often puzzle me, and I tell them so. But
be assured, the struggle when Communism comes will not be less, but
greater; but achievement will be certain. You say, "unless the Lord build
the house"; well, isnt the Lord building the house? "All things were made
by him; and without him was not anything made that was made." The
Holy Ghost isnt only with those who go about crying, Lord, Lord. I dont
see why you should have scoffed at NISI DOMINUS FRUSTRA. I dont
know Latin; but I'd say it meant "You Cant Cod God." Well, neither can
you, or I, or anyone else. The Hound of Heaven has sung that song for
us; and G. B. Shaw has told the story in "The Showing Up of Blanco
Posnet"; and St Paul mentions it in his "Be not deceived, God is not
mocked." Your problems of today arent mine of yesterday; theyre equally
mine of today. But I believe, and have no reason for adding help thou mine
unbelief. That, it seems to me, is the one difference between us. And dont
you think that this war can be a terrifying thing to an old codger like me,
too? Of course it can; and of course it is. I hope it may mould the ES-
SENCE of life into new channels. That is bound to be; and there's no
reason for being afraid of it. The big thing now is the terrible economic
immorality under which we live and suffer and die. That controlled, all
other things will reach a healthy and vigorous level.

　　I know nothing of Kalidasa. Candidly, I've never even heard of him.
And we've a lot to learn from every culture—from our own first, though. If
we cant learn from our own, we can learn nothing from other fountains.
And, lastly, I think, we can learn nothing if there is nothing in ourselves.
Not in the Vedic Scriptures, nor the Hebrew sages, nor the Evangel of the
New Testament. Nor in the Keltic Sagas, can we find comfort or safety. We
must seek it in ourselves. The Kingdom of heaven is within us. Not yonder;
but here. And, to me, Communism is the gateway. Believe me, there is

loveliness in the hand of the craftsman hammering out sheet metal as there is in the hand of the craftsman hammering out gold.

Yours very sincerely,
[Sean O'Casey]

To Jack Carney

MS. NYU LIBRARY
[TOTNES, DEVON]
22 MARCH 1942

Thank you,
My dear Jack,

for saying you'd send me your copy of "Curtain Up." [1] It is a book I should very much like to read; &, indeed, I had put it down on my waiting list as a probable future purchase. I shall be very glad to get it. Thanks, too, for the papers. "The Nation" is interesting reading. What a puzzle Eire is! All for her, & all against her. I wonder what the outcome of it all will be? There's no doubt that if Germany was where England is, the question would have been settled long ago; but England, throughout the years, has created such an indissoluble feeling in Eirinn & elsewhere, that she is now where she was bound to be—on the high horns of a dilemma.

Young Jim's [2] long letter is a revealing one. I do hope that Big Jim will be able to take his essential place in the fight, unified fight for the integrity of the Trades Unions. But it will be a hard job to keep them out of the suave silky hands of the Church. The whole trend is towards an instant & unquestioning obedience to the Catholic Social activity of the Church—the Wireless, the Government—Cosgrave & Dev—& 9 tenths of the Press. And this will be, if possible, a link with the Catholic Bloc of Petain France, Franco Spain, & Salazar Portugal, to be followed by an effort to hook in all Latin America. I think this to be one strong reason why Dev is anxious to preserve neutrality; &, curious enough, he is being splendidly helped by the stupid careerists of Protestant side N. Ireland.

I had sent on a note to "Plebs" [3] before I got yours suggesting I should

[1] Lennox Robinson, *Curtain Up* (1942), an autobiography which contains two letters from O'Casey to Robinson, 9 October 1922 and 11 November 1922, the latter quoted partially. Both are complete in Vol. I, pp. 104–6.

[2] Jim Larkin, Jr. (1905–69), labor leader and member of the Dail, succeeded his father as head of the Workers' Union of Ireland.

[3] See O'Casey's unpublished letter to *Plebs*, 6 March 1942.

ignore Bill [O'Brien]. I enclose a copy which you might let me have back; for, in case, I like to have a copy of what I've written. Anyway, I don't think Bill should get away with it. I certainly don't give a damn about Bill. I'll let him have an answer, good and proper, to anything he says about me.

I have been busy with my new play.[4] I've done 3 acts, finally, tonight; & the 4th, roughly written out, remains to be hewn into a proper form, finally typed, & the play's finished. I hope the result may be good.

The cake is simply splendid. Breon has found the kid gloves you sent a little tight; so yours truly wears them now on cold days. My love to Mina. And to you.

Sean

Myles na gCopaleen sent me his book.[5] I haven't read it yet—working till two every night with play; but will write to thank him; & will read it when play is done.

[4] *Red Roses For Me.*
[5] *An Beál Bocht.* See O'Casey's letter to Brian O'Nolan (Myles na gCopaleen), 2 April 1942, note 2.

To Jack Carney

MS. NYU LIBRARY
[TOTNES, DEVON]
28 MARCH 1942

My dear Jack:

Thanks very much for Robinson's "Curtain Up" which I have just read. To me it seems, nay sir, it is, a disappointing book. It, in my opinion, gets only to a mediocre level. I may be predg biassed—forget for the minute how to spell prejudiced—; but all his people are too lovely altogether, Higgins, Hazel, & the whole of them. He leaves a few things out: one the award of a first Tailteann prize by him & J. B. Fagan to a 15 minute thing (they called it a play) called "The Passing." [1] Jasus! And because it got the prize, the Abbey had to do it, with Sally Allgood killing herself trying to put

[1] Robinson and Fagan were on the committee which awarded the 1924 Tailteann prize for drama to *The Passing* by Kenneth Sarr (District Justice Kenneth Reddin), performed at the Abbey Theatre on 9 December 1924. This obscure one-act play was chosen over *Juno and the Paycock.* For O'Casey's earlier comments on *The Passing,* see his letter to Lady Gregory, 17 December 1924, note 2, Vol. I, p. 120; see his undated letter to Lady Gregory, included in the series of letters in the *Irish Statesman,* 9 June 1928, Vol. I, p. 270; see his letter to Gabriel Fallon, 21 June 1928, note 1, Vol. I, p. 286.

something into it, after having gone on her adorers to be excused. That was one of the shots I sent into the Ship of the Abbey when they jettisoned "The Silver Tassie." [2] And his statement that my first plays "were divided into two compartments—selfish, licentious Capitalists, & noble & pure proletarians" is either false, or shows a woeful lack of memory. My first "The Frost in the Flower," [3] dealt with a chap, utterly incompetent, who, by soliciting votes (largely through the I.R.B.) got a job as teacher of English & Elementary Mathematics in Capel St. Technical School. The whole family were in glee—except himself, who was sure he wouldn't get it. But he did, stuck it for a week, resigned, & came back to a glowering family. That was No. 1. of the "licentious Capitalists." No. 2. "The Harvest Festival" [4] dealt with a strike in which a Protestant clergyman stood up, against his Vestry, for one of the leaders. The "noblest" character in the play was the clergyman. He appears in the present play I'm writing; a much finer play, of course, but with a theme something the same. No. 3. "Crimson in the Tricolour" [5] was really a "play of ideas" moulded on Shaw's style. It had in it a character posed on A. Griffith, a Labour Leader, mean & despicable, posed on whomsoever you can guess, & the "noble proletarian" in it was later "The Covey" in the "Plough & the Stars," as was a carpenter who developed into "Fluther." Funny enough, the second scene in the "Plough"—the "pub scene"—was first sent to the Abbey as a one-act play, by the name of "The Cooing of Doves," and rejected! They took a thing of mine instead, called "Kathleen Listens In," only in the ½' [ha' penny] place to the one they refused.

By the way, who's Francis Macnamara, mentioned in his prologue as the writer of Diminutivus Ululans? [6] Never heard of him. Heard of Francis MacManus—a friend of mine who writes poetry, & who is a Neo-Thomist, & likely to write such a thing. Robbie seems to have mixed them up; as I think he does Sherwood Anderson with Maxwell Anderson; & calls Ernie O'Malley "Eric"; & comes out badly with his

> Cover her face. Mine eyes *glisten.*
> She died young.

This about Hazel [7]—; but the word glisten should be dazzle. [8] But he never liked the Elizabethans. And what a bad drawing—the arms & hands, the

[2] See O'Casey's series of letters on *The Silver Tassie* controversy in the *Irish Statesman,* 9 June 1928, Vol. I, pp. 265–75.
[3] See the Abbey Theatre's Reader's Opinion of "The Frost in the Flower," Vol. I, pp. 91–92.
[4] *Ibid.*
[5] See Lady Gregory's critique of "The Crimson in the Tricolour," ? October 1921, Vol. I, pp. 95–96.
[6] In the prologue of *Curtain Up,* Robinson quotes a poem by Francis Macnamara, "Diminutivus Ululans."
[7] Lady Hazel Lavery.
[8] John Webster, *The Duchess of Malfi* (1614), Act IV, sc. 2.

legs—Oh O'Sullivan, O'Sullivan! [9] I can hardly bear it. There seems to be
something pathetic about the book. He certainly was lucky in getting jobs
without the knowledge of knowing technically how to do them.

And [St. John] Ervine, too! They all seem to want to have a slap at
me. They'll never forgive me for being made of common clay. And the
commonest of common clay, too! Not even a bricklayer or a carpenter—
only a tradesman's helper, an unskilled labourer, a fellow that muled with
his hands. Well, Breon mules with his hands, too, thank God, cutting down
trees, cleaning out rabbit hutches & pig byres, & chopping wood; doing
"useful work" it is called; & damned useful work it is, too.

Some time ago, Ervine did a mean thing on me: he wrote a private
letter to G. J. Nathan, exclaiming against Nathan's good opinion of me.
And Nathan replied in an article,[10] which I'll look for, & send it on to
you, when I finish this; asking you to let me have it back. He has put the
most of what he said in a preface to "Five Famous Irish Plays," [11] issued
by Random House, N. York; so Ervine's got his answer. Eileen's got
Ervine's last book "Sophia" [12] from the Library, & I've just read it. Seems
to me he's going soft. Says all things "written by the Ancient Gaels is terrible sludge," & goes all out for the destruction of S. Ireland.

Personally, I'm afraid, his own Ulster (of the non-Gaelic element)
has given us nothing for the past 50 years but screaming blatherers. James
Douglas; J. L. Garvin; himself now; & the twilight nonsense of George
Russell. Ulsteria. If Yeats wasn't a great writer, I'm no Gael; if Joyce wasn't
a great writer, I'm a balls; if Shaw isn't a great writer & thinker, too, you're
a balls, too.

That was a beautiful sentence from Moscow. "Console our frightened
children" is worthy of the Soviet Union, may God strengthen her mighty
arm.

I'm glad you have the flat. I long ago guessed all about poor Wyn.
She's wrapped up in herself, keeping warm a poor piece of goods. She
can't help it. In her last article on Films in "Tribune," she says the Cinema
can do a Dream better than the Drama. She's never read Strindberg's "The
Dream Play"; & I hope she never will. The day's ending for these poor
people, & night is close at hand—pray for them.

My love to Mina & to you.

Ever yours
Sean

9 The frontispiece of *Curtain Up* is a drawing of Robinson by Sean O'Sullivan.
10 See George Jean Nathan's "The Best of the Irish," *Newsweek,* 29 January
1940, Vol. I, pp. 838–39.
11 See O'Casey's letter to Nathan, 22 September 1941, note 1, Vol. I, p. 904.
The relevant passage in Nathan's foreword to *Five Great Modern Irish Plays*
(1941) is reprinted in note 1.
12 St. John Ervine, *Sophia* (1941), a novel.

To Mrs. Grace McCormick [1]

MS. MCCORMICK

TOTNES, DEVON

30 MARCH 1942

Dear Mrs. McCormick:

It was very nice to hear from you. It is rather difficult to get books now on account of scarcity of materials. Besides, dear lady, my book [2] is a pretty tough one, & there is fierce writing in it. I would be the last to give a shock, or offend in any way, the dear little girl I knew so well long ago. If you think you can stand it—and, for all I know—you may have had worse shocks than any book can give; then I shall be very pleased to do my best to send you a copy. Your sister, Alice, wrote some time ago, asking for a copy. I can't send books to Erinn—the law doesn't allow it. I've mislaid her letter, & don't know whether her Bank of Ireland is in Newry, Portadown, or Lurgan. Will you please tell her this? By the way, you say "Suffolk" in your address, & "Norfolk" in your letter. Gillingham's in both shires, maybe. I, too, am married, & have three children. My old love to the child of a very scholarly & lovable father.

Ever yours,
Sean O'Casey

[1] Mrs. Grace McCormick, one of the daughters of the Rev. Edward M. Griffin, rector of St. Barnabas Church, Dublin, was then married to a Church of England clergyman and living in Gillingham, Suffolk.

[2] *Pictures in the Hallway.*

To Irish Freedom

APRIL 1942

Correspondence

In his most interesting article on the origin of the Irish Republican colours in February's issue of "Irish Freedom," [1] Mr. T. A. Jackson seems to have made one mistake by attributing the revival of these colours as an Irish emblem to Padruig Pearse and Jim Connolly.

[1] T. A. Jackson, "The Green, White, and Orange," *Irish Freedom,* February 1942. A cordial letter of reply from Jackson appeared in the April issue along with O'Casey's letter.

Green, white and orange badges were worn by Republican Committees and Stewards at all National Concerts and Anniversaries under Republican Club control, years before Jim Connolly or Padruig Pearse came into intimate touch with the Republican Movement, and I, at a meeting of the '98 Memorial Committee pointed out that these badges were made of imported satin, and caused the material used to be changed to Irish poplin.

The Republican flag was carried in the processions to Bodenstown, and saluted at a point in the Sallins Road by marching contingents. One of these demonstrations, particularly that part of saluting the flag—was filmed by a Mr. Jamieson, who used the Round Room of the Rotunda as a cinema, and this film was attended by crowded houses.

This was well before either of the two mentioned Leaders identified themselves fully with the I.R.B. The badges, I think, were sold to all members at threepence each. In point of fact, when Jim Connolly took over the I.C.A., the flag he had hoisted over Liberty Hall was not the green, white and orange tricolour, but the conventional green flag of an earlier Irish nationalism.

Sean O'Casey

3 March 1942

To Brian O'Nolan [1]

TS. O'NOLAN

TOTNES, DEVON

2 APRIL 1942

Dear Brian O'Nolan:
Many thanks go to you from me for sending me a copy of your Beal Bocht.[2] Lots of things come my way, loudly or silently calling for a good word (though I seriously declare before God my word is no more

[1] Brian O'Nolan (1912–66), novelist, playwright, columnist, who wrote under the pseudonyms of Flann O'Brien and Myles na gCopaleen (the latter from a character in Dion Boucicault's *The Colleen Bawn*, 1860). As Flann O'Brien, he wrote the novels *At Swim-Two-Birds* (1939), *The Hard Life* (1961), *The Dalkey Archive* (1965), and *The Third Policeman* (1967). As Myles na gCopaleen, he wrote *An Béal Bocht* (1941); *Faustus Kelly,* a play produced at the Abbey Theatre on 25 January 1943; and his popular satiric column "Cruiskeen Lawn" (the title of a well-known song in *The Colleen Bawn*) in the *Irish Times,* collected in *The Best of Myles* (1968).

[2] Myles na gCopaleen, *An Béal Bocht* (1941), a satiric novel which mocks the Irish-language enthusiasts. Translated into English by Patrick C. Power as *The Poor Mouth* (1973).

than the opinion of an intelligent man), and rarely deserving one (in my opinion); but yours is a happy exception; though, I'm sure, many in Chorca Dorcha [3] wont say the same. There is, I think, the swish of Swift's scorn in it, bred well into the genial laughter of Mark Twain. It is well that we Gaels should come to learn that Gaels do not live by Gaelic alone, though, of course, no Gael can really live without it. The birth of the boy is well done, his home and all that therein is—a vicious bite at the hand that never fed it; with the Sean Duine Liath in the middle of the moil, a Gaelic Polonius, with his creed of "As it was in the beginning, is now, and ever shall be": the reek of the Penal Laws and all that followed them, over the lot. The chapter on the coming and going of the Gaedhilgeoiri [4] is delightful, and the Feis [5] that followed grand. How often have I seen and sensed things similar! The scene and the description of the scene where the young man stands to watch the sea, on page 62, is fine. I like your book immensely.

I often read your column in the Irish Times. By the way, I'm not sure you're right in saying there's not a line of Literature in anything written by O'Leary. [6] It must be thirty years, and more, since I read Seadhna, but I seem to have a recollection of a fine description of the playing of the Union Pipes; but, generally speaking, you're right. In spite of O'Leary's lovely Irish, he wasnt much; and Niamh was pretty bad. But better than Edgar Wallace who, I see, is cracked up by Roddy the Rover [7]—whoever he may be—. A "writer of best-sellers, not best-smellers," says Roddy. I think the same boyo said some time ago that a street fiddler did better work than those who stand high in musical creation. Maybe he's right; though I dont think he is.

Anyway, thanks again for sending me your cleverly written book. I wish it every success.

Yours sincerely,
Sean O'Casey

[3] The name of the imaginary Irish-speaking village in the novel.
[4] The Irish-language enthusiasts.
[5] Festival.
[6] See O'Casey's letter to Jack Carney, 2 March 1942, note 2.
[7] Aodh de Blacam (1890–1951), Irish journalist and author, editor of the *Standard* in the 1930s, and writer of a regular column in the *Irish Press* under the pseudonym of Roddy the Rover. See O'Casey's comments on him in his letter to Gabriel Fallon, 11 September 1930, note 2, Vol. I, p. 420.

To George Jean Nathan

MS. CORNELL

TOTNES, DEVON

3 APRIL 1942

My very dear George:

I've sent, first, the 1st & 2nd acts of "Red Roses For Me," &, a week later, the 3rd & 4th acts to Dick [Madden]. They were (as usual) badly typed. He will, probably, get a few copies done fairly, & I've asked him to let you have a copy when he gets it. As I said before, it makes a breach in the Canons of deprecation in your article on us Irish in your recent book.

The article "In This Tent, Saroyan" [1] is a grand one; a really unique tribute to a Dramatist. I hope he'll go on getting more from you; for such as he are bound to be scarce. I only wish the younger Irish would read your article. G. J. N. doesn't get to them. I wonder could it go into what is called "The Irish Digest"? If it could, a lot of them would read it; & be able to benefit by the warning as I have done.

I don't think the subject of the Church has really been squeezed dry yet. At present there's a P.P. being tried for murder. He tried to get a man sacked from his job for leading an immoral life, by living with a woman he wasn't married to; & when he didn't succeed, drew out & gave him a skelp that sent him so to the ground that his skull was crushed.[2] I have a bit I wrote about another incident, meant for Purple Dust, but kept out of it, because it didn't suit there; but I hope to use it in another play.

Bad luck about Eddie Dowling. I do hope he soon gets well again. It's years since I heard from you—but the book came, & that answers a lot of questions, in a lovely way, too.

I'm afraid I've given Dick a lot of trouble for nothing. I daresay, he gets less out of me than any other Dramatist. He is a very kind & lovable man.

I hope "Pictures in the Hallway" came safe to you.

Ever yours with love.
Sean

[1] George Jean Nathan, "And in This Tent, William Saroyan," Chapter III in *The Entertainment of a Nation.*

[2] O'Casey used this incident in *Cock-a-Doodle Dandy* (1949) at the end of Scene II when Father Domineer strikes and accidentally kills the Lorry Driver.

To Jack Carney

MS. NYU LIBRARY

[TOTNES, DEVON]

9 APRIL 1942

My dear Jack:

Rain everywhere here, too; Dart flooding the fields & creeping nearer to the houses ajaycent. And a thick wind blowing. Nice Spring Devon weather. Thanks for the papers, & the terror shown by anyone thinking of keeping a theatre open during Holy Week. "People will have to learn that they live in a Christian City," well the mountains around it may be called delectable—but a Christian City—well, we know our own know about that.

Thanks, too, for the cutting about "End of the Beginning." [1] I've had a bit of bad luck—& so has [Eddie] Dowling—about the production. Dick Madden, my agent, writing on the 19th March—I got the letter more than a week ago—says, "Plays were given four performances in all, ending in Princeton, N.J., then they were to do Boston for a week; & then come to the Booth Theatre, New York. Unfortunately, Dowling was taken severely sick, & had to abandon the whole venture. The company got 2 weeks salary, & were disbanded." Well, I get $100.00 out of it anyway. And I hope for better fortune next time. My new play, 2 acts 3 weeks ago, & the last 2, last week, are on their way to the U.S.A. I hope. And I do hope they'll get there!

I sympathise with you listening to the Dublin man telling you that "this is the position." Quite a lot of people know the position of most things. Political astronomers. If you get any copy of "Time & Tide," keep an eye out for the correspondence page. I sent in a few remarks on Gwynn's remarks, & he may reply. Particularly the curious remark that "an Arann man was as big a stranger in Dublin as a Welsh-speaking miner would be in London." What a curious thing to say. Of course, it's nonsense.

I forgot to thank you & Mina for the tobacco jar. It looks lovely on the mantlepiece beside the photo of George Jean. By the way, Jack, aren't you gathering a library together? Won't I send back "Curtain Up" to you? I have a book of yours, too, by Wernher; & maybe others that you may remember yourself. Or do you want to wait till you have a place of your own?

---

[1] The ill-fated production *Life, Laughter, and Tears,* a triple bill of O'Casey's *The End of the Beginning* and William Saroyan's *Coming through the Rye* and *Hello Out There,* presented by Eddie Dowling, with Eddie Dowling and Julie Haydon, directed by Schuyler Watts, was performed at the McCarter Theatre in Princeton, N.J., on 28 February 1942. It had previously opened at the Court Square Theatre, Springfield, Mass., on 25 February. See also O'Casey's letter to George Jean Nathan, 2 December 1947, note 2.

Eileen & I have been admiring the Dress Mina sent to Shivaun—I've a good eye for clothes—except me own—, & the dressing-gown with the really charming coloured fringe on the belt ends. Mina has very fine taste.

I've read Nolan's "Beul Bocht," & it's not going to please a lot of people. Risteard O'Foley has already gone for it. I think it curious and clever; a blend of Dean Swift with Mark Twain; but a savage onslaught on the romantic conception of the Gaeltacht, its poverty, its dirt, & its glamour—to all who haven't to live there. I've written to the author thanking him for sending it to me.

Well glory be to God. Niall is learning "Hallelujah! I'm a Bum," & seems to like it.

All the best.
Yours ever
Sean

P.S. 2 more Cruisers gone! Will the dead ever awaken?

To Time and Tide

11 APRIL 1942

Dear Sir:—

While fully appreciating the generous review of PICTURES IN THE HALLWAY by Mr. Gwynn,[1] will you give me room for a few remarks? His "Sean O'Casey is a Protestant," should be "was a Protestant," for like an ancient Gaelic bard, I have to say "I'm neither a Protestant nor a Papist now." "Uncle Tom" was not an infantryman, but a horse-soldier, not a Dublin Fusilier, but a dragoon; and it was he who was "high in the Orange Order," a Purple man, and not his warder friend. When he says that "O'Casey is often coarser in his utterance than Dublin workingmen generally permit themselves to be," he is asserting an elegant ignorance. They can be just as coarse as Shakespeare. His remark that "an Aran man would be just as much a stranger in Dublin as a Welsh-speaking miner in London," is astonishing. The comparison is, indeed, an odious one. It isnt so at all. I myself, thirty-five years ago, have jumped about the rocks at the base of the Howth cliffs, snatching at edible Slat Mhara [2] with an Aran man, Michael MacRuary, then gardener to Padraic Pearse; two Aran men were in my hurling club, the Ard Chraobh,[3] and so far from being strangers, they were sought for because of their fine Irish; and, lastly, when I was

[1] Stephen Gwynn, *Time and Tide,* 28 March 1942.
[2] Seaweed.
[3] The high or central branch of the Gaelic League.

down and out, and had no place to go to, it was an Aran man who shared his room with me till things improved.[4] No Aran man could be lonely in Dublin city. And, as far as I know, Liam O'Flaherty [5] never felt himself to be a stranger in Dublin either.

I am, Yours etc.,
Sean O'Casey

Devon

[4] O'Casey shared a room at 35 Mountjoy Square in 1920 with Micheál Ó Maolain (Michael Mullen), the Gaelic-speaking Aran Islander who became the model for Seamus Shields in *The Shadow of a Gunman* (1923). See O'Casey's letter to Ó Maolain, 17 December 1945.

[5] Liam O'Flaherty (1897–), the novelist, was born on the Aran Islands in a Gaelic-speaking community.

To Francis MacManus [1]

MS. MacManus

Totnes, Devon

12 April 1942

Dear Frank,

A greeting to you. I've seen you have had "a few words" with Frank O'Connor [2]—or was it Sean O'Faolain? I can rarely extinguish between the two—over poetry and literature in general. Well, it's a good sign when men have even life to argue. I thought your poem had some rough life in it somewhere—but I'm no judge of these things. But I don't think you should be so scornful of the hob-nailed boot and the black porter, or the sweat on a man's body after a dance.[3] Maybe this remark has a personal

[1] Francis MacManus (1909–65), was a writer of novels, short stories, biographies, history, as well as a school teacher, until he became Director of Talks and Features at Radio Eireann in 1947, a post he held until his death. O'Casey had met him in Dublin in September 1935.

[2] A poem by MacManus, "Pattern of Saint Brendan," had appeared in the *Irish Times,* 21 February 1942, and was attacked in a letter by Frank O'Connor, *Irish Times,* 25 February. MacManus replied on 28 February, and O'Connor on 3 March.

[3] O'Casey alludes to the following lines in MacManus's poem, which had offended O'Connor:

> This is the evening. The bleat of melodeons
> buckleaps fandangos and whips
> up the hobnails to belt at the floorboards.
> Thirst gravels the gullet; lads with puffed faces
> muster a yowl for slopped foamy porter
> and grope for the pence in fist-hoarded purses.

In his 25 February letter, O'Connor had said of these lines: "That reminds me inevitably of a head-hunter of Borneo who has lighted upon a shipwrecked cargo of Woolworth's best jewellery."

reason; for when I danced, & I danced often and danced long, I always had on a pair of hob-nailed boots. They were the only ones fit to work in; & the money didn't run to the buying of a more elegant pair for a dance. And is black porter any worse than golden wine? Are we to condemn a thing because it is the thing beloved by the poor? I must say, I don't like the taste of it myself, having had but one—no two—bottles of stout in my life; but, then, I don't care for the taste of wine, either. I haven't heard from Gaby for a long time. Macmillan's sent him a copy of my last book, which I hope came to him safely. I hope he, Rose, & the family are well. We are all—you there, & we here—are going through a tough time of it; & God knows what'll be the outcome of it all. So do I know; or, believe I do: the burning of hay, & straw & stubble, leaving lasting things free to live.

Anyway, greetings to you; & every good wish to you in your everyday life.

Affectionately yours,
Sean O'Casey

To Jack Carney

MS. NYU LIBRARY

[TOTNES, DEVON]
18 APRIL 1942

My dear Jack,

No, I don't want "Time & Tide" that has my little letter in it; but I should be obliged if you kept an eye out for a possible reply. The Aran man who, with me, jumped about the rocks on Beann Edair beach was oul' Miċeal MacRuary, Pearse's gardener in Scoil Éanna. The Aran man who gave me a shake-down in his room was Micheal O'Maolain (Mick Mullin),[1] who, to this day, calls himself "Miċeal O'Maolain, as Arrainn," M. O'Maolain out of Aran. Bill O'Brien's right this time—[Francis] Cruise O'Brien was always Cruise O'Brien. I've never known a Brien yet who hadn't an O. W. O'Brien, M.P. Johnston, Mooney, & O'Brien. Barrie O'Brien, who wrote Parnell's Life. The Bryan or Breen form, yes; but never the Brien form.

I've written an article for "I. Freedom": "Empty Vessels,"[2] complaining of the Socialists & Communists indifference to Literature. "I.

---

[1] See O'Casey's letter to Micheál Ó Maolain (Michael Mullen), 17 December 1945.

[2] "Empty Vessels," *Irish Freedom*, May 1942; reprinted in *Blasts and Benedictions* (1967), ed. Ronald Ayling.

Freedom" asked me to write on "The Trend of Irish Literature"—whatever that may be; but, I may do that later. Also a message to Council of Action for a May Day number. Owen Sheehy-Skeffington [3] asked me to do it. I doubt that it will pass the Censor.

And thank you for the cake. And thank Mina for me for the cake—which seems to be a Dublin way of sayin' it. My love to Breon.

And all the best, oul' Swaddy. Know what "Swaddy" means? [4]

Yours as Ever,
Sean

[3] Owen Lancelot Sheehy-Skeffington (1909–70), son of Francis and Hanna Sheehy-Skeffington; nephew of Francis Cruise O'Brien, father of Conor Cruise O'Brien; member of the Irish Senate for sixteen years; lecturer and reader in French at Trinity College, Dublin, for thirty-five years, having followed Samuel Beckett in the post as lecturer in 1935. O'Casey wrote many letters to him for over thirty years, but so far only one has been found—that of 22 July 1961, Vol. III. For further information about him, see the news story about O'Casey's public debate with Mrs. Hanna Sheehy-Skeffington on the riots at the Abbey Theatre over *The Plough and the Stars,* in the *Irish Independent,* 2 March 1926, note 2, Vol. I, p. 179.

[4] See O'Casey's letter to Carney, 8 May 1942.

To George Jean Nathan

TS. CORNELL

TOTNES, DEVON
18 APRIL 1942

My very dear George:

I have written to you several times about your last book which came safely, as did, also, the volume of Irish Plays issued by Random House.

Some time ago, I sent on to Dick [Madden] the four acts of a new play—RED ROSES FOR ME—two acts under one cover, and the other two under another, a week or so later. I asked him when they came, and he had them typed in a sensible manner, to let you have a look at it. I didn't like to send you a thing so badly done; typed, that is, not the material and spiritual content of the play. I had the whole play roughly typed, and half of it done for the third and last time, before I got your book holding forth on THE CONTRIBUTION OF THE IRISH. The play is built in a wholly new way on a theme sent many years ago to the Abbey Theatre by the name of THE HARVEST FESTIVAL. [1] Of course, there was little or nothing then to the play; though I think this one isn't bad. Everything—

[1] See the Abbey Theatre's critique of *The Harvest Festival,* 26 January 1920, Vol. I, pp. 91–92.

almost—you criticise in your chapter is in the play of mine, though the Clergyman doesn't happen to be either a Canon or a Catholic. And there is no drunken sponger in it either; and the ingenue has an important part in the play, I think even an integral part; and the miracle isn't a miracle at all; and, I think, the "mysticism" flows naturally from the characters in the play—by God, George, I seem to be making a rare defence of myself!

The Arts Theatre Club in London—a group to be run on the system of your Group Theatre, though, I fear, not so cleverly, has asked me for PURPLE DUST. I have—today—sent a note of refusal, on the chance of the play being done, maybe next season in New York. Anyway, I'm not very sure, much less enthusiastic, about them; and so I have refused without any regrets.

By the way, George, if you happen to like the new play, and Dick succeeds in getting a backer, I imagine it would be better held back till the Fall. On account of the delay in the appearance of PURPLE DUST, Dick might try to get it on as soon as possible. If it's done at all, it will take some planning; though, of course, nothing like that of WITHIN THE GATES.

I hope you are well, and that you'll take a fine holiday. My love to Carlotta and Eugene. My love to you.

Ever yours,
Sean

To Daniel Macmillan

T.S. MACMILLAN LONDON

TOTNES, DEVON
21 APRIL 1942

Dear Mr. Daniel:
I'm sorry you dont know about T. Rokotov. My God! what have the Society of Cultural Relations with the USSR been doing? One would have imagined they'd have made every British Publisher known to International Literature. Rokotov isnt a Publisher. He is Editor of the International Literature Magazine, published in Moscow by the USSR Government, published in English, Russian, and, I think, in French and German—or used to be published in those languages. He is also a fine critic of literature, the kinema, and the drama. He doesnt want the books to translate them into corresponding Russian volumes, but to keep pace with International literature; to review them; and to quote from them in Russian Magazines. He had this done to "I Knock at the Door." They also published part

of "The Star Turns Red." I enclose two examples of letters sent to, and received from, the USSR, which may give you an idea of the way I was in touch with Moscow; also two copies of the I. Magazine—English Edition. The Russian equivalent is much bigger, usually. They rarely reprint—never to my knowledge—plays, stories, or anything else without the Author's permission; and, I think, pay for what is published, though this is, I believe, contrary to the general law. They are passionately interested in what is being written here and in Ireland; and I have written for the Russian Edition of I. Magazine a long article on Irish Literature,[1] beginning with the Gaelic writers, and going on to Yeats and the contemporary names in Irish Literature. They are also intensely devoted to drama, and the enclosed copy—special Shakespeare number—of Sovietland will, maybe, give you an idea of how much they are interested in things theatrical. Without knowing much about it, I'd suggest that the Publishers' Association should keep their eye on the USSR; get into touch with Mr Rokotov, for, when this terrible war is over, the USSR may be a wide field for literary activities. My connection with Messrs Rokotov and Apletin have been going on now for a long time, and I'm sure their one purpose is to make the Russian People acquainted with what is going on here in the world of literature and the drama.

With all good personal wishes,
Yours sincerely,
Sean O'Casey

Thank you very much for sending a copy of "Pictures in the Hallway" to Mr. Rokotov.[2]

[1] O'Casey's article first appeared in a Russian translation as "Literatura v Irlandii" in *Internatsional'naya Literatura,* December 1939. It is reprinted in a fuller version in English as "Literature in Ireland" in *Blasts and Benedictions* (1967).
[2] Added in longhand.

To Sunday Times

26 APRIL 1942

The New Challenge

Dear Sir: Mr. Agate was in so much of a hurry to say what he was eager to say that he didnt ask Mr. Clunes if permission had been given to put

PURPLE DUST in his programme.[1] It hadnt then; and it hasnt now. An unsigned letter was sent me saying it was down for production, to which a polite answer of refusal was written; but before this was sent, another letter from Mr. Clunes told of Mr. Agate hurrying off to write about the new venture, so the polite note was changed to a curt telegram refusing permission to perform my play. So O'Casey leaves Mr. Agate free in his desperation to fly here and fly there to revel in great drama; or to lie down at rest and in peace with his own dear Ego. I suggest to the New Challengers that they open their venture with Pinero's LETTY, or with Mr. Agate's own "Jack Hughes." [2]

Yours sincerely,
Sean O'Casey

[1] In an article titled "A New Challenge," *Sunday Times,* 19 April 1942, James Agate announced that Alec Clunes had formed a New Arts Theatre Group, and indicated his displeasure over the report that Clunes intended to open his season with *Purple Dust.*

[2] A jesting reference to Agate's play about the Dreyfus case, *I Accuse* (*'J'accuse'*), adapted from the German of Hans Rehfisch and Wilhelm Herzog, produced on 25 October 1937 at the "Q" Theatre.

To Irish Freedom

MAY 1942

"I.R.B. and the Flag" [1]

It was I who changed Mr. Jackson's name to Wilson. I had mislaid *Irish Freedom,* and had to rely on memory, which, for the thousandth time, failed me. I think P. H. Pearse came into the I.R.B. rather later on; for there was a feeling of doubt about him because of his support of the big Home Rule meeting held in Dublin in 1912. Pearse, of course, in his great heart, was always an I.R.B. man. He was a great deal more than that, too: He was an artist as he showed in the creation of the pageant, Tain Bo Cuailgne, performed in Jones's Road in, I think, 1913: [2] more than an artist, even, for he was a great humanist, stretching out his deep affection for all men. His execution was a sad loss to Ireland. But, for some time, there was an I.R.B. doubt about him. So was there a doubt

[1] A reply to T. A. Jackson's letter, *Irish Freedom,* April 1942. The May issue also contained an article by O'Casey, "Empty Vessels," on the failure of Socialists to be concerned about literature, reprinted in *Blasts and Benedictions* (1967).

[2] See O'Casey's report on Pearse's pageant, "The Irish Fete in Jones's Road," *Irish Worker,* 7 June 1913, Vol. I, pp. 27–28.

about Sean Connolly [3] because, for religious reasons, he wouldnt join the I.R.B. I had many an argument before he was invited to appear on the stage at National Celebrations; but when he did appear, he charmed everyone with his "The Men From God Knows Where"; and "Paudh O'Donohoe." He was, I think, a natural actor, and one of the handsomest and truest young Irishmen then living. He, too, was a sad loss to Ireland. I'm afraid I must, most amiably, disagree with Mr. Jackson on the question of the Flag. The Republican Flag was prominent long before either P. H. Pearse or Jim Connolly became active in the National political movement. The point, of course, is of very little importance; but it is interesting. Personally, from an aesthetic point of view, I dont like the flag. The rising sun on a green field, however sentimental the symbol may have become, is a finer conception than the three horizontal stripes; and, in the dim ages of the past, must have been connected with the worship of the sun. A finer conception, too, was the flag of the Irish Citizen Army, the Plough and the Stars. Indeed, I hope, some day, that this banner, like the Soviet Hammer and Sickle, will become the National banner of a united Ireland. I assure Mr. Jackson that his remarks on these things interest me greatly, and I send him my warm regards which I trust he will be good enough to take from me.

Sean O'Casey

6 April 1942

[3] Sean Connolly, actor and nationalist, who was killed in the 1916 Easter Rising. See Mrs. Hanna Sheehy-Skeffington's letter to the *Irish Independent,* 15 February 1926, Vol. I, pp. 167–68.

To Puck's Fare [1]

MAY 1942

"Still More Ideals . . ."

There is no such thing (that I know of) as an ideal play and an ideal caste. All fine plays are ideal and all fine actors are ideal—that is all there is about it, in my opinion.

There is such a thing as an ideal theatre in a particular sense, having a good stage, lighting, and auditorium—an ideal that neither Dublin nor London knows yet. There is, I suppose, such a thing as an ideal theatre in a general sense, one producing only plays worth producing, and having a

[1] The editor of this Dublin magazine, which appeared for only one issue, had asked O'Casey to comment on his "ideal play and ideal cast."

fine acting group, each having a vocation for his or her work. Such a one was the Moscow Art Theatre, and there are now many such in the U.S.S.R., with the one drawback that the plays are by no means as good as they could and should be.

Every city and town should aim at having at least one such theatre to its credit: that would be an immense step forward.

Sean O'Casey

By James Agate [1]

3 MAY 1942
Sunday Times

MR O'CASEY: A REPLY [2]
By James Agate

"I suggest to the New Challengers that they open their venture with Pinero's 'Letty' or with Mr. Agate's own 'Jack Hughes.'" Mr. O'Casey has asked for it, and Mr. O'Casey shall have it. On his own ground. I Jack Hughes him of overweening vanity and, in his letter last week to the Editor of this paper, underweening courtesy. I Jack Hughes him of being so desperately afraid of the SUNDAY TIMES standard of criticism that he must fly to the telegraph to prevent production. Lastly, I Jack Hughes him of making a pun half of which seems to have dropped into the Irish Sea.

"What is the reason that you use me thus? I loved you ever," says Hamlet to Laertes. Why should Mr. O'Casey misuse a critic who has loved his work ever since a November evening at the Royalty Theatre in the year 1925? The critic who wrote " 'Juno and the Paycock' is as much tragedy as 'Macbeth,' but it is a tragedy taking place in the porter's family." [3] Who, about "The Plough and the Stars" wrote, "Mr. O'Casey has done what Balzac and Dickens did." [4] Who said, apropos of "The Silver Tassie," "This author's dramatic sense sticks out like a bull's-eye on a target." But held that the second act didn't quite come off. "The trouble, I imagine, is Mr. O'Casey's

[1] James Agate (1877–1947), drama critic of the *Sunday Times*, 1923-47. See his controversies with O'Casey in *The Flying Wasp* (1937); see also Vol. I.
[2] A reply to O'Casey's letter, "The New Challenge," *Sunday Times*, 26 April 1942.
[3] James Agate, *Sunday Times*, 22 November 1925; reprinted in *Sean O'Casey: Modern Judgments* (1969), ed. Ronald Ayling.
[4] James Agate, *Sunday Times*, 16 May 1926; reprinted in *Sean O'Casey: Modern Judgments*.

failure to be a great poet." [5] Who regretfully noted that "a dramatist who can write all kinds of great stuff, from the scrumptious-majestic to the overheard bar-parlour should in 'Within the Gates' give his characters nothing except groans, moans, grunts, sneers, snarls, yells of rage and whoops of despair." [6] Six years later finds the critic still pursuing Mr. O'Casey, this time into the fastnesses of Camden Town, where a company of amateurs produces "The Star Turns Red." He writes: "A masterpiece." [7]

Now what does Mr. O'Casey want? Is he like that *diva* before whom Berlioz imagines some critic bowing low and stammering: "Your voice has the sublimity of the Heavenly Choir. Your trill is more amazing than the sun. Saturn's ring is unworthy to crown your head. Before you humanity can but prostrate itself; deign at least that it embraces your feet." In reply to which poverty-stricken meed the singer shrugs her beautiful shoulders and says "Qu'est-ce qu'il me chante, cet imbécile?" Is the model Wordsworth, who, according to Miss Mitford, demanded that his admirers should be "admirers *en masse*—all, every page, every line, every word, every comma; to admire nothing else, and to admire all day long." Must every word about Mr. O'Casey be jam scooped out of a silver tassie with a golden spoon?

This distinguished dramatist has thought fit to sneer at a play which brought to the stage, integrally and textually, burning speeches made at the trial of Dreyfus by Zola, Jaurès, Clemenceau and Anatole France on behalf of freedom of the mind. If Mr. O'Casey's "Purple Dust" had contained any passages as worthy of to-day as those dead yet living speeches were worthy of yesterday I should have encouraged Mr. Alec Clunes to stage his play. But it does not, and I hold that this is not the moment to produce a witless lampoon at the expense of the English, too busy fighting for freedom to answer back. I have done my duty faithfully by the drama of Mr. O'Casey at its best. I shall do it faithfully by that drama at its poorest. It may interest Mr. O'Casey to know that before Mr. Clunes received his "curt telegram" he got from me one even curter. It ran: "Purple Dust all dust and no purple stop leave alone stop."

[5] James Agate, *Sunday Times,* 13 October 1929.
[6] James Agate, "Beyond the Agates," *Sunday Times,* 11 February 1934, Vol. I, pp. 492–96.
[7] James Agate, "A Masterpiece," *Sunday Times,* 17 March 1940, Vol. I, pp. 849–51.

To George Jean Nathan

MS. CORNELL

TOTNES, DEVON

5 MAY 1942

My dear George:

Dick has cabled saying he got the 4 acts of the new play safely, also, by the time you get this, you may have read it. I hope, of course, you may like it. I enclose cutting (2) showing what Agate thinks of PURPLE DUST, and a copy of what I have said to him. It may interest you. He has lost his temper, and, I think, a critic, above all others shouldn't do that. He makes a bumball of patriotism to shy at me; and unfurls the banner of the higher criticism of the SUNDAY TIMES. And, at the same time, he seems to think that fine speeches by Clemenceau, Anatole France, Zola, and Jaures make a play. Curious example of higher criticism. "Jack Hughes" is a corruption of a play called *J'Accuse* which he wrote himself, and which had a tryout in a suburban theatre here called the Kew, or "Q." You may have heard of it. Anyway the main point is that this Group were determined to do the play, and had a lot already done (selection of cast), without my knowledge, and went very angry because I wouldn't let them go on with it. They would have, I think, given as bad a performance as that given to WITHIN THE GATES, and that was pretty terrible. We have had a few uncomfortable nights here. Hundreds of incendiaries, and a few high explosives, one of which shattered a row of houses a little up the road. One of our windows was blown in, and the ceiling fell from the garage. I was afraid we'd have to bring our first-aid equipment into use; but, fortunately, all passed off without injury, though our seven year old boy was a little frightened—and so was the sixty year old boy, too, I can tell you. I was working at a new part of the biography, but since then, I've found it hard to get back to the old concentration; but I daresay it'll come allright again soon. I have to do a bit of work about the house and garden too; but that cant be helped; and only wish I was fit to do more.

Ever Yours, my love.

Sean

To Jack Carney

TS. NYU Library

[Totnes, Devon]
8 May 1942

My dear Jack:

Thanks for the papers, and the cutting containing Mr Agate's coup de grace to your friend. I wanted to keep my copy, and yours has already gone on its way to George Jean Nathan so that he may share in the fun. Agate wrote a play called "J'Accuse" [1] which appeared in the "Q" [Theatre], and never appeared anywhere else. That was the play, under the alias of Jack Hughes I suggested should be given as a first offering by the T[heatre] Arts Group. I'm convinced "the old boy" as Alec Clunes calls him, guessed they hadn't told me, and was burning, like a good-hearted Englishman, to have a rap at one who dared to criticise a couple of them. All merry to laugh at the criticism of the Irish, but the English—no, no sir. Stoke and Poges must have stung him badly.[2] I'm the only wan able to get him into a Paddy, and make a patriot of him. "England fighting for freedom, me man, and unable to answer back," [3] and he answering back for all he was worth. And he thinking that magnificent speeches by Clemenceau, Zola, Anatole France, and Jaures made a play. A book of recitations, right enough, but not a play. But there's the higher criticism for you. Next, I'll be writing a play made of the "Speeches from the Dock." I have sent a short reply, for I'm too busy to spend much time on the withered mind of Agate; but, by the way, him calling "The Star Turns Red" a masterpiece shows him down; it isn't anything like one; I wish it were. It has a fine third scene, and good bits, here and there; but a masterpiece—no. However, let him find out that for himself: I'll argue with him, but I'm not going to educate him.

£1500 isn't much when you say it quick. Where in the name o'God, would you get that sum, may I ask? You'd hardly get that now, if you robbed a bank. They don't know much over there in Eirinn. They think too I make a fortune out of every book I get published. Owen Sheehy-Skeffington wrote to say he got my message for Action only on the sixth of May, though the postmark showed it had been posted on the 11th of April; so it wasn't in time, even for reading from the platform. He says it's sickening; but you and I know those things well, and it doesn't make us turn a hair. Rokotov has cabled again for more books, and "articles by English Dramatists on the war." He wants them sent by airmail. Who are the Eng dramatists writing on the war? Hard to get as that £1500. A few of them are horning in on what they think the people will like; and the rest of the stage is full up

---

[1] See O'Casey's letter to the *Sunday Times,* 26 April 1942, note 2.
[2] The satirized Englishmen in *Purple Dust* (1940).
[3] See Agate's reply to O'Casey, *Sunday Times,* 3 May 1942, reprinted above.

with silly musicals, or sillier plays. Moscow doesn't know London. He has cabled me £14.0.8. to spur me on. I'll write to J. B. Priestley to see if he couldn't send some of what he has written; and, maybe, Shaw and P. V. Carroll would send something, too, though they don't stretch into English dramatists. I'm glad you like Breon; he's a fine fellow, though a bit shy. I think after this war, more than Wilno will go to the USSR; probably the whole of Poland—another family of the S.S. Union. Niall was a bit frightened with the bombing, but he's a young boy—I may say that the old boy was a wee bit frightened too. Eileen was calm and steady; but I'm not such stuff as hayros are made on. No wrapping of a flag round me. It's a rotten way to be, but there it is.

Love to Mina and to you. Swaddy?
Sean

Isn't "Swaddy" the way Indians say "Soldier"? [4] How close it is to the Gaelic Sodger. The Sanscrit is close to the Gaelic.

Yours, Mr. Sean O'Casey, D.D.C.L.
F.R.S.L. Ack. Ack.

PPS. Righto. Mums the word about WH. I don't want her fluttering near me, like a wooden butterfly. I hope Peter Newmark won't prove to be a nuisance—two visits a week is going it strong. I shouldn't worry about that £1500. Neither you nor I could give, beg, borrow, or steal it, & that's the end o't.

So that's what "The New Republic" thinks of "P. in the Hallway"! [5] Et tu Brute! Well, I'll have to do better next time, wid the help o' God.

Ever yours, Sean

[4] This sentence and everything that follows were added in longhand.
[5] James Stern's review in the *New Republic,* 30 March 1942.

To Mrs. Grace McCormick

MS. McCORMICK [1]

TOTNES, DEVON
9 MAY 1942

My dear Mrs McCormick—who used to be Grace—, here's a copy of "Pictures in the Hallway" for you. We have two boys—one fourteen, the other seven; & one girl two years & eight months old; all three sturdy & vigorous. They may be a blessing, but, my dear Grace, they are a pretty

[1] Postcard.

heavy responsibility these times, especially to one who has fought most of his life for a children's charter. Think of Charlie—what a small boy he was when I knew him!—having four of his kind now. Give him my love, born out of my love for his father. My love to you, & affectionate remembrance.

Sean O'Casey

P.S. I loved your dear mother, too.

To Sunday Times

10 MAY 1942

Mr. Agate: A Curt Reply [1]

Dear Sir:—

If it wasn't for overweening vanity, after Mr. Agate's terrible deenoomong, I'd spend the rest of my days telling my beads; but, God forgive me, in the midst of a chill of trembling, I see a funny picture of Mr. Agate running for shelter to the Union Jack to save his critical face from critical scars. He finds discourtesy everywhere, save in the handling of a play of mine, and the public declaration of its early production without my knowledge or consent, by the New Arts Theatre Group.

If he thinks Stoke and Poges (though Poges isn't such a bad fellow) to be types of Englishmen, then he doesn't know much about his people. They aren't, I hope, typical even of the small class they belong to; though they may be of those in Mr. Agate's own little world. Certainly not in that of mine, textile, building, engineering, fire, shop, shipyard, and transport workers. If he shirks the show of them making fat profits out of national danger, then I remind him some are in jail for this, and many have been heavily fined for it; and as for the sanctity of shares, let him read what his own Dickens thinks of shares written down in the tenth chapter of his "Our Mutual Friend."

Mr. Agate seems to think that the word "curt" necessarily means rude: it doesn't (I wish he knew English as well as he says he knows French). Mr. Agate's following me about, even up to Camden Town, has nothing to do with my objection to the publication of a production of a play of mine, without my knowledge. If "Jack Hughes" be a play due to the collaboration of Zola, Clemenceau, Jaures, and Anatole France, and I

---

[1] A response to James Agate's "Mr. O'Casey: A Reply," *Sunday Times,* 3 May 1942, reprinted above.

do not doubt his word, then what finer firstling of the flock could be offered on the altar of The Arts Theatre Group? Finally, Mr. Agate "Jack Hughes" me of being "desperately afraid of the *Sunday Times* standard of criticism," meaning, I daresay, its standard of Dramatic Criticism. I'll not say a word about that—there it is, and there I'll leave it.

Totnes.

Sean O'Casey

Mr. Agate writes:

I was not responsible for what turned out to be the premature announcement of Mr. O'Casey's play. I wrote in strict accordance with the letter of my information that Mr. Clunes "hoped to start off with" "Purple Dust." In the matter of English Mr. O'Casey has only to consult Webster's Dictionary to discover the word "curt" defined as meaning "rudely concise." I agree that "J'Accuse!" would be an admirable choice.

To Sunday Times [1]

TC. O'CASEY

TOTNES, DEVON
11 MAY 1942

Mr. Agate: A Reply.

Dear Sir:

Allow me one or two words more, please. Mr. Agate's dignified statement about writing in accordance with the letter of information given by Mr. Clunes doesn't seem to fit in with what Mr. Clunes wrote to me, saying that, after a conversation, "Mr. Agate dashed straight to the Sunday Times office, bent on mischief."

Mr. Agate says Webster says Curt means Rudely concise. So he does; and says too it means Short, Brief, Condensed. Telegrams are invariably curt, but rarely rude; letters written by Editors rejecting MS. are invariably curt, but rarely rude. The other day I heard an officer giving orders to his Home Guard comrades: each order was curt, but none was rude. In fact a letter that is anything but curt, may be very rude; one very curt, may be coldly polite. There's more in the English language than is dreamt of in even the philosophy of the great Webster.

Yours sincerely,
Sean O'Casey

[1] This letter was refused publication by the editor.

To J. B. Priestley [1]

TS. TEXAS

TOTNES, DEVON
12 MAY 1942

Dear Mr Priestley:

Mr Timofei Rokotov, Editor of The International Magazine, once published in German, French, and Spanish (I think), now in English and Russian, and dealing with the Literature and Art of most Nations, has cabled to me asking for articles on the war that have been written, or may have been written, by English Dramatists. I know that you have given many excellent broadcasts about the life of the people during the war, spiced by some venturous opinions of your own. I am therefore asking you should you have any article you think might interest Moscow, to send it to me; or, if you like, to

Mr T. Rokotov,

Editor, International Literature, Box 527, Moscow. USSR.

He wants these articles sent by airmail; but there's no usual airmail to the USSR, and the only way to get them quick to him is to send them through the Russian Embassy, which, I'm sure would be willing to do this for you. Should you know any other English Dramatist who has written about the war, I should be glad if you could possibly let him know about Mr Rokotov's request. I sincerely hope you yourself will be able to do something for him in this way.

I am,
Yours sincerely,
Sean O'Casey

[1] J. B. Priestley (1894–   ), English novelist, critic, and playwright.

To George Jean Nathan

TS. CORNELL

TOTNES, DEVON

17 MAY 1942

My very dear George:

I got the books of plays sent by Random House, acknowledged in a letter before, and a finely turned out volume it is. No need to say how I feel about your preface; I feel fine, and will do my best to keep it fresh with good work, which is the best thanks to give you.

I am so glad that you liked my new book, "Pictures in the Hallway," and how much rest your fine opinion of it gave to me. I have started notes for a further volume; but I am so much occupied with many things that only God knows when it'll be well on the way. I am working to help bring about a fuller co-operation between us here and the people of the USSR there. The Editor of International Literature, Timofei Rokotov, cabled me some time ago asking for the finer books in English for review in the Russian Edition of the Magazine; but it is very hard to get the publishers here interested. So far Macmillans—a Conservative Firm, is the only one who has replied, and have sent books to Moscow. Rokotov has also cabled for articles on the war written by English dramatists, but, as far as I know, no English dramatists are writing about the war—bar Priestley, who seems, however, to be more interested in forming a new political party. However, one can only go on, and, at any rate, I've written a new song to the tune of "The Green Bushes," which I think you'll like. We are all working and walking in a worried way now—the great white way has given place to the great red way, and it will be, I fear, a long one. I didn't get your Bachelor Life yet; but it may be on its way—sometimes a lot of American mail comes in a rush. I hope it does. You know, I hope, that I got your last grand book on the theatre—I sent several letters to you about it. To keep my head from flying too high, I see James Stern, in the New Republic, has said some stern things.[1] "It is hard to believe that this book, P in the H, has been written by the creator of Jack Boyle and Donal Davoren." Donal Davoren, mind you! "An amateurish, clumsy, broth-of-a-boy book, and a wearisome story of Johnny Casside's adolescense . . . various rather banal and painful experiences reminiscent of D. Copperfield." He's kind enough to say that the chapter "I Strike a Blow" has grand writing, but "the road leading there is monotonous and mighty long in which O'Casey dismally recalls the years." There's me for you! thinking the years recorded grand effort and the will to live. If I ever go to New York again, I'll have to sit at the feet of Stark Young, and learn of the mysteries of the Chekhov

---

[1] James Stern, *New Republic,* 30 March 1942, a review of *Pictures in the Hallway.*

Theatre Studio. Some think that the talk of St. Patrick to the Irish [2] and the Protestant Kid's Idea of the Reformation [3] was got from Finnegans Wake; but I have a recollection of writing the latter fourteen years ago, and of being encouraged to go on by a fellow named G. J. Nathan publishing it eight or nine years ago in THE AMERICAN SPECTATOR; and saying it was good.[4]

Ever yours, with my love.

Sean

[2] The "Exordium Purgatorius Patricius" comic-fantasy passage in "A Coffin Comes to Ireland," the first chapter of *Pictures in the Hallway* (1942).

[3] "The Protestant Kid Thinks of the Reformation," *I Knock at the Door* (1939).

[4] In other words, he wrote the supposedly "Joycean" chapter, "The Protestant Kid Thinks of the Reformation" in 1928 and had it published in Nathan's the *American Spectator* in July 1934, five years before *Finnegans Wake* appeared in 1939.

To Jack Carney

MS. NYU LIBRARY

[TOTNES, DEVON]

20 MAY 1942

My dear Jack:

Thanks again for the papers, & for the notices about "Pictures in the Hallway." I have been compensated for the blasting notice of "The New Republic" by a letter from G. J. Nathan saying: " 'P in the H' is a grand book! I have read it with the highest delight, am enchanted by it, & offer you my congratulations & warmest thanks." So there you are—Ni ha duine 'n a baramhail: Persons are no more numerous than opinions. So the book has been banned in Eirinn.[1] Canon Harry Fletcher [2]—written of in "Death on the Doorstep," has written saying he couldn't get "I Knock at the Door" [3] in The National Library; but was told to "try Trinity." Couldn't be got there, either; but when he said he was mentioned, & should know what had been said about him, he got a loan of it. The National Library, the

[1] Irish newspapers reported in May that the Irish government had seized all copies of *Pictures in the Hallway,* published in March 1942, but the book was not officially "prohibited" by the Censorship of Publications Board until 16 December 1942. The ban was "revoked" on 16 December 1947.

[2] See O'Casey's letter to the Rev. Canon Arthur Henry Fletcher, 1 December 1941, Vol. I, pp. 911–12.

[3] *I Knock at the Door* was "prohibited" by the Censorship of Publications Board on 16 May 1939. The ban was "revoked" on 16 December 1947. See O'Casey's letters to Richard Madden, 6 February 1948, note 2, and to Sylvia O'Brien, 19 December 1952, note 3.

National University, & Trinity afraid of a book! What's Eire comin' to, at all?

I'm quite sure the Vatican is very busy; and it is apparent that they are out to horn in on the bewilderment of war. What a world it would be if we were taught the things of life (this, or, the next one) by the almost illiterate popular Catholic Press. The ignorant buggers banning books not half as bad as Shakespeare or the Holy Bible. Macmillans have already sent books to Moscow; Faber & Faber & Constables are to follow, so that's a beginning. Priestley writes to say that he has already sent articles to the S[oviet]. Press; & that, if he writes another, he'll send it on via the Embassy.

Tom Kelly was a rare old skin; & that's his best epitaph—though he once refused me a pair of boots on the shilling a week plan; didn't trust me, I suppose. I don't blame him. So poor oul' Milenkov's writing still—& is bitterly anti-Soviet—I don't blame him, either. They took everything away from the poor old balls.

We'll have to keep our eyes open for anything dirty played on the USSR. Last Sunday, a Secretary of the Workers Education Association, came to see us—wanted me to "LECTURE." Curse o' God on anything he knew about the Soviet Union, & what he did know, he didn't like. As bloody a little Bourgeois as ever you saw. Didn't like modern education, because Eton & Harrow were bound to remain ever powerful, & so we'd have to adapt ourselves to THEIR ways. The sons were to go into the civil service, & administrative posts, & there seemed to be no further vision in the world. And this a Secretary of the W.E.A.

There I'll leave you, Jack. We'll be seeing you shortly, anyway.

Love to Mina & you.
Ever yours,
Sean

PS. I hope you feel betther, & know more, afther the long talk with the Economist. P.EIP. All plan an' no performance.

To Gabriel Fallon

MS. TEXAS

[TOTNES, DEVON]
23 MAY 1942

My dear Gaby,

Sorry to have hurried you into a 2nd acknowledgment—these things are a nuisance to a busy man, as I know well. I got your letter shortly after

I had sent the card. With yours, I got one from Frank McM[anus], to whom I had written over a literary argument appearing in the Irish Times. The burying of a mother—if she has been anyway decent—is always a sad task. Good job it has to be done only once in a lifetime. It is interesting to hear of your opinion about Carroll's latest.[1] All I have heard from sound an opposite note. I always thought—from S[hadow] & Substance—that there was stuff in Carroll, & Nathan thought highly of that play, & of his "White Steed." "The Strings are False" is shortly to go into rehearsal in New York,[2] & I shall be interested to hear what Nathan has to say about it. Anyway, Carroll, must go his own way, & do his own work, for better or worse, according to what is in him. I'm glad he did well in the Olympia, & I do hope L. D'Alton will do as well after him.[3] I rush to admit that 70 articles per annum's enough for any poor white man. I have heard of W.A.A.M.A.[4] In fact, I am a member of the Writers' Guild of the Association—paid up to the end of the year. By the way, mention to the Sec he needn't bother sending me notices, etc, & so, save time (a lot) and money (a little).

I daresay you are right about Joyce & O'Casey—you know what I mean; but partly wrong, I think. Certainly Finnegans Wake had little to do with me this way. Fourteen years ago, I wrote a thing called "A Protestant Kid Thinks of the Reformation" see "I Knock at the Door"; & four or five years after, a fellow named G. J. Nathan wrote asking an article for "The American Spectator" which he had started. After a while, I thought of "A P. T. of the R." & sent it to him. Back comes a glowing letter of praise from him & the other 4 Editors of the Journal; so I said there's something in that way of writing. But far earlier still, 1908 or so, I wrote an article called "Sound the Loud Trumpets"[5] (an ironical skit on Birrell's Irish Education Bill) for a Gaelic League MS. journal; & got such praise that I sent it to J. P. O'Ryan's Irish Peasant & Nation; & lo & behold, it appeared. It was written in a laughing mocking rush, so that sort of thing must have been in me ab initio. I see by the Irish Times that the book has been banned. And, at the same time, bread is rationed & the trains can hardly move. God doesn't seem to be rewarding the Censors for their vigilance. Why they don't ban Shakespeare, I don't know. Never read him, probably. Agate's praise isn't worth a damn. He'd say of "Journey's End" & "The

[1] Paul Vincent Carroll's *The Strings Are False* opened in Dublin at the Olympia Theatre on 16 March 1942, directed by Shelah Richards, and ran for two months. Fallon wrote a glowing review of it, "Greatness and Paul Vincent Carroll," *Irish Monthly*, April 1942, stating: "Paul Vincent Carroll has written five plays, and the greatest of these is *The Strings Are False*."

[2] Under the title *The Strings, My Lord, Are False,* the play opened in New York on 19 May 1942, and closed after fifteen performances.

[3] Louis D'Alton's *You Can't Be Too Careful* opened in Dublin at the Olympia Theatre on 18 May 1942.

[4] Writers, Artists, Actors, and Musicians Association in Dublin.

[5] "Sound the Loud Trumpet," by An Gall Fada (The Tall Foreigner or Protestant), O'Casey's first published work under his first pseudonym, appeared in W. P. Ryan's *The Peasant and Irish Ireland,* 25 May 1907; reprinted in *Feathers From the Green Crow* (1962).

Combined Maze" what he said of "Juno." He doesn't know as Drama per se a bad play from a good one. I am busy helping to form a Branch of Anglo-Soviet Alliance here (with Eileen), & getting publishers to send some books to Moscow, who have cabled for them; & articles on the War by English Dramatists; as well as house work & my own speciality of Authorship—a curious word.

My love to Rose, the young family, & to you. We are all well.

Ever Yours
Sean

To Lillian Gish [1]

TS. GISH

TOTNES, DEVON
15 JUNE 1942

Dear Lillian:

This afternoon your parcel and your letter came safely to us—after a long, long journey, though why it was kept so long away from us would be hard to say. Eileen and I were very glad to hear from you once again, and in such a very acceptable way. It wouldn't be possible to leave England now; and for many reasons, I think it would be better to stay here. I should like to remain here—having been here from the beginning—till the Nazi menace is cut away from the world forever. Then there will be a general sorting out of things, and we know not what may happen, what we may do, or where we may go. That is, if we be spared, and the airplanes that flutter over us so often do not come too close. I try to think of the U.S.A. as little as possible in a personal connection; for the days spent there were too pleasant and exciting to dwell upon the fact of being so far away from them now. Indeed, I believe that the U.S.A. is the land of the future; but I believe that after the war every land will be a land of the future. If we can put into the peace the energy put into the war—and it can be done—then the future will be a profitable, and, I believe, a gay one.

I have read that your last season was a poor one, and that the Critics' Circle didn't award any prize to any American play—a sad state of affairs. I am doing my best, anyhow: I have three plays in New York City awaiting production, possible production, I should say—The Star Turns Red,

---

[1] Lillian Gish (1896–   ), American actress, played the role of the Young Whore in the American premiere of *Within the Gates* in 1934; see O'Casey's letter to George Jean Nathan, 17 October 1934, note 1, Vol. I, p. 522. See also O'Casey's letters to Miss Gish in Vol. I.

Purple Dust, and Red Roses For Me. Not bad going in the midst of a war.

I am glad to hear that Eugene [O'Neill] is doing well and that his lovely Carlotta is close by his side. Perhaps he is right in saying that men's minds are too confused, now, to listen to what he has to say. Perhaps the voice of the Lord is not in the great wind, or in the earthquake, or in the fire, and that the still small voice in his new plays should stay silent for the time being. I doubt it. Eugene should go on speaking. The Lord hath a way in the whirlwind, even in the whirlwind of war.

The things in the parcel showed that you guessed right, Lillian, and I and Eileen thank you warmly for your kind thought. We left London some time ago and are down in Devon now, where our three children go to a school that we and they like and to which they shall go as long as we can afford to send them. The war, of course, is making things very difficult for thousands of people and we are of their number; but I am hoping that one of my plays may go on, and possibly pass another year or so safely by us. Should you get this, if you are ever in touch with Brooks Atkinson, thank him for me for his article in the N.Y. Times praising me so well that I wondered if I was the man he meant.

We have gone thru tough times, but we are all well and fighting on as well as we can. As well as giving a hand to promote cordial connections with the U.S.S.R., I am trying to get together another volume of biography. Thanks again, dear Lillian, for remembering us. My love and Eileen's to you; and the best of wishes to you and to your sister, Dorothy.

Yours most sincerely,
Sean

PS. I'm typing this that it may be read by the Censor easily.

To Jack Daly [1]

MS. DALY

TOTNES, DEVON
26 JUNE 1942

My dear Jack.

Forgive me for not writing before this to thank you very much for G. W. Foote's grand book on grand men.[2] It is fine to read men who write

[1] Jack Daly, a close friend of O'Casey's when they were in Dublin early in the century in the St. Laurence O'Toole Club, now living in Oxford. See O'Casey's letters to him in Vol. I.

[2] George William Foote, *Flowers of Freethought* (1893).

in enjoyment of writing, out of love for what they have received, rather than those who write to show how much they know.

I have been very busy trying to get English Publishers to send books to Russia. A Timofei Rokotov, Editor of "International Literature," has cabled me numerous times to get them sent to Moscow; & it has been a job to get the publishers interested. A few responded willingly; but a lot of them seemed to think that it should be a business deal. And, my boy, some of the Authors too. Some of these Christians forget that if they cast their bread upon the waters, it will return to them after many days: they want it to come now. Rokotov wants, too, articles by English Dramatists on the war. What a hope! [Herbert] Farjeon has nothing to write; [J. B.] Priestley, if he writes one, will send it on himself thru the Soviet Embassy; [Paul V.] Carroll is hitting the botttle, because of a flop of a play of his in New York; & writes commissioned articles only; & [St. John] Ervine hasn't replied: so I gave that up as a good job. I am also busy helping the wife to start a Committee of the Anglo-Soviet Alliance here in Totnes. There is still a lot of half-hidden, quiet enmity to the U.S.S.R. I have been in touch with Moscow now for nearly ten years; & of course, with what they were doing since Lenin led off in 1917, & Hands Off Russia meetings were held in Dublin. No fear of meetings like that there now. All busy crowding round respectability, hunger, and the Sacred Heart. Jim Larkin comes down here to see me tomorrow.

Aren't we in a nice mess in Libya? The guttersnipe, Rommel is doing it to my Lords and Gentlemen. The sooner our Army gets a few guttersnipes into it as leaders, the better. Do you ever hear from the oul' Homeland now? From Billy Kelly,[3] with his consequential strut, and his wild sweeping leap on to his motor-cycle—keep your seat, keep your seat, Kelly! And Mrs. Stanley whose nodding head solved the problem of perpetual motion. I wonder, now, where's "Charlie Russell," with his "Should the Workers Support Sinn Fein" in one hand, and the lead of a red-bowed pekinese in the other. And poor Sydney Arnold who became Semyon Aronson, the Bolshevist, when the Revolution came to Russia; & he trying to get Billy Kelly to read Rousseau's "Social Contract." And Wally Carpenter nearly extinguished, & utterly weighed down under his big, broad-brimmed, black revolutionary hat. And poor Tom Egan chanting "The Red Flag" in a dark corner to himself.

Them was the days. We'll never look upon their like again.

I'm sending "Irish Freedom" under another cover.

> *Love to Floss*
> *Ever Yours*
> *Sean*

What a grand kind face is that of Foote's.

[3] O'Casey's first visit to the Abbey Theatre was with William Kelly in 1917. See O'Casey's letter to Fergus O'Connor, 13 February 1918, note 1, Vol. I, p. 69.

To George Jean Nathan

TS. O'CASEY

TOTNES, DEVON

26 JUNE 1942

My very dear George:

I got your letter dated 2nd of June the other day. I'm glad you got two from me. I'm more than glad to hear from you, fearing you weren't well. I'm delighted that "much that is fine is in RED ROSES FOR ME." That's a lot of praise from you. You are probably right about the superiority of PURPLE DUST. Somehow or another, I never could go into raptures over it. But then, I got to dislike every damned play I write. It's a penalty even to have to read the proofs. I do hope you liked "I Tucked Up My Sleeves for to Tie Up Her Shoe." [1] It is curious to hear that the play travels some of the same road travelled by KINDRED.[2] It is certainly familiar ground to me; for I was in the midst of a lot of it. I saw (and laughed, God forgive me, at the poor boyo buried in the big bugle) all of what I wrote about, and I dressed up like a cockolurum in full Gaelic dress, kilt, shawl, sporaun, and all. I kept close to an I.R.B. man armed with a six-shooter who, I knew, would use it before he'd let a baton fall on his head. We got away allright. I was an I.R.B. man then, myself full of fight and glory. By the way, I wrote to P. V. Carroll asking for an article about the war (Moscow had cabled asking me to get these, if I could, from British Dramatists), and in a reply refusing, he wrote gloomily that he had had an elaborate flop with his newest play [*The Strings, My Lord, Are False*], saying that after the Nathan pack had finished with it, it littered the East river. So, he goes on, this makes one take to the bottle. Well, a bad way to meet a reverse. Better to start on another play. I wouldn't tell you this, did I not know you'd be all out for a good play, caring not a damn who wrote it, even had the writer called you a son-of-a-bitch. You are a Critic, and you couldn't do anything else. I'm afraid it will be some time before the Nazi planes begin to fade. However, we must go on, "putting the day today towards the day tomorrow"—an Irish proverb. I'm real sorry to hear about Eugene, dear Eugene.[3] A big great man, if

[1] The song that Brennan o' the Moor sings in the third act of *Red Roses For Me*.

[2] Paul Vincent Carroll's *Kindred* opened at the Abbey Theatre on 25 September 1939 and in New York on 26 December 1939. See O'Casey's letter to Gabriel Fallon, 18 January 1940, note 2, Vol. I, p. 836.

[3] Eugene O'Neill was suffering from a rare disease similar to Parkinson's, in which the cells of the cerebellum were subject to a slow, degenerative process. The main symptoms were speech impairment and trembling hands. First afflicted by the

ever there was one. A big great child, rather, as a great man should be. I do pray that he will have strength to complete his plays. There are so few O'Neills in the world. Give him my deep love again when you write to him.

In the midst of many interruptions, I'm trying to get together a few chapters of the 3rd volume of biography, which I think I'll call Drums Under the Window. I do hope your prayers for PURPLE DUST may be answered—a production of any kind of success next Fall would be a god-send. We can but hope for the best. Did you read the Interview with that bloody Alfred Noyes in the N.Y.T[imes]. Book Review of April the 12th? He finds "great danger in the literature of the age." He does, does he? Condemns Lawrence and Joyce, though he wouldn't be fit to unlace the latchet of Joyce's shoe. The bags that withdrew his good word for Voltaire when some Cardinal told him to do so. He's the danger. We're all well here, so far.

I, too, wish I could look on you again, George, my dear friend—comrade rather. In the meantime, my love be with you.

Ever Yours,
Sean

---

disease in 1937, he suffered a severe attack in 1942, and was subject to chronic attacks until he died on 27 November 1953.

To Jack Carney

MS. NYU LIBRARY

[TOTNES, DEVON]
29 JUNE 1942

My dear Jack,

Here's the book, signed for Tommy, as requested. What a remarkable talker Jim [Larkin] is! A bubbling fountain of vitality. On Sunday, Leslie & two of his pals dropped in; they didn't know Jim was here. They had a long talk, Jim leading the way. He sent some shivers down their spines. In the middle of the discussion, one of them, the best-off of the three, was calling him "Sir"! It was delightful to me to see sometimes the flash in Jim's talk that I so often met during the old days in Liberty Hall. What a damn pity William O'Brien—not the politician,[1] for, take him for all in all, he was a man—but the other, what a pity he wasn't born dead. He has set

[1] William O'Brien (1852–1928), Irish writer and politician, M.P. for Mallow and Cork. The "other" William O'Brien (1881–1968) was the Irish labor leader and bitter rival of Jim Larkin.

back the Irish Labour Movement for a generation. To set Jim on the one side & Bill O'Brien on the other—good God, what a contrast—the lion and the mangy rat.

I am very busy getting into touch with publishers about sending books to Moscow. They are still discussing it. However, the question is now before a Committee representing all publishers, bar Gollancz—he refuses, evidently, to have anything to do with collective action. I'm busy, too, helping Eileen with this new Committee she's trying to get going in Totnes. I hope it may be a success.

I hope you'll like your new abode. I see Eileen managed to get some provender for the Buderdigregar—I'm not quite sure about this spelling; but you'll know whom I mean—Micky.

> *Love to Mina & you*
> *Sean*

To Lovat Dickson [1]

MS. MACMILLAN LONDON

TOTNES, DEVON
29 JUNE 1942

Dear Mr. Dickson:
    With this you'll find a few words about RED ROSES FOR ME, which, I hope, may be suitable for the Jacket. It is a job I don't like. The last phrase is what has been said by a famous New York Critic,[2] so it isn't self-praise.

> *Yours,*
> *Sean O'Casey*

Red Roses For Me [3]

Here is a new play by Sean O'Casey, and in it we find a lot of what we expect from this dramatist—tense scenes among a blossom-filled wilderness of words. Though in this play he is in a gentler mood than is usual, there are fierce things in it as well as gentleness. The play is woven out of many moods, forming a coloured pattern of lively life, especially we note the Dublin Street scene near the River Liffey. A thing of black and scarlet,

---

[1] Lovat Dickson (1902–   ), editor, publisher, writer; a director of Macmillan, London. See O'Casey's first letter to him, 10 March 1941, Vol. I, pp. 879–80.

[2] George Jean Nathan.

[3] This statement was typed.

silvered with song. The characters are clearly and vividly painted in rich, dancing dialogue. It shows how many things, thoughts, and activities cross and recross the minds of the Dublin people; and shows—though some be blind to it—how all, from the Protestant Rector down to the street flower-seller, are correlated in a strange, sometimes sad, and always vigorous rela-tionship. The Dublin of myth and misery, of darkness and light, of the shrinking sigh and the aggressive shout stands there, and beckons us to come and have another look at her; stands there with her Civic Crown balanced rakishly on her stately head, with Eblana, Ptolemy's name for Dublin, carven deeply into its golden rim. There is, indeed, much that is fine in this latest play of O'Casey's.

To Timofei Rokotov [1]

TS. INTER LIT, MOSCOW

TOTNES, DEVON
29 JUNE 1942

My dear friend:
      This is a note about what you asked me to do in getting new English books sent to you. You should have received a number of them by now, from Macmillan's, Faber's, Methuen's and other Publishers. Among the books that went to you were Atlas History, Modern Short Story, Philosophy for our Time, Topolski's Britain in Peace and War, The Irish Countryman, An Irish Journey, and others, some fine, some fair, some damned poor. But this to me seemed a slow way of doing things, so I sent letters to publishers telling all about you and your Magazine, trying to get them interested in the matter in a general and lively way. The question is now before the Publishers' Advertising Circle, and, I'm sure, it will mean that books will be forwarded on to you at regular periods. If the Publishers in assembly dont take to the idea, then I'll get going some other way; but I think they will, and this will be the most effective way of carrying out your wishes, and a good way, too, I think, of making the Soviet Union, and all it stands for, better known to many more people. I have written to a number of English Dramatists asking them for articles they may have written about the war. I'm afraid they are too busy with other things to do that. However, if I get any, I shall send them on to you. Here, I and my wife, at the moment, are busy getting together a branch of the Anglo-Soviet Committee for, as

---

[1] Timofei Rokotov, editor, *International Literature*, Moscow.

you probably know, aims at deepening and broadening the Alliance that now is a settled thing at last.

At this stage of our mighty struggle, there is not much in me sending you my best wishes as ucht mo chroidhe—from the bosom of my heart, as we say in Irish; for I have walked in the way of the Soviet Union since Lenin first sounded the trumpet in 1917; and today the only difference is that these wishes are riper and stronger than ever before.

My love to you, your Leader, your great Fighting Forces, Military and Civilian, and, before the year be out, may the Red Star shine day and night everywhere, even to the core of Berlin.

Yours very sincerely,
Sean O'Casey

To Winston Churchill [1]

TC. O'CASEY

TOTNES, DEVON
4 JULY 1942

Dear Sir:

I have had the honour of meeting you once, a time when you were wearing a Bronze Ark in the centre of a Stuart tartan ribbon bow.[2] We are all, mixed up every way, in the Ark of War now, and the Soviet Bear is a welcome friend—to most, anyhow. We are, as you have said, fighting for our very lives, Conservative no less than Communist, and we are being put to the pin of our collars to keep the things going. You know that better than anyone. So no atom of energy should be left lying round unused. It

[1] Winston Churchill (1875–1965), British politician and prime minister.
[2] They probably met in 1928 when O'Casey was living in London, and the reference to the "Bronze Ark" suggests that the occasion was one of Lady Londonderry's Wednesday parties at "The Ark," Londonderry House. There Lady Londonderry's friends were made members of the Order of the Rainbow, a symbol of hope, and were given code names of birds, insects, beasts, or mythical figures—names which matched the first letter of their Christian or surnames. For example: Lady Londonderry (Edith Helen Vane-Tempest-Stewart) was Circe the Sorceress; Lord Arthur Balfour was the Albatross; Lord Edward Carson was the Eagle; Lady Hazel Lavery was the Hen; Sir William Orpen was the Ortolen; Winston Churchill was the Warlock; Sean O'Casey was the Spider. See Lady Londonderry's *Retrospect* (1938), "The Ark," pp. 236–50. See also the "Rose and Crown" chapter in *Rose and Crown* (1952), where O'Casey describes his meeting with men like Carson, Churchill, and Stanley Baldwin, then Prime Minister, at a party in "a great Conservative Mansion," most likely Londonderry House. That must have been the first and only meeting between the Warlock and the Spider. See O'Casey's first letter to Lady Londonderry, 13 June 1928, Vol. I, p. 279.

should be added to the blaze of the guns. I enclose a page taken from the Soviet Daily War News. It is a Pravda call to the intimate leaders of the workers. We have no equivalent to it here. We might have. We should have. But the atom that is the "Daily Worker" is lying idle.[3] Worse still, those who want it back are using energy that should be confined to forcing on the work for victory. These can do this work so trenchantly called for by Pravda. Its influence wouldnt be a mighty power at your elbow; but it would be a remarkable force behind you. It would have, in physical energy and spiritual inspiration the force of an army with banners, and you, and all of us want all the banners that can be flown. It would add another horse to your chariot of war, a good one, too, one that would make the pace, and urge the others on. Those who in the Labour Movement are sceptical, are those officials who, on account of their jobs, are afraid of offending higher officials, so they put officialdom before the Nation. They are of little account; for they will have to work just the same; Worker or no Worker; but the Daily Worker will create pioneers (so I fervently believe) that will make a lot of these people look like snails; for these pioneers will go on till they drop, and seek no job, no reward, save that of putting new strength into the blow against Hitlerism. There's no use in arguing about it: one sees it, or it is hidden from one; but I venture to suggest that you might give it another thought, crush it in someway between those multitudes of anxious thoughts whirling forever in your busy brain. I hope you may see it, and release this restless power into the ordered channel of renewed energy for the production of all arms for all our fighting men.

Yours sincerely,
Sean O'Casey

[3] The *Daily Worker* was suppressed by the government on 21 January 1941, and the ban was lifted on 7 September 1942. See O'Casey's letter to the *New Statesman and Nation,* 2 August 1941, Vol. I, pp. 900–901.

From Lord Simon [1]

TS. O'CASEY

HOUSE OF LORDS
9 JULY 1942

Dear Mr. Sean O'Casey,
Your rollicking letter of June 24th [2] is worthy of the author of "Juno and the Paycock" which Mr. Asquith used to declare (and I agree with

[1] Sir John Simon, 1st Viscount (1873–1954), Liberal politician; Foreign Secretary, 1931–35; Lord Chancellor, 1940–45.
[2] In this letter, which has not been found, O'Casey explained how he had originally been encouraged by the landlord to leave the flat at 49 Overstrand Man-

him) was one of the best plays ever written in the world. It is hard to come down from these heights to the horrid business of writs and sealing wax, and I feel quite apologetic when you tell me that my name was on the writ against which you protest.

I enclose on a separate piece of paper the note that was made for me on your eloquent and pitiful appeal. I do not feel at all sure that it will be of any help or relief to you, but at any rate it states the situation in matter of fact terms. I am afraid I must leave you to take advice from your solicitor, if you wish, as to whether you are likely to get relief under the Courts (Emergency Powers) Acts. The Lord Chancellor has many and curious duties, but he has no dispensing power.

Yours sincerely
Simon

Sean O'Casey, Esq.
Lord Chancellor

Mr. Sean O'Casey

The facts of this case are not clearly stated in Mr. O'Casey's letter. He seems to have been under the impression that he had successfully negotiated a surrender of his lease; but on a claim for rent due to an amount of £124. the court decided that there had been no surrender and that the rent claimed was then due. Since the date of the judgment, further rent has been accruing under the lease, which may or may not have now been determined by effluxion of time. It seems probable that Mr. O'Casey has no defence to an action for the instalment of rent now claimed. If what he states as to his financial circumstances is true, I think he would be in a position to claim relief under the Courts (Emergency Powers) Acts. Under those Acts, he will not be relieved of his ultimate liability to pay the sum found to be due, but if the court came to the conclusion that his inability to pay was due to war circumstances, it would be able to refuse leave to the landlords to proceed to execution on the judgment for the debt.

The solicitor for the landlords are said to be asking for £5. down and £5. per month until the £22. is paid. Having regard to Mr. O'Casey's position in the world of letters this does not seem particularly harsh, and it may be that the court, in exercising its discretion under the Courts (Emergency Powers) Acts, would enforce terms not less onerous. If Mr. O'Casey's financial circumstances are as stated by him, the Acts do afford him relief.

---

sions, Prince of Wales Road, London SW 11, when the family moved to Totnes in September 1938. Subsequently, however, the landlord changed his mind, after the flat remained empty, and demanded additional rent on a claim of a broken lease. For the background on this dispute, see O'Casey's letter to Mrs. Charlotte F. Shaw, ? September 1938, note 2, Vol. I, p. 742; Bernard Shaw's letter to O'Casey, 17 October 1938, Vol. I, p. 752; O'Casey's letter to George Jean Nathan, 4 April 1939, Vol. I, p. 791; and O'Casey's letter to Gabriel Fallon, 25 August 1939, Vol. I, p. 812. In the first paragraph of the letter to Fallon, O'Casey sets out the whole case, which was still in the courts in 1942, and which he eventually lost.

If this particular debt is the only financial embarrassment with which Mr. O'Casey is faced, it seems hardly worth while suggesting that he should seek the protection of the Liabilities (War Time Adjustment) Act, which would involve some little publicity and a complete investigation of his affairs by the Liabilities Adjustment Officer.

2.7.42.

To Jack Carney

MS. NYU LIBRARY

[TOTNES, DEVON]

25 JULY 1942

Dear Jack,

Thanks for the navvy's plug. I'm getting used to its strength, & am a little afraid, when I do, that then all other brands will be but small beer. Your pound on Moore's works for such a price was a fine capture; & Lady G's "Poets & Dreamers" [1] a better one. I have a copy with "To Sean O'Casey, Poet & Dreamer, from the writer, Lady Gregory 1924." So there you are now! It's not as good as it might be, but it is, worth reading, especially what she says about Raftery.

I have yet another letter from Moscow asking for "War plays written by English (& Americans) about the heroic struggle of the British against Hitlerism." And, as far as I know, not a one of such a play on in any theatre in London!

Isn't it the black & bitter news about the big German break through at Rostov! And the others, seemingly, not able even to make an advance in Libya as long as a cock's step. That little Ryecroft [2] book on Parnell was a quaint thing. The photo inside of our Uncrowned King is a fine one. What a lot of poor faded things the Irish leaders seem now compared with him—all but the one and only Jim Larkin. At the moment, & for the past week, I'm trying to clip the garden hedge—trying to keep my mind off the news from the U.S.S.R. I expect the new play "Red Roses For Me" will be published in the Fall. I've just finished the final proofs. But there seems to be little chance of it or of "Purple Dust" going on in N.Y. [Richard] Watts, Junr. in the "Herald-Tribune" says they want trivial plays to take their minds off the war. And so do we; & so to bed. I'm reading the Capuchin

---

[1] Lady Gregory, *Poets and Dreamers* (1903).
[2] Dr. F. S. L. Lyons, Provost of Trinity College, Dublin, has assured me that O'Casey must have had the wrong name here, for there is no book by a Ryecroft on Parnell.

Annual for 1942. It has a long article giving Canon Sheehan [3] a literary canonization; and James Joyce, a get thee behind me, Satan, valedictory malediction. If they could only lay hold of his bones! A pity they can't read "Finnegans Wake"—neither can I; but enough to show me what he says, & the flame in it burning up the ecclesiastical hay & stubble & straw. It looks as if Shelley was right: all the cods in heaven; all the men in hell.

Well so much for the present.

Love to Mina & to you.
Yours as Ever,
Sean

[3] Father Michael, O. F. Cap., "Twilight and Dawn," *Capuchin Annual 1942* (Dublin), an article on Canon Sheehan and Padraig Pearse.

To Boris Sutchkoff [1]

TS. INTER LIT, MOSCOW

TOTNES, DEVON
12 AUGUST 1942

Dear Mr Sutchkoff:

You should have received some books long ago, those sent by me, and those sent by various Publishers. I have already forwarded list of those sent (1st parcel) to M. Rokotov. Since then, I have sent the following: Owen Glendower (the great Welsh Leader, Tudor Times) by J. C. Powys. Cornish Tales. Charles Lee.
You Cant be too Careful. H. G. Wells.
The Time of Your Life. Plays by Saroyan, the Armenian-American Writer. Bernard Shaw. Art and Socialism.
E. Straus. The German Witches Sabath.
Twilight of France. Alexander Werth.
The Bow and the Wound. (criticism) E. Wilson.

Books were also sent by *Macmillan's, Faber & Faber, Methuen, Nelson & Sons, Michael Joseph, Jonathan Cape,* and others. Several of these Publishers said they were writing to Mr Rokotov. On July the 5th, I wrote to M. Rokotov, through the Soviet Embassy, who wrote saying they would forward the letter at the first opportunity. With this, I enclosed a letter from the Secretary of the Publishers' Advertising Circle showing their interest in what you wanted me to do. These books from the Publishers will not mean any expense to you. When my book, PICTURES IN THE HALLWAY, came out, in Feb, Macmillan's sent a copy to you. If you havent got it, I'll

[1] Boris Sutchkoff, Editor in Chief, *International Literature*, P.O. Box 527, Moscow.

let you have another. I am very sorry I cannot become a regular Correspondent to Interlit. I wouldnt be competent to do what you ask, for I have few means of collecting the details of the themes you mention as a matter for writing. Unfortunately, too, I am not a facile writer. However, I will ask some of my Press friends, and see if anything can be done about it. Here, there isnt the unity of endeavour yet that there is in the U.S.S.R. Youth, for instance, is divided into many camps of thought; but there is a definite hardening towards a united war effort, but there's still a lot of work to be done. Many prejudices about your country have still to be met and overcome. Enclosed cutting from the Catholic UNIVERSE will show you something of what I mean. These pious praters strive to keep back a full and free understanding between the two countries. I knew the C.Y.M.S. in Ireland, and, on the whole, a gang of ripe ignoramuses the most of them. By Christ, if they get the full smack of the German Force, they'll lose their heads, their memories, and a lot of their reason!

I enclose another cutting from FORWARD showing the reluctance on the part of some (Lord Camrose and his henchmen) to reveal what your Country is doing in the way of interest in British Literature and Dramatic Art.

The war plays here have been few, and not much good; not good enough to trouble to send any to you.

I confirm the acknowledgement in cable of the receipt of royalties. £8 and £14, sent to me through the Narodny Bank. Stamped and personally made out receipts for these amounts were sent to the Bank, and I thought that this would be sufficient acknowledgement.

Of course, most of the writers, actors, and dramatists are in either the army or the navy; everyone else is busy with a thousand different jobs, trying to make the night joint labourer with the day, and so this scattering makes it difficult to concentrate on any one thing. But as it means hard work to win the war is being done, it doesnt matter much. The Question of the Second Front is now taking first place in the thoughts of the people, even in rural districts. They seem to be wakening up to what will happen to them should the Red Forces be forced back beyond the Volga—and nearly time too. But, to me, it seems there are still a lot of wooden heads in important positions. The foundation of a Classical Education doesnt seem to have worked too well. But things inevitable are forcing a wider choice of leaders on us, and a selection among a million will be bound to be more effective than a choice among a ten, an "upper ten," too.

It seems ridiculous irony to send you and Mr Rokotov greetings in the midst of the appalling sacrifices your people are making for the world's benefit; but I venture to do so, coupled with all the help I can give here to hurry up the people's minds towards effective comradeship with the people of the Soviet Union.

Very sincerely yours,
Sean O'Casey

To Jack Carney

MS. NYU LIBRARY

[TOTNES, DEVON]
20 AUGUST 1942

My dear Jack,

Thanks, and more, for your letters, papers, books, & tobacco. Have been very busy clipping the hedge & making bonfires of the rubbish, & was upset for a few days by something in some tinned food—me curse on Woolton! [1] Yes, I saw Barney [Conway] was standing for Municipal dishonors. I do hope he'll win; &, of course, Jim [Larkin], too. The incorruptible Jim and incorruptible Barney. I'm glad you're starting on another Library; but don't make it mainly political, economical, & critical. Put a rich leaven of pure writing into it. If you like, any book I'd like to have myself, I'll suggest to you—on condition you buy but one for yourself only; though should I want it badly, I'll ask a loan of it from you. I'm sure (in The Bow & the Wound [2]) the essay on Joyce is very interesting; anything about H. C. Earwicker, the Everyman Dublin Scandanavian Irish pub-owner of the Hole in the Wall, Phoenix Park, & all the history, politics, economy, Science, Religion, & Philosophy—not forgetting Legend—of Ireland & the known world from before the year of one till now! And all in a half dream as he lay with a wide multitude of thoughts running through his brain. Anyway, the USSR has got to win; but how? To win into weakness isn't good enough. Perhaps Churchill's visit, & the Dieppe raid is a harbinger of mightier things to come. God grant it. I do hope the new Irish C. in Chief in Libya will move his men in the right direction. Anyhow, the Germans risk a heavy defeat in the Caucasus. I hope it comes. You're right about Courtaulds. Col. Raynor, member for Totnes, [3] is a son-in-law. A bright spark, too. "You may safely leave Libya in the hands of Auch," he says. Auch [4] Ay! Whours your old Auch noo? Raynor is silent.

There are no "excesses" in Finnegans Wake. Wilson is wrong there—wasn't it Wilson who wrote the B & the W.? Or maybe, as Wilde said, "There's nothing succeeds like excess."

There is nothing sinister in Lady Astor. I'd take my oath on that.

---

[1] Woolton, 1st Earl, Frederick James Marquis (1883–1964), Minister of Food, 1940–43, in Churchill's wartime National Coalition Government.

[2] Edmund Wilson, *The Wound and the Bow* (1941). The chapter on Joyce is titled "The Dream of H. C. Earwicker."

[3] See O'Casey's letter to the *Totnes Times,* 31 October 1942, a reply to a speech by Lt.-Col. Ralph Raynor, M.P. for Totnes.

[4] General Sir Claude J. E. Auchinleck.

She wouldn't be so open-mouthed, if there were. If the Communists only paid more attention to the silent ones, they'd do more wisely and well. But as the English can't understand us Irish, so they can't understand a Virginian.[5]

Love to Mina & to you.
Yours as ever,
Sean

I sent back the book, signed, to your comrade, Somain.

[5] Viscountess Nancy Astor. See O'Casey's letter to her, 25 December 1943.

To Jack Carney

MS. NYU LIBRARY

[TOTNES, DEVON]
21 SEPTEMBER 1942

My dear Jack,

Thanks for the papers, & for Gallagher's Condor Plug. You've had a full house now for awhile, & must be a little tired of it all. I know, I would be. It would be a fine yarn & full of edification to hear the real things that Stalin said to Winston. Anyhow, how could any responsible Allied official expect a cordial welcome from Moscow? There is, I daresay, a gang here uninterested in a Soviet Victory, & some of them labourites with a vision of a customary top-hat as the peak of their lives, or maybe, like Snowdon, a two-times procession round the H of Lords in a crimson gown, & a two-time-three-time bows to the Speaker.

What do you think of the D. Worker? The Editorial Depart wired for an article on the Second Front; & I sent a short one,[1] reluctantly, for I'm not good at that sort of thing—not near as good as Ilya Ehrenburg.[2]

It is really shocking about that balls, Cripps.[3] He's crippled the Indian Problem, without a doubt. And all that was thought of him when he headed the storm (stage storm) for a Popular Front. And backed out of it, afterwards. I don't know about distrusting all that aren't in the ranks of the masses. Ireland, God be thanked, had a few fine men: Tone, Emmet, Russell [4]—not AE—, Parnell, others. It's really the men from the masses

[1] "Further They Go, Nearer They Come," *Daily Worker*, 24 September 1942.
[2] Ilya Ehrenburg (1891–1967), Soviet novelist and journalist.
[3] Sir Stafford Cripps (1889–1954), served briefly as the leader of Commons in Churchill's war cabinet.
[4] Thomas Russell (1767–1803), prominent member of the United Irishmen; responsible for organizing Ulster during Emmet's Rising of 1803. Hanged for treason.

that really sell, figuratively, their own class—Citrin,[5] Snowdon,[6] [William] O'Brien, & that vulgar thick, Jimmy Thomas.[7]

By the way, did you ever hear that W. B. Y. wrote a marching song for Duffy's Blue Shirts? [8] Someone told me this—if I remember right, it was Paul Potts, Canadian Corporal in the Royal Ulster Rifles, who wrote proletarian verse for the D.W. & has published a thin volume of them. A fine fellow, but too much of an anarchist to be sensible. I certainly never heard of W. B. Y. doing anything of the kind.

I'm afraid Stalingrad is gone. And afterwards, they'll try to blot out Murmansk, I suppose, so the U.S.S.R. will be as bad off as China. They'll let every road go, before they get their coats buttoned straight.

> *Love to Mina & to you.*
> *Yours as ever,*
> *Sean*

[5] Walter McLennan Citrine, 1st Baron of Wembley (1887–   ), right-wing trade union leader.

[6] Philip (Viscount) Snowden (1864–1937), British politican; served as Chancellor of the Exchequer in the Labour governments of 1924, 1929, 1931.

[7] James Henry Thomas (1874–1949), British trade union official and politician; leader of the railway union; served in J. Ramsay MacDonald's Labour government in 1931.

[8] W. B. Yeats wrote "Three Songs to the Same Tune" as a result of his brief interest in General Eoin O'Duffy's Fascist Blueshirt movement. These songs appeared in *A Full Moon in March* (1935). Yeats later recanted and rewrote the songs which then appeared as "Three Marching Songs," in *Last Poems* (1939). John Unterecker, in *A Reader's Guide to W. B. Yeats* (1959), made the following comment:

> But General O'Duffy's rebellion soon proved, Yeats felt, more comic than heroic. Six months later, by the time the second edition of his book was ready for the press, he had decided O'Duffy's cause was a lost one and he rewrote the songs: "I increased their fantasy, their extravagance, their obscurity, that no party might sing them." (p. 244)

To Timofei Rokotov and Boris Sutchkoff

TS. INTER LIT, MOSCOW

TOTNES, DEVON
30 SEPTEMBER 1942

Dear Friends:

Enclosed is a brief article appearing in the Daily Worker. It may interest you to have a copy of it. With it are copies of cartoons appearing in American Journals that may interest you, too, dealing as they do with the necessity of a second front. The call for this is getting quite loud and becoming fierce among the workers, and, indeed, it is high time that a shower of steel should be falling on the Germans from the West side of the battle-front. God knows there is a wide choice from which to hurl it. These cheers of ours for the men fighting in Stalingrad, and the roll of drums in their honour arent enough, arent good enough, arent damn well good enough. I'm afraid some of our leaders are something like dishes of skimmed milk, and that some of them could be brained by a clout from a lady's fan. Here, among the rural workers, a Second Front is being called for too. It is so silly to think of the Germans as something superhuman, as if a fiercely thrust bayonet wouldnt run through their flesh as readily as the flesh of any other man; or that a grenade wouldnt shatter a German's bones as effectively as the bones of any other man. One would imagine by now, after what the Red Army has done, that we would all realise that these Aryan warriors fit a grave as finely as any other man. Maybe, some of our experts are more afraid of losing a reputation than of losing an army corps or two, as if the bubble reputation mattered a damn in this fight for life, or the loss of an army corps either. A lot of things besides reputations will have to be lost before this war is won. Surely the great German war machine has been well tested and well shaken by now by the amazing fierce-ness of the Red Army, and, though its guns still fire, the cranks cant work so smoothly and the wheels must be wobbling a lot. Now is the time to sail in at the rear and crack the cranks, shoot the wheels flying, and lay the damned machine low.

I do hope you have got the books that have been sent to you. You will have heard already about the mistake I made in acknowledging the amounts sent to me by you. I am very sorry for this, but the circumstances merit an excuse.

My most deep wishes to you both, to your great Leader, Stalin, and to your brave and indomitable People.

Yours sincerely,
Sean O'Casey

To Jack Carney

MS. NYU LIBRARY

[TOTNES, DEVON]
12 OCTOBER 1942

My dear Jack,
Many thanks for the papers, tobacco, & Barney's letter. After reading the papers, anything suitable, with the D.W. Eileen leaves in the Y.M.C.A.

Rest Room here—the tobac I keep for meself. I imagine You're right about the D.W. There isn't enough of emotion in it. There's no one writes like Ehrenburg for them. But I can't say much, for they'd say, you write. That's impossible, unless I gave up everything else. I have to try to do a little from 10 to 1.0'c; & this, even (the quietness of the place) is broken into now, for Nannie has a damned soldier in the kitchen most nights till 12 midnight. Try as I may, I can't forget they're there, & they come into my head, crossing thoughts & turning them into exploding expressions of blasphemy.

If you are still looking for autographs, the enclosed one of a real live Princess will interest your collector friend.

I see the Bishops (in Eirinn) are now literally laying down the law as to how, when & where the maids & boys will dance. Four long ones in a year, & none on Saturdays or the Vigils of a Saint's Day. I remember in the Gaelic League more than 30 years ago, they invariably had their long dances on Saturday nights, & a Gala one on what they called "Easter Saturday"—the day before Easter Sunday, which wasn't Easter Saturday at all, but the Vigil of the First Easter morn, E. Saturday being, of course, the Sat *after* Easter Sunday. When I first pointed this out to a Ceilidh [Dance] Committee—I was Secretary—they were astonished, & would hardly believe it, saying, anyway, that there were few Catholics as well up as I was in the Church Calender! Practising Catholics.

I see H. G. Wells has made a fool of himself in a new book [1] by associating the Holy Ghost with the first vision of first St John, "In the beginning was the Word," saying that, or giving the title of the Holy Ghost to the Word or "Logos" as he called it.

Doesn't look as if the 2nd Front was coming to the front, does it? I was reading a little about the Indian Mutiny [2] in a book brought home by Breon from your place, & find them then, 1856, just the bloody god damned same as they are today. I'll leave you to guess who "they" are— not the R.I.C.[3] anyway.

All the best, and many thanks again, with love to Mina & you. I see Cripps is forming a new army with the cross of Jesus going in before. Jasus help the Germans now! Well, in "Major Barbara," we saw which was the more powerful—Sign of the Sword, or Sign of the Cross.

Yrs, Sean

[1] H. G. Wells, *You Can't Be Too Careful* (1941).

[2] Sepoy Mutiny, the revolt of the Sepoys, the native Indian troops, in 1857–59, against the British empire. See also O'Casey's comic account of an Irishman in the British army during the Sepoy revolt, "the bould Mulligan" in "There Go the Irish," *They Go, The Irish: A Miscellany of War-time Writing* (1944), compiled by Leslie Daiken; reprinted in *Blasts and Benedictions* (1967).

[3] Royal Irish Constabulary, the police force in Ireland under British control before 1922.

To Daniel Macmillan

MS. MACMILLAN LONDON

TOTNES, DEVON
12 OCTOBER 1942

Dear Mr. Daniel:

Thank you for your very kind letter of the 23rd September. The missus should have said that International Literature cabled asking me to become their English Correspondent; but I cabled declining, for I felt I wasn't up to the job. A song or dance would be more in my line; &, at any rate, my articles might prove to be too critical. So I thought it wiser to refuse. I'm afraid, too, English periodicals wouldn't publish my letters, let alone articles. Unless one has a facility, like "the way the waters come down at Lodon," writing articles is a wearing work; & I am too old now to try to wear out that way. I have written a review of Mayakovsky's Poems for the Anglo-Soviet Review,[1] & have been told that "it is a lovely thing," & "only I could have written it." That's something, anyhow.

As for Novels, my dear Mr. Daniel, I find it hard to read a novel, much more to write one! To me, it is a dead art after Ulysses & Finnegans Wake; & was, even before they were written. As for a "story," a story is being told now that won't be forgotten in our time. Of course, you are right about its popularity; & some of them deserve it. But take, say Priestley & Dickens: I'm reading, at the moment, to one of my boys, Our Mutual Friend, & would hardly think of reading a Priestley novel, or story, to him. Why? Just a bare few can equal the best of the past; & Joyce was one of them—a genius. But all this is in the nature of Literary Controversy, & gets us nowhere, as far as business is concerned.

I am, of course, trying to go on with my "biography," an O'Casey history of latter-day Ireland; & hope it may be a good book when the work is finished. Although, I'm a damned rogue in many ways, in the way of Literature, like the noble W. B. Yeats, there is something of the damned Puritan in me.

I will think over your suggestion, for, from a business point of view, you are wise, & I should like to make a bit of money just now, if possible; but I fear the feat of writing a "novel" is beyond me.

This appears to be a letter decrying all your kindly suggestions; but it isn't really so, & I shall remember them all. But most of the things on the war, & on all Nations woven into the war, as you know well yourself, will, in a short span of time, be as if they had never been read by man.

I do hope you & yours are in good hope & in good health.

Ever yours,
Sean O'Casey

---

[1] "A Flame in Overalls: Mayakovsky and His Poetry," *Anglo-Soviet Journal,* October-December 1942; a review of *Mayakovsky and His Poetry* by Herbert Marshall.

To Jack Carney

MS. NYU LIBRARY

[TOTNES, DEVON]

13 OCTOBER 1942

My dear Jack,

No apology needed for asking return of "Irish Republic." [1] I have kept it too long. Here it is back, with many thanks. Please give your Kind Comrade my warm thanks for the loan of the book. Strange Mrs. McArdle, neither in book or index, mentions Dr. O'Hickey! He who battled for Essential Irish in the "New University," was expelled from Maynooth, badgered & silently bullied at the Vatican, & died poor, without a parish, of a broken heart. A man to make ten of Ireland's Hyde, the "Sweet Little Branch." [2] I gave 10/– of hard-earned money towards his expenses in Rome. Oh, Ireland, Ireland! Curious, too, she credits Sean MacDermott as Editor of Irish Freedom. Bulmer Hobson was Editor. Still, for dates, etc., it is a fine book to have; but entirely devoid of life and imagination.

Thanks again.

Yours ever,

Sean

[1] Dorothy MacArdle, *The Irish Republic* (1937).
[2] Douglas Hyde (1860–1949), founder of the Gaelic League, first president of Ireland, 1937–45, wrote under the pseudonym of An Craoibhin Aoibhinn (the Sweet or Pleasant Little Branch).

To Macmillan & Co. Ltd.

TS. MACMILLAN LONDON

TOTNES, DEVON

28 OCTOBER 1942

Dear Sirs:

The Landlord is hammering at the door for his quarter's rent, due three weeks ago, and some other bills quarterly, have to be met, so, if it doesnt come to a great inconvenience to you, I should be real glad if you'd let me have a £100 on account. I know how you must be put to the pin of your collars to get things in shape, and keep things going, and am sorry that I have to trouble you in this way.

Yours sincerely,
Sean O'Casey

To Jasper Deeter and Mahlon Naill [1]

TC. O'CASEY

TOTNES, DEVON
31 OCTOBER 1942

Dear Jasper Deeter and Mahlon Naill:

With conscientious objection I have naught to do, for I have been a fighter all my life, finding some wars to be just ones, and especially this present fight to the death to destroy the spiritual and temporal horror of Fascism; and it might be over bold of me to venture a criticism of the clauses flourishing in the Selective Training and Service Act of 1942 as passed and practised by the U.S.A., Ours and the Soviet Union's great Ally in this desperate fight for life waged against a common enemy by decent men and women the wide world over. But the curious attitude of mind (hardly due to selective training) shown in the letter you quote from, Col. Lewis F. Kosch is a horse of another colour. What the devil does he mean by saying that "the maintenance of a theatre is certainly not a thing of National importance." Does he mean that such an activity is but of Local importance? I thought we had all learned by this that nothing, however insignificant, is only of local importance. A lot of glossy fools here, some time ago, thought, and got others to believe, that the Japanese irruption into Manchuria was but a local incident with which the rest of the world had nothing to do: we know to the differ now. We know now that Manchuria is on the border of Australia and not very far from the U.S.A. In a war, life is a thing of national importance as well as death. If it be that the theatre is of no use, then why not turn every art gallery into a munitions works? Because of the use of oak, beech, elm, and ash, I suppose we should rush out to hack down every rowan tree whose milky blossom and scarlet berries promote a smile on many a barren hillside; because of the

---

[1] Jasper Deeter and Mahlon Naill, of the Hedgerow Theatre, were conscientious objectors. Deeter was the founder and director of the theatre, a repertory company which he established in 1923 at Moylan, Rose Valley, Pennsylvania.

bodily need for vegetables, we should blast away the daffodil that comes before the swallow dares to take the winds of March with beauty. If we did these things, we not only do not deserve to win, we do not deserve to live. In London where a great space of useful buildings were laid low by fire and brimstone, not showered down by heaven, but by Hitler, a well-known church escaped. No guns were being hammered out in it; no shells fashioned there; it had no runway for planes to take off to seek the skies; but thousands of Londoners, and many outside the city, sighed happily when they heard St. Paul's still stood. We need the great wind, we need the earthquake, we need the fire in this terrible war, but there must be a place for the still small voice too. In the future, what we save from this struggle will be of more importance than what we have destroyed, and the theatre will not be the least of all these things. Where can the necessities of the war effort be felt and known more than in war-entangled Russia? Do they say to hell with culture in our effort to save it? On the contrary, the theatre is busier than ever there. I know that, for I've been in touch with those activities for the past eight years. Look at the "International Magazine," published in Moscow (it can be got, I think, in Four Continent Book Corporation, 253, Fifth Avenue), and see what they say there. The Moscow Art Theatre, safe in Saratov, is as great a treasure as ever. Though the audiences have changed, consisting of Red Army men and War Workers, the Theatre remains the same, producing the great European masterpieces as vividly as ever. The Moscow Gorky Art Theatre is hard at work, too, producing The Pickwick Club, Ostrovsky's Ardent Heart, and A. L. Tolstoy's Tsar Fyodor Ivannovich. The Moscow Academic Theatre is at work on the production of one of Shakespeare's tragedies, having already done Hamlet, Julius Caesar, and Othello. They say "the war has not compelled our workers in the field of culture and art to suspend their activities. On the contrary it has welded them into a more closely-knit family. The lights still shine brightly in our crowded theatres. In the first eight months of war thirty concert brigades gave over 19,000 performances on the shores of the Barents Sea, in the Arctic, in the forests of Karelia, in besieged Leningrad, in Sebastopol, in Kerch, and other parts of the front."

So far from the theatre losing its importance, it has become more important than ever. And the Hedgerow Theatre is in the centre of this importance for the work it has done in the past, and the work it may and should do in the future—if Col. Kosch doesnt foolishly close its door and put out its lights. Sure the stars in your banner symbolise something more than so many acres of land? I, myself, sometimes see them flare into the faces of your great statesmen, poets, sages, dramatists, and pioneers. And in one of them, that for the State of Pennsylvania, I see because of its work for National and International Drama, the sturdy light of the Hedgerow Theatre holding up the torch of the drama, a torch that should shine, must shine, clearly throughout the smoky flame of the war.

Long live the Abbey Theatre of Dublin! Long live the Art Theatre of

Moscow! And long live the Hedgerow Theatre of Moylan, in the State of Pennsylvania!

Ever yours,
Sean O'Casey

To Totnes Times

31 OCTOBER 1942

"Mr. Sean O'Casey and Lt-Col. Raynor's Speech"

Dear Sir:—

Lt-Col. Raynor's recent speech, as reported,[1] seems to be very fluid and a little confused—to use a phrase of the experts writing on the war. His chief remark, made vehemently, was that "this ballyhoo of a Second Front is a poor advertisement for the Democracy for which we are fighting." That is one view from a military and political expert of a sort. Not very long ago, Mr. Winston Churchill hailed this "Ballyhoo" as a fine advertisement of the courage and determination of a democratic people—so we have one expert opinion against another.

This "clamour," as Col. Raynor calls it, is really the drums of the people beating to battle; and though the sound tightens the ear, it isn't half loud enough yet, as the speaker admitted himself (a slight contradiction, apparently) when he said "we havent our whole heart in this war. Germany has, so has Japan, so has the Soviet Union, but England hasn't." So the other side of his mouth condemns the very people who are showing signs of putting their whole heart into the war. It isn't as if those who did were content to send others to take all the risk, while remaining themselves behind safe among the lotuses, for where is the safe habitat today for anyone still drawing the breath of life? But why aren't the whole of the people wholehearted in the waging of the war? One reason is that Col. Raynor and many like him seem to go in fear of such a spirit developing, as he shows himself by declaring that this desire on the part of the people to get into closer grips with the enemy is a parade of ballyhoo. I wonder what he'll feel like when the desire becomes a passion as it must, if Hitler is to be defeated! Much as he seems to dislike the sound (and few of us love it), the drums of war must be hammered harder, even though they disturb those who prefer to play nicely and more delicately on the dulcimer.

The speaker seemed to have a superstitious reverence for what he called "experts," forgetting that an expert is none till he proves himself one. All of us, in one way or another—if it be but diving under a table—

---

[1] "Second Front Ballyhoo," *Totnes Times,* 24 October 1942, a report of a speech by Lt.-Col. Ralph Raynor, M.P. for Totnes.

have to become experts in this war, and till each of us excels in this way or that this war will not be won. Expert knowledge this time can't be lifted happily out of books or brains in war office or admiralty, but in, and only in, the field of experience. The Soviet Military Commanders weren't long discovering that the war wasn't going according to the principles focussed on the students in the military academies.

The Germans, thank God, are finding this out too; and today gunners teach gunners, snipers snipers, tank attackers tank attackers co-operatively together from experience gained on the field of battle. And experts have done curious things in the war. "The astonishing inadequacy of our equipment when the British Army was pushed into Belgium to meet the whole weight of the German Army" wasn't the result of a "ballyhoo clamour," but was wholly organised by the experts of that time. It was Col. Raynor's experts who declared day after day for years that the Red Army was ragged, rotten, and ridiculous (against popular clamour, too); and that the German Army would in a few weeks of fighting go through it like a knife through butter. If I remember right, Hitler's experts destroyed the Red Army several times in one week, and have now discovered it was but an expert's dream.

In an article some time ago, Col. Raynor told us a lot about his friend, General Auchinlech, saying, at the end, that "we may safely leave everything to Auch." Though since then, and not through any ballyhoo that I am aware of, we lost 80,000 men, with numerous tanks and guns to boot. No, experts have yet to become infallible. So far, everything done in this war has been done, not because of ballyhoo clamour, but under the direction of the experts, and few will deny that many things, at home and abroad, have been done very badly. Not with us alone, but by the Americans, too, as in Pearl Harbour. We mustn't be too timid to say boo to an incompetent, even though he wears the feather of an expert in his cap. In the Soviet Union, after the fall of Kiev, Budyenny, who, evidently, wasnt up to the job of the time, was removed (though then, and now, a personal comrade of Stalin's), and Timoshenko put in his place. So must we do—Churchill did it after a visit to Libya—in criticism and ever vigilant watchfulness, if we are to come out of this conflict alive and kicking.

In his wonder at the fact that Britain in the war isn't as hot as her ally or her enemy, he asks, "is it because we, unlike Russia, have never been invaded, or is it because many believe we fight but for preservation (the first law of nature, by the way), with nothing to hope for after victory. . . . We have forgotten to be proud of being British. Patriotism has been out of fashion for far too long." It certainly isn't because we have never been invaded (we have been, several times, as a matter of fact—the Col. has forgotten his history), for France has been invaded I daresay, as often as Russia; yet France collapsed while Britain stood. Patriotism has been out of fashion—why? One thing, I imagine is, because profits became holier things than love of country, making many Christians even forget God.

And it is strange that Col. Raynor in his speech fails to mention one thing about which England might be proud. Nothing whatever of her heritage in music (Purcell, Elgar); painting (Gainsborough, Turner, Constable, Raeburn, John); Science (Faraday, Darwin); Literature (Shakespeare, Shelley, Keats, Milton, and a host of others); Religion (Coverdale, Wickliffe, Sir John More, Wesley). The British people's leaders have forgotten those who have given the nation a lasting fame and an eternal glory. A sad evidence of this was given when, at the end of Gen. Smuts's speech, a united Parliament, Lords Spiritual and Temporal, with His Majesty's Faithful Commons (Col. Raynor was probably there), sang as a fitting finale the soul-stirring chant of "He's a Jolly Good Fellow." Britain has more noble anthems than this sort of thing; but the leaders (or experts) seem to have thought patriotism to be out of fashion.

Lastly, the way the Anglican Archbishop talked recently about the future seems to have made the Col. a little hot under the collar. He calls it "airing his opinions," which, says Col. Raynor, "in a democracy he has a perfect right to do, and it is the Archbishop's duty to formulate a Christian basis in which our activities should move, but—". Ah, that "but"! The Col., I presume, is an Anglican, and he should know that neither this nor that Archbishop can formulate (as he calls it) a Christian basis. That was "formulated" nearly 2000 years ago, for all men by the Church's One Foundation; and for the Col. personally, at his baptism when he was made a child of God, a member of Christ, and an inheritor of the kingdom of heaven.

It is the Archbishop's duty, as far as in him may lie, to see that his flock be given every chance to grow in Christ, so that as they grow in years they may grow in wisdom, daily increasing in God's Holy Spirit (not weekly) more and more, till they come into their everlasting peace through life eternal; and to refuse to let them rest in the damning belief that this can be fulfilled by a formal visit to a church on Sundays, supplemented by jingling a coin for the poor and needy on a silver plate. There can be, conceivably, a brotherhood of man without a fatherhood of God; but there can be no fatherhood of God without a brotherhood of man; and no wave of a cheque book, be it never so large, can set it aside: it is, for Christians, an eternal fact. This land, if she is to continue to be worth fighting for, must become a land of hope and glory, not alone in song, but in all the daily round of all the common people of the Commonwealth.

Yours sincerely,
Sean O'Casey

To Jack Carney

MS. NYU LIBRARY

[TOTNES, DEVON]

4 NOVEMBER 1942

My dear Jack,

Thanks, oul' son, for Laverty's "Never No More," [1] & Cross's "The Tailor & Anstey." [2] I've read the first, and I'm afraid there isn't a greadeal in it. I think O'Faolain has rushed in too quick; & from what I've read of the 2nd book—67 pages, I think O'Connor has rushed in as quick as O'Faolain. Neither of these books (in my opinion) can come anyway near "The Green Fool" [1938] by Patrick Kavanagh; &, even his, staggers occasionally. We must be wary of what O'Connor & O'Faolain praise; they, quite evidently, have assumed the purple cope of the Irish Academy of Letters; & are determined to canonise only those whom they lay their own hands on. Since I read in O'Faolain's "Irish Journey" [3] that only when he & O'Connor are together can he feel the surge of great things to be done. The two of them, it seems to me, to be a double dose of AE. They are quite as pontifical as Yeats, though the two of them together, mounted on each other's shoulders, can never reach higher than his knees. Yeats—with all his faults—was greater than even he thought himself to be; these two as little (in my opinion) as they think themselves to be big. Wasn't it O'Connor who wailed that they lacked the grace given by an intimacy with the Big Houses? I'm afraid neither Laverty nor Cross will do any remarkable things. There's a good chance for Francis McManus, possibly a better one for [Roibeard] O'Farachain & Kavanagh, but a small chance for these two. They will, I'm afraid, be like Teresa Deevy & P. V. Carroll—their best will be their first efforts. Anyway, we must beware of the choice of those two who are panting to present their hand-picked geniuses to the world. However, we can talk a little over these things when you & Mina come down. By the way, I hope you got "The Irish Republic" all-right. I sent it on the day after you asked for it. I hear there's a good Pelican book published on English Music—by Blom,[4] I think. How'd you like the song in the D.W.? I've written a review of Mayakovsky's poems for the Anglo-Soviet Magazine [5]—this is good writing, I think. I hope they may send me a copy when it comes out. They say "it is a lovely thing." I hope they're right. I've just written an article for the D.W.'s

---

1 Maura Laverty, *Never No More* (1942), her first novel.

2 Eric Cross, *The Tailor and Ansty* (1942). The book was banned by the Irish Censorship of Publications Board in 1942; the prohibition was revoked in 1948. Frank O'Connor wrote an introduction to the first edition, and a new introduction to the second edition in 1964.

3 Sean O'Faolain, *An Irish Journey* (1941).

4 E. W. Blom, *Music in England* (1942).

5 See O'Casey's letter to Daniel Macmillan, 12 October 1942, note 1.

R[ussian] Revolution Anniversary Number [6]; & a long letter to the Totnes Times in reply to a speech made by the local M.P., Col. Raynor—a good letter. I've signed a contract with the Abbey for "Juno" [7] who are going to put it on again—they did it last in 1940—so I hope this may bring in a few quid. And they've translated "The Plough" into Irish, & are to put it on in Galway! [8] March on, march on! That won't bring in much, £1. or so; but, strangely enough, I feel rather elated about it!

I believe Niall & Breon told you of the local blitz. Oh, it was bad enough, now, you that came outa the flames of London. The old town, men and materials, got an untidy shakeup. They seem to be constantly circling round the Sou'-West. I have just finished reading "Charles O'Malley," [9] & it was strange reading an old-fashioned yarn written a hundred years ago; the book itself, is nearly as old as the yarn. What a lot of travels the old book had. I remember Shaw saying somewhere that Lever wrote the first realistic book about the relations of husband & wife in a story called "The Ride," [10] a yarn no-one could bear. I see Niall going about with the George medal on his breast.

I hope you'll have a good time at the Soviet Embassy. Thanks for the papers. An Irish article says that "the Gaedhilge [Irish language] is the one shield protecting Christianity from Paganism."

Love to Mina & you.
Yours as ever,
Sean

[6] "Twenty-five Years Ago," *Daily Worker,* 9 November 1942.
  [7] *Juno and the Paycock* was revived at the Abbey Theatre on 9 November 1942, directed by Frank Dermody, and ran for four weeks, until 6 December 1942.
  [8] The Taibhdhearc Theatre in Galway produced *An Chéachta is na Réalta* (*The Plough and the Stars*), translated into Irish by Buadhach Tóibín, directed by Walter Macken, on 5 November 1942. Two years earlier the same theater produced *Scáil an Óglaigh* (*The Shadow of a Gunman*), translated into Irish by Pádraig O Finneadha, directed by Walter Macken, on 16 May 1940. Both productions ran for four nights. See O'Casey's letter to Walter Macken, 24 November 1942.
  [9] Charles Lever, *Charles O'Malley* (1841), a comic novel based on the author's student days at Trinity College, Dublin; one of his most popular works.
  [10] Charles Lever, *A Day's Ride* (1864).

To Jack Carney

MS. NYU LIBRARY

TOTNES, DEVON
8 NOVEMBER 1942

My dear Jack,
    Many thanks for the papers, the grand little cake, & the tobac; thanks to you and Mina, for I guess she had a hand in it too. I am enjoying a

nice smoke at the moment. I see Eileen has told you about our new shop—buy away, buy away—new shop opened. I have had a little argument in the Totnes Times with Lt-Col Raynor, our local M.P. Keeping my hand in, I suppose. The T. Times printed it in toto. I'll show it you, when you come down. Jack, I'm afraid "The Tailor & Anstey" is a very poor book. I don't like to say this; but nothing else, I feel, can be said about it. It is away below "Never No More." The yarn of them cutting the rope round the bent-up corpse was told to me by my brother, Mick, 56 or so years ago; he said *he* done it at a wake. As far as I can see, there is no folk-lore in the book from cover to cover. Not a word about the "West Room" or the power of "the curse." The West Room, attached to the modern term of going West, is also attached to Tir na nOg, to Avalon, to the Hesperides, to the Land of the Dead, towards the place where the sun sets. And the humour of the book doesn't come near the humour of "An Baile Seo 'Gainne," written by An Seabhac [1] many, many years ago; old tales told round the fireside, some of them the world over, like the one on which I founded "The End of the Beginning." No, I'm afraid Eric Cross won't go far; & I wish a protest had been made against the banning of a better book. If I remember right, I don't think he tried to give an explanation of the "straw men."

Well, coming back to Tir na mbeo, [2] the news is a lot better, & Germany seems now to be in something of a fix. It is hard to guess what may be in the minds of the big fellas about the world of the future. It is almost certain to me that the USSR will meet with opposition; but she will be well able to take care of herself. From the landing in N. Africa though, of course, as a threat to Rommel's rear, is, maybe, an effort to get Italy out of the war, & so create a great Latin Catholic Southern block of States, in spiritual union with Catholic America, & so, naturally, a powerful bulwark against the spread of Bolshevism—the first, the Pope's (Vatican's) dream; the second, the Pope's (Vatican's) nightmare. I agree with you about Garvin; [3] I don't know why they got him to go. A big mouth he was, & a big mouth he'll die. Curious, Jack, how modern Ulster writers think so much of themselves—did this ever strike you?—Ervine, AE, Garvin, Jimmy Douglas. More dogmatic than the veriest Vatican-controlled Ecclesiastical Council proclaiming a tenet of faith.

I hope Mina & you had a good time at the Soviet Embassy: I wish I could have been there.

I'm sure Shaw's Life [4] is interesting. There's no doubt, in my opinion, about Shaw. He is one of the great men of our time. A great man in every way. It is hard lines in Eire that she has to say farewell to such souls.

[1] See O'Casey's letter to the *Irish Times,* 23 February 1937, Vol. I, p. 651, for his comment on *An Baile Seo 'Gainne-ne* (1913), a book of short stories (*This Town of Ours*), by An Seabhac" (the Hawk), pen name of Pádraig Ó Siochfhradha (O'Sugrue); the source of O'Casey's one-act play *The End of the Beginning.*

[2] The land of the living.

[3] J. L. Garvin, editor of *The Observer.*

[4] Hesketh Pearson, *Bernard Shaw: His Life and Personality* (1942).

"Saoghal fada agus bas i nEirinn." Long life, & death in Ireland, the Irish-man's hope. Shaw has got the long life, but, I suppose, Kensal Rise will receive his bones.

I wonder if you could get me the following Penguin Books.
Pelican Book. History of England. Halevy. 2 Vols. [1924]
Growth of Civilization. W. J. Perry. [1937]
Medieval People. Eileen Power. [1924]
Psychopathology in Everyday Life. S. Freud. [1922]
Back to Methusaleh. Shaw. [1921]
Music [in England] by [E. W.] Blom. [1942]
The Common Reader. V. Woolf. [1938]
I'll let you have a PO. for the cost.

Love to Mina & you.
Ever yours,
Sean

When shall we see you?

To Miss S. D. Lange [1]

TC. INTER LIT, MOSCOW [2]

[TOTNES, DEVON]
8 NOVEMBER 1942

Dear Miss Lange:

My good Christ! Isnt it a pitiful thing that some publishers are worry-ing at such a time about the copyright of their books that the blood-dabbled Soviet People are asking for? Do not these gentlemen realise that the Soviet Union is a signatory to more important things today than the Berne Con-vention? [3] Dont these gentlemen realise that no personal profit will be made by anyone by the gifts of books of literary value to the reading Russian people? They are asking for bread, and these gentlemen wont even send them a stone. The people—not a little group here and there, mind you, but the people—are asking to be sent books that will show them what the British people are doing in literature, art, and the drama; and you

---

[1] Miss S. D. Lange, Secretary, Publishers' Advertising Circle, London.

[2] O'Casey enclosed a typed copy of this letter with his letter to Boris Sutchkoff, 15 December 1942.

[3] The Berne Convention, an international agreement on copyright principles, was established in 1886, and revised periodically up to 1971, when fifty-nine countries affirmed the reciprocal rights of authors in member nations to copyright protection. Neither the United States nor the Soviet Union has ever been a member.

are asking them if they wear the badge of the Berne Convention in the lapels of their coats. I have told them, as I have told him who preceded you in the Secretaryship, that Mr Timofei Rokotov is not a publisher; that he is a well-known film and drama critic in Moscow, and is one of the Editors of the International Magazine that circulates now in China, Iraq, Palestine, The U.S.A., Great Britain, Persia, Turkey, Australia, New Zealand, Mexico, Cuba, Uruguay, Chile, and Colombia. He has nothing whatever to do with the question of payment of royalties ala the Berne Convention. That is a question that must be taken up with other authorities, but not just now. The People of the USSR have something else to do, as the British publishers should damn well know. Instead, they should be glad that the Russian people are taking an interest in British literature. I should certainly be glad, if they took a greater interest in what I try to do. At the moment a well-known Writer in the USSR has made a new translation of Romeo and Juliet, and, if Shakespeare be in the land of the conscious, he'll be glad of the honour done to him, and glad he was able to bestow the honour to the writer in translating his play, without asking him anything about the Berne Convention. When peace comes, I shall be one who will be interested in helping any way I can to get the USSR to treat our copyright in the way we prefer; but, even then, should that way be declined, I shouldnt like to keep back a book from a people who ardently wished to have it when I knew there was no personal profit to be made out of the transaction. And, if an agreement should be reached, what a market for our books—for some of us, anyhow; for it is only fair to say, on my own behalf, that mine arent first favourites with the R people. Now it is a disgrace for publishers to talk in this way, and, I pray you, try to get a little sense into their British heads.

Yours sincerely,
Sean O'Casey

To Totnes Times

14 NOVEMBER 1942

"Mr. Sean O'Casey Replies to Lieut.-Col. R. Raynor, M.P."

Dear Sir:—A few remarks on Col Raynor's very courteous reply [1] to my criticism. I should like to drop a few flares of thought upon his strange analysis of the Indian problem, but as the Col. has left the field, it would

[1] A letter by Lieut.-Col. R. Raynor in the *Totnes Times,* 7 November 1942.

be silly to gallop out to tilt at the insubstantial air. I fail to see that the "clamour" for a second front has any political motive behind it. To me, it seems to be a genuine out-cry from the heart. Its partial happy realization has already sent a much-needed thrill through the veins of the people. One powerful reason, I think, why the "public were pleased to starve the army for twenty years" was because they felt it wasn't a people's army; now it is, and, giving the people their due, they have in equipment moulded it pretty near to their hearts desire.

The remark of mine relative to a previous invasion was parenthetical, and so didn't enter the argument. My point was that invasion or non-invasion didnt seem to have anything to do with the British people's "lack of heart in the war." France had been invaded, and collapsed; Greece had been invaded and even conquered, but she fought with the combined valour of Achilles and Hector. My reference to the Colonel's remark about Auchinlech was simply used to emphasise the danger of worshipping what were called "Experts." That he, personally, didn't succeed was likely due to the uncertain fortunes of war. But the experts have done a lot of harm. Negatively, in proclaiming the utter inefficiency of the Red Army; positively for so long in implying the invincibility of the German Army.

Very recently, some of them seemed to be insinuating the invincibility of Rommel. Well, the clever German General seems to have met his match now. In a war of this magnitude, more than expert knowledge is needed; imagination must go with it, and this gift is reserved for the unfortunate few. Lastly, those who fill high places and have high names shouldn't be afraid of criticism, even stupid criticism (this will very quickly find its level), or of "treading on one another's toes," as the Col. calls it.

Moscow has seen the production of a play called "Front," which denounces the smugness and self-satisfaction of certain older officers with a fine record in the Civil War, but who are unfitted for the programme of efficiency and enterprise needed today; and calls for the introduction of younger men with competence and drive into all branches of the war machine. Though, of course, it doesn't always happen that the young are efficient or the old incompetent, yet it is natural, I suppose that older leaders with fine records, like old actors and actresses, don't like to move out of the limelight; but in times when even little things mean life or death to us all, fine records must be satisfied with a secondary honour, and, if they aren't ready to be resigned to this, then they must be pushed heart-lessly out of the way.

Thanks, many thanks, Mr Editor, for your courtesy to me and to my opinions.

Yours sincerely,
Sean O'Casey

To Jack Carney

MS. NYU LIBRARY

[TOTNES, DEVON]
16 NOVEMBER 1942

My dear Jack,

In bed—Influenza has got me in the bag.

This is to say just that I didn't say R. Roses For Me had been published because I didn't know. Officially, I don't know yet, Macmillans haven't said anything about it.[1] They are "tre na cheile" [2] with things now because of lack of staff. I didn't get my year's pay till the 25th of Oct, due on the 1st, & had to ask for it. But the publication is, of course, the main thing; & to do that they must have toiled like hell. As soon as copies come to me, I'll send on one to you & Mina at once.

All the best,
Sean

1 *Red Roses For Me* was published on 17 November 1942.
2 "Confused."

To Jack Carney

MS. NYU LIBRARY

[TOTNES, DEVON]
23 NOVEMBER 1942

My dear Jack,

I have got the 17 books now. I got them for 4/9 each, so it will save you £1. They will be set (the cost) in a contra account deduction from my royalties next time. If there be any you would really like inscribed, let me know as soon as you can, & I shall be glad to do this for you. The rest I will autograph in the usual way. I will ask Breon to do what you suggest. I've sent to you & Mina, under another cover, a copy of the play. Seventeen copies seems a lot to give away. It's good for me, of course, for (I think) I get royalties even on a trade price, though I'm not sure.

The news continues to be good. But I think we'll be up against a hard fight in Tunis. They'll strive like hell to hold on there—make another Odessa of it. I'm glad Juno goes on for another week—it's very welcome. Capt Holdsworth, a big-gun here, has entered the field of debate (Raynor cantered off) & has challenged the term of "a people's Army" to the present fighting force. He says England's Army was always a people's army—oh yeh?

I'm better of the Influenza now; but uncomfortable with the damned catharrh it left behind.

Did you see the reference to the fight between National University & Trinity over N. University Degree Day in Dublin? "The police had to make a baton charge, but though many got superficial injuries, no-one was obliged to go to hospital."

No, indeed; I wonder if the workers had been part of it, would all of the wounds have been so superficial? No, sir; they wouldn't.

Well, all the best.
Love to Mina & you.

Sorry you had to postpone your visit; but I daresay "the wires are hot" these days. I'll send you Laverty's book back with a consignment of the play. Later on, "The Tailor & Anstey," when Eileen reads it.

Ever yours,
Sean

To Gabriel Fallon

TS. Texas

Totnes, Devon
24 November 1942

My dear Gaby:

I put "Esq" on letters now just to show to whom the letters have truly been written. I put it on letters to Communist friends who address me as comrade. There's no more in it than that. I'm glad to hear that you are all well. I've just crept from an attack of Influenza, and feeling the usual hilarity that follows it. I see Frank MacM has written another book; [1] I hope it's a good one, and that it will have a fine sale. Rose's belief in an American production, was, I'm afraid, a very kindly dream. She probably saw a reference to a production of three one act plays there by [Eddie] Dowling, one of which was the E[nd] of the Beginning.[2] It started off well, but after three or four nights, Dowling fell seriously ill, and all were or was abandoned: better fortune next time.

---

[1] Francis MacManus, *Watergate* (1942), a novel.
[2] See O'Casey's letter to Jack Carney, 9 April 1942, note 1.

Thanks, Gaby, for your telegram and letter. I should like to let Shelah [Richards] have a go at RED ROSES FOR ME, but the Agent here might advise against it (not that I'd care, if I decided myself in favour of her doing it). We'll see. Another point: Louis D'Alton asked me for the play while I was doing the proofs; but as well as fearing it might be too much for him, I was fearful he'd lose money on it, and he earns what he gets too hard to lose it that way, lose it on me.

I daresay Shelah has, by now, read the play, and knows what she thinks of it. If she likes the play, after reading it, and doesn't think production too much trouble, and that it could be done well, let her, if she wishes, write me out a draft agreement, and we'll see—she and I—what we can do about it. No option can be given, Gaby, without a contract, or, at least, agreement on the main parts of a contract. The play's production wouldn't be as hard as that of W the Gates, or the S. Tassie, but harder than P. Dust. So let Shelah tell me what she thinks of it. Since she has formed a first opinion of it on what has been written in the N. Statesman,[3] let her read an opposite opinion that appeared in Reynold's News on Sunday the 22nd.[4]

I will write to Macmillan's to send you a copy, as it is forbidden for me to do so. It may be some time before it gets to you, for Macmillan's are understaffed, and trying to carry on with workers who are either too old or too young. I first knew it had been published by friends telling me of what was in the N. Statesman.

I met V. Connell here. He was staying in a hotel near Totnes, and came to see us twice. Throng O'Scarlet [5] is an odd play, and I don't know enough to comment upon it, I haven't read his other one: He writes to say that many think it to be first-class. He tells me some Managers who have read it say that it is a great masterpiece. So there should be something in it.

In haste to catch a post.

My dear love to Rose, the children and you.

Sean

---

[3] G. W. Stonier, "Mr. O'Casey's New Play," *New Statesman and Nation,* 14 November 1942, a favorable review of the published text of *Red Roses For Me.*

[4] H. A. Milton, "Tragedy of a Comedy," *Reynolds News,* 22 November 1942, an unfavorable review. See O'Casey's letter to Jack Carney, 26 November 1942, note 4; and his letter to *Reynolds News,* 6 December 1942.

[5] Vivian Connell, *Throng o' Scarlet* (1941).

To Walter Macken [1]

TS. MACKEN

TOTNES, DEVON

24 NOVEMBER 1942

Dear Walter Macken:

Thanks very much for your cheque, receipt for which goes with this letter. Taking everything into consideration, £14 isnt too bad for one performance of a play in Irish.[2] Towns in Ireland have given less for a performance in the vulgar tongue—the English. Tell me have you ever read An Beul Bocht? [3] It was written by him who writes as Miles na Coppalleen in The Irish Times. I understand that it caused a lot of anger among the Gaels. I have read it. It is, undoubtedly bitter, but some of it excellently written, and a good deal of it is true. There are a few Corcha Dorchai [4] in Ireland still. The thing, in my opinion, that weakens the Gaelic Movement is the same thing that weakens every movement here— too select a selection of leaders. Here, Harrow and Eton (though these are wobbling a bit now; the guns of Stalingrad are weakening the walls); there the Colleges, Tourmakeady, Rinn,[5] and the like. What a pity Jim Larkin wasnt an Irish Speaker; and what a pity Pearse died in Easter Week. I read that the Gaelic League the other year got but a little more than £400 for its revenue. Seems incredible. It has lost its colour, its sparkle, and its punch. I dont know that our enthusiasm was entirely due to the antagonism of the then government. In Wales the same Government wasnt so bitter against the language because, I suppose, it wasnt firmly connected with any "rebel" movement; yet the Welsh tongue held its own, and grew, and, I believe, is still growing. There are, as you say, many lovely things in the Irish language—indeed, the language is beautiful—, and it would be a great loss if it perished. If England had any savvy for the good things of life, she'd allot a few millions a year each for Welsh, Irish, and the Gaelic of the Scot. Under a Communist Government she would, as the Soviets do to the many tongues living in their land. Some of them, spoken by a few millions, hadnt even an alphabet or grammar, and they just sat down, created both, so that the people's folklore might be preserved forever, and the people made proud of their spiritual possession. My warm regards to

---

[1] Walter Macken (1915–67), novelist, playwright, actor; director of the Taibhdhearc Theatre, the Gaelic-speaking theatre in Galway. Later he served as Assistant Manager and Artistic Advisor of the Abbey Theatre, 1965–66.

[2] *The Plough and the Stars* was produced in an Irish translation at the Taibhdhearc Theatre on 5 November 1942. See O'Casey's letter to Jack Carney, 4 November 1942, note 8.

[3] Myles na gCopaleen, *An Béal Bocht* (1941).

[4] The imaginary Gaelic-speaking village that is satirized in *An Béal Bocht*.

[5] The Gaelic-speaking colleges, Tourmakeady in Galway and Rinn in Waterford.

you and your friends and to Galway—my mother spent a number of years there when she was a kid.

Yours sincerely,
Sean O'Casey

To Jack Carney

MS. NYU LIBRARY

[TOTNES, DEVON]
26 NOVEMBER 1942

My dear Jack,

I'm feeling a little more at home in the world now, thank you. I think I like the thick twist best. When I get any, I do a little Alchemycal job: I cut it up, roll it, tear it into shreds, mix a little other kind with it, place the mixture in the jar, cover all with a moist cabbage leaf, & leave simmering for a few hours, then I have a lovely cruiser-weight smoke. Stalingrad, & round about it, is great news. I must admit that I never expected a push here; & being human, & liable to err, expected the call often that the "Red Army had evacuated Stalingrad." It just amounts to the fact that the Red Army is even better than I thought it, & that's saying a lot. Thank God I was in the wrong.

I don't think I'd like your job in Éire, Jack. You have your work cut out for you. She was always a shy young lass, & she's shyer now. However, you can but do your best. And, as you say, the best stories in Ireland have got to stay there. Is Rhys Davies the author of "How Green Was My Valley"? [1] Anyhow, whether he is or no, he's not wise to pass by a chance of £20 a week, though I doubt any theatre would guarantee anyone £1 a week, much more £20. If in Ireland you'd get me a catalogue of publications by An Gúm. [2] I like to have one; & if you see a second-hand copy of Hyde's Love Songs of Connacht, [3] I'd like to have it too.

I do hope you'll have a successful time. I made out your cheque for £4.0.0. minus (Latin for within) the cost of 5 Penguins a copy at 9d each, making the cheque £3.16.3 I think, or is this correct?

I am keeping the books here till you send me the list of names you want put in them.

Those were two lovely tartan skirts Mina made for Shivaun. She has lovely taste in these things.

[1] Richard Llewellyn, not Rhys Davies, wrote *How Green Was My Valley.*
[2] *An Gúm,* the government plan for publications in the Irish language.
[3] Douglas Hyde, *Love Songs of Connacht* (1904).

So Milton, H. A. is H. Fyfe,[4] is he? Now I know. If you remember what I said in P. in the Hallway about Northcliffe [5] & his henchmen, you'll get the reason for his curious remarks. I've sent a comment or two. Curious why he should think a Protestant Anglican a queer thing in Dublin. He's right there (and wrong at the same time) for there's no Anglican Protestant in Dublin. The Church of Ireland (Protestant) isn't Anglican. And there are 100,000 members in Dublin Diocese; so one "walking down Sackville St" wouldn't really be "the queerest sight." Oh, he knows, he knows—in me arse.

Love to Mina & you,
Sean

PS. And "Life of Hyde" written by Himself, in Irish.[6]

[4] H. Hamilton Fyfe (1869–1951), author and journalist, political writer for *Reynolds News,* 1930–42. He used the pseudonym of H. A. Milton for some of his reviews. See O'Casey's letter to *Reynolds News,* 6 December 1942.

[5] Lord Northcliffe, Sir Alfred Harmsworth (1865–1922), publishers of *The Times* and the *Daily Mail;* described in the *Encyclopædia Britannica* as the "most successful newspaper publisher in the history of the British press." He was born in Chapelizod, Co. Dublin. The young O'Casey and his brother Archie worked for the Harmsworth Irish Agency in Dublin at the turn of the century. See "All Heaven and Harmsworth Too," *Pictures in the Hallway* (1942).

[6] Douglas Hyde, *Mise agus an Connradh* (*Myself and the [Gaelic] League*) (1905).

To Dr. Joseph D. Cummins [1]

TC. O'CASEY

[TOTNES, DEVON]
26 NOVEMBER 1942

My dear Joe:

Et tu Brute! Oh, God! am I in for another row over RED ROSES FOR ME! When I was writing the play, and, indeed, till I got your letter such an implication in the incident of the missing statue never entered my mind.[2] But now, since you have placed it before me, clad in a grumble,—

[1] Dr. Joseph Dominick Cummins (1882–1959), 38 Merrion Square, Dublin; ophthalmic surgeon; was head surgeon at the Royal Victoria Eye and Ear Hospital, Dublin, in 1923 when he first met and treated O'Casey for an ulcerated cornea. They remained close friends and exchanged many letters until the doctor's death, but unfortunately none of O'Casey's letters have survived, except for this typed carbon copy and another written on 30 October 1944. O'Casey dedicated the published text of *Red Roses For Me* "to Dr. J. D. Cummins, in memory of the grand chats around his surgery fire."

veneration versus worship—, I suggest that you were thinking of the theory and not the practice. For more than forty years I have lived among these "simple, poor Catholics"; I have been, and am, still one of them in all but the faith, and I know them to the bone. Now, Joe, do you really know how they think, and what they do in this matter of holy image veneration? As a matter of fact, the incident happened, bar the singing of those particular verses, which are, of course, my own coinage, but represent the actual feeling of those rejoicing over the return of their Patroness. Did you know, or do you know (She may stand there still) Our Lady of the Tolka? Below Drumcondra Bridge, on the miry bank of the river, at the back of a group of miserable cottages, flooded in the winter by the Tolka waters, on a pedestal stood a statue of Our Lady in white gown and blue mantle. I knew Her well, knew the people who lived in the cottages, and sometimes watched them spending a few precious pennies to buy flowers for the shrine. They never asked for much, the necessaries of life; daily bread, or, maybe a cure for something brought on by hunger and rottenness of home life; and maybe that the river wouldnt flood too much when the rains came. No petition for a contract or success in an examination to provide a job in the Civil Service, Railway Clerkship, or one in Guinness's Brewery. I tell you the devotion to that statue was, in my opinion, nearer than next door to worship—and what the hell harm anyhow? She represented to them the colour and loveliness they craved for, and they worshipped what was, in their opinion, beyond their reach in this world. That is where I fell from them. It was within their reach in this world, only they wouldnt stretch out their hands far enough to get it. But their devotion was always a beautiful manifestation to me: they adored something above themselves. So do they in the play, and it is not to be condemned, or deprecated, by a fairly comfortable, safely-placed professional man. It strikes me, dear Joe, that it is you rather than I who are unjust to the simple Catholic poor.[3]

[2] Dr. Cummins, a devout Roman Catholic, had just finished reading the copy of *Red Roses* which O'Casey had sent to him, and in a letter of 22 November 1942 to O'Casey he made the following comment on the statue of the Lady of Eblana incident:

> The Catholic uses statues of the Saints and the members of the Holy Family to evoke a pious mood, as an aid to religious zeal and fervour, but he does not worship them. I confess I do not like the incident of the missing statue and the attendant behaviour of the simple poor Catholics of the house. Is it possible to present fairly the religious aspects of contemporary Ireland? For centuries the Catholics were oppressed by a system that aimed at destroying their self-respect as well as their material prosperity; while, under the system, indeed as an essential part of it, the Protestants, a small minority, were protected and favoured and made the lawful receivers of the looted Catholic property. (MS. O'Casey)

[3] In part of a letter to O'Casey on 4 December 1942, Dr. Cummins made the following reply:

> You are quite right . . . I have become irritable from being too much absorbed in my own affairs and have grown morbidly touchy. Forgive me for imputing to you a lack of sympathy with those simple people. I am shocked at having done so. I have never known a man so free from bias, so white-hot in the face of injustice as you. (MS. O'Casey)

On the other hand, the "bleeding statues" of Templemore was an ugly and sordid business, receiving hurried acceptance from the lower middle class who rushed in droves there, whether belief in them was genuine or not. It was turned into a profitable market for the letting of lodgings at advanced prices (Republican police went down to keep order), and the rapid and profitable sales of bundles of Rosary Beads. Lourdes is but a gargantuan expansion of Templemore, and Fatima in Portugal is taking its place since the war. I dont for a moment believe (I know they dont) bother their heads about the fine difference between Latria, hyper-doulia, and Doulia. And why should they? Havent they enough of problems to face without facing those in theology? But this attitude is just as prevalent among the "respectable" and better-off Catholics. Do you ever read the more popular C. Press and Catholic Literature (as it is called)? What about the Imeldist and its Miraculous Medal? And the blood of St. Januarius, liquefying when the proper time comes. Shaw mentions it in his preface on Miracles in "St. Joan." Freud mentions it in his book on everyday Psycho-analyses,[4] and you mentioned it one evening at your surgery fire when you were trying to get me interested in Freud's idea of the sub-conscious in the nature of man. Did you read the goings-on when Mother Maddelena (I think that is her name) was being canonised? The Nuns in her titular convent have an image of her made from leather and straw, with a wooden belly (they call it, I think, an abdomen) in which—for it is hinged—is the holy relic. Lately there have been some disquieted letters in the C. press about The Legion of Mary, intimating, in a gentle way, the danger of going too far with this devotion; the writers (and the paper) got a sharp rebuke from Father Heenan, the Director (I believe) of the Legion. As well, church authorities had to exclaim against a lot of clients who were eager to constantly wear chains as a sign of their captivity to the Blessed Virgin. And look at the cult of that Matt Talbot[5] going on in Ireland, led by persons rich comparatively in this world's goods, and anxious to keep that way, with the help of the Blessed Matt. No, Joe, my only mockery of the poor simple Catholics is that they are content to stay simple and remain poor. I dont think the Penal Laws had so much to do with it all. Certainly they arent responsible for the Dublin Slums. And, as well as fighting for the Faith, they were, we must remember, fighting for the Stuarts. Without Penal Laws, the Catholics are as badly off in Spain and Portugal as they

[4] Sigmund Freud, *Psychopathology of Everyday Life* (1922).

[5] Matt Talbot (1856–1925), a Dublin laborer who had been a dissolute drinker until the age of twenty-eight, when he suddenly reformed and went on to live a life of extreme mortification and holiness. During the 1913 General Strike he continued working on the Dublin quays and was accused of being a blackleg. When he died chains were found around his body, rusted into the flesh. In recent years many unsuccessful attempts have been made to canonize him. O'Casey mocks him as "Mutt" Talbot in "In this Tent the Rebubblicans," *Drums Under the Windows* (1945). Interest in Talbot remains high in Dublin. Thomas Kilroy's play on his life, *Talbot's Box,* was presented at the Abbey Theatre during the Dublin Theatre Festival on 13 October 1977; and in 1978 the new Matt Talbot Bridge over the River Liffey was dedicated.

are here. And the good Protestants of England, the millions of them, arent much better off than either. I've seen them often, and lived with three of their children when they came to us here after or just before the London bombing. It was a revelation to Eileen (and to a lot of other people), for she hadnt come up against anything like it before. And Ireland isnt so poor as some think (part of it). At the opening day in Cavan Cathedral they took in £7,000, a good start off, to sày the least. Of course the Catholic gentry didnt like to lose their property when the planters took it off them, and they wont like to lose it when the workers take it off them either. No, Joe, the Bank is more to them than the Temple, except in so far as they use the sanctity of the Temple to hold on to what they have. Well, that's enough for tonight. It's just as hard to project a play on to the stage as writing it. One would want to be able to rehearse, or experiment before publication; but where would I get that chance? So one has to use one's inner vision as well as one can.

Except for a recent touch of Influenza, I'm O.K. And we're all going strong. The eldest boy is just six foot now, and broad chested. He's not fifteen yet. The younger boy is big and sturdy too; and the girl, now three, is a grand kid. Eileen is fine. She's busy helping on a local branch of the Anglo-Soviet Council, and has opened a shop where books are sold dealing with the USSR, and for the sale of toys made by local workmen and women, the profit to go to the USSR Medical Fund. And, then, she has to keep an eye on me, for this war food makes it hard for me to live happily. I do some digging—there's no one else to do it; cut all the hedges, keep the garden trim, and various odd jobs about the house, as well as answering letters, doing an odd article for the "Daily Worker"; and I've written an article on Lady Gregory for the "Saturday Book." Well, that's enough for today.

My love to you.
[*Sean*]

To Totnes Times

28 NOVEMBER 1942

A People's Army

Dear Sir:—

No sooner does Lt-Col. Raynor gallop from the field than Capt Holdsworth [1] gallops on to it, troubled and anxious about the term of a

[1] Captain F. J. C. Holdsworth's letter, "A People's Army," *Totnes Times,* 21 November 1942.

People's Army. Of course all armies are made up of individuals, but the army of yesterday may be very different to that of today, and that of today very different to that of tomorrow. Armies, like all organisms, grow, and as they grow, they change. It doesn't follow that because an army is composed of individual units it must therefore be a people's army. It doesn't follow either that because an Army is part and parcel of the people of the nation, it must therefore be a people's army.

The army that followed Wat Tyler and Father Ball (a formidable force) differed in ideal and outlook very much from that which followed the Young King and the Mayor of London, though each side formed part and parcel of the nation. The army that fought behind Cromwell differed very much in outlook and ideal from that which fought for King Charles, though both were part and parcel of the people of the nation.

Capt. Holdsworth's low-brow disregard of the relativity of time in assuming that the Boer War was of the olden time seems to imply the belief that the British Army, like a fairy flower in a pantomime, suddenly bloomed into full existence when forty thousand horse and foot sailed for Table Bay. The then army had evolved from a thousand impulses and activities of the past. The Clan armies who followed their chiefs, the feudal armies that followed the liege lords, in which the soldier couldn't look upon himself as an Englishman, but only as a vassal of his master, and then, finally, out of the system of scutage, came the mercenary army from which the standing army was eventually evolved. As a matter of fact, relatively, the standing army is practically an innovation.

With the advance of military science (the discovery of gunpowder, the invention of cannon, for instance), the scope and nature of the army gradually changed though they remained part and parcel of the nation. Yet some of the problems of the past remain the problems of today—unity of command, for example, was a problem in the time of the Crusades. As the army grew in science, a better education became necessary for the soldiers, if they were to be of the fullest use.

It isn't necessary for me to point out how many things a soldier must know above what he knew "as long ago as the Boer War," and so his nature has become a fuller one. But a long journey through life had to be made before the army could become an army of the people. It had to be used first to add to the wealth of England's industrial lords by conquest of land and exploitation of peoples, forcing cotton into India, and opium into China, and drink everywhere. Indeed, the army that subdued India was for a long time, not an army under the British Government, but was formed and armed and paid by a private company, the valour of the men making huge profits for the owners of the company.

The South African War was one of conquest, pure and simple, and the British "Absent-minded Beggars" who fought in it werent very conscious in any social or political way. "They came from every walk of life," says Capt. Holdsworth, Cook's son, Duke's son, and son of a belted Earl—forty thousand of them. Quite; but the son of the Duke, and the Earl were all officers, and the sons of the cooks were all privates.

Then came the big change in the first World War. It was too big for the dukes' sons and the sons of the belted earl to go round and furnish leaders, so they had to call on the cook's son to lend a hand. It was in this war that a people's ideal became plain and evident. It wasn't any longer possible to write of the soldier, "his not to reason why; his but to do and die." One phrase of the Nation's leader will furnish the ideal: "We fight to make England a land fit for heroes to live in." It didn't come off, and our last state was worse than our first. A wave of indifference and cynicism swept like a blight over the land, indeed, over the world. But there was a difference: out of the vast wreckage rose a red star. It was the symbol of a tremendous achievement by a people, determined through community service, to build as no nation ever built before, and beset by hostility all round, and hurt by many mistakes, rose up what is now known as the Union of Soviet Socialist Republics.

Today, more socially and politically conscious than ever, the people are united more than ever before. The whole people are in the fight, with the consciousness of what must be done when the fight is over. The cook's son is more dominant than ever—not because he is a cook's son, but because he has a talent the nation needs. The nation will need that talent more than ever when peace comes, and he will see he has a chance to use it, or know the reason why. There will be no sigh of cynicism then, but the cry of labour to make England a fit place for decent men and women and sturdy children to live in. A big change is bound to take place, to enable the British people to bring this about.

Indeed, the change has well begun. It is not I who am shouting this; it is not being said by Moscow: it is being said by Washington, by London, and wherever the fighting French have their headquarters. Lt-Col. Raynor, even, has said as much. The people know it, and knowing it, the army knows it, for in this war the people and the army are one and indivisible. Otherwise the war could not be won. That is why the present army is a people's army as it never was before. When this fight ends, the needs of the people will come before profits. The big monopolists will no longer be permitted to take much and give little.

One thing only stands in the way—Hitler and his German army. Economic security for all has got to come. The people demand it; and the people's army are aware of the demand made by their mothers, wives, sisters, fathers, and children. The change may not be a comfortable one for Capt. Holdsworth. Certainly, not for me, for I am over old to readily adapt myself to such a change in life. But there is no escape, and he and I must but do our best to fall in with it. Finally, I don't believe Capt. Holdsworth is as low-brow as he says; certainly not so bad as that high-placed fool mind who recommended the Home Guard should be armed with pikes. Another reason calling for a change.

Yours sincerely,
Sean O'Casey

To the Hogarth Press [1]

TS. TEXAS

TOTNES, DEVON
DECEMBER 1942

To:—
            The Hogarth Press
      Messrs . . . .
Dear Sirs:
      The Chief Editor of International Magazine, printed and published in Moscow, has sent me the following cablegram:

> O'Casey, Totnes, Devon.
> Will you kindly forward following cable to publishers who consented to send books to Interlit (International Magazine): We have learned that by arrangement with Mr O'Casey you are kindly sending our address. International Magazine, Moscow. Post Office Box 527, you publish. Sure close relations between British and Soviet Editions will be extremely valuable in strengthening ties between our great nations. Unfortunately, books not yet received. Kindly forward list of books sent, it would help checking delivery. Please inform what may we do for your honorable edition.
>
> *Yours. Editor-in-Chief.*
> *Boris Sutchkoff.*

And to myself, personally, the following:

> ELT O'Casey, Totnes, Devon.
> 12 December 1942
> Your two most interesting letters received. No books save several from Faber & Faber yet reached us. Earnestly request PICTURES IN HALLWAY again, (a book of Mine which Macmillans kindly sent). Many thanks all you've done for Magazine. Letter following. Royalties remitting. Greetings. Sutchkoff.

[1] This was one of many such form letters O'Casey had drawn up; he wrote in the name of the Hogarth Press on the dotted line. Besides this letter, which is in the University of Texas Library, I also received a copy, without a name added, from *International Literature,* Moscow. O'Casey had included the second copy in his letter to Boris Sutchkoff, 15 December 1942.

The International Magazine, published in Moscow, contains stories from many nations, and reviews the literature, art, and cultural activities of all peoples. It was formerly, before the war, printed in English, French, German, with a bulky edition in Russian and other tongues of the USSR. Of course, it is no longer printed in either French or German; but it appears now in England, U.S.A., Iran, China, Turkey, Palestine, Australia, New Zealand, Mexico, Uruguay, Chile, and Colombia. So you see it is penetrating to quite a number of countries. At the moment, it deals principally with war activities from a literary point of view. Recently, I received a letter from the Secretary of your Advertising Circle which suggested that I should do something about bringing the USSR under the wide wing of the Berne Convention.[2] In times of peace, this would not be possible for me to do, much more impossible in time of war. I venture to suggest that the Soviet Parliament has a lot of other things to think of now. This is an inopportune time to solve this problem. But I further suggest that this shouldnt prevent us from sending books of quality that might interest the Soviet Peoples. It may lead to big things after the War. I myself hope that British Publishing will be represented in Moscow as it is now represented in New York, Canada, and the Dominions (other). With a population of 200 millions there is a fine chance for British Books. If I'm not mistaken, the U.S.A. isnt in step with the Berne Convention either.[3] But these things cant be rectified now; so because of what to us is an imperfection, we shouldnt miss the chance of doing what Mr Sutchkoff asks us to do.

I do appeal to you to give **Mr Sutchkoff's** cable your careful consideration, and hope you may come to a favourable and unanimous decision to do all you can to supply and satisfy his wants. If we cast our bread upon the waters, it may return to us sooner than we imagine.

Yours very sincerely,
Sean O'Casey

Please acknowledge so that I may show Mr Sutchkoff I sent you his message. Thank you. S. O'C.[4]

---

2 See O'Casey's letter to Miss S. D. Lange, 8 November 1942, note 3.
3 *Ibid.* O'Casey was right about the United States not being a member.
4 O'Casey added this final comment in longhand.

To Reynolds News

6 DECEMBER 1942

"Real Dubliners" [1]

H. A. Milton, reviewing a play of mine, "Red Roses For Me," writes: "A young man wants to be an actor, makes wild revolutionary speeches and is killed in a brawl. He is—of all queer things to be in Dublin—an Anglican Protestant, and his great friend is a clergyman."

Now the young man does not "want to be an actor"; but specifically says that he "would give anything to be a painter." He is not killed in a "brawl," unless, to Mr. Milton, a meeting held by workers on strike to voice a claim for a shilling a week increase, which meeting is proclaimed, and on which the soldiers open fire, be a "brawl."

I must ask your reviewer why an Anglican Protestant should be the "queerest of all things in Dublin"? So far from it being "queer" that one should be found in Dublin, there are, as a matter of fact, upwards of 100,000 of them in the Dublin Diocese.

If he be ignorant of this, as he shows himself to be, and so knows little of the life there, how does he know that the characters in the play are "real Dubliners"?

Sean O'Casey

Totnes, Devon.

[1] This was a reply to a review of the published text of *Red Roses For Me*, by H. A. Milton (H. Hamilton Fyfe), "Tragedy of a Comedy," *Reynolds News*, 22 November 1942. Milton stated that O'Casey was a comic writer who shouldn't try to write serious plays like *Red Roses*, about which he went on to say: "The picture drawn is true to life; the characters are real Dubliners, police inspector and all; but nobody in Dublin or out of it ever talked as they talk." See also O'Casey's letter to Jack Carney, 16 December 1942, where he complains that "the damned Editor of Reynolds edited my comments so as to make me say what I didn't say."

To Boris Sutchkoff [1]

TS. INTER LIT, MOSCOW

TOTNES, DEVON
15 DECEMBER 1942

Dear Friend:

I am sending a copy of your cable to each publisher listed on Official Notepaper of Publishers' Advertising Circle—55 of them. I hope the

[1] Boris Sutchkoff, editor, *International Literature,* Moscow. With this letter O'Casey enclosed a copy of the form letter similar to the one sent to the Hogarth Press, December 1942.

message from you, and a note from me may have a good effect. I enclose (I type it now) extract received from Circle's Secretary some time ago, in reply to a letter of mine:

Extract.

Dear Sir: I write to apologise to you for the long delay in replying to your letter. . . . I am glad to have the information you give about the International Magazine. I understand that some London publishers are responding to your requests for review copies, and that others have not responded. The reason for this is possibly that publishers fear that the copyright of their books will not be honoured in the USSR, as the Soviet Union is not a signatory to the Berne Convention, and I think that possibly there would be a better [response] if Mr Rokotov would obtain some assurance that the laws of copyright regarding English books would not be disregarded.

Yours, etc. S. D. Lange. Hon. Secretary.

I was ashamed to send you this information. I attach reply I sent to this Secretary.[2] I am still probing at them. Now I will forward your message when it has been typed to 50 copies.

I'm sorry you got only the books forwarded by Faber & Faber. Certainly, more than that lot went to you: I sent a number myself. But the way is long and, I suppose, dangerous. I got but two of the Interlit sent to me. If we can but get a grip on the Mediterranean Sea, we shall be nearer a touching of hands. Heaven send it soon. I enclose with this letter a copy of a review I wrote on a slender vol of Mayakovsky's poems published here recently. It appeared in the Anglo-Soviet Magazine, and it may interest you. I also enclose a number of verses recently written that may interest you, too. I am very busy with many things. We have opened here a depot attached to the Central Anglo-Soviet Committee, and, so far it has been a great success—far greater than I thought it could be among a rural people. We sell a lot of books dealing with the USSR, the local workers make toys which we sell, and give the money to The Soviet Medical Aid Fund. The profits on the books go to the same Fund. The soldiers here have given us a hand, painting and decorating the premises. My wife gives a lot of her time to it, in spite of having 4 children to mind (including myself), and we have given lectures, film shows, etc; and things are going well for a stronger knowledge of what the USSR is doing and has done.

As my cable has already told you, I have decided to do some regular correspondence for Interlit till a better man or woman turns up. All writers are very busy here in the way of articles for the Press, and in writing books about military and political problems—there's a military expert in every street. The SOCIETY FOR CULTURAL RELATIONS BETWEEN THE PEOPLES OF THE BRITISH COMMONWEALTH AND THE USSR might put you in the way of finding a suitable correspondent. I dont like to ask them, before acquainting you. Should you think well of this idea, I

2 See O'Casey's letter to Miss S. D. Lange, 8 November 1942.

shall be pleased to write to them. Anyway, if what I send to you doesnt do, just send a cable saying "You are no damned good: for God's sake get someone else," or something like that, and I will do my best to get a better correspondent.

By the time you get this, each British Publisher of any standing (there are about fifty of them) will have received your cable message, supplemented by an explanatory appeal from me. The extract from the Publishers' Secretary given in this letter, will show you that there is quite a lot of persuasion to be done yet. None of them seems to have heard of Interlit, and I cant understand why the Society of Cultural Relations hasnt told them about it. I have spread my copies far and wide through the district. The latest person to get a copy is the head mistress (a prim person) of our County school for girls; and she has already lectured, and lectured well on the USSR.

The master of another school here is a Pacificist, and he is very hard to move. A fine fellow, but he doesnt believe in war. Neither do I—it isnt part of my faith—but I'll defend myself, my family, and all other families the world over as strongly as in me lies against any attack on their security; much more so, then, against this slimy saurian violence of the Hitlerite thugs.

Please give my warm regards to Mr T. Rokotov, and to Mr Apletin of the Moscow News. The Mayor here is the Chairman of our Anglo-Soviet Union, and the Vice-Chairman is the Rev R Edwards, Anglican Rector of Dartington, and our Treasurer is the daughter of the Wesleyan Minister. She is Latin teacher in Torquay Grammar School. I just mention these things to show you that I do many things besides writing not to mention digging our plot, and various things about the house to help the wife.

There's no use of me praising the Red Army—no praise can add to its greatness. May the final destruction of your enemy, and ours, be but a few moments away from us all. If it be not too presumptuous, please give my deep respects to M. Stalin, your mighty Leader.

Ever yours, with warm regards,
Sean O'Casey

P.S. YOUR CABLE CAME YESTERDAY, 14 DEC. 1942.

To Jack Carney

MS. NYU LIBRARY

[TOTNES, DEVON]
16 DECEMBER 1942

My dear Jack,

I can't find the letter I wrote criticising Col. Raynor. Anyhow, after saying a few words in reply, the Col said "he had no intention of continuing the controversy, & would leave a clear field for Mr. O'Casey." A brave lad! A week later, Capt Holdsworth wrote the letter in enclosed clipping, & I send you my MS reply to his remarks. He has answered never a word, nor has anybody else. Totnes Times printed every word of the two letters. So far so good. You can send the MS back when you've read it. Thanks for the papers. Pity the anti-censorites took their stand on "The Tailor & Anstey." Pat Dooley of I. Freedom phoned asking me to write about what happened in the Senate, so I wrote one called "The Virtue of Erin Censorship." [1] I think it is a good one. It is to appear, I believe, in I. Freedom's next number. I've got two more cables from International Magazine, Moscow, with a message appealing for British books from the Editor which I have to send to England's 55 Publishers. There must be a good deal of ships going down: up to now, he has received only the books sent by Faber & Faber. My poor P. in the Hallway must be at the bottom of the sea. It was I suggested to Macmillans that 7/6 was too much for "The Star Turns Red"; & I think they reduced it to 6/–. Since then, the plays have been 6/– per vol. I daresay it is cheap nowadays. But I'm not sure the small sale justifies the price to Macmillans. Oh, for the day when they can be bought for a bob!

International Magazine has asked me to do an article of notes for each of their issues, & I have promised I would till someone more suitable is found. So if you come across anything you think might be of interest, let me have it, if you can, & if it doesn't cost you too much trouble. I have written them saying if I'm not suitable they're to cable "No damned good; for God's sake get someone else." I daresay I'll have to cable the article. Does one do this on or over the ordinary telephone? The cabling will be a bigger job than the writing. I see the Trades Congress turned Jim [Larkin] down as a candidate for the Dail. I do hope Jim will stand. I'd love to [see] him, & his boy, & the big Barney [Conway] in Teaċdairé Daile.[2]

Hamilton Fyffe is what you call him. And the damned Editor of Reynolds edited my comments so as to make me say what I didn't say, hav-

---

[1] The title was changed to "The Irish Busy-Bodies," *Irish Freedom,* January 1943.
   [2] In the new spelling, Teachta Dála, Dail Deputy, or T.D., member of the Irish Parliament.

ing first sent me a letter asking if I wanted the letter published, & that he had sent it to Fyffe for his comments. Catch Fyffe commenting! He knows a thing or two of that.

Did you get the Laverty book?

All the best to Mina & you.
Sean

To Peter Newmark [1]

MS. NEWMARK

TOTNES, DEVON
18 DECEMBER 1942

Dear Peter—

I'm glad you are satisfied with your [writing worn away] the barrage. I daresay, you'll be an officer soon. I think you should have been one long ago. And all, or almost all the Sargeants should be officers too. I daresay you're right about R. R. for Me. But autobiography has nothing to do with whether the play's good or bad—& you should know this. How did you know it had anything autobiographical? Because I had read. . . . A friend of mine (he who introduced Nathan to me 20 years ago) says the very opposite to you. He is an old Abbey Actor, was a fine critic, & producer. "I like your play. It is far & away ahead of P. Dust. & the S. T. Red. The best since W. the Gates." [2] So there I am, balanced delightfully between the two of you. Nathan said—"I like your P. [writing worn away] notwithstanding the many fine things in R. R. for Me. P. D. is more imaginative, & much more original." I know Ayamonn was intolerant—& rightly so. So was Sheila, & cowardly, too. But I agree: I think P. D. better than Star T. Red. Anyway, there's no use arguing. I don't think the D.W. [*Daily Worker*] likes my way of writing. I'm afraid the standard isn't very high; but I've no time to argue that toss either. I don't know why they don't take a fuller interest in Art & Literature. Irish Freedom, that comes out but once a month, takes a far better view of these things. Pat Dooley,

[1] Peter Newmark, then a soldier in the British army, later a teacher in London, was an undergraduate at Cambridge University when O'Casey wrote the first of many letters to him, 25 February 1936, Vol. I, pp. 610–11.

[2] This praise of *Red Roses For Me* by Gabriel Fallon in a letter to O'Casey should be contrasted with Fallon's changed attitude toward the play and O'Casey, mainly on religious grounds. See O'Casey's letter to Fallon, 20 February 1943, notes 4 and 5.

the Editor is a fine skin. There's an article of mine on the Eire Censorship in next month's issue.[3]

The Editor-in-Chief of Moscows Magazine [writing worn away] to become a "regular correspondent," & I've agreed to do so for a while. He wants me to write on British Art, Drama, Literature, Youth, & the Intellectuals in relation to the war. If you come across anything you think interesting about Intellects, Art, Drama, or Literature in any paper or magazine, or prayerbook, let me know. Breon is better; but Niall is down with them now.

> *All the best.*
> *Eileen sends her love.*
> *Yours as ever*
> *Sean*

[3] Sean O'Casey, "The Irish Busy-Bodies," *Irish Freedom,* January 1943. The opening sentence reads: "All the snakes that Patrick banished from Ireland have returned in the form of books."

To Daniel Macmillan

TS. MACMILLAN LONDON

TOTNES, DEVON
21 DECEMBER 1942

Dear Mr Daniel:
Thank you very much for your letter telling me you would send another PICTURES IN THE HALLWAY to Mr Sutchkoff, and that you wouldnt charge it to me. That is really very kind of you.

I do like your edition of WAR AND PEACE; it is a fine production in the heat and battle of a war at such a price. I have read [Constance] Garnett's translation a dozen times; now I shall have the joy of reading [Aylmer] Maude's.

I think your news about the Book Club wishing to reproduce I KNOCK AT THE DOOR very good news indeed, and readily agree to the terms mentioned, only provided the copyright remains with us.

I wish we could have a big workers' Club on these lines. Gollancz's Left Book Club didnt do anything at all for literature. I hated his vulgar, cheap-looking editions, without the least semblance of taste on cover or contents. His dearer books are just as bad in this way: ugly covers, and uglier jackets. I never joined his Club, but I have a few copies here, and never take one down without a grimace. In this way, I'm afraid, he did for book publishing what Harmsworth [1] did for the Press. And he confirmed the workers' habit of reading books for information alone, and never for joy. They feed on pamphlets. A first-class machinist was taking tea with us the other evening, a fine fellow, mannerful and intelligent; yet he had never read what I would call a book. Never even read about Mr Pickwick.

I wrote an article on this called EMPTY VESSELS for Irish Freedom lately; [2] and intend to touch the question again when I've time.

Many thanks again for your kindness.

Yours sincerely,
Sean O'Casey

[1] See O'Casey's letter to Jack Carney, 26 November 1942, note 5.
[2] See O'Casey's to Jack Carney, 18 April 1942, note 1.

To Peter Newmark

MS. NEWMARK

TOTNES [DEVON]
27 DECEMBER 1942

Dear Peter.

Here's a play [1] I'd like you to read, & then tell me what you think of it. Not one of your Cambridgean theses, but just a few sentences showing how the drama tale struck you.

I am very busy sending copies of a Moscow cable to 66 British Publishers asking for books; while the publishers hem & haw & hum about the Berne Convention & the payment of royalties. They suggested I should get the USSR to join the Berne Convention! Good Christ!

Well all the best.
Yrs
Sean

[1] The manuscript of Vivian Connell's *The Nineteenth Hole of Europe* (1943). See O'Casey's letter to him, 8 January 1943.

To Jack Carney

MS. NYU LIBRARY

[TOTNES, DEVON]

31 DECEMBER 1942

Dear Jack,

Many thanks for papers. I have, or am to have, an article in next issue of Irish Freedom on "The Virtue of Erin Censorship." [1] At the moment, I have my hands full writing to 66 English Publishers asking them to honour an appeal cabled by the Editor of International Literature for English books. I am sending a few to you to address them for me, for neither my official—ahem!—book has them, & the London Directory I have is too old. It is a hard job trying to get them to respond—except Methuens, Macmillans, & Faber & Faber. I am very glad to see Jim has a good chance of standing for the Dail. Christ, isn't he needed there. To think of Colgan (he was our first Pipe-Major in our O'Toole's Pipers' Band, & a cantankerous fellow he was) & others being selected before Jim, and Barney or Pat Mooney shows the condition of the Irish Labour Movement. I daresay Colgan sleeps in a friar's habit. "We want no Reds here," spouting out of him at a Pioneer Temperance meeting; crushed between a crowd of clergymen. Fionn McCool must have been a myth.

Things don't look well in N. Africa. Wireless just announced arrest of twelve people in Algiers. [Gen. Henri H.] Giraud is, I'm afraid, going to make trouble. A French Eoin MacNeill. [2]

I haven't started yet on my job as Correspondent of International Magazine. I'm afraid I won't be a flaming success. I get tired too damn quick.

Ay, Lady Astor's handwriting isn't as clear as the writing on the wall. When you went to see her from here, she wrote, after you had gone back, saying something about you. To this day, I don't know what it was. Lady Gregory was the same. Every letter I got from her had to be decoded.

Your letter in Tribune around Harris, Shaw, & Wells, [3] was a fine one, well written, clear, & to the point.

If you're still buying books of criticism, I think Raymond Mortimer's "English Packet"—I think that's the title—would be worth getting.

Well, I'll leave the rest, & say it when you & Mina come down. I shall be glad to see you again. And, if you think of it, bring H. P.'s Life of Shaw with you. Thanks for Two Hyde Books, & Love Songs of Connacht. Hyde's

---

1 See O'Casey's letter to Carney, 16 December 1942, note 1.

2 Eoin MacNeill (1867–1945), scholar and nationalist; Professor of Early Irish History at University College, Dublin; Chief of Staff of the Irish Volunteers from 1913. O'Casey is alluding to the fact that MacNeil opposed an army revolt against England and missed the 1916 Rising.

3 *Tribune*, 11 December 1942.

books confirm my opinion of him—a bit of a bags, & a writer of dull & dead Gaedhelghe.

Love to Mina & you,
Sean

"Channel Packet" 's the name of Mortimer's Book.

II

OUTSIDE EIRE
AND EDEN,
1943-44

E IRE is, of course, now little more than an enlarged sacristy,
with Christ outside and all the doors locked.

I've done a bit in our garden—hedge-clipping, & sowing of
beans, peas, & onions—and, be God! I don't like it! The spade
is a damned primitive tool. Brings you back to the outside of
the Garden of Eden. No; for me, let a mist go up to water the
earth, & make it fruitful.

For a quick-triggered and quarrelsome fellow, O'Casey always remained
high-spirited and even cheerful in his contentious encounters, for the
pleasure he took from verbal battle reflected his basically optimistic view
of human nature and his confident belief in the ultimate improvement of
the condition of life. He may have been disturbed by temporary setbacks
in the war effort, but he never doubted that Germany would be defeated.

In an exchange of letters he crossed swords with his local M.P. and warned him that working people would demand a more equitable share of cultural as well as material benefits when the war ended. He envisioned the voice of the people as "A Halleluyah chorus sung in overalls." He tried to hasten the day of that liberated proletarian choir by helping the Russian people obtain books from Western publishers in a literary lend-lease campaign that he himself had undertaken by writing close to a hundred letters to British and American firms. In the midst of all this dedicated and exhausting labor, his sense of humor was there to save him from discouragement when he wrote to Jack Carney about the urgent requests in Moscow for what amounted to a Russian rosary: "They want a litany composed to please them, with all the Russians saying it—as the Irish—a few of them— say the Rosary—at nights. 'For all the tanks delivered safely—We praise thee & bless thy name; for all the guns, shells, lorries, & aviation oil. We praise thee & bless thy name. Mirror of Democracy. Send us more. Shield of Justice. Send us more. Sword of Righteousness. Send us more'; & so on, ad infinitum."

Meanwhile, he himself was on the receiving end of a lend-lease supply of newspapers, pipe tobacco, and food packages sent regularly by the generous Carneys in London. He exchanged Marxist sympathies with Leslie Daiken in Dublin; he worried about the indications that "The Irish are being blitzed into holiness"; and he also complained that some Marxist intellectuals were blitzing him with their fanatical abstractions to the point of ignoring the important influence of literature: "Jasus! They drive me mad sometimes. I tell them to read Pickwick and they stare at me." For all its imperfections, he says, he reads the *Daily Worker*—"the only daily I do read"—though his friends regularly send him some of the daily papers and cuttings of interest from London and Dublin. Although his career still suffered from the taint of Yeats's rejection of *The Silver Tassie,* he was not vindictive and seldom mentioned the poet without stressing his nobility and greatness. After reading Joseph Hone's biography he stated that Yeats deserved a more honorable tribute than this undistinguished book. Avidly he read William Carleton's powerful peasant stories and William Prescott's epic account of an exploited people, *The Conquest of Mexico.* And the by now ritualistic writing and reading of letters continued to absorb his interest and keep him in touch with the world of people outside Totnes.

None of his letters to Eugene O'Neill have survived, but there are two letters from O'Neill in O'Casey's private papers—one appears in Volume I, and one is reproduced here. In the second letter of 5 August 1943 O'Neill reveals some significant information about his later cycle plays, and we see how deeply both men admired each other's work. In response to O'Casey's praise of *Mourning Becomes Electra,* O'Neill writes: "As for the envy you felt about the play, hell, don't you know I want to bite off one of your ears in jealous fury every time I think of—Well, of

'The Plough and the Stars,' to mention one of several." He also says he has read and enjoyed *Purple Dust,* and he adds that he believes his own two best plays are the then unproduced *The Iceman Cometh* and *A Long Day's Journey into Night.* There is little doubt that if O'Casey could have read or seen the O'Neill plays performed he would have wanted to return the jealous compliment by biting off O'Neill's ears in envious admiration.

In the spring of 1944, however, almost twenty years after the first production of *The Plough and the Stars* and the riots of protest it had touched off in the Abbey Theatre, O'Casey still had to defend his play from attack by a Dublin critic, Aodh de Blacam, who, in a bitter comment that reflected an attitude that was still prevalent in nationalist circles in Ireland, lamented that it was disgraceful that O'Casey had exposed Padraic Pearse and the 1916 martyrs to "abominable slander." Ironically, at the time of De Blacam's protest, O'Casey was finishing the third volume of his autobiography, *Drums Under the Windows,* in which he had already expressed his praise of Pearse as a noble teacher, poet, and rebel, even though the dramatic context of his mock-heroic play had demanded an irreverent view of Pearse's messianic call for blood sacrifice from the long-suffering people of the Dublin slums. O'Casey's countrymen have seldom been able to appreciate the double-edged sword of thought which impelled him, according to the precise nature of the provocation, to desecrate as well as to celebrate certain aspects of Irish heroism. Dramatic techniques seldom coincide with national sanctities. O'Casey was not against the martyred Pearse; he was for the tenement people. Another side of this dualism emerged in his comical row with St. John Ervine over the relative merits of the people in Eire and Ulster. O'Casey is quick to expose the frailties of his countrymen, but when anyone else, particularly a pro-British Ulsterman like the dour Ervine, makes what he considers an unfair attack on the Irish, he brandishes his sword with a mighty and somewhat flutherian rage and uncharacteristically defends the honor of Cathleen Ni Houlihan.

If it is difficult to understand how O'Casey found the time to enter into so many controversies, it soon becomes evident that word fighting helped keep his mind clear and active. He would not suffer fools under any circumstances, and yet they helped him sharpen his thoughts and avoid their folly. He moved rapidly to defend himself and his work, to protect the honor of Ireland or Russia, with the same conviction that prompted him to defend his five-year-old daughter, who he felt was being terrorized in school. Only the right words could put things right. And while he was busily engaged in so many necessary battles, he somehow managed to find the time to finish another volume of his autobiography and a new play, *Oak Leaves and Lavender.* The act of writing was apparently a natural catharsis for him.

To Totnes Times

2 JANUARY 1943

"Lt.-Col. Raynor's Three Things"

Dear Sir,—

In the last letter of the old year written by Lt. Col. Raynor [1] to his constituents, touching on the Beveridge Report, he says:

"All the workingman asks for is work and security—a steady job, an adequate home (probably meaning a house, for a home can be built only by those living in it. S. O'C.), and sufficient means for the days of old age."

If the Lt. Col. really believes in this "all," he is deluding himself. A dog would expect as much, and get it. His remark is a curious vindication of a commonplace materialism, a strange vindication coming from a Christian. He evidently thinks that a workingman is all body, and is destitute of a mind and spirit. I'm afraid a workingman is just as complex a being as any other member of the human family. Does he think that matter has cohered together from its diffuse float, that the soil is on the surface, that water runs, and vegetation sprouts for him and his friends only, and not for the workers too? And so all the things of the spirit, the mind, and the imagination are as much the heritage of the workers as they are of any other section of the community. And though C.E.M.A. hasnt done a lot yet for the encouragement of Music and Art, it, at least, recognises the principle that these things are for all the people. So as well as a job, a house, and old age security, we want an education that will lead us to understand and enjoy these things, for they will be a dear part of what we learn, and dearer they will become as we grow, for we will be in touch with them from our youth up, sharing fully both in their creation and their enjoyment. What the Beveridge Report or Plan [2] offers will be a step forward; but when the step is taken, no voice from heaven will call out halt; rather will the voice from heaven say in the hearts of the workers, speak unto the children of England that they go forward.

Yours sincerely,
Sean O'Casey

---

[1] Lieut.-Col. Ralph Raynor, "War Letter," *Totnes Times,* 26 December 1942.

[2] William H. Beveridge (1879–1963), British economist who wrote an influential report on *Social Insurance and Allied Services* (1942), thereafter known as the Beveridge Report.

To Peter Newmark

MS. NEWMARK

TOTNES, DEVON

5 JANUARY 1943

Dear Peter.

Thanks for prompt review of Connell's play. A good criticism, tho' I dont agree with it. It isn't "beautiful writing," for a start. But there is something in the play—it's not his first, by the way. [James] Agate praised his "Throng o' Scarlet." You are right about the character—puppets they are—and damned dismal puppets at that. To me his philosophy isn't alive, hasn't even been born yet. Never once, if I remember, has he mentioned the working-class, unless those who "roll out the barrel" be such. Connell, I think, has a kink towards the gentry. We, he, I, & Herbert Marshall—it was comic to hear Herbert & him at it—talked here one evening, & he always jibbed at the mention of the working-class, & especially the Soviet people. He—to me—misses everything that is happening in the world; & sees only what twitters about in his own head. Not only is he trying "to say the last word on life"; but the last word on death, too. And he is totalitarian wrong when he alleges no-one would go to the aid of men & women stricken by plague & famine. The instinct to preserve the race, even, would prevent that indifference. I'll send him your remarks, for they are much more impartial than mine could be. I've been writing to over 60 publishers, asking for Books for Moscow. I'm not glad to hear you are going away: you certainly bring with [you] all the good wishes of Eileen & myself for a speedy & safe return. And don't be asking your poor conscience so many damned questions. Waste was sinful in peace as well as it now is in war: more so, for if we had had the sense of the value of things in peace, there would have been no war. George-Jean has to take his place in the turmoil as well as anybody else. And he'll do it—better than a lot of tougher guys, for he has always lived simply. Glad your brother liked R[ed] R[oses]—better sense than you have. Anyway, oul' son, my affectionate regards, & thanks again for your fine review of Connell's play.

Yours as Ever
Sean

To Boris Sutchkoff

TS. Inter Lit, Moscow

Totnes, Devon
7 January 1943

Dear friend:

With this letter goes an article of comments, which I have called
(being an Irishman) Green Searchlight.[1] I hope it may please you, but if
it doesnt, please let me know without hesitation. By the time you get this,
some books should have reached you. Macmillans have sent another copy
of Pictures in the Hallway. Fred Warne & Co say they will send on any
book published in the future, Gollancz is sending [James Landale] Hod-
son's WAR IN THE SUN, [Alan] Dent's THE SAMPLER and will send
other books, they say, from time to time. I have asked G. Bernard Shaw,
a dear friend of mine, to get the publishers to send you [Hesketh] Pearson's LIFE OF SHAW. Martin Secker and Warburg, Chapman & Hall
are also sending you some. I have written, enclosing your cabled message,
to over 60 publishers, so that we should get something out of this effort. I
have also sent an English and a Russian copy (the one containing article
on Chaucer and a chapter from I Knock at the Door) to the Secretary of
the Publishers' Advertising Circle, and have asked her to put the matter
before her members, which number fifty or so. The Oxford University
Press are sending some books in a day or so. The Lutterworth Press, 35,
John Street, Bedford Row, London, W.C.1, say "We shall gladly co-operate
with Mr. Sutchkoff in the manner suggested. I am having a selection of
our books, adult and juvenile, despatched without delay. J. Gun-Munro."
They are also to send to you monthly periodicals, published for Women,
Girls, Boys, and Youngsters. They say "These deal with the youth of
other countries, and Women's Magazine recently dealt with the women of
other countries, and I think that work can be further extended. We have
been in contact for some time with The Anglo-Soviet Youth Friendship
Alliance London. The Anti-Fascist Youth Committee, Moscow, and the
Anti-Fascist Soviet Women's Committee, Moscow, from whom we have
been promised literary material and pictures describing the lives of Soviet
Women and children in their own territories. In the case of one Magazine,
we have already been supplied with excellent pictures and material. J. Gun-
Munro." This latter note is from the Lutterworth Periodicals Branch of
the Lutterworth Press, and the address is the same as John St, Bedford
Row. London. W.C.1; or Doran Court, Reigate Road, Redhill, Surrey.
England. It would be a good thing to let the Lutterworth people have as
many pictures and material as possible; and some of these things would be

---

[1] O'Casey intended to write a series of essays, based on life in Ireland, to be
called "The Green Searchlight."

very welcome to us for use in our own Anglo-Soviet Unit here. The D. Appleton Century Publishing Co, 34, Bedford Street, Strand. London. W.C.2, in a letter to me say, "We are issuing few books at present, but any applications we receive from the Editor of Interlit, for review copies, will receive favourable attention." So you'll have to write to them personally. Their reference (given on letter to me) is: GN/TB. E. J. Arnold & Son, are sending some, as also are Messrs Chapman & Hall. Some publishers have simply acknowledged receipt of my letter, without promising to [do] anything about it. I will get into touch with these again. I await replies from the other publishers. I enclose copy of the letter I have sent to the various publishers. I hope the various books sent come to you safely. In my last letter, which I hope you got, I sent a few verses, and a short article about the poems of Mayakovsky which appeared in the Anglo-Soviet Journal.[2] I do hope your belief in final victory during the present year is a certainty. Certainly your gallant Red Army and Navy and Airforce are doing more than their share to bring it about. It is amazing the way they are striking the Nazis in the frosts and the falling snow, and the biting blasts of the wind. I do hope that the war may finish with complete victory this year so that we may get on with the gigantic tasks that wait to be done when peace is here. And to help this hope on, I hope they get going in North Africa—Tunis—soon, so that a bigger blow may be given to the Nazis—buile chun chroidhe, a blow to the heart as we say in Irish; a blow that will stop them breathing forever.

I am looking forward to receiving the Soviet Book and Document you mentioned as having sent to me in your last cable.

My love to you all. Please give my regards to Mr Rokotov and to Mr Appletin of the Moscow News.

> *Yours very sincerely.*
> *Sean O'Casey*

[2] See O'Casey's letter to Daniel Macmillan, 12 October 1942, note 1.

To Vivian Connell [1]

TC. O'CASEY

TOTNES, DEVON
8 JANUARY 1943

Dear Vivian Connell:

I have been busy writing to fifty publishers, and had no chance to write sooner. I dont like your play [2] at all. I dont like its philosophy, and

[1] Vivian Connell (1903–   ), novelist and playwright.
[2] *The Nineteenth Hole of Europe* (1943).

almost everything in it is utterly alien to my way of thinking. To me, what
was done before by the USSR in famine and plague, can be done again,
with greater success and power when this strife is over. However, it is only
fair to say that there is something in the play as a play. What it is, I havent
the analytic knowledge to say. Besides, I am biassed in my social beliefs,
and biassed, too, insofar as I am inclined to lean my way of playwriting. I
sent your play to a close friend of mine,[3] at present a range-finder in the
artillery. He used to be a critic on the Cambridge News; I met him in that
town, when, at a talk, he argued against some of my remarks. We then
became friends, and I know him now for seven years. He has a fine way
of looking at plays, and I wanted to get you, or try to, an impartial
opinion. Here is his: "I think the play good; very theatrical and vivid,
and beautifully written. That's the first thing to say. If it be produced, its
production would be a fine thing for any theatre. Some of the speeches
should be skilfully compressed, but Connell has a sharp ear for the spoken
word, and he can invent moving and dramatic situations. The combination
of modern and legendary imagery is excellent. This is the best first play
I've read for years. I say that without reserve. The play, however, is limited
by its insufficient appreciation of character (apart from Punchus, they are
all mere puppets of the author), and a vague wild wooly philosophy (as an
example, of a weak passage, take Mark's speech on page 95). I think the
play has quite a bit of nonsense in it (e.g. on relations between church and
state p. 65), and I think Connell misses a good deal of what is happening
in the world (hear, hear—O'Casey). He's really saying the same as Sherwood's feeble 'Petrified Forest.' What Eliot said well in WASTE LAND,
and Coward badly in CAVALCADE. Still that doesnt prevent the play
from being a fine one, technically advanced and imaginative. The trouble
is, he's already trying to say the last word on life, though he hasnt quite
got sufficient observation of contemporary manners or affairs. There's too
much of the tough modern American sophisticated dramatists (Hecht,
Anderson, Odets, etc) in it; unless he limits himself severely, and tries to
say a little less next time, through more carefully observed characters, I
doubt whether he'll ever write another good play."

Well, there you have a criticism and a half. Whether it's all so or no, I
cant tell. But the critic is no fool, and his words are, in my opinion, worth
considering.

All the best,
Yours sincerely,
Sean O'Casey

[3] Peter Newmark.

To Picture Post

9 JANUARY 1943

What Sean O'Casey *Says* [1]

Your special number is a fine issue and a brave one. Long we laughed at the Soviet Union's "Blue Prints." Now England is being carpeted with them—and so much the better. It is a grand thing when brains begin to stir. Even God had to make a plan for the future when in the beginning He "Sat, brooding o'er the vast abyss," before it became pregnant. Our own last child is the same as she on your cover—wakened by the shrill of the siren, or by the shaking of the house, not yet knowing the taste of a banana. But she will, and she will live when a siren calls only to productive labour, and her house stands firm. That is why we and our Allies fight this war. That is why PICTURE POST is planning now. For the day when the tremendous energy of all able people working for the common wealth will be released. A Halleluyah chorus sung in overalls. Listen. Lieut.-Col. Raynor, our local M.P. says: "All the working man asks for is work and security— an adequate house, a steady job, and sufficient means for the days of old age." This is his plan. Take it away. It's no good. Give me Huxley's instead. Even now, a dog would expect as much from Lieut.-Colonel Raynor and get it. We want a helluva lot more. We want, as you say, all the necessary things first, all the fine things to follow, the theatre, music, literature, fine cities and towns to walk in, and fine gardens in which to rest and play. And we must get the education that will allow us to enjoy all these things. We want the young man's and young woman's vision. God (or natural force) is making the world pregnant again. Life is moving and Heaven help him who gets in the way of it. This particular issue of PICTURE POST is, in my opinion, a much brighter banner than your last special issue. May it wave over the head of an army of vigorous people.

Sean O'Casey, Devon

[1] The editor had asked O'Casey to comment on the special New Year issue of the magazine, 2 January 1943, based on the theme of "Changing Britain."

To Frederick May [1]

MS. MAY

TOTNES, DEVON
11 JANUARY 1943

Dear Frederick May,

Well, Eileen & I listened in to your Prison Songs. It would be just ridiculous for me or her to give you an opinion on what we heard. Just a guess or two will have to do: The reception wasn't particularly good—it is often bad down here; something seemed to be wrong with the conducting, at least during the first half, and the Singer wasn't good, or rather, didn't sound good here. The latter part of the composition pleased me well—when the voice was silent. Eileen liked it a lot, & she knows much more about music than I do. Mine goes no further than jigs, reels, hornpipes, marches, & laments—though today I could have a good laugh at the bould St. James's Brass & Reed Band playing the Battle of Waterloo—big guns an' all—in the Hollow of the Phoenix Park, a "number" I've heard them play several times. Of course, they played it as well as any band could play it, & many's the pleasant hour this band gave me as it played to all who wanted to hear it in the Dublin Parks.

I'm sorry I can't give you a better review of your work; but it isn't in me to do more.

And all good wishes.
Yours sincerely,
Sean O'Casey

[1] Frederick May, c/o Abbey Theatre, Dublin. Irish musician and composer, May was then a member of the Abbey Theatre orchestra. He is the brother of Sheila May.

To Gabriel Fallon

TS. TEXAS

TOTNES, DEVON
20 FEBRUARY 1943

My dear Gaby: I got yours yesterday morning, and oh, what a woeful letter! Don't forget, dear friend, that there's a war on, and that, though not in the centre, still within one of the outer rings. I have a lot to do, Gaby now that I hadn't to do before. With chopping wood, digging the garden, clipping the hedge (grows here like a bloody jungle), work about the house, and other chores, I never know even what time o day it is. Just now I've been doing an article on something about my life here, impressions of place and people, etc, for the next issue of the SATURDAY BOOK, to get a note when it was two thirds done, that this feature had been cancelled, and would I do one on the theatre? [1] That I'm trying to do now. As well I am trying to get British publishers (60 of them) to send their best books to the Editor of Moscow International Magazine who is anxious to know what we think and what we do; sending an odd message to the India League, this meeting and that meeting; and now to write a short article about Eirinn for the Glasgow Communists who are holding a special meeting and celebration about our old land next month. Since Shelah [Richards] wrote, Eileen had a bad attack of Influenza, with a cough; I escaped with a touch of the Influenza, but got a whirlwind of a cough. Now Breon is to deliver an hour's lecture to his schoolmates on the ART OF THE EIGHTEENTH CENTURY, and as Yeats has gone, I have to do my best to help him. These are but a few of the things—the nightly cloaking of the windows [2] is another—of the things one has to do; so you see, I find it hard to get time to write a letter. I've owed one to Joe Cummins for months. I forgot: workmen are in putting back ceilings that fell down; and that's another bother. The plasterer's a young man from Clonmel—maybe you've heard o that place before. Now to your letter. Shelah has carried no objective, main or minor, till she and I sign a contract. [3] I sent her the draft of one, but she didn't send it back; I sent her another a week ago, registered; but have heard nothing since. So, as far as I am concerned, There is nothing doing. She hasn't been very courteous to my concessions. I don't care a damn whether she does it or no; and if it leads to quarrelling, I'd rather no-one did it. After I had mentioned over the phone to her that I wouldn't mind a few small cuts, I recollected the Censorship, and grew afraid that she'd cut the bowels out of it; so, in my last draft of contract, I decided to make myself overseer to any cuts made. As far as you are concerned, Gaby, I don't want you to be responsible for anything. I shouldn't care for you to take any risk with the play. I have a great regard for your literary acuteness, and grace, though, to be perfectly frank, I

[1] Sean O'Casey, "The Curtained World," *Saturday Book—3* (1943), ed. Leonard Russell; reprinted under O'Casey's original title, "Behind the Curtained World," *Blasts and Benedictions* (1967).

[2] For the blackout regulations during the war.

[3] The contract was signed, and *Red Roses For Me* was first performed on 15 March 1943 at the Olympia Theatre, Dublin, presented by Shelah Richards and Michael Walsh, directed by Shelah Richards, sets designed by Ralph Cusack and painted by Cusack and Anne Yeats, with the following cast: Ann Clery as Mrs. Breydon; Dan O'Herlihy as Ayamonn; Sheila Carty as Eeada; Gertrude Quinn as Dympna; Cepta Cullen as Finnoola; Sheila May as Sheila Moorneen; John Stephenson as Brennan o' the Moor; John Richards as a Singer; W. O'Gorman as Roory; Seamus Healy as Mullcanny; Michael Walsh as the Rev. E. Clinton; Luke McLoughlin as Samuel; Austin Meldon as Inspector Finglas; John McDarby as Dowzard; Wilfrid Brambell as Foster.

imagine what are called Catholic connections are having an effect on you.[4] Indeed, they are bound to have this effect, just as my connection with the gospel of the proletariat effects me. But don't forget, please, that even if you wore frock and cowl, I'd still have the same affection for you, with all your faults; and you have a few (for my many), and one of them is that of being suspicious of me. Having written that—Quod scripsi—let me challenge a sentence of yours: you say, "One passage might give grave offence to Catholics." [5] Honestly, I'm a little tired of these "offences to Catholics." Who are they above anyone else to him who doesn't believe in the Catholic Faith? I have hardly written a line that hasn't been offensive to someone or other, then why should I single out the Catholics for special consideration? Some might whisper, The Box-office. I'm as fond of the box-office as the next, but it isn't my first principle. More important still, why in the name o' God should the Catholics care a damn of what I may say about them? If what they believe be true, that attitude—resentment or offence at what I may write—is like a man going about afraid that a touch of a butterfly's wing would bring him concussion of the brain. And what Catholics would likely be offended? Not many of those in the Labour Movement, certainly. Those on the Censorship Board? Well, let them. The Silver Tassie offended some of them; Within The Gates others. One cleric upbraided me for allowing a Bishop to have an illegitimate child! And he couldn't understand that the play showed no such thing. He failed to see that a Bishop cannot be judged as a bishop till he becomes a Bishop, till he is consecrated one; and that anything he may have done before can't be set down to him as an offence during his office as a bishop. But the whole thing tires one. One thing is certain: the Church—Catholics, if you like— have more to puzzle them now than anything I may say, actively or incidently, about them. Between the two of us, I'd like to be shown the passage that you think might be offensive. I haven't the slightest awareness of it, or of any other, except that I feel almost anything might be capable of offend-

[4] At this time Fallon was writing regular theatre reviews for the *Irish Monthly,* a magazine edited by the Jesuit Fathers, and *The Standard,* a Catholic weekly newspaper with a well-earned reputation of sensational pietism. What O'Casey called the "effect" of these "connections" probably contributed to the break in their twenty-four-year friendship three years later when, writing about a second production of *Red Roses* in Dublin, Fallon accused O'Casey of "coldly-calculated bigotry." See Fallon's review in *The Standard,* 28 June 1946, reprinted below in chronological order; O'Casey's letter of reply, *The Standard,* 26 July 1946; and the replies of both Fallon and O'Casey, *The Standard,* 9 August 1946.

[5] Fallon clarified the passage of "grave offence" in his review of the first production of *Red Roses* in *The Standard,* 26 March 1943, when, after finding little dramatic merit in the play, he raised a religious objection:

'My own quarrel with the work lay in its excess of sentimentality and in the inclusion of one particular scene which attempted to brand Dublin's Catholic poor as ignorant idolators, a scene in which the author is being as false to himself as he was to his characters.'

This was perhaps the first warning of trouble between the two men. Most Irish reviewers had attacked the play, but none had done so on religious grounds.

ing some one or two of them. It's strange to me how those who are continually mocking their Beliefs in their own lives are so very contentious
about anything said may, in the slightest, give offence to their quiet, indifferent, and often, mechanical devotion.

Well, well, my dear Gaby, that's enough for one day! To end up, since
Shelah hasn't sent on the signed agreement, I take it that all plans have
gone awry, and that RED ROSES FOR ME won't be seen in Dublin just
now.

I am just beginning to read Hone's LIFE OF YEATS.[6] Do you EVER
hear anything about Will [Barry Fitzgerald]? I've asked Mr [Eric] Gorman,
but he didn't notice the question. I've asked Shelah, but she didn't notice
the question, either. So I don't know whether the boul' Will's alive or dead.
I've never had a word from him since I saw him in New York. It's all very
strange. The three mousketeers have been scattered.
Alack aday! Well, love to Rose, to your children, and to you. And don't
think because I don't write for awhile that I've forgotten you.

Yours as ever,
Sean

[6] Joseph Hone, *W. B. Yeats, 1865–1939* (1942).

To Jack Carney

MS. NYU LIBRARY

TOTNES, DEVON
[23 FEBRUARY 1943]
MONDAY, 2 A.M.

My dear Jack,

Just time for a few remarks. I am trying to write an article for the
next issue of Saturday Book. The Editor asked first for one on my impressions of myself, life here, etc; & when it was 2/3rds written, changed
over to asking for one about the Theatre, Past & to come.

I was very sorry to hear of Mina's fall. It's remarkable how you can
hurt yourself by falling off a chair. Once here, in bed, a bomb went off
near; I sprang out in the dark, tripped over something, fell recklessly, dint-
ing my back into the coal-scuttle; & lay there, careless of the falling of a
thousand bombs. I went about like that for a week or more. I am glad she's
better. Thanks ever so much for the papers, & Davitt's speech—what a
speech! Aren't we doing well in N. Africa! I'm afraid Eisenhower's a bit
of a failure. What a lot of chocolate generals we've had.

Could you find out for me who published Robert Greenwood's "Mr Bunting in Peace & War"?[1] Moscow wants me to get in touch with the author. A sizeable part of his book is in a recent issue of International Mag. (Russian edition). I thought it was written by Walter Greenwood—Love on the Dole author—, & wrote to him! He hasn't replied, & I don't wonder. Did a lot of digging today—no-one else here to do it.

Love to Mina, & a warning to take
more care; & to you.
Yours as ever
Sean

[1] Robert Greenwood, *Mr. Bunting at War* (1941).

To Jack Carney

MS. NYU LIBRARY

[TOTNES, DEVON]

12 MARCH 1943

My dear Jack,

Thanks for papers & for information about Bunting & Greenwood. A good deal of his work is in the last number of International Literature. I have written to him, % Dent's. I'm writing, or will be, now to 30 American Publishers asking them to send books to International Literature—a literary Lease & Lend Measure. Nice Ambassador, that one in Moscow. They want a litany composed to please them, with all Russians saying it—as the Irish—a few of them—say the Rosary—at nights. "For all the tanks delivered safely—We praise thee & bless thy name; for all guns, shells, lorries, & aviation oil. We praise thee & bless thy name. Mirror of Democracy. Send us more. Shield of Justice. Send us more. Sword of Righteousness. Send us more"; & so on, ad infinitum.

You are right about Hone's "Life of Yeats." I got it from Macmillans. I had it on order a year ago. It is a dull book, & altogether unworthy of the great man's memory. But he is the official biographer, & that settles it; the chosen, I daresay, of Mrs. Yeats, or George as she is known to her friends. George never liked me; &, I believe, she had a big hand, & gave a big putsch to the rejection of "The Silver Tassie." It doesn't matter much now. The thing is the book doesn't let us see Yeats at all—even through a glass darkly. I certainly could—without any of the official or private letters—have done a better one myself. But as D[esmond]. McCarthy was forced to say "it isn't the last biography of Yeats." Others will write of him, & use this as a static guide, "or something to that effect," as the Dublin Polis say. It's a failure, a colourless failure, too.

"Red Roses For Me" is to be played soon by People's Theatre, Newcastle-upon-Tyne,[1] perhaps, too, by the W.E.A. in Bristol; & by, I hope, Shelah Richards (wife of Denis Johnston) in the Olympia, Dublin— you know where that place is—"oul spot be the river." I've written an article on the Theatre past & present for the coming Saturday Book, & Leonard Russell says its fine & rousing. I hope he's right. Is Mina allright again? I've just declined to do a scenario—whatever that may be—for a Viennese hilarity theme transposed—or is it transfigured?—into a real Irish hilarity one. Isn't the Cavan affair a nice thing.[2] Cheap labour for the holy laundry. An illuminated end to the Song of Bernadette. These nuns!

> *God be wi' ye.*
> *Sean*

---

[1] In its English premiere, *Red Roses For Me* was produced by the People's Theatre, Newcastle upon Tyne, 25 March 1943.

[2] The *Irish Times* of 24 February 1943 reported a tragic fire in a dormitory over the laundry at St. Joseph's Orphanage in Cavan, conducted by the Poor Clare Order of nuns, in which thirty-five children were burned to death, most of them locked in their rooms in an old building that had no fire escape.

To Jack Carney

MS. NYU LIBRARY

TOTNES, DEVON

26 MARCH 1943

Dear Jack,

Could you keep an eye on The Catholic Times? I sent a reply, last Monday, to it, commenting on the report of an address given by E. M. Delafield to Women's Conservative Sunderland Club, in which the Director of Time & Tide laid down the law on the Soviet Union. I should like to know if the C.T. referred to my reply.[1] I've just read your review of Life of Jaures:[2] by God, you've got it all in the oul' head! Viscount Castlereagh many years ago, was trying to interest himself in the Labour Movement. He, like us all, must submit to the changes; & with him, & his sister, they began long before the war. Twenty years ago, the life of the young in the big houses was changing. They no longer lingered within the smell of

---

[1] O'Casey's reply was ignored by the *Catholic Times.*

[2] "Jean Jaurès," *Tribune,* 5 February 1943; Carney's review of J. Hampden Jackson's *Jean Jaurès.*

the lavender. The Lavender Lady was dead. 1917 began the big change; slow, gradual, but sure, & gaining now in proportion & speed. Of course, we can't blame Churchill for his son; or is it a new saying that the sins of the children will be on the fathers unto the third & fourth generation? I shouldn't wonder if the second front began in the Balkans—they might try to kill 2 birds with the one stone. We can't blame them; there's no use blaming the inevitable; but, of course, we can fight it. I don't think it matters—politically—where they fix the 2nd front. The Soviet idea will grow, for one can't prevent the growth of a living organism. They are grafting their ideas here; even Churchill's speech showed that.

I think, Jack, myself, the failure in N. Africa was mainly due to bad generalship—Eisenhower. A blower, and a Dubliner knows what that means. The Allies—apart from the USSR—can't stop. Like Macbeth, they must go on; to go back would be more difficult than to go on, so they're had! "Oh! silver trumpets, be ye lifted up, & call unto the great race that is to come!" [3] Yeats could stand on his toes occasionally. Thanks for the hard tack. It was very acceptable, & will make a sturdy blend.

Love to Mina.
All the best
Sean

[3] W. B. Yeats, *The King's Threshold* (1904); the Youngest Pupil's speech at the end of the play.

To Jack Carney

MS. NYU LIBRARY

[TOTNES, DEVON]
22 APRIL 1943

My dear Jack,

This is written on some stuff you left behind you—nice soft paper for a Hard pen. Thank you deeply for the papers & the book by poor Carleton.[1] I am very glad to have that. It is supposed to be a classic, but I don't think it is a favourite in Éirinn. It's curious the way he sets down "The King of Ireland's Son," for "The Three Tasks" is quite evidently a somewhat more homely version of that story. It is a book to read when one is quiet, & the place is still, & no work to be done is worrying one. That's the way I'm doing it.

You are possibly right that the inclusion of the C.P. into the Labour

[1] William Carleton, *Traits and Stories of the Irish Peasantry* (1830–33).

Party would cause a split. But even if it should, I think it should be worked for; it gives a fine chance for propaganda among the Unions; & those who leave, should the union be consummated, will be well rid of: they aren't worth much to militant Labour. Auld Col. Raynor here is against the union; so is the Universe, & these objections seem to me to be the strong reasons for the affiliation. "It will disrupt the Labour Unions," says the Universe. Sweet solicitude! What's the address of the Catholic Times? I want to write to the Editor asking why he didn't publish my letter, & to make a casual inquiry of him if he be on the side of truth. Veritas. Ye shall know the truth, & the truth shall make you free. Very well, Veritas. Joyce had them taped. Glad to hear you are keeping in touch with the Labour Union Movement. Rust [2] spoke in Belfast recently, & got a fine reception. I hear in the year 600 new Branches of the Labour Movement were formed in Ireland. Aiseirgh will have to look out. It's grand to hear Jim [Larkin] is President of the Trades Council. He is to speak at a United Front Labour meeting in Belfast shortly. I'd love to be there. The Border is withering away.

Why didn't they want to publish or broadcast the report of Cowles' speech in Washington on learning & literature in the USSR? [3] Are they afraid they'll be found out? Moscow has more books—twice as many—as Congressional Washington! But isn't Dorothy Sayers punching Christ over the wireless? Plugging religion into the people. And damn the bit of music in the plugging. I listened to one episode tonight—Jesus before the High Priest, the denial by Peter, & the crowing of the cock. God help poor Jasus! She didn't put any of the "And he began to curse & swear, saying . . ." No, no: Dorothy is too respectable for that, & so's the B.B.C. It was pretty bad: there was no drama in it—or so it seemed to me.

I've read Capt. Miksche's book,[4] & it seems he's got the right end of the stick. I've often laughed at the astronomical times they've shattered wharves, moles banks, buttresses—in fact, if all that was said was done, the world would be in bits by now.

Strangely enough, Jack, I well remember a discussion I had more than 20 years ago with a member of the I.R.B. Supreme Council, Seumas Deakin, a chemist who did business a little up from Blaquiere Bridge, in Phibsboro! In a room, back of the shop, he showed me pictures & diagrams of Airplane stations & Zeppelin sheds in the Rhineland facing Britain. They were in, if I remember right, Stead's Review of Reviews. He, Deakin, was quivering with excitement. The airplane was going to win the freedom of all little subject nations, & make them secure forever—including our own homeland, of course. "An airoplane" says he "will cost only £50, & so, from a military point of view, every little nation will be as mighty as the

[2] William Rust, editor of the *Daily Worker,* London. See O'Casey's first letter to him, 12 March 1942.

[3] Gardiner Cowles, Jr., gave a speech on the distrust of the USSR in Washington, D.C., on 29 March 1943.

[4] F. O. Miksche, *Is Bombing Decisive?* (1943).

biggest." Then he paused for breath. "England," says he, when he got it again, "is going to go up in dust." When I demurred, saying I dunno about that, & that, like everything else, aeroplanes were bound to go up in price, he said "Nonsense; you'll see, Sean." By now, I've seen pretty clearly, though all the way home I couldn't help thinking how easy it was for a man to believe what he wished to believe. When I said to him, It'll take thousands of them to do much, he just said, "You'll see, Sean." I have seen.

But some don't seem to have seen yet. It would be grand if the problem could be solved by the Bomber. If they multiply by a hundred what they do now, so that they'll have to have traffic control in the skies, & Belisha Beacons to show the pilots where to cross, there'll still be a mighty German Army ready for eventualities in Europe. They might as well say the war will be won by the snipers.

I see Red Roses For Me has gone into another print—a second edition; meaning in all, I think, 3,000 copies. Star Turns Red stops where it was—curious, isn't it. I thought the Red Star would have the best sale of all. Ni mar siltear bitear.[5]

I have written to 20 U.S.A. publishers asking them to send books to Moscow. Moscow is bobbing about everywhere. I don't think Moscow will be pleased if there isn't a Second Front soon. And in Tunisia, they seem to be leaving everything to Montgomery.

Love to Mina & you.
Sean

Got an airgraph from P. Newmark. He's in Egypt.

[5] Expectation is not realization.

To George Jean Nathan

MS. CORNELL

TOTNES, DEVON

11 MAY 1943

My very dear George:

At last I have had a letter from Dick telling me you are, practically, yourself again after the villainous attack upon you.[1] I had written to you & to him several times about it, and asking for a word about you. A Pressman, here, a friend, told me about the attack, & I was very anxious about you, for my own sake, & for that of the theatre. You'll have to be more

[1] Nathan was mugged on Fifth Avenue in New York during the early morning of New Year's Day, 1943.

careful of yourself in the dim out. I understand it isn't altogether safe in London either, and the sooner these thugs, who attack men & women in the dark suddenly, are laid by the heels, the better.

I read your note about Gene [O'Neill], saying he was much better, & working on his cycle of plays again. It was fine to read that. I've written to him saying I was so glad to read your joyful tidings. The theatre is bare enough, without losing him or you. It is very consoling to know you are both at work again.

I have written five chapters of a new volume of "biography," but it is hard to keep close to it. So much to be done now in house and garden, &, as well, to share in the activities & studies of the three children. Our eldest fifteen years old, handsome, near as you are, & over six foot tall—is very interested in the theatre—without any incitement from me. I don't like to try to enforce anything on anyone. He's a scenic designer for the school, & his nose is often deep in a book about the Drama. He says when war is over, he's for America, again no incitement from mother or me. He likes American comics, films, & their Broadcasts. Anyway, they're better than ours.

I see Brooks Atkinson is in Chung King now,[2] & R[ichard]. Watts in Dublin. Left their jobs to get on with the war, though to do that, it seems to me, one would have to fight, dig the earth, or make munitions. No use of leaving a job to take another of the same kind. However, they know best. I just got Mrs. Turk's book about you—reading it; & it reads well so far; more anon.

All that matters at the moment, George, my boy, is that you're allright again, & back in the old seat, with those keen eyes fixed on the stage.

> *My love,*
> *Ever Yours*
> *Sean*

[2] During World War II, Atkinson took a leave of absence from his job as dramatic critic of the *New York Times* to serve as that paper's war correspondent in China and Russia.

To Jack Carney

MS. NYU LIBRARY

[TOTNES, DEVON]
17 JUNE 1943

My dear Jack,

A line to thank you for the papers. We are very busy here looking after the crops. Each of the children got some kind of a germ that made them sick; but they got over it in a day. Then Eileen went down suddenly, & got a bad night of it with a temperature. Dr. [George] Varian was rather anxious, thinking it was some kind of a fever, & that made me anxious, too; but on the fourth day, it suddenly went, & Eileen got allright, except for a little grogginess when she moved about. Nannie has got her papers, so I'm trying to get as much of the next vol of biography done as I can before she goes; for then, heaven only knows what we'll have to do.

Did you see that the Directorship of Ireland's National Bank carries a salary of £500? Good for Bill! [1] I do hope Jim & young Jim will get into the Dail.

Thanks again for papers, Jack.

Will write again when I have a minute or two. I'm handing on the Irish papers to an Irish neighbour here, who reads every word in every one of them.

> *My love to Mina.*
> *Ever yours*
> *Sean*

[1] William O'Brien, the labor leader, served as a director of the Central Bank of Ireland, 1943–67.

To Jack Carney

MS. NYU Library

[Totnes, Devon]
9 July 1943

My dear Jack,

Many thanks for the papers, magazines, etc, & the lovely tin of Yankee doodle tobacco. It's a pity you couldn't smoke it, though I say it as shouldn't. It does me, allright. Nannie's away, & the household duties have increased 50%. I'm hoping more than ever that the war will end soon, though it doesn't look like as if they were in a hurry to bear a hand with Russia's burden. And General de Gaulle seems to be a bitter pill to them. Too friendly with the USSR, perhaps. And the Vatican, who holds the keys of heaven & hell, and a few belonging to this world, prefers Giraud. Now that Petain's in a cage, they like the bird on the tree—or is it the bird in the bush better than the bird in the hand?

I've just got a copy of "The Bell" from a L. H. Daiken, B.A. of Denstone School, Staffs. He mentions your name. You know him?

At the moment my eyes are closed, or almost so, with a whoreson inflammation that comes on them periodically—a tearing painful business while it lasts—and it is a work of superpurgation—is this word right? It's a good honest Catholic word, & the last Gael to which it could rightly refer is, or was, Matt Talbot, of immortal mummery.[1]

With this, I enclose your "Dublin Magazine," thanks for the loan. I don't know Shelah May.[2] I also enclose book, "Windfalls" for Eric Baume. Daniel Macmillan has just told, in a letter, Eileen that no copy of "I Knock at the Door" or "Pictures in the Hallway" are to be had. That's hard lines. To come, too, when the sales were good. So we also serve who only stand and wait—like the Allied Armies. And isn't there a petition going round London asking, praying, that the bombing be stopped? The Germans don't like their land to be scorched. Who's getting up this petaintition?

Have you heard from Jim since he became a T.D.? Is the new Lord Mayor any good? And Mick Colgan seeking a seat in the Senate. How he used to mock me when I wheeled from the O'Tooles towards Liberty Hall! And Sean O'Faolain's studying Marx—so Mr. Daiken says. I'd like to think it was all due to the love of labour; but I doubt it. Colgan's probably looking for a nice comfortable seat; & O'Faolain is feeling the pressure of canons minor & major, shoving him out of the busy Catholic hive.

Oh, well, there's nothing to do, but to go on trying to get together another biographical volume for printing when the war is over. I do hope the USSR won't be left to fight it out alone. Don't bother Eric about pricing "Windfalls." Didn't think a great lot of 7 winters—did you?

Love to Mina & to you.

Sean

P.S. Mina dear thank you for the biscuits. I am sorry not to have sent tea before, the folk have visitors & I couldn't take it away. Nannie has gone. Enclose cheque for £2. Love Eileen X.

[1] See O'Casey's letter to Dr. Joseph D. Cummins, 26 November 1942, note 5.

[2] Sheila May had recently finished playing the role of Sheila Moorneen in the premiere of *Red Roses For Me,* which opened at the Olympia Theatre in Dublin on 15 March 1943; see O'Casey's letter to Gabriel Fallon, 20 February 1943, note 3. She had also written a review of the published text of the play in the *Dublin Magazine,* April-June 1943, a review which O'Casey had just read, in which she praised the play but pointed out some flaws in the characterization of Sheila Moorneen. Here is the relevant passage, which apparently led to O'Casey's uncharacteristic silence:

Sheila is the latest addition to that dreary procession of Mary Boyles and Norah Clitheroes and Iris Ryans, weak and clinging, hugging security rather than her lover, with his dreams and aspirations, losing him to clammy death and realizing too late, etc. At least she isn't "wronged"—we are spared that. Why is it that neither Sean O'Casey nor Paul Vincent Carroll can draw a decent, sensible, full-blooded young woman? There must be a few Pegeen Mikes still left in Ireland.

See also O'Casey's letter to Sheila May Greene, 12 October 1946. She was then married to Professor David Greene, the Celtic scholar at Trinity College, Dublin.

To George Jean Nathan

MS. CORNELL

TOTNES, DEVON

12 JULY 1943

My very dear George:

It was good to get your letter, though not so good to hear that the old neuralgic pain was in you again. I daresay the hooligan attack had a lot to do with bringing it on. Heaven be praised, you have recovered from those injuries. You seem to have had a very narrow escape. You will be wise to watch out during the coming black-out. There are, I'm told, thugs like those knocking about London, too; &, I suppose, in all big towns. Our boasted civilization, George, is still stern up, & head down. I do hope, by the time this gets to you, the pain will be gone, & that you can stare into the curtained world with comfort again. I have written an article of that title—the curtained world—for the next issue of The Saturday Book, to be published in October, & will send you a copy when it comes out. I'm afraid it is, in a large way, a very hopeful article. The Editor said it "thrilled him"; but looking over the proofs today, though it doesn't seem too bad, I failed to be thrilled by it. I shouldn't worry too much over Purple Dust. I daresay, it will go on sometime. Strangely enough, the book hasn't sold well—a little over a 100 copies U.S.A. & about 700 here; though Red Roses has sold out a 2nd Edition.

The one girl we had here to help us in the house, has been called up for military service, so with the children & all the household jobs to do, I and the missus have a time of it—the time of our lives. God knows when I'll be able to sit down to settle on another story. I am trying to get another part of the biography done; but whether or no it can be published is another question. There are no copies here of I Knock at the Door or Pictures in the Hallway to be had—they are awaiting to be bound. I have composed a little love song called "Down By the Green Bushes"; [1] one I'm sure you'd like. I wish I was in 44 West 44th [2] to lilt it to you. Our eldest boy—over six foot & broad in proportion; a handsome lad—is still stuck to theatricals, & I'm very anxious about him. I don't like it. But he must go his own way; that way is the only way, & the best one for him. The Abbey, I understand, is gone away from its third glory; a showplace now of harmless pietistic plays.

I got an offer some months ago for changing a scenario of a Viennese Theme into an Irish one, with a catch of some hundreds a week during the progress of the work—the father of two children who go to the same

[1] This song appears under the title "The Green Bushes" in O'Casey's *Under a Colored Cap: Articles Merry and Mournful with Comments and a Song* (1963).
[2] The address of the Royalton Hotel in New York, where Nathan lived.

school as ours offered it to me; but I refused. I couldn't see myself doing it. [Paul Vincent] Carroll took on the job, &, I believe, did it well. He is having a new play produced in Dublin shortly. I'm afraid for Carroll. In an interview, he talked a lot of nonsense—so it seemed to me—about the needs of the future. I don't exactly know how to place him. He has funny ideas about Communism. He's all out for a change—that'll come, anyway, whether we're out for it, or no—, but when I asked him to write an article about the war for the USSR press, he refused, saying he wrote plays only. Heaven grant he won't keep on writing bad ones. I'm just saying this to you, & would say it to no-one else—about the plays. I'm afraid his first visit to N. York did him some harm. And Denis Johnston seems to have merely become a B.B.C. reporter. I have read a few plays sent me from youngsters in Ireland; but they weren't much good; though in one instance a play has been published with a preface by Lennox Robinson, contradicting the opinions I wrote to the author (at his own repeated request) of the play.[3] I've decided to read no more for God or man. Anyway, I'm not good at this job. One has to have a special gift for it, & that I haven't got.

I'm just going to have a shave—2 o'clock in the morning—so that I shall be free to help in the house when we all get up to face another day.

Remember me to Eugene. I do hope he will rally into more permanent vigor, & that Carlotta is allright. Eugene would be a big loss to the U.S.A., & to us all.

> *My love.*
> *Ever Yours,*
> Sean

[3] Vivian Connell's *The Nineteenth Hole of Europe* (1943).

To Louis D'Alton [1]

TS. HOGAN

TOTNES, DEVON
24 JULY 1943

Dear Louis D'Alton:

Thank you for your letter and for the M[oney]. O[rder]. enclosed, receipt for which goes with this letter. It was good to hear from you again. On the road again! It is odd how Ireland likes the strolling player. Totnes

[1] Louis D'Alton (1900–51), popular Abbey Theatre playwright, and producer-actor in his own touring companies.

three times the size of Letterkenny, never sees anything like one. The nearest is Torquay—occasionally—or Exeter, forty-five miles away. Curious combination that—MacLiammoir and Edwards. Havent heard from Clopet since the performance.[2] I have written to him asking to give me a formal note of the venture's ending. In real life, though, I could see Juno sandwiched between a variety show and a band. I knew about this, and wondered what would happen. And the fee tempted me. I read in the Dublin papers that the house was sold out fortnight before the show. Maybe that wasnt true. But of course, playing for laughs is a common thing—common now as in the time of Shakespeare. [Arthur] Sinclair, Molly O'Neill, and even Sally [Allgood] did it often and often. So when they—! We are having rain, rain, rain here, night and day, soft rain, gentle rain, gentle dew from heaven, but damned irritating.

What's happened to Tom McGreevy?[3] Do you know him? A friend of L[ennox] Robinson. Worked with him long ago in the Carnegie books trust, and resigned with him the time of the row over the paper TOMOR-ROW.[4] I see McGreevy has written an article in the FATHER MATHEW RECORD on St Francis de Sales,[5] seemingly comparing him favourably with Shakespeare, only that while S was full of the love of man, St F was full of the love of God. Oh, well—as Jack Yeats would say.

All well here, but for the fact that I and the missus have a lot more work to do, inside and out. We dont have a second till nine at night. And the three children are on holiday, though the eldest, a big fellow, six foot one, and only fifteen, is to work most of the time.

God be wi' us all.

All good wishes to Mrs D, Sheila,
and me sweet yourself.
Sean O'Casey

[2] Carl Clopet's ill-fated production of *Juno,* which opened in Belfast on 3 May 1943, was, as O'Casey goes on to say, "sandwiched between a variety show and a band." The following advertisement in the *Northern Whig,* a week before the opening of the triple-header, probably explains the nature of the misadventure:

Three Shows in One for the Price of One, May 3rd, Daily for six Days Only, at the Royal Hippodrome, G. L. Birch presents, First Time in the World, A THREE AND A HALF HOUR SHOW, First Time in the World, 'Pla-Vaude-Band': [1] Sean O'Casey's Famous Irish Play, produced by Carl Clopet, *Juno and the Paycock.* Diana Romney, Ronald Ibbs, with the Clopet Company, including many Abbey Players. [2] Nine Big Acts!!! Black & Richardson; The Doyle Twins; Ursula & Noel; Morelli Bros. & Angelina; Annette the Skipping Rope Wonder; The Comerford Troupe of Irish Dancers; The Merry Macs; Joseph McLaughlin; Will Duffy, Gentleman Comedy Cyclist with Pearl. [3] Music for All, by Peggy Dell and Her Band, first time in northern Ireland.

[3] Thomas MacGreevy (1893–1967), poet and critic; Director of the National Gallery of Ireland, 1950–64.
[4] For the background of the *To-Morrow* controversy in 1924, see O'Casey's letter to Lady Gregory, ? January 1925, note 2, Vol. I, p. 123.
[5] Thomas MacGreevy, "Saint Francis de Sales," *Father Mathew Record,* June 1943.

To Totnes Times [1]

TC. O'CASEY

[25? JULY 1943]

Religion and Life

Dear Sir:—

It seems to be a pity that the Church, standing forth as a mirror of humility, is becoming a trumpet of boasting, over boasting, too, by associating the theological, cardinal, and all human virtues with Christians only: "excellent ideals that wouldnt have been taught at all but for Christian revelation"; ideals kept alive by those who worshipped God; "others able to live up to these ideals largely because they live in an atmosphere created by these worshippers." Noble thoughts were uttered, noble lives lived long, long before Christ was born. The Christians werent, and arent now, such fine fellows they sometimes set themselves out to be. Their sins of commission and omission—as an organised body—are pretty bad. They have been the friends of the high and mighty, while the poor have been sent empty away. They have condoned—sometimes encouraged—the economic exploitation of the people. They have remained indifferent to the ignorance of the masses. Only the other day in the *Tablet,* Monsignor R. Knox told a story of how he had asked a friend, who knew these parts well, why such places as Slovakia and Ruthenia always chose a priest for their Prime Minister, to be told that in these parts only priests and lawyers could read, and the people preferred the priest to the lawyer. So Monsignor Ronald Knox is pleased to make a joke about a people's illiteracy—an up-to-date one, too. And even if all their claims to all the virtues were accurate, that wouldnt prove the actuality of the poetical miracles of Galilee, or the prosaic miracles of Lourdes. As for "the bogey man in the skies," we have but to read the Old Testament to see that the Deity shown there was something more terrible. If that testimony be too old, then we have the Crusades, the Inquisition, the Conquests of Mexico and Peru, the story told by Dante—guided through Hell, by the way, by a noble-minded Pagan, and, if all these be ancient things, then read the record of the Jesuit's sermon on hell in James Joyce's *Portrait of an Artist.* I dont like to go against Mr Edwards,[2] for I have a great respect

[1] This letter was refused publication by the editor, A. P. Copplestone, who on 28 July 1943 wrote to O'Casey: "I have no desire to start a fierce religious controversy locally at this time. . . . I fear your letter will do that and therefore I would rather not publish it." (MS. O'Casey)

[2] The Rev. R. A. Edwards, Vicar of Dartington Parish, whose speech, to which O'Casey alludes throughout his letter, was reported in the *Totnes Times,* 24 July 1943.

for him as a fine man, but I dont think he is either fair or just when he lifts Hitler into the front rank of Freethinkers. Hitler isnt one, for he is a Christian, probably, too, in a state of grace; for but a few weeks ago, in answer to a question asking why Hitler had not been excommunicated by the Church, the Catholic *Universe* said through its Inquiry Bureau, "Hitler had not been excommunicated by the Church because he had infringed none of its canons."

Yours sincerely,
Sean O'Casey

To A. P. Copplestone

MS. COPPLESTONE

TOTNES, DEVON
31 JULY 1943

Dear Mr. Copplestone:
Thank you for your letter.[1] Doubtless, you are right. Now that I begin to think of it, what the hell good would it do, anyhow? The heresy of Nazi-Fascism is enough to confront & destroy at the moment.

With all good wishes,
Yours sincerely
Sean O'Casey

[1] See O'Casey's letter to the *Totnes Times,* 25? July 1943, note 1.

To Jack Carney

MS. NYU LIBRARY

[TOTNES, DEVON]
2 AUGUST 1943

Dear Jack,
Thanks ever so much for the papers. I hope you are right about the Guerrillas. It sounds very likely. They should be a power after this war is over: a kind of fully-armed trades unionism, inclined to take no nonsense.

The condition of things after the war will be a nice problem for everyone—
Churchill, Pollitt, Bevan, Lord Halifax, Carney & O'Casey. How it is going
to be straightened out, God knows. A few will be flattened out before that
can be done. Perhaps, The House of Savelery will rise up, and settle all
things to all our satisfaction. I'm afraid Eisenwhore is something of a clog.
A mind that loves the long ago. Heaven knows where he'd be now, if
Alexander hadn't been close to his elbow, getting in his way, and stopping
him from doing things.

I'm afraid that the nice notice of [Michael] Todd doing Red Roses in
New York before the leaves fall isn't worth much. He was to sign a contract
6 months ago, via my agent, Dick Madden, but didn't; & I haven't heard
from Dick since. A letter from George Jean—however, says "he was to do
the play in April, but didn't, & so I'm looking for a Producer that will keep
his word." Perhaps it's just as well. George has been laid up with head
neuralgia for weeks. Got it when he'd got well of an injured thigh &
broken ribs from the attack made on him in the blackout.

The Carl Clopet Productions has failed with the production of the
Irish Plays in the Hippodrome, Belfast. So it seems. I've been told "Juno"
went down & down as the week went on, & the Directors wouldn't let him
do any more. I've written to Clopet telling him the contract is over; but the
letter to the Hippodrome came back marked "Not Here." Where is my
wandering boy tonight? Where, oh, where can he be? Not in the Hippodrome, anyway. He wanted me to give him the rights for all Ulster, but,
fortunately, I refused this to him; so I'm lucky, after all.

If by any chance, you can let me have a loan of Foxes Book of
Martyrs—R. M.'s Citizen Army,[1] I shall be glad. I don't think R. M. will
ever write anything very alarming.

> *Well, all the Best.*
> *Love to Mina & to you.*
> *Ever yours,*
> *Sean*

Enclosed is a very encouraging review of Red Roses from Australia. Ni lia
duine ná baramhail. "People are no more plentiful than opinions."

[1] R. M. Fox, *The History of the Irish Citizen Army* (1943). See O'Casey's letter
to Fox, 27 October 1924, Vol. I, p. 120.

To William Rust

MS. DAILY WORKER

TOTNES, DEVON
3 AUGUST 1943

Dear Mr. Rust:

Thank you for letters & all else. I have a lot to do here now, & have little time to bless myself, much more write, or even ponder. Besides, as I think I told you before, my eyes limit my activity a lot, & they aren't getting younger. One can but do what one can, &, at times, what one can't.

I have no suggestions to make, not knowing enough about things you meet every day. I can but repeat my opinion that the Vatican will prove to be the biggest, & most subtle, obstacle before us in the future. I see the Pope's address to the Italian Workers (a blitz of platitudes), warning them against "the deceptive enticements & seductions of false prophets who call evil good & good evil, boasting of being friends of the people who do not agree with those mutual agreements between capital & labor, employers & employed, which maintain & promote," etc. etc. . . . "Again hear them in the public streets, in clubs, in congresses, you recognise their promises on handbills. You hear them in their songs and anthems." You know whom he means?

Here is the gospel of the White Star: Faith in Christ and Fidelity to the Church the Deep Roots of True Brotherhood. The Church meaning the Vatican, Popes, Cardinals, Bishops, Priests, & Deacons, with the people and Jesus working for a pittance in the back garden. It wouldn't be so bad, if this appeared only in the Roman Observatore, or whatever the Pope's paper may be; but I am reading it now from The New York Times of June 14th 1943. So you see.

I enclose article on Ireland's part in the war which I shall be glad to see published, if it suits you. But dont cut or amend it. I'd very much rather you'd let me have it back.[1] I won't mind, though the general idea that Ireland only stands aside, looking after herself, is a vain & foolish acceptance of a false fact. I wish Ministers would think a little more deeply, & realise that the Irish are more than those in Eirinn. That they must number now about 30,000,000 & that however they differ, when the mother is attacked, 95% of them ask Why?

Yours as ever
Sean O'Casey

[1] The article was not published.

From Eugene O'Neill [1]

TS. O'CASEY

TAO HOUSE, DANVILLE
CONTRA COSTA COUNTY
CALIFORNIA
5 AUGUST 1943

My dear Sean:

This is a hell of a late reply to your May letter, but the O'Neill household has suffered so many upsetting ordeals in the past two months that, while promising myself I would surely write you to-morrow, when to-morrow arrived I always felt too dull and depressed to attempt it. Carlotta has been ill with bad arthritis. This has made it particularly hard for her because she is now doing all the housework and cooking. Impossible to get a servant. I can't be of much help, except as dishwiper, what with my ailment. The matter of merely keeping the home fires burning is a problem when it is complicated by inexperience and illness. If we were both a bit younger and physically fit it would be easy enough.

It seems silly even to mention our troubles when civilian life in this country is such a bed of roses compared to what people have to endure, sick or not, in so many other countries. But my tale of woe does explain why I have done little or no work recently. Too tired the flesh and spirit— and too damned many worrying interruptions of one kind or another to nag at the mind and distract concentration.

All I've done since Pearl Harbor is to rewrite one of the plays in my Cycle. "A Touch Of The Poet" [2]—(an Irish play, incidentally, although located in New England in 1828). This is the only one of the four Cycle plays I had written which approached final form. The others will have to be entirely recreated—if I ever get around to it—because I no longer see them as I did in the pre-war 1939 days in which they were written. I have also (in the past two years) written a non-cycle play entitled "A Moon For The Misbegotten." [3] In this, too, the important characters are Irish, although it is less remote in time (1923) than the Cycle play. Beyond these two plays—and they both still need a final touch of condensation—I've messed around with another play, "The Last Conquest" but haven't got beyond writing the Prologue and a scenario of its eight scenes. It kept dying on me, after each brief burst of enthusiasm. In many ways it could be

---

[1] Eugene O'Neill (1888–1953), American playwright. Mrs. Carlotta O'Neill informed me that all of O'Casey's letters to O'Neill were destroyed. Only two letters from O'Neill to O'Casey have been found in O'Casey's papers, this one, and that of 15 December 1933, Vol. I, pp. 482–83.

[2] *A Touch of the Poet* was first performed in New York on 2 October 1958.

[3] *A Moon For the Misbegotten* was first performed in New York on 2 May 1957.

better done as a picture than a stage play—that is, if Hollywood ever could treat a subject of depth and integrity with depth and integrity—which, of course, is a fantastically impossible notion.

You would like "The Iceman Cometh," [4] I know. It was written after I stopped going on with the Cycle in '39 and is one of the best things I have ever done. And the play I wrote immediately after it, (in 1940) "Long Days Journey Into Night," [5] is *the best*. No one, except Carlotta, has read this play yet. I have a strong feeling against letting anyone see it now. For that matter, no one has seen the two Irish plays I've mentioned. Because they are still in longhand, and my secretary (Carlotta) has had to resign as such for the duration (except for letters). She simply has not the strength or time to keep on that job, too. Typing my longhand is tough work. A magnifying glass is part of the necessary equipment. I couldn't hire anyone else to do it, even if there were anyone to hire.

I'm delighted to know you saw the "Mourning Becomes Electra" production in London [6] and liked it. I saw all the press comments on it, of course. And they sent me a lot of photographs. Beatrice Lehman looked the part of Lavinia more than Alice Brady who played it in New York. But I doubt she could have given as fine a performance. Alice, at her best, was hard to beat.

As for the envy you felt about the play, hell, don't you know I want to bite off one of your ears in jealous fury every time I think of—Well, of "The Plough and The Stars," to mention only one of several.

The next time your write, tell me about yourself and your recent work. (God knows I have wished a bellyful of information about mine on you in this letter, and you ought to retaliate!) I've read "Purple Dust," of course, and there was grand stuff in it for me. [Richard] Madden wrote me several times he hoped he had found a good producer for it but, if he succeeded, he never told me and I have been so entirely out of touch with the New York theatre, I wouldn't know unless he or George mentioned it.

Carlotta joins me in love to you. And much gratitude for your letter. It bucked up my spirit a lot. Here's hoping we may have an opportunity to get together again in New York, as we did once when there was no war.

Very sincerely,
Eugene O'Neill

[4] *The Iceman Cometh* was first performed in New York on 2 September 1946.
[5] *A Long Day's Journey into Night* was first performed in New York on 7 November 1956.
[6] *Mourning Becomes Electra* opened in London on 19 November 1937; it was first performed in New York on 26 October 1931.

To Leslie Daiken [1]

MS. DAIKEN

TOTNES, DEVON

17 AUGUST 1943

Dear Mr. Daiken.

Thank you for your kind card. I'm glad you liked the article.[2] A great many Irish Workers were pleased with it. It may make things easier for them. Even the staunch Catholics in factories took & read the D.W. because of it—so I've been told by a Welsh Shop Steward in a big factory. Over the wireless tonight I heard that the V.C. has been given to a fellow named Connelly who came from a place called Tipperary. He attacked an army with a Bren gun! I sent The Bell [3] off to Pat Dooley the moment I got your request. Yes, Walter Macken asked me to write a play in Gaelic; but I've no time in which to think it out. It would be a terrible job. I havent spoken a word of G for more'n 20 years; & my tongue & mind are a little rusty, now. Even if I tried, & succeeded, it wouldn't be put on. I've had experiences with the tory Gaelic League long before I thought to write a play. Some of it—I hope—will appear in the next vol of Biography—Drums Under the Windows. Macken, I hear, has left the Gaelic Theatre. I can't see any first-class writers rising in Ireland while she's in the embrace of the Vatican; closer than ever before. There wont be a soul soon that wont have the sprinkle of holy water on it. The Vitamins (Spiritual, of course) will be poured down everybody's throat. The Irish are being blitzed into holiness. Its very hard for the middle-class or professionals or intellectuals to get into a deep touch with the workers. They'd have to do a few years of it themselves, & live as the workers live. Still, a lot of them are grand men & women. Oh, those arty-arty boys & talky-talky girls! But you'll find these among the Communists too—not on art; but on Marx. Jasus! they drive me mad sometimes. I tell them to read Pickwick, & they stare at me. They've barely heard of him; but that's all. Of course, when a worker rises, he wants to be like the fellow who lives in a better street; he wants all the veneer that middle-class culture gives; but the war is tumbling a lot of it down. The Gaelic League was full of it.

I can't go into all (or any) of your thunderings at the D.W. Of course I read it—the only daily I do read. Of course it's not perfect. Bill Rust is always asking me for articles; but my eyes allow me to write but a small amount a day, so I have to be satisfied with a little now & again—& so has he; & so will you.

---

[1] Leslie Daiken (1912–64), Dublin-born poet, playwright, author, broadcaster, teacher, authority on children's games and toys.
[2] Sean O'Casey, "False Witness Against the Soviet Union," *Daily Worker,* London, 3 April 1943.
[3] *The Bell,* Dublin literary magazine.

Who is this Shean Mahan who is worrying you?

By all means let me have any instances of Irish activity in this war. I have a hunch they may be needed when it ends. Fools—as far as Ireland is concerned—like [Herbert] Morrison will probably try to injure her when the time comes to count the cost. I've sent a much longer article on the same lines to the USSR Committee of Foreign Writers as a preliminary for their possible help when the cannons go silent.

Why not have a shot at Dartington? I understand they need teachers badly. William Curry is the Head. Dartington Hall School. Dartington, Totnes, will find him. Though even at Dartington it isn't all beer & skittles.

Well, all the best, & the D.W. is doing a good work, however you may roar at it. I wish I could do more for it.

Jim Larkin has been with me here for two days. A grand man. Know him now for well over 30 years.

All the best again
Sean O'Casey

To Jack Carney

MS. NYU LIBRARY

[TOTNES, DEVON]
26 AUGUST 1943

My dear Jack,

Jim has come, and gone again. The same old Jim, the Lion of the Labour fold. I daresay he's back in Dublin now, sitting opposite Trinity College.[1] Thanks for the papers, & for the "History of the Citizen Army." I'll return it to you in a day or two. I've read it. It is very useful; but not very thrilling. Of course Fox was handicapped by not knowing the men & the circumstance then. He came over, I think, just before the outburst of fire between Republican & Free Stater. I remember bringing him to the Grand Orange Lodge, 10 Rutland Sqr, then held by Republicans—there wasn't one there who understood the least one of the principles of Republicanism, as, say Tone did, or Emmet, or Miles O'Byrne, or Tristram Shandy—, & was sheltering the refugees from Belfast. Jim tells me he "designed the flag of the Plough & the Stars." The book by Fox says Megahy; [2]

[1] The office of Jim Larkin's Workers' Union of Ireland was on College Street across from Trinity.

[2] R. M. Fox quotes the *Irish Worker* in April 1914, commenting that the new labour flag, the Plough and the Stars, "was the work of Mr. Megahy." *The History of the Irish Citizen Army,* p. 68.

AE told me HE done it; & I, who was Secretary then,[3] don't know who done it! I'm inclined to think Jim's fancy first thought of a design like it, suggested by W. P. Ryan's "Plough & the Cross"[4] of which he sometimes spoke; that AE was asked to draw it & paint it—being a painter of sorts—, that Megahy was asked to do it, then. Anyway, he knocked out a design (I have it here),[5] but it was just a plough shape sprinkled with stars, crudely representational. Finally, if I remember right, Dun Emer[6] did the flag, & gave it a stylistic touch which really made it very beautiful. It was the finest flag—in design & execution—Ireland ever had. It's a great pity that flag was lost. The fellow who carried it—an Espell—was six foot three. It was I who first drew the plan for the strap carriage (or harness) to enable the banner-bearer of the O'Toole Pipers to march with ease; & this I got copied for our Citizen Army. It had, instead of a spearpoint, a green dragon (Capitalism) being choked by a brilliant sturdy Red Hand (The I.T.G.W.U. [Irish Transport and General Workers' Union]).

I got a copy of "I Knock at the Door" from you. No slip came with it, so I suppose it was meant for me because no copy could be got. It was Eileen who wanted one (for Nannie, I think), & she wrote to Macmillans, who told her none was available at the moment: they were awaiting binding. So I don't need it. Shall I return it, or shall I wait till you select a friend to have it for a present?

The enclosed cutting explains itself. Have you heard of the pamphlet? I wrote an article for the D.W. on these lines. Since I have had letters from Shop Stewards in Oxford, Plymouth, & Bristol, commending it; but none of them mentioned the pamphlet, so they couldn't have heard of it either. Seems strange, that. Has it been quietly shelved?

Capt. F. O. Miksche's article, "What Europe Fears," in the Tribune, is a very fine, & a timely one. He hits more than one nail on the head. I seem to see my own thought in everything he says. Clerical Fascism is what we have to fear, & fearing, fight. I've been trying to tell this for weeks to the D.W.

They call it Christian Socialism; but it isn't. It's neither Christian nor Socialist. They aim, even, at bringing it to being in the USSR. The Vatican has more than a Skibereen Eagle eye on Moscow.[7] This world-wide broad-

[3] O'Casey, then O'Cathasaigh, was secretary of the Irish Citizen Army in 1914. See his statements and letters, written as secretary, April to June 1914, Vol. I, pp. 50–56.

[4] William Patrick Ryan, *The Plough and the Cross: A Story of New Ireland* (1910).

[5] In 1954 O'Casey presented this original design of the Plough and the Stars flag to the National Museum of Ireland in Dublin, where it is now on display. See O'Casey's letters to G. A. Hayes-McCoy, 11 and 19 November 1954.

[6] The Dun Emer Press and handicraft industries in Dundrum, founded in 1903 by the sisters of W. B. Yeats, Elizabeth Corbet and Susan Mary Yeats. See Oliver St. John Gogarty's letter to O'Casey, 8 February 1929, note 2, Vol. I, p. 336.

[7] The Rev. Francis S. Mahony, S.J., in his *Reliques of Father Prout* (1836), wrote that Jack Montesquieu Bellow, editor of the *Cork Chronicle,* "kept an eye on Russia, an eye of vigilant observation, which considerably annoyed the czar." Later

cast of "The Love of God" is a bit terrifying, coming as it does through the blast of the hatred of man. The new departure; or is it the new arrival? This Quebec Conference is a curious event. No one seems to know what it may bring forth. So far we are just hearing Roosevelt & Churchill blowing through two trombones. A blast of "Onward Christian Soldiers."

Have you heard at all from Peter Newmark? He wrote to us once from Egypt on an airgraph. The thing has disappeared, & I've lost his number, etc; so I should be glad if he has written to you.

I am doing a little with a new volume of "biography." I've got about 9 chapters done, which leaves me about 14 more to do. It's a bit more difficult since Nannie left. No word yet from New York about P. Dust or Red Roses. I've given up thinking about them. [Louis] Dalton is still hawking Juno through Ireland. The few pounds regular are immensely useful. That was a good victory for Labour in Australia; & a good beginning in Canada.

Hope you are well, & of course, Mina, too. Love to her & you.

Sean

P.S.O.S. If you come across any of the black stuff, I'd be glad. It seems years since I had a tough smoke.

---

in the 1880s the *West Cork Eagle,* published in Skibereen and known as the Skibereen Eagle, had on its masthead a drawing of a large eagle peering over a globe of the world—hence, the well-known comic saying in Ireland, "The Skibereen Eagle has its eye on Russia," or "on You."

To Jack Carney

MS. NYU LIBRARY

[TOTNES, DEVON]
27 SEPTEMBER 1943

Dear Jack,

All are at school this morning, so there is a slight space in time left to thank you for the papers and the black tobacco. Things seem to be moving quick now. For their own sakes, they'd better shove on this 2nd Front as soon as they can. It looks to me as if the Nazis were getting out of the USSR with all the men & equipment they can save so as to concentrate towards the West. Even after the last man has got away from the Borders, there will be a sizeable army left; & if this gets going, plus the planes, we will be in for a bad time of it, especially if the USSR is determined to take a holiday when they have freed the Baltic States, the Ukraine, Bessarabia, Belorussia, Poland, & put Finland in a corner. They will, God knows, deserve a rest. I shouldn't be a bit surprised if we find ourselves calling for a 2nd Front— not in the West—but in the East to relieve the pressure on us. I should like to have seen the Battle Exhibition. Not much to be seen here—not even up there, up the hill to the city set on the hill—Dartington. I understand Imogen Holst,[1] who is up there now, is trying to make the musical side of the show more popular. She is doing what I have argued should be done (years ago), namely to bring the local people into touch with music and literature. That pretentious fool Oppenheimer,[2] with his German songs—sung in German, mind you! Just imagine the simple Devon people with their simple dialect trying to get round the German Lieder. And he tried Opera here that would certainly require fine artists & a good many rehearsals in La Scala, & even in Bayreuth. The fool couldn't see that "To Be a Farmer's Boy" or "Down by the Old Bull & Bush" sung well and heartily are much better & brighter things than those that cannot be sung at all. To produce opera among those who've never sung anything above "I'm Sitting on Top of the World" takes time & training. And all the lovely British Ballads there are too, good enough for a beginning. I hope Imogen Holst will be a success.

Before I forget it—a young lass here attending the Girl's County School is seeking to become a doctor, & is working for a scholarship—God help her. She is poor, but most intelligent. I understand, if she wins the S, Mrs. [Dorothy] Elmhirst is to help financially, which is good of Mrs. Elmhirst. Well what I want from you is that if any copies of The Lancet or B. Medical Journal are knocking about, send them on to me for her. I've given her already those you have sent. She is a great lover of the USSR, & buys the Soviet News Weekly; reads the D.W. & a good number of the magazines you so kindly send, which I pass on when I have read them, & Breon & Niall, & sometimes Eileen—who looks at the pixstures.

Dickie Fox is a strange animal, if I remember him rightly. I never liked conscientious objectors, & I like them less now—except one like [Francis] Sheehy-Skeffington who was the grandest fighter I ever knew. So I am inclined to be biassed against Dickie, though, honestly, his book isn't worth much.

I missed your article on Curten. Papers get mixed here, & I'm never certain of getting what I want—rather certain of getting what I don't want. S. Dispatch instead of the Observer; S. Express instead of the S. Times. Yesterday it was S. Dispatch instead of the S. Times, but there's no use of commenting on it. It is part of our proud sense of efficiency.

A lot of good may come from the friendship between the Orthodox &

[1] Imogen Holst (1907–   ), musician and composer, director of music at Dartington Hall, 1942–51; assistant to Benjamin Britten at the Aldeburgh Festival, 1952–64.

[2] Hans Oppenheim (1892–1965), director of the Dartington Hall Music Group, 1937–45; conductor of the English Opera Group, 1946; associate conductor of the Glyndebourne Opera at the Edinburgh Festival, 1949.

the Anglican Churches. Each now is, I think, much more communal & democratic than the Roman one, the bitterest & most reactionary power the poor world has ever seen. I have suggested this to the D.W., & have thought of writing a short article on the Vatican & its politics. However, it is now between the devil & the deep sea. I touch on it in the chapter on Dr. Mac-Donald & Dr. O'Hickey in my Biography. I have begun writing one about Jim—Red Avatar.

I hope you are all well. Love to Mina & to you.

Ever yours
Sean

To Daily Worker

4 OCTOBER 1943

IRISH BADGES [1]

I don't see why the Irish fighting Fascism shouldn't wear a distinct shoulder badge as the others do. If the English were wise, they'd do as the Soviet land does, call them by one of their national heroes. Emmet or Wolfe Tone Brigade, or Michael Davitt, or Parnell Division. I imagine the Royal Irish Regiment wear an Irish symbol—the Harp. Anyway, they are fighting the common foe of man, and that's the main thing. When the war is over, I hope they'll go on doing the same thing—fighting the common foes of man, namely, those mentioned by Beveridge in his half-forgotten Report. Anyhow, we'll have to fight them, I'm afraid, and a good job, too. As the people have shown they can fight like men, it's too much to ask them, when all is won, to live like sheep.

Sean O'Casey

[1] In response to O'Casey's article, "The Irish," *Daily Worker,* 12 August 1943, Royston Green of Leicester, in a letter in the 4 October 1943 issue, asked if O'Casey would agree that Irish soldiers, sailors, and airmen serving in British uniforms in the war should wear shoulder badges bearing their country's name. This is O'Casey's reply.

To Lennox Robinson [1]

MS. ROBINSON

TOTNES, DEVON

25 OCTOBER 1943

Dear Lennox:

The job you have in hands is enough to bend anyone's back.[2] It's hard enough to write, or try to write, one's own life, but to do justice, or injustice, to another's, is harder still.

The play you are puzzled about—since it isn't the Crimson in the Tricolour—must be either The Frost in the Flower, or, The Harvest Festival,[3] for these were the three plays submitted before "The Gunman."

I shall look forward to reading both Letters & Life. It was a shame to demolish the House. And now I see [Henry] Grattan's home in Tinahinch is to be done away with too. If it were Matt Talbot's!

To save you possible trouble, should you want to quote any letters of mine, you can go ahead. I don't think they have any importance—even from an Irish, or a Dublin, point of view. We are all well, here, so far; but necessarily cramped a lot by the war. At the moment, we—Eileen especially—are working to collect funds here to endow a "Totnes" Bed in the British Stalingrad Hospital. Already, we have enough for two. We have here a very vigorous branch of the Anglo-Soviet Friendship Committee, with the Irish working the hardest on it.

My good wishes to Mrs. Robinson & to you.

Yours sincerely,
Sean O'Casey

[1] Lennox Robinson (1886–1958), Irish playwright, actor, director; served as a director of the Abbey Theatre, 1923–56. See the first of O'Casey's many letters to him, 5 August 1921, note 1, Vol. I, p. 93.

[2] Robinson had planned to write the "Life and Letters of Lady Gregory," but he abandoned the project. Later he edited *Lady Gregory's Journals, 1916–1930* (1947).

[3] See the Abbey Theatre's Reader's Opinion of "The Harvest Festival" and "The Frost in the Flower," 26 January 1920, Vol. I, pp. 91–92; and the critiques of "The Crimson in the Tricolour" by Lady Gregory and W. B. Yeats, ? October 1921 and 19 June 1922, Vol. I, pp. 95–96, 102–3.

To Jack Carney

MS. NYU LIBRARY

TOTNES, DEVON
21 NOVEMBER 1943

Dear Jack,

A short note to thank you for the tobac & the papers. An attack of Influenza out-flanked me, got me on the run, & downed me. I'm just trying to crawl out of No Man's Land. It always leaves me with a congested chest which lingers on for weeks. It is a nuisance. Even the siren doesn't interest me. The other day in the middle of the early morning, there was a sharp attack on Plymouth, & they were flying low around us for hours. Eileen got up, & dressed; but I stayed put where I was in bed, indifferent even to a block-buster.

By the way, have you heard from Daiken recently? He has rather a fine poem in this month's "Our Time." "Shamrocks For Mayakovsky." I think it damned good. I hope the Red Army will be able to hold the Germans in the Dneiper Bend. Isn't it bad about Leros, Cos, & Tomas. Seems to me that Maitland Wilson is another one of those "might-not-have-beens." With Eisenhower & him, poor Montgomery has a lot to do. I hope Mountbatten won't be another of them. And Stillwell doesn't seem to be much better. McAteer, had he had a chance, would have made a good general; & had such as he got the favours of fortune granted to a swarm of duffers, we'd be well on our way to Berlin now. –'/–*— that was just a fit of coughing. We have collected £400 here for a Stalingrad bed.

I'll write again as soon as I get back some way into the shape of a man.

Love to Mina.
Yours as ever,
Sean

To Jack Carney

MS. NYU LIBRARY

[TOTNES, DEVON]
23 NOVEMBER 1943

Dear Jack,

Your letter must have gone via Stalingrad, as enclosed envelope will show. What I want to say is that no letter from Young Jim [Larkin] came with it. The P. Atlas came allright. In my last letter, I forgot to mention the R. Blades. They were especially welcome. They ration them here to one per calendar month. I've been going over ones abandoned twenty golden years ago. I've given a few to Brian who shaves once a week now. I hope you are right about Krivoi Rog. The Red Army can't afford a defeat on that side of the Dneiper. Oh, wouldn't I like to be there to listen to Stalin chatting to C. & R. To be there; oh, to be there!

[Herbert] Morrison seems to have lost his head since he became a Cabinet Minister. That is a weakness a lot of one-time workers, & left-wingers, have. Prominence does it first; then power to that finishes the job. And such as Morrison would be much more dangerous than poor R[amsay] MacDonald who was, at least, a cultured fellow, fond of art & literature.

Glad you got a rise. It's work, work, Jack, all the time for all of us now, & forevermore I'm afraid. Looka me, even. I get up at nine, & can't start my work till nine, or maybe ten, when the house is asleep. In between I am always trying to do something—when I write this, I have to go out to sweep the garden path a little of decayed rubbish. From nine or ten I try to work till two o'clock. Take two hours a day off for a doze, and you have well over 100 hours a week in some kind of work or another. It's not work, it's the kinda work we have to do that unravels our spirit; but there's no escape till this fever of war dies out of our blood.

Gone are the richer days of steak and onions! The workers now feed on Income Tax Credit Notes, & Savings Certificates. They'll be taxed at the end of the war to pay themselves back again.

What a Commissar of some kind of Industry Jim [Larkin] would have made! He'd have made a hell of a lot of big mistakes, but big things would have crept out of the errors.

I have very little respect for those who spring to work for Beaverbrook because he gives big money (maybe this is because he's never asked me). They get what's coming to them: Everyone does in the end. Karma, I think, AE called it. As a man sows . . . is S. Paul's way of putting it.

If you ever pick up a simple book of elementary Russian—simple lessons in Irish style—send it on. I'd like to put it under Brian's nose. He might become interested in it; & Russian is, & is going to be an important language to us all.

Love to Mina.
Yrs
Sean

To Gabriel Fallon

MS. TEXAS

TOTNES, DEVON
20 DECEMBER 1943

My dear Gaby:

A few words of greeting to you, Rose, & all the children—one of them must be near out of childhood now. Our eldest is 16. For the past year I haven't had time to bless myself. We've no help, & there's a lot to be done about the house to help Eileen who has to do a colossal lot now. I don't get time now to think of work till 9 or 10 at night. I usually stay at it till 2 am; or, if thought doesn't come, to read a little. I'm writing this at 1–30., just after finishing a chapter of "biography." Do you know Leslie Daiken? He knows F. McM[anus]. He's getting out a book of articles, stories, etc by Irish writers; & I've written one called "There Go The Irish." [1] Just read "Puck Fare." [2] Not so bad. God be wi' the time when Old Hummel chaired the stage of the Abbey! [3] It must be a long time ago. One of your best parts, I think. You really didn't get a fair hunt. Deegan, for instance, in "P. Twyning." [4] Waste be God! And you should have done Peter Flynn in The Plough.[5] And Needle Nugent in Juno.[6] Ah! I didn't know then what I know now—which is all too damn little still!

Many are beginning to feel a little strain from the war now—or, maybe, it's getting old I am. Anyway, we've got a few paper chains left—three years old; & they'll put some colour into the rooms of the two young ones. And two Christmas Trees, each as big as a Dublin geranium. The young one—4¼ chants around it

> Oh! Christmas tree, oh Christmas tree,
> How are your branches, Christmas tree?

And I join in, seriously; for it is a big question. How are your branches! How indeed? Well, as far as I'm concerned, not too bad, for the Red Army has done well. How are the branches of Ireland's Xmas tree? After the

---

[1] Sean O'Casey, "There Go The Irish," the leading essay in *They Go, The Irish: A Miscellany of War-Time Writing,* ed. Leslie Daiken (1944); reprinted in *Blasts and Benedictions* (1967).

[2] See O'Casey's letter, "Still More Ideals . . . ," *Puck's Fare,* May 1942.

[3] Fallon played the role of Old Hummel in a Dublin Drama League production of Strindberg's *The Spook Sonata,* performed at the Abbey Theatre on 19–20 April 1925, Sunday and Monday, when the theatre was not used by the regular company.

[4] Fallon played the role of James Deegan in George Shiels's *Paul Twyning,* which opened at the Abbey Theatre on 3 October 1922.

[5] Fallon played the role of Captain Brennan in *The Plough and the Stars,* which opened at the Abbey Theatre on 8 February 1926.

[6] Fallon played the role of Charlie Bentham in *Juno and the Paycock,* which opened at the Abbey Theater on 3 March 1924.

war? Will there be a boycott? Well, we'll fight it. I've defended her already, here, & in the USSR. The dead who died for England. A lot. I'm just reading Conquest of Mexico.[7] Never read it before: only that of Peru.[8]

Remember me to all friends—and enemies.

Love to Rose, all the children, & to you.

Sean as ever

[7] William H. Prescott's *A History of the Conquest of Mexico* (1843).
[8] William H. Prescott's *A History of the Conquest of Peru* (1847).

To Lady Astor [1]

MS. ASTOR

TOTNES, DEVON
LÁ NA NODHLAG [2]
25 DECEMBER 1943

Dear Lady Astor.

Your kind card has prompted me to beseech you to take thought before you wave your fists in defence of Mosley,[3] who was, when the limelight shone on him, & bugles blew him on to a platform, little less than "a foolish prating knave." So said Hamlet of Polonius, & that poor old fool, who "was for a tale of bawdry" was far wiser than Mosley. I was shocked when I read of your defence of him. What's Hecuba to him, or he to Hecuba? If you still want to oppose Communism, oppose it by defending finer things than that peacock-feathered jay.

I do hope all yours & Lord Astor's sons are well & safe.

Give my best wishes to him.

Yours sincerely
Sean O'Casey

[1] Viscountess Nancy Astor (1880–1964), born of an old Virginia family, married Viscount William Waldorf Astor in 1906; became an M.P. in 1919, the first woman to sit in Parliament. See the first of O'Casey's many letters to her, 4 December 1931, note 1, Vol. I, p. 442.

[2] Christmas Day.

[3] Oswald Mosley (1896–   ), leader of the British Union of Fascists.

To Peter Newmark

MS. NEWMARK

TOTNES, DEVON
26 DECEMBER 1943

My dear Peter:

Things to do & think of, are so pressing and so many that I havent had a minute to say a word to you. We have no help here, now; & with three children, there's a lot to be done about the house. I don't be able to start even thinking of work till ten o'clock, & usually keep thinking & trying to get down a few of the thoughts till 2 o'c in the morning. It's fine to hear that you are well and sound in limb & mind. I don't know what papers what I write take, which is good Irish grammar, in Soviet land—a Magazine of great importance, I suppose. Seriously, I don't know, not having seen them myself, or if I have, didn't know them. But appear they do, sometime, somewhere, for a young lass here, on the Anglo-Soviet Committee, a Wesleyan teacher in Torquay Grammar School told Eileen that a Russian Professor (who teaches her Russian) (Dubhairt bean liom go ndubhairt bean lei) (Irish proverb of A woman said to me that woman said to her) told her of some fine remarks on Youth appeared in a magazine, which he gave the Grammar School teacher so that she might read O'Casey's remarks; which she couldn't do because her Russian wasn't good enough; so she asked Eileen to ask me to give her the original English version which, I couldn't do, either having mislaid the typescript or destroyed it. So now, Peter you know all about it. I've written an article on the Theatre, copy of which I enclose; some biography, an article for a forthcoming book. "There Go the Irish." And that's about all; & by God, considering the circumstances, enough, too!

I haven't read your play. I can't read MS. It drags my eyes out. And your God-damned penmanship is terrible. Eileen, it was who, in a snatched moment, read your letter to me. I tell you what I'll do; Vernon Beste is Editor of Our Time; he's on a C.E.M.A. Committee; & he knows something about the Theatre. I'll write to him asking him to read it, & if he thinks it worth while, to place it somewhere. He'll do this for me. I've just sent him a message saying good luck to Our Time, & if he wont do what I ask, I'll send another saying Bad Luck to Our Time. Let the Bourgeoise [writing worn away] try how they will to keep the world sober, they can't do it. Things happen & times change, when God pulls against them; & there he is pulling everywhere with Croce, with Tito, with The Red Army, with Harry Pollitt, with the furore O'Casey, yelling out (God, not O'Casey) Now boys, a good pull, altogether, & over they go! And Bloomsbury's Lady Rhonddas & the rest of them are beginning to see that God isn't quite the respectable old gent the Churches made him out to be.

I do hope you're well rid of the jaundice by now. It's usually a tedious thing, & by no means to be disregarded as trivial. Nathan's allright again—got a [writing worn away] ribs; but fought back, & they got [writing worn away] off him, but a fright. Scawen Blunt is mentioned in Shaw's preface to J. Bull's Other Island, where Shaw gives a fine official account of the Denshawai horror. Blunt was a friend, I think, of Lady Gregory's. I've never read anything by him, but, like all true Irishmen, knew about the Egyptian pidgeon shooting. We in Eire were used to these things. But "black rages" aren't any good. Progress is terribly slow, & never uniform; but it goes on, all the same. Eileen & all send their love to you. And so do I.

Yours as ever.
Sean.

From Lady Astor

MS. O'CASEY

CLIVEDEN
30 DECEMBER 1943

Dear, dear Friend,

I *never* stood up for Mosley. He practically murdered his first wife, who was one of my dearest friends.

As you know, I hate dictators—whether they are from the Right or Left. Like St. Paul, I was born free. All I know is that that outcry about Mosley was an organised affair. When I see you I will explain exactly what I mean. Anyhow, it's not the British way to keep dying people in prison, particularly if they are uncondemned. We don't keep people in Princetown and I am sure you would be the last to do it, for in spite of all you say—no one has a tenderer heart.

I do long to see you again. I have had such an amusing letter from G. B. S. which I will bring down to show you.

Please don't class me as a Mosleyite, Stalinite, Hitlerite or Musso-ite; I am not among the "ites" and you shouldn't be either!

What about coming up and paying us a long visit here? Please think about it.

My sons were all here on Boxing Day. Think of it. I pray God this war will soon be over—& we shall meet. With love to you both.

Yrs.
Nancy Astor

To Bernard Shaw [1]

MS. BRITISH MUSEUM
TOTNES, DEVON
1 JANUARY 1944

My dear G. B. S.

Greetings for what is called another year, though where or when Time begins, sorra bit of me knows.

I see Eire won't leave us alone, wondering why our "propaganda" is so successful there. They think a few full houses at the Abbey is a wonderful thing. Very important and gratifying—I was often glad of their full houses—, but not what could be called extraordinary successes. Thanks be with God they haven't forgotten us anyway.

Totnes collected £414. for Stalingrad Hospital—more than Exeter or Torquay. Eileen worked very hard for it. I did a little.

Very glad to hear Cosgrave [2] wrote to you. Curious De Valera didn't. A far more "pious" man than Cosgrave, but not half so human. The Irishman in him drained away the Spaniard; & the Spaniard in him drained away the Irishman, leaving De Valera. [3]

We are very busy here, having no help, so community singing has gone west, & community work has come to stay.

An appallingly bad C.E.M.A. [4] Company playing—trying to play—here. They'll ruin the theatre. I do hope it's the worst Company they've got. Thanks be with God for the Red Army. The Diehards here are speechless. I told one of them that I had it on good authority that Michael when he fought Satan, carried a red pennon on his spear.

My love, & Eileen's
Sean

[1] George Bernard Shaw (1856–1950), Irish playwright and man of letters. See the first of O'Casey's many letters to him, 29 June 1928, Vol. I, p. 293.

[2] William T. Cosgrave (1880–1965), head of the Irish Free State government, 1922–32, under the Cumann na nGhaedheal, later the Fine Gael Party.

[3] Eamon de Valera (1882–1975), born in Brooklyn, New York, of an Irish mother and a Spanish father. His American birth saved him from being executed after the 1916 Easter Rising. During the Civil War in 1922 he led the fight against the Free State government and founded the opposition Fianna Fail Party. He was head of the Irish government in 1932–48; 1951–54; 1951–59; and was elected President of the Irish Republic in 1959.

[4] Council for the Encouragement of Music and the Arts; now the Arts Council of Great Britain.

To The Macmillan Company

TS. MACMILLAN, N.Y.

TOTNES, DEVON
I FEBRUARY 1944

Dear Tim:

I am sending you the following chapters of an additional number of biography,[1] which, of your charity, I trust you won't mind minding for me. Here we never know when a bomb may fall, or a Commando drop from the skies; & I don't want to have to write them all over again, if I remained to do it even. They are:

> Poor Tom's acold
> Home of the Living
> Home of the Dead
> Drums Under the Windows
> Sign of the Pick & Shovel
> Behold, My Family is Poor
> Song of a Shift—Seven in all, with more to follow.

Yours sincerely,
Sean O'Casey

[1] *Drums Under the Windows* (1946).

To Jack Carney

MS. NYU LIBRARY

[TOTNES, DEVON]
7 FEBRUARY 1944

Dear Jack,

It's near time I'm telling you for me to acknowledge & thank you for the present of tobacco sent to me at Christmas, & for the showers of papers & magazines you have sent to me since.

I have been very occupied, wishing, if at all possible, to get done another volume of biography so as to have, if at all possible, it published sometime this year.

I have about two-thirds of it done—Drums Under the Windows, & I hope it may be as good as the last one. I have good hope of signing up for

a London production of Red Roses, at long last. I've read the contract
(not so good as I'd like; none ever is), & bar one point of difference, which
I hope the Licensee will grant, have decided to accept it. It will bring
Eileen & me some much needed relief for another short spell; & if it should
succeed, then Ireland, Boys, Hurray!

I'm afraid, I don't think much of Michael Foot writing a stinging
article when he knew he was to say farewell; but he knows his own know
best. Well, isn't the Red Army doing well! The stone all the builders re-
jected has become the head of the corner. "Where are they to find their
Generals?" said Tabs & Debs in 1933-34-35-36-37-38-39-40 & 41.
And nobody knew, except themselves. Where's the great Gooderian now? [1]
"Here Come the Thanks!" he wrote in a book of his; but where is he now?
There must be consternation in the War Office; & in the Vatican; and in
Leinster House. I haven't seen sign or light of Father Russell [2] since the
Red Army turned about to march back the way they came. We can't
count their generals now. They're as many as the sands of the seashore. A
good old ex-Colonel said to me some time ago, "I never expected this. It
is incredible—they must be getting some kind of help from our Staff." I
wouldn't doubt it, said I. I daresay they'll soon be in Poland. I'd nearly bet
the Polish Government in London will never see Poland again—never the
Poland they knew—except in old motion pictures.

Eileen tells me you are working very hard, & doing a seven-day week
of it. Don't do it too recklessly. One must have an occasional stretch.

I imagine Bill O'Brien has made a false step this time. I'd say it was
a dying kick. The Labour Movement can't stick that sort of bullying. Even
[Richard] Corish has to kick back. Bill's beard will soon be white. Like
G. Borkman [3] in The Master Builder, the young are knocking at poor
Bill's door, & he's afraid to open it. It's a pity he can't see how things are
moving. Even without Jim [Larkin], they'd move. No man can keep control of things forever; & such as Bill, least of all. Is he in the Senate? It must
be a bitter thing for him to see old Jim & young Jim members of the Dail.
But he's behind the counter of a Bank,[4] & that's something.

A lot of people here are very anxious. They expect heavy raids here
as soon as the 2nd Front takes shape. It could happen, as Roddy the
Rover [5] says. What a strange throw-up of the Gaelic Movement! I see the

1 Heinz Guderian (1888–1954), German general and leading authority on tank
warfare; responsible for the notorious *Blitzkrieg* strategy. O'Casey is punning on his
name and his book, *Achtung-Panzer!* (1937).

2 Father E. Russell, the Dublin-born parish priest of Totnes. See O'Casey's comments on him in his letter to Gabriel Fallon, 17 July 1941, Vol. I, p. 897.

3 He meant Halvard Solness in Ibsen's play.

4 See O'Casey's letter to Jack Carney, 17 June 1943, note 1.

5 See O'Casey's letter to Brian O'Nolan, 2 April 1942, note 7.

6 *The Wolfe Tone Annual,* written and published by Brian O'Higgins, which had
appeared annually since 1932, was suppressed by the Fianna Fail government in 1944,
probably because O'Higgins had attacked the Roman Catholic hierarchy for its role in
the dismissal of Dr. Michael O'Hickey. The 1944 edition later appeared in 1945. See
O'Casey's letter to Roger Hayes, 24 November 1945, notes 3 and 4.

Government wouldn't let Brian O'Higgins' book about Tone be printed.[6] A lot of them would like to forget Tone. I'd love to be in Ireland, & hear some of the things that are said there.

Well, all the best; and many thanks again; with love to Mina. Have you heard from Daiken lately? Did I tell you I wrote an article to be included in some Irish collection he thought of getting printed? You were to write a Fleet St Sketch. Mine was called, "There Go the Irish."

Adieu,
Sean

To George Jean Nathan

MS. CORNELL

TOTNES, DEVON
8 FEBRUARY 1944

My dear George:

Greetings again. I'm sure things are very strange in New York now. But you remain the Champion of the Theatre. I am very busy here, doing a lot of things beside my usual & favorite work—more or less—as St. Paul would say—a serving of tables. However, it's my own table, & Eileen can't do everything.

I hope to finish another volume of "biography" for publication this year, if the Lord, & the war, allow. Then, I might start on a play, possibly a war-play—that's how my thoughts go at the moment.

I see by a N. Y. Times Book Review Magazine that you have sent out another book.[1] I hope I may have it. The Review printed a fine photo of you, too. It was very pleasant to see an image of your fine, pleasant, critical face again.

Ireland is becoming more virulent than ever over my books, "a venomous expatriate" is the latest. The whole of Ireland has become a Boston, a Boston without any Americans.

I had a letter from Eugene sometime ago,[2] saying things had changed his mood about his Cycle of plays, & that he would have to begin all over again. I am reluctant to write and suggest he shouldn't do this; but go on in the way set out by himself at first. What do you think of it?

The New York Season seems to have been a pretty poor one. Here, God help us, we are as we were—forsaken & almost lost. A Jewish actor of the USSR came on a visit here lately. Asked "now what would you like

[1] George Jean Nathan, *The Theatre Book of the Year, 1943–1944* (1944), *A Record and an Interpretation.*
[2] See Eugene O'Neill's letter to O'Casey, 5 August 1943.

to do." "Visit every Shakespeare play in London." There wasn't one. "Pity" said the Shakespearean Jewish actor, "well, we'll go to see the ones in Memorial Theatre." It was shut. There wasn't a Shakespeare play anywhere. And one of Stalingrad's main streets was Shakespeare Street! I wish I was there, or you were here.

Ever Yours,
Sean

To Lady Astor

MS. ASTOR

TOTNES, DEVON
9 FEBRUARY 1944

Dear Lady Astor.

Oh; my friend, my friend! You say "it is not the British way to keep dying people in prison, particularly if they are uncondemned." May I say, I am an Irishman, & have seen uncondemned men die in British prisons? Ireland knows a lot about Virginia; Virginia very little about Ireland. I suppose each of us has been born free (and equal, as the American Constitution says), but that's no good, if on the day after we become a slave. My dear lady (and friend), I have been pro-Stalin ever since Lenin died. I am pro many things; & you are, must be pro-something, if only pro-Lady Astor; &, I think, you are pro-Shaw, & needn't be ashamed of it. I know you are pro-Lord Astor, & pro-Mr. Will, David, Michael, & Jake; & quite rightly so.

Thank you for asking me to visit you. I should like it very much, but things forbid. We have a tremendous lot to do here now. I have to give a hand in the house, & can't start work (my own) till 8 or 9 at night. Eileen never has a second, looking after the house & the children. When things get better, maybe we shall all meet again.

I've just signed a contract for a play of mine for a London Production, & this will make me busier than ever; as well as working at another volume of biography, & various articles.

I am really glad you had all your children with you on St Stephen's Day. That was something. I do hope they are all well.

Yes, most of us, I daresay, wish the war over. I do, so that the real war may begin, to do away with the iniquities of peace, no less renowned than war.

Eileen sends her love to you & Lord Astor, & so do I.

Yours sincerely.
Sean O'Casey

To Leslie Daiken

MS. TEXAS

TOTNES, DEVON
10 FEBRUARY 1944

Dear L. Daiken.

I'm no critic, so what I may say is but a personal opinion. I think your monologue very good. The vernacular's caught grandly. Whether it will get over to England or Scotland's another question. One thing I'd recommend: some punctuation. This isn't purely O'Casey advice. When I Knock at the Door was in MS, it wasn't pointed as it is now. Harold Macmillan came to see me, & we had a long discussion on the question. After a good deal of thought, I decided he was mainly in the right, & I amended the MS by a good deal of punctuation. But that's your pidgeon, & I don't like to say yea or nay to any writer old, or a new commencer.

I have written to John Singer, Editor of Million, saying I had your piece, that I liked it, thought it worth a place in a new Million, if any more were to be published, & sent a stamped addressed envelope for his reply. By the way, they don't pay well. I got £2.11.6 for "The Dog." [1] But that was much better than nothing. I haven't seen a Bell since you sent me the last copy. How does that keep going?

I'm not conscious of ever having done anything to hurt Hugh Mac-Diarmuid. He went through a hell of a time when I knew him—I saw him but once—we went with some friends to a Revue in Chelsea Palace. I thought him a grand fellow. He was in great poverty at the time—I was but a little better myself. His wife [2] left him & went with another. A long time after he wrote to me from the Shetlands saying he had another woman [3] whom he loved, & who loved him; but his mind was on the bairns, & asked me if I thought he should leave the woman he was with, & go back to the first wife. I didn't answer the letter, for I knew this was not for me to say. That he, & he alone, must decide such a question. And that is the one & only injustice I did to Hugh. But he is a poet. His "A Drunk Man Looks at the Thistle" is grand.

Well, all the best.
Yours
Sean O'Casey

[1] "The Dog," a short story, in *Million: New Left Writing,* December 1943, published by William Maclellan, Glasgow. Reprinted in *Blasts and Benedictions* (1967).
[2] Hugh MacDiarmid's first wife, Margaret Skinner.
[3] Hugh MacDiarmid's second wife, Valda Trevlyn.

To Irish Independent

7 MARCH 1944

THE INTERNATIONALE

Sir—In a recent issue of your journal, "Spectator," in one of his paragraphs dealing with the new Soviet Anthem, says that "the Soviets have scrapped that very martial rabble-rousing song, 'The Internationale.' " This is not correct. Having achieved might and power through Socialist energy and labour, the old song was no longer suitable, and so an anthem acclaiming what had been done and what remained to do, was substituted for "The Internationale." But "Spectator" forgot to say that "The Internationale" remains the anthem of the Communist Party.

Sean O'Casey

To George Jean Nathan

MS. CORNELL

TOTNES, DEVON
[? APRIL 1944]

My very dear George:

Just a line or two to say your book [1] (one of them) came safely to port a day ago. And it was welcome. And it is being read with eagerness and gratification. Indeed, I've already quoted from it. A new magazine is about to come out (so it's said), and the Editor asked me for an article on "Theatre & People." [2] I quoted your remarks about what foreign Producers have done in the U.S.A., to season remarks that the English Theatre, to be good of its kind, must first be English. Your summing up of Emlyn Williams as a dramatist is, I think, grand. What a pity the chapter can't be done in leaflet form, & dropped over this little hoodwinked land of ours.

I'll write again soon. Eileen (the wife), our younger boy, and an old servant we had ages ago in London, who came down to escape the fly-

---

[1] George Jean Nathan, *The Theatre Book of the Year, 1943–1944* (1944).
[2] Sean O'Casey, "The People and the Theatre," *Theatre Today*, March 1946; reprinted in *Under a Colored Cap* (1963).

bombs, are sick with a germ of a chill knocking about here; so with very little help, I've got my hands full.

Some time ago, I sent to Macmillans the MS of the 3rd Vol. of biography—Drums Under the Windows & hope the printers may be able to tackle it soon. And I have written & typed out roughly 60 pages of ideas and dialogue for a new play, & when I've done near as many more, I'll try to put it into shape. It's what you call a "Boom Boom" play, though there are no "Boombs" in it. I imagine, in ways, it may be an odd play. I was going to call it "Roll Out the Barrel," but have decided to change it to "A Warold on Wallpaper." [3]

There will be a good deal of what I think to be humour (I hope I'm right) in it; and this will be painted with a few attempts at seriousness. However, be it good or bad, I'll, of course, send you on the first MS as soon as it is finished. When that will be, God knows, for many interferences now jerk themselves in between me & any work I may try to do. But I do try to do a little every night, working from 10-30. (when all are abed) till about 2 a.m. though its hard to get one's thoughts deep in the work, after a long day of distractions.

I hope you are keeping fit, & have taken a long American holiday, though it's little you seem to need to enable you to go on writing your fresh, delightful comments on Theatre & Drama.

All the best, with love, for the present.

Ever yours,
Sean

I didn't thank you for your book. But I read & love it, & that's the best I can give. I hope we may have many more of them.

[3] Sean O'Casey, *Oak Leaves and Lavender: or A Warld on Wallpaper* (1946). The subtitle is an allusion to Yeats's rejection of *The Silver Tassie:* ". . . the whole history of the world must be reduced to wallpaper in front of which the characters must pose and speak." See Yeats's letter to O'Casey, 20 April 1928, Vol. I, p. 268.

To Jack Carney

MS. NYU LIBRARY

[TOTNES, DEVON]
5 APRIL 1944

My dear Jack,

Greetings foremost to Mina & you. It isn't pleasant to hear that you have had again the trying experience of bombs falling about your ears. It is hard to say whether one should count you fortunate or unfortunate. Unfortunate to have them so close to you so often; fortunate that they missed you both, however near the miss may have been. But however fortunate, it is a terrifying experience. Life at its easiest is hazardous enough; in the midst of flame and bursting bombs it ceases to be life, & becomes just a struggle for self-preservation. The Civilians are getting it this time as bad, or worse, than the front line. And those who retain the civvy suit, who bear the burden & heat of the night, won't get any ribbon to stick in their coats. Moscow does it better with its Leningrad medal. But the English aren't really part of their cities. Birmingham, Liverpool, London don't seem to have the effect on an Englishman that Moscow, Kiev & Kharkov have on the Russians; or, indeed, that Cork, Belfast, & Dublin have on us. Here the city is part of the fact, vice versa in the USSR.

We have had a little stir here the other night; on the queui vive from 11 to 1-30, with bombs dropping at Ipplepen & Berry Pomeray, 2 or 3 miles away, &, of course, the drone of the damned things in the sky over us. I wonder, now, how do the prayers of the people get through to God? We are all cut off from heaven; the Church Militant is isolated from the Church Triumphant: a state of seige, or is it siege?

Some three weeks ago, I gave myself a knock on the chest (knock knock), which grew into a swelling like a bird's nest. Could hardly breathe, & went about hunched like a Toby jug. Then Breon near got an eye knocked out with a wallop from a base-ball bat; & Niall shoved a fist through a window-pane, barely escaping a cut artery. Yes, life at its easiest is dangerous enough for Sean O'Casey, Esq. of Totnes, Devon, nee Dublin, in Eire of the Sorrows. Glad you liked the comments on Eire & the Vatican.[1] They didn't put the whole of the Vat article in, which was a pity. I've just sent in a few comments on two usual letters received in reply to the Vatican article.[2] And I'm still working at the next edition of "biography," as well as circumstances allow. Daily Sketch rang up about Eire & so did Reynold's; but I referred both to the D.W. I don't think either was pleased. I can't forget Reynold's hatred of the USSR a little while ago, & their refusal to publish anything I tried to write in defence. Well, for good or evil, now, they all have to make a gangway for the entry of the Soviet Union into the world's Council. "The USSR has no desire for any territorial extension in Roumania"; but the Roumanians we know won't be the Roumanians we don't know when the Red Army has gone through, & returned to its own homeland. And they all know it, though they don't say so.

Many thanks for the papers & magazines.
My love to Mina & you.
Yours as ever,
Sean

Have you Pat Mooney's address? Barney [Conway]'s is, of course, Townshend St. or "Moscow" as we used to call that district.

[1] Sean O'Casey, "Shadow of the Vatican," *Daily Worker,* 23 March 1944.
[2] "The Vatican Dictates: Sean O'Casey Replies to His Critics," *Daily Worker,* 10 April 1944.

To William B. Curry [1]

TC. O'CASEY

[TOTNES, DEVON]

22 APRIL 1944

Dear Mr. Curry:

Thanks for your kind letter. In some respects, you have either misunderstood me, or I have failed to make myself quite clear. I didnt mean to attach the Shivaun [2] incident to any general or particular principle; to me it seemed too simple for that. In some way or another, the teacher's attitude to the will and egoism of Shivaun—common to all youngsters—was a wrong one. That is my main point. Whatever it was it terrorised the child. That is quite clear to me. It gave the child a psychological shock from which, regarding the school, she hasn't recovered; and, I'm afraid, it will extend to future school connections, because whatever it may have been couldn't have happened here, and so, for the time being at any rate, naturally fixed a preference in the child's mind for (to her) a safer life at home. My letter meant nothing about preferential treatment for one child, or for all—it was the teacher who brought this to the front in her report. She, not I, harped on that string. To connect the tears and terror of the child about going to school with the commonplace one of wanting her own way is just nonsense. The claim for "preferential treatment" (Latin, I suppose for wanting her own way) evinced by Shivaun was clumsily tackled, both when the first incident occurred, and afterwards during the attempt to humour the child back to a normal feeling for the school again. My letter does not "disapprove of Nora's unwillingness to accord preferential treatment," but it does disapprove of something done to frighten the child—a very different thing. There can be no excuse even in an overcrowded school (though we may understand it there) for frightening a child into meek obedience; and least of all is there an excuse for the school of Dartington Hall.

I hope that what I have said above is clear now.

Now, I'd like to say a few words on the general remarks in your letter. First, I'm a Communist, not a Socialist—a very different thing. This isnt said in any arrogance of spirit, for many Socialists are finer fellows, personally, than many Communists, as indeed are many Tories, for that matter. But the ideal aimed at by Communists is, in my opinion, a much higher one, and it is this which counts in the end. I dont agree that the

---

[1] William B. Curry, headmaster, Dartington Hall School, Totnes.
[2] Shivaun, O'Casey's five-year-old daughter.

youngest member of a household "usually gets preferential treatment." Certainly not in most working-class families. There they are often thought of as a nuisance, always in the way. As a Communist, I am in favour of preferential treatment to all in all schools—that is the adapting of 'educational methods to each child according to its needs. Oddly enough (not oddly, really, but naturally) you are out for that too. Each particular, or peculiar, gift in every individual child should be fostered in its own peculiar way so that each can enjoy life in its fullest, and give of his best to itself and community companions. Many would be inclined to call this preferential treatment, but I dont think you would.

Let me say, too, that this is no sudden Shivaun interest in these things. I have been staring into them for over 35 years, since Padruig Pearse founded St Enda's School in Dublin, which would "teach modern languages orally; which should be bilingual in method; which should aim at a wider and humaner culture than other Irish Secondary schools; which should set its face like iron against 'cramming' and against all the evils of the competitive examination system, which should work at fostering the growth of the personality of each of its pupils rather than at forcing all into a predetermined groove."

Indeed, I am at the moment, writing, or rather, referring, to this great man, Pearse,[3] who, unfortunately, was executed as a "rebel" by the British Authorities in 1916, in the next volume I hope to have published.

Finally, a strong will and a desire to have one's own way are not necessarily evil things, you will agree, I think, provided they are linked with a sane humility, and intense feeling towards all men of goodwill, a proper respect for human life, and an intelligent realization that no-one is infallible. So they should be encouraged and guided, rather than suppressed in the young by either psychological or physical intimidation, if we are to have the enlightened leaders humanity will always need.

Well, there you are, now; and let me end up with my warm regards to you, and my best wishes with you in your work.

Yours sincerely,
[*Sean O'Casey*]

---

[3] Padraig Pearse (1879–1916), teacher, writer, nationalist; one of the leaders of the 1916 Easter Rising, for which he was executed by the British. He founded St. Enda's School in 1908. In the dramatic context of *The Plough and the Stars,* O'Casey's tenement characters mock Pearse's glorification of bloodshed; but in "In This Tent, the Rebubblicans," *Drums Under the Windows,* O'Casey celebrates the memory of Pearse as a great teacher, poet, and rebel.

To Time and Tide

22 APRIL 1944

Eire's Neutrality

Sir:—Mr Ervine's hatred of Eireann is almost too pronounced to give seriousness to his attacks on her.[1] He cannot find even one good word for her. There is none righteous, no, not one, there—according to him; and *Time and Tide* seems to be happy in agreeing with him. But after all, the "Eireans" have something to their credit. St John Ervine's homeland [2] hasn't yet given us a thinker of the calibre of Shaw; a poet anything like Yeats; nor have they anything to equal the Abbey theatre, nor even anything to come up to that of the Gate. They gave us AE who was something of a humbug as a novelist, a poet, and a painter. The Ulsterians can certainly build ships, weave linen, make tobacco, and cord ropes; but they seem to be strong in neither poetry or play. Martha was a grand woman, we all admit; but Mary has a place in the household, too. There is a lot to be said for Hilary Boyle.[3] She is as near a fact as is St John Ervine, or *Time and Tide*. There are other countries where neutrality is more dangerous than that of Eireann. Eire doesn't send wolfram or chrome to Germany, as far as I know. Hasn't sent her so far even a sack of spuds. Mr Ervine doesnt mention this. Cordell Hull does. "A sensible and loving people think less of favouring either side in the catastrophic disturbance that cleaves the world than of preserving their own invaluable neutrality and peace. She is gloriously neutral; that is its gift from the Gods and to Europe." So Rose Macaulay in *The Spectator*—of Eire? Oh, no, thank you; of Portugal. How many of these fellows are fighting for the Allies? How many Eireans? Tens and tens of thousands; and if we count the men of the Merchant Fleet, then more thousands must be added. The Irish Press have printed sad sheets of Eireans lost in the fight to bring goods to the USSR and to Britain; almost every week there is a list of men lost, men who will never again hear the ticking "of the old clock on the stairs." When Hilary Boyle says four millions of minds are at one with hers, she isn't far out. She hasn't numbered them all—that's all. A good many of Ulster's one and a quarter million agree with her. Mr Ervine evidently hasnt heard of the great meeting of Irish in America who have voiced agreement with De Valera; or those in Australia, presided over by Archbishop Mannix,[4] who have done the same thing. These are facts, and it is as well to face them. Rightly or wrongly (wrongly, I think, over the

[1] St. John Ervine, *Time and Tide,* 1 April 1944, a letter.
[2] Ervine was born in Belfast.
[3] Hilary Boyle, *Time and Tide,* 19 February 1944, a letter in support of Ireland's neutrality, which provoked Ervine's letter.
[4] The Most Rev. Daniel Mannix (1864–1963), Archbishop of Melbourne.

question of deporting the enemy Legations to their own townlands) there are four millions (probably more) who are at one mind with Mrs Boyle.

What Mr Ervine calls "treachery," others would dub patriotism, opinions as good, at least, as those of Mr Ervine. Reckon up the Irish in the Australian, Canadian, and American Armies, and he will find a mighty host on the side of the Allies, a host that no other "neutral" has contributed. If he objects to this, then let him remember that one of the very recent V.C.'s was credited to Australia; but the lad had been but seven years there, and his family lived in Kerry. And let him remember that Ulster's finest leader since King Billy, [Edward] Carson, was the son of a Dublinman, and educated in Portarlington School. Finally, let him try to remember to be fair.

I am, etc,
Sean O'Casey

To Irish Times

24 APRIL 1944

"THE PLOUGH AND THE STARS"

Sir,—In a recent issue of the *Irish Press,* Roddy, the Rover, tealogian, antiqueerian, playwrong, jennyologist, litterary and dhrimin dhu [1] dreama critic, hystorian, and heaven knows what else, says: "Sarsfield has been written of with honour, but how have we treated Pearse? We have depicted, in our National Theatre, his men coming off parade, with the colours of Ireland, to a sodden pub (something wrong with the sintext here?) and we have crowded to applaud this abominable slander: shame on us who, if we did not die with Pearse, did not honour him!" [2]

Leaving aside the feeling that Roddy doesn't seem to realise the meaning of either "abominable" or "slander," we are not told whether Pearse or the flag suffered the slander, or why any flag in a pub should feel uneasy. But, if only Roddy had stopped to think, he'd see things worse now than they were then, for now during any event calling for a show of bunting, the pub has as much right to display the flag as any shop, bank, or detached villa. And, as a symbol, it guarantees security to the pub just as much as it guarantees it to the temple. Isn't it a fact, too, that these pubs contribute a tidy sum to the State revenue, and, in that way, help to keep the old flag flying?

---

[1] *Drimendru,* Dublin slang for an insipid fellow.
[2] Roddy the Rover (Aodh de Blacam), "Seen, Heard, and Noted," *Irish Press,* 5 April 1944. He was indignant about the scene in Act II of *The Plough and the Stars* where the patriotic words of Pearse are spoken outside the pub.

As I write this, I am looking at a picture that appeared in an English paper some years ago. Under it, we are told, it shows "Mr. de Valera addressing an immense open-air meeting in Dublin to protest against the proposed Coercion Acts, introduced to curtail the activities of the Republicans." And what background has Mr. de Valera behind him? The Old House of Parliament? The General Post Office? No; he's standing right in front of a pub! No! Yes! There he is, framed nicely in the doorway, with the sign of "Private Bar" on his left hand, and the striking coloured sign of "Bass" on his right one. And forms, inside the pub, pressing against the window looking out at the meeting—just as it is in the play! History repeating itself. The righteous men who made our land a Nation Once Again are becoming a little too righteous for poor ould Ireland, if you ask me. It could happen!—

Yours, etc.
Sean O'Casey

Totnes, Devon,
April, 1944

From St. John Ervine [1]
To Time and Tide

6 MAY 1944

Eire's Neutrality

Sir: How foolish is Mr O'Casey's staggering statement that "there are other countries whose neutrality is more dangerous than that of Eireann. Eire doesn't send wolfram or chrome to Germany, as far as I know. Hasn't sent so far even a sack of spuds." Ireland has scarcely any minerals to export to anybody. But even if it has, how could it send them to Germany? There is, however, another point to be considered, one which has not, apparently, occurred to Mr O'Casey; and that is that Eire, in some degree, is a member of the British Commonwealth. Portugal and Turkey are not. Mr O'Casey is an Eirean, but he is able to live in Great Britain without let or hindrance, and is under no more restraint than I am or than any Englishman, Scotsman or Welshman. Does Mr O'Casey suggest that a nation can belong to an accociation, so far as the rights are concerned, but not belong to it, so far as concerns the responsibilities; and that a member of the Commonwealth can, if she wishes, render aid to an enemy of the Commonwealth?

[1] St. John Ervine (1883–1971), Ulster-born Irish playwright and novelist.

Mr O'Casey's letter is a typical example of the sort of Eirean argument against which I warned your readers: a collection of unproved assertions and irrelevant ascriptions. He ascribes hatred of Eire to me. Why? There is nothing in my letters to show love or hatred for it. A man does not hate his brother because he criticizes him, however caustically he does so. I am accused of unfairness. Will he cite a single example of unfair statement in my letters? Mr O'Casey seems to suggest that the words *Eirean* and *Irish* are synonymous and that all the Irishmen in the Australian, Canadian and American forces are of Eirean origin. This is a common Eirean trick. Has Mr O'Casey not heard that Ulster Protestants emigrated in thousands to Canada and the United States a couple of centuries before a single Southern Irish Roman Catholic had set his feet on American soil? If the Eireans may take credit for their remote kindred in the Commonwealth who have joined the Allied Forces then Ulstermen may do the same; and I shall not fear the balance between them.

"What Mr Ervine calls 'Treachery' others would dub patriotism," says Mr O'Casey. Would they? Well, I would rather starve than take wages from a man whom I meant to betray, no matter what high-sounding title I gave myself; and John O'Leary, the famous Fenian, would have agreed with me. But that was not the point I was making. I was anticipating what I feel certain was the absurd argument about non-employment of Roman Catholics in the Six Counties which Mrs Boyle said she could use if she were in the mood; and I asked the simple question, has a Government the right to defend itself from those who seek, even by foul means, to overthrow it? If I run around the town telling people how skilfully I stole Mr O'Casey's money and caused the death of his kindred, will Mr O'Casey take me into his employment the next time I want a job?

What really staggers me in his letter is the fatuous reference to culture in Ulster as compared with culture in Eire. "St John Ervine's homeland hasn't yet given us a thinker of the calibre of Shaw; a poet anything like Yeats; nor have they anything to equal the Abbey Theatre, nor even anything to come up to the Gate." He then proceeds to belittle AE describing him as "something of a humbug, as a novelist, a poet and a painter." Humbug is a singular word to apply to AE who never wrote a novel in his life. But let that pass. I doubt if Mr O'Casey will find many, if any, people, to share his opinion. Certainly Bernard Shaw will not subscribe to it. Has no one ever told Mr O'Casey of Sir Samuel Ferguson, a poet who was not far short of Yeats, if he was short of him at all? Ferguson was born in Belfast. Has no one told him that the Group Theatre is at work in Belfast, building itself up much in the way the Abbey was built up, but building without a subsidy from an Englishwoman, Miss [Alice] Horniman, or a subsidy from the Government. The Group receives no money from anybody but the playgoing public. If the Abbey had depended on the support of Dublin, it would have perished in its infancy. It was started and chiefly maintained on English money. Whenever a crisis in its financial affairs occurred the English passed round the hat to save it. The Group Theatre depends on nobody but the people for its funds, and it is drawing crowded houses every night.

Mr O'Casey seems to think that there is only one kind of genius in the world that is worth mentioning: literary genius; and that a Darwin or a Stephenson is nobody in comparison with a Wordsworth or a Shelley. I do not agree with him. But if a list of Ulster men and women of high distinction in all arts and crafts were to be made, it would, I think, compare more than favourably with a similar list of Eireans. Lord Pirrie, the shipbuilder, was only one of a host of industrial men of genius, none of whom was ever equalled or even approached in Eire. I have already mentioned Sir Samuel Ferguson, whom the young Yeats hailed as a great poet, but whom Mr O'Casey has strangely failed to note, and I shall insist on AE, despite Mr O'Casey's shabby belittlement of him. Yeats had Ulster blood in him. I am not a passionate admirer of Mr Louis MacNeice, but who, among contemporary poets in Eire, is as good? Is there an essayist in Eire equal in quality to Stephen Gwynn, the Donegal man, or Robert Lynd, from Belfast? Forrest Reid is a novelist who commands the respect of Mr E. M. Forster. I will put him and Mr Joyce Cary against any two novelists the Eireans can mention; and then have room for Lynn Doyle and George A. Birmingham. Fault can be found with Sir John Lavery, but what painter in Eire is as good as he was at his best, or can put Paul Henry and William Conor and Humbert Craig to shame? Will Mr O'Casey kindly name the Eirean who surpasses the late Sir Hamilton Harty as a composer?

Need I mention our soldiers? In our own times, they have ranged from Sir George White, who defended Ladysmith, when an Englishman, Sir Redvers Buller, advised him to surrender it, to Alexander, Auchinleck, Sir John Dill, Brooke and Montgomery. The late Sir Joseph Larmour, a most famous scholar, was Professor of Mathematics at Cambridge, a National School boy from Magheragall. He was an Ulsterman. So was Lord Kelvin. Nine Presidents of the United States were of Ulster Protestant origin. Not a single Irish Roman Catholic has ever come near that position. The Regius Professor of Greek at Oxford, E. R. Dodds, is an Ulsterman. One of the best Latinists, who are rare birds, in this country, Professor R. M. Henry, of St Andrew's, brother to Paul Henry, the painter, is an Ulsterman. Our record in the academic world is far superior to Eire's. One of the best mediaeval scholars today, Miss Helen Waddell, is a native of Ulster. The present editor of *The Times* is an Ulsterman. So is its Military Correspondent. The most interesting religious writer among young men today, C. S. Lewis, who wrote *The Screwtape Letters,* is a Belfast man. Here is only a selection, made from memory, of notable Ulster men and women. They can stand up without a quiver in the company of the most select Eireans.

I am, etc.,
St John Ervine

To Time and Tide

20 MAY 1944

Eire's Neutrality

Sir: Of your kindness, allow some last remarks on what Mr Ervine has written. I'm glad he who was attacking Eire, is now defending Northern Ireland. There's little need of it: we of Eire are proud of Ulster's deeds in the past, of her achievements in the present, and hope to be prouder of her in the time to come. We do not grudge her the glory of building great ships, of spinning fine linen, of cording strong ropes, or of making good tobacco—[I'm smoking some of it at the moment, Gallagher's Condor Twist.] [1] But we do resent Mr Ervine's evil report of things in Eire's other three provinces. We may be poor, but he would make us out destitute. There are things which we have done which seem to be beyond Ulster. God has given us a few gifts. The Six Counties, while doing a lot, and some things better than Eire, hasnt produced a Shaw, a Yeats, not to mention a Joyce, a theatre anyway equal to the Abbey, or even a Gate. These are not tricks, they are facts. I know something about the Group Theatre, enough to know that it cannot compare with Abbey or Gate, though I sincerely hope it may equal either soon, and later surpass both.

Mr Ervine has kept silent on the fact that more than four million stand, not only for neutrality, but for De Valera's stand over the question of enemy Legations. This is no trick, for it is as unwelcome to me as it appears to be to him. It is a fact, and we must face it. And quite a number of these millions are Ulster people; Mr Ervine forgot to mention that. He seems to believe that all Ulster is like himself. In the March issue of the magazine called *The Bell,* there is an article on the Ulster question, written by The Committee of the Ulster Union Club which describes itself as "an Association of Ulster Protestants devoted to the emergence of an Ireland that will transcend the present unnatural divisions of our country." Here is part of what the article says about Ulster's hilarious (according to Mr Ervine) participation in the war: "The end result of Ulster's insistence on partition has been to exclude any possiblity of Ireland entering the war as a whole; while at the same time Ulster merely 'goes through the motions' of being at war, but in reality remains at home without even making a large-scale effort to defend her corner of the island." That is an expression of a Committee of Ulster Protestants, having their home there, in contradistinction to Mr Ervine hopping about England "without let or hindrance." Can he call this a fatuous statement, or a trick of argument on the part of O'Casey, the Eirean?

The same article maintains that persecution is meted out to Catholics in Ulster, not because they are Catholics, but because they are Nationalists,

[1] All passages in square brackets were omitted by the editor.

adding that Protestant members of the Club had had their share of police attention. This certainly agrees with my opinion, for Irish history shows that the rope hanging a Protestant Nationalist was always as thick and strong as that hanging a Catholic. [The article says that "In Derry City, 27, 162 Nationalists get 8 seats, while 18,079 others, the majority of whom are Unionists get 12. In Fermanagh County 32,455 Nationalists secure one seat at Stormont, whereas 25,529 others get 2." Perhaps, Mr Ervine will remember that in Eire proportional representation prevails. Are these facts, or are they "typical examples of Eirean arguments against which he warned *Time and Tide* readers"?]

Mr Ervine asks me to cite a single unfair statement in his letter. First, it is unfair for him to expect Eire to be an enthusiastic member of the Commonwealth (to say the most of it), when one remembers what happened in Eirinn to the knowledge of us all, when—as Mr S[tephen]. Gwynn reminded us a few weeks ago in this very Journal—England was behaving in Eire as the Germans were behaving now in Poland. Does he think—though it be possible to forgive—that it is possible to forget? It is most unfair for him to say that Eire as a member, renders aid to the enemies of the Commonwealth, when he must know that she does nothing of the sort, for he admits that, "even an she would, she couldn't," thereby proving the fact that she doesn't. [He laughs at the statement that Eire sends no metals to the enemy, saying that she has none to send, and, even if she had, she couldnt get them there, ignorant of the fact that an Irish paper had a Leader protesting against an English Sunday Journal, with a circulation above a million, which had attached Eire's name to those neutral countries who did. But what proof has Mr Ervine that Eire would, if she had metals, and could get them to Germany, send them to Germany? None, but his own spiteful opinion. And this is the man who prates about moral uplift-ment in argument!] And he says these things in face of the fact, which even he can scarcely deny, that thousands of instances of positive help to the Allies in Airforce, Army, Navy, Merchant Service, and Factory can be placed before his eyes, and under his nose. Again, has Eire the right— even under the canon laws of the Commonwealth—to remain neutral, or no, if she wishes to do so? Then, if she has the right, Mr Ervine is not only unjust, but unfair, for condemning her for exercising that right under a free partnership, apart from it being a foolish or a sensible policy. No wonder that Mr Churchill suggests that we should search our hearts: Mr Ervine would do well to search his.

[Mr Ervine asks me if I havent heard of "the thousands of Ulster Protestants who emigrated to Canada and the U.S.A. centuries before a single Irish Roman Catholic set foot upon American soil." Centuries before . . . Not a single one . . . there's a flash-back for you! If he reads the American *Humours of the Deep South,* he'll find they were there early enough. And since America was known to the Irish for centuries under the name of The New Island it must have been fairly familiar to them. He doesnt tell us, though, why these thousands of Ulster Protestants left a land so rich and rare as he makes it out to be.

As for "treachery" to those who paid a man his wages—who furnished the funds to pay the Civil Service, the Constabulary, and the great sum given to the Viceroy? It was got by taxing the Irish people as it is got now. The Irish were just getting less than some of their own back; and, as a good Protestant, Mr Ervine should know there is holy Scripture warrant for spoiling the Egyptians.

I never said, nor do I think, that the genius of man is confined to literature. Eire thinks as much as Northern Ireland, at least, of Science, and the last postage stamp issued was one commemorating the centenary of Rowan Hamilton, the mathematician—a thing, by the way, never done in Mr Ervine's townland to honour Kelvin. Whether Eire has a composer to equal Harty, I dont know, for I am not qualified to give even an opinion on music. And Samuel Ferguson wouldnt fit in to Stormont's idea of an Ulsterman, for if there was an "Eirean," he was one. One can see what he thinks—not of the Six Counties—of Ireland in the song (a translation from the Gaelic, by the way) The Fair Hills of Holy Ireland. Mr Ervine hops over the border into Donegal to gather in that fine fellow, Gwynn, who, if his books betray his thoughts, has a kindlier feeling for his whole country than has his friend, Mr Ervine. And, if I mistake not, over into Monaghan, too, to get Gen. Montgomery.

There was nothing "shabby" in my reference to George Russell—I said the same to himself when he was in his bloom. His poems are there for all to read—I suggest Mr Ervine writes an article on them for *Time and Tide.* We'll find, I think, that their purple has faded fearfully. Novel is a wide term, and *The Interpreters* was AE's attempt at one; the second— *The Avatars,* was far worse, though a very comic book, if you dont take it seriously. If Mr Ervine reads *Tales of Old Ireland and Myself,* by [Sir William] Orpen, he'll see what that painter thought of them. Of course, Mr Ervine can go on insisting on AE till doom's day, and will, I daresay, for he is a sentimentalist, as most Ulstermen are; indeed, I think I once heard his voice shouting "Yes!" when Tinkerbell asked him if he believed in fairies, so belief in AE is but natural. Just to show there's no coolness, I remind Mr Ervine that Eire's greatest hero was an Ulster warrior, the Hound of Ulster, a memorial to whom can be seen in Dublin's General Post Office.]

But the main points are these: Other neutral countries, Spain, Portugal, Turkey, and Sweden have given long and valuable help to Germany. Is this a trick, a fatuous statement or a fact? Has Eire given any (apart from neutrality)? No. That is the negative side of it. Has Eire given any help to the Allies? Yes; considerable, in energy and blood; and many of her sons and daughters have been decorated for valour by the British Government. Mr Ervine can read a list up to March 1943, issued by the Government, if he thinks O'Casey is trying it on. Is this a trick, a fatuous statement, or is it a fact? [Let Mr Ervine answer, and answer too the remark of the Ulster Protestant Committee about the Six Counties "going through the motions of being at war"; and let him be fair, if only even out of respect for the Irish dead who died for the Commonwealth.]

Finally, neither Mr Ervine nor the Royal Ulster Constabulary can prevent the grace of God from trickling over the border into Eirinn.

I am, etc.
Sean O'Casey

To Jack Carney

MS. NYU LIBRARY
[TOTNES, DEVON]
29 MAY 1944

Thanks, ever so much, dear Jack, for the "twist" & the papers, especially for Time & Tide with its Ervine screw-papers. I don't think I'll write again to T. & T. They let Ervine quote Samuel Ferguson, & suppressed my remark about him; & many more remarks too. Ferguson—Ervine's "Northerner" wrote "The Fair Hills of Holy Ireland" (God forgive him), & his home was in North Great Georges St.[1]

I'm afraid Jim's in for a hard fight, though [General Richard] Mulcahy's absence should lighten the burden. What a crew Fianna Fail is becoming! It is an extraordinary fruit of "Easter Week." Could there be evolved a meaner or a shallower pack? And isn't [Michael] Colgan a shit! A ruler, I daresay there aren't fifty of them in the whole of Éire. He wants to be another kind of a ruler now. In with Bill, Ora et Labora O'Brien. He has played his cards well. He has helped De Valera no end. And Mick McQuaid[2] behind him.

News-Chronicle has asked me to write an article 700 words on Eire's Neutrality. I'll try it anyhow. They say there's a wall of thick prejudice rising up against Eire. That wall was always there.

I seem to have no time to spare these days. Something to do all day. I can't begin any work till nine at the earliest. However, I've finished 18

---

[1] Samuel Ferguson, Irish poet, was born in Belfast in 1810, and died in Dublin in 1886. "The Fair Hills of Ireland," one of his best-known songs, is a translation of an anonymous eighteenth-century Gaelic song. It is sometimes called "The Fair Hills of Holy Ireland" because the refrain line of each stanza is "On the fair hills of holy Ireland."

[2] The Most Rev. John Charles McQuaid (1895–1973), Archbishop of Dublin.

chapters of the next biography volume, & about two more should be
enough & to spare for a thick volume. I have got up to Easter Week.

We had a nasty raid near here—too near—last night. I really thought
things were going to happen. The children (Niall & Shivaun), & Eileen
stretched themselves in the Morrison shelter; Brian & I stood or sat in the
Hall—our hall, not Dartington. At each explosion I could see the door
bending its belly inwards, while the house shook like a thing infirm; and
Sean O'Casey felt that heroism was a thing of naught; a bubble. Then our
guns spat out at the planes, & made things livelier. The youngsters took it
splendidly, & Breon, as usual, acted as if he was just waiting for his pretty
girl to come as per appointment. The old man wasn't a bit perturbed, not a
bit. But he was damned glad when the "All Clear" sounded. Life was worth
living again.

The Phaidon Book on Vermeer is a lovely volume.[3] I haven't heard
any more from London about Red Roses. Tigheann Jack maith le cáirde.
All things good come by waiting—even the All Clear.

My love to Mina, & all the best to you, & many thanks.

> *Yours as ever,*
> Sean

[3] *The Paintings of Jan Vermeer* (1940), with an Introduction by Thomas
Bodkin.

To Daniel Macmillan

TS. MACMILLAN LONDON

TOTNES, DEVON

9 JUNE 1944

Dear Mr Daniel:

It seems a little odd to trouble about one's own affairs when the 2nd
Front is in full swing; but I daresay we have to go on with what we find at
hand to do.

I have roughly estimated the number of words contained in the chapters already forwarded to you, and guess that they are about enough to
form a volume—with one addition on which I am working at present.

Perhaps, when there's time, one of your staff might give them a run
over to confirm my opinion, or contradict it.

I have almost chosen the title of DRUMS UNDER THE WINDOWS
for this number. I will send on the other chapter as soon as it is done. I
was thinking of writing a short FLASH FORWARD to describe my

thoughts at the present (some of them anyway), and so give an unusual end to it. I think I shall finish it off with a fourth volume to be called THE CLOCK STRIKES TWELVE.

God prosper our men in France.

One more idea: some time ago, I wrote a six or seven thousand word article for an Irish book a friend of mine roared about having published. But I havent heard from him for a long time, and presume he has had to give it up, unable to get the other work he sought—stories, poems, etc. I think the article is a good one, and would make an interesting little booklet (might make one). It is called *Here Come the Irish,*[1] and deals generally with them in relation to England and the world. What do you think of it? the idea, I mean.

I have written a short article for The News-Chronicle (at their request) on *Ireland's Neutrality.*[2] This question is bound to be an interesting one—or rather Eire's connection in the Common-Wealth—after the war. Britain cant afford an hostile Eire on her flank; & Eire cant afford a hostile neighbour on the step of her back-door. There's no reason now or in the future for either to be an enemy of the other.[3]

I hope you are well, & Mr Harold, too.

> *All good wishes.*
> *Yours sincerely,*
> *O'Casey*

[1] The article was printed as "There Go the Irish," in *They Go, the Irish: A Miscellany of War-time Writing,* compiled by Leslie Daiken (1944); reprinted in *Blasts and Benedictions* (1967). See also O'Casey's letter to Leslie Daiken, 17 August 1943; and his letter to Gabriel Fallon, 20 December 1943, note 1.

[2] The *News-Chronicle* didn't print the article, but the material appeared in several letters to *Time and Tide.* See O'Casey's letters on "Eire's Neutrality" in *Time and Tide,* 22 April and 20 May 1944; and St. John Ervine's reply, 6 May 1944.

[3] This paragraph and the conclusion of the letter were written in longhand.

To Jack Carney

MS. NYU LIBRARY

[TOTNES, DEVON]

10 JUNE 1944

My dear Jack,

Well, Eire's well planted now. De Valera's on the pig's back.[1] And Labour biting its nails in a corner. One of their leaders appealing to the

[1] Eamon de Valera's Fianna Fail Party won the 1944 election.

Bishops to hold an inquiry & clear him from the charge of having touched a Communist in a crowd. What a lot of bitches' gets they are! And the old warrior, Jim, out too.[2] Colgan did it to him. And, I daresay, a crowd of his followers over here working for a Second Front. I'm very glad young Jim got in—more important, in a lot of ways, even, than that Jim Senr should go in. The young fellow represents the youth knocking at the door, with old Bill inside behind it, the heart beating unsteadily. Well, Bill's days are numbered anyhow, though he be in the parlour counting out his money. It might have been better, though, for Dev to have been defeated. He has a rocky furrow to plough. It will be interesting to see how the R.C. Church stands after this war. The new government won't be very (Italy) friendly to the Vatican, and Poland won't be so ardently pro-Vatican as she was when Joe is done telling them things. He's setting the Orthodox Church to bark at the Cardinals. And the American Hierarchie, North & South, will start to play their own game, I think, demanding full representation in the Conclave, so that we may have something other than an Italian in the Ex Cathedra. Maybe Downey,[3] or MacRory,[4] or even Father O'Flynn[5] as Pope, & Sean T. OK [O'Kelly] as Duce of the Immaculate Conception, after getting a dispensation to marry his deceased wife's sister.

I do hope the first attempt of the Second Front will prosper. Seems they'll be hard put to it. News-Chronicle has postponed my article on the head of it,[6] though I don't think it could hamper the boys. Perhaps, they want space for the news. We won't get much to bite on.

Do you know where Daiken is? I'd like to have that thesis, There Go the Irish, back, if it can be got. It's evident he failed to get the book together in which it was to sit enthroned—vide his letter to me years ago. I've written to Macmillan's telling them about it, & suggesting they might publish it as a booklet. If you know where Daiken is, let me know. He needn't be shy over having failed. I'm used to that sort of thing myself, & won't say a word.

Love to Mina & you.
All the best
Sean

[2] Jim Larkin was defeated in his attempt to retain his seat in the Dail, but his son, Jim Larkin, Jr., was elected.

[3] The Most Rev. Richard Downey (1881–1953), Archbishop of Liverpool.

[4] Joseph Cardinal MacRory (1861–1945), Archbishop of Armagh and Primate of All Ireland, 1928–45.

[5] Father O'Flynn, the idealized and jovial Irish priest in the popular ballad of that name.

[6] This article was not published.

To Jack Carney

MS. NYU LIBRARY

[TOTNES, DEVON]

21 JUNE 1944

My dear Jack & Mina,

I was glad to get the copy of [Alexander] Werth's dispatch about the Red Army advance on the Karelian Isthmus because its receipt showed Mina & you were safe.

One can't say what one thinks about this pilot-less bombing. Maybe it will show the [Harold J.] Laskis & the [Henry N.] Brailsfords what the Germans are like. Christ! it does annoy me to hear these lambs bleating out peace and good-will to the Germans! Bleating their abstract & moral principles while the bombs are falling. The Germans our long-lost brothers! Prodical sons of Eve! By God, they'd hail plague, pestilence, & famine on us, if they could. May it rain up a flood of hate among the Allied Forces. This is what they need to give punch to their blows. They will add to their stature if they look upon the Nazis as Churchill looks upon the Nazis. Stalin is right—death alone can keep them quiet. The Pope hasn't said anything yet about these bombs. Rome is safe in the arms of Jesus, so all's well with the rest of the world.

Well, I'm glad you & Mina are safe. God keep you both so. Eileen wrote to Mina yesterday.

All the best, & death to the German bastards!

Yours as ever,
Sean

To Horace Reynolds

MS. REYNOLDS

TOTNES, DEVON

6 JULY 1944

Dear Horace.

Just a line to give you a hello! I've often wondered how you are, & Kay, & John & Peggy. How are you faring these turbulent days? I haven't seen a review of yours for some time now in the Book Magazines—we get a copy occasionally.

We are all well here, so far, though we have passed through some noisy moments. But life is very different, with a hundred interferences where before there was but one. We have no help now—all gone to the War effort, & I have to give a lot of help in the house, which means I can't commence my own work till ten o' nights, & then keep going till 2 am., if nothing happens in the meantime. But, all the same, I've just finished another biographical volume, & have written the first few words of a new play. But let's hear how you all are. I daresay all the boys I met at Harvard are away in far-off points of the earth now. I've met quite a lot of Americans—all the States are roaming around England—a lot of them Irish.

Remember me to all yours—Kay, John, & Peggy.

All good & warm wishes

Yours as ever.
Sean

To Jack Carney

MS. NYU LIBRARY

[TOTNES, DEVON]

12 JULY 1944

My dear Jack,

Got the acidol-pepsin all right. Thanks, ever so much. Sat down in dead of night several times to write to you, & fell asleep. "When I am old and grey & full of sleep"—full of sleep especially. However, here's my acknowledgement & thanks at last. I use the pepsins occasionally, when I've eaten something that Woolton [1] has kept in his pocket too long. And the water here reeks of chlorine. Strange that such a squeamish belly doesn't mind the strong tobacco, & stands dauntless in a storm at sea on the main-deck! I see Jim [Larkin] & Barney [Conway] refused to vote on the election of Lord Mayor. Seems to me the Labour Movement—or members of the movement—are a necklace round Dev's neck, with a Sacred Heart badge dangling in the centre. A curious place Eire must be now—worth a visit, with priests & friars pathrollin the streets instead of Tommies. "Ireland" says The Bell, "is locked up in a Sacristy." The Standard is advising all the people to buy a Breviary, & read the Daily Office. I wonder do they bless the Dublin Sweep Drum with Holy Water? Bad an' all as it is, The Orange Drum is a more decent thing than that. Ireland's up-to-date Crom Cruach. [2]

---

[1] See O'Casey's letter to Carney, 20 August 1942, note 1.
[2] He probably meant pagan drum, but crom cruach could mean a pagan hill, or the expletive By Jove!

I guess you are all having a severe time in London. To me, it seems the only way to stop it is a bold sweep over France, & a push that will send the Germans back too far for the V's to be effective. They are painfully slow there. Lack of imagination in the commanding officers. I hope they will go forward a trifle quicker, & bring to an end the strain on London. There seems to be no other way.

Wilson Barrett Co. put on "Juno" for a week in Glasgow, & brought in some badly-needed coins. I've sent in the MS for another vol. of biography & comment—Drums Under the Windows, & have started work on another play. But I feel tired. One cannot, or one would, banish the thought of the war away. As in the last war, so in this, I follow the armies foot by foot, & wonder when will they see the lights of Berlin. Anyway, The Red Army is moving, quick as Master McGrath! [3] What a shock they have been to the Wehrmacht! But what a world of desolation Hitler has brought about, & still at it. I see the Tablet is yapping about the "most Catholic independent Republic of Lithuania." I'm afraid the Catholics—bar those of Portugal & Ireland—will be running wild for a bit, though His Holiness opens his door to audiences of thousands. "Hello, Buddy!" motto under the Crossed Keys. [4]

Not much use sympathising about the pilotless bombs. Sympathy can't keep them away. I do hope you sleep well in your shelter. That's about all that can be done. And chance the rest; but it must be damned worrying. I hope it may soon end.

Love to Mina & you.
Sean

[3] The famous Irish greyhound in the song "Master McGrath."
[4] The keys of St. Peter in the papal insignia.

To Irish Times

11 AUGUST 1944

SHAW, O'CASEY AND CARROLL
ON "ABBEY'S" DECLINE

George Bernard Shaw, Sean O'Casey and Paul Vincent Carroll, all of whom have had plays produced in the Abbey Theatre, have commented on the theatre's decline in reply to telegrams asking their opinions.

Mssrs. Shaw and O'Casey live in England, Mr. Carroll in Scotland. Declaring that "mediocrity must be the staple of all daily enterprises,"

Mr. Shaw described as "thoughtless" a question as to whether the attempt to found an Irish-speaking National Theatre justified mediocrity. Mr. Shaw declined to suggest how the Abbey might be saved.

He did not reply to a question asking him if, in his opinion, an attempt should be made to save it.

Declaring that he did not know what the Abbey language policy—past or present—was, Mr. O'Casey asked how the theatre could avoid the inclusion of plays in Gaelic in their programme, "seeing they get a subsidy from a Government that is free as well as Gaelic and Gaelic as well as free. There is no reason why a fine play (what some call a masterpiece) should not appear in Gaelic, though no sign as yet is showing.

"However good or fine a playwright might happen to be, however the Abbey Theatre might encourage him, it could never give him any kind of a living—decent or indecent. And, it seems to me, there will be even a less chance for a Gaelic playwright, unless he gets a Government job or a Government pension. Then, of course, he must write nothing to displease the powers or the nominees who place the powers there. There is the crux—for Eire. She will be, is now in fact, in the condition of control of thought so often attributed to the Socialism of the U.S.S.R. It's funny."

Mr. O'Casey says there is a world movement of the peoples which will shape the world to the people's desires. He says: "Eire won't be even mentioned. She can go on singing her 'Song of Bernadette,' or listen to the champions of Catholic thought—Belloc and Chesterton, the present-day summer of Eire's faith. . . . What the Abbey does is a small thing. If Ireland can become freely Gaelic so much the better—that is singing bawdy songs as well as hymns. If not—."

Paul Vincent Carroll, when asked whether he considered the present Abbey policy destructive of the theatre's heritage, replied: "Dublin's censorious, provincial and pietistic attitude is chiefly responsible for the Abbey débacle. The introduction of foreign puritanism has proved inimical to native art. Ireland has shed immortality and clothed herself in the rags of a bogus, bombastic freedom. Here lies the ruins of the glorious Anglo-Irish European tradition."

To Harry Cowdell [1]

TS. MACMILLAN LONDON

TOTNES, DEVON
4 SEPTEMBER 1944

Dear Mr Cowdell:

With this letter, I enclose a caption to go beneath the frontispiece picture of Mr. Griffin; [2] also a dedication to the late Dr O'Hickey. [3]

And a roughly-sketched diarama for the jacket. I think I like the idea of an indication of buildings to the right of the picture (where a figure meant to be Yeats stands), as if the turbulence of the marching drummers and pipers was hurrying them out of the picture. The main idea, I think, is the dominance of the drummers and pipers, in stature, over what looks like a toy town. The pillar in distance is meant to be Nelson's in Dublin; and the figure, on left, looking over the buildings, is meant to be that of G. B. Shaw.

For the "Spine" is a sketch of a drum, flanked by Easter lilies—symbol of Rising in Easter Week—a crossed pick and shovel, and a rayed circle, cap-badge of the Irish Volunteers; if a right Red Hand—which would symbolise the Irish Citizen Army—could be inserted in centre of rayed circle, I should be glad.

I hope these may be satisfactory. I imagine that a vivid red should be the note in the picture, not necessarily put in as I have shown, though, maybe, that way would be best. I leave that to the artist.

Usually, if I remember right, I didnt get these things to do till proofs had been finished, and mention this in case you didnt know the proofs hadnt come. I daresay, many things have delayed them. I just refer to them in case you think they may have come.

Yours sincerely,
Sean O'Casey

[1] Harry Cowdell, art editor, Macmillan & Co. Ltd., London.

[2] The frontispiece photograph of Griffin in *Drums Under the Windows* is described as "The Rev. E. M. Griffin, B.D., M.A. who by refusing to be either Orangeman or Freemason, kept the door of the Church open for all to enter." O'Casey also dedicated *Pictures in the Hallway* to Griffin: "To the memory of the Rev. E. M. Griffin, B.D., M.A., one-time Rector of St. Barnabas, Dublin. A fine scholar; a man of many-branched kindness, whose sensitive hand was the first to give the clasp of friendship to the author." For further information about Griffin, the father figure of O'Casey's formative years, see O'Casey's letter to Fergus O'Connor, 6 April 1918, note 4, Vol. I, p. 80; and O'Casey's letter to Daniel Macmillan, 1 July 1941, notes 3, 4, and 5, Vol. I, p. 888.

[3] For the final version of the dedication to Michael O'Hickey in *Drums Under the Windows,* see O'Casey's letter to Lovat Dickson, 8 July 1945, note 2.

To Beatrix Lehmann [1]

MS. LEHMANN

TOTNES, DEVON
6 SEPTEMBER 1944

Dear Beatrix:

Fancy the M.O.I. being interested in me! However, go ahead, & write whatever you like. A few quarters in Moscow know of me fairly well—I have been in touch with them now for about fourteen years. I sent them my plays (first three) in 1924, but they were too busy to take notice; or, maybe the British Post of that period failed to deliver them. They held an inscription praying that the USSR would go on & prosper, grow in strength, & drive a wedge into the Capitalistic hell around them: they're more than a wedge now. I hailed them, hungry & shoeless in Dublin, when Lenin first climbed on to the armoured car in Leningrad, crowned with his old cloth cap; & I hail them now; and, God forgive me, feel proud, as if I had anything to do with their glorious conquests. But it is out of what we have here, & not out of what they have there, that we must build a new nation. There's no use of admiring Tolstoy, if we haven't first learned to admire Dickens, Keats, & the rest of our fine souls.

A new magazine called "Counter Point" is, they say, to come out soon; & at its request, I've written an article on "Theatre & People." I hope it may appear, though I haven't heard anything for a month.

You're right about the Theatre. It could hardly be worse; but we must be patient. The boyos on this C.E.M.A. seem to be a poor bunch. Why aren't you there? C.E.M.A. sent a group down here—"Pilgrim Players" or some such name—by God, they were terrible!

We are all well, here; but with three children, & little help, there's a helluva lot to be done; & I don't start work now till 10 or 10:30 o'nights, when all's silent & still. But I've managed to send another volume of MS to the publishers—"Drums Under the Windows"—but God only knows when it'll be published.

Perhaps, one day, we may get a chance to talk; though I'm too old to be of much use: the young must take up the job now.

> *All the best to you.*
> *Yours sincerely,*
> *Sean O'Casey*

[1] Beatrix Lehmann (1903–79), English actress.

To William Rust

TC. O'CASEY

TOTNES, DEVON
11 SEPTEMBER 1944

Dear Mr Rust:

Thank you for your letter acknowledging mine. I think I mentioned in it that there was a possible movement towards the discontinuance of the Vatican remaining a preserve for Italian clerics; that the clerical centre of gravity was moving away from Italy towards America and other lands where Catholics were numerous. I now enclose an article from the "Tablet" called "The Future of the Curia" which bears out what I tried to say to you. It is very significant. The Vatican has been flooded out with visitors—including the Bishop of Lichfield, he who so frequently protested against the bombing of Rome; representing—possibly with the Church Times—a strong section of the Anglican Church who would step along with the Vatican, and, incidentally, be opposed to anything friendly to the USSR. As I see it (only a guess of course), an attempt, a powerful one, will be made to weave round the USSR, after the war, not a military, but a Catholic clerical cordon sanataire to keep "Bolshevism away from us all"—they forget that, like the kingdom of heaven, Communism is within us, and cant be kept out. But they may hinder and perplex us for a long time—that is the danger. An American (or English) Pope wouldnt mean a more democratic Church; it would mean a few external changes, while the influence—more powerful than ever—would be more reactionary than ever. (Another guess) With a Poland after the heart's desire of whom we know of, Spain, Portugal, and a clerically controlled Germany and Austria—possibly even France—, the people would be up against a big opposition, especially with the wealth of Catholic America thrown in. Eire is, of course, now little more than an enlarged sacristy, with Christ outside and all the doors locked. With the Christian creeds, of course, we have no quarrel—they constitute no danger as such to any forward march of the people. It is those who use these sacred things to hold on to the means of life for their own mean ends that we fight against; those who set "the rights of property" against the rights of life, and mingle their animosity with the Virgin Birth, the Resurrection, and the Redemption of man, so as to tighten their grip of what is the property, not of this or that fellow, but of all. Of course, your Party, as far as I can see, can do little about this clerical "revolution," but it is well to be aware of it as much as possible; and that is why I send you from time to time these cuttings which tend to show the way these clerical activities are inclined to go.

By the way, it isnt that "we shant be troubled with the evacuees any more" that matters; but that the children should become familiar with country life by coming down for a long spell each year—not only in the summer, but in Autumn and winter as well so that they may get in touch with nature in most—if not all—of her moods. I hope to write about this when I've time.

[*Sean O'Casey*]

To George Jean Nathan

MS. CORNELL

TOTNES, DEVON
8 OCTOBER 1944

My dear George:
Greeting. I hope you are well, & still to the front in every theatre with whip in one hand, and crown of bays in the other. I expect to finish my new play—A Warold on Wallpaper—in a fortnight or so. I hope, of course, you'll like it. I don't imagine it is in any way like most plays (like any) written around the war. It is largely a comedy (or Farce), & is (will be) inscribed to Cuchullain, the legendary hero, who, having tied himself to a stake that he might die upright in front of his enemies, laughed long at the comic aspect of a raven slipping about in the blood that had flown from his wounds. The play opens with a prelude, shades of eighteenth century sparks & their ladies dancing a slow minuet, & wondering in a ghostly way at what is happening. They end the play, too; & between these two appearances, the major play is written. There is ne'er a bang in it anyway: I don't care a lot now for these bangs, though I had them often enough in my earlier plays; & can't cavil at anyone having them in his. As soon as I write finished, I'll send you on a copy; but I'm afraid it'll be a toussled one; & it'll be too long to read; don't strain your eyes over it. And, if it comes, please *don't* send it on to Dick [Madden]. I'm not taking this attitude because none of my last three plays haven't been produced in the U.S.A., but because of financial reasons. When one has to pay 34% Federal tax, 10% agent's fee, & 30% or so here, one doesn't get very much for oneself. So, if an English production be possible, it will be much better for me.
    I have met quite a lot of your countrymen lately—the last, Tom Quinn Curtiss, whose opinion of you appears on the jacket of your Theatre Book of the Year. He spent a day & the night with us. Things are very difficult still, but the present military situation gives some hope.
    I'm waiting for proofs of Drums Under the Windows; but God knows when they'll start to print it. I've sketched out a rough design for the kind

of a jacket I'd like—I did that with each of the others. I'll post a copy pronto to you when it comes to me.

Our three children have taken grandly to the Americans who visit us; & it's a job to get the two younger ones to bed when there's an American uniform—military or naval—knocking about.

Tom Quinn Curtiss brought a letter from Ernest Boyd. Do you ever see him now?

I wonder how is Brooks Atkinson doing in Chung King? [1] Someone told me he was tired of it now. Fine fellow, Brooks; but I don't know the hell why he wanted to go to China. Join the army, & see the warold, I suppose.

> *My love.*
> *Yours as ever,*
> *& still longing for New York & the*
> *sky over it.*

[1] Brooks Atkinson was war correspondent for the *New York Times* in Chungking, China, 1942–44.

To Horace Reynolds

MS. REYNOLDS

TOTNES, DEVON

14 OCTOBER 1944

My dear Horace:

Thank you very much for the candy, the soap, and the gay-coloured wiping-cloths. They were very acceptable, & it was very kind of you to send them. The soap that floats was a magical thing to our youngest—Shivaun. It is hard to realise that the youngster who rode the mechanical horse in the Britannic [1] is now galloping about in a jeep under a hot sun & the coconut trees in the Pacific Islands. God keep him safe. And your young lady must be a lady indeed be now. I'd like to see her; & say a few words; but not many, for the young get tired of the old quick. Listen to what they have to say; look at what they do, are the best ways to win their affection & confidence. And often they do better than the older ones, & often say things most wise and astonishing. You are still among them, I see, who go their way singing. A week ago, listening here to the Radio's Children's Hour— the best thing they do—I heard a "hill-billy programme"; & what did I hear near the end but "Brennan On the Moor!" Brave, bold, an' undaunted stood

[1] The ship that took O'Casey back to England after his American visit in 1934. See his letter to Lillian Gish, 22 December 1934, note 2, Vol I, p. 524.

bold Brennan on the Moor. In my new play, I've written a few songs; but the best one, "Kate Kindly Kiss'd Me," I'll have to leave out. This air is "The Green Bushes," & I daresay, you've heard it. I'm glad Barry [Fitzgerald] has had such a success on the Film; though I think he made a mistake leaving the theater. I've never had a line from the rascal since I saw him in New York.

We have had a lot of Americans here with us from time to time—Thomas Quinn Curtiss for one, whom you may know; & David Greene whom you certainly know well. He was with us last night with his friend, Burt Cumming. Talk! We heard the bells chime at midnight. He tells me I met him at that meeting in Cambridge long ago. He lives in Dorchester, Boston. He has paid us six or seven visits; but he will soon I believe, be shifted some where else. I think all the States have passed through Totnes.

And Harvard's a Camp now! Good God, the whole world's a tent sheltering armed men. The siren's silent here at last; & the children no longer have to dive under their steel-topped shelter; while their bold undaunted dad sat on the stairs found it damned hard to keep firm while fancying the house was sure soon to come toppling down on them all.

I was delighted to hear the "Old Grey Mare" still keeps her tail up. David tells me she is a "Hudson." He is a grand fellow (as is his buddy), & I'm very fond of him.

Don't go too hard with the farming. It's a job that puts a strain on the muscles. In fact it's very like work. I've done a bit in our garden—hedge-clipping, & sowing of beans, peas, & onions—and, be God! I dont like it! The spade is a damned primitive tool. Brings you back to the outside of the Garden of Eden. No; for me, let a mist go up to water the earth, & make it fruitful.

All my love to Kay, to John, Pegg, & yourself.

Ever Yours.
Sean

To Beatrix Lehmann

MS. LEHMANN

TOTNES, DEVON
15 OCTOBER 1944

Dear Beatrix:

Thanks for the copy of the article. It is a grand one from my point of view. And a godsend, in this way: a naval officer at Plymouth comes here occasionally—when he has an evening off; and asks me question after question after question about why I did this, that, & the other. At home, he is a professor in a Boston College. I have never been able to answer him, never, as you know, having had a fierce apprenticeship in the God Almighty Brains Trust. But your article, it seems to me, answers for me splendidly; & so I've sent it on to him to read.

I agree with you that Moscow should know as well as words can tell how we stand here. I'm writing myself to try to show we may have a fight about the USSR when this war is apparently over. Not only with Tory powers & Tory papers; but with those who should know better—The Tribune, Forward, and that strange woman group who run Time & Tide. I agree, too, that it is time to stop every Tom, Dick, Harry, & Jane, who can memorise a line of poetry from forcing themselves in front of the footlights. They're turning the theatre into a drab, dull, & deadly Bedlam. Thanks be to Christ the Red Army hadn't the scientific religion of Edith Evans! Had they had, we wouldn't be thinking of the theatre now.

Was it I told you about the article for "Counter Point"? I sent it long ago, but never was told they got it. A week ago, I wrote to the Editor at Oxford, saying if he wasn't going to use it, to let me have it back; but he hasn't replied, so far.

And who is this "British Council"? And what do you think of the British Drama League? Their report of their work for years, recently issued, is a terribly poor thing; & their monthly Bulletin is beyond reproach—too bad to blame.

I may have a production in London of "Red Roses" after Christmas. Would you fancy a part in it, if it should go on? The mother or Dymphna?

I am putting finishing touches to a new war play now; hope to have the last word satisfactory (as far as in me lies) in a few weeks.

All the best.
Yours as ever.
Sean

To Lord Longford [1]

TC. O'CASEY

[TOTNES, DEVON]
30 OCTOBER 1944

Dear Lord Longford:
Soviet theatrical and literary circles are eager to know something of what Ireland is doing in the way of drama, and of her general activities in the theatre. I am getting together a few notes about these things, and about

[1] Lord Longford (Edward Arthur Henry Pakenham, 6th Earl of Longford, 1902–61), playwright, translator, a director of the Gate Theatre, Dublin, and founder-director of Longford Productions, 1936–61.

the theatre in England, so as to send them a descriptive article, with a few personal comments.

I should very much like to have from you a few words about your own adventure, what you have done, and what you aim at in the future. I will send it on to my friends in Moscow just as you have written it, making no comments, for, of course, I know very little about the work of the Gate outside of the brief references found in the Irish papers. I shall be glad if you would do this for me.

With all good wishes.
Yours sincerely,
Sean O'Casey

[*To Dr. Joseph D. Cummins:*] [2]

Some months ago I wrote to the gentleman asking a few words for Nos. about Chekhov; but got no reply; though replies came from Des. Mac-Carthy, Shaw, Brown (I), Eliot, & Masefield. I'm writing above to see if he answers; not to find out anything about the Gate. There's not much to know about it. It will never be like the old Abbey, though L. Longford's very much better off than were L. G. [Lady Gregory] or Yeats. Longford's a pompous man, I'm afraid.

S O'C.

[2] At the bottom of the typed carbon copy of the letter to Lord Longford, O'Casey wrote this draft in longhand of a letter to his old friend in Dublin, Dr. Joseph D. Cummins.

To Jack Carney

MS. NYU LIBRARY

TOTNES, DEVON
7 NOVEMBER 1944

My dear Jack,

A line or two to inform you I am still alive. Thanks ever so much for the papers & the Condor Plug. We have had some sickness here—Shivaun, Niall, & Breon; & I have had an eye out of action for a week or two. But, as well, I've finished a new play—Warld on Wallpaper.[1] It was the one I long ago contemplated under the name of "Roll Out the Barrel," though

[1] This was the original title of *Oak Leaves and Lavender,* and he later made it the subtitle of the play—*A Warld on Wallpaper.* See O'Casey's letter to Jack Carney, 17 January 1945, where he decided to change the title. The subtitle is an ironic allusion to Yeats's letter of rejection of *The Silver Tassie* in 1928, in which he stated that "the whole history of the world should be reduced to wallpaper in front of which the characters must pose and speak." For the context of Yeats's remarks, see Yeats's letter

the play now never even mentions it. I hope it is as good as I hope it is. So far, no proofs of "Drums Under the Windows" have come to me, so labor must be scarcer than ever. I hope none of the flying bombs come near where you live & work! [Tom Quinn] Curtiss was a rather fine chap; & I hope he does well when he goes back to the USA. The labour Conference seems to have been a good one this time. The C.P. here is picking up, & a number of new members have joined it; but, I fear, few of the Totnes people. A few in Dublin tried to pull me into the controversy over the Abbey; but I kept out of it. The few words of mine that did appear were taken from a private letter, never meant to be published. I'm afraid the Abbey is on the rocks. By the way, Pat Dooley rang me up some time ago, & asked me to appeal to you to allow him to explain about your articles. Anyway, he appealed to me to appeal to you to make it up. I promised I'd do so; but my eye got bad, & the pain drove Pat out of my head. I know it's irritating to have one's articles tampered & tempered, but most Editors do it. Last one of mine to the D. Worker had a title of "Oh! For God's Sake, Lady Gibbs"; but it came out as "Don't Talk Nonsense, Lady Gibbs!" [2] And there's no use of complaining. Pat's a good fellow, & he tells me you are very useful to him; & he is really doing a good work. Now, I've done my duty, & I'll leave it to your honour. If you see a Pelican called "Life in Shakespeare's Time" by Dover Wilson,[3] could you get it for me? I asked Smith & Sons today to order it; but was told they couldn't order it; & if it came by chance, & they remembered, they'd keep it for me. Very kind indeed! Bronson Albery says: he hopes to do "Red Roses" sometime after Christmas; so light a coloured candle in front of your favorite saint. Have just read "Beefy Saint" [4]—nice title, wha'?—& "Boys of St Declan's" [5]— Oh, boys, oh, boys!—published by the C.T.S. [Catholic Truth Society] of Eireann. Mother o' Jasus! will nobody tell them about these! The worst of stuff written in the worst way. I've never read anything like them. They were sent for Brian. I daresay these are nix jobs—done for the glory of God, if not for the honour of Eireann. It looks as if it was going to be a close fight between Dewey & Roosevelt. A success for Dewey, I imagine, would harden the fight the Germans are making. They'd have more hope of a division between USA & USSR; though I daresay, if that appeared likely, the USSR would plunge into the war with Japan?

Well, all the best, as ever, with my love to Mina; & thanks again for paper & for plug.

Yours as ever,
Sean

---

to O'Casey, 20 April 1928, Vol. I, p. 268. See also O'Casey's letter to Daniel Macmillan, 2 October 1945, where he discusses the changing of the title.

[2] *Daily Worker,* 31 October 1944.

[3] J. Dover Wilson, *Life in Shakespeare's England; A Book of Elizabethan Prose* (1910; Pelican, 1944).

[4] Fergal McGrath, S.J., *The Beefy Saint* (1922), a fictional pamphlet.

[5] "A Christian Brother," *The Boys of St. Declan's* (1942), a fictional pamphlet.

To Daniel Macmillan

TS. MACMILLAN LONDON

TOTNES, DEVON
15 NOVEMBER 1944

Dear Mr Daniel:
    I have written another play (which is another way of saying that I
have created more trouble for myself and for you). It is called A
WARALD ON WALLPAPER. I think it good work, if my judgement be
worth a damn. Mr [Bronson] Albery of the New Theatre is very interested
in it; Michael Redgrave, one of his Directors, is enthusiastic about it—
Mr Albery says; and Beatrix Lehmann thinks it fine. What I would like to
know is—will there be any use in sending the MS on to you for possible
publication?
    By the way, I have a contract with Mr Albery for RED ROSES FOR
ME, and he says he hopes to have the play produced after Christmas. He
is waiting to get a Producer over from Eire, and he says a permit is likely
soon.
    I was glad to hear of Mr Harold's promotion, though he might have
been happier among the books. Things now must be a great strain on you.
I know they are on me. I do hope you are keeping fit and well.
                                        With all good wishes.
                                        Yours sincerely,
                                        Sean O'Casey

To Beatrix Lehmann

MS. LEHMANN

TOTNES, DEVON
23 NOVEMBER 1944

Dear Beatrix:
    Since writing last, I caught a cold which has snuggled down into my
chest, & the back of one lung, so this mysterious Universe has, for the time
being, become a shivering cough.

I've sent the amended form of play to B. A.[1] I don't think I'd like [John] Gielgud's good offices. I'll write again soon as I feel better.

Yours as ever,
Sean

[1] Bronson Albery, and the play was *Oak Leaves and Lavender,* at this time still tentatively titled "A Warld on Wallpaper."

To George Jean Nathan

MS. CORNELL

TOTNES, DEVON
4 DECEMBER 1944

My dear George:

Under another cover I am sending you a dishevelled copy of a "boom boom" play, without a boom from first to last. Be indulgent about the condition of script; but if it be too bad for your eyes—don't bother.

Since writing last, I got a cold dodging about here, & it nestled in the chest, & a shoot of it went to the base of a lung. I'm just crawling back to normal again; but it tires me now to look out of a window & even glance at other people working.

Some weeks ago, I sent an article to Moscow's "Novy Mir"; & in it I said a lot about you, recommending them to get your books & read them. I quoted you a lot, especially about war plays, & about the intrinsic value of Drama generally, for I think it good they should hear a prophet speaking. I think they'll listen to me, for I've been in touch with Moscow now in the way of literature & drama for near fifteen years. I hope you don't mind me quoting from your wisdom—all, of course, acknowledged as from you.

I've signed a contract for A WARLD ON WALLPAPER with a London producer here; & so I can't be free to give it to Dick. I will be writing him in a day or so. The producer doesn't like title, nor does the missus—it's from a remark made by Yeats years ago in a letter [1] to me—so I'll probably think of a new one.

Forgive shaky lettering & short letter. Will write more full when the world gets bright again, & the Universe ceases to be a cough.

Ever Yours
Sean

[1] See Yeats's letter to O'Casey, 20 April 1928, Vol. I, pp. 267–68.

To George Jean Nathan

MS. CORNELL

TOTNES, DEVON
6 DECEMBER 1944

My dear George:

Got the Book of Great Plays. Thank you. I've never seen, nor had I read, Lysistrata, & I must say, it disappointed me. But then all translations of Classical plays have seemed dull to me. Gilbert Murray's Greek plays in his English clothes, are, to me, dull and void of influence. To me, [Robert] Turney's Daughters of Atreus was high above them all. Yet I can read & re-read all these major & minor Elizabethan playwrights. Neither had I seen, nor had I read, Cyrano de Bergeraic; this was a grand treat to me. I revelled in it. The others I know well, one too well—my own.

I have sent on a ragged copy of the new play to you. You may have it now; if not, it should be on its way to your door. I am sorry to hear that Eugene is still very ill. We all feel it when he's down. I do wish he'd let his plays go on; & do try to prevent him from destroying any of his first Cycle plays. After all, these things don't really belong to him. We all have a claim on them. I do hope your opinion about the war is a correct one. I doubt it, George. Things have gone deeper than even the defeat of Germany & Japan. I think the war's end will usher in a European Revolution, though, of course, it may, probably will, be a bloodless one. When Eugene comes to New York, give him my love; & Carlotta, too. I am trying to pull out of a spot of illness myself; but it's hard going.

I enclose two cuttings about the Abbey, taken from Irish papers. Ernest Blythe was first Minister of Finance to the Dail, & then to the Free State Government, & is now Managing Director to the Abbey, for, which, I hear, he gets £700 a year. Anyway, he's made far more money by staying in Ireland than I have by coming out of it. It seems the Abbey is in a bad way. Efforts were made to pull me into the dispute, but I'm too damned busy with other things. I am looking forward to your latest book on the New York Theatre. From what I saw & heard myself when I was there (them was th' days!), & from what I've read in your books since, I know far more about the theatre 3000 miles away than I do about the one in my own townland. Give my best to Brooks Atkinson & Dick Watts. Reading your letter again, I see Eugene can't travel til April; so when you write give him my best love.

My love to you.

I have signed a contract for W. on Wallpaper, so that's a bit of luck.
Ever Yours.
Sean

To Miss Beatrix Lehmann

MS. LEHMANN

TOTNES, DEVON
7 DECEMBER 1944

Dear Beatrix—

Thanks for your letter. I have signed a Contract with B[ronson]. A[lbery]. for Warld on Wallpaper. Neither he nor [Michael] Redgrave likes the title. They think it would be meaningless to the public. Eileen agrees with them, so I perch a bird alone. I am trying to think of a new title, but find it hard to think at all just now. However, some things like thought now & again trickle through my mind. For instance—"Mobled Morning" is a good title for a play, but I'm not sure it suits this one; at the moment I think it might.

Ah! who will play Feelim! I haven't a ghost of an idea. Barry Fitz-gerald would; but he is away over the sea in Hollywood, never out of sight of the camera—the morning & evening star to him now. It is one of the handicaps of those who try to write good plays that by this work they cut themselves off from the theatre, & know little about them who tread the stage.

I hope Redgrave asks you to help him—that is if it wouldn't inter-fere with your work. Redgrave is, apparently, to produce. The play is to open in the Provinces.

Are you still on the Editorial Board of the D.W. [Daily Worker]?

Nice goings on in Greece! Finnegans Wake isn't over yet—the morning is still mobled. The Labour Leaders are a curious lot, with Ellen Wilkinson President of the T. Congress. Lady Astor, politically, is a gem of purest ray serene to some of them. And up North, Ethel Mannin is complaining that if she knocked at the Kremlin door, she wouldn't be let in, because Stalin's a Dictator, & won't have anything to do with a person having an opinion of her own.

So now you know the news.

I'm not so sure about these hurryings to France, Italy, Burma, & the rest of it. [Noel] Coward, dripping with sweat, keeping the troops from thinking! Curious love of country—& hiding the dollars in a handkerchief. Anyway, let us leave something worth while in the old townland.

Yours as ever
Sean

To J. B. Priestley

TS. TEXAS

TOTNES, DEVON
29 DECEMBER 1944

Dear Mr Priestley:

Thank you for your letter received this morning.

I, of course, shall be very glad to serve on the SCR Council of the Writers Group [1]—though it be only to stand and wait—, and will do all I can to help. We have a very active group for Anglo-Soviet Unity here in this ancient Borough.

My best personal wishes to yourself, and many more for the good work.

Yours sincerely,
Sean O'Casey

[1] Priestley was president of the Writers Group of the Society for Cultural Relations with the USSR.

III

CONTROVERSIES
AND PLAYS,
1945

I SHOULDN'T call dislike of "conceited amateurs, arrogant homosexuals, & impertinent dilettantes" a prejudice. I hate them—except when they're comic, like most of the Irish ones. We don't hate enough in England. The English don't know how. They think it a virtue. It isn't. It shows a lack of life force.

And don't talk to me in the jargon of "holding up the play's action." Turn to Act II, Scene 1. Julius Caesar, and see how the action is held up there while the conspirators argue as to the point where the sun rises: "Dec. Here lies the east: Doth not the day break here?" etc. I am not a writer of the "well-made play."

There were hard and lively times ahead in 1945 when O'Casey was trying to recover from the war years. Early in the year his brother Michael in Dublin wrote to say he could use any old clothes that might be discarded, at a time when O'Casey himself was wearing his eldest son's cast-off coat and trousers. All he could afford to do was send his brother a pound note. At the same time, ironically, he was tempted by a Hollywood offer of up to $100,000 to write the film script of Thomas Wolfe's *Look Homeward, Angel,* which he refused. He was too busy with his own writing, he claimed, but he also knew in all honesty that he wasn't right for the task; and more important to him personally, he couldn't allow himself to be seduced by money, particularly when he was in great need of it. Several months later, writing to Gabriel Fallon, he sadly recalled that he had not heard a word from Barry Fitzgerald during the nine years he had been in Hollywood, and O'Casey concluded that it was "not a place for a conscientious artist."

Still as rigorously quarrelsome as he was conscientious, O'Casey seemed to believe that the life force was manifested in his anger as well as in his inspiration. He simply couldn't resist the call to arms against censorship vigilantes, and in a little-known article in *The Bell* he summed up his views on this urgent theme—which he was to dramatize in many of his later comedies. He turned his wrath on the Irish censors, who were fearful, they claimed, about the "need for protecting adolescence against a warped mental bias," to which O'Casey pointedly replied that the saved would have to be protected from their saviors: "The protecting angels themselves may have a warped mental bias, and so the adolescents will have to have an additional protection against these, and so on, *ad infinitum."* But since infinite controversy can sometimes lead to unexpected reversals, O'Casey was soon forced to defend the Ireland he had attacked so fiercely when George Orwell and St. John Ervine entered the field to mock O'Casey and his native land.

The occasion was the publication of the third volume of the autobiography, *Drums Under the Windows.* In his petulant review, included here, Orwell was guilty of a number of inaccurate and insensitive comments that led to a quick and corrective reply from O'Casey, which the editor of *The Observer* refused to publish and Orwell decided to ignore, but which at long last is printed here for the first time. Orwell had accused O'Casey of devoting his "life-work to abusing England," overlooking the fact that he had spent much more of his lifetime abusing Ireland when she deserved it; he accused O'Casey of being one of the hypocritical Irish nationalists who "enjoyed a special status" in England, though the indigent and ignored playwright whose plays remained largely unproduced in England was hardly in a position to enjoy any status, special or otherwise; he accused O'Casey of suffering from "blatant nationalism," though there was probably no Irish writer who was more anti-nationalistic than the irreverent O'Casey; he accused O'Casey of being an example of the "worst extremes of jingoism and racialism," though there was no one less patriotic and more tolerant of all races than O'Casey; and, finally, he accused O'Casey of resorting to cheap poetry of romantic bombast in honor of Cathleen Ni Houlihan, though the verse in question was actually from one of Tennyson's more chauvinistic poems. Perhaps it was therefore not surprising that

Orwell chose the discretion of silence. When the wronged and frustrated O'Casey finally had a chance to present his rebuttal nine years later in the last volume of his autobiography, "Rebel Orwell," *Sunset and Evening Star,* some defenders of Orwell accused O'Casey of cowardice for waiting until his adversary was dead and couldn't defend himself. The appearance of the censored and ignored letter now, however, should clear up that misconception. O'Casey could be ruthlessly aggressive in controversy, but he was also scrupulously fair.

The cross-grained St. John Ervine was not so silent or inaccurate in his unyielding defense of Ulster at the expense of what he called the "shabby back-street Republic" of Eire. In different circumstances O'Casey might have agreed with Ervine about the Ireland which he felt de Valera presided over like "a lay bishop"—to use his own phrase—but now he couldn't ignore the northern sneer. And though he had made his tenement characters laugh at the blood-sacrifice words of Pearse in *The Plough and the Stars,* he again defended the 1916 martyr as a great teacher and visionary. The one issue, however, on which he himself remained unyielding, was his idealistic view of life in Soviet Russia, which he defended against all critics, including the formidable Bertrand Russell, an Oxford don, and a Jesuit priest. He might ridicule pompous Marxists, but he felt he had to defend the hope that Russia was a noble Socialist experiment. In other letters he lectured his friends: on his anticipation of the Women's Lib movement by predicting that women were on the move toward "full equality with men"; on the egotistical excesses of "arty" people in the theatre; on his new and unorthodox method of writing plays. And he had sent his latest play, *Oak Leaves and Lavender,* to his publisher while he waited patiently for a producer, a play which presents a visionary approach to the redemption of England during the Battle of Britain, yet another corrective to Orwell's misconceptions.

Perhaps the most surprising turn of events was the beginning of his extensive correspondence with a young Irish Catholic girl named Sheila who wrote him first, and provoked him to write five-thousand-word letters on religion and politics, mainly Catholicism and Communism. When she told him she had, on the advice of a Jesuit priest, taken a lifelong vow of chastity, he apparently set out to save her body as well as her mind, and he insisted he had no intention of shaking her religious faith, only of liberating it. Though she worked at a lowly job in a London factory, he gradually learned that she was "highly connected" to one of the influential Catholic families of England, and he was soon involved in controversy with the Jesuit member of the family, who was trying to rescue her from the double damnation of O'Casey and Communism. For his part O'Casey tried carefully to be a kind and trusting confidant, maintaining that he wanted to bring her to common sense not Communism. He was considerate but firm in his reasoned arguments, but when she once played the shocked lady and urged him to act like a gentleman, he warned her, "Don't be romantic about O'Casey," and then he revealed his true colors in a characteristic passage that sounds like a speech from one of his plays: "So far from being a 'gentleman,' I am an artist, & such a being, as touching his art, is ruthless; so, lady, beware! I am entirely indifferent as to what people say of me, or think of me; being myself always, I care of no other, & am not afraid of myself. Oh, Sheila, what would it profit me to gain the whole world, & lose my own soul—lose myself?"

To Lord Longford

TC. O'CASEY

TOTNES, DEVON
1 JANUARY 1945

Dear Lord Longford:

The literary and drama circles of the USSR are eager to know all there is to be known about the theatrical activities here and in Eire.

I should be very grateful if you could spare the time to send me an account of LONGFORD PRODUCTIONS, all that you have done in the past, and all you hope to do in the future. I shall be glad to forward it on to the Soviet Society for Cultural Relations with Foreign Countries, for publication in INTERNATIONAL LITERATURE, or Novy Mir.

I wrote twice to the Gate Theatre for this favour, but, apparently, you didnt get either of the letters.

I am venturing to send this to your private address to make assurance double sure, with apologies for troubling you.

> *With all good wishes,*
> *Yours sincerely,*
> *Sean O'Casey*

To Michael Casey

TC. O'CASEY

TOTNES, DEVON
? JANUARY 1945

Dear Mick:

Sorry to hear about the Arthritis, but when one goes over fifty years, pains and aches become fairly common; and you must be a pretty old man now;[1] though your writing seems to be as young-looking as ever.

Just to think of you living away from city life is strange, but I'm sure it's much better for you. Anyway, the city must come close up to "The Thatch" now.[2] In my days there, when I played hurling in "The Thatch" field, it looked like the country, but before I left, Whitehall was becoming a suburb of Dublin, something like Clontarf.

By "gear," I suppose you mean clothing; but where is such a thing to [be] got here now? At present, strange and all as it may sound, I am wearing the eldest boy's coat and trousers which became too small for him—he's just six feet two. Both the missus and I have to give all the clothing coupons to the children—three of them, and even then these arent enough. Everything here now has to be worn as long as possible— not a trial to me, for I always hated new things. The war has done a lot of harm, and production now is very scant. And will be for a long time to come. You can, of course, get anything you really want, if you are able, and prepared, to pay the price for it; but few can do that. I enclose a quid for you to get something for yourself. I cant send more, for I am by no means well-off. Indeed, I have been often up against it. My books dont bring in a lot, and never will. I could do a lot better, if I wrote to please people, but I dont do that, and I dont think I ever shall. There is a play of mine to be put on in London next month, I think; and, if this be success- ful—which is very doubtful—, I'll let you have a little more.

The missus and I are pretty tired after the years of war what with the nights of wailing sirens, the black-out, and the occasional bombing, with the children prone under a Morrison shelter, we have had our fill of it; but, all in all, we have been very fortunate. My ears are well attuned to gun-fire now, after Easter week, the time of the Black and Tans, the Civil War, and then, the World War, they ought to be.

Well all the best.
Yours as ever,
Sean

[1] O'Casey's brother Michael was seventy-nine years old. He died two years later. See O'Casey's letter to Mrs. Isabella Murphy, 20 January 1947.

[2] The ailing Michael had gone to live in Whitehall, a suburb on the north side of Dublin, with his niece, Mrs. Isabella "Babsie" Murphy, the daughter of Isabella Casey Beaver. Mrs. Murphy's home on Ellenfield Road was alongside "The Thatch," an athletic field.

To M. J. Kane

PC. *Irish Press*

10 JANUARY 1945

SEAN O'CASEY'S FINGAL DAYS

Seán O'Casey, in a letter to the Rush C.Y.M.S. Players, recalls meetings with Tom Ashe,[1] hero of Ashbourne in 1916, and events in Co. Dublin in pre-Easter Week days.

The Rush Players had been in communication with Mr. O'Casey before their production of "The Shadow of a Gunman." From Totnes, Devon, the playwright replied to M. J. Kane, N.T., Rush, as follows:—

"How well I remember Rush and Lusk, Donabate, Balbriggan, Malahide, Man O' War, Gormanstown!

"How often have I worked with the men of Fingal who manned the ballast train on the G.N.R.[2] And I have played hurling in Lusk—a great match in which we were beaten. And the lovely walk from Skerries to Balbriggan along the coast!

"I spoke to meetings there during the big lock-out of 1913. And Loughshinney and the curious little village of Ballisk. Ah, well! God be wi' those days! And Tom Ashe—solas Dé da anam [3]—a great friend of mine. And the Lusk Pipers—their big white banner with the broad-winged black raven on it."

The reading of the letter by Mr. Nagle, producer, at a performance of the play in Skerries in aid of the memorial fund to honour Skerries men killed in the War of Independence, was loudly cheered.

---

[1] Thomas Ashe (1882–1917), teacher, Gaelic Leaguer, and Republican martyr, commanded the Irish Volunteer forces at Ashbourne during the 1916 Easter Rising; was sentenced to death by court martial, but the sentence was commuted to life imprisonment in England. He was released in the general amnesty of 17 June 1917, but was shortly rearrested for making speeches against the British authorities in Ireland. As a prisoner in Mountjoy Prison, he went on a hunger strike for a week, was forcibly fed, and died shortly after, on 26 September 1917. See O'Casey's tribute to Ashe in the *Dublin Saturday Post,* 6 October 1917, Vol. I, pp. 64–65. See also O'Casey's pamphlets on Ashe: Sean O'Cathasaigh, *The Sacrifice of Thomas Ashe* (1918); and a slightly expanded second edition, *The Story of Thomas Ashe.* The former is reprinted in *Feathers From the Green Crow* (1962).

[2] From 1903 to 1911, O'Casey worked as a common laborer on the north-side Sutton branch of the Great Northern Railway of Ireland. During these years he played on the St. Laurence O'Toole hurling team, and also played the pipes for the club's pipers' band.

[3] The light of God to his soul.

To Jack Carney

MS. NYU LIBRARY

[TOTNES, DEVON]
17 JANUARY 1945

My dear Jack,

Thanks ever so much for the papers, & for the tobacco Curtiss left, & which Nannie has forwarded on to me. I am nearly all right after the chill; the spot on the lung kept me coughing for weeks, & the tablets of M & B I swallowed made me feel alone in the world for a long time. I have signed a contract with Bronson Albery for "Warld on Wallpaper," & am thinking of changing the name to "Oak Leaves & Lavender." So now I have two contracts for plays, & two for publication—the third vol. of biography, & "Oak Leaves & Lavender." As soon as "Drums Under the Windows" comes out, I'll send you a copy. I've sent an article (reply to one appearing before) on the Censorship to The Bell, at Sean O'Faolain's request; G. B. S. is sending another; & the two are to be in next month's issue. What's all this I hear of your going to Paris? Are you going gay, or what? I don't suppose there's much gaiety there now, though. It will be a long time before France dances spontaneously again. Possibly, a long time before we do it either—if the English have ever danced spontaneouly before. Well, all the old British poise is loose again in Greece. Showing the ignorant world the way things should be done. Yes, George Jean knows about the theatre. He complains a lot about the poverty of last year's season. There's no English critic like him; & none here or there half so courageous. I hope he'll like my latest play.

Well, the Red Army seems to be moving again! Jásus, isn't it comical, after so many asking if they were going to stay stuck on the Vistula forever! An' what about the Rhine? These Soviet Generals! It's damn odd, isn't it, when we remember the poor devils hadn't a chance to go through Sandhurst. With Stalin playing possum for months, with his mouth shut; & suddenly shouts Now Boys! And the Red Army's off like a horse into Full Gallup, with the B.B.C. playing the Russian National Anthem "in honour of our great allies!" Between you & me, Jack, I'm afraid "Wrap the Green Flag Round Me, Boys" is getting a little out of date. And "God Bless the Pope" too! What wailing and gnashing of teeth there will be in the Editorial offices of the Catholic Press. His Holiness blessing the world with two fingers; & the Red Army blessing it with their guns. No starving children any more, any where—the first message in the boom of their artillery. Which shows that guns may bring bread, if they happen to be the right ones. All Hail to the Soviet Union! Three Shouts on a Hill [1] for them.

> *Love to Mina & to you.*
> *Ever yours*
> *Sean*

---

[1] The title of one of O'Casey's early manuscripts; see Bernard Shaw's letter to O'Casey, 3 December 1919, note 1, Vol. I, p. 87.

To William Herndon [1]

TC. O'CASEY

[TOTNES, DEVON]
17 JANUARY 1945

Dear Mr Herndon:

Many thanks for your letter, dated 29th Dec. 1944, received yesterday, asking me to take on the task of adapting Mr [Thomas] Wolfe's LOOK HOMEWARD, ANGEL, for the Films. I am, indeed, indebted to Mr Arthur Ripley's kind opinion of me when he says that I would be the "right man" for the job; and I thank him for his offer to make a "most lucrative deal with me immediately, paying my transportation to, and from, England." And for your offer that, should I agree, you would get me from between $50,000 and $100,000, if I undertook to do this screenplay.

A very tempting offer, by God! And the chance of making a fine Film from a fine work. But, all the same, I'm afraid I must refuse. Yes, undoubtedly, I must refuse. I have too much of my own work to do, to take up the big task suggested by you.

Believe me, I dont scorn money. I know no-one who does; nor do I know why anyone should, though we may sometimes have too much of a good thing.

I need money badly, for my work doesnt bring me in a fortune, or anything like one; but, all the same, thinking it over carefully, I have to repeat the refusal I gave before.

And, perhaps, the work would be done better by an American who knows well the work of Wolfe, and, certainly, is more alive to the life he wrote about than I would be. Oddly enough, it is only just a week ago that I read LOOK HOMEWARD, ANGEL. It was given to me by an American

[1] William Herndon, John McCormick Agency, Inc., 9730 Wilshire Boulevard, Beverly Hills, California.

naval officer whom I met when I paid a visit to Harvard—he was a student there then—and who came a good many times to see me here.

Thanks again. I hope you will make a great Film of the work.

Yours very sincerely,
Sean O'Casey

To Beatrix Lehmann

MS. LEHMANN

TOTNES, DEVON
24 JANUARY 1945

Dear Beatrix:

I am very glad indeed to hear you are well over the trial of an operation, & look forward again to be before the footlights; but stay in the dark as long as you can—till you are sure you are quite yourself again. If I were you, I shouldn't think too much of your "troop show." Think only of getting well, & then face front once more; but get well first. It is one of the first wisdoms of life to know when we are able & fit to do what we set our hands to.

I have changed, or am changing, the name of the play to "Oak Leaves and Lavender; or a Warld on Wallpaper." As for production, heaven knows when that will come; but I'm too busy to care. I'm just doing the proofs of the 3rd vol. of biography. I've just got an offer of $50,000 to $100,000 to turn [Thomas] Wolfe's "Look Homeward Angel" into a Film story. The Selznick Co. of "Rebecca" & "Gone With the Wind" fame has said "I'm the right man for the job, being a poet as well as a dramatist." So now we know—a dramatist with four plays still unproduced by professional actors. The one thing I hate most in our Social life is the curious animation shown in trying to get one to do what one doesn't want to do; & these are they who say "there's no personal freedom in the USSR"! I'm afraid there's more than a kick left in the Nazis yet—abroad & at home. But the Red Army will always be there. Anyway, you got well—that's your first job.

Ever yours sincerely
Sean

To Daniel Macmillan

MS. MACMILLAN LONDON

TOTNES, DEVON
27 JANUARY 1945

Dear Mr. Daniel:

I have fixed on the title of *Oak Leaves and Lavender; or, A Warld on Wallpaper* for my new play; & I have so written it down on the agreement.

I have signed it, & send it on with this note.

I hope London isn't so tight in the grip of snow and frost as we are here. It must be terribly hard on the men at the Front. It was sad for me to hear of the death of our latest V.C. Lieut. Grayburn.[1] When he was a youngster of six, he came to our place in Chalfont St Giles; & on our little lawn, I often played football with him. A handsome, virile youngster. It is very unfortunate that he is here now only in the shape of a copper cross with a gold centre. It is dreadful to think of the hosts of the young that them damned Germans have robbed of life.

I hope you and yours are all well.

My Warm Regards.
Sean O'Casey

[1] O'Casey dedicated *Oak Leaves and Lavender* (1946) "To little Johnny Grayburn, who, in his sailor suit, played football with me on a Chalfont lawn and afterwards gallantly fell in the battle of Arnhem."

To The Bell, *Dublin*

FEBRUARY 1945

CENSORSHIP: COMMENTS BY READERS

We now have, here, a Literary Censorship, a Film Censorship, the Censorship of the Common Law, the Censorship of the secret reports of the Librarians' Association, and the private censorship which any citizen irrespective of class, education, age, or sanity may exercise over any book in a public library merely by objecting to it.[1] Last month we printed an

[1] Ireland's first Censorship of Publications Act was passed in 1929, establishing a board whose function was to recommend books to be banned by the Minister of Justice. In 1946 the act was amended, giving the board itself the power to ban books, and an appeal board was set up. In an appeal, six copies of the banned book, accompanied by £5, must be sent to the board, but only the editor, publisher, author,

article by Mr. Monk Gibbon, poet and man of letters, "In Defence of
Censorship."

The following specially invited comments have been received.[2] *We
will conclude the discussion in March with other opinions, and a brief
reply from Mr. Gibbon.*

by Sean O'Casey

Mr. Gibbon's defence of Censorship is, it seems to me, a comic
medley of fright, fear, superstition, faint piety, Greek fire, and a cool desire
to keep on the lee side of the counts, knights, and esquires of the Holy
Roman Empire. He starts out by conceding that "a reasonable censorship
is almost a contradiction in terms," and then proceeds to debate "whether
censorship is, or can be, justifiable." This contradiction in terms seems to
end the matter for Mr. Gibbon, but he hurries on to defend the indefensible.
"A commonplace," he says, "is—every community defends its young, for
what youth thinks matters at least as much as what it eats, perhaps more."
Oh? Thirty years ago, or more, when I was speaking at meetings about
"Meals for Necessitous School-children," there wasn't much of a sign about
of communities defending the young; and only the other week, an article
in *The Economist* said that on enquiry among many homes in Crumlin,
among families in the favoured position of having the head of the house in
permanent employment—that is in a position better than thousands—
eighty per cent. of the children showed definite signs of under-nourishment.
Curious way of protecting the young. To me, the mind that thinks thought
as important, or more so, than food to the young is away behind the back
of beyond. Food was, and is, and will be, life's first need, always. And as
for thought, children for a good many years drown their minds in the
thought of their elders. That is why it is so hard to make the Irish language
the common tongue of the people. And it is a mistake to associate a change
in community life with deterioration. It is nonsense to connect the corruption of the controllers, the grandees, the kings, the courtiers with the virile,
everlasting life of the people. The change from tribal life to feudalism
(changing thought too) wasn't deterioration; it was a step forward. So, too,
the change from feudalism to mass production, to capitalism, wasn't
deterioration; it was another step forward; and so, too, will the change—
taking place now—from the control of the means of life by the few, to the
ownership of these things by the people who created them. We are a little

---

or a group of five members of the Oireachtas (the combined legislature of the Dail
and Senate) might submit an appeal. Any member of the public could recommend
books to the board for prohibition, and this was the most common procedure. In
1967, the act was further amended and liberalized for the first time, when all books
prohibited prior to 1955 were unbanned, and all books prohibited after 1955 were
to be unbanned twelve years after their initial prohibition.

[2] Besides O'Casey's comment, statements appeared from Bernard Shaw, T. C.
Kingsmill Moore, and Professor James Hogan, University College, Cork.

too fond of harking back to the Greeks and the Romans as ones selected by God to show the way to the world. Our life, socially, scientifically, and even morally, is altogether different from that of Roman or of Greek. We might as well look back to the life of Aztec or Inca. What is it to present-day man or woman in field, factory, or workshop that Ovid was sent away while Virgil stayed at home? We're getting a bit tired of this three hundred men and three men business. Even the Brehon Laws wouldn't fit our social life now. And what has all this got to do with determining what book must be pooh-bahed out of Ireland?

Mr. Gibbon tells us that "writers influence current mentality, if not current morality," thereby hinting, though he won't say so definitely, that they do influence what he thinks to be morality. But he doesn't tell us what influenced the writers to write as they do. They take, in their writing, their cue from the life around them. Those two fine men, Shaw and Wells, who have written numerous books, haven't influenced thought and life one ten thousandth part as compared with Hitler who has written but one.

Mr. Monk Gibbon says, "Two realistic institutions, the Roman Catholic Church and the USSR, have consistently made it plain that in their opinions certain authors and certain books are better left unread." As far as the Catholic Church is concerned, this is true enough, God knows; and not only the Catholic Church, ex officio, but every bishop, priest, deacon, and confraternity man, from the centre to the sea, is bursting with anxiety to have special books banned from the sight and sense of all other men— having first read the books themselves. But where did Mr. Monk Gibbon get his news about the USSR? I have re-read, a week ago, the History of the USSR Communist Party (Bolshevik), which is mainly the history of Russia from 1917 to 1940, and I have seen no reference whatever to the censorship of poem, play, or novel throughout the whole of that historical period. I myself have been in touch with the USSR, regarding literature and the drama, since 1925, nearly a year before I left Dublin, and I am still in touch, closer touch, today, and I have never yet heard a whisper of the banning of play, poem, or novel by the officials of the USSR, good, bad, or indifferent. On the contrary, just a year ago, I put in a lot of work writing to all the British publishers, and the American publishers, too, appealing to them to forward all the books they could to Moscow and Leningrad. Indeed, at the request of Moscow, I wrote a long article on Irish Literature, and was surprised in the acknowledgment to read that they were surprised I hadn't mentioned Phelan's *Green Volcano* [1938]. So, at least, I have some reason for asking Mr. Gibbon where he got the news that officials in the USSR have declared that some books are better left unread?

The case of the young girl who became "hardboiled," because she had "read practically nothing but Maugham for a whole year," may be passed over. That attitude of mind was fixed, not by dangerous literature, but by the aftermath of the first world war. It has passed away, and even Maugham, himself, has changed.

To me, it doesn't seem a question of what we have lost or gained in Ireland by the censorship (most of those who read have read the books that have been banned); but a question of how long intelligent people are going to stand this pompous, ignorant, impudent, and silly practice that is making Ireland a laughing-stock among the intelligent of all lands.

Signor Benson's (is this Monsignor Benson, one of the Champions of wholesome literature, in the same row with Belloc, Chesterton, and Noyes?) monologue on the novel, quoted by Mr. Gibbon:—"Fiction in the hands of new and distinguished authors was undergoing a corresponding sea change . . . it made its studies of morality in the monkey-house and followed its heroines to the water-closet. The mirror which it is the function of Art to hold up to nature (as if the water-closet wasn't part of poor human nature) seemed to be always adjusted to reflect to what lies below the belt; the heart and the brain (with the exception of the department of the sexual urge) were outside the field of vision . . . and the most unsatisfactory feature of these coitions was that the partners in them seemed to care for the act so much more than they cared for each other." Well, that's Benson failing to see anything in the works he read save what a gentle soul like his should keep away from. But this criticism is mainly a lie; a mean, desperate lie, uttered with forethought. No distinguished author would, nor could, make the water-closet, and its spare parts, a main, or semi-main, theme in a novel, play, or poem. Such a thing would be impossible in the first place; and, in the second place, were it possible such a work would knock the author off his claim to be distinguished. As for the morality of the monkey-house, to go by a lot of the clergy, that kind of morality is to be found rather in a dancing-hall than in a book. It is a remarkable and enlightening thing that the clericals and their followers concentrate so ardently and so persistently on these kinds of thoughts, more so by far than the worst writer with which they themselves are acquainted. At least, no author whom I have read, and I have read a few, made such things the theme of his work; but possibly, Benson, keen on the track of these things, nosed them out far more successfully than I did.

And how are we going to satisfy the "need for protecting adolescence against a warped mental bias"? The protecting angels themselves may have a warped mental bias, and so the adolescents will have to have an additional protection against these, and so on, *ad infinitum*. But surround youth with protectors, as the Light Brigade were surrounded by guns, yet no power of wisdom, age, or piety can damn a physiological urge; and books, or no books, it will have its way, as strong in those who cannot read as in those who can, for life comes first; and a good and fine thing, too, provoking in man the urge to create some of the most beautiful things in art and literature that have justified the ways of man to God.

Mr. Gibbon, assuming the mantle of censorship, says to Anatole France, Rousseau, Voltaire, and Maupassant, You can go out to play, boys; your marks are good; and to Strindberg, he says, You must stop in—you are really a bad boy. This of a man who is one of the greatest playwrights of his time and ours. And why? Strindberg frightens him. He finds the playwright a little spurious, a little windy, and a little rhetorical, just as each of us is at some time or another of our little day of life. Well, Mr. Gibbon has a perfect right to banish Strindberg out of his own life, but none whatever to banish him from the life of others. Besides, if the others got away from Gibbon, someone would seize on France, another on Rousseau, and a third on Maupassant, leaving Voltaire to the clericals, who, when Noyes wrote a book about him, came rushing and roaring together, till Noyes took the book back to hide it from the sight of men. I notice Joyce wasn't mentioned—too far down for Gibbon to reach. Joyce, the bravest and finest soul in literature Ireland has had for many years; who made of Dublin a dancing Hecuba, and, at the last, wrote the most extraordinary and wonderful *Everyman* the mind of man could conceive. But, if not mentioned by Gibbon and the rest of them, the stars themselves move over the Dublin sky to figure out the name of Joyce there. Mr. Gibbon complains about the "propagandists" dismissing religion with:—"The great mythologies of the past (including the Church) are deprived of enough facade even to launch good raillery against." But surely one ought to be free enough to say a thing like that? And isn't it the clerical who is the biggest propagandist of them all? Not alone in matters of religion, but in politics (see the Catholic Press for Poland, Yugo-Slavia, and Greece; and we all remember the hullabaloo for Franco), literature, art, family life, schools, and what not; each of them insisting that he, and he alone, has all the truth there is to be found in what he says about anything whatsoever. It's a bit of a cheek to hear the princes of propaganda complaining about the humble yeomen. And Mr. Gibbon forgets that Chesterton is full of the very remarks he condemns in his writings about those who challenge the creeds. But Chesterton's a privileged person.

And where did Mr. Gibbon pick up the brilliant thought of "The artist goes his own way. He is content, if necessary, to wait for recognition." Content to wait, eh? There isn't an artist who hasn't, or who doesn't, make a fight for recognition, in one way or another. Mr. Gibbon should read the Introduction to the American edition of Joyce's *Ulysses* (perhaps the bravest and proudest artist of them all), where he will learn something of the fight Joyce made for the publication of *Dubliners*. And what about WAAMA [3]? Not only for recognition do artists strive, but, willy-nilly, for a living too. But then Mr. Gibbon believes that—"literature in our time has almost ceased to think in terms of art. Writers are not artists, they are propagandists for a particular point of view. Poets tend to be Communist firstly and poets, if at all, secondly." There you are! Saying exactly of art what he condemns writers for saying about religion. But a poet always remains a poet, though he be an aristocrat poet like Byron; a democratic poet

---

[3] Writers, Artists, Actors, and Musicians Association in Dublin.

like Burns; a middle-class grandiloquent poet like Yeats, or a Communist poet like Mayakovsky.

Authors must always fight these enemies of free thought be they publicly commissioned censors or self-appointed guardians of morals, like the National Organization for Decent Literature, presided over by the Catholic bishop of Fort Wayne, Indiana; the Watch and Ward Society of Boston; or the Society for the Suppression of Vice in New York. There they are being licked in one fight after another, and let us hope they will soon disappear from Eire. And Mr. Gibbon seems to agree with his officer friend about rapes and murder in literature, while forgetting that he will find both in the Bible and Shakespeare; plenty of murder in the poet's best plays, and the plays of his Elizabethan comrades; and, to me, the vilest story of a murder I have ever read appears in the works of the Christian bravo, G. K. Chesterton. It is just as well that Mr. Gibbon decides to stand aside. He would be a responsibility rather than a help to sturdier writers determined to fight rather than to be submerged under the standard set up by the Eire Censorship Board, or the Legions defending Decent Literature scurrying about the streets of Boston and New York.

To Daniel Macmillan

MS. MACMILLAN LONDON

TOTNES, DEVON
6 FEBRUARY 1945

Dear Mr. Daniel:

Enclosed is a copy of a letter I got from George Jean Nathan, the leading American Drama Critic. I am very pleased, for he is the only one of the Drama critics, here & there, whose opinion is, in mine, worth trusting. No friendship, however fond, would make, or tempt, him to say a different thing from what his inner mind thought.

Yours sincerely,
Sean O'Casey

Copy of Letter from George Jean Nathan [1]

> Royalton Hotel,
> 44, West 44th Street,
> New York City.

> 13 JANUARY 1945

My dear Sean:

The Script,[2] long delayed in transit, arrived yesterday. I read it at once, and love it. It is a fine play—far and away, to my mind, the best play on war I have encountered in years; and I offer you my hearty handshake.

What is the state for America? Is it available for production here? I should like Eddie Dowling to read it.

Again my congratulations.

> *Yours always,*
> George Jean Nathan

[1] This letter was typed.
[2] *Oak Leaves and Lavender.*

To Geoffrey Grigson [1]

> TC. O'CASEY

> TOTNES, DEVON
> 7 FEBRUARY 1945

Dear Mr Grigson:

I'm afraid, I cant do what you ask of me. To my mind, it wouldnt be worth while. I'm certain no-one, bar Mrs O'Casey and, maybe yourself, would listen to it. And, even were I sure a host would listen, I'd be still of the same mind.

I'm tired of talking about the theatre. To me, the English theatre is without hope and God in the world. One has only to read the weekly remarks of the drama critics, or, best of all, attend one of their dinners given by the Circle, or, better still read their private monthly bulletin. I have written of the theatre in a book which had a sale of a few hundred; for the Saturday Book, and the article was reviewed as the "usual O'Casey repetitive, cantankerous diatribe on the English theatre"; months ago, at the editor's urgent request, I wrote one for a new Magazine called "Counterpoint," sent it on, but got no acknowledgement; I wrote about it,

[1] Geoffrey Grigson, Talks Producer, West Region, BBC, Bristol.

got an apology, and a promise of payment in a week's time; that's more than a month ago, and I have heard nothing since. I have now three plays—no, four—written, but ne'er a one of them has had a professional performance, though two of them, through the kindness of Mr Bronson Albery, are under contract; and a one, previously written—WITHIN THE GATES—got a production that gave me a horrifying experience of the English theatre. So I know something of what I am talking about.

Some years ago, I joined in an "impromptu discussion" on the theatre, but the rehearsals of this impromptu discussion wearied me, and the number of copies of the talk printed frightened me away, so that I refused all subsequent invitations to broadcast. Some years ago, too, I was asked to give a snappy three-minute talk on "The National Theatre" when that question was in the air. Reluctantly I consented, wrote the talk, after spending hours trying to compress what I wanted to say into a few words, sent it in, and got word that it was fine. A day before it was to be given, I got a long telegram to say that the talk would be cancelled, unless I agreed to praise Miss [Lillian] Bayliss and her Old Vic as equivalent, or as something better, than the proposed National Theatre. I refused; they sent a courier to argue; Fleet Street got wind of it, and I was persecuted all that day and all that night escaping from inquirers who didnt care a rap about the theatre, national or otherwise. I made a vow never to have more to do with the theatre as exemplified by the B.B.C. No, my friend, forgive me when I say I cannot do what you ask regarding request No. 1.

About No. 2 [an interview] there is difficulty too. With things as they are, and with three children attending day school, I fail to find a chance to do any work till nine or ten at night, and so have very little time for anything else. At the moment, I am reading the proofs of a third biographical vol., and hope to be reading the proofs of the last play I've written when I've done those; besides doing odd work for the local British-Soviet Unity Council. As well, I am working—when I get a chance—at the 4th and last biographical vol, so have more work in hand than I can comfortably do.

And anyway, you could not sanction what I should say. To say what should be said about the theatre today and its critics demands a fierceness that would terrify the B.B.C., C.E.M.A., the British Council, and the Drama League.

> *Regards,*
> *Yours sincerely,*
> *Sean O'Casey*

To Leslie Daiken

MS. DAIKEN

TOTNES, DEVON
8 FEBRUARY 1945

Dear Leslie Daiken:

Thank you very much for your gift of "They Go—The Irish"; with
my own article in the vanguard.[1] I've read it from end to end, anyway—the
book—, & that is a compliment to the Genii who produced it. It is an odd
production, & I don't know what to say about it. It is definitely interesting,
& that's saying a lot these days. The book has a woeful cover, and a charming
jacket. The harp looks very graceful; & no Irish landmaid blossoming out of
its breast. Flann Campbell [2] could be a lot better; but the dramatization by
Phelan of his little youngster's impressions of the Blitz is fine.[3] That was
a frightful blow to Jim. And yet there are those who would forgive the
Germans. I didn't quite get the article a la Joyce,[4] & I'll have to read it
again. Margaret Barrington has a close touch of O'Flaherty about her
style—or was it that O'Flaherty had a touch of Margaret? [5] I often thought
she used to give him a hand, but I may be mistaken. Anyway, the book
was well worth producing, & it gives a lift to a few who do not get much of
a chance to get going. I was sorry I couldn't see you the time you rang up:
I had really a nasty chill that descended to the tip of a lung; & at the age of
88 or 98 or thereabouts, such is very uncomfortable.

I have contracted for a new play—"Oak Leaves & Lavender," &
Nathan has written to say "it's fine—far and away the best play on war
he's met for years." When it'll go on, the Lord only knows. What are you
doing up in Malpas? Jack [Carney] hasn't mentioned you in his last few
letters—I thought he was to write something for "They Go—The Irish".

All the best, & a hope I'll see you sometime

Sean O'Casey

[1] The leading essay by O'Casey, "There Go the Irish," in *They Go, The Irish*
(1944), edited by Daiken, is an historical and comical account of Irish fighting men.
[2] Flann Campbell, "Jottings From a Campsite," a description of life in a labor
camp for the Irish in England.
[3] Seamus Boy Phelan, "An Irish Child Meets Nazism," peasant-writer Jim
Phelan's six-year-old son's account of the night his mother was killed in a London air
raid.
[4] Bernard Abarbanel, "Variations on J for Bray," a story written in an imitation-
Joycean prose style.
[5] Margaret Barrington, "Village Without Men," a story of an Irish village where
all the fishermen are drowned at sea, by the wife of novelist Liam O'Flaherty.

To George Jean Nathan

MS. CORNELL

TOTNES, DEVON
8 FEBRUARY 1945

My dear George:

A line to say I got your letter saying how you liked my latest play. Your liking of it was better to me than wine from the Royal Pope. The name "Warld on Wallpaper" didn't seem clear to some, so I have changed it to "Oak Leaves and Lavender; or, A Warld on Wallpaper." I have sent copies of your letter to Bronson Albery, who has the play under contract, & to Macmillan's. Bronson Albery has an option on the American license; but he has told me that he will give every facility to any sensible American offer. I have told this to Dick [Madden] in a letter I hope he got.

I hope you got my letters (2), one of them telling how your book on the Theatre had come at last, & how I was enjoying it. A good & gay book. I have quoted you quite a lot to the USSR. I do wish they would read your books. They have a habit there (I'm afraid) of writing too much & too learnedly about what they love. Stanislavsky's book [1] for instance—so much in it that the thing bewilders. I have some magazines here published in 1924–25, on the theatre, & they are full of scintillating thoughts from many minds that lead one in a hurry everywhere, so that the learner grows old & dies before he can sit down to think. I think they will listen a little to me now; for I have many friends there. I have been in touch with them now since 1925; & am closer than ever. I'm certain their plays will grow big after the war has ended. The theatre here is very bad. I enclose an article by [Ashley] Dukes, "Theatre & Life," with neither the one nor the other near it. All the criticism seems to be the same—no bite nor substance in any of them. Curious man, [Maxwell] Anderson. I never could get any warmth from his work, even from "Winterset." And I'm sorry to read about L[illian]. Hellman. Give my deep love to Eugene & Carlotta.

My love
Ever Yours
Sean

[1] Konstantin Stanislavsky, *An Actor Prepares* (1926).

To Bernard Shaw

TS. CORNELL

TOTNES, DEVON
17 FEBRUARY 1945

Dear G. B. S.:

I am about to bother you with a question—two as a matter of fact: Have you got in your library the following books—Cambridge History of English Literature; Volumes 4 and 5; and History of English Literature by Legouis?

Should you have them, could you lend them to me? Brian, our eldest is preparing for some examination under the aegis of Dartington, and he has been called upon to memorise most of these books. They are in the Dartington Library, but there is such a call on them that they rarely can come into his hands. If you have them, and let me have them, I shall warn him to take great care of them, though unable to guarantee their return in perfect condition. He is a lad, however, who takes great care of books, and has still even the childish ones got for him when he was a kid.

If you havent them—and I imagine, like myself, you havent, having had little use for them—dont bother your sage head about the inquiry, but forget it ever came.

I have just finished correcting proofs of third vol. of semi-biography— Drums Under the Windows—which is to appear in the Spring. And I've written a war play—Oak Leaves and Lavender; or, a Warld on Wallpaper which Bronson Albery has taken for production when he can get a Cast. Nathan says it's a fine play, far and away the best play on war he has encountered for years.

I am sending a cutting from International Literature—No. 3, 1944, showing reproduction of an engraving of yourself, which looks to be a fine one. And a cutting from the New York Times Book Review showing a photograph of yourself which, I think, cant compare with the engraving. You have probably got both of them, but then you mightnt. And a cutting from I. L. giving a review of your Pygmalion. We are all well here, the children growing apace, and staying healthy and strong. It is easier here now since the bombing stopped—it was a nuisance hurrying the children down to the Morrison Shelter in the middle of the night, particularly when your own mind wasnt feeling too steady at all. The workers seem to be coming into some of their own at last. This new International of Labour should be a force for good among men and women.

I do hope you are well and feeling fit. Recently, I had a bad chill which got into the chest and crept down to a lung, but I fought a way well out of it all, and am "all gay" again as the soldiers used to say. I see we were together in the last number of "The Bell."

Eileen sends her love, and so do I.

Ever yours,
Sean

To Jack Carney

MS. NYU LIBRARY

TOTNES, DEVON
22 FEBRUARY 1945

Dear Jack,

Thanks very much for the papers. I have got a photo from Elliott & Fry, & have sent it on signed to Mina. I have written a sympathetic letter to the bold Barney.[1] It is a pity that he has been knocked down with Rheumatic Fever—a dangerous thing to hit a man of his bulk, for it usually weakens the heart. However, Barney has a stout will, & should have a few years in front of him still. I dearly hope so.

Yes; I can see (or hear) the members of the Irish Labour Conference threatening young Jim if he even mentioned the USSR in his prayers. Relatively, it doesn't matter much how this Labour Conference thinks, for its days are numbered, as are all of those charitable, religious, political, & social institutions that fail to add the USSR bead to their rosaries. I daresay, the Skibereen Eagle[2] is busy with a Press excommunication of the Bolshevik Party. But I imagine their right & left Irish flank will soon be turned by the departure of Salazar & Franco. How safe & serene these two vatican vultures looked a few years ago! And now the thunder of the Red guns is heard in old Madrid & just as old Lisbon. Even Dublin's windows rattle a little; for a new & a queer blessing is in the sound of this cannonade *urbi et orbi* benediction. I can quite see that Ireland is panicking with the dint of each trying to say more prayers than the other fellow; for it has to do now with getting on in the world of Gaels. I shouldn't be surprised if there were competitions soon of endurance & speed in the recital of rosary & litany. Catholic Stakhanovites.[3] The Campaign of Emulation. 150 per cent today over quota in prayer & penance.

---

[1] Barney Conway (1882–1965), loyal assistant of Jim Larkin. Apparently all of O'Casey's letters to Conway have been lost, except for one, 9 May 1962, which appears in Vol. III. Conway was the model for the character of Brannigan in *The Star Turns Red* (1940).

[2] See O'Casey's letter to Carney, 26 August 1943, note 8.

[3] The mass Stakhanovite movement in Russia began in 1935 as a result of the extremely zealous example set by such young Russian workers as the miner Aleksei

Who do you think will be our next Uačtarán [President]? Shawn Tee [Sean T. O'Kelly]? He is said to be the choice of F.F. [Fianna Fail] He'd make a comic President. And would [Sean] Lemass then become the Tanaiste [Deputy Prime Minister]? What's the betting on Stephen Gwynn? [4] He's gone back to Ireland, & is writing quite a lot in the Press. And all the intelligentsia recently gave him a welcoming supper. And Roddy the Rover [5] has given him a blessing. I shouldn't be surprised to see Stephen in the Vice Regal.[6]

Yes; it was a fine conference, & looks like we're going to have a Labour International at last.

And imagine the Catholic Archbishop of Westminster [7] having to hob nob with Communist Kuznetzov [8]—your health, Tovarich! Slainte! Where it goes, boys! Pity there wasn't a representative of the Grand Loyal Orange Lodge there, too. He could tell Kuznetzov all about the Boyne. Pity you didn't ask his Grace did he think next year would see an Irish Pope. It's a wonder they don't give Downey of Liverpool [9] a Red Hat as compensation for passing him by twice. What a sweet little, tight little bourgeois is Griffin.

Of course there's no chance of the London Polish Government, per se, going back to Poland. The most of them will never see a government office again. These Stakhanovites are dead. They always were dead, anyway. Now the blast from the Red artillery has blown them into the grave, with The Tablet on top of them.

Bronson Albery, of the New Theatre, has signed a contract for "Oak Leaves & Lavender; or, A Warld on Wallpaper." I heard the other day from George Jean. He says, "Delayed long in transit, I got your play yesterday. I read it at once, & love it. It is a fine play—far & away above any play on war I have encountered for years; & I give you a hearty handshake."

Well, that's something.

I'm glad you got out of the snag. Be careful what you say about these people; & more careful how you say it.

> *All the best to Mina & you.*
> *Yours as ever*
> *Sean*

Stakhanov and many others who exceeded their production quotas. In the context of O'Casey's remarks, a Stakhanovite would be any over-zealous believer.

[4] Stephen Gwynn (1864–1950), Irish writer and nationalist; authority on eighteen-century Ireland.

[5] See O'Casey's letter to Brian O'Nolan, 2 April 1942, note 7.

[6] Vice Regal Lodge, the official residence of the President of Ireland, in the Phoenix Park, Dublin; formerly the residence of the Lord Lieutenant, the British representative in Ireland.

[7] Bernard Cardinal Griffin (1899–1956), Archbishop of Westminster.

[8] Alexis A. Kuznetsov, Communist official, appointed secretary of the party by Stalin in 1945; fell into disfavor at the time of the Stalingrad purges in 1949 and, along with a number of discredited associates, was shot.

[9] See O'Casey's letter to Carney, 10 June 1944, note 3.

To Mina Carney [1]

MS. NYU Library

Totnes, Devon

22 February 1945

Dear Mina,

Inside this envelope's the spaced-out photo sent to me by Elliott & Fry, signed as requested for Tom Curtiss.

I am very glad Jack has got well away from his bout of Influenza—a tough job to do.

I wish they would put a spurt on in the West, & end this damned war once for all. One can't get one's mind away from it, while it lasts. There should be a good chance now to burst ahead. But, of course, I'm no military expert, & don't know the facts. Probably, were I there, I'd be the last to council a push forward. It's all right for the guy in the inner or outward seats to shout; but not so good for the fellow fighting in the ring.

All the best & more. Will be writing to Jack soon.

Yours as ever,
Sean

[1] Mina Carney, sculptor, wife of Jack Carney. Her well-known bust of Jim Larkin is in the Hugh Lane Municipal Gallery of Modern Art, Dublin. She died in 1974 in her early eighties.

To Beatrix Lehmann

MS. Lehmann

Totnes, Devon

23 February 1945

Dear Beatrix:

Very glad to see you are back in Chesil Court. I sent a letter to the Nursing Home, but found out you had gone the day or so before; maybe you got it. It advised you to take things easy (if you could) for some time, & not to worry about faraway contributions. London now, I daresay, is a "Distant Point," [1] but remains very important: Wherever we may be, that is the important place—such is my philosophy.

Bronson Albery has the licence of "Red Roses For Me." He wrote asking for it some time before I had finished "Oak Leaves and Lavender; or a Warld on Wallpaper" (that's its name now), and renewed the contract a few weeks ago, on behalf of the "Una Players." Anyway, I'm not keen to have a connection with them who revel in "Art for Art's sake." I had an experience with "Within the Gates" that I shan't forget in a hurry. Never did I meet with such gigantic conceit with nothing at all behind it. I've seen one who was active in Glyndbourne—Hans Oppenheim [2]—conductor or something; & I don't want to see a second. A for A's sake is all right with one like Yeats or even O. Wilde; but Jasus deliver us from most of the others. Of course I don't include the various Societies who give time and money [to those] struggling to do dramatic work against a thousand obstacles, & generally doing it badly; but this is effort, & has my profound respect.

I should like to get conclusive evidence that Curtis Brown said "I asked exorbitant fees"; I would get into touch with them at once, & remind them of a few things. This—if they said it—is born of malicious spite, for they know I have nothing but contempt for their agency.

I have received the following from G. Jean Nathan who read the MS of "Warld on Wallpaper": "Long delayed in transit, I got the Script yesterday. I read it at once, & love it. It is a fine play—far & away above any play on war I have encountered for years, & I offer you a hearty handshake."

So, according to George Jean you were right (and he's a good judge) about "Warld on Wallpaper."

All the best, & keep as quiet as you can for a time.

Sean

[1] Allusion to Alexander Afinogenov's play, *Distant Point* (1937).
[2] See O'Casey's letter to Jack Carney, 27 September 1943, note 2.

To Beatrix Lehmann

MS. LEHMANN
TOTNES, DEVON
28 FEBRUARY 1945

Dear Beatrix:

Lectures, articles, committees—of course this is not your job; never was; never will be. Your job is circumscribed by the four walls of a theatre; & the main part of your job is acting—a thing damn few can do. Oh, God! When I think of them now strutting the stage! And the bloody British

Council behind them. And the Drama League in front of them; Cema [1] on their left hand, & Ensa [2] on their right. It reads like a worn-out chapter from an early edition of the Old Testament. I, too, am pestered for articles, short stories, & in my "leisure moments" to write appreciations of some book or other; or to read a play, & give the author my "honest opinion" about it. And all for nix! Were I even to read all the play MS I am asked to, I'd have time for neither meal nor sleep, let alone an odd prayer or two. Here before me's the latest book, written by "a workingman." The publishers say "We are enthusiastic about. . . . We think he is a discovery. Irish peasant by birth, Lancashire workingman by upbringing." Well, they haven't made a discovery; but they must find that out for themselves. If I said what I think of the book, I'd make the author an enemy for life. He'd think I was envious. So he will have to make his own discovery too. It is all a great weariness of the flesh. Like those who think they have but to step on a stage to become an actor, so these think they've but to dip a pen in ink to become writers.

I wish I could get conclusive evidence that Curtis Brown said I demanded advances of £500. I have never asked such a sum; never thought of asking it; never was in a position to ask for it. Curtis Brown in my experience, is a most careless and incompetent Firm. To give one instance: A time ago, I was in a bad financial way (I often was) & had to sell out World Amateur rights of Irish plays to [Samuel] French's. This time C. B. were acting as my agents. By accident I got a cutting telling of a production of a play of mine by a Canadian Rep. Co. I wrote asking why they did it without fee or permission. They replied saying French of New York had given permission, & that the fees had been paid to them a month ago. I wrote to French, & discovered that this Firm had more than £350 which they had collected from time to time (some of it 8 months previously), &, as they "didn't know where the author lived, they were keeping it safe for him." And C. B. knew nothing about it. Then it was suggested that both agents should be paid Commission; but the Author's Society intervened. But it was too late to save the World Amateur rights from French.[3] I daresay, I'd ask it, if I thought I'd get it; but as I know I wouldn't get it, I don't ask. But C. B.'s statement is bound to be a harmful one, & I'd like to write to them to tell them what I think.

I shouldn't call dislike of "conceited amateurs, arrogant homosexuals, & impertinent dilettantes" a prejudice. I hate them—except when they're comic, like most of the Irish ones. We don't hate enough in England. The English don't know how. They think it a virtue. It isn't. It shows a lack of life force.

[1] Council for the Encouragement of Music and the Arts, now the Arts Council of Great Britain.

[2] Entertainments National Service Association.

[3] See O'Casey's letter to George Jean Nathan, 28 September 1932, note 2, Vol. I, p. 449, for the reference to the sale of half the amateur rights of *Gunman, Juno,* and *Plough* to Samuel French for £300. Apparently the unfortunate sale was unnecessary.

And don't overdo the work, particularly after an illness. Try to separate what can be done from what can't. Then don't waste time & energy on trying to do the impossible.

All the best,
Sean

To Gabriel Fallon

MS. TEXAS

TOTNES, DEVON
10 MARCH 1945

My dear Gaby & Rose.

Many thanks for the remembrances of Christmas. It seems—I have been so busy—only an hour ago since I wrote last. First, I hope all in a particular house in Whitworth Road are well & thriving. So far, here we are fine, though pretty tired with the many difficulties we had to face during the last five years or so. However, the sirens haven't shrilled now for a long time, and our Morrison shelter hasn't been used for more than a year, and looks rather pathetic in the middle of a room. It was a nasty experience for a time to hear the Heinkels and Focke Wolfes droning, droning overhead, on their way to Plymouth, & to feel the house rocking with the concussion of bursting bombs. I was never a very brave fellow, & it near shook the guts out of me. It wasn't a joyful thing to be sitting on the stairs (there was no room for me or Brian in the shelter) at three or four of a cold morning waiting for the house to fall in on you, & make an end of things. First, we used to climb down to an old cellar, dank & cold as a tomb; but we soon decided it was better to die quick by a bomb than slow by a dose of pneumonia. And days were packed with fears after Dunkirk when everyone saw the German in field and road. And it was a very narrow escape. We decided, whatever happened to stay where we were, & to take with our neighbours all the hardships that might be going. I busied my thoughts for hours thinking out the best way to shelter the children & Eileen (and me-self) from the gunfire that we all felt would soon be echoing along the valley of the Dart, though I knew, sooner or later, the Nazis would go for the USSR, & that there they would find their first deep grave. But I also guessed they'd go for us first, & why they didn't, God alone knows. I felt more than ever my poor eyesight that would leave me helpless when darkness fell. But at least I had had the experience of the war in Dublin with Tommy & Tan, & afterwards our own foolish one, just as deadly; & I knew how easy it was for Life at times to run through, or crawl by, imminent dangers. But, all the same, it wasn't very precious, or pleasant. Strange, though how the mind has to get used to things. At first, we all lepped up at the shrill of the siren; but we soon got tired of that; then I became the "Knocker-up," when I heard the throb of a German Airplane overhead; we got tired of this, too, & then got up in a damned hurry when a falling bomb shook the old house; though I continued to awake Eileen when the siren went so that both could be on the Qui Vive. However, I managed to do a lot of work, even when the airplanes were overhead. Indeed, I got so thoughtless that one night I was so absorbed in work that I forgot the siren had gone; and heard in a distant, vague way the hum of the planes, when suddenly what I would say was a terrific bang near lifted me out of the chair, rumbled the house, sent the windows of one room flying, & the children racing down for shelter. I kept a strict guard for sometime after. However, it would seem to be over now.

I suppose you are still doing drama criticisms? I read that Eire is rapidly becoming the Island of Actors & Authors. By the way, why don't you whisper friendly, as a critic, to A. de Blacam to give up trying to write plays? Didja read his Apologia for King Dan? [1]

Your eldest boy, Francis isn't it?—must be a big fellow now; & all your children must be getting on, & putting Da & Ma into the shade. Our youngest, Shivaun is going on for six; the next 10; & the eldest 16. And the "oul' fella" is 65. Good God! d'ye tell me that, now! Aye, do I, so I do.

Long ago, I corrected the proofs of the latest biographical vol.— Drums Under the Windows, but haven't seen sign nor light of the page proofs; & I don't know when the book will appear. Scarcity of labour.

Well, here's to Kelly & Burke & Shea.

Not forgetting the Fallons & O'Caseys.

> My love to Rose, you, & all.
> *Yours as ever.*
> *Sean*

---

[1] Aodh de Blacam, "What It Feels Like to Be Damned," *Irish Press,* 3 January 1945, an article in defense of his play, *King Dan,* which had been attacked by the Dublin critics. *King Dan,* "An imaginative Drama on the life of Daniel O'Connell and his wife Mary," was produced by Longford Productions at the Gaiety Theatre in Dublin on 4 December 1944, and ran for one week.

To Gabriel Fallon

MS. TEXAS

TOTNES, DEVON

3 APRIL 1945

Dear Gaby: It was most interesting (and gratifying to read your polite thunderbolt launched at de Blacam.[1] What a bluffer the fellow is! His

[1] Gabriel Fallon, "DRAMAMADEASY," *The Standard,* 15 December 1944, a review of Aodh de Blacam's *King Dan.*

distinguished friends & experts behind the green bushes. He hides their
extinguished heads, & does a little private censorship on his own account.
What a player to the gallery he is, exploiting everything—holy angels, holy
nuns, St Patrick, Irish Ireland, and St Stephen Gwynn! But he can't write a
play: not even in the same rank with poor Father [Michael H.] Gaffney. I
daresay he thought—ay, he thought!—he'd be an Irish [Henri] Gheon or
a [Paul] Claudel; well, he won't, not while seamar's the Irish name for
clover. Like him once proving that G. K. C[hesterton]. lived among the
humble workers when he had a flat in Battersea—Overstrand Mansions. I
lived there myself, & I know the "humble workers" are well behind the
flats.[2] I've been behind, among the Communists, & mine eyes have seen
the glory of the Lord as manifested in His own image, living under conditions bearable only to those used to nothing else from their day of birth.
And I can tell you the most snobbish, bourgeois locality in London is the
same row of residential flats that form the face of Battersea, fronting the
Park. The sort that, if they were presented at Court, had a dinner in full
evening dress, with the table flanked by two uniformed footmen hired for
the evening. Park Lane was the home of Democracy compared to it. De
Blacam est de clenda!

Yes, we are a little easier now, though not much. The black-out is
gone; & the danger from bomb-burst and bomb-blast is over for good, I
think; though I won't do any shouting till the last German hands in his
gun. Peace will be very difficult, & the food question will long be a bit of
a worry to those who have children! However, we've managed for six years,
&, I daresay, we can float through another ten. It will take 25 years—maybe
50—to build up England; & as for Europe, outside of the USSR, another 50
or so before the bells can ring with any confidence. But if the people are
the owners & rulers, it won't be so long; & it is likely that the USSR will
pour its energy into the peoples next door to it.

I'm afraid there's a lot of stories knocking around about Shaw that
aren't quite genuine. I've been with him many times, & never once have I
seen him attempt any trick associated with hilarious youth: he has always
acted the part of a man of his age. Indeed, I've got letters from him (before
Mrs. Shaw died) saying "we are terribly lonely, & feel damnably old." I'm
glad you're away from statistics, & hope it means a better job for you.[3]

The case of Frank is a common one—the selfish fearful outlook of the
"craft Unions." Not so very long ago these were the only Unions in existence—it was Jim [Larkin] who first organised the unskilled, & the craft
unions never took kindly to them. The A.F.L. of Labour never did anything for those outside these "favoured unions," & when the I.C. was
formed, did, & are doing, their best to weaken it. I'm afraid it will be like

[2] See O'Casey's comments on Chesterton in Battersea, "A Drive of Snobs,"
Sunset and Evening Star (1954).
[3] After twenty years as a civil servant in the Department of Commerce and
Industry, Fallon had retired on a small pension and was earning his living as a drama
critic and journalist.

that till the conditions become so that life, far from having too many workers—will have too few. Those conditions can come only in collective ownership, a threshold to Communism. And coming it is: it is already doing wonders in the USSR, & soon will, I think, be dominant in Poland, Czecho-Slovakia, Roumania, Bulgaria, & Yugo-Slavia—not to mention Hungary, Italy, & France.

It amuses me to read the Bishops' Pastorals declaiming against "atheistic Communism." No such thing exists. Whether a man (or woman) cries out for belief in the Incarnation, & all that this implies, even from the popular Catholic view, or cries against it, is a matter of indifference to a Communist per se. And that Communism began & ends with Marx! They forget Fintan Lalor; &, having never read, "Das Kapital," don't know that Marx acknowledges his scientific views were largely built on the arguments of a Corkman.[4]

I do hope Frank will be able to make his voyage. Couldn't Jim help you in any way? Why not ask him?

I daresay the Censorship does give an excuse to the mediocre. Any writer who cares a damn about the Censorship is damned himself. How about Frank MacManus? By the way, Barry Fitzgerald is going strong in Hollywood—he, they say, is to get $75,000 for his next picture. Reports say he is going to marry. I'm very much afraid for Will. Never once has he sent me a line for the last nine years. Timid of my advice, I suppose. He gave a glowing interview lately, of how he sprang out of his job, regardless of risk, to plunge on to the stage. Wouldn't let a man plunge! Ne'er a word of your or mine endeavours to convince him of his talent. I may be wrong; but to me, Hollywood, as at present constituted, is not a place for a conscientious artist.

I have written a play called Oak Leaves & Lavender, & Geo. Jean [Nathan] has read the M.S.

He says "a fine play, Sean; far and away above any play on war I have encountered for years. I offer you a hearty handshake."

God knows when it will go on. I have now four major plays that haven't yet had any professional production [5]—if we don't count Shelah's R. R. for Me.[6] However, two of them—the last & R. Roses for Me—are under contract with Bronson Albery of the New Theatre, & that has helped to keep things going.

Recently I saw that Earnan de Blaghd [7] said I was making a pile of

[4] William Thompson (1775–1833), Irish Socialist born in Cork who anticipated the views of Karl Marx. Although he was a wealthy landowner, he was an active force in the Co-operative movement.

[5] *The Star Turns Red* (1940); *Purple Dust* (1940); *Red Roses For Me* (1943); *Oak Leaves and Lavender* (written in 1944, published in 1946).

[6] Shelah Richards directed the premiere of *Red Roses For Me* in Dublin at the Olympia Theatre on 15 March 1943; see O'Casey's letter to Fallon, 20 February 1943, note 3.

[7] Ernest Blythe (1889–1975), Irish politician, Gaelic language enthusiast, and a director of the Abbey Theatre from 1935, managing director, 1941–72. See Blythe's

money, &, naturally, enjoyed the parties organised for me by the Duchesses of England. There you are; though, truth to tell, he's made more money by his patriotism & by staying in Eire than I've made by coming here or by my play-writing.

How's Brinsley [Macnamara]? Has he written anything lately? I see my old friend, Tom Ennis, has passed away.

Well, God be wi' you all.

> *Love to Rose from Eileen & from*
> *me; & to the family.*
> *Yours as ever*
> Sean

---

letter to O'Casey, 29 October 1928, Vol. I, p. 316; and O'Casey's letter to Lady Gregory, 1 November 1925, note 2, p. 154.

From Miss Sheila————[1]

TC. O'CASEY

[TOTNES, DEVON]
9 APRIL 1945

Dear Mr O'Casey,

I read your article "Clericalism Gone Looney" in the *Daily Worker,*[2] and was thoroughly disgusted. It is sad to think that the English public should be given such foul trash to read. If people administer poison causing death they are hanged, and when a person like *you* administers poison that kills the souls of the workers, nothing is said or done. The abuse in your letter shows you are a very low type; by using such language you do harm

---

[1] Miss Sheila————, a young Irish Catholic girl, who had connections with some highly placed Catholic families in England, worked in a factory in London. See O'Casey's linking comment at the end of this typed carbon copy, leading into his reply of 14 April 1945, which indicates that he intended to use the exchange of letters for some future writing, particularly a series of essays about Irish people that he had been collecting under the title "The Green Searchlight." See also his letter to Brooks Atkinson, 17 October 1946, where he describes Sheila as being "too wild to be educated," and mentions her father, an Irish major in the British army who was killed fighting in India. I met Miss Sheila in 1963 in London, and after a considerable time she kindly allowed me to make copies of O'Casey's letters to her, only after I agreed to maintain her anonymity. Eileen O'Casey believes that Sean based the character of Foorawn in *The Bishop's Bonfire* (1955) on Sheila: "I know what prompted Sean to create in it the part of the girl, Foorawn: he remembered a young Irish girl who wrote long letters to him over the years in Totnes, telling him that she had taken a vow of chastity and therefore could never marry." See Eileen O'Casey, *Sean* (1971). pp. 236–37.

[2] "Clericalism Gone Looney," *Daily Worker,* 20 March 1945.

to yourself and to your cause, and every man of honour will despise you for it.

But what is calculated to do enormous harm are the awful lies circulated by such writers as you, and unfortunately believed. The workers believe everything they read in the *Daily Worker,* and that is why it is a crime to write such lies. The Curzon Line was never intended to be the permanent boundary line. And when it was discussed between Poland and Russia, it was the Russians who said the Line would be unfair to Poland! And so they agreed to the *Riga* Line. What's more, in the great Soviet Encyclopedia it is stated that the Riga Line is 50 to 100 kilm. west of the line suggested by Poland in 1920, before Russia and Poland fought, and in your article Russia really won the war when Germany invaded Russia. Stalin and Co. signed a solemn agreement to retire beyond the Riga Line, and release the two million Poles he had seized and carried off to Siberia. He never released them. They are still there. And as soon as the tide turned, and the Russians began to get the upper hand, he broke all his solemn treaties, claiming all that part of Poland he had invaded in the most cowardly way, when Germany had invaded the other side of the country. Now, Mr O'Casey, that is the *Catholic* answer to your article. You make fun of us Catholics believing in the priests, and you say "Archbishop Griffin and his ecclesiastical boyos." Don't you realise how very ignorant you are? Is that the way for a gentleman to speak? Incidentally, you Communists are "yesmen" to Stalin; you take your orders from Moscow, do you not? I will now close. I will not call you comrade; I think of you as my brother in Christ Jesus, and will pray for you. The talents God has given you are being abused. The brilliant literary gifts you possess are wasted. It is a pity—God gave you those gifts, and one day He will ask you to account for them.

> *I remain,*
> *Yours sincerely,*
> *(Miss) Sheila*

A Catholic factory worker—not a *Communist*.

Well, I said to myself, this factory lass is, at least, honest, and she has abused me to my face, appending her name and address to her attack. For my own sake, and for hers, I must reply. So I sent her the following letter:

14 APRIL 1945.

Dear Miss Sheila:

Thank you for your letter. I'm sorry my article disgusted you, though I cant see any reason why it should. It was neither trash, nor was it foul. How in the name o' God could that article kill any worker's soul? Think again, my friend. Dont you see that your own letter confirms what I said that Catholics are all too ready in the use of extravagant language against those who venture to differ from them? What else can one think of "Foul,"

and "Trash" and "Poison for workers' souls"? If a soul be poisoned by
such a simple thing, then the Catholic soul must be a poor thing indeed.
And I am "a low type, too"! That isnt a Christian statement, is it? Just because I countered a Catholic prelate on a political question. Now, maybe,
you see why we have to face and fight the political influence of the Vatican.
Your letter shows how this influence has gripped you, and made you unaware of your relationship with Labour. My article didnt deal with abstract
truth, but merely with facts round a political question. What I wrote about
were facts, and facts cannot be denied. Lord Curzon was no friend to the
Soviet Union, yet it was he who fixed the Curzon line as fair; Churchill is no
friend to Soviet Communism (he did his best to destroy it by aiding the
White Guards under Denikin, giving them a hundred millions to buy arms),
but he, too, says the Curzon Line is a fair one; so does [William] Henry
Chamberlin in his book, THE RUSSIAN REVOLUTION, published by
Macmillan's, and Chamberlin then was, and is now, a bitter enemy of the
Soviet way of life. These are simple facts, and cannot be disputed. The
Riga Line was formed under duress, just as was the boundary line separat-
ing Northern Ireland from Eire. The White Russians and the western
Ukrainians were cut off from their kin, just as the Northern Irish are from
theirs; the former have come back to their brethren—thanks to the might
of the Red Army—; and the Irish will be reunited, sooner or later. As for
breaking "treaties" signed under duress, De Valera broke the Treaty with
England when he abolished the oath of allegiance, refused to pay the
Annuity Tax, and did away with the Governor-Generalship—though he
and his Party took the oath themselves on entering the Irish Parliament;
and no Bishop or Priest said a word against him. Why? My dear girl, to
understand something of the guile of ecclesiastics, particularly Catholic
ones, and even of the Holy Roman Rota, itself, you should read
REMINISCENCES OF A MAYNOOTH PROFESSOR (Maynooth is the
great Irish College for the training of young men for the priesthood.
S. O'C); by Dr. [Walter] MacDonald, Professor of Theology in the College
for forty years. An eminent theologian, he expressly left this book to be
published after his death so that he should be free from the bullying of his
superiors from which he suffered so much during his life in the Seminary.
You should read what he says about Cardinal Logue, Archbishop Mannix,
and many others. Here you have a Catholic, a Professor of theology, an
eminent man in every way, saying far more than I ever said about the
chicanery and deceit of fellow-ecclesiastics. You say factory workers have
no time to read. When I was an unskilled labourer—for forty years—, I
found time to read. So can most workers if they want to. They are reading
more now, and the world's workers are asking many questions of the
clergy, though the clergy dont like it. But they will have to answer.

Yours sincerely,
Sean O'Casey

To Jack Carney

MS. NYU LIBRARY

TOTNES, DEVON

14 APRIL 1945

My dear Jack,

Thanks again for the papers. Since writing last (I wrote last), Eileen & I were down (or rather up) with some kind of Influenza; but had to keep going, though both of us had it together. When she fell down, I got up, & staggered about, till I fell down, then she got up—a vice-versa time of it. Afterwards, I got a feverish attack of colitis, that left me sorry for myself for some time. I'm feeling better now; & through it, all but a day, I managed to write a thing for a new Quarterly—The Mint—, to come out in a few months; a chapter or two for the next biographical vol.;[1] & corrected half of the page proofs for "Drums Under the Windows." So I didn't do too badly.

I can hardly credit that yarn about P[atrick] Kavanagh. Are you sure it's true? You know, when I came to London first, it was published that when I went into some Lady's house, at once I roared for bacon & whiskey! Another report said I went about with a black clay pipe stuck in the band of my hat. Neither—to use a phrase of Tass—story in any way corresponded to the facts. It may be the same about Kavanagh. Looks as if Bill O'B. was going to have his own way with Labour in Ireland. I'm afraid it's the one country in the world that will work the miracle of putting the clock back. And the Libel Act saves Bill from criticism. And, of course, he's got the Government, the clergy, & the Banks behind him—Ireland's latest triad.

By the way, what has happened to Peter Newmark? I've sent three letters to him since he went away, & got no reply to any of them. Is he going to disappear like Frank Ryan?

A big blow to us all, the sudden death of F. D. R.[2] Feels like one of the family has gone; or so it does to me. I hope Truman will be worth his name. Churchill and Stalin must be feeling it badly. He was badly needed for another few years.

Since I had the article "Clericalism Gone Looney" in the D.W.,[3] I've been getting letters from the Irish in London about the "foul lies," "poison

[1] "The Raid: An Autobiographical Sketch," *The Mint: A Miscellany of Literature, Art, and Criticism* (1946), ed. Geoffrey Grigson; reprinted with some minor changes as "The Raid," *Inishfallen, Fare Thee Well* (1949).
[2] President Franklin D. Roosevelt died on 12 April 1945.
[3] "Clericalism Gone Looney," *Daily Worker*, 20 March 1945.

for poor souls," etc, till I'm more convinced than ever of the ignorance that can spawn from the cult of the Vatican—as bad as any from the Loyal Orange Order. What a cold sweat they're in over the advance of the Soviet Union; & now Micolaczjik [4]—chance spelling—even, lets them down.

Eileen & I will be very glad to see you & Mina in May. Hope you are doing well. It is fine that the V Rockets will hardly be flying again over your heads. That's a relief that was a long time coming.

All the best.
Yours as ever,
Sean

[4] Stanislas Mikolajczyk (1901–66), leader of the Polish Peasant Party; Prime Minister, 1943–44. Perhaps O'Casey was referring to Mikolajczyk's meeting with Stalin in Moscow in 1944.

To Sgt. Peter Newmark

MS. NEWMARK
TOTNES, DEVON
23 APRIL 1945

Dear Peter.

It was fine to get your letter & to read that you were safe and well. In the Engineers now, eh? [1] Well, you'll have a good job for a good while, building houses & making the crooked ways straight. Such a long time went by without hearing from you that we had become anxious, & felt something had happened. So it had, indeed, a Sargeant, but not, I hope, a fell one. Glad you liked my article on Branson.[2] We are all well here, & easier now since the Sirens ceased whistling. We all feel strongly about Greece; but these things don't get right with the suddenness of a clap of Thunder. Life has to build up, not out of new life, but out of the old life remaining. We can't build life as we'd build a new house out of new materials fresh from the quarry. We have to use the old life with a lot of its follies & ambitions & conceits remaining. However, I don't think we'll have another Chamberlain or Baldwin, & that's a step forward. I don't think many of the war criminals will escape. They're in an ugly position even now; & none, such as they, escape the bitterness of failure; & nothing can be more bitter than the failure of evil. We shall welcome the piece of alabaster. I've asked Eileen

[1] Newmark was now a sergeant in the Engineer Branch, British army.
[2] "Red Grave in Burma," *Daily Worker,* 21 October 1944, a review of Clive Branson's *British Soldiers in India* (1944).

what she'd like that she hasn't got, &, like meself, the list is staggering, from boots to tobacco, from lingerie to lipstick. I heard Eileen murmuring something about a yard of silk, or a pair of silvereen stockings but, for God's sake, because of this dream dont go entering some house at dead o' night to murder the man, & take the silk stockings off the woman's legs.

I've just finished correcting the page proofs of "Drums Under the Windows" 3rd vol. of biography; & I've written a war play, called Oak Leaves & Lavender; or, a Warld on Wallpaper. I sent it to George Jean N——, &, replying, he calls it "a fine play—far & away above any play on war he has encountered for years, & offers me a hearty handshake." But where will it be done? I've now 4 major plays, & none of them have as yet got a professional performance. And yet J. Gielgud, in Theatre Arts Monthly for this April says "We've got the actors and the producers, but where are the plays?" [3] He wouldn't know even if they were sticking up in his arse.

Don't you worry; even amid the ruin & devastation, man has taken a step forward, however indifferent some of them, many of them may appear to be when they are off duty. What we have to do, as Eire, in the shape of a beautiful maiden, told the sad-hearted poet, is to "Keep leathering away with the wattle O!"

Brian is just six foot two now; & Niall's growing so as to be even more at Brian's age; & Shivaun is changing into a slip of a girl, and Eileen is as vigorous & active as ever, and Sean is becoming an old, old, old man. Salud! Saalam! Dumminy Vobiscum.

Well, Hitler is caput. Fascism is destroyed everywhere, save at home by our ain fireside. Here's to seeing you soon on the plains of Totnes.

All the best, with love from Eileen & Brian.

Yours as Ever
Sean

[3] John Gielgud, "The Haymarket and the New: London Flocks to Repertory," *Theatre Arts Monthly,* March 1945.

To George Jean Nathan

MS. CORNELL

TOTNES, DEVON

25 APRIL 1945

My dear George:

I got a letter from Dick [Madden] telling me that Eddie Dowling was out of the question regarding "Oak Leaves & Lavender" (Warld on Wallpaper) because of "Glass Menagerie" [1] becoming a smash hit in N.Y. He seems eager about getting the play for a Mr. [Edward] Choate, to be done by [Edward] Chodorov, two men about which I know nothing. Dick cabled to [Bronson] Albery here, who has the American option, & Albery tells me he thinks Choate wanted to put the play on at a Summer Theatre. I certainly don't like that idea. What do you think of Choate & Chodorov? I'm afraid, I'm getting a little tired of the funny way plays are welcomed in the theatre. In this month's T. Arts Monthly, Gielgud has an article which says "We've got the actors & producers, but where are the plays?" It's funny for me to read this when I remember I have written four major plays,—the worst of them, I'd say, as good, or better than any recently produced here— that have had no professional performance here, nor any sign of one, either. So far, I've got about nine pounds from "Purple Dust" & thirty from "Red Roses"—not a lot for four years. So, in the nature of things as they are, I'm afraid I'll have to give "the back of me hand" to the theatre. I've written an article—by urgent request—on "People & Theatre," [2] but the asker-for-it wouldn't publish it when it came to him. It's extraordinary how hard it is here, in this land of free & open thought, to get a chance to say a free word. As far as support goes, the London theatres are packed; but this is due, admittedly, in the Press—to the fact that fifty per cent of the audiences are Americans.

Our eldest boy, going on 17, has plunged deep into your books. He read an article in an American magazine on Saroyan, previously having heard some talk about "The Beautiful People." I told him of your comments on the playwright in "In This Tent William Saroyan," & gave him the book which held the article.[3] Well, he went from the article to the book, & from that book to others. He's read four of them, now. I've often heard a gurgling laugh from his room as he read. He likes your style. I have never pressed any book on him; nor any of my own ideas; I just talk & comment on things as they come before us; & then let him discover things for himself. Anyway, his Truth is bound to differ from mine, for his world will be, is, different. Selznick's, the Film people, some weeks ago; wanted me to write the scenario from Wolfe's "Look Homeward, Angel," & offered, through McCormick, who got my address from you, a fee of anything from $50,000 to $100,000. It was a big temptation; they wanted a "poet-dramatist"; but I declined. I don't think Hollywood could be good for me. Dick says Chodorov & Choate are O'Casey "fans," but I'd found that some "fans" are a danger, rather than a help. I'd like to know what you think. Edward Choate has been waltzing round "Red Roses" for some time; but has now put it aside till the "end of the war." There are quite a lot of things going to be done at "the end of the war."

[1] Tennessee Williams's *The Glass Menagerie* opened in New York on 1 April 1945, directed by Eddie Dowling, who played the role of Tom.

[2] "The People and the Theatre," *Theatre Today,* March 1946; reprinted in *Under a Colored Cap* (1963).

[3] George Jean Nathan, "And in This Tent, William Saroyan," *The Entertainment of a Nation* (1942).

I've just finished correcting proofs of "Drums Under the Windows," thank God! A job I don't like.

My love as ever
Sean

To Gerald O'Reilly [1]

TC. O'CASEY

[TOTNES, DEVON]
26 APRIL 1945

Dear friend:

You ask me a big question; one that I can only partially answer. At the time of the coming of the Plough and the Stars, I was up to the neck in organising The Irish Citizen Army, and, as well, was suffering from beri beri, partial and painful paralysis, brought about by what is still called, pleasantly enough, mal-nutrition, but whose proper name is starvation. However, I remember the Flag well, and an account of its arrival is given in a chapter of my new biographical book, called DRUMS UNDER THE WINDOW,[2] to be published by the Macmillan Co—I have just passed the Page Proofs for printing. To give you a replica of the flag isnt possible just now. I have a sketch of the banner done by him who did it for a guide to the makers, but to find it would mean a long search, and, at the moment, I havent the time to do this. The sketch is a little too realistic, and the actual design of the banner was more formalised, and much finer looking than the one shown in the sketch. It had a blue field (some say the field was green), on which was the formalised framework of a plough, a rich brown colour, edged with a dark red; over this the constellation called The Plough was superimposed; the banner was edged with deep yellow fringe, and on the top of the staff was a Red Hand—then the badge of the Union—strangling a green Dragon, typifying Capitalism. Its size, I should say, was about eight feet by four. It was carried at the head of the Citizen Army, which was followed by the members of the Irish Transport Union, usually headed by its creator, the redoubtable Jim Larkin. Its meaning, or significance, was, of course, the Union of Heaven and Earth, the Dignity of Labor uniting itself with the Stars; that the workers were one with the highest things of the Universe—which, of course, they are. The origin of the Design is disputed: some say it was designed by George Russell, known as AE. but he himself told me that this wasnt so. Jim Larkin had often complained about

---

[1] Gerald O'Reilly, Transport Workers Union, C.I.O., New York.
[2] See "Under the Plough and the Stars," *Drums Under the Windows* (1945).

the common, dull, and gaudy banners carried by Labor Unions, all vulgar oilpainted things, done badly, and without much imagination. He mentioned that the Irish Citizen Army should show an example of what a flag could be like; and I, for one, assign the suggestion of the design to him. No-one knows where the banner went to during the Rising of Easter Week. Some say it was burned in Liberty Hall, the Union's Headquarters, when it was shelled by the British warship from the mouth of the Liffey; some that it fell from the top of a building held by the I.C.A. when the building went up in flames; some that a British Officer took it away with him after the surrender of the I.R.A. And, by the way, it was Jim Larkin who created the Irish Transport Union, and first made Labor a fighting force in Ireland. Without him, there would never have been the great force which the un-skilled workers became under his great leadership. Of course, Connolly was a great fellow, too, dogged, true, and incorruptible; but he hadnt the amazing magnetism and lovable personality of Larkin. My best wishes to your Union, and a prayer that the workers, the world over, will be the arbiters of their own fate in the coming peace.

[Sean O'Casey]

To Jack Lindsay [1]

PC. S. O'CASEY REV [2]

TOTNES, DEVON

I MAY 1945

Dear Mr. Lindsay,

Your letter confirms my thought—your visit would probably have been a waste of time—yours. I had no idea I'd be lifted up on to the Writers' Committee; I deliberately neglected to notice the preliminary letter so that I might be safely and easily forgotten. I can't work with the New Movement; at best I can but hobble behind, cheering, with the old voice quavering. It is the younger who must go ahead now. My work has been done. I've told Bill Rust many times that my participation in things must be limited to looking out of the window at the fellows who do the work. I have been battered about so much in early times that the effects are apparent now, leaving nothing sound but head and heart. For instance, I must rest my eyes after each little spell of work; one is gone west, & the other isn't like the eye of an eagle. And with three children home every day

---

[1] Jack Lindsay (1900–   ), English writer; active in the Communist Party. He had placed O'Casey's name on the party's Writers' Committee.

[2] This letter was printed in the *Sean O'Casey Review,* Spring 1975.

and little help, I can't conscientiously leave everything to the missus. This eats into one's energies, and takes time, so that I have no chance to sit down to think—much more work—til ten at night; and go on till two in the morning. I am not complaining; I take these things, since they are inevitable, in my stride; I just mention a few facts so that you and others will not take silence and slowness for indifference.

Your letter is glittering with possibilities but the good writer will always be rare. And try to get your workers to accept the fact that a play must be regarded, must be criticised as a "play" and not as a piece of propaganda. Gorki stressed this often and some of his ringing words and advice appeared in "International Theatre" published in Moscow in 1924. And don't let them try to break away from the great and gracious things of the past. The Soviet writers and play producers tried to do this; but it didn't work. TRAM, for instance, tried a "new art" completely cut away from everything "Bourgeois"; but it was a hopeless failure. The Soviet People have realised their error; and it would be a grievous waste of time and energy for us to travel the same insane byway. Try, too, to get me off the Directorship of "Fore Publications." I'm not competent for anything like that now. At present I'm just finishing page proofs of 3rd vol of biography, and expect shortly to be working on the proofs of my new play—Oak Leaves and Lavender.

All the best
Sean O'Casey

To Miss Sheila———

TS. PRIVATE

TOTNES, DEVON
7 MAY 1945

Dear Miss Sheila:
Your big letter has certainly given me a few questions to answer. To reply to some of them would take a large vol. or two; indeed, libraries have been written around them. But I shall answer one or two, and try to answer some of the others.

I was never a member of the Catholic Communion; but was born into, and reared, in what is known as the Protestant Church of Ireland. You will find all this set down in my book, called, "I Knock at the Door." I wont venture into a discussion of what the Catholic Faith may be, the "Pearl of great price," but, I'm afraid, it differs a good deal from the popular conception of it held by so many Catholics. But it would be neither fair nor judicious for me to discuss that question with you. I have no desire to try to wean you from your Faith. But dont for a moment think that everything a priest may say is bound to be part of, and a wise remark, the irreducible minimum of what a Christian Catholic is called upon to believe. Even a Cardinal may talk through his hat, as did Cardinal Logue when he condemned a play which he had never read, written by Yeats; a play that is now universally accepted as a beautiful piece of poetic work. Cant you see, for instance, that an educated man, as every priest is supposed to be, who says of me, or anyone, that "He is an agent of the devil, sent to tempt our immortal souls," must be either a knave or a fool? Not a single thing I have written, as far as I know, could be construed into an attack on the theory of the Catholic Faith; though I often have, and will again, come out against the practice by which it is manifested in the conduct and speech of its believers, or, indeed, of any section of the Christian Church. Too many of your clergy are far too fond of calling down fire and brimstone on simple men, while they leave the mighty ones, mighty because of their exploitation of the workers, high and snug in their fine places. They have changed the word of the Blessed Virgin to "He hath filled the wealthy with good things, and the poor He hath sent empty away." Well, I have done something to show that the Blessed Virgin said the very opposite. If that be the work of the devil, then, as far as I am concerned, so be it. Whether, as you put it, the Catholic Church will "ever be restored in Russia?" I dont know. You might as well ask me if it will ever be restored in England. But the Catholic Faith is not, and never was, since the schism (long before the Communists appeared in the world) the dominant faith in Russia. It was, and is, the faith of what is called The Orthodox Church, which your Church recognises as a valid faith, though schismatic in so far as it refuses to agree to the supremacy of the Pope, and differs in a few other points. There are all kinds of religions in the Soviet Union as well as these; Methodists, Mahommedans, among others; all equal before the law of the state. But, my dear, that isnt a question for me to try to solve.

I'm afraid I cant agree that "the Russians are terrible people." Leave aside your religious doubts for a second, and think of what they have done in a few short years. They havent hidden a single talent in a napkin, and buried both in a field, anyway. From an illiteracy of 85% of the people when the Communists took over, they have created an educated people, with an interest in art and literature that is, as yet, utterly unknown here. I know this, for I have been in touch with Moscow in this way since 1924. One can be content to say that, for instance, for every performance of a Shakespeare play here, there are half a hundred given in the USSR. From a country carrying on agriculture in a most primitive way, they have made of it an industry and a science second to none in any country. And I think we all realise now that the heavy industries of steel and iron and coal were such when the war began that its might staggered and finally routed the then mightiest army in the world—the German Wehrmacht. I enclose a little book, written by Sir Bernard Pares,[1] who isnt, by any means, an out and out admirer of the Soviet system. But you will see from it the amazing things done by a fervent and united people under Socialism in a few short years; and remember it was begun when they were starving, when the whole country had been devastated by the first great war, when these hungry and ragged people had driven from their land half a dozen armies, and when many diseases were rife in the land. So they had to clear away the ruins first before they could start to build; but never daunted, they made of their land a power now second to none the wide world over. Would you say that these were terrible things to do?

As far as I know, and I try to get to know as much as I can, Communists dont "persecute Catholics." In spite of the Pope's encyclical (not infallible, you know) that a "practising Catholic cannot be a Communist," thousands, tens of thousands are. Just as in Ireland, even in my time, the Catholic Church declared that no Catholic could be a Fenian, tens of thousands were, not caring a snap of their fingers for the bishops' condemnation. I know this to be a fact, for I was a Fenian myself. As a matter of fact, in thought I am still a Fenian. No, Communists dont persecute Catholics per se; they dont care what a man may believe; but they will fight Christian and Pagan and Jew who stand to prevent them from overthrowing the power of privilege, the power of property, the right of one man, or a group of men, to exploit the masses. That is all they are concerned with—the conquest of the earth for man's security and comfort, that he may have leisure to enjoy the lovely and fruitful things of life. Of course, in the throes of any revolution, excesses are bound to be committed, or in civil wars either; but bad deeds in these turmoils are not confined to Communists; indeed, the Communists come well out of them. Hitler, for instance, is a Catholic (or was till he died, if he be dead); and when a reader asked the "Universe" once why he wasnt excommunicated, he was told that "Hitler had never encroached, or offended against, the Canonical Laws"! And, remember, the Church herself, did slaughter on no small scale; "liquidating" without mercy, when she had the power, everyone who ventured to differ from her. And remember that during the Irish Civil War, many horrid things were done on both sides, shootings, tortures, and executions. Were these Communists? No, dear lass, they were Catholics fighting Catholics. The creed of Communism—or Socialism for the matter of that—is not destruction; but creation. And nothing can keep it back. I dont like to hurt your feelings, Sheila (since you call me Sean, why shouldnt I call you Sheila?), but Communism doesnt need the sanction of the Holy Father; it is a process of materialistic evolution that neither he, nor any other power can prevent. It is simply a development of human society—first the tribe or clann, then feudalism, then the bourgeoisie revolution, followed by the Industrial revolution, introducing the developing Capitalism, which will finally give place to the ownership of all things

[1] Bernard Pares, *Russia and the Peace* (1944).

by all the people; production, not for profit, but for need. Now, Sheila, dont tell me the silly story that "if a Catholic child was to be educated in Russia, it would be taught the Soviet religion, which is atheism." The child wouldnt be taught any religion. The State as a state has no religion; but tolerates all—a bigger toleration than Catholics show when they have the power. And atheism is neither the religion of the USSR, nor of the Communist Party. Of course, there are atheists in the Communist Party, just as there are among the Conservatives and the Liberals. None of these parties ask as a sine qua non a certain religion to be believed by those seeking membership. For good reasons we Communists dont like Gen. Franco. I'm afraid the "miracle" worked by that general was a wily and unscrupulous one, the employment of the Mahommedan Moors and the ruthless Nazi bullies of Germany, and those of Fascist Italy, too. But dont think it is the Communists alone who are against this Gen.; Jacques Maritain took the side of the Spanish Republicans, and I'll readily make a bet that Maritain knows more about Catholic philosophy than any priest or prelate in your diocese. No, my friend, the Vatican is too wise to canonise Gen. Franco. They will do their best to forget him now. Think again, Sheila, when you say that "all Communist minds seem to think about is the world's goods." Where are the big shareholders, company promoters, company directors, press lords, property owners among the Communists? You'll find these people all good Christians, many of them "practising Catholics," too. Are the treasures, beloved of these, in heaven, where rust nor moth doth corrupt, and where thieves do not break through and steal? No; they are in the strong rooms of the banks. And all of them are hail fellows, well met, with most of the clergy. You wont find many hob-nailed boots treading the Vatican floors—not till the dread circumstances of the war burst open the silent, secret doors for the crowd to enter. And believe me, my dear, there's a fight going on there at the moment for fuller representation among the Cardinals, by the distribution of Red Hats to other countries, rather than to have all the power and privilege retained by an Italianate Conclave. It is the place of aristocratic intrigue, and will continue to be so till the workers of the world take over the power and the glory of the earth.

Surely your own have seen something of the favour shown to wealth and money privilege by ecclesiastics? My own wife was shocked profoundly when she saw the poor Catholic evacuees arrive here, and compared their condition with that of the richer ones. You should have seen how the Catholic workers children were treated in comparison with that lavished on the pupils of the most select Convent of Sharpham, where big fees were paid, of course. Dr. [Douglas] Hyde, the Irish President, in his book, Mo Thuras go hAmerice—My Journey to America [1905], tells us, page 92, that "the Archbishop gave a big, gorgeous, very costly dinner in his honour. There were just Twenty at the dinner, and their united wealth must have represented at least Fifty Million dollars." How much were their workers worth? We arent told.

"Every man is born equal." That was written long ago, before Communism appeared, and it stands today. It is a phrase in the Constitution of the U.S.A. Communists—and Socialists but fight to make its implication a fact.

I am a busy man in more ways than two. With three children going to a day school, so home every afternoon, I and the missus have a lot to do. As well as trying to write I try to give a hand with the house.

You neednt apologise for anything you say or said: Your name and address attached to your letter showed you had the honesty and courage of your convictions; and fully deserved any attention I could give them. And I'm afraid my remark about being a labourer wont be counted for righteousness to me: there was more of conceit than of humility in it. I am rather proud of being able to reckon myself one with the commoner people.

I send you a copy of "I Knock at the Door," which you may, or may not, read, just as you like. It has been banned in Eire.

Whether you ever become a Communist or no, be true to your comrade workers. You will never offend The Sacred Heart by being loyal to your class.

With all good wishes,
Yours sincerely,
Sean O'Casey

P.S. If Pares's book seems tiresome—it's a bit dry, maybe, take it easy. Don't try to read too much at a time. Reading this sort of a book comes only with practice. And when I go to the Quarters of the Anglo-Soviet Unity Council we have here, I'll try to get some simpler books, & send them on to you. *S. O'C.* [2]

[2] The "P.S." was added in longhand.

To Lovat Dickson

MS. MACMILLAN LONDON

TOTNES, DEVON

11 MAY 1945

Dear Mr. Dickson,

I am sending you with this note, the Contract from the Macmillan Co. for "Drums Under the Windows," signed as requested; & as received, save that I have put in the word "Two" instead of "One," in Clause 13; & an additional Clause saying that "the copyright of the book is to be taken out in the name of the author."

I, of course, readily take your word that, in the case of "Cheap Editions" the rights are limited to an edition of a certain size. I want the copyright taken out in my name, because I remember there was trouble with a Film Co. when they did "The Plough" [1] (and what a sorry job they made of it!), & discovered the copyright was in the name of the Company. Not, indeed, that I revere Hollywood—a few weeks ago, I refused an offer to write a Scenario for one of Wolfe's books—"Look Homeward, Angel," though a fee of $75,000 was dangled under my nose.[2] But Hollywood, like us all, must, sooner or later, change with the changing world. Look at the change that has taken place in five years! Lady Gregory said a true thing when she wrote in "The Risin' of the Moon"

> Them that are up shall be down; & them that are
> down shall be up.

Well, when "the down shall be up" I hope they will be well fit for their elevated state. They will be, if all men of intelligence make themselves men of good will. Anyway, one thing at a time: it is good to see that Nazism has turned to dust and ashes. But we had a damned narrow escape. The Swastika near took the place of the Cross of St George—though why the English chose St George instead of St Edward beats me! Though it's just as strange that the Irish think more of St Anthony of Padua than of St Finnbarr of Cork.

I am glad quiet has come to London. No more of those damned sirens. Give my good wishes to Mr. Daniel.

All the best to you.
Sean O'Casey

[1] For information about the film version of *The Plough and the Stars,* made by John Ford in 1937, see O'Casey's letter to Horace Reynolds, 15 February 1937, note 1, Vol. I, p. 648.
[2] See O'Casey's letter to William Herndon, 17 January 1945.

To Miss Sheila———

TC. O'CASEY
TOTNES, DEVON
26 MAY 1945

Dear Sheila:

The news in your last letter has surprised me. I assumed you were a simple Irish girl who had gone to do war-work in an English factory—indeed, you said as much in your first letter to me. Now, though you still are a simple girl, I imagine, very sincere, very charming, and very bewildered at the thoughts in your own mind and those in the minds of others, I find you are very "highly connected." We are all a little bewildered at times. Well, let me first try to deal with what you say in your letter. I am sorry you found my book "very horrid in some parts"; but, then, so is life. Why should a few sentences be worse, or even as bad, as the things in thousands we see in civilised Christian communities? In the lovely greenery of life, the slug is to be seen as well as the butterfly. No, Jennie [1] isnt my wife. She went out of my life when I was eleven, and I neither saw nor heard of her afterwards. Life isnt quite so romantic as all that, Sheila. The "thought equal to the deed" needs a lot of qualification. Curious thoughts arise from the stream of subconsciousness, unsought and unbidden; they are there before we are aware of them. But you know the thought isnt as bad as the deed. The thought may be overcome; the deed, once done, is done forever. All these things are related with man's development; some find it easier to sublimate these things than others. We must be careful how we judge. "Neither do I condemn her." And quite a lot of them are related to the vigour and virility of life. A celibate would be uneasy when a lusty young person would be exhilarated. And immorality isnt all connected with sex. The clerics seem to think so now. But there are Ten Commandments. If the Catholics are to ban books because of authors recording actions of life, then Shakespeare and the Bible—to mention but two—must be banned immediately. But the "Catholic" censors are too cute to venture to do this. It is amusing to read that you had to "cross yourself and pray hard for the devil to leave your soul." It seems a very easy thing for the poor devil to find an entrance into the Catholic soul! Shakespeare's "lover and his lass" are bad examples to us all, but, unfortunately, they are among the immortals. So Father C——— is afraid that if you write to me, you will perish, for, as he saith (and the Holy Ghost) "He that playeth with fire shall perish by the fire." Well, isnt that just laughable. What does the Rev. gentleman mean by *"The* fire"? There are various kinds of fire: fire that consumes and fire that cleanses. Moses wasnt afraid to approach the burning bush. Ashach, Shadrach, and Abednego walked unharmed in the midst of the fiery furnace. Tongues of fire descended on the heads of the Apostles on the first Pentecost; and Elijah went to heaven in a chariot of fire; and a prophet's lips were touched by a live coal from the altar of God. Well, Father C——— doesnt fit, evidently, into any of these categories. An icy refuge is the refuge for him. He seems to be a sorry soldier of Christ. Not for him to advance to meet the foe. They are all, I'm afraid, like him. An ice age has descended upon the guardians of the Faith. There, it seems, they are content to perish. Why doesnt he point out something definite in what I have done, in what I have said, or written, that consigns me to the worm that dieth hot, and the fire that is never

---

[1] Jennie Clitheroe, the girl O'Casey knew as a boy and wrote about in the last chapter of *I Knock at the Door*.

quenched? If he doesnt, or cant, then, by the implication of silence, he is bearing false witness against a neighbour. Perhaps he would tell you what he thinks of a Catholic Archbishop guaranteeing immediate entrance to heaven to young airmen killed in action, provided their parents sent 49 dollars to some Church Fund. Or Cardinal Gasquet's deliberate lying on historical questions to suit his own party ends? But with the world as it is, it seems a waste of time to fling questions at this ecclesiastical antique.

Then, again, he thinks—as you say—I dont know the difference between religion and politics. Maybe I dont. Does he? But what kind of politics, and which religion is in the centre of his mind when he makes this statement? The politics of Aristotle, Plato, Locke, Bentham, or Karl Marx? The Christian Faith, or that of Mahommed, Buddha, Confucius, or Zoroaster? What a world of opposition he can sweep away with those ten words of his! How far away does he sweep it though? A few inches from his own mind only. There he is, his head covered with an ecclesiastical belisha beacon, standing at a point where no-one crosses. Does he mean that as politics are not connected with life though religion is, then religion and politics can have no relationship? Or though religion has a relationship with politics, politics have no relationship with religion? Let me quote two sentences which your reverend friend will readily recognise: "Man does not live by Bread alone"; and "Give us this day our daily Bread." Now the word "alone" makes Bread a very important thing, for it implies that man cannot live without it. Now when Christians say "Give us this day our daily Bread," how do they expect to get it? Is it going to fall in showers of loaves from heaven? Of course not. We have to sow the seed, care the plant, reap the corn, thresh and grind it, carry it from place to place in ships, bake it into Bread, and then distribute it among those who need, and can pay for it. Quite a hard, anxious, and complex job of work, involving the co-operation of tens of thousands of workers. Is your reverend friend going to tell me that this activity—only one of thousands—which not only regulates, but determines, the life of man, has nothing to do with politics; or, if it has, then it has nothing to do with religion? When we, or you, rather, pray for bread, then you have as much right to pray for all other reasonable and necessary things as well—the shelter of a decent home, the wherewithal with which to clothe yourself and your children. But will prayer do it? No; it is useless without work. Houses have to be built, clothes have to be woven, each a hard and serious job, involving millions. With work, but without prayer, these things may be done; with prayer, but without work, they cannot be done. Miracles will never replace hard work. And that is why I am out to give the first place in life to those who do these hard, sacred, and wonderful things. No, my friend; politics may differ from religion, just as one tree may differ from another; but they are both sacred; both inextricably intertwined—from the Christian point of view, and not from mine—, for they are in the fullest sense (politics) the way in which a man can do his full duty to his neighbour, and love him as he loves himself.

When you quote your reverend guardian as saying, "If a rich man exploits a poor man, he can be punished. You can punish individuals, but if a Communist Government were in power you would have no redress; you cannot overthrow the Government"; I get impatient. The man seems to know nothing of present-day economic and industrial life. The rich man now exploits, not one man, but millions. And who's going to punish him for it? Concerning this assurance of the punishing of a rich man who exploits a poor one, let me just quote, not a Communist, but a well-known Catholic apologist. Your friend will find the quotation, I think, in G. K. Chesterton's *What's Wrong With The World*.[2] Here it is: "They jail the man who steals the goose from the common, and exalt to the House of Lords the man who steals the common from the goose." Well, I am out for the restoration of things that will give both common and goose back to the poor man, and land the robber peer in jail. Now consider the position of the workers in a Soviet factory. What they get in labour rewards depends solely on their own competence, energy, and enthusiasm. Socialist competition—not Capitalist cut-throat competition, mind you—between worker and worker, between factory and factory is a very important and sacred thing in the USSR. Each factory that excels in production for the people's needs—not for private or personal profit, mind you—is honoured by the award of the Red Banner of Labour. The victory carries not only glory, but handsome financial rewards. One factory secured 80,000 roubles for the improvement of living conditions in the factory; and 100,000 roubles for distribution as a living conditions in the factory; and 100,000 roubles for distribution as a premium among the workers who contributed to the victory. And the only one who isnt eligible for a share in this premium is the *Director of the factory—the boss*. Now the discipline in a Soviet factory is very strict, and rightly so for the work of every toiler when it is good, conscientious, means a better life for the community and for himself. If he comes, say, ten minutes late to join his shift through any cause within human control, the worker gets an individual warning the first time. The Superintendent or foreman says unpleasant things to him. A bulletin in all shops of the factory names him, and so informs all the other workers of his fault. If the worker commits the same offence within a month, he gets, not only a warning, but a reprimand, and a bulletin again posts his name in all the shops. If he is late again within one month, he faces trial in a people's court. The sentence is usually one of "redeeming labour," of from three to four months, during which a percentage of from 15 to 25% is deducted from his wage during the time the sentence is effective. As for the protection of the worker against the decisions of his Director, supposing one is dismissed for drunkenness, demoralization of other workers, or, above all, for laxity and incompetence, he has the right to appeal to the controlling committee of his trade's Union. If he gets no satisfaction from this committee, he can carry the appeal to the central committee of the

2 Gilbert K. Chesterton, *What's Wrong with the World* (1910).

union. If they agree with the Director, the charge usually remains in force, though the dismissed man may seek reinstatement through court action. So you see the worker has quite a number of channels through which to apply for a fair deal. When if the workers ever objected, a Director replied, laughing, "Why should they? It is for their own good, and for the good of the community. No-one derives any personal profit from it. By diligence, they earn more money for themselves, and if the factory shows larger profits, these are used by the government as capital investment for new factories as a means of lifting the material and cultural standard of living of the community, which, in the last analysis, means the worker and his family. Why should any of our people object to our labour policy when it is all, not for the enrichment of an owner or an investor, but for their own advancement." And dont forget that, in the Soviet Union, work is not considered a curse, but, well done, a glory; that workers there are honoured as they are honoured in no other country. There the landgirl, the miner, and the factory worker appear on the postage stamps as well as the statesmen, the warrior, and the poet. Again and again, one can see in Moscow, and other cities, a row of decorations on the coats of workers, men and women, as rich as those on the tunic of the soldiers. Again your friend says "If a Communist Government were in power you would have no redress. You couldnt overthrow the Government." Isnt this a ridiculous statement! Does he know anything about Communism over and above its name? Why under Communism, even the State would gradually wither away. And it isnt Communism that is the system of life or that of Government in the Soviet Union. It is State Socialism which is the gateway, and will become the leading path, to Communism. Communism isnt a "government." It is a scientific, a planned order of life, an advanced state of social life reached through the material evolution of man, sometimes shoved forward suddenly by revolutions, such as the French Revolution, the Industrial Revolution, and the Bolshevik Revolution of 1917. Communism is for the people, the whole people, and it is not peculiar to a government. If it were a government alone that held the opinion of the government, then that Government could never come to power. It would be still-born. If the people of the USSR had not accepted, and then assimilated the theory of Socialism as put forward by Marshal Stalin and his comrades; more, if the people had not put that theory into vigorous practice, adapting it to the circumstances around them, and outside of them—that is, beyond their frontiers, then, great as Stalin is, and great and persistent as his colleagues were, and are, Socialism could never have grown into the power and majesty and might of the Soviet State. And, by God, fortunate indeed was it for the Soviet people that they could share in the astonishing vision of Stalin, or, if they couldnt, at least, that they had faith to trust in it. Had not the bulk of the people (though many at first opposed the plans), especially the young and enthusiastic, thrown their brain and muscle into the Five Year Plans, then today, the Soviet Union might have been the sorriest Nation under the sun; for the German might, had it succeeded, would have ruthlessly tried to exterminate this old, generous, cultured, and lovable people. Take one thing for instance—the Tractor. This is what is said in the book called MOTHER RUSSIA: "The tractor made the forest-minded muzhik engine-minded, and, in time, as with a surgeon's scalpel, scraped out of him every trace of muzhik spirit. Deep and mighty have been the powers of the tractor in transformation. Above all, it was the tractor that prepared peasant youths by the million for the tank and other mechanised weapons of warfare. And it was this power that so strongly helped to halt, and then destroy, the brilliantly mechanised, the superlatively trained, and merciless Nazi Wehrmacht. The heroic spirit of the Soviet people behind the machine in the airplane, the artillery, the tank, the tommy-gun, and in the factory that finally laid the proud vaunting of Hitler and his murderous gang a thing of dust and ashes."

When you talked of Soviet Life at your dinner among your friends, you quote a Polish Countess as saying "But think of Poland Miss Sheila." Well, think of her, and then think of Poland! What is she doing for Poland? And which Poland does she mean—that of the people, or that of the Pans? She is certainly having a good time of it with her emigre companions. They can have what they conceive to be a good time on fifteen millions a year, given by the Government, all of which is raked from the pockets of the men, women, and children of Britain. But Poland is working out its own destiny, and it is very unlikely that these in London wont get much of a hurrah if they venture to go back to their own townland. And, you tell me, Lady C——— chirupped in with "The Russians (or Russia, but in the first and last analyses, Russia is the Russian People) are terrible; think of their morals!" Aha! think of that, now! But wait a minute: are Tolstoy, Lermontov, Turgeniev, Gogol, Pushkin—to mention a very few— terrible people? Look at the pictures contained in the little book I am sending to you, and then tell me if you think a "terrible people" could do such things? Certainly, the Russians, and the other Nationalities in the Soviet Union are terrible people when they are wantonly attacked, as the Germans found out before Moscow, Leningrad, and Stalingrad; and we have reason to be damned glad that they are terrible people to meet under these circumstances. As for the question, of morality—read the chapter on MORALITY in the book, MOTHER RUSSIA, which deals with facts, and not with venomously fantastic opinions. Isnt it obvious, for instance, that a people so immoral as Lady C——— would like the Russians to be, that it would be impossible for them to put the passionate energy into the Five Year Plans that made Russia mighty in the face of Germany and the whole world? No, my dear, a people sunk in immorality cant do these amazing things. Let me give a few quotations from the book I mentioned: "Morality," says Lenin, "serves the purpose of helping the human society to attain new heights of development, and to rid itself of exploitation of labour." When the writer of the book said to a leader of the Konsomol of

Moscow that the people were growing surprisingly puritanical, she laughed, and replied, "No, we are not puritanical. We do not like the word *puritanism*. We do not condemn sex as a sin. We only advocate sex decency based on the individual's responsibility to himself and to society." When she was asked what she'd do with a boy in her organization who was enjoying himself with one girl after another, she said he would be expelled; and another leader said, "We'd not only expel him, but disgrace him in public and in the press, perhaps even in the *Komsomolskaya Pravda*." Brothels are banned by law. "Were anyone," says the book, "to conduct such an institution secretly, the penalty would be severe—most likely 'the highest measure of social defence'—death by shooting." And divorce is far harder to manage there than it is here. I wonder, now, if some rich man or woman, who gave a money gift to the church now and again, did anything like one of these young people, would his bishop have him publicly condemned, and print his name in the Catholic Press? Not damned likely! These people who say these things about the Soviet Union are just shamelessly and brutally lying, and no measure of truth is in them. As for the Lady's "Ruling Class," in a lot of places they rule no longer, and will never rule again. And it looks as if in some land where they still live and hope, they are going to lose this privilege soon. Their rule here, for instance, is meeting a tremendous challenge. They could never have countered the challenge of the Nazis effectively, couldnt have met it at all, without the united brains and brawn of the whole people. At the moment they are bewildered, knowing not what to do in India, in Burma, in Syria, in Ireland, or about Poland. They either cannot make up their minds, or they havent any longer any mind to make up. And for a long time, it hasnt been the aristocrats, as such, who "ruled," but the big Industrialists, the boyos who act as Directors over a dozen companies either in land, in factory, or in the Press. The only independent daily in the country is the *Daily Worker*. All the others proclaim, not the opinions of the people, but those of Lords Kemsley, Camrose, Beaverbrook, Rothermere, and the rest of them. Not the old Caste, dating from the coming of William of Normandy, but the new money lords rule now. And they will go on ruling till a truly democratic people sweep them away to hell. You remember in Shaw's *Major Barbara*, when Stephen says to the Owner of the Undershaft Munitions Combine, "I am an Englishman; and I will not hear the Government of my country insulted"; Undershaft replies, "The Government of your country! I am the government of your country. You will make war when it suits me; and keep the peace when it doesnt. When I want anything to keep my dividends up, you will discover that my want is a national need. When other people want something to keep my dividends down, you will call out the police and military." The poor, mouthing "Ruling Class" is but the timid and subservient lackeys of the money lords and big industrialists. The rule of the "Lady Britomarts," charming, elegant, and forcible as some of them were, is over forever. The march of events, of man, has put them in the far background. You say "They have a great regard for the priest, Father C———, the Jesuit, because he is like our blessed Lord to them." How is he? Now, how is he like unto him whom you call "our Blessed Lord"? From what you say of him, he apparently has nothing either of poet or Artist in him. Jesus had. Consider the parables, his delight in "the lilies of the field," and many other touches in his talk that proclaimed the artist. He hasnt done anything that anyone has heard of in driving the "money-changers out of the temple," so he hasnt the courage of Christ. He hasnt the broadmindedness, either, for, from what you say, he would be afraid of his life to go about "with publicans and sinners." Whether we believe in the divinity of Christ or not, he was certainly a humanist, and that is a nature denied to your "spiritual guide," or, if he got it as a gift, he has obviously buried it deep in a field, rolled up tightly in a napkin. No, my dear; your Jesuit is evidently a spiritual lath painted to look like iron. In my last, or first letter to you, I said that Churchill, in the days of Intervention against the early Soviet Union, donated a million pounds to helping those who tried to overthrow the establishment of the people's rule; that sum should have been One Hundred, not One, Millions. By the cutting enclosed, marked with a blue X, you will see (referring to an earlier remark) that The Orthodox Church is the power in the Middle East, in Bulgaria, Yugo-Slavia, Romania, and Greece, rather than the Church which acknowledges the jurisdiction of the Vatican. Now, I think I have said enough for the present, and so all the best to you.

Yours very sincerely,
Sean O'Casey

To Jack Carney

MS. NYU LIBRARY

TOTNES, DEVON
27 MAY 1945

Dear Jack,
Mo mhile buidheachas to you for the present of the grand American & Irish tobacco. (The strange words above mean "my thousand thanks"). Both together will form a fine and lasting Irish-American Alliance. I hope things are well with you. Things concerning news must have undergone, or will undergo, a big change since the European war ended. News will hardly come so readily now; or there won't be so much to choose from. But I daresay the Election will give you plenty to do; for a time, anyway. And maybe

the peace will be more strenuous than the war. It looks that way in places. I have seen a few gasp when they learned that the rations were to be further reduced. They were polishing up their gold and silver slippers in expectation that when the lights went up, there would be nothing left to do but dance gay life away. It will be a long time before life becomes gay again. What with coupons & lack of supplies, it looks as if a lot of us would be without a shirt on our back. Back to old times again—for us; not for them. I got used to going without a shirt, as, I suppose, you did; so we won't feel indecent, if the best comes to the worst. But the others! What will they do? Offer their poverty up to God? Lay up treasures in heaven where neither moth nor rust doth corrupt, & where thieves do not break through and steal. That's what a lot of them will have to do. It is odd (not to me or you to whom a little rag had to do for a cambric handkerchief) how precious insignificant things are becoming. An old shirt now, with a button on it is a thing to be prized. I think the middle-class is going; & the "lower" middle-class is gone.

I see the ikey Archbis. of Westminster [Bernard Cardinal Griffin] is lining up with the returning soldiers. We must do justice to the heroes who defended us, & they must not be suffered to sink into beggary again. That's his policy—the troops. But what about the civvies? Doesn't mather a damn if they sink into beggary, I suppose; though they form the bigger part of the people. And the damned injustice of the discrimination! As if the civvies, out of uniform, & in it, weren't in the war, too. What about those who lived & worked in London, Coventry, & all the other Towns? Weren't they in the war? Aye, were they, & for a long and terrible time too. Why even to this day, even Totnes carries about a few scars on her body. But it serves Griffin to use his slimy arguments & tongue-in-the-cheek devotion to the Tommies so as to create, if possible, envy & jealousy between the proletarian who was at the front afar, & the proletarian who was at the front at home. But I don't think Westminster, with a mitre on its head, has a lot of influence now—save among the half illiterate confraternities.

I do hope, if they don't win, that Labour will win enough seats to form a barricade to Tory power. And that, at least, half the Communists standing will get home.

Love to Mina & you.
& thanks again
Sean

To Miss Sheila————

TS. PRIVATE

[TOTNES, DEVON]
[? JUNE 1945]

Comments on a letter from [Father C————]
S.J., and on Sheila's [1]

Stand away from all your beliefs and thoughts, and just regard this Jesuit's letter, unattached to any feeling of friendship for him, or preconceived tendency to think everything he says must necessarily be profound, or even important.

"If you go on as you are going (that is, asking me, O'Casey, questions and reading the answers), you will be in great danger of losing your Faith." Ecclesiastical gunfire, but it's blank. He takes it for granted that your faith is a poor thing. Why not go around wearing pads on your ears and blinkers over your eyes? What is your "Faith" anyway? Neither he nor you seem to be very sure about it. Apart from its decorative features, confraternities, legions of Mary, apostleship of Prayer, and the like, doesnt the Athanasian Creed contain its salient beliefs, with the additions of those dogmas developed from the "Deposit of Faith," and the ordinances instituted by the Church, namely the Seven Sacraments, the Immaculate Conception, and, under very special and peculiar circumstances, the Infallibility of the Church (The Pope, if you like) on questions of dogma, or Faith, and morals? Now what have any of these things to do with the belief that the Transport System, the mines, the means of life should, or should not, be under public or private ownership? Or, to put it as we do, what have they got to do with the control of the Means of Production and Distribution and Exchange; whether these be owned and controlled by private or by public powers? If you say that they should be left in the hands of private ownership, then you argue, not as a Catholic, but as a Conservative. Is that what the Reverend C———— calls the "Church" is concerned [with], not with the greater glory of God (which you so often quote), but with the safety of its colossal pile of wealth in the shape of rent, interest, and profit? Are you in danger of losing your Faith if you venture to say a word about these things? Now, Father C———— (I assume that he is a priest), obviously, isnt destitute. If he were, he couldnt be talking of leaving you in his Will. Therefore, he is an interested party. I notice, too, he is staying at Craigarn Hall, Bridge of Allan—quite a nice place, far away from the sinister, slimy slums of Glasgow. On the Banks of Allan

---

[1] This title appears on the first page, and at the top of each succeeding page the following is repeated: "Comments on a Jesuit's letter and some notes on Sheila's." She had told a Jesuit priest, a close friend, about her correspondence with O'Casey, and she sent the Jesuit's letter of warning on to O'Casey.

Water! A "beauty spot." Why doesnt he, for a change, spend this time in these slums, or in those of Stepney, Bermondsey, or even those of St John's Wood? He'll preach at the workers right enough, but wont live with them. My friend, believing in the right of public ownership need in no way, as far as I can see, prevent you from believing in God, the Father, God, the Son, and God, the Holy Ghost. Friendship with the Soviet Union isnt going to separate you from the friendship of heaven. Your friend says "It is for theologians and philosophers, who have gone through the necessary training, to read and answer such books." Well, isnt this nonsense. On the Censorship Board of Eire that tells the people what they may, and what they may not read, there isnt a single theologian or philosopher. And who differ more among each other than theologians and philosophers? One has given us a proverb: "Odium Theologicum," the enmity peculiar to contending theologians; and it isnt necessary to emphasise the differences that are apparent between one system of philosophy and another. You should have read what Father MacDonald, Professor of Moral Theology for forty years, said about the theologians in Rome. Some of them, unknowingly, contradicting the philosophy of St Thomas Aquinas! If your friend thinks that theologians are the men to deal with questions of social life and economic problems, then he doesnt quite know what he is talking about. I really dont know why I'm wasting my time dealing, or trying to deal with his letter. It is just a medley of whirling statements without any sign of proof whatever behind them. At least I do try when I make a statement to support it with a fact, or a reason in which I thoroughly believe. He's still on about the "bad books." You can see if these thinkers had the power there wouldnt be a book worth a damn left in a library. I can see him hurrying to a huge bonfire, a mass of "bad books" in his arms, sweating under their weight, mad to pitch them into the fire. Oh, let him be about the books.

Next he says "Not one Catholic in the world is a Communist. Anyone who becomes a Communist ceases to be a Catholic." Does he now?

When a Catholic commits a mortal sin, does he cease to be a Catholic? When he happens to be disobedient to one, or more, of the commandments of the Church, does he cease to be a Catholic? I dont think so. And what exactly is the Communism that the Pope has deprecated? He usually qualifies the term with the preface of "Atheistical." But that term doesnt apply in any way to Communism. When the Pope deprecates "Communism," does he include the communism that demands the transference of the ownership of public utilities from private persons or Capitalist Boards to community ownership? That would be impossible, for it is already in force as in armies, navies, roads, bridges, street lighting and paving, policemen, the Post Office, dustmen, officers of health—all familiar and obvious instances. What then is the "Communism" that is in the mind of the Pope? No-one knows. He is careful not to definitively declare what he exactly means by the term he uses. So many Catholics not aware of the definite mind of the church, because the mind isnt definite itself, plunge into what

Father C——— says automatically deprives them of their Catholic connection. I remember in Ireland when the Bishops condemned Fenianism, saying exactly what your friend says of Communism, and some members became troubled. A meeting was called by the Centres, and there on the platform were four priests who were themselves Fenians. These stressed the noble motives of Fenianism, maintaining that as it was no sin to be a Fenian, there was no necessity to mention the matter in confession; and so the question was settled. Does belief in the public ownership of things overthrow the sacramental mystery of baptism? I should like to get the theological opinion of Father C——— on that question.

As for Catholics who have been Communists, I enclose a list of the names of 48 Irishmen (by no means complete) who fell fighting against Franco in Spain in spite of the tirades of bishop and Pope. Not all, but most of them were Catholics, and ten of them were known personally to me. Quite a number survived.

Quite a number of them are still to the fore—you can see the picture of one, Paddy O'Dare, in the enclosed copy of THE IRISH DEMOCRAT; all active in the Labour or Communist Movements; and all Catholics. Would Father C——— say that all of these young men were outside the pale of the Catholic Church, that the Church had no longer any claim on them because they fought against Franco, the church's pet, on the one hand, or were Communists on the other? In the parable when the father said to one son do this, and the son said, I go, sir; but went not; and the second son said, I will not, but afterwards repenteth, and went—during the time of disobedience, did these sons cease to be the sons of their father? Yet Father C———, with a lordly wave of his ecclesiastical hand, would cut off from all communion with the Church Militant all those young and hearty fellows who ventured to think that all the means of life should be owned and controlled by the people. That is what the Socialist Party aims at, and a good many Catholics are members of it, some of them representing it in Parliament. Doesnt Mr Tinker, M.P. agree with Mr Attlee, M.P.? Father C———'s demi-divine fiat wont work.

Your friend says "Hitler a Catholic!!!!!!!" (seven of them!!!!!!! Tell him from me, that one is quite enough; that to overdo a thing is not to do it at all). He goes on: "I fear your friend with all his show of knowledge is either very ignorant indeed or is deliberately trying to take you in."

Now what is one to think of that? How can he prove from a statement that Hitler was a Catholic the deep ignorance of the one who makes it, or that he who makes it is deliberately trying to deceive for his own purposes? Why hasnt he the decency or the charity to ask first for the source of that particular statement? Where or how does he suggest I am "trying to take you in"? Does he mean that I am trying to coax you into becoming a Communist? He can free his tortuous mind from that fear. It is obvious from your letters that your mind is too confused, too undecided to be a Communist. Cant he realise that what I have been doing all along is to defend myself and my convictions from mean and lying charges leveled against me and them by persons of his type? Is he to say anything he likes about me, and I never to reply by a word? Is this to be our idea of freedom of thought? Not mine, certainly. I take this from the July issue of THE IRISH DEMOCRAT: "Commenting on Adolf Hitler's death in Berlin, "Spectator" writing in the Leader Page Parade of THE INDEPENDENT (an Irish paper, daily) claims to have met Hitler several times. He says that the Leader's only private life was an occasional mountain walk. The writer also reveals this "curious" fact. A year before the world war a new German Who's Who was published. The fuehrer had the first page all to himself, of which, obviously, he must have authorised the proof, the long summary of his birth, career, distinctions, etc, ends, laconically, with the words "Religion. R.C."

But it wasnt the "Spectator" who told me the news. It came from a higher authority still. Some time ago, an inquiry asked of him who conducted the Inquiry Bureau of "The Universe," a Catholic professional paper, as you are doubtless aware, "Why was it that Adolf Hitler had not been excommunicated by the Church?" The answer given by this professional Catholic weekly was that "Hitler had not offended against any Canonical Law, and so was not a subject for excommunication." I quoted this in an article for "The Daily Worker," and, of course, it wasnt denied. I took it for granted that Hitler was a Catholic, for "The Universe" would hardly say he was, if he wasnt. So you see, I did not deliberately make a false statement in order to try to "take you in," nor was it deep ignorance that prompted the statement. Father C——— and "The Universe" will have to settle this matter between them. As for "all his knowledge," well, I have little, but what I have, I have had to search it out myself: it wasnt given to me; but though I have little knowledge, I am far from being "ignorant indeed." It is your friend who parades his knowledge, for he is above discussion, and makes every phrase he uses into an ipse dixit.

Let me try, now to murmur a few words about Father C———'s hatred of the Soviet Union as expressed in his reference to what he calls "The Anti-God Front." He builds his animosity up on a public speech alleged to have been made by a Soviet Commissar of Education. But he doesnt say who was this Commissar, or where or when the speech was delivered. I assume that the "copy" of the "Anti-God Front" is a pamphlet published in England in the English language, for he advises you to forever keep on quoting its "words of hatred against the love of a neighbour"; but he doesnt tell us where it came from, when it was translated, who translated it, or how competent the translator may have been in his knowledge of the Russian language. He just makes another ipse dixit of it. In the first place, it is foolish, not to say un-Christian, to condemn a whole people for the speech of a single man, and that man not named, or the time or place given in which the words were spoken. Was Father C——— listening to the Commissar speaking, or whosoever wrote the tirade in the English pamphlet; and, if so, did they take the words down verbatim? If the speaker, as alleged, said "Down with the love of our neighbours," then he, inevitably, set all who listened to him on fire with hatred against each other (supposing they accepted the speaker's admonition), for each in the crowd was neighbour to his fellow—a result that would be palpably absurd. But I daresay there is a Secular part in the Soviet Union (just as there is here); and rightly so, for if men and women are permitted, or have the freedom to preach and adore Deity, then they ought to have the same freedom to deny the existence of Deity, if they wish so to do. This is a deep question around which there must be a lot of liberty; but to say, or imply, that the whole Soviet people was a mass anti-God front is just to be ridiculous. There was difference on these questions even between the leaders—between Lenin and Gorki, for instance; but this didnt prevent them from working in delightful harmony for the common good.

It is childish for Father C——— and his ecclesiastical pals to pick out the Soviet Union as an example of a country in which Atheism is found. It flourishes here just as strongly, and it isnt quite a Communistic growth. Surely Father C——— has read Reade's "Martyrdom of Man," the poems of Shelley and Swinburne and Byron to mention but a few. And, I daresay, he has heard of "The Freethinker," edited by Chapman Cohen, a very able writer, whether we agree with him or no. And the works of Anatole France are there, in English, for anyone who wants to buy them. And Renan, too. And many others. In England it isnt necessary to speak only in private opinions denying the existence of a God—Father C——— doesnt rule the land yet. So his yell against the law of free speech and thought in the Soviet Union is of no account against her.

And Communism doesnt go in for killing priests. If in a revolution, priests are found on the opposing side, they are bound to suffer; but a revolution isnt Communism. The revolution that killed Archbishop Laud wasnt Communistic; nor was it they who did away with Becket. Evidently the priest wants an immunity denied to everyone else: if he speaks as a re-actionary politician, you mustnt contradict him; if he fights as a re-actionary partizan, you mustnt fire at him. Heads, I win, tails, you lose. As for killing, maiming, and torturing, in all common decency, the advocates of Christianity ought to keep their mouths shut. The Church has done more than her share of these things in her time; and, from what Father C——— says, seems to be quite willing to start all over again. The Inquisition in Spain, the Star Chamber, under Laud in England, and Calvin in Geneva— they were all busy. "In the name of religion," Shaw says, "citizens have been stripped of all they possessed, tortured, mutilated, burned alive, by priests who didnt spare even the dead in their graves, whilst the secular rulers of the land were forced, against their own interest and better sense, to abet them in their furious fanaticism." And they are still running fast and furious after the rule of theocracy so that they may have again all the plenitude and the power, to (Shaw again) "take on themselves powers of life and death, salvation and damnation; dictate what we shall all read and think; and place in every family an officer to regulate our life in every particular according to the priest's notions of right and wrong." What Totalitarianism could be worse than this? Well, it's not good enough for me, thank you.

His venomous statement that "Fifty per cent of the Soviet children under fourteen are afflicted with acquired syphillis," is a dirty libel disproved by the facts of what has been achieved by the people. No people in such a woeful condition of disease could have evolved the Red Army that smashed into bloody bits the greatest military power the world had ever seen and felt; nor could they have achieved the colossal amount of work in the field, factory, and workshop that kept that heroic Army fully efficient, and made its power eventually invincible. But oughtnt Father C———, while he's at it, try to dig the beam out of his own patriotic eye before he tries to pick the mote from his brother's? While it has been stamped out of the Soviet Union, the horrible disease is on the increase here, close to his own doorstep.

But tell me why all you pious, loquacious Catholics are so occupied with the question of sex; preoccupied with it, so that you seem to see it everywhere, and think, or dwell on it, morning, noon, and night? Is it because of the Freudian idea of frustrated jealousy, or what? Is it that you cannot help forever thinking of what you think you have renounced? It doesnt seem to me to be healthy. Well, enough of Father C———'s letter except to say he hasnt said anything about the Catholic Archbishop who offered the kingdom of heaven as a going concern for forty-nine dollars.

Thanks for your personal letter which, among other things, tells me you are unsettled in mind, and that you "arent feeling very happy now-a-days." We're all a little unsettled: we cannot hope to come out of a terrible war, and feel elated. We must just meet things as they are bravely, and try to arrange them in a more sensible way for the good of all. You say that Father C——— explains the "difference" between politics and "religion" is that one permits "murder," and the other Doesnt. But first we have to decide what is "murder" and what isnt. Does the Church allow that the secular power has the right and the authority to punish certain kinds of criminals with death, and those also convicted of treason against the State? Did the Church allow that Franco had the secular right and authority to execute those whom he thought to be guilty of attempts to oppose the authority established by him? A number of "Communists" were executed by the Falange State only a week or so ago; quite a crowd of eminent people, here and in other countries, appealed for a reprieve, but the appeal was ignored; and no protest was made by the Church in Spain, or anywhere else. William Joyce is to be tried soon for "adhering to the King's enemies," and, if found guilty, will surely be put to death. Will the Church oppose this sentence? If the Christian State of England has the right to do this, hasnt the Soviet State an equal right to do the same? If this be done by what Father C——— would have to call "Christian and religious" men, then how can he decently blame those whom he would call "anti-God and irreligious" from following their example? It is a "most Christian" act, I suppose for a Christian to put an enemy to death; but a highly reprehensible thing for a "Communist" to do the same kind of thing. The statement that, like Hitler, Stalin is a "murderer of the deepest dye," and that Stalin, "who professes to be the friend of the working-class, has done more to crush the working-class than all the Czars put together," is such as to make one impolite, and say that your Father C——— must be a damned fool. But there's no reason why you should be another. Dont let yourself slide down among the dead men. Dont add to the Athanasian creed, the additions of "I Believe that Stalin is a murderer of the deepest dye." "I believe that there are fifty per cent of Soviet children, under fourteen, suffering from syphillis." "I believe that the Red Army was made into a mighty force by the Soviet Union's encouragement of illegitimate children." "I believe that the Communists, with malice aforethought, slaughtered thirteen thousand (an unlucky number) priests in Spain, which is proved by the fact that all their names are set down, written in a fair hand, and grimly chronicled in Rome"; and all the rest of this tomfoolery. Laugh at this nonsense, and you remain as good a Catholic as ever you were.

I am amused to read that one of your friends said, "If O'Casey were to write to Father C———, on politics and religion, the Jesuit would wipe the floor with him, because the Jesuit has the qualities O'Casey doesnt possess—class, breeding, and spirituality; and he is highly educated, an ascetic." Let the bugles blow! Tell your friend from me that if the said Father C——— is clamorous to argue about religion and politics, any Communist leader will take him on with joy and acclamation. But I write to those only who first write to me—as you did. I value the advice of Polonius about being cautious of entering into a quarrel; but once being forced into one, I can tear and bite as fiercely as an Irish wolf-hound that feared not to face the biggest wolf, and tore the throat out of him. And dont you be awed into dumbness before a panorama of names of teachers and colleges, Louvain, Salamanca, Heidelberg, the Sorbonne, Valladolid, Oxford, and Cambridge. They are on their last legs. And even were each one of them all that it should be, none can give a man what a man hasnt got. No man can become either a fine scholar or a great thinker by simply sleeping and eating for a certain time in a certain building, or by going through a certain ritual under the direction of priestly tutors and priestly dons.

And, by the way, before I forget, success as such is nothing to me; I am indifferent to it. And I dont get any pay, salary, or honorarium for being a member of the "Daily Worker" Editorial Board;[2] nor do I get anything whatsoever for anything I do for Labour or Communism; nor have I ever

[2] See O'Casey's letter to the *Daily Worker,* 10 June 1940, note 1, Vol. I, p. 864.

got a red penny from any of these movements; or from the Gaelic League, or the Republican Brotherhood for which I gave up the leisure of years. All I get is earned by my work as an author.

And dont forget that the O'————'s, [Irish clan of Sheila's family] northern or southern, are far and away an older and nobler family than any the Father C————s, the H————s, and the rest of them can claim to be. If that be worth anything, and it cant be worth a lot, then you and I can say to them, We have been from the beginning; you have appeared on the earth but the day before yesterday.

For God's sake, woman, dont go about repeating what old fossils of aunts say, moaning, "you deserted our Divine Lord"; old fossils who have never looked higher than over a hedge all their lives, and who think they get credit in heaven by having a connection with someone who is a priest or a nun; and so they may go on having a good time in the world outside, while others do the spiritual work for them, as their tenants or workers do the temporal jobs for them. They, I daresay, belong to that oligarchical gang typified by that Duchess of yours who holds the God-given belief that she and her clique are specially adapted by God and nature to rule all the others. Read what Bernard Shaw says about them:

"Their plan is to take one person every ten (say), and make her rich without working by making the other nine work hard and long every day, giving them only enough of what they make to keep them alive and enable them to bring up families to continue their slavery when they grow old and die. This is roughly what happens at present, as one-tenth of the English people own nine-tenths of all the property (These are they who accuse us Communists of ever thinking of the world's goods! S. O'C.) in the country, whilst most of the other nine-tenths have no property, and live from week to week on wages barely sufficient to support them in a very poor way. The advantage claimed for this plan is that it provides us with a gentry (the class gifted for government. S. O'C.); that is with a class of rich people able to cultivate themselves by a rich education; so that they become qualified to govern the country and make and maintain the laws; to officer the army for national defence; to patronise and keep alive learning, science, art, and literature, philosophy and religion, and all things distinguishing great civilization from mere groups of villages. . . . Most important of all, as men of business think, by giving them much more than they can spend, we enable them to save those great sums of spare money that are called capital and are spent making railways, mines, factories, and all contrivances by which wealth is produced in great quantities. This plan, which is called Oligarchy, is the old English plan of dividing us into gentry living by property and common people living by work; the plan of the few rich and the many poor. . . . But the abuses that arise from this plan are so terrible that the world is becoming set against it. With the best intentions, the gentry govern the country very badly because they are so far removed from the common people that they do not understand their needs.

They use their power to make themselves still richer by forcing the com- mon people to work still harder and accept less. They spend enormous sums on sport and entertainment, gluttony and ostentation, and very little on science and art and literature. They produce poverty on a vast scale by withdrawing labor from production to waste it in superfluous menial service. They either shirk military duties or turn the army into a fashion- able retinue for themselves and an instrument of oppression at home and abroad. They corrupt the teaching in universities and schools to glorify themselves and hide their misdeeds. They do the same with the Church. They try to keep the people poor and ignorant and servile so as to make themselves more indispensable. At last their duties have to be taken out of their hands and discharged by Parliament, by the War Office, by the Civil Service, by Parish, District, and County Councils, and institutions of all kinds. . . . The old reasons for making a few people rich while all the others work hard for a bare subsistence have passed away." Bernard Shaw's AN INTELLIGENT WOMAN'S GUIDE TO SOCIALISM; page 30.

It has passed away, and the old fossils of countesses who bleat about "culture and class of the gentry" have all but passed away too. In the times that suited them, they had charm, and did many fine things, and these with the charm shall live forever; but they charm no longer; they have lived too long, and must yield up their power and privilege to sturdier and more energetic life.

When you say you work in L———'s factory, do you mean the one in Greenford? If that be the one, I know the factory as well as you do, but not the workers. I was all through it, and watched the workers working; looked into the First-Aid clinic, and took tea in the restaurant; stood in the tropical heat of the cocoa factory, and stared at the man sweating as he tore open the chests of tea in his frantic effort to keep the filling-machines on the move. And all for whom? A few idle, rich, unmoved by either human being, art, or literature. So it's there you are, is it? Why dont you suggest to Father C——— that he should take a spell of work there? There would be the chance of mortifying the flesh! A work of supererogation. No, not a life of it, to be sure; but just a year of his life spent in a hectic unbuckling of the tea chests to keep the filling-machines going. That's what would bring him into touch with a strange reality. Better by far than wasting his time on the banks of Allan Water. Say I suggested this to him as a work that might add to his own spiritual development, and help to add to the greater glory of God. It would be hail and farewell with him for a time.

The Taylor you mentioned in a letter is surely the Frank Taylor I knew when I lived in Chalfont St Giles. I know him well—a delicate chap whose nerves are a little awry, which makes him somewhat timid; but a fellow with a lot of good qualities. If you should see him again, remember me to him. But what are you doing in a place like that? Are you, too, mortifying the flesh? Seems like it, Sheila, when your spiritual advisers—

God help you—tell you not to murmur, but to store up your weariness and
toil as treasure in heaven. The gang of hypocritical curs! Would they do
it? Why they'd even hurry past the gateway. If you work there, and continue to, then it's for you to join with them who are trying to abolish such
miserable, selfish, savage things from the face of God's earth forever. Otherwise, you are a brake, a clog, a hindrance to the efforts of better and
braver people. If you cant be one with them, then leave them alone. Leave
them to fight their own battle—the last fight they face—in their own way,
unhampered with pious moans about resignation, patience, and nebulous
rewards in heaven. Had I been "Red Mullard," you wouldnt have escaped
so easy. Your place is with the workers in all they do, in all they hope to
do; or, to stand out among their enemies against them. Think carefully,
think long, of the path you want to choose; but having made up your
mind, walk steadily along it to the last hour of your life.

I am a little doubtful as to what to say about your more intimate con-
fidences; but I unhesitatingly say that it is, to my mind, a dastardly thing
to coax, or seduce, a good-looking young girl to pledge herself by a vow to
life-long chastity. And not only to herself does this mean torture, but it
means the same thing to young men attracted towards her in a lovely and
very human way. Dont forget the beautiful story of Romeo and Juliet; and
dont forget that by far the most beautiful of our literature, poetry and
prose, concerns itself with the story of the strange ways of a young man with
a maid. And if you want to choose something from our own country, there
are Dermot and Grannia, Deirdre and Naisi, Cuchulain and Emer, Sarah
Curran and Robert Emmet.

But enough for the present, for this has grown into an epistle, rather
than remaining a letter. I hope the brother with whom you live will grow
into a staunch Socialist.

And dont forget that even Father C. cant keep life from changing,
and that even the teacher has to give place to the pupil.

> I am the teacher of athletes,
> He that by me spreads a wider breast than my own
>   proves the width of my own,
> He most honors my style who learns under it to
>   destroy the teacher.

But your Father C. isnt that kind of a guide. He wants all to throw
a narrower breast than his own; but many there are now, among his own,
who are refusing to comply with him.[3]

I am returning the book G——— C——— & R———'s "Poems",
both autographed, & so, doubly yours. Maybe later on I shall try to say
something about the first book. The second is already judged by Desmond

---

[3] The typed part of the letter ends here, and what follows is written in longhand.

MacCarthy, a far better judge of poetry than I. But one thing—I wish your poet would put more passion into his love lyrics—such as "my love is like a red, red rose; Drink to me only with thine eyes." And I do hope he will go the road of life as bravely as he trod the road of death. And for Christ's sake don't you try to *study* art: enjoy it, or leave it alone. And now, my warm wishes to you, always.

Sean O'Casey

To Miss Sheila———

MS. PRIVATE

TOTNES, DEVON
[? JUNE 1945]

Dear Sheila,

This is a reply, or attempted reply, to your more personal questions. I'm afraid you'd find it difficult to buy most of my books at the moment—shortage of labour makes a reprint difficult. This makes things pretty hard for me; but it cannot be helped. I've just heard a third vol. of biography—"Drums Under the Windows"—that was to come out in Spring, is now listed for the Summer, or, maybe, Autumn. I am, at the moment, at work on the 4th vol (the last, I think), to be called "The Clock Strikes Twelve."

We have three children, the eldest sixteen, the next ten, the third, five. The eldest are boys, the last a girl. The first is named Brian—pronounced Breé-on, the second, Niall,—pronounced Nee'ull; the third Siobhan, pronounced Shiv'aun. Both physically & mentally, they are fine kids. The eldest is 6 foot 1, deep-chested and broad-shouldered; & both of the others promise to be similarly vigorous. My wife, Eileen, is the Secretary of the local Anglo-Soviet Unity Council. Her mother is a Mayo woman; her father was a Westmeath man; & she, herself, was born in Dublin. I am sending you their photos. I haven't a single one of mine own. I have been asked by photographer after photographer to give them a free sitting—they sell them to the Press, etc—but have done so twice only—once here, & once in America. If I ever get one, I'll let you have it. As for having a patron, or having had one, I never had one, & have none now. All my plays were put on in the usual way, by contract between the manager & me. I haven't had a professional production for ten years now; though I have written four major plays since the last one produced, two of them "Purple Dust" and "Oak Leaves and Lavender" claimed as first-class by America's leading Drama Critic. The only "patronage" I have ever had was, when I went to America ten years ago, & hadn't enough money to permit my entrance, & had to get a reference from the Bank, that a friend of mine went Guarantee for £200.[1] The Guarantee was never touched, & was sent back (with many thanks, of course) to my friend as soon as I returned; & once, when I was on the rocks, Bernard Shaw lent me £100,[2] fifty of which I have returned to him; & hope, if I get any success in a production, to send him back the remainder; & that is all.

But what about yourself? I can't quite get how you are placed. I wrote first to you as a simple-minded "factory girl," & now you talk of ladies, Countesses, & duchesses; and quote Shaw & Shakespeare. How do you live? On your factory wage, or what? And where were you educated; & were you another of those who won a Scholarship, God help you! And what are your, or your people's association with Ireland? Your photograph shows the countenance of a very lovely young girl, so why aren't you married? "Answer every man directly; ay, & briefly; ay, and wisely; ay, and truly, you were best."

You see, my friend, we should know the circumstances under which we live, & act within them. There is no reason to be as harmless as a dove; but it is prudent to be as wise as a serpent. If the antagonism of the C———'s would take away your livelihood, or even endanger it, you must go warily. Each of us has to live first of all. Believe me, these kind people—and I assume they are *really* kind—to preserve their privileges, would hesitate at nothing. They would, an' they could, if they thought they were really threatened, soon show you the "love to your neighbour" business, in no uncertain way, in spite of Father C———'s blather. They are threatened, of course; threatened by this dreaded force they call "Communism," which is the upsurge of the Common people—Communism is but its spearhead; & so they rush around, & wail, & smother you with pleadings about your immortal soul. I am sending you a few simple books about the Soviet Union, "the head & front of the offending," though I'm not sure a "battle of books" will convince many. Each, in his own mind, must decide the issue for himself. The books will come under another cover. Later on, I will try to answer some of your reverend friend's delirious exclamations, though, by the way, it wasn't I who said Hitler was a Catholic—it was "The Catholic Universe."

All good & fine wishes.
Yours very sincerely,
Sean O'Casey

1 See O'Casey's letter to Lady Astor, 17 August 1934, note 1, Vol. I, p. 517.
2 See O'Casey's letter to George Jean Nathan, 28 September 1932, note 2, Vol. I, p. 449.

To Guy Boas [1]

TS. BOAS

TOTNES, DEVON

12 JUNE 1945

Dear Guy,

I was, indeed, very glad to learn by your letter that you and yours were safe and sound "saved so as by fire." We, of course, had a taste, a bad taste, of it here; but nothing fell on the hearth. We had windows blown in, slates shattered, two ceilings knocked down, and some crockery broken, before it passed away into "old, unhappy, far-off things, and battles long ago." But it was very trying, and tensed nerves weren't things to be proud of. Eileen and I are feeling a little weary after it all. And, for us, the Home Front hasn't changed. We have still to do most of the housework between us; and will so continue, I fear, for a long time to come.

You are, I think, right about Yeats—he was a bit dictatorial, but it didn't work with me. He wasn't altogether to blame. Those adulatory fools who clustered round him led him on and into it. He and I became fine friends for some years before the end. Whenever he came to London, he sent for me, and we chatted for hours in his lodgings in a street off Lancaster Gate in Bayswater. And when I was in Dublin last, I spent a day in his home at "Riversdale," and played a game of Croquet with him for the first and last time.[2]

At the moment, I am working out a 4th vol. of biographical incidents. The 3rd vol. "Drums Under the Windows" has been passed for Press; and a new play—"WARLD ON WALLPAPER" patterned in "Oakleaf & Lavender" is under contract with Bronson Albery of the New Theatre. I understand that the man who carried on Glyndebourne Opera before the war is to back it, and open up the Lyric Theatre (which he has bought), Hammersmith, with the play. G. J. Nathan, the American critic, has read the MS, and says it "is by far the finest play on war he has encountered for years." I think, myself, it is the best of my last 3 plays; and I am carrying on a correspondence about Catholicity and Communism with a factory girl (who is aided by a Jesuit), as well as writing on the theatre, art, and politics for VOKS, the USSR's Soviet Literary and Art Society—that seeks

---

[1] Guy Boas (1896–1966), teacher and writer; headmaster of Sloane School, Chelsea, 1929–61, where he produced fifteen of Shakespeare's plays, several of which, including *Twelfth Night* and *A Midsummer Night's Dream,* O'Casey saw; see O'Casey's essay, "Shakespeare Lives in London Lads," *The Flying Wasp* (1937); reprinted in *The Green Crow* (1956). Boas was also editor of the educational books department at Macmillan, London. See O'Casey's first letter to Boas, 9 October 1939, Vol. I, p. 747.

[2] See O'Casey's account of that last visit with Yeats in September 1935 at the poet's home in Riversdale, Rathfarnham, in the opening pages of "The Friggin Frogs," *Rose and Crown* (1952).

companionship with similar activities here. So I am busy—too damned busy, if you ask me!

Well, well! to think of Robin in the Rifle Brigade! and but yesterday, I was watching him, a kid, playing Monopoly. Well, God be wi' him. Breon will be registering in another seven months or so. I'm afraid, I don't agree about Eton. Of course, its walls aren't thick enough to keep Socialism out; but it doesn't ring the bells to welcome it. Where are "the sincere Socialists" who have come from Eton? Of course, good-natured and charming lads come from Eton, though the school does its best to ruin them; but nature is hard to beat.

Aw, for God's sake don't you try to tell me you know all about women! They are only beginning to get going. We'll see something more of them in the future, and learn a lot, now that they are pushing their way into full equality with men—and it's damn near time they did it. I'm only beginning to realise what's in Eileen now, and we've been together now for 20 years. She and Breon were the calmest when the German planes were soaring over the trees and towns; and, in my more sober moments, I felt heartily ashamed of my agitation. However, in one of the worst, when the house was rocking, we stopped our dodging from room to room to have a damn fine hearty laugh together at our ridiculous capers. I don't know when I may be in London again. It's hard to get away. I haven't been from the house for six years or seven, and Eileen has been away for a fortnight only during that time. However, we'll see each other some time. And now give my sincere love to Cicely and to Robin, and take a share of it yourself.

All the best,
As ever, yours,
Sean

To Sgt. Peter Newmark

MS. NEWMARK

TOTNES, DEVON
22 JUNE 1945

Dear Peter.

We got the big block of alabaster all right; it came safe and sound and smiling. It has a look of immortality about it. Eileen is to write to thank you for sending it. It must be a fine thing to be in the Intelligence Dept. It should be a cushy job; easy to find the Department; not so easy to find the Intelligence. Here we are in the midst of the Election fight, with Churchill waving a Red Light in everyone's face; & chanting, "Workers beware;

workers take care!" asserting in his spare time that the Tories are the best nurses & nannies the childlike workers can have. I am carrying on a correspondence with a girl, working in a factory, who wrote condemning me furiously for an article in the D.W. on the Vatican. She's Irish & a Catholic; but she has become very friendly, & writes now to "Dear Shawn" while a Jesuit writes to her warning her she is playing with fire when she writes to me. I thought, when I first wrote, that she was a simple factory girl, over from Ireland; but she is well-connected, & spends her week-ends with big nobs. She quotes my letters to them; & I am giving them something to think about—I've just sent her a 5,000 word note!

I hear the man who ran Glyndebourne Opera is interested in Warld on Wallpaper; & may take it on for production. Do you know it is ten years now since I've had a professional production—never since New York's "Within the Gates" production; though I've 4 full length plays in hands since then. How England loves the Arts. And Gielgud writing in the "Theatre Arts Monthly," says "We've got the producers & the actors, but where are the plays"! I see be the papers, that Cema—like the alabaster—is to become immortal. The only note I ever [had] from the British Council of Art & Literature was a request to allow "Juno" to be done into Chinese by the people of Chungking—and no fee offered. But they can have it, & all, & welcome. It's not there the disease is—it's here, right here at home. Yes; his Holiness, the Pope has thundered out against Nazism, now that it is in pieces, & Hitler's safe moling a way somewhere under ground.

Well all the best, & we hope to see you soon.

Eileen sends her love.

Aha, Red Star arise,

The wide world over.

Yours as ever
Sean

To Miss Sheila——

TS. PRIVATE

TOTNES, DEVON
26 JUNE 1945

Comments on Letter from Miss Sheila, enclosing one
from a member of S.J.

Dear Sheila:

You say "My Father C—— is leaving Scotland and coming to London, and I know I shall fight like the devil with him." It looks as if, in thought and feeling, you were his, instead of him being yours, my dear Sheila. Why dont you shake this foolish, ranting fellow off, and be yourself for the rest of your life? And why fight, why try to fight with a fossil? The man is dead to the world, dead in himself, and dead to the meaning and audacity of a living God. Let him go on putting his trust in Franco, now beset on all sides, repudiated even (at the San Francisco Conference) by the Catholic countries of the world; though he saved Spain for Christ the King, with the aid of the Barbarian, Mahommedan Moors, who, according to St C———, loved and trusted him; and the braided bullies of Mussolini and Hitler. "He could tell you (St C——— says) hundreds of stories of the barbarism of the Reds and the heroism of the Crusaders." Dont you see how childish that sentence is? The Bad Boys and the Good Boys. On one side (his) only virtue; on the other (theirs) nothing but guilt. The man must have a childish, melo-dramatic mind. Heroism isnt peculiar to Christians, even to the Catholic ones. Thousands of Christians have died to testify to what they believed to be true, and thousands of Communists have done the same thing. Barbarism and deceit and cowardice arent always on the side of Socialists. Compare the meanness and deceit of Jacob's character—beloved of God—and the generosity and broadmindedness of Esau; of David's duplicity—another one beloved of God; and what about the classic example of Peter's denial of his Friend, when, cursing and swearing, to make it better, he said "I know not the man"!

Imagine any educated or intelligent man advising that when your brothers or anyone else speaks of Germany as a Catholic country, "You should laugh outright, and say 'really! I did not think you were so ignorant.'" Good God isnt it terrible! That's the way this scion of Louvain, Salamanca, the Sorbonne, and God knows where else, clinches an argument. What sort of a man is Father C——— at all, and how did this tiny squirming mind put the comether [1] on you? Your brother wasnt so far out in declaring Germany a Catholic country, that is Germany as a whole and not Germany as distinct from Prussia. In last week's "Universe" we are told that in the Soviet controlled Germany and Austria alone are nearly eight million Catholics. Add those in the parts controlled by the U.S.A. and Britain, then add those in the Rhine Province, plus the minority in Prussia, and you will have, I guess, nearly half—if not more—of the whole German population. Then remember that the Protestants arent unified as are the Catholics, who have forged themselves into one bloc (bar those who are, or will become Communists, growing every day), and is it very much of an exaggeration to say that Germany is preponderately Catholic? "Prussia is Protestant," this learned cleric says, "and Prussia rules Germany." Prussia hasnt ruled Germany for the past ten years. She was ruled, from top to bottom, by Hitler and his gang, and he, according to the "Universe," was a Catholic and an Austrian. It seems that Father C——— doesnt stop a

---

[1] Comether: an Irish expression denoting a sort of spell brought about by coaxing or wheedling; derived from "come hither."

second to think before he ventures to pour out his childish statements. And "Prussia" isnt the Most Protestant country in Europe; it is no more Protestant than Sweden, or Norway, or Denmark; and no more Protestant than England herself, for in normal times, the Catholics of Germany exercised a far more potent influence on politics than the Catholics were ever able to do here since the final settling of Protestantism on English life.

Whether Protestantism be the villainy Father C———— alleges it to be; whether it has been responsible for the war just over, or no, is a question that I have no intention of studying. But if he thinks Catholics cant do a bit of this business on their own, he should read a little history of man's life on this earth when Catholicism was the one religion (Christian) known; books such as CATHERINE, written by one in full sympathy with the sad wife of Henry the Eighth, or GREY EMINENCE by Aldous Huxley, who has full sympathy with Father Joseph. All I would add, in words, to this onslaught on Protestantism by this fierce Jesuit is only the Bible phrase of "How these Christians love one another!"

And isnt he inconsistently Christian, and how does he reconcile it with a pure conscience when he implies that Italy's attack on Abyssinia is to be excused, or even condoned, because England did the same thing a hundred years ago? Is that the Jesuit way of looking at things? What England did, others may do. Oh, Father C————, Father C————! And Selassie, King of the country, is naught but a murderer, a usurper, an unscrupulous nigger chief! Oh, Father C————, Christian charity, Christian charity! I thought all were equal before God? And, if I'm not very much mistaken, he isnt a Negro. But anyway, has a Christian priest any call to refer so contemptuously to any man having authority, even though he be what the priest calls a "nigger"? The Communists could teach this cleric a lesson in politeness to a dark-skinned neighbour. And a dark-skinned Christian, too. Oh, Father C————, Christian charity, Christian charity!

And where has his gospel of "loving your neighbour" gone? Is the "unscrupulous nigger" outside the pale of Christian love? Is this an English outburst rather than a Catholic one? I remember once Lord Salisbury, then Prime Minister of Britain, contemptuously referring to us Irish as "hottentots." Had we been black, he'd have called us "Unscrupulous niggers." In the Soviet Union, Father C———— would be arrested for referring to a citizen as an "Unscrupulous Mongol." There no discrimination between race and race is allowed. All men are equal there: black, yellow, or white; believer or atheist, Christian, Mahommedan, or Parsee.

And imagine the wide scope of his Christian charity when he calls "English Protestantism the Devil's masterpiece." Oh, dont these Christians love one another! I at first thought that he imagined Communism to be the devil's masterpiece, but apparently, I was wrong; or, maybe, there are two of them. The devil is evidently having a fine time of it. And after two thousand years of conflict too.

What a fine idea is that he gave you from the famous example of

Pope Honorius. "If what people say is clearly nothing but abuse, the best answer is absolute silence." This from a man who, in letter and sermon, uses nothing but abuse with which (as he imagines) to confound his enemies. Has he no sense of humour at all? But let him go on: "That is how I should treat Denis' (sic) attentions. If he tries it on again, act the statue. Say absolutely nothing." Mind you, youre not to say nothing, but absolutely nothing; nothing, nothing at all. Imagine a grown man—even apart from any education—thinking like this, writing like this, and the world the way it is. Some (one of them C——) seem to have made not one step forward in thought since God's hand first fashioned them. Here we have the world in the throes of a social, political, and psychological revolution; most of the peoples of the world—in spite of the Vatican and its scarlet-robed and purple-robed boyos—wheeling bravely to the Left; Clericals, Landowners, and Monopolists fighting for their very existence; modern thought from the popular secular books to the monumentous "Golden Bough" of Frazer, turning the popular and scholastic conceptions of Christianity upside down, questioned even by some of their own theologians; the Pope no longer the force he once was, for he is frantically appealing for help, half buried in the ruins of Fascism, which he backed, though it happened to be the wrong horse; the political power of the clergy, so long used for the propping up of money and privilege, going, going, and soon to be gone forever, everywhere; the once despised Red Army victorious on every field, its battalions now standing from Lubeck through the core of Germany, by the borders of Italy, down to the waters of the Helespont and the most lamentable ruins of Troy. And yet Father C—— babbles advice into your ear to "act the statue, and say absolutely nothing," if any Denis should fling a question or two at you. Pygmalion and Galatea in reverse. Well, let's hope, fair Galatea, that even on the counsel of a foolish Jesuit, you wont shrink away into your cold marble again. But cant you see that anyone giving any such advice to the questioning world is utterly unfit, if not utterly unworthy, to take a place among sensible, questioning men and women.

Again, listen to the old, old wail: "If your brothers continue in the same vein they will lose their faith altogether." What faith? That you will lose it if you ask a question about God or man; that you must believe Franco to be a noble, most virtuous gentleman, who fought to make Christ a King; that youngsters in the Soviet Union are riddled with Syphillis; that you must regard Protestantism as a masterpiece of the devil; that there isnt a Catholic Communist from the world's one end to the other; that the gentle Franco waited till he could wait no longer; that Prussia is the most Protestant country in Europe; and so on: unless a man or woman believes all these things, and keeps them whole and undefiled, without doubt he shall perish everlastingly. Jasus! isnt it all very funny! And what is a faith worth that is so easily lost?

Again: "Loss of the faith is the greatest of calamities. Once lost it is seldom recovered. (Lady, beware!) So long as a Catholic retains his faith, even though he has committed all sort of crimes, there is a chance of his recovery." A remarkable, if not a dangerous, statement, surely. So we learn that a man may commit murder, but if retaining his faith, he has a good chance; but—and, lady, mark this well—if he helps a Communist, or believes in any of their sayings, he is damned everlastingly. A Catholic murderer is nearer God than a Communist—the latest tenet of the new dispensation. Well, Father C——— can have it his own way; but were I a Catholic, I'd refuse to be saved that way.

Again: "You mustnt be astonished if religion to worldly people is 'a red rag to a bull,' as you say. 'If you were of the world,' said the Master, 'the world would love its own, but because you are not of the world, the world hates you.' " Well, there's a bit of self-complacent, self-righteous blather for you. Who are, and who have seen, the most hated persons in the world? Who are the most unworldly people among us today? Who are the persons most secure, most comfortable, most prone to seek the things of the world, the honours, the privileges, and the good things that go with them? The most hated, the most unworldly, are the Communists; the rest that love the world are the Christians. In defence of their Socialist country, who are the first to go into the fight, the last to leave it? The Communists. Who are the foremost in every effort, every personal sacrifice to increase the security, to add to the brightness and glory of living of the people? The Communists. These are their privileges and their honours: not big balances in the bank; not sumptuous houses at home and ornate villas abroad; not rich food and gorgeous clothing—they leave these to the holy, sanctified Christians. The people before privilege is their slogan; and so they are not of "this world," and so the worldly, like Father C——— hate them. But they dont give a God-damn for Father C———, even though they were to number a thousand where now there is but one. And they have suffered for it.

> Five-pointed stars were branded on our backs by White Guard bands,
> With our live bodies Japanese engines were stoked,
> Manontov's band buried us alive head downwards in the sands,
> With lead and steel our mouths were choked.
>
> Recant! they commanded in paroxysm;
> But just three words burst from flaming throats
> Long Live Communism!

And for what? For a bright reward hereafter? Not a bit of it. It is done by the Communists because they simply think it right to do so. Additional responsibility is the one reward they seek. Now do the Christians, do the Catholics do likewise? Not on your, or their, life! Have I any tangible reason for saying this? Ay, have I. Here it is: A little while ago, and it is being continued now, a great protesting wail went up from prelate, priest, and layman about the hardship inflicted on Catholics by the fact that, to maintain their own schools, they would have to gather in a great amount of money. They pointed out that to send their children to any other school other than those owned and controlled by Catholic authorities, was to endanger the faith of the children. Now this danger, if the protest be a true one, and the Catholic bishops, without exception, say it is so, then the question is of first importance to all Catholics, rich and poor alike. I have no doubt that the poor will do their best; will the rich ones do likewise? If the faith of the children, even of one child, be lost through having to attend a school other than their own, then these rich ones will be responsible insofar as they may not have given all that they had to save them. Will the H———s, the D———s, the B———s, and the C———s sacrifice their wealth for the sake of these little ones? Will they surrender their Arundales and their Billings to save the faith of the children; will they not only be satisfied, but glad, to live poor, even indigent lives, that the faith of these little ones be made safe? It is their bounden duty to do this; as it is the bounden duty of the rich bishops to live on pure water and bitter bread that this great work may be done. They can say to themselves—as you were told to say to your mother when you entered the convent—Our reward shall be great in heaven; there shall we place our treasure whether neither moth nor rust doth corrupt, and where thieves do not break through and steal. Just think of that glory reserved by God Himself for them! Will they do this really little thing for God? For Christ the King, about whom they so often blather? They have given no sign as yet. Theyre rather fond of the place where moth and rust doth corrupt, if you ask me. Now is their chance to prove how good and pious they are. Will they take it? I'll bet a hundred, a thousand to one, that these unworldly persons will continue to hold their fine homes, add to their balances in the banks as best they can, without losing much sleep over the children of the workers whose faith may be endangered by attendance in secular schools. They'll agitate to get me and others to pay tax to save the children, but curse o' God on the bit they'll tax themselves to do it. They are just a gang of mouthing hypocrites, yelling Lord, Lord, but willing to keep as far as they can from the implications of the call.

Well, so much for Father C——— and his letter. I'm done with him, now. I darent waste my time commenting any more on his childish, hysterical philosophy, piety, and theology that would turn the revelation of his own, and all other, religion into a Punch and Judy Show. So hail and farewell to him.

I dont so much want to convert you to Communism as I do to commonsense; and to realise that you neednt accept as gospel everything said to you by priest, bishop, or even pope. It has for a long time seemed strange to me that while you Catholics give God the attributes of almightiness, allknowledge, omnipresence, mercy, justice, truth, you never associate the name of artist with Him, nor allow that He must have commonsense. As Shaw says in BLANCO POSNET, "you cant cod God"; though that is what Father C——— is trying his best to do; and you are helping him. If you are going to live on in the world, you'll have to listen to all kinds of arguments, and why not? That is one way of learning part of the truth of life.

Oh, for God's sake dont go on telling me that Richard C——— is "profoundly spiritual." And that "all the worship and passion in his soul belongs to his Blessed Lord!" How can you tell? How do you know the thoughts of the man's mind? Does he go round telling people this? How does he show his great spirituality and his passionate love for his Lord? From the picture in the front of his slender book of poems he looks pretty prim; well fed; and trimly dressed. I'm sure he is a very decent man, possibly very charming, even kind and thoughtful; but these things dont make him a saint: thousands have as much and to spare. It would seem that all the C———s have all the grace that God can give. That's a mistake, my lass. They protest a little too much. The Church is making it all too easy to become a saint: the Little Flower, Bernadette, and the rest of them. Evidently, every community, every order must have its quota. If what you say about his mother reviewing his poems before they are published (I presume you mean she would emend them, if she thought it necessary), damns him as a poet. His vision—if he has one—is his alone, and cannot be hers; and as for the passion of love, why that commends itself to our loveliest literature and finest poetry: like Byron's She moved in beauty like the night; Marlowe's picture of Helen, Oh, thou art fairer than the evening air, clad in the beauty of a thousand stars; and Jonson's Drink to me only with thine eyes, and I will pledge thee mine; and all the lyricism of Shakespeare, not forgetting the Bible itself when it sings the Song of Solomon. Richard C——— would do well to give his mother the go-by, as you would do well to listen more to yours. And of course, the holy decision of Simon not to paint any ugly thing or a nude is his own business; but the self-denial doesnt make him a "Great" painter. He paints, you say, holy pictures and society people—a rich and suitable combination for a "great" painter. Oh, dont let this fellow cod you; he's as much a great painter as I am.

Well, so the C——— family helped Hinsley to the purple.[2] Tell them they'll have their reward in heaven for it. I've spoken to the late cardinal— when he was but an archbishop—a big, heavy, lumbering man, whose mind seemed to be anything but that of a brilliant theologian and philosopher. All your swans, sweet lass, seem to be geese. You'll find very few great theologians wearing the purple. They have something better to do. Even Newman—a far, far greater man than Hinsley—you know, wasnt a great theologian; a brilliant controversialist, yes; but theologian, no. So an eminent Catholic theologian says. I'm glad you discovered how delighted

[2] Arthur Cardinal Hinsley (1865–1943), Archbishop of Westminster; appointed Cardinal in 1937.

the convents are when they get a suitable novice with a suitable dowry. It is odd how all these religious, secular and regular, love material things, the dross of this world, the stout cheque, and the tinkling coin. If youre clever, and have got a good education, and have certificates, then they use your talent, give you nix, and devote what you earn to the greater glory of God. In the possession of the wealth of this world, there is no monopoly existing that can stand beside the Vatican. It owns more than two thirds of Spain, it owned vast properties in Germany and Poland; it has huge sums invested in the U.S.A. It owns banks in Southern America, and gigantic properties as well; and why shouldnt this enormous example of international financial power and influence stand out against, and condemn the Communist movement, or any movement of the peoples that would minimise its money power and influence? And this excludes the private investments of priest and prelate who have shares in every industrial and financial activity under the sun; and all the lay Catholic families come a close second; so why shouldnt Lady C——— dread Communism, and call them hooligans, while the Rev. Father C——— tells the world he loathes the men and women who threaten his substantial accounts in the banks, certainly something more than Saving Certificates. These are left for me and you. Of course love of Jesus is behind the bonds. Holy Mary, Mother of God, keep our dividends up! These are they who have devoted their hearts and minds and bodies to the love of Christ, but keep a fine house around it all. And dont you get into believing me to be any kind of philosopher, but just one who is no fool, and has an uncommon share of commonsense.

No, my lass, I wasnt a "problem" child; neither were you. There's no such thing as a problem child. It's fellows like Father C——— and women like Lady C——— who are the problems. Adults just use these words about children to cover and conceal their lack of responsibility and sympathy. It's our teachers, spiritual pastors, and masters who are the problem, who look on punishment as the one way to keep children in fear of them, so that they can enjoy their own selfish ways in life. Lay the lash on their backs, is the common call of the clerics. By God, I'd like to be present some day when a cleric or a schoolmaster was laying the lash on a child's back! "You beat your children," said Stalin scornfully, to Lady Astor when she visited him in the USSR. What a commentary on the followers of Him who said Suffer the little children. The sadistic dastards! And for God's sake dont burden yourself with Father C———'s "dearest wish that you should become a Carmelite before he dies." What the hell's his dearest wish to you? Who the hell's this fellow who goes about with his "dearest wishes" hanging round his neck? There's no more godly sense in such a wish than that of a kid wishing a new toy over the wishbone of a chicken. What is of some importance is the dearest one you wish yourself. My dearest wish is that you get well away from this C——— priest, from the crowd of them, if you can; and live a normal and healthy life, instead of running with every complaint to God for help and advice. Like Catholics torturing priests with every little thing that assails them; having "scruples" about everything they do, and every thought that comes into their heads. For God's sake, dont be a nuisance to God.

A thought has just "come to me like a full-blown rose": Ask Simon, the great painter, who refuses disdainfully, with a prayer for help on his lips, to paint nudes, if he thinks God pulled Adam and Eve fully clothed from the dust of the earth; or were they naked. Doesnt it seem a little supercilious conceit on his (Simon's) part to be embarrassed, or superior to, nakedness, when God didnt mind it, so at all? Naked, we are always ourselves; clothed, we often look like another; the king with his robe; the priest in his vestments; the soldier in his uniform; the judge in his gown; all very grand and dignified, but strip them, and they become themselves, all dignity gone; poor and shivering human beings; unless fine qualities— distinct from fine raiment—of mind and soul illuminate their mortal bodies. Doesnt it look a little blasphemous to regard with scorn the bodies that the Lord God has fashioned?

As a concluding clause, let me try to say a few words on the books and pamphlets you have sent to me. The Chapter, taken from the NINE- TEENTH CENTURY MAGAZINE [3] presents now a pitiable appearance, scored deeply with red and blue by Father C——— hunting for knowledge. The booklet has the aspect of last year's autumn leaves decaying quietly in a heap by themselves. Douglas Jerrold has proved to be a poor prophet. Bet- ter for his fame had he stood with me alongside the USSR; for the stone the builders rejected has become the head of the corner. "We (England) are afraid of a new Spain under Franco. We want a weak Spain allied to France and Russia as a make-weight for our loss of prestige in the Medi- terranean and to provide harbours for our fleet. We are being not only wicked but foolish. There will be no harbours for the allies of Moscow in the Mediterranean, and there will be no Englishman willing to fight the battle of Moscow over the ruins of Christendom. The Spaniards know this, and so do not fear us." Well, time has changed things, and today Madrid is down, while Moscow is up, with her allies having harbours in the Mediterranean. Today, the Leader of the Russ, Stalin, meets Truman, Leader of the Americanos, and Churchill, Leader of the Englishry—but where is Franco? Again "The great South American Republics (Catholic) will not tolerate the League unless and until it recognises the Government of Franco." But these very American Republics, (Catholic) have all re- pudiated Franco, and all that goes with him. Now Franco is making fran- cotic efforts to sort himself in with the new situation. Today, I read, he has sacked a prominent Phalangist from his Cabinet; and the Franco Junta has passed a "new Bill of Rights." But, I'm afraid, it wont do. The day is over for Franco sitting, uniformed and defiant, at his big desk, with a

---

[3] Douglas Jerrold, "Things That Are Not Caesar's," *Nineteenth Century,* May 1938, a review of F. A. Voight's *Unto Caesar.*

crucifix on one side and a huge bottle of champagne on the other. All the loving Fascist encyclicals from the Vatican havent saved him. He is despised and rejected of God. The Republican forces are being brought together by Negrin to get ready for the fight to come. He is meeting all the Republican leaders in Mexico. Doesnt that strike you as strange? Mexico you know isnt a Protestant country; never has been; never will be; but it stands for democracy the world over, a democracy, not only in name, but in content as well; Franco wont even be let say a word as to whom is to control Tangier where he marched his troops so jauntily when he was sure Hitler was winning. Ask Father C——— why the plan against Franco is taking place in a Catholic country rather than in a Protestant one. He'll tell you the Mexicans are Reds, and that he loathes Mexico. He'll soon have to begin to loathe the whole world. Yes; the Champion of Christ the King—Franco—will soon cease to be seen at his big desk, the crucifix at one side of it; a big bottle of champagne at the other. Read the pamphlet of the NINETEENTH CENTURY—scored all over with marked passages to make a Jesuit's sermon—and see for yourself how forlorn and deserted it looks today.

The same can be said for FOR GOD AND SPAIN, written by Aodh de Blacham for THE IRISH MESSENGER.[4] Well, for a start, very, very few, even in Eire, take any notice of the MESSENGER. De Blacham was once a lusty Socialist, but is now something of a professional Catholic; a man who is well-known in Eire for his bad plays, and so takes every opportunity he can get to belittle better plays. He contradicts Douglas Jerrold on the matter of Atrocities. D. Jerrold says, page 17, "There have been no atrocities on Franco's side." "It has been charged against Franco that his men shot their prisoners after victory, and at Badajoz, especially, killed many hundreds. This also is deplorably true. Both sides in this hideous civil war have shot their prisoners." Did Father C——— see this? Which of the two, Jerrold or de Blacham, are we to believe? So we see, according to de Blacham, the Crusaders, fighting for Christ the King, murdered their prisoners, while, according to Mr Jerrold, they did no such thing. And these arguments of these boyos are what the Jesuit builds his sermons out of; shouting about the truth, but ignoring the facts. This is on page 26 of GOD AND SPAIN. Well, it doesnt matter very much now which was right.

De Blacham on page 23 says, too, "Things bulked as Fascism work under the dictatorship of Mussolini, one of the most popular leaders of history." Another foolish prophet! Where's Mussolini now? Ask de Blacham. And the Pope's Benediction at the end of the booklet, bestowing the papal blessing, with knobs on, on the Fascist Gangster, Franco, and his Nazi collaborators, Hitler and Mussolini, for it was their armed forces, in conjunction with the infidel Moors (I daresay, the benediction was

---

[4] Aodh de Blacam, *For God and Spain: The Truth about the Spanish War* (1936).

spread over these, too), that won, for the time being, the struggle for Franco, has proved to be a foolish prophecy too. His darling infant, Franco, is tottering from power; and Franco's comrades, Hitler and Mussolini have disappeared forever from this world.

The book, GUERNICA,[5] proves nothing, except that the town was destroyed. We are wiser now than we were then. We *know* that squadrons of Italians and German planes aided Franco; and the war has shown us that they would spare nothing they could destroy, so it was a small thing for them to put an end to Guernica. Time has told the truth. By the way, this book comes from Eyre & Spottiswoode, of which Douglas Jerrold is a Director.

Concerning the pamphlet, RUSSIA'S WORK IN SPAIN,[6] I need quote but one paragraph from the very last page: "This story is a chapter of modern history, which is still far from being appreciated in this country, where few people recognise the peril from which we so narrowly escaped in 1936–37. At a time when the Government of Spain was being directed from Moscow, France was in the hands of a Popular Front Government, the creation of the Communist Party, whose secretary had described it as 'the prelude to the armed rising by the proletariat.' The plot nearly succeeded. The creation of 'a United front against Fascism,' deliberately recommended to the seventh World Congress of the Comintern as one of the transitional stages to the proletarian revolution, came very near to the realization of Lenin's dream of a Europe red at both ends. It was the national rising in Spain which defeated the plot. That is why we are entitled to hail in General Franco, not only the saviour of Spain but the saviour of European civilization." Well, there's Reginald J. Dingle, of the Western Mail, for you! Well, the plot to form "a united front against Fascism" had to come later; and well it would have been for many had it succeeded then. It was the like of these prophetic fools, Blacam, Dingle, and the rest, that were, insofar as they could, were responsible for the rise and growth of Fascism, the bloody death of millions of men, women, and children, the destruction of numerous cities, and sorrow and shame the wide world over. How can this Father C——— have the damned impudence to send you such things to read now? Is he so woefully ignorant that he cant see their wretchedness and falsity now? Franco the saviour of Europe's civilization! Rather Stalin is the name and Stalin—if any one man did it—is the man who first saved Europe when his gallant Red Army destroyed the German Armies around Stalingrad. Dingle and Blacam will be silent about Franco now. They are hardly the sort to stand up for him now; but maybe C——— will go down fighting by his side. You'll find, my dear Sheila, that these sanctified writers, fighting against "a soul-destroying materialism," got more

[5] *Official Report of the National Government Committee on the Destruction of Guernica* (1938).
[6] Reginald J. Dingle, *"Democracy" in Spain* (1937), a 36-page pamphlet. He also wrote a book, *Russia's Work in France* (1938).

pay for doing it than does Sean, an unbowed materialist, for being a member of the "Worker's" Editorial Board.[7] They have either something to gain for what they do; or something to lose if they refrain from doing it. That's their glory to God in the lowest.

I am sending you back the books, and thank you for letting me read them. For some time on, I shall be very busy with proofs, and with writing out rough draft for new vol. of biography, and, possibly, notes for a new play; so I shall be able only to send you an odd, hasty, short letter in reply to any you may send to me. For the present, Goodnight, Sheila.

Sean O'Casey

[7] See O'Casey's letter to the *Daily Worker*, 10 June 1940, note 1, Vol. I, p. 864.

From Rubinstein, Nash & Co. to Lovat Dickson

TC. O'CASEY

TOTNES, DEVON
3 JULY 1945

COPY LETTER FROM RUBINSTEIN, NASH & CO., 5/6, RAYMOND BUILDINGS, GRAYS INN, W.C.1.

Dear Rache,[1]
re: "DRUMS UNDER THE WINDOWS"
I have now read this book, and would call attention to the following points:
Pages 1 & 18
Is it possible that Messrs. Mahon, Harvey, Jones or Smith, referred to on these pages in derogatory terms, might have a nuisance value?
Pages 24–50
Is the Author's sister-in-law Agatha still alive? If so, she might claim to be defamed in this second chapter of the book.
Page 61 et seq
The Doctor in charge of the asylum, although not mentioned by name, is described in some detail and would presumably be easily identifiable. If alive, he might claim to be injured by this account of an interview with him.
Pages 151–165
In case of any inaccuracy of fact in this story of how Dr. O'Hickey, in the words of the dedication "was driven to poverty and loneliness by arrogant Irish Bishops and the sly deception of the Roman Rota," one or other of the Catholic officials implicated might make a claim. Possibly the Author

[1] Lovat Dickson.

can give you an assurance that the whole story is common history and that all the villains of the piece are dead.

Pages 166–167

Is Miggins a real name? If so, it would be prudent to substitute a fictitious one, as also for the other names mentioned in the anecdote.

Page 172

The unnamed Secretary of the Central Executive referred to on this page might object to the account of his technical assault on the Author.

Page 174

Can D. P. Moran safely be called a "bounder"?

Page 179 et seq

I believe Douglas Hyde is dead, but if not it might be prudent to consider some modification of the references to him.

Pages 193–195

Is Bonem a real name? If so it would certainly be desirable to disguise it and the firm concerned.

Page 224

The middle paragraph contains allegations against Murphy and other employers which would be actionable, if any of them thought fit to seek a vindication of their reputation. I do not know whether this is a practical risk.

Page 226

The same applies to Bimperton, if that is a real name.

Pages 242–243

Dr. Donnelly (if that is a real name) could claim to be defamed on these pages.

Pages 300–301

Lady Oxford might object, if she could deny having made the statement attributed to her. I imagine this is most unlikely.

    I return the book herewith,

Yours ever,
[Rubinstein, Nash & Co.]

To Lovat Dickson

MS. MACMILLAN LONDON

TOTNES, DEVON
8 JULY 1945

Dear Mr. Dickson:

    With this note go the comments made on the points raised by your solicitor on passages in "Drums Under the Windows"; and a fresh dedication of the book to Dr. O'Hickey.

I shouldn't care to have that Solicitor looking over my shoulder while I wrote, even were I writing prayer or hymn.

Reluctantly, I let the little "bawdy" song go, as you suggest. It makes me wild at times to listen to Broadcasters slinging smutty innuendoes out to the listening crowd—smut for smut's sake, sans wit & sans humour. Why isn't this stopped?

> *All the best & thanks.*
> *Yours sincerely,*
> *Sean O'Casey*

TS. MACMILLAN LONDON

8 JULY 1945

Dear Mr Lovat Dickson:

Prefatorily, let me say that in DRUMS UNDER THE WINDOWS, I primarily aim at doing something that Yeats might call "unique"; that the whole work will be a curious biography, entirely, or almost so, different from anything else of its kind; and, in its way, a kaleidoscopic picture of the poorer masses as they surged around one who was bone of their bone and flesh of their flesh. Now I shall try to deal with your solicitor's fearful criticisms.

Pages 1 to 18. These may be put out of our mind. There isnt any fear of them becoming even a nuisance value.

Pages 24 to 50. There isnt the slightest chance of "Agatha" [1] reading the book, and a very remote one, indeed, that she will ever hear of it. I heard that she is dead, but I have no proof of it. If she be alive still, she must be a very old woman. There is nothing said of her that isnt a fact, and most of them were the subject of gossip by the neighbours who lived around her. And it is almost certain that the book will be banned in Eire. Your solicitor doesnt know anything of the things said in a neighbourly way among people living closely together. It happens even in convents among nuns. I dont think there is the slightest danger here.

Page 61 et seq. The "doctor" here described never existed. He is purely a phantom of my imagination, as is most of the chapter. He couldnt be "identifiable" since he never lived. And anyway, the incidents, fantastic, took place forty years ago. The whole thing, bar the account of Benson's madness, is, of course, pure sardonic fantasy.

[1] Agatha Casey, widow of O'Casey's brother Tom (1869–1914); see "Poor Tom's Acold."

[2] The account in "Lost Leader" about the Rev. Michael P. O'Hickey, D.D. (1861–1916), Professor of Irish at St. Patrick's College, Maynooth; President of the

Pages 151–165. The whole story is common history;[2] it was a wild time in the Gaelic during the period of the controversy; and the details of the dispute and the subsequent trial before the Roman Rota is given in Dr. MacDonald's REMINISCENCES OF A MAYNOOTH PROFESSOR.[3] Dr. MacDonald was a professor of theology in Maynooth for forty years. However, it might be prudent to soften the dedication a little. As far as I know, the "villains of the piece" are all dead, bar Monsignor Mannix,[4] who is now the Catholic Archbishop of Melbourne. Nothing I have said down, however, is as bad as the things said of him, and published, by Dr. MacDonald. I will send a modified dedication (probably with these comments) to you.

Pages 166–167. As far as I can remember, Miggins is the real name. I can change that, and also the name of the estate which he had charge of.

Page 172. The words show that this is but a bantering account of the interview, just as in the case of a pictorial cartoon.

Page 174. I think so? Curious thing a solicitor asking a question instead of answering it.

Page 179 et seq. Douglas Hyde is not dead.[5] He has the other day retired from Presidency of Eire, giving his bed and board to S. T. O'Kelly.[6] Isnt it like the English not to know anything about a country next door to them; a country theyve governed for seven centuries, and which is still a member of the British Commonwealth. Imagine an educated Englishman not knowing whether Eire's President was alive or dead! Is it any wonder Eire stayed "neutral"? All the main incidents related about Hyde are told with gusto by Hyde himself either in his "Mise agus an Connradh," or in "Mo Thurus go hAmerice";[7] and a good many of them were known to us all golden years

---

Gaelic League, 1898–1904; author of many articles and pamphlets in support of the study of the Irish language; dismissed from his Irish Chair at Maynooth in 1909 over his militant fight for "compulsory Irish" at the National University. After a prolonged and unsuccessful appeal of his case to Rome, he died a broken and forgotten man.

[3] See "The O'Hickey Case" and "Death of O'Hickey" in Dr. Walter McDonald's *Reminiscences of a Maynooth Professor* (1925), ed. Denis Gwynn.

[4] The Most Rev. Dr. Daniel Mannix (1864–1963), Archbishop of Melbourne. Mannix was President of St. Patrick's College, Maynooth, when O'Hickey was dismissed from his Irish Chair.

[5] See O'Casey's letter to Jack Carney, 13 October 1942, note 2.

[6] Sean T. O'Kelly (1882–1966), second President of Ireland, 1945–59. See O'Casey's postcard to him [20 July 1913], Vol. I, pp. 29–30.

[7] Douglas Hyde, *Mise agus an Connradh* (1905), Myself and the [Gaelic] League; *Mo Thurus go A hAmerice* (*My Journey to America*) (1905).

Pages 193–194. "Bonem" isnt the real name of the firm, nor are Jim and Jerry the real names of the brothers who owned it. Bonem, however, is a Latin approximation of the name; but I dont see that that would connect it with identification of the two brothers.

ago; and these, "public property," are just surrounded by me with bantering, and sometimes satiric comments.

Page 224. The allegations against Murphy[8] and other employers are nothing to what has been said and published about them elsewhere. It was known to all men, in Eire and here. There was a public inquiry held in Dublin Castle where Tim Healy, the employers' Counsel, and Jim Larkin, the Labour Leader, had a battle royal, and Tim got the worst of it. It is all old history. I suppose your solicitor, his nose buried in vellum and parchment, never heard tell of it.

Page 226. "Bimperton" isnt the real name of the Firm. This question of signing a declaration not to remain a member of Jim Larkin's Union, on pain of dismissal,[9] was a public matter, and became the reason for the biggest labour fight in history. Everyone in Eire knows about it.

Pages 242–243. Dr. Donnelly is the real name. He has been dead a long time. He was forced to resign as Dispensary doctor on account of the many complaints against him.

Pages 300–301. Lady Oxford avows all this in her own biography.[10]

Note. I'm surprised the solicitor didnt say anything about St Patrick objecting.

Well, I can see nothing in the above that would evoke any inclination on the part of the persons concerned, living or dead, to take any action.

Sean O'Casey

Amended Dedication for DRUMS UNDER THE WINDOWS

To Dr. Michael O'Hickey

A Gael of Gaels, one-time Professor of Irish in Maynooth College. In a fight for Irish, he collided with arrogant Irish bishops, and was summarily dismissed without a chance of defending himself; taking his case to Rome,

[8] William Martin Murphy (1844–1919), conservative Irish Catholic, owner of the *Irish Independent,* the Dublin trams, and many hotels; leader of the employers' association and chief opponent of Jim Larkin and the Irish Transport and General Workers' Union during the 1913 General Strike and Lock-out.

[9] O'Casey himself was dismissed from his job as a common laborer on the Great Northern Railway in 1911 for being a member of Larkin's union. See O'Casey's letter to the *Irish Worker,* 7 December 1911, note 2, Vol. I, p. 10.

[10] In the chapter "St. Vincent Provides a Bed," *Drums Under the Windows.* O'Casey used exact quotations on John Redmond and Rufus Isaacs, Earl of Reading, from Lady Oxford's two-volume *Autobiography* (1920, 1922).

he was defeated there by the subtlety of the bishops, helped by a sly Roman Rota, ending his last proud years in poverty and loneliness.

Forgotten, unhonoured, unsung in Eire, here's a Gael left who continues to say Honour and Peace to your brave and honest soul, Michael O'Hickey, till a braver Ireland comes to lay a garland on your lonely grave.

To Lovat Dickson

TC. O'CASEY

TOTNES, DEVON

14 JULY 1945

Dear Mr Lovat Dickson:

Dealing with DRUMS UNDER THE WINDOWS

What a damned lot of work there is about a book!

The name of MIGGINS has been changed, or marked to be changed, to Caocaun, which is Irish for a blind man; and the words MORE O'FARREL ESTATE (this might identify Miggins) altered to the Eire Gobrath Estate, which might be anywhere in, or outside, Ireland. Page 167. I have altered the name of BONEM to that of Dilish, Irish for reliable and trustworthy. Pages 193–194–195. I have altered the name of BIMBERTON to Gomarawl. Pages 225–226.

and I have marked the bawdy song, WHITE-LEGGED MARY to be deleted. Page 150. I think that is all.

I am enclosing the page proofs, marked as mentioned.

I dont like to bother you further, but venture to ask you if the MS of my play—WARLD ON WALLPAPER, or, Oakleaves and Lavender is anyway near being tackled by the printers? If this query is too much of a bother at the moment, dont trouble to reply till you find it more convenient.

Yours sincerely,
Sean O'Casey.

To Miss Sheila———

MS. PRIVATE

TOTNES, DEVON

22 JULY 1945

Dear Sheila,

What do you mean by "I'm sure you wont abuse—or words to that effect, as Father C——— would say—my confidence, for you are 'one of nature's gentlemen' "? Make no mistake: I am no gentleman born, nor one naturally, nor have I acquired such an accomplishment. I have no interest in the implication. I've never set out to try to be one; & I never will. I am just what I told you I am in my last note to you, so don't be romantic about O'Casey. Is it that you are afraid of what you say? Dont be. Look you, I've taken you into my confidence, too; but I'd be glad if you shouted what I said from the housetops. So far from being a "gentleman," I am an artist, & such a being, as touching his art, is ruthless; so, lady, beware! I am entirely indifferent as to what people say of me, or think of me; being myself always, I care of no other, & am not afraid of myself. Oh, Sheila, what would it profit me to gain the whole world, & lose my own soul—lose myself?

Don't you lose your own soul; don't lose it in that of Father C———, or in that of Lady C———, or of Richard, or of Simon, or of O'Casey. Be yourself at all costs.

Affectionate regards to you & yours.
Sean O'Casey

To Bernard Shaw

TC. O'CASEY

[TOTNES, DEVON]

12 AUGUST 1945

My dear G. B. S.

Greetings. I hope you are well. All well here, except that I am under a periodic week or two of trouble with my eyes. I am, however, well used to it, and, so far, doesn't do much harm, bar the discomfort of the pain.

I want to ask your permission to use, in a future work, your letter to me when I asked you for a preface to THREE SHOUTS ON A HILL,[1] and,

---

[1] See Shaw's letter to O'Casey, 3 December 1919, Vol. I, pp. 87–88.

maybe, one or two of the others, including the letter you sent to me commenting on the play called THE SILVER TASSIE.[2]

Breon has, apparently, got over the difficulty of getting suitable history books. The reason I asked was that he is a mortally shy fellow (mostly), and either too timid or too independent to ask for what he needs. He is near as tall as you, now—six foot one. Looks as if the war would soon end, and that, at long last, we may have something to thank God for. By the way, I'm afraid De Valera's heart isn't so warm as you think it is. He was one who stopped poor schoolchildren from getting meals, because that would be "the thin edge of the wedge of Communism." All the best.

Ever yours,
Sean O'Casey

[2] See Shaw's letter to O'Casey, 19 June 1928, Vol. I, pp. 284–85.

To George Jean Nathan

MS. CORNELL

TOTNES, DEVON
22 AUGUST 1945

My very dear George:

It's sometime since I wrote to you. I've had a painful few weeks with my eyes, & activities had to be controlled. I get these set-backs periodically; they are a bit of a nuisance, but I'm used to them now. Anyway, I think we may regard the war as over, & that is something to be thankful for.

Your Dorothy Thompson can take a rest. Your book hasn't come to me yet; and, of course, I'm waiting for it with postponed enjoyment. I've lent one of your vols. containing an appreciation of Eugene to a friend [Guy Boas]—he's Editor of Macmillan's Educational Books Depart; a Schoolmaster; a lover of Shakespeare; & a fine fellow—the last's important, or most important, item—, who is writing a book on the Theatre. He has, I believe, never read a book by you—, so when he returns the one I lent, I'll send on another.

I think you asked me for a copy of my reference to your criticism on various matters. I enclose a copy here of that particular article, so that you may cast a critical eye over it. I think I asked you if you'd send some of your books to Moscow. If you think well of this; would you send one, or more, or all, to my friend there, whose name & address I append:

M. APLETIN
Vice-President of the Foreign Commission of the Union of Soviet Writers.
POST OFFICE BOX 850
KUZNETZKI MOST. 12
MOSCOW

Mr. Apletin has just sent me some verse by "one of the best of their Ukranian poets, Pavlo Tuchina" eulogising me as man and writer. So, if I'm without honour in me own country, I have found it elsewhere.

I daresay, you've heard of the Old Vic. Theatre. I've just consented to give them a three & a half week's performance of Purple Dust in Liverpool,[1] with an option of a London production, if they think fit. I'm not sure about the nature of the production. The producer is a young & new man who has done work for Unity Theatre, London, & the Citizens Theatre, Glasgow; neither of which means that he is bad or good. Anyway, it will bring in a few pounds till times get better,—& I can stretch out in my own lazy and particular way. The theatre here is no better than it was. Brinsley Macnamara has had a new play on in the Abbey—seemingly, a sequel to "Look At The Heffernans," called "Marks & Mabel," [2] but, I hear, nothing singular about it.

My love
Yours as ever
Sean

[1] See O'Casey's letter to Beatrix Lehmann, 30 September 1945, note 1, for details on the first performance of *Purple Dust* on 31 October 1945.
[2] Brinsley Macnamara's *Marks and Mabel* opened at the Abbey Theatre on 6 August 1945, directed by Frank Dermody.

To Nan Archer [1]

TS. ARCHER

TOTNES, DEVON
25 AUGUST 1945

Dear Nan,

About your request for a reduction in the fee charged for The Gunman—it's this way: Some years ago, I found it necessary to sell out the Amateur rights of The Gunman, The Plough, and Juno; and the firm to which they were sold fixes the fees.

However, in your case, on the understanding that you keep the matter

[1] Nan Archer, Rush, Co. Dublin.

to yourself, you can do this particular performance for, say Ten Shillings and sixpence.

That's curious about the Archers of Galway or Wicklow.[2] My mother's mother came from Wicklow, and, I think, my own mother was born in Delgany. And I have heard when I was a kid that she spent some years when she was young in Galway—possibly with some relatives. But I had friends named Archer who came from Kerry, the same place that gave Ireland Thomas Ashe, though, as far as I know, they weren't relatives. I understand that the Archers were with the Normans when they came to Ireland. Alderman Tom Kelly once told me that they were an old Dublin family of 800 years standing there. My father was of the Limerick branch of the O'Caseys.

All good wishes,
Yours sincerely,
Sean O'Casey

[2] O'Casey's mother's maiden name was Susan Archer, from Wicklow; Nan Archer's family, no relation, came from Galway.

To Horace Reynolds

MS. REYNOLDS

TOTNES, DEVON
27 AUGUST 1945

My dear Horace,

I hadn't a chance to send a line sooner. Busy as hell, for there is no change on the Home Front, here; & we have to do near everything ourselves. I've had a spot of trouble with the eyes, & have had to limit writing a bit for awhile. I get these periodic bouts, but am well used to them by now. Isn't it a fine thing that the Rising Sun has set forever; & you'll have your John & Peggy safe home some day soon; & the thousand other Peggies & Johns everywhere; though the first ten years of peace aren't going to be too hilarious. Macmillan's are to publish "Drums Under the Windows" next month, & I'll send on a copy to you pronto. I return the cheque you so kindly sent to me, feeling that a book is due to you as from one buttie to another. By the way, a lot of "American" curiosities of speech are Dublin. "Quickern" for instance—"I can run quickern t'n you," & "I should of done it" is my own idiom when young; & our youngest, Shivaun, uses it as if to the manner born, though she has never heard it from her "educated" Pa. And Huck Finn's "You dont know about me without you have" etc. is joined to the Irish word "gan" "without"—"Is truagh gan mise i Sasana" I wish I were in England; literally It's a pity without me (to be) in England, and the word "twyste" in your song of the old woman of Slapsadon is as Dublin as they make them. "He's twyste as strong as you" was said by me a thousand times, long, long ago. Ireland has forced her way to many places, without a gun or a saber; merely by her talk.

I do hope you are all well, & as happy as wise persons can expect to be. Here, the Old Vic is to do "Purple Dust" in October, first in Liverpool, & then, maybe, in London—after 5 years of waiting, the play gets a little chance. A new war play of mine, which Nathan thinks is fine, is waiting too. All in good time.

My love to Kay, Peggy, & John, & you.
Sean

To Shelah Richards [1]

TC. O'CASEY

[TOTNES, DEVON]
1 SEPTEMBER 1945

Dear Shelah:

I'm afraid Bronson Albery has made his choice for a producer.[2] He has had the play for some time, and, I think, the Irish producer he first had in mind for RED ROSES was Frank Dermody.[3] He went to the Abbey when he was in Dublin, and was so shocked by the play, MARKS AND MABEL, that he didnt bother to see Frank Dermody. A little illogical, for Dermody cant be held responsible for the plays written by Brinsley Mac-namara; but there you are, and that is the way the human mind works. Bronson certainly didnt think much of Brinsley's play. It would appear that you didnt impress him as a producer; and that, again, is the way the human mind goes.

[1] Shelah Richards, Abbey Theatre actress who played Nora Clitheroe in the first production of *The Plough and the Stars* in 1926, now an independent actress, director, and producer; she produced and directed the first performance of *Red Roses For Me* in Dublin at the Olympia Theatre on 15 March 1943. See O'Casey's letter to Gabriel Fallon, 20 February 1943, note 3.
[2] Albery chose Ria Mooney of the Abbey Theatre to produce (direct) the London premiere of *Red Roses For Me,* which opened on 26 February 1946. See O'Casey's letter to Mrs. Una Gwynn Albery, 6 March 1946, note 1.
[3] Frank Dermody (1907–78), producer (director) at the Abbey Theatre. In 1938 he came from the Taibhdhearc Theatre in Galway and joined the Abbey, where he directed many revivals of O'Casey's first three plays.

Managers usually select their own producers, as they do in America. As for me "putting in a good word for you," I didnt even know that Bronson was going to Dublin; and the first inkling I had of it was the letter from you. I then wrote to him, and he replied saying he had been there; mentioned how bad he thought Brinsley's play was, and added that he had selected the producer who would be most likely to put across the play satisfactorily. So there you are. I am busy at the moment with a production of PURPLE DUST that The Old Vic are arranging for the end of October in Liverpool, to be followed by one in London, if a theatre can be got. Tell the Abbey that they have a poor chance of a 15% share of possible film rights, if they go on doing poor plays.

All the best.
[Sean]

To Gabriel Fallon [1]

MS. Texas

Totnes, Devon
[? Sept. 1945 ?]

. . . They offered $50,000 to $100,000 for the job.[2] It was a bit hard to refuse, but I managed it. So you see, it isn't necessary to strain an eye after Hollywood; for, whatever they may say of me, I don't imagine anyone would say I wrote with an eye cocked at Hollywood. I quite agree with you, that the young Irish writers should bother about the censorship. They have as good a chance to be published here—or will, when the paper gets more plentiful, & workers in the trade more numerous—as any new English writer. Is Frank [MacManus] living at Carysfort Ave yet? It's years since I wrote him about a poem of his in the Irish Times. Did his little child recover? And has he had another since? Of course, Frank teaches in a school, & that may force him into caution. The clergy have it all their own sour way in Eire now, I imagine. Of course, Maritain is right. What other could be the accusation? It isn't Communism, but Christianity that has ruled for twice a thousand years. Or what was, & is, called Christianity. But Maritain remains unread to the general & the particular. Fear has overtaken the clergy. Chesterton & Belloc have joked themselves into Church Doctorates, & joked St Aquinas out of his. Some little time ago, a factory worker wrote

1 The first and last pages of this letter are missing.
2 A reference to the offer from Hollywood to write the scenario for a film version of Thomas Wolfe's *Look Homeward, Angel*. See O'Casey's letter to William Herndon, 17 January 1945.

me a furiously abusive letter; & as she sent her name & address, I replied as quietly & sensibly as I could. She became friendly & sent me several letters on politics & the Catholic Faith as she knew it. Then along comes a letter from a Jesuit to her warning her of hell-fire, if she continued to write to me, or read any of "O'Casey's bad books." (I had lent her a copy of "I Knock at the Door," which, as far as I can see, won't lead anyone into hell—or heaven; but that's another question.) This sort of thing simply stuns me. So you had better take care!

By the way, what's wrong with Shelah R.? I read of her hysterical raptures over the scenic wonders of a production of "Journey's End," where they had "real grass growing on the sandbags." Hasn't the Dublin Drama League saved her dramatic soul yet? What a pity the performers didn't use "real ball cartridges" so that they could kill themselves in earnest. I daresay, that would be going too far. But Shelah Richards! after all her experience.

Has Robinson finished his "Life of Lady Gregory" yet? Long, long ago, he wrote me asking permission to quote letters of mine to the Old Lady, saying "According to accounts (or words to that effect) of what she left on record, I came out with flying colours." I'd like to read the book, but haven't seen it announced anywhere.

I haven't heard anything yet of a production of "Warld on Wallpaper, patterned in Oak Leaves & Lavender"—there are a few shamrocks in it—, but am living on hope. D'ye know (barring Shelah's production of "Red Roses," & the Abbey revivals), I haven't had a professional production of any of the four lately-written plays for ten years! [3] I wonder is that a record? Those "idiotic audiences of London & New York" that Brinsley [Macnamara] [4] denounced must all be dead. Well, all we can do is to "Leather away with the Bottle O!" Is the hoisting of the new flag of green over the Uachtaran's [5] Residence a prelude to the creation of a new national flag? Republican as I am (and always was), I hope so. The Irish Tri-colour is the most dejected-looking flag of all the flags of all the nations. I do be ashamed to see it flying, though I was the one who organised the first military salute to be given to it (marching to Bodenstown) more than 20 golden years ago. It's all set down in the next Biographical Vol. "Drums Under the Windows."

I should like to come to Ireland again, but things don't point that way. I'd like Breon & Niall & Shivaun to see their own countrie, "it's glory and its shame" as Connolly wrote; though, on the whole, sardonic critic as I am, I'd say more glory than shame; far more glory. But it seems to me that Ire-

[3] The last professional performance of one of O'Casey's plays was exactly ten years earlier, the Abbey Theatre's production of *The Silver Tassie* on 12 August 1935, barring the exceptions he mentions.

[4] See Brinsley Macnamara's letter to the *Irish Times*, 7 September 1935, Vol. I, pp. 583–84, objecting to the Abbey's production of *The Silver Tassie*.

[5] The President of Ireland.

land has now no outstanding personality, bar Jim Larkin. To me they're all a little, tame, bourgeois crowd, far away from Tone & Parnell, & farther still from Jesus Christ.

Enough, Sean; don't you get going again. I enclose a pixsture of the bould Barry [Fitzgerald] with a golden lady behind him. Isn't it all over the place that she's going to marry him; though Barry hums & haws, & is very nervous. . . .

To Miss Sheila————

MS. PRIVATE

TOTNES, DEVON
7 SEPTEMBER 1945

Dear Sheila,

I'm afraid that my last letter frightened you—I guessed it would. My remark about the ruthlessness of an artist gave you pause, did it? Dear, dear! Why? Isn't it odd how you Christians fear the opinions of men, though you flout God more than three times a day. It is, of course, good that men should think well of us; but, in the fight for humanity, if they think ill of us, it doesn't matter a damn. Well, farewell to you, & all the best to you that this world has yet got to give.

You've mixed up the titles of my work in your last letter—"The Star Turns Red" is the name of a play; "Pictures in the Hallway," 2nd vol of biography; "Red Roses for Me," is a play which may be produced in London after Christmas; "Purple Dust" a play, to be done next month by The Old Vic in Liverpool; & then in London.

It was a little pathetic to read Father C————'s complaint about the rejection of his book by eight publishers; & that he now leaves it "in the hands of the Little Flower." Hardly fair to the Little Flower. If how he writes in his letters & speaks in his sermons be any guide to the kind of stuff in his book, then it will never see the light of earth or light of heaven either. I see the Pope has declared for equal pay for equal work done by women in field & factory! He's coming on! And glance at the cutting attached below: His Holiness gives audience to a Communist! What will Father C———— think o' that?

Yours as ever,
Sean O'Casey

POPE MEETS COMMUNIST

The Pope yesterday gave a private audience to Eugenio Reale, Italian Ambassador to Warsaw. Signor Reale, a member of the Communist Party, is leaving for Moscow shortly.

B.U.P.

P.S. I hope you aren't ill, or anything.

To Beatrix Lehmann

MS. LEHMANN

TOTNES, DEVON

30 SEPTEMBER 1945

Dear Beatrix:

There's very little news "of a concrete nature," as the politicians & journalists say. Bronson A[lbery]. still has "R. Roses" & "Warld on Wallpaper." He has written to say—after I had had a letter from Dublin from a friend telling me he was there—that he had chosen Ria Mooney as producer for "R. Roses"; but that she wouldn't be able to come over till after Christmas. I wrote asking if my information was true, & he replied telling me about Ria Mooney. The Old Vic are to do "Purple Dust" in Liverpool for 3 & ½ weeks, beginning on the last day of October; [1] & may bring the play to London. For the past number of weeks, I have been surrounded with proofs—and still am—of "Drums Under the Windows," biographical; & "W. on Wallpaper," as well as a biographical sketch, "The Raid," [2] to show itself in "Mint," a new Quarterly to come out soon, edited by Geoffrey Grigson. I have had to do most of the work handicapped by my good eye troubling me (the other one went blind long ago), but managed to get over it, & chant a song when the worst was passed. I do hope your estimate of the Arts Council will prove a correct one. It's near time we had something to make the theatre life worth living. It is most interesting to hear of your

---

[1] The professional premiere of *Purple Dust* was presented by the Old Vic Company in Liverpool on 31 October 1945, directed by Eric Capon, with the following cast: James Cairncross as the First Workman; David Garth as the Second Workman; Harry Locke as the Third Workman; Maurice Jones as Cyril Poges; Joan Geary as Souhaun; Charles Keogh as Barney; Sheila Mullin as Avril; Cyril Luckham as Basil Stoke; Lucille Steven as Cloyne; Kieron O'Hanrahan as O'Killigain; Alfie Bass as the Yellow-Bearded Man; Stanley Howlett as Canon Chreehewel; Edward Burnham as the Postmaster; Peter Varley as the Figure. The production did not go to London. See O'Casey's letter to Eric Capon, 9 December 1945.

[2] See O'Casey's letter to Jack Carney, 14 April 1945, note 1.

production of "School for Scandal." [3] It's near time we got rid of these lispers of fine words. And haven't we quite a lot of green acid faces pouncing about life? Citrine is one of them. Oh! don't tell me about RADA [Royal Academy of Dramatic Art]! Pouring poison on any bud of life that ventured to show itself. The one & only academy of dramatic art is the theatre, where a thing is learned how to be done by doing it. Perhaps, the Arts Council will bring us nearer to the fact that the Theatre is one of the playgrounds of the people. God! I hope so! How good is it; how well is it produced; not how much will it make. I always had a suspicion that L. Casson was no hero ever since I saw him play "Jason" many years ago. [4] A very amiable fellow, but no-one to carry sword or spear.

All the best,
Yours very sincerely
Sean

[3] Richard B. Sheridan's *The School for Scandal* opened at the Arts Theatre, London, on 21 September 1945.
[4] Euripides' *Medea,* with Sybil Thorndike in the title role, and her husband, Lewis Casson, as Jason, opened in London on 30 May 1929.

To Miss Sheila———

MS. PRIVATE

TOTNES, DEVON
[? OCTOBER 1945]

This booklet—"The Labour Charter for Franco's Spain" [1]—says it "was enacted in 1938" seven years ago.

Why, if this be such a lovely guarantee of a lovely life for the Spanish workers, has Franco had to enact another "Bill of Rights," the other day, in an effort to provoke a smile on the starry face of watching Democracy?

You can cod the English, but you cant cod God.

S. O'C.

[1] An eight-page two-penny booklet published by Spanish Press Services, London, given to Sheila by her Jesuit friend and sent by her to O'Casey.

"Mint" to be out soon. The Old Vic are to do "Purple Dust" in Liverpool at the end of this month; [1] & I hear that Albery is to do "Red Roses" after Christmas; & Unity to do a production of "Juno." I see Koestler has become a Yogi; [2] & has seen visions of how things are in the USSR. And Bertrand Russell has become his Sacristan. And Bevin [3] has set himself the task of putting a break on Stalin's ambitions; so we've all got a lot of work before us. And Auntie Ellen [4] is going to raise the school-age after the Robins nest again. I was told by an eminent man recently that Bevin will be a far better man than Churchill in getting Stalin to know his place; but I'm afraid Big Ernie has put his foot in it.

I see poor Pat Fox has died. Did you know him—Pat Fox from Drumree? Barney & Pat did.

All are well here save for colds afflicting Eileen & myself.

All the best.

Yours as ever,

Sean

[1] See O'Casey's letter to Beatrix Lehmann, 30 September 1945, note 1.

[2] Arthur Koestler, *The Yogi and the Commissar* (1945).

[3] Ernest Bevin (1881–1951), politician and one of the leaders of the British labor movement in the first half of the twentieth century; Foreign Secretary in Clement Atlee's Labour governments, 1945–51.

[4] Ellen Wilkinson (1891–1947), Minister of Education in Atlee's government, 1945–47. In the 1945 election, Labor had pledged to raise the school-leaving age.

To Eric Gorman

MS. CHRISTINE GORMAN

TOTNES, DEVON

10 OCTOBER 1945

Dear Eric Gorman.

Thank you for the cheque & for your very kind letter. It is very gratifying to hear of the good houses for "The Plough." [1] I'm sure the Americans are having a good time of it in Dublin. I hope they will continue to go there: the more friends we have from the 48 States, the better for us in the days to come. We haven't a lot here, though many Irish are most vital in the newer Labour or Democratic Movement. Many Americans have come here on a visit—two naval men careered here last night in a jeep from Exeter to see us. Since the Americans came to England, I must have

[1] *The Plough and the Stars,* directed by Frank Dermody, was revived at the Abbey Theatre on 2 October 1945 and ran for six weeks, until 10 November.

I should also like to have Nine additional copies of the book—Fifteen in all.

The weather hasnt been too bad; but today, it is just a moist canopy of fog. As a matter of fact, the glorious climate of Devon is a sad delusion. Eight years of it has proved that to me. When we came first, we were told that Devon didnt know what frost was like. They werent long finding out! That winter, all the precious trees perished with the dint of the frost, and it wasnt safe to look out of the window. As a rule, most of the days were full of wet mist, and when it is cold as well, human nature isnt very enthusiastic about life. But—and this is a big but—the people are lovable and charming, and extraordinarily talkative for English people. I wouldnt let a one say a word against the Devon people. Of course, the haphazard methods of production and distribution, so common in many places, is common here too—and the sooner we begin to do a little planning the better.

I am glad to say, we are all well, though, like most people, getting a little shabby looking, and a little tired of hunting—all of it done by Eileen —out clothing for the children. However, the eldest fellow, Breon, is six foot one, so what became too small for him, did me nicely.

I hope you and yours are all well; and, should you see Mr Harold, please give him my warm regards.

My warm regards to you.

> *Yours sincerely,*
> *Sean O'Casey*

To Bernard Shaw

TC. O'CASEY

TOTNES, DEVON
15 OCTOBER 1945

Dear G. B. S.

Oh! why did you write such a kind, if bewildered, letter to Dr. Newman? He has sent his book [1] to me, accompanied by an explanatory letter in which he says that "the book must be read straight through and at one go." The tale of 250 visits to the one play,[2] and a very bad play too. Since I got the book, he has rung me up twice. Eileen answered to say I was out, in the hope that he would understand that I was unwilling to say anything. But

[1] Dr. Keith O. Newman, *Mind, Sex and War: Blackouts, Fear of Air-Raids, Propaganda* (1941). Newman was a psychiatrist at the Oxford County and City Mental Hospital.

[2] Terence Rattigan's *Flare Path* was produced in London on 12 August 1942 and ran for 670 performances. Rattigan dedicated the play to Newman.

he is to ring up again and again and again I suppose till he forces me to tell him what I think of it.

Any man who would venture on a work like this ought to be psychiatrised himself—there must be something astray in him. He says "please keep the book, if only as a memento of the kindness of heart of G. B. S." Your kindness of heart has brought sin into the O'Casey fold, and a lot of woe.

Here's one sentence about the play written by G. J. Nathan: "They come pretty bad at times, these English imports . . . but they do not often come quite so entirely bad as this one." [3] That's the play Newman went 250 times to see! God forgive him—and you.

My warmest regards.
Sean

[3] George Jean Nathan, *The Theatre Book of the Year, 1942–1943* (1943), review of the New York production of *Flare Path,* which opened on 23 December 1942 and closed after fourteen performances.

By George Orwell [1]

OBSERVER

28 OCTOBER 1945

THE GREEN FLAG

Drums Under the Windows. By Sean O'Casey. Macmillan. 15s.

W. B. Yeats said once that a dog does not praise its fleas, but this is somewhat contradicted by the special status enjoyed in this country by Irish nationalist writers. Considering what the history of Anglo-Irish relations has been, it is not surprising that there should be Irishmen whose life-work is abusing England: what does call for remark is that they should be able to look to the English public for support and in some cases should even, like Mr. O'Casey himself, prefer to live in the country which is the object of their hatred.

This is the third volume of Mr. O'Casey's autobiography, and it seems to cover roughly the period 1910 to 1916. In so far as one can dig it out from masses of pretentious writing, the subject matter is valuable and interesting. Mr. O'Casey, younger son of a poverty-stricken Protestant family, worked for years as a navvy, and was at the same time deeply in-

[1] George Orwell (1903–50), pseudonym of Eric Blair, English writer; author of such notable books as *Homage to Catalonia* (1938), *Animal Farm* (1945), and *1984* (1949).

volved in the nationalist movement and the various cultural movements that were mixed up with it. Several of his brothers and sisters died in circumstances of gaunt poverty which would excuse a good deal of bitterness against the English occupation. He was the associate of Larkin, Connolly, the Countess Markievicz, and other leading political figures, and he had a front-seat view of the Easter Rebellion in 1916. But the cloudy manner in which the book is written makes it difficult to pin down facts or chronology. It is all in the third person ("Sean did this" and "Sean did that"), which gives an unbearable effect of narcissism, and large portions of it are written in a simplified imitation of the style of "Finnegan's Wake," a sort of Basic Joyce, which is sometimes effective in a humorous aside, but is hopeless for narrative purposes.

However, Mr. O'Casey's outstanding characteristic is the romantic nationalism which he manages to combine with Communism. This book contains literally no reference to England which is not hostile or contemptuous. On the other hand, there is hardly a page which does not contain some such passage as this:

> Cathleen ni Houlihan, in her bare feet, is singing, for her pride that had almost gone is come back again. In tattered gown, and hair uncombed, she sings, shaking the ashes from her hair, and smoothing out the bigger creases in her dress; she is
>
>> Singing of men that in battle array
>> Ready in heart and ready in hand,
>> March with banner and bugle and fife
>> To the death, for their native land.

Or again:

> Cathleen, the daughter of Houlihan, walks firm now, a flush on her haughty cheek. She hears the murmur in the people's hearts. Her lovers are gathering round her, for things are changed, changed utterly: "A terrible beauty is born."

If one substitutes "Britannia" for "Cathleen ni Houlihan" in these and similar passages (Cathleen ni Houlihan, incidentally, makes her appearance several times in every chapter), they can be seen at a glance for the bombast that they are. But why is it that the worst extremes of jingoism and racialism have to be tolerated when they come from an Irishman? Why is a statement like "My country right or wrong" reprehensible if applied to England and worthy of respect if applied to Ireland (or for that matter to India)? For there is no doubt that some such convention exists and that "enlightened" opinion in England can swallow even the most blatant nationalism so long as it is not British nationalism. Poems like "Rule, Britannia!" or "Ye Mariners of England" would be taken seriously if one inserted at the right places the name of some foreign country, as one can see by the respect accorded to various French and Russian war poets to-day.

So far as Ireland goes, the basic reason is probably England's bad conscience. It is difficult to object to Irish nationalism without seeming to condone centuries of English tyranny and exploitation. In particular, the incident with which Mr. O'Casey's book ends, the summary execution of some twenty or thirty rebels who ought to have been treated as prisoners of war, was a crime and a mistake. Therefore anything that is said about it has to pass unchallenged, and Yeats's poem on the subject, which makes a sort of theme song for Mr. O'Casey's book, has to be accepted uncriticised as a great poem. Actually it is not one of Yeats's better poems. But how can an Englishman, conscious that his country was in the wrong on that and many other occasions, say anything of the kind? So literary judgment is perverted by political sympathy, and Mr. O'Casey and others like him are able to remain almost immune from criticism. It seems time to revise our attitude, for there is no real reason why Cromwell's massacres should cause us to mistake a bad or indifferent book for a good one.

To The Observer [1]

TC. O'CASEY

DEVON, 29 OCTOBER 1945

Ignored by "OBSERVER." A letter from Mr. Trewin says it was sent on to Orwell. But the reply was not published. Orwell's freedom of thought! [2]

Dear Sir:

Orwell and the Green Flag

It is sad to think that my book filled Mr. Orwell with such fury, so it isnt any wonder that he contradicts himself, and makes misstatements. He

[1] This letter was refused publication by the editor.

[2] O'Casey added this note in longhand at the top of the carbon copy. He had to wait nine years until his reply to Orwell was printed, in an expanded version in the chapter "Rebel Orwell," in *Sunset and Evening Star* (1954), the sixth and last volume of the autobiography. In that chapter O'Casey attributed the tone of Orwell's review partly to the fact that ten years earlier O'Casey had refused to give a pre-publication puff to Orwell's *A Clergyman's Daughter* (1935); see O'Casey's letter to Norman Collins of Gollancz, 11 February 1935, Vol. I, p. 541. O'Casey also alludes to this motive in his letter to Jack Carney, 31 October 1947. Some critics of *Sunset and Evening Star* complained that O'Casey had unfairly waited until Orwell was dead and could not reply to the attack; however, O'Casey was informed that his letter had been sent by the editor to Orwell, who presumably read it and decided to remain silent.

writes like a spiteful kid when he says that my "life-work is abusing England," and that she is "the object of my hatred." What England has he in his troubled mind? Is it the England of poets, painters, scientists, saints, and great warriors, the England of those who till her fields, sail her ships, herd her cattle, carry her transport, weave her textiles, and hew her coal? If this be the England he has in his mind, then, simply, he is libelling me, and he knows it. Does he think that those who ruled so long in Dublin Castle, and those who sent them to rule there, are England, the whole England, and nothing but England? Is this England, his England? Doesnt he know that "England" is wider than herself, and that within the broader circle are Scotland, Wales, and (by England's own force and determination) Ireland, too? It is certainly a queer evidence of "hostility to England," on the part of one who has built up the greater part of his educated view of life on Shakespeare, Marlowe, Webster, Herrick, Milton, Shelley, Keats, Blake, Dickens, the English Bible and prayerbook, Hogarth, Gainsborough, Wilson, Turner, Constable, and Crome (let Mr. Orwell read Sir Charles Holmes to see how some of these great men were treated by his England), Darwin, and Huxley. So leaving out all Welsh poetical tinges and the prose, poetical, and scientific influences of Scotland (Scott, Burns, and James Frazer), and confining my choice to pure English influences, there stands a fair array to show an admiration for England's achievements that Orwell himself could hardly excel. I'll venture the statement that I know far and away more about England than he knows about my country. Mr. Orwell complains that in my book, Cathleen ni Houlihan appears in most chapters (he is seemingly unaware that this is a name for Ireland), and that in the book "Sean does this and Sean does that," which is hardly surprising, since the book is part history of Ireland seen through the vision of this irritating "Sean," and that the fellow wasnt, happily, born deaf, dumb, and blind. But a laughable thing is that the name of Cathleen ni Houlihan was forced on us by Mr. Orwell's England, who, for many centuries, made it a penal thing to write down the name of the country, so her poets were forced to adopt the allegorical ones, one of which so annoys the reviewer. It looks now, if Mr. Orwell has his way, that the use of the name will again become a penal offence once more. In one breath he snarls at O'Casey as "a blatant nationalist," and in the next tells everyone that "he has managed (managed, mind you!) to combine his nationalism with Communism," thus telling us (through the term "combine") that the Nationalist is an internationalist, too. The fact is, Mr. Orwell doesnt know the difference between nationality and nationalism. Again, Irish writers "enjoy no special status" in England: Yeats tells us that he never got more than two hundred pounds a year for his books. Less than Mr. Orwell gets for his reviews, I'll wager. And what about Joyce? Let Mr. Orwell read James Joyce's letter to his American publishers, and he will see something about the "status" of this great writer in Orwell's "England." How often have Synge's plays been performed here? How long ago is it since even the

Abbey Theatre has toured his England? Apart from Mr. Bernard Shaw, will Mr. Orwell give us the names of Irish nationalist authors who "enjoy a special status" here? Perhaps, Mr. Orwell thinks we shouldnt get published at all; or, if we do, then we should be careful not to say what we think; that we should not portray life as we see it, even in our own country; or that we should write to please him. Where, then, is the principle of freedom of thought, which, I daresay, Mr. Orwell holds in honour, like red wax berries in a glass case. As for O'Casey living in England, the plain facts are that he gets near as much from his own country as from England, and much more from America; so that, actually, he has often given back in tax more than he got. But this is an odd thing to be brought to the fore by a critic.

In the end of his article, he quotes from my book an example of what, to him, is "blatant nationalism," but he doesnt give the sentence that follows —the very last in the book—which shows that what has gone before is meant to be sadly ironical. Why doesnt he give this last sentence? Because, if he did, it would go to disprove his point. He is out to prove O'Casey a "blatant nationalist" at any cost.

But what are we to think of a critic quoting the poem,

> Singing of men that in battle array . . .
> Marching with banner and bugle and fife
> To the death for their native land,[3]

as those written by an Irish nationalist, when as a matter of fact they were written by a famous and most respectable poet who was English of the English! Well, that's maudern English literary criticism for you!

Yours sincerely,
Sean O'Casey

[3] From Tennyson's "Maud."

By St. John Ervine

SPECTATOR

2 NOVEMBER 1945

Mr. O'Casey Continued

Drums Under the Windows. By Sean O'Casey. Macmillan. 15s.

Those who, like myself, have not read the first two instalments of Mr. Sean O'Casey's serial story of his life, may feel, like the celebrated "Captain"

Jack Doyle in *Juno and the Paycock,* that he is "in a state of chassis." What is this serial story, which is to be concluded in the next number, about? Ostensibly, it is Mr. O'Casey's autobiography, but it is manifestly fiction. No one could possibly remember everything that anybody ever said to him or that he ever said to anybody with the particularity with which Mr. O'Casey here reports conversations that took place over thirty years ago; so Mr. O'Casey, professing to record them exactly, must be drawing on his imagination. The reader may well wonder whether he is not inventing, especially when he finds that the book is untidily set out: a chapter full of wounded soldiers from the first World War is followed, as if in sequence, by one describing the gun-running at Howth which occurred immediately before the war began. As a bitter invention, the book is entertaining. As an account of events, it is nonsense. The reader is treated to a description of the way in which Patrick Pearse surrendered to the British Forces at Easter, 1916. One might imagine that Mr. O'Casey had witnessed the surrender, so neat are his details. "He comes steadily, in no hurry; unafraid, to where two elegant British officers are waiting for him," and, having heard a demand for unconditional surrender, "hands over his sword; bows, and returns to marshal his men for a general surrender." So writes Mr. O'Casey.

It happens that I received an account of the surrender from the late Lord Basil Blackwood, who was private secretary to the Lord-Lieutenant. It was given to me as we both crossed from Kingstown to Holyhead soon after the Rising was suppressed. Blackwood said that Thomas MacDonagh had gone to the surrender with his head high and his step firm and without the slightest appearance of qualm, but that Pearse had reeled there like a drunken man, his great head, made hideous by a squinting eye, lolling from side to side as if it were about to fall off. I ought to add that his account was not in the least unsympathetic. His admiration for MacDonagh's calm and courage was obvious. He showed no contempt for Pearse, though he might well have done so, but seemed to think that the first President of the Irish Republic was suffering from wrecked emotion. Remembering his account of the surrender, and comparing it with Mr. O'Casey's, I find myself wondering how much there is in this autobiography that is veracious. In a postscript to a letter to his nephew, Charles O'Malley, Godfrey O'Malley, in Lever's novel, remarks that one Considine had called out and shot "a fellow in the knee, but finds out that after all he was not the candidate" for Parliament, "but a tourist that was writing a book about Connemara." And in another postscript, he complains that "Old Mallock is a spiteful fellow, and has a grudge against me since I horsewhipped his son in Banaghar. Oh, the world, the world!" A vast amount of *Drums Under the Windows* is like that; and we are left with the impression of very few good men on this earth, Mr. O'Casey being about the best of the lot.

The style is a mixture of Jimmy O'Dea and Tommy Handley. There are thousands of invented words, bad puns, and stuff that nobody outside a

Dublin slum will understand. "There's nothin' like hitchin' your flagon to a bar!" might have been said by That Man Again. There's a piece like it on almost every page. But no one who knows Mr. O'Casey's work can fail to expect vivacity in it, nor will his expectation be disappointed, though I found much of the eloquence wearisome. Some fearful blows are dealt at heads of all sorts, especially heads of the Roman Catholic Church, and many of the blows are deserved. Mr. O'Casey, giving rough hands to Madame Markievicz, tells a good deal of the truth about that odd lady, but forgets to consider the supreme fact about her, that she was out of her mind. He spends many pages in cussing the hierarchy of the Church of Rome in Ireland for its unjust treatment of Father Michael O'Hickey when he demanded, and the hierarchy declined, compulsory Gaelic in the New University. That cunning old peasant, Cardinal Logue, receives some sharp smacks, but not for a second does it penetrate Mr. O'Casey's head that the hierarchy were right, and Dr. O'Hickey was wrong. Mr. O'Casey, indeed, positively maunders about this obsolete lingo, just as he maunders about Communism, and the ould, ancient days in Ireland, when, it seems, all was exceedingly well until the thick-skulled English abolished Grattan's Parliament. He does not realise that the Act of Union was a supreme blessing to Ireland. Under it, the entire social structure of the island was changed enormously for the better. Before 1800, not a single Roman Catholic could sit in Parliament or practice a profession on terms of equality with Protestants. At the end of the Union, the majority of the representatives of Ireland were Roman Catholics, and the whole power of the landlords in the counties had passed from grand juries to elected bodies. And every farmer either owned, or was in process of owning, his land. It was Cosgrave who abolished popular government in local authorities, with, indeed, ample warrant for abolishing it. All sorts of people, Bernard Shaw, Yeats, A. E., Dr. Douglas Hyde (who receives fearful slaps), Arthur Griffith, James Connolly, James Larkin, and one Bulmer Hobson figure vividly in the book. But among them all only two continuously shine with grace: Mr. O'Casey's mother and his Protestant Rector, the Rev. E. M. Griffin. *Drums Under the Windows* will be understood by Irishmen whom it will enrage; it will not enrage Englishmen because they will not understand half of it, and will not want to understand the rest.

St. John Ervine

To George Jean Nathan

MS. CORNELL

TOTNES, DEVON
4 NOVEMBER 1945

My very dear George:

Your book [1] came yesterday. Splendid. I put a hundred thousand welcomes before it. Breon has it now up in his little room reading it, while I write this to you. I have already quoted some of it in an article [2] just written about the theatre here. It was the comments on "The British benefactions in the later seasons," in the review of Rattigan's "While the Sun Shines." [3] A most worthy comment, & a palpable hit. Of course, I quoted as from the one & only George Jean. Indeed, when I write to the "new commencers" in theatrical activities (and there are a lot springing up), I always suggest that Nathan's book should be read. No-one I know (not even myself), nor anyone I have heard of, loves the theatre in such a persistent & unerring way as you do. With all your deadly criticism, you are so patient; & so ready to pull any God-touched effort into prominence. That is a superb characteristic in you. You are as eager to plank a good play on the stage as you are ready to pull a bad one to pieces. No critic here does that; would do it, either. I daresay, [James] Agate is as good as we've got, but the man isn't able to see a good play from a bad one till others—or time tells him. Shakespeare, of course, is good; so is Chekhov— he tells us what we all ought to know by this. But try him with untried plays, & he collapses into stupidity. He raved about "Journey's End," [4] & made me & Eileen go to two plays—"Combined Maze" [5] and "As Others See Us" [6]—when we had very little money to spare, on the strength of his comments on their value & glory. "Exquisite" he called "As Others See Us." I've never forgiven him for that sin: I never will. Lost money, & lost hours. I know of no-one of them who has caused the production of a meritorious play in a new MS. That's where you shine over them all. A lot here, who went to London to see the play, those in Dartington, don't agree with your estimate of T. Wilder's "Skin of Your Teeth" [7] & there's a holy row on in

[1] George Jean Nathan, *The Theatre Book of the Year, 1944–1945* (1945).

[2] Sean O'Casey, "The People and the Theatre," *Theatre Today*, March 1946; reprinted in *Under a Colored Cap* (1963).

[3] George Jean Nathan, *The Theatre Book of the Year, 1944–1945*, a review of Terence Rattigan's *While the Sun Shines*, which opened in New York on 19 September 1944, and closed after thirty-nine performances.

[4] R. C. Sheriff's *Journey's End* opened in London on 10 December 1928.

[5] Frank Vosper's *The Combined Maze*, adapted from a novel by May Sinclair, opened in London on 13 March 1927.

[6] Ronald Jeans's "As Others See Us," a sketch in Jeans's revue, *One Damn Thing After Another*, which opened in London on 19 May 1927.

[7] Thornton Wilder's *The Skin of Our Teeth* opened in London on 16 May 1945. The original production opened in New York on 18 November 1942, and Nathan attacked it in his review in *The Theatre Book of the Year, 1942–1943* (1943).

Eire between the producer there, Hilton Edwards, & the local critics, who, oddly enough, took the same view as you did.[8] Hilton Edwards has proclaimed T. Wilder one of the greatest living dramatists.

Purple Dust has been done by the Old Vic in Liverpool. I enclose a criticism of it which you might send to Dick. "Red Roses" is to go on next February, followed by "Oak Leaves and Lavender;" or "Warld on Wallpaper."

God keep you fit. I wish we could do something for Eugene. Is an improvement possible?

Yours as ever
Sean

[8] Hilton Edwards and Micheal MacLiammoir presented Thorton Wilder's *The Skin of Our Teeth,* starring Hilton Edwards, in Dublin at the Gaiety Theatre on 8 October 1945. The play was attacked by all the Dublin critics, the anonymous reviewer in the *Irish Times,* 9 October, calling it "pretentious nonsense." Immediately a controversy developed in the letters column of the *Irish Times* when Denis Johnston defended the play on 10 October; the anonymous reviewer replied on 11 October; Gabriel Fallon replied to Johnston on 12 October. On 15 October Hilton Edwards stated that the poor notices had affected attendance, and the play had to be withdrawn after one week.

To Beatrix Lehmann

MS. LEHMANN

TOTNES, DEVON
5 NOVEMBER 1945

Dear Beatrix:

Thanks for your kind letter containing so much news. I knew B. A. [Bronson Albery] was concerned with my play through Una Plays, Ltd., with [Robert] Helpmann & [Michael] Redgrave as fellow-directors; but didn't know that the money came from tax-free profits. I thought it came from backers in the usual way, & I wondered. Pity Redgrave is so conceited —it is a baneful thing in any man; worse in one with talent. I don't remember insisting on an Irish producer—Massie [Raymond Massey] did the Tassie [1]—; but B. A. is anxious to have Frank Dermody who has been producing at the Abbey for some time. I certainly shouldn't welcome Hugh Hunt. He isn't an Irish producer, anyway. I met him in Ireland years ago when he was a guest producer for the Abbey; but I don't think he managed to get the best from the players there—a hard thing for anyone to do, when they decide to go against a new-comer. But I don't think he and I would make a perfect fit.

[1] See Lady Gregory's letter to O'Casey, 11 October 1929, note 2, Vol. I, p. 368.

I'm very glad you like the play [*Oak Leaves and Lavender*], & hope it is really as good as you think it to be. I'm not quite satisfied with some of the last act, & have told B. A. so, asking him for the play back for alterations there. Some of Feelim's speeches are too long & tedious; & I want to bring "Abe" in once more; & I have made the "Chant for Shelters" better, & more dignified; &, I think, more poignant, too.

I am writing for B. A.'s final opinion. If he doesn't decide to put it on within a reasonable time, I shall send it on to the U.S.A., & take my chance there. I don't agree that it is too "painful for audiences to stand at the present." They've stood more than that. Barry Jackson said same of "Tassie:" "a great play, but daren't try it: too painful; people couldn't stand it!" It's all very amusing! Well, I'm used to this now: "Juno" was the one play over which there was no row. Anyway, I've another biographical vol. to write, &, with many other things to do, won't have time to brood over things too deep for laughter.

All the best, Beatrix.
Yours v. sincerely,
Sean O'Casey

To Roger Hayes [1]

MS. HAYES

TOTNES, DEVON
6 NOVEMBER 1945

Dear Mr. Hayes:

Thank you for your letter, telling me a lot about meself. I daresay "Jason's" [2] is still going strong—just as they used to, presiding over Evangelist meetings, & selling Keys of Heaven & Gardens of the Soul like cold cakes. I don't care a damn whether Magennis [3] banns the book or no. He may have thought well of Joyce in "his early days," but would hardly

[1] Roger Hayes, an administrative officer in the Department of Justice, Dublin.

[2] The name O'Casey used for Eason's, a newspaper, stationery, and bookselling firm in O'Connell Street, then Sackville Street, where he worked in 1896 as a van boy when he was sixteen. See "Work While It Is Not Yet Day" and "The Cap in the Counting-House," *Pictures in the Hallway* (1942).

[3] William Magennis, Professor of Metaphysics at University College, Dublin; Chairman of the Irish Censorship of Publications Board from 1934 until he died in 1946. Under Magennis, the board banned *Windfalls* on 4 December 1934, *I Knock at the Door* on 16 May 1939, and *Picture in the Hallway* on 16 December 1942. A year after the death of Magennis the ban on the latter two works was "revoked" on 16 December 1947

stand for him now; but Joyce is greater now than he was then, & so shows us what metal is in Magennis. Old Hancock [4] of Birmingham mustn't have been much of a fighting Hancock if he let Magennis puzzle him. England's Empire—nearly dead now—& the British people (Scots, Irish, Welsh, Cornish, & Manx) are two very different things. Why, where I am—Devon —100 years ago, was known to us as East Ireland, & hurling matches took place between the two peoples. Almost all West England is Celtic—Hardy's Wessex—, & in Cumberland they still count the sheep as haon, dho, tri, etc. Arthur Griffith was a lath painted to look like iron. There was no man amongst the chattering crowd around the Treaty big enough to lead, or drag, Ireland from the fatal Civil War. They are still paying for the betrayal of Parnell. I don't suppose a lot will agree about Hyde, but when he stood for the Senate after the Treaty was passed, I remember Lady Gregory complaining to me, with tears in her eyes, in Coole, "dat no-one would vote for An Craoibhinn; [5] & dat dee Irish forget their best friends." No-one bothered about him. His choice as President was DeValera's dodge to prove toleration by having a Protestant-President. But [George] Moore calls Hyde a "Catholic Protestant." Read his "Hail & Farewell." Certainly to me, his two books in Irish, "Journey to America" [6] and "Meself and the League," [7] are two of the dullest & most commonplace books in Irish I have ever read—& there have been a few of them. "Irish" was always popular. Hyde had the people & the Church behind him when he went for Mahaffey & Atkinson; [8] but a word for O'Hickey, [9] & the "Church" would be against him; so Hyde remained silent. Dr. Walter McDonald was Professor of Theology in Maynooth for 40 years—till he died in 1920, four years after O'Hickey. A book of his, "Reminiscences of a Maynooth Professor," published after his death by Constable's, contains revelations of Maynooth that are astonishing. For instance we learn that the most vicious enemy O'Hickey had was The Rev. ——— Mannix,[10] now the Patriotic Archbishop of Melbourne! I daresay, the book is out of print now; & you will hardly hear it mentioned in Ireland. The veil of "Catholic" silence. Writing of Theology, McDonald says "Our books are stuffed with arguments based on principles in which no man of Science believes—which

[4] Sir Keith Hancock, Professor of History at the University of Birmingham, who gave a lecture at University College, Dublin, and became involved in a dispute with Magennis.
[5] See O'Casey's letter to Jack Carney, 13 October 1942, note 2.
[6] See O'Casey's letter to Lovat Dickson, 8 July 1945, note 8.
[7] Ibid.
[8] Sir John Pentland Mahaffy (1839–1919), Provost and Professor of Classics at Trinity College, Dublin, noted scholar and wit. Robert Atkinson (1839–1908), Professor of Romance Languages and Sanskrit at Trinity College, Dublin, noted philologist and Celtic scholar. Testifying before a university Commission on Education in 1902 with Hyde, Mahaffy and Atkinson attacked Hyde's plea for "compulsory Irish" at the National University.
[9] Michael P. O'Hickey. See O'Casey's letter to Lovat Dickson, 8 July 1945, notes 3 and 4.
[10] Ibid., note 5.

would be laughed out of existence if paraded, in the language of daily life, where men of Science could hear what we say and ridicule us. . . . We produce first-rate missionaries, but men who can work parishes, or even dioceses, well, may be utterly unable to influence the higher thought of the world." Magennis Abú! [11] followed by the scholarly gillie, Chesterton. "The Catholic Press, as I think," adds McDonald, "is a very good index of how feeble we are in this respect." . . .[12]

[11] Long live Magennis!
[12] Mr. Hayes could not find the last page of this letter.

To Jack Carney

MS. NYU LIBRARY

TOTNES, DEVON
9 NOVEMBER 1945

Dear Jack,

Thanks for your letter. I have returned the books, under cover, signed as requested and shown. Macmillan's tell me the book is "selling very well." I was surprised that the Irish Press gave such a favorable review. I'd love to see that of the Standard. Yes; I remembered that Orwell was with the Tribune, & drew my own conclusions. I've written a reply which Trewin, the Literary Editor acknowledged, saying he was sending it on to Orwell. Whether it will be published or no, is another question. But listen: the patriot Orwell quotes

> Singing of men that in battle array,
> Ready in heart & ready in hand, etc.

as a blatant example of Nationalism. He thinks it was written by an Irish Nationalist; but it was written by a famous poet, & most respectable Englishman, English of the English. He didn't know!

It's bad news about the Dublin Trades Council. The Church is at the back of [William] O'Brien. Now with a Labour Government in, they'll be more frightened than ever; though why, God only knows. If things go on, you'll find Griffin of Westminster with his arms around Bevin. Swing low, sweet Chariot! Well, if the Labour Party hasn't got a Ulysses or a Nestor, they've got a Stentor, anyway. Yes, Plough has had a good time at the Abbey—the Americans in Dublin are, I'm told, all going to it. Purple Dust in Liverpool is, I hear, not doing badly; & there's a chance they may show it in London. Oak Leaves & Lavender & Red Roses are down for performances in either February or March next: it never rains, but it pours. D'ye know it must be ten years now since I had a professional performance of a play—not since Within the Gates was done to death by Norman McDermott [1]—bar Unity's show of "Star Turns Red." [2]

Everyone seems to be worrying about the atomic bomb. I think it's the best thing yet. It's too dangerous for anyone to use. "I dar you! You blow me up, an' I'll blow you up!" No boxer would fight, though he knew he'd knock out the other fellow, if he knew, too, the other fellow was bound to knock him out. There'd be no fight in that, so there wouldn't. When they didn't dare to do it with gas, they wouldn't dare with the atomic bomb. It puts Capitalism in the worst position ever: here they are with the power to blow Communism out of life, & they daren't use it! Why? Because in blowing out Communism, they'd be blown out too; & the one & only thing a Capitalist values more than his money is his life. Without the money, life may be of some use to him; without life, money is no good. There's the philosophy of an Irish Spinoza for you.

Love to you & Mina.
Yours as ever,
Sean

Who is—Winston of Ayot St Lawrence? He wrote asking an article on Shaw among others to form a book to be presented to the sage on his 90th birthday. So did a Elkan Allan who is, apparently getting Heineman to do the same. Is there a competition, or what? I have refused both requests. If an article would lift 50 years off the 90, I'd do it quick.

[1] For the opening of *Within the Gates,* see Gordon Beckles's "Challenge to Sean O'Casey," 8 February 1934, note 1, Vol. I, p. 491.
[2] For the opening of *The Star Turns Red,* see James Agate's "A Masterpiece," 17 March 1940, note 1, Vol. I, p. 849.

To Daniel Macmillan

TS. MACMILLAN

TOTNES, DEVON
16 NOVEMBER 1945

Dear Mr. Daniel:

And amnt I glad to hear you saying that DRUMS UNDER THE WINDOWS is selling very well. It is very gratifying to me. Oddly enough, I wasnt so sure of this book as I was of the previous two—shows you what a fine judge I am. There is rather a comic connection between the book and George Orwell's review in The Observer.[1] He sets down the verses

> Singing of men that in battle array,
> Ready in heart and ready in hand,
> March with banner and bugle and fife
> To the death for their native land.

as an example of blatant nationalism (Irish). Well, these verses were written by a poet, English of the English, but he didnt know it. Tennyson, no less!

It is very kind of you to suggest another advance to me; but I think I prefer to wait till after April—I hope it may be later, even; not so much because of the reduced tax—though that is a lot to me, but because a good deal of money brings about a temptation to spend. I have enough at the moment, have always dreaded debt. We have lived fairly simply, and it is better to be on the safe side. Things are better with me now than they have been for ten years or so—that is enough to banish anxiety; so I'll wait. But of your kindness, if I should want it, I shall not now hesitate to ask you.[2]

Thank you again.

Yours very sincerely,
Sean

[1] See George Orwell's review in *The Observer,* 28 October 1945; see also O'Casey's reply, 29 October, which was refused publication.

[2] This sentence and the rest of the letter were added in longhand.

To The Forward

17 NOVEMBER 1945

SEAN O'CASEY REPLIES [1]

Dear Sir,—

Please permit me a few phrases in reply to Mr. Highet of Balliol. Mr. Highet must try to pardon me if I prefer the logic of life to the logic of the

[1] Originally Bertrand Russell had written an article, "What Is the Truth about Russia," *Forward,* 22 September 1945, in which he used Arthur Koestler's new book, *The Yogi and the Commissar,* for an attack on Russia. This prompted O'Casey to write a reply to Russell in an article, "Bertrand Russell and Russia," *Forward,* 13 October 1945, in which he challenged the truth of the bitterly anti-Soviet statements by Russell and Koestler. Then John Highet, a don at Balliol College, Oxford, in a letter to *Forward,* 3 November 1945, attacked O'Casey for attacking the great Russell: "Next time O'Casey sets out to 'advise' a man of Bertrand Russell's intellectual calibre, let us have a little more Irish intelligence and less totally-inept shilly-shallying." What follows is O'Casey's reply to Highet.

Academy. According to the very best logic of the military art, Germany should have won the war; should have taken Leningrad, Moscow and Stalingrad in its stride; but the logic of life in the Soviet Army and people interfered with the logic of the military academy and made hash of the military dons.

That's one of the facts that distresses Mr. Highet. It was not I who said Koestler's book was a "Yogi" fantasy—he avows it himself. The book is even named "Yogi and Commissar." If the conditions in Britain are a matter of indifference to him (since he is in Balliol, he probably hadn't to handle them); if the mote in his brother's eye is more important to him than the beam in his own, then there is something wanting in the logic of Balliol.

He counters my opinion that if the conditions in the Soviet Union were such as alleged by Russell, then the people there would never have fought so heroically, by the statement that "O'Casey must admit that the Germans lived a fulfilled life under the Nazis, for they fought every bit as enthusiastically as anyone else."

The fact is: they didn't. The Soviet stand in Moscow and Leningrad shocked them from head to heel and, after the defeat of Stalingrad, the slogan of the German Army became "Caput Hitler"; just as after Alamein they didn't stop running till they gave themselves up at Cape Bon; to be followed later on by the surrender of about five million well-armed Germans, mind-lost and panic-stricken.

That is another fact that Mr. Highet can hardly find fault with in all his Balliol logic. As another matter of fact, all these tales of Soviet decrepitude are pretty musty now. They are all to be found in a clerical garb in the book "The Gates of Hell" (meaning, of course, the U.S.S.R.), written by Erik von Kuhnelt-Leddihn, and published by Sheed & Ward in 1933. It is the tale of a "Catholic" sent to Russia, underground, by the Jesuits, to preserve and propagate the "Catholic" Faith. Unconsciously, a great comic book.

Stuff like "Easy to distinguish the people from the tourists. Everything the people wore was cheap, bad and dirty. Women were to be seen in filthy, ragged slippers, with blouses showing the remains of their last meal, and woolen stockings that failed to disguise their ugly legs. The most terrible thing was the expression on these people's faces—it betrayed their complete paralysis of any sort of soul-life." These were they who smashed the German Wehrmacht!

Again, "the atmosphere is of a God-less catechism-morality, a slimy, idolatory of work, the parading of technical and scientific snobberies. Ghastly! In the Five Year Plan they are grinding themselves to death. The room was full of the smell of decayed food refuse. On the walls were hung innumerable red pennons with mottoes inscribed on them . . . Shuslova had a round, tubular mouth, like a blood-sausage in longitudinal section. Popov wore long pointed side-whiskers and gave the impression of a morpho-maniac. He was hugging Shuslova to him, executing tango figures, fixing his mouth by suction to the tubular mouth of his partner, making movements with his knees, the meaning of which was unmistakable."

Now the author of this stuff is an accredited Catholic apologist, and his book ran into four editions. Sheed & Ward would hardly publish it now.

The last I heard of this von Kuhnelt-Leddihn was that he was "writing a trilogy on the Devil, the real Devil, with claws, horns and a tail; the first part to deal with Austria of 1889, the second with England, and the third with Soviet Russia in 1970"!

I suggest to Mr. Highet that he should read this book. I never said there was a "black-out" of information about Russia. I simply pointed out that facts known to all contradicted Koestler and Russell, and that both these gentlemen contradicted themselves. I could say much more. For instance, when I was searching the booksellers for a book of Mayne Reid's for a son of mine and couldn't get one, the Soviet Union was printing sixty thousand copies of his works!

Lastly, Mr. Russell's "intellectual calibre" (like the big gun on the "Queen Elizabeth") doesn't awe me. He showed very little of this calibre in his article, or in the thought of building a policy of antagonism to the U.S.S.R. on Koestler's Yogism. To me, this couple, along with the Catholic von Kuhnelt-Leddihn, set down what they would like to see in the U.S.S.R.; but I'm afraid the Commissar is far away ahead of the Yogi.

Yours sincerely,
Sean O'Casey

To Eric Gorman

MS. CHRISTINE GORMAN

TOTNES, DEVON
23 NOVEMBER 1945

Dear Mr. Gorman.

If my memory serves me right, you & your wife were very appreciative of the art of Music. I send you some slips, one of which you might be able to put up in the theatre vestibule, of a Recital to be given by Agnes Walker.

Her husband, W. McLellan,[1] has asked me to introduce this Pianist to friends in Dublin. I have no personal interest in the matter, never having clapped eyes on the artist or her husband; & have no acquaintance with

---

[1] William Maclellan, publisher, Glasgow.

them other than reviewing a book of poems published by McLellan's, & of getting an article, sent by a Dublin friend to me, published in a magazine of theirs. McLellan is a friend of Hugh MacDiarmuid, who wrote "A Drunk Man Looks at the Thistle"; & he is a Scot, a brother Gael; & this is the beginning & end of my interest & my knowledge of the matter.

If you could, I'd like you to forward one of the slips to Dr. Larchet, who I hope is well, with his good wife & children; & to give one to the Leader of your own Orchestra.

This is about all I can do—many think, or seem to think, that I have enough influence to move Croagh Padruig.

All good wishes.
Yours sincerely
Sean O'Casey

To George Jean Nathan

MS. CORNELL
TOTNES, DEVON
23 NOVEMBER 1945

My very dear George:

Well, I've read your book,[1] & a very fine one it is, in spite of the poor season. It is an odd thing to read notice after notice of play not worth the trouble of writing them. It has always been a puzzle to me—one of the mysteries of the universe—why so many set themselves down to write plays. It's not so often done in the other arts. Everyone seems convinced that there is nothing in the writing of a play, a story, or a criticism. It would seem they're right, too, on the strength of the plays produced, the stories read, & the criticisms encouraged. Take here, for instance, in the matter of criticism: bar D[esmond]. MacCarthy, who very seldom writes for the theatre now, there isn't a single drama critic I would trust. [James] Agate just is a jester; I[vor] Brown a condescending mind; & the rest of them imitating jingles of these two. But there are signs of braver and more enthusiastic minds being born among the younger folk; but they've no chance yet of getting in the regular Press. It's not that the critics are ignorant; they're far from that; they know better, far better than they say; & that makes matters worse. Frankly, their job is more to them than the drama.

It was very amusing to read your criticism of the production of "Dark

1 George Jean Nathan, The Theatre Book of the Year, 1944–1945 (1945).

of the Moon" [2]—what a fine title. It is maddening the way a lot of good plays are handled; when producer & actors are determined to make a good play better than it is. Your review of "Foolish Notion" [3] is grand fun— & so bitterly true, too. That "No" to Miss Bankhead [4] is splendid. And the review of Dodson's "Garden of Time," [5] man & the universe! It is very trying to meet those who have "the arbitrary determination to write a play, come hell or hot water." I'm often plagued with them here—sending me scripts, all of which are inconceivably bad. I never read them now. I used to, till I got wise. Breon read the book before I could get it. Before it came, the usual inquiry each morning was "Is Nathan's book here, yet?" Well, you've one more admirer any way. The Index of Plays & Authors is a great help in the quick arrival to the place one is seeking.

I am glad to hear Eugene is allowing his play "The Iceman Cometh" to go on; [6] & that he has written a lively one around the Irish.[7] America has been blessed in having a great & fearless playwright living alongside with a great & fearless critic. May God be with the pair o' You, & give yous both a long life.

I am sending an extraordinary book to you, descriptive of what it is like to see the same play 250 times.[8] The author sent it to me, asking for my opinion; then, when it didn't come, he kept ringing up daily—sometimes twice a day—for a week. The wife answered. I was going to write; but decided against it. To me, the book is appalling.

> *My love to you & Eugene &*
> *Carlotta.*
> *Ever Yours*
> *Sean*

[2] Howard Richardson and William Berney's *Dark of the Moon,* with music by Walter Hendl, opened in New York on 14 March 1945.

[3] Philip Barry's *Foolish Notion* opened in New York on 13 March 1945.

[4] Nathan's "No" is aimed at Barry's play and its starring actress, Tallulah Bankhead, who had praised it and tried to explain its meaning.

[5] Owen Dodson's *Garden of Time,* a modern version of *Medea,* produced by the American Negro Theatre in New York on 7 March 1945.

[6] Eugene O'Neill's *The Iceman Cometh* opened in New York on 2 September 1946.

[7] Eugene O'Neill's *A Touch of the Poet,* which was not produced until 2 October 1958.

[8] Keith Newman's *Mind, Sex, and War* (1941). See O'Casey's letter to Bernard Shaw, 15 October 1945.

To The Spectator

23 NOVEMBER 1945

MR. O'CASEY REPLIES

Sir,—St. John Ervine in his review of *Drums Under the Windows,*[1] says he got it straight from the horse's mouth of Lord Basil Blackwood, private secretary to the Lord Lieutenant of Ireland (a great man by all accounts) that, when Paudruig Pearse came to announce surrender, "he reeled like a drunken man, his great head, made hideous by a squinting eye, lolling about from side to side as if it were about to fall off." I hereby warn Englishmen if they want to learn anything about Eire to keep a couple of miles away from all private secretaries of lords lieutenant of Ireland. Though O'Casey wasn't there on the exact spot, Press photographers were, and took pictures of what happened. I am looking now at a reprint of a photo showing the exact scene. In Great Britain Street, at the northern end of Moore Street, stand two elegant British officers while Pearse, in his top-coat, stands before them. He is standing more erect than the two officers taking the surrender, and, oddly enough, it is Gen. Lowe who seems to be a bit uneasy. In a note to Pearse (spelling his name incorrectly), this Gen. commanded him to come alone, allowing him no comfort of a comrade, though the victor General takes care to have a companion himself.

Pearse, though he had a very slight cast in one eye, was a very handsome man, and always carried himself with grace and dignity. After a week of blood and fire, grimed with the dust and smoke of the blazing Post Office, unshaven, and tired, he couldn't look so trim as the elegant officers, but Pearse was by far the finer man. As for death, Pearse feared it no more than the legendary hero, Cuchullain. Nor did any of his comrades, to give them no more than their due. I don't think it was Pearse who was called the first President of the Irish Republic, but Lord Basil Blackwood should know. It is very nice to read that Mr. Ervine believes the Bishops were right, though he doesn't make it clear whether he thinks them right because they opposed compulsory Gaelic in the University, or because they caused O'Hickey to be dismissed without a chance of defending himself. Mr. Ervine says of the book, "Englishmen won't understand the half of it, and won't want to understand the rest." Possibly not the elegant Lord Basil Blackwoods, though their want of understanding Irish activities doesn't speak well for these gayboys who ruled the country for 700 years. When Mr. Ervine says that neither O'Casey nor anyone else could re-member "conversations that took place thirty years ago," he seems to be ignorant of the fact that O'Casey was writing of these very things in Gaelic League and Sinn Fein Manuscript journals, in the Irish Worker and in

---

[1] St. John Ervine, *Spectator,* 2 November 1945; reprinted above.

The Irish Nation. But then, even St. John Ervine can't be expected to knew everything—*Yours sincerely,*

Devon   *SEAN O'CASEY*

To Roger Hayes

MS. HAYES

TOTNES, DEVON

24 NOVEMBER 1945

Dear Mr. Hayes:

It would be hard to get a copy of "Drums Under the Windows" now, for the edition is sold out, & it is hard to say when the next one will be able to appear on account of labour shortage. You should have held on to the one you had. Bruno Nolan's [1] attitude doesn't trouble me much. Of course, Maginnis is a joke, & as such I treated him in my book. No, I never read Binchy's book.[2] You'll hardly find Dr. McDonald's book in any public library in Ireland. The Church's big bosses seem, in some way, or another, to have managed quietly to limit its circulation. I have never met a one who had it. I wouldn't let it go from me for love or money. Denis Gwynn edited it. If you can find out his address from Stephen Gwynn, & then write to him, he'd be the one to let you know. Or, if you got his address, & sent it to me, I'd write to him. He asked me once to spend a week-end with him (years ago), but I didn't go; & haven't heard from him since. I have heard of the "Wolfe Tone Annual," with its article on Dr. O'Hickey; [3] but I understood (there was a letter saying so by B. O'Higgins in the Irish papers) it had been banned.[4] I daresay, you're right about the Irish section of U.C.D. Once these Irish enthusiasts get a job, they grow careless, & lose any enthusiasm they once had. I hope Irish doesn't die out before these

[1] See O'Casey's letter to Brian O'Nolan, 2 April 1942. O'Casey is making a Joycean double allusion to Browne and Nolan, the Dublin stationery and printing firm, and to Giordano Bruno (1548–1600), the Italian philosopher, born near Nola, who was burned as a heretic.

[2] Daniel Binchy, *Church and State in Fascist Italy* (1941).

[3] "A Fight For Nationality: Dr. O'Hickey and the West Britons," *Wolfe Tone Annual* (1945), written and published by Brian O'Higgins.

[4] In the lead article, "The Story of the *Wolfe Tone Annual*," O'Higgins explains that this was actually the 1944 issue, which was originally "Stopped by the Censor," specifically by Frank Aiken, Minister for the Co-Ordination of Defensive Measures in de Valera's Fianna Fail government. No specific charges were given for the ban, but it is likely that the politicians were sensitive about O'Higgins's strong attack upon the Roman Catholic hierarchy, especially Cardinal Logue and the Rev. Mannix for their roles in the dismissal of Dr. O'Hickey. See O'Casey's letter to Jack Carney, 7 February 1944, note 6.

jobbers can be hunted out of Irish life. Of course "is mo thóin le falla"[5] is
what Rafteri would say & sing. Against a cold wall, too, I'll back. Not like
the hot one in Back Lane.[6] No-one thinks of ranking [H. G.] Wells as a
Scientist, nor as a philosopher; but he's a great man, all the same. His best
work few can equal; & his opinions are worth hearing. [C. E. M.] Joad is
not to be compared with Wells either as an artist or as a man of political
integrity. You are wrong, I think, when you say Joad attacks Christianity.
At the Cork Rotary Club recently, he congratulated Eire on her Faith,
& before this, he was quoted as a champion of morals by the recently late
Cardinal MacRory. Not Joad, but Frazer, France, Renan, Joyce, Reade,
the little books of "The Thinkers Library," Shaw, & the Catholic Bishops,
here & over there, are far more important enemies than the pathetic Joad.
I have a fling at Joad's philosophy myself in the character of Stoke in
"Purple Dust." In Eire, my friend, Maynooth is stronger than ever, make
no mistake. You let some member of the Dail propose to send a minister to
the USSR, & see what would happen. It amuses me to think how the USSR
has burst upon the world; & how frightened all tall-hats, the bowlers, the
wigs & gowns, & the chasubles are to see the Hammer & Sickle every where,
except in Eirinn. Strange how they all failed to see it! I have just sent an
article for the next number of the Anglo-Soviet Journal, called "Rise o' the
Red Star," [7] though I daresay you've neither seen nor heard of this
magazine. Parnell founded the Independent [8] to oppose the Freeman, & a
good paper it was then. When Parnell died, Martin Murphy got a grip on it,
& so, in its mean manner, became, unconsciously, an avenger of Parnell's.
The Irish People are still paying the price for that wretched and stupid
betrayal. If "NN" be a barrister, what is he doing writing literary criticism
for the Independent? Hyde's Irish, prose & verse, is bad. Is it Irish at all?

[5] "With my back to a wall," a line from Raftery's poem, "Mise Raifterí" ("I
am Raftery"). O'Casey is alluding to the fact that in his translation of the poem,
Douglas Hyde modestly changed the word "thóin," back or bottom, to "aghaidh,"
face, thus altering the line to read, "And my face to a wall," in *Songs Ascribed to
Raftery* (1903). The word for wall, "balla," is written as "falla" in the Munster
dialect. Anthony Raftery (c. 1784–1835) was the blind minstrel poet of Mayo and
Galway whose poems survive in oral versions among the peasants, for whom he sang
them. See Colm O'Lochlainn's "Mise Raifterí," in *Eigse: A Journal of Irish Studies,*
edited by Gerard Murphy, Vol. VIII, Part I, 1956–57, pp. 18–20. O'Lochlainn agrees
with O'Casey, and says: "I imagine that if the words really uttered by Raftery had
survived, they would have run something like this:

> Mise Raifterí a's mo thóin le balla
> Ag seinn ceóil do phócaí falmha."
> [I am Raftery with my arse to the wall
> Playing music for sweet damn all.]

[6] A street in the Liberties area of Dublin near Christ Church, a slum where
there was a night shelter for derelicts.

[7] Sean O'Casey, "Rise o' the Red Star," *Anglo-Soviet Journal,* spring 1946.

[8] Charles Stewart Parnell (1846–91), leader of the Irish Parliamentary Party;
repudiated by the Irish Party, the Irish hierarchy, and Gladstone, when his relationship with Mrs. Kitty O'Shea was disclosed. Parnell died on 6 October 1891; the first
issue of his long-planned new newspaper, the *Irish Daily Independent,* appeared on
18 December 1891.

Mise agus an Connradh is the dullest book, the worst written, & to me, the worst Irish I have ever read. All his songs are bad. "Mairín" and his "Féac Sinne, Clann na hÉireann!" [9] a verse of which, with the chorus, he shoves into "Mo Thuras go hAmerice"—Good God! I've read An Beal Bocht, allright. Now there's Irish for you, if I'm not mistaken. Old Hyde couldn't write like that. And Torna! [10] O'Conaire [11] was coming along well; but he was very trying to meet. He wasn't a natural hobo; he made too much of it. But he had the makin's of a fine writer. Years & years before, I remember reading a piece of his Irish in An Claidheamh Soluis [12]—about Paul's journey to Damascus, & it was fine. But at that time I couldn't buy the paper often, & so lost track of the story. I don't wonder Beal Bocht wasn't liked. I read a few of the letters denouncing it. Certainly, there's little romance about it. To me, some of the writing suggested an Irish Swift.

I wasn't aware that "They Go—the Irish" aimed at putting red, white, & blue ribbons in Cathleen's hair. I certainly had no such notion. The colours, anyhow, are shocking, & the Union Jack—Patrick's Cross and all—is, esthetically an ugly flag. So is the G. W. & O.[13] I couldn't say why the Irish joined the fight, except that there are more Irish anti-Fascists than many imagine. We are a funny people, but that's no reason why we shouldn't be a great people too.

The letters R. T. D. on the stamp mean "Russia Today" the organization that prints them; & carries on the propaganda for friendship with the USSR.

With all good wishes
Sean O'Casey

[9] "Behold, We Children of Ireland."
[10] Torna, pseudonym of Tadg O'Donoghue (1874–1949), Irish-speaking poet and Professor of Irish at University College, Cork, 1916–44.
[11] See O'Casey's letter to Jack Carney, 2 March 1942, note 3.
[12] *The Sword of Light,* journal of the Gaelic League.
[13] Green, White, and Orange, the Irish tricolor flag.

To Jack Carney

MS. NYU LIBRARY

TOTNES, DEVON
26 NOVEMBER 1945

Dear Jack,

Thanks for Spectator. If Ervine replies, please let me know. He may have something to say about Pearse's bravery as compared with that of Cuchullain. This I should like to answer.

Yours as ever,
Sean

From St. John Ervine to The Spectator

30 NOVEMBER 1945

MR. ERVINE RETORTS

Sir,—Mr. Sean O'Casey, who prefers to live in this country rather than in his shoddy, backstreet Republic, gives, in your issue of November 23rd, a perfect example of the lopsided and fallacious statement which Eireans regard as argument. Adjectives become missiles when used by an Eirean. The word "elegant," for instance, is used by Mr. O'Casey as if it were a synonym for unmentionable crimes. It is applied to every non-Eirean he mentions. Sneers and defamation are part of the Eirean case. They are, indeed, often the only case an Eirean possesses. A private secretary to a Lord Lieutenant must be a liar, from whom all Englishmen would do well to shrink. General Lowe seemed "uneasy" when he met the high-minded Pearse, who was, "by far," a "finer man" than the two "elegant" officers who received him. How does Mr. O'Casey know this? Has he the slightest personal knowledge of these two "elegant" officers? I shall not affront your readers, Sir, by defending Lord Basil Blackwood from Mr. O'Casey's street-corner gibes. He was killed in France in the last war at a time when Mr. O'Casey was, he candidly confesses, taking to his heels every time he heard a pistol fired. Lord Basil saw MacDonagh and Pearse surrender. Mr. O'Casey did not. All he has to bolster up his servant-girl's romance is a Press photograph and his florid imagination. The photograph obviously is of a different scene from that observed by Blackwood: the scene when Pearse began negotiations for surrender, and not of the surrender itself. By that time Pearse was in a state of nervous collapse.

Mr. O'Casey says, "I don't think it was Pearse who was called the first President of the Irish Republic." One of Mr. O'Casey's most dangerous delusions is that he thinks. He does not think, never has thought, cannot think: he can only splash about in his emotions. But, Sir, a man who claims to be able to repeat exactly conversations which were held over thirty years ago, should surely know that Pearse was, in the words of Miss Dorothy Macardle, in her work, *The Irish Republic,* which must be read with the greatest discretion, for Miss Macardle is another typical Eirean, "chosen to be President of the Provisional Government" which was constituted on Easter Monday, 1916. That Government proclaimed the establishment of an Irish Republic. Mr. O'Casey next professes to find me obscure in my reference to the hierarchy of the Roman Catholic Church in Ireland. He cannot tell whether I am praising the prelates for refusing to sanction compulsory Gaelic in the new University or for dismissing

Dr. O'Hickey, an advocate of compulsion, without allowing him to state his argument. Mr. O'Casey is not quite so thick as he here professes to be. My meaning is crystal clear. I mean that the Bishops were right to oppose compulsory Gaelic, and that Dr. O'Hickey was wrong to advocate it.— Honey Ditches, Seaton, Devon

Yours Sincerely,
ST. JOHN ERVINE

To Jack Daly

MS. DALY

TOTNES, DEVON
6 DECEMBER 1945

Dear Jack.

The book inscribed as requested is here. Glad you liked it, & that you found a laugh or two in it. Any book you have, or may have, will, if you wish, be gladly inscribed by me—& don't be makin' me tell you this any more. Just send them along. I've read Robertson's article,[1] & it is just what I've been telling the Left Boys all along. The next fight will be with this power backed by all its concomitants—Wealth, big business, ignorance, slyness, and the power of the oft-repeated lie. I wish the D.W. would realise this. They do, maybe, but they're reluctant to hurt the Catholic members of the Trades Unions. Well, these Catholic members won't hesitate, one of these days, to hurt them.

All good wishes to Floss & You.
Sean

[1] Archibald Robertson, "Gods and Devils," *Rationalist Annual, 1945.*

To The Spectator

7 DECEMBER 1945

O'CASEY v. ERVINE

Sir,—Mr. Ervine says my use of the word "elegant" is "a synonym for unmentionable crimes." Not common crimes, but unmentionable ones. He's certainly giving meaning to an English word. How he drags it down into such lower depths only he and God can know. My bad memory cannot

remember calling Lord Blackwood "a liar." I said that no Under Secretary
of Ireland (or Over Secretary, for the matter of that) can be regarded as
a reliable historian of an Irish event. Most Englishmen, I imagine, will
have realised that by now. If my contention amounts to calling Blackwood
a liar, then it will have to go. Mr. Ervine's contention that Lord Blackwood's saying must be protected from criticism because he was killed in the
last war is just comic Ervinian logic. He says: "O'Casey's photograph is
obviously of a different scene from that observed by Blackwood." Obviously, a very different scene. As for "O'Casey taking to his heels every
time a pistol was fired," well, O'Casey errs in quite good company—the
Apostles took to their heels, too, as Mr. Ervine, who, I understand is a
sincere Anglican, must know. While Mr. Ervine rebukes me for "sneering,"
he seems blind to the fact that almost all his letter is a screeching sneer from
end to end. Dr. O'Hickey wasn't dismissed from his Professorship because
he stood for Compulsory Gaelic in the University, so he never sought an
opportunity "to state his argument." He was dismissed for "lack of proper
respect to the bishops and Senate." Of course, I never knew (till Mr. Ervine
told me) that Miss McArdle's *Irish Republic* mentioned Pearse as first
President, nor did I know the same thing was mentioned in hundreds of
other places. But there is more in it than that formal mention. It struck me
as very odd that all the rancour was poured over Pearse (McDonagh was
a fine fellow—to balance the bias), while the name of Tom Clarke was
never mentioned by Basil Blackwood or Mr. Ervine. Most probably Blackwood did not even know of his existence. Yet here was the man who was
the very head and front of the Rising: the real President of the Irish Republic. If Pearse was the nominal fact, here was the living substance. It was
this fiery, shy man, careless of any prominence so long as the work went on,
who shattered the moribund Republican Brotherhood when he came out of
jail, and revived it into a power and a menace; and if Mr. Ervine looks at
the Proclamation, he will see his name in the place of honour (dishonour,
if the critic wishes), in a line to itself, above all the others, including that of
Pearse. Pearse was a late-comer into the revolutionary movement; when
he came, most of the work had been done, though he crowned it with a
brilliant life and a very gallant death.

I am asked how do I know that Pearse was a "finer" man than either
of the officers who received his submission, and if I had "the slightest personal knowledge of these two officers." No, not the slightest personal knowledge (incidentally the word "finer" is comparative, and leaves the word
"fine" behind it). No one would say fine to a fellow guilty of "unmentionable crimes"; but I'll give my reasons for my belief. First, Gen. Lowe's
officer companion has passed out of our ken; Gen. Lowe nearly so, for his
name nowhere appears, unless it be conjured up by that of Pearse. These
two officers, as far as I know, are associated only with gunfire and bloodshed, and not world-famous in that; so is Pearse, but his name is associated
with many more things, and is known to millions, many of them not

"Eireans" either. Forty years ago Pearse became a pioneer in Education, and founded a school in face of prodigious difficulties and decided opposition, a school which has become historic in Ireland, America and Australia. He was a born man of the theatre in its widest sense of song, story, play and pageant. Pearse had left behind him a testimony of his faith in article, poem and play. He was a "foreseer" as were neither Gen. Lowe nor his superior, Gen. Maxwell. They thought the executions would put the fear of God in the people; Pearse believed they would arouse them to resentful action; Pearse was right. More than thirty years ago, in his article *The Sovereign People,* he anticipated the events that have, and are, taking place the world over. Gen. Lowe's name is fading. Pearse's is growing, and these be some of the reasons why I think Pearse to be a "finer" nature than either of those who caught him for death to hold forever. When Mr. Ervine says "O'Casey doesn't think," he means that no one thinks except one thinks as Ervine thinks. Thank you, no. The fact is, I think, that Mr. Ervine hates the Irish. He will find this thought confirmed by a pointed reference to his "dislike of the Irish as much as St. John does" by George Jean Nathan, the American drama critic in the well-known New York paper *Newsweek* for January 29th, 1940.[1] And Nathan is no "Eirean."

As for, finally, his "O'Casey lives in this country rather than in his shabby, back-street Republic" (a sneer?), well, God and a lot know I have criticised things and men in my own country; but has Mr. Ervine done so to his Northern Ireland? To him Ulster is a second Canaan, overflowing with milk and honey; but—and it is a big but—he, too, lives here all the same. But that is a low way of arguing, I'm afraid.—Thanking you, Sir, for your courtesy, I remain, yours sincerely,

Devon   *Sean O'Casey*

[1] See Nathan's article, "The Best of the Irish," reprinted in Vol. I, pp. 838–39.

To Eric Capon [1]

PC. COLBY L.Q.[2]

TOTNES, DEVON
9 DECEMBER 1945

Dear Eric Capon,
    Thank you very much for your clear and eloquent report of *Purple Dust's* production. And thank you for all your work in producing it. It is a

[1] Eric Capon directed the professional premiere of *Purple Dust* at the Liverpool Playhouse for the Old Vic Company on 31 October 1945. See O'Casey's letter to Beatrix Lehmann, 30 September 1945, note 1.
[2] Richard Cary printed this letter in his article, "Two O'Casey Letters," *Colby Library Quarterly,* June 1972.

hard job to produce a play of mine, after the strutting little things now seen half-dead on the stage. Next issue of *Common Wealth Review* is to have a short article by me on Theatre and Politicians.[3] I hope *P. D.* may come to London.[4] It may be easier there, for I see by an Irish paper that the actors, playwrights, and producers there are restless, many of them streaming over here to film and stage. Ria Mooney, who is to do *Red Roses For Me*[5] is bringing over some with her; and it would, I think, be worth your while to keep an eye on them; though, I daresay, most of them will be after big salaries and big names and little plays. *P. D.* is far better than *R. Roses*. This isn't the egoistic dictum of O'Casey. G. J. Nathan first told me this, and he's no bad judge. I believe him now, and have done so for some time; so that is why I'd like to have *P. D.* done in London—and, of course, everywhere else, too. The main thing in the play is good actors for O'Killigain, Avril, Souhaun, Stoke, Poges, and the principal workmen. Strange how Barney's talk went so well—I always thought this the dullest part of the play. Actors, I agree, are so demoralised with scanty plays, that, when they find themselves in one with guts and gusto, they become lost souls. It was at once laughable and maddening while we were rehearsing *The Silver Tassie*.[6] Indeed, that play has never yet been *acted*. It never will, I daresay. Such is our English stage.

Thanks again, and all good wishes to you, your wife, and little one.

Sean O'Casey

[3] "The Theatre and the Politician," *Common Wealth Review,* January 1946; reprinted in *Blasts and Benedictions* (1967).

[4] O'Casey had to wait seventeen years for the London premiere of *Purple Dust* at the Mermaid Theatre on 15 August 1962.

[5] See O'Casey's letter to Ria Mooney, 22 December 1945.

[6] The world premiere of *The Silver Tassie* was presented in London at the Apollo Theatre on 11 October 1929. For details on the production, see Lady Gregory's letter to O'Casey, 11 October 1929, note 2, Vol. I, p. 368.

To The Forward

15 DECEMBER 1945

SEAN O'CASEY AND RUSSIA [1]

DEVON
5 DECEMBER 1945

Sir,

About the U.S.S.R. Mr Highet and I could never agree, so I, too, shall say no more, except to suggest that life can neither be measured nor pre-

[1] This is a reply to John Highet's letter to *Forward,* 1 December 1945, in which he had argued, in part, that if Russell and Koestler were unable to get the true facts about Russia, how did O'Casey obtain his own facts.

dicted by little a's and b's; that I don't think I have sold my mind or soul to Moscow. It might as well be said that because of my admiration for the U.S.A. from the Revolution to the T.V.A. I have sold mind and soul to Washington. I assure Mr. Highet that I had no intention whatsoever of reflecting on his character as a man, or on Balliol, except that I resented the rebuke for countering a man of Bertrand Russell's "mental calibre," when he was writing on a matter about which he knew no more than I did.

Finally, if Mr. Highet ever happens to be in Totnes, and he be willing, I shall be delighted to meet him, and give him a grand cup of tea brewed with the cunning of my own two hands.

Yours sincerely,
with thanks for your courtesy.
Sean O'Casey

To Jack Carney

MS. NYU LIBRARY

TOTNES, DEVON
17 DECEMBER 1945

My dear Jack,
Thanks for the Book of Ballads, the razor & blades. And for the papers. I have been told by Macmillans that Drums Under the Windows is sold out. Curious that, for neither of the previous two had such a quick sale. I understand all Ireland's looking for it. Enclosed is a letter from M. Mullen, asking me to send it on, & he'll forward the money. His is the third request of that kind I got from Dublin. He evidently doesn't get on with Jim now. He has another scheme on foot to bring the Old Age Pensioners to clover—four-leaved clover too. You will see by the letter that Mick's eternal—he never changes. Everything is split, false, pretense, bar Mick himself. He speaks well of Pat Fox now that he's dead. Mick, like meself, must be growing grey hairs now. And still in the same old place—35 Mountjoy Square—near Gardiner Street Church. I enclose the letter to let you have a look at it. You can let me have it back when you've taken a copy for presentation to the N. Library.

I am working now on the page proofs of Oak Leaves & Lavender.

Eileen has told me of a cough you got in Paris. I hope it is gone, or near gone, now. Take care of it anyhow. You aren't made of iron.

All the best to Mina & you,
Sean

To Micheál Ó Maolain [1]

TC. O'CASEY

TOTNES, DEVON

17 DECEMBER 1945

A chara:

There isnt a copy of DRUMS UNDER THE WINDOWS to be had anywhere, and heaven only knows when there will be. The paper and cardboard shortage here is great, and the shortage of labour in the printing and book-binding trades just as bad. No writer can know when a book of his may be published. For instance, DRUMS UNDER THE WINDOWS was advertised to come out last March, but didnt appear till November. An edition of a book like this isnt a large one—not like one of a more popular kind, the sale is usually a slow one, and so the size of an edition is limited. This one sold more quickly than the last ones, and so no copy can be had by anyone till a further edition is printed. Publishers now do not like selling books direct, but only through the booksellers. It saves them a lot of trouble, and at the moment, booksellers can get rid of most of the books they get. The number of books given free to a writer is limited to six copies; after that the writer has to pay for any copy he may want. No copy of the first two volumes can be got either; and most of the plays are out of print too. The other day, Lars Schmidt of Gothenburg asked for copies of two plays for translation into Swedish, but I had neither, and even Macmillan's had to lend him one of the two which they had on their file. You didnt miss much, anyway. I dont think the book would interest you much. It isnt written in detail, but in an impressionistic way. To write down the details would mean five volumes for each of the one that did me for my purpose. The review of the "Independent" was, as you say, "rather critical," [2] but the world outside Ireland doesnt care very much about the

---

[1] Micheál Ó Maolain (1881–1956), the Irish-speaking Aran Islander with whom O'Casey shared a room in the tenement at 35 Mountjoy Square in 1920, was the original for the character of Seumas Shields in *The Shadow of a Gunman* (1923). Ó Maolain (Mullen) was the founder of Coisde na bPaisde, the scheme which has enabled the children of Dublin to spend summer holidays in the Gaeltacht, the Irish-speaking districts in the west, for the past twenty-five years. He met O'Casey in Dublin during the 1913 General Strike, and over the years wrote many articles for labor, nationalist, and Gaelic papers and magazines. In one article, "An Ruathar Ud Agus An Deachaigh Leis" ("That Raid and What Went With It"), *Feasta* (Dublin), May 1955, he gives his version of what happened in the tenement on the night of the Black and Tan raid, the incident O'Casey used in his play. When he died in 1956, Ó Maolain was still living in the same little "return room" at 35 Mountjoy Square. See O'Casey's letter to Ronald Ayling, 26 January 1960, note 8, Vol. III.

[2] "Mr. O'Casey's Memoirs," *Irish Independent*, 12 November 1945, a review of *Drums Under the Windows* by "N. N." The last sentence of the review reads: "It is

opinion of the "Independent," and I dont care a tinker's damn. No author
published here bothers about the "Independent." I dont know anything
about the practices of the "Irish Press," of course, but it is certainly edited
much more effectively, I think, than its rival. As for getting down your
own memories of what happened around you and to you in Dublin, that
would depend for publication on how you set them down—not an easy
thing to do. But the Ireland of 30 years ago cant be dead, for the past
always lives somewhere in ourselves, and in what follows after us. I heard,
or rather read of, poor P. Fox's death. But then Pat was a bit unmanage-
able, looking for a "post of trust and responsibility." Now for a job like
that, one has to have experience, and maybe a degree in trade or commerce. Yes, of course, the labour trouble is a pitiful thing, but it will all
come right in the end. I hope your Old Pension Association will bear fruit,
but I'm afraid that a drastic economic change in Eire's life will have to come
before each gets even a pound a week. There's no harm in trying, though.
All good wishes.

[*Sean*]

---

a book which, I think, no Irish Catholic could read without feelings of pity and
disgust."

To Ria Mooney [1]

TC. O'CASEY

TOTNES, DEVON
22 DECEMBER 1945

Dear Ria Mooney:

I am going to be quite candid with you about this matter of RED
ROSES FOR ME. I don't like most of your proposed cuts at all. You
don't seem to be aware that you are trying to get rid of some of the play's
best passages. Why do you want to cut on page 10 Life and all her vital
changes, etc? Not only is it a good phrase, but a fine prophecy—it is happening all around us. And don't talk to me in the jargon of "holding up
the play's action." Turn to Act II, Scene 1. Julius Caesar, and see how the
action is held up there while the conspirators argue as to the point where

[1] Ria Mooney (1900–73), Abbey Theatre actress and director, who had played
the role of Rosie Redmond in the first production of *The Plough and the Stars* at the
Abbey in 1926, had been engaged by Bronson Albery to direct the London premiere
of *Red Roses For Me*, which was to open at the Embassy Theatre, Swiss Cottage,
on 26 February 1946. See O'Casey's letter to Mrs. Una Gwynn Albery, 6 March
1946, note 1.

the sun rises: "Dec. Here lies the east: Doth not the day break here?" etc.
I am not a writer of the "well-made play." On page 13, your cut makes
Ayamonn's action a little ridiculous, though I allow the whole speech might
be too long; so I have left in, "The face, the dear face, that once was
smooth is wrinkled now." The lower cut on page 24 must stay, and so must
that on page 40. On PPs 41 & 42, there must be only two "choruses" of Our
Lady of Eblana's gone—another would make the plaint ridiculous; indeed,
I think one is enough. Why do you want "I hope the Blessed Virgin'll come
to live with us all again," on P. 44 cut? Cuts on PP 48, 66, 72 to stay.
Those, too, on PP. 76. 78. 84. to stay. Cut on 92. allowed. Cuts on P. 130
to stay—why did you want to cut these? Surely they don't hold up the
action—though I have never yet known what that term "action" means.
P. 150. quiet action here, as you suggest—the laying of the roses on the
bier by Sheila—may be better. Rehearsal would show that. Cuts on 150 to
stay. If you want to produce the play, get out of your head all the nonsense
of conventional production; and take the play as it is, without trying to
force it into some little traditional mold that I have smashed long ago.
About the "references to mythological characters which will mean nothing
to English ears," how do you know this? How do you explain the fact
that Lady Gregory's Cuchullain of Muirthemne [2] ran into five editions,
and her Gods and Fighting Men; [3] the Story of the Tuatha de Danaan and
The Fianna of Ireland did the same? I'm afraid our own people know little
about them either. Well, I'll do something to let the English know about
them; and no reference to them can be taken out. Let me give you a bit of
advice, if you want to be a producer [director]: whenever you have a play
to produce, let the one thought in your mind be about the play; and banish
every thought about a career. The less you think of your career and the
more you think of the play, the better for the play, and so, too, the better
for your career. Lastly, you are under no obligation to me for being chosen
as producer of RED ROSES; Bronson Albery is he who chose you, it is
only fair to him to tell you this.

> *Yours sincerely,*
> *With all good wishes,*
> *Sean O'Casey*

2 Lady Gregory, *Cuchulain of Muirthemne* (1902).
3 Lady Gregory, *Gods and Fighting Men* (1904).

To Roger Hayes

MS. HAYES

TOTNES, DEVON
31 DECEMBER 1945

Dear Mr. Hayes:

I have been very busy since, having had no time to bless myself. You are right in saying McDonald was "an amazing man." He amazed Maynooth, & made Rome uneasy. He was a thinker, & traditional religion doesn't like thinkers. Long ago a heretic was one who thought the wrong (so they said) way; now a heretic is one who ventures to think at all. Certainly, there was thought in the idea that Theology should be brought into line with the tremendous new Knowledge gained by man during the last century. As St. T. Aquinas based his speculations on the Knowledge of the day, so the present-day Theologians should base their ideas on what we Know now. But where is the one of them all who would venture forth into thought as St. T. Aquinas did? They are but office-boys of the Roman Rota. And the Vatican is concerned only with the power of the world, ignoring, altogether, the power & majesty of God. That is why the 32 new Cardinals have been selected so as to imitate the Universal aspect of the C. Church. The Pope has Himself declared that this mass creation shows this to be so. Well then, did the Church lose its Universality during the centuries the Council was dominated by the Italianate Cardinal Council? The fact is, in my opinion, the Vatican is bewildered, & knows not where to turn, or what to do. Months ago, I told an American Naval Officer, a fine fellow, & a most sincere Catholic, this creation was sure to happen, & in a letter he sent a few weeks ago, he reminds me of this, & says he "is looking forward to welcoming an American Pope in Peter's Chair." Well, that's by no means impossible. I see by a Sunday paper that Spellman's [1] name is mentioned as the next Vatican Cardinal Secretary of State—the real Pope, the Red Pope, the Pope of Power. So, you see, some day soon, we may have the Dollar Vicar of Christ head of the Church! So America may become the world's political, economic, & Spiritual guide, philosopher, & friend—if the USSR would only step out of way. Britain leads no longer. U.S.A. in the Western Hemisphere & USSR in the Eastern Hemisphere are now the two great powers; with the U.S.A. by far the wealthier of the two today, but with the USSR unimaginably powerful by reason of its Labour affiliation every where, & by the determination of Labour every where—even in U.S.A.—to overcome all obstacles in the way of the march of men. This isn't meant to be impudent egoistic prophecy, but simply opinions on what is happening around us.

McDonald failed "to develop political science" because that wasn't his

[1] Francis Cardinal Spellman (1889–1967), Archbishop of New York.

job. He looked at it from the point of view of the Catholic—obedience to authority that came from, or was allowed of, God. Of course a former colleague would deplore "the publication of his 'Reminiscences.' " They revealed too much. Concealment is the strong weapon of the ecclesiastics, & all who have reason to fear their influence. Only the other day, in a review of a book,[2] I referred to the burning to death of the 33 little "delinquents" in Cavan School, under the care of the Poor Clares.[3] The review was published, but the reference to the horrible roasting alive of the 33 children of the workers was cut out of it. The ecclesiastical members—women & men— must never be asked to answer, & pay, for their misdemeanors. The way they whine these days whenever they happen to be martyrs! Kill a bard, a soldier, a philosopher,—worker—anything; but kill a priest, & the Keen goes out to the world.

My dear friend, DeValera returned to power [4] because he himself is a lay bishop, following the rest, step by step; because of a National halo around him, & the Irish haven't yet discovered that this halo may be a romantic will o' the wisp; & because the Labour Movement has (having abandoned Larkin) no leader beyond the cold and calculated W[illiam] O'Brien. But Mayo & Wexford have recently shown that a breeze is blowing up against him. In your instance of the charges [of] a priest, it all depends on what way the case went. Perhaps, you remember the case of a priest striking a man so that he died? Of the one, too, who had a woman of "bad character" dragged to him by the hair of her head, whom he threatened to put in a coffin if she didn't leave the place; of the case of the blind boy who died in his bed, & was subjected to violence an hour before he went his way; of the young man & girl who were fined forty shillings or a month's imprisonment for Kissing; & of the case here when a case was tried to be concealed by Magistrate & Court Clerk because the accused was a priest. And these only are the ones that couldn't be hidden. You know, as well as I do, that it would go hard indeed with any Catholic before he would take a priest into court. Of course there are good priests & good bishops & good popes—moral, chaste, humane, generous, thoughtful; but that doesn't alter the fact that the organization has become corrupt, worshipping Mammon, greedy for power, & control of world affairs. I'd make a big bet that the next fight (begun already) will be what is called the Church & all the Socialistic organizations the world over. Indeed, even the Anglican Church is splitting on the question; numbers of clericals, in their hatred of the USSR, ready to join up with the Vatican against the common enemy. Yes, I agree with you about such men as Dr. Boylan & Canon O'Keefe; but my contention is that even these two men—fine & all as they are—wouldn't

[2] Sean O'Casey, "Spirits in Prison," *Spectator,* 28 December 1945, a review of *I Did Penal Servitude,* by D. 83222 (Dublin, 1945).

[3] See O'Casey's letter to Jack Carney, 12 March 1943, note 2.

[4] Eamon de Valera's Fianna Fail party won a majority in the Dail, and he became head of the government in 1932, ending the ten-year reign of William T. Cosgrave and the Cumann na nGaedheal, later the Fine Gael Party.

come out publicly in defence of free thought—not free in respect of dogma, mind you; but free in respect of politics, art, literature, & of all those things about which even Catholics can't be certain. What, for instance, have these men ever said in criticism of the "Catholic Press," a thing that any intelligent Catholic should be ashamed of? Examine the Bishops' Pastorals—if anyone even reads them—and it is clear that a youngster of fifteen in a Secondary School would think as deep & write as well. I have a number of letters written by a Jesuit, & if you were to see them they would shock you. This man died recently, & now there's a move on to make him a Saint—He comes from a very rich & influential family, who were largely instrumental in getting a cleric an Archipiscopal Chair, or Throne. I happened to say in a letter to a friend, whom he knew, that Hitler was a Catholic. He replied with a laugh, & a deliberate statement that I was wilfuly lying; though he never replied when he was given date & place for the statement—not made be me—but by the Catholic Universe. You must know something of the things published by the C.T.S. here & with you. The Protestants are, of course, equally as bad. Their publications, too, are pretty awful—particularly those of the Evangelicals. And [J. Arthur] Rank, the Film Magnate, owns all the Methodist publications! He, too, wants to teach religion through the Cinema—going my way!

I quite believe some Bishops support Dev. & others Fine Gael because there's no difference between them. What Bishop is a member of the Labour Party, or is there one a Communist—or even a Socialist? Archbishop Griffin,[5] I understand, was at a Reception given by the Labour Party some time ago; much in the same way as Chamberlain stole into the Soviet Embassy. Or can you name a single Catholic prelate who has ventured to say a word in defence of the USSR?

My friend, there is no similarity between Communism & Fascism. One is an organised effort to defend Capitalism, the other one to overthrow it. How could these be alike? Surely you have heard of the German business bosses—the Krupps, Thyssens, etc, who have recently been arrested. Where are their likes to be found in the USSR? And it is State Socialism, not Communism, that is the present system of life there. You have heard of the great factories owned by Goering, the property—all the great publishing firms—owned by Hitler. What great firms do Stalin or Molotov own? There is no such thing as private property in the USSR, only personal property. The things that mean life to all are owned, either by the State, the great Co-operative Combines, or the Trades Unions. Of the two great National daily papers, Isvestia is owned by the State, & Pravda by the Communist Party. No-one can exploit the labour of another man from one end of the USSR to the other—bar the Mongolian Republic, which is now rapidly becoming Socialist too. I see Dublin has at last its Anglo-Soviet Friendship Council, & I hope this activity will soon be able to give Eire the

---

[5] The Most Rev. Dr. Bernard Griffin, Archbishop of Westminster, who succeeded the late Cardinal Hinsley in January 1944.

information she so badly seems to need. Of course, sooner or later, you'll have a Russian Minister in Dublin—speaking Gaelic maybe! Ireland might do worse than have a trade pact with the USSR.

Communists, as such, have no "attitude to religion." They leave that to the private conception of their members. They collide with clerical & layman only when these interpret religion as the authority allowing them privilege, & the power to exploit their fellow-man.

It isn't quite fair to expect [H. G.] Wells to know the difference between the dogmas of The Virgin Birth and The Immaculate Conception; &, anyhow, this ignorance doesn't do away with his case. I suggest that quite a crowd of Catholics don't know the difference either. But it would be better (as McDonald suggests) for these Theologians to deal with Salmon's attack on "Infallibility" [6] (a dogma, too), than to bother about Wells's mistakes. And, of course, one has the right to think how he may about Caesar & Napoleon. Certainly, Anatole France, a countryman, didn't think a lot of Napoleon. I quite agree that Catholics aren't "harmed" by the ban on Trinity.[7] It is, as you say, "no great shakes." Which of them is? But it does seem odd to me that a number of Irishmen are banned from entering a College that gave Ireland T[homas] Davis, & the man who wrote Ireland's best patriotic ballad—Who Fears to Speak of 98.

Of course, Dr. McDonald's book did you no harm. How could it? He was a loyal Catholic, if ever there was one; & if the ecclesiastics of the Church flung away ambition (in its lowest sense), they'd set about his canonization pronto. But to loyalty, he added intellectual courage, & that is what they don't want, for they are mortally afraid of it.

Well all the best, & all good wishes for the New Year.

Yours sincerely,
Sean O'Casey

Addendum

My reference to Maynooth's influence is not prompted by any thoughts of bigotry, but on the warm words of Dr. McDonald, whose hope was that Catholic Ireland, with its core & intellect in Maynooth, would become an influence in the Catholic world, not second, even to Rome.

The Dr. says "A California friend of mine, a priest who knows the American Church well, once told me that we in Ireland did not realise the position which we hold, as a centre of Catholic thought; did not know or

[6] George Salmon, *The Infallibility of the Church* (1888).

[7] In his Lenten pastoral of February 1944, the Most Rev. John Charles McQuaid, Archbishop of Dublin, announced that all Catholics within the diocese of Dublin were forbidden to attend any non-Catholic school, primary or secondary or university, and anyone who disobeyed would be guilty of a mortal sin and unworthy to receive the sacraments. For a critical comment on the pastoral letter, especially the ban on Trinity College, see Sean O'Faolain's leading article, "The University Question," *The Bell*, April 1944.

bear in mind how many ears are strained, from the Atlantic to the Pacific, day after day & year after year, to catch whatever message of faith or doctrine may be transmitted from the Irish shore. It is so in Australia, too, which is practically an Irish Church, & in South Africa, of which the same may be said . . . ; so that for them, there are two Matres et Magistrii— Rome & Ireland." And again, on the appointment of a Dr. Owens to be Professor of Theology: "Whatever one may think of him—who was my confessor & true friend, & for whom I have the highest respect—one who knew his capacity as a Theologian could not but regard his appointment to the Chair of Theology as a job." A job! And to the Chair of Theology! And in Maynooth! Christ help us. Is there e'er a bishop today in Eire who thinks in these terms—of an influence—not for jobs—in the world, not even second to Rome, to be used—not for mean & trivial ends; but for the greater glory of God & fuller freedom of man? No: McQuaid (is his name Mick?) excommunicates any young man (Catholic) who enters Trinity, while all Ireland honors Davis, a man who came out of it! An American Naval Officer, a Catholic, came here to see me once a week when he was stationed in Plymouth—I've just had a long letter from him, from Annapolis, in Maryland—, who told me of a Jesuit who tried to prevent him from going to Harvard, on the grounds that the College would undermine his Faith. He went to Harvard, & added that this Jesuit tried to do several "dirty tricks on him afterwards." Yet this young officer, now married, was one of the few genuine Catholics I've met, who believed in his Faith as evenly and as romantically as P. Pearse did. We had many discussions on politics, literature, & religion, & he was a staunch, & I must admit, an eloquent Defender of the Faith.

At the end of the long letter I am looking at now, he says—"Well, Sean, it seems that writing a letter is a poor substitute for the wonderful evenings I had, sitting by your fire, & arguing about religion with you and Eileen." (Eileen is my missus) It seems to me that the Bishops are making the people so fearful of talking about their Faith to others, in case they'd lose it, that the Bishops themselves are not well established in their own belief. And no wonder when the matter of a Maynooth Professorship of Theology is made the subject of a job.

S. O'C.

(See over page)

Addendum Secundum

I enclose two little examples of what the Russia Today Society (R.T.S.) distributes. Both of course are a bit out of date now. Voroshilov, Buddenny, & Timoshenko have given place to a host of military leaders second to none any where. The biggest events held recently in honour of Swift were held in the USSR. Lately I looked for a book by Capt. Mayne

Reid [8] for my eldest boy, but could get it nowhere. The USSR was, at the time, printing 50,000 copies of his works, & in a Russ Magazine, they gave his life, from the day he was born in Co. Down to the day he died.

S. O'C.

[8] Thomas Mayne Reid (1818–83), novelist, born in Ballyroney, Co. Down; lived an adventurous life in America, 1840–49, serving as a Captain in the Mexican War in 1847; published his first novel, *The Rifle Rangers,* in 1850, and thereafter wrote many popular romances and tales of adventure for boys. The National Library of Ireland has over forty of his books.

IV

FROM LAST WORDS TO LAST JUDGMENTS, 1946

COURAGE is what we all sadly need. Goethe's last words were "More light, more light." Mine will probably be "More courage, more courage."

Dante, the great Italian, and the great Christian, put his enemies in hell, and I, no Christian, and much less of a poet, will not hesitate to do the same thing.

Religion and politics are common concerns for most Irishmen, and these two conflicting subjects were often in the forefront of O'Casey's mind throughout 1946. His letters indicate that he was busy defending his plays from those who denounced him for not being more sympathetic to Catholicism and those who demanded he should be more Marxist in his themes. In a May letter to someone who was searching for political "messages" in *Purple Dust,* he wrote: "There may be messages in the play, if you like to look for them. But I never have, and never will, just put plain slabs of propaganda in a play." He had to insist once again that he was his own kind of nondoctrinaire Communist; that he was anticlerical, not anti-Catholic. Perhaps he summed up his reaction to some of his critics most effectively in a September letter to Honor Tracy when he wrote: "Twenty years ago, and more, after JUNO and THE PLOUGH had appeared, 'The Universe' referred to me as a (a correspondent to the paper) Judas; and the 'Sunday Worker' called me a Pontius Pilate; the first for ridiculing Catholics, and the other for ridiculing the workers. And, I daresay, you know how Dublin took the second play. But still and all, I love Dublin, I dont hate Catholics, and I look upon myself as a friend of all workers." In the same letter, he also expressed his impatience with "Marxian fanatics who are so full of theory they would not stop to have a look at a lily or a rose." In an earlier letter to Francis MacManus, who had just written an article praising Canon Sheehan, the Irish priest who wrote homiletic little novels for decent Catholics, O'Casey protested that the cautious canon was too painfully virtuous and frightened of life: "Poor Sheehan's heart was always troubled, & it was always afraid. He wanted to go to Heaven without making a single mistake; & in avoiding mistakes, he made the biggest one of his life."

No such fear ever troubled the bold O'Casey, who courageously took his risks and made his mistakes. For example, he was right about Canon Sheehan's limited talent as a novelist, but he was too severe on the naïve priest's cloistered virtue. In his bristling determination to defend the power and glory of Jim Larkin, he went to the unnecessary extreme of denigrating the magnificent contribution of James Connolly and "stirred up a hornet's nest" in the camp of labor. He continued to indulge his moralistic reaction against "cissies" or homosexuals in the theatre, instead of simply judging them, like anyone else, on the basis of their artistic ability. He was in a more characteristic mood of fair play, however, when he wrote cheerfully to MacManus, a devout Catholic: "I like your reviews—I disagree with most of what you say, but I like the way you put things down." Understandably and inevitably, he was unable to be so open-minded when Gabriel Fallon made the mistake of accusing him of "coldly calculated bigotry" in *Red Roses For Me,* an unjust indictment which led to the breakup of their twenty-year friendship.

O'Casey was not angry because Fallon had attacked the play and called it, among other disappointments, an unsuccessful mixture of realism and expressionism. He had heard this kind of criticism often in the past, and he was prepared to grant his friend the right to disagree with him. But the cruel accusation of premeditated bigotry from one so close to him was too much to bear for a man of his known compassion for his poor Catholic neighbors and friends in Dublin. Several years earlier, in a 20 February 1943 letter to Fallon, there had been a slight hint of worry when O'Casey quoted Fallon's timid warning that "One passage might give grave offence to Catholics," but that was a far cry from what now became "coldly calculated bigotry." On that earlier occasion Fallon had hinted at the offensive passage, and it now became clear that he meant what he called the "hocus-pocus" of the disappearance and recovery of Our Lady of Eblana's statue. In a previous encounter with Dr. Joseph Cummins over the same incident in the play, in a deeply moving letter of 26 November 1942, O'Casey had convinced his friend Cummins that he was so dedicated to the fight against injustice of any kind that he was incapable of bias against Catholics; against the reactionary clergy, yes, but not against the people of any faith. Now Fallon, after twenty years of close observation, should have known better than anyone else that if O'Casey could sometimes be an imperfect playwright, he was an unwavering champion of religious and political tolerance. Fallon supported his charge of premeditated bigotry by claiming that the Catholic characters of the tenements were all presented as "liars and hypocrites and fools." He preferred to overlook the fact that such terms could be applied only to the Protestant vestrymen in the play, although O'Casey also makes it clear that no religion holds the monopoly on folly or hypocrisy. After Fallon's initial hint of offense, O'Casey, in his 1943 letter, had scolded his once freethinking friend for becoming too narrowly Catholic, alluding especially to his "connections" with *The Standard,* the sensationally pietistic newspaper for which Fallon now worked as drama critic. O'Casey had reason to suspect that his old friend was becoming a frightened Catholic, and that he was telling his frightened readers, who had long been conditioned to recognize O'Casey as an enemy of the people of Ireland, precisely what they wanted to hear. Originally, back in the early 1920s in Dublin, O'Casey and Fallon and Barry Fitzgerald had been the three inseparable "butties" at the Abbey Theatre, when Gaby and Barry worked regularly as clerks in the civil service and were part-time actors in the evenings, and Sean, the promising new playwright from the tenements, was still working as a common laborer and writing in the evenings. Now O'Casey, isolated in Devon with his Dublin memories, had lost both friends; Fitzgerald had presumably defected to the materialism of Hollywood, and Fallon had apparently defected to the pietism of *The Standard.* Perhaps they had created their own hell without any curse from O'Casey.

The two American drama critics, George Jean Nathan and Brooks Atkinson, whom he had met in New York in 1934 when he made the journey for the production of *Within the Gates,* were now among his most loyal friends and judges of his work. It was the more skeptical Atkinson, often teasing him about his Communism, who forced O'Casey, in a defensive and touching letter of 17 October, to justify what he had done with his pen during the war years. And it was the caustic Nathan, in a comment on an inept dramatization of *The Song of Bernadette,* who helped O'Casey remember what he knew, but sometimes overlooked, that political dogma can be as deadly as religious dogma when it is superimposed upon a work of art. In a reply to Nathan at the end of the year he wrote: "It is frightening that a bad play about the Immaculate Conception should be hailed as a great one; just as it is frightening that a bad play about 'Left' principles should be hailed as a good one." In his own case it was the political more than the religious theme which tended to make some of his later plays too didactic, especially when he departed from his saving grace of comedy.

To Sgt. Peter Newmark

MS. NEWMARK
TOTNES
2 JANUARY 1946

My dear Peter.

Grand to get your letter, & to learn that you still wandered under the glimpses of the moon. We were all wondering what had happened to you. I wish I were young enough to gallop about among the new, inquisitive life everywhere. I'm sure your experiences should do you good, & that you've learned more in the wild parts of Europe than you ever did, or ever could, in the tame groves of Cambridge. It is going to be a hard fight, though, against what you call "financial interests"—why the hell do you use such worn-out phrases?—, in Trieste, Pola, London, & Totnes. Old things take a long time to pass away. I have changed the name of the last play from W. on Wallpaper, to Oak Leaves & Lavender; or, a W. ôn W. Nathan thinks it a fine play, & so do I: much better than Red Roses for Me. I hope it may go on in Feb. or March. Red Roses is down for Feb. Purple Dust went well in Liverpool. I wish, too, you, or someone could translate The Star Turns Red into Croat, or Schlavic, for, bad as it is, it, as Nathan says, "is oddly invested with what may conceivably turn out to be a poet's prophetic vision." Nathan seems to have been right, for the star is turning red in a lot of places. Even Dublin has just started an Irish-Soviet Council of Friendship. Workers & Peasants are out for more than "a decent way of living" (though a lot of them dont know that yet); they're out for a full way of life—an hour a day among the stars. I have been very busy since— writing biographical sketches, articles for The Mint, Fore Publications— new ventures—Common Wealth, & a long one for the Anglo-Soviet Magazine—Rise o' the Red Star, corresponding about Socialism & the USSR with an Irish factory girl & a Dublin University Student; defending the USSR against attack by Bertrand Russell, & doing work about the house. Breon is bent on entering the London School of Economics. All well; & we shall be glad to see you in the Spring, when the Apple-blossoms & the frost come.

Ever yours.
Sean

To Gabriel Fallon

TS. Texas

Totnes, Devon
6 January 1946

My dear Gaby:

Thanks for the remembrancing card of Christmas. I sent part of your letter to Bronson Albery, with Miss O'M's—she should always add her full name to a letter like that; I didn't know it, and so couldn't pass the name on; but B. A. remembered, so that's allright—, and he says "I don't think Miss O'Mahony read the part of Mrs Breydon at all badly, and I know Miss Mooney has a considerable opinion of her. We decided on Ethel O'Shea by a narrow margin. The part of Eeeada has become vacant, and perhaps Miss O'Mahony would do for that." [1]

That's how it is, and all I can do for Miss O'M.

Well, well, your character of Christian Eire, my boy, is a very bad one. The same thing applies to each of the Christian countries. There isn't much use, in my opinion, in thinking that the condition of things around us flourishes because Christianity isn't put into practice. Christians will be always judged for what they do, or don't do; just the same as Communists—the whole world is a tiptoe looking over the walls of the Kremlin to see what's going on there; and eager to see, and comment upon, the slightest flaw. The burst-up has already come; the whole world is aflame for a new life. A young soldier, a friend of mine, tells me that in Yugo-Slavia, every Slovene, Macedonian, Croatian Serbian, and Albanian flag has one thing in common—on each is the tiny red star of the militant workers and thinkers in each of the lands. And though it hasn't come on to it yet, it will appear on the flag of China; and, maybe on that of Japan, too. The Vatican is alive to the danger as the latest selection of Cardinals proclaims—an attempt to unify the political church against the common enemy. And no Cardinal for Eire! And Mannix [2] passed over; and Downey,[3] too—a far abler man than Griffin [4] is, or ever will be; but Downey hasn't got the influential and rich Catholics behind him that Griffin had, and has; a big house where all the leading Tory politicians are welcome; and old English Catholic family, rich, powerful, influential, but

---

[1] Nora O'Mahony played the role of Eeada in the London production of *Red Roses For Me*. See O'Casey's letter to Mrs. Una Gwynn Albery, 6 March 1946, note 1.

[2] The Most Rev. Daniel Mannix (1864–1963), Archbishop of Melbourne.

[3] The Most Rev. Richard Downey (1881–1953), Bishop of Liverpool.

[4] Bernard Cardinal Griffin (1899–1956), Archbishop of Westminster.

dead in thought and vision for the last hundred years. But these things would take weeks to argue upon, and so per amica silentio luna. My dear Gaby, ever since I started to write publicly, I have been confronted with the big word WHY? Why this, why that, and the one answer to each and all is I'm damned if I can tell. As for the Eire Censorship, I'm afraid it is more powerful, if not in fact, in influence, on Irish writers than you think. I've seen its influence a lot of times "A Statue for a Square" [5] or a square for a statue; Macnamara; and I've just read a pitiful short story by one called Daniel Corkery, called "The Boy Saint," [6] in a recent issue of The Irish Press. Is this the Hidden Ireland man? And Macnamara's article on the theatre, from the playwright's point of view, in a recent Independent; [7] and its shadow dims the sound of The Bell; [8] and Sean Tee [9] broadcasting, "Trath so ne Feile beannaithe, is cuibhe dhuinn smaoineamh ar mhifhortuin ne ndaoine bochta ata creachta ag an gcogadh." [10] There's Irish for you! This blessed time, Mhfhortuin,[11] mind you! The Irish of S. Tee, Dev. and Hyde go together, dry and dead, sere and yellow leaves drooping from the Gaelic tree of life. I'm glad you liked The Time of Your Life—there's drama in Saroyan. I've neither read nor seen Skin of Your Teeth, but Nathan doesn't rank it very high, thinking that it is built up on Joyce's Finnegans Wake, without acknowledgment.[12]

I do be very busy these days. The three children put in on me a lot, & I don't like (I never have) to make the room I work in, a prohibited parlour. But still I manage to do a little. I have an article on the Theatre & the Politicians in Common Wealth,[13] & a longer one on Theatre & the People to appear in a new paper [14] coming out this month; and one on Synge for British Ally,[15] a magazine circulated by Britain in the USSR; & one on

[5]Francis MacManus, *A Statue For a Square* (1945), a novel.

[6] Daniel Corkery's "The Child Saint," *Irish Press,* 19 December 1945, originally appeared in Corkery's collection of short stories, *A Munster Twilight* (1916). Corkery (1878–1964), Professor of English at University College, Cork; teacher, scholar, author; wrote *The Hidden Ireland* (1925), a study of the Munster Gaelic poets of the eighteenth century.

[7] Brinsley Macnamara, "The Future of the Irish Theatre," *Irish Independent,* 29 December 1945.

[8] *The Bell,* literary magazine in Dublin edited by Peadar O'Donnell and Sean O'Faolain.

[9] Sean T. O'Kelly.

[10] "In this time of the Blessed Feast, it is fitting for us to think on the misfortunes of the poor people who are afflicted by the war."

[11] Misfortunes.

[12] The typed portion of the letter ends here, and the following paragraphs were added in longhand.

[13] Sean O'Casey, "The Theatre and the Politician," *Common Wealth Review,* January 1946; reprinted in *Blasts and Benedictions* (1967).

[14] Sean O'Casey, "The People and the Theatre," *Theatre Today,* March 1946; reprinted in *Under a Colored Cap* (1963).

[15] This is probably a reference to O'Casey's article, "John Millington Synge," commissioned by the British Ministry of Information and published in *Britansky Soyuznik,* Moscow, 23 June 1946; printed in English for the first time in *Blasts and Benedictions* (1967).

Rise of the Red Star in the Anglo-Soviet Journal;[16] as well as doing an
odd page for the next biographical vol. That article by Brinsley seemed to
me to be a poor one—that one on the playwright & the Theatre. Why on
earth did he fling up his job over Skin of your Teeth? Perhaps, there was
more work than pay in the job—as there is in most of them. But hasn't he
some kind of a Post in The N. Gallery?[17] I see old Bodkin,[18] now in
Birmingham, has yelled out that Picasso should be prevented from showing
pictures where decent men live. I'm afraid Picasso'll live longer than the
bare Bodkin. And McColl,[19] too, the friend of Steer,[20] Tonks,[21] & G[eorge]
Moore. Well, Picasso'll live longer than poor McColl the poor painter.

I daresay, all your boys & girls—five of them, isn't it?—are grown up
be now. Has Frankie left you? Our Breon is "going on" 18, now; Niall 11,
& Shivaun 6. I hope all of them—yours & mine—will do fine in the world
before them. Rose must have had a time of it bringing them all up. I know
what it is, for I'm home all the day to see it. Housewives never get a fair
do. Give her my (& Eileen's) love; the same to all your children, & to
yourself.

A late Picture Post has been full of pictures showing Barry Fitzgerald,
also known to some as Will Shields, being hauled out of a river of "icy-cold
water" by Barbara Hutton, in a Film called "The Incendiary Blonde." Going
every way but his own. He needn't do it, you know; he has enough to keep
himself safe, & satisfy his art. Had he ever any? I'm afraid Barry would
do anything for the dollar. There's a lot like him. Even Brinsley, who jokes
at Hollywood, might find it hard to refuse a chance there. There's some
consternation here over Shaw's "Julius Caesar."[22] Rank poured it into a
golden mould, & it seemed to come out crooked. The hand of the potter
shook, or something.

Well, all the best.
Yours as ever.
Sean

P.S. I am sending back with this the letter you got from Miss Nora O'M.

[16] Sean O'Casey, "Rise of the Red Star," *Anglo-Soviet Journal*, Spring 1946.

[17] Brinsley Macnamara held the position of Registrar at the National Gallery, Dublin, from 1925 to 1960. James Stephens held it from 1915 to 1925, and when he left, O'Casey told me, Lady Gregory wanted to obtain it for O'Casey but he refused.

[18] Thomas Bodkin (1887–1961), Director of the National Gallery, Dublin, 1927–35; became the first Director of the Barber Institute of Fine Arts, and Barber Professor of Fine Arts, at the University of Birmingham, 1935–53.

[19] Dugald Sutherland MacColl (1859–1948), painter, critic, and keeper of the Tate Gallery, London.

[20] Philip Wilson Steer (1860–1942), painter and teacher at the Slade School of Fine Arts, London.

[21] Henry Tonks (1862–1937), painter and teacher at the Slade School of Fine Arts, London. Tonks, Steer, and MacColl were members of an intimate circle of artists and literary figures, including George Moore, J. S. Sargent, and Sir Augustus Daniel.

[22] The film version of Bernard Shaw's *Caesar and Cleopatra*, made in 1945, produced by Arthur Rank, directed by Gabriel Pascal, with Claude Rains and Vivien Leigh in the title roles.

To Ria Mooney

TC. O'CASEY

[TOTNES, DEVON]
7 JANUARY 1946

Dear Miss Mooney:

It would seem that there is little more for me to say to you, bar reminding you that it was you yourself, in your very first letter who wrote prominently about your "career"; that nothing was said by me without a reason; that, though you say you "assure me you could have made your letter longer," you didn't; that I gave you valuable instances where "holding up the action" added to the fineness and magic of a play; that the fact of you being "a middle-aged woman, with a family to support," has nothing whatever to do with the production of a play; and to express the hope that you see that now.

In fact, to avoid all unnecessary arguments, I have allowed most of your "cuts," [1] and added some of my own, though your last letter is very irritating. You are the second fortunate person with whom I have come into touch who knows all there is to be known about the Theatre. I confess that, directly or indirectly, I have been in touch with the theatre for nearly fifty years, and it is as much a mystery to me as ever it was. But since I have no desire to dispute the estimate you may have of yourself; and since the Theatre is your "job," as you put it; and since you know so much about it, it would seem that it would be a waste of your time to come down here to talk about things concerning the production of the play.

But it is the custom here, wisely or unwisely, to submit all questions of doubt and difficulty in a play to the consideration of the author before any change or alteration is made.

Yours sincerely,
Sean O'Casey

[1] In the script of *Red Roses For Me*.

To Jack Carney

MS. NYU LIBRARY

TOTNES, DEVON
10 JANUARY 1946

Dear Jack,

We said all we could to persuade Jim [Larkin] to stop the night; but he was obstinately determined to go back. He doesn't realise yet that a man of 70 can't do what one of 25 can do easily. I daresay, he'll die with harness on his back. Of course, Jim was always religious—in the good sense of the word. I don't think he acted quite justly to Mrs. L.[1] After all, it must have been a tough job to have been tied to Jim. He had very little time for any home-life. I think he made a mistake in not living with her when he came back. But I never said so to him—that sort of thing's too private to be discussed with anyone. Of course, he would dream about her, for his mind is full of her now; & all associations would come into the dreams—there's nothing supernatural in these things.

Ay, have I seen the articles on the Theatre in the I.I.,[2] & bloody poor ones they are too; as if the things happening everywhere didn't send a ripple of sound to Eire's ear. I've just written an article on Synge for "British Ally" which, they told me "would bring me into touch with the Russian people." And me in touch with them for over 20 years!

The name of him who does my Tax—I daresay it was he I mentioned—is

A.W. Mills, F.C.A.
Farrow, Bersey, Gain, Vincent, & Co.
Chartered Accountants
53, New Broad Street
London, E.C. 2

Love to Mina & you.
Sean

[1] Jim Larkin had lived apart from his wife since 1923, when he returned from America. See O'Casey's letter to William O'Brien, ? November 1921, note 3, Vol. I, p. 97.

[2] The *Irish Independent* ran a series of six articles, on "The Future of the Irish Theatre," from 28 December 1945 to 3 January 1946, written by Lord Longford, Brinsley Macnamara, Micheál MacLiammoir, Thomas J. Collins, Piaras Beaslaoi, and Harry O'Donovan.

To Francis MacManus

TS. MacManus

Totnes, Devon

14 January 1946

Dear Frank,

By now, you're an old married man, with a family, I daresay. I just write to say a word about you and your "An Scriobhnoir a Ciapadh," [1] appearing in the first number of An Iris. Well, well, the Gaels have at last, published a magazine worth reading. Of course, I can't read it, having no Gaelic—you know that—, but, all the same, it looks well, anyway. Now let me give an opinion or two (not dogmas, mind you) in a very friendly way. Yours is a most interesting article—for a critic—but is it a good thing for an author to be diving so deep into the relatively shallow mind of Sheehan? "Claoidheadh leis na sean-mhodhanna" [2] . . . By God, he did, ri' enough. He hadn't one ten-thousandth part of the courage of [Walter] McDonald and he a prisoner in Maynooth,—jail for a theologian more fiercely barred than even the Vatican. "B'eidir go raibh eagla air uaireannta (always) eagla roimh an saoghal, eagla roimh a comh-shagairt, agus eagla roim an buafacht!!" [3] eagla roimh [4] everything, Frank. Afraid of the humanism of Shakespeare, & frightened of the Paganism of Goethe. How terribly unlike his Master. Yes, how terribly unlike his Master's Servants— him of Assisi, Francis, of Dominic, of F. Xavier, of our own Colmcille, Aidan & Brighid, & the rest of them! "Let not your heart be troubled, neither let it be afraid." And—according to your Faith—Christ nearer to them now than He was to the Disciples at that time. Poor Sheehan's heart was always troubled, & it was always afraid. He wanted to go to Heaven without making a single mistake; & in avoiding mistakes, he made the biggest one of his life. And as for the "Buafacht" [5] you mention, he could have found it everywhere in Ireland in the horrifying slums, in the neat houses of the middle-class, in the bigger ones of the well-to-do, ay, and in Maynooth College itself, in the desire for promotion rather than the love of honesty and truth.

I'm afraid Canon Sheehan's a bad guide to the coming Irish writers.

---

[1] Proinsias MacMaghnais, "An Scriobhnoir a Ciapadh" ("The Writer Who Was Tormented"), *An Iris,* Samhain (November) 1945; an article by MacManus about the Rev. Patrick Augustine Sheehan (1852–1913), parish priest of Doneraile, Co. Cork, made Canon in 1903, who wrote a number of popular novels under the name of Canon Sheehan. *An Iris,* an Irish-language monthly magazine edited by Séamus Ó Néill, ran from November 1945 to April 1946.

[2] "To cling to the old traditions."

[3] "Perhaps he was always afraid, afraid of the world, afraid of his fellow priests, and afraid of malice."

[4] "Afraid of."

[5] "Malice."

In the article "An Coras Oideachais," [6] striding stoutly in No. 2, and you will see some of the Buafacht you mentioned in your own article. I hope Fear na Dhuthaigh [7] will read it. And, if you meet him, say something of what happened when Fr. M. O'Flanagan [8] of Cliffoney, told his shivering people to go & gather the turf from the bog, even if it were private property, so that they could bring a ray, of heat towards their icy bodies. I'm afraid there's more truth in the satire An Beal Bocht [9] than there is in any of Sheehan's genteel yarns, or were in Corkery's Bantry Bay, I'm-sitting-all-alone-in-the-gloaming peace & quietness of Munster Celtic Twilight.[10]

And I hope "Maire" isn't going to imitate O'Henry, as he seems to be doing in "Miorbhail Cholum Cille." [11] He is much more at home with skin the goat, though it wasn't poor Kitty O'Shea who put her little feet on Eire's fate, but the brogues of the Bishops; & Parnell never did false by the Invincibles, never knowing about them till the attack took place. But it is, I think, right that these men, very rough & ready in their love for Ireland, should have a niche, at least, in the porch of Ireland's temple to her heroes. I remember my mother spoke respectfully of the big man Brady, how brave & true he was, however mistaken his policy, & she showed signs of grief whenever she mentioned the name of handsome Dan Curley. I wonder is there left any where one of the black-edged cards, dropped into the letter-boxes of the Press, morning after the killing, bearing the words (in Curley's writing it was said) "This deed was done by The Irish Invincibles." They had a terrible time of it, for there was no sympathy anywhere. And yet, these men stood to gain nothing personally from it—their motive, at least, was not an evil one.

Well, anyway, I've read the two numbers of Iris (getting them translated first) with great interest, & some surprise. How poky, matter-of-fact is the Irish notes appearing in the Irish Press. The horrid I. Independent is better in this regard than the I.P. I think.

I do hope you and your wife are well, & that you are doing well. We are so so here, a bit tired after the years of black-out, wailing sirens, & some bombing, with the airoplanes buzzing over us night after night; & the comforting of our two younger children, when I wanted all the comfort

---

[6] Seán Ó hUrmoltaigh, "An Córas Oideachais" ("The Education System"), *An Iris,* Samhain 1945.

[7] Roibeárd Ó Faracháin, "Fear 'na Dhúthaigh" ("A Man in His Own Land"), *An Iris,* Samhain 1945, a regular feature in all issues of *An Iris.* In the issue of Nodlaig (December) 1945, "Seachain do cheann, a Éireannaigh!" ("Watch your head, Irishman!") O Faracháin reviewed O'Casey's *Drums Under the Windows.*

[8] Father Michael O'Flanagan (1876–1942), the Republican priest who was censured and silenced a number of times, and who told the starving and shivering peasants to cut the turf in a bog which had been declared private property.

[9] Myles na gCopaleen, *An Béal Bocht* (1941).

[10] See the reference to Daniel Corkery in O'Casey's letter to Gabriel Fallon, 6 January 1946, note 6.

[11] Máire, "Miobhail Cholum Cille" ("The Miracle of Colum Cille"), *An Iris* Samhain 1945. Máire is the pseudonym of Seámus Ó Grianna.

myself. Eileen was great; ready with her box of First Aids to see to any injury that might suddenly appear on any of us. I often wondered what the hell I'd do if it were she who happened to be hit first.

I'm not a bit frightened of the atomic bomb. No-one will dare to use it; though by the way, its making isn't a question of money, as S. Mac-Cnaimhin [12] thinks. It is a question of labour alone; & so the difficulty of money doesn't apply to the USSR. Socialist Labour can always create the thing it thinks it needs.

All good wishes to you & to Iris.

Yours very sincerely,
Sean O'Casey

[12] Seámas MacCnáimhin, "An t-Adamh—Priomh-Námha an Phobail?" ("The Atom—Public Enemy Number One?"), *An Iris,* Samhain 1945.

To Paul Vincent Carroll [1]

TC. O'CASEY

[TOTNES, DEVON]
15 JANUARY 1946

Dear Mr. Carroll:
Thank you for your kind invitation to have a chat. I am not in London at the moment, for the rehearsals of my play havent begun yet. I was surprised to hear that you were living permanently in London. I thought you were busy with the affairs of the Civic Theatre that gave such promise for an active theatre in Scotland. The last I heard of it, some months ago, it was doing well. But, of course, you could hardly think of writing plays if you continued to be busy with other things.

I hope your new play [*The Wise Have Not Spoken*] will be a great success in Bristol. I hadnt heard of it before. The last play of yours that was in the news was THE STRINGS MY LORD ARE FALSE which had such a success in Dublin when produced by Shelah Richards.[2] I daresay she will be doing the new one there, too, for you. I will try to see you, if I come to London, but I have to see so many—Unity Theatre people, friends of the

[1] Paul Vincent Carroll (1900–68), Irish playwright, born near Dundalk, Co. Louth, educated in Dublin; went to Glasgow in 1921 where he worked as a teacher in a slum district for sixteen years. His early play, *Things That Are Caesar's* (1932), was awarded a prize by the Abbey Theatre; among his other plays were *Shadow and Substance* (1937), *The White Steed* (1938), *Kindred* (1939), *The Strings, My Lord, Are False* (1942), *The Wise Have Not Spoken* (1944), *The Devil Came From Dublin* (1952), *The Wayward Saint* (1955).
[2] See O'Casey's letter to Gabriel Fallon, 23 May 1942, note 1.

Daily Worker, some members of the Soviet Embassy, and others that it may be hard to find the time.

However, all the best anyway.

Yours sincerely,
Sean O'Casey

To Horace Reynolds

MS. REYNOLDS

TOTNES, DEVON
17 JANUARY 1946

Dear Horace:

A line or two to let you know we got the two parcels safely, and the sugar, tea, meat, & candies were admired & carried away. Thank you & Kay, very much, for thinking in such a kindly & practical way of us. But, personally, whisper, I dont altogether like the idea of you sending us these things. I know Kay & you well, &, I think, your circumstances, too; & that you have two children to guard and cherish. Now I know that you, like myself, are anything but a rich man, & that, on the last day of an old year, Kay & you start the New One with more courage & hope than money. No, my friends, your Bank will never be able to build a new wing with what you deposit in it; so be careful, oul' son, and take a chance, but never two.

We are fairly well here; just a little tired after the years of black-out & sirens blaring. Lucky, we were to be out of range of the robot bombs. Your boys' capture of Cherbourg & its surroundings saved Devon from them. We still have to [do] most of the housework ourselves, for nothing better can be got at the moment than a woman to come in the morning on odd days to do a little for us. It's not so bad when the children are at school; & they go back on Monday next after 5 weeks' holidays. So God is good.

Red Roses goes into rehearsal next February. The Manager has got an Irish woman (Ria Mooney who was with Eve le Galliene for some time, & knows it!) to produce. She began by writing airily asking for cuts to prevent the "holding up of the play's action." When I wrote asking how this or that held up the action, & asked what was "action" anyway, she replied that she was "a middle-aged woman with a family to support" & that "the theatre was her job." But the theatre has to suffer fools gladly. I'm just completing page-proofs of "Oak Leaves & Lavender", & when it comes out, I'll send you on a copy. A new monthly Irish Magazine, "An Iris," has appeared, &, at last, articles in Gaelic worth reading have come before us.

There is a gleam of new thought & sharper questioning of life in it; & I hope it is the first swallow of a fine flock of them to herald an Irish Summer.

I daresay, your boy, John is with you again. I hope he is. Remember me to him, though he'd hardly remember me now. And Peggy: she must be a fine lass now. To her my fond remembrance. And my love to Kay & you. God be wi' you all.

Yours as ever
Sean

To Miss Sheila———

MS. PRIVATE

TOTNES, DEVON
18 JANUARY 1946

Dear Sheila,

I haven't had a second since to acknowledge your last letter—what with proofs of a play, articles, Christmas & the children, I and the missus haven't had time to say How do you do to ourselves.

Not even time to give a thought to the hope the Jesuits have of turning Father C——— into a saint. I, of course, can judge him only from what you said of him, & what he, unconsciously, said of himself in his letters. I shouldn't be surprised if they succeeded, for the day of the saint is ended. Decadence is to be seen every where in religious circles. You are not going to have a Frances, a Dominic, a Teresa—not she who is called "The Little Flower"—a Xavier, or even a John Bosco again. They have all gone over to the Communists. Why even St. Nicholas has become a valuable asset to the money-makers.

You are wrong about the impossibility of Catholics marrying Protestants. It occurs often. The Ne temere decree tried to stop it; but didn't succeed. And animosity among C.'s & P.'s in Ireland is, as far as I know, almost unknown, except the ports of the North, where one side is as bigoted as the other.

All the best for the New Year.

Yours sincerely,
Sean O'Casey.

To Ria Mooney

TC. O'Casey

[Totnes, Devon]
23 January 1946

Dear Ria Mooney.

Very well; you didn't understand me, and I didn't understand you, so we won't mention these things again; we'll forget all about them, and begin right from the beginning when you come down to us.

The week-end is a little awkward, for our children are day scholars and are home all the week-end; and, since the war, help is hard to get, and very uncertain, so a lot of the work has to be done by my wife and me. But we can make you fairly comfortable in a simple way, and, I'm sure you won't mind, if, at times, we have to leave you by the fire so that we may do a thing or two in the house.

I hope the Cast given you will be a good one, and that the play may be a success.

Let us know by what train you will come to Totnes from Paddington.

All the best,
Yours sincerely,
[Sean O'Casey]

To Alfred Jordan

MS. Jordan

Totnes, Devon
29 January 1946

Dear Mr. Jordan,

It doesn't matter if a play be "technically amateurish," so long as there is vigor, originality, & vision in it. Technique can be learned; the other features are gifts from nature or from God. Don't mind the things that are "billed" as "good successes." No good man writes to be "billed" or to be a "success"; he writes because he feels he must. So I think, anyhow. Your wife, you know, may be right. Very often things written long ago, contain the germ of a fine work. I hope your novel may be a good one. "Great success" is a relative thing. Marie Corelli, Charles Garvis, Edgar Wallace, & Noel Coward are "great successes"—or were—, but they have added nothing to life's literature.

As for withholding your plays from production because of a personal resentment—that would be foolish. Any way, you wouldn't do it: no human being would. You might do it, if you thought the production not to be good enough, but that's a different thing. If you think of persisting in play-making, read all the finest plays you can get—not for their technique; but for their meditation, their valour, their exuberance, their pity, & their beauty. But why not send a copy of your play to one of the Repertories? Newcastle on Tyne—The People's Theatre, is one; or, maybe, the Old Vic. Write a preliminary letter first, asking them if they be interested. If they reply to say they are, they will be almost certain to read it. Many managements return plays without reading them. There are so many, & so little time.

Your sincerely,
Sean O'Casey

To Irish Democrat

FEBRUARY 1946

"Larkin vs. Connolly"

In his very flattering review of my book, in December's issue of your important Irish Journal, "E. M. B." makes the comment, "The author does no service to the Irish Labour Movement (particularly at this time when the O'Brien breakaway elements are trying to claim Connolly as their own) by extolling Jim Larkin at the expense of his greater associate." [1] Again "E. M. B." refers to Connolly as "the outstanding figure in the Irish Labour Movement." "E. M. B." is sadly mistaken—Jim Larkin is the outstanding figure in the Irish Labour Movement; it was he, and he only, who created it. "The greatest Irishman since Parnell," said Bernard Shaw, once in referring to him; and Bernard Shaw was right. It was the excessive devotion to Connolly, at the expense of Larkin, that gave O'Brien his chance; a thing I warned the Labour Movement of fifteen years ago. That Connolly was, relatively, a great man, there is no doubt, but to say that he had the magnetism, the strange organising power, the eloquence of Jim Larkin, or anything like these qualities, is in no way warranted by any fact whatsoever.

"E. M. B." will naturally say these are the opinions of O'Casey, and

---

[1] E. M. B. (E. M. Boyle), "Dublin Days of Hunger, Fear, and Wrath," *Irish Democrat,* December 1945, a review of *Drums Under the Windows. Irish Freedom* (1939–44) had changed its name to the *Irish Democrat* in 1945.

opinions are not facts, and "E. M. B." is, of course, right, though the opinions are based on knowledge and personal experience. But they will be found set down in *The Irish Labour Movement,* written by W. P. Ryan, and published by The Talbot Press twenty-five years ago. I should advise "E. M. B." to read chapter XIII, called "Larkin's Youth in the Depths," and chapter XIV, called "The Rise of 'Larkinism' "; not "The Rise of Connolly," mind you, but the "Rise of Larkinism." Now W. P. Ryan was a deep personal friend of Connolly's, and was also one of his faithful disciples, so that his opinion has a meaning that can't be over-rated. Ryan was one of Ireland's great men, too, though Ireland didn't know it, and doesn't know it yet. Here is a quotation: "I well remember the swift, strange growth of the marvel, the dire magic of the sinister, tremendous 'Larkin' of the legend, several months before I met the human 'Jim' in the actual world. We have seen already a good deal of the long and patient toil, the serious teaching, the deep convictions of Connolly. Now and then his doctrine had heartened or antagonised elements in Ireland, but his personality had not really come home to the popular mind, had not taken any definite place in its consciousness. Like sensations that are read of in newspapers or novels, Connolly's light and logic had passed, leaving no ultimate trace. Neither friend nor foe had felt any sense of mystery on the one hand, or diabolism on the other. Then Larkin came, agitated Belfast, and set to work in obscure quarters of our Irish world, and soon there was a sense of something sinister and haunting in the background of life." One more: "Towards the close of Connolly's American term, Jim Larkin had begun his mission amongst Irish toilers in deeps that Connolly had never reached or attracted so far. Labour comrades themselves had the feeling or the fear that Connolly was overmuch of the theorist. After his prompt and hearty association with Larkin they began to see him in a new light." (Page 169.)

In other words, Larkin made Connolly more human, and so more effective. The flame that burns in the heart of the Irish Labour Movement, whether we like it or not, was lit by Jim Larkin, and lit by none other.

We should not forget, either, that others died in Easter Week, besides Jim Connolly. Peadar Maicin was one; Richard O'Carroll was another; so was Sean Connolly and so was [Michael] Mallin, not forgetting the spendid Bill Partridge, who died after doing penal servitude. And who wants to forget the indomitable little figure of the valorous [Francis] Sheehy-Skeffington who fell at the hands of a frantic British officer? These I hope, some day, will form a group of statuary in some Irish park.

Connolly was greater than these—bar Sheehy-Skeffington, who was as great as any in his own way; each was great in his own way, but Jim Larkin, from the Labour point of view, was, by far, the greatest of them all; and still is.

Sean O'Casey

Totnes, Devon.

[We are glad to publish this letter by Mr. Sean O'Casey, though not agreeing with his viewpoint. At a time when the whole future of the Irish Labour movement is in the melting pot, it would be interesting to hear other reader's opinions on the relative contributions made by Larkin and Connolly in building up the movement. Mr. O'Casey has probably stirred up a hornet's nest. Will readers please note that stings should be brief and written on one side of the paper only.—Editor]

To Lovat Dickson

TS. MACMILLAN LONDON

TOTNES, DEVON
19 FEBRUARY 1946

Dear Mr Lovat Dickson:

This is a note to say that RED ROSES FOR ME is to be produced on either the 26th, or 27th of this month, at The Embassy, Swiss Cottage.[1]

I thought, perhaps, you might like to know this in order to place some copies in the Theatre; or that the production of the play might possibly result in some additional demand for the book of the play in the booksellers.

After the Embassy, the play is to go on tour—to Brighton, I think, first; but when I get the names of the places, I'll let you know.

Thanks for the letter asking about the French license for JUNO.

One thing more: when you send out review copies of OAK LEAVES AND LAVENDER, as I daresay you will, please send no copy to either *The Universe* or *The Irish Independent* of Dublin. The critics of these papers are, in my opinion, destitute of thought, either for or against a work.

All the best.
Yours sincerely,
Sean O'Casey

[1] *Red Roses For Me* opened in London at the Embassy Theatre, Swiss Cottage, on 26 February 1946. See O'Casey's letter to Mrs. Una Gwynn Albery, 6 March 1946, note 1.

To Bernard Shaw

TC. O'CASEY

TOTNES, DEVON
19 FEBRUARY 1946

Dear G. B. S.

Greetings and congratulations on becoming a Freeman of Dublin's fair city; Ptolemy's Eblana (or was it Strabo), the Danes' Dyflinnisk, and the Gaels' B'lah Cliath of the Golden Goblets.

Sooner or later, we'll see you in stone in one of the parks or erect in one of the streets—in stone or bronze.

What a pity about CAESAR AND CLEOPATRA.[1] Apparently, too much money has spoiled it all. I'm sorry you didnt go in for THE DEVIL'S DISCIPLE first. This play would have lent itself to a grand film production, I think. I remember mentioning it years ago, years and years ago, but Mrs Shaw didnt like the idea.

All the best to you.
Yours very sincerely,
Sean O'Casey

[1] See O'Casey's letter to Gabriel Fallon, 6 January 1946, note 22.

To Jack Carney

MS. NYU LIBRARY

TOTNES, DEVON
22 FEBRUARY 1946

Dear Jack,

Enclosed letter for you came here this—Friday—morning. Looks bad in Egypt & India—the old, old story of Ireland: & Bevin looking out of a Triplex window at it all. And Brigadin Rigadoon Raynor telling us "When he came into contact with the Russians, he found they were Orientals." I wonder what are Orientals? Fellas that cause trouble, I suppose. Didn't oul' Salisbury[1] call us Irish "Hottentots"? I wonder why. Because we caused trouble, I suppose.

[1] James Edward Salisbury, 4th Marquis (1861–1947), British politician, extreme right-wing Conservative.

"Red Roses" is to appear in London next week. I was to go up, but my eye got inflamed & painful, so Eileen went up alone.

Thanks for papers. Can't write more: eye too painful.

Love to Mina.
Yours as ever
Sean

To Mrs. Una Gwynn Albery

MS. ALBERY

TOTNES, DEVON
6 MARCH 1946

Dear Mrs. Albery:

A thousand thanks to you for all you did to get my play, "Red Roses" from the book into the added life of a production.[1] I am glad that it proved worthy of being a choice made by "Una Plays."

Eileen has mentioned to me a book you have holding within it many reminders of a Golden Past, when Gaelic Ireland first began to rise from a too-deep sleep; & that you would be glad to lend it to me. I shall be delighted to get a loan of it from you.

It will be pleasing to me, too, to autograph any book of mine you like to send me. Apart, entirely, from your interest in my plays, a daughter of the scholar & poet & Gael, T. W. Rolleston, would always command my most respectful attention and affectionate regard.

With all my warm wishes,

Yours very sincerely,
Sean O'Casey

[1] *Red Roses For Me* opened on 26 February 1946 at the Embassy Theatre, London, presented by Bronson Albery's Una Productions, directed by Ria Mooney, with the following cast: Ethel O'Shea as Mrs. Breydon; Kieron O'Hanrahan as Ayamonn; Nora O'Mahony as Eeada; Sheila Carty as Dympna; Norrie Duff as Finnoola; Maureen Pook as Sheila Moorneen; Eddie Byrne as Brennan o' the Moor; Dermot MacDowell as a Singer; Alex Dignam as Roory; Victor Wood as Mullcanny; Tristan Rawson as the Rev. E. Clinton; Robert Mooney as 1st Railwayman and Lamplighter; Michael Healy as 2nd Railwayman; Harry Webster as Inspector Finglas; T. J. Hurley as Samuel; Charles Blair as Dowzard; Terry Wilson as Foster.

To Mrs. Una Gwynn Albery

MS. ALBERY

TOTNES, DEVON
6 MARCH 1946

Dear Mrs. Albery,

Thank you so much for the book & the tea which came this afternoon. No two things could be more welcome to a sober Irishman than a good book and a package of good tea. I daresay you know the Irish proverb: "Marbh le tae agus marbh gan é—death with tea, & dead without it" I am convinced that there is an undiscovered vitamin in tea.

I'm sure I shall enjoy the book. Ay, indeed, O'Leary [1] had a fine Tolstoyan head, broader a little, & not quite so long; but very like that of the Russian. Strange, how he was such a poor writer. My knowledge of him was but a stare or two as I watched him teasing the second-hand books on the Book-barrows—old, tired books, looking as if they needed a rest & desired one too. I daresay we must put up with Agate a little longer.[2] A friend of mine tells me in a letter that he believes Agate never saw the play. That may be so. I remember he wrote mockingly of "Murder in the Cathedral," play and production in the S. Times. Afterwards, Ashley Dukes wrote to me to say Agate hadn't set foot inside the Theater to see it. Of course what he said won't matter in the long run; but it matters now; & now is our time only for life & work. The man is no danger to me as a dramatist: I couldn't be led by him; but he is a danger to the younger men & women of the theatre: and that concerns us all. However, I'll think more of this anon, when I'm drinking a cup of your grand teeo.

Love from Eileen, & every good wish from

Yrs very sincerely,
Sean O'Casey

[1] John O'Leary (1830–1907), a leader of the Fenian movement; editor of the *Irish People.* John B. Yeats's portrait of him in the National Gallery of Ireland reflects his very impressive and "noble head." (W. B. Y.)

[2] James Agate, "A Poet's Play," *Sunday Times,* 3 March 1946, a review of *Red Roses For Me.*

To Peter Newmark

MS. NEWMARK

TOTNES, DEVON

6 MARCH 1946

My dear Peter,

Many thanks for the tobacco. It was very kind of you, though I don't remember you knew I smoked a pipe. Glad you're home again, & I hope you'll soon be able to settle down. I don't like the idea of Rochdale very much. I imagine more thought should be given to the country, where the Tories hold on fast. Besides, I think, you'll be up against the Vatican there. It is up North that the attempt of creating Catholic Trades Unions is strongest. Isn't it in Manchester that the "Catholic Worker" is printed & published? I'm glad "Red Roses" turned out better than you expected. I hope it may run long enough to make things safe for a year or so. I shant bother about Agate. I haven't seen what he wrote; but from what you have written, I can guess it. I shouldn't be surprised if he hadn't seen the play. He criticised, mockingly, "Murder in the Cathedral," in the S. Times, & Ashley Dukes wrote to me later saying he hadn't come near the play. I wanted Dukes to kick up a row about it; but he thought it better to let it go.

I'll write you more when this eye of mine improves. I've just corrected proof of article—"Rise o' the Red Star"—for Anglo-Soviet Magazine,[1] & the eyes is damned painful.

I hope they publish your letter.

Affectionate Regards
Sean

[1] See O'Casey's letter to Gabriel Fallon, 6 January 1946, note 16.

To Jack Carney

MS. NYU LIBRARY

TOTNES, DEVON

8 MARCH 1946

Dear Jack,

Thanks ever so much for the tobacco & the papers—including Agate's sonata. I should love to have seen Bevin yelling for his wife, & looking for his teeth. Clapham amok in Moscow. The Labour Movement is bound to throw up a blossom like him now & again. We're far from being half-way home. Agate evidently doesn't know the difference between a shunter & a platelayer. I wonder what they'll think of an article of mine appearing in a New Magazine on the Theatre [1]—I've forgotten its name. It's in charge, I think, of Montague Slater & Reynolds, or the Co-op. I wrote it months & months ago.

I'm very glad the Play got a good reception, & hope it may hang on till it makes the coming year a sure one for us. The small stage handicapped the movements.

Curious about old Bill O'B. retiring from the I.T.G.W.U.[2] I simply can't believe it. I'm certain he'll control it some way or another. Unless he saw his time was up, & the game lost. Jim must be feeling bucked up over Shaw's letter. Bill O'B. must be furious. I wonder what sort of a book Bill will write.

Why did you send the copies of Drums Under the Ws.? Do you want them signed? No slip came with them. The copy Macmillan sent to Moscow never got there. Are they holding things back? British Iron Curtain—guaranteed noiseless?

I've still got the whoreson cough, & the eye's still painful. Had to get it treated, & it's a little better now.

Shivaun fell off her bike & got slight concussion, & a torn-up face; but she's allright again—a narrow escape.

Isn't it odd the Government should rent the Abbey to show visitors a play of mine! [3] The note in the D. Tel. is the first I heard of it.

Love to Mina & Jack.
Yours as ever
Sean

[1] "The People and the Theatre," *Theatre Today,* March 1946; collected in *Under a Colored Cap* (1963).

[2] William O'Brien retired from his position as leader of the Irish Transport and General Workers' Union.

[3] *The Shadow of a Gunman* was revived at the Abbey Theatre on 11 March 1946 for a two-week run, directed by Frank Dermody.

To Gabriel Fallon

MS. TEXAS

TOTNES, DEVON
8 MARCH 1946

My dear Gaby,

This has to be a brief note, for an eye of mine is out of action, & very painful; so I have to do as little as possible. However, the doctor's treatment is making an improvement.

I enclose some cuttings showing "Will" [Barry Fitzgerald], going his way, from several angles. Last I heard was from Horace Reynolds of Cambridge, in Massachusetts. Reynolds tells me he hit on Will doing a bad broadcast for Ballantine's Ale. "When Punker's Ale was new, me boys." Look at the picture showing Will with his "staunch man, Friday." Will's guardian angel. And Will with Ingrid Bergman. The look on his kisser: amiable, but cautious—thus far shalt thou go, but. . . .

The play is going well, so far, but it will be hard to get another theatre when the four weeks run ends. Eileen went up, & helped with the rehearsals. My eye was too bad to stir. Eileen says Ria [Mooney] didn't do badly at all. Indeed, she did very well. I'm concerned now with the new play—written near two years ago.

By the way, Horace Reynolds tells me he got a book by Gogarty to review, & that it was so bad, he sent it back. He, on account of friendly relations, didn't like to have to slate it. Says it read like a cheap film scenario. What is happening to us all!

All the best to you all.

Love to Rose & to the big and the little children. But, genuinely speaking, Rose must be tired looking after you all. I know what it is, for I'm never out of the house, & so see all. Children are the biggest job anyone can tackle. It may be a grand job; but it is a damned wearing one.

All the best again to Rose & to you.

Yours as ever
Sean

To George Jean Nathan

MS. CORNELL

TOTNES, DEVON
20 MARCH 1946

My very dear George:

Greeting. I have been very busy, & one eye crocked up, so that I had to go canny. I daresay you have heard "Red Roses For Me" went on here in a Suburban Theatre,[1] & —so they say—created great interest, &, so far, has been a "success." The production (I've just come back from going up to see it) was three-fourths good, & one-fourth bad; &, as no trouble was taken with it, compared with a commercial West-Ender, I was very fortu-

[1] The Embassy Theatre, where *Red Roses For Me* opened on 26 February 1946 for a one-month run, was in Swiss Cottage, a London suburb, and had 687 seats.

nate. The critics here were divided—some for, some against. Anyway, the "success" has aroused great interest in the other play, "Oak Leaves & Lavender," or, a Warld on Wallpaper; &, by present accounts, this is to get a much more important & careful producation: when, no-one knows.

Have you heard from G. B. S. yet about the book you sent him? I haven't seen him since we came to Devon. I've written a number of times, and—up to say a year ago—invariably got a reply. But my last half-dozen letters remain unacknowledged. Even one congratulating him on getting the official freedom of Dublin, and sympathising with him over what so many are saying about the costly film—"Caesar & Cleopatra." Since he writes to the Press often, it can't be because he's too old to do it. Eileen & I often wonder why; for, as you know, it would not be possible for me to offend Shaw in any direct way. I sometimes think he may not like my biographical books (Mrs. Shaw wrote once to say my Dublin "wasn't the Dublin they knew"—which I knew myself); or because of my steady admiration for James Joyce, whom he dislikes, & whom he has never once mentioned, as far as I know.

I enclose cuttings about the opinions on Saroyan's play.[2] The English critics don't seem to like Saroyan. My eldest one, Breon, is a great admirer of Saroyan's; likes him better than he likes his dad. He'll soon be in the army; today passed medical board as A1; he's but 17, & is six foot two—a guardsman!

I send a cutting of an article by Denis Johnston on the theatre in Dublin. It seems to be an extraordinarily poor one to me.

It is astonishing to me how the critics here seem to reject everything delicately artistic, or virtually so, which comes from the U.S.A. Surely, it should be plain to them that there is something in Saroyan that isn't in anyone else? If you saw some—many—of the plays on in London, now, you'd be ill at ease to think of Saroyan getting a show in the suburbs, to be afterwards railed at by the critics for writing & feeling something above & beyond them.

Quinn Curtiss writes to say he has been talking to you. I see Agate dedicates one of his "Ego's" to him.[3] "Red Roses" may come to the West End, but it is very doubtful. Bronson Albery put it on in conjunction with the Arts Council of Britain; and it was Mrs. Una Albery who pressed for its production; & in pressing for "Purple Dust" too. She is an Irishwoman, daughter of T. W. Rolleston, the scholar & poet, who founded the Irish Literary Society.

My love to you.
Ever yours,
Sean

[2] William Saroyan's *The Time of Your Life* was revived at the Lyric Theatre, Hammersmith, 14 February 1946, directed by Peter Glenville.

[3] James Agate, *A Shorter Ego* (1945), with a "Dedicatory Letter to Thomas Quinn Curtiss, Sergeant, U.S.A."

To Mrs. Una Gwynn Albery

MS. ALBERY

TOTNES, DEVON
24 MARCH 1946

Dear Mrs Albery,

Here are the two books signed. I have written to some of the Caste to thank them for their help in presenting the play; & have asked Eddie Byrne to thank them all for me. In a letter to Kieron O'Hanrahan, I forged a few words of advice (as suggested by Mr. Albery) about leaving the Films alone for a time.[1]

On the last night of my stay in London, one whom I know insisted on coming to the Hotel for a half-hour's chat (He had got into touch with me the very first day I came to the City); &, I, at last, consented. During the "chat," he coughed hilariously in my face, remarking he "had a cough"; & the result was, I carried home with me an acute bronchial attack which I am trying to climb out of now.

I have typed an alteration in the last act of "Red Roses," for a possible West End production, & an further possible production in U.S.A. Something is missing in the spacious cut in this part of the play; &, to me, it doesn't suitably link up with all that follows. So I have, I think, managed to bring it closer, & to keep the unity safe to the end, without adding very much, or changing it in any appreciable way. I have decided to abandon the "Tuba" and the "Drum" incident; so that, with a few minor links, the play is as it is now being presented.

If you'd like to read it, I'll send it to you. I'd like to know what you think of it.

Breon passed Medical Exam as an A1 item.

Warm regards to Mr. Albery & to you.

Yrs sincerely,
Sean O'Casey

PS. Heard nothing since from Mr. [Anthony] Hawtrey about "Juno."

---

[1] Kieron O'Hanrahan later became a film actor under the name of Kieron Moore.

To Corporal S. S. Segal

TC. O'CASEY

TOTNES, DEVON
27 MARCH 1946

Dear Cpl. Segal:

I'm afraid this note must be a disappointing one to you. If I were to write a Foreword [1] for you, I'd be deluged with applications. Besides, it would take me a month to do it, and I find it a hard enough job to do my own, with all the needs surrounding the activities and needs of three children attending day-school.

Twenty-seven years ago, I asked Bernard Shaw to write a foreword for myself. He replied "I'll do nothing of the sort. If I did so, of course you would be published. But why? Because of my Foreword, and not because of anything you wrote. We all have to go through the mill. Go on writing till you are published for your own sake, and not for anything I may add to what you do." [2] It was disappointing; but it was sound advice. I followed it. You can see from my work that not a single one of them has a preface by another. I advise you to do as I did.

Will Gallagher [3] should be ashamed of himself—he was just getting rid of you by handing you over to me.

By the way, a poem must do more than just "serve a useful purpose." A broom or a poker could do that much. A poem, to be a poem, must have something unique in it in thought or wording. I really dont think (though I am not a critic) the verse you sent to me had either. Why dont you steep yourself in the verse of the greater poets—Shakespeare, Shelley, Burns, Whitman, Keats, Byron's Childe Harold; ay, or even Tennyson, for he wrote many lovely things, and was a master of words. I'd advise you to do this; and, then, try again; or, give up trying, then, if you think the greatness of these beyond you.

With all good wishes,

Yours sincerely,
Sean O'Casey

[1] Segal had asked O'Casey to write a foreword to his book of poems.
[2] See Bernard Shaw's letter to O'Casey, 3 December 1919, Vol. I, pp. 87–88.
[3] William Gallacher (1881–1965), one of the leaders of the British Communist Party; Member of Parliament for West Fife, Scotland, 1935–50.

To L. C. Carroll

MS. MACMILLAN LONDON

TOTNES, DEVON
29 MARCH 1946

Dear Mr. Carroll,

Ay, I got the letter you mention; but I had to go to London, came back with a bad cold, & forgot everything except the bit of life left me.

Here's the reply to Mr. Woodington's query: John did two pictures of the same kind. The first having a dark background, the figure seated on a hard chair with formal polished back. From the breast pocket part of a vivid orange handkerchief. This picture is in my possession.[1] The second— from which that appearing in "Observer" is taken—has a reddish-purple background, & the colour motive here is the vivid piece of chintz, covering the chair, seen between the figure's arm & the body. I understand this picture was sold by the Chenil Galleries, Chelsea, to an American; but whose it may be now, or who bought it, I don't know. I hope this slight amount of information will be satisfactory. Perhaps, Augustus John himself could say where the second picture is.[2]

> *Yours sincerely,*
> *with regrets for the delay*
> *in replying.*
> *Sean O'Casey*

[1] This portrait is now in the possession of Mrs. Eileen O'Casey.

[2] The second portrait is now in the possession of the Metropolitan Museum of Art in New York, and in November 1978 negotiations were in progress to present it on permanent loan to the Abbey Theatre.

To Irish Democrat

APRIL 1946

"Scientific Socialist" [1]

The messages sent to the *Irish Democrat* condemning my remarks concerning Connolly and Larkin, leave the question exactly where it

[1] O'Casey's original title for this letter was "Larkin and Connolly." He is replying to letters in the March issue by Malachy Boyle, Barry O'Meara, and Paddy Clancy, which were responses to his letter, "Larkin vs. Connolly," in the February issue. The editor reversed the order of the names in the first sentence, placing Connolly before Larkin.

stands. There can be no doubt that the flame lit, a great flame too, in 1913 was lit with the torch held by Jim Larkin. It was "Larkinism" that put the fear into the mean hearts of the employers of that time, and "Larkinism" alone. So says W. P. O'Ryan, in his History, and so say all who took part in the struggle who are not interested in what Labour has got to give in the nature of a job. The writers contradict each other. Barry O'Meara says "nationalism and internationalism just dont mix"; while his comrade, Paddy Clancy says "Connolly proved himself a scientific socialist" by mixing the struggle for national liberation with the struggle of the working-class. He is right, of course; but what my friends fail to see is that I resented Connolly doing this because I knew when he separated himself from the Labour Movement per se, the power would pass to the hands of a clique who cared, not for their class, but for themselves alone. I felt then that while Connolly stayed there, this could never happen, and, as it fell out, I happened to be right. My friends must remember too, that half, or more, of what I wrote then, was suppressed by the then British Censor. No, I don't put "fiery oratory" before everything. Parnell was a poor orator; Redmond a fine one; but we all know which was the greater man. Larkin was far more than just a fiery orator; he had a soul of flame, and lighted every other one that touched his—bar those who were out for their own interests. Not only the workers, but many of the intellectuals, too.

Barry O'Meara says that "when the roll is called, there will be the great Lenin and on his right hand James Connolly—the rest will only make up the congregation." Oh, Barry, Barry! Have you even forgotten Stalin? If you ask me, there will be a great crowd at Lenin's right hand; and the Gael will have a hosting of his own. Lalor, Mitchel, Davitt, William Thompson (a landowner to whom Karl Marx owed a lot), Goldsmith, and a cloud of poets, sages, saints, and soldiers. I hope to God to be there myself, close to the right hand of the redoubtable Jim Larkin; and, of course, Connolly will be to the forefront. Paddy Clancy says that in his valuable book, W. P. O'Ryan states "Connolly was a convinced Marxian Socialist, an Industrialist Trades Unionist, and a Devout Labour Leader." Why, of course he was; but so were most of us. While remembering leaders, let us not forget the crowd of men and women who made them. As Stalin said the other day, without these unknown, unmentioned in Press or on Platform, we Leaders wouldn't be worth a tinker's damn. That forcible phrase was changed by the *Daily Worker* into the very respectable one of "a tinker's cuss," which was a sin against the light. My contention is simply this: As a leader, Connolly was secondary in power and magnetism to Larkin; and that the death of Connolly was, not a Gain, but a Loss to the Irish Labour Movement.

Totnes

Sean O'Casey

To Bronson Albery

TC. O'CASEY

TOTNES, DEVON
6 APRIL 1946

Dear Mr. Albery:

By all means, call me O'Casey, or Sean. I dont care a lot for Mister.
Anyway, there's no Mister in Irish. In Eire I would be Sean, or Mac Ui
Cathasaigh—son of O'Casey.

Thank you for the letter from B[eatrice] Straight, and for the Brochure
of Theatre Inc. It all looks very imposing, though I dont think such a lot
was necessary for Pygmalion,¹ about which everyone knows so much
through play and film.

As George Jean Nathan, the New York Drama Critic, has approved
of the Theatre Inc. for the play (As Mr. [Richard] Madden, my Agent,
said in his cable), I am quite satisfied to let it go to them, providing I, or
Nathan, approves of Producer and Principals in the Caste. Mr. Nathan is
a dear friend of mine, and takes a great interest in my plays, not because of
the friendship, but because he admires my work. He does the same for
Saroyan and for P. V. Carroll. Unfortunately, Carroll wouldnt take Nathan's
advice about the three plays written before THE WISE HAVE NOT
SPOKEN, and suffered for his mistake.

I cannot say about Mr. [John] Burrell as Producer, though WITHIN
THE GATES was done by Melvyn Douglas splendidly in N. York; ² and
THE SILVER TASSIE was done in a terrible way by an Irish fool, named
O'Farrell.³ Raymond Massey,⁴ on the other hand, though handicapped
with a bad Caste—bar [Sidney] Morgan, [Barry] Fitzgerald, and Lehmann
(Beatrix), did a very fine job indeed. A good producer remains a good
one, whether he or she be English, Irish, or Jew. If Eddie Dowling could
be got, it would be grand; and he'd make a splendid Brennan of the Moor; ⁵
but I suppose he's still playing in "The Glass Menagerie." Surely, Mr.
Burrell, after seeing the play, should have a good idea of its spirit. I dont
agree that a producer should necessarily know all there is to know about

¹ Bernard Shaw's *Pygmalion* was revived in New York on 26 December 1945
by Theatre Inc., with Gertrude Lawrence as Eliza Doolittle and Raymond Massey as
Henry Higgins.
² Melvyn Douglas directed the New York premiere of *Within the Gates,* which
opened at the National Theatre on 22 October 1934. For details of the production
see O'Casey's letter to George Jean Nathan, 17 October 1934, note 1, Vol. I, p. 522.
³ O'Farrell's Irish Theatre company produced *The Silver Tassie* in New York
on 24 October 1929 at the Irish Theatre, Greenwich Village, directed by Miceal
Breathnach.
⁴ Raymond Massey directed the London premiere of *The Silver Tassie,* which
opened at the Apollo Theatre on 11 October 1929. For details of the production, see
Lady Gregory's letter to O'Casey, 11 October 1929, note 2, Vol. I, p. 368.
⁵ One of the main characters in *Red Roses For Me.*

Dublin. I imagine, there's more than Dublin in the play. Looks as if there was, anyway. I may be wrong, of course.

I should, if I were you, go canny about sending Ria [Mooney] to America. I like her, and dont like to say much against her; but to my mind, she has a weakness for putting a difficulty behind her. I fear she mightnt be able to stand up to the Committee running the venture, (by the way, I've written to her thanking her, and saying that the disappointment wasnt anything like what I expected it might have been.)

I certainly dont want David O. Selznick to have the producing of the Play. If he takes the play—after it has been done well by someone else—allright; but not the play. The same Firm, a few months ago, wanted me to do the scenario of [Thomas] Wolfe's LOOK HOMEWARD, ANGEL, offering a huge fee; but I wouldnt have anything to do with it.[6]

I enclose the emendment I have made to the latter part of the last act,[7] making it as simple as possible. I think it connects events together in a better way than the version now running. I dont think you ought to hurry the change on to the version. Better to do it quietly, and so not disturb the actors. You will see that there is to be no dancing on the floral wreath. I dont think this necessary. Let the actor just fling the cross scornfully away, and then, if he will, dance around the Rector. I have sent a copy of these changes to my American Agent, Mr. Madden, with a marked book of the play, which together are to form the script of the play as produced by the American Co. interested. By the way, if it isnt too much trouble, I'd like you to get me a few copies typed; I've tried everywhere here, but, though they do printing, they dont do typewriting. I shall be much obliged, if you can do this for me; or, rather, get it done.

I enclose a letter from a J. J. Hayes of Dublin, who writes as Dublin correspondent for THE CHRISTIAN SCIENCE MONITOR. Long ago, he gave permission for performances of JUNO without my knowledge, and tried to keep the fees; but his girl has nothing to do with that. So she may be useful to you later on. I have written to her—c/o the Interval Club, Dean St. Soho—, telling her you have all to do with engaging artists.

I also enclose a letter from Hopkinson of PICTURE POST; and two for Mrs Albery.

Also a receipt for the latest cheque.

Lastly, to be quite clear, I vote for Theatre Inc.

All good wishes and warm regards to you both.

Yours sincerely,
[Sean O'Casey]

P.S. I daresay there's no danger of them asking [Arthur] Sinclair or Molly O'Neill to join the Caste? They would overthrow the balance completely.

[6] See O'Casey's letter to William Herndon, 17 January 1945.

[7] *Red Roses For Me* was originally published in 1942; for the changes in the last act, see the modified version in *Collected Plays* (1951), Vol. III; and the acting edition (1956, Dramatists Play Service, Inc.).

To Corporal S. S. Segal

TC. O'CASEY

[TOTNES, DEVON]

8 APRIL 1946

Dear friend:

I just tried to write a commonsense letter, without thinking of Shavian wit or Marxian science. What has either got to do with the question of writing a preface? I havent read either Aragon or Mayakovsky, not being familiar with the languages in which these two wrote. I have read the translations by H. Marshall,[1] excellent, forcible, and acceptable as far as they go; but no-one could say these were the full and hearty expressions of the Russian poet. But they do show forth the tremendous (in shadowy form) figure of the great man. Dont run away with the idea that because one is a Marxist, one must be a good critic. Lenin who was something of a Marxist, himself admitted that he wasnt competent to judge Mayakovsky's poetry. Poetry will live when there is no longer any need of Marxism. In the verse you quote there is a simplicity and a beat and a beauty, irrespective even of any message it may have. "In order to attain beauty of Form the artist must cast aside everything superfluous, hindering the expression of his idea, and find the form which will enable his work to arrest the ear and stir the imagination." An ideal; but we must ever aim at it. I am sorry I disappointed you.

With all good wishes,
Yours sincerely,
[*Sean O'Casey*]

[1] *Mayakovsky and His Poetry* (1942), compiled and translated by Herbert Marshall. O'Casey wrote a review of this book for the *Anglo-Soviet Journal*, October–December 1942.

To Peter Newmark

MS. NEWMARK

TOTNES, DEVON

9 APRIL 1946

Dear Peter:

I've written to Mr. Foster of Skipton's Grammar School, & you should hear from him requesting an interview.

Now, if you want the job, spruce yourself up a bit; for these Grammar School Masters (all Masters, in fact; even those at Dartington) have to keep up a certain dignity to escape derision from the boys. Be as alert as you can, till you get to know the ropes; time enough then to relax a little. I do hope you may get the job. It all, I think, will depend on yourself. My note should bring an invitation for an interview.

Yours as ever.
Sean

To Michael Casey [1]

MS. MURPHY

TOTNES, DEVON
10 APRIL 1946

Dear Mick,
Here's a pound for you. I haven't got much out of the play [*Red Roses For Me*] yet—it is performing in small theatres.

If it continues to go, I'll send you some more.

All the best,
Jack

[1] Michael Casey (1866–1947), O'Casey's brother, who was living in Dublin with their niece Mrs. Isabella Murphy, the daughter of their sister Mrs. Isabella Casey Beaver. See O'Casey's letter to Michael, 18 December 1938, Vol. I, p. 762; and his letters to Mrs. Murphy, 20 and 24 January 1947, on the occasion of his brother's death.

To Ria Mooney

TC. O'CASEY

TOTNES, DEVON
27 APRIL 1946

Dear Ria:
Thanks for your inquiry about my latest play, OAK LEAVES AND LAVENDER. Put the idea of performing it in Dublin out of your busy

mind—at once. I wouldn't dream of letting it be done there. I believe this play to be the most imaginative one I've done for years (I may be wrong, of course, though G. J. Nathan of New York thinks so, too), and the handling of it will be a very anxious time for me. I am too positive about the quality of the play to have any such thing as a "try-out." For a long time now, I haven't been anxious to have anything of mine done in Dublin. Very reluctantly indeed, I gave RED ROSES to Shelah Richards. I prefer to leave the Dublin stage as free as possible to the Irish dramatists.

In any case, I wouldn't let this play be produced anywhere without long and anxious thought about the whole method and manner of its showing. I daresay, T. C. M.'s article [1] stimulated this idea into your head. I doubt very much that this review should have appeared so early; as far as I am aware reviews appear only on, or a day or so before, the day of publication. What about Carroll's THE WISE HAVE NOT SPOKEN. I'm sure, or almost sure, he'd consider any offer from you. OAK LEAVES AND LAVENDER is out of the question.

And all the best, with an encore, to you.

Yours sincerely,
Sean O'Casey

[1] T. C. Murray, "Mr. O'Casey's New Play," *Irish Press*, 25 April 1946, a review of the published text of *Oak Leaves and Lavender*.

To Flight Lieutenant G. F. Parker [1]

MS. PARKER

TOTNES, DEVON
2 MAY 1946

Dear Lieut. Parker,

I couldn't tell you "how far" the language of "Red Roses" corresponds with the common speech of the people. No dialogue in any play does, you know—even in those termed "realistic."

There is the truth of imagination, & there is the truth of actuality; but the first transcends the second, for it is new, original, and often poetic. There is no such thing in a play as dialogue exactly the same as that spoken by people in the streets or at home. Even the worst play must have some selection, some shape, & so, to that extent, it is altered from actuality.

[1] Flight Lieutenant Parker was in charge of education at an R.A.F. bomber command station, and the question about the language in O'Casey's play had arisen in one of the discussion groups he conducted for the airmen.

But very often one hears a fine phrase from the people. For instance when Churchill was raving about the "Irish Ports," a wag said "Poor old Churchill—a few little ports have gone to his head." When Tim Healy, K. C. was made Governor-General of the Free State, and given the Vice-regal lodge to live in, a wit referred to it as "Uncle Tim's Cabin." Again, as well as having traces of Shakespeare's language in our talk, there is the influence of the Gaelic which gives the English we speak a curious lilt & a strange twist sometimes. When the Irish say "I axed him a question," or a "sup o' tay" or "a slice o' mate," they are giving the sound of ea as Elizabethans gave it, & as it is given in many Gaelic words. For instance again, Shakespeare's "Daffodils . . . and take the winds of March with beauty." Take Irish "He took to the wather (an Elizabethan pronunciation, like Murther) like a duck." "He didn't take to it at all," etc. I could go on giving examples, but I haven't the time. Over all this, is the dramatist's own selection of words, his own grouping of them to form a picture. Few dramatists do this, for they are concerned first with a financial success, & don't bother (or are incapable of it) about a literary creation. In any poet you may read, you'll find hundreds of examples. There is certainly a freshness about the way we Irish speak (or a lot of us, anyway) that the English language has lost. So say Moore & Yeats, too. Yeats' "Plays & Controversies" is well worth reading. But the playwright, even with this advantage, has to labour hard if he is to succeed in creating something new & imaginative. It is Per ardua ad astra [2] with him as it is with you.

> *My best wishes to you*
> *Yours sincerely,*
> *Sean O'Casey*

[2] The R.A.F. motto, "The way to the stars is hard."

To George Jean Nathan

MS. CORNELL

TOTNES, DEVON

5 MAY 1946

My very dear George:

Very, very glad to hear from you. Your new book [1] will be welcome to me and Breon. It's Nathan and Saroyan Abu [2] with Breon now. Well, he could do a lot worse. And he found them out himself.

I've sent you a copy of "Oak Leaves & Lavender" under another

[1] George Jean Nathan, *The Theatre Book of the Year, 1945–1946* (1946).
[2] Long live Nathan and Saroyan.

cover. Thank you for taking an interest in production of Red Roses. Dick [Madden] writing to [Bronson] Albery, says he has asked Sally Allgood to play part of Mrs. Breydon. I am altogether against using any of the old Irish Players in any play of mine after "The Plough," or even in that one, or "Juno." To me they have passed away into the oblivion of Filmland. The company doing it here, do excellently, all "New Commencers." Eddie Byrne, a Music Hall actor, gives an exquisite performance of Brennan. I've never seen anything like it. It is a jewel-like portrayal. One critic here suggested [Arthur] Sinclair for the part; but Sinclair would have roughed it off the stage, &, in my opinion, destroyed the balance of the entire play. The Irish old school tie is well faded by now. I do hope Theatre Incorporated will see this. Dick is inclined to be impulsive, and, good and fine fellow as he is, he isn't, I fear, a first-class hand in judging a play, or the acting of one. S. Allgood, too, would want to be too dominant; want too much attention, & the part doesn't allow that.

I am glad you are so often with Eugene [O'Neill]. I wish the third musketeer could be there too. I suggested Eddie Dowling as producer for R. R.'s; not knowing then he was doing Eugene's. Had I known, I, of course, shouldn't have mentioned his name. I am real glad Eugene has such a fine fellow to help him. It's fine that Eugene is letting one of his plays be seen. Granted the chance of a good production, I think everyone who loves the theatre should push the expression of that love to the fore.

At the moment, I'm revising "Within the Gates"; trying to knit it closer together. As you know, I was never satisfied with it. I have already altered the first two acts a lot.

My eyes have been troublesome recently. I went to an Eye-surgeon to get some ingrowing lashes pulled out. He pushed some of them in farther, & took a neat piece of flesh out of an eyelid. Eileen (the wife) it was who cleverly pulled them out with her woman's tweezers when I got home in great pain. She would have made a damned fine surgeon.[3]

"Purple Dust" has been done in Glasgow by a Labour Group.[4] Their producer, C. Mitchel, is a fine fellow, & gave it, I understand, a gay & rousing production. I quoted him your "a poetic theme, orchestrated with slapstick," & he went all out for that idea. He is bringing the play to Edinburgh. I think he is a producer of the right kind—imaginative & fearless. God be good to him! And to you, to Eugene, & to me, & to all who love the theatre, from a good Punch & Judy Show to Shakespeare & Sophocles.

My love.
Ever yours
Sean

[3] Throughout his lifetime O'Casey suffered from ingrowing eyelashes, which pricked his eyes like needles and had to be pulled out regularly.

[4] O'Casey's *Purple Dust* was performed by the Glasgow Unity Theatre in Glasgow on 9 April 1946, directed by Robert Mitchell.

To Jack Carney

MS. NYU LIBRARY

TOTNES, DEVON

10 MAY 1946

Dear Jack,

Here are the books signed as requested.

I understand Red Roses goes to the West End in a few weeks. When Oak Leaves will be seen, the Lord only knows. The Gaiety Dublin wanted it, & then Red Roses, but they can't be given either. As you say, Politics are in a curious way, and all are against the USSR who were for her when the guns were booming, including the little, strutting, whining Cardinal Griffin. Once again I'm wearing the little five-pointed Red Star with its Hammer & Sickle, feeling that someone should show that the USSR has an Embassy here.

My eyes are not too good yet. Went to a Specialist to get some lashes pulled out. He shoved some in, & took a neat piece of flesh out of the lid. It was Eileen, when I came home, who, with her simple toilet tweezers, took the damned things out.

Glad to know you are both well. All well here, too.

All the best.
As ever,
Sean

To Alec Donaldson [1]

TC. O'CASEY

TOTNES, DEVON

13 MAY 1946

Dear Mr. Donaldson:

No National Theatre excludes the classics of other countries. The Abbey Theatre has done various dramas; but it has to keep within the

[1] Alec Donaldson, director of Scoop Books, Glasgow, and a member of the International Brigade during the Spanish Civil War, had seen the Glasgow Unity Theatre production of *Purple Dust,* and wrote to O'Casey about the play.

terms of its Covenant which prevents it from interfering with the security of the ordinary commercial theatres. In Lady Gregory's OUR IRISH THEATRE you can read about the fight it had to get permission to produce plays at all. If I remember right, a special act of Parliament had to be passed.

At the moment, and for a long time past, the opposition in front of Irish Labour isnt either the bosses or the church, but the break-away from the Labour Congress by large numbers of the workers themselves, led by William O'Brien (since retired, though the half-dead hand is there still) and his clique of followers. English Capital is still very powerful in Ireland, though the politicians have left, leaving a good garrison in Northern Ireland.

The English arent made the Butt in the play. Your remark begs the question of Who are the English? The dockers, railwaymen, wood-workers, miners, transport workers, etc; or those typified by the two men in the play? Answer this question, and you'll see I dont make a butt of the English. You should remember, too, that there are many still alive who bear the marks of the Black and Tans on their bodies. This was only the other day; but you seem to think we can forget it.

The Irish kings, or most of them, were far from uncouth. They spread their conquest over Europe as far as the Black Sea—not like England's Empire, or the Roman State; but caring little about vigorous government, leaving the conquered peoples to live their lives their own way. The Georgians are cousins of the Irish, so you can see how far we travelled. We make a mistake, I think, by imagining that all civilization came from Greece and Rome. My friend, there is no doubt that the Lineage of the Irish goes far farther back than does the English; just as that of Chicherin, first Sov. Ambassador, went far farther back than those who looked down on him when he came to London. My own name O'Cathasaigh, comes from a very old sept of an older Clan. There is no reason to be ashamed of "the fathers who begat us."

There may be messages in the play, if you like to look for them. But I never have, and never will, just put plain slabs of propaganda in a play. That can be done better in an article. In THEATRE, published in Moscow during the Twenties, Gorki came out against this sort of thing. The other day a new magazine of criticism has been published in the USSR to combat the poor stuff so often published during the war years. One of the Soviet writers, reproached for not having enough of propaganda in his work, replied that Literature to be literature had to make discoveries, which propaganda wasnt required to do. Are we never to feel the thrill of a song well sung? Is there to be P. in a love song say like "Drink to Me only with Thine Eyes"? After all, the lark has to hunt out its food, has to build its nest, and has to feed its mate and young ones, but it doesnt cease its song, all the same.

There are quite a number of city girls who dont know much about bulls.

I myself was twenty-seven before I saw a field of corn or a plough in action. And your remark that Avril should have left what she had to an hospital or a Workers Home is, pardon me, sentimentality mixed with an outworn puritanism. Now, now, Mr. Donaldson!

You call the two women in the play "prostitutes," not because they werent married to the men, but because they didnt love them. I daresay you have heard of the Catholic church. It must number more than 300 million members. Now what is the circumstance that makes marriage sacramental in this church? Is it that the partners MUST be in love with each other? Not at all; it is Consent. You should read Mon. Claudel's THE SATIN SLIPPER, and you will get some information about the fact. It is an odd thing that so many Communists know so little about these things. This morning I got a letter from one of the most prominent members admitting she was wholly ignorant between the Catholic Church and the one called Orthodox; though this matter is plainly of importance seeing now that the latter has been officially recognised by the Soviet Government. Why? You say my criticism of the C. church takes a minor part in the play. So it does; but if you read DRUMS UNDER THE WINDOW, you'll find more criticism than the play holds. One cant be forever harping on the one string. When you say it is going "too far to have a garden roller that Ten men couldnt move," you are writing in terms of naturalism or realism, with which the play has little to do. You must take a play for what it is intended to be. It is odd too what men like Poges will endure in order to show off. When sending the play to Unity [Glasgow] I quoted George Jean Nathan, the famous American Drama critic as saying, "This play is based on a poetical theme, orchestrated with slapstick." Unity acted on the hint, and I agree with them. That's just what the play is.

I notice at the end of your letter, you say, "I like you as a man and a dramatist, but I dont like "Purple Dust." Well, that cant be helped. I wrote the play because I liked it myself, and spent little time wondering how others would like it. If you want that class of playwrights, you must go after what Nathan calls, "The Cowards, the Novellos, and the Rattigans." However, to be fair, I dont think youd like these boyos at all; and so I do wish you'd try to understand drama a little more than you apparently do.

All the best, anyway, whether you liked it or not.

Yours sincerely,
Sean O'Casey

To Horace Reynolds

MS. REYNOLDS

TOTNES, DEVON

19 MAY 1946

My dear Horace.

Greetings. I hope you are all well, & that John & Peggy are beside you. I expected bad things from Gogarty. I warned him 15 years ago, that he should try to look at a few things seriously, or, look at all things with genuine savagery. Afterwards, his hatred of, & contempt for, Joyce were too much for me. He could never come up to Joyce (who could?), & so he envied & hated. But I think you did wrong in [not] reviewing his book [1] because you were his friend. What has friendship got to do with it? And it might have done Gogarty good. G. J. Nathan would never hesitate to criticise a friend. Why the hell should he? A critic must, in my opinion, be above (or below) friendship. It is a pity about Gogarty—the man has a unique talent, if he'd only use it.

Have you heard from David Greene lately? I've written a long letter to him, long ago; but he didn't answer.

I'm told Dublin is asparkle with cleanliness, & trim with new paint, & fairer buildings. Was in London recently about Red Roses, &, oh, my! how shabby she looks! And soiled—like one who had slept in their clothes for weeks, & had lost the heart to care! But it's a false dawn, I think; for, if England sinks, we sink with her.

My love to Kay & you and to Peggy & John.

Yours as ever
Sean

[1] Oliver St. John Gogarty, *Mr. Petunia* (1945), a novel.

To Jack Carney

MS. NYU LIBRARY

TOTNES, DEVON

1 JUNE 1946

Dear Jack,

Here's the book signed. Vlademir's Vlademir, & not Valdemir as you tried to lead me to believe. So I waited till Vlademir came to make sure.

He's a fine fellow. I think we had a good talk; though I'm too old now to go through the turmoil of a tour of the USSR. But I'd like Breon to go some day. The day is with the young; & no longer with the poor old lingerers in life.

I am getting a pasting from the Dublin writers at the moment—"Every book I write now is worse than the one that went before" etc. The same was said of Gorki & of Dickens; I daresay of everyone; though that doesn't prove it wrong about me. However, the critics aren't a Unity. Trewin of Observer & John o' London said the part in Oak Leaves & L. of the Dame & British-Israel, "was terribly tedious, & should be cut"; [1] but Stonier in The New Statesman says "The high point of comedy is reached in the discussion of B. Israel by Feelim & the Dame" [2]; so what am I to do? Cut it, or leave it there?

Ireland is clamouring for me to go back to "Juno" & the "Plough"; but I have old cuttings showing that these were condemned in their time as "photographic, disorderly, not plays at all"; & definite dismissals by [Liam] O'Flaherty, A. E. Malone, Fred O'Higgins, the poet, Austin Clarke, et al. So what am I to do? Just go on in my own way, not caring a sweet damn at all for any of them. So help me God!

All the best.

Star Turns Red is, I think, to go on at Unity.

Love to Mina.
Sean

[1] J. C. Trewin, "A Rush of Words," *John O' London's Weekly,* 3 May 1946, a review of the published text of *Oak Leaves and Lavender,* which Macmillan of London brought out in May 1946, a year before the play was produced. Trewin's review was mainly favorable, but he felt that the episode of Dame Hatherleigh's vision of Britain as one of the ten lost tribes of Israel in Act I should be cut from the play.

[2] G. W. Stonier, "Poetry and the Theatre," *New Statesman and Nation,* 25 May 1946, a review of *Oak Leaves and Lavender.* Stonier praised the "British Israel" episode, and the comic scenes, calling the play O'Casey's *Heartbreak House,* but he objected to some of the didactic and pseudo-poetic passages.

To Bronson Albery

TC. O'CASEY

TOTNES, DEVON
10 JUNE 1946

Dear Mr. Albery:

Miss Straight has written to me, and I enclose a copy of her letter to you.[1] It is, to me, something of a silly letter. The art of a producer isnt that of visiting plays to see how he will or will not produce these plays later on. A bad part of a play may be in the play itself, and no better acting will make it shine; on the other hand, a good part of a play may appear bad by bad acting or bad production, and the producer who goes to note things may think this part should come out too. A producer's guide is the script, helped by the dramatist—if he be there. This last advantage was denied to Ria Mooney, and I am telling this to Beatrice Straight; for, though I dont agree with Miss Mooney on a lot of things dramatic, she did, in face of many difficulties, including my absence, a good job. Miss Straight has the advantage of Nathan's advice—better than mine—but she doesnt appear to be eager to use it.

I want you to tell me definitely what you think of this [John] Burrell business; for we must make a decision some time. Should we let it pass, and chance it? I can say to Miss Straight that I have left the matter to you. But I think we should hold fast to the agreement that Nathan should have the power to veto or accept the proposed principals—I dont like her remark about "getting the best actors possible." It may be all production and no play. However many "shortcomings" there were in Ria Mooney's conception, she brought a play out of it anyhow. If I were financially in a secure position, I'd just tell Theatre Inc. to go to hell, and take Burrell with them. It was Eric Capon,[2] and not John, who was always eager to do PURPLE DUST. And it was an ordinary "commercial" Manager, and not John, who first aroused an interest in my plays after a good many years of silence.

I'm quite sure what the Tass Representative told me was true. He had no reason for taking the part of the Old Vic, or of going against it; but I'm equally sure that the Old Vic, on the whole, got a "good Press" when the Critic of the New York Times lost his job for venturing to say they didnt deserve it. The same sort of thing is common in Dartington Hall—everything done there is the work of gods and goddesses, and everything said

---

[1] After its one-month run at the Embassy Theatre, Swiss Cottage, beginning on 26 February 1946, the Albery production of *Red Roses For Me* was moved to the West End, and opened at the New Theatre on 28 May 1946, where Beatrice Straight saw it. She now wanted to convince O'Casey that John Burrell of the Old Vic should direct the New York production.

[2] See O'Casey's letter to Eric Capon, 9 December 1945, note 1.

is as if it were ripe wisdom coming from the mouth of divinity. I will write a reply to Miss Straight, and then no more—when I hear from you as to whether we shall chance Mr. Burrell or no. I have too much to do to continue arguing with Miss Straight. Rightly or wrongly, I believe she will never grasp the true import and impact of the theatre, stretching from a good Punch and Judy Show to Shakespeare and Sophocles.

Yours very sincerely,
[*Sean O'Casey*]

Copy. Letter from Miss B. Straight, dated May 31, 1946

Dear Mr. O'Casey.

It was so nice hearing from you, and you probably don't remember a long time ago at Dartington, when you and your wife were there and I was so thrilled to have a chance to talk with you then.

With regard to RED ROSES FOR ME, I want to say first how much we *love the play,*ˣ and then to explain a little our points with regard to the producer. I know Eddie Dowling and his work here, and admire him for what he's done, and I think he understands the idiom of RED ROSES, and though he's never been to Ireland would have a natural flair for the play.

Our reasons however for preferring John Burrell are that he is a brilliant producer, to our mind, and has such wonderful ideas for the play. He has always been an admirer of yours and was *responsible for getting PURPLE DUST done* in Liverpool.º He's also done some fine productions with the OLD VIC COMPANY. He has imagination, sensitivity, which are essential for your script. He's also lived in Ireland and is part Irish, and so has a very definite [feeling] for the Irish idiom, and has worked with Irish actors before.

In stating that "Mr. Burrell has the added advantage over Eddie Dowling of having seen the play before," of course I agree with you that no producer is a good producer if he copies a production he's already seen. The advantage of seeing a production is to get an idea of what *not* to do, and it can be extremely helpful, I think.

I gathered that the London production had many shortcomings, and it was with this in mind that we considered it an advantage to have seen it.

Of course we will get the best actors that we possibly can in this country, and I believe the production will be a very exciting one. Theatre Incorporated's future depends upon the quality of each production that we do, and we will aim always for the best setup we can and try to make as little compromise as possible. I can assure you that Mr. Burrell will be the ideal producer for your play, and that Mr. Dowling would be a very good second.

All the best wishes to you.
Beatrice Straight.

^x balls! The play was there in the book for years, & they began to love it only when the "commercial manager," B. Albery made a success of it in London.
    ^o balls again! It was a younger, assistant, Eric Capon, who was enthusiastic about P. Dust, & persuaded them to let him have a shot at it in Liverpool.[3]

    [3] *Ibid.*

To George Jean Nathan

.

MS. CORNELL

TOTNES, DEVON

11 JUNE 1946

My dear George:

    I was sorry to hear you had been down with the Grippe; & glad to know you were better, & in full view of a holiday soon. By the time you get this, I hope you will be in the sun beside a cool sea.

    Red Roses is still on here; not doing a roaring trade, & not doing too badly.[1] It looks as if the London Theatre has passed away from its torrid financial summer—mainly, & think, because the Americans have gone home. It looks like that Eddie Dowling won't do Red Roses in New York. Aldrich, the Managing-Director of Theatre Inc. was agreeable at first; but Beatrice Straight, one of the Directors, &, I daresay, the one who put in the dough, has evidently fallen for John Burrell of the Old Vic., & has come to believe him to be the one and only God-chosen producer in the world we know; & maybe, in the world we don't know. For a long time, I've been fearful that this young lady would meddle with a play of mine; & now it has come to pass. From what I saw & heard of her here, with Michele Chekhov, & their "Chekhov Studio," [2] convinced me that here was not the theatre, but a tinselled tomfoolry. I don't believe the woman knows even a thing or two about the Theatre. Anyway, in the case of Red Roses, she has evidently shoved Aldrich aside, & jumped into the breach herself; & so we hear a million pounds talking. Bronson Albery here has the American option, & is in favor of Theatre Inc. doing the play. As he has been very kind by doing Red Roses here, & contracting for Oak Leaves and Lavender

    [1] *Red Roses For Me* was transferred from the New Theatre to Windham's Theatre on 24 June, and continued there until it closed on 10 August, after a total run of five and a half months in three theatres, since its opening at the Embassy on 26 February.
    [2] Michael Chekhov (1891–1955), director and actor, nephew of Anton Chekhov. With the help of Beatrice Straight, daughter of Mrs. Dorothy Elmhirst, he established the Chekhov Theatre Studio in the 1930s at Dartington Hall, Totnes. For O'Casey's comment on the venture, see his letter to Nathan, ? November 1938, Vol. I, p. 760.

—so delivering me from a difficult financial position, I don't like to roar out an opposition; & am inclined to let Burrell do the play, & chance it.

By the way, a Soviet Press Representative was down here visiting me, the other day, & we talked of the Theatre. He didn't care a lot for the Old Vic. Productions, & told me they got a "bad Press" in America; &, also, that Nicolls of the N.Y. Times didn't like them, & wanted to say so; but the Editorial Depart. commanded him to give a favorable report. Rather than do this, the Pressman said, Nicolls resigned his job. Is this true? If it be, it bodes bad for Theatre Inc. I wrote a letter to Beatrice Straight pointing out my reasons for favoring Dowling, & got a reply back, a copy of which I enclose.[3] It is, to me, both silly and inaccurate. But what can one do against the power of a million pounds. It was just the same here when she was fooling around with that chancer, Chekhov—no-one dared, or would venture, to voice a word of criticism. I did, though, & told her & Chekhov & the lot of them exactly what I thought of them.

I enclose a curious article (to me) written by Priestley, telling me to give up experiment, and go back to Kathleen Mavourneen. It may interest you. There seems to be a conspiracy of goodwill here and in Ireland to save me from myself; which is very kind & flattering; but which only provoke a raspberry from me.

I do hope you are allright again. We here had our share of Influenza during the winter; & I had a cough for months and months! But we drifted out of it, & are in harbour of health again—for the time being anyway.

> *My love to you and Eugene,*
> *Carlotta, an' all.*
> *Sean*

[3] See the copy in O'Casey's letter to Bronson Albery, 10 June 1946.

To Jack Carney

MS. NYU LIBRARY

TOTNES, DEVON
20 JUNE 1946

Dear Jack,
Thanks for papers. I send back the books, signed as requested. The Labour Conference seemed to be a poor one. Big Ernie [Bevin] is to have it all his own way. "What More Can I Do" should be the slogan now.

It is possible that Red Roses may go to Wyndham's. It is holding out well; better than I expected. I haven't heard yet how Ria Mooney's production (as against that of Shelah Richards) went in Dublin.

I shouldn't advise Phelim Byrne to go back to medicine. As a Foreman he can be much happier (and safer) than if he were a doctor. Hundreds, thousands, of doctors haven't £12 quid a week. All well here; except for my own eyes that have been very painful for weeks. I should rest them; but this is very hard to do; so it is difficult for them to try to get well.

Love to Mina & you.

PS. I think Theatre Inc. of New York will take Red Roses for the American production.

All the best,
Sean

By Gabriel Fallon

THE STANDARD, JUNE 28, 1946
THEATRE . . . . . by GABRIEL FALLON
ROSES WITH THORNS [1]

A week or two ago an Irish poet wrote: "I am still young enough to feel sorry—and a little angry—watching genius being squandered and frittered away upon ephemeral concepts such as Mr. O'Casey has elected to promulgate." [2] But sorrow and anger in such circumstances are not solely the prerogatives of youth. Even middle-age may drown an eye unused to flow on being compelled to witness the incandescence of genius doused in an overflow of its own wilfulness.

Red Roses For Me is not a good play, and no amount of second-hand cheering can make it one. One reason for this lack of goodness is that the author mixes his modes. Here is expressionism staggering with realism, realism reeling with expressionism; a heavy tide of sentimentality bearing against both. The result is that the work never rises, seldom strides; but for

[1] A review of *Red Roses For Me,* which opened on 17 June 1946 at the Gaiety Theatre, Dublin, directed by Ria Mooney, with the following cast: Cathleen Murphy as Mrs. Breydon; William Foley as Ayamonn; Rita Foran as Eeada; Twinkle Forbes as Dympna; Barbara McGilligan as Finnoola; Joan Wall as Sheila Moorneen; Noel Purcell as Brennan o' the Moor; Joe O'Dea as Roory; Seamus Forde as Mullcanny; Hamlyn Benson as the Rev. E. Clinton; Philip Flynn as a Railwayman; Dermot Kelly as Samuel; Michael Duffy as Dowzard; Pat Fay as Foster.

The production ran for three weeks. As a contrast to Fallon's review, it might be noted that Seamus Kelly of the *Irish Times,* who had little love for the works of O'Casey, wrote a generally favorable review on 18 June, in which he deplored the sentimentality and praised the comedy, concluding: "Over all, however, I would assess 'Red Roses' as one of the very few worth-while productions Dublin has seen in the past five years."

[2] Valentin Iremonger, "Rude Mechanicals," *Irish Times,* 18 May 1946, a review of the published text of *Oak Leaves and Lavender.*

the greater part of its journey lumbers and flounders along. One feels that it is the play which Sean O'Casey *insisted on writing,* rather than the play which Sean O'Casey could have written. The folly of genius lies in the distinction.

Red Roses is, in many respects, an autobiographical work. It is, besides, the story of a Protestant hero living and loving and preaching and fighting his (always aesthetic) way through the strike of 1913; lifting up his eyes to the glory that might have been Dublin, had striking workers the grace to glimpse a Protestant hero's conception of it. Defeat and death prevents the desired fulfilment.

Being autobiographical and deliberately didactic, *Red Roses* lacks that objectivity which is essential to all good playwriting. Instead of steadily observing his world and allowing his audience to draw conclusions from his observation of it (as in his earlier great plays) the author of *Red Roses* not only jumps onto the stage himself, but, being there, creates a world largely stuffed with his own conclusions concerning it. This, of course, is the work's fundamental fault, the source from which the inevitable mixture of modes and the rivers of sentimentality flow. The result is ersatz, phoney, froth and bubble, shadows without substance, a tree lacking roots.

One of the author's conclusions about Dublin life has always made me pause—and take a deep breath. I refer to the conclusion which he attempts to enshrine in the hocus-pocus concerning his "Our Lady of Eblana."

Faced with it, I find myself forced to recall the kindliness and the understanding of the personality I once knew in order to assure myself that this is not a piece of coldly-calculated bigotry.

Protestant heroism does not necessarily postulate Catholic ignorance. Yet, for reasons best known to the author, the work is heavily weighted in this direction, despite the castigation administered in the interests of low comedy to an aspect of Orange intolerance.

How is it, some may ask, that a number of English critics have described this play as a magnificent piece of dramatic poetry, beautifully conceived, and written, "with an Irishman's passion and a poet's fervour" (as one puts it), its central character a fiery idealistic figure, a Shakespearean student and a strike-leader? Well, anyone who knows anything about the present condition of the English theatre, and, in addition, knows his Englishman through *John Bull's Other Island,* will be able to find the answer to that question.

Like the fact or leave it, Sean O'Casey is one of the world's greatest playwrights, a dramatic genius of the first order, but it is not on works like *Red Roses For Me* that posterity will establish its verdict. Unless there is a return to first principles, we shall all be forced to join our young poet in his anger and tears. THE CURRENT PRODUCTION at the Gaiety Theatre inevitably challenges comparison with the play's first presentation at Olympia during the emergency years.

On the whole the Gaiety's second act is the better of the two, and Ria Mooney, Carl Bonn, and Harry Morrisson between them manage to make something akin to poetry in movement and setting and lighting. On the other hand, Bonn's finely realistic setting for Act I in the Gaiety presentation hardly gives the play a fair start. Ralph Cusack was wiser at Olympia when he threw the room open to a background of expressionism. But, then, the work itself presents frightful problems for both designer and producer, particularly in the matter of its mixed modes. The Olympia acting was more professionally effective.

Noel Purcell at the Gaiety gives a magnificent performance as Brennan o' the Moor. His speech, with its rich Dublin accent of tarnished velvet, his excellent timing, his gesture and movement (what Americans call his bodily plastique) are all that the author himself could desire for the play. Purcell's performance is outstanding.

The rest of the playing is amateur, but to me not unpleasingly so. I liked the freshness of most of it, and in particular the work of the ladies of the cast. Some of the men might have made more of their opportunities, particularly that usually sound actor, Joe O'Dea. I would prefer, too, a slightly less cantilating cleric than the one which Hamlyn Benson saw fit to play.

But, taking the whole production into consideration with particular attention to the well-devised positions and movement and the total effect of that memorable second act, I would say that the Gaiety presentation was a triumph for Ria Mooney.

To Peter Newmark

MS. NEWMARK

TOTNES, DEVON

1 JULY 1946

My dear Peter.

Have it your own way. There is little profit in trying to refute a critic. To refute one, you would have to refute all. For instance, Trewin says the British Israel episode "is tedious, tiresome, & should be cut"; [1] Stonier says this episode reaches to the "peak of humour." [2] Which is right? You & Priestley are both critics: which of you is right? You see, the dramatist can only go his own way.

[1] See O'Casey's letter to Jack Carney, 1 June 1946, note 1.
[2] *Ibid.,* note 2.

I'm sure you are having a busy time with your pupils. To have 50 to control isn't easy; nor is it even possible. A good idea to give them comics. As fine a way as any as an introduction to literature. But it isn't enough. The C.P. have let themselves down badly by this affiliation business. Rust wanted me to write in its favour; but I told him it was very bad tactics at the moment. So it proved to be. Most of the Internat. Brigadiers are fine fellows. One of them, a Dublin man, has just stayed the night with us. He's a Plymouth worker; far more imaginative than the S. Devon Com. Organiser. By the way—this organiser, too, is a critic; didnt like the ending of R. Roses; not hopeful enough; didn't have a plain enough message. I made him feel a little uncomfortable.

Carroll's "White Steed" is good. He can write; though his last four plays don't seem to have penetrated into acceptance.

Eileen sends her thanks for the coupons.

All the best.
Yours sincerely,
Sean

To J. C. Trewin [1]

MS. TREWIN

TOTNES, DEVON
9 JULY 1946

Dear Mr. Trewin:

You're asking a lot of me! To set down definitely impressions of Totnes would be a dangerous job, for it is old, & utterly unsuited to modern life. But the Devon people who live there, & in the surrounding districts, love it; & I love the Devon people, & wouldn't care to offend them for all the gold in the Indies. I'm not a clever hand at this sort of work either; but I'd like to say something around my affection for the kindly, warm-hearted, gossiping West country folk—so like my own people. They are a different race to the English who dwell in the East. No wonder Hardy wrote about them; & no wonder Dickens seemed to be so fond of them.

I'll try to write something, & if you think it suitable—well and good; if you don't, just send it back, and I won't mind a bit—I like the West country brethren too much to be indignant with a West-Country man,

Yours sincerely,
Sean O'Casey

[1] John C. Trewin, dramatic critic of *The Observer,* had asked O'Casey to write an article on Totnes for the *West Country Magazine.* See O'Casey's 28 July 1946 letter to Trewin.

To The Standard

26 JULY 1946

RED ROSES FOR ME

SIR,—Permit me to make a few comments on the review given by your Drama Critic recently to *Red Roses For Me,* and to ask him a question. The play has nothing to do with the strike of 1913. That labour upheaval was not a strike. It was a fight by the workers to win the right to belong to the Union of their choice. "Leave Jim Larkin's Union or leave your job," was the ultimatum presented to them by Martin Murphy, C. Eason and the other Catholic and Protestant and Quaker employers massed as one man in the Employers' Federation. The "glory that might have been Dublin" was not a Protestant vision, but a proletarian one, held by Catholic and Protestant worker alike. I'm sure Catholics want to rid their city of things ugly and common and mean just as much as Protestants do; though a lot of well-placed in both churches don't bother much about it. We workers do, for it is we who have to live in the bad places.

The question is: What coldly-calculated bigotry has the critic in his mind, when he mentions what he calls "the hocus-pocus concerning 'Our Lady of Eblana' "? I am not aware of any, either coldly-calculated or warmly-calculated.

SEAN O'CASEY

"Tingrith," Station Road,
Totnes, Devon

Our Theatre Critic writes: So far as I am concerned, Sean O'Casey is too important a playwright, too old a friend, too earnest a questioner to be answered in haste and a footnote.

If he is prepared to wait until I have both time and space at my disposal (I am rather busy this week rehearsing his *Gunman* for the Gaiety) [1] and if he is still hankering for a public answer—then I'm his man.

I suggest he should in the meantime (a) read his play again, (b) read my review again, and (c) recall that we discussed this matter in letters which passed between us on the occasion of the first Dublin production of *Red Roses For Me*. So, till the bell goes, and the seconds leave the ring—

G. F.

---

[1] *The Shadow of a Gunman* was revived on 29 July 1946 at the Gaiety Theatre, Dublin, directed by Gabriel Fallon, with Noel Purcell in the "starring" role of Seumas Shields. One of Fallon's colleagues at *The Standard* protested in the 9 August issue that the Dublin critics had ignored this production.

To Michael Casey

MS. MURPHY

TOTNES, DEVON
27 JULY 1946

Dear Mick,

The photograph was fine. You look very venerable in it—like G. B. S.[1]

I hope you have quite recovered from the weakness in the legs; or recovered enough to let you go around the world easily.

All well here, bar the youngest, who has an attack of tonsilitis.

I enclose cheque for a quid.

All the best,
Sean

[1] O'Casey's brother Michael had grown a Shavian beard during his illness.

To J. C. Trewin

MS. TREWIN

TOTNES, DEVON
28 JULY 1946

Dear Mr. Trewin.

Enclosed are a few remarks about Totnes [1] & "the adjacent vicinity" —as a Dublin polisman would say. I should have liked to have said more, critical of Town, industries, pleasures, education; but hadn't room in a 1000-word article; besides it is from the Devon mind & soul expansion must come, & not from these things born in Dublin.

I have sent the article early so as to get it off my mind, &, secondly, to give you a chance to get a substitute, should you think it no good, or unsuitable. What a difference between Devon—the West Country—and Buckinghamshire, Kent, or Essex! To me a different race. Plymouth has had a bad blow, but not a knock-out.

[1] The article enclosed in this letter, "Totnes of Gentle Mien," was published in the *West Country Magazine,* Winter Issue, 1946; reprinted in the *Sean O'Casey Review,* Spring 1976.

So you are a Cornishman? I had a suspicion, all along, there was something "wrong" with you. Devon, too, is mainly Keltic. 100 years ago Ireland knew Devon as "East Ireland," & hurling matches took place between them. We are all very "matey" with the Devon people; & a fine lot they are—to me, anyhow; & to the missus—she knows them better even than I do.

By the way, what has happened to St. John Ervine? He doesn't seem to write anything now. You may remember he used to fire a critical salute of big guns in the Observer every week.

Well, all the best, & warm regards to the Cornishman.

Yours sincerely,
Sean O'Casey

To Jack Carney

MS. NYU LIBRARY

TOTNES, DEVON
2 AUGUST 1946

Dear Jack,

Thanks for the journals. Evidently G. B. S. got a new lease of life on his last Birthday.[1] He certainly seems to have hopped about a bit. Have you a television set? Has he signed the roll yet? I wish I had some of his energy. I'm having a little discussion (or trying to) with Gaby Fallon (an old friend of mine), Drama Critic of the Dublin Catholic Standard. He called the episode of "Our Lady of Eblana" a bit of "hocus pocus that showed a coldly-calculated bigotry." I've asked him to tell me why, how, where! He suggests "a public discussion," but I just want a few words of explanation, or explanatory proof. The world will move along its own way, no matter what Byrnes or Bevin can do. Like the doctors, they think they can keep things from happening. But collective life, and collective activity, is growing stronger, & nothing can hold it back. Just think of us in 1913, & then look at us now! The only place left soon to God will be the Pope's Green Island. I should like to have seen those pictures of Ireland's History, shown at the National School of Art. [Sean] Keating's one of "A Republican Court," as reproduced, is pretty bad. And Kathleen Fox's one's nearly worse.

All seem to be going to foreign lands now. Breon's away in Holland, the Lowlands Law. I hope your niece, her husband, & Mina will have a good time in Switzerland. You'll feel odd on your own.

1 Bernard Shaw was ninety on 26 July 1946.

All the best, & thanks again for the papers. I've written an article on Shaw for "Our Ally," the British-Soviet Journal.[2] They sent it to G. B. S., who said it was "superb." I wonder was he joking? Central Office of Information swears he wasn't.

Yours as ever,
Sean

[2] O'Casey's article "A Whisper about Bernard Shaw" appeared in a Russian translation in *Britansky Soyuznik*, 21 July 1946; an expanded version in English was published in *The Green Crow* (1956).

---

9 AUGUST 1946

The Standard, Dublin

Theatre . . . . by *Gabriel Fallon*
CALLING MR. O'CASEY

My Dear Sean: You at least will understand why I address you thus. Old friendship and long custom both demand it. Yet here I sit in the sultry August afternoon wondering what sharp winter of discontent has suddenly frosted that clear perception you once had, what cutting east wind has lashed into you the pompousness of believing that letters to "Mr. The Editor" concerning "Your Critic" could make any difference to that "Gaby Fallon, whose Friendship and Talent was and is a wonderful gift to his affectionate friend and buttie, Sean O'Casey."

Your play, *Red Roses For Me,* was first produced here some years ago. On that occasion I said as much about it as I said last month. Possibly more. Yet you found no occasion then to write to "Mr. The Editor" about it. I wonder why; and why you should do so now?

Blandly enough you declare that you are not concerned with the criticism of the play as a play. The neutrality of *"Your Critic is as likely to be right there as he is likely to be wrong"* is obviously intended to divert attention from what (for me, as critic) was the major issue. You go on to say that you will be very glad if Mr. Fallon tells you the reason he had for giving the name of "hocus-pocus" to the episode of Our Lady of Eblana and why he thinks the treatment of this episode an instance of "cold calculated bigotry."

Well, Mr. Fallon will tell you. But why should you choose to think that *"a quarter of a column"* will serve the purpose? Why should you want to cabin and confine my answer in a matter which you with your unmistakable dramatic genius have raised to a wide-flung and compelling power of theatre? Why, too, should you declare that there is neither time nor reason for what "Mr. The Editor" called "a public discussion." No time? Perhaps. But, *no reason?* There I very grievously beg to differ with you.

You know your play: who better? Hundreds of thousands of playgoers and readers in the English theatre know it perhaps as well. But for the sake of those who know it not at all, let us recall the episode of "Our Lady of Eblana" which begins in Act I.

Into a dilapidated room in a poor working-class locality come a group of women and men carrying a statue of the Blessed Virgin "more than two feet high." *"Could you spare a pinch of your Hudson's soap to give the Blessed Virgin a bit of a wash?"* Thus one of the women to the kindly Protestant room-keeper, Mrs. Breydon. In a lengthy speech we are told about little Ursula (an inmate of the tenement) *"savin' up odd pennies to bring Her where She'll find a new blue robe, an' where they'll make the royalty of th' gilt glow again; though whenever she's a shillin' up it's needed for food and firin'; but we never yet found Our Lady of Eblana averse to sellin' Her crown an' Her blue robe to provide for Her people's need."* So far so cryptic; or should it be, so crystal clear?

In the action of the play the statue is removed from its niche in the hallway by the Protestant Mr. Brennan Moore, in the eyes of his Catholic neighbours, *"a decent oul' blatherer; all bark and no bite."* Mr. Moore has the statue re-painted and returned to its niche in the hallway. Then suddenly at a point little over half-way in Act 2, we are informed by the Protestant Hero of the play, Ayamon Breydon, that *"th' Blessed Virgin has come back again."* He invites us to *"Listen."*

Men and women now appear at the door singing a hymn softly, "staring at the Image shining bright and gorgeous as Brennan made it for them." After the singing of the hymn, three of them speak. EEADA tells us *"She came back; of Her own accord."* DYMPNA declares that *"From her window little Ursula looked, and saw Her come; in the moonlight, along the street. She came, stately. Blinded be the coloured light that shone around Her, the child fell back; in a swoon she fell full on the floor beneath her."* This is followed by the FIRST MAN'S speech: *"My eyes caught a glimpse of Her too, glidin' back to where She came from. Regal and proud She was, an' wondrous, so that me eyes failed; me knees thrimbled an' bent low, an' me heart whispered a silent prayer to itself as th' vision passed me by, an' I fancied I saw a smile on Her Holy face."*

Now, what can anyone with eyes to see, ears to hear, and common-sense to reason with, make of this scene? What do *you* want to make of it, Sean O'Casey? Are these liars and hypocrites and fools your chosen representatives of the Catholics living in the poor working-class districts of Dublin? You asked me why I called this scene a scene of hocus-pocus, why I feared the possibility of a cold-blooded bigotry. Knowing me as you do, knowing that I know (and that you know) a great deal about the Catholics in the poor working-class districts of Dublin—I am amazed you should ask me!

You will hasten to point out, of course, that you dealt far from tenderly in Act 3 with Orange ignorance and bigotry in the persons of your Dowzard and Foster. But you took care, did you not, to provide throughout your play a carefully dramatised corrective in the dignified bearing and the dignified words of the Rev. Protestant Rector and in the characterisation of Ayamon and Mrs. Breydon? What corrective did you provide for the lying and the hypocrisy and the folly of your representatives of working-class Catholics?

In your first letter to this paper you tell us that you feel sure that *"Catholics want to rid their city of things ugly and common and mean just as Protestants do."* Now will you allow me to tell you in return that I defy anyone to see and hear or read your *Red Roses For Me* and detect even a jot or a little of that feeling of yours? We may take your letter's word for it, Sean O'Casey, but in deference to our understanding, we must reject your play's.

Make no mistake about this. I am not so foolish as to expect that you ought to write plays to suit a pattern of thought other than your own. But, for integrity's sake, do stand by that pattern and do not assume amazement if some other—even an old friend turned critic—should elect to stand against it. Let us be faithful to the light that we have. It is your own affair that you have chosen to leave that way of theatre in which the drama is allowed to convey its own lesson without the dramatist insisting on coming before the footlights to correct it. But it is also the affair of the critic.

Let the scoffers say what they will. I am not so damnably lost in intellectualism as to pretend that public criticism of an old friend's work has been a disporting place of thornless roses for me. Sitting here in the cool of the August twilight I am thinking of our long and valued friendship, of the fundamental differences of opinion which that friendship has so far survived, of your many public and private kindnesses to me, and of that deeply-rooted affection for our native city which we share in common. But how could I honour that truth and frankness which you have always respected in friend and foe, how could I face you again, or my good friends and neighbours again (of every description, without any exception of persons) if I did not boldly deliver myself of the opinions that are in me. These opinions may be right or they may be wrong, but they are undubitably mine, mine as a drama critic, mine as a Dubliner, mine as a Catholic, mine as an old friend of Sean O'Casey.

Such as they are then take them.

With every good wish and all the old affection,

Yours sincerely,
Gabriel Fallon

To The Standard

9 AUGUST 1946

AND SEAN O'CASEY WROTE [1]

Sir,—There is neither time nor reason for what you call "a public discussion." I am not concerned with the criticism of the play as a play. Your Critic is as likely to be right there as he is likely to be wrong. I am concerned only with the charges made during the course of the criticism. So I shall be very glad if Mr. Fallon tells me the reason he had for giving the name of "hocus pocus" to the episode of Our Lady of Eblana; and why he thinks the treatment of this an instance of "cold, calculated bigotry." Less than quarter of a column will, I'm sure, serve the purpose. It is but just, that, since the charge appeared in your journal, the reason for it should be given there.

[1] This letter was written before Fallon's open letter, "CALLING MR. O'CASEY." Many years later, in the summer of 1963, O'Casey and I discussed his break with Fallon. "In those reviews and letters in *The Standard,* Fallon said so much, you said so little. Why?" I asked him. He answered:

> How do you reply to an "oul' friend" who has just called you a coldly calculated bigot? Does he deserve the dignity of an outraged denial? And what was the point of replying to a holy slander-sheet like *The Standard* when all its crawthumping readers already believed I was a coldly calculated bigot, and worse, before Fallon told them the great secret; though he probably got it from them, the poor pious and gutless Gaby. There he was in his sanctimonious glory, telling his readers I had written a terrible play because I was a terrible man. All my life I've been attacked and vilified, but never for want of integrity. And I've been called a lot of nasty names, but never a coldly calculated bigot. One thing I am cold and calculated about is bigotry; and perjury, and cowardice.

See also O'Casey's letter to Fallon, 20 February 1943, notes 4 and 5. For Fallon's version of what happened, see his *Sean O'Casey: The Man I Knew* (1965), pp. 152–57.

To Francis MacManus

TS. MacManus

Totnes, Devon
11 August 1946

My dear Frank,

I have had to rest my eyes a lot lately, & haven't been able to write sooner. I've had a lot to do, too, in the house and outside of it—at home and abroad.

I am sorry to hear about your elder youngster. It is odd that these things happen; they shouldn't. They do, because we never ask the reason why, saying, to escape bother, that it is part of God's will. This God's will is a dangerous ejaculation. Can't anything be done for the lad? Can't treatment & care not strengthen the heart? It is very hard on the mother who has to be with him always. There is joy, of course, in the fact of the lad's intelligence. Little, after all, is lost once the mind stays bright. Now I call *that* God's will. My sympathy to Mrs. MacManus & to you.

So Iris has departed—just when I had made sure of getting it. It seems strange that such a magazine couldn't keep going. I am very much afraid for Ireland. You're hard on the Gaels, but a lot of them deserve it. Certainly Irish wont come back if it depends on the Irish quips of Roddy the Rover,[1] or the Nuacht business in the Irish Press.[2] The Irish all seem to be coming over here. There's another new doctor from Dublin practising here now, with his wife from Crumlin Road, Belfast. I remember [Cardinal] Hinsley—clad in scarlet and purple—once telling me, in his unctuous way, that this exodus was the special will of God. You meet it everywhere there are Irish—this will o' God.

Divil a word more I'll say about Canon Sheehan. But [Walter] Mac-Donald was no cranky egoist. He was a man, if ever there was one, who tried to learn something about the grace o' God. He aimed at making theology a living thing, & not a dead embalmed body, held up, now & again, for veneration, like a bit of the true Cross. He wanted to unwind her from the embalming cloths of easy piety & surpliced jobs; to send her out from the deadening air of balsam & sulphur, into the free airs of heaven, to live and grow, & be fearless and lovely.

Yes, I'd like to have a go at Mo Bhealach Fein.[3] I'd have to read it slow, for the Gaelic characters tire my eyes; so I might have it some time before I'd send it back to you. I hope MacGrianna will get his annuity. No original writer should be bothered with translation.

We had our share of the war down here. The house is a bit shook. We lost windows & two ceilings went west, put up again by a Tipperary man. Hardly a night that we weren't up out of bed, listening to Dornier & Messerschmitt flying overhead, & then the odd sickening thud of the things falling in the near distance; Eileen & the two younger stretched out under the steel-topped Morrison shelter; & our eldest sitting on the stairs with me, well aware now that I had a heart. The eldest, Breon, was the best of

[1] Aodh de Blacam, who wrote a regular column under the pseudonym of Roddy the Rover in the *Irish Press*. See O'Casey's letters to Brian O'Nolan, 2 April 1942, note 7; and to the *Irish Times,* 24 April 1944, note 2.

[2] A reference to the column of news printed in Irish in the *Irish Press*.

[3] Seosamh MacGrianna, *Mo Bhealach Féin* agus *Dá mBíodh Ruball ar an Éan* (1940), *My Own Way* and *If the Bird Had a Tail*. The first work is an account of MacGrianna's adventures during a walking tour of Wales, and the second is an unfinished satire on General Eoin O'Duffy's Fascist Blue Shirts. See O'Casey's comments on both works in his letter to MacManus, 17 September 1946.

us, taking it all very coolly, & giving courage to the younger ones—a thing, I'm afraid, I did badly, though I did my best. Yes, I am going on with my "Biography." Why the hell shouldn't I? Oh! Those verbal tricks of mine! They're a worry to a lot. But you may be right, all the same.

Something has happened to the *Bell,* too. It's going to be changed and made bigger. Peadar O Donnell has written to me, asking for a contribution; but I've nothing at the moment. And another! From Cork, too, this time. *Irish Writing,* to pay "fees as good as the English journals of the same kind". With a galaxy of names for the first number—O'Flaherty, James Stephens, F. O'Connor, S. O'Faolain, Bill Naughton, L. MacNeice, Lord Dunsany, R. Farren, P. Kavanagh, Sean Jennett (Who's he?), M. na gCopaleen, Edith Somerville, L. A. G. Strong, and Vivian Mercier (Who's that fella?); & a constellation for the second no. Padraic Colum, E. Bowen, C. Day Lewis, Mary Lavin, Jim Phelan, & Oliver Gogarty. Your name isn't there. Why? They've asked me to do a one-act play of 4,000 words, & offered a fee of £15 15s od for it. I couldn't take the offer for various reasons. Their address

David Marcus, or,
Terence Smith,
Irish Writing,
15, Adelaide Street, Cork.

You might like to get into truck with them. A few pounds, now & then, come in useful. Sell them the first publication rights, which leaves what you write with yourself after six months or so from publication. But where are they getting the paper? Macmillan's have over a 1,000 titles waiting publication. All my books—bar O. Leaves & Lavender—are "out of print."

What's the Irish Press printing "Rocky Road to Dublin" for? Is it the answer to the prayer of "Holy St. Patrick, dear saint of our Isle. On thy dear children bestow a sweet smile"?

All the best to Mrs MacM. to your two boys, & to you.

Sean

To Jack Carney

MS. NYU LIBRARY

TOTNES, DEVON
20 AUGUST 1946

Dear Jack,

The little Bretagne lass in her gorgeous dress, is sitting grand on a chair in the nursery; & the gallant French soldiers are fighting battles brave on the table.

I should be glad to read MacLiammoir's book.[1] I hesitated to get it myself, guessing it wouldn't be deep enough to warrant the parting of a guinea, & they so hard to get. I'll send it back to you, soon as I've read it. The reference to "Hecuba" is taken from Hamlet; the scene between him, the Players, & Polonius. The leading player, at Hamlet's request, recites a piece about the tragedy of "the mobled queen" in tragic style; & when they go, Hamlet, alone, compares the actor's fervent pathos over Hecuba to his own hesitation to avenge the death of his father. Referring to the player, Hamlet asks himself, "What's Hecuba to him or he to Hecuba?"

The weather here continues to be most unkind. I daresay, you've heard of the New Bell to sound in November? An English edition as well as an Irish one—total printing of 13,000, much enlarged. And Cork is publishing another magazine, "Irish Writing," [2] both offering fees comparing favourably with English ones. "I. Writing" offered me £25 for a one-act play of 5,000 words! I couldn't do it; but they have appealed for something from me. I asked them in a letter "Where th' hell are you getting the money?" but they didn't say. Moscow, be God!

All the best to Mina, Francoise & her man, & to you.

Yours
Sean

[1] Michael MacLiammoir, *All For Hecuba: An Irish Theatrical Autobiography* (1946).
[2] *Irish Writing,* based in Cork, was to begin publication in November 1946. See O'Casey's letter to David Marcus, 31 October 1946, note 1.

To Francis MacManus

TS. MacManus

Totnes, Devon
20 August 1946

Dear Frank,

Thank you for sending me Mo Bhealach Féin. I'll tell you what I think of it as soon as I have read it.

My last letter forgot to mention the book you had in your mind to write—the various influences that control the Eire of today. I am very chary of suggesting anything to a writer—it is always such a precarious job—but your idea is (to me) an intensely interesting one. You certainly should consider it well and deeply. It needs courage, and, if ever you do it, try to get an English publisher for it. Take your time thinking; but if you decide to do it, do it with all your might. "Whatsoever thy right hand findeth to do, do it with all thy might" St. Paul.

I am sending you a copy of "Oak Leaves" as a slight return for your kind thought of sending me MacGrianna's book.

All the best.

Sean

To Jack Carney

MS. NYU LIBRARY

TOTNES, DEVON
24 AUGUST 1946

Dear Jack,

Thanks for the loan of "All For Hecuba," which I now return to you. I'm afraid it doesn't do a lot to honour Priam's wife and Hector's mother. Such a flutter of a tin, tinselled butterfly I have never read before. They're all the same—these shadow-souled Cissies. Well, the Hilton Edwards-Liammoir pregnancy won't give birth to much more than an artificial drama-mouse. They never will—not even with the Ponderous help of [Lord] Longford—do even as much as a ghost-like resemblance of what Yeats & Gregory did at the Abbey. A squeal done up in satin & silk, damp with the perfume of false violets. Well, well, & 21 bob!

Thanks again.
Yours as ever,
Sean

To R. L. De Wilton [1]

TS. DE WILTON

TOTNES, DEVON
24 AUGUST 1946

Dear Mr. De Wilton:

Thank you for your kind letter. With this note, I return the contract, signed, as requested.

[1] R. L. De Wilton, Macmillan Company, New York.

I am, of course, naturally glad that you like the play, Oak Leaves and Lavender. George Jean Nathan, the New York Drama-critic thinks very well of it too. It is an O'Casey tribute to the hardships borne, & the big fight waged here against Nazi domination. I had a slight share in it all myself. Didn't like it at all; but we all had to stick it. I saw more of your Countrymen here in Totnes than I ever saw when I was with you some years ago. From all states, from Alabama to Maine. Totnes people feel rather lonely since your boys left.

Well, maybe, in the future, when the planes really get going, Alabama won't be very far from Totnes—the state comes nearer to Dublin daily.

All the best to you all.

Yours sincerely,
Sean O'Casey

To Miss Sheila———

MS. PRIVATE

TOTNES, DEVON
26 AUGUST 1946

Dear Sheila,

I haven't had a chance to write to you, & now but a minute for a hasty note. I will try to write more fully later on. I couldn't advise you about the job of Welfare Officer, for that question must be answered by yourself. I'm inclined to think, though, you may have acted too hastily. It may not have been good "tactics" to fling the job away. What about your Union, & haven't you Shop Stewards to advise you there? Surely, they should have been by your side to tell you what you should do. I don't know that you should be breaking your back on a job that may not suit you. You won't serve the workers' cause by killing yourself. Has no effort been made to abolish the Bidaux System? Is it applied only to the work done by L———? You aren't paid for the amount of work you do, are you, above a certain norm, as in the USSR? You should draw the attention of your Union to anything you think amiss, & not try to rectify it yourself. Surely, the officials of your Union could do something; or is L——— mainly a blackleg factory—mostly non-Union hands?

I write again as soon as I can; meanwhile try to take it easy.

Yours very sincerely,
Sean O'Casey

To George Jean Nathan

MS. CORNELL

TOTNES, DEVON
1 SEPTEMBER 1946

My very dear George:

I got your letter allright, telling me about Billy Rose's interest in Purple Dust. That is very good; & I hope it may mean a fine production in New York City. "Red Roses" had a fair run here—good enough to lift me from financial worry for maybe a year; and that's good, too. We are all well.

Cork is issuing a new magazine called "Irish Writing"; they begged & begged me to write for them; so eventually I wrote an article [1] connecting myself (I think) with the Theatre in general. I ventured to quote the opening remarks of the Preface to "Five Famous Irish Plays" [2] (Random House) holding your tribute to the Irish Theatre (I said nothing of what you said about me), so that I might let the Irish dramatists know the high standard they had to face. I wish they had your book to read. Your "Critic & the Drama" [3] should be in the hands (and head) of every dramatist—I've just been reading it again. What Ireland lacks is a Critic. There isn't one from one end of the land to the other. Lots of chaps write about plays for a guinea or two—for the guineas; but not for the theatre. I enclose an Agate article appearing in "Theatre Today" No. 2, & a poor thing it is—to my mind. And a "snap" of myself an clan.

[Paul V.] Carroll has written a new play; but I don't know how it goes. He's busy now on some scenario. I wish he wouldn't give so much thought to the films.

My love as ever.
Sean

[1] See O'Casey's letter to David Marcus, 31 October 1946, note 2.
[2] *Five Great Modern Irish Plays* (1941), with a Foreword by George Jean Nathan. See O'Casey's letter to Nathan, 22 September 1941, note 1, Vol. I, p. 904.
[3] George Jean Nathan, *The Critic and the Drama* (1922).

To Honor Tracy [1]

TC. O'CASEY

TOTNES, DEVON
1 SEPTEMBER 1946

Dear Miss Tracy:

Thank you very much for sending me the copy of THE BELL, containing Sean O'Faolain's comments and criticism of my DRUMS UNDER THE WINDOWS.[2] A mutilated copy, alas!, for Two pages—17 and 18—are missing. What a pity! But it cant be helped; and, anyway, it means only the delay of a few days, for I have written to the American critic (whom I know) to send me his copy.

Well, well; A Joycean phrase seems to set Sean O'Faolain's teeth on age. Of course, he may be right, but I am inclined to think that "dustiny" is a good word. "Dust thou art, and to dust shalt thou return." "Stop! for thy tread is upon an Empire's dust"! "Caesar dead, and turned to clay" etc. And, even in this very number, he writes of "those last verbal echoes of buried towns and time-erased gardens, and forgotten cosmogonies." An odd coincidence. Destiny, sooner or later, comes to dust, like golden lads and lasses. Yes, it seems to me to be a good word.

It isnt so hard for a mind to look at things through reflections (the full comment is missing, so I dont know the context from which the comment is made); for the mind can look through a reflection—contemplation—to a thing beyond it. I dont rightly know how one can think of the church in Ireland as an "abstract thing." To me the church was always "concrete" enough—too much so sometimes.

I think, too, "bankum" a good word; but minds differ; and I think—from the worker's point of view, at any rate, Mutt Talbot [3] to have some meaning.

However, I'll see more clearly when I get the full copy.

In the meantime, thanks again for the trouble you took for my sake.

Yours sincerely,
Sean O'Casey

[1] Honor Tracy, Irish novelist, was an assistant editor and reviewer for *The Bell* in 1946.
[2] Sean O'Faolain, "Too Many Drums," *The Bell,* December 1945.
[3] See O'Casey's letter to Dr. Joseph D. Cummins, 26 November 1942, note 5.

To Brian Hurst [1]

TC. O'CASEY

TOTNES, DEVON
4 SEPTEMBER 1946

Dear Mr. Hurst:

Thank you for your letter in which you say you are interested in the filming of THE SHADOW OF A GUNMAN.

I dont think it is a "great" play; but there are, I think many good things in it; and I think, too, with good handling it would make a fine film—possibly, a stirring one.

As for helping in the scenario, etc, I'm not so sure I'd be an excellent partner now. There is a tale to that: Twenty years ago, and more, I was eager to try my hand at a film of Hyde Park, which was to begin by the opening of the gates at dawn and end with the closing of the gates at midnight. I had visions of fine scenes—pictorially—of the swimming of swans; of two lovers overwhelmed with an advancing pyramid of Evangelistic placards like enveloping slogans, of a football match to the singing of a song, etc. I wrote to Mr Hitchcock about it; he came to see me, and over dinner, we talked of it, and he was very enthusiastic. He left, leaving warm words with me, saying I was to come to dinner to his place, and we'd finish the scheme. I'm still waiting for the invitation. I imagine his wife (who was with him) talked him out of the idea.[2] Anyway, I came to the resolution never again to have anything to do with the Films, and I never have—bar to write some additional dialogue for the silent show of JUNO AND THE PAYCOCK. Or was it a silent one? I dont know; for I never saw it.

I shouldnt mind trying to write additional dialogue, if it happened to be necessary, I suppose. I fancy some good shots could be made of things only suggested in the play—deserted streets, with the Cars and the Black and Tans cruising through them, for one.

For business arrangements, mine is usually done by Miss M. E. Barber, M.A. The Dramatists' League, 84, Drayton Gardens, London, S.W.10.

Yours sincerely,
· *Sean O'Casey*

[1] Brian Hurst, Kinnerton Studios, Belgrave Square, London.
[2] See O'Casey's account of the meeting with Alfred Hitchcock in "A Long Ashwednesday," *Rose and Crown* (1952).

To Honor Tracy

TC. O'CASEY

[TOTNES, DEVON]
5 SEPTEMBER 1946

Dear Miss Tracy:

Now dont come to such a hasty decision over the change in your article by the Editor of OUR TIME. We have to put up with such things occasionally. And a few guineas are a few guineas, after all, Honor Tracy. I have had changes in articles of my own, and, at times, deliberate refusal to publish them. I wrote a reply to a Mr. Orwell's review of DRUMS UNDER THE WINDOW which hasnt yet appeared anywhere.[1] It will one day. Patience. This fellow quoted a verse I put into the book as an example of "doggerel nationalistic poetry," but he didnt know that the verse he condemned was written by Tennyson, and taken from that poet's MAUD. My reply was sent on to him, so no wonder it didnt appear. But it will some day. Twenty years ago, and more, after JUNO and THE PLOUGH had appeared, "The Universe" referred to me as a (a correspondent to the paper) Judas; and the "Sunday Worker" called me a Pontius Pilate; the first for ridiculing Catholics, and the other for ridiculing the workers. And, I daresay, you know how Dublin took the second play. But still and all, I love Dublin, I dont hate Catholics, and I look upon myself as a friend of all workers. TIME AND TIDE refused to let me say a word against the late Dicky Sheppard,[2] one of the greatest cods that mighty England ever produced. OUR TIME is doing good work, and it has a hard fight against some Marxian fanatics who are so full of theory that they would not stop to have a look at a lily or a rose. I have long and bitter letters from one condemning PURPLE DUST because it is likely to "inflame Irish national passions, and so injure the Socialist Movement." There is a Communist Party here; but the only Communist I know who wears the Red Star in the lapel of his coat is your unhumble servant, O'Casey. Ewart Milne,[3] reviewing OAK LEAVES AND LAVENDER, says that the dialogue of the play is more reminiscent of Usnagh than it is of Devon. He doesnt know that that isnt surprising seeing that there is a close kin between Devon and our Irish past. The very name of Devon is from a Keltic tribe; that Devon years ago was known as East Ireland; and that West and East Ireland used to be opposed in hurling matches. And, for God's sake, don't

[1] See O'Casey's letter to *The Observer,* 29 October 1945, a reply to George Orwell which was refused publication. He had to wait nine years until his extended comments on Orwell were published in "Rebel Orwell," *Sunset and Evening Star* (1954).

[2] See Phoebe Fenwick Gaye's letter to O'Casey, 20 January 1936, note 2, Vol. I, p. 606.

[3] Ewart Milne, *Irish Democrat,* August 1946.

send my next book to a reviewer "anxious to discover all its excellence." I must prefer that it should be sent to one burning to pick out all its faults. This would be much more fun. And dont forget to be patient; so take any chance to write about any book OUR TIME may send you. Thanks for the magazine. All the best. I see Barry Fitzgerald has gone back to Hollywood. Not, I daresay to B. Crosby, who seems to be a little jealous of him.

[*Sean O'Casey*]

To Jack Carney

MS. NYU LIBRARY
TOTNES, DEVON
12 SEPTEMBER 1946

Dear Jack,

I am returning the bould Jim [Larkin]'s letter with this note. He is right about Delargey. But how is one to answer him? The Irish papers won't print a reply, or a comment, favorable to the USSR, or to the workers. I tried it twice. You see that what I feared was true—Bill O'Brien's as potent as ever. More now than ever; for he has the "democratic" fame of resignation behind him. O'Brien resigns from nothing. That mask he calls a face looks over, & into, everything. I wrote Jim, at the request of Peadar O'Donnell—now new Editor of "The Bell" [1]—asking Jim to see [George] Gilmore, who wants to write about him in the new "Bell," to be much larger than the old one; & to have a wide English circulation.

I hope you will have a fine time in Dublin. I understand the city is flooded with all sorts of Nationalities; & that it is very hard to come across an Irishman. Where the real Dublinmen are, God knows.

Love to you & Mina.
Yours as ever
Sean

[1] Peadar O'Donnell became editor of *The Bell* with the April 1946 issue and continued until the magazine stopped publication in December 1954. Previously Sean O'Faolain had been editor, from the first issue, October 1940, until March 1946.

To Michael Casey

MS. MURPHY

TOTNES, DEVON
14 SEPTEMBER 1946

Dear Mick,

Here's another quid that may be of some use to you.

I see by the Irish papers that you are getting a bellyful of rain in Eirinn. We are having our full share of it here too.

All well here,
All the best,
Yours as ever,
Sean

PS. I can't bring to mind the "Murphy" who is in the Hospice. Who was he? [1]

[1] A neighbor of the Caseys when they lived in the Abercorn Road.

To Francis MacManus

TS. MACMANUS

TOTNES, DEVON
17 SEPTEMBER 1946

My dear Frank:

I have read MacGrianna's Mo Bhealach Fein along with Da mBiodh Ruball ar an Ean,[1] and like both very much, and think a lot of them, though the second be incomplete, which is more than a pity.

There's no doubt, in my mind, that this boyo can write. It's a long, long time since I have read a long thing in Irish without feeling bored. I got more from this book—not only did I not feel bored, but often felt exhilarated; and I dont often feel this way even with books in the king's English. Mo Bhealach Fein seems to owe something to [George] Borrow. Borrow began the journey through wild Wales from the upper end; MacGrianna from the lower one. His story is so well done, not anything like so scholarly as that of Borrow's; but he has humour which Borrow doesnt seem to have had. It's a great shame that he gave up on the second story, which seems to be a satire on the Blue Shirts. He must never do this again. Better even to end the thing badly. He mustnt let the lines

[1] See O'Casey's letter to MacManus, 11 August 1946, note 3.

Bradan breagh me is luthmhar leim,
Acht faraor, ta an t-eas ro-ard [2]

get on his nerves or mind. A salmon like that would lep anything. He has but a faint idea about Communism, but that doesnt matter a damn. His name for it is far better than that of Cummanacht—a clumsy, ugly-looking, harsh-sounding title. Like that terrible one of Poblacht. It is fellows like him, writing out of themselves, who will give all new things a local habitation and a Name in the Irish—if they are only let alone; like Dante to the Italian, about whom, or his tomb and body, you wrote recently. I hope you havent fallen out with the editor of the Irish Press.

By the way, our friend Seosamh shouldnt think that a drinking life is essential to art. That is just a myth. Some of the artists are given that way; but so are thousands of the ordinary people. We never hear anything about these, but an artist is always prominent. If an artist commits suicide, the old, whole world talks about it; tens of thousands of ordinary folk may slit their throats without a soul bothering. There have been more suicides among business men than among artists. P. O'Conaire's [3] devil-may-care life—part of it a pose to get away with things—wasnt essential to his art. This sort of thing isnt bohemianism. Bohemianism has always a dignity and grace of its own. O'Conaire's "bohemianism" was often a nuisance; it was simply hooliganism at times. I've seen some of it, and I didnt like it. He practised it mostly on those who were little better off than himself. The rich escaped him. But Grianna's a good fellow, and should try to take care of himself, for as a writer, he owes it to man to live as long as he can, and write as often as he feels he must. Thanks again for letting me have the book.

> *All the best to you and yours,*
> *Yours as ever,*
> *Sean O'Casey*

[2] I am a fine salmon with an agile leap,
   But, alas, the waterfall is too high.
[3] See O'Casey's letter to Jack Carney, 2 March 1942, note 3.

To William Rust

TC. O'CASEY

TOTNES, DEVON
23 SEPTEMBER 1946

Dear Mr. Rust:
    Since it seems evident that your Journal is connected with the activities of Unity Theatre; since Mr. Ted Willis, Unity Theatre's producer, is evi-

dently one of your Staff, and since the aims of the Theatre seem to be identical with your own; it is meet that I should put the following matter before you:

You are doubtless aware that this theatre performed my play, THE STAR TURNS RED [1] for a period of six weeks recently, and that this production was, of course, the subject of an agreement between me and them. I gave permission very reluctantly, and only after several appeals by Mr. Collier; for, since John Allen had left the job as Producer, I was very doubtful about the ability of Mr. Willis to produce the play. However, I gave it after getting a letter from Mr. Collier implying that John Allen was still there to help with advice—it was J. Allen who produced on the first occasion; [2] I know him, and have a sincere admiration for him.

On July 30th, 1946, I got a letter from Mr. Collier saying he would send photographs and fortnightly accounts on the box-office receipts, and payment of royalty agreed upon. Since that date, I have received no word from Mr. Collier. Not only have I received no royalty, but I havent been able even to get a reply to letters sent to this gentleman. Very recently, Mr. Willis rang me up when he was on holiday in Cornwall, asking if he and his wife could come to see me. When I said by all accounts received from friends, the production was a bad one, he rather indignantly replied that it was a great success, and "I had only to look at the box-office receipts to see that"; so it was a little ironical to hear this when I remembered that I had received no royalty, and couldnt get an answer to letters sent to Mr. Collier.

I would like to mention that when this play was published, the sales were so slow and so poor that Macmillan's reduced the advance from £100 to £75 on all future play publications.

I am handing over the matter to the League of Dramatists, for it is necessary that other dramatists should be cautious about giving their work to Unity Theatre.

I am also writing to the Theatre demanding that my name be removed from the list of members of the Council.

Yours sincerely,
Sean O'Casey

[1] *The Star Turns Red* was revived at Unity Theatre, London, on 31 July 1946, directed by Ted Willis.

[2] The premiere of *The Star Turns Red* at Unity Theatre, London, on 12 March 1940, directed by John Allen.

To Bronson Albery

TC. O'CASEY

[TOTNES, DEVON]
12 OCTOBER 1946

Dear Mr. Albery:

Thank you for your letter. As far as I can judge, we are entitled to no more money from Theatre Incorporated till a year has passed by. The $2500.00 covers, I think, a period of a year. There is an alternative method in which the advances are divided into months, more in the season of production, and less in the summer time, when the season has ended.

But maybe you havent heard that the double tax has been cancelled by an arrangement between Britain and the U.S.A. This agreement is retrospective to the 1st of Jan. of this year, 1946. So you can get the tax that was withheld from the advance. So the Author—organ of the Authors' Society—says. A Form has to be got from the Inspector of Taxes has to be signed, and sent to the Agent—in your case and in mine—to Mr. Madden. The Macmillan Co. of Ameria has sent me two forms, which I have signed and returned. I have sent to the Inspector of Taxes for forms which I want to send to Mr. Madden and to Samuel French of New York. If you havent heard of this, then I should see about it—that is you should see about it. The "I should see about it" is the Irish way of saying YOU should do it.

About Michael Benthall's two years imprisonment for the play—well, I certainly [do not] consent to that, for it holds no wisdom in my opinion. What magic is there in Two Years? If Two Years enhance the play's chance of success, why not wait Five? He gives no reason for his opinion, so I guess that he is afraid of the psychological impact of the play on the people. (Or thinks himself that this is the reason). But honestly, I believe this to be ridiculous. After all that "the great human soul of England" has stood, the little play wont kill them. We Irish had plays going on, damned critical plays—during the Civil War. In the USSR a play THE FRONT was produced when things were very, very bad, criticising the Generals who, because they had fought in the Revolution, thought they knew everything, whereas they were utterly incompetent to grapple with the newer aspects of military strategy and tactics. This play, THE FRONT, said so bluntly, and many of them were removed, and fresh ones chosen with magnificent results. We had the same intolerable vanity in Ireland. If one said anything about economics, art, religion, etc., one was asked, "Were you out in Easter Week?" And if you hadnt carried a gun then, you were silenced at once.

But, quite frankly, I think that, either consciously, or sub-consciously, Benthall is afraid of the production, rather than of the people. He realises its difficulty, and wants to put it off, as another might a visit to a doctor. He would like to do it, but wants to put it off from him as far as possible. I believe that if the play isnt put on at an unsuitable time—near Christmas, or in the heat of the summer, for instance—it will do well.

[*Sean O'Casey*]

To Jack Carney

MS. NYU Library

Totnes, Devon
12 October 1946

Dear Jack,

Just a line to say I got the jersey—Tip an' all, & to thank you for it, & Ireland who knitted it.

Can't write a lot. Eyes still bad. Treating them now to Penicillin, so that should do something; and Dr. Tivy, of Plymouth—a Cork man!—has sent Eileen a pair of Oculist's goggles so's she can see better to pull out the lashes. So I'm well away.

Love to you & Mina.
Yours as ever
Sean

Sheila May Greene [1]

TS. GREENE

TOTNES, DEVON

12 OCTOBER 1946

Dear Miss Greene:

No. I cannot let any minus matter be introduced into my article.[2] It goes as it is, naked and unashamed, or not at all.

I am amused to read that the article "would be harmful to the Labour Party." Since the Labour Party are evidently afraid to say anything against the biggest enemies of their Movement, then there is no Labour Party. Dont you see that if Griffin be allowed to say what he likes, without question; and anyone who ventures to question him is refused publication—that is, permission to speak—, then there is no freedom of speech; and that cowardice is as big a censorship as that of the Censorship Board, or Kemsley, or any of the powers standing against democracy. And remember that Dr. McDonald was a theologian for forty years; and in Maynooth College; and an Irishman; whereas Griffin is no theologian, an enemy of free thought, and an Englishman. Yet you try to bury McDonald deeper, while you fix Griffin more securely on his episcopal throne—not of divinity or ecclesiastical leadership, but of dictatorship.

If these people—like Stepinac [3]—stand against the people, then, unless the people have the courage to stand against them—as they have stood against Stepinac—, then the people will remain as they are. And, sooner

[1] Sheila May Greene, editor of *Irish People,* journal of the Irish Labour Party. She had played the role of Sheila Moorneen in the first production of *Red Roses For Me* at the Olympia Theatre, Dublin, 15 March 1943. See O'Casey's letter to Gabriel Fallon, 20 February 1943, note 3. She was now married to Prof. David Greene, the Celtic scholar of Trinity College, Dublin. For her review of the published text of *Red Roses For Me,* see O'Casey's letter to Jack Carney, 9 July 1943, note 1.

[2] In a letter of 7 October 1946, Mrs. Greene had asked O'Casey to cut out an attack upon Cardinal Griffin, Archbishop of Westminster, in an article on labor and religion which he had been asked to write for *Irish People.* She wrote in part:

> Now I am in a most painful and embarrassing position, because I cannot print your article as it stands. Without putting a tooth in it, it would be harmful to the Labour Party. I like it immensely for its political urge. So much, indeed, that I am going to have the colossal nerve to ask if it would be possible for you to alter it in one particular way. Your political argument is unfortunately interwoven with theological disputation and I am afraid that the readers would get so worked up about the rights and wrongs of Cardinal Griffin's theology that the social message would be obscured and lost. I think that if you lived over here you would understand what I mean. Will you please try to forgive me and if you can, let me have either this minus Cardinal or another.

[3] Aloysius Cardinal Stepinac (1898–1960), Archbishop of Zagreb and Primate of Yugoslavia; arrested by the Tito government in 1946, charged with collaborating with the Croatian underground, and sentenced to sixteen years at hard labor for "crimes against the state." He was released in 1951 and appointed Cardinal in 1952.

or later, by someone, somewhere, sometime, this stand will be taken in Ireland; as Parnell took the stand against them, even to death.

To allow my article to be changed as you suggest would be to make it an article by you, and not by me. And, though not actually living in Ireland, I know something about it. If you mean that I would take no risk, were I living there, you are woefully mistaken. Here in the book of THE FLYING WASP, critical of the critics, I risked my living, even with a wife and family looking to me. Courage is what we all sadly need. Goethe's last words were "More light, more light." Mine will probably be "More courage, more courage."

Well, that's enough for the present. I am not out to force the Labour Party of Ireland. Their ways rest with their own conscience. Please let me have the article back. No wonder Bill O'Brien [4] has had his way.

All the best to you.
Yours sincerely
Sean O'Casey

[4] See O'Casey's letter to Jack Carney, 13 February 1942, note 1.

To Brooks Atkinson [1]

TS. ATKINSON

TOTNES, DEVON
17 OCTOBER 1946

My dear Brooks:

It was fine to hear your voice once more in The New York Times of Sept. 22nd, and all about me too.[2] It brought back the evening in your City when I and George Jean had dinner with you and your wife up in Twelvth Street—if I am not mistaken. A long, long time ago, but seemingly but a wee yesterday's step away from my memory.

Thank you for your kind references to my last book about the way we tried to live in Ireland some time ago. In your own gentle way, you imply a soft reproach for the small amount I have written. I've done more than you think, however, and against big obstacles. During the war years, we had no one to help us here, and the family of myself, wife, and three children gave me and the missus a lot to do. I have been washing up, helping with

[1] Brooks Atkinson (1894–), American drama critic and author; drama critic for the *New York Times,* 1926–60. For the first of many letters O'Casey wrote to him, see that of 4 November, 1934, Vol. I, p. 523.

[2] Brooks Atkinson, "O'Casey's Own Story," *New York Times,* 22 September 1946, a review of *Drums Under the Windows.*

breakfast and dinner, making beds, and all sorts of janitorial and domestic work for six long years. Then there were the siren calls to notice, often three in the night; to awaken those who were asleep, and get them down under the stairs, or beneath the morrison shelter. Then there was the black-out, seeing that no slit or chit of light crept through the curtains hanging over God only knows how many windows. During that time, we had to let the garden—not a great one, but still a garden—take its own way so that it became a devonian jungle. I've been working at it now for some months, for there is no-one to be got yet to do it for me; so me and the elder boy have done a little; if we haven't made it another Eden, we have, at least, brought disorder out of chassis. And all this has had to be done—as far as I am concerned—sideways, as it were, for one eye has been blind now for some years, and the other is set in a minor key, though it must be used for all it is worth. At the moment I am having penicillen treatment to keep it oiled. So you see, I have had a lot to do besides writing plays and things. During this time, I have written Purple Dust, The Star Turns Red, Red Roses for Me, and Oak Leaves and Lavender—plays; and Pictures in the Hallway, Drums Under the Windows, and part of the next vol., as well as numberless letters and articles—for instance, on Synge,[3] Yeats,[4] and Shaw [5] for the B.B.C., and one on Gorki for the Tribune; [6] some paid, and some unpaid. I have a suitcase full of letters from an Irish girl [7] working in a factory in replying to which, I must have written a little book. She sent me a violently abusive letter because I had criticised the Vatican in an article; but she added her name and address, so I replied, and we became fast friends, though I have never seen her. She has had a curious life, too wild to be educated, though I found out from her (a long time after we had begun to correspond—that she was the daughter of an Irish Major who was killed on the N.W. Frontier of India. We wrote and argued about Spain, Labour, religion, communism, and literature; I on my own; she helped by a Jesuit who acted as a kind of guardian to her.

But it is a little hard that since Within The Gates, I have had but one professional performance of new plays—Red Roses, and that came only because an Irishwoman,[8] daughter of T. W. Rolleston, the Irish poet, co-

[3] Sean O'Casey, "John Millington Synge," commissioned by the British Ministry of Information, published in Russian in *Britansky Soyuznik,* Moscow, June 1946; reprinted in English in *Blasts and Benedictions* (1967).

[4] Sean O'Casey, "Ireland's Silvery Shadow," commissioned by the BBC Spanish Service for broadcasting in Spanish in 1946; reprinted in English in *Blasts and Benedictions.*

[5] Sean O'Casey, "VPOLGOLOSA O BERNARDE SHOU," commissioned by the BBC Russian Service for broadcasting in Russian in 1946; published in *Britansky Soyuznik,* Moscow, 21 July 1946; reprinted in English in an expanded version as "A Whisper About Bernard Shaw" in *The Green Crow* (1956).

[6] Sean O'Casey, "Great Man, Gorki!" *Tribune,* 3 May 1946; reprinted in *Blasts and Benedictions.*

[7] See O'Casey's letters to Miss Sheila ———.

[8] Mrs. Una Gwynn Albery.

founder of the Irish Literary Society with Yeats, never stopped supporting it till she got her husband to put it on. I had a hasty, semi-Old Vic production for a few weeks in Liverpool; [9] and that is all since I saw the sky of New York overhead. I know they are difficult of production, but what's the good of doing anything that comes easy to one? Except routine things, of course, that must be done, that we may live. One of the exhilarating things in the reduction of our garden to disorder was the difficulty of doing it. You couldn't do it with a brush and comb; it had to be done with hack and spade, with nears and shashers. Here in England that fought so well and so tremendously, they are afraid that the People couldn't stand the impact of Oak Leaves and Lavender! Not for another two years! Bomb and blast they could stick, but not a play. Well, we are mighty with our little pens, it seems.

With you, The Theatre Incorporated took on RED ROSES FOR ME, but some hitch has happened; the Directors and Advisory Council have had a difference about it, and now it is a question whether it will go on or no. The Abbey sticks to Juno and The Plough, and wouldn't do anything else of mine, so I have to publish before rehearsals give me a chance of discovering whether the plays run right everywhere, and so have to wait a time for some future publication of a play in which to make any alteration in the play a rehearsal shows it may need.

I'm not grumbling; only showing you the facts that make things more difficult. And, of course, this is all confidential and friendly and off the record. Just an effort to justify myself to you, and to show you there is more in me than meets the Atkinsonian eye. I enclose an example (unpaid) of the things I write occasionally, aside from those on Synge, Yeats, et al. I also enclose a copy of the latest play—not for comment, but as from a friend who, from all you have written about him, thinks you are interested in most of what he is trying to do. It is to be published by the Macmillan Co. this year.[10]

My warm regards, Brooks, and best wishes to your wife and you.

Yours as ever.
Sean O'Casey

P.S. I am sending this to The N.Y. Times, instead of Twelvth St., because, since you have raced from one end of the world to the other, I haven't an idea where you may be unsettled now.[11]

---

[9] For the Liverpool Old Vic production of *Purple Dust,* see O'Casey's letter to Beatrix Lehmann, 30 September 1945, note 1.

[10] *Oak Leaves and Lavender* was published by Macmillan of London in 1946 and by Macmillan of New York in 1947.

[11] Atkinson was a war correspondent for the *New York Times* in Chungking, China, 1942–44.

To Francis MacManus

TS. MacManus

Totnes, Devon
21 October 1946

My dear Frank,

No, of course, I shouldn't mind you showing what I said of Mac-Grianna to a friend of his—or an enemy either. But the poor fellow's case looks a bad one. How could he write in Grangegorman? [1] I can comprehend your meaning about his wife and her nagging. I know a lass like that who brought a cruel nervous breakdown on a sensitive, cultured man, who never really recovered from it. She was a good, aggressive Catholic too, making him miserable for the glory of God. He was a Catholic, too, of course, so it wasn't a question of dogmatic differences. It is a great pity about MacGrianna; but there doesn't seem to be much chance for him. I didn't like that sudden break off in his second story.

Well, I am glad you came safe from the waves of Clear Bay. Though I am a good sailor, even in a storm, I never like the look of big waves, though I watch them, fascinated; & shudderingly remember them a long time afterwards. I was near drowned once, though I was born with the caul. [2]

Evidently, you don't like Dunsany! I wonder why, now? I heard—indeed she said it to me, when I had mentioned his name—Lady Gregory say of him "Oh, dot derrible man!" I never met him. He's a Plunket or a Packenham, isn't he? I noticed in a recent article [3]—I. Press or Independent—he referred to AE as "the poet of the century," (or was it in The Bell, I saw it?), never mentioning the name of Yeats. A back-handed slap at Yeats, I daresay. I don't know that you were wise to refuse the job of a leader-writer in the Independent. Because you didn't like the paper's politics. Oh! Frank! What's the difference, in politics, between I. Press, Independent, & Irish Times! They're all armoured to defend the same things—God, the law they make themselves, and the sacred rights of private property. Is there such a thing as Catholic Literature? Catholics creating literature, right enough; but the other is only to be found in things written by

---

[1] Grangegorman, a well-known mental hospital in Dublin.

[2] The caul was supposed to be a symbol of good luck against drowning. O'Casey told me his mother sold it to a sea captain to keep in his cabin.

[3] Lord Dunsany, "A Mountainy Singer," *The Bell*, August 1946, an article about the poetry of Joseph Campbell. Dunsany pointedly ignored Yeats and singled out A.E. as the main influence on Campbell and all modern Irish poets:

> But no young poet writing in Ireland near the beginning of this century can easily have escaped the influence of A.E., not only because his work was that of the greatest Irish poet of this century, but because he had the largest heart of a poet, without which a poet's work must be as difficult as the work of a blacksmith to a man with weak arms, and he helped all the young poets of his time.

Chesterton & Belloc, who did more harm to Catholic "literature," than any I know. You needn't have been so meek about your "After the Flight." [4] I've read a lot of H. B's, The Eye-Witness,[5] & like yours much better; & I don't say that because you're a Protestant.[6] When I read Maritain or Mauriac, & then look at the other two Flat St. boyos,[7] I feel angry. And that man, too, Hugh Benson! [8] He is recommended by some of the friars at Buckfastleigh here to anyone whom they think to be outside the Church. Enough to make Dr. Walter MacDonald turn in his grave. I like your reviews—I disagree with most of what you say, but I like the way you put things down.

All the best to you & yours.

Sean

[4] Francis MacManus, *After the Flight* (1938), "Being eyewitness sketches of Irish History from AD 1607 to 1916."

[5] Hilaire Belloc, *The Eye-Witness* (1908), "Being a series of descriptions and sketches in which it is attempted to reproduce certain incidents and periods in history, as from the testimony of a person present at each."

[6] Intended as irony. MacManus told me that O'Casey meant here: "because I know bloody well you're not a Protestant."

[7] G. K. Chesterton and Hilaire Belloc.

[8] Robert Hugh Benson (1871–1914), novelist, son of the Rev. Edward Benson, Archbishop of Canterbury, took Anglican orders in 1894, and became a convert to Roman Catholicism in 1903.

To Sgt. Frank McCarthy [1]

MS. McCARTHY

TOTNES, DEVON

27 OCTOBER 1946

Dear Sergeant McCarthy,

I never read the MS. of other writers, for I am no critic. Anyway, I wouldnt like to encourage anyone to try to cut a living out of authorship. It is too uncertain. Besides, most of those who send MS. say the same thing: "Throw this in the fire," and I won't mind. They do—always. Say what they say they wont mind, & one makes an enemy forever.

[1] Sergeant Frank McCarthy, born in Drumcondra, Dublin. As a soldier in the British army during World War II, he had been a prisoner in Japan. For an account of the torpedoing of his troopship and his rescue after floating in the sea for twenty-six hours, wearing a "Bernard Shaw scapular," see O'Casey's letter to Daniel Mac-millan, 11 November 1949. McCarthy had sent O'Casey a copy of a short story, "If the Blinds Are Down," which he wrote about his experiences in a Japanese prison camp. He later became General Secretary of the Christian Socialist Movement, and worked as an assistant to Donald Soper at the West London Mission.

However, I've read your short impressionistic—or expressionistic—story, & had no inclination to "throw it in the fire." There is something in it. I liked it. There is a strange vein of sadness—child-like (not childish) sadness running through it. Its one fault seems to be that it is a little hard to follow, & might, I think, be made a little clearer, only a little. I gave it to my elder boy (18, he joins up next week, and is trying to write himself), & he liked it too, saying he "found it just a little hard to follow." I hadn't said to him any more than that I had liked it.

Perhaps you might send it to "The Bell," 2 Lower O'Connell Street, Dublin. They might publish it. You can say I read it and liked it, if you like.

A last word—tell no other that I read your MS. I don't want to be pestered with bundles of MS. in every post.

My good wishes to you,
Yours sincerely,
Sean O'Casey

I enclose your MS.

To David Marcus [1]

TC. O'CASEY

[TOTNES, DEVON]
31 OCTOBER 1946

Dear Mr. D. Marcus:

You neednt have been so anxious. Illness in myself, or in one very close to me, is the only thing that would prevent me keeping a promise—that is why I dont like making them.

The article [2] I have written goes with this letter.

I'm afraid that the article is longer than 2000 words. If it be unsuitable to your Magazine, let me have it back. Be assured, I shant mind. You certainly have a fine collection of writers for your 2nd Number. I do hope it may go well, especially in Ireland so rich in potentiality, so poor in opportunity. I understand *The Bell* is coming out in a bigger way to Cork and Dublin! Well, I have as big a wish for Cork in this matter as I have for Dublin.

I am sure you worked hard on the venture, and that it is very dear to

---

[1] David Marcus (1926–   ), Cork-born Irish writer and editor; founder-editor with Terence Smith of *Irish Writing* in November 1946.

[2] Sean O'Casey, "Tender Tears For Poor O'Casey," *Irish Writing* No. 2, June 1947; reprinted in *The Green Crow* (1956).

you, so I venture on a little advice from a dog who has travelled a rocky road. Dont ever be panic-stricken when an author neglects to send a promised article—there's always as good as he somewhere about. And dont pump too much praise in to an author when you write to him. Believe me, too many authors think too much of themselves, and if you praise them too often and too well, they'll be beside themselves with conceit. They'll begin to think these fellows cant do without me, and act accordingly. Indeed, it is hard for an author who gets any notice at all to keep himself clear from vanity; so dont you add to it. It is bad for you; it is bad for him. All you can do is to get an author to say definitely whether or no he will do a certain work within a certain time. If he agrees, and doesnt do it, then his omission cant be on your conscience.

Dont forget that if my article shouldnt be suitable, send it back—there'll be no coolness.

Yours sincerely,
[Sean O'Casey]

To Miss Sheila ———

MS. PRIVATE

TOTNES, DEVON
11 NOVEMBER 1946

Dear Sheila,
If I were you, I should at once accept the long holiday to Oxford. It is near time you got a rest from adding to the profits of Messrs L——— & Co. The workers there will have to combine & fight the Firm, if they want to be something higher than Bidaux' slaves. You have done your share, & now it is time for you to have a chance to sit down & quietly view the work of the past. So go to Oxford, & don't worry that brain of yours too much with study for a Social Science Degree. Take things easy; use the things given to you—eyes, ears, brain, & tongue—incessantly; & you'll come closer to knowledge this way than you ever will by books alone. If you read all the books in the world, & use not your senses, the books profiteth nothing; but if you use these, you will have a factual, & often delightful, correspondence with life, even without the aid of a book. If you can combine the two, then, of course, you become a finer and fuller personality. Go to Oxford.

No, Sheila, I'm not a Fabian; I never was one. I don't fit in with them. They are too much for the bookways. They pave the road to life with books & booklets. The road to life is through life itself. A book can show us how other minds see life, how they understood this & that; & how beauty showed herself to them, here & there. But, while enjoying their visions, we must—if we are to live—have our own.

Of course I believe Card. Stepinac to have been a menace to the upsurge of the workers & peasants. They all are. They always have been. I've seen so much of this in Ireland. The Bishops were always toadies to whomsoever happened to be in power, so long as that power left episcopal power in their hands—not the power to bless; but the power to curse any-one who ventured to differ from them on any question whatsoever. Look at what they did to poor Dr. O'Hickey! And what they did to Parnell—threatening to excommunicate any poor peasant who voted for him. And, by God, poor Ireland payed a terrible price for this betrayal of Ireland's Leader. They condemned De Valera & his Party, till that Party got into power. When Rory O'Connor, & Liam Mellowes, who had been in jail for months, were executed by the Free State, as a reprisal—dirty murder, if ever there was one—not a Single Bishop protested; not a single one of them cried out against it—their own countrymen,.men of their own faith. The Bishops were afraid then that De Valera's crowd would be too much to the Left, so the more of them that perished, the better. When they found that Dev was harmless, they put their arms around his neck.

Don't you believe everything Griffin says. Cardinals can often lie a damn sight better than laymen. Look at Cardinal Gasquet who, as a his-torian, deliberately falsified the reading of documents to serve his own version of things. Look at the Archbishop of Winnipeg offering a guarantee of safety & of heaven to the parents of airmen for the payment of forty dollars. History is full of the false nature of the Churchmen. Read what Dr. McDonald—who held the highest scholastic position the Irish Church could give him for forty years—Professor of Moral Theology in Maynooth —read what he said about the bishops of his day. Why only the other month I read a young Catholic's article in an Irish Journal, lamenting the low state of the Épiscopal mind at that time. To get nearer to what these Cardinals & Bishops should be thinking, one should read Jacques Maritain. He, at least, is Catholic in the full sense, & the mind of such as Griffin is but a whiff a sour air to the scent of an orchard of apple-blossoms, or the perfume of a thousand roses.

Anyway, dont you bother your pretty head for a time. You go to Oxford, & have a rest.

Yours as Ever.
Sean

To Bronson Albery

TC. O'CASEY

[TOTNES, DEVON]
14 NOVEMBER 1946

Dear Mr. Albery:

Eileen came back to us with a severe cold, which explains the delay in replying to the suggestions made for alterations in OAK LEAVES AND LAVENDER by Mr. Peter Ashmore.

As a matter of fact, there is no reply. I wouldnt consider his suggestions for a second. I'd rather wait for ten years, wait a lifetime, than do as he says I should do.

The time and the spirit of the play is the time and spirit of the Battle of Britain, and I cannot consent to change the time or alter the spirit.

Dante, the great Italian, and the great Christian, put his enemies in hell, and I, no Christian, and much less of a poet, will not hesitate to do the same thing.

Frankly, I have neither sympathy nor feeling for these super-benevolent people, these "dishes of skimmed-milk," as Shakespeare called them (there's quite a little crowd of them up in Dartington Hall), who go around teaching gentleness to Jesus Christ.

I am herewith returning the book of the play which Eileen brought back to show me where and how the alterations were to be made. I understand it belongs to Mrs. Albery.

Since last writing to you, I havent had a word from Madden about RED ROSES.

My love to Mrs Albery and to you from the two of us. Breon is a little nearer to us now—he has been sent to a camp in Taunton. He is, I hear, to come home for Christmas.

Yours very sincerely,
Sean O'Casey

To George Jean Nathan

TS. Cornell

Totnes, Devon
14 November 1946

My very dear George:

Your book of the theatre [1] came the other day, fresh as a new-born rose, surrounded safe with pointed critical thorns. I have been reading it, though for the first few days I had to hand it over to Breon (for days before he had been asking me, "Heard anything from G. J.? Did the book come yet? It should be here by now."), who seems to drink in American activities—You, O'Neill, and Saroyan. However, Breon is now gone to his training-camp, and I have the book to myself. It seems to have been a poor season, though that doesn't interfere with the criticism. Thank God there's something left alive with us. You are still hard on M. Anderson,[2] who certainly doesn't fail for want of effort. I wonder what is really lacking in him? Lack of human warmth and humour I think. And, maybe, a little too much vanity. Both O'Neill and Saroyan have got these, and to me they are delightful, whereas Anderson is always chill, and I read him because I think he should be read. Duty! It is a pity that a play less than the customary length has so little chance of succeeding. Even the Dublin Abbey now rarely puts on a play that doesn't run the full length of the evening. I think this is partly due to the fact that this means the author gets full royalties; in the other case, he gets only two thirds. Whatever the cause, it is a pity, for many may be able to do well in a short play, who couldn't do so well in a longer one. So far the best in the book that I have come across (it makes me sit up, and cheer!) is the criticism and the comments going with the review of the play "A Sound of Hunting."[3] Those who write about the drama in mystic and mystified chatter are often maddening. What can anyone make of Eliot's definition? [4] A fine chap, a finer poet, and yet he

[1] George Jean Nathan, *The Theatre Book of the Year, 1945–1946* (1946).

[2] Nathan wrote a negative review of Maxwell Anderson's *Truckline Cafe,* which opened in New York on 27 February 1946, and closed after thirteen performances.

[3] Harry Brown's *A Sound of Hunting,* which opened in New York on 20 November 1945, and closed after twenty-three performances.

[4] In his review of *A Sound of Hunting,* Nathan considers and rejects a number of "confusing" definitions of art, and at one point he says:

> To the flames next will be conveyed, in the interests of the public weal, T. S. Eliot's *The Sacred Wood* for this example of prime double-talk: "In a peculiar sense he (the poet) will be aware also that he must inevitably be judged by the standards of the past. I say judged, not amputated, by them; not judged to be as good as, or worse or better than, the dead; and certainly not judged by the canons of dead critics. It is a judgment, a comparison, in which two things are measured by each other. To conform merely would be for the new work not really to conform at all; it would not be new, and would therefore not be a work of Art. And we do not quite say that the new is more valuable because it fits in; but its fitting in is a test of its value—a test, it is true, which can only be slowly and cautiously

blathers in this way about the way an artist looks at life. And Komisarjevsky's "The unliterary theatre is the only genuine form of theatrical art." [5] That was what Michele Chekhov wrote to me when he was turning the men and women he was teaching into demented souls at Dartington. So signs on it, he did nothing, and never will do anything. I lost my temper, and replied with verve and a burning, and never saw or heard from him again. These who write elaborate and soul-deep disquisitions on art frighten away the people, who, if they just sat down to enjoy it would comprehend it as well as those who write long and complicated sentences about it. To me, it seems to be propaganda of the worst type. I wish you were read in every family, for you are a god-send.

I have had a letter from Dick telling me that Theatre Inc. has almost given up the thought of doing RED ROSES, because it is "commercially" uncertain. I'm not terribly sorry. I didn't like the idea when I heard Miss Beatrice Straight was a prominent figure in it. With the best intentions in the world, she knows nothing about the drama. Another of those who have been disqualified and confused by the abstract disquisitioners of our times. I imagine that "commercial" is a veil hiding other reasons. I don't think she liked my frank letters to her—the very rich can't bear to be opposed. They think their wealth confers infallibility on them. Her mother and step-father, Mr. and Mrs. Elmhirst here called on me long before I heard of Theatre Inc. and asked me about my plays. I told them they were under contract, for, honestly, I didn't want them to have anything to do with production. By the way, it was Mr. Elmhirst who financed JOURNEY'S END,[6] and made a bundle out of it; all lost, I think, on further production. Mr. Elmhirst didn't know anything about the theatre, and Maurice Brown, who did the business end of it, went wild, putting on plays that were no good, after declaring that Sherriff was "the hope of the English Theatre."

---

applied, for we are none of us infallible judges of conformity. We say: it appears to conform, and is perhaps individual, or it appears individual, and may conform; but we are hardly likely to find that it is one and not the other." (p. 192)

[5] Nathan on Theodore Komisarjevsky:

Consider, for another example, Komisarjevsky, whose *The Theatre* goes on the bonfire without delay if I have my way about it. "The unliterary theatre is the only genuine form of theatrical Art," pontificates Komy, who gallops on to observe that "the Art of the theatre is an Art of actors and directors and not of writers." . . . So the only genuine form of theatrical Art is not the literary theatre of anyone like Shakespeare, Molière or Shaw but the theatre of Owen Davis, Anne Nichols or Phoebe and Henry Ephron! (pp. 192–93)

Among the other critics that Nathan consigns to his "bonfire" are W. Somerset Maugham, George Santayana, and Ludwig Lewisohn.

[6] Nathan drew the following comparison between two war plays, *A Sound of Hunting* and R. C. Sherriff's *Journey's End:*

But simple as the narrative thread is, the playwright has woven [*A Sound of Hunting*] into a drama which, while intermittently and perhaps unavoidably a little monotonous, flowers with honest pathos and honest humor, and one which compared with its British all-male counterpart, *Journey's End,* is in its avoidance of sentimentality a relative masterpiece. (p. 189)

So you see, I was very nervous when they came to see me, for I knew what they had done, in a commercial way with JOURNEY'S END, and in an art way with Chekhov and his Chekhov Studio down here in Dartington Hall. So I was glad to be able to say my plays were under contract, and you may imagine my unsettled mind when I learned they had a hand in Theatre Inc. So maybe it's all for the best that things are as they are. Eddie Dowling, if he can be got, will be preferable to me than John Burrell who "knows the Irish character and idiom and conduct" according to Miss Straight; though how she knows he knows is beyond me.

Sorry to hear about Billy Rose's difficulty in getting suitable characters for the Two Englishmen.[7] It can't be helped, and the play can wait a little longer—that's one of the good things about a good play—it can afford to wait, if the author can't.

There's a play on in the Abbey now that has broken all records—14 weeks to packed houses, with the police still keeping in order all who want to get in to see it.[8] A writer in THE BELL says it is terrible and stupid.[9] It is a kind of a Dybbuk play, demonic possession, I imagine, rather than a human soul entering another's body—I amnt sure, having forgotten what was said about it. A girl comes back to Mayo, the priest there writing first to the Local P.O.[10] conveying details about her, which trouble him, and he tells some of it to the parents. When she comes back to the old house, the light before the statue of the B.V.M.[11] goes out. When the mother goes to relight it, she is stopped by her daughter hissing, "put out that light." She then gets frenzied, rushes to the statue, spits on it, and smashes it on the floor. The doctor and the priest argue about obsession and possession, and the priest is the victor in the argument. It appears that the family is affected by the devils too. There are it appears, eleven of them. The son gives vent to a lot of freethinking, egged on, it is said, by the devil speaking through the Girl. The exorcism begins, offstage, through the help of gramaphones, but ends in full view of the audience. The devils are driven out, and the priest dies. Like the Boy Who Lived Twice, I suppose, though here we have real devils wild and free on the plains of Mayo. Well, I'd love to see it myself.

All of us—bar myself—have had a time with the grippe; but are all well again.

All the best, with my love,
Sean

---

7 Basil Stoke and Cyril Poges in *Purple Dust.*

8 Frank Carney's *The Righteous Are Bold* opened at the Abbey Theatre on 29 July 1946. It was a sensational and very popular play about a young Irish girl who is possessed by devils, which cause her to have mad fits and smash holy statues, until the evil spirits are exorcised by a priest.

9 Thomas Hogan, "Dublin Theatre," *The Bell,* October 1946, a review of *The Righteous Are Bold.*

10 Police officer.

11 Blessed Virgin Mary.

Many thanks, deep thanks for your book, giving Breon & me a most enjoyable time.

To Peadar O'Donnell [1]

TC. O'CASEY

TOTNES, DEVON
21 NOVEMBER 1946

Dear Peadar:

I'm not a reviewer. I've commented on a few books, but the art of reviewing does not take kindly to me—in short, I'm not good at the job.

But if you like to send the book on Lady G. by Robinson, I'll try to make a shot at reviewing it.[2] If I think it beyond me, I'll send it back. I was wondering what happened to it. Mr. Robinson sent me a letter long, long ago, asking permission to print extracts from my letters to Lady G.—though, oddly enough, he didnt ask for any letters from her that I might have.

By the way, where are you boys getting the money for THE BELL? I heard you were backing IRIS,[3] but that the Gaels let you down. They would, as they let down Dr. [Michael] O'Hickey, and set up [Douglas] Hyde on the Presidential throne. I hear [Liam] O'Flaherty has gone to Paris. Faolain's article on [Wolfe] Tone was a damned fine one.[4]

> *All the best,*
> *Yours sincerely,*
> *Sean O'Casey*

---

[1] Peadar O'Donnell (1893–   ), Irish Republican soldier, novelist, editor; fought on the Republican side in the Irish Civil War; a leader of the left-wing faction of the IRA during the 1920s and 1930s; wrote a number of novels on peasant life and the Irish revolution; founder-editor of *The Bell* in October 1940, with Sean O'Faolain.

[2] Sean O'Casey, "A Protestant Bridget," *The Bell*, February 1947, a review of *Lady Gregory's Journals, 1916–1930* (1946), edited by Lennox Robinson; reprinted in *Blasts and Benedictions* (1967).

[3] *An Iris*, an Irish-language magazine in Dublin.

[4] Sean O'Faolain, "Rebel by Vocation," *The Bell*, November 1946.

To Jack Daly

MS. DALY

TOTNES, DEVON
26 NOVEMBER 1946

My dear Jack.

Here's the book back, signed as requested. Well, the oul' Orange Lily O
is still a fine flower, & has a right of a place in the Irish vase as well as the
White Madonna one.

Breon is now in the army, in a camp at Taunton, among West Country boys, Shropshire Lads, & London Cockneys. "I Knock at the Door" has
been out of print for quite a time, & will be, I fear, for some time to come.

Macmillan's had ne'er a copy to send for a Continental translation;
neither had I, so I had to give them Eileen's copy.

I am working at the "last" vol. of Biography.[1] It will end at the time
when I leave Ireland for England. "The last glimpse of Eireann."

I have to go warily now with my eyes. The left one has been dark
for a long time—a vivid lightning-flash would look like a match that
wouldn't light well. The other is only about a third in value of a normal
eye. I have been under treatment of Penicillin by a Cork Oculist in Plymouth, who said "It's a wondher to me how much you see with that good
eye." It's an eye that can see around corners. The D. Worker is now beginning to realise the pressure of the Vatican. I warned them of this years
ago, but they thought, I think, that it was "a bee in my bonnet," & were
half afraid of offending "comrade Catholic workers." Now the Dublin
Teachers have gone meekly back to the schools because the Archbishop
of Dublin courteously requested them to do so. He was getting afraid of
the growth of Parents' Committees, who were beginning to ask untidy questions about the way their children were treated.

All for the love o' God.

Ever Yours
Love to Floss
Sean

[1] *Inishfallen, Fare Thee Well* (1949).

To Sgt. Frank McCarthy

MS. McCarthy

Totnes, Devon
27 November 1946

Dear S. Frank McCarthy,

I've just come across your letter (which got lost), & so am now able to thank you for sending me the book which seems curiously to reveal a dead, if not altogether gone, Ireland.

It was kind of you to think of me; but you mustn't do anything like that again. Put your money in the Bank.

Our boy is doing his drill well with the others; but the authorities have a silly custom of giving them exercises in pants & vest under pouring rain, so that they get coughs & colds, & a few of them worse things. It is, of course, the British dumb way of making men of them. There seems to be no possibility of making an Englishman think different from his father. You see the typical Englishman in the odd brazen, bullying manner of [Ernest] Bevin. Knows everything, understands everything, the centre of wisdom & goodwill; & determined to make all races like his own. Utterly destitute in Bevin's case, of any knowledge or liking for art or literature.

A new magazine—quarterly, I think—called "Irish Writing"; Editors, David Marcus, Terence Smith, "Irish Writing" 15 Adelaide Street, Cork, to whom you might send your MS, if Bell doesn't take it. An article of mine will be in No. 2, out in Feb. The first number of I.W. is out now. Not bad; not as good as it should be. Some of the stories or sketches are very bad— and all Big Names! I've told the Editors not to always trust a B.N. We do damn bad things at times, if not often.

All the best.
Sean O'Casey

To Bronson Albery

TC. O'Casey

[Totnes, Devon]
28 November 1946

Dear Mr. Bronson Albery:

Thanks for your letter of the 25th of this month.

I'm afraid that Mr. Peter Ashmore is a washout as far as I'm concerned. From what Eileen said about him, I take it I'd never be easy with him.

From what he wants to do with the play, I'd surmise he's something of a Cissy, and Cissies arent welcome with me. Indeed, I simply cant stand them, or anything like them. To change the "mood" of a play would simply mean writing it all over again, and Ashmore should have known that, if he is anything of a producer. Most people now reject the old idea of a hell-fire, but we dont rub out the vision of hell pictured for instance in the paintings of Signorelli. Indeed, the value, artistically, of the play is that the mood of the day is held there; just as, in a picture the mood or aspect of part of a day is held forever there.

I have written to John Allen,[1] have sent him a copy of the play, and have asked him what he thinks of a production. Should he think favourably of it, I told him I'd tell you, and maybe you could spare a half-hour to see him. As a matter of fact, he likes the play. I, of course, havent committed you to anything with him.

I amnt very sorry about RED ROSES. I never felt easy when I heard that a daughter of Dartington Hall had something to do with it. To me, a lot that goes on in Dartington Hall is bloody humbug.

I've forgotten all you said about [Robert] Henderson, and cant lay hands on your letter; and I've forgotten all I said about him too; I've even forgotten the name. I must be getting damned old.

By the way, I've had a letter from Brooks Atkinson telling me he thinks highly of the play—OAK LEAVES AND LAVENDER—, and that with a good production, it would have a haunting effect on an audience.

And, now let me say, that I am quite content to forego any further option fee on the play, say for a year, rather than that you should have to seize on some producer who mightnt be the man you'd select, if you had more time to look around.

Lastly, our love to Mrs Albery and you.

[*Sean O'Casey*]

[1] John Allen had directed the first performance of *The Star Turns Red*, which opened at Unity Theatre, London, on 12 March 1940; see James Agate's review of the play, *Sunday Times*, 17 March 1940, note 1, Vol. I, p. 849.

To Richard J. Madden [1]

TC. O'CASEY

[TOTNES, DEVON]
3 DECEMBER 1946

Dear Dick:

Thank you for your letter and enclosures—the Agreement with the SPUR people and the article by Brooks Atkinson. Some days before, I got a cheque from Guaranty Trust Co. but guessed it was the tax on royalties restored. Now I know it's from the Spur people.

I am enclosing with this letter the alterations made in "The Silver Tassie." [2] I had sent you these a good while ago, but it looks as if you hadnt got them. I cant remember whether they were registered or no. However, here they are again, and with a few ADDITIONAL changes; so you can cancel the first sample, if by any chance they should happen to reach you.

I amnt very disappointed over the lapse of RED ROSES. I guessed nearly all along that that would happen, though I wish they hadnt had anything to do with it. It seems a mean thing to me to take it up, and then drop it without a word to the author. And the author too who knows [Beatrice] Biddy Straight; and her mother [Mrs. Dorothy Elmhirst] regarding herself as a great friend of the author's. And the children going to Dartington Hall School. Theyve never forgiven me for warning them that the Theatre they tried to build up here would never succeed, with the way they were going. They wanted me to act as an Assistant, but I wasnt having any, thanks; nosir. I dont know much, but I knew enough about the theatre to know that they were making fools of themselves and others. But there was sickening flattery all around them, and so they went on, and failed.

I think I remember you telling me you got the dual tax forms that I signed (which you sent me), but the memory's going—getting old, Dick, me son. I had a long delightful letter from Brooks a few days ago. He tells me George looks as young as ever. I'll be writing to George and him as soon as I get a minute.

My love to Tessa and to you. And, if you see George or Eugene [O'Neill], give them my love. And Carlotta.

Yours as ever,
[*Sean*]

[1] Richard J. Madden (1880–1951), author's agent and international play broker; O'Casey's American agent. Among his clients were Eugene O'Neill, T. S. Eliot, and W. Somerset Maugham. For the first of O'Casey's many letters to him, see that of 14 March 1934, Vol. I, pp. 508–9.

[2] *The Silver Tassie* was published in 1928; for an indication of the "alterations" O'Casey had now made, mainly in Act II, see the "Stage Version" in *Collected Plays* (1949), Vol. II.

To Miss Sheila ———

TS. PRIVATE

TOTNES, DEVON
7 DECEMBER 1946

Dear Sheila:

I think you should go to Oxford, if you are given the chance. It's time you got away for a spell from L———'s. The Union will get there in time. And dont be telling me of the way you offer up your pain to heaven. The Confessor who tells you to stick it for the glory of God must be a damned fool. Why doesnt he do a bit of it himself? I know quite a lot of these boyos. Dont do what I do, do what I tell you. God doesnt want that kind of glorification. He surely got more than enough of it during the reign of the Nazis. You exaggerate the physical sufferings of your Lord, and give them too much emphasis. They werent by any means the important part of His Mission. Many and many a man and woman has gone through just as much psychically. His great gift was the taking of human nature upon Himself, and his suffering was spiritual rather than physical. And He never welcomed it, never put Himself in the way of getting it; and He shrank from death as we all do—all who are healthy in their mind. "Why smitest thou me?" "Let this cup pass from me." You know this as well as I do. And He must have been a strong and a most healthy Man. He walked a lot, kept in the open air, had worked with His hands, and could bear a great deal; but, like all sensitive natures, He didnt welcome pain. Neither should you, or anyone. So give up this nonsense of welcoming suffering that, had we common sense, wouldnt be inflicted upon us. And take care that it doesnt lead you into spiritual pride.

You dont get Maritain writing about this kind of thing.

The "Daily Worker," I believe, is printing an article of mine early next week on the case of Stepinac.[1] Maybe you will see it, so I wont say anything about it here.

No, Breon isnt going to Oxford or Cambridge, or any other University. In the first place—even were we desirous of it—we havent the money to spare for that glorious achievement. He is at the moment a private in the British Army, and we expect him home next week on his first short leave. He is taking his place among all sorts and conditions of men, and has a great cockney friend with whom he scrubs out the floors, and who gives him tips as to [how] hard and uncongenial work can be done fair and square. His mother, who went to see him when he had a few hours off, tells me, she saw a group of his soldier friends waving for him when he left her to join them. He will learn of life this way. Let me say, though, in

---

[1] Sean O'Casey, "Vatican and Red Star in Yugoslavia," *Daily Worker,* 12 December 1946.

all fairness, that there are some fine scholars among the men of the Universities, and many of the young students are gallant lads. I met them myself in Cambridge and Oxford. But there are gallant lads everywhere, and everyone must get a full chance to fulfil himself so that the community may benefit to the full.

And now farewell, for the present.
Sean [2]

When you asked your S. [Spiritual] director should you go to Oxford, and he said "In the spirit of humility, stay where you are" etc, did you really swallow that pietistic nonsense? There may be as much humility in Oxford as there is in Greenford. You have a duty—if you want duty—to make as much as you can of whatever talents have been given to you. If you stay at L———, you may be just burying the one you have in the garden. (See parable of the Talents.) That spiritual Director of yours is a decadent—he is a Kiss from death. Life is the loveliest thing God has given to man, & we should guard it as a precious thing. And enjoy it too. No-one loved life more than Christ. I'll back you a lot, your S. Confessor wouldn't say that to me. You'll find he keeps himself warm when he has a cold; & when ill, sends for a doctor. Even St Paul, who said of death that it was "absence from the body, to be present with the Lord," said it only when he knew he had to go. And only after he had had a full life of it.

S. O'C

[2] The typed letter ends here; the following paragraph was added in longhand.

To Bronson Albery

TC. O'CASEY

[TOTNES, DEVON]
8 DECEMBER 1946

Dear Mr. Albery:
Thanks for your letter of the 3rd of Dec. We seem to be in a bit of a tangle over the plays. About OAK LEAVES AND LAVENDER: First, if you are tired of this, please dont let any friendliness towards me cause you any hesitation in abandoning it. I assure you I wont mind, and that I will understand. However, if I be wrong, I suggest that you hold it for another three months, without any further advance. That will bring us to February, and, if things go well, it should be near production by March. If it cant be done in March, then I prefer to wait till the following season,

for I am, naturally, anxious that it shouldnt be put on in, or towards, the summer when its chance of success would be lowered.

The American proposal: I dont like the idea of [Edward] Choate doing the play at all. I have told R. Madden this in a recent letter. Choate ran after PURPLE DUST a good while ago, gave me a lot of work writing letters, cost me a lot in cables, and then left it lying in the street. Nathan doesnt care for him either. He told me Choate is a kind of snapper-up for the Shuberts, and Nathan says he doesnt know where Choate gets the money.

Dick (Madden) naturally thinks first of the Advance and his fee; I think of that too, but I also have to think of the kind of production to be given the play, and, on this point, I invariably take the advice of Nathan, than whom there is no one in the theatre knows so much about it from the acting and production points of view. Of course, I should prefer that the play should first be done here. That would give me a chance of knowing how rehearsals go, and also, if it should be necessary, to make one or more technical changes, which I could pass on to the American production.

About RED ROSES: Mr. Robert Henderson seems promising. I dont know anything about him, and I'd have to be sure that he is in "good standing" with the American League of Dramatists. I will write to Madden to ask him about this. I certainly like the colour of what he has written to you.

I should like to assure you that I have no personal interest whatever in my suggestion about John Allen, other than that he did a fine job with THE STAR TURNS RED, using amateurs. And he had to train two companies to play on alternate nights, for they were all workers, and couldnt act every night without a break. He writes very well about the theatre, and is in love with all connected with it. He served in the Navy during the war, and as you know is in charge of the Glyndebourne Children's Theatre at the moment. Apart from my play, I think you should keep an eye on him. While doing THE STAR, he spent a few nights here, and we thought him a fine fellow. I will write to tell him to ring you up so that he may call when you are ready to receive him. My love to Mrs Albery.

[*Sean O'Casey*]

To Robert Goldie [1]

TC. O'CASEY

TOTNES, DEVON
10 DECEMBER 1946

Dear Mr. Goldie:

Thank you for your letter. It must, indeed, have been disappointing to your Company, after all their work, to have to abandon the performance of THE PLOUGH AND THE STARS.[2] It is very distressing that this interference should be allowed. I am quite used to this sort of thing now. I had a tour of a play of mine stopped in America by the combined agitation of the Jesuits and the Methodists.[3] And they talk about the censorship of the Soviet Union!

It would be interesting to me to know what team won the prize at the Feis,[4] and what play they performed. I daresay the Feis Committee was an important and a representative one.

Of course, the Press doesnt want to offend "the powers that be," and so those who want to suppress the ideas of others have their own sweet way with things. You have to be careful too, unless you happen to have an independent income, and neednt care about anyone. If, on the other hand, you have to earn your living, and earn it in Cahirciveen, you must walk warily. It has been always strange to me that the clergy should go on thinking that they know everything. In the Middle Ages, when all knowledge was held—or almost all—by priest and monk, it was understandable; but now when so many laymen know so much more than they, even about their own particular vocation—Jacques Maritain, for instance—, it is laughable, though in Ireland, where it isnt questioned, it is very annoying. Look at the way the clergy ranted about the paintings of Picasso. The damned cheek of them! A picture postcard would be more in their line.

But never mind, time is with us, and their ways have caused the peoples of Poland, Croatia, Roumania, France, and partly in other countries, to put them in their proper places. You and your Company go on with the good work, but I'd strongly recommend you to give my plays a miss, for your own sakes. It doesnt do me a lot of harm, for I get most of my income from America.

All the best to you and to the members of your Company.

Yours sincerely,
Sean O'Casey

[1] Robert Goldie, director of Iveronian Productions, Cahirciveen, Co. Kerry.
[2] The play was rejected by the Cork Drama Festival.
[3] For the banning of *Within the Gates* in Boston, see O'Casey's letter to Richard J. Madden, 17 January 1935, note 1, Vol. I, p. 531.
[4] Festival.

To George Jean Nathan

MS. CORNELL

TOTNES, DEVON
14 DECEMBER 1946

My very dear George:

I've just got your letter of Nov. 30th. A letter travels slow now from America to here. I am a bit doubtful about your attention to "The Silver Tassie." Please don't do too much—you've your own work to do; work no-one else can do for you. Just you keep that in your mind.

I am, in a way, sorry to hear of Theatre Inc.'s difficulties, though I was afraid from the first that it wouldn't do, basing my fears on what I saw happening here in Dartington Hall. A heap of money is a hard thing to climb. There is so much flattery, so much curious fear, so much lick-spittling even by followers with fine talents, that it near comes to ex nihil nihil of it—if this be the correct Latin. I thought Inc. had done well with "Pygmalion" and "The Doctor's Dilemma"; but I daresay, as was the case here, so much was spent in largesse salaries, that nothing was left for the child—the fathers & mothers ate everything. I wish Beatrice Straight wasn't so rich. She is a charming lass, good-looking, & good-natured, & no fool; but she is human, & like most of us, ready to listen to too much praise. But while we love to earn it—hard, too—, she can command it, & that's very bad for one. Good God, am I preaching!

I wish more (especially in Catholic Countries) could get a hold of your chapter on "The Song of Bernadette." [1] It's maddening the way Christians hail as great a "Christian play," a play about "religion." It is frightening that a bad play about the Immaculate Conception should be hailed as a great one; just as it is frightening that a bad play about "Left" principles should be hailed as a good one. That no-one, except ignorant "Leftists" hesitate to condemn a bad Labour play; but most hesitate to condemn a "religious" one. I remember a bishop of Welles over here jumping on a London stage to disclose that "The Tents of Israel" [2] was "a great

---

[1] In *The Theatre Book of the Year, 1945–1946* (1946) pp. 344–46. *The Song of Bernadette,* a dramatization of the Franz Werfel novel by Walter and Jean Kerr, opened in New York on 26 March 1946, and closed after three performances. Nathan wrote in part:

> There is obviously no reason in the world why a playwright may not concern himself with religious life. That is not the point. The point more often is that playwrights, however incompetent, who do concern themselves and who do produce plays however incompetent still and nevertheless believe that their incompetent plays should be accorded the same reverent and respectful critical attitude which out of the theatre is reserved for their subject matter. As a play, *The Song of Bernadette,* for all that it deals with the Immaculate Conception, deserves nothing better from drama criticism than any other bad play.

[2] Gladys B. Stern, *The Matriarch,* a play which she adapted from her novel, *Tents of Israel,* produced on 8 May 1929 at the Royalty Theatre, London.

play because it showed a whole nation on its knees." I wrote a letter to the papers asking if a play would be great if it showed a whole nation, standing on its toes, cheering, but it wouldn't be published. There seemed to be a curious feeling that to say anything against the bishop's praise would be an offence against God.

Breon is now a gunman in the artillery, & the only book he has asked to be sent to him is one of yours! I tell you this to please you, but only because it is a fact that Breon has an amazing regard for you since he started to read your books, & loves your sense of humour. But he seems to like everything American—the Comics when he was a kid, & now, Nathan, the Marx Bros, O'Neill & Saroyan. He's more American now than his Da.

I had a charming letter the other day from Brooks [Atkinson]. He seems to be a bit disturbed about my being a Communist, though why he should be, I don't know. He suggests I should be banned in the USSR, though he forgets I haven't had an altogether free time of it here.

It must be fine to be with Eugene so often. I, too, wish I was in the middle or at either end of the triangle. Give him my love, & the same to Carlotta.

A young Jew, Sidney Benson, third officer on a Cargo ship, visited me today. He is, he says, leaving the Merchant Service in a few months time, & then proposes to go into theatrical productions. He wants to do "Purple Dust." He certainly knew a lot about the theatre, & could hardly talk of anything else. A clever & charming fellow. He came while I was having a bout with my eyes, & the pain kept me from being at my best; but Eileen did well, for—so she says—in receiving one of these boys, one feels one is showing hospitality to the USA. Of course she is right.

A Robert Henderson is coming over here to do Saroyan's "Beautiful People," & Bronson Albery tells me he is anxious to do "Red Roses." I've never heard of him, & am writing to Dick. Choate—who wanted a play before—is now asking for "Oak Leaves & Lavender," but I've told Dick I don't cherish the idea. I hope you are having a good season this time— "The Iceman Cometh" has given it a good start.

I am working on my "Biography," [3] intending to end the Irish life in the last chapter, when, on the boat, I get "The Last Glimpse of Erin."

I hope you are well. With all the affection begun in the great City of New York.

Sean

[3] *Inishfallen, Fare Thee Well* (1949).

V

FROM O'NEILL TO STRINDBERG, 1947-48

I THINK you're right in saying [Eugene O'Neill] goes far deeper than either Shaw or I do. I've often envied him this gift. I've pondered his plays, & tried to discover how he came by it, &, of course, never could; for the man doesn't know himself. He's got it, & we just have to leave it with him. It is a powerful gift, & Gene, thank God, uses it with power & ruthless integrity.

Strindberg is one of the giants of drama. Even in English translation, by which only I know him, he is splendid. His THE DREAM PLAY is one of the loveliest plays I have ever read. It has all the tender, beautiful sadness of a dying rose. And yet through its sadness, we get the murmur of hope saying that soon another rose, as fair as the first, will be budding again. He is said to have been full of bitterness, but this bitterness was the man's noble revolt against the harshness, the stupidity, and the hypocrisy of life around him.

Now in his late sixties, suffering from chronic influenza, silicosis scars on his lung, a weakened heart, and near-blindness, the stubborn O'Casey was far from giving up the fight on all fronts. He remained as argumentative and creative as ever, fortified by his own determination to go on living and writing, as well as by the courageous example set by the titans in his life, Strindberg and O'Neill, Joyce and Yeats, Larkin and Shaw, and those three great Socialists, as he called them, Byron and Shelley and Dickens. Sometimes his survival seemed like an act of sheer willpower. At the end of 1948, he wrote to the ailing George Jean Nathan: "Resolve to live on. . . . Never let yourself say goodbye to life. The will is mightier than any opinion of any doctor, & often prevails over their decisions: only, if you can, don't let yourself down." He certainly took his own advice and never let himself down; he went on writing new plays, new volumes of autobiography, and endless letters full of heated argument and gritty encouragement. It was part of his nature to sound outraged and comical when he was angry, and often when he wasn't. He could sound like a blustering Captain Boyle when he tore into R. M. Fox and accused him of trying to make the Socialist Connolly a respectable son of the Church merely by calling him James instead of Jim. He continued to wage his crusade against excessive respectability and religiosity, because he believed they made people too timid and subservient to authority, particularly the reactionary hierarchy of the Catholic Church. The demeaning effect of that authority was most noticeable in his native land, he felt: "Everyone in Ireland now goes about in a friar's cowl." And he once told Edgar Deale, of the Irish Association of Civil Liberties, "In Ireland they wear the fig-leaf on the mouth."

Early in 1947 he received a different kind of sad news from Dublin. First, his brother Michael died; eleven days later, the mighty Jim Larkin fell. He lamented his brother's death quietly, but he was moved to a heightened tone of socialist and biblical incantation in his tributes to "the lion of Irish Labour"; one of the first men "who brought poetry into the workers' fight for a better life. . . . There was a man sent from God whose name was Jim, and that man was Larkin." His feeling of heartbreak was profound, yet the experience of sorrow or disappointment never drove him to despair. When the London production of *Oak Leaves and Lavender* failed in May, mainly, he believed, because of the overcautious and unimaginative director, who happened to be a "Cissy," he wrote to one of the actresses in the play: "The battle has gone against us, but we haven't lost our swords." Bloodied but still on his feet, he was in the field again several weeks later when the controversial *Silver Tassie* was successfully revived in Dublin. A month later, in a July letter to Miss Sheila, he expressed his determination "to go on writing foolish plays"; and in an August letter to Daniel Macmillan, he said he was working on a new comedy, "a play with a curious title—COCKADOODLEDOO!" The play was finished in three months, and turned out to be one of his most satiric and affirmative works.

While he was in the midst of writing his new play, he took the time to wield his pen on another front by striking a number of eloquent blows for the I.R.A. prisoners who had been jailed in England since 1939 as a result of bombing incidents. Although he made it clear that he was against the I.R.A. methods of violence, he shared the idealistic principle of fighting for a united Ireland free from British rule. He felt it was unjust punishment for these young political prisoners to be treated as common criminals, and he turned the sharp edge of his wrath on the British and Irish governments, which had ignored all reasonable pleas for amnesty, particularly the voices of power in Ireland that had remained hypocritically silent—"the Bishops— who are forever talking about mercy and forgiveness"; and the famous Republican leader of the government: "How can this man, de Valera, and his followers, good Catholics as they deem themselves, be so callously indifferent to men who continue to practice what they so long and so ardently preached?" By coincidence, the theme of his new comedy was aimed at this same target, which he called Nyadnanavery (a Nest of Knaves masquerading as a Nest of Saints), in an Ireland "that bites away some of th' soul." Since he was laughing at repression in his play, it was appropriate that those Irishmen who had the deepest appreciation for O'Casey's sword of conscience were political prisoners. One of them, Martin Clarke, in a Christmas letter of thanks, praised the playwright for his "prodigious moral courage in saying what you want to say without fear of the consequences in the face of heavy but narrowminded, stupid and bigoted odds." A year later O'Casey was gratified to learn that his stinging words of protest must have helped contribute to the embarrassment of the authorities and the release of the men. No doubt it also confirmed his belief in the power of words over bombs.

Throughout 1948 he was forced to defend his new play, *Cock-a-Doodle Dandy,* before it could be produced or published. His American agent, Richard Madden, was afraid it might offend Catholics, and the devout Eddie Dowling decided he could not produce it, though O'Casey argued that nothing in the play conflicted with Catholic doctrine. When he learned that the star-chamber Tenney Committee of California, spawned by McCarthyism, had listed him as a dangerous subversive, he wrote: "Anyway, Tenney is right. I am a subversive writer; always have been, and I hope, always will be. I take my place with the other subversive writers—Dickens, Milton, Shelley, Byron, Joyce, Shaw, and a shining host of others, not forgetting Tenney's own Walt Whitman." And so he carried on with his art and letters with indefatigable energy, defending Ireland's moral right to the Hugh Lane Pictures; helping Irish writers seek publication of their works in America; arguing with the Totnes M.P. over the shocking gulf between the rich and the poor; brawling with Douglas A. Hyde over Catholicism and Communism in a five thousand-word letter that even the *Daily Worker* would not publish; assuring a Russian friend that the West and the East were part of one great world and must never wage war against each other, and making a special point of defending the work of Picasso and Eliot from Russian prejudice. Also worried about Irish prejudice, he wanted to protect Francis MacManus by telling him: "I wont write to you again, except for a very special reason. It would do you, a Catholic, no good, if it became known you were corresponding with a hardened Communist, the way things are now." In spite of these remarks he really was quite a softened Communist, though the ultramontane Irish then looked upon all Communists as hardened.

Toward the end of 1948, he wrote to Nathan: " 'Blessing and victory!' as we say in the old Irish Pagan greeting, usually adding 'and the killing of many enemies.' " He had scotched some enemies, and if he was blessed as a man he had won few victories as a writer.

To Liam Shine

TC. O'CASEY

[TOTNES, DEVON]

5 JANUARY 1947

Dear Mr. Shine.

I am in no way vexed with you, though I dont think you should use such an impressive word as—appalling—in connection with the word—tripe—. I cant see how you expected your letter to be published, for it didnt even make a secondary effort to answer any question put forward in the article written by me.[1] Some of your facts about me, personally, are wrong: I was never a Roman Catholic; and I am still an Irishman. One doesnt cease to be an Irishman because one ventures to contest airy statements made by Card. Griffin. It seems to me a silly way of conducting a discussion, but it is a common practice of R. Catholic apologists. This sort of argument appears again in—this picture of a soul, spleened, soured, and shrivelled; tis not so much Vatican and Red Star, this rambling *raimeis,*[2] but the vacuum and the black scar in Comrade O'Casey—. These things have nothing to do with the questions put in the article. Spleen, etc, even bias, are irrelevant. The point is, are the statements made in the article accurate? Did Dr. McDonald say what is attributed to him? He did, and wrote it down, and said many more things as well, far deeper and far more cogent than the Clergy's petty passion for promotion. Did Card.

---

[1] "Vatican and Red Star in Yugoslavia," *Daily Worker,* 12 December 1946. Shine's letter, refused publication by the editor of the *Daily Worker,* was forwarded to O'Casey.

[2] Rubbish or nonsense.

Gasquet deliberately distort and falsify historical records to suit his own ends? [3] He did. Did Dr. McDonald say that—he would recommend no clergyman to trust the Roman Rota? Did Card. Logue condemn a play by Yeats, COUNTESS CATHLEEN, admitting, at the same time, that he hadnt read the play? [4] Did a priest kill a man with a blow of his fist because the man was living with an unmarried woman? [5] Did you read the accounts of the fire in a Poor Clare's School for delinquent children from 5 to 10, in which 33 were burned alive [6]; and the fact that these kids were locked in their dormitories, with the light cut off, so that rescue work was made nigh impossible; and did you read of the kindly expressions of sympathy to the Sisters? You read Dr. McDonald's REMINISCENCES OF A MAYNOOTH PROFESSOR, my friend; and when youve read it, put it all down to McDonald's spleen, black scar, etc. You say—you have twisted the words of Dr. McDonald to make him speak for something that in truth he never spoke for—. In manlier language you would have called me a liar. Well, if the Universe challenges what I have quoted from Dr. McDonald, I'll give it chapter and verse, and a lot more to go with it (if they guarantee to publish what I write). Who wrote this? "Card. McCabe took the place against the Fenians which had been held by Card. Cullen. In opposing this agrarian revolution in Ireland, he and the bishops were acting quite in conformity with the Catholic tradition, which had opposed the revolution in France, Italy, and elsewhere. The Catholic schools of theology are almost the most Tory bodies in the world; and, strange as it may seem, Ireland is the most conservative country in Europe, through its being so much under the influence of the Catholic schools." Dr. McDonald did. Now Card. Griffin, true to type, is opposing the revolution in Yugo-Slavia. But we have marched a long way since the Land League, and the peasants now wear the Red Star in their caps; and Card. Griffin wont find the going so easy as his brother McCabe. Indeed, Dr. McDonald seems to have anticipated your letter to me, for he has written down,—Are the Russians, however cultured they may become, bound for all time to autocratic Czars?—. Again, in reference to an article of his—To get at me, they (the bishops) must hit at Rome, and no-one who knows the higher ecclesiastics of Ireland would ever deem them capable of such folly as that—. Again, referring to Dr. Moran's rejection for a professorship at Maynooth —If you wish to succeed, my students, you should take care either not to write at all; or to write good commonplace; above all not to do anything original, however excellent it may be—. Again, on the question of Presbyterianism in the Early Church—Two of their Lordships told myself that it

---

[3] The main source for O'Casey's comments on Cardinal Gasquet was George Gordon Coulton's *The Scandal of Cardinal Gasquet* (1937), a sixteen-page pamphlet.

[4] Michael Cardinal Logue (1840–1924), Archbishop of Armagh and Primate of All Ireland, condemned Yeats's play in 1899 without having read it, because he heard that in it the countess sells her soul to the devil to save the starving people of Ireland.

[5] He used this incident in *Cock-a-Doodle Dandy* (1949).

[6] See O'Casey's letter to Jack Carney, 12 March 1943, note 2.

was wrong on my part to say that the P. had some right on their side, one
of the two adding that, even though they might have, it was a mistake to
admit it, and to give them an opportunity of crowing over us. That, as I
think, may be good politics, but it is not the scientific spirit, which does
not hesitate to admit any error that has been proved. No small part of our
theology is due to this, that we persist in maintaining positions, that have
been long since shown to be indefensible—.

Now is it a fact (never mind truth) that The Universe said Hitler was
never excommunicated because he had not offended against the Canonical
Law? Tito has, of course, because he stood up for the poor people. Is it a
fact that Dr. McDonald asked the Irish Catholic Church to publish a
balance sheet? Is it a fact that Card. Newman said, when discussing the
foundation of an Historical Review—All historical facts will have to be
doctored if we are not to be called bad Catholics? Are the things Lord
Acton said about the Ultramontanes and the Jesuits facts? That is, apart
from their truth, did he say them? Did the Irish Bishops issue their statement, mentioned by me, on the murder of Free Staters on the one hand,
and of Republicans on the other? And are all these things said by these
men evidences of a spleened, soured, and seared nature? Remember that I,
in most instances, said what others had said, and by men who had some
right to claim authority for what they said. And remember that Card.
Gasquet did, in a far, far greater way, the thing condemned by Dr.
McDonald—he refused to correct errors, and deliberately distorted and
altered records to build up a thesis, which the confutation of these mis-
statements destroyed. One can understand this sort of thing coming from
the Chesterton-Belloc duo, with their got-it-from-God airyness of manner,
but Card. Gasquet! I dont know what you mean by the bad manners of
not giving some persons their C. names. We dont always call Stalin Josef,
nor Churchill Winston, nor Shaw Bernard, nor Wells, H. G., nor Newman
Henry. Isnt this a very silly quibble on your part? If that sort of thing is
to be used by a defender of the faith in Prelatial Toryism, then the faith
wont last long. It's going fast anyway, for the common people are destroying it. What do you mean by saying—all history is false?—Do you include
the Acts of the Apostles? All the chronicles, testimonies, records, and
dialogues of the earlier ages? All false? Now, now, Mr. Shine. If it were all
written in the way of Card. G. you might well say so. And, by the way
Gasquet was something more than "a poor Benedictine scribe." May I ask
what had Kitty O'Shea got to do with Parnell as a Leader of the Irish
people? Was he the one man who ever got into bed with a woman? Who
made the Plan of Campaign a power? The Boycott? And who condemned
them? Did you read the Meath Petition? There was no statement made by
me that The Pope or the Bishops had "concocted a Parnell Plot." And well
you know this, but like a minor Gasquet, you can twist and distort with
the next. What I said was that the Bishops were against Parnell's methods,
as they always have been against the uprisings of the people, as Dr.

McDonald knew as well as I. And that when these Bishops got a chance—after the English Gladstone and Morley had written saying they'd support Parnell no more—they seized their chance, because, not of Kitty O'Shea, but because they knew the sort of man Parnell was, and that with the people behind him, he'd stand no nonsense from them. He was not a Douglas Hyde. So like the mean men they were, they used poor Kitty O'Shea to down the one man who could have solved Ireland's trouble. Well, they've paid bitterly for that, and are paying bitterly for it still, and will go on paying for it for a long time, and sorrow mend them. Why dont you try to learn a little about Communism, instead of implying the question of what I would write about the aristocratic Landowner were he alive today. That would depend on where he stood, and since he could abandon his property to serve the Irish peasant (and get damn little in return for it, save cement in his eyes in Kilkenny),[7] he'd do the same for the workers, for what are the peasants but workers too. Remember that Thomson [8] was a Landowner too, and that Engels was a rich business man. Who is the biggest landowner in Eire now, I wonder? The R.C. Church must have a few broad acres in her pocket by this time. I'm glad, anyhow, that you read the Daily worker. So do the Dublin workers—quite a lot of them, and I understand they are busy talking now about Stepinac. So you see, somebody is talking about him. The fact is that another Revolution has taken place in Europe, and the ecclesiastical prelates are blue in the face condemning it as they did all the others; and the terrible disappointment to them is that they cant get at the USSR to take the Red Star down from the tower of the Kremlin. Well, this letter has gone on long enough. I take it you will have no objection to the publication of your letter to me, if I should, at some future date, include it with others from others along with my own.

> *All the best,*
> *Yours sincerely,*
> *Sean O'Casey*

[7] When Parnell was forced to resign as leader of the Irish Nationalist Party in 1891, as a result of pressure from the Irish bishops and British Prime Minister Gladstone, he was attacked in Castlecomer, Co. Kilkenny, by people who threw quicklime in his eyes. See Joyce's "Gas From a Burner" (1912):

> This lovely land that always sent
> Her writers and artists to banishment
> And in a spirit of Irish fun
> Betrayed her own leaders, one by one.
> 'Twas Irish humour, wet and dry,
> Flung quicklime into Parnell's eye.

[8] William Thompson (1775–1833), the Irish Socialist born in Cork who anticipated the theories of Karl Marx. Although a wealthy landowner, he was an active force in the Co-operative movement.

To Jack Carney

MS. NYU LIBRARY

TOTNES, DEVON
8 JANUARY 1947

Dear Jack,

Another year down on top of us! And not half done with the gone year
yet. Wirrastrue! [1] as they used to say in the old "Irish" plays—better than
Bing Crosby's "Irish Lullaby" in the Balls of St. Mary's. Thanks for the
Turkey, though it was so long delayed in transit that it came bad. A pity,
but no fault of yours. And thanks for the tobacco—the hard tack, as
brother Tom used to call it—; it was fine. Eileen tells me you saw in the
Irish papers notice of the "S. of a Gunman" to be made into a Film. The
Dramatists League gave Bryan Hirst [2] an option months ago, but I never
thought it would come to anything. I hope the notice is true. "The Silver
Tassie" may go on in New York—a tentative arrangement has been made
with a new Company—if they can get the money to produce. Next month's
"Irish Writing," published in Cork, is to have an article by me "Tender
Tears for Poor O'Casey," [3] on what was said about the Irish plays—"Juno,"
etc, when they first appeared. It is, I think, something of an eyeopener.

Important: Attention! Could you get me a book or pamphlet containing
the Names, Offices, & Constituencies of the present members of the Government? Breon has asked me for these, but, bar Bevin & Atlee, I don't
know—and Strachey of course. I shall be glad, if you could do this. I'm
still working on the last few chapters of the "Biography."

> The weather here is very bad.
> Eyes not too good.
> Coal is hard to get.

but,

> Stare fate in the face;
> Sure the heart must be aysey
> When it's in the right place.

Miles na Copaleen, I think, used to sing this in the Mechanics Theatre's (Abbey T. now) edition of "The Colleen Bawn."

Love to Mina, & all the best.
Yours as ever,
Sean

[1] A Mhuire is truagh, Oh Mary (Mother of God), what sorrow! A common
expression in the Irish plays of Dion Boucicault.
[2] See O'Casey's letter to Brian Hurst, 4 September 1946.
[3] "Tender Tears for Poor O'Casey," *Irish Writing,* June 1947; reprinted in a
slightly revised version in *The Green Crow* (1956).

To Jack Carney

MS. NYU LIBRARY

TOTNES, DEVON
10 JANUARY 1947

Dear Jack,

Here are the books, autographed as desired. I'm not sure that your "Williamena" is quite correct—should it be "Wilhamena"; but you should know better nor me. Not surprised to hear about the way R. M. Fox wrote about Jim [Larkin] by making Connolly cock o the South as well as the N. That is the safer way to write today, and, to me, from the first day I met him, & brought him to Fowler Hall, held by the Republicans, he was always a little shit. And he doesn't even know how to write badly well. Yes, let's have a look at it. I'll send it back. I have Robinson's book on Lady G. I've reviewed it for "The Bell" Feb. issue.[1] Why doesn't someone get Fox to write the life of Bill O'Brien—the big sharp shit?

Yours as ever
Sean

[1] "A Protestant Bridget," *The Bell,* February 1947, a review of *Lady Gregory's Journals, 1916–1930* (1946), ed. Lennox Robinson.

To George Jean Nathan

MS. CORNELL

TOTNES, DEVON
14 JANUARY 1947

My very dear George:

I am sending you a copy of "Irish Writing" at the request of those who publish it. It's done in Cork, & I hope it may be a success. There's a heavy clamp down by the clergy on anything that hasn't a crib, a candle, or a cross in it. The whole land is being pelted with prayers. Your attention is drawn to the play by Katie Roche.[1] I'm afraid you won't get much excite-

[1] Teresa Deevy, "Strange Birth," a one-act play, *Irish Writing,* No. 1, November 1946. O'Casey had confused Miss Deevy with the title of one of her plays, *Katie Roche* (1936).

ment out of it. Katie Roche will hardly write another good play; nor, I'm afraid will [Paul Vincent] Carroll, for he is too fond of rushing hither & thither after films.

I'm sending you the magazine simply because I was asked to do it. There's a work in it by James Stephens [2] which I'd like your opinion about —as we say in Dublin. A good exchange of Dublin is, I think, in Miles na Copaleen's contribution.[3]

Breon is now a gunner in the artillery, looking handsome in his beret, white lanyard, & yellow flash. Isn't it odd how the years bring changes! The old Fenian has a son an artillery gunner in the English army. What will the Irish saints think!

I'm seeing a Producer (your Director) here on Saturday about a production of Oak Leaves & Lavender. I understand he wants me to take out the chant, "Oh, give us Shelters," alleging that the people had no fear of the bombing. Holy God, grant us patience!

> *All the best to you.*
> *Yours with my love.*
> *Sean*

& to Eugene

[2] James Stephens, "A Rhinoceros, Some Ladies, and a Horse," a short story, *Irish Writing*, No. 1.

[3] Myles na gCopaleen, "Drink and Time in Dublin," a short story, *Irish Writing*, No. 1.

To Jack Carney

TS. NYU LIBRARY

[TOTNES, DEVON]
15 JANUARY 1947

Dear Jack,

Thanks for the loan of Fox's book JAMES CONNOLLY [1]—why not the name by which he was known—"Jim"? Fancy calling Jim Larkin "James"! It just shows you the sort of writer Fox is, or is it part of an effort to respectablise him and make him more a son of the church? But what a little lowser he is. Connolly has now, through the transmutation of what a man really stood for, has become the accepted labour idea of Ireland's church and state, and so this dish of skimmed milk, Fox, joins them, and pinnacles Connolly at the expense of Larkin. It is the meanest

[1] R. M. Fox, *James Connolly* (1947).

book I have ever read, and thank God, the dullest too. It is practically a rehash of what has already been written by Ryan, Liam P.,[2] and Ryan, Desmond,[3] with almost all the tributes to Larkin, given by these two men, left out. One has only to read Liam O'Ryan's book to see how, quite unconsciously—for Connolly was Ryan's friend as Larkin never was, and so Ryan gives every possible tribute to Connolly he can, but he happened to be an honest man—he places Larkin first. In his references to the two men, he always places the names thus—"Larkin and Connolly," Larkin's coming first, so proving which of them led in the tremendous fight for Labour. They are put in their proper and fair order, for undoubtedly, Connolly followed Larkin in stature in the Irish Labour fight; and it is no small thing to rank next to Jim Larkin. But Connolly's qualities were limited, and in the matter of literature very much so. His best work, LABOUR IN IRISH HISTORY,[4] was largely the work of the modest, saintly Sheehy Skeffington,[5] that strange Pacificist who was one of Ireland's finest fighters; who refused to sanction violence, but allowed himself to be a Vice-President of the I. Citizen Army—the Irish Gandhi! In his book, Fox makes Markievicz [6] responsible for a resolution at the moulding of the I.C. Army Constitution, making it, where possible, obligatory on every member to be a member of a T. Union; but the louse, though he must have taken the incident from my book,[7] deliberately avoids quoting the fact that it was Larkin who framed the resolution, first thought of it, and asked that some one present should propose it. That's the sort of thing this fellow does to try to blot Larkin out of his due. Did you notice that, on the book's jacket, the press notice, the 2nd one, on his GREEN BANNERS,[8] is given as from "Ch: Le: Monitor, Boston."? What is "Ch: Le: Monitor," but The Christian Monitor, showing the shit was afraid to quote it as praising him to an Irish public! (The Christian Science Monitor) Well, that's about enough. He gives himself away, too, when he tells, apropos of Connolly going to America, that his party gave him a banquet before he left. Not a dinner, but a banquet; and follows that up by saying that when Connolly embarked, there wasn't anyone to say farewell! That was Connolly's party for you. So numerous, so powerful, that there wasn't one to say good-bye ee. The fact is, whether we like it or not, that Connolly had to call on Nationalism to make him famous, and were it not for Easter Week Connolly would

2 W. P. Ryan, *The Irish Labour Movement* (1919).

3 Desmond Ryan, *Remembering Sion* (1934).

4 James Connolly, *Labour in Irish History* (1910).

5 Francis Sheehy-Skeffington (1878–1916), pacifist and champion of women's rights; a Vice-President of the Irish Citizen Army in 1914 when O'Casey was Secretary; brutally executed during the Easter Rising, in which he took no part, by a British officer who was later declared to be insane.

6 For the background of O'Casey's confrontation with Countess Markievicz, see his letter to *Plebs,* March 1942, note 3.

7 P. O Cathasaigh, *The Story of the Irish Citizen Army* (1919); reprinted in *Feathers From the Green Crow* (1962). The "P" was a misprint.

8 R. M. Fox, *Green Banners* (1938).

have remained as insignificant as he had been before Larkin came to Ireland.[9] Connolly had that weakness—he passionately wanted fame, & did everything he consistently could to achieve it—the parading of the C.A.; the natty uniform he had made specially for himself; the hoisting of the "Green Flag" over L. Hall; the companionship of the Countess; the writing of a Play [10]—a terrible, silly, sentimental thing, as it was found to be, for he hadn't a glimmer of the artist in his whole make-up; the guards on the roof of L. Hall, & all the rest of it, photographed & ready for such serving shits as Fox. And as for military skill—well, Connolly showed how little he had of it.

However, I don't think Fox's book will do much harm to Jim. It is too dull to live, save, perhaps, in Ireland. Sooner or later, things reach their proper level.

I hope Mina is allright again. Thanks for cuttings. Some months ago, Miss Barber of the Dramatists League gave B. Hirst an option on the S. of a Gunman for 6 months for £100, on behalf of Rank. Since then, I've heard nothing, bar what the cuttings say. I certainly am not writing a script for this, or any other play.

Yours as ever,
Sean

PS. No, when in Dublin, I didn't foresee that one day I'd have a son a gunner in the British Army. He could do worse—be on the staff of the Standard.

[9] The typing stopped here; the rest of the letter was written in longhand.
[10] James Connolly's *Under Which Flag?* an unpublished three-act play about the revolt of 1867, was produced on Sunday, 26 March 1916, by the Irish Workers' Dramatic Company at the Workers' Concert Hall, Liberty Hall, Dublin.

To Mrs Isabella Murphy [1]

TS. MURPHY

TOTNES, DEVON
20 JANUARY 1947

Dear Babsie,

I am very sorry to hear about your daughter, Mary.[2] I don't remember ever seeing her, but she must have been a young woman. What happened

[1] Mrs. Isabella Murphy, O'Casey's niece, the daughter of his sister Isabella Casey Beaver.
[2] Mary Murphy Dunn died of diabetes on 12 January 1947 at the age of twenty-six. She was O'Casey's grandniece.

to her? It doesn't matter about Mick; [3] he was an old man, and had his day. But Mary's death is quite different. I am writing tonight to the Prudential Agent here to tell him about the death of Mick. The premium has been paid up to the end of the first week of Feb. next. As well, I have the record of another Policy, which, as the Companies say, has "matured." This will amount to £8.16.10. which, when I hear from the Agent, I will send on to you. There is, I think, another sum to be paid as well, on another Policy, so that you should get something like £15 or more.

Don't send me the policies till you hear from me. You may be able to draw what's due on Mick's policies in Dublin, and so save me the trouble of getting it and forwarding it on to you. A letter from me (this one even), when brought to the Prudential Office (I suppose they have one in Dublin still?) should be sufficient authority to allow you to draw the money.

I remember meeting a young girl in the Standard Hotel when I was last there (Bridget [4] was her name I think and she worked there) who said she was a niece. Who was she? Yours or Susan's? Trying to bring my memory back to Abercorn Rd, I remember Susan having a baby that was afflicted with very painful abscesses—what happened to her? And Tom's three kids—Joseph, Christie, and Josephine, I think?

I will either send you on the policy money, or tell you how to get it, as soon as I settle with the Agent. In the meantime, I enclose a cheque for £2 for immediate emergency.

Yours sincerely,
Sean O'Casey
(Uncle Jack)

[3] Michael Casey, O'Casey's brother, died on 11 January 1947 at the age of eighty-one. He had lived in Mrs. Murphy's house for many years.

[4] It was not Bridget but Mary Murphy that he met at the Standard Hotel during his last visit to Dublin in September 1935.

To Mrs. Isabella Murphy

TS. MURPHY

TOTNES, DEVON
24 JANUARY 1947

Dear Babsie:

I have seen the Insurance Agent. He tells me, I have to get a Death Certificate; [1] that I must claim the amount due as the next-of-kin.

So let me have a Death Certificate, with the Policy, if you can find it.

[1] For his brother Michael.

If you can't find the Policy, never mind, I can get the amount due by signing a special form, but the D. Certificate is necessary.

Then as soon as I receive the money from the Insurance Society, I shall send an equivalent cheque to you (I assume you were in charge of the burial) to cover the expenses.

This is done in haste as I am down with influenza.

Yours sincerely,
S. O'Casey
(*Uncle Jack*)

To Bronson Albery

TC. O'CASEY

[TOTNES, DEVON]
31 JANUARY 1947

Dear Mr. Albery.

Glad you got back the American Tax. We dont get the market value of the dollar. The Treasury takes that from us, and, I suppose, this explains the difference. Anyway, it's a lot better than nix.

Glad to hear that you are starting auditions [1] on Saturday. I am not quite easy in my mind about [F. J.] McCormick. My choice, failing Victor, would be Eddie Byrne, whom we know, and who gave more than satisfaction. You think he mightnt be authoritative enough, and you may be right. I hope McCormick wont be too authoritative. I saw him—more than twenty years ago—in the part of Tanner in *Man And Superman,*[2] and he played the rest of the Cast into insignificance, including Barry Fitzgerald, who played Roebuck Ramsden. I'm afraid, what with the film parts that he has played, that he may be more so now than he was then. I'd suggest you should think once more of Eddie Byrne. Once an actor gets any kind of a name on the film, it's wallops, your worship!

We are snowbound here, and have to collect from the town the things we need, for deliveries are held up. I daresay it's near as bad with you.

All good wishes,
Yours very sincerely,
Sean O'Casey

[1] For the production of *Oak Leaves and Lavender.*
[2] See O'Casey's letter to M. J. Dolan, 13 August 1925, Vol. I, pp. 138–40, for his comments on that production of *Man and Superman* at the Abbey Theatre.

Daily Worker

31 JANUARY 1947

LARKIN DEAD

James Larkin, Irish Labour leader, died yesterday. He was 69 years old.[1]

Four days before his death, despite a succession of collapses, Larkin was still working, fighting for better conditions for the workers on the Grand Canal.

Then, unwillingly, he allowed himself to be taken to the Meath Hospital, Dublin.

SEAN O'CASEY writes:

Jim Larkin is dead. The lion of Irish Labour has gone on his long holiday.

"The greatest Irishman since Parnell," as Bernard Shaw called him, has left the Irish workers to fight the battle without him.

They will miss him. It is a sad blow to them, and a bad blow to us all.

Over wherever he may be laid to rest will be written, Here Lies the Hero of Socialist Labour.

No less, for he was the man who lifted the prostrate, helpless Irish worker to his feet and made him say to all the world, I am a Man, and gave the Irish worker the power to prove it.

But Jim Larkin is not dead. Such as he can never die.

His spirit will be forever at the forefront of every forward movement of Irish Labour, and the world's fighters for man's freedom.

He is with us always, never absent; with us always.

Others have on their brow the mark of Cain's treachery to their class. On Jim's forehead is the stigmata of the Red Star.

Irish workers, let not your hearts be troubled, neither let them be afraid; Jim Larkin is not dead; he will be with you always.

---

[1] Jim Larkin (1876–1947) died in his seventy-second year. He left only £4.50 and some personal belongings. Besides the tributes in the *Daily Worker* and the *Irish Times*, O'Casey wrote two similar pieces in the *Irish People*, 8 February 1947, and the *Irish Democrat*, March 1947; the latter is reprinted in the *Sean O'Casey Review*, Spring 1975.

Irish Times

31 JANUARY 1947

"JIM" LARKIN DIES

Sean O'Casey Tribute [1]

Mr. James Larkin, internationally-known Irish labour leader, died in a Dublin hospital, after a short illness, yesterday morning. He was aged 72. Revolutionary, journalist, orator, "Big Jim" will be remembered chiefly for his work among the unorganised dock labourers of Belfast and Dublin early in this century.

"A man of seething energy . . . of remarkable oratorical talent . . . a talented leader . . . he performed miracles among the unskilled workers" —this was how he was described publicly by Lenin.

Sean O'Casey, last night, paid the following tribute to Mr. Larkin:—

It is hard to believe that this "lion" of the Irish Labour movement will roar no more. When it seemed that every man's hand was against him the time he led the workers through the tremendous days of 1913 he wrested tribute of Ireland's greatest and most prominent men. Yeats, George Russell, Orpen and George Bernard Shaw proclaimed him to be the greatest Irishman since Parnell. And so he was; for all thoughts and all activities surged in the soul of this Labour leader. He was far and away above the orthodox Labour leader, for he combined within himself the imagination of the artist, with the fire and determination of a leader of a down-trodden class.

He was the first man in Ireland—and, perhaps, in England, too—who brought poetry into the workers' fight for a better life. Lectures and concerts, and other activities, he brought into Liberty Hall, and the social centre he organised in Croydon Park coloured the life of the Dublin workers, and was a joyous experience they had never known before, and won for Jim the admiration of many who had but scanty interest in the labour movement.

Before all others, Jim Larkin brought into the Dublin labour strife an interest in the hearts of humanity never associated before with the life of those who had to work hard and long for a living; and to-day this interest has grown to tremendous proportions, and the workers are swarming to enjoy and to understand the finer things of life.

So Jim Larkin, as well as being a great leader of men and an imaginative artist himself, was a foreseer of things to come. He was the man who first introduced to me the great name of Eugene O'Neill just after that playwright had had his "Hairy Ape" produced in New York. He fought for the

[1] Reprinted in the *Sean O'Casey Review,* Fall 1976.

loaf of bread as no man before him had ever fought; but, with the loaf of bread, he also brought the flask of wine and the book of verse.

He had the eloquence of an Elizabethan, fascinating to all who heard him, and irresistible to the workers. He was familiar with the poetry of Shakespeare, Whitman, Shelley and Omar Khayyam, and often quoted them in his speeches. In all his imaginative speeches there ran the fiery thread of devastating criticism not only of the employers, but of the workers themselves.

Jim Larkin never hesitated to expose and condemn the faults of his followers. No man ever did more since the days of Father Mathew to persuade the workers to live a more sober and sensible life than this Jim.

Many were jealous of his great fight and of his influence on the working class, and many still are, but the life of this man, so great, so unselfish, so apostolic, will live for ever in the hearts and minds of those who knew him, and in the minds of those who will hear of the mission to men, and of all he did to bring security and decency and honour to a class that never knew of these things until Jim Larkin came.

There was a man sent from God whose name was Jim, and that man was Larkin. Jim Larkin is not dead, but is with us all, and will be with us always.

To Miss M. E. Barber [1]

MS. LEAGUE OF DRAMATISTS

TOTNES, DEVON
1 FEBRUARY 1947

Dear Miss Barber
Enclosed are the folios of forms from the French Authors' Society, giving an account of myself from the year of one, to the best of my ability.

I hope they will satisfy all whom it doesn't concern. What made them forget to take our finger-prints? I enclose Birth Certificate. If the name "John" be commented upon, it is simply that "Sean" is the Irish form of the name.

We are snow-bound here. The frost is enveloping our very souls. The wife has to go to the town knee-deep in snow to fetch bread, spuds, etc, while I bring in wood for the fires we try to keep going. People say they've

---

[1] Miss M. E. Barber, League of Dramatists, London.

never seen the like, but they always say that when the snow falls, or the wind blows.

All the best
S. O'Casey

SEAN O'CASEY

(ne Shaun O'Cathasaigh), dramatic author; born Dublin 31 March, 1884; [2] son of Michael O'Cathasaigh and wife Susanna; educated Dublin; Married Eileen Carey (Katherine Reynolds). Was formerly in succession, a builder's labourer, railway labourer, and general labourer.
First play was "The Shadow of a Gunman," 1922; "Cathleen Listens In," was produced at the Abbey Theatre Dublin, Oct. 1923; has since written "Nannie's Night Out," Abbey Sept. 1924; "Juno and the Paycock," which was his first big success, produced at the Royalty, Nov. 1923; "The Plough and the Stars," Abbey Theatre Dublin, Feb. 1926; also Fortune, London, May 1926; "The Shadow of a Gunman," Court, May 1927; "The Silver Tassie," 1929; "Within the Gates," 1934; "The End of the Beginning," 1939, was first performed at the Theatre de l'Oeuvre, Paris, May 1939, and at the "Q" Theatre London, in Oct. 1939;
Later plays are "The Star Turns Red," 1940; "Red Roses For Me," 1943; "Purple Dust," 1945; "Oak Leaves and Lavender," 1946; "The Flying Wasp" (book) 1937; published his autobiography "I Knock at the Door," 1939, which was banned in Eire; followed by "Pictures in the Hallway," and "Drums Under the Windows"; gained the Hawthornden Prize, 1926.

2 He was actually born on 30 March 1880.

To Brooks Atkinson

TS. ATKINSON

TOTNES, DEVON
4 FEBRUARY 1947

My dear Brooks:
First let me say how glad I am to hear you are back in your favourite & most suitable haunts—the office desk and the rose garden. Why the hell you ever left them, I don't know. They are your natural places, & you do there (in my opinion), your best work for humanity. What we can best do is the best thing we can do. I hope Mrs. Atkinson will chain you up now. It is fine to see you spreading yourself out once more in the N.Y.

Times. I don't agree with a helluva lot you say, but you are always interesting, & that's the main thing.

As for the rest of the "biography," I am ending it (for the present) on the morning of my departure from Ireland for England. That episode meant, not only another day, but a new life; so I put the fife in my pocket for awhile, till I learn a new tune or two in the new places I visit, & the new life I live. I haven't yet decided on the title for this vol., but I think it will be "The Long Day Over." [1]

Preparations are going on here for a production of "Oak Leaves & Lavender," but I'm afraid I won't get it done altogether in my way. The Producer (your Director) talks about making it "as normal as possible," which means, I daresay, that whatever imaginativeness may be in the play should, as far as possible, be taken out of it. And you twit me with the Soviet Union! My dear friend, you may be right, but I have endured so much repression here that, no matter what you may say, I feel there is just as much (and more) repression here than there is in the USSR. You just read the Preface to Joyce's N.Y. Edition of "Ulysses," & see what he went through before "Dubliners" would be published. The present Court Censor here, Lord Clarendon, banned my "Star Turns Red," because "he didn't like the theme." As if I cared a damn whether he did or no; or as if, when I sat down to try to write a play, I asked myself the question— "Now what kind of a play would Lord Clarendon write?" You yourself must remember what the Jesuits (father O'Connell) [2] & the religious said about "Within The Gates"; and how the Abbey Theatre treated "Silver Tassie." I see by Lady Gregory's "Notes" [3] recently published, that she thought the Abbey had made a big mistake, & blames Robinson for its final rejection. But more of this anon.

Only the other day, a Cahircrvien Drama Co. selected "The Plough" as a play for a Drama Festival in Cork. After months of rehearsal, the Committee of the Festival banned the play.[4] I tried to get the names of this Committee, but all to whom I wrote, remained silent. They were afraid to write to me. I don't blame them, for their very livelihood was in question. Look at what James Agate said about "Purple Dust"![5] I could give you

---

[1] He finally called it *Inishfallen, Fare Thee Well* (1949).

[2] He meant Father Terence L. Connolly, S. J.; see O'Casey's letter to Francis MacManus, 21 March 1948, note 3.

[3] *Lady Gregory's Journals, 1916–1930* (1947), edited by Lennox Robinson. Lady Gregory made the following entries in her Journal:

> 10 June 1928 . . . I asked Yeats and Lennox Robinson, when we went up to the office on one of the last nights of the *Plough and the Stars,* if we might consider putting [*The Silver Tassie*] on. Yeats inclined to do it, but L. R. said "No. It is a bad play." (p. 110) 23 October 1929 . . . But my mind goes back to *The Tassie*—we ought not to have rejected it. We should have held out against Lennox Robinson that last evening the order to return it was given. (p. 124)

[4] See O'Casey's letter to Robert Goldie, 10 December 1946.

[5] James Agate, "Mr. O'Casey: A Reply," *Sunday Times,* 3 May 1942; reprinted above.

many more instances of oppression. I have put down some of them in my new book—not about myself, but of others. Perhaps, you've never read "Reminiscenses of a Maynooth Professor," or Coulton's references to Gasquet,[6] Belloc, & Chesterton? A Catholic Naval officer, visiting me here during the war,—I had met him at Harvard, when he was a student there —told me Belloc came to the U.S.A. to lecture, shortly after the run of "Within the Gates." At Harvard, the following conversation took place:

Student: What do you think, Mr. Belloc, of "Within the Gates"?

Belloc: Never heard of it.

Student: The play, you know, written by Sean O'Casey.

Belloc: Never heard of him.

A palpable lie, for he had heard of "Juno," & his butty Chesterton, had written a long article on O'Casey in the paper he then owned & edited, "G. K.'s Weekly." [7] Well, by now, he has heard of me, anyhow, for I wrote about him in the Daily Worker,[8] but, like all these shallow controversialists of the Vatican, he preserves his reputation by silence. These fellows attack others, but when the others reply their answers are suppressed, & are, the devotees believe, lost forever in silence. Believe me, all the opposition to Poland & other countries, isn't due to the influence of the USSR. There is a tremendous revolt rising against the tyranny & obscurantism of clericalism everywhere; & it is near time, too. Since the clerical row in Dublin over "The Silver Tassie," no new play of mine has been done—or even asked for—by the Abbey. I'm afraid, Brooks, afraid for the Abbey.

Well, so far, so bad. If you like, I'll send you a copy of the next biographical vol. when it comes out. I am working now on the two last chapters—interrupted by many things intruding—, but God knows when it may appear on account of the shortage of Labour in the printing-trade.

It is said that the Theatre slump has begun here, and that the day of constant notices, proclaiming "House Full," is over. Maybe, that is why they are handling "Oakleaves & Lavender." I hope for a production of "The Silver Tassie" in your great City soon. I was sorry to hear of Ernest Boyd's death.[9] A curious man.

My love to Mrs. Atkinson & to a fellow called Brooks.

Ever yours.
Sean

[6] George Gordon Coulton, *The Scandal of Cardinal Gasquet* (1937).

[7] Probably a reference to J. K. Prothero, "The Glory of the Paycock," *G. K.'s Weekly,* 28 November 1925, a review of the first London production of *Juno.*

[8] Sean O'Casey, "Vatican and Red Star in Yugoslavia," *Daily Worker,* 12 December 1946.

[9] Ernest Boyd (1887–1946), editor and author of books on the Irish literary renaissance, died on 30 December 1946.

To Jack Carney

MS. NYU LIBRARY

TOTNES, DEVON
8 FEBRUARY 1947

Dear Jack,

Thanks for letters. It must have been a dreadful Journey there and back. I hope you're feeling no ill effects from it. I'm, at the moment, creeping out of a depression induced by a bout of Influenza. And the other night, Eileen coming home stepped on a patch of ice, & came down on the back of her head, giving herself concussion, a bad bruise, & a nasty cut. Dr. Varian, however, ventured out, dressed the wound & stitched it, and she is much better now. How she struggled home, I don't know. There wasn't a soul about, when she came out of the black-out, so there was nothing to do, but pick herself up, and stagger home. All seems to be well now, however.

I don't like that of Church and State at Jim's funeral. Imagine S. T. O'Kelly [1] praying for Jim's soul! And the slimey McQuaid.[2] The Church has horned in on the Labour Movement.

And that shit, Fox, asking you in such a place, at such a time, about his book! I've rarely read a duller one. By the way, you didn't say if Delia [3] was at the funeral?

Flann Campbell of "The Irish Democrat" has asked me to write about Jim for his next number.[4] I forced myself to write something, & sent it on to him.

Will write again when this "depression" declines.

Love to Mina & you.
Yours ever,
Sean

Addendum.

Snow-bound here again! Last week had to plod to town to get what we could of bread, milk, & spuds. Pipes on top burst; water cascading down the stairs—a lovely sight.

Can't focus my thought on Jim's death. Seemed to me, he'd live a long time. Wonder will it weaken or strengthen O'Brien and his gang? Will young Jim manage to keep the Union going? Poor Barney! He will feel it first & last. I'll write when I get a second.

Yours
Sean

Thanks for the Buckingham Palace ribbon—I'll keep that.

[1] Sean T. O'Kelly, President of Ireland.
[2] The Most Rev. John Charles McQuaid, Archbishop of Dublin.
[3] Delia Larkin, Jim's sister.
[4] "James Larkin, Lion of Irish Labour," *Irish Democrat,* March 1947; reprinted in the *Sean O'Casey Review,* Spring 1975.

To Jim Kavanagh [1]

MS. KAVANAGH [2]

TOTNES, DEVON

9 [FEBRUARY?] 1947 [3]

Dear Jim.

I was glad to hear from you, & to know that you were still active in the land of the living—though, maybe, Ireland is now the land of the dead. I don't know that the "old quarters" are so good for you. These tenement basements should no longer exist in any country, much less in a Christian one. It is an extraordinary thing that your mother held on so well, for she hadn't a very easy time of it. I still remember when you went through the floor-boards of your room that had rotted away with the damp. Vera [4] must be a young woman by now. I am very occupied with many things, & am now giving a hand to try to get the I.R.A. prisoners out of jail. Of course, you know I'm married, & have three children—one of them, the eldest, now a gunner in the Royal Artillery. The other two go to day school, so, as I was in 422, I am still always to be found not far from children. They bring in friends occasionally, & we have, maybe, five of them tearing about. When all are asleep, & everything quiet, I begin work, & stay at it usually till two in the morning. I daresay, you remember me keeping you awake typing, & how you hammered the ceiling with the broom as a definite signal for me to give over!

I remember well, most of the lads of the hurling-club—Paddy Callan & his brother Phil; O'Reilly, Michael O'Murchadhu, Leo Rush, Brown, Bennett, the Dunshaughlin lad who broke a leg & thrust a spike through his hand, trying to reclaim a ball beyond the chevaux-de-frise of the Magazine Fort. The Hanrattys & Joe Scully; and the lads & lasses from St Margarets. All scattered now, and old; faintly remembering the past. I had a few letters from Proinnsius O'Kelly, but hadn't time to keep up the correspondence; for the past is gone forever, & there's little use in trying to awake or renew old acquaintances. I do not remember the girls so clearly as I do the boys, but I have a happy recollection of those who formed the

---

1 Jim Kavanagh was still living in the basement flat at 422 North Circular Road, Dublin, where O'Casey had lived as his neighbor and friend in the first-floor front room from 1921 to 1926.

2 An imperfect copy of this letter appeared in the *Sean O'Casey Review*, Fall 1975, reprinted from the *Irish Democrat*, November 1964.

3 O'Casey dated this letter 9 January 1947, but he must have made a mistake, since he refers to the death of Jim Larkin, who died on 30 January 1947. I have therefore suggested a 9 February 1947 date.

4 Vera Tully, Kavanagh's niece, who was staying with him.

Camogie team. I remember Lawless with his home-made fiddle; & poor blind Daffy.

As for me, Jim, I, too, grow old; & have to try to take things easy because of—of all things—Silicosis that has, so an X ray says, pulled the heart a little from its right place.

We live here in Devon, near the Dart, an old town called Totnes, founded, it is said, by the Trojans. A pleasant enough place, but a very damp climate.

I realise how you miss the big-hearted Jim [Larkin]. A few months before his death, he spent a few days here with me. Irish Labour will wait a helluva long time before she gets such another Leader. I see the clergy & the business folk are very anxious about the growth of Communism. The Red Star is plainly visible from all countries now—even from Ireland.

Well all the best to you, to Mrs. K., & to Vera; & to all the old warriors of Gaelic League & hurling-team.

Yours sincerely,
Sean O'Casey

To Horace Reynolds

MS. REYNOLDS

TOTNES, DEVON
18 FEBRUARY 1947

Dear Horace,

The box of good things came allright & hearty & secure. But I wish you and Kay wouldn't send it. I know you are far far from being well-off, and, like myself, can never say Well, life has no financial uncertainties for me now. It was kind of Kay and you to think of us. The "Noodle" soup came in very handy when we were snowed up. For days, we had to trudge to the town through deep snow to gather what we could of bread, milk, & spuds. One snowy night, coming home by herself, Eileen slipped on an icy patch, fell on the back of her head, & cracked it open a bit. After lying in the snow for a while, she managed to rise, & totter home, & a long way it was. Fortunately, our doctor—a Duublinn man—risked the bad road, & heavy snow, and came. He stitched & dressed the wound, & she is almost allright again. She had a damned narrow escape—and so had I, for I'd be fairly lost without her.

Our elder boy, Breon, is now a gunner in the Royal Artillery, has learned how to use a rifle, a sten-gun, & handle a cannon; & finds it a bit monotonous.

I liked your article on the elder Yeats,[1] father of W. B. The old boy was a gay talker, a rich letter-writer, a middling painter, & a bit of a humbug. He talked a lot about family life, & kept away from his own as far & as long as he could. Is Gogarty with you in America still? It is odd how the litterateurs of Dublin fell away, & were lost, when Yeats and Lady Gregory died. A new kind of circle is forming now, all bound, or nearly all, together with scapulars & Rosary beads. The Bell is the one Journal or magazine that has any kind of Liberal views. I'm afraid the Abbey is done for. All who can (and who cant?) are panting after the Films. Holywood is the Holy City.

I am writing out now the last two chapters of biography Vol 4. I daresay you've heard of Jim Larkin's death. He had a great funeral. That's one thing we Irish can do excellently—give a man a great funeral.

I hope your John has done well, & has won his Doctor's Degree. Imagine the youngster I saw with you on the "Brittannic" [2] a Doctor! And the little lass with him, a blooming young lady now! It's all a great worry, but I think it is good to grow old in the midst of such worries. It must be rather a lonely thing to get grey thinking only of oneself. God be wi' the two of them. And with Kay and you.

> *All the best from*
> *Eileen & me.*
> *Yours as ever.*
> *Sean*

[1] Horace Reynolds, "Successful Mr. Yeats," *Christian Science Monitor,* 30 November 1946, an article on John Butler Yeats, father of the poet.

[2] O'Casey left New York on the *Britannic* on 12 December 1934, after a three-month visit for the American production of *Within the Gates.*

To Lennox Robinson [1]

TC. O'CASEY

[TOTNES, DEVON]
18 FEBRUARY 1947

Dear Mr. Robinson:

Thank you for your letter asking me if I should allow my name to go forward for Membership of the Academy.

Some fourteen or fifteen years ago, G. B. S. wrote and asked me the

[1] Lennox Robinson, Irish Academy of Letters, Dublin.

same thing, but I refused.[2] I'm afraid I must do the same thing again. After all, the Academy has done splendidly without me, and I have done fairly well without the Academy; so, in my opinion, the farther we keep away from each other, the better for both of us.

With all good wishes,

Yours sincerely,
Sean O'Casey

[2] See O'Casey's letter of refusal, "The Academy of Letters," *Irish Times,* 11 October 1932, Vol. I. pp. 451–52.

To John Lehmann [1]

MS. TEXAS

TOTNES, DEVON
19 FEBRUARY 1947

Dear Mr. Lehmann.

I wonder would you do me the favour of saying what you think of the little sketch enclosed. It is from a young soldier, aged 18. As I see it, it is a symbolical representation of a young lad's turn from an impossible lass (Jazz) to a more sensible and genuine—& so more alluring—girl (Beethoven).

To me, there seems to be a promising lilt in the piece, & the imagination of it might conceivably grow into something far finer. I should like to know what you think.

I get a good deal of these things—mostly wretched attempts—, but don't like to pass over anything that has a hint of imagination in it. Recently, I got a sketch from another young soldier—"The Blinds are Down"—a rather poignant sketch of a mother's death, seen thro' the eyes of her child.

So if you can—and if you find time—

Yours sincerely
Sean O'Casey

[1] John Lehmann, founder and editor of *New Writing.*

To Bronson Albery

TC. O'CASEY

[TOTNES, DEVON]
27 FEBRUARY 1947

Dear Mr. Albery:

Thanks for your letter. Now that [F. J.] McCormick has refused the part of FEELIM,[1] I can say that I'm not sorry. I didnt want to come close to any of the old Abbey actors again. I've got enough of them. Anyway, with the film aroma around him, he mightnt be able to fit into the character. I am sure we made a mistake in not asking Eddie Byrne first. I should have liked to have had him. I am not surprised to hear he has refused. I guessed he would. The asking of McCormick first went all over Dublin, and of course Byrne knew about it; and Eddie Byrne is a proud fellow, if I'm any judge of men. So he said, "to hell with them; let them get whomsoever they can now." Well, that's a fellow after mine own heart. It is a disgrace to the English Theatre that Byrne should have been allowed to go quietly back home. We've lost, in my opinion, an exquisite artist. I dont think you'll get [Noel] Purcell. He has a fine job in Dublin, and is very popular with his audiences. I dont think it wise to appeal to Ria Mooney. She's a charming lass, and I like her well; but she has definite, very definite limitations with regard to knowledge of fine acting and original production. She is one of the big crowd who take the line of least resistance. That is fatal in the realm of imagination. On the whole, there is no-one more likely—not excepting McCormick—who could do the part with Eddie Byrne.

Breon is doing well. He looks a fine figure in uniform, with his white lanyard cord, his yellow flash, and the red and blue insignia of the Royal Artillery. He has had a tough time of it, on account of the weather. They have had to leave their huts because all the pipes burst, and the place was a rolling river; and they sleep all together now in the gym. First thing, every morning, they have had to do for weeks is to dig the guns out of the snow. But he looks fit and bronzed. We have had our share of it here, having to plod, plough, and plunge through deep snow to get whatever bread, milk, and spuds we could gather together. It's a little better now. One dark, snowy evening, returning from the town, Eileen slipped on a patch of ice, fell on the back of her head, and cracked it open. She lay unconscious for a time, but the cold awoke her, and she managed to totter home, dazed, and bleeding (before coming in to me, she took off her rubber boots at the door, for fear of spoiling the hall—oh, these women!) Fortunately, our doctor very generously braved the snowy night and the icy

[1] Feelim O'Morrigun in *Oak Leaves and Lavender*. The role was finally played by Fred Johnson of the Abbey Theatre.

roads to come to us. He stitched her head, dressed it, and, after some days in bed, she got better, and went about with a bandage. She's allright again, now; but it was a very narrow escape. So take care of yourself and of Una in Switzerland. All are well here, bar meself, who has had influenza some months ago, and hasnt been able to shake off a whoreson cough since; but I manage to split a few logs daily to keep a few of the home fires burning. At the moment, I am doing the last few chapters of my 4th vol. of biographical experiences, and, of course, various odds and ends of articles.

Regarding Miss [Margaret] Webster: I think it might be well to wait a little to see if anything better should turn up. [John] Golden's fear is a common one. No-one can tell about a play. 20 managers refused TOBACCO ROAD, but it afterwards ran for seven years; and GLASS MENAGERIE was refused by as many, and it afterwards ran for three years, or more. I'll write again. . . .

[*Sean O'Casey*]

To Cynthia Walsh [1]

TS. MACMILLAN, N.Y.

TOTNES, DEVON
4 MARCH 1947

Dear Miss Walsh:

I enclose two photos done by the Black Star Photographic Co., which may be of interest—one of meslf and one of the whole family. I presume that they will have to be paid for, or a fee given, if used. I am writing to them to say I'm sending them to you.

As for additional biographical stuff, what am I to say? Well, "I am just now working at the two last chapters of the fourth biographical vol.[2] which ends on the note of my departure from Ireland to fresh woods and pastures new. As you may be aware, we are all having a stiff time of it here— literally a stiff time, what with the venomous frost and the cold, cloying snow. Sun, moon, and stars have been hidden for a long time. And, as you know, fuel is very scarce. Some time ago, we had to plough our way through snow, knee-deep, to the town to get what we could of bread, milk, and spuds. When I say "we," of course, I mean all as well as ourselves. And we have to go canny now with firing; sometimes, when current has to be saved, to sit in top coat—and gaiters, if we had them. And we have

[1] Cynthia Walsh, Macmillan Company, New York.
[2] *Inishfallen, Fare Thee Well.*

to make full use of every fire we happen to have. For instance hardly a night goes by that there aren't things hanging before the fire I have that they may be dry for those who need them. As I write this, the fire is hidden by socks and singlets drying for one of our boys. One night, black with frost, my wife was coming home from the town when she slipped on an ice-patch, fell on the back of her head, and cut it open. There was no one around, but the cold shook her out of her coma, and she managed to get up, and stagger home. But, at the door, she halted to take off her thick boots so that she would not soil the hallway—and she bleeding badly and half unconscious! However, our doctor risked the blizzard and the icy road to come to us, stitch the wound and dress it; and she's OK again. The bright, careless days are gone, and we won't have them again for some years. There is nothing to be done, except our best to meet problems as they arise, and solve them.

All Americans who come close to here, usually ring me up, and ask to come over. The other day, an officer on a merchant vessel, whose ship ran into Plymouth out of a storm, came to see me, and we had a long talk about the theatre, there with you, and here with us; and about painting, and about books. He lives in 8th Street, N.Y. (The big boy in the photo, Breon, is now a gunner in the Royal Artillery; the younger, Niall, and the girl, Shivaun, are at school. My wife, Eileen, never has a minute, what with rations, coupons, and points, and with all the work to be done; but she is hearty and courageous, and faces a busy—sometimes a hard—life well.) I can't think of any more to say except to send my love to all my friends in your great City.

Yours very sincerely,

A Big PS. The address of the Firm that took the Photos is: The Black Star Publishing Co., Clifford's Inn, Fleet Street, London, E.C. 4.
P.T.O.
overleaf
I think the Black Star Co. has a Branch—or Headquarters—in New York.

Official notices say milder weather is a cumin in. Hurrah! We won't miss the scarcity of coal so much—when it comes.

It is now 1:45 in the morning. All the family are fast asleep, and it's near time I had a doze too. I have just typed 2000 words of a biographical chapter; written a number of letters; looked up some passages in Dr. Coulton's "Five Hundred Years of Religion," [3] and feel inclined to call it a day.

I enclose the remarks on the flap of the English Edition of "Oakleaves & Lavender," and think that what is said there (or something like it) would do well for what you might think of saying about it.

So, my dear Cynthia, good night, and peace be with you.

Yours very sincerely again,
Sean O'Casey

[3] George Gordon Coulton, *Five Centuries of Religion* (1923–50), 4 vols.

To D. L. E. Curran [1]

MS. CAMB. U. HIB. SOC.

TOTNES, DEVON
7 MARCH 1947

My dear Mr. Curran.

Can't come to you. I wish I could. Too old now to be running around, & too, too much to do. And not all "literary" work either—just split a lot of logs to keep the poor home fires burning.

Indeed, and I'd like, if I could, to come & spend an hour or two among the Cambridge Hibernians. I did go once there to speak—some 12 years ago,[2] but never met an Irishman. Anyway, what do you want a "literary" talk for? What is "a literary subject"? God forgive yous! And why "non-political"? D'ye mean that Ulster can sit down & talk to Connacht; or that, in the Union, Free State and Sinn Fein join hands together? Surely, you're all interested in life, & don't politics deal with life? A damned sight more than literature, I'm afraid.

From your letter, I take it you're all young fellows. Well, then, the world's with you to make or mar it. And literature, too. Don't bother about what I think. What you think is of much more importance. And each of you know as much about literature as I do; & maybe more.

But I would like to go among you, not to air my views, but to have a chat, & hear what you are thinking about Eire and the wide world—but that isn't possible now.

Please thank Mr. Barnes for his offer of entertainment, & if he be ever my way, or you, ring me up, & we'll have a cup o' kind tea together.

With all good wishes to the Cambridge Irish,
Yours very sincerely,
Sean O'Casey

[1] D. L. E. Curran, Cambridge University Hibernian Society.
[2] See "The Holy Ghost Leaves England," Vol. I, pp. 603–5, a draft of the talk O'Casey gave at the Shirley Society of Cambridge University in 1936. See also the chapter "Cambridge," *Sunset and Evening Star* (1954).

To George Jean Nathan

TS. CORNELL

TOTNES, DEVON
14 MARCH 1947

My very dear George:

I was sorry indeed to hear that you had been down with illness. Of course, you must be often surrounded with infection at the theatre—people will come with colds on them. However, it's possible to pick up these damned viruses anywhere—even on a quiet country road. I was down myself with a touch of influenza, and have neither been in theatre nor church for many, many years. I hope you went into an hospital or a nursing-home while you were ill. It isn't nice to be lying alone when one is ill. I don't think you could expect to get proper attention at the Royalton. Anyway, try to take care of yourself in the future.

We have been snowbound here for quite a time; had to trudge (or the wife had) through deep snow to the town to gather what we could get of milk, bread, and spuds; and every damned pipe in the house spraying jets of water everywhere. As you say, things aren't too good here, but they could be worse. Ireland is ten times worse off; in fact, she couldn't be in greater trouble. I have had a letter from one saying armchairs were broken up to give a little heat for a little while; while all the bishops are proclaiming that the ills of the world come out of the brains and bowels of Communism.

There's to be a production of OAK LEAVES AND LAVENDER here in early spring, so it is planned. I am in no way enthusiastic about it. It was to be a grand thing; but it has been decided that it is "a short-run play," and so comes under the Arts Council policy of no profit, no taxation. The Producer [1] is a curious fellow—alert, overwhelmingly confident, and over sure of his own opinions. He is what he calls "a realist," and doesn't like anything puzzling or picturesque or what might be too imaginative for an audience to grasp; so he is striving to "make the play as normal as possible." I have let him cut quite a lot out—I am getting too old and too tired to argue—, but have just refused a request to change the figure of Young Son of Time from an expressive costume to fit him into a modern one—overalls or dress-suit, I suppose. Taking out as much as possible of the very thing I laboured so hard to put into it—and before any rehearsal had taken place. I had the same thing with RED ROSES. Both of the producers are teachers of dramatic art, especially production and acting, so one can't oppose a teacher. It is very annoying but it can't be helped. I don't doubt Oakleaves and Lavender will get a very competent

[1] The director, Ronald Kerr. See O'Casey's letter to Mary Hinton, 19 May 1947, note 2.

production; but it won't be the play I wanted to see on the stage. Sorry that the young lads who were interested in The Silver Tassie couldn't gather enough to put it on. Better fortune next time to them and to me.

I have just finished another vol. of biography, which ends this work for awhile. I end it when I leave Ireland, and am calling it (I had a trying time thinking of a title; Clock Strikes Twelve was used as a title a few months ago here) Goodbye At The Door.[2]

I am sending you a curious review of Drums Under the Windows by Sean O'Faolain,[3] of whom you have probably heard. He is a clever writer, but doesn't like my work. Years and years ago, he wrote to me asking me to write an article round Countess Markievicz [4]—he was editing a series of articles on her for some English big weekly; and also he wanted me to write four or five articles on Famous Irishmen for the same Journal, for which I was to get £200, or £250, if I demanded it. Faolain added that if I did this, it would give him a leg-up to a job on the paper's staff. I wanted the money very badly at the time, but couldn't conscientiously write about famous men in the popular way the paper desired, and so I refused. I'm afraid Faolain, either consciously or unconsciously remembers this against me. I may be wrong. But why he should have added a private letter to his public criticism, I can't understand. It seems to me to be a crawling letter, full of apology for a criticism that he should have let stand, or not written at all. But the point that amuses me is that while he blames me for my bad English, his own in the review is as bad, or, maybe, worse than mine. The "mutilated" copy he mentions is one that was sent to me by The Bell—after I had asked for it—with two pages of the review missing, including the worst example of his own bad English. He has followed me since AE sent him over, or asked him to go to it, to write a criticism of The Silver Tassie, then running in London. You should have seen the criticism![5] Funnily enough, apropos of Faolain's contention that [George] Moore's English or art got better as he practised and studied it, Desmond McCarthy in The Sunday Times, the other day said it got worse.

But the fact is, as far as I can judge, O'Faolain is keeping within the borders of the Canonical Law; and, with things as they are in Ireland, few can blame him. But I am not in Ireland, and, even if I were, I wouldn't give a damn about them.

By the way, George, can you give me [Thomas] Quinn Curtiss's address. I owe him a letter for a long time; I have searched high up and low down for one of his letters to me, but can't find one. I shall be very much obliged if you can send it to me.

[2] *Inishfallen, Fare Thee Well.*
[3] Sean O'Faolain, "Too Many Drums," *The Bell,* December 1945.
[4] See O'Casey's letter to O'Faolain, 10 August 1932, Vol. I, pp. 446–47.
[5] Sean O'Faolain, *"The Silver Tassie* Staged," *Irish Statesman,* 19 October 1929. It is a hard review which condemns the play and urges O'Casey to come back to Ireland to his old themes and techniques.

I will send you a copy of Irish Writing, containing my article [6] (it mentions you) when it comes. But I'm afraid the coal shortage has shut down nearly all the printers of Ireland, bar the dailies.

I have just got a letter from that Producer saying "Fundamentally I think we are in agreement as to the symbol of the Young Son of Time. The interpretation, however, still worries me, and, at the moment, intrudes in the prologue rather than assisting it." He can't see the figure is meant to "intrude" on the shadowy dancers, and isn't meant to be an assistant. I have let him cut a lot in the rest of the play, simply because I am too tired of it all to argue; but it is a mistake to be amiable. He has said in the letter that he "proposes to brave the blizzard, and pay a flying visit to Totnes." I have telegraphed him not to come, and that the Prelude must stand. But it is very wearying. It's a divine pity that there aren't more like you, who judge a work as a whole, rather than by a chip here and there. But there's only one Nathan.

> And I send my love to him.
> My love, secondly, too, to Eugene,
> hoping he is keeping fairly fit.
> Ever yours,
> Sean O'Casey

[6] Sean O'Casey, "Tender Tears for Poor O'Casey," *Irish Writing* No. 2, June 1947; reprinted in *The Green Crow* (1956).

To Bronson Albery

TC. O'CASEY

[TOTNES, DEVON]
27 MARCH 1947

Dear Mr. Albery:
Thank you for your letter, dated the 24th of March. I dont think there should be any reference in the Press, or in the programme, about the revisions in the text [1] for the purpose of production, as distinct from the full measure given in the printed book of the play. There are good reasons why I couldnt agree to this. Although I have consented to the revisions, or, rather deletions, I have never agreed to them; nor did I agree to them in the case of RED ROSES FOR ME. To allow them is one thing, to be satisfied with them is quite another. Mr. [Ronald] Kerr (as in the case of Ria Mooney) is a teacher,[2] and likes everything to be extremely accurate

[1] *Oak Leaves and Lavender,* which had been published on 30 April 1946.
[2] Ronald Kerr was a teacher at the Royal Academy of Dramatic Art, London.

according to his own ideas of accuracy, which is natural; but nevertheless doesnt fall into line with my view of the way things happen, or the way in which things should be done. All teachers of drama are mad on what G. B. Shaw calls "the well-made play." Now I have no respect for what Mr. Kerr regards with profound reverence. Indeed, I have laboured to undermine it, and make something of a laugh of it. I agree that the "well-made play" makes it easier for producer and for actor, but I am not out to make things easy for either the one or the other. No-one who aims at writing good drama can be, and that's the end of it. Mr. Kerr (and Miss Mooney) thinks that what he likes is "realism," but it is simply the common-place carpentry of dove-tailing things very neatly together; a thing that any competent craftsman can do. I give an instance of what I am driving at—You may remember Ria's statement to you in a letter, which said that "Eddie Byrne wasnt a good actor." Of course she's right—he is neither a good nor a bad actor. He is a first-class artist. One can get thousands of good (and bad) actors; but the artist is a rara avis indeed. Byrne would—from what he did in "Red Roses," be a splendid Polonius, a Capt Shotover, an Uncle Vanya, and maybe, a fine Lear. It was a shame to the English Theatre that he was allowed to go. But there you are. Think of what "Red Roses" would have been without him! But teachers of dramatic art have to concentrate on the little men and women; the big ones are a nuisance.

We have been having a spot of trouble here; I've had influenza which has left me with a whoreson cough, and the little girl, Shivaun, is recovering from lumbar pneumonia. She was very bad, but Penicillin pulled her out of danger. Had an experience last night: a second officer of a ship (Desmond Brannigan) driven into Plymouth by a heavy gale, came to see me, and stopped the night. He was reared up in an Irish Industrial School—a place, governed by Christian Brothers, where little is learned, and boys are knocked senseless for not showing sufficient reverence to catechism and saints; where the world, the flesh, and the devil are beaten out of them by main force. Well, here was this fellow, well read, having taught himself trigonometry, and all navigational problems, sailing the world's seas; and I learned quite a lot of the secrets of the deep sea sailors. All the night before, he had been up to his waist in the sea swamping over the deck, helping to get his vessel safely into Plymouth Port. The world doesnt go too well for sailors. Hope you both are well. All best wishes.

Sean O'Casey

To Mrs. Isabella Murphy

MS. MURPHY

TOTNES, DEVON
31 MARCH 1947

Dear Bella,
    Enclosed please find twelve One Pound Notes, which I hope may be of some use to you.[1]

Yours sincerely,
S. O'Casey

Delay caused by influenza and pneumonia in the family. Please acknowledge.

    [1] The insurance money for O'Casey's brother Michael's death. See O'Casey's letter to Mrs. Murphy, 24 January 1947.

To Jack Carney

MS. NYU LIBRARY

TOTNES, DEVON
16 APRIL 1947

My dear Jack,
    A line or two of greeting from "a feeble tongue." During the past few months I have had influenza three times—three times, mind you! The first & the second, light—just a day or two in bed. And then came the third, a wallop that laid me low, lower, lowest. It became bronchial, & the cough bugling through the house still. On both of Breon's last two leaves, I've been in bed, and not a very bright spark there either. Thanks ever so much for being so kind to him during his stay in London. And give my best thanks to Mina for receiving him, & giving him a chance to feel less lonely. It's not so attractive to be in London, & have nowhere but a barracks to sit at home in. Montgomery's army is in toyland still. And all such a waste, too. 800 millions a year to keep a sword in England's hand! And what is it going to cost to keep a pipe in her mouth? Cigarettes will soon be worth a guinea a box. Our "high standard" will soon be a dream.
    And all the little Conservatives here are foaming at the mouth. They all thought we'd at once go back to the silken dress & the golden slipper. God, if the Tories ever get back, they'll be in a nice pickle! They daren't

go back. They must keep the workers quiet & active; & to do this, they will have to give up Toryism as they knew it, & we knew it.

One of them started on me, before I got ill, but I suggested that what he thought was "Communism," was but a change of life. I told him things were just as bad in Ireland, where no Communist existed, & where everything was Conservative & pure and holy. He didn't like it, & went away muttering.

I hope your digestive muscles are better by now—you shouldn't have gone to Dublin. You & I are getting a bit too old for these activities.

Thanks again to Mina & you for your kindness to Breon.

Yours ever,
Sean

To Lovat Dickson

TS. MACMILLAN LONDON

TOTNES, DEVON
18 APRIL 1947

Dear Mr. Dickson:

Thank you for your kind letter of the 16th inst. Under another cover, registered, I have sent you the MS of the latest vol. of biography—INISH-FALLEN, FARE THEE WELL; eighteen chapters in all.

As well I have sent with the MS, list of contents, and photo for possible frontispiece, and sketches for a possible Jacket, with three additional thumbnail ones for the Spine.

If you could, if it wouldnt be too much bother, I'd like you to let me have back the Cardboard wrapping. This is hard to get now; and we use the piece wrapping the MS to protect stuff we send to our elder boy who is now a gunner in the Royal Artillery.

I suppose you know that OAK LEAVES AND LAVENDER is to open in Cambridge (the Arts Theatre, I think) on the 28th of this month, April; going from there to Bournemouth; and, afterwards, I hope, to the West End.[1] Maybe you'd like to send some of the books of the play to these places. Best wishes to Mr. Daniel and to you.

Yours sincerely,
Sean O'Casey

PS. I have also enclosed, with MS, a description of the sketches, so that the artist will get an idea of what the Hieroglyphics are all about.[2]

[1] The play opened in London at the Lyric Theatre in Hammersmith on 13 May 1947. See O'Casey's letter to Mary Hinton, 19 May 1947, note 2.
[2] The PS was added in longhand.

To Herbert Marshall [1]

MS. MARSHALL

TOTNES, DEVON

15 MAY 1947

Dear Herbert—

No; count me out. I have too much to do, & no time in which to do it.
I have already written an article on "Theatre of the People" [2]—can't remember for what or for whom; & I can't find the mood to do the same
again. I think it was for "New Theatre."

My eyes force me to limit my work, & they have to do all that they
can safely do at present.

I've been in London, & found your letter waiting here for me last
night—hence the delay in replying.

I hope you are doing well. Where's Britten now?

All the best.

Sean

[1] Herbert Marshall (1906–   ), film, theatre, and TV director; author and
translator.

[2] Sean O'Casey, "The People and the Theatre," *Theatre Today,* March 1946; reprinted in *Under a Colored Cap* (1963).

To Mary Hinton [1]

TC. O'CASEY

[TOTNES, DEVON]

19 MAY 1947

Dear Mary:

Many thanks for your very kind letter. The battle has gone against
us, but we havent lost our swords.[2] I wasn't surprised at a lot of what some

[1] Mary Hinton, Lyric Theatre, London.

[2] *Oak Leaves and Lavender* opened on 13 May 1947 at the Lyric Theatre,
Hammersmith, presented by Bronson Albery, directed by Ronald Kerr. It received
poor notices, and closed after twenty-three performances on 31 May. Mary Hinton
played Dame Hatherleigh, one of the leading roles; other members of the cast were:
Fred Johnson as Feelim O'Morrigun; Sheila Sim as Monica; Charles Lamb as Mark;

of the critics said. Few of them like an experimental play, and are frightened at anything new, as many are frightened by a new note in a painting, or even a new note in a symphony. I think some of the criticisms are just a little too harsh. The play didnt present itself so badly as they would make out. It is hard after so much hard work by the actors to meet with such determined opposition. I am used to it, and suffer it now with the patience and unconcern of a Stoic. So many of them are so bad themselves even in simple exposition, that it is to me comical to hear them telling others how to do things well. There isnt one of them would be able to sit down and write a harmless one-act play. I enclose two poems by I. B.[3] (you can guess the personality these initials cover), and yet there is none able, none afforded a chance to tell him to stop. He is king in his dominion, absolute and disdainful and minor.

The play, of course, is far from flawless; but it was marred in the very beginning by the choice of a most unsuitable producer. I guessed that when he first came down here to talk about it. "We must make the play as normal as possible," he said, and then the bell tolled. With an experimental play one has got to encourage, not only encourage, but emphasise, the newness, or leave it alone. To modify it, as was done with ours, is to harass it, twist it, distort it from its new shape till it has no shape at all, or very little. I am indeed sorry for the artists. They didnt, in my opinion, get what we in Ireland call Fenian justice—bare and impersonal judgement on what is said or done. You were grand, and got less than you deserved; Drishogue, Edgar, and Monica were good; Jennie and Joy less so, but not bad; and Pheelim or Feelim did his best. But, it seemed to me, [Ronald] Kerr had got them into a nervous state; and, though I did my best to give them confidence, the nervousness had gone too deep. Oh, those speeches! Destitute of fury, full of sound, and signifying nothing! And the Design was flat and without any imagination. I should have tried my hand myself, but I didnt get a chance. I wanted a young producer—him who did the first show of THE STAR TURNS RED for Unity,[4] and afterwards served in the Navy. A fine chap, and one with whom I could have ventured with confidence. But he hadnt name enough, and wouldnt be chosen. At present he is the Producer for the Children's Theatre. He certainly would have been a less risk than Kerr; for he loved the play, and was very anxious to do it. A puzzle to me is why the weakness wasnt spied

Joyce Marwood as Jennie; June Whitfield as Joy; Reynor Healy as Constable Sillery; Kenneth Brown as Constable Dillery; Edward Golden as Drishogue; Alec Ross as Edgar; Marjorie Ziedler as Mrs. Watchit; Bertram Shuttleworth as Michael; Janet Borrow as Mrs Deeda Tutting; Oliver Burt as Abraham Penrhyn; Robert Urquart as Mr. Constant; June Whitfield as a Seller of Lavender.

O'Casey made one of his infrequent trips to London for several days to attend final rehearsals and the opening night.

[3] Ivor Brown, drama critic of *The Observer,* wrote an unfavorable review on 18 May 1947.

[4] John Allen directed the premiere of *The Star Turns Red* at Unity Theatre on 12 March 1940. See James Agate's review of the play, Vol. I, note 1, p. 849.

out in the book, printed more than a year before the play was done. The book got good, sometimes glowing, notices; but something went wrong, and I can put my finger on one of the reasons. Well, we must live through the disappointment, Mary. At least I share in the hard work that went in the making of the play, working on it for near two years; so the actors dont suffer alone. Kerr gets out of it the easiest.

One good, very good thing the play did . . .[5]

[5] Page missing.

To Jack Carney

MS. NYU LIBRARY

TOTNES, DEVON
24 MAY 1947

My very dear Jack,

When I got back here, I found a pile of letters waiting—oh, these letters! I answered a few of them anyway.

I have to thank you for that fine book of Mencken's on the American language; [1] & for Maxwell's odd and most interesting one on the "98" Rebellion,[2] about which no-one fears to speak of now since Sean T [O'Kelly] . . . to quote himself . . . declared that "He was the Authorised Version showing St Patrick's prayer had been answered," and Ireland was free. Eire's Authorised Version! Where is Wolfe Tone, where is Pearse?

Mina's and your home made a fine and enjoyable resting place for us all while we were in London; & I've written my thanks to Mina (who had all the trouble) for her kindness.

Yesterday, I got from Moscow the Russian translation of "I Knock at the Door," [3] the first of mine to be printed. I am sorry, in a way, that they did it, for I don't see how the translator could capture the Irish idiom. It would be better for me if they had waited till they knew more about us, & the ways of Eire, with her Authorised Version of Freedom, in top hat and frock coat, trotting after the clergy.

I let the S. Graphic man come down here to have a chat. He was a

[1] H. L. Mencken, *The American Language* (1919; enlarged and rewritten, 1936).
[2] William H. Maxwell, *History of the Irish Rebellion of 1798* (1891).
[3] *Ya Stuchus' V Dver'. Na Poroge* (1946), a Russian edition of the first two volumes of O'Casey's autobiography: *I Knock at the Door,* translated by V. Toper, N. Daruzes, M. Lorie, O. Kholmskaya, N. Volzhina, E. Kalashnikova, and I. Kashkin; and *Pictures in the Hallway,* translated by N. Volzhina, O. Kholmskaya, N. Daruzes, V. Toper, E. Kalashnikova, and M. Lorie.

rather decent chap, a little timid; but listened to my ideas of what life was, & what it could & ought to be. He had an Irish mother, so there was a kinship between us inasmuch as I had one, too.

I hear there's a difference between Dartington's new Drama Organiser, & Mrs. E[lmhirst] over a production of "The Trojan Women." All who saw it, that I met, said it was "terrible"—or a word to that effect; & so said all the Dartonians who were present; & the Organiser said so too. Suddenly, Mrs. E. said it "was a most artistic production," & all Dartonians said so suddenly too; leaving the Organiser agape & gawking! Now he doesn't know whether to agree with the crowd, or go.

Sweet Jesus, have pity on us!

All the best,
Sean

To Mina Carney

MS. NYU LIBRARY

TOTNES, DEVON
[24 MAY 1947] [1]

My very dear Mina,

Well, here we are at home again, after a spell in a home away from home, which, of course, means your home. There's no thanks competent to deal with your kindness, practical and complete, which we so much enjoyed while we were in London; and which has been so generously extended to Breon, too, during his stay in the Army there. It is all very kind of you and Jack, & we are all very grateful to you both.

I hope the pain in your ear will have gone by the time you get this. Do your best to take it easy, & stay as long as you can in Margate, if you & Jack like it (There's no reason you should, just because we did), for the air is bracing; and, if only the weather be kind, it should do you both a lot of good.

The play, I believe, hangs on still. There's a fine article (from my point of view) in this week's "Cavalcade"; [2] sent to me, I think, by the

---

[1] This letter probably accompanied O'Casey's letter of the same date to Jack Carney. It indicates that O'Casey and his wife stayed with the Carneys in their Cliffords Inn flat near Fleet Street while O'Casey was attending rehearsals and the opening of *Oak Leaves and Lavender*.

[2] Hayter Preston, "O'Casey and the Critics," *Cavalcade*, 24 May 1947, had some favorable comments on the dramatic technique in the later plays, following the production of *Oak Leaves and Lavender*.

writer. But of course it can't do the play any good—[Ronald] Kerr did his work too badly.

Don't entertain too much. Get your rest. We all need what rest we can get to soften the effects of the years of war.

Many thanks again for your dear kindness.

Love,
Sean

To Jill Howard

TC. O'CASEY

TOTNES, DEVON
5 JUNE 1947

Dear Jill Howard:

Harry was right not to go to see the play [*Oak Leaves and Lavender*]. It was just a fine dream turned into a nightmare. I am largely to blame myself. When the Producer came down here first, I saw plain that he wasnt the man for a play of mine, but I hadnt the courage to tell him to go off, and keep to plays that were trite and inconspicuously bad. He was an odd fellow, a one who could keep talking for hours without saying a single thing. The first thing he aimed at was "to make the play as normal as possible" and in trying to do so, quite evidently made it the most abnormal play performed in London for a very long time.

With an imaginative play, having new ideas in it, the thing not to do is to try to banish every new feature from it, in fear and trembling; and the thing to do is to boldly set them forward, emphasise them even, and produce the play in a new manner, as Raymond Massey did with THE SILVER TASSIE, and Melvyn Douglas did with WITHIN THE GATES in New York. But the producer of OAKLEAVES was afraid of every-thing novel, and ran away from it; and so harassed and cut the play, making the Caste as nervous as himself, that it appeared as a frightened thing, apologising for its appearance on the stage. Unfortunately, the Man-ager took the side of the producer, and contested everything that I pro-posed when I got well enough to go down to Eastbourne to see the play.

The worst thing is that such productions make it harder than ever to have a good play produced; and audiences fight shy of anything they think is to be other than what they are used to.

But it is all over now, and I shall, I hope, be wiser next time.

I wont be in London for some time, but thank you for your very kind invitation. I am sorry to hear about Harry's handicap. These damned wars! I dont think the people will allow another war. We have too much to do with life to be bothering about death. I do hope Harry may soon be all-right again.

I am sending back the B[ook] Token you so kindly sent to me. You will understand that having signed the book quite readily, it would trouble my mind if I took advantage of your kindness.

With all good wishes to you both,
Yours very sincerely,
[Sean O'Casey]

To Arthur Calder-Marshall [1]

TC. O'CASEY

[TOTNES, DEVON]
9 JUNE 1947

Dear Mr. Calder-Marshall:
Thank you for your letter. Imagine meeting for the first time at a Lady Rhondda Party! A hen-head and cocktail party. My first and last one. It is rarely that I go to London, so you may knock me out of your idea for interviews. Besides, I dont like to, and I dont know how, talk about my work.

When I get an American production, it is a good one; one about which there can be no complaint; but they come seldom.

I certainly never met a Backer "loving the theatre so much that they are prepared to lose money putting on good plays." Experimental plays will never get a dog's chance under the commercial way of the present-day theatre. The only chance I ever got here was when C. B. Cochran put on THE SILVER TASSIE. But then Cochran really loved the theatre, and had knowledge and genius to make that love effective. It is he who should be at the Head of the Arts Council. If this Council goes on, as it is going on, putting on plays badly done, miserably helped, it will kill all chance of newness in the theatre, and will rest a humbug and a sham.

Oddly enough, this play at the moment, has been enthusiastically [received] in Dublin at the Commercial Theatre called The Gaiety, has been retained for another week, and may run into a third.[2] Last time

---

[1] Arthur Calder-Marshall, BBC, London.

[2] *The Silver Tassie* was revived at the Gaiety Theatre, Dublin, on 26 May 1947 for a two-week run, directed by Ria Mooney, starring Noel Purcell as Sylvester Heegan and Pat Nolan as Harry Heegan.

(done by the Abbey years ago, and never touched again) it caused a hell of a row. Actually, I got more from the production of my plays from Ireland than I do here.

All the best wishes, and tell Lady Rhondda that the USSR is still going strong, and the Red Star fills a bigger space in the sky.

All good wishes,
Yours sincerely,
Sean O'Casey

To Jack Carney

MS. NYU LIBRARY

TOTNES, DEVON
10 JUNE 1947

My dear Jack,

Thanks for the ribbon which came safe and sound.

Oakleaves had a horrible last week—only a few coming in each night. It was as bad as the fate of "Within the Gates," when it was done here.

Strangely enough, the Dublin Gaiety has just put on "The Silver Tassie" (of all plays!), and it has been "enthusiastically received." Put on for a week, it is to have a second week, and—according to the owner, Mr. Selby, may have a third. And looka the row there was over it before—priests & friars denouncing it; B. Macnamara declaring it an outrage, & resigning from the Abbey;[1] & the Abbey itself leaving it severely alone when the one week ended. That was in 1935; so twelve years later, on it goes at the Gaiety, & is "enthusiastically received."

You never know!

I hope you & Mina are having a good time. The weather hasn't been too good. It has been cold & rainy here; but today—Tuesday—looks better. On cold days seaside places aren't happy. But the English climate is a perjured bitch.

You never know.

Anyway, the air should do you good; & I hope your typewriter has ceased its clicking for a spell.

All the best to you & Mina.
Sean

[1] See Brinsley Macnamara's statements on *The Silver Tassie* in the *Irish Times*, 3 September and 7 October 1935, Vol. I, pp. 583–84, 588–89.

To Herbert Marshall

MS. MARSHALL

TOTNES, DEVON

11 JUNE 1947

Dear Herbert,

I can't remember any of the "New Theatre" article; [1] but you can use it, if you like. Enclosed is one I wrote long ago for a thing called "Counterpoint" which never appeared. It might suit you better. If it does, or if it doesn't, let me have it back on your life. I like to have a copy of everything I may have said about people & things; & this I send you is the one copy I have.

My "agents" are, in America—The Richard Madden Play Co. (Richard J. Madden), New York, in England, The League of Dramatists.

All the best,
Sean

[1] See O'Casey's letter to Marshall, 15 May 1947, note 1.

To Jean E. Smith [1]

TC. O'CASEY

[TOTNES, DEVON]

16 JUNE 1947

My dear Miss Jean:

Good God, what is it you are telling me! That "under the terms of the endowment of the College, no political activities were to be allowed." What endowment, whose endowment? When was it made? Did God Almighty whisper it to Moses on the top of Mount Sinai when He was handing over the Ten Commandments? Or is it one of the clauses in the Atlantic Charter; or is it a sentence in the Bill of Wrongs, of an amendment of the Magna Carta? Who is responsible for it? Is the endowment to turn the graduates and undergraduates into a group of dummies? Why if this is to be the case, and the young people of Exeter College decide to abide by the "terms of the endowment," then the very stones of your city will cry out and mutiny. Did the Endower think that his (or her) little bag of coins

[1] Jean E. Smith, Honorary Secretary, Literary Society, Guild of Undergraduates, Exeter College, Exeter, England.

would form a barricade against thought, and the blossoming of thought in living speech? If he (or she) did, then you young people let it be known that coin cant stop the tongue from moving. Some time ago, we heard a lot of "let the people sing," now it would appear that they arent to be let to even speak. And of all persons, college lads and lasses! These have no excuse for remaining silent as to what they think about the ways of life, for, from an educational point of view, they have had all or most of the advantages life can give them. If they be afraid to speak, then let the stones speak out; for these can allege no excuse either to God or man. They remain silent at the peril of their souls welfare. If those who receive the best knowledge education can give elect to sing dumb, then who is to lead us? What shall we think of intellectuals who have nothing to say about the things that concern life?

Let ye be full of courage, and let ye care not a tinker's damn for the terms of any endowment if such a thing stand in the way of human thought and bold expression. Fight it till it dies, and then bury it in an unknown grave.

Of course you have my permission to publish my letter, and may it strengthen you to do what you think well to do in the problems of life that confront us all.

Yours very sincerely,
Sean O'Casey

To George Jean Nathan

MS. CORNELL

TOTNES, DEVON
[? JUNE 1947]

My very dear George:

I am sending you, with this letter, the magazine holding the article [1] I mentioned long ago, & which I said I'd send you. The magazine was to appear last Feb., but the English banned the sales of periodicals & magazines from Ireland (to give preference to those from the U.S.A.), & so plans had to be altered, preventing its publication till this month.

I daresay you've heard something about the London production of "Oak Leaves & Lavender." It was a ghastly thing; but it was so bad that it was partly comical. The Producer was the most conceited, self assured mortal I ever met; & the very first interview I had with him, it didn't need

[1] See O'Casey's letter to Nathan, 14 March 1947, note 6.

God to tell me he wasn't the man for me. A Cissy, too, be God! But he had been chosen by the Manager, & there he was, telling me "that he was a stern Realist; that the imagination in the play should be tempered down as much as possible; and that he would labour hard to make the play normal." Actually, he made it one of the most abnormal plays ever appearing on the English stage. I was intermittently ill (thank God!) at the time, & couldn't attend the first rehearsals. When I got down, I found the play in an awful state, the actors half out of their minds, all the intricate parts left to their own devices, and the Manager ready to pounce & condemn any criticism or suggestion I had to offer. I stayed three days, where the company was, & during that time was allowed 3 hours' rehearsal. I just had to let the play go to hell, straight there it went, in a violent hurry, too.

I haven't been too well lately. The doctor thinks it may be a spot on a lung, so I am to have an X ray examination. I have sent in the MS for the fourth vol. of biography, calling it "Inishfallen, Fare Thee Well".

"Oklahoma" [2] is having a great time here. Eileen (the wife) and our gunner son saw it, pronouncing it "superb."

Give my warm regards to Eugene & to Carlotta. Eugene must be mad about his play; but his dismay was nothing to mine.

My love.
Sean

[2] *Oklahoma!* a musical play based on *Green Grow the Lilacs* by Lynn Riggs, music by Richard Rodgers, book and lyrics by Oscar Hammerstein II, opened in London on 30 April 1947.

To Miss Sheila ———

MS. PRIVATE

TOTNES, DEVON
12 JULY 1947

Dear Sheila:

This to thank you for your letter I got some time ago. I've been troubled with a cough for some time (this prevented me from attending rehearsals of my play, which with a producer as "stupid" as your golfing Father C———, made a production that was appalling), & an X Ray examination has shown the lungs badly scarred with silicosis. Now one doesn't contract silicosis by playing golf. Anyway, my doctor says these scars have wrenched the heart a little, & I must take things easier. It is a nuisance, but it can't be helped. I won't be able to swing an axe to chop wood any more, quoth the raven, nevermore! But I hope to be able to go on writing foolish plays; & I've sent in the MS for another biographical volume, & so give more pain to the C—— Clan. I wonder from what group of sweating workers do they derive their income? They certainly dont pick it off the trees. And certainly blokes with four or five pounds a week can't play golf. I daresay Card. Griffin has blessed the sticks!

Anyway, keep caring for yourself, & don't stay in that factory much longer. Why don't you look for a healthier job?

We expect our elder boy home tonight—the artillery gunner—on leave. He is intensely interested in painting, & tells a Picasso from a Braque, a Manet from a Renoir at a glance. The younger one, 12, is a big fellow too, & the girl, 8, is now getting to be a fine swimmer and a good horsewoman.

All the best to you.
Sean

To Jack Carney

MS. NYU LIBRARY

TOTNES, DEVON

17 JULY 1947

My dear Jack,

A line to thank you for the newspapers, home and colonial. Dr. Varian came the other day with the report from the X ray examination: the lungs are scarred by—what d'ye think? By silicosis! I must have had it for years, and didn't know. The scars have wrenched the heart a little from its right place, so I have to go easier. Farewell to the axe & chopping of wood. Well, I have the marks of the proletariat on me anyway. However, I'm told I can use the brain as much as I don't like.

We have Breon with us for 10 days. I see be the papers that the Soillse, Mrs. S. T. O'Kelly, has ladies-in-waiting after her now, wherever she goes. She shall have ladies wherever she goes. A Land of Lords an' Ladies. And d'ye know what "a Soillse"—pro. Súlsheh—means? "Her brightness"! Her man—Sean T. is called "a Shoillse"—"His Brightness"—pro. húlsheh. Are we losing our sense of Humour? An' well His Brightness looks in his frock-coat an' his tall-hat, so he does, says Mick McGilligan's daughter, Mary Anne.

Poor Patrick Pearse!

I hope Mina & you are well. Love from Eileen & me.

Yours as ever,
Sean

To Jack Carney

MS. NYU LIBRARY

TOTNES, DEVON
19 JULY 1947

My dear Jack,

I forgot to add to my letters to you that of course my name can be added to those proposing a Memorial to Jim. If you send me the name to whom a cheque should be made out, I'll send a Pound. I'd rather send something when I give my name. I'm sorry I can't send more. I don't know how this year will go. No word yet about MS of 4 vol. of biography sent to printers long ago.

I thoroughly agree with you about memorial demonstrations. It is inevitable that Jim isn't known to the younger generation. Bill O'Brien & Holy Church saw to that. But these youngsters don't even know much about Easter Week—they were born when it had passed. Some other way should be chosen by which to remember Jim.

Ever yours,
Sean

To Jack Carney

MS. NYU LIBRARY

TOTNES, DEVON
26 JULY 1947

My dear Jack,

I couldn't find the article by [M. J.] McManus in the I.P. [*Irish Press*], but it doesn't matter much. I sent the mag. to George Jean N., & this is what *he* says: "My most dear Sean, I am delighted to have the article on the Irish critics, a deserved and finely murderous job. What a crew they must be! Their opinions of your plays are sorely biassed and supremely absurd." And George Jean knows more about drama than McGilligan McManus.

I am fairly well, though the cough still troubles me a little. I send my love to Barney and Paddy [Larkin]. I didn't write to them as I promised to do; but the fact is I get tired very easily now, and the flesh isn't in any way equal to the spirit. The Fabians are down in Dartington Hall again, & with them is [Dr. C. E. M.] Joad of Joad Hall. Isn't it a pity A. Bevan jokes about the H. of Lords? Why the hell do they keep these fellows going? And making Lords of Labour too. If they had guts they'd turn the lords into Labour, instead of turning Labour into the lords. A group of Dartington students, on their way to the station to go home for the holidays, passed our window, carrying a Red Flag and singing "The Internationale"! Well, it's the one and only thing that can unite the human race—they're right there. Bishop Browne of Galway & Archbishop McQuaid of Dublin can't do it. They can't even unite Ireland.

> *My love to Mina & to you.*
> *Yours as ever,*
> *Sean*

To Daniel Macmillan

TS. MACMILLAN LONDON

TOTNES, DEVON
29 AUGUST 1947

Dear Mr. Daniel:

Greetings. It is some time since I wrote to you, but I know the old Firm is going strong still. I am writing this to put forward a proposal I thought of long ago, but circumstances prevented me from doing so till now. When I was in London for a few days about the production of OAKLEAVES AND LAVENDER [1] (a ghastly time), I intended to ask if I could call on you; but I wasnt well at the time, and was glad to get home. Since then, I have had an X Ray of my chest, which showed the lungs scarred from silicosis which was the cause of occasional pneumonic trouble. This (they say) has wrenched the heart a little from its right place, and I have been told to take things as easy as I can. This is just to explain why I didnt try to see you.

The proposal is this: Would it be good to issue a vol. holding the three plays—"Within the Gates," "Silver Tassie," and "The Star Turns

---

[1] The play opened on 13 May. See O'Casey's letter to Mary Hinton, 19 May 1947, note 2.

Red"? [2] I have rewritten "Within the Gates," making a stage version of it, and so, I think, simplifying its production a good deal, and improving it. The alterations are so many that, I think, it would need a new printing. That was one big reason why I wished to see you. There would be far less alteration of the other two plays. A number of people have written asking for "The Silver Tassie," as the enclosed letter will show.

I dont like to bother you, but I should like to know if there's any chance of a reprint of any of the biographical books, and if there be any other chance of the last one going into publication this year? I was thinking of writing a further vol. dealing with my arrival in England, and carrying it on, maybe, to the day that now is. I'd like to know what you think of this? The last vol. was named "Inishfallen, Fare Thee Well."

On the strength of the royalties last year, we bought a little Ford Car, and now it looks as if we would have to hang it on the Christmas Tree next December. During the war, we got a car, second-hand for £60, but shortly after, had to hang this up too. But we were fortunately able to sell it for exactly what we gave, which was something of a miracle. The one we have now is practically the only one we have ever had. It was very useful last year in bringing the children to school every day during the winter; but this winter, we'll have to get them the best way we can. Eileen, of course, drives it. I dont get into it often, staying quietly here, and getting as much rest as I can. It is hard lines to have to hang it up, but no harder than many more have to bear.

If you happen to be too busy, dont worry to answer these questions. I can wait. At the moment, I am trying to hammer out another play—one with a curious title—COCKADOODLEDOO! [3]

All good wishes,
Yours very sincerely,
Sean O'Casey

[2] This proposal led to the decision to publish the four-volume edition of his *Collected Plays:* Vol. I, *Juno and the Paycock, The Shadow of a Gunman, The Plough and the Stars, The End of the Beginning, A Pound on Demand* (1949); Vol. II, *The Silver Tassie, The Star Turns Red, Within the Gates* (1949); Vol. III, *Purple Dust, Red Roses For Me, Hall of Healing* (1951); Vol. IV, *Oak Leaves and Lavender, Cock-a-Doodle Dandy, Bedtime Story, Time to Go* (1951).

[3] This was the first indication that he had started to write *Cock-a-Doodle Dandy.*

To Jack Carney

MS. NYU LIBRARY

TOTNES, DEVON

10 SEPTEMBER 1947

My dear Jack,

I understand your mind in returning the little we sent to help care for Breon during his free days. It is very good of you and dear Mina. Breon has had a fine pied de terre (is this the correct Latin?) in London, since he went away to do his time.

One can't say much about the Government. Lost sheep who haven't gone astray. They couldn't go astray. Atlee will always have the ermined edge of a peer's robe dangling round his neck. He'll always hold out a pleasant hand to a Knight of the Garter. I see a nice leader in last Sunday Times, saying how sweet were the old days, when, though a rich man would have his Rolls Royce, the worker would have his motor-bicycle; when the rich one went to the Riviera, the worker, at least, went to Calais. Oh, them were th' days, Jack, me son; & well we remember them! I often admired you speeding along on your mother-bicycle—£40, & paid it easily. And d'ye remember me bidding you au revoir, with the ticket in me hand, on me way to Calais or Boulougne? The god-damned liars! Why, we often hadn't the wherewithal to pay our fare from the Pillar to the Phoenix Park. Tuppence it was then, & we hadn't a penny! The unflinching, lousy liars! And these are the boyos to whom Atlee, Bevan, & the rest hold out a friendly hand. "I met th' Earl of Kemsley, & he tuk me by th' hand."

I've set meself down to do another play, & have a good deal of it drafted out. I'm not sure yet how it'll go. Its mise en scene—grand things, these foreign phrases—is Ireland, & I think I'll call it "Cockadoodledoo."

Will you thank Mina for the trouble she is taking to get Breon on his train for a brief visit to us in the week-end? My sincere thanks to her for this, and all. And to you for the ever-welcome papers.

I refused this week a big offer to do a film job for [William] Wyler who did "Mrs. Miniver," & "The Happiest Days of Our Lives." After a telegram, formally refusing, I sent a polite letter. He rang me up (a soft, attractive American voice), & appealed to me. To get out of it, I said I wouldn't be free for a year. He replied he'd willingly wait a year, if I'd promise! I liked his voice, but I had to refuse, for I've more work of my own than I can do. He said I was held in high honour in the U.S.A., & I said I wished they'd play my plays oftener. I was sorry I couldn't take it on, for I liked the gentle, but penetrating, voice.

Ever yours,
Sean

PS. Hope you're allright after Southport. A long trip!

To George Jean Nathan

MS. CORNELL

TOTNES, DEVON

10 SEPTEMBER 1947

My very dear George:

A line to let you know I'm still alive; if not running out in the fields, at least looking out of the window. The X Ray showed lungs scarred by Silicosis, & this (they say) has wrenched the heart a little out of its right place; so (they say) I've got to take things easier. In consequence, I've been very busy. I told you, I think, I'd sent in the MS of another biographical vol.; [1] but, I'm afraid, there's no chance of it being out this year. I am, at the moment, trying to hammer out another play—"Cockadoodledoo," which will, if it be successful, hit at the present tendency of Eire to return to primitive beliefs, & Eire's pre-occupation with Puritanism. I hope it will be gay, with a sombre thread of seriousness through it. Macmillan's propose to print a vol. holding "The Silver Tassie," "Star Turns Red," & "Within The Gates"—a stage version; & I'll send a copy to you when it comes.

We have had a spell of terrific heat here, which left me gasping, but which the children enjoyed. We have, for the first time, a little Ford car in which Eileen (the wife) brings them to the sea, while I potter around trying to escape from thinking of work, but ever forced, groaning, to run to do it.

All the best to you.

Love.

Sean

PS. I enclose cutting of criticism by Agate's successor on "Point Valaine." [2] Read it, and you'll know something of what we suffer here.

[1] *Inishfallen, Fare Thee Well.*

[2] Harold Hobson's review in the *Sunday Times* of Noel Coward's *Point Valaine,* which opened in London on 3 September 1947. Hobson was the successor of James Agate, drama critic of the *Sunday Times* since 1923, who died on 6 June 1947 at the age of sixty-nine.

To Eoin O'Mahony [1]

TC. O'CASEY

TOTNES, DEVON

24 SEPTEMBER 1947

*30 I.R.A. Prisoners in British Gaols
Since 1939* [2]

The Labour Government, if not the Labour Party, will have to be jeopardised if they go the way they are going. There is nothing more pitifully mean than one who seeks power and is afraid of the power when he gets it.

Whether the Irish Government is willing, or not, to take back the imprisoned I.R.A. men is not the point—it is that a Socialist Government should not keep these political prisoners a single second longer in jail. They were moved by idealistic principles, had nothing to gain and all to lose. It is a shocking thing that they should have been treated as criminals. I think their policy was a mistaken one; I thought so all along; but there was nothing of self-interest in it anyway. If the Labour Government have any sense, they would go with bands and banners to the prisons where these men are, open the gates for them, and ask them to join in the fight for human political and economic freedom.

I am not well enough to speak publicly for these fine fellows, but, if my name is of any use to you, it is yours and theirs.

And, by the way, why don't the Bishops—who are forever talking of mercy and forgiveness, speak a word for them? Or the "Republican" Government of De Valera?

Oh what are some of those on the Government benches here, on the Government benches there, and on the benches where the Bishops sit!

All good wishes, and if I can do anything more I'll do it.

Sean O'Casey

[1] Eoin O'Mahony (1904–70), Cork-born barrister-at-law, noted Irish genealogist and popular figure, affectionately known in Ireland as "The Pope O'Mahony"; devoted much of his life to Irish causes, such as the release of IRA political prisoners from British prisons.

[2] O'Casey sent a mimeographed copy of this letter to O'Mahony, who used it, and others from O'Casey, in the campaign to free the thirty Irish Republican Army men serving up to twenty years' imprisonment in Parkhurst Prison, Isle of Wight, for bomb offenses in 1939 in an attempt to dramatize the need to end the partition of Ireland. A slightly shortened and modified copy of the letter appeared in the *Irish Times*, 13 October 1947, with the last two sentences and the phrase about the "Bishops—who are forever talking of mercy and forgiveness," omitted.

To Daniel Macmillan

MS. MACMILLAN LONDON

TOTNES, DEVON
30 SEPTEMBER 1947

My dear Mr. Daniel,

I thought I'd be able to answer your two kind letters long ago; but I've had to leave them aside for the present.

The maid we have had for a year has saved up some money, & she's "off to Philadelphia in the mornin' ' "; or will be off on the 10th of October. This will mean a return to wartime help about the house; so I've used all the time between in getting on with the draft of my new play as fast as possible. When this is done, I shall reply to your two letters. I am sending this as a reason for the delay.

Good health to you & yours.

Yours very sincerely,
Sean O'Casey

To Guy Boas

TS. BOAS

TOTNES, DEVON
14 OCTOBER 1947

My dear Guy,

Fine to hear from you again. I've often thought of you, Cicely, and your boy, Robin. I hope you are all well.

"Boney's Oraculum" [1] was a booklet published by millions in my young days, and sold for 2d. (I think) containing all sorts of oracular statements. It explained the meaning of playing cards, expressing the future fortune of those who shuffled and dealt them; it interpreted dreams; the formation of various things as expressing the coming events in the life of the individual. It was consulted by almost all the poorer people, and of more importance to R. Catholics than the "Key of Heaven"; and to Protestants, more imposing than the Bible. What did it in, I don't know. It gradually lost favour, and died out. It was as good as anything else, any-way, in making the way of this world and the next plain.

[1] Mentioned by "Captain" Boyle in *Juno and the Paycock,* Act II.

The "Clawhammer" coat [2] had nothing to do with a hammer. It was, at first, I think, the colloquial name for a swallow-tail dress coat; but this gave place to a coat worn by respectable tradesmen—especially carpenters —on Sundays, and which was worn at work when it became too faded for festive wear. The pocket behind always held the handkerchief, and sometimes the pipe, and, usually the purse. It was a damned clumsy garment of, invariably, a sombre black. It had nothing to do with nails either. These are carried in a front pocket of the apron.

"Boney's" of course is a shortened form of Bonaparte, probably given to the booklet because this General was alleged to be superstitious, and had a lot of faith in the stars, particularly his own.

I hope this is all clear to you now. I hope Robin will soon be back with you. Wish to God I knew Russian. No, the Russians won't say much; but they do a damned lot; and it's coming home to ourselves now that we've a lot to learn from them in making both ends meet. I've not been too well—silicosis trouble; but I am working on another play. Love to Robin, Cicely, and to you.

Ever,
Sean

[2] Worn by Fluther Good in *The Plough and the Stars,* Act I.

To Jack Carney

MS. NYU LIBRARY

TOTNES, DEVON
31 OCTOBER 1947

My dear Jack,

Hope you are keeping fit & hopeful. I've almost finished a new play— "Cockadoodle Dandy." Possibly cause a row. I daresay you've seen that the Abbey, after a long spell of forgetfulness, have put on the "Plough" again. It's odd they never try one of the more recent plays. I've often tried to determine why, but never could. They never mention them either. They seem to be determined to believe that nothing worth a damn followed the "Plough." Yet in his last book, G. J. Nathan, writing about Barrie's "What Every Woman Knows" says, "O'Casey's 'Red Roses' & 'Purple Dust' make Barrie's play look like a counterfeit penny." It's odd, isn't it?

D'ye remember George Orwell's yelping attack on "Drums Under the Windows"? Well, recently, I've moved from the bottom to the top of the house, Doctor saying "more air at the top." Things became confused, &

straightening out letters, etc, I came across a letter, dated Feb 11th 1935, from Gollancz.[1] He'd sent me a book, asking me to give an opinion, & guiding me by saying that part of it was a piece of literature's best for years, equal to Joyce's best. (He was looking for a free review & advertisement.) I wrote back telling him what I thought, which didn't please him. But the odd thing about the book—"The Clergyman's Daughter"—was that the author was a fella named George Orwell! Now we know where we are.

I see Mr. O'Mahony doesn't quote what I said about the Irish Bishops. Aren't they frightened about these bishops!

Love to Mina & to you.
Yours ever,
Sean

[1] See O'Casey's letter to Norman Collins, 11 February 1935, Vol. I, p. 541, in which O'Casey refused to write a testimonial for George Orwell's *The Clergyman's Daughter*.

To Daniel Macmillan

TS. MACMILLAN LONDON

TOTNES, DEVON
31 OCTOBER 1947

Dear Mr. Daniel:

This is a reply to your letter of the 4th of Sept., and to the one following on the 15th of the same month.

I am enclosing herewith the new tunes for the revised copy of *Within the Gates,* & the old ones, too. I am in a quandary about *The Silver Tassie,* and, to a lesser degree, about *The Star Turns Red.*[1] The revisions I wish to make to these two plays are not very extensive; but I dont quite know how to do them. That is, how I should present them to the compositor for setting up. Can I send the printed book, with the deleted parts marked out, and send the revised version typed out in the ordinary way? Or must the play be done, typed out, in toto?

Perhaps the best thing to do is to do it my own way, then forward it to you, so that you can see what I mean; and you can then tell me if that way be wrong, or unsuitable, and suggest, or tell me, the proper way.

I was a little disappointed to hear that you didnt believe a reprint of a biographical vol. would sell; but you know better than I do about such a question; and it wouldnt be much good putting it forth if it didnt march.

[1] Revisions in these three plays were for the "Stage Versions" in the *Collected Plays,* Vol. II (1949).

The vol. on my impressions since I came to England will take a lot of thinking about; but I may try to start it soon in a rough way. It would be, I think, a more thoughtful one, and less exciting, which may be a good or bad thing. I'm not sure.

I have almost finished my new play, and have decided to call it *Cockadoodle Dandy*.

Thank you very much for your kindness in offering me an advance on the new biographical vol. I dont like the idea of advances very much before the book appears—it seems to me something like running into debt—, and I wont ask for one, unless I need it badly. But should I do so (and I hope I shant), I shall ask you for one, since you are so kind as to suggest it.

Yours very sincerely,
Sean O'Casey

Please see over-leaf.[2]

7 November 1947

Two cases of suspected Infantile Paralysis happened in the school, & our children had to come home, which upset us a little (they come home, anyhow, after school-hours; but this meant they were home all day), & prevented me from finishing the marking of the music.

I have cancelled that part of the music which forms an accompaniment, & have left in only the straight tunes, which, I think, is the best thing to do.

What a number of books you have temporarily out of print! All Dickens' works, too! Bad, bad. I do hope things may be better soon, or a race will grow up knowing very little.

S. O'C.

[2] The remainder of the letter was added later in longhand.

To George Jean Nathan

MS. CORNELL

TOTNES, DEVON
31 OCTOBER 1947

My very dear George:

I am very sorry to hear you have been ill, & do hope you are much better by now. Of course you find it hard to escape anything that may be going, for a crowded theatre carries infection when colds are about. Even I got one in New York when I was there. People will go to the theatre when they should be tied up in their beds.

Your 1946–1947 Theatre Book [1] came sailing in the other morning, and, from what I've read of it, carrying a grand cargo. Richer, I think, than last year's argosy. I haven't read more than a small fourth of it yet. Our Breon (the lad in the artillery) got to know it came, & clamoured so long & so loud for it, that I sent it on, on loan, to him. He has an odd affection for Nathan. Your reviews are the only ones he likes—as far as I know. He went to Holland recently—when he was still at school—, & has written an article on his visit. And topping the article is a quotation from G. J. Nathan, & he begins "The gentle philosophy of George Jean Nathan." And he picked you out himself. Well, he could have a literary affection for many a worse one, anyway. I personally think the lad must have good wit to make such a choice.

I've read your review of O'Neill's play,[2] & a damn fine tribute to Gene it is; and all deserved. I think you're right in saying he goes far deeper than either Shaw or I do.[3] I've often envied him this gift. I've pondered his plays, & tried to discover how he came by it, &, of course, never could; for the man doesn't know himself. He's got it, & we just have to leave it with him. It is a powerful gift, & Gene, thank God, uses it with power & ruthless integrity.

I've almost finished my play, & am calling it "Cockadoodle Dandy." I'm afraid it's a kind of morality play, with Evil & Good contending with each other; but, I think, on different lines. In fact, I'm thinking of giving it the sub-title of "An Immorality Play in Three Scenes." I don't quite know what to think of it myself; but I'll send it on to you when I have it properly typed. I don't imagine Eddie Dowling would tackle it (if he be a good practicing Catholic), but, I imagine there are some characters in it would suit him well.

Mr. [William] Wyler—he who did "Mrs. Miniver" and "Happiest Days of our Lives," wanted me to change a Marseilles play by Pagnol into a Dublin background. He was in London, &, when I refused, came on the phone & appealed to me to let him come to Totnes to talk. It was hard going—he had a very charming American voice—, but I had the hardihood to refuse finally.

My love.
Sean

---

[1] George Jean Nathan, *The Theatre Book of the Year, 1946–1947* (1947).

[2] Eugene O'Neill's *The Iceman Cometh* opened in New York on 9 October 1946 and ran for 136 performances.

[3] In his comprehensive review of O'Neill's play and his career, Nathan made the following comment:

> In a broader sense, [O'Neill] is certainly in no remotest degree the mind that Shaw is—his is an emotional rather than an intellectual; he is not by far the poet that O'Casey is, for in O'Casey there is the true music of great wonder and beauty. But he has plumbed depths deeper than either; he is greatly the superior of both in dramaturgy; and he remains his nation's one important contribution to the art of the drama. (p. 105)

Irish Times

2 DECEMBER 1947

SEAN O'CASEY URGES RELEASE
OF REPUBLICAN PRISONERS

Mr. Eoin O'Mahony, who is campaigning for the release of the 28 I.R.A. prisoners serving sentences at Parkhurst Prison, last week received a letter from Mr. Sean O'Casey, the playwright, on the subject. Mr. O'Casey wrote:

I don't think stress should be put on "deportation to Eire." They should be released as honest men who embraced, maybe, a mistaken policy, who have abundantly paid in punishment for what they did years ago, and should now be released forthwith; released if hearts were honest—with a deep apology and a low bow.

I am surprised Acland [1] hasn't declared in favour of their release; because Acland is a good fellow, and has a warm heart as well as a fair mind.

The Conservatives and Liberals, of course, are seeking the Irish votes because they need them. The Labour men are indifferent because they think they don't need them; but it doesn't matter a damn who gets them out so long as they go free.

It is an extraordinary thing that the Irish Government doesn't ask for their release now. Surely, if they have any wit, they should know that these young fellows have seen—not the errors of their ways or principles, but the error of their tactics, and that when released they will fight for what they believe is right for fatherland and faith in the way we all do—by argument and by vote.

But the Irish Government has a lot to learn. They were as indifferent about the Lane Pictures as they are now about their own imprisoned boys; to keep in power is their Kingdom of God. Is there a single one of Eire's Government, past and present, who hasn't avowed the very principles for which these men are in jail?

As far as I know, de Valera has never expressed regret for heading the civil war, which did so much material harm to Ireland—a harm a million and more times more terrible than all that was done, and all that was thought to be done, by these I.R.A. lads. How can this man, de Valera, and his followers, good Catholics as they deem themselves, be so callously in-

[1] Richard Ackland (1906–   ), Labour M.P.

different to men who continue to practice what they so long and so ardently preached?

To George Jean Nathan

MS. CORNELL

TOTNES, DEVON

2 DECEMBER 1947

My very dear George:
    I have read your Book of the Theatre for 1946–47, and a grand book it is. It is the best of the last three or four—& that's saying a lot. It is a sparkling book, and very serious, with all its sparkle. I'm glad you liked Brigadoon,[1] & didn't find the pipes & kilts so terrible. I used to play the pipes myself—An Piób mór—the War Pipers—, & wore a kilt for years. Now I haven't quite the same veneration for them, though the kilt is a handsome dress. But the Pipes aren't as good as an organ; but they are a grand marching instrument. The Producer of Brigadoon, by the way— Cheryl Crawford—asked me to write a play about Parnell—through Dick [Madden]—, but I was in no mood to do it, & declined. It is maddening to read what was done to "End of Beginning"; &, indeed, to Saroyan's "Hello, out There." [2] Surely, these two things are simple enough to be played simply. Oh, these Directors! Surely what was to be done was to get the humour out of one & the pathos out of the other. The Director with too much "imagination" is as bad as the fellow with none. The boyo [3] who did "Oak Leaves" set out to cut the imagination from an imaginative play; & now, your boyo cut the realism—pathetic & funny—from plays that should have been faced straightly. And when I think of the two common commercial Directors I had once—[Raymond] Massey, for the "Tassie" &

---

    [1] *Brigadoon,* a musical fantasy with book and lyrics by Allan Jay Lerner, music by Frederick Loewe, opened in New York on 13 March 1947.
    [2] In his review of a double bill of Shaw's *Androcles and the Lion* and O'Casey's *A Pound on Demand,* produced at the American Repertory Theatre in New York on 19 December 1946, Nathan objected to the incompetent direction that undermined both works; and this reminded him of an unfortunate project of "about a half dozen years ago," to which O'Casey refers, when he saw a similarly disastrous production of a triple bill of O'Casey's *The End of the Beginning* and two short plays by William Saroyan, *Hello Out There* and *Coming Through the Rye.* See O'Casey's letter to Jack Carney, 9 April 1942, note 1. Nathan attributed the failure of the Shaw play to the youthful and inexperienced director, Schuyler Watts. (*Theatre Book of the Year 1946–47,* pp. 231–39)
    [3] Ronald Kerr.

[Melvyn] Douglas for "Within the Gates"; I offer a prayer to God to give the poor theatre more of them.

[4] . . . "undulating" laughter! Well, as a consistent Christian, I pray God's curse on the Watts with you, & the Ronnie Carr with me.[5]

You give O'Neill a lovely—and a well-deserved—tribute. I think you're right about him going deeper than Shaw or I. And his drawing of a character who never appears is amazing. When I first began playwriting— "Crimson in the Tricolour"—I had a clash with Yeats about this.[6] He said it was impossible to put a Character in a play who never appeared. I contradicted, & now, many years after, O'Neill proves I was right. (I read "The Iceman Cometh" a week or so ago).

I'm quoting your remarks on Father Nagle's play, "On the Seventh Day." [7] It's a lovely description of the stupidity of conceit. We've another in Ireland, a Dominican, who's called "The distinguished Dramatist," who has written two appalling things, and goes about as an infallible critic, & unerring judge of what Drama ought to be.

Thank you so much for sending me your sparkling, splendid book. Your right-hand will never lose its cunning.

I expect to be sending you a copy of "Cockadoodle Dandy," in a few days.

> *I hope you are fit & well.*
> *With my love to Gene & you.*
> *Sean*

[4] A page of this letter is missing.
[5] Schuyler Watts and Ronald Kerr.
[6] See Yeats's critique of *The Crimson in the Tricolour,* 19 June 1922; Lennox Robinson's letter to O'Casey, 28 September 1922; and O'Casey's letter to Robinson, 9 October 1922, Vol. I, pp. 102–5.
[7] See O'Casey's letter to the *Irish Times,* 30 December 1949, note 3.

To John Swift [1]

TC. O'CASEY

TOTNES, DEVON
5 DECEMBER 1947

Dear Mr. Swift:

Thank you for your letter holding the remarkable story of what you have done to establish such an impressive headquarters for your Union.

[1] John Swift, General Secretary, Irish Bakers', Confectioners' and Allied Workers' Amalgamated Union, Dublin.

It is certainly a very fine achievement. I hope the workers will make good use of the treasures in books you have gathered together for their benefit.

I have always thought that Socialists didnt know enough about what their own great men and woman have said—without in the least knowing that they were Socialists—Dickens for one; Byron; Shelley; and I've never met one who had read the trenchant and remarkable things said by the Hero of Khartoum—General Gordon; and the way he was backed up in what he said by General Butler, showing how good men—one from Ireland, the other from Scotland—werent afraid to speak their minds when it was harder to do so than it is now. There is no necessity to mention Tone, Emmett, Mitchel, Lalor, or Pearse; though the nationalist sides of these men are exaggerated at the expense of what they said about social conditions.

I will send you the books autographed as you request. But I wont send you a photograph. I do not want my kisser to shine from any wall.[2] It would greatly embarrass me, and I beg you to put it out of your mind completely.

From the point of view of decoration, let me say, too, that the room will want to be a big one if it is to take on mural decorations. If the room isnt spacious enough, they will look bad, however well they may be done. Dont put them on the wall just for the sake of doing it; if it doesnt add dignity and grace to a wall, then leave the wall alone. The murals in the refreshment room of the Tate Gallery in London, done by a first-class artist (it is said), to me, look horrible. The walls are plastered with them, and there are so many of them that one cant see anything but numbers. Anyhow, whatever be done, my face isnt to appear there.

All the best wishes to your Members and to you.

Yours sincerely.
Sean O'Casey

[2] The union wanted to include a painting of O'Casey in the murals for their new assembly hall, dedicated to the history of bread and labor in Dublin.

To Tribune

5 DECEMBER 1947

I.R.A. PRISONERS

Thirty I.R.A. prisoners have been in British gaols since 1939. Here is a list of them:—

Leo Duignan, Leitrim, 10 years. Michael Fleming, Killarney, 12 years. Charles Casey, Belfast, 14 years. Patrick Deveney, Mayo, 14 years. James

Morgan (McGowen), Belfast, 14 years. Patrick McBrine, Belfast and Birmingham, 15 years. Peter Walsh (Stuart), Glasgow, 15 years. Nicholas O'Cleary (Michael Mason), Ennisworthy, 17 years. Rory M. Campbell, Belfast, 20 years. Martin Clarke,[1] Belfast, 20 years. Joseph Collins MacNessa, Dunmarway, 20 years. Vincent Crompton, Liverpool, 20 years. Patrick Donaghy, Dundalk, 20 years. Patrick Dower, Waterford, 20 years. Dennis Duggan, Tipperary, 20 years. John Duggan, Tipperary, 20 years. Laurence Dunlea, Cork, 20 years. Gerry Dunlop (Lyons), Belfast, 20 years. Joseph Gavahan, Mayo, 20 years. John Glynn, Mayo, 20 years. Gerard Kerr,[2] Belfast, 20 years. Patrick McAleer, Belfast, 20 years. John McCabe, Shercock, Cavan, 20 years. Timothy Murray, Waterford, 20 years. James O'Brian (Evans), Dublin, 20 years. Edward O'Connell, Dublin, 20 years. Patrick O'Connell, Tipperary, 20 years. Eric O'Neill (Thomas Nelson), Belfast, 20 years. Daniel O'Regan, Greenmount, Cork, 20 years. James F. O'Regan,[3] Sunday's Well, Cork, 20 years.

The Labour Government, if not the Labour Party, will have to be jeopardised if they go on the way they are going. There is nothing more pitifully mean than one who seeks power and is afraid of the power when he gets it.

Whether the Irish Government is willing or not to take back the imprisoned I.R.A. men is not the point—it is that a Socialist Government should not keep these political prisoners a single second longer in jail. They were moved by idealistic principles, had nothing to gain and all to lose. It is a shocking thing that they should have been treated as criminals. I think their policy was a mistaken one; I thought so all along; but there was nothing of self-interest in it anyway. If the Labour Government have any sense, they would go with bands and banners to the prisons where these men are, open the gates for them, and ask them to join in the fight for human political and economic freedom.

I am not well enough to speak publicly for these fine fellows, but, if my name is of any use to you, it is yours and theirs.

And, by the way, why don't the Bishops—who are forever talking of mercy and forgiveness, speak a word for them? Or the "Republican" Government of De Valera?

Oh what are some of those on the Government benches here, on the Government benches there, and on the benches where the Bishops sit!

Totnes.   *Sean O'Casey*

P.S.—Christmas cards, letters, books, weekly papers, and periodicals may be sent to the prisoners, addressed to Parkhurst Prison, Isle of Wight.

[1] See Martin Clarke's letter to O'Casey, 22 December 1947.
[2] See Gerard Kerr Bradford's letter to O'Casey, 30 December 1947.
[3] See O'Casey's letter to Frederick May, 29 September 1948, note 1.

To Denis Johnston [1]

TC. O'CASEY

[TOTNES, DEVON]
11 DECEMBER 1947

Dear Denis:

A week ago, I had a letter from a big Trades Union saying that they had built a new headquarters costing £60,000 having many qualities besides a library of 8000 volumes. One big room, they said, was to have mural decorations, and part of this was to consist of the heads of those who (they thought) had, in one way or another, helped the workers in their fight. One of the heads selected was mine.

I refused to give permission, though, if they like, of course, they can paint the thing without it. They had asked for photographs, however, which I wouldnt send, and so they will hardly carry out this threat against my wishes.

This is just a prelude to the refusal of the Third Programme request too.[2] I am not sufficiently interested to do the speaking myself, and not interested at all in the idea of anyone else doing it. The plays are already well enough known without giving a voice to them on a record. And only a snip from one, or two, of them too. No, Denis, I must refuse.

We're all well here, waiting for the Gunner to come on his Christmas leave, and a bit restless with the Xmas stir growing strong all around us.

Best wishes to Betty and to you.
Yours sincerely,
Sean O'Casey

[1] Denis Johnston (1901–   ), Dublin-born playwright, best known for his early successes at the Dublin Gate Theatre, *The Old Lady Says No* (1929) and *The Moon on the Yellow River* (1931); BBC war correspondent, 1942–45; BBC Director of Programs, 1946–47.

[2] A radio program based on readings by writers from their own works.

To H. A. Evans

TS. MACMILLAN LONDON

TOTNES, DEVON
15 DECEMBER 1947

Dear Mr. Evans:

Thank you for your letter about neglected corrections in THE SILVER TASSIE.[1]

The Soldier Characters should have been numbered as you say, and I have done so now. I have brought the 1st Soldier and the direction "chanting, and indicating . . . of the R.C. Station," down to the verse, beginning "The perky bastard's cautious nibbling," and have numbered the others your way. Page 52.

I have corrected (properly, I hope) the numbers on the chants too at back of the book. The music can be left as it is. The first chant—page 133 —is given full as an example of the way the others go. The dots . . . indicate that the note preceding them is to be kept up till the music script shows a change.

We usually say and write "Tommie" in Ireland—as in "Mollie"—, but Tommy is better, and I have made the change.

WITHIN THE GATES: Cut out, please, the "Notes on Production," page v. It will always depend on the Producer. If he be an imaginative and practical fellow, all will be well; if he be (as often happens) what Dublin would call a "cod," then, if one was a Christian, there would be nothing left to do but to offer up perpetual supplication to heaven to have mercy on the play. Please retain the description of what the Front curtain should be like—page xvi; and the divisions called "acts," should, preferably, be called "scenes" as at first, with their added aspects "Within a Park. On a Spring Morning," etc.

Yours sincerely,
Sean O'Casey

[1] These corrections in *The Silver Tassie* and *Within the Gates* were made for the "Stage Versions" of the plays in the *Collected Plays*, Vol. II (1949).

From Martin Clarke [1]

MS. O'CASEY

22 DECEMBER 1947

In replying to this letter, please write on the envelope:—
Number 301   Name   Clarke

PARKHURST, I.W. PRISON

Dear Sean O'Casey,

Many thanks for your kindness & thoughtfulness in sending on to me a copy of your play "Red Roses for me." I can assure you that it will be one of my most treasured possessions.

I have read all of your works, the last being "Drums under the window" and it may or may not interest you to know that your mention of the "Golden Bough" made a few of us so curious that we determined to get the book by hook or by crook, and after numerous applications to the Seely Library, some of us are fortunate enough to be members, we eventually succeeded in having it sent in.

I only mention this to show how deep an interest all of us here take in what you have to say, and to make known also that our search for knowledge and truth is unceasing, as I'm sure it is no secret to you that most of us belong to that unfortunate class from whom education and knowledge—outside of life's experience—have been very deliberately and expertly kept.

I take this opportunity to wish you long life, happiness and good luck, and remain one of the most ardent admirers of your prodigious moral courage in saying what you want to say without fear of the consequences and in the face of heavy but narrowminded, stupid and bigoted odds.

I remain yours respectfully
Martin Clarke

---

[1] Martin Clarke, imprisoned for IRA activities. See O'Casey's letter to *The Tribune,* 5 December 1947. In a letter to O'Casey, 13 December 1947, Eoin O'Mahony, who was leading the campaign to free the prisoners, wrote: "Thanks for your latest letter. What a tower of strength you are to the prisoners." (MS. O'Casey) See O'Casey's letter to O'Mahony, 24 September 1947.

To Daily Worker

22 DECEMBER 1947

OPEN THE PRISON GATES! [1]

In 1939, thirty young men, members of the Irish Republican Army, were sentenced to periods of up to twenty years' imprisonment for bomb offences. Nobody was killed, and there is no war on now to excuse the severity of those sentences. A growing movement is asking for their release.

SEAN O'CASEY *here argues trenchantly that to keep these men longer in prison is vindictive and senseless.*

There are 30 Irishmen in Parkhurst Prison, Isle of Wight, squeezing out the ripe youth of life behind iron bars.

Young men whose one fault was that they loved Ireland not wisely but too well.

And 22 of them are to serve 20 years' penal servitude, while the easiest sentence on the other eight is ten years.

They have already spent an irretrievable time in prison, and it is high time that they were let out, to live as they deserve to live.

The changing circumstances in politics, here and everywhere else, have rendered the old tactics useless: they will never resume them, and so there isn't the slightest reason for keeping them where they are.

If prison be (as so many think) a corrective, then, since they will not go back to their old activities, and since they have languished long enough further imprisonment will simply be vindictive, just cold and bitter vindictiveness.

Vindictive conceit on the part of authority calling itself democratic, broad-minded and fair.

There isn't one among the present Government of Eireann, or one of that Government which preceded the present one, who hasn't avowed the principles for which these chaps are now in jail.

And these members of the Government of Eireann have met, and will continue to meet, in amiable discussion, the members of the Government of Britain who are keeping these lads in prison.

Indeed, between them, the two Governments of Eireann, the past one and the present one, have done more damage, have caused more suffering, than these lads, were they multiplied by a thousand, could carry on for the next ten hundred years.

It is a hypocritical policy to keep these young Irishmen another day in jail.

These lads got a good deal of their inspiration from W. B. Yeats, the great Irish poet. Like the poet, these young men had

---

[1] A shorter and milder version of this letter, probably softened for Irish consumption by the editor, appeared in the *Irish Press,* 16 December 1947.

> *hidden in their hearts the flame out of the eyes of*
> *Cathleen, the daughter of Houlihan.*

And not from Yeats alone. Reviewing a book of mine, George Orwell [2] got very angry because he thought there was too much Irish nationalism in the work; and he selected passages to prove this, quoting the following verse:

> *Singing of men that in battle array,*
> *Ready in heart and ready in hand,*
> *March with banner and bugle and fife*
> *To the death for their native land.*

But it wasn't Finn McCool, or even Thomas Davis, who wrote it. It wasn't even an Irishman.

It was an Englishman, well-known and famous: it was Tennyson, but the learned George Orwell didn't know.

But the romantic flame has gone from the eyes of Cathleen, the daughter of Houlihan, and she looks at life now in a realistic way; and so do these lads in prison.

We are greatly troubled by the state of peoples in many countries (and rightly so), but we mustn't forget those we have at home with us here.

These young lads are badly needed in our struggle towards a better life. They are being wasted where they are. This isn't either right or sensible. They must be brought forth to freedom.

They must be delivered from bondage so that they may do their share in the fight for a finer and a safer life for all.

It is time that the workers of Britain called for the release of these fine lads.

Workers of England, of Scotland, of Wales, of Ireland, call for the quick release of these, your comrades, that they may take their place in your ranks, to march with banner and bugle and fife, to march for the great cause of Labour.

---

2 George Orwell, "The Green Flag," *The Observer,* 28 October 1945, a review of *Drums Under the Windows.* See also O'Casey's reply, *The Observer,* 29 October 1945, which was refused publication.

To Sean O'Rourke [1]

TS. O'ROURKE

TOTNES, DEVON
24 DECEMBER 1947

Dear friend:

So Frank [2] is about to retire and join the order of the contemplatives.
Well, after fifty years, he deserves a rest. I see you are in the old street still
—beside Stanley's shop, if it be still there. Far away and long ago! I daresay there has been a great scatter since I walked beneath the glimpses of
the moon in the streets of the Parish of O'Toole. Tommy Lynch and his
brother of the dour face—Feardorcha; [3] M. Lawless, Mackey, called Lar,
Colgan—a very devoted labour man now, and a baiter of the poor communists; Carroll, the well-dressed, who married Miss Wisely—Molly to her
friends; Fitzharris, gone the way of all flesh; Seumas Moore of whom I've
heard nothing for a long time, though he visited me several times years ago
when he came to London; Frank's sisters, Martha and Mrs Pollard; Sean,
Michael, and Tom, the clarinetist; and last, but by no means least, the
bould Kevin O'Lochlainn: I can see them all, and remember them well. All
grey-haired now, I daresay; that is, all who still live.

I'm not a rich man, and though I was all against testimonials when
one was proposed for myself, the time I was very ill, I'm not so sure now
that the opposition was justified. Here's a guinea for you, all I can spare,
and with it my best wishes to Frank, and to you all who still walk the old
streets and live in the old, old houses.

I daresay you know I've three children now—the eldest a gunner in
the Royal Artillery, home on leave with us for Christmas; a fellow of six
feet two.

I suppose the Clan O'Neill is scattered too. The Hendersons and the
Murphys. The Murphys should be well away now, for their mother was a
relative of your very comic President—Sean T. [O'Kelly]

All the best to you,
Yours sincerely,
Sean O'Casey

Don't bother to reply.

[1] Sean O'Rourke, 2 Seville Place, North Strand, Dublin; one of O'Casey's
friends in the St. Laurence O'Toole Club during the first decade of the century.

[2] Frank Cahill, one of O'Casey's friends in the St. Laurence O'Toole Club and a
lay teacher in the Christian Brothers School, St. Laurence O'Toole parish.

[3] The dark man.

To Francis MacManus

TS. MacManus

Totnes, Devon
26 December 1947

Dear Frank,

A friend of mine, a young married man with two children—two years & one—, who is a Professor in New York University, & will be next session, lecturing on Irish Literature, has written to ask me about Irish writers of today. He lists a number with whose work he is familiar, & asks after a Denis Devlin, [Valentin] Iremonger, a H. L. Green; but doesn't mention you or Peadar O'Donnell. I've written to Peadar O'Donnell; & now I'm writing to you. It might be worth while sending him copies of your best work—including your book on Boccacio—is this spelled right?—I met this Professor first when he was a kid at Harvard, &, later, when he became a naval officer in the war, he & his friends came to see us regularly whenever they were in Plymouth, or often near Devon harbour. His address is:

DAVID H. GREENE,
244 HILLTURN LANE,
ROSLYN HEIGHTS,
NEW YORK. U.S.A.

And all the best to you & yours.
Sean O'Casey

To George Jean Nathan

TS. Cornell

Totnes, Devon
30 December 1947

My very dear George:

I am so glad that you think so well of "Cockadoodle Dandy." Your good opinion is very gratifying & very exhilerating too. But I amn't easy about your not feeling well. Don't you think you should leave the theatre for awhile, go away & have a rest? Are you sure you're taking proper care of yourself? And have you a doctor to come & give, at least, an occasional look at you? You do want someone to look after you a little. And please don't bother yourself about either "Purple Dust" or "Cockadoodle Dandy" any longer—not till you feel quite fit & yourself again. You are probably trying to do too much. Give things a miss for a few months. It is really a mistake to overtax oneself. Why not (if you can afford it) go way South more into the sun for a month or more, till you get rid of whatever may be troubling you. And are you sure that your "Theatre Books" are not a bit of a strain on you? It's no easy job, writing the way you do in the keen exercise of mind & witful thinking. We sometimes forget that the use of the mind is as physical a thing as the use of the hands, & far more wearing. It is wise to take stock of what we can do with fair ease, & what we can't do without a strain.

Do have a look at yourself, and try to take things easier for a while anyway.

Gene should never have endorsed the film of his play.[1] What has he got to do with kindness in relation to his art? It is really a dreadful thing that such a play, such a regal play, should be turned into a ragamuffin on the screen; & sealed, too, with the monogram of Gene. He mustn't do it ever again. He wouldn't let anything loose from himself, if he didn't think it good; so why should he give a signed liberty to another that he wouldn't dare to give himself?

And do take things easier, George, till you are allright.

Ever yours, with love,
Sean

[1] Eugene O'Neill's *Mourning Becomes Electra,* the film version, released in November 1947, produced and directed by Dudley Nichols, with Rosalind Russell, Michael Redgrave, and Raymond Massey in the leading roles.

From Gerard Kerr Bradford [1]

MS. O'CASEY

30 DECEMBER 1947

In replying to this letter, please write on the envelope: o
Number 598   Name   Bradford

PARKHURST, I.W. PRISON
New Year's Eve.
1947

Mr. Sean O'Casey,
Totnes,
Devon.

Many thanks for the gift which you very kindly sent along a few weeks back. It is one that I will treasure with the utmost care, not because of

[1] Gerard Kerr Bradford, imprisoned for IRA activities. See O'Casey's letter to *Tribune,* 5 December 1947.

your unequalled success in the literary world, as your consistency in revealing the hypocrisy and deceitfulness which exists among certain functions and societies of reputable standing.

Most of your works I have read and many weary and lonesome hours of prison life were dispelled by your wit and humour, and the joys and tragedies of life which you portray so vividly. For this also I send you my thanks.

We had lectures here last year on yourself and on your plays with Mr. Eugene O'Neill and G. B. Shaw included; by one who knew his job of work well. They were the most interesting and most enjoyable lectures I have ever attended.

I'm afraid I am lost for something more to say so I will end here in thanking you once more and wishing you long years of health & happiness.

Gerard (Kerr) Bradford

To Mina Carney

MS NYU LIBRARY

TOTNES, DEVON

1 JANUARY 1948

Dear Mina,

Enclosed is a cheque for £4. for Niall, which we have divided into 10/– a day for him. We'd be glad if you would do the Almoner to him. We fear he might lose it, if we gave it all to him. We've given him a pound as a prelude. I hope Jack is enjoying himself in Paris. I'd like to get a quiet photo of him under the Arc de Triomphe. So different from Jack on the Dublin Quays; & yet the same man. Well, good luck to him; & may he keep well while he's absent from you.

George Jean Nathan says my new play is "a superb piece of work," & that he "is absolutely delighted with it."

My love & Eileen's to you.
Sean

To Tribune

9 JANUARY 1948

"ODD MAN OUT" [1]

Neil MacIntyre, in his "Odd Man Out" poem, has a laugh at me (which doesn't matter), and another laugh at the Irish prisoners who have already done nine years in jail, which matters a lot to humane minds. In the first place, these prisoners are not "Odd Men," for they have but fought for the principles avowed by De Valera and his followers a day or so ago; and which have been avowed by the Labour Party since it was born; a principle they have been putting into practice in the restoration of independence to India and to Burma; and which they hold, presumably, regarding the nationalities nearer to their own particular home.

If the Englishman has the right to think in his own way, so has the Irishman, so has the Welshman, and so has the Scot. Even as the Australian, the New Zealander, and the man from Canada. Unity around diversity is surely the proper and sensible way to live; and, if we be wise, the Commonwealth of Nations, the British Commonwealth, will soon have its Council of Nationalities. If this Council existed now, these men of Ireland would not be let stay another day in jail. And it would not be foolishness on the part of the Labour unions to go with bands and banners to open the gates for them; and it would not be foolishness for Chuter Ede [2] to lead the unions there.

Mosley and his followers were reckoned to be a danger during the war years; but they had an easy time of it in quod, with daintily-cooked food and a suite of rooms, with many privileges, and quick release when the war ended. Our lads have now been closely confined within all the rigours of prison life for nine long years. Doesn't Mr. MacIntyre think it time to cry enough? Does he think that vengeance should go on having its own sour way till the life of these lads is swallowed up for ever in the waste of lonely and useless time? Apparently he does, for all he can think of is a laugh at the fate of men who had the courage to face danger for what they believed to be true. Well, let him have his laugh, though, for me, I'd rather be one of the jailed than have a laugh like that.

Devon   *Sean O'Casey*

Neil MacIntyre writes:
Sean O'Casey does me an injustice. My motive in writing the poem

---

[1] The 26 December 1947 issue of *Tribune* printed a poem by Neil MacIntyre, "Odd Man Out," with an introductory comment explaining that the author had been inspired by O'Casey's appeal for the release of the IRA prisoners in his letter of 5 December 1947 in *Tribune*. Apparently O'Casey felt the poem was a bit of misplaced doggerel, too flippant in its comic approach to a serious problem.

[2] Home Secretary in the Labour government.

was, I thought, the same that made him write his plea for the release of the I.R.A. men:—pity, and a desire to see mercy done them. God forbid that I should laugh at injustice.

From Patrick Kavanagh [1]

MS. O'CASEY

62 PEMBROKE ROAD, DUBLIN

14 JANUARY 1948

Dear Sean,

I am about as good a Catholic as yourself. Thanks for the advertisement. I am not interested in what the "good Catholic" Yankee [2] says, however. I was glad to see that our pious censors had removed your intensely Irish Catholic books from the list.[3] I remember meeting yourself and delightful wife and children with much pleasure. *La France Libre* asked me to write an article on you but wouldn't use it, I gave you such a slating. Your work has given me much pleasure and I thank you. With warmest regards to yourself and wife and children

From
Patrick Kavanagh

[1] Patrick Kavanagh (1906–67), Irish poet, novelist, journalist. His best-known poem is *The Great Hunger* (1942). He is also the author of *Collected Poems* (1964); *The Green Fool* (1938), an autobiography; *Tarry Flynn* (1948), a novel.
[2] Professor David H. Greene, New York University.
[3] On 16 December 1947 the Irish Censorship of Publications Board "revoked" the "prohibition" against *I Knock at the Door* (1939) and *Pictures in the Hallway* (1942), which had been banned at the time of publication. See O'Casey's letter to Jack Carney, 20 May 1942, notes 1 and 3.

To Patrick Kavanagh

TC. O'CASEY

[TOTNES, DEVON]

19 JANUARY 1948

Dear Patrick Kavanagh:

Very well—have it your own way, though at the risk of irritating you, I'd recommend you again to consider sending all the information you can about your work to David Greene. He knows a lot about literature, loves it, and is, in every way, a very fine chap. I know him intimately, for, with friends, while he was in the U.S. Navy, he came frequently here when he was stationed in Plymouth. I had met him first as a youngster-student in New York. I have written to Peadar O'Donnell about his work, and have asked him to get Iremonger to forward whatever of his that may have been published. I wrote as well to Francis McManus. D. Greene knows already about O'Faolain and O'Connor, so there was no necessity to write to them.

I'm sorry "La France Libre" didnt publish your article, though I cant think of any special reason as to why you should "slate me." Why not send it to one of the English magazines? Or were you anxious to hide it in French? You seem to be developing a gift for slating, and I would very much like to see how you set about doing it to me.

Has "The Standard" [1] any idea when Spellman will become Cardinal Secretary of State? There's a big intrigue going on to plant him into that job, which, if it happens, may mean for the Catholic people an American Pope. Italy may go Communist before they agree about it, if they dont hurry up; and then we'd have a Communist Pope maybe!

I think you must be mistaken about my books. I understand "an appeal" can be made by the author now (so the bold broadminded Dev boasted recently) to have a ban removed. I made no appeal, so they must be still banned. I'd die a lot of painful deaths before I'd make an appeal to that little bunch of religious louts.

I hope you are well.
from
       Sean O'Casey

[1] Kavanagh worked as film critic of *The Standard*.

To Francis MacManus

TS. MacManus

Totnes, Devon
21 January 1948

Dear Frank,

I'm glad you wrote to David Greene—he's a fine fellow. I'm glad, too, you're with Radio Eireann, seeing that you, evidently, dont like teaching. I can't understand, though, your mention of "unreason, foolishness, & unreality" in the education of the children. I have my own, & I can't see foolishness in what they are taught, or what they teach themselves. Our boy of 13 still likes "comics," & why shouldn't he? When a chap, writing about the Abbey Controversy asked in a letter condemning my "treachery," "What would I say, if, as a teacher, I came on a pupil reading a cowboy yarn, instead of the book of literature with which he was covering it," I was tempted to reply that I'd say he was a very sensible young lad. I've just sent a little subscription towards a testimonial to a Dublin boy Christian Brother teacher in St. Laurence O'Toole's School. He was with them for fifty years! So you have escaped a terrible fate.

I daresay the young poets who lectured the Abbey [1] did it partly to attract attention. I wish they'd chosen someone else's play. The phone here was ringing hour after hour, day after day, asking me what I thought about it; but Eileen answered the calls, though I was caught once, & did a girlish voice, saying I was the maid, & informing the inquirer that Mister O'Casey had gone to Bristol, & no-one knew when he'd be back.

I've written to Peadar O'Donnell telling him to tell Iremonger about Greene; and to Patrick Kavanagh, advising he should get into touch with him. But P. K. has replied saying "he wasn't interested in what the American Yankee would say"; & puts, in his letters, on the back of the envelope "SAINT ANTHONY GUIDE." Well, the Saint didn't guide him well this time. I've written again suggesting he should change his mind.

I'm busy now on the proofs of the biographical vol. "Inishfallen, Fare Thee Well." I am doing a few things to help get the I.R.A. lads out of jail. The [harp] [2] looks well on the note paper. Dulanty [3] has a green—why always green?—one on his. It's on the flag over the Arus too; so it should be taken off the beer bottle. [4] If the English did that, they'd say it was "defaming poor Ireland."

All well, so far, here. Breon was with us for Xmas; but I and Eileen had to put Influenza from us on our feet.

It's bitterly cold here too—and damp, & depressing; but the Devon folk are a charming crowd; the farmers & labourers, & workers.

Hope all yours are well.

Yours,
Sean

[1] On 8 November 1947, Valentin Iremonger, the young poet who had won the AE Memorial Award in 1946, and Roger McHugh, two of whose plays had been produced by the Abbey, protested in the Abbey against the current revival of *The Plough and the Stars*, which had opened on 13 October 1947. Just before the curtain rose for the last act, they stood up and addressed the audience, protesting against the poor quality of the performance and the policies of the Abbey directors, and then walked out amid a confusion of other speeches and outcries. The incident was reported in the *Irish Times,* 10 November 1947, and on 18 November a joint letter from Iremonger and McHugh appeared justifying the protest. In a review of the opening performance, *Irish Times,* 14 October 1947, "B. I." commented: "If you have ever seen the play before, the present production will be 'torture.'" He objected to the "lamentable mis-casting" of Brian O'Higgins as Fluther, Brid Ni Loinsigh as Nora, and Eileen Crowe as Bessie Burgess.

[2] A drawing of a harp, which appears on all Radio Eireann and government stationery. O'Casey drew a small harp here.

[3] John Whelan Dulanty, Irish High Commissioner in London.

[4] Bottles of Guinness stout have a picture of an Irish harp on the label.

To Brooks Atkinson

MS. ATKINSON

TOTNES, DEVON

31 JANUARY 1948

My dear Brooks:

It was a very pleasant thing to me to get the book [1] you so kindly sent to me. Times Square & Broadway lights came close again. But I don't care for the title—the work is a lot more than a Scrapbook. That's a weakness you have, Brooks, to think a little too little of yourself. You are inclined to be over modest, & there's hardly an article you write that hasn't an indication of it. I wish you had more of the "I am Khayyam" of the recent James Agate, who hadn't anything like the deeper love for the drama that you have. He was always readable, often entertaining, but never farseeing; never a prophet; never able to see intrinsically into a new work. He could be grand on works praised by hundreds before him; but the day-to-day drama eluded him. He really thought Walpole's play, & the plays others made from his novels, greater than O'Neill. And yet his whole demeanour shouted infallibility. To him Agate was the theatre. Now, you could never be so thoughtful, with more love & far more knowledge, so you could, with benefit to yourself modify your modesty, & thrust that old face out further to say, I know. I often wondered why you didn't write oftener about the theatre in book-form. You know more about the theatre than you do about the U.S.S.R. Quite a lot read your articles. I do, anyhow, for there aren't a lot I miss. I missed you when you knocked your desk over, & packed off to China. Why, God only knows, for I don't think you know yourself. Broadway is your stance. I read your article on Connell's "Nineteenth Hole," with special interest. He, years ago, sent the play to me; but I refused to comment, for I do not think it wise for one playwright to comment on the plays of another—except in fireside conversations, or on plays so bad that no-one can take a wrong turning. I didn't like the play & got a friend to comment on it, who gave a very favorable criticism.[2] There is something in Connell of an odd, macabre, woeful spirit; but how to analyse it is beyond me, for I have neither the knowledge nor the experience as critics must have in dealing with plays beside the ordinary. I liked your

---

[1] Brooks Atkinson, *Broadway Scrapbook* (1947), illustrated by Al Hirschfeld, a collection of Atkinson's articles published originally in the *New York Times,* 1935–47.

[2] See O'Casey's letters to Peter Newmark, 27 December 1942, and Vivian Connell, 8 January 1943.

article on the rules of Aristotle.[3] I wish it could be read by Irish "critics," who are always looking for a "beginning, a middle, & an end." I liked them all, & the book will go up among my books on the theatre, among which there is no-one undeserving of a place there. The critics here are duller than ever. The fellow in Agate's place is as commonplace as a puddle long standing. It's sad to think I've never had a meal or a drink with a critic here—so different from your American friends; yours and mine, I'm glad to say.

I'm just in the middle of correcting galley-proofs of a new biographical vol—"Inishfallen, Fare Thee Well." how there seems to be no end. And I've sent in the MS of a new play—"Cockadoodle Dandy"; so I'm not idle; as well as helping in an effort to get young I.R.A. lads out of jail.

Warm regards to Mrs. Atkinson & to you. I'll send you a copy of "Inishfallen" when it comes out. My love to New York, in spite of the snow.

Yours very sincerely.
As ever.
Sean

[3] Brooks Atkinson, "Aristotle's Rule-Book," *Broadway Scrapbook,* pp. 143–46.

To Jack Carney

MS. NYU LIBRARY

TOTNES, DEVON

4 FEBRUARY 1948

My dear Jack,

Thanks for the papers. We'll soon know how Ireland stands. McBride or De Valera.[1] Jasus! What a spate of warring, useless words have been blowing & flowing over Ireland during the past few weeks! And not a thought that is new; not even an old thought said in a new way among them all. A wholesome Christian country's Ireland. It's funny how frightened they are of a Communist. I sent the message, but doubt it will be given. They all know what I am. I'll give them something more to think about in the next biographical vol. I am working on the galley proofs now. Ireland, boys, hurrah! God, the clergy are turning the lot of them into sly shits. The "Universe" wails last week over a Moscow announcement that "the last of

[1] In the Irish election, held on 4 February 1948, Sean MacBride's new Clann na Poblachta Party won ten seats in the Dail, weakening Eamon de Valera's Fianna Fail Party, which had been in power since 1932. This led to a failure of confidence and the new coalition government of John A. Costello in 1949, in which MacBride served as Minister of External Affairs.

the Units have now been liquidated." The Pope's lost 8,000,000 followers! More than double the population of Ireland. Bill O'B[rien] is, I'm sure, at the back of [Sean] MacEntee. And McBride & Co don't know enough to answer him.

I signed a contract for "Red Roses" last week. They say it'll be done next season. I hope so.

The level of the dollar doesn't effect me—that is the upward movement —a downward one would, I suppose. All dollars I get are sold by the New York Guaranty Trust Co to the British Treasury, & they give an English price for them.

You remember the great & glowing patriot, Noel Coward—"In Which We Serve"—all of us?—"It's a grand, proud thing to be an Englishman!" Sez you—was fined, first £1000, & second, £2000, for hiding his share of dollars from the Treasury.

All the best & love
to Mina & you.
As ever,
Sean

Hope things are allright again with Eric Baume.

To Richard J. Madden

TC. O'CASEY

[TOTNES, DEVON]
6 FEBRUARY 1948

Dear Dick:

I'm sorry the new play [1] puzzled you a bit. It shouldnt. Apart from being a play in substance and in fancy, it is a loud laugh at present tendencies of thought and action in Eirinn. The killing of a man by a priest because the man was "living with a woman" happened recently in holy Ireland. The priest demanded that the man should be dismissed; the employer refused, because the man was a fine worker; the priest struck him in a fury so that he died. The incident around Loreleen happened recently too. I have the account before me now. The woman "caught in a car with a married man" was dragged along the road to the priest, who threatened her with a coffin if she didnt leave the district—almost in the same way as is depicted in the play. The incident of lovers getting fined forty shillings

[1] *Cock-a-Doodle Dandy.*

or a month in prison happened recently as well. There was nothing indecent alleged against them. Simply that they had kissed each other as they sat on a grassy bank bordering a country road. "Kissing in a public place" was the charge. I have the account before me now. The case excited interest here in England as well as in Eirinn. It was an utterly silly and appalling example of puritanism gone mad. The pilgrimages to Lourdes go on eternally. They expect two millions this year. I've seen hundreds go from Dublin. Two of my friends were "brancadiers"—those who carried the sick on stretchers on to the boats. Of all the hundreds, thousands, in fact, who went, I never yet knew of a cure coming back to Dublin. If doctors had such a small percentage of cures, they'd be driven from practising. You know, of course, about the Censorship. For instance, every book of mine, from "Within the Gates," no, from "The Silver Tassie" to "Drums Under the Windows," has been banned.[2] That means that no copy can be found in a Library; that no book-seller is allowed to stock them; and anyone coming to Eirinn having one of them in his possession, loses it, for it is confiscated by the Customs. The young are leaving the country in droves. There are wide districts in Eirinn in which there isnt a single girl from eighteen to twenty-five. The marriage rate is the lowest in the whole world. The idea—rapidly becoming a belief—of demonic possession is spreading over the land. A play put on some twelve months ago, called "The Righteous Are Bold," had the longest run ever held by a play in the Abbey; and, produced recently, had another long run, playing to crowded houses, even when it had to be taken off to make room for a Gaelic pantomime. This play depicted a girl coming home after working in an English factory, behaving "queer." Soon it was discovered that she "was possessed of a demon," and it took the priest a long time, much effort, eventually costing him his life "to exorcise the evil spirit" from the young lass. It is hardly credible, but it is a fact. Had she returned from an American factory, she would, probably, have been possessed by ten devils. In a Gaelic story, telling of terrible happenings in a house to which a priest came to say Mass, and drive away "the demons," the following talk is recorded: The priest, after staring long at a young lass sitting crouched by the fire:—Who's that girl there in the corner by the fire?

Old Man of the House:—Me own daughter, father.

Priest:—My advice to you is to get her off to America. First thing tomorrow, get her to Galway, and pack her off to America, for she it is who's at the bottom of all this evil. And keep all this a secret.

And the man of the house sent the troublesome one to America. And oddest of all, no tale or tidings of her was ever received by any from America;

---

[2] Only three of O'Casey's books were officially banned by the Irish Censorship Board: *Windfalls* in 1934, *I Knock at the Door* in 1939, and *Pictures in the Hallway* in 1942; the "prohibition" against the latter two works was lifted in 1947. It was probably true, however, that an unofficial ban against most of his works was enforced by booksellers and librarians in Ireland, especially outside Dublin.

and no-one ever could give any account of the poor possessed one—she just disappeared!

And do you think this yarn appears in some ignorant, obscure journal? Not at all, but in a leading Dublin Daily; in the paper bossed by De Valera, and representing De Valera's Party. It appeared in "The Irish Press," with a good many more of the same kind.

It is needless to stress the idea a lot of clergy have on woman's vicious effect on virtue. I understand that at one time, theologians held that woman had no soul! Once dancing in the hall of our Gaelic club in Dublin, it was suggested that a glass partition should divide the room into two so that the girls could dance at one side of it and the boys at the other. And when my new biographical book comes out, read in the chapter called "Silence," what a laugh Father McDonald, D.D. Professor of Theology in Maynooth for forty years, has at the bishops trying to regulate the length of the cut in the neck of the bodices of the lasses going to a ball; and that the men partners must dance with the ladies with their hands behind their backs.

These few remarks, out of many, may give you an idea of what "Cockadoodle Dandy" has been built on, apart from the fancy and the song O'Casey has added to the play.

Apropos of "Red Roses," I suppose you havent forgotten the emendations I made in the play for production, and which I sent on to you, the time "Theatre Inc." was thinking of the play. If you havent these changes, I can send another copy on to you. And, I hope, you wont forget my mention of Eddie Byrne for the part of "Brennan." If you should meet anyone interested in "Cockadoodle Dandy," I'll send the airs for the songs along to you. I am soon to have issued a new three-play vol.—"Star Turns Red," "Within the Gates," and "The Silver Tassie"—and I'll send a copy to you. All plays have been amended. "Within the Gates" has been altered considerably, and made, I think, much more tight and easy.

Love to Tessa and to you.

[*Sean*]

To Jack Carney

MS. NYU LIBRARY

TOTNES, DEVON
7 FEBRUARY 1948

My dear Jack,

That's definitely bad news about your resignation. I hope you haven't acted too quick. You have a hasty streak in you, you know. I do hope it won't end in your leaving the office. I'm sure Baume is trying at times. All bosses are. I never yet met a boss who wasn't (in my opinion) a bit of a bastard. But I had to stick most of them till the jobs were done. I flung one to hell once—after near knocking the foreman silly—, & felt proud as Lucifer after doing the good deed; but I often looked back on it all, to come to the conclusion I was a god-damned fool. It meant hardship for quite a time till a new job was found—after a long, trailing, weary search.

When I knew Margaret Stewart,[1] she wasn't as you call her. She was rather charming, intelligent, & really tired of the "aristocratic" life. But we must always remember that such as she is (as we are) the product of circumstances she couldn't control, & of environment in which she had to live so long. The Big House was bound to produce the aristocrat; the tenement, the proletariat. Both have their limitations; are bound to have them, till a generation appears which knew neither what all mean by "The Big House," or the "tenement." She is not to blame for being a "lady" as we are not to blame for being "guttersnipes." Both categories are unnatural, & have to go.

It may be a good sign that E. Baume is being nice to you now. It may mean that the storm will "blow over"; &, if it does, you don't go raising the wind again. It would be a great pity if all you have gathered together should be threatened again. Even if your going did "seal Baume's doom," what good would that do you?—unless you got his job. That's the realistic way of looking at it. The romantic way of being proud & independent exists only to a degree. None of us is independent; none of us can afford to be too proud. This is a pity & a damned nuisance; but it is a fact. I couldn't tell Albery all I thought of him over my recent play. Albery's a man with many good qualities; I like him; but he ruined my play, & was lousy to me in the ruining of it. We just have to put up with these things—for the present. If you have to go, Jack, go; but don't try to shove yourself out. I do hope all will come straight again.

Well, Dev is on top again—not quite so high, but high enough. McBride is a papier-maché cannon. They are still clinging to who fears to speak of '98—all of them do, for the principles of '98 were but the brave precursors of the principles of today. Not one of them—even McB. or [William] Norton, gave a word from the ghost of Fintan Lalor.[2]

> *All the best, Jack, to you & Mina.*
> *Yours as ever,*
> *Sean*

[1] Margaret Vane-Tempest-Stewart (1910–   ), daughter of Lady Londonderry.

[2] James Fintan Lalor (1807–49), Irish political writer and early socialist. A strong influence on the young O'Casey, Lalor advocated the expropriation of the landlord class and the nationalization of the land, insisting that the rural proletariat were "the true owners of the soil."

To Francis MacManus

TS. MACMANUS

TOTNES, DEVON
16 FEBRUARY 1948

Dear Frank,

You may have seen the enclosed cutting from "Herald-Tribune"; &, again, you may not. I don't think you are quite so close to Chest. or to Belloc as the critic alleges. You may say "take it, or be damned," but not in Chesterton's or Belloc's way.

You certainly have yourself behind you; but those two had nature, tradition, the Church, and God Himself. And yet they were cowardly. The Levity, the free-and-easy manner of the soul afraid.

In the list of "Young Writers" given by Bain in "Review" your name's not mentioned. I think it should have been.

Well, the Election is over, and De Valera has felt the first push. It is the beginning.

Don't bother to reply to this.

All the best to you & yours.
Sean

To George Jean Nathan

TS. CORNELL

TOTNES, DEVON
9 MARCH 1948

My very dear George:

Well, so Eddie D. wont crow with the cock.[1] I guessed he wouldn't, but had a hope that he might as an artist cancel his fear, and do the right thing by his art. It can't be helped. Of course, the play doesn't deny that

---

[1] Eddie Dowling had decided not to produce *Cock-a-Doodle Dandy* because of what he considered to be its anti-Catholic theme. On 2 January 1948, Nathan had written to O'Casey:

> My very dear Sean: As you anticipated, Eddie Dowling, who otherwise likes the play greatly, says that his devotion to the Catholic church prevents him from doing it. In addition, he seriously alleges his own sister was cured at Lourdes, which theoretical fact further alienates him. What do you wish me to do next with the script? I'd like to let Billy Rose read it, though I fear that that Catholic note will frighten him, even though he is to the synagogue born. The theatre here seems to tread gingerly in the Holy Roman Direction. But I still say that 'Cock-adoodle Dandy' is a mighty fine thing—and I'll work hard on it. My love always. George (MS. O'Casey)

See also O'Casey's letter to Horace Reynolds, ? February 1942, note 3.

his sister was cured; it just declares that the lass of Nyadnanave failed to get the ear of the B. Virgin. The funny part of it is that belief in Lourdes isn't an article of faith. Although even Zola, in his LOURDES,[2] grants one of the central characters a miraculous cure, if we depended for our medical and surgical needs on Lourdes, we'd be in a damned bad way. If man doesn't find a cure for cancer, and other hideous ailments outside of Lourdes, then a cure will never be found for them. Eddie Dowling, Catholic and all as he may be, must, if he thinks for a second, must realise this. I've seen thousands from time to time leaving Dublin for a cure (at £50 a time), and never once have I known a sufferer to come back whole. We even have a minor rival to Lourdes called Knock, but it hasn't caught on, and the "patriots" go to Lourdes without giving a thought to the Vision of Knock; just as St. Anthony of Padua is more important to them than St. Columbus of Derry. Our friend, Dick [Madden], is disturbed by the play. He seemed to be a little puzzled by it, so I sent him an explanation of the facts in the play. I've just got a letter from him saying that Laurence Langner told him that "It was the best play he had read for years, yet, for the world, he wouldn't think of doing it, because of the onslaught he'd get from the Catholic Church." Freedom of thought! Dick says of the play himself, "The instances you cite—the killing of a man by a priest, the woman in a car with a married man—are written into the play with great feeling and power, but do they really contribute a dramatic value to what you have to say? I'm sure you will be the first to admit that life translated in terms of theatre does not always make effective playwrighting." This, after him saying they have been woven into the play with great feeling and power! What is one to think of such criticism? Just not to think of it at all. I have given poor Dick a lot of trouble with my plays, and he hasn't made much out of them—they were more trouble to him than they were worth. I'm really sorry for this, but I can't help it. I am very fond of Dick, and ready to forgive him anything he may say. Anyway, it's the Producers who should have the guts to do the things they think are good. But it seems that under a free democracy, one must be damned careful of what one says. The funny part of it is that there isn't a single instance in the play of any attack whatsoever on the doctrines which every Catholic is obliged to believe. But singularly few Roman Catholics—even priests— know intimately the facts of their own Faith. In my next Biographical book, there's a chapter called SILENCE,[3] which I hope Eddie will read— it may astonish him. The fact is that the clergy—from cardinal to deacon— have divorced themselves from all knowledge of, and feeling for, art or literature. Their pastorals and speeches are primed with dullness and mummified phrases; their churches are dens of vulgarity and their accessories are but rowdy atrocities in paint and plaster.

[2] Emile Zola, *Lourdes* (1894). O'Casey had an undated English translation of this book in his library.

[3] "Silence," *Inishfallen, Fare Thee Well* (1949), a chapter on Dr. Walter McDonald.

Brooks sent me his BROADWAY SCRAPBOOK. It was very interesting, and the illustrations were very good. Brooks is a fine fellow, very
honest, very wise, but I wish he was a little more lively and a little more
vicious.

Our elder boy, the artillery gunner is home on leave. He has, apparently, set his mind on becoming a painter. I tried to dissuade him, but it
was no use. Thank God, he didn't choose the role of a dramatist.

The fellow who has taken the place of Agate on THE SUNDAY
TIMES is a dull devil. I daresay you've heard of the protest made by two
young men against the Abbey Theatre's present way of life.[4] They choose
my play to demonstrate about. I wish they had chosen another one. The
Abbey brings in about £150 a year, which was a great help; now, I'm
afraid, they'll not put on any of mine again for a long time to come. What
the Abbey needs, of course, is another Yeats and another Gregory—things
that won't come Ireland's way for a century, if they ever appear again.
I enclose a few cuttings about the row. And a picture of James Stephens in
his robes as Dr. of Litt. James seems to do little now but give an occasional
broadcast. It is a great pity. Everyone in Ireland now goes about in a
friar's cowl. They're developing special muscles with the dint of crossing
themselves. And as they grow more spiritual, they grow more worldly.
Even the Abbey thinks now only of the affections of the box-office. They
won't risk anything. Soon most of them'll be afraid to get up in the
morning. Ireland has undergone a See change.

I hope you have recovered, and are your own dear self again. I have
still to take care; and always will have to now. But, anyway, we'll go on till
you are the last rose of summer there, and I'm the last one here.

All the best with my love.
Sean

[4] See O'Casey's letter to Francis MacManus, 21 January 1948, note 1.

To Francis MacManus

TS. MacManus

Totnes, Devon
21 March 1948

Dear Frank,

Yes, I daresay these lists of established and promising writers are
compiled by the few, maybe by the Academicians, for, I suppose, the Academy is still to the fore. Some little time ago, Mr. L. Robinson wrote asking

me (I don't know why) to let him put my name forward for election; but I am too far gone in the horn now to want to do that.[1]

Things will get worse for you with the Jesuits of America the more your work is original and provocative.[2] I suppose it was AMERICA that tossed your work up so that the theologians would see it; or was it THE NATION? I suffered the same attack from the Jesuits over WITHIN THE GATES. The principal descryer of immorality was a father O'Connell.[3] He came to Ireland while I was in London. Gaby [Fallon] and father Senan made him promise that he would pay a visit to me. They wrote, asking if I would see him. Of course, I said ay, and fortify him with a cup of tea. So F. O. C. was to ring me up, make an appointment, and visit me. I never heard another word from him, or about him, from the father himself, or from Gaby or from F. Senan. One of the things he had said was that the Bishop of the play had an illegitimate kid, and worded the complaint so that meant that the bishop per se was guilty. He didnt seem to know (or pretended not to, which would be worse) that a bis. becomes a bishop only from the hour of his consecration, and that anything done before cant be laid to his charge as a bishop. He forgot, too, about St. Augustine. But I didnt.

I wish you would let me have a copy of that famous encyclical on AMERICANISMUS. If you have it, I'd be glad of a copy. I am interested in most things, heresies included. I hope you have replied to David Greene. You should keep in touch with him. He may be useful to you.

I wont write to you again, except for a very special reason. It would do you, a Catholic, no good, if it became known you were corresponding with a hardened Communist, the way things are now. Even only on literary matters.

So my warm wishes to you and yours,

Sean

[1] See O'Casey's letter to Lennox Robinson, 18 February 1947.

[2] MacManus's *Boccaccio* (1947) had been attacked as heretical by the Jesuit magazine *America*.

[3] The Rev. Terence L. Connolly, S. J. (1888–1961), Professor of Philosophy and Librarian at Boston College; occasional contributor to drama and Catholic magazines. He led the attack against O'Casey which caused the banning of *Within the Gates* in Boston in 1935; see O'Casey's letter to Richard J. Madden, 17 January 1935, note 1, Vol. I, p. 531; and O'Casey's telegram to George Bushar Markle and John Tuerk, 21? January 1935, note 2, Vol. I, p. 535. Father Connolly also attacked Yeats's *Purgatory;* see O'Casey's letter to the *Irish Times,* 29 August 1938, note 1, Vol. I, p. 731.

To Joseph MacColm [1]

TC. O'CASEY

[TOTNES, DEVON]
26 MARCH 1948

Dear Joe MacColm:

Penny Starr will have to find some other play.[2] Al Tamarin has the sole licence for the play in America, and I dont intend to ask him to share it with anyone else. The play has been there for a long time, and Penny Starr didnt even notice it. Besides, I dont let my plays go on to enhance a sensation. If the plays are not to be produced as plays, then they wont go on at all. You can tell Penny Starr this, and add that O'Casey doesnt care a tinker's damn what the Tenney Committee [3] think of him; or what anyone else either thinks of him, be it pope, prince, or pauper.

Anyway, Tenney is right: I am a subversive writer; always have been, and I hope, always will be. I take my place with the other subversive writers—Dickens, Milton, Shelley, Byron, Joyce, Shaw, and a shining host of others, not forgetting Tenney's own Walt Whitman.

And Penny Starr can tell the Tenney Committee that I am a friend to the USSR; that I have been one since 1917; that I am a friend still, and no less a friend of the people of the United States because of my friendship for the Soviet Union. And let Penny Starr tell the Tenney Committee that even Christ was crucified for being a subversive talker; and that a chance of the world's life is here, and a thousand Tenney Committee's cant stop it.

That is all, bar repeating that she cant have RED ROSES FOR ME.

With all good wishes,
Yours sincerely,
Sean O'Casey

[1] Joseph MacColm, Unity Theatre, London.
[2] Penny Starr, of the Actors' Laboratory, Hollywood, California, wanted to perform *Red Roses For Me*.
[3] The California legislature established a joint "Fact-Finding Committtee on Un-American Activities" in 1941, with Jack B. Tenney as chairman. The controversial Tenney Committee held hearings and issued reports against "un-American" writers and individuals, and denounced O'Casey's plays as "subversive." In 1949 Tenney was forced to resign as a result of his star-chamber methods.

To Manchester Guardian

30 MARCH 1948

THE LANE PICTURES [1]

Sir,—The Lane pictures were left not to the Tate Gallery or the National Gallery of London but to the Municipal Gallery of Dublin. Lane's last written words say so, and there is no getting away from them, except by a pretence that is a sham and shameful.

At first, in a fit of temper, "wrongly," Lane left them to London; later, when that temper had gone, he "rightly" left them to Dublin; for it was for Dublin he intended them all along, and few would venture to deny it. Those who knew him most intimately have sworn to it. The committee set up by a British Government during the controversy said decidedly that it was undoubtedly Lane's last wish that these pictures should find their home in Dublin; but the British Government then, and the British Government now, do not honour the decided declaration of their own committee.

As for the lousy quibble about the "illegality" of the codicil, it may be remembered that all wills unsigned by witnesses made by British soldiers, Irish soldiers too, were perfectly legal, and their requests and bequests were loyally carried out. Tens of thousands of them must have been honoured; so, since Lane died in the heat of the war, was a war casualty, then his last will and wish would have been honoured too, if it had not fell among thieves. And what a mean and paltry theft it is! Not the poor robbing the rich, but the rich, the very rich, robbing the poor. And what a mean reason is implicitly given for keeping them: they "were worth £200,000 in 1938." The costlier they become the tighter the hold London will keep on them.

As for the retention being "legal," the legality is signed and sealed in the bonds of dishonourable and dishonouring morality. It is no less than legal theft. Theft not from one but from the whole people of Ireland, from Belfast as much as Dublin. Dublin was the last choice of Lane; he set this down clearly and precisely. The dead man still speaks; he says the same thing; no legal quibble can change his last words; we hear them still; they

---

[1] Sir Hugh Lane (1875–1915), art collector and critic, nephew of Lady Gregory, lost his life on the *Lusitania,* which was torpedoed off the coast of Ireland by a German submarine on 7 May 1915. In February 1915 he had written the controversial codicil to his will, giving his collection of modern paintings to Ireland on the condition that a gallery be provided for them within five years of his death. But the codicil was unwitnessed, and it was contested by the British National Gallery, which had possession of the paintings. After forty-four years of controversy the British and Irish authorities finally reached a compromise plan in 1959: the Lane pictures were divided into two groups, one to be held in London, and the other in Dublin, and they were to be exchanged every five years for the next twenty years. The Municipal Gallery in Dublin, which holds the Irish share of the pictures, was officially renamed the Hugh Lane Municipal Gallery of Modern Art in 1975.

can never be altered now; it is still Lane's last testament, his last will that these pictures should go to Dublin.

I fought for these pictures when Lane first brought them to Dublin; I fought for them in London, with Lady Gregory, more than twenty years ago; [2] I fight for them now, and will always fight for them till they go back to Dublin. Lane has the last word, and his last word is that Dublin is the only place in which they can find an honourable home.—Yours, &c.

SEAN O'CASEY

Tingrith, Station Road,
  Totnes, March 24.

[2] See O'Casey's statements in defense of Ireland's rightful claim to the Lane pictures, beginning with his letter to Lady Gregory, 12 July 1924, note 4, Vol. I, p. 112.

To George Jean Nathan

MS. CORNELL

TOTNES, DEVON
30 MARCH 1948

My very dear George:
    Enclosed are two notices reviewing "The Righteous Are Bold," [1] which I'd like you to pass on to Dick. If this kind of pietistic hokum can be produced—a travesty of the Catholic Faith—, I don't see why "Cocka-doodle Dandy" can't strut the stage. I've neither read nor seen the play; but the reviews—even some of the Irish ones—show it to be shockingly bad—and hysterically sensational. I don't know what to say about the Abbey now—or about Ireland—a waste land, lit up by holy candles. I hope you are yourself again.

Ever Yours
With my love.
Sean

[1] See O'Casey's letter to Nathan, 14 November 1946, note 8.

To P. J. Clancy [1]

PC. *Irish Democrat*

April 1948

Dear P. J. Clancy,

I am indeed sorry I can't come to your meeting. To "make a very special effort" I'd need a new heart and I can't get that anywhere. All who know me, and almost all who don't, know what I think about the continued confinement of our Irish comrades in Parkhurst Prison.

The De Valeras, McBrides, Nortons, Costellos, and Mulcahys should be there themselves to see how they'd like it. When some of them were, they had all Ireland howling at the British to let them go; and now when as good, if not better, men are there, they're silent themselves.

Of course, with £600 as a Deputy, £500 as a pension and £1,000 as Leader of the Opposition, De Valera may well think the geraniums in his window are of more importance than men who are flesh of his flesh and bone of his bone, who tried in their own way to defend a Cause De Valera had sworn to and then abandoned.

To me, leaving these men in jail by the De Valera Government and now by the present Government is just cold, calculated political villainy.

May the curse of every Irish saint fall heavy on every Irish head that refuses to lift itself and say a word for these fine men wasting away in jail.

Yours very sincerely,
Sean O'Casey

[1] P. J. Clancy was on the committee of the *Irish Democrat* organizing a rally at Holborn Hall in London on 18 April 1948 to demand the release of all Irish political prisoners in British jails. In the April issue of the *Irish Democrat,* in which O'Casey's letter appeared, the committee stated "their disapproval of the terrorist methods the prisoners had used in the past," and claimed that nine years' imprisonment was sufficient punishment.

To Francis MacManus

TS. MacManus

Totnes, Devon
2 April 1948

Dear Frank,

I have to write you again. I've had a long letter from Dave Greene, saying he is embarrassed because he has read none of your novels, not

being able to lay his hand on them, &, that, as he is lecturing on Irish poets &
novelists, he can't include your book on Boccaccio.[1] Can't you send him a
few of your novels? Say a "Candle for the Proud," [2] & "Stand and Give
Challenge." [3] I've read your "This Was My Home," [4] but don't think it's
Frank at his best. I haven't read "The Greatest of These" [5]—a bad title,
boy. Don't give a title that is but part of a sentence—but, maybe, you'd
send him that one. It's for you to choose, of course. I'd like you to be
known in the U.S.A. I've written to Kavanagh again, suggesting he'd send
"The Great Hunger" [6] and I'm writing again to [Peadar] O'Donnell. So let
yourself be shown among the company. I've written to Dave, & said a lot
about you (as you appear to me), not so technically good as O'Faolain,
but more sincere, &, I think, deeper. I've told him you were a lover of
Aquinas's idea of the world, this one & the next, though I think myself
that Aquinas has been left behind by the advance of knowledge. This isn't
impudence—I got it from McWalter.[7]

Anyway, if you can, send some of your novels to Dave.

All the best,
Sean

1 Francis MacManus, *Boccaccio* (1947).
2 *Candle For the Proud* (1936).
3 *Stand and Give Challenge* (1935).
4 *This House Was Mine* (1937).
5 *The Greatest of These* (1943).
6 Patrick Kavanagh, *The Great Hunger* (1942).
7 Dr. Walter McDonald, *Reminiscences of a Maynooth Professor* (1925).

To Harry Cowdell

TS. MACMILLAN

TOTNES, DEVON
8 APRIL 1948

Dear Mr. Cowdell:

Thank you for sending me the sketch for the Jacket of INISHFALLEN,
FARE THEE WELL.

It is fine, and I have but a few comments to make.

I think the face of "St. Patrick" ought to be more masklike, more
stern-looking; a face indifferent to all things outside of its own thought—
if it can be done.

The face of "Chesterton" is inclined a little to the left; I think the face
of "Belloc," on the opposite side, should, to balance the picture, be a little
inclined to the right.

The colour scheme is fine, too, I think.

Please give my thanks to the artist. I return the sketch with this note.

Yours sincerely,
Sean O'Casey

To Jack Carney

MS. NYU Library

Totnes, Devon
11 April 1948

Dear Jack,

How are things with you? Have you left the office, & if you have, has anything else turned up?

It is a hard time to be looking for anything—for each & all of us who haven't a steady income rolling in from shares. Months & months ago, I corrected the galley proofs of the new biographical vol., but so far, no page proofs have come, & god knows when they will. Yesterday I got the first batch of galley proofs of the new play! Starting on the play before the other's half finished! The publishers have to seize the chance of getting anything they can done when the chance comes. Time & the Calendar have gone out of existence.

I hope you haven't left the job; but, if you have, I hope there's a good prospect of another job presenting itself.

I've just heard from George Jean Nathan that he doesn't like the way they're thinking of doing "Red Roses" in N.Y., & that [Boris] Tamarin, who has the play, hasn't yet collected the money to do it. So maybe it won't go on at all. The costs of production there are enormous now. The least a new, straight play can be put on for is £9000 or 10,000 pounds.

We'll all have to go out and sing carols at Christmas.

Love to Mina & to you.
Yours as ever,
Sean

To Manchester Guardian

12 APRIL 1948

THE LANE PICTURES

Sir,—Perhaps you will allow one more note about Dublin's claim to these treasures. Mr. MacColl [1] was always opposed to the return of them to Dublin; why, only himself can know. Lane was not a "burning patriot" in the nonsense of running around with a green rosette in his coat and a green flag in his hand; but he was a patriot in the sense of going about with lovely pictures under his arm which he wanted to bestow on Dublin. The last words written by Lane do not make Mr. MacColl sole trustee of the wish of the codicil, but his aunt, Lady Gregory, who understood him as Mr. MacColl never did, and loved him as Mr. MacColl, of course, never could. He did not even mention the name of MacColl in the codicil, but the name of "his friend, Tom Bodkin," as the man he wanted to help Lady Gregory. And if Lady Gregory is not enough there is the sworn declaration of his sister, Mrs. Shine.

All Ireland, North and South, Catholic and Protestant, wanted, and wants, the pictures back. At a mass meeting in Dublin the voices among many others, of Lords Granard, Decies, Midleton, Mayo, Desart, Rossmore, and Powerscourt, Dr. Bernard, Protestant Archbishop of Dublin, the Moderator of the Presbyterian Church, Mr. Justice Madden, the Lord Mayor, and General Sir Bryan Mahon were heard demanding the return of the pictures. Artists John, B. Tree, Orpen, Clausen, Kelly, W. Rothenstein, Shannon, W. Nicholson, and Wilson Steer requested their return. Lord Glenavy said that "all the evidence makes it clear that the testator intended the pictures to return to the Dublin Gallery." So said Alec (now Sir Alec) Martin,[2] who knew Lane well.

Sean O'Casey is not a bit too hot about the pilfering of the pictures. He was not the first to say that it was a question of honour rather than one of law. So said Lord Ribblesdale. So said Augustine Birrell. There are many more testimonies from eminent and well-known persons in "The Case for the Return of the Lane Pictures" which prove without doubt that Lane's heart was set (set, mind you) on fixing the pictures on a Dublin wall.

When the pictures were first in the possession of London's National Gallery Mr. MacColl's expert friends did not know how to value them, for instead of fastening them on the wall they shoved them into the cellar. Mr. MacColl's "The pictures must go by gift, if at all," is, indeed, a cocky order. It is not a question between him and Ireland, or between England and me: it is a question between two nations. The holding fast of the Lane

---

[1] Dugald Sutherland MacColl, Keeper of the Tate Gallery, London.
[2] See O'Casey's letter to Sir Alec Martin, 1 September 1948.

Bequest is a scurvy transaction. It was one when they were held in spite of Lane's last will; it is as scurvy, more so, to-day; and each day they are withheld the deed grows meaner.—Yours, &c.,

SEAN O'CASEY

Totnes, Devon, 8 April

To William Rust

TC. O'CASEY

[TOTNES, DEVON]
16 APRIL 1948

Dear Mr. Rust:

The article by Harry [1] is good as far as it goes, though it isnt trenchant enough, in my opinion. But it is useless for one writer to try to tell another how to write. Each has his own way, as we say in Dublin, "Every cripple has his own way of walkin'." Anyway, sooner or later, somewhere, by someone, the fight against the Vatican Church—not the Catholic Church— must be begun by the Communists, indeed by anyone seeking freedom of thought and expression, if we are not to be deprived of a life worth living. The Rerum Novarum is all, and more, than Harry says of it. A string of platitudes from start to end. It was promulgated more than half a century ago, and it has had no effect whatever on the lot of the Catholic workers. In all countries ruled by Roman Catholic thought, the workers are in the last state of poverty and depression—Ireland, Portugal, Spain; it is only in the countries where the workers have gone ahead, in spite of encyclical and pastoral, that they have found time to look at the light in front of them. "Christian Trades Unions" are the one fruit of the Rerum Novarum, and these are remarkable only for the facts that they are not Christian and they are not Trades Unions. Harry will have to be careful to know what he is writing about, and be sure of any fact he may set out to prove—I assume he is a Catholic, and should know something about the Faith, though few there be who do.

All these encyclicals are, as Harry says, just efforts to ensure that in all conditions the ecclesiastics will have the real power, and so maintain what they are so eager to hold, the treasures of this world—in other words, private property; for the Roman C. is the greatest property-holding institution in the world. They are not likely to forego this delight without a

[1] Harry McShane, Scottish correspondent of the *Daily Worker*.

struggle to the death; for the victory of the workers would mean the death of the church as it is now known to men—a purely worldly institution, seeking its one power, privilege, and wealth; and, as well, the right to distribute charity to millions which is another potent way to hold on to power over the wretched and the poor. That is another reason why they hate militant labour—the workers would depend—not on charity, but on their own might and imagination (as they are doing now in the USSR), and so do away with the curse of charity doles forever. It wont be an easy fight, but it is an inevitable one. At the moment there's a great flutter in the Vatican as to who should be Secretary of State—it has been vacant for a long time—and so who will be the next Pope. The American R.C. ecclesiastics want Spellman, but, of course, the other Vatican Prelates are dubious and frightened about this. It is almost certain that the next P wont be an Italian, though, if the Christian Democrats win, this may be set aside, and an Italian elected. The V has its own troubles, and it is up to us to add to them. It is very hard to advise you, but I think Harry's article should be published as a preliminary shot, so that we may see what will be the response.

Could you direct the enclosed letter—I cant make out . . .[2]

[2] Page missing.

To Jack Daly

MS. DALY

TOTNES, DEVON

10 MAY 1948

My dear Jack.

Thank you for your letter. I'm glad you liked the article.[1] You read, I suppose, about Hyde.[2] How they didn't see through him long before, I don't know. His articles are to be published in pamphlet form, & Harry

[1] Sean O'Casey, "Study Course for a Vatican Recruit," *Daily Worker,* 4 May 1948.

[2] Douglas Arnold Hyde, who had been a Communist for twenty years, 1928–48, and a member of the editorial board of the London *Daily Worker* 1940–48, suddenly resigned from the Communist Party and the *Daily Worker* on 15 March 1948, and announced that he had become a convert to Roman Catholicism. He was the "Vatican Recruit" in O'Casey's article. Hyde wrote a series of articles for the *Catholic Herald* on his "journey from Communism to Catholicism," which were published as pamphlets for the Catholic Truth Society, *From Communism to Catholicism* (1948) and *Communism From the Inside* (1948). See also Hyde's autobiography, *I Believed* (1950).

[Pollitt] promised to send me a copy, adding that he hoped I'd write a reply. The article I sent (before I got Harry's letter) seems to satisfy them. It shouldn't. In his first letter, Harry wanted something that "wouldn't offend Catholic workers." Now how is one to fight without hitting someone? They'll have to rid themselves of this fear of offending, if they want to oppose the Vatican effectively. They even changed the title of my article, which was "Cardinal Griffin's New Recruit." The fear of giving offence to "Catholic workers" is an obsession with them. Now they send me a Brochure on the answers given to questions asked as to how Soviet Writers work, live, move, & have their being. But my forte is a peculiar knowledge of the Catholic Theory & of its practices from many angles; & to write what they are asking of me is just a waste of time. I've just written a letter [3] replying to an article in the "Totnes Times," by Brigadier Raynor, M.P. for Totnes, quoting—not Marx or Lenin—Disraeli to confute and confuse him. You see, Jack, these Tory—or rather, Conservative—Leaders read little, & have forgotten what they saw on the notice—boards in Cambridge & Oxford; so it is easy to give them a jolt. But I wish Communists would read more. Harry evidently thinks he knows more about Catholicism than he does. They should have a special library dealing with the Vatican, & all its works & pomps. Years ago, when I warned & warned them, they thought I had a "bee in my bonnet," a thought enough to show how little they knew the force they were up against.

Don't bother returning enclosed letter. If I had known it would become a leaflet, it would have been better done.

All the best to Floss and you.
As ever.
Sean

[3] See O'Casey's letter to the *Totnes Times*, 15 May 1948, written on the 10th.

To Frank McCarthy

MS. MCCARTHY

TOTNES, DEVON
12 MAY 1948

Dear Frank McCarthy,
Here's the book [1] signed. I see you managed to get a "first Edition"— these must be scarce now. Indeed, it has been out of print for some time.
Mrs. O'Casey is keeping the bag allright. She says it will be fine for

[1] *Pictures in the Hallway* (1942).

carrying lunch for two for a day's trip to the seaside. That is how we take our holidays with the children—day trips. The hotels are far too costly now to allow even a week's stay in one. I didn't know you had been a P.O.W. in the hands of the Japanese. That must have been a tough time. Lovely cherry trees in full bloom aren't much of an inspiration to a prisoner.

Yes, I know most of [James] Stephens' verse; and it is a pity that he has ceased to write. His son's death, I think, had a bad effect on him. Well I know Stoneybather [2]—the Road of the Stones, in Irish, Constitution Hill, and Parkgate. The chocolate box was red for the Army & blue for the Navy [3]—if I remember right. An old Devon man, who does an odd bit of gardening for us, has one. He was a "Vidette," a mounted scout during the Boer War, & fought against the tribes of North West India. He & I sometimes have lunch together. Well I remember the Soldiers' Home, &, when a kid, often watched the red-coats coming out & going in, wishing I was one of them.

Yes, our boy is still in the army—a gunner. But he is a clerk, too, & doesn't like it. He is back now on general duty. He is to go on a farm for a few months, and looks forward to the harder work, for he is longing for exercise. Another couple of years, & our younger boy will have to be off too; so we'll only have the girl left; for by that time, though out of the Army, our elder boy will probably be on his own.

What an odd choice to make—a lighthouse keeper! But as good as any other.

All the best.

Yours very sincerely,
Sean O'Casey.

I enclose a book you might like to read.[4]

[2] Stoneybatter, a working-class district on the north side of Dublin.
[3] Queen Victoria presented boxes of chocolate in red and blue tins to soldiers who fought in the Boer War.
[4] *Looming Lights,* a book about lighthouses.

To Totnes Times

15 MAY 1948

Sean O'Casey's Reply to Brig. R. Raynor, M.P.[1]

Sir,—Brigadier Raynor is, I'm sure, a very busy man, maybe making the night joint labourer with the day, but however busy he may be, when

[1] Reply to an article by Brig. R. Raynor, M.P., "Totnes M.P. and 'Russian Myth,'" *Totnes Times,* 8 May 1948.

setting down to write an article, he should pause for some time to take thought. His article is a breathless one, consisting of hundreds of statements shouted out without rhyme and very little reason. He says "all this wrack and ruin has been brought in less than 36 months." A very bad sentence, and untrue as well. The wrack and ruin we suffer from now, and not we alone, but all Europe, was brought about by the war. Some of it has lingered with us since the first world war. There is always ruin, more or less, after every war. There were difficulties in England even after the battle of Crecy; and these difficulties bring changes, be the government what it may be. There is no escape from it, and the last war was the biggest bringer of calamity the world has ever known. Even the rich and mighty United States hasnt escaped it. Prices are mounting there, though, as yet, Labour isnt the governing power in that part of America. Indeed, things arent looking too well in other ways. For instance "Over two million children of school-age are not in school (How many of these are swelling the ranks of juvenile delinquents?). Millions of those in school (perhaps yours among them) are receiving inferior education. Many of the good teachers who remain faithfully in their jobs are underpaid and overworked. School enrollments are greatly increasing. Class rooms are overcrowded. Outmoded equipment and obsolete text-books are in use in many schools. Many buildings are in sad disrepair. Do you wonder why 350,000 teachers have left their professions since 1941? Why 70,000 teaching jobs are unfilled? Why fewer and fewer students are preparing to be teachers? What chance have your children of becoming good citizens under whom our democracy can prevail?"

What chance indeed! The above quotation is a statement issued by the Macmillan Company of New York, and appears in the New York Times Book Review, Feb. 1st, 1948.

But Brigadier Raynor would solve the problem by sending out our children to earn. No high school, no chance of a University for them. Would a son of the Brigadier be sent out to earn the minute the clock struck the fourteenth year of his age? Well, whatever the Soviet Union may be, it hasnt over or under two million of children running round wild, with no school to go to.

We get Brigadier Raynor's attitude of mind about "Russia" (meaning the Soviet Union), when he says, "At the end of hostilities, talking in our Senior Mess, we most of us agreed that a move forward by the British and American Armies to push the Russians back behind their own borders offered the best hope for world peace."

Well, let us thank God there must have been wiser minds in the Senior messes than those in Brigadier Raynor's. He evidently saw nothing dishonorable in suddenly turning on an Ally immediately hostilities ended. He wanted hostilities to begin again, never thinking, like a good democrat, of what the Rank and File would say. And the mothers, the wives, and sweethearts of the rank and file would say. Indeed, he seems to be eager for a war again, this time with the Soviet Union. Soldier beware; soldier take care! We have had enough of war for a long time to come—forever, if you ask me. Totnes mothers lost their sons, Totnes wives lost their husbands; they are not eager to make any more of these sorrowful sacrifices. "And this in spite of the Conservative pack that infest clubs, chattering on subjects of which it is impossible they can know anything, barking and yelping, denouncing traitors, and wondering how the leaders could be so led by the nose, and not see that which was flagrant to the whole world": Disraeli.[2]

The Red Army is no myth. Indeed, the tenacity, the bravery, the almost supernatural endurance of the Russian soldier never was a myth. If Brigadier Raynor will read [George] Borrow's *Wild Wales* [1862], he will get some information there about this fact, brought about by an opinion held then, similar to the one the Brigadier holds now, during the progress of the Crimean War.

Changes have come, changes are coming, and they are headed by the Young—even the young of his own Party; and, if Brigadier Raynor persists in blocking the way, he will be swept aside. The Young hold the field. To again quote Disraeli: "We live in an age when to be young and to be indifferent can be no longer synonymous. We must prepare for the coming hour. The claims of the future are represented by suffering millions; and the Youth of a Nation are the Trustees of posterity." [3]

Yours sincerely,
Sean O'Casey

[2] Benjamin Disraeli, *Sybil; or, The Two Nations* (1845), a novel on the causes and nature of Chartism.
[3] *Ibid.*

To Richard J. Madden

TC. O'CASEY

[TOTNES, DEVON]
19 MAY 1948

Dear Dick,
Thanks for your two letters, one as big as a petition to the House of Commons. What a wilderness of words from [A. R.] Houghton! With his elaborate financial scheme I wont deal, but confine my remarks to what is embedded in his pile of sentences.

1. He wants to get the film done as cheap as he can, outside of what will be given to Barry Fitzgerald. His remarks about the other characters show

this; but what about "Juno"? And what about "Joxer"? I'm not going to have the film simply a glorification of Fitzgerald.

2. This is what Fitzgerald wants, I'm afraid. His brother [Arthur Shields] wrote to me some time ago about the film, and I simply gave him your name and number. It was my plays that lifted Fitzgerald up, gave him his chance. He seems to be getting bad stuff to do, and, in my opinion, is eager to do something which will give him back a big name so that the demand for him may be clamourous again. I dont blame him, but this doesnt interest me, as you will understand. This is confirmed by the statement of Houghton that they propose to keep to the play as much as possible—meaning to keep as close as possible to Fitzgerald.

3. I gather from the letter that the royalty offered is $10,000; with a further $7500. deferred; but I'm not sure about this, and you dont comment upon it in your letter.

4. The market value of "Juno" is, I think, increasing. I have just been asked to sign a contract for a London production, which offers £100 advance on royalties—as much as if it were a new play; and £50 advance for a provincial tour, after the London production. It is almost certain that a film of the play will be done, whether Houghton does it or no.

By the way, isnt THE PLOUGH AND THE STARS back with me again from RKO? Arent the ten years up? [1]

I should like your comment on Houghton's plan, besides your advice to give it "careful consideration."

And all the best and more to Tessa and to you.

[*Sean*]

P.S. I'd very much like to know how much Fitzgerald expects to get out of it. Very much more than the offer made to me, I warrant. He looks to me to give him fame and make his fortune too! Well, I'm not eager to do either.

[1] The film version of *The Plough and the Stars,* directed by John Ford for RKO, was released in March 1937. See O'Casey's letter to Horace Reynolds, 15 February 1937, note 1, Vol. I, p. 648.

To Peter Hughes [1]

TC. O'CASEY

[TOTNES, DEVON]
25 MAY 1948

Dear Mr. Hughes:

Thank you for your letter, in which you say my idea of the middle ages is all hayswire [sic]. But what I said had nothing to do with any idea of mine own, but quoted the opinions of those who lived through them—Froissart, Langland, Chaucer; and from him who wrote the *English Social History* [1944], Trevelyan [G. M.], the scholar and historian. If you want more, then read Exordium Magnum, and St. Bonaventura's wail about the failure of the friars, "Therefore when these younger men come to rule in the Order, they bring up the next generation in their own likeness, so that the early friars are now become a laughing stock, rather than a model for the rest." And this of the Cistercians! You can find out hundreds of instances, if you wish to look for them. No R. Catholic preacher would today dare to teach his flock what was taught to them and told to them then, and retold by the great Massillon but two centuries ago with placid and childish orthodoxy. Read, if you wish to learn a few things about your Church, *Reminiscences of a Maynooth Professor,* written by Dr. Walter MacDonald, for forty years Professor of Theology in Maynooth's R.C. College of St Patrick; but dont go then and say these are only O'Casey's opinions. All these things have astonished me, for they utterly sweep away the rosy rottenness of all that Chesterton said and sung about, praising what never existed.

Supposing I did "wilt, and embrace the symbol of the cross," that even wouldnt prove anything to be other than it was and is. Did it never strike you as strange that so many flags of "Protestant" nations had a cross on their banners, and so few "Catholic" nations use it?

I'm afraid I'll have to leave with you the miraculous "smile" and "a little help here and there". I still prefer The Communist Manifesto.

I dont quite know what you mean by "my patrimony." All that I know I have are a wife and three children. The churches and their orders could tell you a helluva lot more about "patrimony" than I can. And as for Rowton Houses, I thought the Rerum Novarum was out to do away with these dreadful things? Is this the fruit and blessing we are to have from the Pope's Social Encyclicals; or do you mean to suggest that these places are hot-bed cultures towards saintship?

1 Peter Hughes, 322 Casterknowle Road, Sheffield.

As for Mr. Hyde's Pamphlet[2]—do you really believe this to be a document of merit, either of spiritual values or literary achievement?

Oh, Mr. Hughes, Mr. Hughes!

> *Well, all the best to you, anyway.*
> *Yours sincerely,*
> *Sean O'Casey*

[2] Douglas A. Hyde, *From Communism to Catholicism* (1948).

To Totnes Times

29 MAY 1948

O'Casey's Reply to Brigadier Raynor

Sir,—Of your courtesy, please allow a last reply to Brigadier Raynor's reply to me.[1] The Brigadier is breathless still. The present Government is far from perfect—all governments are—but it is not responsible for the ruin and dislocation left behind by the great war. Some could point to the Government of Chamberlain as being responsible for the things that brought the war into being; but it is useless to fight about things past when the present is so pregnant with problems. The United States hadn't a single brick disturbed by the violence of the war, yet she is in a very disturbed state just now. Like our pound here, the dollar there hasn't the value it had some little time ago. Thousands of returned G.I.'s can't get a house to live in; even men in well-paid jobs find it hard to make both ends meet. I know this, for they have written to me about it. One, a professor, got a rise of four hundred dollars a month, but rising prices soon left him where he had been before. There is, too, the woeful state of schools, the scarcity of teachers, the hopeless out-of-date condition of the text-books, so plaintively commented upon in the bulletin issued by the Macmillan Company of America. The Congress is now arguing in a turmoil of words about the indifferent quality and ugly taste of margarine, which has to become a substitute for butter in many American homes now. Half of the middle-west is a dust-bowl, worse now than when the film of *The Grapes of Wrath* appeared; and the Oklahoma at home in America isn't quite as gay and lovely as the Oklahoma now in the Drury Lane Theatre. All this, and much more, hasn't been brought on the American land by a Socialist Government, but by one, probably after the Brigadier's own heart.

[1] Raynor's letter to the *Totnes Times*, 22 May 1948.

It isn't quite true to say that everything soon became all sagarnio after the first World War. The children of the Nation weren't fed as well then as they are now. I saw the evacuees myself, and many of them were in a shocking condition. The Conservatives near had a fit when it was proposed to increase the Old Age Pensions. Britain could not repay the debt she owed to America; couldn't even continue to pay the interest on it, and had to default. Indeed, when speaking at a meeting once in New York, I was interrupted and bitterly attacked for not paying back the debt we owed to the U.S.A. And, though the income tax wasn't then so high as it is now, it was much higher than it had been before the war, and, if the Government had improved even the schools then in the land, it would have been higher still. The Brigadier has but to look at his own Grammar School to see that it isn't in any way suitable for the crowd of boys who attend it; hasn't been for years, but the Labour Government isn't responsible for that neglect. The Conservatives think more of their Club than they do of their school; the Club, where, as Disraeli said, they chatter of things about which they know nothing.

My question about the schools his own children went to, was in no way personal. His remarks simply say that he sent his children to schools in which he thought they would get the best education. Sensible man. I did the same. My point is that the best schools should be available for all capable of using the advantages they offer. That all schools should be public schools; and that the existing ones should be brought to face the newer outlook on life. That there should no longer be Two Nations in England; "between whom there is no intercourse and no sympathy; who are as ignorant of each other's habits, thought, and feelings, as if they were dwellers in different zones, or inhabitants of different planets; who are formed by a different breeding, are fed by a different food, are ordered by different manners, and are not governed by the same laws—The RICH AND THE POOR." This was said, not by a Socialist, not even by a Labour Leader but by a British Prime Minister—Disraeli.[2] Now we are moving towards that end, and the Brigadier is growling; protesting, even, because of the inconveniences caused, though his Party never tried in any way to make the way straighter for the newly-risen men of the people. If we haven't enough schools for our children, then we must build more; if we haven't enough teachers, then we must provide a system by which more will come to take up teaching as a vocation. These are the only ways to meet the irresistible demand of the new life.

To discuss the question of Czechoslovakia, and the other lands friendly to the Soviet Union, would require the whole of the Totnes Times, and the Editor, naturally, couldnt allow that; but if the Soviet Union were, as the Brigadier maintains, "a land of serfs, slave camps, and torture," she could never have defeated Germany, Austria, Roumania, Hungary, and Finland,

[2] See O'Casey's letter to the *Totnes Times,* 15 May 1948, note 2.

combined; and neither would she be now the "menace" that the Brigadier thinks her to be.

Devon is a beautiful county, and the West Country Folk a grand lot, but I may remind the Brigadier that Devon wasn't always a secure place to live in. After the retreat of Dunkirk, Invasion seemed imminent, and even the Brigadier's comrade military expert, Capt. Liddel-Hart, thought it so certain that he went away to the Lake District, after telling me to get away, too, for a man of my ideas would be "particularly objectionable to the Nazis." Well, after living with the Devon people, we decided that we would share anything coming to them, while I personally decided that, though I would probably die in a ditch, I would never die in a concentration camp.

When I mentioned age, I did not mean the age of years, but the aged mind that will not allow adaptation to the eternal law of change. There are many old who do not permit age to weary them, or the years to condemn them, while some, young in years, treasure minds fashioned fast in the past. But in passing, I'd remind Brigadier Raynor that many hardy men play golf, and hardier ones played bowls, for the great Captains who fought the mighty and magnificent Armada, loved to ply the brown or black woods along the green sward towards the waiting white Jack.

The Member of Totnes seems to be very much afraid of "the East," as uncivilised and savage, for he says that the Soviet Union is "an Eastern race and uncivilised" only understanding force. Well, they understand Shakespeare too, and honour him far more than we do. And we've learned a lot from the East: the origin of chemistry, improvements in trigonometry, the invention of Algebra, numerals of arithmetic, and many discoveries in astronomy. The East measured the height of the atmosphere, and explained the twilight, the twinkling of the stars. Three of the world's great religions—Christianity, Islam and Buddhism—were born in Asia. No, the West cannot separate itself from the East, and why, in the name of God should it? We are all one.

I have little to say to "True Marxian." Brigadier Raynor pays the respect to his readers by putting his name to what he says, and I pay the respect to him by doing the same. The first faculty of a Marxian—much more a True Marxian—is that of having the guts to put a name to what is said by him or her. His letter is useful in proving one thing: That there are pathetic fools to be found, even among "True Marxians."

I thank you, Mr. Editor, for your courtesy.

Yours sincerely,
Sean O'Casey

To Daily Worker [1]

TC. O'CASEY

TOTNES, DEVON
31 MAY 1948

Mr. D. Hyde and O'Casey

Dear Sir,

Permit me one reply to Mr. Hyde. Mr. Hyde is very excited, and in it, he seems to be bearing false witness gainst a neighbour. There was no personal abuse in my comments on his change of mind and conscience. I simply challenged from quotations from others, who knew better than I, that the faith and culture of the Middle Ages meant a rosy life for men. Does he dispute the fact of the great Peasant Rising in the reign of Richard the Second? Did not the Hundred Years War take place during the Middle Ages? And the Wars of the Roses too? And werent all who took part in these fights a part of the unity and faith of the Middle Ages? Are these facts personal abuse? And didnt the Black Death devastate England and Europe periodically then, once sweeping away half of England's population? Does he dispute the fact that, at the time of the French Revolution there were still three hundred thousand ecclesiastical serfs in France alone? Are these statements "sneers," or are they facts? Dont these facts prove that in the Middle Ages the members of the Catholic Church didnt hold the faith in the unity of peace?

Mr. Hyde is, apparently very angry with me for saying that what he said in his articles suggested he hadnt a knowledge of the faith he had accepted as his own. There is nothing in them to show that he did, or does. There is not only no spiritual grandeur in them, there isnt even spiritual poverty apparent in any of them. I took what his words said; what they were meant to mean is another matter. And perhaps it would be wiser for those, who set about instructing Communists in the faith, to set about, instead, instructing the others who have been with them since they were born. Mr. Hyde is evidently unaware that the Hierarchy has recently declared publicly, that Catholics are pitiably ignorant of the teaching of the Church, saying "that many are ignorant of even the elementary truths of their religion," and the Catholic *Universe* of June 27th, 1947, writes a leader about this "Tragic Ignorance." And if Mr. Hyde takes the trouble to read Dr. MacDonald, he'll find that some of the clergy are as bad as the laymen. I'm afraid, from the words of the Bishops themselves (not O'Casey's), the instruction given

---

[1] This letter was refused publication because of its length. It was a reply to Douglas A. Hyde's article, "Red 'Anger Frustration' over Hyde, Ex-Communist Replies to Sean O'Casey," in the Catholic *Glasgow Observer*, 14 May 1948, which was in turn a reply to O'Casey's article, "Study Course For a Vatican Recruit," *Daily Worker*, 4 May 1948.

to young Communists is more effective than that given to young Catholics by their Catholic instructors.

I was not "commissioned" by the *Daily Worker* to reply to Mr. Hyde. If he knew anything about me, he'd know I criticised Christian practice long before I even heard his name—the play *Within the Gates,* for instance, written in 1931, published in 1933.

His contention that England is in a state of violence comparative to that of the Middle Ages is either an ignorant statement or a lie. Here now it is illegal to carry a weapon; then it was necessary for all men in order to defend house and home. Indeed, somewhere, his friend and guide, Chesterton, reminds us that the walking-stick is a survival of the club all men—not having a finer weapon—had to carry to protect themselves from attack.

And—apart from its unfairness and irrelevancy—how could I rest "so comfortably in the backwater of Totnes," if, as he says, England today is filled with rapine, beatings, murder, and robbery? The one difference of the criminal of today and that of the Middle Ages is that the one today has to say, as suggested by Mr. Hyde himself, "Can I get away with it?" and the criminal of the Middle Ages knew, in most cases, that he could. Since he has brought up the "comfort" idea, "far away from it all," I can say that, if he had read what I had written, he'd know something of the Comforts with which my life has been dotted; and that my body will carry to its grave the badge of my tribe, the marks of the battling proletariat.

Mr. Hyde recommends to me the works of William Morris, "a Socialist and medievalist"; and he adds that "O'Casey remains discreetly silent about him." Well, I'll mention Morris now. Morris was a poet—and not in the front rank either—and an artist-craftsman. When Mr. Hyde calls him a "medievalist," does he mean by this term that Morris was an authority, an historical authority on the cultural, social, and ecclesiastical life of the Middle Ages? Mr. Hyde can answer by a simple yes or no. And even his ballads about life then arent all complimentary to the life lived then. Was he any more an authority on that time, and all its activities, than Sir Walter Scott, author of Ivanhoe, The Talisman, and Lay of the Last Minstrel? And, since we are about it, let Mr. Hyde read Morris's *News From Nowhere,* his most imaginative work, his vision of what he thought the world should be like. If I remember right, in it, no priest appears, no hymn is sung, no prayer is offered. And, as an afterthought, let him read Sir Thomas More's *Utopia.* In it, I think he'll find the following, after describing the happy place it was: "They have priests of exceeding holiness, and therefore very few." Very few, even in St. Thomas More's *Utopia!*

If he wants modern examples of Christian violence, let him remember that it was Hitler, a Roman Catholic (according to the *Universe*) who wasnt excommunicated, because he never encroached upon the Canon Laws (according to the Catholic *Universe*), who led the Nazi Terror; and that the German Army was crowded with Catholics attacking Catholic

Poland. And, nearer home, apart from all this, the bitterest violence was shown, not in Protestant (Pagan, if he likes) England, but in Catholic Ireland, when, in the Civil War Catholics were busy for quite a long time murdering each other.

Hilaire Belloc is quoted as a guide; but he isn't such a fine one as Mr. Hyde seems to think. As an authority, he has been weighed in the balance, and found wanting. He has been referred to by one opponent as "that happy-go-lucky journalist," which seems to fit him fairly well. For instance, writing about the use of the word "Roman" as a prefix to "Catholic," he says, "The term 'Roman' Catholic is a provincial term invented for political purposes by the Westminster Crown Lawyers of the late sixteenth century to safeguard the remaining claims of the English Monarchy to be Catholic. It was invented to be used in England as a protest that the Church of England could be Catholic without the Pope. It no longer corresponds with reality . . . The phrase is peculiar to our official system. The term is even more of an absurdity than a falsehood." Yet at the same time, the Pope, in the person of Cardinal Gasspari, was publicly proclaiming the exact opposite. The Cardinal condemned General Strickland for suppressing the word, saying "The religion of Malta is the Roman Catholic Apostolic Religion," and by trying to suppress the word, the General "could only disgust and offend the Catholics, for whom the word 'Roman' was precisely the expression which distinguished the Catholic religion from all other confessions." Indeed, the Marriage Certificate of my own wife is signed by Percival Howell, Roman Catholic Priest; and the official notepaper of Maynooth College bears the title of "St. Patrick's Roman Catholic College of Maynooth." That's H. Belloc for you, going against the Cardinals when it seems to serve his purpose. But I dont ask Mr. Hyde to take my word for this. Father J. B. Code, in his *Queen Elizabeth and the English Catholic Historians* [1935] (and such a writer wouldnt want to be hard on Belloc), says, "Unfortunately, he (Mr. Belloc) refuses to give authorities even for statements whose very novelty makes it impossible to accept them without further investigation. . . . It is impossible to know what facts Belloc has mastered, what evidence he has gathered to substantiate his statements." Well, there's Belloc for you, according to a priest of his own Church, twirling his slender stick, dismissing all questions with a wave of the hand. A better guide for Mr. Hyde on Ecclesiastical History would have been the unbeliever, Gibbon, for according to Cardinal Newman, "Perhaps the only English Writer who has any claim to be considered an ecclesiastical historian is the unbeliever Gibbon." But what does the name of Belloc mean to the worker—Catholic or Protestant or unbeliever? It doesnt mean a damn, save insofar that it allies itself with those who, using special and plausible pleading, try to lead the militant workers from the ranks of militant labour, which alone can bring them to security, deliver them from want and fear, and restore them to dignity and honour.

Mr. Hyde says "Having tasted of the servitude of Communism for twenty years, and now the freedom of the Catholic Faith, I know which way lies peace and freedom." A curious sentence. Surely twenty years were more than a taste; and why did such an intelligence endure this servitude so long? And, as a matter of fact, no one yet has lived for a day, much more for twenty years, in a state of life in which Communism is its practice—not even in the USSR. And what is the "freedom of the Catholic Faith"? Is it something separate from the tyranny of the Church authorities? Does it embrace freedom of thought? What about the case of Alfred Noyes, the Roman Catholic poet? Some time ago, he published a book on Voltaire [2] aiming at (his own words) "persuading or convincing the sceptical non-Catholic world (especially the literary section of it) that the solution of its present difficulties and bewilderments is to be found in the Catholic Faith and there alone." Noyes is, of course, a far, far greater writer than Mr. Hyde, with a more extensive knowledge of, and a finer conception of what is the Catholic Faith. It was condemned by the Vatican, and the poet had to withdraw it. Freedom for Hyde! And the Denunciator attached to the Holy Office of the Vatican, who condemns the book remains incognito, so that Mr. Noyes didnt know who accused him, and, to make it worse, didnt know what was wrong with the book, for no instances of error were given, while the poet was asked to "write something that would be equivalent to a reparation." Books even that are universal are on the Index; and if the Holy Office had its sway now, as it had in the Middle Ages, neither the faithful nor the unbeliever would be permitted to read anything that hadnt on it the sign and signature of a bishop. And how many books of the first order are on the Index? Books which no Catholic is permitted to read, without special permission? What about the Clerical-sponsored Censorship in Eirinn? There, no writer, unless he has already a sale outside the country, can write without a vision of the Censor looking over his shoulder. Almost all my own books have been banned by this clique aflame for the glory of God, the safety of souls, and the honour of Eireann! When my play, *The Silver Tassie,* appeared it was greeted with a roar from members of the Catholic Young Men's Clubs, and one fool Dominican, in elegant and priestly manner, referred to the play as "Sewage," "Filth," and "Cesspool." [3] W. B. Yeats's play, *Countess Cathleen,* was condemned offhand by an ignorant Cardinal as anti-Catholic, though the prelate admitted that he hadnt even read the play.[4] If Mr. Hyde (who apparently knows me so well that he calls me "Sean") takes the trouble to dip into my book, *Drums Under the Windows,* he will see how shabbily a Roman Catholic priest, Dr. M. O'Hickey, was treated by the notorious Roman Rota, not on a religious question; not even on a political one; but merely on that of making Irish an essential subject in the

[2] See O'Casey's letter to Daniel Macmillan, 26 August 1948, note 5.
[3] See the letter from Father M. H. Gaffney, O.P., to the *Irish Press,* 14 August 1935, Vol. I, pp. 576–77.
[4] See O'Casey's letter to Liam Shine, 5 January 1947, note 4.

University just then established in Dublin. He can follow up this by finding out the way the theologian, Dr. MacDonald, was treated by the same authorities. If this "taste" of Roman Catholic freedom isnt enough for Mr. Hyde, then I shall be happy to give him a mouthful; and, if a mouthful shouldnt be enough, then, I'll give him a hearty meal of it.

Mr. Hyde and his co-adjutorial instructors are mightily fond of declaring that Communism is a materialistic faith, that its leaders are hot on the trail of the things of this world; that they are after, not only the flesh-pots of Egypt, but also, those of the whole world, implying, of course, that his Bishops and priests are high above that sort of longing. But, when I went to America, I noticed that a bishop and all the priests travelled as "Cabin-passengers," while the great bulk of the Catholic laity travelled steerage. I was down there, and there wasnt a single priest among them. Now, if his new comrades are so unworldly, why dont they publish yearly a balance-sheet, showing the properties they possess and the revenue they gather year by year.

Since he saw the light, Mr. Hyde has even turned prophet, prophesying that by eighty years, maybe, Beaverbrook's black building, the architecture of Kharkov (what a thorn in the flesh is anything achieved by the Soviet Union!), and O'Casey's plays—all gone west by a blast from an atomic bomb. True Christian thought, true son of the wish; but, in passing, I may remind the Christian well-wisher that cathedrals as well as cinemas can be tumbled down by the atomic bomb. But a prophet came before Hyde—Dr. MacDonald, Theologian of Maynooth College. Listen to him, a Roman Catholic priest and a theologian to boot: "You English Radicals, what political method do you believe in? Was it immoral to pull down the Hyde Park railings; and were it not for that threatened outburst and others like it, would your trade unions be legal now? You know full well that, if your masters could, they would put you in jail for strikes and picketing. And they could, and would, only that you learned to disregard their law. . . . Is it not our Irish experience—is it not the lesson of history?—that unjust rulers, masters, holders of every kind, laugh you to scorn, working-men of England, unless you can take them by the throat. . . . Are the Russians, however cultured they may become, bound for all time to autocratic Czars? (This was answered in 1917. S. O'C.). . . . My books, if published, might do a little to withstand the Revolution, which the official guardians of our religion will not see coming, or will endeavour to keep out with their broomsticks." And, now, Mr. Hyde is, apparently, one of the broomsticks!

Most English workers have heard of the fight the Irish tenant-farmers made through the Land League, using the weapon of the Boycott, to break the power of the absentee landlords, and free themselves from the power of feudalism. The Irish clergy didnt like this weapon, for, as Dr. MacDonald says, "Boycotting is a revolutionary weapon, and—unfortunately, as I think— the rulers of the Catholic Church have been opposed to revolution in any shape. Leo the XIII condemned boycotting, as practised in Ireland, at the time of the Land League, towards which his whole attitude was so hostile." And, Catholic workers, this Pope, who condemned the one weapon the Irish tenant-farmer had, was the one who issued the Rerum Novarum, which Mr. Hyde says is the charter of the workers!

And, in passing, Dr. MacDonald gives this jab at the hypocritical bishops, "There isnt a Bishop on the bench that does not some time or other squeeze those with whom he deals, to secure more favourable terms. The pressure applied is the fear of losing this contract, perhaps, others too. The pressure is sometimes considerable, as everyone knows who has experience of trade: it is the oldest and commonest form of the boycott." Oh, ay, the Bishops can squeeze the contractors ruthlessly, but the workers must go gently at the peril of their souls' salvation! No wonder the name of MacDonald is never mentioned in polite or impolite Catholic higher circles today!

Well, Catholic fellow workers, there's a man for you, a Professor of Theology in a Roman Catholic College for forty years, for forty years; a man beside whom Hyde is but a bewildered, blundering pigmy.

Now listen to what the same theologian says about the Catholic Press and Catholic journalists. A students' debating society had been set up in the College, and was doing well, till "the superiors began to fear that it was getting out of hand—that at times the members turned from art and literature to criticise their superiors. Fear of criticism, on the part of superiors, seems to argue a certain lack of confidence—self-reliance—on their part. The rulers of states, surely, have been improved since the time when no one dare criticise their actions, under pain of imprisonment, confiscation, or worse; and it is possible that the ecclesiastical state, too, might flourish even though the citizens, without usurping apostolical authority, were allowed to speak their minds more freely both as to men and measures. A debating society or journal that is kept in leading-strings will do little good to its members or readers. If the Catholic Church has in her service hardly one strong, well-conducted newspaper or periodical, that is the price she pays for *keeping all her journalists in bondage;* (italics mine) no really strong man will continue to serve under the strictures that prevail."

That, my comrades, isnt the opinion of O'Casey, but of Dr. MacDonald, Professor of Theology in St. Patrick's College of Maynooth, for forty years. All her journalists in bondage! And this is the liberty that Mr. Hyde loves! Indeed, a very chilly freedom in which to sun his talents— if he has any. It looks, from what Dr. MacDonald has said of Catholic journalism, that Mr. Hyde has hastened to wrap his one talent in a napkin, and buried it in a field.

And Father Yorke, Doctor of Divinity, said the same thing to this very Theologian about the Catholic Press of America. "With all its thick, well-bound and much-ruled books, the many pigeon-holes, one for every parish, convent, and other institutions; the apparatus of seals, stamps, typewriters, the Chancellories of the Bishops were little more than a great business office, well managed, but nothing done there that would be beyond the capacity of a Market Street clerk who might be got for seventy-five dollars a week. Collecting money is the business of most of the clergy of the United States, so they have little time for reading, or even for thought, except as to how to get in the dollars."

We all know how very recently two Roman Catholic dignitaries, employed by the Vatican itself, were concerned with the theft of some millions of lira, and how, if the Italian authorities hadnt laid hands on one of them, no one would probably have heard a word about the matter, which shows that the love of money, which is the root of much evil, clings to the skirts of Popes, Cardinals, and Monsignors, just as the love of money did in the Middle Ages, so much admired by the Bellocs, Chestertons, and the Hydes. "The only protection that is worth a straw," says Dr. MacDonald, "in money matters is publicity—publication of accounts—as experience proves. There is a feeling that conversion of public funds to private uses, if not inconceivable, is, at least, so rare as to be negligible in the case of Churchmen. Would that it were so, but, unfortunately, the history of the Papacy alone proves that it is not. For, if the Roman Catholic Curia lost the hold it had on Europe during the Middle Ages it is mainly because of misappropriation of Church funds. (The Middle Ages again, so beloved of Chesterton, Belloc, and Hyde!) Not only was the wealth of Rome the cause of all the scandals that shocked the conscience of Europe, but it was in itself, perhaps, the greatest scandal of all. In reading Dr. Pastor's history of Pope Alexander the sixth [5]—no very edifying churchman—I was more shocked at the misuse of public money than at the personal irregularities of the head of the Church. Twenty-seven benefices including the Archbishopric of Amalfi, were held by the Pope, Leo the tenth in his youth. Even the good St. Charles Borromeo was loaded with benefices from his youth, and Cardinal Mazarin received the incomes from twenty-seven abbacies, besides a number of bishoprics; and these are but a few examples." The Middle Ages were a golden age right enough—for some people. And they're at it still, as the recent pinching of Vatican money by Vatican dignitaries proves. Ay, indeed, "The history of the Papacy justifies the faithful in being on their guard against maladministration in the Roman Curia"; so, Catholic workers, warns—not a Communist—but an eminent theologian of your own Catholic Church.

And as for the arguments used by such as Chesterton, many priests standing by the altar, speaking from the pulpit, or on public platforms; arguments so glibly used everywhere, let us see what Dr. MacDonald, the theologian thinks of them. He says "Our books are stuffed with arguments based on principles in which no man of Science believes—which would be laughed out of existence if paraded, in the language of daily life, where

[5] Ludwig Pastor, *History of the Popes: From the Close of the Middle Ages* (1891–   ).

men of science could hear what we say and ridicule us." And it is precisely because these arguments are received and answered by ridicule and laughter that many are denounced as "atheistic Communists" by those who are ignorant and silly enough to use them.

We often, too, hear about an "iron curtain," and Mr. Hyde in his reply to me, mentions it frequently. It has always puzzled me that those who breathlessly proclaim that all is hidden behind it, that no one knows what the "enigma" of the Soviet Union is up to behind its steely protection, yet seem to be able to tell us of every detail of life "endured" and "suffered" by the Soviet people; indeed, able to reveal everything that happens there, from the numbers in the "concentration camps" to how many times Stalin looks at himself in the mirror. But they never say a word about the Iron Curtain of the Vatican sheltering it from the outside world. The Soviet Union publishes a balance sheet; we know from its published budget what is spent on the various activities making up the life of her people. What do we know of the revenue of the Vatican, or what is spent by the various departments on its many activities. We dont even know what the revenue of the Roman Catholic [Church] of Ireland is; or even what monies are gathered in yearly by the same Institution in England; dont know what the Archbishopric of Westminster costs, or the Bishoprics of Birmingham, Liverpool, or Plymouth. Indeed, we dont know what Mr. Hyde is getting for his services; he certainly doesnt live on air. How quiet and orderly was the investigation into the fire in Ireland which roasted to death forty-four little delinquents, locked in their dormitories, light cut off, so that they had to blunder about in the dark, screaming; an old woman of seventy in charge, while the nuns slept safe, a long way off from where their little charges died the death. And quiet too the case of the priest who killed a man with a blow, because he refused to leave a woman he was living with; and we all recollect the recent matter of a priest caught meddling with a boy, whose case was to be tried in private so as to prevent a scandal. I remember myself in a Buckingham town the case of a Prior being removed quietly because of an affair with a woman. Indeed, I shouldnt have known a thing about it if a member of the Order hadnt been a visiting friend at the time. The Roman Catholic Church has its own way, a very quiet and effective way of silencing clergy who say too much, or think too deeply. A bitter and ruthless way, if the authorities think that was necessary, as Bishop Hefele and Dellinger—not to mention the name of Tyrrell—found out when they ventured to contradict the "Holy Office." If such strong men are made to suffer, of whom we hear, what happens to the weaker men of whom we hear nothing? We can gauge the extent of the tyranny by remembering the Index and by the fiat that goes with it forbidding the reading [of] each book 'throughout the world and in every translation." Well, the Kremlin wouldnt venture to go as far as that; but Mr. Hyde and his friends see in the Vatican power, not only "freedom," but sweetness and light!

As for the "hatred" provoked by Communists in encouraging "class war," let us mention one incident seen with our own eyes. When the Roman Catholic Evacuees came to Totnes, they came in three Class-divided contingents; the children of the rich were conducted to a place with "beautiful" surroundings—lawns, lovely house, orchard, gardens, and, I believe, a lake with swans on it. The place was named "Sharphams"; the lower middle-class children went to a large house, called "Plym House," on the upper Plymouth Road; a house about one-fifth the size of "Sharphams," and with but scraggy surroundings; the kids of the working-class Catholics were shoved into any place they could get. But all are equal in the sight of God, but not in the sight of Bishop, monsignor, or even priest. Do you approve of this class-war, fellow Catholic-workers? Are not your children as the others are! If you prick them, will they not bleed; if you tickle them, will they not laugh; and if you do not feed them well, clothe them sensibly, and give them good places in which to sleep, will they not languish, if they do not die? Are you going to condemn the Communists for working towards the end of providing a decent and safe life for your children; to abolish the difference between the conditions that provides a place for one child to abide beside swans, and for another to abide beside dustbins?

The Catholic *Universe,* every week, has a column called "Apostolate of the Countryside," which aims at bringing Catholics to pretty places in England where they are scarce. The moment a place becomes vacant, and is for sale, the fact is announced, and details given. The places range in price from two thousand pounds to ten thousand, and usually have orchards, walled gardens, acres of woodlands, and all amenities. Comrade Catholic workers in factory, field, and workshop, how many of you could dash your name down on a cheque for even the lower of these figures, pack up your troubles in your old kit-bag, and hurry off to these pleasant woods and pastures new? Not one of you, even were you to take out all you had in savings certificates. You are all equal in God's sight, but even a thousand pounds go a long way to confirm this faith!

Here is a taste of Roman Catholic propaganda on the problem of falling in love, about which so many of the poets have sung their rarest and richest songs. It was given by Fr. Joseph Manton, the radio priest, to six hundred young members of Boston's League of Catholic Women:

> Dont marry a man for his handsome profile. It may develop into two mezzanine chins.
> Dont marry a set of circumstances, marry a man.
> Dont marry for wavy hair—wavy hair soon may fall out.
> Dont marry a gambler and put yourself in the position of being a rival to a horse.
> Dont marry a younger man—he'll want a rhumba when you are a rheumatic.
> Ask your mother before you stick your finger out for his ring and end up wearing it in your nose.

The above is so beautiful, so unique, so original, that the Catholic *Universe* of May 28th, 1948, couldnt resist the desire to publish it, and make it known to the astonished Catholic world. But what sort are the members of the Boston Catholic League of Women to submit to this kind of mind-stupefying inanity!

But what do the clerics care—get the money in, get the money in, is their godlike slogan, though they lay the sin of "materialism" at the door of Communism. The Vatican is ever ready to make a bargain with the highest bidder. In 1929 it sold itself to Mussolini and Fascism for sixteen million pounds—see R[obert] Sencourt's *Genius of the Vatican* [1935] (Sencourt is a Roman Catholic who has recently published the life of Newman). In this connection, R. Sencourt says, "It provided the Vatican with a new and splendid endowment, greater than that of the greatest emperors or kings. The agreement with Mussolini regularised the Vatican's position in the Modern World, and left it free to engage in larger tasks and new schemes. At the same time the new emolument freed it from the dominating influence of America. The dependence on America ceased just in time." But that lovely "endowment" has now gone west and once again the Vatican is under American domination (Cardinal Spellman can see the Chair of Peter from his higher sky-scraper, bedroom window), and it is calling for lend-lease and martial aid from America. I noticed that Douglas Hyde's article in the *Glasgow Observer* is marked, "world copyright reserved." He, seemingly, wants a fee for a reprint. This reminds me of a celebrated Roman Catholic Apologist, who, when he was asked by the *Saturday Post* for an article defending his faith, demanded a fee of fifty guineas in return for one.

Well, we see, now, the Roman Catholic Church adopting the laughed-at policy of the Salvation Army parading its converted pugilists; changing, not the manner, but the man; instead of the "converted pugilist," we see the "converted Communist" paraded on the platform to give testimony against us. I'd love to hear him talkin'. There he goes, wearing the Rerum Novarum before him, like the embroidered bib on the body of a freemason, preceded by horn, sackbut, and psaltery. There he is, shaking hands with a Monsignor, or kissing a bishop's ring; never leaving off the bib of the rerum novarum, fifty-seven years old, with Cardinal, Bishop, and Domestic Prelate studying it still to find out what it means; while the Catholic workers wait outside to hear the news, or hunt for a home to live in; while in purely Roman Catholic countries, Portugal, Spain, and Latin America, the workers remain in the worst state of poverty and the best state of illiteracy, so that when they go to vote, pictures have to be put on the papers, instead of names, so that they may have a shot at trying to put their marks down in the right places.

Comrade workers, in the midst of the Revolution of 1917, Blok,[6] the

---

[6] Alexander Blok (1880–1921), Russian poet and playwright; one of the leaders of the symbolist movement in Russia.

poet, saw twelve Red Guards marching through the streets of Leningrad; heads bent to fight the bitter wind; saw them marching silently through the silently-falling snow, and, looking again, he saw Jesus marching at the head of them. And, today, if Jesus Christ be anywhere, He will hardly be found at Epsom that we hear so much of, with its crowd of morning suits and grey toppers; He wont be found in the Stock Exchange, listening to the ticking of the tapes; he will hardly be found among the gorgeously-robed Cardinals; if He be anywhere, He will be found among the fluttering red flags, at the head of the people marching towards a more abundant life.

Sean O'Casey

To Harry Pollitt [1]

TC. O'CASEY

[TOTNES, DEVON]
2 JUNE 1948

Dear Harry,

The D.W. [*Daily Worker*] has sent me an article by [Douglas A.] Hyde which appeared in the Glasgow "Observer," a Catholic paper. It is a reply to me. It would be useless, I'm sure to reply, for it wouldnt be published. One has but to read Coulton's works to realise how cute these R.C. apologists are in controversy. They simply refuse to publish in their Press answers to their statements. Hyde's is a long, rather hysterical outpouring of his weak and exhibitionist spirit, without a single quotation from the works of those he quotes. But, all the same, he is going to do a lot of harm. Mr. Rust, when it first happened wrote saying he didnt think it would affect the readers of the D.W. I told him that there wasnt a pulpit or a platform directly connected with the R.C. community that wouldnt bellow out everything Hyde said; and one like Hyde is bound to be more venomous than an ordinary R.C. He is making a good thing out of it; a cod-hero; able at last to display himself; full of pride; in a position of honour now, shaking hands with cardinal, bishop, and monsignor. And all this has been conferred on him by the D.W. A bad job, Harry.

What are we going to do? I suggest this, anyway: I am writing a reply to what he has said, with additions—at present it runs to about 3000 words, and may have, say, another 1000. It is, I think, a murderous onslaught on what Hyde is standing for now. It should be made into a pamphlet or a brochure—whatever the latter word may mean; booklet in English. It has quotations from Morris (whom Hyde quotes against me, very ignorantly, for he claims that Morris is a "Medievalist," which, in the sense

---

[1] Harry Pollitt (1891–1960), one of the leaders of the British Communist party.

of scholarship, Morris never was), from Card. Newman; St. Thomas More; from the celebrated Dr. MacDonald, Professor of Theology in the R.C. College of Maynooth for forty years; a grand fellow, whose name is never mentioned by the The R.C. authorities. He kept the MS. of his Reminiscences till he died, so that there could be no bar to its publication. The Bishops and monsignors are afraid of their shit of him. He even prophesied the rise of the people long before it happened. He was a seer and a true democrat, though a loyal Catholic—not to tradition or authority, but to the spirit of Catholicity. All the quotations are from those whom Hyde couldnt dispute.

Connolly's old pamphlet [2] isnt of much use. Connolly really didnt understand the C. Faith, either in theory or in practice; and he wrote always under the shadow of clerical domination. He wasnt free enough to take an uncompromising stand. Besides, he has been accepted now as a pure Catholic labour leader, blessed by the church; so his influence is now nearly nil. If any worker quoted Connolly to a cleric, he would be sympathetically told that Connolly died a true churchman, and that all the more extreme views he may have once held, had been repented of, and forgiven. You can see by Fox's book on him—Connolly the Forerunner,[3] that C. has been saved from the grip of Marxianism. Connolly has been successfully used now by the most reactionary labour leaders in Ireland, and it was Connolly's prestige that kept Jim Larkin from resuming his militant actions when he came back from the American jail. It was a dastardly thing to use the influence of such a man as Connolly was for such a purpose; but these things are done, and we can but fight them the best way we can.

We must face the fact that the policy of the U.S.A. has tremendously aided the R.C. position. They are getting back their breath and their courage everywhere—in Czechoslovakia, Roumania, Poland, and in England. And it is an added trouble that the Anglicans are trying to link up with them; worse still that the Nonconformists seem to be going the same way. If you decide to get what I have written into a pamphlet, then it should be placed in the hands of the Nonconformists, sold to them (or given away) as they come out of their churches; and even the same thing might be done with the Catholics in the working-class districts.

In Hyde's reply to me, he makes a point of the title given to the article which appeared in the D.W. Now this title wasnt mine, but was given by Mr. Rust, or someone else who didnt know a damn of what it dealt with, or why it was written. The D.W. has a bad habit of changing my titles, for I think long before choosing them, and it is reasonable to think that I know best in these things.

I sent a subsequent article, containing a reply to an opposing letter

[2] James Connolly, *Labour, Nationality, and Religion* (1910), a reply to Father Kane, S.J., who had denounced Socialism in a series of Lenten discourses delivered at the Gardiner Street Church, Dublin, in 1910.
[3] R.M. Fox, *Connolly the Forerunner* (1947).

which appeared in the D.W. It didnt appear, and was neither acknowledged nor returned to me. I hope there isnt another Hyde blossoming out in the D.W. There may be some who would like to share the loaves and fishes with Hyde, so be careful.

Well, then, shall I send my effort to you when I have finished it?

I hate writing letters, and I am very busy, and this is a damned long one, so I'll shut up.

All the best.
Yours sincerely,
Sean O'Casey

To Peter Hughes

TC. O'CASEY

[TOTNES, DEVON]
14 JUNE 1948

Dear Mr. Hughes:

Chesterton's views on the Middle Ages dont clash with mine, for I *know* nothing about them, being no scholar. His views clash with the views of those who do know—the scholars who have made this period their special study; and one of them is your own—Lord Acton; another is the Roman Catholic Theologian Dr. McDonald. I have quoted such authorities; I havent used my opinions (which would be ridiculous), and you must either accept them or reject them as you wish; only, if you do, you will be revealing yourself as somewhat ignorant of the very question about which you are so dogmatic. And you should read what Acton thought of the Jesuits, not to mention Pascal. Chesterton couldnt look up any of the prime authorities, if he had tried, for the gentleman simply hadnt the scholarship to enable him to do so. I have read all about Chesterton's White Horse, and about the White Horse of the Peppers too. I have read the encyclicals you mention,[1] two of which were referred to as a collection of platitudes by the Theologian, Dr. McDonald, mentioned a moment ago. It looks as if you regard these opinions as articles of faith. Do you? I am not conscious of "attacking Catholicism." If you think so, well, go on thinking it, but it shows that you dont know so much about your faith as you seem to suppose. As for two world wars in our time, you should remember that things

---

[1] Encyclical Letter by Pope Leo XIII, "Rerum Novarum," 1891, On the Condition of the Working Classes; Encyclical Letter by Pope Pius XI, "Quadragesimo anno," 1931, On Reconstructing the Social Order; Encyclical Letter by Pope Pius XI, "Divini Redemptoris," 1937, On Atheistic Communism.

are relative, and, that, if you regard the then population of the world, and the population now, you'll find that the Hundred Years War—a hundred years!—was as bad, relatively, as any that have taken place now; worse, for it was fought by those who pretended to hold the faith—your Faith— in the unity of spirit and in the bond of peace! The Roman Catholic work- ers today have to thank the Communist Manifesto for whatever they have won rather than the Encyclicals, full of sound, signifying nothing. The two world wars at any rate, in spite of the evil in both of them, gave birth to two fine things: the first to the Soviet Union; the second to the spread of a militant labour movement over Europe, and the awaking of the people of China—the Red Star has grown a lot bigger. Since you have a hunch that I will, ere long, gravitate "painfully towards the penetential bench"— were you a Salvationist ever?—, there's no more for me to say. You are a romanticist, and discussion would be a waste of time for both of us. But arent you somewhat self-righteous?

> All good wishes, all the same,
> Yours sincerely, from Sean O'Casey in the bosom of his Patrimony.

To Richard J. Madden

TC. O'CASEY

[TOTNES, DEVON]
12 JULY 1948

Dear Dick:

In a letter dealing with the overtures of Mr. Houghton sent by ordi- nary post, and which you will probably receive after this, I said that in the Agreement now under negotiation here that there was NO commitment as to Film rights. In case you might assume that this assurance was an im- plication to go on with talks to Houghton, I am adding now the assurance that I think Houghton's circumlocutory offers arent worth anything, and continuance with him isnt worthwhile.

Also, that, in any event of the offer coming to anything, I want to say what I forgot to say in the letter mentioned above. It is this: Should the thing come to anything, I MUST be satisfied with the Caste, particularly with the choice of those who will play in the parts of JUNO and JOXER. You will remember that Houghton in his first letter thinks only of CAPT. BOYLE, evidently anxious to boost Fitzgerald. I shouldnt be surprised if

Barry F. hadnt promised to put some of his dough in it himself so as to have a chance of renewed Glamour.

One more thing: I assessed the minimum Fee in the letter mentioned as £3000. Now Mrs. O'C. reminds me that the first offer reached this figure nearly; so let us make the minimum figure one of £4000 for a ten years' licence.

That's all, except to add that I dont think it worthwhile for you or for me to continue the discussion.

Yours as ever,
[*Sean*]

To Richard J. Madden

TC. O'CASEY

TOTNES, DEVON
12 JULY 1948

Dear Dick:

I have been busy at the proofs of a new biographical book, and with this, plus housework, I hadnt a second to answer your last letter referring to Houghton's high-flown effort.

Yes, this man is full of windy words, sounding grand, but signifying nothing. I have little patience with this kind of fellow. I dont even remember what he said to me, and I'm too sensible to try to read it again. I did say that I had said what I wanted to say to you, and that you dealt with the American end of my affairs.

I havent yet concluded arrangements for the proposed revival of "JUNO," but expect to do so soon. There is NO commitment regarding Film rights in the agreement whatever.

But some time ago, the Rank organization took an option of six months for £100 on SHADOW OF A GUNMAN, through the British League of Dramatists, and the Secretary of the League, should the option have been exercised, intended to ask £4000 for the film licence. I dont think we'd have got so much; but probably would have got £2500 or so. This leaves me certain that JUNO is a valuable asset. But to be less "verbose" than our friend, this is what I think:

a. I wont consider letters, however eloquent; but must have a sober contract set before me to consider.

b. I refuse to be just a lever to hoist up Barry Fitz. again.

c. I wont consider any contract that doesnt set down a good price for the play, in set words, without any equivocation about the matter. The price is, of course, a matter of arrangement, but, between you and me, I wont take less than £3000 for it; and I and you might strive for a higher figure.
d. Anyway, whatever the terms be, they must be set out in a contract form with assurance that whatever Fee be asked for, it will be paid as soon as the contract is signed.

I think the above is clear, anyway clearer than that written by Mr. Houghton.

All the best to you and Tessa. Cold and rainy weather here; never remember a colder summer.

[*Sean*]

To Jack Carney

MS. NYU LIBRARY

TOTNES, DEVON
18 JULY 1948

Dear Jack,

I've had a bad eye, & the little power in it, I used to correct the page-proofs of the 4th biographical vol. "Inishfallen, Fare Thee Well."

In their latest list, Macmillan's have listed it for publication in November next—a long, long trail since I first sent in the MS.; but, in these times, it is good to get anything going.

Thanks so much for the "Mick McQuaid" plug. It gave a lot of sweet smokes.

I hope your article brought in a tangible reward to you. You should try, I think, to get a contract for any future ones.

The Labour movement in Eire seems to have gone west. Everyone there cowers before the clergy; &, over here, they're a little afraid of them. My pamphlet, giving a few theological kicks to D. Hyde, won't be published [1]—a week's work, & more, gone west.

Looks black around Berlin. Another war will bring world revolution. Bevan isn't good for us. Will write more when the eye gets normal. All the best to you & Mina.

Yours as ever,
Sean

[1] See O'Casey's letter to the *Daily Worker,* 31 May 1948, reprinted above in chronological order, which was refused publication because of its length. For the background of his dispute with Douglas Arnold Hyde, see O'Casey's letter to Jack Daly, 10 May 1948, note 2.

To Jack Carney

MS. NYU LIBRARY

TOTNES, DEVON

2 AUGUST 1948

Dear Jack,

You send very bad news about yourself & Mina. There's little use in saying one's sorry.

I guessed that Syndicate business would bring in nothing. The Author's Society wouldn't allow any of us to do such a thing without a contract. I'm afraid the N.U.J. [National Union of Journalists] is a very poor Union. It is, I think, just as well you didn't take on the job of writing Larkin's life. The sale here wouldn't be great; & the Irish sales not enough to grant you much of a reward. Jim waited too long to have it done. I often told him in Dublin that he should keep records; but Jim was always too occupied with fighting for his men—not like O'Brien who had time to index everything.

The thing to do now, is to try for a regular job; the freelancing can be done in spare time. It would be sad to have to leave the flat; or, rather, to break the home up. The present one of course would be too dear to hold on to. Couldn't you try for a post in the provincial Press? That might keep you going for a while. But I suppose these are hard to get nowadays. I heard yesterday they are economising in Exeter by lessening their staff— one, an Irishman—has gone back to Erinn.

I do hope you may soon hear of some way out of the difficulty.

Ever yours,
Sean

To Peter Newmark

MS. NEWMARK

TOTNES, DEVON

12 AUGUST 1948

Dear Peter.

The Carneys are wrong. The book of the play [1] wasn't remaindered. It didn't sell as well, at first, as the previous books; but it sold itself out

[1] *The Star Turns Red* (1940).

long ago. There isn't a copy to be had anywhere that I know. I have had
a number of inquiries, even one from the USSR, but had no copy to send
to anyone. Macmillans are to publish a vol. containing Red Star, Silver
Tassie, & Within the Gates sometime. The music has been printed, & I have
made a few alterations in each; but when it will come out, God knows. All
my books, bar school editions of Plough & Juno, are out of print. Sorry I
can't give a copy to your "Brown Priest." [2] But, I'm afraid, it doesn't matter—in the R. Catholic Church, discipline would soon make an end of any
Brown Priest who opened a mouth to say a word. I've seen too many
instances in Ireland not to know this: Father [Michael O'] Flanagan, Father [Morgan] Sheedy, Father [Donal?] Sullivan, & Dr. W. McDonald,
Professor of Theology in Maynooth for 40 years. I have a lot to say about
the last one in "Inishfallen Fare Thee Well". The B. Priests have a chance
now in the Middle E. Countries & in Czechoslovia, but none where no
spiritual-materialistic revolution has taken place.

We are glad to hear that you are going to be (or are) married; & wish
you and your lady good fortune & patience with each other, till riper
knowledge promotes a contented and useful companionship.

It was a repertory theatre that did "Within the Gates" in N.Y. "a
travesty of O'Casey's play," said R. Watts in Herald-Tribune. I've made a
good many changes in the "stage version" of the play for Macmillan's new
vol. We are all well, bar the fact that I get older and older & older; & the
effects of silicosis prevents me from being as active as I'd like to be. Breon
starts studying painting in the Anglo-French Centre next month.

I return the P.O. with this letter, which I am sending to the Bristol
address.

All the best to you and Mrs. Newmark.

Yours as ever.
Sean

[2] The name of the working-class priest in *The Star Turns Red*.

To Bernard Shaw

TC. O'CASEY

[TOTNES, DEVON]
17 AUGUST 1948

Dear G. B. S.
Enclosed is a letter from a friend in Dublin. He was for a time the
Editor of THE BELL. He has asked me to write to you to see if you would

write a preface to a book written by Tom Barry [1] on what happened during the I.R.A.'s fight with the Black and Tans and the Auxies. Barry was a Brigadier of an I.R.A. Cork Brigade. The writer of the letter to me— Peadar O'Donnell—complains, as you can see, that letters to you from him get no reply. I am writing to tell him that he isnt a bird alone. That you have more important things to do than answering letters; and, that, even if you do, you wont be likely to agree to his request.

I shouldnt forward this letter of his to you if it didnt appear that you seemed to be more interested in things Irish now than you used to be; and so I didnt like to withhold the letter to prevent you from being bothered.

Well, there it is: for you to answer, to ignore, or to write the preface, as you will.

All the best with our love.

Yours as ever,
Sean O'Casey

[1] Tom Barry, *Guerilla Days in Ireland* (1949).

To Daniel Macmillan

MS. MACMILLAN LONDON

TOTNES, DEVON
20 AUGUST 1948

Dear Mr. Daniel,

Thank you for sending me the copies of the Scholar's Edition of my plays.[1] They are charming little volumes. I hope they won't be used to bore the students. I dread the danger of having to study things—never having had to do it myself; though, in order to learn, having no guide, I took many a road which led nowhere, & wasted a lot of precious time. Our friend, Guy, makes one mistake in his Preface—the dispute between Dublin Castle & the A. Theatre was over "Blanco Posnet," not "John Bull's Other Island." "Blanco" was refused a licence because it was "blasphemous"! [2]

[1] *Juno and the Paycock* and *The Plough and the Stars* (1948), Scholar's Library edition, Introduction and Notes by Guy Boas.

[2] Bernard Shaw's *The Shewing-up of Blanco Posnet* was banned in London by the Lord Chamberlain's office in 1909, because of Blanco's irreverent comments about God: "He's a sly one. He's a mean one. He lies low for you. He plays cat and mouse with you. He lets you run loose until you think you are shut of Him; and then, when you least expect it, He's got you." Yeats and Lady Gregory promptly offered the Abbey Theatre for a production of the play, and it was presented there on 25 August 1909.

I should be glad if you would kindly send me 2 copies of each of the volumes.

> *Warmest Regards.*
> *Yours very sincerely*
> *Sean O'Casey*

P.S. I hope you have taken a good long holiday.

To Daniel Macmillan

TS. MACMILLAN LONDON

TOTNES, DEVON
26 AUGUST 1948

Dear Mr. Daniel:

I am sorry to hear that The Macmillan Co. [New York] dont wish to print COCKADOODLE DANDY, because they think it will not have a large sale in America. They may be right, but I dont think this is the real reason. Rather is it because of their fear of it giving offence to the Roman Catholic Prelate and priest. They feel, I think, and rightly so, that its publication would hurt their connection with R.C. schools and convent schools in the matter of supplying them with educational books. Cardinal Spellman is becoming a big boss in the U.S.A., and he has his eye on the Papal Secretariat of State—the Red Pope, more powerful than the elected Pope himself. An ignoramus, if his speeches, his pastorals, and the book [1] he published during the war are anything to go by.

I feel that I should do all I can to get this play as fair an audience in America as possible. There is nothing in it controverting any theory of Catholic doctrine—Anglican or Roman; but it is with me a question of free thought and free expression in the art form of the drama. I remember the bitter things said and done by these curious clergy when the SILVER TASSIE was done by the Abbey; [2] though when it was done again, twelve years later, in Dublin's biggest theatre, The Gaiety,[3] to crowded houses, there wasnt a murmur from a single cleric. They had apparently decided to be ashamed of themselves. The younger writers are chittering with fear before the censorship and the clerics. One of them wrote a book on Boccaccio

[1] Francis Cardinal Spellman, *The Road to Victory* (1942).
[2] *The Silver Tassie* was first produced in Dublin at the Abbey Theatre on 12 August 1935. See the letter of Father M. H. Gaffney, O.P., in the *Irish Press*, 14 August 1935, and O'Casey's reply, 20 August, Vol. I, pp. 576–80.
[3] *The Silver Tassie* was revived in Dublin at the Gaiety Theatre on 26 May 1947.

some time ago; [4] and a finely-written work from the point of view of an ardent Catholic, a neoThomist. The Jesuits of America, in their Journal, recommended that the book be brought to the notice of the Holy Office; which, if done, would probably mean an order for the book's withdrawal, as was the case of Alfred Noyes' book on Voltaire.[5] Recently, a young author sent me a book, TONN TUILE [6]—Floodtide—for an opinion. It was a simple story of two newly-married people; but, to me, this was a writer of promise, one who was touched with the Holy Ghost. And a poet too, in Gaelic. But he wrote to me to say that his book was called blasphemous! And he darent say much, for he teaches in a R.C. Secondary School or College. These, and such as these, I'm afraid, look to me as a kind of a leader; and, maybe I am. Anyhow, to give the play of mine a chance, I suggest that I should ask another American publisher to do it—say The Random House publishers, which Firm would be my preference. I'd like to know what you think of this. I enclose copy of a tribute from G. J. Nathan, writing about the play in a New York Journal.

Yours very sincerely,
Sean O'Casey

Enclosure

George Jean Nathan [7]
New York Journal-American
9th August 1948

Another recommended script is Sean O'Casey's new fantasy, COCKA-DOODLE DANDY, which, unless my critical equipment has gone to seed, is one of the finest plays of its kind to have come hopefully to the attention of the modern theatre.

The theme here is the rightful joy of life and the proper dismissal from all consideration of those who would fetter it. Employing a mixture of gay symbolism and wild humour, some of it as rich in laughs as anything I've read for a long time, O'Casey filters through his natural cynicism as lively and amusing a slice of fantastic drama as one can imagine.

The embodiment of his central idea in the figure of a rooster, his two boozy counterparts of the memorable Fluther and Joxer out of THE PLOUGH AND THE STARS and JUNO AND THE PAYCOCK, his fancy in such scenes as those in which the fairest and most delicate of his females suddenly sprouts devil's horns, and in which the stern males madly

---

[4] See O'Casey's letter to Francis MacManus, 21 March 1948, note 2.

[5] In 1938, the second edition of Alfred Noyes's *Voltaire,* originally published in 1936, was suspended by the Supreme Congregation of the Holy See because it contained "destructive ideas." After Noyes agreed to write a special preface defending and explaining some statements in the book, the suspension was lifted in 1939. For his comment on the situation, see Noyes's *Two Worlds For Memory* (1953), pp. 271–73.

[6] Seamus O'Neill, *Tonn Tuile* (1947).

[7] Nathan's article was titled "Let 'Em Stop Grousing and Read."

try to bag an innocent little fowl which they superstitiously imagine is a creature of prodigious evil—these and more, all coated with the brilliant writing for which the author is famous, combine to provide the kind of evening we too seldom are privileged to enjoy in the theatre of today.

To Sir Alec Martin [1]

MS. MARTIN

TOTNES, DEVON

1 SEPTEMBER 1948

My dear Sir Alec,

Many and true thanks from Ireland & from me, & from the memory of that grand old woman, Lady Gregory, for your honest and splendid letter to "The Burlington Magazine." [2] I have written a short note to the Editor, giving the opinion that now he has no reason for shying away from the demand to restore the Lane Pictures to Dublin. If anyone knew [Hugh] Lane, you did, and there can be no honest questioning of your decisive declarations. Recently, I had a letter from Dr. T[homas]. Bodkin saying that one of those who objected to the return of the pictures (I've forgotten the name, & haven't time to look it up) used as an argument against their return that "Lane's Codicil was written in pencil." They'll be saying soon it was written in invisible ink. The Burlington Editor didn't catch my reason for using the word "fell" instead of the word "fallen"; namely that the retention of the pictures in London was a fell deed as well as a lousy theft.

Of course, I remember our meeting in Lady Gregory's flat, & the luncheon in the Ritz, too.[3] I was a very raw recruit then; but I have learned a lot about many things, & a great deal more about pictures since I came to live in England. Our elder boy, Breon, now a gunner in the Royal Artillery, is beset with a love for painting; and, after demobilization this month, goes as a student to the Anglo-French Centre, St. John's Wood, to study Painting. I didn't encourage him—for the artist's life is a precarious one—, but my own interest in painting had, I daresay, an influence on

---

[1] Sir Alec Martin (1884–1971), intimate friend of Sir Hugh Lane; Managing Director of Christie's, London, 1940–58; for nearly sixty years a Governor and Guardian of the National Gallery of Ireland.

[2] Sir Alec Martin, *Burlington Magazine,* August 1948. Sir Alec's letter was a reply to a leading article, "The Lane Bequest," *Burlington Magazine,* June 1948, in which the editor objected to the return of the Hugh Lane paintings to Ireland.

[3] They met in 1926 when O'Casey received the Hawthornden Prize. See the news story, "London Honours O'Casey," *Irish Times,* 24 March 1926, Vol. I, pp. 183–85.

the boy. However, it's his own way, & one's own way is the only true one.

You have a big family, for I remember my visit to East Sheen many years ago; and the wetting we got in Richmond Park when a lovely English evening suddenly changed into a downpour. I have three children, the boy mentioned, another boy of thirteen, & a girl of eight; so my wife and I have many things to think of outside ourselves.

I rarely go to London now. Years & years of gradual silicosis has pulled the heart a little from its right place, so I have to take things as quietly as may be; but, if I do go, I shall certainly take advantage of your very kind desire to see me again.

My thanks to you again, and warm regards to yours & you.

Yours very sincerely,
Sean O'Casey

To George Jean Nathan

MS. CORNELL

TOTNES, DEVON
[? SEPTEMBER 1948]

My very dear George:

Thank you so much for the news-clipping calling out the name of Cockadoodle Dandy. Your clipping has reached Dublin, & I've had several appeals to let it go on there. They know not what they're asking for. Of course, I've courteously refused the offers. But it's odd the Abbey rigidly ignores all the plays I've done since "The Tassie." One would think they'd have done "Red Roses" and "Purple Dust." I'm afraid, they won't put on now even any of the first three plays. The biographical volumes have, I imagine, got them thinking in terms of a boycott. Well, we'll live without them.

I daresay, you've read of Yeats' body being brought back to Ireland.[1] But a live jackal now is greater than the dead lion. He won't have any influence on the Abbey. He will be quiet enough near Ben Bulben.

G. B. S. has sent me a postcard—the first line I've had for years. A young I.R.A. leader wanted a preface on a book about the B. & Tans fight; & asked me to ask Shaw. He couldn't get a reply. I knew Shaw couldn't do it; but I passed on the request. So the postcard came saying he had written

---

[1] W. B. Yeats (1865–1939) died on 28 January 1939 in the south of France and was buried at Roquebrune. On 17 September 1948 his coffin was brought back to Ireland by the corvette *Macha* and was reburied in Drumcliffe churchyard, Sligo.

to the I.R.A. author setting down reasons for refusal. The Dr. [F. E.] Lowenstein who is with him now is G. B. S.'s Iron Curtain. I don't think he will do G. B. S. any good. He calls himself Shaw's Bibliographer and Remembrancer, devoting his time to keeping the great man's name before all the peoples. To me, always a weakness in Shaw. Linked to his love of photography, he used it copiously to keep himself familiar with the public. In "An Unsocial Socialist," read 35 years ago, I remember being shocked at his belief in Photography as a great art; and he holds this opinion still. He never seemed to have any response in him to painting, bar a conventional interest in academic art. I enclose samples. A ripe lot of bearded pards! Curious he doesn't seem to realise that if his works don't make him immortal, pictures of him won't—unless done by a great artist.

A few weeks ago, Transatlantic pictures wanted me to do the dialogue for a Film showing a priest martyred because he refused to reveal the "secrets of the confessional." They are all trying to horn in on "religious" pictures since "Song of Bernadette" was a day. Allright as touching individuals, but if they touch the Church's power & security, that power & security become greater than the secrets. Anyway, I can't summon up the courage to lend a helping hand to these things, though the reward tempts.

I hope you are keeping fit. Breon and I are looking forward to your latest book of criticism. I am taking down a few notes for another biographical commentary. Inisfallen, Fare Thee Well, is promised for November. Breon is now attending, as a student, the Anglo-French Centre in London, though liable to be called to the colours if another cursed war breaks out. But there won't be war: we've no longer any money to burn.

My love,
as ever.
Sean

To Jack Carney

MS. NYU LIBRARY

TOTNES, DEVON
22 SEPTEMBER 1948

My dear Jack,

Thanks very much for the papers. I do hope you have found some solution of your difficulty—that you have managed to get a job, or, at least, enjoy a good prospect of getting one soon. The paper shortage seems as bad as ever; and the life of a Journalist, and of anyone who hopes to make a living writing, is a damned hard & heavy one. I am promised publication of Inishfallen, Fare Thee Well in November; but it isn't certain even then; nothing is these days. God knows when Cockadoodle Dandy will appear—I must have done the galleys a year or so ago. At the moment, I'm struggling with Income Tax returns—or rather Eileen is, for my eyes are too misty to see figures; &, heaven knows these were ever a torment to me.

I daresay, you've read the account of "Yeats's Homecoming." It struck me as odd that none of the younger writers appeared to be present; they were all the old grey-heads (like myself) who had clustered round him in the days of his younger power. Perhaps, the invitations were limited; for it is said Yeats desired a plain quiet funeral. Though to a dead man, a funeral, however noisy, is bound to be a quiet one. Anyway, it will be long before we look upon his like again. There's no-one now to take even a second place. Curious how suddenly poor Ireland has become—first Yeats of the aristocratic writers; then Jim Larkin of the people; yet neither left a soul behind to take his place; & so signs on it, drama, literature, & labour now look like weeds. Neither had a Tanaiste.[1] Well, the land deserves it; for neither got their due when living.

I do hope you have something in sight.

My love to Mina & to you.

As ever,
Sean

[1] Deputy Prime Minister or, in this context, an heir presumptive.

To Miss M.E. Barber

MS. LEAGUE OF DRAMATISTS

TOTNES, DEVON
24 SEPTEMBER 1948

Dear Miss Barber.

I am glad to hear that Liam Redmond has signed the contract; & that the accounts from Australia have arrived safely.

That's the worst of Cornwall and Devon—the climate. The sea on both sides sends the rain down too often. It is like the West of Ireland—"the friendly Irish rain" is always falling. I never found it very friendly. A great number of people think Devon is always laughing & never surly. On the posters the sky is always golden & the sea is always blue; and frost unknown. But in the bad winter the snow was as deep here (and as cold) as anywhere else. Indeed, my wife coming home on a dark evening, slipped on a patch of ice, fell so that the back of her head struck the road. When the cold shook her out of unconsciousness, she just managed to stagger home, her hair & blouse soaked in blood. Fortunately a doctor risked the icy roads, & stitched the wound, so that a week in bed made her O.K. again. When the frost comes & the snow falls, we have to go canny here as anywhere else. But the Devon folk are a grand lot.

But this summer has been a very poor one. Holidayers had a very unhappy time; & things so expensive made it worse.

I hope the bad rain will do you no harm. It is really irritating to have the few days one can spare out of a year's work wet and unresponsive.

All the best, & thanks for your letter.

Yours sincerely
Sean O'Casey

To Frederick May

MS. MAY

TOTNES, DEVON
26 SEPTEMBER 1948

Dear Mr. May:

My head and hands are full of work at the moment, & will be for a long time to come; so it won't be possible for me to write a foreword about one-act plays. Anyway, I don't know enough about them to do any-thing worth reading. One-act plays are good, I imagine, to beginners in Play-writing, insofar as they help to keep the authors close to a sense of brevity; & learn them how to keep within the bounds of theatrical technique. And they are admirable for those who've begun to act, for they do not put too much of a strain on emotion, or high concentration of thought for a long time in the portrayal of a character. But if one has the essence of a playwright in him (or her), they soon become unsatisfactory, for the compass in which to display the meaning, emotion, & action of a play, is too confined. The playwright wants to expand, & so, to him, the one-acter becomes a thing of the past; except when some episode interests him, which is not important enough to demand the fulness of a full-length play. Besides, there's practically no chance on the ordinary stage for a one-act play now.

All the best to your young students, & remember, what you think and do is of far more importance than anything I say.

Yours very sincerely,
Sean O'Casey

To Frederick May

MS. MAY

TOTNES, DEVON
29 SEPTEMBER 1948

Dear Fred May,

I am so glad that J. R.[1] is out of jail at last; & I feel sure the rest will be out before long. What a rancidly stupid thing it was (and is) to hold these men in so long; & bloody cut-throats in high positions, with salaries bulging their pockets, acclaiming the power and venom of the atomic bomb. Is it any wonder that in a Revolution the death-rate is high!

If you can, please tell J. R. how pleased I am. The last magazines I sent were returned from the prison, per the Governor, with a note that J. R. had already "received his entittlement." Concern for him, & his comrades prevented me from telling this bostune what I thought of him in good O'Casey language. It was very hard on me to have had to keep silence when there was a chance to fight fools; fools in power lording it over better souls than their own. However, I expect they will all be out before the year ends.

And how are you? I haven't heard of you since you were to undergo an operation on your ear. I do hope it was good and effective; & that deafness has been removed to a long way off.

All good wishes to you & to your sister, Shelah.

Yours very sincerely,
Sean

[1] James O'Regan, imprisoned by the British for IRA activities. See O'Casey's letter to *Tribune,* 5 December 1947.

To Sir Alec Martin

MS. MARTIN

TOTNES, DEVON
14 OCTOBER 1948

Dear Alec,

Thank you for your letter. I have no doubt that, in the end, the Lane Pictures will go back to Dublin. If Dublin wanted them badly enough, they would be there now. If the Eire Government, past or present, knew anything of the art, or cared something about it, the pictures would be there now. I'm afraid a lot of the artists don't wish them back, for fear the pictures would show up their own bad art.

You certainly have a lot to think about—your own family and your children's children. It is distressing to hear about your youngest boy. He probably had a bad time of it in the army. It is really appalling to think of the waste of valuable life that goes in the senseless work of using weapons. We should be skilled enough in sense by this time to give this useless business up forever. There is no room for a sensitive nature in either army or navy. I have met so many who hate it, but who have to go on with it; till, when they escape, are not the same balanced boys, &, possibly, never will be again. I pray that your wife & you may, by now, have had better news of your boy. The last war did more damage than is generally thought. We have had many broken lives as well as broken buildings. Another one, & we will be completely done for. However, I, for one, don't believe it could come. It is, of course, the mothers who suffer most. I believe if a vote was taken of the world's mothers, there would be almost a unanimous declaration against war & its evils.

Should I ever go to London, I shall be very glad to get into touch with you.

My warm regards to Lady Martin, & to you, & all who are dear to you.

> *Yours very sincerely,*
> *Sean O'Casey*

To Harold Macmillan [1]

TC. O'CASEY

[TOTNES, DEVON]
15 OCTOBER 1948

Dear Mr. Harold:

After searching high up and low down for the page-proofs of INISFALLEN FARE THEE WELL, I remembered that I had sent them to Mr. Lovat Dickson to be forwarded on to your American House. So I had to search through the Galleys.

---

[1] Harold Macmillan (1894–   ), British publisher and statesman; Prime Minister, 1957–63. See O'Casey's letters to him in Vol. I.

1. Pages 35–37, My brother, Michael died a year ago or less.[2] He wouldnt have taken any action, for he would never have read the book. He never read a line I wrote. To be fair to myself, I may say we were friendly after separation. When he was down and I was up (in a job), I helped him to many a bit of tobacco and many a drink; and when I came to Eng., I sent him many a quid, finally paying the funeral expenses.

2. Pages 56–56 (sic) I cant think there would be any response here. Anyway, the story [about Mr. and Mr. Ballynoy] was published two years ago (or more) in an issue of THE MINT, edited by Geoffrey Grigson.[3]

3. Pages 114–116. The Bishop referred to is the B. of Waterford, and "Blarney" may be too near; but I dont think the Church would take action. His remarks were, as you see, published in *The Cork Examiner* and the Republicans' reply in their Journal called EIRE. These Republicans were then the followers of De Valera's Party, and some of them now have good jobs. The Bishops actually did issue a united declaration condemning what they called "unauthorised murder," meaning the shooting done by the Republicans; thus implying that "authorised murder" was to be allowed, meaning the shooting down by the Free Staters. There was such an outcry that they immediately withdrew the declaration, and sent out a modified one. I enclose a galley proof of the part mentioned with suggested alterations—for instance, calling the gentleman the Bishop of Ireland's Eye, a tiny island off the Dublin coast.

4. Pages 132–133. After a long search of the galley-proofs by myself and Eileen, neither of us could find the reference to the "Englishman from Kingston-on-Thames." And I havent the slightest recollection of the incident.

    All well here, as we hope you and yours are.

Yours sincerely,
Sean O'Casey

[2] Michael Casey died in Dublin on 11 January 1947 at the age of eighty-one. See O'Casey's letter to Mrs. Isabella Murphy, 20 January 1947.

[3] Sean O'Casey, "The Raid," *The Mint: A Miscellany of Literature, Art and Criticism* (1946), edited by Geoffrey Grigson.

To V. Ermilov [1]

TC. O'CASEY

TOTNES, DEVON
16 OCTOBER 1948

Dear Comrade:

Many thanks for your letter. I have to be careful in the use of my eyes, and now confine myself to writing what I feel should be written, in the best way and for the best purpose. You should know well what my views are on Peace and the People. I have set them down often enough. What I think of War is, to me, expressed best in my play THE SILVER TASSIE, and of the aspiration of the People in the play THE STAR TURNS RED. And there will be references to these things in my biographical fourth volume, which is called INISHFALLEN FARE THEE WELL, to be published by Macmillan & Co. some time next month, if all goes well. Apart from political opinions altogether, War now would be inconceivably horrible; and War with the Soviet Union would be far more horrible still. It would be utterly senseless and utterly inhuman. It would be War for War's sake, and that is the last stage of lunacy. We have had enough of War forever. I am of the thought of the American Philosopher, Emerson, when he says "War, to sane men at the present day, begins to look like an epidemic insanity, breaking out here and there like the cholera, infecting men's brains instead of their bowels." Touching myself, it would not matter so much, one way or the other; for I am a man well spent in years and have but a short way to go now. I have had most of my life. But I think of the young who have the best of life before them. Their first right—the first right of the Young is the liberty to grow old. That is the one way, the only way, in which they can give full value back to the land that bore them; to the life that nature gave them. The healthy and intelligent young aim at giving back to life more than life gave to them; and they have the right to do this, with every encouragement the older ones can give them; and, especially, without the bloody interruption of a senseless War. Mothers too dont want their children cut down in the flower of their youth. They want to see their children happy at play; doing well at school; doing better at work; doing things for the good of all, and winning honour for the energetic use of their talents. These alone are the true and everlasting activities, bringing security and glory to the name, and dignity to the stature of man. Man can mould life nearer to the heart's desire, but only when we obey nature's fundamental law, namely, to seek out peace and follow her forever.

My warm regards to you and your People, and joy to you in all your efforts for peace and good-will among all men. Although I am not with you

---

[1] V. Ermilov, Moscow U.S.S.R.

in all you say (for instance concerning Picasso as a painter and T. S. Eliot as a poet), I am with you in all you have done, and what you are doing to make your great People greater still in the striving world of men. And in all things we shall reason together as sensible beings, knowing, however we differ superficially we are bone of each other's bone, flesh of each other's flesh—that we are brothers.

[*Sean O'Casey*]

To Thomas Mark

TS. MACMILLAN LONDON

TOTNES, DEVON
19 OCTOBER 1948

Dear Sir:

This is in reply to your letter of the 18th of October, concerning suggestions of alteration in parts of INISHFALLEN FARE THEE WELL.

Page 200. The names are fictitious. Fedamore is a town (England would call it a village) in Limerick from which a famous team of hurlers came, who held the Championship for years. Errishcool is a manufactured name from two words often appearing in the Irish names of places.[1]

Page 278. By all means put in "the Catholic Press" instead of the "Universe," though what has been said is actually a R.C. Canonical Law.[2]

Page 279. Very well; leave out the name Leahy; though the whole letter written by Leahy (Maurice) appeared in the Irish Press.[3] After Leahy had made his onslaught on my work at the Abbey Theatre Festival, I accidently came across his letter to me (which I had completely forgotten), and, with a covering criticism, I sent a copy of it to the Irish papers, and so silenced the bould Leahy. But I've no objection to the elimination of the name. I dont want to hurt Leahy; he is but the expression of his environment.

[1] See "Dublin Gods and Half-Gods," *Inishfallen, Fare Thee Well*, the incident where O'Casey goes to visit Yeats in Merrion Square and two Free State CID men are guarding the poet's house, since he is now a member of the Irish Senate and all senators are being guarded against Republican attack. The fictitious names are "Senator Fedamore" and "Jim Errishcool."

[2] See "Silence," *Ibid.*, pp. 223–24.

[3] See O'Casey's letter to the *Irish Press*, 17 October 1938, Vol. I, pp. 751–52, which contains a copy of the original letter Leahy wrote to O'Casey in 1928. For the O'Casey-Leahy controversy on Christianity and literature in Ireland, see O'Casey's letter to the *Irish Times*, 29 August 1938; Leahy's reply, 2 September; and O'Casey's reply, 6 September; Vol. I, pp. 731–35.

I am assuming that Mr. Harold will deal with the previous answers I sent to his inquiries. I still cant remember the incident connected with "the Englishman from Kingston-on-Thames." I cant remember writing anything like this name of this town.

I am returning the proof-pages to you with this note.

> *With all good wishes,*
> *Yours sincerely,*
> *Sean O'Casey*

To Harold Macmillan

MS. MACMILLAN LONDON

TOTNES, DEVON
21 OCTOBER 1948

Dear Mr. Harold,

Though I haven't found the reference to "The Englishman from Kingston-on-Thames" in the proofs, I have found it in the Press-cutting. He was a boyo—a Mr. Edwards—who, writing 20 years ago, called me a "Judas Iscariot," & "a renegade"; who said I had "sold myself to the Bourgeoise," & was busy "exploiting the workers to make money." If there be any "defamation," surely it is I who have been "defamed." But I don't feel it, and, whenever I read the cutting, I get a good laugh out of it. The gentleman would hardly take an action.

> *All the best.*
> *Yours very sincerely,*
> *Sean O'Casey*

To Ward Costello

TC. O'CASEY

[TOTNES, DEVON]
22 OCTOBER 1948

Dear friend:

Thanks for your letter.[1] I have had quite a lot of letters from the U.S.A. lately—all from young, lusty, and striving lads and lasses. All eager to go out and do things. The banner of youth is a bright one, and I hope it will never be dyed in the sombre colours of Sartre's sickly hues, who would find death even in the laugh of a little child.

What I am doing now, or trying to do, is the Fifth vol. of the curious biography of mine; the fourth one is to be published some time next month, if present scarcity of labour and material will allow it. By an odd coincidence, before getting your letter, and since I have been putting together a chapter on "The Silver Tassie." It is astonishing what vehement controversy this play provoked from the first day of its rejection by the Abbey to the time when the Abbey, at the instigation of Yeats himself, produced it, seven years afterwards. And here it is cropping up again, thirteen years later. I think Lady Gregory changed her mind earlier than Robinson would admit, for I have just read a letter from Bernard Shaw to me in which he says that "Lady Gregory has been on your side all the time." But she couldnt overcome both Yeats and Robinson, and, of these two, I'm sure that it was Robinson who confirmed the rejection; who was the head and front of the refusal; and, indeed, Lady Gregory confirms this in her Journals.[2]

I spent many happy days with G. J. Nathan when I was in the U.S.A., and a few with O'Neill and him—a delightful couple. I hope both of them may be long spared to add to the delight and depth of American Drama.

And, now, all the best to you.

Yours very sincerely,
Sean O'Casey

[1] O'Casey made the following comment on Costello's letter in "The Friggin Frogs," *Rose and Crown* (1952):

Nearly two years later, Sean gets a letter from Mr. Ward Costello, an airman in the last World War, now a student of drama at Yale University, Connecticut. He wrote to say that he had defended O'Casey during an attack made upon him in a lecture given by Mr. Lennox Robinson to the University's students of drama, with Marc Connolly in the Chair. The young student asked Mr. Robinson "if *The Silver Tassie,* since it had not been produced by Yeats because of his prejudice, had been produced, or considered for production, since his death?" And "Mr. Robinson had answered with a flat 'No,' adding that it was a bad play; even though Lady Gregory had changed her mind about it." The old lady had said Yes, when the Huntingdons brought her to see the London production of the play.

[2] See O'Casey's letter to Brooks Atkinson, 4 February 1947, note 2. See also Lady Gregory's letter to O'Casey, 23 October 1929, Vol. I, p. 372.

To Jack Carney

MS. NYU LIBRARY

TOTNES, DEVON

4 NOVEMBER 1948

Dear Jack,

Are things any better for you in the way of a chance of a job? Or are you making anything out of a freelance effort? If not, why not see if you could get a job on the new D. Worker? Or is it a closed shop?

I do hope you have something in view. It is pretty difficult to get things going. I've just heard from the Author's Society of America that [Boris] Tamarin has handed in his option on "Red Roses," after holding it for a year & 130 days. So now I have five plays that haven't had a day's performance on an American Stage. Good for you, O'Casey! Did you read Michael Straight's article on H. Wallace in "Reynold's News"? [1] He has slung out of his sympathy the fighting Wallace. [2] "Wallace threw away his chance," he said, "by opposing the Marshall Plan & gathering in the Communists." He may be right. I thought there was something changed when Wallace resigned from the Editorship of the "New Republic." Wallace's day is not yet.

"Scots wha' hae from Wallace fled."

Well, Truman may be better than Dewey—that wad be easy, ses you.

I do hope you are in the way of getting something.

Yours as ever,

Sean

[1] Michael Straight, "Wallace Has Missed His Chance," *Reynolds News,* 31 October 1948. Later editor of the *New Republic,* Straight summed up the prospects for the presidential election on 2 November 1948.

[2] Henry A. Wallace (1888–1965), U.S. government official: Secretary of Agriculture, 1933–40; Vice-President, 1941–45 Editor of the *New Republic,* 1946–47. Unsuccessful Progressive Party candidate for president, 1948.

To George Jean Nathan

MS. CORNELL

TOTNES, DEVON
15 NOVEMBER 1948

My very dear George:

"Blessing and victory!" as we say in the old Irish Pagan greeting, usually adding "and the killing of many enemies." A good wish, when we attach it to the Drama. I've just read your last book [1] (Breon on a visit from London, took it with him, so I had to wait. I am always eager to give the young the first chance of gaiety & wisdom), and, of course, enjoyed it immensely. It is very odd how you manage to saunter through so many poor productions, & yet furnish them with comments which make them all worthwhile. Shaw had that gift, too. It is a rare one, I'm afraid. God is very niggardly with his best gifts. But He is wise, for He gives them only to those who have courage to use them. Your "Lamentable suspicion that you are usually right & others usually wrong" is fully justified. Breon & I had a loud laugh, when I read this out to him. He has a great gradh [love] for you. Eileen (his mother) tells me, when they are out together, he often says "Nathan says this; or Nathan says that." He loves anyone who can make him laugh. And this is all to the good, when there's wisdom in the laughter.

"Inishfallen, Fare Thee Well" is announced to come out this month. I hope it does. I'm working now on another volume.

Dick [Madden] has written to me saying "A young, forthright group, Norman Rose and David Heilweil, are actually interested in the play, 'Cockadoodle Dandy.' This group is responsible for an unusual double bill at the Cort—Sartre's 'The Respectful Prostitute,' and 'Hope is the Thing with Feather.' " [2] He wants me to agree. The commercial terms are ok, but I am anxious about the spiritual side of the question. Do you think the group would make a good effort? I am writing to Dick to say that if you think this group would make a good effort, to go ahead with it. I'd love the play to be done, but I don't want it spoiled. I've had enough of these sad experiences here.

What did you think of H[ilton]. Edwards and [Michael Mc]Liammoir? Pity they are Cissies. They've done good work, which makes me feel even worse about them. [Denis] Johnston, I'm afraid, won't do anything more. He runs about from place to place; from thing to thing; never setting anywhere. The Abbey, of course, is non est now.

> *All the best to you, with*
> *my love.*
> *Sean*

[1] *The Theatre Book of the Year, 1947–1948* (1948).
[2] Richard Harrity, *Hope Is the Thing with Feathers,* a one-act play produced in New York on 11 April 1948 as part of a triple bill called *Six O'Clock Theatre,* with *Celebration* by Horton Foote and *Afternoon Storm* by E. P. Conkle.

Did you ever read "The Nineteenth Hole [of Europe]," by Vivian Connell? Brooks [Atkinson] had an article about it some time ago. As despairing as Sartre's plays, but, I think, a good deal better. And did you come across Ewan MacColl's "Uranium 235" [1948]? I'll send it to you, if you like. A "documentary play," but written, I think, by a poet.

To Edgar M. Deale [1]

MS. DEALE

TOTNES, DEVON

19 NOVEMBER 1948

Dear Mr. Deale,

Here's the book with the jewel of the autograph attached—a poor jewel in a fine setting, for the "Plough" is well ahead of "Juno" as a play.

Barry Fitzgerald might as well be dead; for he is now, of course, a lost soul in Hollywood. It is a great pity, & a great loss.

All the best,
Sean O'Casey

[1] Edgar M. Deale, Irish Association of Civil Liberties, Dublin. Deale told me he had received several other letters from O'Casey, which he had not been able to find, and in one of them, commenting on censorship in Ireland, O'Casey had written: "In Ireland they wear the fig-leaf on the mouth."

To David Marcus

TC. O'CASEY

[TOTNES, DEVON]

20 NOVEMBER 1948

Dear Mr. Marcus and Editors of IRISH WRITING,

If you do not publish what you term correspondence—which isnt correspondence at all—you should not publish articles or comments of the nature sent in by Mr. Colum.[1] If you and everyone else were to act

[1] Padraic Colum, "The Narrative Writings of Sean O'Casey," *Irish Writing* No. 6, November 1948. The editors eventually agreed to publish O'Casey's previous letter in reply to Colum's review of O'Casey's autobiography—it appeared in *Irish Writing* No. 7, February 1949.

in this way, anyone could say of the work and statements of others whatever they liked without any fear of contradiction or of refutation. Perhaps, this is the newest way in Ireland.

Mr. Colum made a statement in his article definitely assuring your readers that what I said about Griffith's effort at poetry was a deliberate invention—simply meaning I was a liar.

I have sent you, him, and your readers evidence to show that what I said was indisputably a fact, and, now, you tell me that you refuse to publish it. What am I to think of this?

If I were to let this go, then there is no reason to doubt that all I have said of Griffith, or of anyone else, is in the same category of falsehood: so your readers would naturally believe.

I am not concerned with placing this information before Mr. Colum— as a writer about these things, he should have known; for this matter proves that it is I, and not he, who is the more careful about what he says in print. But I am very much concerned with your readers knowing the facts as they lie between me and him.

I must, therefore, request you to publish my letter. If you are still determined not to do so, let me have the letter back, and I will get it published elsewhere.

Yours sincerely,
Sean O'Casey

To Francis MacManus

TS. MacManus

Totnes, Devon
21 November 1948

Dear Frank:
Thank you for your invitation to speak over Radio Eireann. Perhaps, as you say, quite a number would be interested in what I'd be allowed to say. But I am interested only in what I think I should say. At present, I am writing down for a future vol. a few things that show how interested many were—rather prominent persons, too—in things I ventured to say not very long ago. A few other interested remarks will be shown in the vol. about to be published—"Inishfallen, Fare Thee Well." I am not anxious to come into personal contact with Ireland—even through Radio Eireann, having love left only for Ireland's dockers, factory workers, farm labourers, clerks, housewives, railway workers, postal workers, ship-yard workers,

workers in the publishing trade, in the ship yards, sailors and soldiers up to the rank of sargeant, telephone operators, boys, girls, and little children. The rest are among those to be kept at a distance. I have dipped deep enough in Ireland, and now am content to watch her gadding to church and state arrangements from a distance. The rest, particularly the writers, who ought to be leaders, it seems to me, lack the courage even to act fair. I have an instance before me now. You may have read P. Colum's article about me in last issue of IRISH WRITING. In this he said, touching my criticism of Arthur Griffith, "O'Casey puts down some absurd verses which he says Arthur Griffith wrote. On my word, he never did." Here is an implication that I composed the verses and set them down to deliberately belittle Griffith. Now Griffith not only wrote the verse I quoted, but others which were worse, and sang them at a public meeting in Mayo. The whole of the incidents is set out—not to belittle him, but to glorify—in GRIFFITH AND HIS TIMES, written by his life-long friend and follower, Geo. Lyons, and published by The Talbot Press in 1923. I sent this information to IRISH WRITING in my own defence, and this morning got a letter from the Editors saying "They do not publish correspondence."

Well, Frank, there you are there, and here I am here. I may add that I have refused to broadcast over the B.B.C. numbers of times, even when appealed to, and promised that the microphone would be brought into the back garden. I dont like the method of censorship. Did you ever hear the boyo who controls Children's Hour prayers? Oh, Jesus of the adorable mind and gentle hands, give us grace to keep our hands from murthering sanctimonious fools!

> *My love to you and yours,*
> *as ever,*
> *Sean O'Casey*

To George Jean Nathan

MS. CORNELL

TOTNES, DEVON
25 NOVEMBER 1948

My very dear George:

I was very, very sorry to get your letter this morning telling me of your illness. It is very distressing & disconcerting, for one ever expects the great to be free from the ills of the flesh. I do hope by the time you get this, there will be an improvement in your condition. It is a very painful thing to have anything wrong with the kidneys. I do hope your doctor is a good one. Couldn't you see a specialist, & go to an hospital for a good rest & continuous treatment? You've no-one to mind you where you are. Do be sensible, & look after yourself in the first & best possible way.

I sent you a letter recently, not knowing you'd be ill. Don't bother about it. Don't read it; & if you have read it, forget all about any request I've made in it for advice. Keep yourself quiet; do as little as you can; do nothing at all, except to rest and amuse yourself with a book. Why not give the present season a miss? Going to theatres uses energy, & you should conserve all you've got till you are better. Diet and rest are very important.

God grant you may soon be well again.

> *Ever yours with my love,*
> *Sean*

To Ivar Ohman [1]

TC. O'CASEY

TOTNES, DEVON
27 NOVEMBER 1948

Dear sir:

Strindberg's dramas are not played, nor are his novels read here. Even his name is rarely mentioned. I have never read a novel of his. They are, as far as I know, unobtainable. They may be found in some remote, select library; but I have never heard of any place holding them. His plays are a little better known, but they are very rarely performed, and when done, done badly. During my experience I have seen but two done, and done splendidly—THE FIRST PART OF THE DANCE OF DEATH and THE FATHER. But the former play should be done in its entirety, or not at all. The theatre here isnt worthy of Strindberg yet.

Strindberg is one of the giants of drama. Even in English translation, by which only I know him, he is splendid. His THE DREAM PLAY is one of the loveliest plays I have ever read. It has all the tender, beautiful sadness of a dying rose. And yet through its sadness, we get the murmur of hope saying that soon another rose, as fair as the first, will be budding again. He is said to have been full of bitterness, but this bitterness was the man's noble revolt against the harshness, the stupidity, and the hypocrisy

---

[1] Ivar Ohman, editor of *Folket i Bild,* a weekly literary magazine in Stockholm, had asked O'Casey to contribute to a special edition in honor of the 100th anniversary of Strindberg's birth, February 1949.

of life around him. He was a trumpeter of man, not content to weave soft melodies, but to blow a warning against rosy and dangerous indolence, and to sound an advance against the evil remaining in the world. He sought to bring harmony out of selfishness, spite, and indifference. We see this dreadful disharmony, this destructive selfishness in his wonderful play, the DANCE OF DEATH; and we see in the end harmony and hope restored through the young lover and his lass, Allan and Judith: lovely blossoms growing out of clay. Perhaps, Strindberg loved his fellow-men too much; but this was a noble fault. Perhaps he was too sensitive about what they did and what they had to endure; but then Strindberg as well as being playwright and poet, was an apostle too. He is a Prince among playwrights.

Coward is thought more of here than Strindberg. Probably thought more of too in Sweden than your own great poet. Two weeks ago, a critic of a great weekly, THE SUNDAY TIMES, boasted that he had travelled two hundred miles to see a Coward play; probably he would not go five miles to see a play by Strindberg. Strindberg's spirit, however, is in no need of any honour from fools. He has made himself immortal; he is one of the greater souls who will be remembered forever.

Sean O'Casey

To George Jean Nathan

MS. CORNELL

TOTNES, DEVON
[? DECEMBER 1948]

Oh my very dear George:

You send me sad news, but I can't believe it to be so bad as the doctors allege, or as you may think—I've seen doctors disappointed too many times. Our own doctor here, George Varian, fell down with a clot of blood on the heart. Doctors sat by him, night & day for a week; he had to lie motionless on his back for six months; & all, including his wife, expected the end. That was three years ago; and, today, he's driving about visiting & attending his patients as usual. He has to go more quietly; coming up, when he visits us, our seventeen steps of stairs cautiously & slow, & a little breathless when he gets to the top; but he is full of life & spirits, & busy in useful work. And I, myself, had beri beri so bad, from hunger, that all thought I was gone; or that I'd never walk again. That's near fifty years ago; & I'm still here. Don't let what the doctors said prey too much on your mind—Resolve to live on, & take things as slow as slow; and you may have years in front of you. Never let yourself say goodbye to life. The will is mightier than any opinion of any doctor, & very often prevails over their decision: only, if you can, don't let yourself down. Your handwriting looks as strong & as steady as ever. Take as much rest—real rest; lying down— as you can, for once one reaches seventy, one has to prop the body up. I hope to God I'll hear better news from you soon. My deep sympathy & true love to you.

As ever,
Sean

To Jack Daly

MS. DALY

TOTNES, DEVON
1 DECEMBER 1948

My dear Jack.

Thanks for your kind letter. I'm busy putting down things on paper as usual, but felt I had to say a word or two about Professor Russell's whistling his tune for a dance of death.[1] It maddens me to have to listen to those, who are too old to push a button, demanding the young to go forth and destroy themselves. If the Young themselves decide to do it, well, we can but sit back and wonder; but let the old abide by the fire with a book and a pipe, turning aside only to say a word for sense and peace. We can advise the young to build, plant, sow, & mow, for by these things all live—the young just as much as the old; but to shout for things that will bring death is another thing altogether. And, during the war, didn't this old bugger spend most of his time in America? I wonder did he hear the sound of a bomb going off? I daresay, this old shit since he was born has had everything done for him. This old, prating professor never handled an icy rope; never gripped a crowbar, red-hot with the sting of frost. If he was made handle fish in a market this weather, he'd come to work armoured in furry gloves. This very morning here, a fisherman of Brixham, selling fish to the people, warmed his numbed hands by our kitchen fire. The old codger doesn't know a thing about nine tenths of the world. Frustrated, too, I suppose, for who knows a thing about his philosophy? Or who

[1] In a letter to *The Times,* 30 November 1948, Bertrand Russell stated that he had not called for a war against Russia in his "recent address at Westminster School," but that he had warned the democracies that they must be prepared to use force against Russia. If O'Casey sent a reply to *The Times,* it wasn't published.

cares? Hume & Spinosa & Kant & Locke we've heard of anyway; but who hears of Russell? And in Science, what has he done? A big Voice, and that is about all. A Jack the Giant-Killer, aged Seventy-six, out to slay Marx! Anyway, China hasn't heard of him yet. If they had, they'd go home peacefully, & leave the world & Nanking to Chang Kye Sheck.

I'm waiting for Inisfallen Fare Thee Well to come out. It was to be here in November, but I'm afraid it won't come this year now. Scarcity of materials & materials; & Churchill & Russell want to make them scarcer still.

How are Jack & Mina [Carney]? Has Jack heard of anything yet?

My love to Floss & Violet—don't let Violet forget about her vote.

> *And all the best to you,*
> *me Dublin buttie.*
> *As ever, from the midst of a thick,*
> *white fog of mist.*
> *Sean*

To Ralph Thompson [1]

TS. THOMPSON

TOTNES, DEVON
3 DECEMBER 1948

Dear Mr. Thompson:

You ask me some hard questions. So far from knowing a lot about my "general intentions," I know very little about even particular ones. I try not to think of the things of tomorrow, so as to let tomorrow take thought for the things of itself. Just about what every man has to do, if he's straight with himself.

Oh, yes, I had an extended work in mind when I definitely started out on I KNOCK AT THE DOOR. How far, I wasn't sure, but I imagine till Death opened the door softly for me—if it doesn't happen in the midst of an atom bomb. Some of the first vol. was written years before—BATTLE ROYAL, ROYAL RESIDENCE,[2] for instance. I was a bit shy about the idea at first, and took a long time to think it over. I thought that no man liveth and dieth to himself, so I put behind what I thought and what I did

---

[1] Ralph Thompson, book reviewer for the *New York Times*.
[2] "Royal Risidence," the third chapter of *Pictures in the Hallway*, was first published in the *Virginia Quarterly Review*, Winter 1940; see O'Casey's letter to Gabriel Fallon, 25 August 1939, note 1, Vol. I, p. 812.

the panorama of the world I lived in—the things that made me. At the moment, I am jotting down thoughts and incidents for another vol., which will, of course, open up in England, with a pen in one hand and a spy-glass in the other—to take an odd look at Eirinn through them.

I don't know of any autobiography comparable with mine; but, then, I know but two languages well—English and the Gaelic, with a very small smattering of French and German, and a word or two in Latin. I don't very much mind objections to "Joycean phrases" by critics—the Irish "critics" are loudest of all in their complaints. If I wrote less in the way I want to write myself, and more in the way others wish, I'd be a rich man. I've turned down a number of requests, some of them appeals, to write for the Movies; and so I am still a poor devil. Poor, but honest, aha. I don't know why so many are so afraid of Joyce—the greatest writer of his time, and the author of the greatest "Everyman," FINNEGANS WAKE, written by man. He died poor too. It is a shame on the world of letters that he never got the Nobel Prize. As far as I can see, Eire is afraid of her life of me. Plays and books have been banned, bar RED ROSES FOR ME. When *The Silver Tassie* (a play) was in the air, I was accused of subversive activities—not to overthrow a government, but to destroy the Kingdom of Heaven. I have done a lot besides the biography, *Purple Dust,* for instance, and the latest play, *Cockadoodle Dandy,* which G. J. Nathan says is a "brilliant" work. And we've three children, and these take up time. Pity you didn't come to see me when you were near Totnes. Many an American soldier and sailor came. T[homas]. Q[uinn]. Curtiss, for one.

I enclose a notice of INISHFALLEN FARE THEE WELL, printed by Macmillan's here. The vol. ends when I bid goodbye to Eire. And this ends by saying Goodbye to You, a word meaning, simply, God be wi' You.

Yours sincerely,
Sean O'Casey

P.S. I live in Totnes, opposite the Police Station—the constables, sergeants, Inspectors and Superintendent are, however, so far, good friends of mine. Cider, not whiskey, is the drink of Devon.

To Ralph Thompson

TC. O'CASEY

[TOTNES, DEVON]
8 DECEMBER 1948

Dear Mr. Thompson:

When writing to you, I forgot an item that is, at least, as interesting as the ones I recorded. I am just jotting it down now.

The piece called A PROTESTANT KID THINKS OF THE REFOR-MATION, appearing in "I Knock At The Door," was first welcomed by the Editor of *The American Spectator,*[1] George Jean Nathan, and his Associate Editors—who, I think were E. O'Neill, T. Dreiser, E. Boyd, and Sherwood Anderson, years before I began work definitely on the biographical venture. The piece in question is, I think, a Joycean effort, or would be called one, or is pricked with a Joycean influence, though it was written in a full flood of spontaneity. So, it would appear, it was from eminent minds in your Country that I got a first encouraging clap for a "Joycean" indiscretion.

Yours very sincerely,
Sean O'Casey

[1] "A Protestant Kid Thinks of the Reformation," the twelfth chapter of *I Knock at the Door,* first appeared in the *American Spectator,* July 1934; see O'Casey's letter to George Jean Nathan, 8 March 1937, note 1, Vol. I, p. 655.

VI

ON THE WAYS OF
GOD AND MAN,
1949

I DON'T really loathe the Roman Catholic Church. That is a wide term, embracing all the souls baptised into its communion, and even those baptised outside of it. The cardinals and bishops form but a tiny part of it. I loathe those who are turning her liturgy into vulgar nonsense and her temples into dens of thieves. Dante said this about the famous monastery of Monte Cassino—that the monks had turned the place of St. Benedict into a den of thieves. No intelligent man could possibly loathe the dogmas embedded in the "deposit of faith left by the apostles." The idea of the Incarnation, the ascent, the coming of the paraclete, and all the moral philosophy, the poetic tales connected with these, are beautiful; and, though not accepted either in substance or in fact, remain beautiful, and I am not the one to loathe the lovely.

My one complaint against the Creator is that He hasn't given me a mind ample enough to understand most things; that He lets me know so little.

At the end of January 1949 *Inishfallen, Fare Thee Well,* the fourth volume of the autobiography, was published in England, and O'Casey spent most of February replying to reviewers. It is obvious that the smell of literary battle excited him, and probably gave him an opportunity to overcome his insecurities about his career; the word-fighting seemed to stretch his imagination and strengthen his belief in himself. "Indeed," he wrote to Horace Reynolds in February, "it is the reviews that 'go for me' that I linger over, and love." He lingered over the reviews of Padraic Colum, Austin Clarke, and Gerard Fay, mainly because he loved to expose their misconceptions and errors of fact. "Whatever other faults I may have, I do try to be careful of my facts," he replied to Colum, who had wrongfully accused him of fabricating some doggerel verses composed by Arthur Griffith. He also corrected Clarke on a point of fact, relying upon his phenomenal memory of an incident that had taken place thirty-two years earlier, when he had played the role of a stuffy Englishman in a play put on by the St. Laurence O'Toole Club, adding the undisputed fact that he had been miscast and had acted it badly. When Gerard Fay accused him of waging "a private war with the Roman Catholic Church"—it was quite a public war—he pointed out that he was writing in an honorable anti-clerical tradition and was not anti-Catholic: "In criticising these gentlemen [the "dignitaries" of the Church] one does not criticise the Catholic faith."

It was a favorable review, however, by Desmond MacCarthy, which provoked him to make what is probably the most eloquent statement on his attitude toward the basic and beautiful doctrine of the Catholic faith, in his 7 February letter. MacCarthy had praised his book as the work of "a tremendous rhetorician," but he also observed that though O'Casey "is possessed with a loathing of the Church of Rome. . . . Yet his imagination, and his moral judgments, too, are saturated in Catholicism." This paradox possibly contains more truth than O'Casey himself was prepared to admit, for, like Joyce, he was fascinated as well as frustrated by Catholicism. Furthermore, he took exception only to the word "loathing," which he could not associate with the great miracle of the Incarnation, the truth and beauty contained in the dogma; and even though he himself could not accept the faith in "substance or in fact," it remained for him "beautiful, and I am not one to loathe the lovely." He was obviously moved by the poetry of Catholicism, though one would have to add that he was also committed to the poetry of Communism. It would be difficult to imagine a more eccentric and idealistic ecumenism. A day after he made those revealing remarks to Desmond MacCarthy, he pursued the point in a letter to Frank McCarthy, by making a democratic observation about the proper relationship between the laity and the hierarchy, which he felt was too often ignored in Ireland: "Mick McGilligan's daughter is as much a part of the Church as any Pope or Cardinal." A week later he was apparently enjoying himself when he modified the scriptural tenet and wrote that as a Communist he was his brother's equal not his keeper: "You should remember that I am a Communist, and a Communist is bound to think of others, not before, but along with himself." He was indeed saturated with Christianity as well as Marxism, and he should be recognized as a unique believer in poetic and practical Communism.

In his earlier letter to Reynolds, on 17 February, O'Casey indicates that he has been corresponding with young people all over America, from New York to Texas—many of those letters have not been found and collected—and it is likely that this new and intimate audience helped to balance the scale against the unfriendly critics: "It is odd how the young like me; honest to God, though in no way a conceited fellow, I'm very proud of this odd tribute." His autobiography and later plays consistently celebrate the uninhibited glory of youth, and it should not be surprising that he attracted this growing audience of young letter writers. His main objection to old or rigid critics was that they too often contradicted each other and therefore had little to say to him as a writer concerned about his craft, as he explained in a comment to Doris Leach: "The weakness of critics is that no author can learn from them—what one condemns another praises."

Besides Nathan, the one critic he admired, though he sometimes disagreed with him on political matters, was Atkinson, who was dubious about O'Casey's professed Communism. O'Casey often confused as well as amused him, as he probably did in an April letter in which he called upon the Holy Ghost for divine inspiration: "God forgive me, I never shall be satisfied with what I do; I am always demanding the grace from the Holy Ghost to do better"; and then went on to preach his unique doctrine of literary Communism: "Of course, I am a Shelleyan Communist, and a Dickensian one, and a Miltonic one, and a Whitmanian one, & one like all those who thought big & beautifully, & who cared for others, as I am a Marxian one, too." All of this proved that his heart was in the right place, but that exuberant faith didn't help him earn a proper living from his formal writing. His poetic communism and courage were intangible commodities. He didn't gain any material reward from his campaign to help the I.R.A. prisoners, but he expressed his moral satisfaction in an April letter that announced the release of the men from Parkhurst Prison, and he immediately began a new effort to help get the I.R.A. men out of Belfast jails. If his pen was powerful enough to help open the prison gates, it was not powerful enough to help him earn an adequate income, for in the summer he wrote to Jack Daly, "Financially, I've £300 between me and all harm."

Although he had many friends in America, it was fifteen years since he had had a new play produced there, and he was still trying unsuccessfully to have *Purple Dust* and *Cock-a-Doodle Dandy* done in New York. While he waited he moved on and wrote a new one-act comedy, *Hall of Healing,* but in desperation he finally allowed an amateur company, the People's Theatre of Newcastle upon Tyne, to present the world premiere of *Cock,* a quixotic gesture that did little to increase his reputation or his bank account. Nor did it increase his standing in Dublin when Seamus Kelly, the influential drama critic of the *Irish Times,* who believed that O'Casey never wrote a good play after he left Ireland, saw the production and came back to warn the Irish people that O'Casey had once more libeled the national character and wasted his talent. It was a familiar cry, and O'Casey tried to fight back; but perhaps the last word belonged to the Dubliner who wrote an anonymous letter to O'Casey, reinforcing everything the play had presented about repression and hypocrisy in holy Ireland, where he felt he might be persecuted if his name were known. He could have been a character in the play.

True to form, as the year ended he was still fighting, still defending the memory of Yeats and Joyce, when Yeats's body was brought back from the Continent and buried in Sligo: "They brought back Yeats—and, of course, rightly so, for he was a great poet & a great man—, but they left Joyce lying where he fell." He had also taken up the cause of a rebel priest, Dr. Simcox; he had urged the Irish High Commissioner in London to try to stop Bing Crosby from continuing his quaint libel by crooning about a false Hollywood version of Ireland; and he had taken on the conservatives of Totnes in a spirited argument which proved once more that he could be as ruthless with British humbug as he was with Irish folly.

To Richard J. Madden

TC. O'CASEY

[TOTNES, DEVON]
25 JANUARY 1949

Dear Dick:
I got the cheque for advance on COCKADOODLE DANDY from The New Y. Guaranty Trust Company allright, with many thanks.
Got a letter from George Jean telling me he had had pneumonia but was getting better. Thanks again; for I'd miss George bad.
Re PURPLE DUST
No, Dick, I dont feel comfortable about the suggestion made by Mr. [Michael] Todd. I wouldnt be in favour of it at all. It wouldnt show (the production by Amherst, or any other College) whether the play deserved a chance on Broadway or no. No one can say whether a play will succeed there or no. The psychology of a College is very different from that of Broadway. Unless a play be a very, very bad one, there's no saying how it will fare on Broadway, till it be done there. George would tell you that

much. Even he couldnt tell you whether or no a play with anything in it would catch on there or no. All he would say of a play with good in it is that it deserved to go on there. And surely that is enough. I am certain that PURPLE DUST is good enough for Broadway—as a play—and George thinks so too; and so does Richard Watts, Junr; and these should be good recommendations for Mr. Todd—better than any production anywhere else. No-one can tell the result—from the financial point of view; not even George; and, anyway, that isnt his business. And any prophecy of this kind is just stepping from criticism into a gamble. I'd love Mr. Todd to take up the play, and George would like it, too. But I cannot accept the proposal of a previous production in Amherst College. If he'd take an option on it in the usual way, no one would be more delighted than I; and I hope sincerely that he will be willing to do this; and then I will pray for him; but not before.

I have written refusing an appeal that the play should be done at Yale College. The appeal came from a young Student (Hartley) studying there. He may get in touch with you, and I hope you will very softly refuse. He is one of the young, and I am anxious that the young should be treated with as much kindliness as possible.[1]

I hope you may be able to tell me Mr. Todd has taken an option; but if he wont, it cant be helped.

My love to Tessa and to you.

As ever,

[*Sean*]

[1] Several years later he allowed the Yale School of Drama to perform *Cock-a-Doodle Dandy* for a one-week run beginning 1 November 1955.

To Irish Writing

FEBRUARY 1949

ARTHUR GRIFFITH [1] AND PADRAIC COLUM [2]

Dear Sirs:

Of your kindness, please allow a few comments on Mr. Colum's review of my work in the last issue of your Magazine.[3]

[1] Arthur Griffith (1871–1922), Irish nationalist leader and writer; editor of the *United Irishman*, 1898–1906; antagonistic to Yeats and the Abbey Theatre for performing what he considered to be the irreverent and anti-Irish plays of J. M. Synge; President of the Irish Free State, 1922.

[2] Padraic Colum (1881–1972), early Abbey Theatre playwright and poet, wrote a biography of Griffith in 1960.

[3] Padraic Colum, "The Narrative Writings of Sean O'Casey," *Irish Writing* No. 6, November 1948. See O'Casey's letter to David Marcus, 20 November 1948.

Captain White [4] was indeed the son of a general, but that makes him no better than if he had been the son of a gun. I know more about the boots given to those whose broken boots "prevented them from marching." Mr. Colum mentions the incident romantically, but he doesn't add that most of those who got these boots pawned them—some for food, some for drink—a few days later. Captain White had a bad habit of distributing largesse to those who flattered him, and when advised against this practice, resented it. On one occasion, he promised a fine topcoat he was wearing to three different men. No one could depend on his enthusiasm for more than a day. He ordered the uniforms from Arnott's, guaranteeing fifty pounds for them, without a by your leave from the Army Committee; and the collection of this money meant work night and day to promote a festival in Croydon Park that the Captain shouldn't be short. The fact is that Captain White was a noble fellow, but a nuisance.

Mr. Colum says a more serious thing when he writes: "Sean O'Casey puts down some absurd verses which he says Arthur Griffith wrote. On my word he never did." He implies that I composed these myself, and attributed them to Griffith in an effort to "belittle" the man. Now, Griffith not only wrote the verses, but sang them at a public meeting in Mayo during the election contest between John O'Donnell and John McBride. I do not ask anyone to take my word for this. If Mr. Colum is interested, he will find the incident fully recorded—with many more verses, worse than these I gave—in GRIFFITH AND HIS TIMES, written by Geo. Lyons, the life-long follower and friend of Griffith, and published by The Talbot Press in 1923.

Whatever other faults I may have, I do try to be careful of my facts.

Yours sincerely,
SEAN O'CASEY

---

[4] Captain Jack R. White (1879–1947) was hired by Jim Larkin in 1914 to organize and train the Irish Citizen Army, in order to create a labor army to protect the workers against police brutality and victimization. White and O'Casey had worked together in the Citizen Army in 1914 as President and Secretary, respectively. See the Manifesto to the Irish Trades Bodies, ? April 1914, Vol. I, pp. 50–51, signed by "President, Captain White, D.S.O., Hon. Secretary, Sean O'Cathasaigh, Irish Citizen Army." For a recent account of Captain White's exploits in Ireland, see Gerard Burns's article, "Captain Jack White—A Forgotten Figure in History," *Irish Times,* 15 September 1978.

To Irish Times

5 FEBRUARY 1949

"Inishfallen Fare Thee Well"

Sir,—In his review of my "Inishfallen Fare Thee Well," Mr. Austin Clarke [1] makes the statement that "on one occasion he wrote a play for charity which packed out the Olympia."

I said no such thing. I wrote no play for charity. The play produced on that "occasion" was "Nabocklish," by Thomas King Moylan. I merely acted the part of the "Englishman" in the play. The play was a great success; the acting very good; the one failure was myself. [2]

I am sending Mr. Austin Clarke's review to America, for I feel that such a splendid review should receive all possible publicity. [3]—Yours, etc.

Sean O'Casey

Totnes, Devon,
2 February, 1949

[1] Austin Clarke, "Och, Johnny, I Hardly Knew Ye!" *Irish Times,* 29 January 1949.

[2] See "The O'Toole Concert," *Dublin Saturday Post,* 1 December 1917, Vol. I, pp. 65–66, a review of the St. Laurence O'Toole Players production of Moylan's *Nabocklish (Never Mind)*, in which O'Casey acted the role of an Englishman, "George Herbert Chantilly Smith." The reviewer commented that "Sean O'Cathasaigh strove valiantly in a part that was altogether unsuited to him." In fairness to Clarke, O'Casey's original account of the incident, "High Road and Low Road," *Inishfallen, Fare Thee Well,* is vague and misleading: "To keep himself from the sin of idleness, he got together a concert, including a one-act play, in which he himself took one of the principal characters, and persuaded Arthur Armstrong to give them the Olympia free for the great occasion." The Olympia on Dame Street was then known as the Empire Theatre.

[3] This was meant to be ironic since Clarke's review was negative, ending with the following comment: "The present instalment of his serpentine autobiography shows only too plainly that the task of dramatising himself as an author rather than as a man of action is fraught with intricate difficulties. To misquote a famous religious poet—what began with a bang may easily end with a whimper."

To Miss Sheila ———

MS. PRIVATE

TOTNES, DEVON
5 FEBRUARY 1949

Dear Sheila.

You look charming. The photograph is a fine one. Yes, you look
older than in the first one; more important, and, I hope, more sensible;
but just as charming. We are all growing in years, if not in wisdom.

> The years like great black oxen tread the world.
> And God the herdsman goads them on behind,
> And I am broken by their passing feet. Yeats.[1]

A lovely way of phrasing the passing years.

Dont defend Communism to your friends. It is a waste of time. There
are many to whom things are hidden behind the wealth they hold; & some
who sincerely fear the results if Communism comes. It is futile to argue
with the former. Leave the poor C——— family alone. Let them pass
away quietly. It's near a mortal sin to disturb them. As for [Cardinal]
Mintzenty—that is a question for the Hungarians. We have enough to do
with our own. The fact is that many bishops wrap political propaganda in
the cloak of religion. So says Dr. McDonald, D.D., for 40 years Professor
or Theology in Maynooth College. He knew a lot about them—too much
for their quietness.

As for the question of your vow of chastity, I'm not competent to
deal with that big question. A lot depends on what age you are. Why not
apply to your Bishop to absolve you from it? Beyond this, it is impossible
for me to advise you: the question is too personal.

So Father C——— says "the world needs a modern Aquinas"! Well,
I can guess what would happen to him, if he appeared. He did, as a matter
of fact, or the next thing to him—the brave Professor McDonald, I've already mentioned, who held that as Aquinas built his theories on the physical science of his day, so the theory of Theology now should be based on
the greater knowledge of present-day physics. Indeed, he wrote many a
book, condemned as they appeared; and he hoped they would be published
when he died; but no one seems to know where the MSS are.

"Let things stay as they are!" The Bishops don't want to be disturbed; but they are being disturbed, & will be disturbed more in days
to come, as Dr McDonald foretold in his book thirty years ago.

> *Warm regards & good wishes.*
> *Yours sincerely,*
> *Sean*

[1] From Oona's speech at the end of *The Countess Cathleen* (1892).

To Desmond MacCarthy [1]

TS. MacCarthy

Totnes, Devon
7 February 1949

Dear Desmond:

I call you so because my friendship has lasted for a long time, begun before I ever thought of writing a play. Many a scarf of thought I wove for myself out of your comments on literature and drama. And do still and hope I may continue to do so for a long time to come.

So you see, I know my friends, and I think I can feel mine enemies. I don't really loathe the Roman Catholic Church.[2] That is a wide term, embracing all the souls baptised into its communion, and even those baptised outside of it. The cardinals and bishops form but a tiny part of it. I loathe those who are turning her liturgy into vulgar nonsense and her temples into dens of thieves. Dante said this about the famous monastery of Monte Cassino—that the monks had turned the place of St. Benedict into a den of thieves. No intelligent man could possibly loathe the dogmas embedded in the "deposit of faith left by the apostles." The idea of the Incarnation, the ascent, the coming of the paráclete, and all the moral philosophy, the poetic tales connected with these, are beautiful; and, though not accepted either in substance or in fact, remain beautiful, and I am not the one to loathe the lovely.

I got a letter from a friend yesterday telling me that at a gathering of rich R. Catholics, cleric and lay, it was said what was wanted was another Aquinas. Well, they had another, or something very near one, in Dr. Mc-Donald, and he and his thoughts were imprisoned in Maynooth. He wrote the book I quote under sentence from the doctors who told him he had but a short time to live. The book appeared when he had died, when

---

[1] Desmond MacCarthy (1877–1952), literary and drama critic, knighted in 1951 for services to literature and drama.

[2] Desmond MacCarthy, *Sunday Times,* 30 January 1949, a review of *Inishfallen, Fare Thee Well,* in which MacCarthy had written that O'Casey "is possessed with a loathing of the Church of Rome and of any religion as 'the opium of the people,' the instrument of the upper classes. Yet his imagination, and his moral judgments, too, are saturated in Catholicism." It is a very favorable review, in which MacCarthy makes the following comment on the often controversial subject of O'Casey's rhetoric in his autobiography: "O'Casey is a tremendous rhetorician. Personally I love the superb but today despised Art of Rhetoric; and I can forgive O'Casey even when he continues intoxicated with his own, even after I have recovered my sobriety; I wait patiently for the phrase which will be final and quick as a blow—and I am seldom disappointed."

blasting ecclesiastical authority had power over him no longer.[3] And, by the way, his strictures on his own church are much more severe, much more serious than mine. That is, of course, why they buried him and his thoughts so silently. He maintained that theology must develop; that as Aquinas has built up his Summa on the physics of the day, so theology must now be revised to accord with the newer discoveries made and new knowledge known in the activity and phenomena of life. It's a pity you have never read this book. I'll say nothing about the USSR. But there is something, at least, to be said for her. I have been in touch with the USSR now for 26 years. Some years ago, on a Shakespearean Anniversary, they sent me a fine big Magazine, filled with photos of all the Shakespearean plays appearing on their stages. They asked me to write about what was happening here. There wasn't a single play by the poet on anywhere in England, Ireland, Scotland, or Wales. I was ashamed when I wrote to tell them so. Oh, we have a beam in our own eyes still.

And now, my affectionate regards to an old friend.

Yours very sincerely,
Sean O'Casey

And thanks, many of them, for your
fine article about my book.

[3] Dr. Walter McDonald's *Reminiscences of a Maynooth Professor,* edited by Denis Gwynn, was published in 1925, five years after McDonald's death on 2 May 1920.

To Frank McCarthy

MS. McCarthy

Totnes, Devon
8 February 1949

Dear Frank,

The verse on last page is from "Moore's Irish Melodies"; the first lines of first verse of "Sail on, Sail on" written to the air of "The Humming of the Bann." The title is taken from Moore's song "Sweet Inishfallen, Fare Thee Well." No reviewer—even Irish ones who shout love of all things Irish—seems to have had any acquaintance with verse or title. Yes, D. McCarthy's review was fine, but I do not "loathe the Roman Catholic Church." D. McC. evidently thinks the Church to be Conclaves of Cardinals & Benches of Bishops (thought, too, by many R.C.'s) forgetting that the laity, 99% of the Church's members, are the prop & mainstay of whatever the Church may be; that Mick McGilligan's daughter is as much a part of the Church as any Pope or any Cardinal. But that fact is kept hidden by Pope and Cardinal to preserve their own arrogant powers. They are, as Dr. McDonald points out, mortally afraid of the laity. And the Faith is that "Deposit of Faith" left by the Apostles, and defined, once for all by Œcumenical Council; and, as Dr. McDonald points out, precious little has been so defined, so that there is a wide field for criticism of, and laughter at, many things propounded, & popularly regarded as "articles of Faith." I'm sure the book has set the Irish bees abuzzing! I haven't yet seen any Irish comment, bar the two you so kindly sent to me. Those two were gems of agitation. I remember the Tolka Cottages well—I mentioned them & the statue in one of my books.[1] I was in them. One of our hurling team lived there. He was an auxiliary postman at 12/6 a week. It's a good thing they've gone. They were appalling places, flooded every winter, & all in the last stage of rottenness. I collected "pinkeens" often in the waters by the bridge. My father died & was buried from No. 9 Inisfallen Parade,[2] below St. Ignatius Road, beside Father Gaffney's School. One of the chapters in "Pictures in the Hallway" is called "Cat 'n Cage" & deals with the pub.

Long ago, someone sent me, written down, the remarks of T. E. Lawrence about "The Silver Tassie",[3] but it disappeared somewhere. I should be glad if you could let me have a copy, for I shall be writing about the play in another volume.

All the best to you.

Yours sincerely,
Sean O'Casey

[1] "Cat 'n Cage," *Picture in the Hallway:*

Along past numbers of little cottages, the little lights in their windows flitting by them like falling golden stars; on over the bridge crossing the Tolka, giving a fleeting glimpse of the white-mantled Blessed Virgin standing alone among a clump of rain and river-soaked cottages; then a swift, winding turn up into Botanic Avenue, catching sight sometimes of the Tolka waters, singing her gentle song as she went slowly by the elders and willows, away on her short and simple journey to the Bay of Dublin O.

[2] Michael Casey died on 6 September 1886, at the age of forty-eight, and was buried at Mount Jerome Cemetery, Dublin.
[3] See T. E. Lawrence's letter to Lady Astor, 15 February 1934, Vol. I, pp. 498–99.

To George Jean Nathan

MS. CORNELL

TOTNES, DEVON
9 FEBRUARY 1949

My very dear George:

I was so glad to get your letter saying you were recovering again. What an experience to be down with pneumonia and bronchitis. You will have to try to be more careful in future. It is all so damned easy to fall into these illnesses, & so damned hard to climb out of them again. If scientists spent as much time & thought on things to mend us as they do on things to rend us, what healthier mortals we could be!

Under another cover, I have sent you a copy of "Inishfallen, Fare Thee Well," which I hope may be sail safe to New York. I've also sent a copy to Brooks (promised long ago), to R. Watts. Not yet, George, have I ever had a glass of wine or a cup of tea with an English drama-critic. They'd probably say I'm "an impossible man", but, looking at myself, even in Alice's looking-glass, I don't think I'm that. I. Fare Thee Well is to be published in America by Macmillan Co, this month. Did you read "Playwright as Thinker" [1946] by Eric Bentley? I'm reading it now (it was sent to me by a Yale student), and, honest to God, I can't catch hold of a thing in it. One thing seems to cancel another. One is always slipping down as one is climbing up.

I've written Dick to say I'd love [Michael] Todd to do "Purple Dust," provided he's willing to take up the usual licence for a New York production. Todd wants it done by Amherst College—in a scratch way. I'm afraid—to judge if it would be a success in New York.

I've said no-one can judge so. No-one can say whether or no a play will be a success. Not even a Drama-critic. All he can say is whether or no it deserves a success. It is outside the scope of a critic to foretell a "success." When he does, he ceases to be a critic & becomes an old-Moore-Almanack hack.

I do hope you are quite yourself again, George.

My love.
As ever.
Sean

To Manchester Guardian

14 FEBRUARY 1949

MR. O'CASEY

Sir,—Permit me to say a few words on "G. F.'s" comments in his review of my book "Inishfallen Fare Thee Well." [1] Your critic does not seem to know what constitutes the Roman Catholic Church. The cardinals, bishops, and monsignors no more constitute the Church than did the High Priest, the Scribes, and the Pharisees the Jewish Church in the time of Jesus. Because these dignitaries have separated the laity from all say in what she ought to think and what she ought to do does not alter the fact that the laity form 99 per cent of the flock (as Dr. McDonald makes clear in his hidden, but astonishing book).

In criticising these gentlemen one does not criticise the Catholic faith. The "war" with this Church is no private one, as your critic should know, if he had taken the trouble to learn a little about it. The most telling criticism of the Vatican and its assessors in the book comes not from me but from Dr. McDonald, Professor of Theology for forty years in Maynooth Roman Catholic College, one of the best known Roman Catholic colleges in the world. He should read this book before he talks about a "private war with the Roman Catholic Church." And, moreover, this book was written by this brave man under the shadow of death, for he was told by his doctors just as he was ending it that he had but a little time longer to live. It was published after his death when ecclesiastical censorship had power over him no more.

There can be no doubt of its sincerity, and does "G. F.," or anyone else, doubt its truth? In commenting on the "war," why does he not mention this learned doctor of the Roman Catholic faith, or mention his book? Is "G. F." too among the crowd of croziers that would stifle the statements of a courageous thinker? It looks very like it. Indeed, it is obvious that if he could he would stifle mine too. What follows about the "tyranny" of the U.S.S.R. is useless, for in pointing out the mote in a brother's eye he fails to see the beam in his own.—Yours, &c.,

SEAN O'CASEY

Devon. 6 FEBRUARY

Our reviewer writes: "As the cardinals, bishops, and monsignors do not constitute the Roman Catholic Church, so the casuistries, red herrings, errors, and omissions of this book do not, thank goodness, constitute Mr.

---

[1] Gerard Fay, *Manchester Guardian,* 1 February 1949, a review of *Inishfallen, Fare Thee Well.*

O'Casey. After all, I was reviewing his book, not Dr. McDonald's."—Ed.
"Guard."

To Horace Reynolds

MS. REYNOLDS

TOTNES, DEVON

17 FEBRUARY 1949

Dear Horace:

When you say that I was "vexed with you, probably for something I said of your work in a review," you are wrong. None of your reviews about my work would rouse a grumble in me. Indeed, it is the reviews that "go for me" that I linger over, and love. Havent you read "Tender Tears for Poor O'Casey" appearing in the magazine, Irish Writing? [1] Here I published most of what had been said about my work from JUNO to today by various critics—Irish ones; and an article which Nathan said was "murderous." Indeed, in The Irish Times, Austin Clarke reviewing my INISH-FALLEN FARE THEE WELL just finds no good in it at all; hits me hard, and lays me dead at his feet. It was a delightful essay. I wrote to The Irish Times asking for a number of copies, but got no reply. Now, to me, a critic should be prepared to stand for what he says; should be prepared to let all who wish to read it. I am not afraid to declare an opposing review, so why should the critic who writes one be afraid? Dave [H. Greene] knew about, and read, Tender Tears for Poor O'Casey. It's a wonder he [didn't] tell you about it. But the two of you had too much to talk about to find time for a tear for O'Casey.

Now, here's the reason why I didnt write to you—a brotherly one: You seemed to be insistent on sending us parcels. I didnt want you to do this. It's all right for rich ones to do it, but I didnt relish getting things from a chap and a lass who were as badly off as myself in worldly goods, and who had, as we have, to struggle to get their children going. I had written asking you not to, but neither you nor Kay took the slightest notice, so the only thing to do was to break off diplomatic relations. And there you are. You should remember that I am a Communist, and a Communist is bound to think of others, not before, but along with himself. So there you are.

Dave told me about Peggy's marriage. I hope she will have an active

[1] Sean O'Casey, "Tender Tears For Poor O'Casey," *Irish Writing* No. 2, June 1947.

life, the one life worth a damn. May she always be in the midst of the world, and kept from the evil in the world. Give her my love, and give her man my love too. And my love to John, and may he be a true teacher, always teaching himself first; never growing tired of knowing that there is a lot still to learn.

Oddly enough, I have read but snatches of Chaucer, and never the Wife of Bath. To me Joyce is greater than what I imagine Chaucer to be; and, of course, I am very busy, and have to take care of my eyes. Like Pavlov, I cry, oh, life, life—how short it is! And how much there is to do! Yes, I've written a new play called COCKADOODLE DANDY, and G. J. Nathan thinks it fine. Dave told me of a new life of Yeats by an American,[2] which he praises. It was wanted. Hone's LIFE [3] is one of the dullest books I've read, and doesnt show us Yeats at all. I've just written something about him, including my first and last croquet game, played with the poet, for a possible continuance of the biography.[4] I think Kay is wise to work—as long as she doesnt overdo it. You should see to that. Jasus, your writing is terrible! I cant make out what you say youre sending me, but whatever it may be, it will be welcome.

Breon will be twenty-one last day of April. He's in London, in an Art school, studying painting. Niall is fourteen, a keen politician, and a laughing observer of life. Shivaun is nine; Eileen is, I think, forty-five; and I am ninety-nine, ninety-nine, ninety-nine. the heart physically C.3 & morally Al.

I've been getting quite a lot of letters from young Americans, boys and girls, from N. York to Texas, & it takes time to answer them all—in the way they should be answered. It is odd how the young like me; and honest to God, though in no way a conceited fellow, I'm very proud of this odd tribute. I write a lot to the USSR, too, & about and about the great Stir there; so you see (with home affairs thrown in), I'm kept going.

So, Horace, me lad, au revoir, or slán leat, for the present, with love to Kay, John, Peggy, & yourself.

Yours as ever.
Sean

What in the name o' God is my/(your) American. . . . Why don't you try to write like a Christian?

[2] Richard Ellmann, *Yeats: The Man and the Masks* (1949).
[3] Joseph Hone, *W. B. Yeats: 1865–1939* (1942).
[4] See the opening pages of "The Friggin Frogs," *Rose and Crown* (1952), an account of O'Casey's conciliatory and last meeting with Yeats in the poet's home at Riversdale, Rathfarnham, Co. Dublin, in September 1935.

To Mrs. Doris Leach [1]

MS. LEACH

TOTNES, DEVON

18 FEBRUARY 1949

Dear Mrs. Leach:

Yes; if you send along the books, I shall sign them for you. I should like to read what Sean O'Faolain has said.[2] I havent seen the comments he made. Why he refers to me as "Sean," I don't know, unless he wants to imply a familiarity he has no reason to assume—I've never met the man in my life. Years ago, when he was in England, he wrote to me asking me to write a series of articles for a Sunday paper.[3] He added that if I took the job, it would give him an enhanced chance of getting on its staff. Although, at the time, I had to sell the world amateur rights of plays to Messrs French to keep things going,[4] and he suggested a fee of £200, my feelings couldn't allow me to do these low-rate articles (to me) he wished me to write. I sent a letter saying so, and invited him to come to see me for an additional explanation (both of us lived in London then), but he never came. Consciously, or subconsciously, since then, he has never forgiven me. He's a clever fellow, with imagination; but he lacks courage. It is a great pity, for he could be a beacon-like guide and helper to younger Irish writers; but he is, I fear, always concerned with himself alone. And he lacks courage; & lacking courage, he lacks all. It is a great pity. From a sheltered hedge, he watches others ploughing—and jeers.

Yours sincerely,
Sean O'Casey

[1] Mrs. Doris L. Leach, Hurley, Berkshire.
[2] Sean O'Faolain, *John O'London's,* 4 February 1949, a review of *Inishfallen, Fare Thee Well.*
[3] See O'Casey's letter to O'Faolain, 10 August 1932, Vol. I, pp. 446–47.
[4] See O'Casey's letter to George Jean Nathan, 28 September 1932, note 2, Vol. I, p. 449.

To Mrs. Doris Leach

MS. LEACH

TOTNES, DEVON

27 FEBRUARY 1949

Dear Mrs. Leach,

Here are the books signed and all.

And thanks for your very kind and intelligent letter. The intellectuals are a strange band—what with Huxley (Aldous) turning Darwin upside down by declaring that instead of man ascending up from the Apes, he is descending down to them—and he, through the war and all, nicely snug in Hollywood, with Isherwood & Auden.

The weakness of the critics is that no author can learn from them—what one condemns another praises. The one critic who has been a help & a joy to me is George Jean Nathan, the famous American Drama-critic. The others puzzle me.

Sean O'Faolain is really a clever chap, but he is, at heart, afraid of things. I daresay, he finds it hard to live, for reviewing is very poorly paid—but, then, most authors find it hard to keep going, myself included; especially when they've children. I've three—one twenty, one fourteen, & one nine; two boys and a girl. But these additions call for even more courage.

> *God be wi' your husband and you*
> *Yours sincerely,*
> *Sean O'Casey*

P.S. Very busy with proofs, so this letter had to be brief.

To Brooks Atkinson

TS. ATKINSON

TOTNES, DEVON
5 MARCH 1949

My dear Brooks:

Thanks for your kind letter and Review.[1] By the way, two more of your reviews—one from a prominent Labour Leader—came to me the same morning. I am, of course, delighted that you liked so much of the book. The Macmillan Co. say the Reviews are grand; so were those of the last vol., but the sales were small. Anyway, the critics were not to blame that time—nor, for the matter of that, were they to blame for the previous two vols., for the reviews were many and fine. It has been a stiff fight to keep going; but I've managed so far finely, though the O'Casey banner has by now a few rents in it; but it still flies well. I know you don't care a damn whether I am a Communist or not—I shouldn't like you half so much if you did. I don't know what you are, save that you are a dacent man, and that's enough for me. But I was a Communist long, long before I

---

[1] Brooks Atkinson, "O'Casey at Bat," *New York Times,* 27 February 1949, a review of *Inishfallen, Fare Thee Well.*

even heard the name of Lenin. Fintan Lalor, MacConglinne [2]—of the 10th century—and [William] Thompson of Cork—a landowner—and Parnell, with Davitt, with the great Jim Larkin, under whom I served, settled the question of Social Science for me. And Dickens, Byron, Shelley, Milton, Langland, and even Tennyson, helped me along the Road. Look you, Brooks, there is a whole host of Red Stars in our skies. And Strindberg & Ibsen in the North, Red Stars peering out of the Aurora Borealis! There's no use of your blaming me for thrusting the name of Dr. McDonald into what I have written. I know a fellow—a very fine fellow, a fine Drama-critic—who's whole life—bar an hour or so a week among the robes—has been spent watching the stage. Now this fine fellow, one day, kicked his desk down, flung his critical pen out of the window, and, without as much as a kiss-me-arse to anyone, hurried off to a place called Chung King; [3] leaving his duty and his love behind him for a "Distant Point" in which he had no business to be. Maynooth, and all it stand for touches me (and you) far more nearly than the affairs of Chung King touched that fine fellow. It touched us all. McDonald mentions the exile of a beloved friend, Dr. Sheedy; [4] exiled because he dared defend a fellow-priest from the animosity of a bishop. He was sent to Altoona, in Pennsylvania. During the run of "Within the Gates," when I was in New York, I got a letter from a Roman Catholic priest asking me—on account of the play—to "accept the blessing of an old priest." That old priest was Dr. Sheedy, hidden away in Altoona.[5] Dear Brooks, fair and upright opposition will never sour a friendship I have for anyone. The Rev. E. M. Griffin differed from me more than you do; but he held me in affectionate regard to the day of his death, as I hold the knowledge of him, & the remembrance of him still, & will, till the day of my own death. But the fact is that all honest & true and intelligent souls march with the people, though they may know it not. It amuses me to hear voices in the throng murmuring, "I don't agree with this or that"; I look back, & there are the banners of the Rev. E. M. Griffin, Dr. McDonald, Brooks Atkinson, R. Watts, G. J. Nathan, & the rest, waving high as the others in the midst of the People. March on, March on!

You have small idea of the power of the R.C. Church in Ireland. Its hand is around the throat of every thinker, every writer trying to rise higher than mediocrity. What matter, if they could think more kindly, write more attractively themselves. But they don't. Have you read your own Cardinal's (Spellman, with both eyes on the job of Cardinal Secretary of

[2] *The Vision of MacConglinne,* a twelfth-century Irish satire; see *Aislinge MeicConglinne* (1892), edited and translated by Kuno Meyer.

[3] Atkinson was war correspondent for the *New York Times* in Chungking, China, during the war, 1942–44.

[4] Dr. Morgan Sheedy (1853–1939), Rector, Cathedral of the Blessed Sacrament, Altoona, Pennsylvania. See Dr. Walter McDonald's comments on Sheedy in *Reminiscences of a Maynooth Professor* (1925), pp. 67, 210.

[5] See "Only Five Minutes More," *Rose and Crown* (1952), for the account of Sheedy's "fervent blessing" to O'Casey when he was in America in 1934.

State, & the Vatican hoping he'll die before they have to give him the job)
"The Road to Freedom," [6] written to inspire your people during the war?
I've never read a more tawdry and commonplace book in my life. Any
third-rate American journalist would be kicked out of his job had he
handed it in. The fact of a Cardinal writing it doesn't give it God's Im-
primatur—or man's either. And they're all the same. Where is the "distinguished" prelate today—answering to the word as we understand it?
None now like Richelieu, Woolsey, Newman, Gore, Temple, or Trench.
And, I think, never will be again. They've hanged themselves with their
own rosary beads. I've always been interested in "Theology." Many a discussion I've had with Mr. Griffin, & various priests, Secular, Franciscans,
Redemptorists, and Discalced Carmelites. I've read "Newman's Life," [7] but
a month ago, & a poor book it is. I've read "Five Centuries of Religion,"
"The Medieval Visage," "Sts. Bernard & Benedict," & other books by
Coulton; [8] Gore's "Lux Mundi," [9] Stokes' "The Celtic Church," [10] Trench's
"The Parables" [11] "National Law in the Spiritual World," & lots of others.
To reproach me for this stepaside is to reproach yourself for moving among
your Roses in the Garden in Connecticut. Anyway, I like roses, too, so we
agree there. I take an interest in everything, and am now learning a lot
about farming in general. My one complaint against the Creator is that He
hasn't given me a mind ample enough to understand most things; that He
lets me know so little.

I enclose a cutting from the Irish Times of a Review of my book by
A. Clarke,[12] a poet, &, I think, one of the founders of the Irish Academy
of Letters. This is a "surly review," if ever there was one. He was the
poet, who, in the early days of "Juno" & the "Plough" wrote accusing me
of "exploiting Dublin's poor" for money.[13] I have examined my conscience,
& I don't think he was right. This Academy of Letters is a dangerous affair.
I guessed it would be, & wrote so in "The American Spectator" many years
ago.[14] The members are, or seem to be, envious of any young writer who
shows any promise, sensing danger to themselves in any talent outside of the
Academy of membership. Shaw is the outstanding member now. Another

[6] Francis Cardinal Spellman, *The Road to Victory* (1942).

[7] John Henry Newman, *Apologia pro Vita Sua* (1864).

[8] George Gordon Coulton, *Five Centuries of Religion* (1923–50), 4 vols.; *The Medieval Village* (1925); *Two Saints: St. Bernard and St. Francis* (1932), a reprint of a section from *Five Centuries of Religion*.

[9] The Rev. Charles Gore, *Lux Mundi* (1890).

[10] The Rev. George Thomas Stokes, *Ireland and the Celtic Church* (1886).

[11] Richard Chenevix Trench, Archbishop of Dublin, *Notes on the Parables of Our Lord* (1864).

[12] See O'Casey's reply to Austin Clarke's review, *Irish Times*, 5 February 1949.

[13] At the time of the Abbey Theatre riots against *The Plough and the Stars,* Austin Clarke, in a letter to the *Irish Statesman*, 20 February 1926, wrote: "Several writers of the new Irish school believe that Mr. O'Casey's work is a crude exploitation of our poorer people in an Anglo-Irish tradition that is now moribund."

[14] Sean O'Casey, "Laurel Leaves and Silver Trumpets," *American Spectator*, December 1932. See O'Casey's letter to George Jean Nathan, 28 September 1932, Vol. I, p. 449.

Irish Author, Sean O'Faolain, has written in a review [15] that the chapter, "Mrs. Casside Takes a Holiday" should never have been written. So you see how different these thoughts are from yours. Now what should the poor Author do; which point of view should I choose? God helping me, Brooks, I think I'll choose yours.

I'd better close for fear of boring you to tearing this letter up; so farewell for the present, with thanks again for your review & letter; and to thanks, I couple my most affectionate regards & remembrance to Oriana and yourself.

Yours very sincerely,
Sean

[15] Sean O'Faolain, *John O' London's Weekly,* 4 February 1949.

To Frank McCarthy

MS. McCARTHY

TOTNES, DEVON

7 MARCH 1949.

Dear Frank,

Thanks for clipping from "The Standard." Inventions! I was never in my life in the Bailey Restaurant: never saw P. Colum till he came to Dublin from America on a holiday in 1925 or 26; & then visited me (uninvited) to work up an "interview" for the American Press.

I never spoke a single word to Gogarty till I had gone to live in London, & he had come over on a visit. I shouldn't have known him, even, had he passed by me when I was in Dublin; & I very rarely mention my plays to anyone. Certainly, I never discussed them with any of the Dublin intelligentsia; and not at all with anyone, save once, when David Garnett, the English critic came suddenly, with [Liam] O'Flaherty, to me when I lived in the tenement (again uninvited), and, by questions, got me to give a brief summary of the play, "Plough & the Stars" which I was then writing. D. Garnett was a grand fellow. I used to buy cooked pork in Youkstetters, when I lived "on my own" in 422 N.C.R. There's no record of "Pike" in Beasley's book; [1] but quite a number of 4th class "informers" were put in a place of safety by the I.R.A.; poor devils who would sell their own soul and their mother's for a few pints. Is L. A. G. Strong an admirer of Tom Moore? Is it not George Moore he thinks a lot of—and, rightly so? Yes,

[1] Piaras Béaslaí (Pierce Beasley), *Michael Collins and the Making of a New Ireland* (1926).

the poor Irish lap up what the clerics tell them; but what else have they to lap up? They are ignorant and the clergy see they stay so; so it is the clerics who must get the greater blame.

I am very busy with proofs, letters, & God wot, so must finish, for the present.

All the best to you.
Sean

To Richard J. Madden

TC. O'CASEY

[TOTNES, DEVON]
7 MARCH 1949

Dear Dick:

Many thanks for your kind letter and enclosed cuttings. I have had a long, delightful letter from Brooks Atkinson himself. He is a great friend, a good fellow, and I hope all the fine things he says about my work are justified. Indeed, it isnt the American Critics' fault that so few of my plays appear on the American stage. But they dont appear any oftener on the stage here, either; and, worse than that, the Drama Critics here take no notice. There's no G. J. Nathan, Brooks Atkinson, or Richard Watts, Junr. here, me lad. It's a curious thing that I have never had a lunch, a tea, or even a quick drink, with a British critic of the drama. They all go by on the other side of the street, when they see me. However, I get good notices from the English Reviewers of my books, and that's a lot.

About Mr. [David] Heilweil's offer: it didnt come as a surprise to me that the adventure of doing COCKADOODLE DANDY was off; I expected it. Anyhow, I shouldnt like the play to be done in the summer; and I am prepared to wait till the coming Fall, as I have waited so long. It's a pity that Mr. Heilweil doesnt think too of RED ROSES; but one is enough at a time. Well, now, to come to brass tacks—I am quite willing to accept the new idea, contract, or whatever it may be, namely, the terms of Monthly advances as set out in the Basic Agreement, provided, as you say, the same conditions as in the original Agreement—Cast, Direction etc.—apply to the new one.

Perhaps these fine notices will be a means through which the plays may receive more attention, and, finally, be presented on the New York

Stage; and, then, we will have nothing to do, Dick, save hope for a good time with a success, or, maybe, two, to our credit.

Thanks again for the cuttings and for the copy of your fine letter on my behalf. I hope Brooks may be able to get it in [the *New York Times*], though we mustnt expect too much from him. He has done—as far as I am concerned—more than a man's effort for my sake.

My love to you and to Tessa.

I hope business has been good with you, and that next season will be better.

All the best.

Yours as ever.
[*Sean*]

To Shelah May Greene

MS. GREENE
TOTNES, DEVON
11 MARCH 1949

Dear Shelah,

I've got enclosed from Paris. The announcements explain themselves. They've put me down (wrongly) as representing Éire. Ill health keeps me from going, but I cabled a letter of spiritual union (I'll be writing Pastorals next!) Could you, or *Labour Monthly,* or the Irish-Soviet Friendship Society, manage to do anything in the way of helping on this congress for Peace. Perhaps, among you all, someone might be sent to represent even two or three (when two or three are gathered together in my name) of Éire's people, it would be something.

I hope you, your husband, & your little one are well. I don't suppose any of the Irish writers would go over to Paris. [Austin] Clarke? [Sean] O'Faolain, [Frank] O'Connor, or, some other member of the Academy of Letters? No? I'm afraid not. Maybe, some of the lesser-known ones would go.

With all the best wishes,
and warm regards,
Yours very sincerely,
Sean O'Casey

To Roger McHugh [1]

MS. McHugh

Totnes, Devon
15 March 1949

Dear Roger McHugh,

Thanks for sending me "Rossa." [2] Why, though, not send it to someone who has a theatre under him or over him, or beside him? I'm not a
drama-critic—not having the experience nor the training to be fit for one.
I can only analyse safely a very bad play. Any play with good points, I
leave for judgment to the competent. I rather liked your play, & feel there's
something in it. I've told Unity Theatre about it—no commercial theatre
would do it, I fear—, & Unity, a letter tells me, has sent to Tralee for a
copy. I'm sending my copy to Robert Mitchell—a fine producer—

> Glasgow Unity Theatre
> 358 Sauciehall Street
> Glasgow, C.2;

& I suggest you send a copy of the play to

> The Secretary
> Citizens' Theatre
> Gorbals, Glasgow.

[James] Bridie is one of the Directors of Citizens' Theatre. You could say
I suggested consideration of your play.

I am very busy, but hope all the Dans and Donals are well; & that
St. Patrick has some influence over the Gael still.

Yours etc.,
Sean O'Casey

Don't say anything about it. All the great Dramatists from Cork to
Belfast would be bombarding me with plays.

What about America?

---

[1] Roger McHugh (1908–), teacher and playwright, Professor of Anglo-
Irish Literature, University College, Dublin.

[2] McHugh's *Rossa*, a play about the Irish patriot Jeremiah O'Donovan Rossa
(1831–1915), won an Abbey Theatre prize and was produced at the Abbey on 31
March 1945, and published in 1948.

To Jack Carney

TS. NYU Library

Totnes, Devon
16 March 1949

Dear Jack,

I am very glad that you got a job—even only for a short time—on the Evening Standard. Eighty pounds arent to be sneezed at these days. If one could [get] that for eleven months in the year—with a month for a holiday—one would do very well indeed.

Perhaps this, or that, job may lead to something else. One thing often follows another. I do hope something may be got from Dr. Evatt.[1]

We are all well here, except for my eyes that trouble me a lot, which, of course, is to be expected with the passing years and the natural decay of forces keeping one fit. W. Gallagher has written a fine Penguin defence of Communism.[2] I daresay, you have seen it.

About signing the book—I'm afraid I cant sign one for Michael J. Quill,[3] who very recently sold out according to reports from America—the Busmen's demand for a bigger wage. He has been accused by the men of doing what he shouldnt have done, suddenly agreeing with the employers' proposals, so that the men had no alternative but to go back, without their demands being satisfied. So you will understand, I couldnt put my name knowingly down on any book for Mr. Quill, even were he a Dubliner, instead of a son of Corcaigh.[4] So dont send the book to me; or, if you have sent it, I'll have to return it to you unsigned. I hope you havent bought it; but, if you have, maybe you could give it to some one else to whom I could pay more of a conscientious tribute.

I have had a letter from Macmillan's warning me that I neednt expect the sale of Inishfallen, etc, to be anything like the sale of Drums Under the Windows. There's a big slump in bookselling, and, I daresay, it is but part of a general jump down.

I return the stamps. You neednt send stamps with any book that I can sign with a clear conscience.

Yours as ever,
Sean

[1] Herbert V. Evatt (1894–1965), Australian politician. After his dispute with Eric Baume, Carney obtained a job working for a syndicate of Australian newspapers.
[2] William Gallacher, *The Case For Communism* (Penguin, 1949).
[3] Michael J. Quill (1905–66), International President of the Transport Workers Union, New York. He had been sympathetic to Communism in the 1930s, but later his views changed and at a national convention of his union in 1948 he pushed through a resolution that barred Communists or their sympathizers from holding office in the TWU. Perhaps this recent information was still fresh in O'Casey's mind. Carney was upset by O'Casey's rebuke to Quill, and this led to a cooling of their long friendship.
[4] Cork. Actually, Quill was born in Gourtloughera, Co. Kerry.

To Jack Carney

MS. NYU LIBRARY

TOTNES, DEVON

21 MARCH 1949

Dear Jack,

I've sent the book, signed as requested, under another cover to you.
I hope you have heard of something since. This month's issue of "The Author" tells of the bad state of the journal & book world—books because
of the delay in printing & binding, though no scarcity of paper: & newspapers & journals because of short supply of paper—less than half still of
pre-war supplies. So the meagre space gives little chance now to freelances,
& far less, even, to professionals; or, rather none to the F.lances. A bad
way for the men who try to live by the pen.

A cutting was sent to me a little time ago, taken from the "Evening
Standard." In it appeared the story of me, with Gogarty, Colum, & others
in the Bailey Restaurant,[1] Dublin, "discussing our poems & plays," and
drinking "black velvet." The fact is, of course, I was never in the Bailey
in my life; never spoke a word to Gogarty till I met him two years after I
had come to England; & when Colum was in Dublin, writing his plays, I
was elsewhere, never even dreaming I would one day write a play myself.
Who is the gossip writer in the E. Standard?

> *Well all the best to you.*
> *As ever,*
> *Sean*

[1] The Bailey Restaurant in Duke Street, across from Davy Byrne's Pub.

To George Jean Nathan

MS. CORNELL

TOTNES, DEVON

22 MARCH 1949

My very dear George:

Greetings to you. I hope you are keeping fairly fit. I'm not too bad,
but could be better. Tom Quinn Curtiss wrote to me recently saying that

the New York Theatre Season was a poor one. Well, according to all accounts, it was worse here. It is odd how static the English Theatre is in commonplace & stupid shows. Some old classics were given, of course, like "The Wild Duck" and "The Cherry Orchard"; but of new delights—none. Coward here has given place to Rattigan. And the English critics go on in the old dull way, particularly those doing the London Journals. The critic [Harold Hobson] filling Agate's place isn't half as bright or entertaining as the one who, dying, gave him the job. [J. C.] Trewin, second critic on The Observer, is a clever chap from Cornwall—judging from his writings outside The Observer—, but seems to be held in leash by Ivor Brown, whose style & manner he works hard to imitate. I never had a chat with him, never met him in fact, so never had a chance to lead him away from an outside influence nearer to himself.

I sent you a copy of the book, Inishfallen, Fare Thee Well, English Edition, which I hope you get safely. I am enclosing a cutting from the Irish Times, a review of the book by the poet, Austin Clarke, he who, when my first plays appeared, accused me of exploiting the poor workers.[1] It would seem he thinks so still. All the Irish Reviews are in the same strain. Clarke—unfortunately, I think—held fast to the influence of Yeats, and composes verse about the old, old kings & Queens of Eireann, like "Vengeance of Fionn" & "Fires of Baal"[2] done in a minor Yeatsian key, & which few, I imagine, read. He tried a few realistic ones like "The Fair of Windy Gap,"[3] a translation of the Gaelic humourous song "Aonach an Bhearna Ghasta"—a song I've often sung myself—, but he gets none of the lilt & the recklessness out of the original to put into his own. Three-quarters of those who learned the Gaelic seem to have been unable to put the music of it on to their tongues, or even into their thought—like DeValera & Sean T. O'Kelly. It's a pity Clarke didn't decide to remain a minor poet of his own creations; & not one furbished with the skill of another.

We are all well here, & I am looking forward to the Spring & that part of the Summer which isn't too hot. I hope you will take a long & restful holiday when the season ends.

With love.
Yours as ever.
Sean

1 See O'Casey's letter to Brooks Atkinson, 5 March 1949, notes 12 and 13.
2 Austin Clarke, *Vengeance of Fionn* (1917) and *The Fires of Baal* (1921).
3 Austin Clarke, "The Fair at Windygap," *Past and Present* (1936), a free version of Tomás Ó Modhrain's *Aonach Bherna Na Goaithe*.

To Francis MacManus

TS. MACMANUS

TOTNES, DEVON

24 MARCH 1949

Dear Frank,

Enclosed is a Circular from an Irish New York Book Club. David Greene sent one to me, and Gerald O'Reilly, a New York Labour Organiser, sent me another. It may interest you; & may even provide a hint. The "hint" is that you might like to do something to get Devin Garrity [1] interested in some of your books—Boccaccio, for instance. The only thing I knew about Garrity myself—before I got the circular—was a book—a huge anthology—of Irish Poetry, called "1,000 years of Irish Poetry," [2] which I have; a big book, ornamented in Green and Gold, like your Ceann Comhairle's [3] official gown. Why in the name of God, couldn't they think of something more imaginative than green & gold? One would think the Gaelic League had never existed. You may say why does Labour, including the USSR, plaster itself in Red. Why indeed; I don't know. But the USSR is beginning to have banners of other colours; &, of course, the banners of Athletic Unions have symbols of every hue; but there is still too much red.

I hope Seumas O'Neill is well. Has he written anything since Tonn Tuile? [4] And you?

Well all the best to you and yours.
Sean O'Casey

I've just laid hands on a vol. of "The Dublin Penny Journal; 1832–33," and strange reading it is. But, as usual, it had to fight, in its day, against the Commercial Publishing places, who said it was doing them harm.

I hope the Dail will pass a law taking the Harp off Guinness's beer bottles. I see it is the symbol of Eire's High Commissioner here, too, so, I suppose, it is the main symbol for Ireland.

Had a chat the other day with a priest, a Salesian who was "doing" a Mission here. From Galway, worked on a bog for years till the Salesians took him off & gave him an education (Latin Grammar) in exchange for his vocation. There's an ex-nun flitting about here—did a lot of sewing for us—a very comic lass. She was nigh thirty years in a Belgian Order (she's a French lass). She's sixty, & they just shoved her out of the Order (they were down here from Folkstone during the war), with 20 pounds

---

[1] Devin Garrity, publisher of Devin-Adair Company, New York.
[2] *1000 Years of Irish Poetry* (1947), edited by Kathleen Hoagland.
[3] Ceann Comhairle, the presiding officer of Dáil Éireann, the Irish Parliament.
[4] See O'Casey's letter to Daniel Macmillan, 26 August 1948, note 6.

and a few pillow-slips. I don't know what she'd have done only for the Totnes people. Speaks French well (I hope), and English badly. But God Almighty, Frank, she did dress comically when she came into the world. All the colours of the rainbow on her. But she's a damn fine needlewoman, & plucky, by God.

Sean

To Roger McHugh

MS. McHUGH

TOTNES, DEVON

25 MARCH 1949

Dear Roger McHugh,

I've already sent my copy of your play to Unity Theatre of Glasgow, & London Unity's Secretary has written to say he sent to Tralee for a copy of it. I hope either, or both of them, has a shot at it. Regarding America, of course, as you may realise, the end of the play would not, at the moment, appeal to the tycoons of Broadway, for obvious reasons.[1] Some of the Colleges might do it; but, I'm afraid, they don't produce too well, &, in any case, you wouldn't get much out of it.

The only one I can think of as an Agent is my own

> Richard J. Madden
> Richard Madden Play Company
> 20, West 43rd Street
> New York, 18
> N.Y., U.S.A.

a very honest man & an Irishman.

Not a good judge of drama; but a good Agent. He charges ten per cent of royalties received for work he gets performed. It would do no harm, I think, to let him have a few copies. Tell him about Eddie Dowling, for Dowling would be, probably, the first he'd think of. There's a chance, but only a chance. However, dont be discouraged. It is fifteen years since I had a play on in the U.S.A.; & it may be another fifteen years before one goes on.

Would you care to send a copy to the USSR? If you like, & you send me a copy, I'll send it to the Secretary of the Commission (Foreign) Union

---

[1] In the last act of *Rossa*, when Rossa is in New York, he is denounced by both Republican and Democratic representatives with shouts of "Communist!"

of Soviet Writers; a friend of mine now for the last 16 years. I think your play would yield to a ready translation, & Moscow is very eager to know more about Ireland. You would get no royalties, if the play was done; they would be kept in the USSR; but, if you ever visited the USSR, they would be yours to spend. Shaw has quite a considerable sum there, I understand. No play of mine has ever been done there, just a small edition of part of "I Knock at the Door," so I have there only a few roubles, if I've any at all.

All the best,
Sean O'Casey

P.S. Don't think of the USSR, if you don't want to; don't consider you are under the slightest obligation to me for sending your play to the Unities.

To Frank McCarthy

MS. McCARTHY

TOTNES, DEVON

27 MARCH 1949

Dear Frank,

Thank you very much for Lawrence's Letters.[1] A number of them are very interesting. A very remarkable man. I met him once at Shaw's—one would never think him the doughty man he was. The Old Lady who brought you to the Summit must have been a character. I've worked on The Summit often.[2] I helped to build & extend a Railway Restaurant there; and I worked in the Dynamo Room that drove the trams up, & pulled them down, the Hill. But you should keep the books you collect. I never saw the Hitchcock picture of "Juno."[3] He got some fellow to do "The Captain" who couldn't do it; leaving out both [Arthur] Sinclair & Barry Fitzgerald. Jasus, these Film Producers! All as timid as hell, only thinking of what money it will make—with a few saintly exceptions.

You're right to like [George] Moore. It was rather mean of Yeats to try to underrate him. He never forgave Moore's picture of him in "Hail & Farewell"; though Moore gives him many a magnificent tribute. Yes, I

---

[1] *The Letters of T. E. Lawrence* (1938), edited by David Garnett. Lawrence praised O'Casey in a letter to Lady Astor, 15 February 1934, Vol. I, p. 498.

[2] The Summit of Howth, Co. Dublin, where O'Casey had worked as a laborer on the Sutton branch of the Great Northern Railway from 1903 to 1911.

[3] The film version of *Juno and the Paycock,* directed by Alfred Hitchcock, was released in 1930. For details of the production, see O'Casey's letter to Gabriel Fallon, 28 February 1929, note 4, Vol. I, p. 342.

remember well the part in which Moore describes Yeats denouncing the middle-class, & he in a fur coat! And a middle-class man himself, though Yeats thought himself one of the Butlers—Dukes of Ormonde. But Yeats was a very great man, all the same.

Yes, I remember "Proddy Woddy." [4] Those were really bitter times for children.

I am up to the neck now in correcting proofs—I hate the job; but it has to be done.

All the best to you, Frank.
Sean

[4] A street song which Irish Catholic children sang about Protestants.

To Horace Reynolds

MS. REYNOLDS

TOTNES, DEVON
7 APRIL 1949

Dear Horace:

Thanks for your letter. I am glad, very glad, to hear that Peggy is a "fan" of mine. I am with the young all the time. The vote for the young as soon as they go to work or go to war; for if one be able to fight for one's country one is able to vote. So as in the Soviet Union, votes for the eighteen years of age group. They are afraid to give the vote to the young; only when the world begins to be too much with us do they chance the gift. The young here like me. Even the Young Conservatives; and I'm rather proud of this.

I have to return your check. The books you want have been a long time out of print. I wrote to Macmillan's to see if they might have one knocking about in a corner, but they havent even an echo of one. I have no copy of I Knock at the Door myself; and but one copy of Purple Dust which I have to reserve as a file copy for revision when the Collected Plays are published. This is beginning now, and sometime this year two vols will be published. Purple Dust, Red Roses, and Oakleaves and Lavender will come later.

I dont quite agree with you when you say that what my work needs is propaganda and not criticism. I shouldnt like you to think that; or that you should set down anything that you couldnt feel and didnt think.

Gogarty's BLIGHT [1] is, I fear unobtainable. It wasnt Gogarty's, strictly speaking. It was written by two calling themselves A and O—a doctor, who wrote one act, and a solicitor, who wrote the other. It was a two-act play. It was in no way memorable, for I've forgotten all about it. It was produced (I am looking now at the Abbey Souvenir Programme of 1925 giving the lists of plays done to then) in 1917. The play had no influence whatever on me. My thoughts then werent running on plays. Shakespeare and the other Elizabethans, Dion Boucicault, and numbers of "Dick's Standard Plays, Penny Each," insensibly influenced me as I say in one of the biographical books. Gogarty, unfortunately for him, could influence no-one. He had the talents, but he buried them in flippancy and self-conceit. It is a great pity. I havent read MacMahon's book,[2] but I've read a few of his stories that appeared in "The Bell." I dont think he has the poetical glee of Stephens. I wish Stephens would write again. I've dedicated COCKADOODLE DANDY to him.[3] I'm plunging now into a fight for the release of fourteen I.R.A. prisoners held in a Belfast Jail, under sentences ranging from ten years to life. Some have been in since 1942 and all since 1943. We got the lads out who were in Dartmoor and Parkhurst Jails after a hectic battle. I have a telegram from them while they were in Dartmoor thanking me for my part in the fight for them—another thing of which I am proud!

I hope Kay won't overdo the minding. There's no necessity for the body to "crack up." It is the way we live that brings it about. Not till each goes by the hundreth year anyway.

I've a letter from an Irish friend who's cousin is 106. An English reporter was brought to his place—a tiny farm of 3 acres & a cow,—to see him. He was making a rick when they got there.

Do you drink? asked the reporter.

Ay, when I can get it, said the 106.

Do you smoke? asked the R.

Mornin', noon an' night, said the 106.

And That's th' way it should be with us all. And will be under a sensible way of life.

My love to Kay, & don't let her do too much. My love to Peggy & her man; & my love to John.

> *And to you*
> *As ever.*
> *Sean*

---

[1] *Blight: The Tragedy of Dublin,* by "Alpha and Omega" (Oliver St. John Gogarty and Joseph O'Connor), opened at the Abbey Theater on 11 December 1917. O'Casey saw it on his first visit to the Abbey. See O'Casey's letter to Fergus O'Connor, 13 February 1918, note 1, Vol. I, p. 69.

[2] Bryan MacMahon, *The Lion Tamer and Other Stories* (1948).

[3] *Cock-a-Doodle Dandy* (1949) was dedicated "To James Stephens, the jesting poet with a radiant star in 's coxcomb."

To Roger McHugh

MS. McHUGH

TOTNES, DEVON

10 APRIL 1949

Dear Roger McHugh,

I've sent off a copy of the play to the Soviet Embassy to be forwarded
to the Secretary, Foreign Commission Union of Soviet Writers; & copy to
Unity Theatre, London.

Another little snag is the number of scenes in the play. In New York,
for a play of one plain set throughout, it costs £10,000 now to put it on
the stage!

A Glasgow friend has told me there's to be a discussion over Radio
Eireann on "Drums Under the Windows." If you happen to know time &
date, I'd like to know them too.

By the way, did you send a copy of your play to The Citizens' Theatre
Glasgow?

If you didn't, you might send one to

> Winifred Bannister (Mrs)
> 10 Thomson Drive
> Bearsden
> Nr. Glasgow.

She's a great lass for the Theatre, a critic in Theatre News; a writer
of one-actors herself; a broadcaster; & the mother of two children. A clever
woman, & very sincere about the Theatre.

Well, that's all I can do.

Yours etc.,
S. O'Casey

To Brooks Atkinson

TS. ATKINSON

TOTNES, DEVON

11 APRIL 1949

My dear Brooks:

Thanks for your letter. I hope, too, the book sells better than the last
two. If it doesn't, it won't be your fault, or indeed, the fault of any of the

American Reviewers. I couldn't expect more publicity than I got, & nine-tenths of it praise; sometimes even a little embarrassing, for I am not satisfied with what I have done. God forgive me, I never shall be satisfied with what I do; I am always demanding the grace from the Holy Ghost to do better.

Of course, your renegade Catholic correspondent is right—the clergy will do all they can to banish the book silently; just as they prevented the tour of "Within The Gates." [1] I don't know about America, of course, but in Ireland the book won't be admitted to a single Public Library, & this curtails the sale by some thousands of copies. And here, in England, wherever they have the power or the influence, they will do the same thing. The poet, Noyes, had to withdraw his book about "Voltaire," [2] and, I hear, Graham Greene is experiencing trouble now. And this isn't the result of "Stalinism," Brooks. A friend of mine—or he was, for he rarely writes now, for obvious reasons, I fear—, a fine Reviewer, clever and kindly, wrote a meritable book about Boccaccio, which had an American publication. This young man is a sincere and orthodox R. Catholic, & you may imagine his indignation when a Jesuit, reviewing the book in "America" (I think), recommended that the book be brought to the notice of the Sacred Congregation dealing with the matter of the "Index Purgatorius." [3]

Of course, I am a Shelleyan Communist, and a Dickensian one, & a Byronic one, and a Miltonic one, and a Whitmanian one, & one like all those who thought big & beautifully, & who cared for others, as I am a Marxian one, too. We can really move about & play and embrace, when we are tired on a wide, wide space of common ground.

I am sending you a copy of Cockadoodle Dandy under another cover. I hope, of course, that you may like it.

> *And all the best and love to Oriana & to you.*
> *Sean*

P.S. What a fine sketch that is of you, and you running out of a theater to write your Review by Hirschfeld, in your "Broadway Scrapbook"! You have a damned fine jaw yourself.

[1] See O'Casey's telegram to George Bushar Markle and John Tuerk, 21? January 1935, Vol. I, pp. 534–35.
[2] See O'Casey's letter to Daniel Macmillan, 26 August 1948, note 5.
[3] See O'Casey's letter to Frank MacManus, 21 March 1948, note 2.

To Vincent C. de Baun [1]

MS. DE BAUN

TOTNES, DEVON

17 APRIL 1949

Dear Vincent de Baun,

Your letter didn't find me in "good health," for I've been hurried to bed with the Grippe—Influenza, we call it—, so if the writing hops about a bit, you'll know the reason. Your reference to S. Allgood was the first I have heard of her "touring Juno around the nation for the past two seasons." [2] I'd be glad if you'd let me have any credible evidence of it., press-cutting, or any other indication. She got no permission from me or my agent to do it; & I shall be grateful for any information about the tour.

Your questions are hard to answer. I've often heard of, & read about, "naturalism" & "expressionism," but, God's truth, I don't know rightly what either means. I conceived the idea of "The Silver Tassie" when I heard an acquaintance lilting the song in his office—he was a coal merchant. I know it was impossible to depict a war, or even part of a war, naturally or realistically on the stage, without to my mind, making both myself & the play ridiculous. As for instance, in the war play, "Journey's End," of which George Jean Nathan said "all that was wanted was the butter to turn it into a parlour game." So to solve the problem, & to try to give the Spirit of the war, from the rank & file point of view, I developed the 2nd act with the "expressionistic" manner as it appears in the book of the play. T. E. Lawrence was struck with it, & called it "the finest experience he had had in the Theatre"; [3] & Nathan referred to it as a "noble experiment"—see his preface to "Six Famous Modern Irish Plays" [4] published by Random House. I tried to make "Within The Gates" a microcosm of life, and suggest that the virtue we needed most was courage. A lot thought the "Down & Out" to be the "unemployed," but they symbolised those who had lost courage & who were afraid to face life and fight its problems. The Bishop, his sister, and the old woman—young one's mother—were among the other Down & Out; and that what man needed could not be given by ritualism—the Bishop; or by emotional exhilaration—the Salvation Army—but by the will and the fibre of courage; the Kingdom of heaven within us. Nathan has referred to this play as "thrilling song." I have revised it a good deal for the stage, & this new version will be pub-

---

[1] Vincent de Baun was a graduate student at Rutgers University, New Jersey, working on an M.A. thesis on the plays of Sean O'Casey.

[2] De Baun was mistaken about this information.

[3] See T. E. Lawrence's letter to Lady Astor, 15 February 1934, note 1, Vol. I, p. 498.

[4] See O'Casey's letter to George Jean Nathan, 22 September 1941, note 1, Vol. I, p. 904.

lished this year by Macmillan's of London, together with "The Silver Tassie," and "The Star Turns Red," in one volume.

I daresay you are right in your idea of what you call expressionism appearing in The Plough; where you say, & in the outside calls for Ambulance, Ambulance—Red Cross, Red Cross. You are right, I think, in believing this play to be better than "Juno." Nathan thinks so, too. "Red Roses" has its faults, & isnt so good as "Purple Dust".

Don't be too much of a pupil of anyone's. Be yourself as much as you can.

And now, young lad & friend, Goodbye for the present, & overlook the shaky writing.

> *Yours sincerely,*
> *Sean O'Casey*

To R. F. Allen

MS. MACMILLAN LONDON

TOTNES, DEVON

18 APRIL 1949

Dear Mr. Allen.

Most of me has been overwhelmed with an attack of Influenza, so what is left is now in bed, replying to your letter of the 14th of April.

Adding the tax here to the litany of reductions made by you in your letter, there would be sweet damn all left of what might come from the publication of "Drums Under the Windows" in Czechoslovakia; so, to me, the scheme is not worth while, & should be ignored for the present.

Things, dear Mr. Allen, are regimented in other places besides Czechoslovakia:— I've just had word from the Dramatists League that permission to do "Juno" in the Soviet Zone of Germany cannot be given.

This writing is a bit shaky, but the announcement made at the top will convince you that the writer wasn't drunk.

> *All the best to you and all.*
> *Yours sincerely,*
> *Sean O'Casey*

To George Jean Nathan

MS. CORNELL

TOTNES, DEVON

22 APRIL 1949

My very dear George:

I am very sorry to hear about the condition of H. L. Mencken and Gene [Eugene O'Neill]. It is very distressing when old comrades are struck down with afflictions. I have never experienced it, for passing through many movements, though I had friends, I never enjoyed the companionship of what could be called a life-long comrade. But I can understand the way you feel; I'd feel the same if Eileen was hurt, for we have been together now for twenty-three years, the longest time I've spent with anyone, bar my own mother. The one thing left for you to do is to look after yourself. To worry won't serve any useful or useless purpose.

I've just come out of an attack of the grippe—what we here call Influenza—, and it has left me a bit shaky. The flowers don't look quite so fair as they did, but the depression will pass away. The children now are here all the day holiday making, & one has to be resigned to pleasant interference.

I enclose a cutting giving the comments of Austin Clarke on Cockadoodle Dandy,[1] in which he exclaims against the "pernicious influence of Boucicault." Poor Boucicault! With all his faults, he wasn't the worst. Looks like spleen to me. I don't know why. I've never even seen him, so it can't be anything I've done. I'm afraid, though, his gay & flippant manner covers a hearty fear of the powers in Eirinn; & that he whistles to keep his courage up.

Dick [Madden] wants me to [give] John O'Shaughnessy, he who did Command Decision, Red Roses for a four weeks Tour to resident companies during the summer, in the hope this may heat the play up for a Broadway production: "prime the play," as Dick calls it. Doesn't seem very attractive, and I'm not enthusiastic about it. It has waited long, can wait longer. What do you think of it? Don't think long, for I'm interested myself more in P. Dust & Cockadoodle Dandy.

I've dipped into [Eric] Bentley's book, "Playwright as Thinker," and am reminded of Omar Khayyam, hearing great arguments about it and about, & have come out the same way as I went in.

I've read another book on Shakespeare by Edith Sitwell [2] who writes of the poet's magic in his way of associating vowels and consonants to-

---

[1] Austin Clarke, "The Riotous Are Bold," *Irish Times,* 15/16 April 1949, a review of the published text of *Cock-a-Doodle Dandy*.

[2] Edith Sitwell, *A Notebook on William Shakespeare* (1948).

gether to produce effects. I can't believe it. Words, yes, but letters, no. He wouldn't have time. Joyce did it, but his purpose is plain.

I do hope you are keeping fit.

My warm love.
Sean

To Roger McHugh

MS. McHugh
Totnes, Devon
[5 May] 1949 [1]

Dear Roger McHugh,

The enclosed letter will show you your play reached the two "Unities," & what they say about it. I have had Influenza, & couldn't bother to send them to you till I came to myself again. I hope something may come out of what they say.

I am sending Mr. Sharp your address, for it's you he must get in touch with, & not me. I wouldn't agree at all about a "compartment stage" & "spots." These tricks are utterly exploded now, & would do more harm than good. They were always—to me & lots of others—somewhat ridiculous. Thanks about "Drums Under the W." Long ago, in IRIS Mr. Farren reviewing the book,[2] called on old Gaelic Leaguers to refute what had been said in it; & I was curious to know if the proposed discussion was the fruit of his suggestion.

All the best,
S. O'C.

---

[1] O'Casey had mistakenly dated this letter "5 April," but the postmark on the envelope was "5 May"; and the "2 enclosures" were letters to O'Casey from G. Sharp, secretary and general manager of Unity Theatre, London, dated "22 April"; and from Robert Mitchell, artistic director, Unity Theatre, Glasgow, dated "23 April."

[2] Robeárd Ó Faracháin (Robert Farren), "Seachain do cheann, a Éireannaigh!" ("Watch your head, Irishman!"), *An Iris,* Nodlaig (December) 1945, a review of *Drums Under the Windows* (1945). See O'Casey's letter to Francis MacManus, 14 January 1946, note 7.

To Francis MacManus

MS. MacManus

Totnes, Devon

10 May 1949

Dear Frank,

Down with influenza, I couldn't take any notice of your last letter. I didn't mean you should get published by Devin-Adair; but that you might use his Book Club to increase your sales. You could see by the circular I sent that he has my last book on it—evidently by arrangement with Macmillan Co. I didn't know this but D. Greene sent me the circular. Dave says "the Firm will go places," & his guess is bound to be better than yours or mine.

But if you managed to sell 5,000 of your Boccaccio, then I'm not the one to advise you. My own "I Knock at the Door" sold less than 2,000, in America; "Pictures in the Hallway," no more; "Drums Under the Windows," just 3,000, and the last one is not yet recorded. And this even after, in each case, a deluge of fine reviews. So you are not so unfortunate—if you're not exaggerating about it.

By the way, if you haven't placed your last book & you think well of it, why not chance Macmillan's?

Macmillan & Co.,
Publishers,
St. Martin's Street, London. W.C.2.

You could mention my name. I am a friend of the two brothers, Daniel and Harold—Tories, but brave, broadminded chaps—&, if you said I said you should send your book to them, you would be certain, at least of a reading and an opinion.

Mention your other published books, so as to show you are not a new commencer.

Indeed, if you like, I'd write a personal note to them for you. I like your reviews immensely, & think you a lad of promise.

That's all.

All the best to you and yours.
Sean

To Frank McCarthy

MS. McCarthy

Totnes, Devon

13 May 1949

Dear Frank,

Thanks for your letter and enclosure. I am knocking about again, but not heartily. On account of the remains of silicosis, these attacks stay a long time with me. One has just to stick them patiently. "Red Roses" isn't really "magnificent." In fact "Purple Dust" is a more musical, more elegant, more imaginative play. If there were a revival, I don't think I'd pine after O'Hanrahan [1]—a charming chap, by the way; but a bit hard in his acting. The play was actually "made" by the superb acting of Eddie Byrne in the part of old Brennan. I was told the play had to come off because of O'Hanrahan leaving for the Films, but I doubt this: the Manager wasn't very enthusiastic, & I don't think he liked the Leftist Twist in it. The following play was worse.[2] I've never had such a shocking production before— and I've had some bad ones. It seemed to me it was desirable that the play should be made to look as bad as possible. I would never again give a play to this Manager—a charming man, too, with an equally charming wife, who is, oddly enough, the daughter of the T. W. Rolleston, mentioned in your letter. I imagine they were frightened at the reception of "Red Roses."

When was "Saints & Scholars" published? [3] I haven't heard of it. What does he say of McDonald? That's the one essay I'd be interested in. Father Mathew was a great man, a Franciscan friar who made near all Ireland take the pledge.[4] He was influenced by a Quaker. But the reasons for the lure of drink were left—poverty & uncertainty; so the Crusade had no lasting effects. But why they chose such as The Little Flower & Matt Talbot for canonization, and leave out F. Mathew is a puzzle to me. No film value in him, probably. His statue stands in O'Connell St. (Sackville St.), & an atrocious piece of work it is!

It is amusing to read your brother's remarks on the growth of "Joe Stalin's disciples" in Dublin. They're growing much more rapidly in China,

[1] Kieron O'Hanrahan, who later appeared in films under the name of Kieron Moore, played the role of Ayamonn in the 26 February 1946 production of *Red Roses For Me*. See O'Casey's letter to Mrs. Una Gwynn Albery, 6 March 1946, note 1.

[2] A reference to the production of *Oak Leaves and Lavender* in London on 13 May 1947. See O'Casey's letter to Mary Hinton, 19 May 1947, note 2.

[3] Stephen Gwynn, *Saints and Scholars* (1929). One chapter is devoted to Dr. Walter McDonald: "A Maynooth Professor," pp. 207–18.

[4] The Rev. Theobald Mathew (1790–1861), apostle of temperance, signed a temperance pledge in 1838 and carried on a crusade administering the pledge all over Ireland.

you can tell him. Rolleston [1857–1920] was contemporary with Yeats and Hyde. He wrote two lovely lyrics, and was a notable German scholar.

The "Irish Republic" is, of course, a Cod. They're getting out of the linking up with the Atlantic Pact, by joining an alliance with the U.S.A., & handing over all ports, airfields, etc. she needs; so that will preserve their refusal to join it because of partition. More Christian dodgery. It is annoying how unscrupulously clever these Christians can be.

I'll read the book you sent me when I've a free hour.

All the best to you, and a job found quick.

Sean

To H. S. Latham [1]

TS. MACMILLAN, N.Y.

TOTNES, DEVON
18 MAY 1949

Dear Mr. Latham:

Thank you for your kind letter of the 12th May. It is fine to hear that the books "I Knock at the Door" and "Pictures in the Hallway" will be obtainable soon. This morning a letter from a friend asks me where he can get a copy of "Pictures in the Hallway." I daresay, you will send copies to your London firm when they are available.

Though, frankly, I'm no lover of Book Clubs, for I hold that men and women should be fit and able to choose their own books; &, secondly, because the choice of these Book Clubs is very often laughable; yet I am selfish enough (greedy for dollars) to be glad that a book of mine [2] was chosen by the Book Find Club, with your help and encouragement. Certainly, it is, of course, gratifying to feel that 30,000 may have the book, and, possibly, read it.

You probably know that Macmillan & Co., here, are to publish *this year* two vols. of my "Collected Plays"—No. 1. containing the Irish plays; No. 2. Silver Tassie, Within the Gates: and The Star Turns Red.

I have just passed thro' Influenza—the Grippe—, but am O.K. bar a whoreson cough; but able to go about, & even stoop to smell the Spring blossoms.

Yours very sincerely,
Sean O'Casey

---

[1] H. S. Latham, Macmillan Company, New York.
[2] *Inishfallen, Fare Thee Well.*

To Peter Newmark

MS. NEWMARK

TOTNES, DEVON

20 MAY 1949

My dear Peter.

Glad to hear from you—wondered what had happened to you. And gladder to hear you are happily married—may it long continue to be so. So you didn't criticise my last two efforts—well, that's a tribute from Peter to John. I am very glad you like them & think so well of them. There doesn't seem to be much a chance of a production here; but there is in New York. America, I'm told is now taking a "real" interest in O'Casey. That's very gratifying, &, if it be real, will enable me to go on living decently. The other earlier books, long out of print, are to be republished there (in America) this summer. No London Drama Critic has yet mentioned Cockadoodle Dandy. And no religious journal, as far as I know, of any denomination, has mentioned "Inishfallen, Fare Thee Well". Odd, isn't it? I have never attacked the theory of the R.C. Church, but only its practice. Dr. McDonald did both: and no-one has answered him. I have had several inquiries from priests about his book, but it is unobtainable now.

I haven't the energy to comment on your remarks about Communism & heresy hunting (I've just got out of Influenza, but still have a whoreson cough). In a way, I agree with you. Some of the Marxist scholars are just comic. I dont agree with the emotional attacks on T. S. Eliot or [Eugene] O'Neill. Indeed, I've written to a friend of mine for 15 years, T. Apletin, Chairman of Moscow's International Gazette to say so. There is a lot to be said against their way—from the point of the USSR—, but both are undoubtedly poets, and most sincere men. Did you see "Arena"? A quarterly under Jack Lindsay, which, I take it, is out to defend a little more liberty in literary creation. Your friend R. Swingler is one of the Editors. But I can't stand the commonplace, sneering, of that urchin, Sartre. The revolt in the Lab. Party seems to have begun. It was long due. You are right about H[arry] Pollitt going to Dartmouth—he should never had attempted Amethyst or no Amethyst. It is waste of time there and here. The Totnes Secretary, Julia Seyd is very mulish, and utterly incompetent at dealing with questions. She doesn't know how to tackle [Brig. R.] Raynor; & never will, but she wont keep quiet. She makes me wild, & undoes a lot of work I quietly do here. The four Lab. Municipal candidates here were flung out, though they declared before God that they had no truck with Communists! Sorra mend them!

Love to Mrs. Newmark & to you.
Yours as ever.
Tired Sean

To Harold Macmillan

MS. MACMILLAN
TOTNES, DEVON
24 MAY 1949

Dear Mr. Harold.

I am, of course, very glad that you liked "Cockadoodle Dandy," and that it gave you some laughter.

Laughter, if it be genuine, and enjoyed because of a genuine cause and stimulation, is a grand thing. I am very fond of it myself, even at my own expense. We laugh too little—though if one were to listen to the "humours" of Broadcasting, one would think England in the middle stage of idiocy. I've been down with Influenza, & couldn't reply sooner. Just as I clapped my hands when the whoreson thing was vanishing from Totnes, it caught me turning a corner, & laid me low.

I hope you are keeping fit.

Mr. Daniel liked the play immensely, too.

All the best to Lady Dorothy & to you & yours.

Yours very sincerely,
Sean

To George Jean Nathan

MS. CORNELL
TOTNES, DEVON
3 JUNE 1949

My very dear George:

I've just wakened up out of an attack of Influenza, and, like Dickens' little doll-maker, my legs feel queer.

I don't bother personally about Austin Clarke, or anything he may say about me; but only about his influence & power over younger Irish Writers. He is a founder-member of the Irish Academy of Letters, & is now, I think, its President.[1] He assumes a curious imitation of Yeats' in-

---

[1] Austin Clarke was President of the Irish PEN, 1946–49; President of the Irish Academy of Letters, 1952–54.

fallibility, without a titter of Yeats' knowledge, intuition, or generosity. You may remember, I wrote an article on this Academy in "The American Spectator," [2] guessing what would happen; that the members would patronise writers not so good as themselves, and ignore, or injure, any youngster giving promise of throwing a wider chest than their own. Today, should any visitor to Eirinn ask after Literature, he is, of course, led to these academicians, & given the names of the chosen few. Talk about the Soviet Union dictatorship! This, along with the clerical censorship, puts Irish writers in a poor, shivering state of nerves, unless they can break thru to an American or an English publisher. But you are right: neither you nor I can do much about it. Even those outside of it feel its influence— [Paul Vincent] Carroll for instance, who seems to have gone from his first-state, & is beyond recovery. It is sad when one of promise slinks away from his own gifts. Denis Johnston, too.

I shall—and Breon—look forward to reading your new book. Tom Curtiss tells me the season for drama was a poor one. It was worse here. Even with musicals. The only ones worth a damn were "Oklahoma," "Annie Get Your Gun," "High-Buttoned Boots" & "Brigadoon"; all of which Eileen & Breon saw, and reported to me. None of these, I assure you, came bubbling out of an English mind. Dick [Madden] says you are writing an article on "Purple Dust" and "Cockadoodle Dandy." That is very kind of you, and a great honor to me. So far, not a single English Drama Critic has mentioned the latest play—not to speak of recommending it for production. [James] Agate, at least, would possibly have ridiculed it, but that is far better than indifference. I had little respect for Agate—any play written by a Cissy, or acted by Cissies, was a great play to him—but he wrote brightly, & was far and away above the dull fellow now in his place. "Inisfallen, Fare Thee Well," has got into one of the Book Clubs in the U.S.A. Though it won't bring in a fortune—£165—by the time Macmillan's take half, & the tax here is paid; but £165 isn't to be sneezed at these days. Indeed, the U.S.A. has kept me going. The owner of the Club [3] stayed here last night, & did a "little film" of family, in the small garden fronting the house.

Basil Dean wrote to me offering himself as a Producer of "Cockadoodle Dandy," but I courteously suggested he wasn't the man for Galway. I've read "Death of a Salesman,": a good play, but—to me—it hasn't the power & staggering impact of O'Neill's "The Iceman Cometh." I understand a copy of [Ewan MacColl's] Uranium 235 has been sent to you.

I enclose a clipping of [John] Gielgud's "Report on Broadway." He implies complaint of an "all-purpose scene" in "D. of a Salesman"; but I've seen him do first part of "Romeo & Juliet" with half the curtain-sideways-down, which looked very bad.

[2] Sean O'Casey, "Laurel Leaves and Silver Trumpets," *American Spectator*, December 1932. See O'Casey's letter to Nathan, 28 September 1932, note 4, Vol. I, p. 449.
[3] George Braziller.

I hope you are keeping well, & that you will take a long and profitable holiday.

My love to you
Sean

To George Jean Nathan

MS. CORNELL

TOTNES, DEVON

17 JUNE 1949

My very dear George:

Your article has come to me. It is a very fine article—from my point of view. But I worry a little that you should worry so much about the absence of my plays from the American stage. The Theatre Incorporated did a lot of harm to the chance of "Red Roses" by taking it up, and then dropping it. And Agate's onslaught on "Purple Dust" [1] as a "venomous attack on England when she was helpless," was another way of keeping producers shy. Agate really didn't give a damn about England. He was too busy on the look-out for suitable boys. I've no big reason to be angry with the U.S.A. I've had publicity there unknown here. That I'm not on the stage isn't the fault of the critics. Since "Cockadoodle Dandy" was published, not a single Eng. Drama Critic that I know of has mentioned it. So how can I say anything about the USA who, through you, are mentioning it all the time?

And what about my own countrie? It's near three years since any play of mine appeared on the Abbey stage; &, I believe, it will be a long time before one does. There was no reason why they didn't do Red Roses, or Purple Dust, but neither has been mentioned, no ever will be. Had Yeats lived long enough, he would have yearned to put on Cockadoodle Dandy— row or no row. [Lennox] Robinson never had any guts & has less now. The death of Higgins was a sad blow.[2] So what's the reason for blaming the USA, or New York, when this curious boycott goes on at home! The Abbey boycott is particularly hurtful. They produced the plays—"Gunman," "Plough" & "Juno" before publication, & so gave me the power through rehearsals, to amend or alter. Since then, all my plays have had to

---

[1] James Agate, "Mr. O'Casey: A Reply," *Sunday Times,* 3 May 1942; reprinted above.

[2] F. R. Higgins, poet and playwright who became Managing Director of the Abbey Theatre after the death of Yeats in 1939, died in 1941 at the age of forty-five. See O'Casey's first letter to him, 19 February 1939, Vol. I, p. 779.

be published before production; I've had no aid from rehearsals, & so each
—except—"Cockadoodle Dandy," I think—needed touching here and
there. I've done a lot to W. the Gates, some to Silver Tassie & The Star
Turns Red to be issued soon in one vol. I've really gone through a stiff
time with the Abbey, as you will see from next biographical vol.—even
having to fight for royalties due on plays done six months before. Here, they
are always yelling for new plays. I enclose an article by Charles Landstone
writing about this phase. He never even bothers to mention me. It was as if
I had ceased to be, or never had been. However, I have the placid satisfaction of knowing that my name—with all my faults—is there, though never
mentioned. But no American critic would do that. I enclose one of the few
and better comments on Cockadoodle Dandy; & a poor one it is. So, my
very dear George, to me, America is not the bad, bold land, for in many
ways it has done me proud.

I do hope you keep well, & that you will take a long, long holiday.

Ever yours with love.
Sean

I've read "Death of a Salesman," but, to me, it isn't comparable in
power and impact with O'Neill's "Iceman Cometh." But a play, all the
same.

I near forgot to thank you for the article—now gone to Breon to
read. Thank you, dear George.

To Frank McCarthy

MS. MCCARTHY

TOTNES, DEVON
20 JUNE 1949.

Dear Frank,

Yes, I got both book and Pouch safe, & thank you for them. I'll try
the pouch, but please don't make another for me—I usually carry whatever tobacco I happen to have in an old tin. The book was a disappointment.[1] I had imagined better from Stephen Gwynn. I've heard so much
about his writings. Some of his poems are fine; but this book was one of
the poorest I've ever read. And what a mean-spirited thing is his tribute to
Dr. McDonald.[2] God forgive him for his timidity before the violet & the
scarlet robes!

[1] Stephen Gwynn, *Saints and Scholars* (1929).
[2] *Ibid.*, "A Maynooth Professor," pp. 207–18. Gwynn was a close friend of
Dr. Walter McDonald; his son, Denis Gwynn, was McDonald's literary executor and
edited the posthumous *Reminiscences of a Maynooth Professor* (1925).

Thank God, my tribute was better than his. And I didn't know the man. He was one of Gwynn's friends. Oh! Ireland! You give a man great courage, or you take it all away from him! Do you want it back? It's not worth keeping. Don't spend even "a few coppers" on a worthless book. I don't want "devices" to draw the people to my plays. What I want is good acting, Frank, & I don't care where the man or woman comes from who can do it—from music-hall, jail, or poor-house. I have the book about Rolleston, written by his son.[3] A fine book, with, as you say, interesting photos in it. It was given to me by Rolleston's daughter, who is married to Bronson Albery, managing-director of The New Theatre. Yes, I remember Moore's reference to the frothy Hyde.[4] Hyde's Irish is very poor. Hardly any idiom in it, & written in an English manner. His two books, "Journey to America" & "Myself and the League,"[5] both in Gaelic, are terrible efforts. I reported on these in "Drums Under the Windows." "Picture in the H." is out of print. The Macmillan Co. of America are reprinting it (with I Knock at the Door) in the Summer, &, I understand, the London Co. have ordered supplies; so it should be obtainable then.

Poor Kerry! I think I show the spirit of this spirit of repression in my play, "Cockadoodle Dandy."

Well all the best, and thanks again for your kind thought.

I've been (and am) damned busy: An endless queue of letters waiting to be answered. As soon as one goes, two come—sometimes three.

Yours sincerely.

Sean O'Casey.

[3] C. H. Rolleston, *Portrait of an Irishman: A Biographical Sketch of T. W. Rolleston,* Foreword by Stephen Gwynn (1939).

[4] George Moore, *Hail and Farewell,* I, *Ave* (1911), p. 256. Moore describes Douglas Hyde addressing a meeting of the Gaelic League in Irish at the Rotunda, Dublin:

> Somebody called him; a shuffling of chairs was followed by a sudden silence, and whilst Hyde stood bawling I saw the great skull, its fringe of long black hair, with extraordinary lucidity, the slope of the temples, the swell of the bone above the nape, the insignificant nose, the droop of the moustache through which his Irish frothed like porter, and when he returned to English it was easy to understand why he desired to change the language of Ireland.

[5] See O'Casey's letter to Lovat Dickson, 8 July 1945, note 7.

To Drama

Summer, 1949

THE ABBEY THEATRE

Dear Sir,

Mr. MacDonagh's article [1] is interesting, but only partly true. It was inevitable that the death of Lady Gregory and of Yeats would shock the theatre into a long silence. And then followed the unexpected death of the young poet, [F. R.] Higgins, whom Yeats, cute and wise man that he was, placed in the power he had held himself. This was a calamity. Death blitzed out all the chances the Theatre had; and that the "famous—or good —actors of the Abbey are either dead or working for the films" is no fault of the Theatre.[2] It is the crime of the money-seeking "Christian" civilization we have around us.

Yours faithfully,
Sean O'Casey

Totnes

[1] Donagh MacDonagh, "The Death-Watch Beetle," *Drama,* Spring 1949.
[2] MacDonagh had written: "But no famous Abbey actor takes the stage—they are all dead or in Hollywood or Elstree. . . . I imagine that I can hear a small and ominous sound somewhere in the fabric of the Abbey, the tick of the Death-watch beetle, whose advent presages the fall of ancient structures."

To Roger McHugh

MS. McHugh

Totnes, Devon
1 July 1949

Dear Roger McHugh,

You asked me some time ago for J. Stephens' address. I sought it in the valleys low & on the hills high; finally, without a stay, getting it from Mr. Daniel Macmillan.

Here it is—

James Stephens
28 Queen's Walk
London, N.W.9.

"She had the walk of a Queen"

James has been very silent for a long time. I wonder what can have happened to him.

It is a great pity and a big loss.

All the best,
Yours sincerely
Sean O'Casey

To Jack Daly

MS. DALY

TOTNES, DEVON
11 JULY 1949

My dear Jack.

Thanks for sending me the M.G. [*Manchester Guardian*]. I daresay you and Floss and Violet are very busy now. The sun is sending hordes out everywhere, though it leaves me gasping. Time was when I could hop step and lep in it. I enclose a circular that may interest you. I'm getting far better known in the U.S.A. now.

I suppose what you said about giving up the hostel holds good? Will you be leaving your job, too?

Well, if you have enough to live on & on & on, on, then you're a wise bird.

Love to Floss. All well here, full house—Shivaun, Breon, & Niall. Have written a One-act play [1] to keep my hand in—experience of mine in a Dublin Poor Dispensary, the time you & I and Will Kelly were alive on the Dublin Streets.

All the best to you.
Regards to Violet.
Sean as ever

Bloody busy. Within the last two weeks had 7 American visitors here. One of them hopes to do Purple Dust in New York.

[1] *Hall of Healing,* printed in *Collected Plays,* Vol. III (1951).

To Frank McCarthy

MS. McCarthy

Totnes, Devon

12 July 1949.

Dear Frank,

Thanks for the butter. You haven't sent "coals to Newcastle." We get our rations, and no more. During the last year we got two pounds from Ireland, & they didn't last long. I've forgotten the taste of butter, & so has Eileen (the wife), for we give what we get of it to the children. For me, it's a return to type, for Maypole Margarine (when we had the few pence to buy half a pound) was our luxury in Dublin. Very interesting article on the Tolka cottages. So fine to see the place vacant. God, what a collection! Inside they were worse—I had a cup of tea in two of them. It was this Statue of the Virgin that gave me the idea for the change to Her in "Red Roses For Me." [1]

I wouldnt suggest anything to a Film Producer. If any of them wants a play, the play is there, & to hell with them. I am busy with more important work—at least I think it to be more important. I've read Monk Gibbon's book [2]—has he written anything like it about Joyce, a far, far greater man? Who bothers about "AE" now? He wasn't even a "living rush-light." You wouldn't have known him—he wouldn't have let you within an ace of him. He probably never saw a slum. I remember his visit to Liberty Hall & was introduced to AE., by Jim Larkin as "O'Casey—another rebel." But AE didn't stay a rebel long. Dont send me Clutton Brock's "Heaven." [3] I know all there is to be known about "heaven," & a lot more about hell than is generally known. Thanks, all the same, for offering the loan.

Thanks, again, Frank, for your kindness. I feel better now, though the heat is a bit thick. Must be hard to bear in Commercial Road.

All the best to you, lad.

Sean

[1] See O'Casey's letter to Frank McCarthy, 8 February 1949.
[2] *The Living Torch, A.E.* (1937), edited, with an introductory essay by Monk Gibbon.
[3] Arthur Clutton-Brock, *Immortality* (1917).

To The Manager, Glasgow Unity Theatre

TC. O'CASEY

[TOTNES, DEVON]

18 JULY 1949

Dear Sir:

Why dont you write your name clearly, or better still, type it? Neither I nor anyone around me could make out more than "Oscar." I have heard your name before, but I've heard hundreds of others and cannot remember them all.

Wasnt Robert Mitchell [1] able to write for himself? I have a regard for Robert Mitchell, and I think he has done fine work; but I have to think of my play [COCKADOODLE DANDY] first of all. I am hoping to have a production in New York, and, should it or any London production be a failure (I mean a bad production), this would count a lot against me getting the play on in New York. A bad production near ruined my chance with WITHIN THE GATES. The recent production of the play, OAKLEAVES AND LAVENDER (THE WORST EVER), means it wont be done anywhere else. And but for the glorious performance of Eddie Byrne in RED ROSES, that play might have gone west too. So I have to go canny with my latest one. The play just put on [THIS WALKING SHADOW, by Benedict Scott] is a very different one from mine. The News-cuttings are of no use to me. The London drama critics are no guide to anyone. Who are the "people in the profession" who have told you Mitchell is the ideal producer for my play? You dont mention any names.

You have made no business proposals whatever, nor have you made any definite suggestions as to the Caste, yet you want me to give you an option on your words that dont really mean anything at all.

I would have to be much more fully assured on each of these lines before I could venture an option of any sort.

I am a patient fellow, and am prepared to chance a wait for a good opportunity.

There would be no use whatever of Mr. Mitchell visiting me unless I had some idea that he might do; and, as yet, there is no reason whatever for me thinking he might.

Yours sincerely,
Sean O'Casey

[1] Robert Mitchell directed the Glasgow Unity Theatre production of *Purple Dust*, which opened on 9 April 1946.

To Harry Cowdell

MS. MACMILLAN LONDON

TOTNES, DEVON

22 JULY 1949

Dear Mr. Cowdell.

Thank you for returning the photograph of the frontispiece to "Inish-fallen, Fare Thee Well" [1] which came back safe and sound.

The proof of the hymn, "The Ninety & Nine" seems allright, so I return it to you. Odd, you hadn't heard of the hymn. It is a great (or used to be) favourite at Evangelical Missions. I must have sung it myself a hundred times. Now it's the Ninety & Nine that are out astray on the hills, & the hundredth only that's safe.

All the best to you.
Sean O'Casey

[1] The frontispiece of *Inishfallen, Fare Thee Well* is a photograph of O'Casey's room at 422 North Circular Road, described as "The room in the Dublin tenement house where the first three plays were written."

To Jack Daly

MS. DALY

TOTNES, DEVON

26 JULY 1949

Dear Jack.

Thanks for your letter. I didn't see the reference in the Strand Maga-zine; but the writer couldn't know a single thing about me, bar what I have said of myself by myself. I don't know what he means by "Comfortable." Financially, I've £300 between me and all harm; with rising hopes of a production this Autumn in New York; & of royalties from Macmillan Co of New York in October. If I depended on my English Royalties, I'd be a mummer at a street corner, singing, like Raftery, "to the people, with empty pockets, & my arse to the wall." Dr. Hyde very nicely translated the Irish word "tóin" to "back." [1] Even the American royalties dont all come

[1] See O'Casey's letter to Roger Hayes, 24 November 1945, note 5.

my way. Take the Book-Find Club's 30,000 copies of "Inisfallen F. Thee Well." The Club gives £600 for this printing; Macmillan's take £300; & by the time I pay three 45's in tax, I have £165 for myself—or so, I count it up. A big reduction from £600. But we jog along, if not merrily, at least, determinedly. I enclose an article by G. J. Nathan, which I want back. It shows how O'Casey hasn't had much of a show for fifteen years. But, all the same, America has kept me going; & the critics there are much more active on my behalf than the critics here. Not one of them, bar the M.G. [*Manchester Guardian*] has mentioned Cockadoodle Dandy.

But we jog along, & the play will be speaking when the mouth of the British critics are stopped with dust—and not Purple Dust either. I've sent you on a circular—all I've got—& a USSR magazine—this is better propaganda than my circulars—under another cover.

So my love to Floss & You, & warm regards to Violet.

No chance of a house here yet. Will write again about this question.

As ever
Sean

To George Jean Nathan

MS. CORNELL

TOTNES, DEVON
26 JULY 1949

My very dear George:

I daresay you are far away from New York now, lying near the sea, or reclining under a palm tree; so I hope you won't get this letter for a long time. Quite a lot of your countrymen have visited me here—the owner of the "Book-Find Club"; Mr. Bloomgarden, who's thinking of putting on "Purple Dust"; a young chap who produced Saroyan's "My Heart's in the Highlands" in Dartington, two miles away from Totnes; & John Tuerk with the producer of "Life With Father" has written from London, & may come down here. Kermit Bloomgarden wants me to write in a "love scene" between Avril & O'Killigain; he thinks the play repeats itself in jokes too often. I have looked it over—much as I hated the job; & have expanded one incident in the last act; & added a few bits of dialogue; but a "love scene" would, I think overthrow the balance of the play, and hurt its unity. I've written to Mr. Bloomgarden & told him so. If he finally rejects the idea of production, I won't think any the worse of him. He should be free from doubt before he risks his money on the play. So far there is no chance of my production here of "Purple Dust" or "Cocka-doodle Dandy." Neither play has been mentioned by any London critic, bar the onslaught made on "Purple Dust" by Agate eight or nine years ago.

I enclose two cuttings giving Harold Hobson's idea of the American Theatre. He was over there with you recently, &, I daresay, you met him, & had a talk with him. It is over sixteen years since I saw or spoke to an English critic, & longer since I had a letter or a note of any sort from one of them.

Another countryman of yours came over to Dublin to write an article or thesis on Irish Drama. He came down here—Suss[1] was his name—, & told me he had read more than a hundred Abbey Theatre manuscripts. He's to write "Decline of the Irish Drama," a title that gave me something of a shock. I never thought the Irish Drama had declined; but, I daresay, the lad is right.

All the best to you.
My love.
Sean

[1] Irving D. Suss, American lecturer at Rutgers University who was writing a book on modern Irish drama. See his article, "The 'Playboy' Riots," *Irish Writing* No. 18, March 1952.

To David Krause

TS. KRAUSE

TOTNES, DEVON
9 AUGUST 1949

Dear David Krause:
Thank you for your interesting letter. I'm afraid I've no comment to make to you on what you propose to do, knowing that your own comments are of far more importance to you than any of mine could possibly be. I would suggest, however, that you should be a little more critical in your Thesis[1] on my work than you have been in your letter. There are faults in my work—too damned many for my self-satisfaction; for, like you—though very much older—I am still a student of life; a freshman; a hearty love of it all. There is something in what you say about the "subtle and significant relationship of comedy and tragedy" in the plays; but no more than there is in life itself. Sorrow and joy are good things—when they are natural; not when they become unnatural, as in war—, for sorrow keeps

[1] David Krause, "Sean O'Casey: A Study in Dramatic Strategy," M.A. thesis, University of Minnesota, 1950.

us from being too careless, and laughter from being too damned serious.

All I can do is to give you my good wishes, and to hope you will use whatever talents that have been given you wisely and well and bravely too; and that the knock you give to the door of life will sound good in the hearts of others, and echo soundly in your own.

All good wishes to you.

Yours sincerely,
Sean O'Casey

P.S. Don't be discouraged if your knock doesn't sound clear and loud at first—knock again; and again.

To Kermit Bloomgarden [1]

TC. O'CASEY

[TOTNES, DEVON]
21 AUGUST 1949

Dear Kermit:

Thanks for your letter. I'm glad you got the script allright, and that you think the additions and cuts make the play better. I think you are right.

I am not well enough up in the ways of the New York Theatre to comment upon your idea of using American and English actors for the play. But if you could get an Irish actor—as good as any American or English—for the chief parts, you would, I think do well. There is one I would like to mention and fervently recommend—Eddie Byrne of Dublin, who played the part of Brennan in the play, RED ROSES FOR ME, in London here. He was exquisite. There was no doubt about him. Everyone admitted it. Cochran was—and is, I dare say—anxious to lay hands on him. He wrote to me about him. Byrne would make a grand 2nd Workman, or, indeed, I verily believe would make a fine Poges. I would strongly advise you to think of him. I'm sure he'd love to act in New York. He acts very frequently in the Theatre Royal, Dublin. His address is:-

Eddie Byrne, 45, Mespil Road, Dublin. Eire.

As for conferring with me or Dick, I would suggest that you'd get into touch with George Jean Nathan. He thinks highly of the play, and has made many appeals for its production. In a letter he sent me the other day, he says, that he "would be happy to help in the casting, etc, adding "I believe

[1] Kermit Bloomgarden (1904–76), theatre producer, New York.

I could nominate a Caste easily that would help the script admirably." He was tireless in his interest and help when we did WITHIN THE GATES in New York years ago; and, I think, he admires PURPLE DUST more than he did the other play.

I hope you found your wife, David, and Michael fine when you got back home. Dick and Mrs Madden have been here, and we had a long chin-wag on all things except religion and politics.

> *All the best to you, and warm wishes to you and yours.*
>
> *Yours sincerely,*
> *Sean O'Casey*

P.S. What a weird way you take in signing your signature!

To Jack Daly

MS. DALY

TOTNES, DEVON
8 SEPTEMBER 1949

My dear Jack:

About that cottage near the sea, or in the country: There's ne'er a one to be had here or hereabouts. Housing is in a pitiable state. Hundreds are on the list waiting for Council houses as yet unbegun. They also serve who only stand and wait. Dozens of families on the way to Paignton & Plymouth are living in caravans; some even in tents. As for living somewhere here "near me," we are as anxious to change as you are, & more. We hate the present house. It means unending & useless work for Eileen, & a lot for me. It is pretentious, clumsy, cold in winter, hot in summer, and near to the diabolical. There are 27 doors in the damned place. But no suitable alternative place can be got, unless by purchase, &, actually, we haven't the money to move, much more to buy a new one. But should we ever be fortunate, we intend to try to get a flat somewhere—preferably in or near Torquay or Paignton—present mood, though that may change too. Anyway, because of the school, & because of the expense of London, we must keep somewhere within reasonable reach of Dartington. Be careful, if you ever buy a cottage, that you pick a decent one. It is amazing how deceptive these things can be. If you want to know me, come & live in me. If you don't get a decent one, you'll be spending and spending, and spending to keep the damned thing standing. Isn't it grand, Jack, to sit back and think how magnificent the standard of life is here, compared to that of the

USSR? I'm told the angels can hardly be kept in heaven, straining to come down to have a decko at the grand way we live. We have many reasons for thanking God. Thanks for the M.G. [*Manchester Guardian*], though that Journal, too, is bound up in the bonds of money-power. Corresponding with a Father Simcox (from Cork), who was Doctor of Canon Law in Ware R.C. College, he tells me the M.G. refuses to publish letters of his challenging [Cardinal] Griffin about saying that "every parent had the right to decide upon what his or her children should be taught." F. Simcox says Canon Law declares "no parent has the right to teach error," & he has asked [Archbishop] Hinsley & Griffin which be true. They told him not to be a nuisance. He has resigned his job, & lives alone & very poor at Clapham Common. The "Times" won't publish his letters; nor any other paper; even the "Statesman & Nation" refuses; for that, too, is connected with Cadbury. Unfortunately, Father Simcox won't see, or can't see, that no-one gives a damn now about what he calls "truth." All they are concerned with is the defeat of Communism; & the Commissioners of the Salvation Army will readily link arms with the Cardinal to do this. What a gallery of rogues! F. Simcox has now sent his letter to "The Atlantic Monthly," apropos of the dispute between Mrs. Roosevelt & Card. Spellman;[1] but I don't think the letter will shine out there either.

Where's Jack (Carney) now? Has he got a job? Is he at Clifford's Inn? I've not written for some time. I have to limit my writing now as much as possible. Eyes are not getting younger.

Love to Floss & You & to Violet
Yours as ever
Sean

[1] The dispute between Mrs. Franklin D. Roosevelt and Cardinal Spellman arose in July 1949 when the Cardinal accused her of being "an unworthy American mother" because she had defended the clause in the American Constitution on the separation of church and state which says that no public funds shall be given to private or religious schools.

To Joan Littlewood [1]

TC. O'CASEY

[TOTNES, DEVON]
12 SEPTEMBER 1949

Dear Miss Joan Littlewood:
I regret very much that I cannot consider your offer. Evidently, you know next to nothing about the methods of theatrical contracting in the

[1] Joan Littlewood, Theatre Workshop, Manchester.

U.S.A. The American "Impresario" would certainly ask for an option of a British production, and neither he nor the American Guild of Dramatists would allow "two quite separate treatments to run concurrently." You are mistaken if you think an American Director cannot grasp and employ the poetry and movement in a play. There was the recent performance of "Medea" in New York,[2] and an American did "Porgy" here, not to mention my own play, "Within The Gates," which got a lovely production—poetry movement and all—in New York, and by an ordinary "commercial" man, [Melvyn] Douglas. It is sixteen years since I had a chance in New York, and I can hardly be expected to set one aside now. I depend entirely on my work for a living—a precarious one it has been up to now—, and two thirds and more of what I get comes from the U.S.A. There are five of us—not counting Mrs O'C's mother—to keep, and a tough job it has been to do it. Of course, if I had been ready to do work for the films, I'd have a store—one refusal of mine amounted to an offer of from a hundred thousand to a hundred and fifty thousand dollars. So, on the whole, I am out for the sufficiency only; but that much I am forced to keep in front of me—though at times, it has been a long way behind. As for Poland, Czechoslovakia, etc, I prefer—if the play be done at all—that it be done in the language of the land in which the play is appearing. As a matter of fact, copies of the book of the play have been sent to these countries on request. I notice you dont mention the satirical humour of the play. This humour is the banner of the play; the movement and poetry but the tassels and the fringe.

Well, my dear Joan, there you are; I am sorry, but my refusal cannot really be helped.

Yours sincerely,
Sean O'Casey

[2] Robinson Jeffers's adaptation of Euripides' *Medea* opened in New York on 2 May 1949.

To Peter Newmark

MS. NEWMARK

TOTNES, DEVON
15 SEPTEMBER 1949

Dear Peter.

I've sent the book to Mrs. Redhead. You would have waited a long time for Breon to do it. He's immersed deep in his own ego these days, as a young man should be; & can't be bothered with the like of us. Glad to hear you have settled down in a steady job, & I hope you get a decent wage.

I have had no time to myself since the holidays began. No time for prayer or fasting or the meeting with friends. Any time I've had, I give to trying to think out what to say to myself & then to the wide world. A lot of young people have written from the U.S.A. to me; and I try to give an answer for the hope within me. I've written a one-act play on an experience long ago in a Dublin Poor-Law Dispensary—"Hall of Healing"; & have done some additional biographical chapters.

Hugh Willatt wanted "Cockadoodle Dandy," but I had to refuse him. The "Workshop Theatre" & "Unity" wanted it, too; but I had to refuse them. If I don't get a production in New York, I'm done. I've been living on American dollars for a long time, & hope to go on with them till Azrael comes for me.

All the best to Monica and you.

As ever,
Sean

To George Jean Nathan

MS. CORNELL

TOTNES, DEVON
5 OCTOBER 1949

My very dear George:

Your latest testament on the American Theatre [1] came sailing in, all sails set, to me yesterday, bearing a rich argosy of comments. I was delighted to find a few words from me on the jacket. You are, indeed a live man of the Theatre of America, of England, too; indeed, of the wide world Theatre, though you didn't see through the meaning of the Noh plays. [2] Yeats went wild over them having read about them, & couldn't talk of anything else for years. I admire your courage; still as firm, as vicious, and as fair & truthful as ever; and full of fun & fancy; and knowledge, too, a penetrating light from a gayly-coloured lantern. How can a critic abandon his personality, which is his soul, or the manifestation of his soul? God Almighty, what would you be like without your personality? For all things are in it & through it & of it: it is your astonishing knowledge as well as your wit & humour. I like you because you give me a start—at times a

---

[1] *The Theatre Book of the Year, 1948–1949* (1949).
[2] *Ibid.,* p. 5. In a review, Nathan wrote that he was confused by some performances of Noh plays he had seen in Tokyo.

shock—; but I like you just as much because you make me laugh, & always a laugh worth enjoyment. I like what you say about the one-act plays of Gene.[3] Myself, I give all that Coward ever wrote & all he thinks of writing, for Gene's "Moon of the Carribees." I've read it many times, & always it is a lovely song in the silence. A lovely title for a lovely play.

You are right about the importance of little things on the stage. It's amazing the way trifles stand out there, & get in the way of one's perception of the important things—like the louse on the lady's bonnet, seen by Burns. I hope Odets may profit about what you said of his work.[4] A great friend of Odets came here once, & talked of him—how he loved Odets, & how he hoped Hollywood wouldn't destroy him. But I entirely agree with you that anyone with a first-class respect for art of any kind would keep a helluva way from Hollywood. I am still reading, & enjoying your work immensely. I'll finish it this time, before I forward it to Breon.

I'm sorry to read what you say of Margo Jones. However, I've told Dick that I would sign no N.Y. contract, unless she left the choice of Director & chief characters to you. Here, one would-be producer asked me if I "visualised The Cock as a little boy, or as a puppet on strings let down from the flies"! No London paper I've seen has mentioned the play yet. Neither [Harold] Hobson nor [Ivor] Brown has said a word about it. Hobson, after his visit to N.Y. wrote an article wondering why the Americans accepted "South Pacific."

Thanks from my heart for sending me your critical & joyous book.

Ever my love,
Sean

[3] Eugene O'Neill, *S.S. Glencairn,* a revival of a group of one-act plays, *Moon of the Caribbees, In the Zone, Bound East for Cardiff, The Long Voyage Home,* produced by the New York City Theatre Company, opened 20 May 1948 at the City Center Theatre, directed by José Ferrer.
[4] Clifford Odets's *The Big Knife* opened at the National Theatre in New York on 24 February 1948, directed by Lee Strasberg.

To Vincent de Baun

MS. DE BAUN

TOTNES, DEVON
7 OCTOBER 1949.

Dear Mr. de Baun:

I'm sorry you were "able to confound your mentor who is supervising your thesis"—a dangerous thing to do; only what an ardent young soul

like you, & an old careless one like mine, would do. Those who crush
each work of art into a special niche—like dried specimens in bottles—is
a comic figure; & it is just as well to let him go on doing it, if he doesn't
do any harm. How could anyone put a war on the stage; how could anyone
put even a skirmish on it; how can anyone put on stage or in film the
lives of a single family in a single house? Why, even you, young as you
probably are, have forgotten half of the things you have done, or felt, or
seen, or contemplated. That is why selection is so important in anything
we do; & we know this, too, although largely unconscious of it; for selection—as far as we can exercise it—is an important part of each life, &
constantly with us. Each of us has our favourite friends, drinks, foods, &
places where we wish to go. We catch sight of life in glimpses. Fancy
your being a Catholic & taught—like Joyce—by the Jesuits. The Irish are
no more superstitious than any other race. After all, Lourdes isn't in
Ireland—though Bishop, priest, & deacon wish to God it were. So they
have to have the Irish Sweep instead as a halting make-up for the absence
of a Lourdes. They've tried to have one several times, at Knock & Templemore; & they are still trying out Knock as a place of miracles. I am [in]
correspondence with a priest here (he wrote to me in the first instance),
who has been Doctor of Canon Law in Ware R.C. College for twenty
years (Father J. V. Simcox), who has resigned his job; & has practically
left the Church. He has been refused an answer to a simple question on
Canonical Law by Card. Griffin & other dignitaries; asking them if Truth
be greater than Authority; but, characteristically, they told him "not to be
a nuisance." He lives alone in poverty now, &, has accused the church of
being a secret Society. I've met too many R.C. clergy, who venturing to
ask questions in the love of truth, have been summarily silenced, to doubt
that the Stepinacs & Minzentys are all they have been accused of being. I
remember Parnell, the Fenians, the Irish Republican—even de Valera was
threatened till he became obedient. Red Roses isnt so consistent, so well-
knit, so lyrical, or so good in characterization as Purple Dust.

All the best to you,
Sean O'Casey

To the Rev. Robert Saunderson Griffin [1]

MS. GRIFFIN

TOTNES, DEVON
13 OCTOBER 1949

My dear Mr. Robert,

The news in your letter surprised me a little and amused me a lot. I don't know where the "Irish Times" got the information. I certainly know nothing about it. I've had no invitation to attend the re-opening of Chapel at Derrynane, & hardly would expect one, even had I known there was a Chapel to be re-opened there.[2] Of course, I know Derrynane was the head-home of Daniel O'Connell, an Irish Hero for whom I've no great regard.

I know the lad who, I believe, got the renovation of "Derrynane"—a very fine fellow indeed. He was not far from me here for a long time—in Dartmoor Prison, doing a life sentence. I am very glad I had a good hand in getting him & his comrades out of prison.

Your invitation was a very kind one. I know Naas fairly well, having been there on occasions of the commemoration marches to Wolfe Tone's grave in Bodenstown, not very far away. It would be fine and strange to see you again. I sometimes think of the ways to, & the vicinity around, St. Barnabas'; very much changed now, I daresay, with few of the old people living. Years & years ago, on the Dublin-Holyhead steamer, I met Mr. Simpson for a few minutes—a very old, & rather frail man. Tom Glazier sent me a Christmas card last year; but no address on it, so I couldn't acknowledge the kind thought. Tom was a genuine descendant of a Cromwellian Ironside.

I hope all the family are well. Is Miss Jennie with you still? Give them all my love.

Yours very sincerely,
Sean O'Casey

[1] The Rev. Robert Saunderson Griffin, Ballymore-Eustace, Co. Kildare, son of O'Casey's old friend, the Rev. Edward Morgan Griffin, Rector of St. Barnabas Church, Dublin.

[2] On 16 October 1949 the little chapel attached to Derrynane House, the residence of Daniel O'Connell in Kerry, was reopened one hundred years after it was built. According to a report in the *Irish Times,* Sean O'Casey was supposed to attend the event, but it was a Sean O'Casey from Mullingar, not the playwright.

To Seumas Scully [1]

MS. SCULLY

TOTNES, DEVON
15 OCTOBER 1949

Dear Seumas:

Thank you very much for the papers & for the critiques of the two new plays. There is something in "Katie Roche" [2] you know. Each of us has our likings & our dislikings; but the play we dislike may not necessarily be a bad play. I've never seen a play by Lady Longford; but her husband's "Yahoo" [3] has a good deal in it to commend. I saw it done in London by the [Mac] Liammoir-Edwards Group; & done very well, too. I daresay the Dublin critics find it hard to criticize Lady Longford. I never met either of them. Some years ago, a Soviet Magazine asked me to send them news about the Irish Theatre. I wrote 3 times to Lord Longford asking about his theatre (one a registered letter), but never got an answer to any of them. One would think a Lordship would have the courtesy to reply to a letter of genuine inquiry. But the lordly ones, evidently, havent the monopoly of manners. I've never seen the "Irish Sunday Press" before. Looks a bit strained & a little pompous; & hardly reminiscent of "The Gaelic State; or, the Crown of a Nation."

The news item in "The Irish Times" concerning the coming of a Sean O'Casey to Derrynane, cannot be me; or, maybe, it is a Dublin journalist's conception of a joke. Certainly I never "indicated" that I'd be there on the 16th. In fact I knew nothing whatever about the event till a Kildare friend of mine told me what "The Irish Times" had said. Several others have written to me in the same way. I daresay it was put in as an effort to annoy & give trouble. The only trouble of course was the replies I had to send to inquiries; &, in your case, I'd have answered anyhow in acknowledgment of your kindness.

I don't remember getting any inquiry from a Dublin lady about my new play. Anyway, I've linked up with a New York production which is good enough for a start.

I couldn't find any programme of your Debating Society in the package—you must have been gay with wine or something. However, I thank you again very much for everything else; and

With all good wishes
I am Yours very sincerely,
Sean

---

[1] Seumas Scully (1910–   ), Dublin clerk, theatre enthusiast, and secretary of the Technical Students Literary and Debating Society.

[2] Teresa Deevy's *Katie Roche* opened at the Abbey Theatre on 16 March 1936.

[3] Lord Longford's *Yahoo* (1933), a play about Jonathan Swift.

To Totnes Times

The Political Situation

Sir,—With the best intentions in the world, it is clear that Mr. Hiscox [1] and his Conservative comrades know very little of what they are writing about. Socialism is not intrinsically a question of whether the "Boss" is an enemy of the workers—like the late Martin Murphy of Dublin, or a friend like the late Earl Baldwin of Bewdley: it is a question whether the wealth of the country should be held in private ownership or enter into the ownership of the people who create it all. It may be surprising to Mr. Hiscox to hear that Socialism is all around him; and that if Socialism were abolished from the land tomorrow, life would become utterly impossible. Bernard Shaw has shown this to be a fact on numerous occasions, and those who do not know it should read his AN INTELLIGENT WOMAN'S GUIDE TO SOCIALISM. The roads we walk, the bridges we cross, the water we drink (and now the coal we burn), the schools we build, and hundreds of national, county, and district activities are under Socialist control and ownership. Does Mr. Hiscox suggest that the British Navy should be handed over to private ownership? Or the Army? Or the Police Force? Or even the Post Office? If he will glance at the current demand note for rates (I am looking at it now before paying it), he will see that, if he wants to see, many Services socialistically administered by the Borough Council on the one hand, and by the County Council on the other. Socialism is with us, not only on a National scale, and has been for many years; but it is actually sitting under a tree in his own back garden. It isnt the present Government that established Socialism; it is but developing it and extending its power and operation over other necessaries of life and other public services.

Neither is an incompetent Socialist statesman or two any argument against Socialism per se. There have been, and will be, incompetent statesmen in almost every Government. If it were so, the Conservative Party itself would have ceased to exist, for heaven knows that they have had their share of them. What about him who recommended that the Home Guard should be armed with pikes? Or the later one who said brown paper was a sufficient protection against the atom bomb? Let Mr. Hiscox read what Mr. Churchill says about, not only of a statesman, but of a Conservative Prime Minister and his Government, after they had coldly

[1] F. H. Hiscox, "The Political Situation," *Totnes Times,* 15 October 1949.

brushed aside President Roosevelt's offer of assistance, and had refused even to consider an understanding with the Soviet Union. Here it is:

"I have yet to unfold the story of the treatment of the Russian offers of collaboration in the advent of Munich. If only the British people could have known and realised that, having neglected our defences and sought to diminish the defences of France we were now disengaging ourselves, one after the other, from the two mighty nations whose extreme efforts were needed to save our lives and their own, history might have taken a different turn." And this, too, when the issues meant life or death to Britain.

The workers have the right to all the wealth that England holds—not only material wealth, but intellectual, scientific, artistic wealth as well. They are refusing to remain insecure and ignorant any longer. Communism brings with it everywhere it goes a passion for security and knowledge, and an equal passion to use security and knowledge towards greater achievements; and Socialism is but the herald of this advance of man.

Mr. Hiscox does not like the phrase of "soaking the rich." It is a rough phrase, certainly, but as good as any other to denote the change of form that life is taking. The time is past now for any family—like the Wills, the tobacco Combine people—to leave the world possessed of fifty millions, while hosts of others are exhorted to put a shilling in the Post Office Savings Bank for a rainy day. People everywhere are proclaiming their right to live, and even the Conservatives, should they come into power again, will have to answer the call, and fight shy of any attempt to undo what has already been done by the Labour Government of England. They, too, will have to face the fact that the Red Flag is flaunting itself right in the astonished and brazen faces of the banks of Hong Kong.

Yours sincerely,
Sean O'Casey

To Joseph Prescott [1]

MS. PRESCOTT [2]

TOTNES, DEVON
1 NOVEMBER 1949

Dear Mr. Prescott,
      Thank you very much for sending me the copy of your article on J. Joyce in the *Encyclopaedia Britannica*. The first note, in full public, of

[1] Professor Joseph Prescott, Wayne State University, Detroit, Michigan.
[2] Printed in the *Massachusetts Review*, Winter 1964.

the *Last Post* over Joyce's grave. Your article is graceful, fair, sincere, but, of course, far too short. I daresay it's all that the people of the E. B. would release at the moment. Well, Joyce has his niche, & it will widen. In an Encyclopaedia Hibernica, there would be no mention of him at all. Eliot's tribute [3] isn't good enough. Who was a greater master of the Eng. language before Milton? None, that I know of; none I've heard of ever. There isn't a single memorial of him from one end of Ireland to the other. They brought back Yeats—and, of course, rightly so, for he was a great poet & a great man—, but they left Joyce lying where he fell. We'll hardly look upon his like ever again.

Thanking you for remembering that I remember Joyce,

Yours very sincerely,
SEAN O'CASEY

[3] The concluding sentence of the *Britannica* article reads: "A measure of his total achievement, however, may well be T. S. Eliot's remark that Joyce was the greatest master of the English language since Milton."

To Patrick F. Byrne [1]

TS. BYRNE

TOTNES, DEVON
3 NOVEMBER 1949

Dear Patrick Byrne.

Here's a kinda answers to your quiz:

1. Didn't hear B. of "The Plough." [2] Heard Belfast Group in "Boyd's Shop." [3] Good acting, poor play—for such as Ervine.

2. No. Don't listen to any wireless programme, here, there, or anywhere regularly. Don't know how anyone can. Can't always get R.E. clearly here. Don't know programmes, so any effort to hear one is a chance. Heard one of the Sponsored Programmes—it happened to be the B. when I tuned in—it was appalling. Was it for this that Emmet died and Wolfe Tone sunk serene? It was a bad imitation of the worst of England's bad efforts; and their good efforts are bad enough, Christ knows. Anyway, all Radio Eireann broadcasts come to the listeners screened through the Papal Nuncio's robe. You've a new one now, haven't you? I remember a "Hand"

[1] Patrick F. Byrne wrote a regular column, "R[adio]. E[ireann]. Commentary," for *Radio Review* (Dublin).

[2] *The Plough and the Stars* was broadcast on Radio Eireann on 23 October 1949 by the R.E. Repertory Company, directed by Micheál Ó hAodha.

[3] St. John Ervine's *Boyd's Shop* (1936) was broadcast on the BBC radio Home Service on 22 October 1949 by the Ulster Group Theatre.

who came to see my brother Tom when he was ill, and when he lay dead. He would be very old now if still living. "Pa" Monaghan is pulling your leg. I didn't know him. My brother knew a Paddy Monaghan who once went to the U.S.A. for a month: didn't like the place, came back with a billycock hat and a terrible accent, and, as far as I know, never did a day's work afterwards.

Never saw your Review. I don't know what you mean by "highbrow." Was Dan Leno highbrow? Well get some of your comedians to be quarter like him, and they'll do. Or Charlie Chaplin? These are Shakespeares in their own art.

Cheerio.
Sean O'Casey

P.S. Is J. J. McCann a son of the Louth McCann who financed [W. P.] O'Ryan in the Boyne Valley Venture years and years ago, till his eminence Logue came down to stop it for the sake of Virtue and Eireann? [4]

[4] For the account of Cardinal Logue's suppression of W. P. Ryan's newspaper in the Boyne Valley, see Ryan's *The Labour Revolt and Larkinism* (1913), pp. 3-4.

To Totnes Times

5 NOVEMBER 1949

The Political Situation [1]

Sir,—Pray allow me one more letter. Both Brigadier Raynor and Mr. Hiscox loftily ignore the fact that, in many wide and all-important instances, Socialism has been with us for a long time; that it works well; and that life would be intolerable without it. They ignore the facts to wallow in speculation. Instead, we get a sentimental rhapsody from Marshal Montgomery which is, largely, factual nonsense. [The church bells may ring every Sunday, but the fact remains that the British people, according to Church authorities, are seventy per cent pagan. When attendance at church ceased to be compulsory, how many soldiers hurried to church?] [2] Doesn't the Marshal (and the Brigadier) know that the English way of life has changed, not once only, but many times? The individual soldier goes "his own way," but not to church; and, if I be right, it was a Labour Government that gave him this freedom. Does the Marshal and the Brigadier agree that the soldier should have it?

[1] Reply to a letter by Brigadier R. Raynor, M.P., *Totnes Times,* 22 October 1949.
[2] All passages in square brackets were omitted by the editor.

This in itself is a change in the "English way of life." English life changed—not to go far back for other instances—when England began to make cloth of the wool she had previously exported; when the first "capitalist" gathered workers together in one place to weave, instead of distributing the raw material among the hovels to be woven there; it changed when Jethro Tull invented the drill that deposited seed in straight furrows, instead of wastefully broadcasting it; it changed, and rapidly, when the technological revolution came in the eighteenth century, and more rapidly still when this gave place to the Industrial Revolution later on in time; and it is changing still. Whether this law of change is one of the "laws based on the moral code," I don't know; all I know is that neither the Marshal nor the Brigadier can stop its inevitable working. [The Marshal's dictum of "The duty of each is to believe in the English way of life, and to resist any set of circumstances or men that threaten it" is just childish nonsense. The Marshal who makes it and the Brigadier who supports it must know nothing of the history, technological, ecclesiastical, industrial, or social, of their own race. As for the Marshal's "The foe is now more insidious than Hitler"—meaning, of course, the Soviet Union, it is an enjoyable thing to set one Marshal against another. Field Marshal Lord Wavell acting as Chairman at a Royal United Services Institute lecture, is reported to have said: "The Soviet Union is not aggressive. It has no desire to dominate Europe. She has no need for space in which to expand and no arrogant desire like the Nazis to run everybody else's country for them." Which Marshal are we to choose? Follow the one, and we enjoy peace and an active life; follow the other, and it will mean that our way of living will be changed to the way of the dead. And what are "a square deal for everyone"? and "hard work with adequate reward"? They are just clap-trap terms, without Socialistic planning to make these things possible. As for "playing cricket and football," where are the places to play them on? Arent most of us aware of the campaign that had to be carried on before we got the few there are? Even the Totnes Council here finds it difficult to accommodate with fields the clubs that want to play on them; and, even so, Totnes United have to shell out a good figure from their funds to provide themselves with one. In the cities, where seventy-five per cent of our people live, there are hardly any. Our English children, boys and girls, if they want to play, have to risk limb and life among the traffic of the streets. Brigadier Raynor says that Socialism is the "alien invention of a German Jew." This is an uncharitable remark, for there is in it the implication of contempt—if not hatred—for the Jew. This from the upholder of "the worship of Almighty God" Who made the Jews the channel through which came the Christian Faith. Doesnt the Brigadier know that Jesus was a Palestinian Jew? But Karl Marx did not "invent" Socialism. If he read "Amos," he will find it thundered out by that prophet; it was the fire in the Insurrection raised by John Ball, the priest, and Wat, the tiler, in the reign of Richard the II; the flame again in the Peasants' Revolt during the

course of the German Reformation; the logic in the propaganda of the
Levellers during the Commonwealth under Cromwell; it was inherent even
in the attempt at union organization by the Tolpuddle men [3] (not far from
Devon), who got a heavy sentence of transportation because they stood
for elemental rights of man (the Brigadier doesnt mention them). What
Marx did was to gather together all the opinions about poverty, its cause
and cure, including those of Owen, the Liberal manufacturer, and hammer
them into a scientific theory that has revolutionised hesitation and weakness
into power and abiding confidence among the militant workers. Brigadier
Raynor calls us to witness "what happens to the Churches in other lands
as Socialism gives way to red-blooded Communism." What happens other
than what has happened here and in other countries under the older
regimes? Apart from Socialism hasnt there been many instances of revolt
against the tyranny and outlandish claims of the Vatican to demolish us or
govern us by body and soul? Doesnt he know that at one time, all courts
were ecclesiastical? Has he forgotten Henry the Eighth's fight with Rome,
and the consolidation of that fight under the latter reign of Elizabeth (incidentally, it is an odd thought to me that England never commemorates her
greatest queen)? I remember Garibaldi, if he doesnt. What about the Papal
Quanta Cura that fought against any attempt to limit the rights and the
power of the Papacy—not by the Communists, but by the bourgeois governments of the eighteenth century? And the Pope still thinks he can
frighten "red-blooded Communists" with fierce and lavish excommunica-
tions! They are but the snarls from a dying animal. I say again that Communism brings with its power a passion for knowledge. Some few days ago,
a Dr. Somebody (I've forgotten his name), a Missionary to South East
Asia, gave a broadcast. He told us that Christian thought was very anxious
about the sixty million pagans there. These pagans were wholly illiterate,
but were now aglow with the desire for education from the example shown
by the Chinese wherever Communism came to stay. "It was almost too
late" he said, but if we acted at once, we might save them for Christianity.
They must be taught to read and write immediately, for if we didnt do it,
the Communists would. "We have found," he added, "that our efforts at
textbooks are clumsy and uninteresting, so we are copying those created
by the Communists who so swiftly change an illiterate community into a
literary one." There's an instance out of hundreds for you, comrade Brigadier; an involuntary tribute, for you know that imitation is the sincerest
form of flattery. These sixty million people could go to the devil; for
knowledge so long as the Chinese Red Army was a thousand miles away,
but as soon as it came to the border, Christian hearts are stirred to give
knowledge where before there was only ignorance.]

Mr. Hiscox will, I hope, one day learn that Labour is the source of
all value. When the workers stand still the life of England stands still with

---

[3] For O'Casey's comment on the Tolpuddle Martyrs of 1834, see his letter to
Harold Macmillan, 28 June 1934, note 2, Vol. I, p. 514.

them. Millions of workers know this now. And are acting on it. [As for his "Conservatives," I gave a quotation in a previous letter. Here's another—not from Marx, but from Lord Beaconsfield, for long a capable Prime Minister of England: "It seems to me a barren thing, this Conservatism—an unhappy crossbreed, the mule of politics that engenders nothing. A Conservative Government is an organised hypocrisy." If I were to quote what Emerson says of them! Certainly, the present Government, so Socialistically cowardly as it is, is the lesser of two evils anyway.

It is time that these Raynors, ignorant of their country's history, ignorant even of their own Party's policy, should cease to have power, cease to have insolent influence. And it is high time that a Party of at least 50 Communists should appear in the English Parliament, for they represent the young and they foretell the future.]

Sean O'Casey

The letter given above has been greatly condensed. Only contributions of reasonable length will be published—Editor.

To Frank McCarthy

MS. McCarthy

Totnes, Devon

16 November 1949

Dear Frank,

Send the book along, and I'll inscribe it for you. You were fortunate to get clear away from peritonitis. You must have had a rotten time. Keep an eye on yourself for a while. I daresay Kilmainham [Jail]'s changed—if anything ever changes in Ireland. I've played myself in Clonturk—the valley that saw Brian Boru battling with the Danes. Probably, a pity he won. Strange district round the Tolka with its convents, colleges, churches, chapels, institutions, & lunatic asylums. Is the E. Mem. Hostel [1] run by the Government, or by the Missions to Seamen? What a strange organization after 2000 years of Christianity. I knew one cleric—Protestant—who was the missioner for Dublin's seamen. He wore the usual clerical garb, but added a peaked cap—half clerical, half nautical. An insignificant mind in an insignificant body. Smoked Woodbines to show what a man he was. Heard him once singing in The Seamen's Institute—kinda tea-party-

[1] Empire Memorial Hostel.

How are you, how are you?
Very well, how's yourself?
I'm very well, I'm thankful to say,
Never felt better since pancake day! etc.

Appalling example of loutish exhibitionism. I wondered what on earth Jesus would make of the fellow. There were bums there, too—fellows who'd made one voyage, and never again. What's N.A.B.? [2]

All the best to you.
Sean

[2] National Assistance Board, an aid to seamen when on land.

To Daniel Macmillan

MS. MACMILLAN LONDON

TOTNES, DEVON
16 NOVEMBER 1949

Dear Mr. Daniel,

I enclose a letter just received from a friend of mine, F. McCarthy. There is a reference in it interesting to both of us. Perhaps, the difficulty of getting "Pictures in the Hallway" (mentioned) is now past by the arrival of the American edition. I don't like to trouble you, but thought the reference might interest you. The Macmillan Co. were to send me a few copies, but none has come to me yet.

McCarthy is a very interesting man. He was in the army for 12 years, a Sargeant; & has wandered over a lot of the world. He was one of a troopship torpedoed in the Pacific by the Japanese. He floated about for 26 hours before they picked him up, & sent him to Japan, where he was a prisoner till the war ended. He saved nothing but a photograph of Bernard Shaw that he had in an oilskin cover lying on his chest, & tied around his neck. A curious scapular! Bernard Shaw, too, seems to have miraculous power of delivering one from danger.

All the best to you.
Yours very sincerely
Sean O'Casey

To Mrs. Val Dora Frazer [1]

TC. O' CASEY

[TOTNES, DEVON]
20 NOVEMBER 1949

Dear Mrs Frazer:

Well, dear lady, you ask me a lot. It is hard to set down in words simple and few enough to tell what THE SILVER TASSIE is all about. I'll try to say a little.

Apart from the characterization in the play; apart from the humour (if there be humour in it); from the wit (if there be wit); and apart from the poetical use of words (if the use be poetical); there are two implications in the action; that is two main implications. These are the horrible nature of war and the fact that nothing done in this life is hidden from the Christians' Master—the Lord Jesus Christ. That is why the symbol of the Crucifixion hangs over the whole of the second act; and why the singing of part of the Mass is heard behind in the ruins of the broken monastery. That in any evil done to man by man is, according to Christian belief, a crucifying of Christ over again. Although I am not a Christian, I know enough to know that this is the essence of Christ's teaching, of His Cross and Passion; an extension of the gift of man's redemption. When the play was done in London there was an hysterical outburst of condemnation by the priests and apologists of the Roman Catholic church; and, later, when it was done in Dublin by the Abbey Theatre, a greater, a far greater outburst of anger and repudiation of the play as indecent, blasphemous, and insulting. However these boyos may drive sincere exposition off the stage, they cannot obliterate the fact that all things are seen of Jesus, all words heard by Him as touching His co-equalness with the Father. They may hide things from their own eyes, but not from His.

There are minor implications of course, such as the horrible social system that forces persons to permit risk to the life and limb of their loved ones so that they may continue to get the Separation Allowances. I imagine these should have been clear enough to the critics. Also the aftermath of war; the crippled, the blinded, the deafened, the shell-shocked that wander about life till they die; cut off from the full and enjoyable correspondence with life that we all need, and that we should all have. And, again, the necessity for life left whole to go on its way without duly troubling about the less fortunate. Well, so much for the "meaning" of the play.

There is no biographical material of my life after the last book, except what appears in papers and magazines. The row over WITHIN THE GATES in New York—see clipping, enclosed. The row over the Tassie, the first play written in London; and the fact that the biographical vols.

[1] Mrs. Val Dora Frazer, Fisk University, Nashville, Tennessee.

were written in England, as well as the plays RED ROSES FOR ME, PURPLE DUST, OAKLEAVES AND LAVENDER, THE STAR TURNS RED, and, recently, COCKADOODLE DANDY. Then that I got married here, in England, 1927 to an Irish lass, and that we now have three children, Breon 21, Niall, 14, and Shivaun 10; and that I am a lot older. But I'm still writing, and fighting with those who fight for freedom, economic as well as political. . . .[2]

2 Page missing.

To Howard Price [1]

TC. O'CASEY

[TOTNES, DEVON]
22 NOVEMBER 1949

Dear Mr. Price.

Now my lad is it in earnest you are? Do you want to hear of me being locked up in a padded room in an asylum, guarded by armed men night and day? That's the way I'd be if I started to "gather material for a report of the production of my plays in America."

What a job you have given yourself. I cant give you the slightest help. Recently, writing to another American friend, I couldnt remember the date of WITHIN THE GATES's production in New York.[2] Of course, if I dived among press-cuttings, I'd find out; but that would mean suffocation. I dont think productions of my plays were many, and as they were far between one another, the job of finding out when and where is a colossal one.

I remember Augustin Duncan gave the first production of JUNO,[3] and did it very badly; ruined the play in fact for years. And some Irish Company, led by someone named Farrell, did the same for The Silver Tassie,[4] only worse; and ruined that play, maybe forever. That was in 1927–28–29, or thereabouts.

Of course, youve heard of the terrible commotion set up by the Roman

1 Howard Price, 51 Clarendon Street, Boston, a student at Harvard University.
2 *Within the Gates,* directed by Melvyn Douglas, opened in New York at the National Theatre on 22 October 1934. For details of the production, see O'Casey's letter to George Jean Nathan, (17) October 1934, note 1, Vol. I, p. 522.
3 *Juno and the Paycock,* directed by Augustin Duncan, who also played the role of Captain Boyle, opened in New York at the Mayfair Theatre on 15 March 1926.
4 *The Silver Tassie,* produced by the Irish Theatre, Inc., directed by Miceal Breathnach, opened in New York at the Irish Theatre, Greenwich Village, on 24 October 1929.

Catholic Church against WITHIN THE GATES when it was done in N.Y. There's a reference to it in last issue of *Theatre Time*. That was a grand production, but the freedom-loving clerics did their best to down it. It was banned in Boston.[5] I am dealing with this in the future biographical vol.

I wish I could help better; but it's impossible. I havent a minute to bless meself. Horace Reynolds is a very old friend of mine, and, when you see him, give him my love. But I dont think he should have given you this terrible job.

> *And all the best to yourself.*
> *Yours sincerely,*
> *Sean O'Casey*

[5] *Within the Gates* was banned in Boston on 15 January 1935. See O'Casey's letter to Richard J. Madden, 17 January 1935, note 1, Vol. I, p. 531.

To English Churchman

25 NOVEMBER 1949

THE SIMCOX CASE [1]

SIR,—Mr. Arnold Lunn is obviously in a terrible state of nerves. Indeed, quite a lot of the prelates and apologists of the Roman Catholic Church have become hysterical, and have started to shout. Only the other day, Cardinal Spellman ran out of his Archiepiscopal Palace to shout at Mrs. Roosevelt "an unworthy American mother," because the poor woman ventured to defend a clause in the American Constitution. After a long, and partly abusive, letter, the Cardinal declared, "Now my case is closed. Even though you may again use your columns to attack me and again accuse me of starting a controversy, I shall not again publicly acknowledge you." So back the Cardinal ran again into his Palace like a mouse into a hole, determined not to venture out again till times became safer for him. He, too, takes refuge in silence, the hide-bound hide-out for all those who have no answer for the hope that is in them. Though Mrs. Roosevelt gives the Cardinal a gentle answer by saying, "I assure you I have no sense of being 'an unworthy American mother.' The final judgment, my dear Cardinal, of the worthiness of all human beings is in the hands of God," the Cardinal evidently thinks her to be no lady. And in the same way, and for a like reason, Mr. Arnold Lunn evidently thinks that Father Simcox is no

[1] Reply to a letter by Arnold Lunn, *English Churchman*, 11 November 1949. Letters from John V. Simcox and Arnold Lunn also appeared in the 25 November issue; a letter from Simcox had appeared on 14 October. For the background of "The Simcox Case," see O'Casey's letter to Simcox, 3 December 1949, note 1.

gentleman. How does Mr. Lunn know that "very few" of THE ENGLISH CHURCHMAN'S readers have ever seen Mr. Simcox's pamphlet? [2] It can be easily obtained by anyone who wants it (I have just got three to send away to friends). What Mr. Lunn has written seems clearly to bear the construction Mr. Simcox claims it to bear. But surely Mr. Lunn's contention that one who is Irish cannot be a gentleman is a silly kind of an argument. Doesn't it cut both ways as far as Mr. Lunn's hopes and ideals are concerned? Doesn't it cut away the status of a "gentleman" from millions in his own communion, ranging from distinguished laymen to eminent bishops, archbishops, and cardinals? What about the Metropolitan Archbishop Downey? I had the honour of chatting with Cardinal Hinsley for a time. While quite a great gentleman, he seemed to me to be a heavy-minded, unimaginative man. And one could hardly call him a "great" Catholic. Newman of England, yes; J. K. L. of Ireland, yes; but hardly Hinsley. And what can Mr. Lunn gain by such sayings as, "I do not waste money publishing pamphlets in reply to people like Mr. Simcox," or "If I had realised at the time the kind of man with whom I was corresponding"? Surely, from Mr. Lunn's point of view, Dr. Simcox must have been a worthy man in a lot of ways to have been kept as a Dr. of Canon Law for twenty-three years by the Roman Catholic Authorities?

But Mr. Lunn needn't be so frantic about the exposure that Catholic apologists have "one 'academic' truth to be taught in the seminary, and another, its exact opposite, to be professed in public." He is but one of a crowd. If he gets a book published this year in the U.S.A., called *American Freedom and Catholic Power,*[3] he will find, not one, but a hundred and more instances where one thing is said publicly by the Catholic propagandists, and another, the exact opposite, is held hidden in encyclical, theological statement, and clauses of Canon Law. The facts given cannot be gainsaid for each is set down beside the appropriate Catholic authority; and the whole astonishing mass of evidence is built up on what the Catholic apologists say themselves. It is a quietly-written book, evidently written by a "gentleman," so Mr. Lunn need have no hesitation about reading it. The manuscript, we are told, was "scrutinised by a panel of experts, including Professor La Piana of Harvard and Giovanni Pioli of Milan (former vice-rector of the Propaganda Pontifical College for Roman Catholic Missions), and no attempt is made to sway the reader by eloquence or partisan bias."

Anyway, it is not possible to be considered a gentleman, evidently, by some when one has the courage to fight for what some call truth and others know as facts.

SEAN O'CASEY

[2] Dr. John V. Simcox, *Is the Roman Catholic Church a Secret Society?: A Correspondence with the Late Cardinal Hinsley and Others about Parental Rights, with Reports of Speeches by Warren Sandell and Raymond Winch, etc.,* Foreword by G. G. Coulton (1946).
[3] Paul Blanshard, *American Freedom and Catholic Power* (1949).

To Quintin Hogg, M.P. [1]

TC. O'CASEY

[TOTNES, DEVON]
30 NOVEMBER 1949

Dear Mr. Quintin Hogg.

It was really kind of you to answer my letter. I dont want to drag you into a controversy because I dont want to enter one myself, so I selfishly accept the assurance that we should do to others what we expect others to do to me. The *Universe* stated that a hundred Members of Parliament had signified their intention to support the R.C. claim on the Schools Question, and, if my memory is to be trusted (it's a fairly good one), yours was the one name mentioned.

I am not even a Deist, and am content to justify the ways of man to God through the materialistic conception of history—in short, I am a Communist. But I am interested in many things forming life and influencing life, and the religions men accept are some of them. I am interested, too, in brave men, and that is why I stand with Dr. Simcox. This present fight of his isnt a sudden bravery. He came out in 1936 on the side of Dr. G. Coulton when Coulton exposed the deliberate historical falsifications of Cardinal Gasquet so explicitly described in his pamphlet, *The Scandal of Cardinal Gasquet,* [2] which you have probably read.

May I say that I dont think you are quite right about the position of Dr. Simcox? As a Doctor of Canon Law he was *compelled* to teach what the laws say, and, as an honest man, objected to the directly opposite view preached publicly by prelate and apologist. The same thing happened to Dr. McWalter [3] of Maynooth in the matter of teaching theology. Another priest, Father Feeney, [4] has been expelled from the Jesuits for maintaining in the U.S.A. that it is heresy to say that anyone can escape damnation out-

---

[1] Quintin Hogg (1907–   ), 2nd Viscount Hailsham; M.P.; The Corner House, Heathview Gardens, Putney Heath, London.

[2] George Gordon Coulton, *The Scandal of Cardinal Gasquet* (1937), a sixteen-page pamphlet.

[3] Dr. Walter McDonald.

[4] The Rev. Leonard Feeney, S.J. (1898–1978), was deprived of his priestly prerogatives by Archbishop Richard J. Cushing in 1949 for defending four dismissed instructors at Boston College who had accused the Church of teaching the heresy that salvation was possible outside the Roman Catholic Church. In 1953 Father Feeney was excommunicated for preaching that there was no salvation outside the Church. In 1972, through the efforts of Archbishop Humberto Cardinal Medeiros of Boston, and with the approval of Pope Paul VI, the excommunication was removed. Up to the time of his death on 31 January 1978, as far as is known, Feeney never recanted his position that there was no salvation outside the Church.

side the R.C. Church. What these men have aimed at, or are aiming at, is, in my opinion, that the official theological teaching of the R.C. Church should be altered so as to bring it into line with the unofficial (and untrue) statements made in public to cajole and deceive.

I should like to send a copy of your letter to Dr. Simcox, but would not do so without your permission. Can I? Just say yes or no. I ask for this brief reply simply because I know you must be a very busy man hard set to meet the tasks and duties that come clamouring at your door.

Yours sincerely,
Sean O'Casey

To Bureau of Military History, Dublin

TC. O'CASEY

[TOTNES, DEVON]
3 DECEMBER 1949

Dear Mr. Secretary (I cant make your name out)—

To do what you ask, even in a hurrying, mechanised way, would take me months. To record the events I had something to do with, relative to the various National and Labour Movements, the persons I knew; the things they did; the things they said; and to add to all these the dates of years, months, days, would be a job this lad couldnt think of doing.

Indeed, I'm not able to do the work that comes readily to my hands. The day is gone before I've had time to realise that the sun has risen. Anyhow, concerning myself, I'm content to let History do her own telling. Though no historian can be impartial. History itself is, declaring herself in the evolutionary march of things and men we see taking place all around us. Even in present-day Ireland, History is moving towards a new life; a new conception of what man is, what he is to do, how he is to live.

And there, my friend, I'll have to leave you. Most of what I had to say has already been written in my own way. However important dates may be, they are not the candles lighted by life; these are the things said and done within them.

All the best to you,
Yours sincerely,
Sean O'Casey

To Dr. John V. Simcox [1]

TC. O'CASEY

[TOTNES, DEVON]
3 DECEMBER 1949

Dear Dr. Simcox:

I return to you the correspondence appearing in THE MODERN CHURCHMAN and the leading article which appeared in the ENGLISH CHURCHMAN. I am keeping the page holding my letter, to see if Lunn replies; if not, then I'll return to you. Not a very firm leading article. The Anglican Church has a flabby heart. All spiritual bark (and this getting fainter and more timid), and no spiritual bite whatever. Your Church barks as loud as ever, but its spiritual bite is gone. It bites now in a worldly way. The weapon of boycott has become the sword of the spirit. In a book I read long ago (by Rev. Msgr. Donald McClean of Milwaukee, I think), the claim was made for Catholic control, not only of the things of the Faith, but of American foreign policy and of civil aviation too!

I see Lunn's blaming his Secretary again. A fine and a handy thing to have a Secretary who makes mistakes. She was a godsend to Lunn in his fight with Coulton.[2] I shouldnt say you were a goose in the matter of the Atheneum. But you are a childlike man in some ways. To think that

---

[1] Dr. John V. Simcox, 84 West End, Clapham Common, London SW.4. An Irishman born in Cork, Simcox had for twenty-three years been Professor of Canon Law at St. Edmund's College, Ware, the Roman Catholic ecclesiastical seminary for the archdiocese of Westminster, until he resigned in November 1944 as the result of a controversy with Cardinal Hinsley and the hierarchy. The trouble began when Simcox protested that during the 1942–43 campaign by the Church to obtain government grants for Catholic schools, the bishops had misrepresented the Catholic faith in order to get the grants by claiming that any Catholic parent could bring up his child according to his own conscience. He accused the hierarchy of dishonest propaganda, pretending to be liberal when it was in fact rigidly conservative. When Cardinal Hinsley ordered him to be silent, to desist from controversy because he was "an agent of confusion," he resigned his professorship in 1944, though he remained a priest.

He refused to be silent, and began to justify his views in a series of outspoken letters to the *New Statesman and Nation,* 17 March, 7 April, 21 April, 26 May 1945. His letters were ignored by the hierarchy, and in the last one he threatened to take his case to Rome; but on 9 June a letter appeared from George Gordon Coulton (he had also written on 7 April) with the warning to Simcox that "Silence is one of the strongest weapons of the Roman Hierarchy; the silence of military discipline." In 1946 Simcox published his pamphlet, *Is the Catholic Church a Secret Society?* with a foreword by Coulton.

During the time that O'Casey wrote to him, 1949–50, Simcox was living in Clapham Common at a rehabilitation hostel for homeless or destitute professional men run by an Anglican charitable organization. After a period of great doubt and distress, he apparently decided to become silent; he remained a priest attached to the archdiocese of Westminster until 1967 when he retired. In 1969 he was living at St. Anne's House, Manor Road, Stoke Newington, London N.16.

[2] *Is the Catholic Church Anti-Social?: A Debate between Dr. George Gordon Coulton and Arnold Lunn* (1946).

the Atheneum cares a damn about a controversial cheat; or any other kind, for the matter of that, so long as it doesnt appear in court.

Recently, it was said in the UNIVERSE that 100 M.P.'s were ready to stand with your Church in the matter of the schools question; and it gave the name of the Hon. Q. Hogg. I sent him your pamphlet with a covering letter. He sent a very courteous answer. I asked if I might send a copy to you. He consented; so I send the originals (I have so much to do that I've no time to copy them), and must ask for their return at your convenience. The letters may interest you. Q. Hogg, as you know, is a Conservative, and a fine one, though I say it I shouldnt, not having any political opinion in common with him. But I like fine fellows whatever they may believe, even though (were I younger) I might be shooting at them from behind a barricade one fine day. I'm glad you liked the American priest's speech. I didnt think much of it myself. Nothing startling or original in it. All the old blarney. Still, he is a brave fellow too; and that shall be counted unto him for righteousness. I dont believe any "friend" of Lunn's told him you were a "cussed Irishman." Why doesnt he use the word "cursed"? I hate these attempts to make words innocent. All the best to you.

Yours sincerely,
Sean O'Casey

To John Dulanty [1]

TC. O'CASEY

[TOTNES, DEVON]
7 DECEMBER 1949

My dear John:—

You'll have to forgive me for turning the back of my hand to Morath's offer. Every month or so, I'm pestered with persons asking me to come to their studios for light and shade reproduction. I had one done here some time ago, and that is the last, I hope. He came like a thief in the day with God knows what in arc lamps, bulbs, tubes, tripods, and a winning way, so I submitted rather than drive him from the house. But that photographical experience will do me for the rest of my life.

Besides, John, I dont want to be mixed up with the "photographs of

---

[1] John Whelan Dulanty (1883–1955), Irish High Commissioner in London from 1930 to 1950; first ambassador appointed by the Republic of Ireland to the Court of St. James in 1950.

notable Irish people." All the Irish people are notable in one way or another, from Brian Boru to Danny Boy. I suppose youve heard of Dr. Simcox, Professor of Canon Law for 25 years in Ware Seminary, leaving it,
and entering into a controversy by publishing a pamphlet called "Is the
Catholic Church a Secret Society?" And Dr. Simcox is a Cork man! There
he is now living in poor circumstances in Clapham. And a Father Feeney
of New York has been expelled from the Jesuits because he maintained
that the Church taught no-one could be saved outside of it, and that any
other expressed belief by Churchmen was a heresy. I dont know what nationality he is, but the name FEENEY sounds familiar. Maybe he is another Irishman from God knows where. Only a week ago, I refused to sit
for Mrs. Ernie O'Malley who was busy making busts of "celebrities of
actors, actresses and playwrights." I refused very courteously, but she
hasnt written since, so I daresay she is angry. I hope you wont be angry.
But why doesn't this Cultural Committee, commissioned by Sean Mac-
Bride do something to stop that god-damned shit, Bing Crosby, from continuing his Top O' The Morning pictures of what he calls "Ireland"? And
from singing his "Irish Lullaby"? And, Barry Fitzgerald joining in! And
why doesn't this Committee do away with the sign of the Harp on Guinness's beer bottles? It looks well on your note-paper, well on the flag, but
a beer bottle's no place for it. Breon's living in a room of his own now in
Abbey Gardens, and working away. We're all well. Would you like an autographed picture? Of me? Eileen sends her love to you and yours, and so
do I.

[*Sean*]

To George Jean Nathan

MS. CORNELL

TOTNES, DEVON
11 DECEMBER 1949

My very dear George:

It's some time since I wrote to you. I've been down with a touch of
Influenza, &, even when it said goodbye, I was some time getting back to
my usual life.

I am working on the biography, &, as well, I'd like to publish a book
of one-act plays. I've done two already—as you know—I finished another
a month ago—Hall of Healing—& am just finishing the rough M.S. of a
second, with a third simmering in my mind. These, I hope, will keep my

hand and heart in playwriting, while I go on with the biography. I've been busy, too, helping the Peace Campaign, & so you see I haven't spent the time lying on a sofa, or as [Noel] Coward would say, on a chaise lounge.

"Theatre Arts" have written to say they are publishing an article about me by Gabriel Fallon [1]—probably for the January No. There's a photo with it (reproduced for the article evidently) of "O'Casey in his Studio." His Studio! [2] I like that! If you look at it, you'll get a glance of a dim outline of a photo on the edge of the mantelshelf—it is a photo of a dear, very dear fellow named G. J. Nathan.

That was a very noble appeal of yours in your last book for young playwrights. It was, I imagine, badly needed. I saw the Habimah Players [3] years ago in London, & thought them fine. But I heartedly agree with you on the difficulty of judging a play in an unknown language. I've heard— years ago—people, who knew no Irish, judging & acclaiming plays & acting in Gaelic, & the only sensible response to their views was a hearty haw haw.

When did you have the Bust on the back of the cover? I never saw it. It is, I think, fine. G. J. N. on the Seat of Judgement, with, as usual, a smile, gentle, but cynical, in his eyes. Breon didn't like the carved surroundings—he thought it hid a lot of "the delicate & sensitive intelligence of the face." And, maybe, he's right.

I hope you are well, & minding yourself.

With my love.
Ever yours
Sean

[1] Gabriel Fallon, "Pathway of a Dramatist," *Theatre Arts,* January 1950.

[2] O'Casey's one-room bed-sitter in the tenement at 422 North Circular Road, Dublin, where he lived from 1921 to 1926.

[3] Nathan wrote a review of the Habimah Company's productions in Hebrew in New York, 1 May 1948, *The Theatre Book of the Year, 1948-1949* (1949), pp. 3–7.

By "K" (*Seamus Kelly*) [1]

14 DECEMBER 1949
Irish Times

PLAY TO AROUSE BOTH ANGER AND PITY [2]

If I were Joxer Daly or Fluther Good, or even if I were myself trying to parody the playwright who has been at once the adored prodigal and the despair of us all since he shook our dust from his feet more than 20 years ago, I should be tempted to open this review with something like: "Flounderin' and floosterin' in a frantic fanaticism of pulullatin' petunia-coloured propaganda, Shaun the Shaughraun is afther doin' a desperate dangerous drama, didactically destroyin' them that's left afther him in the land he's afther lavin.' . . ."

But that sort of approach is deceptively easy, and I will content myself with saying that Sean O'Casey's "Cock-a-Doodle Dandy," which had its first performance at the People's Theatre, Newcastle-upon-Tyne, last Saturday night (and which I saw last Monday night), is a play that will arouse both anger and pity in any Irishman on first impact. The anger will be *at* O'Casey—the pity will be *for* him.

"Cock-a-Doodle Dandy" is a blindly and bitterly destructive blast against an Ireland that never existed outside the imagination of a lonely and homesick man in Devonshire—a fantastic, mumbo-jumbo land peopled by a race of slaves who kow-tow obsequiously to a jansenistic, authoritarian, clerical tyranny that never could or would be endured in this island. It reflects "John Bull's Other Island" with a distortion of line, colour and character that might be achieved if a sincere, but fanatically warped, party-line draughtsman attempted to caricature a master-artist's "bourgeois" interpretation of his country's life.

The play burns with the insensate ferocity of "Inishfallen, Fare Thee Well" and is full to the brim with those misanthropic misinterpretations of Ireland that have cancerously grown in our best playwright since he shook the bog from his boots, and took to writing crabbed caricatures of the land and the people that made him.

The redeeming points in "Cock-a-Doodle Dandy" are that behind the

---

[1] Seamus Kelly (1912–1979), drama critic of the *Irish Times,* 1945–79; also wrote the "Quidnunc" column, "An Irishman's Day" in the *Irish Times* since 1949. He was Dublin's most influential and capricious drama critic, and he often attacked O'Casey's later works.

[2] A review of the world premiere of *Cock-a-Doodle Dandy,* produced by the People's Theatre, an amateur company, on 10 December 1949 at Newcastle upon Tyne. See O'Casey's reply, *Irish Times,* 30 December 1949. Many years later, when the Abbey Theatre finally presented the Irish premiere of the play on 11 August 1977, Kelly merely quoted from his 1949 review and dismissed the work as "a non-play" (*Irish Times,* 12 August 1977). See David Krause's letter of reply, *Irish Times,* 18 August 1977.

distortion is an eye that sees our flaws—although it magnifies them madly; behind the savagery is a great affection for the land and its people; and behind all is a very great playwright, working at too many miles remove from the source-material he used incomparably well 20 years ago, and viewing it now through the wrong end of a telescope with a flawed and twisted lens.

"Cock-a-Doodle Dandy" is set in a place called Nyadnanave. That its time is during or just after the war is deducible from the fact that two of the principal characters, Michael Marthraun and Sailor Mahan, own a prosperous bog and a fleet of turf lorries, respectively. Michael also owns a young wife (his second), a young daughter (by his first wife) and a sprightly maid-servant.

In the first act, we learn that the powers of darkness, embodied in a demoniacally inspired cock, have misled the young people of the parish into an unwholesome obsession with the undesirable pleasures to be derived from dancing, singing and each other's company. A character called Shanaar, described as "a very wise old crawthumper, really a dangerous old cod," voices the case of "the old and bitter of tongue" against the natural surge of gaiety in the younger people, and puts the spell of his garbled prophecies of doom upon Michael and the Sailor, who are two mendacious old hypocrites like himself, in an uproariously funny scene, written in O'Casey's most brilliant comic style.

In Scene II the struggle develops between Father Domineer (a wickedly caricatured parish priest) on the one side, and the Cock and his adherents on the other. This scene goes to grotesque and extravagant extremes, and unforgiveably travels beyond mere anti-clericalism to a distastefully painful mockery of some of the most dearly-held tenets of the Catholic Church.

In Scene III, the forces represented by Father Domineer and his partisans triumph, and the young people are driven from Nyadnanave. Michael, representing the sitters on the fence among the ageing laity, asks a typically symbolistic O'Casey messenger where they have gone, and is told: "They have gone to a place where it's possible to live." Michael asks further: "What can I do?" (his wife and daughter have gone). He is told brutally and bluntly: "Die!"—and the last curtain falls on a lonely old scoundrel, who has evoked laughter, but no sympathy (in O'Casey's terms, "a man blown about by every wind"), crying in futility in a deserted garden, where no young voices will sound again.

There is a parable here for Ireland, unquestionably, but it is a parable presented with such unnecessary violence that it is repellent to an objective Irish eye (and I submit that mine is at least as objective as O'Casey's). One is forced to the conclusion that the dramatist, in his exile, has been twisted to a malignantly distorted view of his own country by too many, too ardent, anti-traditionalists.

Let us face O'Casey's indictment. There have been, perhaps, in this country clerics whose obsession with a chosen few of the Ten Commandments made them frenetic scorpions against any expression of sensuous pleasure, however innocent. There have been, certainly, and may still be, ignorant lay expositors of a most un-Christian witch-hunt of the natural joys of singing, dancing, youth and those other transient, worldly, but not necessarily sinful pleasures, "the apprehension of which pleases." But it is devoutly to be hoped that at no time in our history did there exist, in fact, characters like O'Casey's Father Domineer, who curses, kills, exorcises and banishes with a ferocity completely untempered by Christian charity, or like O'Casey's Shanaar, who incites Father Domineer's toadying parishioners to torture, violence and brutality of the most evilly sadistic kind in the interests of "faith and fatherland."

Ireland, to-day, has a myriad flaws in her social structure, and possibly the blame for some of them (and for O'Casey's version of them) lies with the too-earnest lay zealots who are often more clerical than the clergy themselves. But Ireland is still a country where life can be very tolerable, and whose people can show, perhaps, a wider tolerance than might obtain if they were remoulded nearer to the heart's desire of Sean O'Casey. Many of O'Casey's sins may be condoned, because his propagandist indignation is so obviously sprung from an enduring love, but I cannot help feeling that, while he might have been equally bitter on this theme had he gained his picture of contemporary Ireland at first hand instead of at one sea's remove, the bitterness would have been tempered with more laughter and presented with a less malign offensiveness. Had he written "Cock-a-Doodle Dandy" in Ireland and from direct observation, he would have realised that Irish humour, Irish common sense and the innate indestructible anarchy which lies somewhere in every Irishman, would never tolerate the lunatic tyranny which he draws as representative of the country, but would have laughed it out of court.

Peter Trower and his players from the Newcastle People's Theatre give this play a performance of infinitely better quality than I had expected to lie in the capacity of mere Anglo-Saxons, unlearned in the tricky inflexions of O'Casey's Nyadnanave.

Michael Marthraun, the Sailor Mahan and Shanaar are characters of the classic mould that made Captain Boyle, Joxer Daly and Fluther Good, and O'Casey gives them some richly alliterative lines to roll out. One that made me laugh deeply (and that I will probably misquote) spoke of ". . . the piercin' pipin' of Bing-Bang Crosby at his heartenin' hummin' o' hymns . . ."—luscious O'Casey, as good as the vintage "Plough" stuff, this!

Tom Rutherford, as the Sailor, manages his lines a degree better than Jack Percy, who plays Michael a shade too jerkily, and without enough regard to the exactions of O'Casey's prose rhythms. Rutherford's performance is solidly rounded and fully flavoured in both speech and movement, and both his and Percy's finely-finished performances made me regret that some of our young Irish actors could not be sent over to Newcastle just to see the amount of really hard work an English amateur puts into the polishing of a good part when he gets it.

John Lilburn's Father Domineer is a performance of sensitivity and force inside the caricatured limits that the part is allowed, and James Garbutt's Shanaar, a latter-day projection of Dolphie Grigson, digging with a different foot, is first-rate buffoonery. Some of the comedy between these three can stand comparison with the great comic passages of O'Casey's early plays.

Margaret Wilson, as Loreleen, the leader of the young women, gives a strong picture of turbulent and rebellious youth, supported by Nancy O'Kane and Helen Paterson. W. R. Nicholson's Messenger is played with an engaging awareness of the demands of Irish balladry. As a character, however, the failure of the Messenger to take vigorous action against the parochial bullies struck me as unreal.

Peter Trower's production grasps all the essentials; it never falters in pace and never puts a foot wrong in movement; and the stage management, which is full of the trickiest kind of pitfalls, is flawless.

After the final curtain on Monday, I learned that the People's Theatre is an entirely amateur undertaking. On what I have seen, I earnestly commend it to would-be professional actors, set-designers and producers in Dublin as a school in which they may learn that the theatre is a place in which good results are produced only by hard work and intelligent forethought.

As for Sean O'Casey, I would exhort him, for the love of Joxer Daly, to come on over and see us for himself—we're not nearly in such a state of chassis as he thinks!

To Frank McCarthy

MS. MCCARTHY

TOTNES, DEVON

26 DECEMBER 1949

Dear Frank,

Thank you so much for the gift of butter, the cuttings about Joyce & "Cockadoodle Dandy." All very acceptable. What a bunch of lice they are who condemn Joyce. They daren't say the same things of the Bible or of Shakespeare. Hell even wouldn't admit such crawling cravens. "K" evidently has a very near-sighted "objective eye." All in C. Dandy happened in

Ireland—the priest ordering a farmer to dismiss a worker who was "living with a woman," the farmer refusing; the priest striking so that the man died—a very quiet inquiry after. A woman dragged by her hair before another priest for "going with a married man"; the priest making her go down on her knees and swear she'd leave the district, or he'd cause God "to coffin her." The couple fined 40 shillings or a month for kissing—no suggestion of any *indecency*—merely the act of kissing in a public place. I have the records (cuttings) of them all here. The gouging out of a lad's eye by a demon; the demoniacal daughter; even the Priest telling the father "to get her off to America"!—were invented, not by Sean O'Casey, but, be God, by the Irish National Daily, controlled by De Valera, "Irish Press." It is all very comic, if it didn't land Ireland in such a woeful mental state.

All the best to you, and many thanks (and Eileen's) again.

Yours very sincerely,
Sean

To George Jean Nathan

MS. CORNELL

TOTNES, DEVON
27 DECEMBER 1949

My very dear George:

Many thanks for your letter. I'm sorry to hear your opinions of Margo Jones' ideas about Cockadoodle Dandy. It's history, maybe, repeating itself. I've had so many horrible productions that I'd begin to feel something was wrong if I got a good one. Even "Red Roses" here, but for the exquisite acting of Eddie Byrne as old Brennan, was a very mediocre affair. "Purple Dust" in Liverpool was worse; "Red Star" worser; & "Within the Gates" worst of all; bar "Oak leaves & Lavender" which was just indescribably bad. Oddly enough, an amateur group up in the North of England gave a very creditable show of "Cockadoodle Dandy." I hope you keep well.

I enclose a review of the book of "Cockadoodle Dandy," written by a Catholic poet, Paddy Kavanagh. It may interest you. The odd thing is that everything in the play "happened" in Ireland—the man killed by the priest for the reasons given; the woman dragged to the priest for "going with a married man," the priest's threat to "put her in her coffin," if she didn't leave the place; the 40 shillings fine for a Kiss; even the gouging out of "Larry's eye" by the thumb of a demon, & the priest telling the father to get his demonical daughter "off to America" appeared in DeValera's paper, "The Irish Press." I've records of them all. Poor oul' Eire! She has been covered with a Cope. The Caidhp Bhais-Kybosh—Cap of Death.

Please give my love to Gene [O'Neill]. Dick tells me Miss [Margaret] Webster wants to do "Red Roses" in an outside New York Theatre, with an option for a N.Y. production. Something on the lines of Margo Jones' production of "C. Doodle Dandy." [1] From what you've said of Margo, I'm hesitant about Margaret. Do you think I should hold out? I remember your review of the arty bastard's production of Saroyan's "Hello, out There" & my one-act "End of Beginning," & I shake with nervousness when I see lights in the eyes of theatrical Directors. I then almost believe in Demoniacal possession.

All the best to you.

My love as ever.
Sean

[1] *Cock-a-Doodle Dandy* opened on 30 January 1950 at the Arena Theatre, Dallas, Texas, the American premiere, directed by Margo Jones.

To: The Irish Times

30 DECEMBER 1949

"COCKADOODLE DANDY"

Sir,—I will not use the slogan of the dear departed Roddy the Rover by saying "It could happen," in reply to the slogan of "K," saying "It couldn't happen here," in his recent review of my play.[1] My slogan is a more memorable one, for it says It Did Happen There. A priest did call on an employer to dismiss a man because he "was living with a woman"; the employer refused; the priest struck the man, and the man was killed. A woman was dragged by "rough fellows" before a priest for "going with a married man," and the priest used the words, put into the play, that "he would see her coffined if she didn't leave the place." A fine of forty shillings, or a month, was inflicted on a young couple for merely kissing in the public street of a country town. Many clerics have denounced the "hells of dancing halls," and one, a Canon, too, declared that after a dance hall had been opened the "place became another Leicester Square"; though how the holy Canon knew the nature of Leicester Square so well always was a bit of a puzzle to me. I have printed records of them all.

[1] See "K" (Seamus Kelly), PLAY TO AROUSE BOTH ANGER AND PITY, *Irish Times,* 14 December 1949, reprinted above.

And the idea of the "demonised daughter" isn't O'Casey's; but the solemnly set down description of a family's life in the blessed national daily controlled by the equally blessed de Valera, set down even to the priest whispering to the father to get "the one off to America," followed by the information that when the ship arrived in port the demonised person was no longer among the passengers. Where did she go? Ah, ask me another. Not only that, but even the gouging out of "Larry's" too far-seeing eye by the thumb of a demon is recorded by the same blessed journal. "K's" objective eye apparently doesn't see everything.

As for O'Casey's aspersions, they are weak, indeed, compared with what the prominent Irish at home say themselves of themselves to themselves. In a recent election we are told in huge letters that shortly before Cosgrave's political warriors were calling de Valera's warriors by the sweet names of Blackguards, Embezzlers, Gun Bullies, Bank Robbers, Ruffians, Communists, Enemies of Religion. And O'Casey hasn't written yet (he may, of course) anything like what the leaders of the Irish call each other in the Dail. "K" should have read the wailing letter of farewell written by the Lad from Largymore [2] on his departure from Ireland to New York, deploring the terrible terms used by the members of the Dail about each other. Listen to this from a Very Rev. P.P.: "The recolonization of the country has made greater headway in 30 years of native government than during the centuries of foreign occupation." Aha, that's a homer! And what about a certain distillery and a certain bacon factory, not to mention a watch, when the Dail was serenading itself with satirical abuse?

What about the rejection by the Clare Co. Council of a proposal to set up a memorial over the grave of [Brian] Merriman? "I would not enther God's acre to knock down any memorial," said one of the enlightened councillors, "but if any memorial is set up in Feakle guards will have to be set over it night and day, the same as is by the grave of Lenin in Moscow." The same again! What about a bishop making the choice of a site for a school a question of faith and morals? Isn't it a fact that a bishop's advice about the ruling of a dance hall was made a rule of law? Didn't a Franciscan Minor advocate a tax on a farm where any man over thirty remained unmarried? Is it a fact that only one woman in four found a husband in Ireland, and that the figure for men was even worse? Didn't the farmers of East Galway refuse permission to the Galway Hunt to pass over their farms because a divorced member had married again during the lifetime of her first husband: an act praised by the local bishop?

These are but a few of the things I have written down in a record covering over 30 pages of tight-packed typescript, which, of course, the Irish Times could not be expected to print, but which shall appear one

[2] Seumas MacManus (1869–1960), Irish writer of short stories and plays (O'Casey refers to him by using the title of one of his popular farces, *The Lad From Largymore*), who recorded his self-exile to New York in his autobiography *The Rocky Road to Dublin* (1938).

day. "K" would be better employed condemning plays delighting in the things laughed at by me. This applies to plays written especially by priests— like the "novel" written by the late Father Finlay. For instance, here's a review by George Jean Nathan of a play by a Father Nagle [3] (who is hard at it still), of the Blackfriars Theatre Guild, U.S.A.

In the stupendously profound work, "The Seventh Heaven," Father Nagle employs an archangel to tell the world and his wife what is wrong with them. I quote from Mr. Nathan's review:

> What is wrong, among eighty or ninety other things, seems to be the Press, the radio, the moving pictures, the late war, the peace, the atomic bomb, the educational system, Communism, the lack of faith, propaganda, military enlistment, present-day society, alien school teachers, the war-time blitzing of Rome, commercialism and the absence of spiritual values. About the only thing Father Nagle forgot to include is bad plays like his own "The Seventh Heaven."

Oh, boys, what a boyo Father Nagle must be.

However, the point is that—bar the "Cock"—all that comes into my play has happened (besides many other things) in Ireland; or has been recorded, first, not by O'Casey, but by other Irish sources of unimpeachable authority.—Yours, etc.,

Sean O'Casey

Totnes, Devon, England,
27 December 1949.

[3] See Nathan's *The Theatre Book of the Year, 1946–1947* (1947), p. 335, a terse and ironic review of Father Urban Nagle's play, *On the Seventh Day*, produced by the Blackfriars' Guild, New York, 6 March 1947. O'Casey called it *The Seventh Heaven*. See also O'Casey's letter to Nathan, 2 December 1947, note 7.

To Sean O'Casey [1]

TS. O'CASEY

DUBLIN

30 DECEMBER 1949

Dear Mr O'Casey,

Your letter in the "Irish Times" to-day suggests that your's is the voice of one crying in the wilderness. You seem to be a little bit out of touch with things in Ireland.

[1] Sent anonymously to O'Casey from Dublin. When I saw him in the summer of 1963, O'Casey produced this letter and suggested I might wish to publish it in support of his reply to "K" (Seamus Kelly). See O'Casey's letter to the *Irish Times*, 13 January 1950, where he quoted from this anonymous letter.

You may have added the case of the young girl living near Collooney, County Sligo. She was acting as housekeeper to a farmer aged about 56 and they lived alone in the house. The Priest objected to her "living" with the farmer. But she maintained and her family backed her up, that she was living a perfectly good and moral life. Despite this the Priest denounced her. And what happened? One night about 9 months ago a party of three or four men burst into the house; gave the farmer a beating and dragged the girl out of the house in her nightdress. The unfortunate girl was beaten; her hair shaved off and she was chained and pad-locked to a telephone post by the roadside. About 6 am she was found still chained by a local postman whose horse shied on seeing the figure slouched by the post.

This is a perfectly true story and the Sligo police have the records. Is there any need to ask why nobody was arrested? Would not such action by the police be unpopular? The action of the Bishop of Galway over the school site is put in the shade by this one.

There was also the case of about 6 or 8 months ago where the motorist priest knocked down and killed a man named Dowling on the road. This was deliberately hushed up. It would be unpopular. The scene of the accident was the North Circular Road, Dublin, a short distance from Phibsboro'.

And then we had the lovely story of boxer-variety artist Jack Doyle. He came to the Theatre Royal Dublin with his divorced actress wife Judeth Allen around about 1937. When Jack and his actress wife appeared on the stage they were pelted with oranges and other missiles on the instructions of the priests. The reason was that Jack had married a divorced woman. They were hounded out of the city. Now the sequel to the story is this: me bowld Jack having refused to join up during the war, came to Dublin with another divorced woman, the Mexican actress Movita. Having learned from expérience, me cute Jack, immediately on landing in Dublin, goes into Westland road church and gets "married." That saved his skin with the boyos and he was able to live in sin and debauchery with Movita in the city until the war ended.

Do you know the reason for the enclosed cutting from the "Irish Independent" of yesterday?

NO MIDNIGHT MASS IN DUBLIN ON NEW YEAR'S EVE.

It is announced from Archbishop's House, Dublin, that, owing to the impossibility of accommodating all the Faithful who would wish to assist at Midnight Mass on New Year's Eve, His Grace the Archbishop has decided not to permit the celebration of Midnight Mass in any Church or Oratory of the Diocese.

The Arch., knowing that it is a Saty night with the pubs open ½ hour later, takes the view that the churches would have too many drunks. The stuff about overcrowding is just twaddle. There were a million visitors here in 1932 for the Eucharistic Congress when there were mid-night masses and there was no talk of overcrowding.

Unfortunately I cannot give you my name. The difficulty is that I have to live in this country. So now you know what it is to live in a "free" republic. You may think that I am anti-Catholic or any religious but I'm not. I happen to be one of the few Catholics whose religion is not exclusively confined to a mere church ritual. I try to make my life a practical Christian reality. I find that a lot of my friends are finished with their Christian outlook after Mass.

VII

ON THE WAYS OF MAN AND LOVE, 1950

I HAVE no knowledge of the "philosophy of sex." Of course it is a need for all normal men and women, just as food is. Hunger and love are two instincts that cannot be resisted without danger to one's health. To me the normal life is the life of the family, healthy, simple, and, on the whole, enjoyable to decent people. Every effort should be made to allow this normal life to be lived. That is one reason why I am a Communist.

Of course, each of us is part of the crowd—Jew & Gentile, bond and free. The day of the Marquis & the Viscount is over. We're all naked, & the M. & the V. look very much like the other fellows—only less hardy. They always did, but the red velvets & ermine made the buggers look more elegant.

O'Casey was still nursing the wound from the *Irish Times* critic's attack on *Cock-a-Doodle Dandy,* his most recent and, he felt, one of his best plays. Within weeks he had rushed a copy of the review to George Jean

665

Nathan and received an immediate and reassuring reply, which he promptly quoted in a January letter to the paper: "The Irish Times review of 'Cockadoodle," Nathan wrote, "is characteristic of almost all Irish reviews of your work; an explosion of patriotism at the expense of dramatic art. Pay no heed to such nonsense." But still O'Casey was hurt and couldn't forget the nonsense. He believed what Nathan said yet he seldom felt confident enough to resist the impulse to gain relief from retaliation. Perhaps, after a lifetime of fighting for survival, it was in his blood and he didn't know how to hold his peace. He should have taken comfort from the announcement that the Belfast P.E.N. Club had just nominated him for the Nobel Prize, but instead he was embarrassed and could only grumble that the noble Joyce had never received that honor. And soon he was once again defending the honor of Eliot and Picasso to his Russian friend Mikhail Apletin, an official of the Union of Soviet Writers. As he did on a previous occasion when he was arguing with a Russian, O'Casey put art above politics and would not allow his proletarian sympathy to divert his critical judgment, saying about Eliot: "I don't agree with his opinions, but I recognize his power as a poet." In his defense of Picasso, he went further and warned the Russians that their approach to modern art was bourgeois and reactionary: "Oddly enough, in your attack on Picasso, the painter, you were at one with the bourgeoisie and reactionaries here who went mad with rage over an exhibition of his held in London a few months ago. Now, I dont care for Picasso's angular and geometrical period, but even in these paintings, the hand of a first-class artist is apparent." He then proceeded to reject Zhdanov's literalistic theory of "Socialist realism" and the Russian propaganda plays as artistic mistakes. One subject of agreement between them, however, was their scorn for the literary figures who had proved to be "false friends," Marxist renegades like Gide and Koestler and Spender. Unlike them, O'Casey doubted the theory of the arts in Russia, but not of politics. He never doubted the divinity of Communism, Communism as he humanistically interpreted it.

At the same time, he was beginning to have problems with a renegade Catholic, Dr. John V. Simcox, the rebellious Irish priest who had challenged the hierarchy of the Church in England and lost the fight. Initially he had turned to O'Casey for aid and comfort, but gradually it became obvious that O'Casey's eclectic Communism was no more palatable for the disturbed cleric than the hierarchy's authoritarian Catholicism. For one thing, O'Casey had begun to enlighten the unhappy Simcox about the great wisdom of Frazer's *Golden Bough,* one of his favorite books, giving him a mythological approach to Christian dogmas, which he suggested were wonderful "as myths; poetical myths, but myths, all the same." Then he grew bold and offered the confused priest an anthropological interpretation of the Resurrection: "There isn't any doubt of the fact that the 'Resurrection' for many centuries and in every country was lapped in the secular thought of a good harvest that man might live. Man was mortally afraid of a failure which he often experienced, with disastrous results to his tribe; and, naturally, he, in his woeful ignorance and fear, added a divine attribute to his hopes—as in the sacrifice of the 'god,' after a year's worship, that the seedtime and harvest should not fail." It was apparent that Simcox, who was having problems with certain Catholics, not Catholicism, preferred the orthodox version of the Resurrection. O'Casey insisted he wasn't trying to convert Simcox to paganism or Communism, but he felt that Simcox was trying to convert him to anti-Communism, particularly when they became locked in a hopeless tangle over who started the Korean War, until they were going at each other like The Covey and Uncle Pether. In an attempt to be reasonable, O'Casey tried to damn both sides: "Korea belongs to the Korean people, not to the Soviet Union or to the U.S.A." But when even this fair statement failed to impress Simcox, the exasperated O'Casey finally gave up the struggle and said he didn't care who started the war, "I dont know, and I dont care a shit."

That earthy four-letter word finished poor Simcox, who was now convinced that the foul heathen O'Casey had lost his mind and his soul; and this inspired O'Casey's parting shot: "Oddly enough, I'm not frightened by the 'austerity' of 'He that saves his soul shall lose it.' To me that is philosophical, and true. It is inevitable that this should be so. I have seen it work in drama, art, literature, and music—not to mention politics. The boyo who is out to save himself is the boyo who gets lost; that is, the kingdom of heaven is within him no more. And serves him god-dam right." He protested that he was writing in great haste and didn't have time to think it all out carefully, but he had made his point with remarkable clarity and conviction. And he sounded like one boyo who would never lose his soul.

For one thing, he was simply too busy to worry about his soul. He finished two more one-act comedies, *Time to Go* and *Bedtime Story;* he was working on the fifth volume of his autobiography; he was preparing the acting script of *Cock* for an American production, hoping that his favorite Irish actor, Eddie Byrne, would be in the cast, but the whole thing failed to materialize; and the letters went on and on. Then there were more of the inevitable controversies. He provided the "facts" to prove to Alan Denson that he had indeed had the "guts" to tell AE exactly what he thought of him while he was alive—showing, "I hope, that I could face a live lion as well as 'spit' on a dead one." (The "spitting" insult was Denson's accusation.) He refused to give in to pressure to cut the Mr. Greenberg passage out of the seventh chapter of *Pictures in the Hallway* for an American book club edition, assuring Daniel Macmillan that there was absolutely no racial prejudice in the passage: "Anyway, I have no racial prejudices—bondman or free, Jew or Gentile are equal with me." He confirmed another aspect of his tolerance in his remarks to Alfred Eris on the blacklisting of Larry Adler and Paul Draper, the musician and dancer who had been victimized by McCarthyism: "A good dance or a good song is neither Communist or Fascist—even if they were, provided they were good, we'd have to forge a good forgiveness." In one of his conciliatory letters to Miss Sheila, he spun out yet another amusing parable on his all-purpose Communist faith: "If your Doctor is a clever one, he may think he's 'Right-Wing,' but he is really a Communist—all men & women who serve the people are Communists—let them call themselves what they may."

This was the year of his great friend Bernard Shaw's death, and in writing to Peadar O'Donnell he recorded some dialogue from his wife's visit with Shaw shortly before he died:

> "I want to go now," he said; "it is better to go now." He added with his usual smile, "It'll be interesting, anyway, to meet the Almighty."
>
> "I'm sure," said Eileen, "the two of you will get on splendidly together."
>
> "I'll have a helluva lot of questions to ask Him," he murmured.
>
> "Take it calmly," said E. "till Sean gets there, and then you can start a row."

To Mrs. P. R. McNabb [1]

TC. O'CASEY

[TOTNES, DEVON]

4 JANUARY 1950

Dear Mrs. McNabb:

Well, thank you for your letter. I am sorry the last chapter didn't please you, but I hope the rest of the book did.[2] I think you are mistaken about the Irish Sea—it is more than a "ferry trip." Its storms can be as bad, or worse, than those of the Atlantic. I have been through storms in both places, and can speak from experience. It is an historical, though legendary, sea, too. This sea, as you probably know, Sruth na Maoile,[3] was the stormy water on which the Children of Lir spent their years of enchantment; and this was the sea Cuchullain crossed to go to Scotia to learn the exercise of arms from Scathach, the Scottish Queen, whose son, by Cuchullain, was afterwards killed, his identity unrecognized, by his father. Yeats has done it into a play called *On Baile's Strand.* I daresay

---

[1] Mrs. P. R. McNabb, Millerton Inn, Millerton, New York.

[2] *Inishfallen, Fare Thee Well* (1949).

[3] The North Channel, between Ireland and Scotland.

the name of Meagher was your own.[4] A fine name; one that goes back a long, long way. It's a pity an O'Casey hasnt found a place in the sympathy of an O'Meagher. As for the "bright Red Star"—this is the symbol of Communism—not only in the USSR—but for all the peoples of the world. I was a Communist years and years before I even heard the name of Lenin; and, indeed, what is called "Marxism" owes a lot of its philosophy and practices to—you'd never guess—Thompson, a Cork farmer, a big farmer, who formed his estate into a Community before Lenin was heard of. And, then, there's Fintan Lalor of 1848; and many another Irishman— O'Donovan Rossa, for instance, who kept strong sympathies for the Communist cause. And the greatest living Irishman today, Bernard Shaw, is a Communist too. So there's more than one villain in the woodpile.

I wont bother you with any more, for, I daresay, you are a busy woman. May I, however, wish you and Mr. McNabb, all the best for the New Year.

Yours very sincerely,
Sean O'Casey

[4] She had signed her name as "(Mrs. P. R.) Elizabeth Meagher McNabb," and O'Casey was obviously thinking of the "fine name" of Thomas Francis Meagher (1823–67), the Waterford-born nationalist leader and writer who took part in the abortive Rising of 1848, and later served as a Brigadier-General in the Northern army, organizing the Irish Brigade, during the American Civil War.

To Guy Boas

TS. Boas

Totnes, Devon
5 January 1950

Dear Guy,
Very glad to hear that you are alive and active.

Thanks for the book about the Garrick.[1] I've already said quite a lot about it in a biographical chapter—not very flatteringly, either. Honour the theatre! They don't give a damn about it. I'll send it as soon as I finish off a pile of American letters. I don't know who did the review in the T. Lit. Supplement;[2] and don't care.

The Abbey Theatre is non est now. That fellow, [Ernest] Blythe, has done it in. I daresay, this was inevitable after the going of Yeats, and—

[1] Guy Boas, *The Garrick Club, 1831–1947* (1948).
[2] "Stars and Paycocks," *Times Literary Supplement,* 9 December 1949, a review of O'Casey's *Collected Plays,* Vols. 1, 2 (1949).

THE LETTERS OF SEAN O'CASEY

so suddenly—of Yeats's choice [F. R.] Higgins, a grand lad; a young poet; didn't know a lot about the theatre, but had the right stuff in him. I've read "Life of Tennyson" by his grandson.[3] A fine book; and he makes Tennyson a fine man. Cicely's right in calling Tennyson a "terrific Chantrey Bequest," but to be that is something. Tennyson was by no means, the worst, and he had a lot to contend against. I've read, too, Chesterton's life (Ward) [4] Newman's,[5] last vol. of Sitwell's "Laughter in the Next Room," [6] and a new vol. of poems by Hugh MacDiarmuid,[7] who wrote the grand "A Drunk Man Looks at the Thistle." Sencourt's "Newman" [8] is a poor, down-at-the-heel attempt. I've tried to read "Canticle of the Rose." [9] Ward's "Chesterton" is good, but what an old charmer the fellow was! Introducing Jesus with a guffaw.

Breon's in London in an art school (painting), Niall and Shivaun are at school; Eileen is going strong; and I'm going weak. But not dead yet.

All the best to Cicely and to you. And a special wish for the youngster, Robin; and another special for your Father, the other youngster of 78.

My love,
Yours as ever,
Sean

3 Charles Tennyson, *Alfred Tennyson* (1949).
4 Maisie Ward, *Gilbert Keith Chesterton* (1944).
5 John Henry Newman, *Apologia pro Vita Sua* (1864).
6 Osbert Sitwell, *Laughter in the Next Room* (1948).
7 Hugh MacDiarmid, *A Kist of Whistles* (1947).
8 Robert Sencourt, *The Life of Newman* (1948).
9 Edith Sitwell, *The Canticle and the Rose* (1949).

To Miss M. E. Barber

MS. SOCIETY OF AUTHORS

TOTNES, DEVON
6 JANUARY 1950

Dear Miss Barber.

I am sorry to hear you have been ill, and very glad to hear you are "almost" yourself again. But, apparently, not quite yourself; so take care how you go for another while. One takes quite a time to recover from an operation. Go slow.

I'm very sorry, I can't do what you ask. I'm working at biography, & a vol. of one-act plays; besides helping in the Peace Campaign, replying to many letters from the U.S.A., and carrying on a correspondence with a

J. V. Simcox (who was for 25 years Dr. of Canon Law in the R. Catholic
College of Ware) on various questions concerning life and thought. He
has given up his job, abandoned the priesthood, & is living now very poorly
(but managing so far to earn a living) in London. So you see, I've me
hands full. I'm afraid, I've little respect for these articles. For instance,
"The life of the Kelt is ultimately a secret life. He wishes to hide himself
from the world"! Jasus, didja ever hear the like? Like Lloyd George, I
suppose; or Aneurin Bevin? Or the great John McClean of the Clyde. On
the contrary, the Kelt, just as much as the Saxon, wants to be known;
wants to get on; wants to influence the world; & why the hell shouldn't he?
This lingering love for the Keltic mysticism that never existed (any more
than in the English—Keats, Shelley, Donne—not to mention Shakespeare)
is laughable. Never mind; we'll get over it.

Yours very sincerely.
Sean O'Casey

P.S. Mind yourself now.

To Miss Sheila ———

MS. PRIVATE

TOTNES, DEVON
7 JANUARY 1950

Dear Sheila,
  I've been very busy in various ways, answering letters, writing messages
to Peace Conferences, adding to my biography, & am now writing one-act
plays to make a volume of them. And then there is the many affairs of
the home to discuss & help Eileen with—I still do a lot of washing up. I
am sorry to hear of your Mother's illness; but glad to hear she's better.
Why don't you stay with her? Isn't Wiltshire a grand County? Ah, indeed,
life is difficult at times to us all; difficult at most times to me; but what the
hell? It wouldn't be much good if it was always easy. It's pleasant to meet
a difficulty, & to overcome it. We'd all soon be bored stiff, if life was all a
song. I don't know what qualities a writer must possess. There are so many
of them, differing in different authors. He must be able to see things no-one
else sees, & hear things no-one else hears; & must be able to put them in
front of readers so that they see & hear them clearly—whether they like
them or not. Yes, my daughter is growing up elegantly—active & vigorous.
She's 5 feet 2 in height, just eight stone in weight, & Ten years and three

months old. Breon is painting away in London. Niall is at school— or will
be in a week's time after the Xmas holidays. I shouldn't dwell too much
on the fact that you haven't married. Many fine women have remained
single; & many married ones are childless. The wife of a police-sergeant,
living opposite—the police station is opposite our house—, has no child: &
she is very sad about it at times; for she loves children & longs for one.
What gave Simon the paralysis? That is a pity. I shouldn't be shocked at
hearing Simon swear. St Peter did it like a genius. But what a gang of
clerics The Lady C——— seems to have around her! I wonder does she
know anything about Dr. Simcox? I don't live in a "lovely house." Eileen &
I detest it, & wish we had the money to chance a change. I'm not one of
the good Catholics who (according to the places advertised in the "Country
Apostolate" chapter in the Universe) can plonk down 2000 or 3000 for a
suitable house. It's enough for me to be able to pay the rent of where we
are.

Well all the best to you & yours. And don't fret, & don't pity yourself,
for self-pity is the worst drug of all.

Again all the best
Yours as ever,
Sean

P.S. I haven't seen Taylor for 14 years now. I wrote to him, but he didn't
answer my last letter written years ago. As you say, he's an odd fellow.

To Miss May Morton [1]

TC. O'CASEY

[TOTNES, DEVON]
12 JANUARY 1950

Dear Miss Morton:
Thank you very much for your very kind letter, and for the strange
news in it, namely that you have forwarded my name to the "Nobel"
Committee, Sweden, as a possible author on whom to confer the Nobel
Award for 1950; supported too by the recommendation of the Committee
of the Belfast Centre of the P.E.N. Club.

Whether or not my name should appeal to the "Nobel" Academy, or
Swedish Academy, or whatever the Gathering that awards the Prize is
called, wont alter me much; but it is indeed pleasant to think and to know

[1] Miss May Morton, Chairman, Belfast Centre, PEN Club.

that you and your comrades of the Belfast P.E.N. Club think so well of what I have tried to do. I have got, and still get, so much abuse from Ireland that it is very enjoyable to hear a good word spoken about me in Belfast.

But whisper, May, I havent a deep respect for the literary wisdom of the Academy that doles out the "Nobel" prize. It has made odd choices in its time, and has passed by some choice names. For instance, James Joyce. If ever anyone deserved (and needed) this award, this was the man. But he wasnt even thought of; too good, too great, for the S. Academy. But— if they ask for them—I'm afraid I wont send them any of my works. I dont go in for competitions. There the works are, and they can either like or lump them.

But give my affectionate regards to the Members of your Committee, and my thanks, too, for their good opinions; these are an award I value highly. And the same to you.

Yours very sincerely,
Sean O'Casey

To Irish Times

13 JANUARY 1950

"COCKADOODLE DANDY"

Sir,—Please allow me one last letter. Why were the things in the play condemned, while the same things in de Valera's holy paper went un-noticed? Do the Stakhanovites [1] of piety in Eirinn really believe with de Valera that "Ireland is the foremost Christian land in all the world"? And yet, an hour or so afterwards, he could say, after listening to some political rival: "When I witness this kind of muck-raking, I think of Geoffrey Keating's reference to the activities of the dung-beetle." Dung-beetles among the members of the Dail! Insects in the apple of heaven's eye! I have had a number of letters from Eire, half-abusive, half-commendatory, but all anonymous. Here's an extract from one of them: [2]

"You should have added the case of the young girl living in Co. Sligo. She was acting as a housekeeper to a farmer aged about 56, and they lived alone in the house. The priest objected to her 'living' with the farmer. She maintained, and her family backed her up, that she was living a perfectly

---

[1] For an earlier reference to the excessive piety of the religious Stakhanovites, see O'Casey's letter to Jack Carney, 22 February 1945, note 2.
[2] See the anonymous letter to O'Casey, 30 December 1949.

good and moral life. Despite this, the priest denounced her, and what happened? One night, about nine months ago, a party of men burst into the house, gave the farmer a beating, and dragged the girl out of the house in her nightdress. The unfortunate girl was beaten, and her hair shaved off. She was chained ànd padlocked to a telephone post by the roadside. About 6 a.m. she was found by a postman, whose horse shied on seeing the figure slouched by the post. This is a perfectly true story, and the Sligo police have the records. Is there any need to ask why nobody was arrested. Would not such an action on the part of the police be unpopular?"

He gives another instance of a case which, was "hushed up" because a priest was connected with it. And he ends: "Unfortunately, I cannot give you my name. The difficulty is I have to live in this country." He has to live "in this country,"—the Eire of Cuchullain, of the Fianna, of P. H. Pearse.

But all these things are beside the point concerning me as a dramatist. "K's" article may have been "splendid," but it was not dramatic criticism. Here is George Jean Nathan's comment on it: "The Irish Times review of 'Cockadoodle' is characteristic of almost all Irish reviews of your work; an explosion of patriotism at the expense of dramatic art. Pay no heed to such nonsense. It is a grand play, and you may well be proud of it." And yet priest, layman, and critic in Ireland yell about the direction of things in the U.S.S.R., indifferent to the fact that they, too, toe a far more dangerous and far more ignorant party line. As Dr. J. V. Simcox, one-time Doctor of Canon Law in a R.C. seminary here, knows now only too damned well!—Yours, etc.,

Sean O'Casey

Totnes, Devon,
11 JANUARY 1950

To Francis MacManus

TS. MACMANUS

TOTNES, DEVON
8 FEBRUARY 1950

Dear Frank,

Your letter came to me in the throes of Influenza. I had got up and gone about too soon, and payed for it by imprisonment in bed, dead to the world, for a fortnight. Up again now, but feel god-forsaken; but the sun is shining—for a few minutes—and the snowdrops are beginning to show themselves. So Spring cant be far away.* Anyhow, Frank, you can see by this that you arent the only one to be bothered with ullagulla ghone illness.[1]

I've written to Des. MacCarthy and to Jim Rose—literary Editor of The Observer—about your forthcoming book,[2] and I enclose their replies, which I'd like to have back when convenient to you. I send them to show I amnt codding you. Dont mention this matter to anyone else, for Id have every writer from Antrim to Cork writing to me about their forthcoming works, and God knows, I get enough of this bother already. Dont take notice of Desmond MacCarthy's ulla gulla ghone about Socialism. He rages against it. He doesnt understand in any way the materialistic conception of history, and that the things he rages against cant stop happening, and that Socialism—stepping forward to Communism—is only a name given to irresistible forces. I told him (and J. Rose) of course, that you werent a Communist; that you were a good Catholic; that you were steeped in what you believed to be Thomism; and that you were a decent chap for a' that and a' that. The two I've written to are important. When I've answered some of the letters that have piled up during illness, I'll write to the New Statesman and Nation about your book. And that's about all I can do. The book must do the rest. And I sincerely hope it may, Frank.

Interested to hear F. O'Connor has found another woman. He's not too old to do so, though it doesnt often turn out to be much better. He seemed happy enough with the first one (was it the first?) when cycling his "Irish Miles" [3] with her. Anyhow, O'Faolain's "reconciliation with the Church" balances O'Connor's naughty deed. An English Journal said this a few weeks ago, that he had returned to the Church, so I suppose it's right. Curious pair. Always together (or were), yet never, seemingly, at one.

I was told a day or so ago that "if the Catholic Church took my advice, it would do her a lot of good"! And it was said by a B.A.,D.C.L., one who had been for 25 years a Professor of Canon Law in St. Edmund's, Ware. There y'are, wha'? He has abandoned his job, left the priesthood, and is earning a precarious living in London—an achievement for an old man. He lives in poverty and hardship different from the eclat, the blowing of trumpets, and the far better job enjoyed by the ex-sub-editor of the D. Worker, Mr. Douglas Hyde, who recommended to me William Morris as a mediaeval scholar! Jasus, the cheek and ignorance of him!

Well, all the best to Mrs. McM, your two boys, & yourself

Sean

---

* Well, I managed to write a one-act play while I was laid down, and this with two other new ones, will go to make a vol.

[1] The lamenting or self-pitying illness.
[2] Francis MacManus, *The Fire in the Dust* (1950), a novel.
[3] Frank O'Connor, *Irish Miles* (1947), an account of his tour of Ireland with his first wife.

To Daniel Macmillan

TS. MACMILLAN LONDON

TOTNES, DEVON
8 FEBRUARY 1950

Dear Mr. Daniel:

Thank you for your letter putting before me questions from Mr. [George P.] Brett concerning proposed alterations in my book PICTURES IN THE HALLWAY. I have carefully read the parts proposed to be cut. As far as I can see, Mr. Russell thinks they might offend Jewish members of his Club. I cant see how they should. Mr. Greenberg is a very acceptable human being.[1] In fact, he was a very decent man, and nothing said of him, shows him to be different. Anyway, I have no racial prejudices—bondman or free, Jew or Gentile are equal with me. I, therefore, cant see my way to cut out the passages named.

Regarding the change of position of the picture—I cant decide that poser. Surely publishers and printers should know more about this question than I? Should it be placed in the beginning, in the middle, or at the end? I dont know. It is a question of publishing taste, and I leave it to them.

I readily allow the change in the word "nigger." I suggest "Trojan," or, better still, "coolie."

A question for you: I've done three one-act plays—"Hall of Healing," "Time to Go," and "Bedtime Story." The first is already with you—I think Mr. Harold got it when you were on holiday; the other two are here with me. I suggest that these, with "End of Beginning," and "Pound On Demand" could make a volume. I'd be glad if you'd let me know what you think of it.

I return the pages of PICTURES IN THE HALLWAY sent to me.

With all good wishes,
Yours very sincerely,
Sean O'Casey

---

[1] For the incident involving Mr. Greenberg, see the opening pages of "Bring Forth the Best Robe," *Pictures in the Hallway.*

To Mikhail Apletin [1]

TC. O'CASEY

[TOTNES, DEVON]
10 FEBRUARY 1950

My dear friend and comrade—

I have had to postpone the effort to reply to your kind letter because of pressure of work, and, worse still because of illness. I had Influenza, got up and went about too soon, and suffered a relapse. Now I am writing a few words more of greeting than of controversy, for all in all, we have very little to disagree about. We are both in the same fight. Although not present at the U.S.S.R. Conference for Peace, I can assure you I do my share in pushing forwards the good cause of peace among all men. The recent number of the Magazine published from Melbourne, Australia, University begins with a letter from me calling for peace. Of course the expulsion of Professor Bernal was a shameful thing, and a stupid thing to do too.[2]

The Wroclaw Congress: You dont seem to realise that writers here have to earn a living differently from the way a living is earned in the Soviet Union. They have to depend for their living on the sale of their books, and, at present, the price of books is so high that only the secure and fairly-well off can buy them. So writers on the whole take the line of least resistance. I for one do not blame them. I would not excuse them, but I can understand them, and most of them manage to convince themselves that they do right—Orwell and those like him. The lure of position, the pressure of the necessity for a living are very powerful things my friend. Your own great genius, Tolstoy, showed that terribly in the character of Selénin. That is just another fact we have to fight against and alter. The workers here dont buy books, or so few that the number is negligible. They call their yielding to toe the line of least resistance their "individuality and their independence," and a great crowd applaud them. But it doesnt follow, my friend, that all of these are poor artists; and some, indeed, because they are great, and, willy nilly, condemn things as they are, meet with persecution, boycott, and abuse—Thomas Hardy, for instance.

Now I dont exactly "take up the cudgels on behalf of T. S. Eliot." I dont agree with his opinions at all; but I recognise his powers as a poet;

[1] Mikhail Apletin, secretary, Foreign Commission, Union of Soviet Writers, Moscow.

[2] Professor J. D. Bernal was barred from reelection to membership to the Council of the British Association in November 1949 as a result of a speech he had made in Moscow on 27 August 1949, in which he stated that "the political and financial direction of science in America and Britain was one towards war." See *The Times* (London), 4 and 8 November 1949.

and I fervently wish he were on the side of the people. Oddly enough, in your attack on Picasso, the painter, you were at one with the bourgeoisie and reactionaries here who went mad with rage over an exhibition of his held in London a few months ago. Now, I dont care for Picasso's angular and geometrical period, but even in these paintings, the hand of a first-class artist is apparent. As for Eliot, I have written something about him for my next biographical volume, putting alongside the poet Hugh Mc-Diarmid,[3] the Scot, who wrote some lovely "Hymns to Lenin." Him you should know about, rather than about Eliot. You say, rightly, that Eliot has declared himself to be a "classicist in poetry (he's a lover of Virgil), royalist in politics, and an Anglo-Catholic in religion." Well, he's honest: he lets us know exactly what he is. He is no renegade; he is but an enemy. Very different from Gide, Koestler, or Spender. These have proved to be damned false friends. They put their hands to the plough, then left it and ran off; not only ran off, but turned to declare that the plough was a useless one and dangerous. You will have to be more careful of whom you embrace as a friend; you will have to see through them who are with you, and them who come to spy out the land. I'm afraid you may have another before long—J. B. Priestley. Already, he seems to have grown cold; and, to me, seems to be looking for a chance to deny all, or most, of what he once affirmed. Give me any time fellows like Eliot in preference to these chaps.

Eliot as an Anglican believes in Institutional religion—as he has a perfect right to do. He sees Christianity as the custodian of the European tradition, and he sees the Roman Catholic Church (not the Vatican, for the Vatican is not the Catholic Church, but only its present leadership) as the most powerful body in the Christian Church. And so she is. She is the biggest and most unscrupulous enemy confronting Communism, and, to me, the biggest enemy confronting all human freedom. I warned Communists here years ago about this, but they seem to be convinced that she is best left alone as much as possible. I, on the other hand, think she should be opposed in every possible way, and on every question concerning the onward march of man. Indeed, my name is known so well to her followers that they never mention it, and no book or play of mine is now ever even condemned in any of her journals. They let themselves down badly in attacks on my plays, THE SILVER TASSIE and WITHIN THE GATES among others, and their stupid ravings will be recorded in the next biographical volume I publish. And, in passing, "Waste Land" is in a way descriptive of England at the moment, and many "Hollow Men" are to be found here.

My dear friend, we could argue all night for weeks about what is and what is not realism. Of course, I agree with you that he who makes plot and technique the be-all and end-all of endeavour is a damned fool. I agree that uniqueness—I dont like the word "novelty"—depends on how

[3] For O'Casey's comments on Eliot and MacDiarmid see "The Dree Dames," *Sunset and Evening Star* (1954).

profoundly it embodies "the spirit of our people"; all the people, or a community or even a family among them. But the spirit of your people may [be], and probably is, different from the spirit of our people here. And there is a bewildering variety between this family and that one, between one man and woman and another. I of course dont know how the training and experience of the late A. Zhdanov fitted him to be a critic of literature. I imagine it did not fit him to be a valuable source of criticism; but, in any case, were he the fittest in training and experience, he would still remain fallible.

You may remember that even your genius, your great poet, Mayakovsky, received abuse about his art from those who probably envied his greatness and his power. The danger is that a unique mind may be frightened away from its creativeness, for lesser writers will always be jealous of it.

Let me make it clear that my words for Eliot are disinterested. I do not know him, and have never met him. When, at the request of Voks some time ago, I wrote to him for an appreciation of Chekhov, he very courteously agreed to write one; so did Desmond McCarthy; so did Masefield; but, oddly enough, Mr. Priestley didnt say whether he would or not.

As for myself, rightly or wrongly, I wish to do work which may last longer than a day; and so I strive to put my best into all I do. Looking over some copies of THE INTERNATIONAL THEATRE, published in Moscow in the Thirties, I find that no play done by the "Blue Overalls," "TRAM," or "Agit-Prop" groups has survived. None of them has lived on even to our day.

But, really, this arguing is a waste of your time, and, possibly, a waste of mine too. We have so much in common, from the earth we stand on up to a high star in the heavens, that there is very little importance in our difference of thought (real or seeming) on what is called "formalism" and what is called "realism" in play and story.

It was interesting to read Colonel L. Borisenko's comments of Capt. Liddell Hart's book, THE OTHER SIDE OF THE HILL. I know Liddell Hart well. He lived for quite a time, during the early part of the war, on the opposite side of the road to me, and I had a number of talks with him. He didnt then appear to be such an enemy of the U.S.S.R. However, when the war became a war, and Dunkirk was in progress—tens of thousands of the rescued soldiers passed through Totnes—he became panic-stricken at the prospect of an invasion, and, like the shit he is, scuttled off to the north of England to the Lake district, where Wordsworth, the poet lived, so as to be as far as possible from any danger that might come to Devon. A right gallant Captain!

To end, let me send my warmest greetings to your great Leader, Marshal Stalin, and let me wish him a long, long, long life; and greeting to your great people; and to you and all your comrades. Long live the U.S.S.R. and all She stands for.

Yours very sincerely,
Sean O'Casey

ADDENDA

Dont be too sure of what is and what is not mysticism—it may be confused with imagination. There's a touch of it [in] your own stories and your own poetry. In ALITET TAKES TO THE HILLS for instance—one of your best stories, I think; and in the scenario PAVLOV, a very fine and moving impression, even though only a scenario. We are all anxious to know what life is, and to live it to the full; and that is the main reason for Communism, because that is the one way in which life can be lived to the full; all life, not only part of it as has been so in the past when life was delivered over to hereditary wealth and hereditary privilege.

And some of us who may have a touch of mysticism in us can be, and are, great friends to the U.S.S.R., standing against the Koestlers, the Gides, and the Spenders, feeling with all our hearts that these, however they may boast of their independence, are not apostles of spirituality, but are but mean vendors of their souls in the world's market place.

All good wishes,
S. O'C.

To M. W. Bennit [1]

TC. O'CASEY

[TOTNES, DEVON]
14 FEBRUARY 1950

Dear Mr. Bennit:

Miss Winifred Carey is very positive and very authoritarian. She is evidently a specialist on drama criticism, on Catholic philosophy, on good taste, on the Catholic Faith, on the significance of Lourdes, on the dominance of clerical power in Ireland, and what is meet, right, and proper to put in a play. It would be dangerous to try to argue with this lady, for she knows too much. But I may just put one question to her as an example of her all-knowingness: How does she know that "No Catholic Pilgrim would ever set off to, or return from, Lourdes in the frame of mind and expressing the sentiments of Julia in the play"? Has she asked all and each of them? "Catholics go to Lourdes for spiritual and not physical regeneration." Well, she knows little about Catholics, and less about human nature, if she thinks any—any, mind you—Catholic afflicted with disease goes to Lourdes without the desire, the hope, and, many, with the conviction, that

---

[1] M. W. Bennit, People's Theatre, Newcastle upon Tyne.

a cure will be their reward. This is what makes the place a gilt-edged source of revenue for the Fathers of the Assumption. When a rival vision was seen a few months ago in a place a few miles from Lourdes, and persons began to flock there, and even priests offered up Mass on the spot, it was quickly condemned, without inquiry, by the Bishop of Tarbes who was [not] going to have any check put on the flow-in of money to his beloved Lourdes. I have it all here, recorded in her own Catholic papers.

As for Werfel and his SONG OF BERNADETTE, well, the less Catholics say about this, the better. I suggest she should read the Augustinian Quarterly, GOOD COUNSEL for July-September, 1949, Vol. V. No. X. published by the Augustinian Fathers, St. John's Priory, Thomas St. Dublin. There she can read a lot about films, especially about her own choice. Here's just one extract: "Some Catholic critics have tied themselves in knots of ecstasy over such productions as GOING MY WAY, BELLS OF ST. MARY'S, THE KEYS OF THE KINGDOM, and THE SONG OF BERNADETTE. The mere sight of a clerical collar is enough to send some American critics into a frenzy of enthusiasms. The fact is that the Church is often acutely embarrassed by what are called religious films." She can read more of this if she looks over my book, INISHFALLEN, FARE THEE WELL. When the "Silver Tassie" was done by the Abbey Theatre, Dublin, nothing was vile enough for the Roman Catholic cleric and layman to say about it. Most of what they said will appear in my next book. But when some years later, the play was done in the Gaiety, the biggest commercial theatre in Dublin, for two weeks to packed houses, there wasnt a whimper from cleric or layman. The years between had shown them what God-damned asses they had made of themselves. That is why the Roman Catholic Press has fought shy of mentioning COCKADOODLE DANDY. They have been warned, and they keep their mouths shut.

Miss Carey's statement that because O'Casey has never been a Catholic, therefore O'Casey can know nothing about the R. Catholic Faith or of Roman Catholic philosophy! Does she not know that Card. Newman said that the most impartial historian of the Church was—who do you think?— Gibbon! Gibbon, the agnostic! In the R.C. Press very recently there was an hysterical scream about the woeful ignorance of Roman Catholics of their Faith, and the R.C. Hierarchy issued a manifesto about it. And Dr. W. McDonald, for forty years Professor of Theology in Maynooth College, in his book laments the number of Priests who were ignorant of facts in their Faith too! Here, now, we have two more examples in the letters from Miss Carey and Miss Adah Brown. I say that "Father Domineer" is typical of the spirit of Clericalism in Ireland, and in Spain and Portugal too; and in Italy, only there are two million Communists there to temper them to caution. It is this clerical tyranny that has brought about the anti-clerical revolution in Poland, Roumania, and Czecho-Slovakia; a revolution on the part of the people which Dr. McDonald foretold thirty years ago.

Miss Adah Brown is another drama-critic. What has what O'Faolain says got to do with the play? What has the Irish Academy of Letters got to do with it either? It was moribund from the start. I refused to be a foundation member, though personally asked by Bernard Shaw to be one. What right has the Roman Catholic community to claim immunity from comment any more than other religions? These assertions made by these complainers—and soul-desiring repressors, had they the power—prove the points of my arguments: they are eager to censor, anxious to repress, if they only had the power. And, if the laity be like this, what way must the clerics feel? What about Alfred Noyes's book on Voltaire which the Roman authorities condemned; and made the poet withdraw all copies from circulation, and called upon him to make reparation! He obediently did as he was ordered to do; but it would take a helluva lot of Cards. Archbishops, and Bishops to make O'Casey do their bidding. But, of course, O'Casey has Protestant England behind him, and that of course gives him a courage he may not naturally possess.

The first fact is that the R.C. clergy are wild with alarm at the new thought arising everywhere, and wilder still at the thought of having to put their hands in their own pockets to pay for their own schools (Card. Spellman roared out at Mrs. Roosevelt that "she was an unworthy American mother" for defending the clause in the Constitution that no grant should be given to any sectarian or privately-controlled school); and so they spout out lies about "the right of all parents to rear up their children in whatever faith the parents choose," a heresy, and contrary to their own Canonical Laws. But they keep the fact of what their Canon Laws say to themselves, and that is why they condemned Father Simcox for daring to reveal their lying practices.

Well, I'm really wasting time. I should be working. So farewell for the present.

[*Sean O'Casey*]

To Francis MacManus

TS. MacManus

Totnes, Devon

23 February 1950

Dear Frank:

I enclose the booklet written by Dr. Simcox (J. V.).[1] It will give you the principles of the case Dr. Simcox has against the church authoritarians. It seems to me to be an unanswerable case. But he finds himself now surrounded by an impenetrable silence. The Iron Curtain has been let down, even on this man. It amuses me to see how brave you all are in denouncing the authoritarianism of the Kremlin, and of the Communists; but ne'er a whiff of a word out of yous against the authoritarianism on your own oul' doorstep. But silence is your one and only safeguard—for a short term policy. I get this silence myself. The R. Catholics have made a concerted attempt to bulldose the Committee of the People's Theatre against producing anything critical of what they call "Catholic Faith and Catholic philosophy"! One lady wrote to say "pilgrims went to Lourdes, not for physical cure, but for spiritual regeneration." I wrote to tell her that spiritual regeneration was found, not in the waters of Lourdes, but in the sacramental waters of Baptism. D'ye think she replied? Took any notice? Not she, though she had written a fierce letter to the Theatre to yell out that I knew nothing about C. Faith or C. Philosophy. These yellers will force so many cults on the C. that it will become (indeed it is, in many places) insufferable, even to R. Catholics. Look at M[att] Talbot. "You make them popular, and we'll make them saints." If the name of Jim Larkin had gone forward for canonization, I'd say the C. was bucking up. I am far from being a "fatalist." I hold, on the contrary, that man can achieve anything, everything; and will go forward, even beyond Communism. But I have no idea in my mind of trying to get you towards such thoughts. You are, innately, a Conservative. And none the worse for that same.

Now—in confidence—why dont some of yous fellas help S[eamus] O'Neill to get the I. Academy of Letters Prize for his Gaelic story (the O'Growney Prize)? And a share, at least, of the Hyde Prize for an effort in Irish to write "modern Literature"? He has written to me to do this for him; but I couldnt write to the Academy of Letters, seeing I'm not a member, and have no profound regard for it either. And a letter to the Committee dispensing the Dr. Hyde Prize would only do harm to him, I'm sure. Couldnt [Robert] O'Farachan help? And S. O'Faolain? I'd like to help him,

---

[1] See O'Casey's letter, "The Simcox Case," *English Churchman*, 25 November 1949, note 2.

if I could; but I cant see any way to do it. Dont let on I told you he wrote to me. He wouldnt like it, I'm sure. I havent noticed any mention yet of your book coming out. But these days, no one dare say when a book may appear.

All the best to you. And to yours.

Sean

To George Jean Nathan

MS. CORNELL

TOTNES, DEVON

1 MARCH 1950

My very dear George:

A letter from Tom Curtiss tells me you've been ill, & are taking things quietly. I am very sorry to hear you have been ill, & glad that you are taking things quietly. We hear many odd things in our rush hours, but just as many odd things in our quieter moments; so we don't lose much in either mood. I've been down myself again with Influenza; got up & went about too soon (they say), & had to fly back to bed again. I'm just beginning now to realise there's such a thing as life. Anyway, in the illness, I managed to finish the one-act play "Bedtime Story." I'll send on the two of them to you as soon as "Bedtime Story" comes back from the typists— my typing is pretty shaky, so I get a fair copy done by professionals. I think "Time to Go" is good, though I'm not sure. It is, again, realism touched with fancy. "Bedtime Story" is out of my usual manner, a comedy, fanciful in a way, too; but wholly unlike either "Time to Go" or "Hall of Healing," which I sent to Dick some time ago.

I have hopes of "Purple Dust" next season; & I've agreed to let Margaret Webster have a go in Woodstock with "Red Roses." Anyway, but for the U.S.A. & her dollars, I'd be in a bad way. I don't get much from England, &, of course, the Abbey doesn't do my plays now. The U.S.A.— between the royalties for biography & here & there performances & monies of performances of plays, has kept me going for the past few years. A town in the North here—a small theatre run by amateurs, who, wonderful to relate, gave a good performance—did "Cockadoodle Dandy." There's been a controversy over it, & R. Catholics have written to the Theatre Committee trying to intimidate them against doing my work. One of them, ironically enough didn't know the first thing about the R. Catholic Catechism. She wrote a letter to me brimful of heresy! She just set aside the facts of Baptism & Penance (R.C. Sacraments) for the fictions of Lourdes. A woeful lot of these apologists are so arrogant & ignorant, it is painful to have to listen to them.

Recently, Eileen went to London, & from there, at G. B. S.'s invitation, went down to Ayot St. Lawrence, & had tea with him. The old warrior is as alive as ever; still gets indignant at stupidity; still has his cascading laugh; & takes an hour's walk every day in the garden, whatever the weather. And him goin' on for 94!

Enclosed is a criticism of a play by Vivian Connell, he who wrote "The Nineteenth Hole." An odd fellow, Connell. I feel there's something in him, but can't say where or how.

> *Take care of yourself, George.*
> *With my love.*
> *Sean*

To Seumas Scully

MS. Scully

Totnes, Devon
6 March 1950

Dear Seumas.

Thanks, ever so much, for the copies of Abbey Programmes, the illustrated "Times," & the silky-voiced Catholic Stage Guild's "Interval." Bing Crosby outdoes himself in it with his comments on "Vocation." He hasn't, after all, a glimmer of a sense of humour. Boosting "this good American way of life of ours, which is founded on a belief in God," he adds "Look at any American coin—'In God we Trust' ". An appropriate union —God and Mammon. He could have quoted the British one, too, "God and my Right"; & the German one as well—"Gott Mitt Uns." Cromwell was, at least, more honest, with his "Put your trust in God, me lads; but keep your Powder dry." Mule Train!

I'd have written before, but mislaid your previous letter, & couldn't remember your address.

Your season's programme [1] is really a fine one—as far as Subjects are concerned. D[orothy] McArdle's chairmanship is over a good one—how did it go? Pushkin says "Only barbarism, villainy, and ignorance do not respect the past, cringing before the present alone." But then, in his time,

---

[1] The Technical Students Literary and Debating Society, Dublin.

Pushkin was something of a "Red," as was Mitchel & Tone, & even Parnell, who struck at landlordism, as the Italian peasants are doing now.

There doesn't seem to be any remedy for the flight from Ireland. Looks like anyone who can is hopping over here. Of course, if you can get a living here, you live a much freer life; and, oddly enough, among the "stolid Saxons," a more exciting life, too. All the excitement had gone from Ireland. The flight stretches a long way back now.

Well, I mustn't start a lecture.

So thanks again.

If you should come a wandering to Devon in the summer, we must try to arrange a meeting.

All the best
Sean

To Joseph Jay Deiss [1]

TS. Deiss

Totnes, Devon
7 March 1950

Dear Mr. Deiss:

I got your book [2] allright. And I've read it. It is very interesting, and, as a novel, there is something in it. It is, I think, very good for a first effort, or, rather, for a first effort to get published. But I am not a critic; I have reviewed no more than half a dozen books in my life, and so have no training and no experience of this kind of work. But as an exposure of the persecution of people who venture to hold any opinion at all, it is powerful, and should be read by thousands. There are, however, even from this viewpoint, some weaknesses—for instance, the fact that Faith cannot prove that she is legally an American citizen; and that Chandler takes up her case (apparently), not because he is determined to fight for justice, but because he falls for her. In the end, Cunningham seems to be the greater man.

But—though I'm reluctant to thrust my opinion on the American scene, being a foreigner—the examinations—and I've read DUE PROCESS IN A POLITICAL TRIAL [3]—seem, nay are, not only a contravention of justice, but a brutal and ignorant abusal of sensible human law. The find-

1 Joseph Jay Deiss (1915–   ), Ridgefield, Connecticut, writer of novels on the theme of political freedom.
2 *A Washington Story* (1950).
3 *Due Process in a Political Trial: The Record vs. the Press* (New York, 1949), National Antipartisan Committee to Defend the Rights of the 12 Communist Leaders.

ings of these "UnAmerican Committees" would make every man and woman who thought for more than a minute an untouchable Red; they would make almost every poet who wrote in the English language a subject to be put behind prison bars, from Chaucer and Langland to many who are singing their songs today. Even Shakespeare would be cited to appear as a dangerous person, and would be silenced by the Daikens of the day; and your own Walt Whitman wouldnt be allowed to ask a question, for he would stand self-condemned as a self-confessed democrat, hailing and applauding the ideals of man, the en-masse.

I hope your good book may be read by many, and that the really ridiculous attitude of mind which would hear unAmerican utterances in the twittering of sparrows will soon be dead and damned there, here, and everywhere else.

Yours sincerely,
Sean O'Casey

PS. Don't tell anyone I've written to you about your book—that you sent it to me to read. I'd be flooded with books. You can't conceive the number of requests I get to read MS., books, poems, plays; & even requests—almost demands—to get them published. *S. O'C.*[4]

[4] The PS was added in longhand.

To Dr. John V. Simcox

TC. O'CASEY

[TOTNES, DEVON]
11 MARCH 1950

My dear Dr. Simcox,
You do well to "paddle your own canoe," but I hope that doesnt mean I shouldnt send any more of your books to friends of mine, or to those who ask questions. I suggest that you should write to Giovanni Costigan and ask him to send you a copy of the book AMERICAN FREEDOM AND CATHOLIC POWER.[1] If you wouldnt like to do this, I could let you have my copy for three months, and welcome—though if your eyes be bad, my conscience will be troubled. Professor Costigan's address—in case you may write to him—University of Washington, Department of History, Seattle 5, State of Washington, U.S.A. A letter, by the way, takes a helluva long time to get there, and the one way to hurry it is to send it via Airmail. I

[1] Paul Blanshard, *American Freedom and Catholic Power* (1949).

THE LETTERS OF SEAN O'CASEY

enclose a stamp and an airmail slip to save you trouble. Even then, it takes a long time. I dont think there is very much that is obscurantist about Communists. A Sunday paper the other day complained that their press didnt admit events of "human interest," which consisted—as they said—of murder, infidelity, theft, and so on. These things happen still in the USSR, but they do not make them matters of "human interest." They think that the things that matter are industrial activity, agricultural liveliness, the things of the theatre, the opera, the ballet, the schools, literature, and art, as well as the building of new greatness in their cities. I think that they are right. As for books from the outside, they say that a mass of triviality is constantly being published which is good neither for God nor man, and again, I think they are right. As for the opposition to my play in Newcastle, that was but a tiny affair. Wait till you read in my next biographical book what was said about THE SILVER TASSIE, WITHIN THE GATES, and other work.[2] A tour of the second play was stopped in America by the agitation engendered by the Jesuits. It was banned in Boston, Cleveland, Chicago, Toronto, and Ontario, so that the tour would have been useless. This meant the loss of a year's income to me. That is the way they work. A Father O'Connell, S.J.[3] was the prime mover, and when I wrote a reply to what he said, it was returned to me with the remark that to publish it would but make matters worse. Recently, the Franciscans, at the Father Mathew Feis in Cork wouldnt allow a Tipperary Drama Society to do THE PLOUGH AND THE STARS,[4] though they had rehearsed it for months before, and would give no reason for the ban. That is the way they work. Edward the VIII's case was a very special one. He made little of all the traditions surrounding the ceremonial of kingship which didnt go down with the respectable English. The real rulers, the Government, wanted this to continue so that privilege and property would hold its sway. The issue wasnt really a moral one at all. Edward from the position point of view, was a very exceptional fellow; the only other one I can remember well was that of Parnell, which had horrible consequences for Ireland. Edward hasnt been missed. Besides, Ed. was submissive. A party among the people to take his side was being formed—the Edward League—they even had a badge; but Ed. let them down, and went off after delivering a very sentimental talk to the people over the wireless. Kingship is used to help to keep the people quiet here, as it still is in Holland, Greece, and maybe again in Belgium, if the King comes back. That is why your Church always supports kingship. The cardinals are always near the throne, either in body or in spirit. It is an effort to keep us still in the track of the lord and the lady, the squire and his privileges. That is why so much is made of the title—

See the chapters "The Silver Tassie," "The Friggin Frogs," and "Within the Gates" in *Rose and Crown* (1952).

O'Casey meant Father Terence L. Connolly, S.J.; see O'Casey's letter to Francis MacManus, 21 March 1948, note 3.

The Plough and the Stars was also banned in Cork several years earlier; see O'Casey's letter to Robert Goldie, 10 December 1946.

Christ the KING. You may remember the quick suppression by the Hierarchy of an attempt made by Catholic workers—in the Catholic Worker, I think—of giving Jesus the title of Christ the WORKMAN. The bishops said they wouldnt allow the name of Christ to be a party one. Well, all these old things are dying, like the wigs, costly gowns, robes of State officials, though they linger on here when parliament opens, and at other state events. Democracy will create new symbols; has already done so, till the old ones are dead and forgotten. There is something ridiculous now in such things as orders of garters or orders of baths, though official, half-slavish labour leaders still take them. But these, too, are perishing.

As for your instance of the prying policeman, this, I think, is trivial. The man and the lass would have a public trial; there wouldnt be the practice of what is virtually lynch law so prevalent in Ireland, as in the case of the cleric in my play, and that of the young lass and the farmer in the letter I received from the Sligo man. The laws can be altered, but not the dicta of the church, and, very often, the worse dicta of individual clerics. Wilde brought it all down on himself. He could have got off if he had gone away for awhile, as advised by G. B. Shaw and others; but he insisted on taking an action against Queensberry, assuring his lawyers that there was no truth in what had been alleged against him; and these lawyers were stricken dumb when witness after witness proved things against Wilde. One was the corruption of young boys. I dont think Wilde was a natural homosexual; but was led into it by that evil rat, Lord A. Douglas. Mac-Liammhoir of the Gate Theatre is another, I'm told—very often trying to corrupt boys; so Denis Johnston told me, who knows him well. If any of these fellows tried this thing on with a boy of mine, I shouldnt feel very friendly about it. These things, to me, are the products of Bourgeois "civilization," and can only be banished when the present way of artificial life is ended.

I cant see how the dramatic technique of my play [5] is above your head. The shaking of the house may be symbolical of the shaking of Ireland, or of the world. Your comment about the trouserless Civic Guard is a good one. Yours may have been the better way of doing it. I wish I had thought of it when I was writing the play. But I didnt. You did. So the technique isnt above your head.

Sex: your fellow-clerks were probably boasting. To spend week-ends with lassies cost money. Lasses who do this sort of thing usually expect "a good time," and a good time costs a lot of money. Hotels, too, are damned dear now. So your brother clerks were probably boasting as clerks are prone to do about these adventurous things. As a matter of fact, those who do spend "week-ends" with women are usually silent about them; they are purely private affairs. I have no knowledge of the "philosophy of sex." Of course it is a need for all normal men and women, just as food is. Hunger and love are two instincts that cannot be resisted without danger to one's

[5] *Cock-a-Doodle Dandy.*

health. To me the normal life is the life of the family, healthy, simple, and, on the whole, enjoyable to decent people. Every effort should be made to allow this normal life to be lived. That is one reason why I am a Communist. Eating is a very important thing, so is sex; but they arent all, nor anything like all of life. Of course, when sex brings forth children, it is very important, and that is why it is such a serious thing to a decent, intelligent woman. I enjoy children. I can get on very well with them. Five minutes with a child, and the child is a friend of mine. I look upon my own children as equals, indeed, the two boys know more than I do. My wife, Eileen, is charming with children, too, and her own love her very much. We have been married now for twenty-three years, and are great companions; and it isnt every girl that I could live with—or every man either. If marriage doesnt bring companionship as well as sex, it's no marriage. We have gone through hard times often, but came through them allright. Of course, the first year or two is difficult, for life has completely changed, and if each doesnt adapt themselves to the change, sharing, and allowing for each other's different thought on different things, then there's going to be trouble. But most people live together quite decently and with proper regard for each other—the "week-enders" dont count much in life. Well, that's all I can think of to say about sex.

I dont know why you assail me with questions about Communism. In one of my earliest letters, I assured you that I had no desire to make a Communist of you, adding that you'd never make one. I was quite frank. Are you trying to make an anti-Communist of me? Mind you, though you would never be a Communist, I hold you are an upright man, liberal, broadminded, educated, kind, and courageous; all splendid qualities. What lack you, then? Nothing, but you have what will always prevent you from becoming a Communist; precisely as Lenin said, you have that bourgeois nature that "can never properly understand Communism, or Social Democracy," which is, properly—not as the bourgeois interpret it—the next step to Communism. Wolfe Tone said the same thing—"merchants make bad revolutionaries," and how often I have heard Jim Larkin say wistfully of bourgeois friends "you can never trust them." If Brogan said in his book what you allege he said, then Brogan is the meanest soul on the planet and the biggest liar God ever sanctioned with life. Question Brogan about his book: [6] anyone who writes villainous stuff about the USSR is sure of a great sale, and a great sale means a lot of money, and a lot of money means a lot of other things. The love of the loaves and the fishes is very much alive today in the hearts of many seekers after truth. Brogan has become a very prominent and well-paid man, and it isnt at all likely that he would be if he supported the USSR, instead of lying about her. Take [Louis] Budenz, one time editor of the American "Daily Worker": he became converted to R. Catholicism, joined, very bitterly the anti-Communists,

[6] Denis William Brogan, *Is Innocence Enough?: Some Reflections on Foreign Affairs* (1941).

and immediately was made a professor in a R.C. college; Douglas [A.] Hyde, one time sub-ed. of the "Daily Worker" here, became converted too, and is now a speaker all over the country with monsignors and bishops, earning what must be twenty or even fifty times what he got from Communism. The R.C. Church can be a very comfortable place to live in. I thought the USSR was only "evil," now, it appears, the USSR is stupid too. Well, its stupidity has given her extraordinary eminence among the nations. I cant see how you manage to say it would have been "all up" with C. if the Imperialists hadnt defeated Germany in 1918. It was the Russian Revolution that defeated the Germans; the spirit of revolt, the rise of the proletariat, the lessons learned by German soldiers from the Russians when they fraternised in the trenches after the truce, infected the German Army so thoroughly that they refused to keep on fighting on the Western Front. Ludendorff, their C. in Chief has not only admitted this, but has proclaimed it. He declared that he called on the civil powers to negotiate for peace, for his soldiers were preparing to leave the trenches and go home; and so peace came. The aftermath showed he was right for risings took place in part of Germany, and a Socialist Republic was proclaimed even in Catholic Bavaria. And then there were the events in Hungary, which led the European to break off peace feelers with the Soviets—though offered extraordinary terms—for they realised that the only thing to do was to crush Bolshevism once for all, everywhere; seeing that when they put barriers up between themselves and the USSR, the movement broke out behind these very barriers. The same thing happened to the French Fleet and French soldiers when tens of thousands landed in Odessa to control the Ukraine. A secret Communist Collegium was set up there, and all kinds of propaganda carried on among the French. When this was discovered, all the members of the Collegium were arrested and shot pronto; but that didnt do, for French soldier and sailor were wearing Red Rosettes, and Fleet and Army had to be hurriedly collected, steam raised, and headway made back to France. You will find all this in Chamberlin's HISTORY OF THE RUSSIAN REVOLUTION,[7] published by Macmillan's. Although he minimises the effects of the R. Rev. on the Ger. troops, subsequent events seem to show that they did; and if they were so potent in undermining the French, why wouldnt they have had a serious effect on the German troops, who must have been equally fed up with the war, and whose people were in a bad way for want of food. No country suffered so much for the past fifty years as the USSR. In the War of Intervention, the Red Guards had to fight, not only their own White Guards, but the Interventionist armies of Czechs, English, Poles, Roumanians, French, Japanese, Americans, and Italians. They were all there, aiding Kolchak coming from the East, Denikin coming from the South, Yudenitch coming from the West, and the English general, Miller, coming from the North; and the Red Guards finally routed

---

[7] William Henry Chamberlin, *The Russian Revolution* (1935), 2 vols.

out the whole damned lot of them. Churchill's intervention equipped a whole army of Red Guards, for they captured it from the army he was helping, just as the Red Army of China has been fitted out with captured American equipment. I daresay you'd call that "meanness" too on the part of the Communists. Taking advantage of their enemies! The Red Guards, during the War of Intervention sang a song that went, "Uniform, British; boots, French; bayonet, Japanese; gun, American." I wonder what you think of the atom bomb being kept secret from an Ally? Or all the new discoveries in Radar kept secret from an Ally? Isnt this the top-notch of meanness, for it meant the loss of thousands of—the secret radar devices—Russian lives. But all their little secrets are of no avail: there's nothing hidden that shall not be revealed, and the USSR has now the bomb, and, probably a better one, and Radar too, and the Jet Fighter, and, probably, a better one, too, for Socialist economy can do these things better—there are no profits to be considered. But this letter has taken on the length of a thesis. I dont want to make a Communist of you, saying this for the third and last time. I have many good and able and true friends who never can become Communists, and I am ready to let them remain what they are—some of them better even than a few Comm. I know. "As long as Communism brings bread to the people," said Lord Boyd-Orr, "Communism will be irresistible." Now, as well as bread, the Comm. bring peace, and so they are more irresistible than ever. To argue with one who cannot be a Communist is a waste of time—his time and mine—and so peace be unto you.

I enclose a review Macmillan's of New York sent me, taken from the Journal AMERICA, Jesuit-controlled (I think), which should interest you —that part I have underlined, which declares that neither Belloc nor Chesterton "claimed special knowledge or authority." Strange statement. Are they throwing them over, or what? Please let me have this review back when convenient. When you mention about "paddling your own canoe" do you mean me not to send any of your books to those I know? I have obtained another dozen, but, if you'd rather I didnt send them to anyone, of course, I'll respect your wishes.

All good wishes to you.
Yours very sincerely,
Sean O'Casey

To The Hudson Guild Players

PC. NEW YORK TIMES
12 MARCH 1950

O'CASEY REPORTS
Irish Author Discusses His Own Play

The following letter from Sean O'Casey was received by the Hudson Guild Players, currently performing in the playwright's "The Plough and the Stars."

DEVON, ENGLAND

Many thanks for your kind letter and pleasant remarks about my work. Well, it's more than hard to give any "significance" to a play written so long ago. And to relate the play to the people of New York today is beyond me. I don't know enough about the American people to do that. It is as much as a playwright can do to relate, imaginatively, with glee or pathos, his work to the life surging around him.

If it has any "significance," it is that a small number—or even one fine mind—may initiate a movement, but cannot bring it to success without the cooperation of what is called "the common people." The gallant men who rose in 1916 to strike for Ireland's independence were defeated, and what they stood for only succeeded, when, years later, the people, as a whole, swung round from opposition to support. It was so with Christianity. It is so with every movement, whether idealistic or materialistic. The mind that conceived the internal combustion engine—which has revolutionized life—couldn't have had much effect on man without the cooperation of thousands of engineers and hundreds of thousands of workers who cooperated in making its use effective, and to changing materially the way in which we live. Life depends on cooperative and collective energy.

Another point is what is called "the looting of goods" in the play. This is usually condemned as a "dastardly insult to the unselfish men who were risking all for Ireland." I don't look at it this way. When they got a chance, they "illegally" seized the brighter goods of life which, with all others, they, too, had the right to have. Here people were usually called "the rats of the slums"; but I, who lived among them for so long, knew they had their own intelligence; they had courage, humor, and, very often, a great zest for life.

Some were irresponsible, but irresponsible persons are just as numerous among the well-to-do. Today, they are nearer to the life they have the right to live; for we are marching toward the realization—in spite of atom or hydrogen bomb—of a government of the people, by the people, for the people.

Sean O'Casey

To Horace Reynolds

MS. REYNOLDS

TOTNES, DEVON

15 MARCH 1950

Dear Horace.

Thanks very much for the Reviews. They were fine. You hit it off—I think—when you compared the play to a folk-tale or fairy story.[1] It was meant as a fantasy, brought into the living world. Seanaar simply means Sean Fear—old man. Marthraun means a crippled or disabled body— evidently derived from martyr. "Ni martradh go daille" = "blindness is the worst martyrdom," actually "no martyrdom till blindness" quite a common phrase in English-Irish—"He's a marthyr to this or that." The Cock has nothing to do with Communism. It symbolises, if anything, the life-force, the sex-call, the "desire of man for a woman & the desire of woman for the desire of man," as Yeats said once or twice. There's but one sin recog- nised in Ireland & in R. Catholic England, & possibly R.C. America—bar the sin of opposing state grant to schools: witness Spellman's yelp at Mrs Rooseveldt "You're an unworthy American mother!"—& that is the sin of sex. Although the play's a "fairy-tale," all the main things are facts, even to the priest advising the father to "get that one off to America," for she was possessed, which the father did, according to the story. There was a yelping protest about the play in "The Irish Times," & objectors were stunned when I wrote in to say that the account of this wasn't really mine, but had appeared in De.Valera's daily "The Irish Press"; but the story was in Gaelic, & no-one, evidently, read it bar myself! I got a letter afterwards from a Sligo man who said a young girl kept house for a farmer in Sligo. The priest denounced the fact, alleging they must be living in sin. The parents of the girl protested, alleging the girl was good, & there was no immoral significance in the business; & no sign of anything bad could be produced. The priest denounced again from the altar. One night, men broke into the house, beat up the farmer & the girl, dragged her out in her night-gown, & padlocked her to a telegraph post, where she was found half- dead the next morning by a passing postman. The case is on the records of the Sligo police; the attackers were known, but no prosecution took place, for fear it would embarrass the clergy. Ireland's in the throes of a sex-mania & a transport of pietistic frenzy. They decorate Christmas trees (I hear) now with rosary beads.

[1] Horace Reynolds, *New York Times,* 19 February 1950, a review of *Cock-a- Doodle Dandy* (1949).

Price [2] sent me a copy of his work, which will be very useful. I have written to thank him for it. Give my love to the little girl who had the courage to read my play seven times. She mustn't read it again for ten years and a day. AE stands or falls by his work—painter & poet & novelist—, &, to me, he falls prostrate. A bad poet, a worse painter, & the worst novelist ever born who claimed greatness. Who reads "The Interpreters" or "The Avatars" [3] now? Who could read them? I fought him over Cezanne & Picasso in 1927 or 1929 till he suppressed my replies to his, which I had to get published in "The Republic," [4] then edited by Frank Ryan, who afterwards perished fighting Franco. I carried the dispute even to the N.Y. Times,[5] of that date, where a column & a half—letter of mine reposes still. He soon left off "fighting" for the workers. Economist! Horace Plunkett took him out of Pim's,[6] where he was a clerk, & sent him into the job of the grand nabob of the Irish Agricultural Organization movement; though before, or after, he never planted even a cabbage or an onion in his life.

I'm so glad that Peggy has a child. She must take care of herself now for a while. Child-birth is a hard time for a girl; & the first birth especially so. She, Kay, & you will be busy all over again in the joyous task of a renewal of life—man goes on into the future. Give Peggy my love with a kiss. And John's to be married too! It seems but yesterday that I saw John & Peggy coming in on the door of 322, in their woolens, home from school. And, anyway, it doesn't seem, it is yesterday. Give John my love, too. My love to Kay, to Peggy and her Art, to Art the younger, to John—may sweet Genevieve be most of what he wishes her to be; not all, though—she must keep some of herself to herself—, & to you.

Yours as ever,
Sean

2 See O'Casey's letter to Howard Price, 22 November 1949.
3 AE (George Russell), *The Interpreters* (1922), *The Avatars* (1933).
4 See O'Casey's letter, "Complicated Controversy," *An Phoblacht (The Republic)*, 18 January 1930, Vol I, pp. 393–94.
5 See O'Casey's letter, "Sean O'Casey and George Russell," *New York Times*, 20 March 1930, Vol. I, pp. 395–97.
6 A Dublin department store.

To Miss J. Franklin [1]

TC. O'CASEY

[TOTNES, DEVON]

17 MARCH 1950

Dear Miss Franklin,

Thank you for your letter. I am, as you can see, still in England, and have been here, now, for twenty-four years. No, I havent been disappointed. I have been in Devon for twelve years, and find the Devon people, and the West Country, charming and lovable. Dublin wouldnt be a foreign city to you at all, unless you ventured to speak Gaelic—then most of the people wouldnt know what you were talking about, which is a pity, but a fact. The Roman Catholic Hierarchy here arent much different from their brethren over there. One sack, one sample. I dont believe any Irish Bishop (or any Eng. Bishop) laughed at INISFALLEN FARE THEE WELL. I daresay the book is banned in Ireland, like most of the rest of mine; [2] I dont know, and I dont much care. If the R.C. Hierarchy here had the power, they'd ban it, too.

You won't be able to get Dr. McDonald's book [3] in any library I know of; it may be in the National Library; and it may be found in an odd corner in some of the R.C. College libraries. One copy was ferreted out by a priest from Fordham University library in the U.S.A. It was out of print shortly after publication, possibly brought up, and destroyed for obvious reasons. Or, maybe, no one was interested in it. I have never met a priest yet, and I've met many, who had read it. One I know, and who writes to me (I have never met him) has read it, and he, too, doesnt know, I believe, of any priest who read it either. It was published by Jonathan Cape, 30 Bedford Square, London, in 1925. I cant say why Irishmen as a whole are not interested in reading—bar the newspapers. Probably, because they get no opportunity, or few, at any rate. The English people, if they do read, mostly read rubbish. I have read most of the R.C. Press—*The Month, The Tablet,* and even *The Colosseum*—a magazine which I used to get, but which, I think, is no longer published; as well, of course, as the popular R.C. Press. I dont think the *Catholic Herald* is a bit better than the others. Its layout—I'm looking at a copy now—is on a par with the *Daily Express;* and its articles are devoid of depth, and full of hesitation; besides being a paper, like the rest, which on many occasions has refused permission for a

---

[1] Miss J. Franklin, 30 Gordon Road, Wanstead, London E.11.

[2] At this time only one of O'Casey's books, *Windfalls* (1934) was still banned by the Irish Censorship of Publications Board. The "prohibition" against *I Knock at the Door* (1939) and *Pictures in the Hallway* (1942) was removed on 16 December 1947. However, there probably was an unofficial censorship of his works in some bookshops and libraries in Ireland.

[3] Dr. Walter McDonald, *Reminiscences of a Maynooth Professor* (1925).

person, criticised in its columns, to reply. However, I dont rely on what I think about them myself. I quote in my book what Father Yorke D.D. thought of them, and of what Dr. McDonald thought too. Presently, I have further confirmation in the booklet written by Father J. V. Simcox, for 23 years Professor of Canon Law in St. Edmund's Seminary, Ware. And from Newman who said "Unless one distorts all one's facts one will not be considered a good Catholic." And Lord Acton (the finest historian the R.C. Church has had maybe for centuries), on the probable result of the doctrine of Infallibility, "Catholics will at once become irreconcilable enemies of civil and religious liberty. They will have to profess a false system of morality, and to repudiate literary and scientific sincerity. They will be as dangerous to civilised society in the school as in the State." He wasnt far out. I could quote a lot more, but I really havent time, for I have a lot of work to do. I return your good wishes tenfold.

Yours very sincerely,
Sean O'Casey

To Alan Denson [1]

TC. O'CASEY

[TOTNES, DEVON]
18 MARCH 1950

Dear Mr. Denson:

You havent answered my question frankly, you know. Youve gone around it, leaving what is in your mind where it is. What you really meant to say was "Had you the guts and the courage to say about A.E., when he was alive, what you have said about him after he was dead." But how would that affect the facts contained in my chapter about him in my last book? [2] The facts there would still be facts; i.e. that he was no poet worth considering seriously, or a painter either; or an economist; or a sage; or anything else you like. I know that he "recorded me due praise for my literary attainments," but would you want me to take this recording as a bribe to say the same of him, when I couldnt believe it? Besides, my opinion of the man left his praise of me cold; I didnt value it in any way. Something like what you say of A.E. was said of a poor dramatist to Nathan, the famous American critic, who replied "The fact that Winter is

[1] Alan Denson, author and bibliographer; he later edited *Letters From AE* (1961).
[2] "Dublin's Glittering Guy," *Inishfallen, Fare Thee Well* (1949).

dead doesnt increase my respect for him in the slightest degree." If you think it was kindness on his part to sit for drawing, painting, and sculpture of himself, then go on thinking it. He was very kind to "young poets" too, and tried to get them published—provided they dedicated their verses to him. Perhaps you may remember what Yeats said of his effort to get Yeats to praise them too—"Later Poems" Macmillan, 1922. Here it is:—

> You say, as I have often given tongue
> In praise of what another's said or sung,
> 'Twere politic to do the like by these;
> But was there ever dog that praised his fleas?

The man set himself up, not only as a critic, but as an authority on art and literature—to mention but two things out of ten; whereas the fact was, he didnt know anything about painting, and, according to Yeats's criticism, above, knew as little about poetry either. You yourself allow this when you say "Your representation may be accepted by many folk wholly ignorant of his character (as recorded in his poetry)." Anyone *wanting* to know about him, would read his poetry, so you, by implication, declare that no-body (or many) will not do so, and so are indifferent to what he was or what he did. He is, in other words, a back number. My facts are undeniable; my opinions, of course, may be wrong, for I do not claim the infallibility that once surrounded A.E., and which, I did a lot to banish. Now for your question, namely, "Did you ever voice your opinions of A.E., prior to his death in July, 1935?" The answer is Yessir, and voiced them very publicly too. In his own Journal, the "Irish Statesman and Nation," and went on voicing them till he himself suppressed them; then the letter he refused to publish appeared in the Dublin Journal "An Poblacht" The Republic, round 1929 or 1930;[3] and letters of mine appear in A.E.'s own paper Nov. 1929 and Dec. 1929.[4] Here is a heading from EVENING POST, New York, 5th Feb. 1930—O'Casey-Russell Debate Enlivens Irish Art Circles . . . Controversy Marked by Strong Expressions. There was also a long letter from me in The New York Times sometime around this controversy.[5] I have no time to look all these things up. These examples will show, I hope, that I could face a live lion as well as "spit" on a dead one. But surely you should be aware of this, and of the controversy I had with W. B. Yeats—a far far greater lion and a far more dangerous one than A.E.—around the same time. These disputes did me a lot of harm—I knew they would—for a long time, for Yeats, and, in a minor way, A.E. had great influence in the literary world of England and America; and I was a beginner, one, too, who had no influence whatever behind him, except his

[3] See O'Casey's letter to Horace Reynolds, 15 March 1950, note 4.
[4] See O'Casey's letters to the *Irish Statesman,* 30 November, 14 December, 20 December, 1929; 3 January, 7 January, 10 January, 1930; also Russell to O'Casey, 6 January 1930—all in Vol. I.
[5] See O'Casey's letter to Horace Reynolds, 15 March 1950, note 5.

own vitality and integrity. Yeats has that influence still—and fully deserves it; but the influence of A.E. is going fast, if it's not already gone.

Now, friend, that is all I can do for you, for I am far away from these things now, and engaged in work which, to me, is more important than any controversy.

Yours sincerely,
Sean O'Casey

To Seumas Scully

MS. SCULLY

TOTNES, DEVON
23 MARCH 1950

Dear Seumas.

Thanks for the clippings. Who is "D. H."? the learned one who reviews Miss McArdle's "Children of Europe." [1] He seems to convince himself that the case against Hitlerian Germany wasn't so bad as represented by Miss McArdle. He cries out for documentation of every sentence. He even questions the evidence given at Nuremberg. But he doesn't need any little date or document to accept the terrible things done—as he says—by the USSR. They're making now the atom-bomb, too. Well, that's a fact anyhow, & explains why the Vatican is so eager to have it banned—the Reds might drop it on curious places. It's a pity D. McArdle wasn't born in the USSR. She's a very talented woman, & deserves a high place in the activities of a nation; but it is hardly to be got in De Valera's or Costello's Eire.

You will, I'm sure, realise, that it would be conceited impudence for me to try to butt in—even by letter—on the Debate "The Critic's Menace to Art." Were I there, among the audience, well & good; but here—to do it would just be damned cheek. I hope it may be a great success.

All the best to you.
Yours sincerely.
Sean

[1] Dorothy MacArdle's *The Children of Europe* (1950), reviewed in "Child Victims of the War," *Irish Press,* 19 January 1950, by "D. H." (David Hogan).

To Francis MacManus

TS. MacManus

Totnes, Devon

25 March 1950

Dear Frank,

I've read your book,[1] & think well of it—for all the good that will do you. It's the best you've done, so far—comparing it in thought with what I've read of yours before. But it could be better, as, indeed, could my own work too. I've written to Kingsley Martin, Ed. of New Statesman, but got no reply. He asked me for an article about the "Theatre of Ideas,"[2] & I took the opportunity of telling him about your book. I've got the proofs of my article, but no letter with them. However, I'm sure he'll remember my request that your book should be given a notice. There's a rule, I think, that no book gets a notice (except a very special one), unless an ad. about the book appears in the journal—all journals, I think, have this unwritten rule. I'm not sure about this, but the guess is a good one. I havent seen your book advertised yet; nor have I seen a notice. Of course, it doesn't follow that all advertised books get notices. I guess your book may be compared with Mauriac, who seems to have influenced you. Another guess! However, we can but wait. The profession of writing is one of waiting for disappointment. Just now a grand scheme of touring a play of mine along the West Coast of the U.S.A. has fallen through, fallen through, fallen through.

Well, we fall to rise again, & lose now today to win tomorrow. Sursum corda. I do hope your book will go fairly well.

Yours as ever,
Sean

[1] *The Fire in the Dust* (1950).
[2] Sean O'Casey, "The Play of Ideas," *New Statesman and Nation,* 8 April 1950; reprinted in *Blasts and Benedictions* (1967).

To Frank McCarthy

MS. McCarthy

Totnes, Devon

27 March 1950.

Dear Frank,

Glad to hear you're allright—last I heard of you, you were in the grip of a cold. Meself, too, had a bad time since—went down with in-

fluenza; got up & went about too soon; went down again, deeper than before. Nearly OK. now.

I've no photograph of meself alone; but could give you a "glossy" of
me talking to Breon—our elder boy as he was before he joined up in the
Artillery—National Service unit. Will this do?

I know Con O'Leary [1] well. A great scout, but childlike; almost innocent; great talents that others knew how, and still know, how to use. For
years he was sub-ed. of "T.P.'s Weekly," really Editor. Drinks far too
much. Years ago, I used all my eloquence with him to give it up, & concentrate on himself, using his talents for his own glory; he listened allright,
& agreed; but Con is too confiding, too childlike to look after himself. He
needed a good wife to hold him in check. The Irish are too fond of keeping together; better if they scattered, & got to know the English thoroughly.

Glad you are so comfortably placed. Its far better & healthier than
Limehouse. The boss isn't running it at a loss. Think what he gets from
lay off—taxation! Productive property—adding to our food supplies—gets
all the costs, your wage & Hans' wage as well, off his Income Tax return;
& so, instead of a loss, there's a decided profit. It's the Authors who really
suffer (and artists). They're not allowed to spread their incomes. If they
made 10,000 this year, & nix for the next five, they can't spread it over the
6 years, but must pay on the 10,000 as a one year's income. Proportion-
ately they pay more tax than anyone else. The business-man can always
wangle.

All the best to you.

Sean.

[1] Con O'Leary (c. 1890–   ), playwright, novelist, journalist; had several plays
produced at the Abbey Theatre, including *The Crossing* (1914), *Queer Ones* (1919).

To George Jean Nathan

MS. CORNELL

TOTNES, DEVON

31 MARCH 1950

My very dear George:
A letter from Dick [Madden] received just now tells me you are not
too fit. I am very sorry I sent you the one-act plays; I hesitated about
sending them, but—from your last letter—thought you were better. Please
don't bother about them at all. Just keep as quiet as you can, and take
good care of yourself. I hope you do try to look after yourself. Don't reply

to this; don't write anything till you feel fit again; & don't bother in any way about the one-acters, or any play of mine, or anyone else's, till you are allright again.

My love to you.
Sean

To Dr. John V. Simcox

TC. O'CASEY

[TOTNES, DEVON]
[? APRIL 1950]

Dear Dr. Simcox:

I find that I have three of your letters to answer. Brogan's book [1] value may be gauged or guaged by his reference to Chiang K. Shek—then, of course, this ruffian was on a high horse, backed by the wealth of the U.S.A., and busy driving the Red Army before him with splendidly equipped forces. That was grand for Brogan, who, possibly, might like to forget what he has written about him. Even Gen Stillwell was recalled for telling everyone the kind of a galoot Kiang Shek was—"the peanut" as he called him. Well, Stillwell happened to be right, and now the U.S.A. and Britain don't know how to get rid of him. Brogan is simply a commercial journalist, watching to see what way the cat'll jump.

"America's" review of Inisfallen: [2] I have, I think, many friends in the U.S.A., but not on or near "America." I could hardly expect it. It seems, though, that they are beginning to see that Belloc and Chesterton are waning. Time was in the Universities, that these men were considered top-hole; hundreds quoting them with enthusiasm. But the young of today are passing away from them; have passed away as the young in Eirinn have passed away from A.E. And so R. Catholic authority, wily boyos, are saying that these chaps really dont represent R.C. thought; they are but popular tassels on a wide-world banner. So it seems to me.

Yes, of course, I agree that there's a lot of silly furtiveness here still about sex. Just before the war, at the Anglican Lambeth Conference, a resolution was proposed—and passed, if I remember right—that contraceptives should be given out only by the Rectors of parishes, after examination of those who asked for them! It was the subject for laughter for a long time. But it was a subject for laughter, not as it would be in Ireland.

---

[1] Denis Walter Brogan, *Is Innocence Enough?* (1941).
[2] Walter O'Hearn, "Sean O'Casey, Fare Thee Well," *America,* 11 June 1949.

There is still a "morality" movement in England; but here, at least, we are subject only to the law of the land; and law that can be altered by the people. There is nothing "wrong" about your "Bourgeois" nature, except that it cannot enter into full intimacy with the life and outlook of the proletariat. It is usually hesitant in a crisis, as it was in Russia during the Revolution—that is as a whole; not always so in the case of individual leaders. Lenin, himself, came of a semi-bourgeois family; but Lenin was a rare kind of a man. So was Marx. We, the proletariat, owe an immense lot to the Bourgeoise in science, art, literature, and economics. It is only in the actual battle, the clash of force against force, that the bourgeois are usually untrustworthy because they have something to lose, whereas the Prol. have nothing to lose, and a lot to gain. You, of course, have nothing to lose now; but your habits, your thought, the whole course of your life have been middle-class, and one cant get away from a life-time of thought and habit. You waste your time writing to Douglas [A.] Hyde—like many another, he has followed those who have the loaves and the fishes. He wont answer you. He cant, of course; but he wont even try. Of course my critic in "America" would say that I have "an anti-Catholic obsession," but, as far as I know, I have never in book or play, criticised any Catholic dogma; nor do I wish to, for I'm no controversialist, and keep away from the theory, though I do know a little about it. Indeed, more than Chesterton knew, and, indeed, I dont believe that either his or Belloc's Catholicity went down very deep, as compared, say with that of Newman, or Dr. McDonald. Indeed, I believe, that it is only the Communists who will eventually see that all persons will be allowed perfect religious freedom—to hold any opinion they like and to try to bring their children up in the faith they conscientiously hold. But no "faith" will be permitted to use that "faith" for any other purpose than their own spiritual needs; they will not be allowed to use it to lay up treasures on earth where thieves might break through and steal, and where moth and rust doth corrupt; they will not be allowed to use it to exploit a brother or a sister. They will not be allowed to use it so as to honour Mammon by calling Mammon God.

I received the Review of Inishfallen—from Macmillan's just as I sent it to you. They collect reviews of the books they publish, and send them on to the authors; the one I sent you was one of many. I sent it to you because I guessed you'd be interested. [Paul] Blanshard wrote only as the Catholic interests and authority concerned America. The prominent secular Press refused to review it. Some of them even refused to accept an advertisement announcing it. All going to prove the truth of the statements in the book itself. However it has had, so far, a sale of near a 100,000 copies.

I got your letter to the Cardinal [Griffin] allright. Of course, it would be hard to get it published anywhere. There are so many questions to be answered now, everywhere. And you dont seem to realise the dilemma of politics—those in the West must (and do) use everything they can lay hands on to oppose the East, and one of the things is the R.C. Church.

Even at home, from a party point of view, if any of the parties thought the R.C. vote would return them to power, they'd give to the R.C. schools all that was asked for them—Liberal, Tory, or Labour; but not the Communists. But each party knows the people would oppose, and so they darent agree; but they waver and equivocate so as to get the R.C. vote if at all possible. Have you tried The Irish Ecclesiastical Gazette—organ of the Prot. C. of Ireland? But, since they receive money from the I. Government for *their* schools, they would jib at publication too. You see how economics work? Truth is left standing. I'd like to keep a copy. May I get a copy typed? I will register it, but there's always a possible risk of a loss, but a small one; but I wouldnt risk even that without your consent.

> *All the best to you.*
> *Yours very sincerely,*
> *Sean O'Casey*

To Howard Fast [1]

TC. O'CASEY

[TOTNES, DEVON]
3 APRIL 1950

My dear Howard Fast:

A short letter in reply to your own. I have to limit my activity in writing now as much as I can because of the state of my eyes. It is an irritation, but as it isnt my fault, I dont fret about it. Every land has its own peculiar loveliness and distinct grandeur, but few of them are as happy as they might be, as they could be, or, as I believe, they will be. I love New York and will never forget my stay in it a good many years ago; neither shall I forget the Hills of Pennsylvania, and many other places I saw when I was in the U.S.A.

I have just read your LITERATURE AND REALITY [1950], and I think it the most reasonable, the clearest, and by far the best essay on that subject which has ever come my way. A good many have come my way, full of "Marxian" fervour, but, to me, destitute of common sense. Even some of the Soviet criticisms have erred in this way. We must be careful of whom we praise, and equally careful of whom we condemn, lest we become as bad as our enemies. I agree with ninety-five, and more, of what you say in your essay. I think that Mauriac and Graham Greene

[1] Howard Fast (1914–), author of popular historical novels and well-known American Communist; later resigned from the Communist Party.

should be let go their own way, for what they write seems, to me, to show what a terrible effect the R. Catholic religion has upon many of those who take it seriously. Out of their own mouths we can condemn them. I dont quite agree about T. S. Eliot. He is a poet just as Picasso is a painter, though we may not like his moods at times. But as you point out the death and decay in such a lot of modern literature is horrible. In Sunday's paper a book is reviewed (American) in which the author's "half-witted Aaron sets out for a walk down the dirt road—the scene is semi-rural U.S.A.— with a pair of garden shears, steals a car, gives a ride to two little girls, outrages and mutilates them, is hunted, tracked down, and blithely confesses." Well, give me the simplest Soviet story of riotous emulation in preference to that sort of thing; for, it isnt life even at its worst. It is significant that the boisterous Catholic laughter of Chesterton is giving way to Mauriac's desperation, and even Spellman can do nothing about it. The R.C. Church is dividing against itself. Even here, I am corresponding with a Dr. of Canon Law who was Professor in the largest R.C. College in Eng. for twenty-three years. Because of the deliberate deception of the Hierarchy in their claims for grants for their schools, he resigned the Professorship, abandoned the priesthood, and is earning, in his old age, a precarious living in the world. A brave man.

My sympathy with you all in the danger that faces you. Maybe it wont be so bad as we imagine. The peoples are waking up at last. [Alexander] Bloc put Jesus at the head of the Red Guard. He is wearing a Chinese blouse now. We have a host of great men with us, and clouds of great witnesses chant the song of the people. When I venture to look back at what I went through, I wonder how I came out of it alive . . .[2]

[2] Page missing.

To Frank McCarthy

MS. McCarthy

Totnes, Devon

20 April 1950

Dear Frank,

Thanks ever so much for the eggs. Only a few were cracked & our younger lad made an omelette of these. I've been very busy—& am still— with the Peace Movement, & various activities of writing—hardly had time to eat one of your eggs. Try as I do, the letters I get keep piling up, & I don't know when they'll be answered. Of course, each of us is part of the

crowd—Jew & Gentile, bond and free. The day of the Marquis & the Viscount is over. We're all naked, & the M. & the V. look very much like the
other fellows—only less hardy. They always did, but the red velvets &
ermine made the buggers look more elegant. There's been another Row in
the Abbey over a play called "Design for a Headstone." [1] A mad religious
patch of persons & a bunch of old I.R.A. yelled & protested. Some tried
to pull the clothes off the author in the Foyer, the C.Guards came, & there
was a fine old packing match. I haven't read about it, but a letter from
Dublin tells me of it. "Thou art not conquered yet, Dear Lance." Thanks,
too, for the booklet about Southwell. And the Photo. All the best to you,
me boy.

Sean

[1] Seamus Byrne's *Design For a Headstone,* opened at the Abbey Theatre on
8 April 1950. Six nights later, a group of protesters in the audience tried to cause a
riot by objecting to the play as anti-Catholic and anti-Irish.

To Margo Jones [1]

MS. TEXAS

TOTNES, DEVON

25 APRIL 1950

Dear Miss Margo Jones,

It's a long way from here to Texas—longer than the way to Tipperary; but, all the same, a word from you can reach me, &, I hope, a
word from me can reach you too. I thank you very much for your kind
words about the book, "Inishfallen, Fare Thee Well"; & for your great interest in the play, "Cockadoodle Dandy." [2]

It was right good to read the pleasant things you said about both the
book and the play.

I hope your gallant little theatre will live long, & bless many good
work in production during the years to come.

With thanks again, & all good wishes.

Yours very sincerely,
Sean O'Casey

PS. Couldn't reply earlier—got Influenza; got up & went about too soon;
was laid flat again. Better, a lot, now. *S. O'C.*

[1] Margo Jones (1913–55), director of the Arena Theatre, Dallas, Texas.
[2] See O'Casey's letter to George Jean Nathan, 27 December 1949, note 1.

To George Jean Nathan

MS. CORNELL

TOTNES, DEVON

25 APRIL 1950

My very dear George:

I hope the sunny weather may come quick for both our sakes. As I write here, a bitter wind blows, & snow & sleet take turns in falling—with all the apple-blossoms out everywhere! I'm not, physically, in "good trim." Eyes, an ear, & a chest give a lot of trouble, & quite a bit of pain. But one has to stick it, & go on.

I'm very glad you liked the one-act plays. Hurrah for the U.S.A. There's not a single indication here of any interest whatever in my plays. They're never mentioned, & the biographical books aren't near the British heart either. So the U.S.A., if they don't put them on, talk about them; and keep the house & home going; &, be God, that's a lot, if you ask me.

I and Breon will look forward to getting your next book. Brooks Atkinson has given me a big hand-up too. He should live a long time. May we all live a long time. I'm only beginning to realise what a fine thing life is. A bit late, but not too late—I hope.

I do trust you will soon be yourself again, George. May God be wi' you.

My love as ever.
Sean

To Jack Lindsay

TC. O'CASEY

[TOTNES, DEVON]

30 APRIL 1950

Dear Jack Lindsay:

I'm not inclined to let myself be entangled in an argument with Mr. [J. B.] Priestley. To me, it is perfectly natural that he has said what he said, and acted as he has done. He was never with us. He isn't now. The Soviet Hospitallers, lay and literary, are, apparently, very childlike. They dont seem to be able to gauge the character of many who visit them. They make a bitter attack on T. S. Eliot and plaster Priestley with praise when he was trumpeting out of him praise of the USSR, which, I verily believe, he never felt. Priestley is a very clever fellow, very plausible, very conventional, and very cautious. He is, too, in my opinion, plump with conceit of himself. So, Ephraim is joined to idols—let him alone. Ehrenburg made a mistake in challenging him in an effort, I suppose, to win him back again. And you and Montagu [Slater] would, apparently, do the same. What use would Priestley be since he is so variable? Months and months ago, writing to Mr. Apletin,[1] Chairman of USSR Commission of Foreign Writers, I warned him (he had sent me a letter, a long one, denouncing Eliot and Gide) that he would have Priestley with the warring ones soon. Apletin upbraided Eliot because Eliot had declared himself "a royalist, a conservative, and an Anglican." So he did, and remains an honest and forthright opponent. And he is a poet as well. To us he is no more than an enemy. He isnt an unreliable friend as Gide and Koestler proved to be. Mr. Priestley's style will, I fear, be cramped by the articles he wrote in—I think— THE DAILY EXPRESS; but we all make mistakes at times. Of course, I am commenting on Mr. Priestley only from the political point of view. Mr. Priestley isnt, apparently, able to see that in an effort to destroy Communism, he may also succeed in destroying himself. There is no such thing as a conservative or Communistic atom bomb. The bomb is no respecter of persons.

> *With all good wishes to you*
> *and Montagu.*
> *Yours sincerely,*
> *Sean O'Casey*

P.S. Your last book was a very fine one.[2]

[1] See O'Casey's letter to Mikhail Apletin, 10 February 1950.
[2] Jack Lindsay, *Song of a Falling World: Culture During the Break-up of the Roman Empire, A.D. 350–600.* (1949).

To Patrick F. Byrne [1]

TS. BYRNE

TOTNES, DEVON
[? MAY 1950]

Dear Patrick Byrne,
    Thank you very much for your letter and enclosure, and for your review of the performance of "Juno" by the C.I.E. Dramatic Society. If you

[1] Patrick F. Byrne, *Radio Review* (Dublin).

are right about Tommy McDonald, then, he should be among the Abbey Players—unless his performance was no more than a strict imitation of Barry Fitzgerald's. Why doesn't he join them as a part-timer?

I see yous have been doing in anyone who ventures to mention the word "Peace" in the streets of Dublin; no clergyman raises a voice against violence. Well, if a war does come, and Ireland's in it, farewell to Shaw's Dublin, Joyce's Dublin, and O'Casey's Dublin, too: It won't even leave a blot behind it.

Thanks again, and all good wishes to you,

Yours sincerely
Sean O'Casey

P.S. Considering what's given over Radio Eireann by the Sponsored Programme, maybe it would be just as well.

To Daniel Macmillan

MS. MACMILLAN LONDON

TOTNES, DEVON
9 MAY 1950

Dear Mr. Daniel.

Sorry I forgot to enclose Mr. Robinson's letter. Absent-minded old age is descending on top of me. A letter I got yesterday from Bernard Shaw says his "legs are a bit untrustworthy, but his head's as clear as ever." My legs are trustworthy still, but the head's not so clear as it used to be. However, I enclose the letter to you now.

I've sent on "Red Roses" to you under another cover.

But please don't bother a lot about the photograph. If it isn't by your elbow, never mind it. I'm not anxious to have my dial staring out of any Irish history.

All the best.
Sean O'Casey

To Joseph Tomelty [1]

TC. O'CASEY

[TOTNES, DEVON]

13 MAY 1950

Dear Mr. Tomelty:

I remember you well and have read several items about you and your work, including a talk you had with St. John Ervine.

Regarding your inquiry, what you ask depends upon your Company's status: if it be an Amateur one, then you must get a licence from French, Ltd., 26 Southampton Street, Strand, London, W.C.2, who own the rights (amateur). Twenty years ago, I had to let them go for a limited sum to this Firm.[2] If, on the other hand, you are professional, then I can deal with you. In the case of French's, the fee would be £3.3.0. for each performance; in the second case it will be ten per cent (10%) on the gross weekly receipts. Or, if more satisfactory to you, the sliding scale of the Abbey, say 7½% up to £40 nightly, and 10% if the receipts go over this amount.

All good wishes to you, and Belfast.

Yours sincerely,
[Sean O'Casey]

[1] Joseph Tomelty (1911–), playwright and actor, Ulster Group Theatre, Belfast.
[2] See O'Casey's letter to George Jean Nathan, 28 September 1932, note 2, Vol. I, p. 449.

To D. M. Doyle [1]

TC. O'CASEY

[TOTNES, DEVON]

15 MAY 1950

Dear Mr. Doyle:

I remember Donnchadh Doyle, Councillor of the Drumcondra Ward, well. I remember how sleek you always looked in your well-cut suit, your natty, rigid bowler hat, your tightly-rolled umbrella, a most respectable

[1] D. M. Doyle, Baile Mhic Siomoin, Gleana Faidhle, Co. Cille Manntain (Wicklow), Eire. For further comments on Doyle, see O'Casey's letter to John Hutchinson, 21 September 1953.

curtain of silky nap separating you from those of us who gathered together
to learn Irish and dance a little in the slum quarters of Seary's Lane. I remember you asking my advice as to what choice you should make in selecting either the woman with whom you had kept company for years, but
who was plain and unattractive, or the good-looking, and dashing (the
term you used) younger lass you had got to know and desire at a later
date. I'm sure you selected the "dashing" lass, and, in some way, quieted
your conscience about the girl you abandoned. I dont blame you; I'd have
done the same myself. I remember how you were careful to keep away
from the tumble-down shack in Seary's Lane as much as possible, just putting your nose inside the door once or twice a year, and then keeping close
to the door so that the cautious nose of yours wouldnt take in too much
of the foul air of the room. You were careful, always very careful, to take
no risks. You had a good job, and you kept it: you were a wise man, a
worldly-wise man. Now, at 75, you have a very pleasant time of it in a
"small farmhouse with 50 acres," with a fine view from the windows. God
has guarded you well. You should be satisfied, and refrain from denouncing those whom you cant understand, and who are incautious enough to
go on fighting for those thousands who can "never hope to break the
bonds holding them in misery." Marx once said, "You have nothing to
lose but your chains, you have a world to gain." You see—or you dont
see—that these miserable ones are breaking their bonds. They have broken
them in the USSR, in the Eastern Democracies, in China, and they will
break them in Cochin-China and in the Malay States too. And, maybe,
for all you say, they will break them even in Eirinn. You dont really understand the first thing about Communism, and it would be a waste of my
time to argue with you about it. Even were I living next door to you, I'd
not spend a minute on this question with you, for you'd be one of the last
I'd try to convince towards Communism: you'd be no damned use to us.
You would do well to go on thinking cautiously on the "Aiseirghe" group,[2]
and give them, now and again, a faint hand-clap from a safe distance. Go
on thinking me an "insufferable cod": it will do you good, and me no
harm. Go on thinking that "the English take to me": it will do you good,
and me no harm. As for The Church, when youve answered, or tried to
answer, the questions put, not by O'Casey, but by a man, a priest, who
was for 40 years Professor of Theology in Maynooth College, you'll be
more interesting to me. But you take good care to shy quick away from
what he said. Perhaps, you'd like to read "Is the Roman Catholic Church
a Secret Society?" written by Dr. Simcox, Professor of Canon Law for 25
years in England's biggest R.C. Seminary—St. Edmund's. who resigned his
Professorship and abandoned his priesthood because of the lying statements made by Cardinals, Bishops, and Apologists of his own Church—
and yours. This ex-Professor of Canon Law is now earning a precarious

---

[2] *Aiséirghé* (Resurrection), a militant nationalist organization with right-wing
tendencies.

living in the world in London. And he states facts. I have here with me a long letter he sent to Cardinal Griffin which I am having typed out into a number of copies; a letter that has never been answered, because it cannot be answered—even by your own *Standard*.[3] I really dont know what you mean by "The Reformed Church." There are so many churches knocking about now, each as good and as bad and as full of dope for the workers as the others; but, from the dope point of view, their days are numbered. Even Excommunication works no longer. There are 5 million Communists in the Pope's own country; and they are all Catholics.

By the way, I didnt say that Lady Gregory "stammered." Nor did I imply it either. I said she had a "lisp," a very different thing.[4] You shouldnt, you know, bear false witness.

And now, my friend, I'm sure you will understand that I am a very busy man. I have a lot of work to do, and more than one letter to write. So farewell to Inishfallen and to you.

Yours sincerely,
Sean O'Casey.

P.S.   If you be such a lover of things Irish, why didnt you write in Gaelic? Is it that you havent learned it over all these years?

[3] *The Standard,* the ultra-Catholic weekly newspaper published in Dublin.
[4] See the account of O'Casey's trip to Gort to meet Lady Gregory, "Blessed Bridget O'Coole," *Inishfallen, Fare Thee Well* (1949).

To Vladimir Phillipov [1]

TC. O'CASEY

TOTNES, DEVON
17 MAY 1950

Dear Vladimir Phillipov:
I am afraid I cannot do much for you. Here are a few details: I was born in Dublin, 1880, Ireland. Father died when I was six years of age. Hunger over the years brought about disease of the eyes which still is with me. Never went to school. At the age of fourteen or fifteen, began to teach myself how to read and write from books left behind by my father who was passionately fond of knowledge, and tried all his life to learn things. He was an educated man, thanks to his own efforts. Mother a great woman, loving,

[1] Vladimir Phillipov, 44 Emil Markov, Sofia 12, Bulgaria, a student at the University of Sofia, studying English literature and writing a thesis on the plays of O'Casey.

patient, and sensible. Went to work at fourteen years of age: Worked from eight in morning till seven at night for three shillings a week. When older, became a railway labourer, builder's labourer, and general labourer, working at anything I could get to do. Bought a number of books cheap, which were cast-outs, for twopence, fourpence, and, at times, sixpence—a great expenditure, this sixpence. Books were Shakespeare, Keats, Shelley, Byron, etc; stole a few of them from the barrows where they were exposed for sale, when I hadnt the money and wanted the books. Left Ireland in 1926 and came to England, where I still am. Went to America in 1934 to help in the production of my play, WITHIN THE GATES, where it was attacked by the Roman Catholic clerics and a tour banned. Have been attacked all along by these fellows, and most of my books have been banned in Ireland. Am getting attacked now by R. Catholics because of my last play, COCKADOODLE DANDY. Used to it all now, and readily attack back when I can. Have written the following plays, as well as those two mentioned: SHADOW OF A GUNMAN, JUNO AND THE PAY-COCK, PLOUGH AND THE STARS, THE SILVER TASSIE, RED ROSES FOR ME, PURPLE DUST, THE STAR TURNS RED, OAK-LEAVES AND LAVENDER, TIME TO GO. BEDTIME STORY, HALL OF HEALING, END OF THE BEGINNING, POUND ON DEMAND: and the following biographical books: I KNOCK AT THE DOOR, PIC-TURES IN THE HALLWAY, DRUMS UNDER THE WINDOWS, and INISHFALLEN FARE THEE WELL. Am at present writing another, ROSE AND CROWN. All these have been printed by Macmillan and Co. London, and by the Macmillan Company, Fifth Avenue, New York City. I am married to an Irishwoman, and we have three children, Breon, 22, an art pupil in London, after he had served his three years in the Artillery; Niall, aged 14, at school still; and a girl, Shivaun, aged 10, at school, too. I hope none of them will have to pass through the horror of war. For advice, I dont know what to give, except to advise you to write about someone you know more about. I enclose some cuttings, which may be a help if you persist in choosing me for your thesis. I send my love to the Bulgarian People.

Yours sincerely
Sean O'Casey

To Patrick F. Byrne

TS. BYRNE

TOTNES, DEVON

18 MAY 1950

Dear Pat Byrne,

Thank you for the R[adio] Review, though I failed to find your review in it. As for the visit—I couldn't say where I'd be when you came. During these months many Americans come to see me, and with the children on holiday, too, I can't place where I'd be any particular time. It wouldn't be worth your while to come so far—I can't see it worth while to cross a street to see me, unless a previous acquaintance has assured you it might be. Is it true that [James] Dillon—instead of a trip to Rome, is setting off for Moscow to tell Stalin off. Dillon confronts Stalin—consternation in Moscow! All the best.

Sean O'Casey

To Dr. John V. Simcox

TC. O'CASEY

[TOTNES, DEVON]

23 MAY 1950

Dear Dr. Simcox:

Your letter to Card. Griffin is with the Typist, and, immediately it comes back, I shall send it to you with a copy of the new typing so that you may check up on the copying. The typist rang me up about it, suggesting paragraphing, etc., for, you may remember, your copy was closely packed together—what professionals would call a very bad copy, something similar to my own amateur way of doing it. I am having three copies done—one top and two carbon copies. For some reason or another, typists are very busy now. When I get any work of my own done professionally, I have to wait quite a time for it. I hope you dont mind the delay; it isnt my fault.

When I said I was "amused" at the arguments still going on about questions of Christian Faith after 2000 years of elucidation, I meant the word to be taken in the sense of ponder or divert; not, as you seem to think, in the sense of a loud laugh. These questions divert me from my customary thinking—away from the questions of Communism, peace, and the making of plays. There seems to be something sad in the thought that 2000 years of examination havent solved these questions, even for those who righteously believe in the dogmas they postulate. So dont be angry with me because I regard them as myths; poetical myths, but myths, all the same. It seems to me that [Peter] Newell is right on the question of "resurrection." The doctrine seems to have been in existence since the beginning of man's life, and is founded on the need for those things which keep life going: the death of life in the winter, the resurrection of life in the spring. This is no myth. It is bound up with the myth of the priest-king, his death and his renewal; the culture of the "god" for a period, then his sacrifice that fertility should come to the earth, and man might go on living. It survives still in the "old man" of the harvest; the sheaf, the last sheaf nailed to the door of the barn till the new crop is sown and the new harvest comes again. Every nation and every tribe has had some form of the belief. The late James Frazer in his great work "The Golden Bough" sets it forth in unquestionable details taken from every known tribe, including the Irish, among men. It would indeed be hard to give a date for the first evidence of the promulgation of any myth. One might as well try to give a date for the beginning of the belief in the myth of Cuchullain or the Red Branch Knights. It has been proved, I imagine, now by the research of the scholar, T. F. O'Rahilly, in his fine book, "Early Irish History and Myth," [1] that Cuchullain is a projection of an earlier god. This is the man who has published a book showing that there were two St. Patricks, one something of a cod and imposter, the other who did all the work. It is the cod who is the popular saint of today. Recently, O'Rahilly resigned from his job of Head of Advanced Celtic Studies; and, it is plain, that he did so because of the resentful reception of his newer discoveries in Celtic Scholarship. Easter was a pagan festival, and its very name is that of an old Saxon goddess. Eire celebrated it in Beltane, whose fires fertilised the land. It is wonderful what men are prone to believe and promulgate to satisfy the desires in their own hearts. To me the myth of the Resurrection is a projection of our desire to live longer; but, to me, it should be confined to the efforts to live longer here. I no more like the thought of death—though I hope I shall "die like a gentleman," as Shaw advocated somewhere—than anyone else, but I cannot associate death with the beginning of a new life somewhere else, which is, itself, associated with a long wait for the time when the "trumpet" will sound, and man will assume again, in a glorified manner, that is, the elect people of God, the body they lost, or which dissolved into dust, when they drew their last breath, and departed from this world. As far as I can see, no plain question can be asked about the problem of the Resurrection, and so no plain answer can be given. It is like a court counsel demanding from a witness a plain Yes or No to a complicated question. The Christians are still asking the question among themselves. It is similar to the question of how and when did God hand the tablets of the

[1] Thomas Francis O'Rahilly, *Early Irish History and Mythology* (1946).

Ten Commandments to Moses. And which of the two Tens did he hand to him; for there were two, one evidently a tribal and primitive bunch of orders; the second—the ones we know—given out when the Israelites had reached a higher moral state of civilization.

It's all very difficult; but just now there's the terrible question of War, the Atom Bomb, that may destroy us all; and which are the weapons of the Christians today instead of the Sacraments and the Sword of the Spirit. The Christians have shoved Jesus into the heavy armour of war, lifted him on to a charger, thrust a spear into his hand, and have shouted into his ear— Have a go!

One whom they mistake for Jesus; or, to be more accurate, they have done this to Barabbas, first putting a surcoat of the Cross around his shoulders.

I return to you the cutting you sent to me; and will send on your letter to Card. Griffin as soon as it comes back to me. You look a handsome, gay lad in the snap you sent to me—thirty golden years ago. Well, however we differ, we are, I believe, both in the battle for truth and humanity.

> *God be wi' you.   My love.*
> *Sean O'Casey.*

To Dr. John V. Simcox

TC. O'CASEY

TOTNES, DEVON
3 JUNE 1950

My dear Dr. Simcox,

Yes, Dr. MacDonald was concerned about the absolute control of the schools by priests and bishops. There is at present a case in Mountmellick where a man had been an Assistant Principal, and had taught in the school for 33 years. The Principal died, and all, Councillors and people, wanted him to get the job; but the Manager—the local P.P., appointed an outsider. The people demurred, the Councillors passed a resolution by a majority in favour of the local man; but the P.P. simply ignored them all; and, indeed, maintained that opposition to him was an evidence of Communistic thought and desire. There was, apparently, no question of the l. man's qualifications; only that he didnt satisfy the P.P., possibly because he was an active supporter of the Labour movement. State Schools must aim at providing educated and efficient citizens, regardless of religion; and, apparently, there is such an amount of time spent by the R. Schools on the teaching of "religion," that, when the pupils come out into life, they are in no way as efficient as they ought to be; even in Religion, for we have had the Bishops themselves (Universe) declare that the ignorance of the faithful of their religion was tragical or appalling, or some such word. Whether we like it or not, each must now take an efficient part in secular life which all must live —even the cloistered monks, for they must eat to live, eat even to preserve the ability to practise contemplation. Yes, you could be happy in Buntingford by allowing the laity to decide themselves; but Buntingford's in England. What about Killorglan? Or a town in Spain? Or in Poland, before the revolution? Could the laity decide in any of these? Canon Law, even Canon Law, is one thing, the Bishop's or the Priest's mandamus is another.

Frazer was, of course, an Anthropologist, and didnt set up to be a teacher of faith. He was, as a scientist, indifferent to any and all faiths. There isnt any doubt of the fact that "resurrection" for many centuries and in every country was lapped in the secular thought of a good harvest that man might live. Man was mortally afraid of a failure, which he often experienced, with disastrous results to his tribe; and, naturally, he, in his woeful ignorance and fear, added a divine attribute to his hopes—as in the sacrifice of the "god," after a year's worship, that the seedtime and harvest should not fail. And this is all very important still; witness the gigantic belt of trees the USSR is planting in the east to protect the crops from the hot sand that blows from the Asian deserts, promoting a drought. Kneel and toss our minds about, in and out of divine things, how we may, we come back to the necessity to provide a living. Frazer doesnt argue that because of the universal desire for, and belief in, the renewal of plant life, there cant be any truth in the resurrection of the Christian God. He doesnt stay to bother about it. But, it seems to me, that because of this universal belief or hope, then it was an easy transition from this belief to the other that troubles so many people; and the early Christians, full of the old ideas, as they must have been, and so ignorant of what we know now, must have wished for, and have come to believe in, the renewal of him with whom they had talked and walked with in the flesh. The pagans believed that without death there could be no renewal of life; their one dread, materialistic dread, was that there might be no renewal of that life which preserved their own. And it is as vital today as it was then. But the Christians are so engrossed in forcing men (for their own material ends) to accept this outworn faith in what they call "eternal spiritual realities," that they will resort to any measure to perpetuate, and, if possible, deepen, it; i.e. roses on an altar that refused to fade; Fatima, Lourdes, Knock; the melting blood of Januarius; and a thousand other shams. The Protestants with their magical texts from the Bible are in the same boat. So it is with the "eating of the god," the fires of Mid-summer, of beltane, the king-god; and all the rest of it; with the church bells ringing out to drive away the evil spirits—the fees to be according to the weight and carrying-power of the bells. That is why in so many R. Catholic countries the peoples are so illiterate; they are kept that way so that they may believe, and keep it up. They are afraid to educate their peoples. But Communism has stepped in, and today the peoples are well on the way to be able to read and write, so that they may soon be able to give an answer for the hope that is in them. I see Ireland has banned Apuleius's "The Golden Ass." [1] And a working woman has just written to say that she cant get "Pictures in the Hallway" in any Dublin library. Small wonder when the book has been banned, since it first appeared, along with "I Knock at the Door." Frazer's "The Golden Bough" has many a long year to go yet. Certainly, the Christian resurrection, according to the Bible account, was a very quiet affair. No one seemed to know anything about it. "He isnt here," said the angels. And who were the angels, may I ask? Have we to believe in them too? There seems to be no end to what a man is expected to believe if he holds to the C. faith. The other week in the UNI-VERSE someone wrote about the existence of man before Adam. The questioner was told that undoubtedly there were men before Adam, but "these men had no souls; man became possessed of a soul only when Adam was created." And, in the same Journal, before this, it was stated that "animals had souls, but these souls were not immortal." And damned be he who first cries, Hold, enough! Oddly enough, I'm not frightened by the "austerity" of "He that saves his soul shall lose it." To me that is philo-sophical, and true. It is inevitable that this shall be so. I have seen it work in drama, art, literature, and music—not to mention politics. The boyo who is out to save himself is the boyo who gets lost; that is, the kingdom of heaven within him is no more. And serves him god-dam well right.

I've some letters from Father Duffy somewhere, but it would mean an allnight search to find them. I simply couldnt find time to go on writing to him. However, at present, he's touring Canada, speaking publicly for the Peace Movement, so would be hard to reach just now. If I come across his address, I'll send it to you.

To me, about the quest of resurrection—it is that the resurrection in a man during this life is the one important thing; that those who are dead join the living; that they do their duty in that state of life until which it shall please life to call them; that they speak, according to their lights without fear or favour; and leave resurrection after death to whatever gods there be.

The C. idea of the resurrection is, I daresay, a superior one to that of the belief held before it came. It gives a far higher conception of a god to many peoples, but no higher than the conception of life given by Buddha. It is but an evolution of the belief in the cult of fertility worship. It gives to a god the attribute of the lord of the harvest—at least in the Prot. church —see their harvest hymns, and, I believe, the Roman clerical blesses the field and the vineyard. Just as the Ten Commandments held by the church, and known as the Only ones given to Moses, are far above the previous ten dealing with tribal law and tribal superstitions for instance, "Thou shalt not simmer the kid in its mother's milk." So it was a step forward; but that step forward is now a step backward; for we cannot stay where we are,

---

[1] Apuleius' *The Golden Ass,* translated by Robert Graves, was banned by the Irish Censorship of Publications Board on 19 May 1950.

however we may long to do so. The divine order changeth, and would change, if Communism had ne'er been born; but those who have "great possessions," and those who live by them, would condemn under another name the change that threatens to undo them; and will undo them. As for Lenin's theory being similar to that of St. Ignatius, well, if it was so, that wouldnt be against Communism, but rather a tribute to Loyola; but, and a big but, the aim, the application, the appeal of Lenin's theory are very, very different from those of the Saint; and I very much doubt that, if Loyola were here today, he would give a loud hurrah for the manner, the means, the actions of his congregation, or, indeed, even for the Church herself. Lastly, if this letter is ever to end, if Jesus be what the Church claims Him to be, and He were here again, if I saw Him making bids in the Stock Exchange, I should be startled and frightened; if I saw Him sitting as a Director of a Trust engaged in the making of the atom bomb; if I saw Him standing quietly watching the burning of "surplus" wheat so that dividends could be kept up; but I wouldnt be at all surprised to see Him marching with the people under the red banners of Communism. And this Stock Exchange, this making of the a. bomb; this burning of things for the sake of dividends are parts, vital parts, of the "civilization as we know it today," acclaimed by Bevin, Churchill, Acheson, and, of course, Card. Griffin.

Lastly again, there never was "false medicine." The medicine men were groping after facts, and were sincere in many things they did—imitative magic, for instance. Those who attended Charles II, though they gave him truly appalling remedies, were sincere enough, and acted according to the poor knowledge they had. Even those who drove their cattle through the fires of Beltane in the hope of ensuring the cattle's health were in deadly earnest. These are, of course, but personal opinions, hastily set down, for I havent the time to think them out quietly; but they are roughly what I believe.

As requested, I return you your MS—four sheets in all.

And now let me wish you a good time while the sun lasts, for you wished for the summer some time ago. May it be all that you may wish in giving you renewal. I dont like it too hot, for I can but gasp when the sun's too strong. My blessing on ye.

As ever,
[Sean O'Casey]

p.s. I once thought that "experts" were anything but trustworthy, and that all, or most, of them wrote wearily; but I have changed my opinion considerably. "The Golden Bough" is a magnificent work, and finely written. So are Frazer's "Origins of Fire" and "Folklore of the Old Testament." Coulton's "Five Centuries of Religion," too, is a great work, and finely written. Eileen Power's accounts of Elizabethan days [2] is a fine one; and

---

[2] *Tudor Economic Documents* (1924), edited by R. H. Tawney and Eileen Power.

Trevalyn's "Social History" [3] is grand; and many more of the "Dons" have
done well. Even in very old age, Coulton was active and intensely alive. I
wish I had known him. And, after all, all the great men were "experts" in
one way or another—Darwin, Faraday, and Shakespeare, to mention but
a few.

It seems to me that all this worrying about oneself in relation to the
cosmos, after life, the possibility of a resurrection, the relationship of man
to God—Aldous Huxley is almost hysterical with it; and T. S. Eliot can
think of little else—is a monstrous projection of the individual ego. It would
seem to make of the cosmos nothing but the vague existence of a God and
of a frantic ego trying to probe out the God's whereabouts.

[3] G. M. Trevelyan, *English Social History* (1944).

To Jack Lindsay

TC. O'CASEY

TOTNES, DEVON

8 JUNE 1950

Dear Jack Lindsay:

No. I cant have my name flying about everywhere, like somebody's
pills.[1] I have already sent a letter to the American Anti-Fascist Committee,
which was published. They then wrote to me for a special letter to be
printed and sent round to all whom they thought would be influenced to
help. This I did for them, and they replied thanking me and saying the
letter was a fine one. I am helping with the Peace Campaign here, and,
just now, embarking on a little help for a similar Campaign just started in
Eirinn. To plaster a name everywhere is just to make the name ridiculous,
claiming a swelled importance which defeats itself.

You know you and [Montagu] Slater jumped me into signing the letter
to Priestley, a letter which wasnt in any way indicative of my manner of
speaking. I've sent a letter, or message to the D. Worker which gives my
feeling about the question of the atom bomb and of peace and of those who
want war with the Soviet Union. I hope the D.W. may publish it.[2]

To see the name of O'Casey, O'Casey here there and everywhere
would gall me, and make me feel ashamed of myself; for it would mean an
importance I dont possess. And I'm no modest laddo either; I know my

[1] Lindsay had asked O'Casey to sign a cable to President Harry Truman from
a group of English writers protesting the congressional Un-American Activities Committee proceedings against Howard Fast.
[2] Sean O'Casey, "Let It Rot Where It Lies," *Daily Worker,* 17 June 1950; reprinted below.

value to myself, but I also know my limitations. The fight for the men and women in America, Japan, Australia, etc., must be carried on, not by a name, but by the combined forces of the people as in the Peace Movement and the Trades Unions; this is the only effective way. When I feel my name can be effective, then it will go down with a bang.

To hang it out everywhere would just be to make it ridiculous, and deservedly so; and, even at the best, it would be bad tactics.

Yours sincerely,
Sean O'Casey

To Eric Gorman

TS. GORMAN

TOTNES, DEVON
10 JUNE 1950

Dear Eric:

Thank you for your letter and cheque, receipt for which I enclose with this note.

I am glad that THE GUNMAN seems to have gone well; [1] after such a long time, it seems odd that everyone isnt tired of it. I am equally glad to hear that you intend to open your season with myself and G. B. S. He is in great form still. Mrs O'C. had tea with him some months ago, and he talked as gayly and as brilliantly as ever. He is really a wonderful Irishman. What with him, Yeats, and Joyce—not to mention Lady G.—Eire certainly gave the stuff to the troops.

I daresay you will have a power of visitors in Dublin this summer, especially from the U.S.A. A number are coming down to see me here. There were between twenty-five and thirty here last season, week after week—from New York, the State of Washington—Seattle, and even up from Texas. They do get about; the very thought of such travelling would make me faint. I hope your Irish Tristan and Iseult [2] was a success.

Thanks for your good wishes, which I return most heartily.

Yours sincerely,
Sean O'Casey

[1] A double-bill of Bernard Shaw's one-act *A Village Wooing* and O'Casey's two-act *The Shadow of a Gunman* opened at the Abbey Theatre on 26 May 1950, for a two-week run. The Abbey's new season began on 3 July 1950 with the same two plays, which ran until 9 August. Doreen Madden and Edward Golden made up the cast of the Shaw play; the featured players in the O'Casey play were: Harry Brogan as Shields; Ronald Walsh as Davoren; Rita Foran as Minnie Powell; Brian O'Higgins as Grigson; Eileen Crowe as Mrs. Grigson,; Philip O'Flynn as Tommy Owens.

[2] *Tristan agus Isialt,* translated into Irish from the classic tale by Joseph Bedier and Louis Artus, opened at the Abbey Theatre on 22 May 1950.

To Seumas Scully

MS. SCULLY

TOTNES, DEVON

11 JUNE 1950

Dear Seumas—

Thanks very much for sending me the "Times Pictorial" & Standard, etc. The fights in the Abbey seem to be losing their first fiery effectiveness.[1] Many more of the people are becoming sensible, & more capable of standing up to criticism built upon observation; &, indeed, a lot of these protesters protest, not out of love for Ireland, or reverence for the Catholic Faith, but to exhibit themselves in the one way their talents will allow—by making a nuisance of themselves. I think you did wisely in leaving the Debating Secretaryship after ten years of labour. It was time to give yourself a wee rest. "Lorna Doone" is curiously dull, though there is a fine account of a great frost. If you come down here, & we happen to be in, we shall be glad to see you. Give us a few days notice. So many suddenly say over the telephone "I'm here outside—can I come along?" which is always a nuisance. You seem to have a fine travelling plan in your head—the Brontes & Long [2] countries. What about Hardy, greater than either—and his Wessex?

All the best to you.

I understand, Sean McBride doesn't mind, or wouldn't mind a dust-up with the USSR. He prides himself on belonging to a country that hasn't a Communist within its borders. Happy man; happy country! But, certainly, there are more than a few Irish Communists outside of it.

All the best.

Yours sincerely

Sean

[1] A reference to the disturbances at the Abbey Theatre over Seamus Byrne's *Design For a Headstone* on 14 April 1950, six nights after the opening. See O'Casey's letter to Frank McCarthy, 20 April 1950.

[2] Longworth, Berkshire, the birthplace of R. D. Blackmore (1825–1900), author of *Lorna Doone*.

To Alfred Eris [1]

TC. O'CASEY

[TOTNES, DEVON]

12 JUNE 1950

Dear Alfred:

Yes, I got your letter and the cuttings safely, and thank you for them. I've been very busy—my own work and a little for the Peace Campaign. The state of things you mention as apparent in the U.S.A. is as common in many other countries as it is there. You have the Communists being banned in S. Africa and Australia; and, of course, anything with even a biblical ring in it cannot be permitted in Spain, Portugal, or Ireland—Communists set aside altogether. The whole world is frightened and suspicious, and no wonder. If the atom bomb—not to mention the H. brother—is loosed on us, then it will be a toss up as to what may happen to all or any of us.

But, all the same, we must try to keep calm, for only by sensible word and sensible action can we avert our own undoing.

To me, it seems, that the hysterical opposition to anything "left" in the U.S.A. will overreach itself, is, I think, already doing so. There are too many diversities of mind and nationality in the U.S.A. to bring about a rigid regimental attitude of mind to things. The white and the Negro question isnt a question sprung suddenly up today; it has been a long time with you, and is but tenser now. This is inevitable, for the Negro is beginning to think of himself, not only with you, but even along the banks of the Congo. The transition is bound to be a painful one.

Now about your proposed [picture] album of Ireland. I havent the time to do what you ask. I can find barely time to do the work I set myself to do long ago; indeed, I'm well behind with it. But if you decide to do it— and the idea seems a good one—I'd advise you to make the "captions" less romantic and less sentimental. Ireland isnt quite so foolishly romantic as she once was. For instance, tens of thousands of children in Ireland arent well fed, nor well housed either. So you can see I would be the last to help towards the success of your adventure. Sean O'Faolain would probably be a lot better; he lives in Ireland, isnt always afraid to write a word or two of criticism; and has been, just lately, "reconciled to the church," so that he would get an implicit nihil obstat for what he might write. Of course, the interference suffered by Adler and Draper is disgraceful.[2] A good dance or

---

[1] Alfred Eris, photographer, Brooklyn, New York. His photograph of the O'Casey family is the frontispiece of *Sunset and Evening Star* (1954); his photograph of O'Casey is the frontispiece of the Braziller edition of the *Selected Plays* (1954).

[2] Larry Adler, the harmonica performer and composer, and Paul Draper, the dancer, who had played concerts together from 1941 to 1950, were accused of being pro-Communist by *Time* magazine in 1948. They brought a libel suit against the wife of an editor of the magazine, Mrs. Hester R. McCullough, claiming that her remarks

a good song is neither Communist or Fascist—even if they were, provided they were good, we'd have to forge a good forgiveness. Of course, an artist shouldnt be asked what politics he holds or religion either; or a good rail-wayman; or a good mechanic; or a good farmer; who would ask a good doctor whether he was a christian or jew or mahommedan, or communist or conservative? No one but a fool; but, unfortunately, there's a score of thousands of fools knocking about today. It's just as well [Dr. Albert] Einstein's called a "red," for this sort of thing shows the fools up. Love to Miriam, Hersh, and yourself.

Yours sincerely,
[*Sean O'Casey*]

---

in a newspaper article and in a talk, based upon the report in *Time,* had injured their professional reputations and resulted in the loss of engagements. The case ended in a hung jury on 27 May 1950.

To Daily Worker

JUNE 17 1950.

SEAN O'CASEY
LET IT ROT WHERE IT LIES

We need a lot of things, we do that; but the first thing of all these things is our need for peace.

We cannot have any of the things we need, if we haven't peace with them. Nothing is any good if we let ourselves be plunged headlong into war.

May God damn the one who raises a voice for war against the Soviet Union.

A war with the Soviet Union would but destroy a lot of the good things of the good earth, and we cannot afford to destroy any of them. We need them all.

Neither old, young, nor little children want to get ready to die, here or in the Soviet Union. And we all want to live generously; we want to build, want to build rather than to destroy.

We refuse to destroy, unless it be to destroy all that is ugly, mean and unhealthy that torments our life.

We want the factories busy, we want the fields fruitful, we want the streets filled with vehicles carrying goods to all the people.

Yes, and the sleeping babe nestling at the breast of its mother must sleep in peace.

To do things, we must be sure of life. To be sure of life, we must first ban the atom bomb. Let it rust away, let it rot away where it lies on its stockpile.

It isn't of heaven, heavenly; it isn't of the earth, earthy; it is of the deeper hell, hellish, so let it rot where it lies.

You young mothers don't want to bear children to have them blown to pieces, or to die in lonely places far from a comforting hand.

We want life, and we are going to have life—life in honour and in peace.

To hell with the atom bomb! On this decision we stand with our robust souls. Shove the skulkers aside. Peace for the whole world, for peace is our first need.

To Joe Papirofsky [1]

TC. O'CASEY

[TOTNES, DEVON]

17 JUNE 1950

Dear Mr. Papirofsky:

Word from the London Unity Theatre tells me of the letter sent to them, and of the requests made in it concerning RED ROSES FOR ME and THE SILVER TASSIE.

It is just as Mr. Madden has already told you—RED ROSES FOR ME is out of the question as a production by your active organization. I rely entirely on Mr. Madden to answer and deal with any inquiry about my plays; and any proposal about them must go to him.

But let me make a few personal remarks. First, if Mr. Madden, on my behalf, made "substantial concessions" on the royalties of "The Silver Tassie," he would, naturally, be expected to make them for any other Society similar to yours. I am a professional playwright; I depend wholly on what I get from my work—I've no income from shares, consols (whatever they may be), property of any kind; so, you will understand, under present cost of living conditions, it's an increase of royalties I'd be looking for rather than a depression. I am, of course, glad to hear that you have been on an "O'Casey jag," but it has come a bit late, hasnt it? It seems,

---

[1] Joe Papirofsky (1921–   ), Actors Laboratory, Hollywood, California. He directed the premiere of *Bedtime Story* and *Hall of Healing* at the Yugoslav-American Hall in New York on 7 May 1952. In 1953, as Joe Papp, he founded the Shakespeare Workshop, which later became the New York Shakespeare Festival; in 1967 he founded the Public Theatre in New York.

frankly, to have come because of the fact that my name has become a bit more prominent than it had been before. When THE STAR TURNS RED was published ten years ago, I went to a lot of trouble persuading my publishers to reduce the price from the usual amount so that it might come nearer the reach of comrades; but, instead of selling better, it didnt sell at all, and the result was a reduction from then on in the advance my publishers give me when they publish a play of mine. But I met, not only negative opposition, but positive opposition as well. When WITHIN THE GATES was on in New York, Mr. Michael Gold wrote in the "Daily Worker," [2] a very venomous attack on me; a very ignorant one as well; an attack on the play, too, though at the time I was fighting an equally venomous attack by the Jesuits against the play, and against me, personally, as well (I understand that Mr. Gold at that time, or before, or later, was in Hollywood trying to earn good money in the Film World. Incidentally, I may say that I have refused many film offers, including one offering a fee of from a hundred thousand to a hundred and fifty thousand dollars—. I dont blame Mr. Gold, of course, for being in Hollywood, but I do blame him for his attack on me, at a time too, when I was fighting Yeats as well as the Jesuits.) And, by the way, THE SILVER TASSIE was printed 22 years ago, and RED ROSES 8 years ago, so you took some time in discovering them. RED ROSES isnt a great play; it has a fine third act, and good bits in other places; but it isnt a patch on THE PLOUGH AND THE STARS. I should like you to do THE SILVER TASSIE, but dont agree that a reduction should be substantial. Mr. Madden, however, might agree to show some favour to you, if you decided to go on with it. I shall let him know that I have written to you. This is written in haste, for I'm very busy with the Peace Campaign and many other things. And, better late than too late that you have found me out, and I thank you for your good words, and send you my best wishes, to you and to your comrades.

[Sean O'Casey]

[2] Michael Gold, "Sean O'Casey and a Film," Daily Worker (N.Y.), 15 February 1937. It was an attack on John Ford's film version of *The Plough and the Stars,* and also denigrated O'Casey. See the comment on Gold in O'Casey's letter to George Jean Nathan, 8 March 1937, Vol. I, p. 655.

To Robert Lewis [1]

TC. O'CASEY

[TOTNES, DEVON]
19 JUNE 1950

Dear Mr. Lewis:

Thanks so much for your letter. It's a very pleasant thought that a play of mine has a good chance of showing itself off on the New York stage this coming season. Needless to say, I hope it may be a rousing success, for I'm very fond of successes. I share humanity's desire that what they do should be successful.

I got a clipping this morning from a friend which says there's a possibility of Barry Fitzgerald taking part in the Cast of COCKADOODLE DANDY. I hope Hollywood hasnt done him in, and that conceit isnt his top virtue. This mention of Barry reminds me of another name of a man who is the equal of Barry, in my opinion, and in some ways, greater. He acted the part in London of Brennan in my play RED ROSES FOR ME, and, by unanimous acclamation, did it exquisitely. He would make a splendid Shanaar, or a fine Sailor Mahan, or a fine Marthraun. I mentioned him a number of times to Dick Madden in connection with the character of a workman in PURPLE DUST; or of Poges in the same play. It is a great pity that this actor doesnt get the recognition he deserves, in my opinion. In case you are interested, here's the details that symbolise the Man:

Eddie Byrne,
45 Mespil Road, Dublin, Eire.

Now for your questions: It is quite obvious that the remark on page 62 is meant for "Michael." How it came to be given to the "Messenger," I dont know. I've just looked up the original script where it is given to "Michael." I get the MS—typed by myself—done by a professional typist, this goes to the Publisher; so it is possible the remark was accidentally given to the "Messenger" by the professional. I'm rather inclined to look over this script in a lazy way, so the fault is my own. I'll correct it in any new issue.

The word "Kyleloch" is the Gaelic word for a cock; pronounced, approximately, as above—Kyle to rhyme with "mile" and loch as in the name Loch Lomond; the accent on "Kyle." The Gaelic form is Coileach, a cock, a male bird. I am very glad you intend to get the fun in the play out of it on to the stage. There is, I think, I hope, a lot of fun in it. God forgive me, but I think the play one of the best things I've written. I'm glad you read "The Flying Wasp." I had a great deal of trouble persuading the pub-

[1] Robert Lewis, (1909–   ), theatre director, producer, and actor.

lishers to print it—they thought it would do me a lot of harm. It did, among the English critics. But I'm alive alive o, still.

All the best to you, and good fortune to us both, and all connected with the play.

[*Sean O'Casey*]

From Robert Lewis

TS. O'CASEY

[RIDGEFIELD, CONN.]
[? JUNE 1950]

MEMORANDUM TO MR. SEAN O'CASEY WITH SUGGESTIONS,
CATEGORICALLY INDICATED BELOW, TO BE OFFERED
TO MR. O'CASEY BY ROBERT LEWIS FOR THE FORMER'S
THOUGHTFUL CONSIDERATION

1. Consult Page 6 re the travel to Lourdes. The front page indicates the progress of the play as of one day. Does this take into consideration the fact that the journey to Lourdes would take more than one day?
2. Page 35—What is Brancardies?
3. Page 37—What is Nyadnanave?
4. Page 38—What is videliket?
5. Page 40—All the information from Messenger about the ruined Holy places is beautiful and informative but Lewis feels it definitely digresses from the mounting action of the scenes that precede and follow and can quite reasonably be cut. He suggests the cut begin on Page 40, after "I don't trust you either" to Page 41 "is your only fun"

    Mr. Lewis suggests that he rehearse it as it is written and if it slows up the action as he suspects, may he cut it?
6. The end of Act 2, page 68 bothers Mr. Lewis because he feels it is not necessary to have Domineer actually strike the lorry driver. He can instead, in his anger viciously grab the driver by the arm and pull him to him and in the scuffle, the driver can lose his foothold and fall to the ground, striking his head severely and the rest follow precisely as you have written it.
7. Page 77—Would the one-eyed "get" be a goat or what would it be?
8. Page 97—The Domineer says—"we'll follow some of the way to

prevent anyone from hurting her" Is this idea of protective cus-
tody a satirical gesture or from whom are they protecting her?

If you will be good enough to return one of these enclosed sheets to
me with your answers it will please Mr. Lewis very much.

To Robert Lewis

TC. O'CASEY

[TOTNES, DEVON]
[? JUNE 1950]

*Replies to Memorandum concerning incidents in play,
"Cockadoodle Dandy"*

1. The play's a blend of fantasy and realism. The journey to Lourdes
   and back again in one day is part of the fantasy. A thousand years
   to God are but as a day, and a day as a thousand years; to a
   dramatist, a year is but as a day, and a day a year. It preserves the
   Unity of the play, one of the three things beloved of Aristotle. It
   also helps to change the *colour* and the *tempo* by allowing the action to have three *aspects*—morning, midday, and dusk. To a sick
   person going to Lourdes to be cured, and to relatives expecting one,
   the time of going and of coming back would be but a second.
2. A "Brancadier" is one who carries the stretcher cases from land
   to the ship or train, or from train to the Grotto where the statue
   of the Blessed Virgin stands. These Brancadiers are, sometimes,
   members of the St. John Ambulance Brigade; but mostly volunteers who take on the job for the time being as a "work of charity."
   They wear the usual *leather harness round shoulders* so that the
   weight of patient and stretcher is spread out equally over the whole
   body.
3. The name of the place of the play. It is a play on two Gaelic
   words—Nead, a bird's nest; and Naomh, a saint. The name of the
   place is in what we call "the genitive plural," and, in Irish, means
   Nest of the Saints. "Naomh" is pronounced Nay-uv; so the name
   may mean either "Nest of the Saints," or "Nest of the Knaves"—
   whatever you fancy.
5. It were a pity to cut it, if, as Mr. Lewis thinks, it be beautiful. I
   dont think it will hold up the action too much; even should it

hold it up a little, it's worth it. There are many examples of this manner in other dramatists—far, far greater than the one now under discussion: Shakespeare, for instance. Let me give one example: In JULIUS CAESAR, the Scene in the Orchard of Brutus when the conspirators come to persuade Brutus to join them (a very serious, solemn moment), Cassius and Brutus enter into a whispering discussion about the projected plot; and the others take advantage of it to introduce a beautiful interruption of the action by a dispute as to where the East lies. It begins with Decius saying: Here lies the east: doth not the day break here? Act II; scene 1. Brutus's Orchard. Another example is the lovely remarks about "the temple-haunting martlet" in Macbeth; and a third (to quote but a few) in the remarks of the crowing of the cock in Hamlet. I think the remarks about the Holy Places should stay in: they are so relevant to Irish neglect. In Dublin, a most historic city, there's but one architectural example of old loveliness left—St. Audoen's Church. All the rest have been ruthlessly removed.

6. As described, the incident actually happened. Indeed, the defending Counsel argued that the cleric had a right "to chastise his unruly member of the flock." The cleric got off. He changed to another job—that was all. If Mr. Lewis thinks it wiser to do it less brutally—that is as he suggests, well and good; I agree.

7. The one-eyed get is the bould Larry himself. The word "Get" in Ireland means one born out of wed-lock in a careless casual manner—within the shelter of some ditch, and who displays most of the despicable qualities of those brought up in this primitive way. Sometimes the phrase is heightened into "You whore's get." Evidently from the word "Beget"; to get in the family way, etc. A term used by the eloquent Dublin worker of one he thinks to be a mean and objectionable character.

8. This remark is used in this way to be partly satirical, but, also, given to Domineer so that the girl mightnt suffer such harm as to get him into serious trouble again. He still remembered what had happened before; and for a second tragedy to occur would mean a serious thing for him. The inner meaning is—"Now that she's going away, and can have no further evil influence in the place, let her go without further harm." The Irish peasants aroused in a moral way (really an immoral way) on what they think to be religious matters, are a dangerous lot; and they dont care where the stones they throw strike. I've had experience of this myself when visiting a town called Balbriggan, Co. Dublin, on behalf of the Irish Citizen Army in 1914, a movement which the clergy didnt like. Showers of stones flew all around me, but, though several struck my body, and hurt a lot, none struck the head, or I should be missing now. No cleric was near, so if a tragedy had taken place, it wouldnt have

been their fault. But, in this case, (the play), Domineer is present, and, if anything happened, he'd have had to share the blame; so he cautions and controls the crowd.

Memo: In a cutting it is said Mr. Lewis is thinking of Barry Fitzgerald. Well and good, though I hope film acting hasnt done B. F. in. But what about Eddie Byrne? A really grand actor; would do any of 3 men fine; do Shanaar splendidly. By the way, the name "Shanaar" is Irish for old man or Ould fella. All critics here—when Byrne acted Brennan in RED ROSES, were unanimous in saying he gave an "exquisite performance," which he did. I think him better than even B. F. In case, his address is:

> Eddie Byrne,
> 45 Mespil Road, Dublin, Eire.

He'd be cheaper, too, I imagine. C. B. Cochran thinks of him as I do. The name "Martraun" means *"a disabled body"; martyr* comes from the same word.

4. Missed out. Eyes not good. "Videliket," the Latin "Videlicet" shortened to "viz"—meaning "namely." Videliket's the way it's pronounced in the play.

To Francis MacManus

TS. MacManus

Totnes, Devon

26 June 1950

Dear Frank,

Enclosed is a cutting from the monthly Journal of the National Book League. In it there's a reference—a good one—to your "Fire in the Dust." You may already have come across it, maybe not. The League has a big membership; each member gets the Journal; & let's hope each member reads it. It's not easy to get a reference here in this Journal, &, I think, it should be valuable to your work. I've never had one in it yet, nor many another, so, you see, it's something of a rarity. Let's hope it helps the sale. Anyway, if you haven't had it already, it should interest you.

I hope the row over "Design for a Headstone" [1] has died down. I've

---

[1] See O'Casey's letters to Frank McCarthy, 20 April 1950, and Seumas Scully, 11 June 1950.

read the various accounts of it in the Press of Dublin. I understand the Government is racking itself trying to think of an Irish Order for the French President. I've suggested a few. One has only to shut one's eyes, stretch out a hand, &, the hand will touch hundreds of ideas at once.

Well, I hope you and the family are doing fine. I had five N.U.I.[2] students here a week ago. And, yesterday, we sat down to tea (the family) & had a cake made—be God, in Finglas! * Land of "Floods o' Finglas & "the Jolly Topers," where I spoke—planks put on beer-barrels—for the I. Citizen Army long, long ago.

Yours as ever,
Sean

* Bought in the grocer's over the road!

2 National University of Ireland.

To Brooks Atkinson

MS. ATKINSON

TOTNES, DEVON
6 JULY 1950

My dear Brooks:
Greetings, one and twenty to you, hoping you are in good condition, & Mrs. Brooks Atkinson well, too. I daresay that you are now among your roses again, trying to keep quiet, and making a holiday out of doing things. There's very little chance of quietness anywhere, now. "Come ye apart into a desert place, and rest awhile." Sounds good, but where's the desert place to be found today? There are bird sanctuaries in every land, but ne'er a one for man. Well, if birds can whistle and sing in peace, in places, I can't see why there's no place for man in which to whistle and sing to his heart's content. Whistle and sing! I'd like nothing better, Brooks.

I've read your writings about me & my work which you set down from time to time, and I thank you for them. They gave me the chance to whistle and sing for a bit—good for the nerves & the heart's content. They helped, too, to bring dollars badly needed—not for any luxury—for the common necessaries that keep life going, keep within us the power and inclination to sing and whistle a bit.

I am working at another book of biography, & have written three one-act plays—to keep the cunning in my hand—"Hall of Healing," "Time to Go," & "Bedtime Story," which, I think, are good, especially "Time to

Go." Quite a number of writers in the U.S.A. have sent me novels, asking for comments; but I've decided not to comply—to give in, rather—, for I really haven't the gift of commenting that way. It needs—beside the Gift— experience & a long training, and I've had neither. Criticism is a big responsibility, & I'm damned if I'm going to plant it on my shoulders—not to mention my conscience. But it's odd how so many think that because one has managed to write a few plays, God has invested one with the disorder of Infallibility! I find that when I've read a number of criticisms of a book or a play, I can build up a good criticism of either from the criticism of others. But before, my mind's a blank. I've ventured a Review of a new book on the Abbey Theatre for your own Journal,[1] & that will do for awhile.

Well, dear Brooks, I hope you have a rest. I send my love to Mrs. Atkinson & to you.

As ever.
Sean

[1] Sean O'Casey, "The Tumult and Pathos," *New York Times Book Review,* 15 October 1950, a review of Peter Kavanagh's *The Story of the Abbey Theatre* (1950).

To Miss Doris Elliott [1]

MS. SOCIETY OF AUTHORS

TOTNES, DEVON

13 JULY 1950

Dear Miss Elliott.

Enclosed with this note go the two Agreements (1. Europa Verlag, Zurich. 2. Dr. Kellerson, France) signed as directed. I don't think I've any comments to make on Mr. Obrecht's letter. A short delay in sending accounts doesn't matter much. If a war comes there'll be a longer delay, &, when they come, we'll all probably be up in the stratosphere mixed up with the scattered remains of an atom bomb: a very disorderly way to enter heaven. I don't think, however, the people will stand for another war. When I was a kid, they were still talking of the Crimea war (an uncle of mine in the Light Dragoons, fought at Balaclava), & now, when I'm old, they're still talking about war! Doesn't make sense, Doris. I do hope the young will rebel. It's always the young who go forth to war. Why don't they send us old fellows out? If they can have an old-age pensioners' race, why not

[1] Miss Doris Elliott, League of Dramatists, Society of Authors, London.

an old-age pensioners' war? It wouldn't matter how we'd finish the tail-end of our life—but the young!

Well, all the best
Sean O'Casey

P.S. I return Mr. Obrecht's letter.

To John Gassner [1]

MS. GASSNER

TOTNES, DEVON
20 JULY 1950

Dear John Gassner,

I've been busy reading (and enjoying) "From 'Ghosts' to 'Death of a Salesman,' " edited by you.[2] You are a most interesting Drama-critic, much clearer & much more to the Point, I think, than Eric Bentley. The Book is a fine one, grandly done, with a dignified & charming cover. Looks fine on a book-shelf. Bentley is trying, I imagine, to be too clever altogether; but this thought may be due to my thickness of mind. Sartre I can't stomach at all. Reading his "The Flies," I'd rather be free from Sartre than free from the gods. After all, Zeus could, at least, sing a song.

I do hope you are well, & that you may strengthen yourself in the Theatre day by day, for, I think, you are in love with Drama—a dangerous attachment.

All good wishes to you.
Sean O'Casey

[1] John Gassner (1903–67), drama critic, anthologist, teacher; Sterling Professor of Playwriting and Dramatic Literature at Yale University.
[2] *A Treasury of the Theatre: From* Ghosts *to* Death of a Salesman (1950), edited by John Gassner.

To Dr. John V. Simcox

TC. O'CASEY

[TOTNES, DEVON]
21 JULY 1950

Dear Dr. Simcox:

My dear sir, I have a lot to do, and not a lot of physical energy by which to do them. I have, first, to try to earn a living for a wife, three children, and myself, which takes a lot of doing. Besides, I take an interest in what my children do, and this takes up a lot of time, which, you might think, might be more profitably spent in writing to you. For instance, yesterday, I spent a good deal of the day at an exhibition of work done by the Juniors (of which my little girl is one) at Dartington Hall, and had a delightful time looking at what these children did (incidentally, I do not wish to see these happy children destroyed by H.B.., or by atom bombs). One boy is interested in biology, and so am I; another is interested in painting, and so am I; they are all interested in music, and so am I; so you see, I am kept busy. Two weeks ago, helping about the house, I thoughtlessly snatched up a basket of laundry and carried it down stairs. I gave my heart a jolt, and, by doctor's orders, had to take things very easy for a week or more. So you can see that a letter from you must, at times, be thought of only as a side line. Your recent letters [1] have put many questions to me, some of which no-one can answer, such as whether or no Jesus Christ was deluded when he assumed to himself the power and nature of divinity. I have been thinking of this question, and have tried to argue it out in my mind to reply to you; but now I have thrown it aside for good, since you are interested only in what I think about things said, or said to be said, in the D. Worker. Another question of yours was whether the dead man, McSwiney had still a right over the way in which his children should be brought up—a gruesome thought to me, and faintly ridiculous. There were others (I have all your letters pinned together ready to be answered when an opportune moment came to me. I shant bother now but content myself in sending you back the copies of letters you kindly allowed me to see. Incidentally, I may say that a letter from Bernard Shaw and from Augustus John—two old friends of mine—received some months ago, have still to be answered, so you shouldnt be surprised when I dont immediately reply to the letters you send to me.

Now, let the "rat" try to reply to the wolf-hound.[2] You may remember that it was you yourself who first provoked a correspondence. You may

[1] Simcox had sent seven letters to O'Casey from 16 May to 20 July full of arguments and accusations, mainly about religion, Communism, and the Korean War.

[2] In some of his letters, Simcox had called O'Casey a "rat-in-his-hole" on the issue of the responsibility for the Korean War.

remember, too, that at the very beginning I explicitly said I had no desire whatever to try to turn you to Communism; indeed, I just as explicitly told you, as courteously as I could, that you wouldnt be worth a damn as a Communist. A mistake the Communists sometimes make is that of accepting persons who are not only worthless, but positive nuisances. Hyde, for instance, who was never, and never could be, a Communist (incidentally, he can never be a Catholic either). My experiences in the Irish Republican Brotherhood made me very wise in this respect. Your recent letters show me that I was indeed right in my estimation of you (in fitness for being a Communist only of course). Many upright, honest, and valuable persons are, and always will be, outside the circle, though, in their own valuable way, contributing to its strength and progress. Many have done so—Dickens, Byron, and Shelley, for instance, of those who are gone; and Sinclair Lewis, Matisse, and Christopher Fry as instance of those who are still, happily, of the living; for Communism is but the good and the security of all—Americans just as much as the Koreans.

Now for your louder questions which will be replied to without prevarication, and which will be answered by me according to the manner of my interpretation, deeper and firmer even than the manner practised by the Daily Worker; and, once answered, then we shall let the correspondence drop.

You ask me if "The Dulles photo's appearance in the 'millionaire' Press proves the initial attack from the South." By the way, though you put the word "millionaire" in inverted commas, it is a millionaire press, isn't it? If you doubt it, read Clifton Reynolds' "Simple Guide to Big Business," Bodley Head (Reynolds isnt the beginning of a Communist, and the Bodley Head isnt a branch of the D.W.), and you will be forced to see that it is. I havent seen the photo in question, and dont know what it seems to prove; and I dont care a shit. The factual truth of the question goes down fathoms deeper than a photo. Whether the North began and the North held on (this phrase should be familiar to an Irishman (southern), or whether the South began it, I dont know, and I dont care a shit. This should be a plain remark, anyhow. The parallel had no right to existence, either from the Soviet Union view or from the American point of view. Korea belongs to the Korean people, not to the Soviet Union or to the U.S.A. And all in Korea, lands, woods, waters, mountains, and all the things created by Korean labour, or may be created by Korean labour, belong, not to this man or that lady, but to the Korean people. That is my belief, and I hope that it is clear to you—that is my statement of conviction. If you talk about the "legality" of the division, then I say I have no regard for any sacramental importance attached to a sheet of parchment with a wax seal on it. The whole of Korea belongs to the Korean people, and the parallel so long dividing the country is good neither in substance or in fact. I care as much about that "legality" as I do about the "legality" of the invisible "Border" separating Ulster from Ireland. It is for the Koreans, the majority of them, to decide how they shall live, and neither you nor I have any business dictating to them the manner of their going. Just as it is for the Irish majority to declare whether Ulster shall or shall not be an integral part of Eireann; and, of course, no other decision could be made than it does. "And for their cruel parchment laws care we not one thraneen" is as true today as it was in 1798, and the parchment law that divides (whether agreed to by the USSR or not) the Korean into two parts is a law that I dont care a damn about. I hope this is plain to you. As for your threat to send a copy of the letter last addressed to me to many persons, including Quintin Hogg, go ahead; more, you can send it to all the crowned heads of Europe if you wish; most, you can have it printed at your own expense, go up in an airplane, and shake it down over all the globe. Not wishing to waste time—for I am genuinely busy with my own work; I must end this once for all; bar emphasising again that I am against young Americans losing their lives in Korea (old enough to die, not old enough to vote); that whether the north or the south "began" it, I dont care a shit; that I stood for the Boers when the Transvaal and O. Free State fought for independence; for India, fighting for the same purpose, as Mr. Krishna Menon, High Commissioner for India can tell you, if you ask him; for the political and cultural independence of my own country; and now for the Koreans fighting for independence and unity. I hope now that my attitude has been set down clearly before you. It isnt to me a matter of what the D. Worker thinks, or what you think, or your friends think: it is alone what the Koreans themselves think that must settle the question.

Anyway, the "aggression" started first in 1947 according to *The Far East* of Vol. XXXIII, No. 6, June, 1950, issued by The Maynooth Society for Missions to China. The priest-in-charge, Fr. Dawson, says that Che-Ju Island, 50 miles off the south-west tip of the Korean mainland was very much in the news of Korea in 1947. From March 1947 for three years, nearly, it was the scene of bitter fighting between guerilla bands linked with the N. Korean Gov. and the army and police of S. Korea. It was estimated that 15000 persons were killed and 90,000 people made homeless. One "Father Carroll visited the Island last year and described the plight of the 300,000 population as 'the worst I have seen in my two and a half year of relief work in Korea.' " How the N. Koreans were immersed in the fighting in Che-Ju Island, 50 miles off the south-west tip of Korea is not told to us. Father Dawson adds, "Thank God, all is quiet now, and there's little talk of Communism; they got enough of that for some time." All Communists, and all who even faintly resembled them were, I daresay, in their graves. The quiet of the grave.

I leave it all there as between you and me. We only, apparently, irritate each other. It is waste of time writing; I, for one, will do no more of it. So farewell, with an assurance that I wish you all the good life can give.

Yours sincerely,
Sean O'Casey.

To Dr. John V. Simcox

TC. O'CASEY

[TOTNES, DEVON]
26 JULY 1950

Dear Dr. Simcox:

I dont understand you: you say two lines of reply would have been enough, but before you call my letter "most interesting." If it had been ten pages, instead of three, it wouldnt have mattered, surely, so long as it was "most interesting"? But maybe you said this just out of politeness. It was you, if you may remember, who by implication referred to me as a "sickening hypocrite" and "a rat in a hole." That was the reason why I made my reply to you as plain as I could. I sent to you words showing frankly and exactly how I felt about the question you put to me; and, I added, I think, a phrase saying you could send it to whomsoever you liked; as a second addendum, I give you permission to print the entire letter—but only the entire letter—anywhere you like—can anything be fairer? Do you want me to have it done as a placard and carried about everywhere on my breast? Please, Dr. Simcox, be reasonable. You are, I think, mistaken in believing that there is no difference between Communism and R. Catholicism—Christianity, if you wish—; we dont claim to be infallible; we dont claim divine guidance; we set out to accomplish a better life by the use of reason, by trial and error; we set no hope whatever as Communists per se on any other life but this one. I have told you before that I claim no special importance for what I say; that I am not a philosopher, logician, scholar; and that what I say is but the opinions of an intelligent human being.

I looked upon you as a friend, and our correspondence as one taking place between two friends, differing on many things while agreeing on some. I had no idea that it was meant to be an official controversy till I received your last few letters. Of course, you can "notify the Editor of the D. Worker that I dont care a shit who began it," if you so desire; though, in fairness, you should put what goes before and what follows that statement. But dont bother to do this, if you dont wish to do so. You have an odd, insensate idea that Communists cant differ among themselves on minor points, or, even, on important points of the ways in which things should be done. If you think that the "Russian Government"—I daresay you mean the Gov. of the USSR—to be a "bloody and intolerant clique," then, of course, you believe it. You may remember that Dr. Coulton bitterly regretted the time he lost in carrying on his controversies, so I dont intend to waste my time and further injure my health by doing the same kind of thing—I am conceited enough to think I have more valuable work to do.

With all good wishes,
Yours sincerely,
Sean O'Casey

To Dr. John V. Simcox

TC. O'CASEY

TOTNES, DEVON

27 JULY 1950

Addenda to letter addressed to you, and dated
the 26th July, 1950

I have received your note enclosing copy of a letter you have sent to the *Daily Worker.* As I thought, you contented yourself with an excerpt of a line from a letter of three pages. I see you think that what I said to you is a "serious 'deviation' from the Party Line." Well, that's a great discovery, and dismays me, and surely dismays the *Daily Worker,* too. We but wait to see what will happen! I know you never said that "I tried to make you a Communist" (it would hardly be possible, after what I wrote about your fitness for the honour or dishonour—whatever way you wish to regard it); but can You say that you have never tried to make me an anti-Communist? You see, the dictatorial propaganda has all been on your side. By the way, I never said that the theory of an initial attack by the S. Koreans was "quite indefensible." It isnt so, but I am not interested in it. You shouldnt misrepresent a body. My letter gave the reasons why I wasnt interested in that particular point.

What interests me really, though, is your reaction to the term of "I dont care a shit." It shows vividly the old Adam flaring up in you. I guessed that you were still immersed in all the old taboos, so I wanted to make sure. I am sure now. It is odd how many still are frightened at a word. Even those who have read the Bible and Shakespeare—to mention but two works. The word occurs in Joyce's "Portrait of an Artist as a Young Man." Perhaps you'd call that a "pot-boiling" book too? Have you read the same author's *Ulysses?* Or Frazer's "Taboo and the Perils of the Soul"? When you say "They sell well. Some modern literary reputations seem to have been built on them," you really become what I imagine would be a Bostonian Roman Catholic Irishman. It is a great pity that a man of your education should be such a one. But then your fear of the phrase "He that saves his soul shall lose it" is part of that fearsome groping after safety. It is a great pity. By the way, when you say that I could have replied in two lines, instead of three pages, you demand not only agreement, but also that the agreement must be set down as you think suitable. This seems to be a kind of egoistic authoritarianism.

Well, goodbye. You really neednt bother sending me notes telling me where you have wafted the phrase you so vehemently object to—you can forward it wherever you like. The world knows me. I am sorry our correspondence ended this way, but I dont think I am to blame.

Yours sincerely.
Sean O'Casey

To Bernard Shaw

TS. British Museum

Totnes, Devon

1 August 1950

My very dear G. B. S.

In a way, I am glad circumstances prevented you from seeing my friend. I dont like the responsibility of sending friends down on other friends. There's a touch of "unfairity" in it. One who may be charming to me may well be a bore to another; and, besides, one cant get intimate with another in an acquaintance of an hour's duration. Tom Curtiss may try to see you when he returns from Paris in six or eight weeks' time, in the forlorn hope that you may have found a maid by then. I have been washing up every day since the war started, and am well used to it now. A letter to me from Desmond McCarthy complains of "creators" having to do such work, and St John Ervine recently complained of the same fact. But why shouldnt we all have to do some useful work, if we're fit for it? I hear our children often talking now of useful work—the seniors are painting the facade of the school; and each junior has to take his or her turn in the kitchen, carrying wood, or serving at tables. Our boy, Niall, is quite a good cook; and the eldest, Breon, who is at an art-school in London, has to do for himself in this way—buy his food, and cook it, before he can eat it. We are all learning a little more about life. And not a bad thing either.

I am very pleased to know that the picture of the family hangs on your wall; and proud, too. It is a long time since I got from you the letter of sharp advice not to depend on Bernard Shaw's preface,[1] but on what I

---

[1] See Shaw's letter to O'Casey, 3 December 1919, Vol. I, pp. 87–88.

wrote myself. Advice which made me curse for a few moments, but which I soon saw to be the one advice to take; and took it resolutely and carried it out; a fierce and fine resolution which brought the picture of myself and family to hang honorably on the wall of Ireland's greatest man. I wont bother you again about a friend. I have been often asked to ask you to see this person, that person. When I decline, they say, resentfully, I thought you were a friend of Bernard Shaw's, and I bewilder some of them by saying That's why I wont bother him; if I were an enemy of his, I'd send you to him readily enough. I see our friend, John Dulanty will be soon leaving his post, outpost for Eirinn.[2] Ireland has few Dulantys, and the chap to replace him will find it hard going to follow Dulanty, much more to keep up with him.

Take care of yourself, great care of yourself—there's no budding Bernard Shaw in Ireland. My deep love to you, and Eileen's too.

Yours most sincerely,
Sean

[2] On 26 July 1950 John Whelan Dulanty, Irish High Commissioner in London from 1930 to 1950, became the first Ambassador appointed by the Republic of Ireland to the Court of St. James.

To Francis MacManus

MS. MacManus

Totnes, Devon

25 August 1950

Dear Frank,

Holidays! and all the children home all day and all night; visitors from the U.S.A. every week, & oftener, mixed with visitors from Ireland every fortnight; so hadn't a second to answer your letter. And the rains falling every day on the evil & the good. 2,000 was, I think, a fine first sale even for a fine first book. I hope you've settled up with the U.S.A. Houghton Mifflin & Harcourt Brace I know, but haven't heard of Holt. They're on the list, though, in the Authors' Guide, just as the others are. Hope you are careful of Film rights & broadcasting and Television. Very important; one never knows. I've just got a suggestion from U.S.A. of a broadcast from biography. Don't give too much away. You should try to join the Authors' Society. I read that Seamas O'Neill went wild over suggestion by "Envoy" to re-assess value of Gaelic Literature.[1] Near time to

[1] John Ryan, "Foreword," *Envoy,* January 1950. Ryan, the editor, mentioned a plan to do a series of articles reassessing modern Gaelic literature. In the May 1950

do it. A lot of it is over-rated. Aodh de Bloucam's estimate. Where's he now? Can't enthuse about Count [writing blurred]. He did a translation of the "Plough". I don't bother much about translations—more trouble than they're worth.

Finglas cakes are sold in hundreds here. Come through Bristol, I think, to the local grocers. And damned fine cakes they are. We all love them: pretty dear, though. Finglas must have changed. I remember standing on planks supported by beer barrels, speaking for The I. Citizen Army & Jim Larkin's Union, many, many years ago; & no car to bring us there or back; walking all the way; & to Swords, Coolock, Raheny, St. Doulough's & adjacent places. Still at it, though I haven't the energy now to speak in public. But I try to write a bit, & am busy now & again, here & there, with the Peace Movement—to try to stop bombs from falling on Finglas & Mt. Merrion [2] as well as Totnes down here. For, if war comes, down they'll fall—everywhere. Why, don't you write for *Envoy*? I heard long ago that "The Bell" was to chime again; [3] but no stroke has been heard, so far. What a brisk controversy that was between Father O'Brien & S. Skeffington about "The Liberal Ethic." [4] I imagine F. O'Brien lost more than his new Sunday hat in it. And John Dulanty's an Ambassador now. Well, he's been Eire's best Ambassador for many a year now. A real grand laddo. I have a very deep affection for him; very able fellow, too, with a delightful sense of humor. A grand Gael.

Love to the family & to you.

As ever,
Sean

---

issue, Ryan remarked that Seamus O'Neill, Gaelic editor of the *Sunday Press,* "foamed at the mouth" over the plan.

[2] MacManus lived in Mount Merrion, Dublin.

[3] The *Bell* suspended publication in April 1948 because of a lack of funds; it reappeared in November 1950.

[4] The controversy over "The Liberal Ethic" took place in the letters to the editor column of the *Irish Times* from 24 January to 15 March 1950, mainly between the Rev. Felim O'Briain, O.F.M., Professor of Philosophy at University College, Galway, and Dr. Owen Sheehy-Skeffington, Reader in French at Trinity College, Dublin, and a member of the Irish Senate. The argument began with Sheehy-Skeffington's reply to a lecture by Father O'Briain, and for the next seven weeks these men and over fifty correspondents debated liberal versus conservative views on Roman Catholicism. All the letters were later printed in an eighty-nine page booklet, *The Liberal Ethic* (1950).

To Seumas Scully

MS. SCULLY

TOTNES, DEVON

25 SEPTEMBER 1950

Dear Seumas.

No, you haven't done anything "wrong." I got all the "literature" safely, & the delay in acknowledging was due to the fact that I and the family were wandering through the wind-swept Plain of Salisbury, lingering long to look at the massive monoliths or trilithons of Stonehenge; & then strolling through the Cathedrals of Winchester & Salisbury—Old & New Sarum, & many other places; so had no chance of sending you a note. A host of letters were waiting for me when I came back, with a request for an article from the New York Times. I've been hard at it since, answering the letters, & finding new ones come every morning, which have to be answered too.

I must ask you to wait for awhile before autographing books—I've to look for them, for I've forgotten where I've stored them for safekeeping. I've other biographical books that I've been asked to autograph too, and a Film Synopsis from a Dublin boyo who expects me to get Rank to do it at once: a very terrible synopsis too. Then there's the future biographical vol. that I have to do; so I've no time to look out of the window to see if it's raining. That was a fine Defence of Liberal thought: I'm afraid the Rev. gentleman came out of it baďly. Dr. Walter McDonald foretold all this nearly forty years ago; but they wouldn't listen to their prophet.

All the best to you from us all.
Sean

To Miss Sheila ———

MS. PRIVATE

TOTNES, DEVON

26 SEPTEMBER 1950

Dear Sheila,

Ay, indeed, the family were away, and I went with them—part business, to see & speak with some Americans in Southampton, where the big

Atlantic Liners come & go; and part holiday, the first I've had for fifteen years. I'm very sorry we weren't in to give you a cup of tea, and have a chat with you. We stayed in Salisbury, & went to a number of places in Wiltshire, including Stonehenge—where Angel Clare & Tess of the D'Urbervilles (Hardy's novel) had their last night together. I prowled through Salisbury & Wincester Cathedrals, for I have something to say about Salisbury's in my next biographical book. I am very sorry I didn't see you. The lad you saw "flash past in a small car" wasn't our Breon—he has no car, big or small. We have a Ford 8 which is a family car, &, when we are all together, it is a big and uncomfortable crush to get into it. Breon is a handsome lad, right enough, six foot two, & powerfully-built; but, if he wants a car, he'll have to earn it. He has a bicycle, an old one, now, but still rides it in London.

I'm glad you enjoyed your visit to the Abbey of Buckfastleigh, though, you know, it is an imitation of a German Monastery from altar to font. If your Doctor is a clever one, he may think he's "Right-Wing," but he is really a Communist—all men & women who serve the people are Communists—let them call themselves what they may.

I'm afraid my plays have gone out of print again. Numbers of persons have written from Ireland complaining; but these days of labour shortage and book binding materials make this a common occurrence. It can't be helped.

Of course, your Lord didn't mind the visitors photographing the altar—He had to, & has, many worse things to hear; though casual photographers often are guilty of bad taste, or worse, bad manners. G. B. S. is a very brave man. If only the prelates of the Church R. Catholic & Anglican had a tithe of his courage & honesty—not to mention his literary power, the world would be better than it is. There is no "brink of eternity," for, if eternity there be, time is part of it; so we are all in it; come into it the second we are born. I'm writing a quotation in the books, for I'm a little shy of being pompous by writing something of my own. When I came back here, a pile of letters waited for me, so I'm busy trying to answer some of them. I think you do well to live with your mother—what part of Wiltshire? And now Seán leat [1] for the present: love.

Sean

---

[1] Seán leat: Sean be with you; a play on the common Irish expression, slán leat: health be with you, or goodbye.

To George Jean Nathan

MS. CORNELL

TOTNES, DEVON

29 SEPTEMBER 1950

My very dear George:

I hope you have been away some where in a consoling sun for the summer, & that you have benefited by the change. Here, we haven't had such a miserable summer for seventy years—rain, wind, & cold airs toning us down instead of toning us up. The slash of constant rain has keened away the season. We can but look forward now, with hope, for the next one.

I suppose you are back again in New York now that the curtain of the theatre rises again. May it be a good season. Here, Eliot and Christopher Fry—with "Cocktail Party" and "The Lady's Not for Burning" seem to be the only ones who parade with any honour over the stage. There is one by Ibsen, "Rosmersholm" and Pinero's "Second Mrs. Tanqueray"; &, of course, the American Musicals "Oklahoma," "Brigadoon," & "Carousel"—high as heaven above the home creations.

I've just got a note from Dick [Madden] suggesting Basil Langton as Producer for "Purple Dust," which worries me, for I don't think he the man at all for the play. I've seen him produce here "Gaslight" and Shaw's "Arms & the Man" at Dartington Hall Barn Theatre. Excellent for the place, but as dramatic creations go, very ordinary things indeed. I am writing to Dick to tell him so. Dick tells me he produced some of [Paul] V. Carroll's plays in London. So he did, and one of them was terrible. Indeed, all that Carroll has done since "The White Steed" [1938] has been done on the borders of the valley of the shadow of death. Langton's producing unit in London was one going about the environs, & no better than hundreds of its kind.

Tom Quinn Curtiss was with us here for a few days, & a good many Americans have visited us this summer. They have an American College Drama Summer School here up in Dartington Hall, with students from England & Ireland attending it. Let's hope it did some good.

I do hope you are feeling fit, & that, during the present season, you'll look after yourself more than usual. Breon & I look forward to reading your latest Book of the Theatre.

My love to you.
Ever yours
Sean

To Brooks Atkinson

TS. ATKINSON

TOTNES, DEVON
9 OCTOBER 1950

My dear Brooks:

It was very kind of you to write to me, advising that I should say "Yes" to a written interlude between Murray Schumach & me. I don't like "interviews" at all, & have refused many requests from persons requesting a visit "to ask me a few questions." I'm not an "Answerer" such as has been depicted by Whitman. After another thousand years of life, I may become qualified. I'm afraid I should have edged away from Murray's request, had he not mentioned your name. I'm very glad I did see him, for I liked him well, &, I think, he liked me. Our lad of fifteen took a great shine to him, & thought him a grand chap. If he be of the same mind about the article, when he gets back to New York, then let him go ahead—for his own sake, for yours, & for mine. But I don't like to be shoved away from the community. Authors, I imagine, Brooks, are inclined to think too much of themselves—light around them a halo of superiority & separation—as seems to be suggested in Sir Osbert Sitwell's "Noble Essences." [1] I must say, I have a great respect for the man or woman who can plough a field with a tractor; or even with a plough pulled by a pair of horses—like Robbie Burns.

You didn't mention your own book. Did you manage to get a publisher? It is odd in Letters how frightened many people become, when a writer changes his tone! They fence us in with the style of our own first work. What matter, if they could be certain of a book's success; but this forecast of the fate of a book is no more certain than a producer's forecast of the success of a play. But there you are, Brooks, & we are helpless under their frightened conceit.

I hope you have recovered from the kill of the woodchuck. Our prime enemies here are slugs, destroying or maiming the few frail flowers we have.

I do hope Oriana's book will be a success in every way, but don't let her work too hard on it. I hope she takes a spell for rest in the weekends.

God give you a good theatre season.

My love to Oriana & to you.

As ever,
Sean

And thanks once more for your very, very kind thought.

[1] Osbert Sitwell, *Noble Essences* (1950), fifth and last volume of his autobiography, *Left Hand, Right Hand!*

To Seumas Scully

MS. SCULLY

TOTNES, DEVON

9 OCTOBER 1950

Dear Seumas.

Here's the books inscribed to Peone Doyle & yourself—what a wretched format they have for 4/–! French's net a pile from these Amateur Companies. Thanks for notices of "Goldfish in the Sun." [1] Critics seem to be divided & uncertain, as the Irish ones usually are. I hope the play is better than you seem to think. The Abbey (and Eire) could do with a new dramatist. But let him not waste too much time on Radio— it's near as bad in effect as films. Alas, that so many die so needlessly & so heedlessly. I'm glad you liked the Bronte country, though it sounds damned lonely to me.

I am working at biography, & answering many letters—mostly American.

Tell any inquirer that Vols. 1 & 2 of "Collected Plays" are "not out of print." Macmillan's have written to say that they are re-printing, & will be on sale again in November. The first Impression was sold out quicker than they thought it would be.

All the best to you from all of us.

As ever.
Sean

[1] Donal Giltinan's *Goldfish in the Sun* opened at the Abbey Theatre on 2 October 1950.

To David Marcus

TC. O'CASEY

[TOTNES, DEVON]

25 OCTOBER 1950

Dear Mr. Marcus,

Thank you for your letter mentioning the possibility of Johnston's article arriving too late for publication in your next issue of IRISH WRIT-

ING, and your suggestion to hold mine over, should that happen, till a subsequent issue.[1]

Personally, I prefer that mine should be published as arranged, with, or without, Johnston's article.

Frankly, I am not eager to appear cheek by jowl with Mr. Johnston, who, according to Mr. [Eoin O'] Mahony, S.C., refused to sign his name to a petition for the release of the Irish prisoners who were rotting alive in Dartmoor Jail. I have very little respect for the bourgeois caution that prevents a man from taking the part of men, brave men, too, however we may disagree with what they may have done, and honest, as well, who were less fortunate than himself.

So I prefer to go in without Mr. Johnston's support, if it be all the same to you. I should like to add that you are under no obligation to publish it at all. I gave it very reluctantly, and would just as well wait till it appears in a future book. And, again, there is the resentment that young writers have to an old hand monopolising space that might be well given to them.

Yours sincerely,
Sean O'Casey

[1] Both articles appeared in the same issue: Sean O'Casey, "A Gate Clangs Shut" and Denis Johnston, "Joxer in Totnes," *Irish Writing* No. 13, December 1950. O'Casey's article was reprinted in *Rose and Crown* (1952).

To David Krause

MS. KRAUSE

TOTNES, DEVON
29 OCTOBER 1950

Dear David Krause:

Bravo! You got your M.A. anyhow. I got the finely bound copy of your thesis,[1] which now stands beside one from Texas and another from Indiana. You mustn't ask me to analyze it, or to give you my opinions about it. Your own opinions are much more important to yourself than ever mine can be. No, you haven't been rash in putting in anything signed by me; though by now (if I remembered them) I might have a different outlook. So will you, as the years go by; if we didn't change, we'd cease to live.

[1] See O'Casey's letter to Krause, 9 August 1949, note 1.

I'm glad you got a job in New York University. I've a friend there—
or he was there, when I last heard from him—David Greene.

Further success to you, young friend, in a full and ripening life.

Yours very sincerely,
Sean O'Casey

Mrs. O'Casey wasn't well, and I have to do many things about the house,
and for our children—hence the delay in writing.

My dear young friend,

I've just had time to read your Thesis. It's fine from my point of view.
I certainly seemed to have builded better than I knew. I enjoyed it immensely.

And I've read my own letters again. I wouldn't alter a line of any of
them.

Good knocking at the door of life to you; and a quick opening; and
brave things done in the House.

S. O'Casey

To George Jean Nathan

MS. CORNELL

TOTNES, DEVON
3 NOVEMBER 1950

My very dear George:

Don't bother at all about any play or thing till your mind has eased a
little. It is very sad about Mencken going,[1] but there's no way out of these
things. The hard thing is that a lively mind is lost to man—a serious thing
when so many herds of bellowing fools are left to live & plague the world.

I have no life-long friend (fortunately, perhaps), & so will, at least,
excape this kind of grief; though I feel very upset indeed at the passing
away of G. B. S.[2] Eileen was with him Saturday last, & sat with him for
an hour—he was very fond of Eileen. She tells me he was woefully thin,
but his humour hadn't abated, & his eyes gleamed as brightly as ever. He

---

[1] Henry Louis Mencken (1880–1956). In late 1948 Mencken suffered a severe
stroke that damaged his power of speech and his ability to read and write. Two years
later, in 1950, a massive coronary occlusion brought him to the verge of death, at the
time when O'Casey wrote to Nathan. But Mencken lingered on in a tragic state of
aphasia for six more years until he died on 29 January 1956.

[2] Bernard Shaw died on 2 November 1950 at the age of ninety-four.

said he was tired, & now definitely wished to go; & that it would be interesting to meet the Almighty. Eileen: I'm sure the two of you will get
on very well together. Shaw: I'll have a helluva lot of questions to ask him.
She says he made her stroke his forehead, & murmured that it was fine to
feel the touch of a soft Irish hand & hear the soft sound of an Irish voice.
Eileen thinks he was back in imagination with his mother, when he was a
young lad. Then he fell asleep, & Eileen stole out. Talking to the nurse for
10 minutes, Shaw rang the bell, & asked if she had gone. On hearing she
was just going, he asked her to be sent in again that he might say goodbye, & give his love to all the O'Caseys. She lingered there till he was off
to sleep again, & then came away. Perhaps his last words were "his love
to the O'Caseys." A great loss. "It's up to Sean, now" was another of his
whispered remarks. A remark I didn't welcome, for I could never be a substitute for G. B. S.; nor would I try to try.

Don't let memories of Mencken dwell too much with you. We have
to go on with life as long as we can, & as well as we may.

Eileen hasn't been well, & went away for some time for a rest &
change; so I've been busy minding house, & getting our little girl to school
every morning. Eileen's back now, & much better. I am working at biography, roughly writing a few things about my visit to the U.S.A. fifteen
golden years ago.

My warm love as ever.
Sean

To Wright W. Miller [1]

TC. O'CASEY

[TOTNES, DEVON]
4 NOVEMBER 1950

Dear Mr. Miller:
It would be impossible for me to write an article about anyone or anything by November the 10th; much more so to write one about such a man
as Shaw. I loved the man, and I am glad and proud that a message to me
was one of the last (probably the last) things he murmured before he sank
into unconsciousness. It is comparatively easy to write about the thing you
hate, much more difficult to do so about a man you have loved.

Another thing, and a very important thing, too: What is the Ministry

[1] Wright W. Miller, Central Office of Information, 62–64 Baker Street, London
W.I.

of Information thinking of when they offer an author these days a fee of 7 guineas for a 1000 words? Are they putting all their spare cash into their own Saving Certificates? I get more from a poor, little Magazine—IRISH WRITING—published by two struggling admirers of literature who live in Cork—15 guineas for 1500 words. Some three or four weeks ago, I wrote an article about G. B. S. for THE NEW YORK TIMES,[2] and got 65 pounds for it. I know you have nothing to do with this, but isnt 7 guineas a lousy fee for the M. of Information to offer anyone?

I get nine-tenths of my income from the U.S.A., and as time goes by swift, I must concentrate on doing what I have set myself to do, rather than waste time writing for next to nothing. I did the article for IRISH WRITING with great reluctance, and only because it was an Irish effort deserving of support.

Indeed, I remember writing an article on Shaw, years ago, for the M. of I., one that was shown to Shaw—a thing I never expected to be done—, and G.B.S. replied saying it was "superb, and ought to be syndicated." It never was, of course, and I have no copy of it, which causes me regret, though I dont at all think it was as good as G. B. S. thought it to be.

You will have to excuse me from the work of doing what you suggest.

With all good wishes to yourself,
Yours sincerely,
Sean O'Casey

[2] Sean O'Casey, "Bernard Shaw: An Appreciation of a Fighting Idealist," *New York Times Book Review,* 12 November 1950; reprinted in *The Green Crow* (1956).

To Peadar O'Donnell

TC. O'CASEY

TOTNES, DEVON
6 NOVEMBER 1950

Dear Peadar:

Sorry I couldnt write about G. B. S. I have just refused to write one for the Ministry of Information here, for their Magazine ECHO. I wrote one some weeks before he died (when I had no idea at all that death was near, and that he would choose to go with him; for that is what happened.) for the NEW YORK TIMES MAGAZINE. His dying was brought much more close to me than I had ever expected—in this way: Eileen (Mrs. O'C.) went up to London recently, and there she got (she says) a curious feeling that she should go to see G. B. S. She had been there before, at

G. B. S's request, with John Dulanty. G. B. S. liked Eileen a lot, so with this feeling on her, she went to see John D. at his office, but he wasnt there; so Eileen decided that she would abandon the idea, though the Secretary suggested she should drop in the following day, Saturday, the 28th October. When Sat. came, the feeling was there as strong as ever; but she resisted it till 12-30, and then went to John D's office, and met him just as he was about to go out. "I want you," he said, and told her G. B. S. had expressed a wish to see her; that she should ring up, and ask the housekeeper if Shaw wished a visit—no-one at this time thought the end was so near. Eileen rang up, and the housekeeper said G. B. S. would like to see her for a few minutes if she came now. So off she set, taking a taxi from Welwyn—for that is the one way to get safely to Ayot St Lawrence (I'm told, for I was never there); and to keep your taxi till the end of the visit, if you want to get back safely, too. The few minutes ran into three quarters of an hour, during which G. B. S. kept chatting intermittently, the musical voice reduced to a whisper. He said he was ready to go, for he had become tired of having to depend for everything on the help of others; and he disliked strongly having "to be minded by those he didnt know." He couldnt stick it, and so he willed his death. He told Eileen so, when she rallied him, and said he'd rise out of it, fit as ever. "I want to go now," he said; "it is better to go now." He added with his usual smile, "It'll be interesting, anyway, to meet the Almighty."

"I'm sure," said Eileen, "the two of you will get on splendidly together."

"I'll have a helluva lot of questions to ask Him," he murmured.

"Take it calmly," said E. "till Sean gets there, and then you can start a row."

"I'll find it hard to take it calmly," said G. B. S., "for I've always been a fighter." He asked her then to stroke his forehead, which she did, and he murmured "It's fine to feel the touch of a gentle Irish hand, and hear the sound of a soft Irish voice."

Then he sank into a sleep, and she softly left the room, stopping without for a chat with the nurse. After a few minutes G. B. S. rang his bell (he had one tucked up near his shoulder somewhere). The nurse, having answered the call, came back to say G. B. S. had asked if E. had gone; and on being told she had not, but was just going, he said he'd like to see her again, to say Goodbye. So she went in to him again, and, she says, with one of his old lovely smiles, he said Goodbye, and gave his love to all the O'Caseys.

"I'm finished," he said, "and now it is up to Sean."

"But, Sean's seventy, now," said Eileen.

"Well, up to one of the boys, if their lives arent wasted by another war."

Then she sat beside him till he fell asleep, and then left for London.

Eileen thinks that part of the time, G. B. S. was back in imagination to the time when he was a lad with his mother. How much this is sentiment, I dont know, for the experience moved Eileen very strongly, and she has in herself a peculiar motherly wisdom and great charm. When she phoned to tell me these things, adding that G. B. S. was dying, I still couldnt believe it, and, like a damned fool, wrote him a letter of "sympathy," adding that if he once passed through the winter, the spring would enable him to look forward to the summer, and be his old self again. When she returned home, the following Tuesday, Eileen convinced me that Shaw's end was very near. I wish now that I had gone to see him sometime in Ayot St. Lawrence, when he was lonely after his wife's death; but I'm a shy lad, and wouldnt risk a visit unless I was certain that a visit would be welcome.

Well, there it is, Peadar; "Up to Sean": He meant it kindly, and as a kind of order of merit, but I have no intention whatever of even trying to try to be another Shaw. Except that as he was a Communist, and so am I (he had a picture of Stalin where he was lying, on the wall in front of him, and one of Gandhi too); as he hated war, so do I; and as he was for the people, so am I. But as for being anything equal to him in wit, valour, or achievement in authorship, I must decline his good and gracious invitation to take up the mantle fallen from his shoulders when he crossed the river of Jordan. In fact, it is up to each of us to see that we use the courage, the wit, and the wisdom of G. B. S. for the achievement of peace in the world, commonsense in international relationship everywhere, and a strong heart with a ready hand to fight on till fear, want, and ignorance be banished from among the nations of the earth.

By implication of your tel. I assume that THE BELL is to appear again, and to ring once more. I am very glad.

As ever,
[*Sean*]

To Vincent Duncan Jones [1]

TC. O'CASEY

[TOTNES, DEVON]
10 NOVEMBER 1950

Dear Mr. Jones,

I am sorry, very sorry, that I cannot be with you during the Peace Congress in Sheffield. The two ideologies in the world today are those who are fighting for peace and those who are fighting for war; it is no longer a question of politics, but a question of life or death: who is for death and

---

[1] Vincent Duncan Jones, Secretary, Sheffield Peace Congress, British Peace Committee.

who is for life—that is the choice each has to make today. At one time it was those who wore the muffler, the manual workers, who suffered most of the agony of war; but war makes a wider swoop now, and anything below the status of a tiara or a mitre will be in the front line of the dreadful devastation. Not only agony and appalling deprivation now, but agony and repulsive mutations among the generations to come. War is no longer led by a bright flag, but by a skull on the top of a staff. The bright flags now are only in the field, the factory and the workshop.

It is criminal the way some interested politicians are trying to assure the people that the atom bomb isnt such a terrible thing after all. In the book, MR STANDFAST [1919], by John Buchan, later Lord Tweedsmuir, a British General caught in a London air-raid, is made to say "The man who says he doesnt mind being bombed is either a liar or a maniac. Bombs dropped in central London seemed a grotesque indecency. I hated to see citizens with wild eyes, nurse-maids with scared children, and miserable women scuttling like rabbits in a warren." And this general was talking about the air-raids of the first world-war; raids that were but the pattering of a few hailstones compared with the hail of bursting, blasting explosions that tore cities to pieces in the war that followed, and which we all remember still. It was more than a mere grotesque indecency; it was a searing, savage horror. We can make a stammering guess at what we shall have in any future war when the atom bombs are falling. Anyone, to me, who says a light word about such an event is a liar, a maniac, or a scoundrel. Over the wireless it was stated that a Unesco Committee had proclaimed that because of the last war sixty million children needed material and psychological help. The children, the children! Well, maybe the next war wont be quite so bad; no child may need either material or psychological assistance, for they will be all blown out of existence. And their mothers with them. Oh, to hell with war!

One of the last things, perhaps the very last thing, said by Bernard Shaw (unrecorded so far, but recorded now), before he sank into unconsciousness, was "I hope the energy and the time of the young wont be wasted in another war." That was his wish; let it be our determination. To hell with war!

Yours sincerely,
Sean O'Casey

To Mort and Irma Lustig

PC. COLBY L.Q.[1]

TOTNES, DEVON
28 NOVEMBER 1950

Dear friends,

Thank you so much for the book by Matthiessen,[2] talking about old American friends of mine, Emerson, Whitman, Melville, & Hawthorn— Thoreau I knew only by name. I am reading it during snatches of leisure I slice from a very busy time. So little time, so much to do, & I grow tired more swiftly than I used to—my head is bending low; but it can shoot up now and again to face things and fight them. I'm writing to the USSR Embassy here, suggesting they should get "American Renaissance" for Moscow Library. Several times they have asked me to suggest books to them; but it is seldom a good one shows a sail. I don't think the American people are "mad." Like us, here, they are stupified at the possibility of another war; & the last one gave them an inkling of what the next would be like. It won't be like anything that has gone before, for, if it does come, it will bring about what the profiteers, the politicians, & the Press want to avoid—world revolution. This will come—is actually here—anyway; but I'd prefer it to come quietly, as it can, if men be sensible. Personally, I don't think there will be a world-war; opinions—even the silent ones—are too strong against it. War has lost all its bright and gorgeous banners, & now carries only a black flag. The bright and thrilling banners are carried now by Peace. It is she who now wears the coloured garments, sings the song, & is loved openly by the many, & secretly by all.

Yes; as with you, the "Left" here has been, and is, very often very stupid. I've never met sillier or more actively stupid minds than the few local Communists here; all Marx and meddling, without sense or tact or understanding. At the last elections, they not only lost all new seats they stood for, but even the two they had, & spent thousands on trying to do what anyone with sense could have seen was foolish & impossible. They should have concentrated on Peace; & so I told them, but they wouldn't listen. They have to do it now. It is the vulnerable chink in the reactionaries armour, for all want Peace; or negatively, do not want war. I have thought from the first that Korea will ruin McArthur. His "our Father" hasn't done the trick yet. More than one Paternoster is needed; & he must be getting tired. I'm sure England will back away from any tussle with China; & that

---

[1] Irma S. Lustig printed this letter and three others from O'Casey (11 December 1950, 29 November 1951, 30 May 1964) in her article, "American and Apollonian Temples: Conversations and Correspondence with Sean O'Casey," *Colby Library Quarterly,* June 1972.

[2] F. O. Matthiessen, *American Renaissance: Art and Expression in the Age of Emerson and Whitman* (1941).

means Europe will follow her. Even the giddy Monsignors preaching to Mothers to give their sons to God and death won't work; the sons have a say in it; & not many of them want to go to Korea; & fewer who are there want to stay. The world is with Peace & us.

My love to you both.
Yours sincerely,
Sean O'Casey

To George Jean Nathan

MS. CORNELL

TOTNES, DEVON
30 NOVEMBER 1950

My very dear George:
   Your book [1] came the day before yesterday, and all I've read of it is grand. Breon when he heard of it, demanded it at once, so, out of my affection for him, I sent it on to him. Thank you so much for letting me have it, accompanied by the glowing tribute from G. B. S.—an order of merit of the first class. I was very glad to read your review of Eliot's "Cocktail Party." [2] Eileen & Breon had seen it done in Dublin, & were puzzled. I had read it, & was more puzzled than they. I couldn't get into it at all. To sit down to write a review of it would have been completely beyond me. But since I've read yours, I could write a lively one. In criticism I am pretty good at following a trail blazed by another. Theologically, I think Eliot is confused. I'm afraid he won't rank as a Doctor of the Church. I don't think "Harcourt-Reilly" is indicative of the "Deity," but of the Church—Anglican-Irish & "Alexander McColgie Gibbs" of the "Anglican-Scots Church plus Dominions"; can't exactly place "Julia." The psychologising of "Celia" seems to be "conversion," & the result of that, the determination to devote a life to God: a "vocation," which some times is a doubtful thing. A vocation fulfilled is a "blessed" thing; unfulfilled, a deeper damnation. But "Celia" goes the right road, & is "faithful unto death." The error is that Eliot seems to believe that saintly sacrifice must be sensational—a heresy. Recently, there was an outbreak of smallpox in Glasgow, and one doctor and two nurses, in caring for patients, contracted the disease, & died. Now this sacrifice in the way of duty was less sensational, but just as glorious as, & much more sensible than, the sacrifice [of] Celia in Kinkanja. Eliot fails,

---

[1] *The Theatre Book of the Year, 1949–1950* (1950).
[2] *Ibid.* T. S. Eliot's *Cocktail Party* opened in New York on 21 January 1950.

in my opinion, in failing to understand, or even interest himself in, the life in his own street. As for the play as a play, I personally much prefer Fry's "Lady's Not for Burning." [3] The poetry is far finer, & the play much more of a song; though it gives a childlike view of the middle ages—Fry hasn't read G. G. Coulton's "Five Centuries of Religion." Your review has given me a fine insight into the play. I know now where I stand. And an insight into Eliot, too, for I've read a lot of his work, & was puzzled—I've touched on it in my present biography, comparing his "Waste Land" with Hugh MacDiarmid's "A Drunk Man Looks at the Thistle." [4]

I got your review of Fry's play, and think he deserves all you say about it. Eileen & Breon saw it, & thought it delightful. And thanks for what you say about me. Naturally, I'm very pleased, & hope I deserve your admiration. In a way, I think I do; though I'm always tormented with a feeling that what I've done could have been done better. And, of course, it could: that's what makes the impression so painful.

A letter from R. Watts, Junr, says you "are looking well these days," which is very gratifying to me. Eileen was with G. B. S. a day or so before he sank into unconsciousness—he asked her, through the Irish Ambassador, to come down to Ayot St. Lawrence. I'll tell you more in my next letter. This is just to say I got your book, & that I will say more when Breon sends it back to me.

> *All my love to you.*
> *As ever.*
> *Sean*

[3] Christopher Fry's *The Lady's Not for Burning* opened in New York on 8 November 1950.
[4] See "The Dree Dames," *Sunset and Evening Star* (1954).

To Frank McCarthy

MS. McCarthy

Totnes, Devon

6 December 1950

Dear Frank,

I've been very busy & my eyes trouble me a lot so that I have to do work in rushes with the head down. Mrs. O'C. wasn't well, & had to go away for a week or so, which made me busier still, getting up mornings to get the children to school. Up in the morning early! See you are back in the old seamen's den. Possibly, as good a place as any other. Dalkey is a lovely place, indeed. Lennox Robinson had a lovely place there on a hill by the sea, with own private strip of beach & all. But he had to give it up— too lovely to last. Like your job in Southall—too good to last too. Ay, indeed, Sally Allgood was a great actress, though not quite the artist her sister Molly, was—if one could keep her from the habit of looking for laughs. I never had a word from Sally from the time she went to America 17 years ago. Yes, she was always whining, & always short of dough, though she must have done well. Odd mixture; one minute primed with prudery, the next one leppin with sex. I knew her very well, but, as I said, heard nothing from her when she left for Hollywood. Nor, for the matter of that, have I had a single line from Barry Fitzgerald either. Odd, that, for, in a way, my plays did a lot to help them. I imagine they guessed I'd go for them for staying in Hollywood.

> All the best to you,
> *As ever,*
> *Sean*

To George Jean Nathan

MS. CORNELL

TOTNES, DEVON
8 DECEMBER 1950

My very dear George:

You've sent me bad news, and after R. Watts, junr. had written me to say you "were looking well these days." I am very sorry to hear of it, but don't let yourself worry too much about it—it would make things worse; though I, myself, when my heart gives a little flutter, rush off into a world of concern. You'll have to limit yourself a lot—give up wine & smoking, & a lot of your usual work. I've had to do it, who could keep up to the stoutest navvy going; or woodman, either, with a heavy-handed axe. All I can do now, in the way of manual work, is to carry an armful of logs or a bucket of coal. A few weeks ago, I forgot, & carried a heavy bundle of laundry upstairs, & then had to lie down for a few days; and send for the doctor. Now I have a special bottle from which I take a few drops in brandy, if I feel the heart tighten too much. It's a nuisance, but it can't be helped; & we've got to submit. If you take reasonable care of yourself, you can live as long as G. B. S. You got the note from him just in time. Eileen (Mrs. O'C.) was with him a few days before he became unconscious—he asked her to come to Ayot St. Lawrence, through the Eire Ambassador,

John Dulanty. She had a long and curious talk with him. I'll tell you about it when I hear you are feeling well again. Why not take—say two hours rest lying down—sleeping, if you can—every afternoon? I do, & find it a great help in keeping alive.

Do try to mind yourself, George. Don't worry about anything—even the war. I don't believe there'll be one: we're tired of burying the young. Take things easy.

My deep love to you.
Sean

To Irma Lustig

PC. COLBY L.Q.[1]

TOTNES, DEVON
11 DECEMBER 1950

Dear Irma,

The letter I sent to you wasnt meant for publication—if it had been, I should have been more careful, not about the content, but about the form. However, if it should (or if you think so) have in it any seed towards checking the rush to war, by all means publish it.

But the question goes deeper than General McArthur's reputation, which is but a bubble; goes deeper than the honour of the disunited nations fighting far from their own countries; goes deeper than any form of "aggression" postered up on all the world's walls: the deep question is—Are we going again to bury our young? That is what war will mean; that is what ever war has meant—even in wars that had to be waged as in the case of the war against the maniacal Hitler. But we have gone a long way into sensible consciousness since that grim time. We want now to create a world conscience in which the young will be allowed to live the widest span of life that they may give of their talents and energy for the common good. The banner of the Young is for life and achievement, not for death and destruction. That Monsignor who declared that God wanted the Young to die is either a blasphemous omadawn [2] or a blasphemous rogue, ready to toady to the rich and the influential. Take away the profits from war, and war would sicken and die. It is a terrible thing that bigger bottles of champagne should be slapped down on tables, richer fur coats worn by rich women, gaudier gatherings of all things should result from the killing

[1] See O'Casey's letter to Mort and Irma Lustig, 28 November 1950, note 1.
[2] Omadawn (amadán), fool.

and mangling of the Young. We do not want our dear young to die; we do not want our dear young to be blinded; we do not want our dear young to limp. We want them upright, bright-eyed, active in all things, always singing the song of life. We cannot make an end of youth. There is no hope for life without the Young, for it is the young who carry life on into the future: the young Americans, the young Chinese, the young of England, and the young of Korea. They are the silver trumpets of life.

> Oh, silver trumpets, be ye lifted up,
> And call to the great race that is to come! [3]

So Yeats wrote, and so say I. Let the Young live!
All good wishes to you, to Mort, and to all friends, and all enemies.

Sean O'Casey

[3] See O'Casey's letter to Jack Carney, 26 March 1943, note 3.

To Joseph Jay Deiss

MS. DEISS

TOTNES, DEVON
12 DECEMBER 1950

Dear Jay Deiss,
Thank you for the clippings. I am well used to now of hearing of the putting on of a play and the putting of it off again.

I'm afraid my comments on your fine book [1] were neither "fine nor discerning." I've no experience of reviewing, for I've always been reluctant to comment upon the work of fellow authors. One is likely to be conceited about one's own work, & so inclined to be cold and unfair to the work of others. I think reviewing should be set aside as a special art, so that the reviewer can have no conscious or unconscious envy of an author writing in a different vein. I have seen so much envy among the Irish writers, each using all the means he can (very often despicable) to lower any estimation of value in the work of another. It's a pity your story wasn't made into a play—it would, I think, have made a fine one. It is sad to think that those, who are battling for "freedom of thought," are so afraid of a little controversy—because, I daresay, it might threaten their interests. And the Churches, who should be in the forefront for free thought, [are] the meanest & most cowardly of them all.

[1] *A Washington Story*. See O'Casey's letter to Deiss, 7 March 1950.

But, dear friend, I don't think you should read my books to your little ones. I'd much rather they read the Comics. They may have been pleased just to please you—children are very wise, & often very eager to please big people. They should never be asked to do this. I've been among children all my life—there were 20 of them in the last house where I lived in Dublin. I have three of my own—one a big lad of 21, another lad of 15, & a girl of 11; so, here, I speak from experience. Don't let them read Sean O'Casey yet. Let the sevens and tens crowd joy & jumping into their lives— they'll never be sevens & tens again. Don't you try to want them to be like yourself, liking what you like, & hating what you hate. Let them be free for the few years of youth. Are they boys or girls, or a boy & a girl? God be wi' them, be they boys or girls.

No discovery of science could restore, or improve my eyes. Thank you, very much, all the same, for your kind thought. Terramycin would never have ended "my childhood's suffering." A good & nourished life would have avoided it. But there are tens of thousands of children still being born to the same ordeal. Irish slums are worse than ever; & there are many here. That is one reason why I strive for Peace. May your new novel be all you hope it may be. With deep good wishes to you & the 10 & the seven.

Yours sincerely,
Sean O'Casey

To David Marcus

TC. O'CASEY

[TOTNES, DEVON]
21 DECEMBER 1950

Dear Mr. Marcus,

Thanks for the cheque and for the magazine.[1] I liked it, but think I've read better issues. I hope it may have an excellent sale. I do hope you wont lose on this venture, for the young Irish writers do need a practice-ground for their literary imaginations. The article by Johnston on me is amusing and, I fear, very ignorant.[2] If the laddo knew more about Ireland, he'd know more about Totnes. As a matter of fact, Totnes is as Irish as Navan or Kells. The very name of the County "Devon" was given by a Keltic

[1] *Irish Writing* No. 13, December 1950.
[2] Denis Johnston, "Joxer in Totnes." For a more detailed account of O'Casey's reaction to this article and to Johnston, see "Deep in Devon," *Sunset and Evening Star* (1954).

tribe who came here from Ireland before the Gaels came to it. Johnston could have learned this, if he had read T. F. O'Rahilly's "Early Irish History and Mythology." The whole district is Keltic, as are parts of Dorset, Wiltshire, and, of course, Cornwall. The Dart which runs through Totnes is derived from the Irish word for an Oaktree, and means "oak-lined." About a hundred years ago, this part was known as "East Ireland"— according to "The Irish in England"; and Ireland proper used to come here to play hurling against them, under the title of West Ireland V East Ireland. And surely he should know Ireland's close connection with Bristol? The district here is packed with crosses quite obviously copied from the "Keltic Crosses" so beloved and hacked to pieces in Ireland. And we are surrounded by the "good people," named "Pixies" who prevent a man leaving a field, lead him astray, and joke with him in the way of the leprecaun and the pooka. There would be many what Johnston calls "arty-crafty" buildings in Ireland had they not been destroyed ruthlessly and thoughtlessly by the Irish, as any number of The Irish Penny Journal would have told him. Totnes is as arty-crafty as Longford or Kilbeggan, caring about art as much as Mat Haffigan in Shaw's play [*John Bull's Other Island*]. The "Civic Centre" is just the Town Hall or village hall of an Irish town. The parish priest here [Father E. Russell] is a Dublinman, and our family doctor [Dr. George Varian] is another; and the Irish are found everywhere, and get on well with the West Country people. The Keltic aspect goes up to Cumberland, where the shepherds still count their sheep in Gaelic—a haon, a do, a tri, etc. I'm afraid Denis isnt quite so knowledgable as he makes himself out to be—the man who didnt know who painted "The Sleeping Venus" shows what he knows about the art of painting. But, of course, there has always been this pretence at knowing among the upper middle-classes of Ireland. As for losing "compassion" for the people, it comes ill from one who refused to sign a petition for the release of the Irish political prisoners from the horror of Dartmoor. This isnt for publication, for I'll probably be writing something like this in a future vol. of biography; and a lot about Yeats, too, things Johnston is ignorant of. All the best to you,

Yours very sincerely,
[*Sean O'Casey*]

VIII

OF REVOLUTIONS AND WRITERS, 1951

You seem to think a "revolutionary" must be a fire, an earthquake, or a big wind, forgetting the still, small voice. G. B. S. was an earthquake, a fire, a big wind, and, also, a still, small voice. He was all, in all, through all, a Revolutionary of the first order. And he was Irish, too, which—to many—made him bewilderingly incomprehensible, especially to the English. But the still small voice has accomplished many revolutions— James Joyce was a revolutionary in literature; Freud one in psychology; Yeats one in the Theatre, ably seconded by the redoubtable Lady Gregory: all working—though they didn't know it—under the Red Flag.

I'm sure that no one can write anything worth a damn without annoying someone: Joyce did; Yeats did; Hardy did; and so did Tennyson. And Jesus annoyed a crowd of people. However, I havent written anything just to annoy, but simply wrote down what I felt I must write down. And that was done, not to annoy any person, but to free myself from annoying God.

The urgent need for world peace was at the center of O'Casey's thoughts now, and he commented on it in most of the letters he wrote. If he had his own way in the world, he would have started a spiritual revolution against war. As a conscientious Communist he couldn't understand how conscientious Christians could appeal to the Prince of Peace and glorify bloodshed; and he was nauseated by the militaristic posing and praying of General MacArthur in the Korean War: "To halt Communism, Christian countries must do better than this, do better than, like MacArthur, recite the Lord's Prayer amidst heaps of dead his soldiers have killed." And again: "Let God rule now instead of MacArthur, says I." He often sounded more Christian than the bloodthirsty Christians. When he was trying to be cautious on a warning from his publisher not to provoke any libel actions in *Rose and Crown,* the fifth volume of his autobiography, which he had just completed, he wrote in March to Daniel Macmillan: "If I be inclined to libel anyone, I'm inclined to libel myself." When the unpredictable Dr. Simcox wrote to him again in a conciliatory attitude, O'Casey replied in June in a gentle and confessional mood: "You are probably quite right about me being a sentimentalist. I am inclined to wear my heart on my sleeve for daws to peck at. G. J. Nathan, the American drama-critic points out that Irish playwrights not only wear their hearts on their sleeves, but their very gizzards too." His sentiments were always out in the open, completely exposed for admiration or abuse. Whether in agreement or disagreement, everyone knew precisely where O'Casey stood on any issue, and he insisted on speaking out on all issues: war and peace, religion and politics, art and propaganda, the Hollywood Ten and McCarthyism, cinema and drama, life and letters in Ireland, and controversial productions of his plays. At one point, in declining to support some worthy organization, he stated that he had written twenty-six messages for various causes over the past ten months, and, though he didn't want to withdraw from the ongoing fight to improve the conditions of life, he felt he had to give it a temporary rest.

He was often suspicious of well-meaning people who wanted to organize his life for him. Early in the year when Lady Astor was trying to arrange a friendship between him and Christopher Fry, whose *Lady's Not for Burning* he admired, he resisted her fussy efforts in a crisp and comic manner that quickly ended the affair: "I don't 'approve' of C. Fry—he may, for all I know, be a bloodier villain than terms can make him out. I like his work in the drama; that is all." A day later he was writing to someone from the progressive Theatre Workshop in Glasgow who wanted him to help sponsor a new type of people's drama, and he sent back the following missile that must have stopped any further talk about the sponsorship: "What's the use of talking about 'drama oriented towards the people'? All good drama's tending towards the people; I dont know what 'oriented' means. Why go on using these damned journalistic words? . . . Cant argue any more—just recovering from Influenza, and so hardly conscious of anything, bar silly journalistic jargon." In the summer when a film producer innocently asked him to help provide some publicity for one of O'Casey's favorite actors then appearing in a new film, the old revolutionary must have sounded old-fashioned when, instead of publicity, he offered a sharp lecture on the artistic advantages of acting in the theatre rather than in films: "No gifted actor should take more than a sip of the films; for kinema art, if it be an art, isnt the art of an actor (that is for the living stage), but the art only of the camera, art of an artificial and mindless eye. The camera is the actor of the Kinema; that is why the films damns an actor."

Nevertheless, his denigration of the cinema as a medium for actors didn't prevent him from publicly defending the Hollywood Ten, the film writers who had been persecuted and blacklisted in America. He also defended Communism as "pro-man" rather than "anti-God," but above all he stressed the right of every individual to earn his living freely no matter what political beliefs he held. His letter to *The Author* then led to a separate controversy with a Major Money, who drew him into the familiar arena of religious and political conflict, where O'Casey exposed the major's muscular Christianity to some of his ironic anthropological barbs: "Surely, you dont expect me to accept the account of Man's Fall as reported in the first chapters of Genesis? That would be to assume that Darwin had ne'er been born. Fossils are facts you know." In another letter to the major a few days later, O'Casey added one of his typical Communist epiphanies: "Communism isnt 'Russian.' I was a Communist years and years before I heard the name of Lenin mentioned; and so was Shaw, and tens of thousands of others. . . . Communists accept the wisdom and imagination and humour of all great minds—Darwin, Milton, Tolstoy, Byron, Dickens, and Jesus Christ, et al." This sort of humanistic appeal to the classics and Christ must have confused many Marxists as well as Christians on the true meaning of Communism. It didn't confuse O'Casey, however, who went on broadening the base of his political faith to include the best of all possible great minds.

His attention was predictably drawn to Ireland on a number of occasions when he thought the country had disgraced itself again. He was shocked when he discovered that the Irish dispensary system of the Red Ticket for the ailing poor, a stigma that he had personally known fifty years earlier, and had just recently used in his farcical one-act play *Hall of Healing,* was still functioning and demeaning the people. He was so angry he publicly berated the pious de Valera for spending too much time on religious devotion while remaining indifferent to the "god-damned Red Ticket." There was another surprise in store for O'Casey, however, when one of the better and more enlightened satiric writers, Myles na gCopaleen (Brian O'Nolan), suddenly launched a venomous attack on the Abbey Theatre's revival of *The Silver Tassie.* A fire had destroyed the old Abbey, and the directors decided to reopen in the Queen's Theatre with O'Casey's play. Possibly Myles was still carrying a grudge against the Abbey since the failure of one of his plays there, and perhaps he was using this occasion for foolish revenge, for he even went beyond the tabloid hysteria of *The Standard* when he called the play "as loathsome and offensive a 'play' that has ever disgraced Dublin's boards." The symbolic second act, he claimed, was "a straightforward travesty of the Catholic Church ritual," and the rest of the play was "bunkum and drool." O'Casey was stunned by this absurd savagery, which he could only associate with the typical "envy, Hatred, & malice" of literary life in Dublin. He had experienced a different kind of surprise earlier in the year when Sean O'Faolain, who for a long time had consistently attacked him in reviews for being too anti-Irish and anti-Catholic, had a change of heart and mind when the Mother and Child health scheme was not so secretly defeated by the behind-the-scene pressure from the Irish bishops, who called such health care Communistic and immoral. Now it was the devout O'Faolain's turn to be outraged by his clerical countrymen, and in his indignant article in *The Bell* he sounded exactly like the O'Casey he had always attacked, declaring that an Irishman "cannot be a good Catholic without being anti-clerical." O'Casey could have told him that if he had been willing to listen.

To Brooks Atkinson

TS. ATKINSON

TOTNES, DEVON
[? JANUARY 1951]

My dear Brooks:
    Very much bright thanks for your fine present. It was received with cheers. It was very kind of O[riana] and you to send it. I hope America may never run short. Once again, me lad, we start around that Sun of yours, day by day going through an epitome of the year. We have our scud, too, chattering at the windows, and ice on the roads, making me long enough for the first daffodil. Even the few birds about are shivering, & we leave a bit of fat (when we have it) about so that they may live and not perish. They have shared the ham, strips of its fat cheering them up while the frost stings. It is odd, when one thinks of it, that Oriana Atkinson & Brooks Atkinson, in faraway New York, should have a hand in giving some comfort to the robins, thrushes, & tits of Totnes. We gave a piece to a neighbour, too,—policeman's wife, who gave us some sugar some time ago. Extraordinary, the barter that goes on here now a curious but necessary Exchange.
    I suppose Betelgense is swinging now over 84th (I think) Street,

rivalling faintly the Light of Broadway. Ah, yes, Brooks, we must recognise the realities though they dazzle us, or dismay us either. I know a Speaker in Hyde Park here who loved Betelgense—always mentioned it in his speeches. He was an independent atheist & amateur astronomer; a book-binder by trade who wouldn't work for God almighty or for Betelgense. Jim Jenner, the Atheist in "Within the Gates" is modelled on him. Had lunch with him a number of times when we lived in London.

> My love to Oriana & to you; and thanks again.
> *Ever yours,*
> Sean

To David Marcus

TC. G'CASEY

[TOTNES, DEVON]
6 JANUARY 1951

Dear Mr Marcus,

Enclosed are the 8/– and the tanner for goods received, with thanks. I hope your Magazine will go well. I cant understand, though, why you go on with it, and risk reputation and life and money. What I think of D. J. [Denis Johnston] or what D. J. may think of me is of no importance to anyone, outside of ourselves, and but of faint importance even to D. J. and S. O'C. And what about your own sweet accusation of my being a "black protestant"? [1] D'ye know what a B.P. is? The things which make a B.P. shiver and shout dont affect me in the slightest degree. Looks like you were trying to "poison the well"; "He is a B.P. therefore unreliable, and a bigot." But what I have said in most instances, was said first by R. Catholics themselves. Indeed, you fine defenders of the faith know damn all about the faith you defend. Do you know that St. Bernard fought against the acceptance of the then theory of the Immaculate Conception, aided by all the Dominicans, and other saints? That it is almost certain that St. Benedict didnt go to Communion more than once a year, and that once it required a miracle to make him realise that it was Easter Day? And what about your own odd ignorance of Duchesne? And Rubens! Was he one of the early Church Fathers? What! Is the work of Rubens, the pageant of buxom materialism even the pictures discerning divine events; are these the gospels

---

[1] In an editorial, "O'Casey's Court," *Irish Writing* No. 13, December 1950, the editors, David Marcus and Terence Smith, described O'Casey as a "Black Protestant."

and the Missal? I wonder what would father mulligan of mullinvat [2] say to
this? Well, we'll leave it at that, though I could have given you many more
names of those who werent B.P.'s, such as Mivart, Tyrrell, Dollinger, with
hundreds of others ranging from the Middle Ages to the day that is with us.
By the way, Duchesne's book was placed on the Index—it was too honest
by half.[3]

As for Strindberg's "sympathy with the Catholic Church," you must
remember that the Church in Sweden is very different from the C. in Spain,
in the S. Amer. Republics, and even in Ireland; that it was the same in
Poland till the Law of the State became more potent than the clerics'
Canon Laws. The Church has to behave itself in Sweden as it has to in
England, and even in Ireland, for there the minority is too strong and
numerous to be ignored. By the way again, not a single priest that I know
of, and certainly not a single Bishop asked for the release of the Irish
Political Prisoners from Dartmoor or Parkhurst prisons. Merciful men!
Another 6d on the magazine shouldnt do any harm. Of course prices are
going up, there and here in spite of D. J.'s pathetic idea and hope that Eire
can keep out of the trouble bustling about everywhere around her.

Well all the best for the present.

[Sean O'Casey]

[2] An imaginary and typical country priest.
[3] Louis Duchesne's Early History of the Christian Church (1910) was placed
on the Roman Catholic Index Librorum Prohibitorum in 1912. Of the other writers
O'Casey mentions above, St. George Mivart's Happiness in Hell (1892) was placed
on the Index in 1893; Johann Joseph Ignaz von Döllinger's The Pope and the Council:
On the Dogma of Papal Infallibility (1869) was placed on the Index in 1869; and the
Rev. George Tyrrell, S. J., was the author of a number of controversial books on
Roman Catholic doctrine.

To Roy D. V. Johnston [1]

TC. O'CASEY

[TOTNES, DEVON]

11 JANUARY 1951

Dear Mr. Johnston,

Thank you for your letter and for offering me the honour of becoming
the President of your Society.

I have to refuse the honour, however, for many reasons. I have as
much to think of and more to do that I can even inconveniently accomplish

[1] Roy D. V. Johnston, honorary secretary, Fabian Society, Trinity College,
Dublin.

for years to come, should I be allowed to live so long. I cannot permit myself to be committed to any other activity in thought or in deed.

I am not attached to any organization whatsoever in Eirinn, and dont wish in any way to alter that unattached condition of participation in any way.

I am a Communist, and have been one now for nearly forty years, so, with all respect, I am inclined to think all Fabian Societies a little old-fashioned.

To my thinking, what is wanted is a more militant outlook in the minds of members of the Irish Trades Unions, and corporate unity to make that outlook strong and menacingly influential.

And the same need is, I think, evident in the minds of the Irish writers, who are, I imagine, fearful of saying anything which might bring down a sacerdotal remonstrance upon their heads.

Please give the Members of your Society my deep thanks for offering me the honour, and say how grateful I am to them for their good opinions of me.

Yours sincerely,
Sean O'Casey

To Lady Astor

TC. O'CASEY

TOTNES, DEVON
14 JANUARY 1951

Dear Lady Astor,

Thank you for your letter, dated the 3rd of this month. It is seven years since I heard from you, a holy number, seven days of the week, seven gifts of the Holy Ghost, seven sacraments, and many others. I'm glad you are as busy as ever, and hope Lord Astor and all yours are well.

Eileen and Breon saw Mr. Fry's play, LADY'S NOT FOR BURNING,[1] and liked it tremendously, much better than RING ROUND THE MOON.[2] I have read the former play, and, indeed, like it a lot. Though not, even by implication, true to the scent and savour of the Middle Ages, it is delightful poetry, and full of very charming fancies indeed. Something worthy has at last appeared—by an Englishman—on the English stage.

[1] Christopher Fry's *The Lady's Not For Burning* opened in London on 11 May 1949.
[2] Jean Anouilh's *Ring Round the Moon,* translated by Christopher Fry, opened in London on 26 January 1950.

Whether Mr. Fry likes my plays or no is his concern, and not mine.

As a matter of fact, I know quite a lot about the last days of G. B. S. The world, indeed, will miss him. To me, he is as much alive as ever—not in the Christian way, or even the Christian Science way; but in the living on of the great mind in the world's life and the world's affairs. Eileen was with him twice for a long time during the last days, and had long chats with him. He sent for her through John Dulanty who was, as you know, Eire's Ambassador, and a great butty of G. B. S.'s. He—G. B. S.—gave the O'Casey's his blessing on her last visit, and tried to hand his mantle over to Sean. "It depends on Sean, now"; but the cloak is far too big for Sean, though he has long ago torn a piece from it, and wears it tightly woven into his own mantle. He was very fond of Eileen, which is something she is very proud of.

I'm not surprised that you disagree with a lot I said about G. B. S.[3] He was, all the same (as well as being a great playwright), a revolutionary saint, or a saintly revolutionary—whichever way you like to put it.

We are all well, all here, (bar our eldest, who is at an art-school in London), and I am busy with a lot of things, including another vol. of biographical sketches.

With all good wishes to you and yours from Eileen and me.

Yours sincerely,
Sean O'Casey

[3] Sean O'Casey, "Bernard Shaw: An Appreciation of a Fighting Idealist," *New York Times Book Review*, 12 November 1950; reprinted in *The Green Crow* (1956).

To Lady Astor

TC. O'CASEY

[TOTNES, DEVON]
19 JANUARY 1951

Dear Lady Astor,

Thank you for your kind letter. I write this in haste to persuade—should you come to Plymouth—not to ask me to come to see you. I am in the midst of writing a further vol. of biographical sketches, and wont permit the entrance of any distraction. It will take me near a year to finish, and more, and more. As well, I have a lot of other work to do and many letters to answer. I have had to refuse a lot of requests—one from the Ministry of Information for an article on G. B. S.; and now I have been presented with a request from the Editor of the American THEATRE ARTS for an article—and the Editor happens to be a friend of mine—so what shall I do, now, oh what shall I do! And a meeting with C. Fry must wait for a future day.

You seem to think a "revolutionary" must be a fire, an earthquake, or a big wind, forgetting the still, small voice. G. B. S. was an earthquake, a fire, a big wind, and, also, a still, small voice. He was all, in all, through all, a Revolutionary of the first order. And he was Irish, too, which—to many—made him bewilderingly incomprehensible, especially to the English. But the still small voice has accomplished many revolutions—James Joyce was a revolutionary in literature; Freud one in psychology; Yeats one in the Theatre, ably seconded by the redoubtable Lady Gregory: all working—though they didnt know it—under the Red Flag.

I dont "approve" of C. Fry—he may, for all I know, be a bloodier villain than terms can make him out. I like his work in the drama; that is all.

There's no such thing as "conversion," except the "conversion" of bonds. There is growth, or, in other words, the never-ending process of evolution.

Now, all good wishes to you and yours,

Yours sincerely,
Sean O'Casey

To William J. Jackson [1]

TS. O'CASEY

[TOTNES, DEVON]
20 JANUARY 1951

Dear Mr. Jackson,

I cant give the sponsoring relationship you ask for, because I really dont know very much about you. What's the use of talking about "drama oriented towards the people"? All good drama's tending towards the people; I dont know what "oriented" means. Why go on using these damned journalistic words? I know the play you mention—at least, I have read it.[2] It is a fine play, in my opinion; but may be destroyed by a bad production; and how do I know that you will give it a good one? I have a pretty good experience of many Societies and Groups "fostering" drama of all kinds, and my experiences havent been happy ones. My own plays have suffered badly.

[1] William J. Jackson, Friends of Theatre Workshop, Glasgow.
[2] Ewan MacColl, *Uranium 235* (1948), a documentary play.

That is the misfortune of a play that has worth in it: it doesnt get what it deserves; indeed, it usually gets a production so cheap and so amateurish that the play is destroyed for the rest of the time the author has to live.

In respect of "Uranium 235," all I can do is to hope it may get the production it deserves; and if it does, then, that you wont be able to find room for all who will flock to see it.

But for God's sake dont keep on about "drama oriented towards the people". This is just jargon; and we have had enough of this god-damned talk that nobody understands, and nobody is interested in. A good play remains a good play, whether it is "oriented towards the people", or not. Read St Joan, Dream Play. And hundreds of others, including Hamlet. And dont talk much about "the culturally conscious sections among the working-class." All who earn a living are of the working-class. Why is it to be "culturally conscious"? If we be conscious of our "culture," then we're just snobs.

Cant argue any more—just recovering from Influenza, and so hardly conscious of anything, bar silly journalistic jargon.

All good wishes,
Yours sincerely,
[Sean O'Casey]

To Elizabeth Sprigge [1]

TC. O'CASEY

[TOTNES, DEVON]
22 JANUARY 1951

Dear Miss Sprigge,
You waste your time and mine writing to ask me to let The Watergate Theatre do COCKADOODLE DANDY. Under no circumstances can I give it to them. That is final.

I have already written to Mr. Billy Gay telling so, and why it is so, and, surely, since he is one of your producers, he told you what I said to him.

For God's sake send down no producer to me—young or old. I have too much to do to even answer a knock at the door.

---

[1] Elizabeth Sprigge, Watergate Theatre, London.

I am glad to hear your book is nearing its completion. I hope it may be a great success—and deserve it.

> *All good wishes,*
> *Yours sincerely,*
> *Sean O'Casey*

To Picture Post

3 FEBRUARY 1951

Stage Censorship

I, of course, agree with everything said by Mr. Monsey about the censor of plays.[1] Arnold Bennett, Granville Barker, and others have protested against the power held by this Court official over the expression of the dramatic mind; and the banning of *Blanco Posnet* here,[2] and its attempted banning by the Viceroy of Ireland from the Abbey Stage, led to the issue of an essay on the censorship by Bernard Shaw, so powerful, so witty, so effectively critical, that no man can add thereto, and no man can take from it. In theory it annihilates the censorship, and, as well, forms one of the higher examples of Shaw's penetrating and delightful prose. Yet few read it now, and the censor is still in his office, as much alive as ever. My own play, at first, *The Star Turns Red,* was banned by Lord Clarendon, who said, it was reported, he didn't like the theme. As if, when I sought a theme for a play, I paused to ponder whether or no it would please duke's son, cook's son, or son of a belted earl, or the belted earl himself, for the matter of that. Years after, the same lord gave permission for public performances. I have been so often banned and denounced, here, in Ireland, and in parts of the U.S.A., that I have become casehardened and almost indifferent to censorship, official or unofficial, when it deals with drama from the view of what it calls "morals, decency, and religion." But there are censorships worse and more dangerous to drama than that of a Court official—the censorship of fine drama by the manager-directors of the theatres, whose one burning thought is the getting of money, who, if they do venture to put their hands on a good play, usually maul it into a minor

[1] Derek Monsey, "Despot in the Wings," *Picture Post,* 20 January 1951, an article attacking stage censorship in Britain, on the occasion of the Lord Chamberlain's refusal to give a license for a London production of Lillian Hellman's *The Children's Hour* (1934), a play about lesbians. E. C. Castle, editor of *Picture Post,* had asked a number of theatre people to comment on Monsey's article, and besides O'Casey's, letters were printed from Alec Guinness, Peter Ustinov, Michael Balcon, and others.

[2] See O'Casey's letter to Daniel Macmillan, 20 August 1948, note 2.

status by a wretched production, and who would, with quiet souls, tear any play to pieces, however high in the canon of drama it happened to be, if they weren't sure that it would make a pot of money for them. The other odious censorship is the coolness of the English drama-critics to higher work, and who never make any effort to promote a good play to the warmth of the established stage. The play in question is an example: I saw *Children's Hour* in New York 16 years ago,[3] and it has taken all that time to reach the stage of London! And then only to a theatre which few know about, and few attend. The better the play, the less the managers will have to do with it, the less the drama-critics will bother about it. These make drama criticism just a way of living, rather than accept it as a vocation.

Sean O'Casey

Station Road, Totnes, Devon

[3] Lillian Hellman's *The Children's Hour* opened in New York on 20 November 1934.

To Frédéric Joliot-Curie [1]

TC. O'CASEY

[TOTNES, DEVON]
5 FEBRUARY 1951

Dear friend,
    I wish, indeed, that my wish could carry me to the Peace Conference to be held in Berlin, or Council, from Feb 21st to the 24th. I wish your meeting every success. It is a shocking thing that the leaders in so many countries, mine own included, seem to be so afraid of peace. I daresay one reason is that in peace, people have time to think, and in thinking, they want things more to their liking—which wouldnt be good for the profit-mongers lingering on in the world, who would be ready to sacrifice millions to preserve their own gains. Indeed, we here are now realising what we shall have to pay for all this lunacy of re-armament for a war that no one wants and no one needs, except those who want to retain out-of-date privi-leges, or foster additional profits into their banking accounts. I have met many people here, numbers of them who look upon Mr. Churchill as pos-sessing minor divine powers, but I have met none who want war. What they say is "We dont want war," or "we have had enough of war," or "War is the last thing we want."

[1] Frédéric Joliot-Curie, President, World Peace Council, 2 Rue de L'Elysée, Paris 8.

But, I imagine, that this mad preparation for war is really aimed at checking the Soviet Union in its progress towards a fuller Socialism. Well, the world's peoples have no objection to the Soviet Union building up life in a sensible and effective way; so any attempt to check the socialistic growth of the Soviet Union is actually an attack on the peoples' life; the people of Europe and the people of Asia, of Africa, and of America too. Those who want war, those who prepare for it are a minor world in armour set against the major world in overalls. The people now hear the voice of God, not from pulpit or from platform, but from their own shouting for peace and brotherhood, for labour and great achievements all the world over. The world of peoples will not have amongst them the bloody maniacs now set free by those in power in Germany. They arent fit to mingle among decent men; and they are not going to be let torment and destroy the German people again. We will not have the world blasted as Korea has been shamefully and shamelessly blasted to preserve the grand prestige of a MacArthur, or a hundred MacArthurs, who take good care to keep out of Korean graves, and more, take care not to be cold in the winter or too hot in the summer. The surety and safety of the world's peoples are more to life and to God than their damned comfort and maniacal ideas of honour and prestige. Peace among the Nations! is the people's war-cry, and a blessed war-cry it is. Let it ring out all over the world like ten thousand bells!

> *My respect and my love to you.*
> [*Sean O'Casey*]

To Patrick F. Byrne

TS. BYRNE

TOTNES, DEVON
8 FEBRUARY 1951

Dear Pat Byrne,

I didn't hear the broadcast of the play, "The Plough." [1] You see, reception here in the evening isn't good. It is fine earlier on, but many interferences occur after 7.30. Indeed, the Sou' West isn't good for most receptions, except West Regional, which comes from Bristol, not far away. Thanks for telling me: and I'm sorry I didn't hear it. I hope it went well. By the way, is Seumas Hughes (Seumas O'h-Aodha) of the long ago—

---

[1] *The Plough and the Stars,* adapted by Norris Davidson, directed by Micheál Ó hAodha, was broadcast on Radio Eireann on 21 January 1951.

he used to be in Liberty Hall, and once refused to put music to a song
of mine (Call of the Tribes), written during the fight against the B. and
Tans; and which I burned in anger at the refusal—showing what a fool I
was then. He refused to put music to it, because I was a follower of Jim's,
then in America, and the Transport Union was under the paternal, eternal
care of Bill O'Brien. All over now, and I sincerely hope S. O'hAodha is
well. An announcer still? When I was in Dublin last 1934 or 35, I caught
a glimpse of him, while the wife was saying a few words on the wireless,

All best wishes,
Yours sincerely,
Sean O'Casey

To Eric Gorman

TS. GORMAN

TOTNES, DEVON
10 FEBRUARY 1951

Dear Mr. Gorman,

Thank you for your letter asking for permission to put on Juno in
consequence of the financial failure of a new play by a young fellow.[1]

I suppose there's nothing to do but give you permission, though it's
hardly fair either to the young playwright or to me. To me, because the play
wont (possibly) be rehearsed well enough, and there wont be time to ad-
vertise in the usual way; to the young fellow because his failure will be
followed by a very popular play. It would have been better for him if a
less popular one (yet one that would have been fairly satisfactory financially) had been selected as a substitute.

Well, you have the necessary permission, and I do hope it may not
do him harm or discourage him. All dramatists, new commencers and old
stagers alike, have failures to bear.

The Influenza epidemic is very severe here in England, and is still
sweeping through the towns and country places. Our elder boy was down
in London with it, but we here havent had it yet, though half the town is
on its back with it. I am fairly fit, though I grow old, Eric, I grow old. As
well, the English are in the throes of a fear that war may come, and

---

[1] When the twenty-five-year-old Maurice Meldon's first play, *The House Under
Green Shadows,* which opened at the Abbey Theatre on 5 February 1951, received
bad notices, the Abbey management announced on 8 February that a revival of *Juno
and the Paycock* would open the following week. A promising playwright, Meldon
died tragically three years later in a road accident.

desperate efforts are going on to scrape a few together for Civil Defence, though all in their hearts know there can be no defence in the next war. I am an Associate of the Atomic Scientists Association, and reading their bulletins, it is clear that neither brown paper nor steel can shield a soul from atomic concussion and flash. The steel table we had here during the last war for the children to shelter under would melt like butter in a red-hot oven in the flash of an atomic explosion. For me, I dont believe there will be a war—for one thing we havent the cash to pay for one.

Well, all the best to you and to Mrs Gorman.

Yours sincerely,
Sean O'Casey.

To George Jean Nathan

MS. CORNELL

TOTNES, DEVON
25 FEBRUARY 1951

My very dear George:

I hope by the time you get this, you will be much better. Rest is the main thing: you will just have to keep quiet for the time being. And when you get better, you'll have to go slow—one book every two years, or three years, instead of a book a year.

Don't worry about arrears of work. There always will be arrears of work facing him who has the gift of writing. If you were one hundred & fifty, you'd still be in arrears. An old Irish song has the title of "Táim in arrears, in arrears," but these were in Tigh na nOl—the tavern.[1] But it's the same with the gifted writer—he's ever singing "Taim in arrears, in arrears." So don't bother too much about, for this bother hinders recovery.

So take it easy, dear fellow, till you can go about again.

My love to you and my blessing on you.

Ever yours,
Sean.

P.S. Breon took your fine picture from Theatre Arts Mag., & has it hanging up in his room in London.

[1] "I Am in Arrears in the Tavern," an Irish drinking song.

To Lillian Gish

MS. GISH

TOTNES, DEVON
6 MARCH 1951

Dear Lillian:

Many thanks for your kind card with its kind greeting which came to us at Christmas. I have had so much to do that I hadn't a second to acknowledge the card sooner. I hope you have had a busy time, too, since "Within the Gates" clanged shut in New York for the last time. I am just mentioning it now, with a few comments about experiences in New York for another biographical volume, that I have prepared in MS for future publication—if Peace isn't put in pirson.

I daresay you are finding it harder to live now—with more to pay for what you need. I don't believe there will be a war—here we are too tired to even bother about it. We need a long, long transfusion of peace into our souls before we'll be able to stand steady on our two poor feet.

I hope you and Dorothy are keeping fit. All the best to you both. Eileen sends her love to you.

As ever,
Sean

To Daniel Macmillan

TC. O'CASEY

[TOTNES, DEVON]
7 MARCH 1951

Dear Mr. Daniel,

Thank you very much for your letter dated the 6th of March, and for your kind interest in the present work [*Rose and Crown*].

I dont think there is anything libellous in it. I certainly had no feeling of writing any thing so derogatory while I was working at it. If I be inclined to libel anyone, I'm inclined to libel myself. But, as you wisely say, it is better to make as sure as assurance can be by getting a lawyer to look over it.

I am sure that no one can write anything worth a damn without annoying someone: Joyce did; Yeats did; Hardy did; and so did Tennyson. And Jesus annoyed a crowd of people. However, I havent written anything just to annoy, but simply wrote down what I felt I must write down. And that was done, not to annoy any person, but to free myself from annoying God. Of course, some of my conceptions may be wrong—nay, all of them may be so—but they are all honest; though that isnt saying that they are true or proper. Let a man examine himself, says St. Paul, and I have done this often, and most often when I am writing, so as to try to prevent anything malicious creeping in to what I am setting down.

I should like, I think, to have the MS back—as I mentioned in my first letter—for I have a few things to add or change in some of the chapters; and, with things as they are, I'm afraid I might get only page proofs from the printers, which would be very embarrassing. Besides, I thought of giving an Inn Sign as title to each of the chapters, and would like to brood a little over the idea. I could let you have the MS finally before a month has passed.

I will send on the Agreement signed as requested later on as soon as I get it witnessed. I presume you will deal with the Macmillan Company of America side of it; or shall I write to Mr. [Harold S.] Latham about it?

All good wishes to you.
Yours very sincerely,
Sean O'Casey

To Frank McCarthy

MS. McCARTHY

TOTNES, DEVON

12 MARCH 1951

Dear Frank,

Thanks for the Irish Times cutting.[1] It isn't really a "forthright" article. Of course, Legal Adoption isn't contrary to Canonical Law; and it is practised in Italy, Spain, & Portugal, as the I. Times says. But there it is just handing over a child from one Roman Catholic charge to another R.C. charge. In Eirinn there is a big Protestant community, & so the Roman Catholic Church acts differently, & opposes, successfully, the practice—

[1] A controversy arose, and continued for many months, when Charles Casey, S.C., the Attorney General, attacked the *Irish Times* for its editorial position in favor of the legal adoption of children. In his remarks, reported in the *Irish Times,* 14 February 1951, Casey, supporting the stand of the Irish hierarchy against legal adoption, objected to the views of W. A. Newman, then assistant editor of the *Irish Times,* who, besides his editorials, had initially called for reforms in an article, "Legal Adoption," *The Bell,* January 1951.

not openly, but through its lay adherents, as per the Attorney General, Monsieur Casey. It becomes in Eirinn (Legal Adoption) for all practical purposes, contrary to Canonical Law; And the I.T. knows this damned well; but sidetracks the issue. This is the R.C. Church everywhere: Where it is all-powerful, or almost so, it just rides roughshod over everyone; Where it is a minority, it goes about secretly, full of tolerance and goodwill to all men.

But it is being challenged now, even in its own heaven—in Poland, Czechoslovakia & Lithuania—even in Italy; and more of that to the power that reigned & resisted so long.

All good wishes to you.
As ever,
Sean.

To Harold S. Latham [1]

TS. MACMILLAN, N.Y.

TOTNES, DEVON
18 MARCH 1951

Dear Mr. Latham:

Thank you so much for your very kind and encouraging letter. It is, of course, grand to hear that you like so much the Manuscript of THE ROSE AND CROWN. Your high praise was unexpected, and was all the more welcome for that reason. I thought you might like it, but not quite so much as you tell me. Hurrah!

One can venture to feel a little younger now.

I hope your stay in London may be a pleasant one, though London isn't the gay spark she used to be before the last war scarred away a lot of her attractions. Probably you will be too busy to notice it, for it must be a big task to fill a coming year up with book publications that will sell, and that will be worth selling. I hope, too, the weather may improve while you are here—we are a very damp people at the moment, for the rain it raineth every day nearly since yesterday was a month. The farmers here look over their hedges on to their fields, and say, My God! A bulldozer couldn't take up a spoonful of earth, it's all so streaming with moisture. But London is paved, so the going there isn't so bad.

All the best to you, and many thanks again for your good opinions of ROSE AND CROWN.

Yours very sincerely,
Sean O'Casey

[1] Harold S. Latham, Macmillan Company, New York.

To Brooks Atkinson

TS. ATKINSON
TOTNES, DEVON
24 MARCH 1951

My dear Brooks and Oriana,

There's nothing to be said but a warm word of thanks for your very fine and most welcome gift. It presented the surprising thing of a feast in a famine. The fire was kindled & the plates set out, and the lamp shone bright. The children—two of them six feet—had a royal time for a fortnight. It was a very kind thought on your part; but now you will have to look after yourselves, for, by all accounts, straight from the horse's mouth, life is harder now with you than it used to be; & will become harder. Still, I believe that we shall eventually learn (the world) to live together in unity, peace, and concord—to use the words of the Anglican Litany.

I am just running my eye over the MS of another biographical vol. to be called "Rose and Crown." Mr. Latham of the Macmillan Co., has read it, &, in a letter, says "It is fascinating, &, in some respects, important." I hope he's right, though I'm puzzled as to how it can be "important." Perhaps, he meant the chapters about my visit to your country. I'm sure these will interest you. The next vols of "Collected Plays" will have 3 new one-act plays. I'll send you them as soon as they appear. I think you'll like "Time to Go" and "Bedtime Story"; &, maybe, "Hall of Healing." Quotations from some of your published remarks are used in Macmillan's, London, announcements.

Look at what I've sent you—an announcement of further activity on the part of "the foremost critic of our day in the theatre"! To me, he knows as much about theatre & drama as say you did when you were thinking of writing your first school essay. You've just got to look at the kisser to say, Ah!

I liked your article "Foreigners Are OK," though I can't think of the U.S.A. as a foreign country.

All the best to you, dear friend, & to my other dear friend, Oriana, with my love to you both; and thanks again.

Yours as ever,
Sean

To Frank McCarthy

MS. McCarthy

Totnes, Devon

24 March 1951

Dear Frank,

Not bad at all. Not so good as some hymns, but better than most; though High Church would call it "emotional." But I wish our Communists would write better than they do, or stop writing altogether. The extracts they gave from their "Here Goes" in the Worker, which they called bitingly witty, weren't witty at all; rather were they dull and commonplace. I'm busy at the moment with proofs of plays & MS. of a new volume of biography—Rose & Crown; & also trying to help a good woman whose husband is to be tried for housebreaking—the 3rd or 4th time. I used to write to him & send him magazines years ago when he was doing penal servitude in Dartmoor. He's an intelligent & rather educated [man]; a kind husband & a good father, with other qualities. Stupid bastards have taken the children from the mother, who is Irish, educated; loves the children who love her; cared for them most carefully; & who is a natural fosterer of children's welfare. In the USSR, she'd have a State job in Nursery or School. Harold Macmillan, thank God, is getting into touch with the Home Department about it all. I know Vernon Av. well.[1] When I was in Dublin, the Avenue was there to look at, & envy—a thousand miles from my reach. Yesterday, I got a note from a young man of Vernon Avenue, saying he couldn't afford them, and would I send him my 4 biographical books for nix! The wheel has gone full circle. All the best, as ever.

Sean

[1] Vernon Avenue in Clontarf, a suburb of Dublin.

To The Author

THE HOLLYWOOD TEN [1]

Dear Sir,

What a roll of drums there was in your last issue against the Hollywood Ten, against Communism, against the U.S.S.R., and against free thought, with Whinny the Pooh beating the big one. After that thundering tattoo, Communism will probably be at its last gasp. There's nothing left now for the Communists to do but to rush headlong into the Roman Catholic Church, beating their breasts, while the others beat the drums. A grand spectacle—the highlight of the Festival of Britain. And such glorious logic roared out loud too! MacGillivray's "Communists are active enemies of the State"; therefore, since the U.S.S.R. is a State, the Communists there must be enemies of their own State; must be trying to overthrow the State they have established. Well, that's all right by us, so we need only stand by and wait; the U.S.S.R. is done for.

Again, "No-one has a right to demand that he be employed by anyone. If for one reason or another, it does not suit an employer to employ him, that is the employer's business, and the business of no-one else." Everyone born into the world has the right to live, and to live he must work; and so, having the right to live, he has the right to work, and no man, king or employer has the right or the power to take the right to work, and so the right to live, from him. And all this ridiculous idea of the sanctity of "law"—the idolatry of parchment scroll and sealing-wax. Thousands of "laws" have been overthrown by revolts of the people, or have been changed because it was realised by those in power, if they weren't, there would be a revolt against them. The long history of life is a story of laws of privilege and inherited power changed or overthrown by a developing consciousness of the whole collective thought of the people.

[1] In the Autumn 1950 issue of *The Author,* the official journal of the Society of Authors, the editors printed a special supplement, "The Hollywood Ten," by Woodrow Wyatt, M.P. "The Hollywood Ten" were a group of American film writers and directors (Alva Bessie, Herbert Biberman, Lester Cole, Edward Dmytryk, Ring Lardner, Jr., John Howard Lawson, Albert Maltz, Samuel Ornitz, Adrian Scott, Dalton Trumbo) who in November 1947 were cited for contempt by the Un-American Activities Committee of Congress for refusing to answer the question "Are you a member of the Communist Party or have you ever been a member of the Communist Party?" Wyatt reviewed the case and concluded that it had universal implications, that no writer in any country should be imprisoned or blacklisted for his political beliefs. In the next issue of *The Author,* Winter 1950, a series of letters appeared attacking Wyatt and "The Hollywood Ten." O'Casey was replying to those letters written by A. A. Milne, E. J. MacGillivray, Warren Tute, R. R. Money, and Norah Burke. The views in O'Casey's letter in defense of "The Hollywood Ten," in the Spring 1951 issue, were supported by letters from E. M. Forster, Rosamond Lehmann, Ethel Mannin, Jack Lindsay, Eric N. Simons (editor of *The Author*), and others.

The Kremlin must be a terrible place—Satanic agency, one contributor calls it—with Stalin as the big devil, his comrades the lesser devils, and all the Soviet people the little devils ready to plunge the Milnes, MacGillivrays, the Tutes, and the rest into a condition of life worse than Purgatory. All the same, it might be wise to make friends with this mass of unrighteousness, for if violent repression be tried, those who try it are in for a bad shock.

Mr. Money tells us that "the foundation of Communism is anti-God, and, in appreciating this, the Roman Catholic Church is in advance in the field of thought." Aha! the Roman Catholic Church is in the forefront to save humanity, to save and deliver (as Norah Burke puts it) free thought, free speech, and free writing throughout the world. Grand crusade, but hardly the one the R.C. Church is destined to join. In England this Church has now to behave herself, but when she was dominant here, what was she like, eh? The most corrupt and persecuting power in existence. Then, under an earlier than Henry the VIII, all the foreign orders had to be driven out because "of espionage against the intentions of the king," and no foreign order before that was allowed to live anywhere near a coast for the same reason. When even the rapscallion but able Wolsey had to suppress many monasteries and nunneries because of theft, corruption, wantonness, and other deadly sins; though many commonly believe that poor old Henry started the racket. It seems to me that the foundation of Communism is, not anti-God but pro-man, his rights first and foremost, as God allows and God approves, which fight the Church has disregarded ever since she was lifted into power by the pagan Emperor Constantine. It is very nice for the business men and the privileged to put their interests under the flag of religion, as was done in the Elizabethan fight with Spain (by both sides), but we, the people, aren't the mugs we once were, and that trick doesn't work any longer.

The fact is that in the case of the Hollywood Ten, it wasn't the Ten who acted illegally, but those who condemned them. Those who are so much for the law should logically support them, for their condemnation was not only against the law, but even against the American Constitution—a much bigger thing.

To halt Communism, Christian countries must do better than this, do better than, like MacArthur, recite the Lord's Prayer amidst heaps of dead his soldiers have killed; must do better than hold the atom bomb in reserve to throw on all who differ from them, and crowds who don't; must put the people before wealth and privilege: till then, Communism will go on spreading its hope and its victory all over the world.

Yours sincerely,
SEAN O'CASEY.

To Eric Gorman

TS. Gorman

Totnes, Devon

7 April 1951

Dear Eric Gorman,

Thank you for your letter asking about permission to do THE PLOUGH AND THE STARS in the Abbey Theatre during May, and to reopen in July with the play.

As far as I am concerned, you can do this, and welcome, if it suits you—a fella cant say more'n that.

I am very busy just now, having finished the proofs of vols III and IV of COLLECTED PLAYS, and am now looking over the MS of a fifth biographical vol, which the publishers are waiting for, here and in America. I wish I had your capacity (and seeming enjoyment for it—if I remember you rightly in older days in Dublin) for work.

The empty spaces here are filled with posters calling on all to join the campaign for Civil Defence, but all turn their heads away from them. But one in a thousand take notice of them, click the tongue, dtch dtch, and pass on. Footman, pass on! A meeting called in a big town in Yorkshire was attended by one citizen. In Bristol a great display was given of the dropping of an atom bomb, with ambulances, an army, doctors, nurses, sirens, navy ratings, wardens; but there wasnt a soul at it bar the participants—all the citizens went to the football matches. They simply refuse to face the possibility of another war. And, by God, they're right! We had our windows blown in and the ceilings down, with the doors bulging in and out so's you'd think they were live animals; and we have had enough. Let God rule now instead of MacArthur, says I.

Well, all the best to you and to Mrs Gorman.

Yours sincerely,

P.S. I hope the young author of the House in Green Shadows isnt taking things too badly.[1]

Sean O'Casey

[1] See O'Casey's letter to Gorman, 10 February 1951, note 1.

To Robert Lewis

TS. LEWIS

TOTNES, DEVON
17 APRIL 1951

Dear Mr Lewis,

Miss [Jane] Rubin, Secretary to The Richard Madden Play Co., has written to say you'd be in London next month, and that you would like to have a talk with me while youre there.

Indeed, I'd like to have a talk with you, too, but I'm afraid I couldn't go to London to have it. I rarely go there now, for I am an old codger now of 71, unable to do a highland fling or take part in a four-hand reel as I used to do in the days that are gone, boys, gone. And when London then will be crowded with Americans spilling out dollars wherever they go—as most think, having the odd belief that Americans can call dollars out of the air, and that there isnt such a thing as an American who has to count his dollars before he spends them—, it would be a harder job still for me to push my feeble way along. I have been chatting with my elder boy, an art student in London now, about COCKADOODLE DANDY when he was here on holiday, and he to pass the time, did a scene and put down his ideas for costuming the characters. Maybe, you'd be able yourself to take a day or two off out of London and drop down here. We could put you up for a night or two, and give you the best of what we have, and show you Totnes, the oldest Borough—bar London—in England; founded, it is said by one Brutus who fled from Troy while it was burning. The residents point to a stone in the sidewalk, and say, There it is, Brutus's stone, the one he planted his foot on thousands and thousands of years ago.

Well, all the best to you. I have written three new one-act plays, and have sent in MS for another biographical vol., so you see I have kept myself from brooding about the intervals between a promise and a practice. And I am, here and there, with a message now and a message agin, trying to persuade people that peace is as good as war any day.

Yours sincerely,
Sean O'Casey

To Robert M. Smyllie [1]

MS. KEATING [2]

TOTNES, DEVON

22 APRIL 1951

Dear Mr. Editor:

In your valuable Journal for the issue of Saturday, the 14th this month, within an article, titled, "Failure of Health Plan Sad Shock," [3] there's a description of Dispensary methods which I thought had died. And the "Red Ticket" [4] has been mentioned in the latest Boomerang from Maynooth. How I remember them all! Eight months ago, I composed a one-act play—"Hall of Healing," describing experiences in one of them—in North William St. The play was sent in some weeks ago to Macmillans, & will appear in the next issue of "Collected Plays." It is an experience of my own, & is true in substance, in fact, and in detail.

I was very glad to see this "Report to Housewives," for it substantiates everything in my play, & I am keeping it for a possible reference.

Yours sincerely
Sean O'Casey

P.S. This is just a personal note, & not for publication—if published, I might be pestered with requests for the play.

[1] Robert M. Smyllie (1894–1954), editor, *Irish Times.*

[2] Mary Frances Keating, wife of Alec Newman, then assistant editor of the *Irish Times,* kindly allowed me to make a copy of this letter, which was given to her by Smyllie.

[3] Mary Frances Keating, in her regular column, "Report to Housewives," wrote a special report on the defeat of Dr. Noel Browne's Mother and Child Health Scheme, "Failure of Health Plan 'Sad Shock,'" *Irish Times,* 14 April 1951. Dr. Browne, Minister for Health in John A. Costello's Coalition government, resigned on 12 April 1951 after his health scheme had been defeated by bitter opposition from the Irish Medical Association and the Roman Catholic hierarchy. On the occasion of his resignation, Dr. Browne released a series of letters from the hierarchy, printed in the *Irish Times,* 12 April 1951, indicating how the Church had worked behind the scenes to defeat the scheme. For a detailed account of the controversy, see Timothy Patrick Coogan's *Ireland Since the Rising* (1966), pp. 97–102, where this church-state fight is described as having "reached heights of emotion unequalled since the Parnellite split."

[4] People who could prove they were poor and sick were given a red ticket, which entitled them to receive free medical care at the public dispensaries. See O'Casey's letters on the Red Ticket to the *Irish Times,* 28 December 1951, 24 January 1952.

To Irish Times

26 APRIL 1951

"World Peace" [1]

Sir,—We writers believe that our civilisation is unlikely to survive another world war.

We believe that differing political and economic systems in the world today can exist side by side on the basis of peacefully negotiated settlements.

As writers we want peace and, through our work, will try to get it; and we pledge ourselves to encourage an international settlement through peaceful negotiation. We condemn writing liable to sharpen existing dangers and hatreds.

As signatories, we are associated with no political movement, party, or religious belief, but are solely concerned with trying to stop the drift to war. We invite all writers to support this declaration, and to tell us of their support, by sending their names to A. E. Coppard, Hillside, Duton Hill, Dunnow, Essex.

> *A. E. Coppard*
> *Alex Comfort*
> *Sean O'Casey*
> *Christopher Fry*
> *Laurence Housman*
> *Roger MacDougall*
> *Compton Mackenzie*
> *Herbert Read*
> *Siegfried Sassoon*
> *Sheila Kaye-Smith*
> *L. A. G. Strong*
> *Frank Swinnerton*

Hillside, Duton Hill,
Dunnow, Essex
22 APRIL 1951

[1] This letter was printed in the *Daily Worker,* 25 April 1951, and in *Pravda,* 26 April 1951.

To Jim Kavanagh

MS. KAVANAGH [1]

TOTNES, DEVON

29 APRIL 1951

My dear Jim,

Thanks for your box of Seamrog [2] & for your kind card of remembrance. I have been very busy getting Manuscript ready for the publishers who were waiting for it, & busy, too, in the effort by the people to keep mad fools from plunging us all into war, as the enclosed cutting shows. I welcome, indeed, the kind greetings from my old friends of the Caman,[3] when Ireland's Hurling Men kept Ireland from wasting away altogether. Of course, I remember them all well; so well, so well. On the whole, they weren't bad days (though you & I had tough times of it, Jim—do you remember the floor of your room, so sodden that it gave way beneath any foot which trod on it?), and I would neither be unwilling nor ashamed to live them all over again. It wasn't our fault that our work helped to pave a smoother way for others to run to jobs, snobbery, and all the opposites of what a Gaelic Nation should be. Give my love to Paddy Callan & to Frances—who embroidered the Silver Lion on the flag of the O'Tooles; & to Leo Rush & to Kathleen. And Tom Russell—good God! is this he with whom I worked so often? If he be the old Tom— young Tom, then—ask him does he ever hear anything of Tom Kennedy, who used to sing Oh, Breathe Not His Name; so well. I think he won a Feis Ceoil [4] medal. A fine singer, but his teeth, rotting in his head, blurred his voice, or he would have been a finer one.

But now you have on a fine row over the Health Scheme. The Bishops again! Remember Dr. O'Hickey? [5] And all that Dr. McDonald, Professor of Theology in Maynooth for forty years said about them? Dr. O'Hickey! Abandoned by the Gaelic League when he was hounded by the "patriot," Archbishop Mannix, then President of Maynooth College. And [Douglas] Hyde keeping well away from O'Hickey's funeral.

Now, the fight is on again, about another & a much bigger question. I wonder how it will go.

Where's Michael Murphy now? Wasn't he literary editor of the Gaelic

---

[1] An imperfect copy of this letter appeared in the *Sean O'Casey Review*, Fall 1975, reprinted from the *Irish Democrat*, November 1964.
[2] Shamrock.
[3] St. Laurence O'Toole Hurling Club.
[4] Music festival.
[5] See "Lost Leader," *Drums Under the Windows* (1945), a chapter on Dr. Michael O'Hickey.

column of the I. Independent? And Cahal Lalley? He came to see me in
London in 1927 or 1928.

> All the happy, far-off things,
> And battles long ago!

Well, Jim, my best wishes to you & yours.

As ever,
Sean

To Major R. R. Money [1]

TC. O'CASEY

[TOTNES, DEVON]
MAY DAY, 1951

Dear Major Money,
  Thank you for your letter. This is a last reply from me, for with all
respect, I still think this correspondence a waste of time.[2] Publish, if you
want to, but, again, I think this is a waste of time and money, for, to me,
the correspondence isnt worth publishing. The earth is not man's "employer," but his property. There is no one but man to own it. The earth
is man's and the fullness thereof; and the collective co-operation of man's
intelligence and labour must be used to make our earth a safe and joyous
place to live in—for all, not for the privileged few. The Religious Orders
kept away from the coast in the early days, for fear that they [who] would
interfere with "the king's intentions" were foreigners. The Irish kept away
from the coast were "British subjects." Whether the first was an unjusti-
fiable or an arbitrary action of statecraft, I dont know. It was a fact. The
second act of precautionary statecraft was stupid, inasmuch while it kept
Irishmen away from certain parts of the country, while building aero-
dromes, it welcomed other Irishmen into high and important positions in
the airforce itself. It was just another example of how ignorant English
officials were about the Irish and how little they knew about them. Surely,
you dont expect me to accept the account of Man's Fall as reported in the
first chapters of Genesis? That would be to assume that Darwin had ne'er
been born. Fossils are facts you know. It was said by some Roman Catho-

---

[1] Major R. R. Money, Royal Air Force Station, Castle Bromwich, Warwickshire.
[2] This correspondence grew out of the controversy over "The Hollywood Ten."
See O'Casey's letter to *The Author,* Spring 1951.

lic theologians that God could have put these fossils in the earth to tempt the faith of man. When Dr. McDonald, for 40 years Professor of Theology in Maynooth College was told that God could have done this, he replied, "He could, of course; but did He?" And there are two accounts of the creation, one by a priest, the other by a folklorist; one declaring that man was created before the other animals, the other that man was created after them. I'll leave you to decide which was right. And, remember that these things werent proclaimed by Karl Marx; he accepted them as most educated men and women do now. Communism had nothing to do with the Higher Criticism of the Bible, nor had Communism anything to do with the discoveries of the anthropologist, James Frazer. You dont say which of the Two Ten Commandments you mean. I suppose you mean those accepted by the Christian Church—who never mentions the other and discarded Ten. But even the C. Church allows that we have gone up from the Ten; that Religion must be something more than a negative force—you must not do this, you must not do that. It has become, or became, a positive force under the New Dispensation as proclaimed by Jesus during his time on this earth. And these fine truths have been proclaimed by other, even by others who came before Jesus. Communism is putting these truths into practice, and the privileged are protesting, and at the same time exclaiming that at the name of Jesus every knee should bow! They want to hold on to their wealth and power. As for my admission that I "dont know what God's priorities are," and your query of "Is that what you are going to tell Him on the Day of Judgement," all I can say is that surely you have a sense of humour? You people opposed to Communism have a happy knack of putting off the Judgement Day to some unspecified date. Every day, my dear Major Money, is a day of judgement.

All the countries you mention—bar those of S. America, about which I dont know surely—couldnt last a fortnight without the Socialism they have established. You have but to look at their budgets to see how much is spent in Public Service—the police, the army, the navy, the postal service, roads, bridges, to mention a few; and then add the expenditures of Local Government Bodies on public services, and you'll see what a gigantic Socialist service in all the countries you mention. It is found even in Persia, and, as you can see by the papers, is developing there. Go where you will, you cant escape it. Communism isnt all theory; there is a lot of common-sense in it. For instance, speaking yesterday, Dalton said Local authorities should have their own architects (he was talking about Housing). There isnt a Soviet town that hasnt its own architect; but, apparently, we havent them. He added a suggestion that houses should be built to suit newly married-couples, others with an extra room so that they could move there when a child came, others with more rooms for families of four and five, and so on; but lousily enough, he didnt add that the Soviet Union has been doing this for years. That may be Communism, but it is also common-sense. I suggest you should read D'Israeli, if you cant stomach

Lenin or Marx. Read what he says about Conservatives, about the Two Nations [3]—The Rich and the Poor, and the great ladies who once governed from Mayfair. Here's just one quotation: "You fine ladies who think you can govern the world by what you call your social influences: asking people once or twice a year to an inconvenient crowd in your house; now haughtily smirking, and now impertinently staring, at them; and flattering yourselves all this time, that, to have the occasional privilege of entering your saloons, and the periodical experience of your insolent recognition, is to be a reward for great exertions, or, if necessary, an inducement to infamous tergiversation." The fine ladies didnt govern the world, but they governed England for a hell of a long time—till Labour tumbled them out of their influence. Well, as for publication, I dont mind mine being printed, as I said, provided that the letters are printed in their entirety, and include this present one. On this condition, I give my permission, though I still think it a waste of paper and of time.

Personally, aside from controversy, I give you my hearty good wishes,

Yours sincerely,
Sean O'Casey

[3] See O'Casey's letter to the *Totnes Times,* 15 May 1948, note 2.

To Brooks Atkinson

TS. ATKINSON

TOTNES, DEVON
2 MAY 1951

My dear Brooks:

I got your book [1] a week ago, and I've been reading it ever since. So far, I've gone round the run with you for eight months—far enough & long enough to know that I thoroughly enjoyed the journey; & will enjoy the rest of the way till the last day of December falls in might over the heads of both of us. I write before finishing to tell you I like your book, like it immensely. It is a grand human account of impression, well seen, and spendidly recorded of a corner of America—Atkinson's corner; &, by and large, a lovely corner, in spite of the dirt here and the sadness there, and the man who brought gold & frankensense to New York, but couldn't get a house to live in. It has been surprising to me how many ways your thoughts and mine have co-incided about New York. In my latest biographical vol, sent to the publishers six weeks ago, there's a fine chapter

[1] Brooks Atkinson, *Once Around the Sun* (1951), illustrated by Don Freeman.

giving my impression of the City,[2] & of the American people I met during my visit there; & many of the impressions seem to be brothers to yours. But I wish I had read this book of yours before I set my foot in New York: it would have been a right royal introduction. I have read it so far with intense interest & grand enjoyment from the Bermans standing by their Kiosk in wind & frost & snow to the dead center of the Summer season when all the birds are molting. Here, Brooks, is the real America, so safely hidden from the films, and, it would seem, from a lot of storytellers, too. I have learned a lot from it about Audubon & his amazing & heroic pursuit of the form & lines & colour of American birds. I'd heard of him; but only a whisper on a breeze; & of Washington, of whom, of course, I'd heard more; but not much more, though a hero to the Irish; and Andrew Jackson, & Jefferson, & the old manor house of stone on Staten Island. I wish I could have seen it. Splendid, too, is your theory that good work with the hands is as much an art as poem, novel, play, picture, or essay; and I, too, give a salud and a saalam or Salaam to the Automobile. A.E. in his "The Aviators," [3] condemns mechanical civilization, does it while his hero, his aviator is sweeping along to the home of a friend in the latest model. "The Gothamite is ignorant of the Bronx." I noticed that, & mention it in my MS: I spoke in the Bronx.[4] I don't agree with all your deductions; I do about the way we fall prostrate before anything with a Greek name. I don't think you're right about Stalin's repression of Music, for instance. The dislike of the present & recent past idea of formal music is evincing itself in other lands. People are going back to the more melodic line: Verdi is coming back into popularity; always my favourite Composer; though, God knows I know nothing about music. And Stalin has written a brilliant thesis on semantics.

Well, Brooks, achara—my friend, in Irish—, I'll write again, when I come to the end of your really fine book. Is this the one some publishers said was crazy? God forgive him. My love to O[riana] & to you & to the Bermans & all.

Yours affectionately.
Sean

[2] See "In New York Now," *Rose and Crown* (1952).
[3] George Russell (AE), *The Avatars: A Futurist Fantasy* (1933).
[4] See "Within the Gates," *Rose and Crown* (1952), for O'Casey's account of his talk at a synagogue in the Bronx when he was in America in 1934.

To Mary Frances Keating Newman

MS. NEWMAN

TOTNES, DEVON

4 MAY 1951

Dear Mary Frances Newman,

It seems incredible that "The Irish Times" should get rid of you for writing such a clear article as that appearing under the title of "Report to Housewives." [1] I could understand "The I. Press," or the "I. Independent" showing you the door; but such a paper as the "Irish Times," one would imagine, could afford to keep a brave writer on its Staff. God Almighty, Eire must be a woeful place in which to live now. The Mother and the Child look well-dressed and well-fed in any picture I've seen of them, & I've seen a lot. But in Dublin, I've seen thousands who were very badly dressed & who looked as if they hadn't been fed at all. I myself must have spent years of my life in cold, drab waiting-rooms on visits to the doctors to get rid of pain for an hour or two, induced by what is called "Malnutrition," but whose true and unholy name is "Starvation." I have pasted your report into the typescript copy of my one-act play, "Hall of Healing." It seems that what I experienced so many years ago is still the experience of thousands. Your Report was supported & confirmed by a woman from Coburg Place—how well I know every house in it; & Wall's Square, than which there were few worse slums in Ireland. This is, or was, at the back of Lower Oriel St. off Seville Place, adjacent to the noted St. Laurence O'Toole's Church. Thanks for the report. It is of great value to me.

I hope your dismissal hasn't done much harm.

Yours very sincerely,
Sean O'Casey

[1] See O'Casey's letter to Robert M. Smyllie, 22 April 1951, note 3.

To George Jean Nathan

MS. CORNELL

TOTNES, DEVON

7 MAY 1951

My very dear George:

I hope you are steadily getting stronger. Recovery needs patience & acute sense to take things easy—the hardest thing in the world for an active spirit to do. It is a trying thing to be in love with work. I have sent in MS of a biographical vol to the Publishers—"The Rose and Crown"; & am jotting down notes for, I hope, the last one—"Goodbye at the Door."

Brooks has sent me his delightful book—"Once around the Sun." It brings America—and, especially, New York, very close to me. In "Rose & Crown," I've written five chapters commenting on my own visit to the City.

England is in the throes of a Festival, though most minds are worried with the possibility of another war. I don't think we could stand one. We are still a quarter—maybe a half—dead from the last one. I am busy myself doing what I can to make peace permanent.

I have heard that Dick Madden is seriously ill with pneumonia. We have enough of natural ills to contend with, without war.

Take care of yourself. I hope you have someone to look after you. I've struggled along fairly well—apart from a touch of Influenza, from which I have just recovered. Watch after yourself, & keep careful.

> *All my old love to you.*
> *Ever.*
> *Sean*

To Major R. R. Money

TC. O'CASEY

[TOTNES, DEVON]
9 MAY 1951

Not for publication

Dear Major Money,

I have no wish to have a last word, nor do I honour the desire to "win" in a controversy, so, as you can see by above note, that this letter isnt for publication. You have plenty to print enough, if you are paying costs yourself, to deprive you of quite a sum, for printing these days is a costly matter. Better to save it for a possible "rainy day"; or a sunny one, for these latter arent much better than those full of frost and bitterness.

If you want to think of the Earth as an employer, go ahead. The right to work is "unqualified," for a man must work to live. If you can accept the "compromise" you mention in the account of man's creation, reputed to be divinely inspired and infallible, you must be a very contented man, indeed. And, I daresay, the same goes for all the multitude of contradictions in the Bible and the many phases of Christian theology. You seem to be awestruck at the "gigantic affair of CREATION," but strangely enough are sarcastic about its highest form—the mind of man; though, forgive me for being so frank, you are in no way modest about your own. Darwin, Marx, and Shaw, however we may differ from what they said or thought, are great minds, living vividly, even though the men, themselves, be dead.

Communism isnt "Russian." I was a Communist years and years before I even heard the name of Lenin mentioned; and so was Shaw, and tens of thousands of others. Communism per se has nothing to do with religious beliefs, with any kind of "faith," as you call it. It is built up on the facts of life and of historical realism, and of historical and social evolution. The English way of life is different from the Eng. way of life of a 100 years ago; and will be very different again 100 years hence. Compare the exhibition of 1851 with that of 1951. It changed when the train did away with the stage coach; when the bicycle came, the combine-harvester, the automobile, the aeroplane. Changed the world over, for these are international alterations in the modes of human living, and the human outlook on life. Look yourself on the way war has changed! Its methods, though its results of devastation have changed only in degree. Communists accept the wisdom and imagination and humour of all great minds—Darwin, Milton, Tolstoy, Byron, Dickens, and Jesus Christ, et al. Judgement is a daily thing, inasmuch as "each day brings forth a noble chance," which was said by Tennyson.

Well, God be wi' you.

Yours sincerely,
Sean O'Casey

To David Garnett [1]

TC. O'CASEY

[TOTNES, DEVON]
[? MAY 1951]

Dear Mr. Garnett,

I have, of course, read about the resignations of the three Directors [2] of The Old Vic, but cant see any reason for signing the protest that you have kindly sent to me.

As far as I know, the resigned Directors didnt protest themselves, so I have nothing to protest about. They havent told anyone a word about

---

[1] David Garnett (1892–　), English author; Hilton Hall, Hilton, Huntington.
[2] Michel St. Denis, Glen Byam Shaw, George Devine.

the reasons prompting them to resign, and it is no good to guess. It seems to me to be foolish to protest about something unknown. Let the Directors take the lovers of the theatre into their confidence, and then we can make up our minds about remaining silent or making a protest.

I have always had my own opinion about The Old Vic from the time I first came to London—as you may read in the next biographical volume of mine—and I have had no reason to change that opinion since. To me it has always been a bit of a cod.

The methods of the British Theatre in toto want protesting against, if you ask me.

Yours sincerely,
Sean O'Casey

To Sean Nolan [1]

MS. NOLAN

TOTNES, DEVON
21 MAY 1951

Dear Sean Nolan,

A message from me! D'ye want to destroy the man? A message from me would be as good as a message from Mars. Michael O'Riordan [2] is his own message. He has all the decent and daring qualifications to represent the people; therefore he'll find it damned hard to win a way for them. There must be a lot of fine fellows in the Union Branch that made him their Vice-chairman. If he's good enough for that, he's better for the Dial. He looks a sturdy lad, &, of course, all those who fought for Republican Spain were sturdy lads. He has nothing to sell but his soul, and he isn't likely to do that; though he'll be told he'll lose it by holding on to it. There's a host of souls in the market-place now, & all of them regulated and well-dressed by the Bishops.

Well, I hope Michael will win; or at least, get so many workers' votes to encourage him on the hard way of fighting for them.

In lieu of a message, I enclose a subscription to the funds.

With good wishes to the mother and child, & to you, & all the Old Guard of "Jim Larkin's Union."

Yours sincerely,
Sean O'Casey

[1] Sean Nolan, election agent, Irish Workers' League, Dublin, used some quotations from this letter for an election handbill, "Sean O'Casey and the Elections."

[2] Michael O'Riordan was the Irish Workers' League candidate for the Dublin South-West seat in the Dail. He received only a handful of votes.

To George Jean Nathan

MS. CORNELL

TOTNES, DEVON

26 MAY 1951

My very dear George:

Thank you for your tribute in the Oklahoma University Press. I don't
worry about the Nobel Prize. James Joyce didn't get it, and so, even the
best of us, those who don't get it are left out in excellent company. There
isn't a book of mine in any Irish Library—I often get requests for copies
from those who "can't afford to buy them"; but giving them that way
would be damned expensive—from one end to the other; so I've no reason to grumble about those in other lands ignoring them. Indeed, I've done
fairly well in your Country, & what I get from the U.S.A. keeps me going.
But your condition is of far more importance, so I hope you are adding
daily to your recovery.

Bob Lewis has been here.[1] He came a fortnight ago, & we had a good
day together. I showed him the sights of Totnes, & we had dinner, en
famille, at an Inn founded in 1630. He is very keen on doing "Cockadoodle Dandy," & proposes that a company should do it in a new Repertory at Cambridge, Mass., first. It could be put on there for a fraction of
the New York cost, & says a first-class New York Company would be engaged. He certainly has tried hard to get money in New York, but failed.
So Cambridge seems, under the circumstances, an attractive proposal.

I daresay you heard of the row in Houston, Texas, over "Red Roses
For Me." [2] I've had a row over every play produced—even "Juno"; though

[1] See Lewis's article on this visit, Robert Lewis, "Visiting Sean O'Casey in
Devon," *New York Herald Tribune,* 29 July 1951.
[2] There were strong protests against O'Casey and his play when *Red Roses For
Me* had its American premiere in Houston, Texas, at the Playhouse, a new arena
theatre, on 25 April 1951, directed by John O'Shaughnessy, with Kevin McCarthy,
Mildred Dunnock, and Joyce Sullivan in the principal roles. A news story in the
Columbia Missourian, 3 May 1951, reported:

> A play by Sean O'Casey split Houston play-goers and critics in a half-
> dozen camps today. But there was this agreement: The play "Red Roses For
> Me" was "shocking."
> The play, which held its American opening here last week, has been
> described as "communistic," "obnoxious," "anti-religious" and "fanatic." The
> *Houston Chronicle* denounced it as "a Communist play by an embittered Irish
> fanatic," in a front page editorial.
> The Catholic Church has taken no official action, but several priests urged
> a boycott of the Houston Playhouse where "Red Roses For Me" is playing. . . .
> Before the play opened the producers rented clerical equipment from a
> Catholic institution. Two days after the play opened the institute recalled its

"Red Roses" was done in Dublin's biggest theatre, ran for 3 weeks, & there was no trouble—bar a few adverse reviews in the Catholic Press. I hope the row won't do any harm to the Houston theatre. The critic of the "Houston Post" stood by the play, so I had a friend, even in faraway Texas.

I hope you are managing to do a little work; but again exclaim, Take it easy, George. Do even simple things as smoothly as you can. I am learning to do things this way myself. Slow motion.

God be good to you.
With my love, my dear George,
Ever yours,
Sean

---

equipment. Producers Joanna Albus and William Z. Rozan said no reason was given. . . .

Effect of the controversy has been the same as banning a book. The Playhouse had numerous empty seats opening night. There has been a capacity crowd ever since. The producers yesterday announced they would extend its engagement for another week.

The play was praised and defended by the *Houston Post.*

John O'Shaughnessy later directed the New York production of the play, with the same principal actors, which opened on 28 December 1955. See O'Casey's letter to David Krause, 3 January 1956, Vol. III.

To Shaemas O'Sheel [1]

MS. O'SHEEL
TOTNES, DEVON
26 MAY 1951

Dear Shaemas O'Sheel

What a frightening letter you send me; frightening when I think of an answer. Yes, I read your Review of "I Knock at the Door," [2] and thank you for it. You were right to give your name a phonetic spelling. I'd do the same to mine, only it is too late now. It's a pity you lost favour with the "Herald Tribune." I lost favour here with the "Sunday Times." They used to give me an odd biographical book to review—because, I suppose, I was writing one of my own; though why a knowledge of my own life should give me a knowledge of others, I dont know—; but they thought so. I

[1] Shaemas O'Sheel (1886–1954), Irish poet and writer living in New York.
[2] Shaemas O'Sheel, *New York Herald Tribune Books,* 23 July 1939.

reviewed "Lives" of Lever,[3] Loraine [4]—the actor, Jack London,[5] and, then, John Mitchel.[6] Then came silence: no publication & no fee. They didn't want me, or anyone else, to remember Mitchel. All the suppression isn't in the USSR. I never was asked to review another book. Just as well, for reviewing to me is a damned hard job—I haven't got the gift for it— & the pay isn't hilarious. As you say "A Pound On Demand" is of no value. Maybe, there may be a laugh or two in it. I hope so, but am doubtful. I am sending you, under another cover, a copy of my latest play—"Cockadoodle Dandy." I remember "The Gael" well—a grand monthly in them days when Irish Ireland was all the world and God as well. But, I fear, the Gaelic language is dying fast. You have had a busy life, and, like myself, I fear, did too much for "Ireland," & too little for yourself. The fight of the Fenians has thrown Ireland, body & bones, into the arms of those solely out "on the make" and under the feet of hordes of clergy, sacred, profane, secular and regular. I don't know what Shane Leslie was doing as a delegate of Irish Fenianism—I never knew he had anything to do with it. [Major John] McBride, of course, was on the supreme Council & so was B. Hobson,[7] & Secretary of the Council, & Tom Clarke's Whitehaired boy, till just before O'Donovan Rossa's funeral, he was discovered to be a "cad," & Tom tried to throw him out of a window in Dublin's Municipal (City) Hall. My first difference with T. Clarke was over this lad. It was pathetic to see Clarke's devotion to this Protestant shit, exploiting his Protestantism in the National movement. Clarke thought him another Tone or McCracken. It was a big tactical error to send Casement to Germany—he had no connection with, or understanding of, the Irish Workers. Larkin or Connolly should have been sent there. The "Bacon-curer" who founded the "Boyne Valley Industries," under W. P. Ryan, wasn't O'Meara, the Limerickman, but J. McCann, a Louthman. Your remarks about not having made a note about Connolly is not surprising: without Larkin, Connolly would have remained a nonentity. His execution was what made him famous. He was incorruptible & able, but very, very limited in mind and imagination. God knows what has happened to Fr Flanagan's data.[8] Like the MSS of Dr. W. McDonald, they

[3] Sean O'Casey, "Charles Lever's Stormy Life," *Sunday Times,* 5 February 1939, a review of Lionel Stevenson's *Dr. Quicksilver* (1939); reprinted in *Blasts and Benedictions* (1967).

[4] Sean O'Casey, "A Prophet in the Theatre," *Sunday Times,* 18 September 1938, a review of Winifred Loraine's *Robert Loraine* (1938); reprinted in *Blasts and Benedictions* (1967).

[5] Sean O'Casey, "Portrait of Jack London," *Sunday Times,* 30 October 1938, a review of Irving Stone's *Sailor on Horseback* (1938).

[6] Sean O'Casey, "Ireland's Tongue of Fire," *Irish Freedom,* March 1939, a review of Seamus MacCall's *Irish Mitchel* (1938). When the *Sunday Times* commissioned but refused to print his review, O'Casey sent it to *Irish Freedom.* See O'Casey's letter to George Jean Nathan, 13 January 1939, note 5, Vol. I, p. 770.

[7] Bulmer Hobson (1883–1969), Irish Republican writer. For further comments on Hobson, see O'Casey's letter to Horace Reynolds, 6 February 1938, note 4, Vol. I, p. 697.

[8] Father Michael O'Flanagan (1876–1942), controversial Republican priest. See O'Casey's letter to Francis MacManus, 14 January 1946, note 8.

have, probably, been destroyed. The clerics are woefully afraid of the light. Fr. O'Sullivan was, I believe, one of the young priests who spoke to the Fenians—the I.R.B. lads in Clontarf. As you say, he was transported to Africa. But why the hell did he go? I know W. Rooney [9] killed himself for "Ireland"; and, incidentally, provoked others—you & me—to go & try to kill themselves, too, for "her." I agree that the Communists should have let [Henry] Wallace alone; kept away as an organization—as the I.R.B. did with Sinn Fein & Gaelic League; but that wasn't the only foolish thing done by C. in the U.S.A., & here, too, by the same token.

All good wishes to Mrs. O'Sheel & to you.

Yours very sincerely
Sean O'Casey

[9] William Rooney (1872–1901), Irish poet; founded the *United Irishman;* worked tirelessly for the cause of Ireland and the revival of the Irish language.

To M. Bassett [1]

TC. O'CASEY

[TOTNES, DEVON]
6 JUNE 1951

Dear Mr. Bassett,

Within the last ten months I have sent 26 messages to various causes and places, and these are enough for a while. To add to them would simply make an exhibitionist of myself, which I have no intention of doing.

Besides, I havent read your Magazine, and so can hardly comment on something I know nothing about, or know it by its name only. I have, or get, as much as my eyes permit me to read, and, even an I would, cannot add to the reading.

I enclose a cutting from the N. Y. Times, which should be quoted by any paper willing to print it. It deals with present facts, human nature, and the opinion of the plain people about the Korean War, those who are being gathered together to join in, and go down, after a brief spell of misery, to an unwanted grave. It was sent to me by a Labour Irish friend in New York.

I suggest you should type a few copies for the Worker, The Irish Democrat, and, maybe, for the Manchester Guardian.

Why dont you use your influence with the D.W. [*Daily Worker*] to try

[1] M. Bassett, *Labour Monthly* (London).

to get it from being so like a Labor edition of the R.Catholic *Universe?*
And advise it to put some limit to its "Musts."

Yours sincerely,
Sean O'Casey

To Frank McCarthy

MS. McCarthy

Totnes, Devon

8 June 1951

Dear Frank,

Glad to hear from you. You last wrote when you were still in the
E. Memorial Hootelhell, but you were about to move, & didn't give the
address you were going to. I've got "The Bell." I'm a subscriber, knowing
Peadar O'Donnell well; &, if your brother doesn't send it to you, I'll send
on my copy to you. Faolain's is a good article.[1] He's a very clever fellow,
but very weak: he can't be trusted. He not only faces both ways, but faces
allways. An agnostic—he never was one—for years, he is now "reconciled
to the Church." It is a pity his cleverness isn't allied to courage. I have been
reading the Browne case as reported in the I. Times, & the whole dispute
is a reflection of Eire herself. I'm glad [Sean] McBride got a sharp rap over
the nut. Whether Dr. Browne and his butties will fight the clerics is doubtful. Everyone in Ireland is afraid of a Bishop's snort. Faolain's opinion is
that the Church has the power because she "got the Sacraments," which,
he says, is "the power of life or death." He wouldn't attempt to combat this,
though in the early R.C. Church—SS. Bernard & Benedict—the sacraments
were of less importance than preaching; & the present Bishop of Shrewsbury
(R.C.) has declared that the practice of "Monthly Communion should be
dropped." The R.C.'s, he says, are content to let everything alone once they
get their "monthly ration" of Their Lord! Faolain doesn't know enough
about his own Faith to criticise it.

Your verses could be better: the rhythm isn't too good. "Frowsy Cafe"
won't do—you must show its "frowsiness."

---

[1] Sean O'Faolain, "The Dail and the Bishops," *The Bell,* June 1951, an article
about the role played by the Roman Catholic hierarchy in the defeat of Dr. Noel
Browne's Mother and Child Health Plan. See O'Casey's letter to Robert M. Smyllie,
22 April 1951, note 3.

For the nonce, au revoir. The MS. of Vol. V biography is in the printer's hands. When it will leave them, God knows.

All good wishes.

As ever,
Sean

(Thanks for "The Guide"—a poor issue, on the whole; poorest about Browne.)

To Lillian Gish

MS. Gish

Totnes, Devon
13 June 1951

My dear Lillian:

First, thank you for the precious parcel. It was, of course, very welcome; but you mustn't tax yourself in this way. Artists' lives are damned uncertain and they must keep particularly prudent. Besides your own country will be soon forced to live less grandly. We shall all soon be thanking heaven fasting. On the road to "Sion" rationed—all of us, except the higher clerics.

"Within The Gates" is, in time, a long way away now, though in my own mind and memory, it seems but a day distant. Well, it was a tremendous experience for me—the play and the City. Since its appearance at the National, I've had close associations with many from your country, from Professors of Universities to workers in the Labour movement. Many Americans have visited us—two came last Sunday; and many more have written.

I am glad that Sherriff's play [1] has done so well, for your sake, & I hope you'll get enough out of it to banish every thought of financial work for life. It isn't easy to score a success in the theatre that way, let the play be important or unimportant. So gather you rosebuds while you may.

Give my love to Dorothy and my pleasure at her deliverance from a most distressing complaint. We'd suffer very little if we thought more about making life comfortable than about making life god-damned dangerous.

[1] Miss Gish had toured America in 1950 playing the title role in R. C. Sherriff's *Miss Mabel* (1948).

George hasn't been well, but he writes to say that he is better, and getting back to normal again.

Thanks again, dear Lillian, for your kind remembrance.

All good wishes to Dorothy and to you.

Yours very sincerely,
Sean

To Otto Brandstädter [1]

TC. O'CASEY

[TOTNES, DEVON]

15 JUNE 1951

Dear young friend,

I have today written to my publishers, Macmillan & Co. St. Martin's Street, London, W.C.2., asking them to send to you the following books: Vols I II III—I Knock at the Door; Pictures in the Hallway; and Drums Under the Windows—of my biographical writings; and, also, a copy of my latest play, COCKADOODLE DANDY.

It may be that Macmillans may not have them all, or, indeed, any; and, in that case, I shall write to you again. I hope they may have them, and that you may get them safely.

With this letter, I enclose some press-cuttings, which may be of use to you; mostly from American Journals. The review given in The Daily Worker was a very good one—in terms of praise—, but I havent a lot of regard for the literary criticisms appearing in that Daily; nor have any more regard for the reviews of Drama appearing there, neither for those written by the present critic, nor for the critic who preceded him. The Drama-critic who has my deepest respect is George Jean Nathan, the famous American Critic and, with him, are Brooks Atkinson of the New York Times, and Richard Watts Junr, of the New York Post. There are many more fine critics there, drama and literary; for the first drama critics here—in England —I havent, and never had, much respect: see my *The Flying Wasp*. This is out of print, and, it is hardly likely that you can get it, which is a pity. I have but one copy myself, and cant let you have that. I amnt aware that The Soviet Union has made much—if any—Bar, *I Knock at the Door*—of my biography or plays. References: Road around Ireland. Padruig Colum.

---

[1] Otto Brandstädter, a graduate student in Berlin, was writing a doctoral dissertation, "Sean O'Casey, Poet of the Working Class." He later published "Ein O'Casey-Bibliographie," *Zeitschrift für Anglistik und Amerikanistik* (1954).

Macmillan Co. of New York. 1937. Gassner John; Masters of the Drama. Random House, New York, 1940. Preface by Nathan to Five Famous Irish Plays. Random House, New York. Allerdyce Nicoll, British Drama. London. George Harrap & Co. 1949. O'Casey's Own Story; Brooks Atkinson, book Review Section, New York Times, September 22, 1946.

But, really, Otto, I'd be jotting these down all night—there are, literally hundreds and hundreds of them, and I am very busy now writing the VI vol of biography—the V—called The Rose and Crown is with the publishers—which I hope may be the last. So you will have to forgive me, for my eyes arent good enough to be peering at these records.

[*Sean O'Casey*]

To Dr. John V. Simcox

TC. O'CASEY

[TOTNES, DEVON]

25 JUNE 1951

Dear Dr. Simcox,

Thank you for your letter and enclosure.

You are altogether wrong about the reason prompting me to refrain from mentioning your work in connection with [Arnold] Lunn's challenge to [Paul] Blanshard. You seem to have forgotten your last letters to me which were very curt and resentful, commanding an end to our correspondence. I did not mention your work because I imagined you might resent any reference to you by me. I do not want to annoy you in any way. To ignore you on such a question because "you think as little of communist honesty as you do of Catholic honesty" would be the act of a fool, and I am not a fool, though very, very far from being a wise one. On the contrary, I was very glad to hear you had written to the Statesman, and equally glad to get your letter for this reason:

This morning, along with your letter, came a letter from a Mr. Hexstall Smith, who, having listened to a Broadcast from a Jesuit, J. Leycester King, of the Newman Association, replied to it, and received a reply from the Rev. J. Leycester King. These he has sent on to me (a quick glance at them shows that they mainly deal with the question of the Inquisition and the penalty of death for heresy), with an implied request for comments. Realising now that you have no objection to the use of your work by me, I am sending a copy of your book [1] with Coulton's pamphlet on "The Death Penalty for Heresy," [2] to Mr. Hexstall Smith.

Though you believe this about Communism, I can see no reason why you should think me to be as dishonest too.

With all good wishes,
Yours sincerely,
Sean O'Casey

[1] Dr. John V. Simcox, *Is the Roman Catholic Church a Secret Society?* (1946).
[2] George Gordon Coulton, *The Death-Penalty for Heresy from 1184 to 1921 A.D., Medieval Studies,* No. 18 (1924).

To Dr. John V. Simcox

TC. O'CASEY

[TOTNES, DEVON]
28 JUNE 1951

Dear Dr. Simcox,

You are probably quite right about me being a sentimentalist. I am inclined to wear my heart on my sleeve for daws to peck at. G. J. Nathan, the American drama-critic points out that Irish playwrights not only wear their hearts on their sleeves, but their very gizzards too. But I had my own feelings to consider, too, as well as yours. You might well have thought that a Communist would be a very questionable ally, and, for all I knew, I might have received an angry letter of protest. I'm sure all sincere souls have a share of the truth; it would be too much for them if they had it all.

I am glad to know that I may send your booklet to anyone interested in the question of official Catholic activity and influence in human affairs.

All good wishes,
Yours sincerely,
Sean O'Casey

To Rod Nordell

MS. NORDELL

TOTNES, DEVON

6 JULY 1951

Dear Mr. Nordell:

Your thesis [1] came a few days ago, and I thank you for sending it to me. Well, I've learned a lot about myself I didn't know before. Although I disagree with a lot of it, I think it well deserves a pass. I hardly thought you had it in you to comment so well. And your quotations were very interesting. I'd never come across most of them before. You may be a writer, & may be even mentioning me again, so I am correcting one statement— that I wrote "S. of I. Citizen Army" under a false name: [2] I didn't. These proofs were the first I'd ever received, &, when they came, the title-page was missing. In my ignorance, I thought these were not usually sent, so never asked for them. When the work was finally printed, I found the "S" had been changed to a "P." There was nothing to be done about it, but to let it go. It was a printer's error which I got no chance to correct.

Thank you for your kind wishes.

All the best to you.

Yours sincerely,
Sean O'Casey

[1] Rod Nordell, "The Dramatic Theory and Practice of Sean O'Casey," M.A. Thesis, Trinity College, Dublin, 1951.

[2] In his thesis, Nordell had referred to O'Casey's "pseudonym of 'P. O'Cathasaigh' " for his *Story of the Irish Citizen Army* (1919).

To George Jean Nathan

MS. CORNELL

TOTNES, DEVON

7 JULY 1951

My very dear George:

I hope you have had a rest during the warmer weather, & that you are feeling fitter week by week. Don't worry too much about the work in progress—I'm trying to get myself to believe I've another hundred years in front of me.

Dick's death [1] will be a loss. He was really a grand fellow; & I had a deep affection for him—apart from his usefulness to me as an upright generous Agent. I was sorry to hear about Carlotta. I still picture her as the handsome woman she was when you & I went to see Eugene & her in Madison Avenue—the time Eugene came forth in his new Daks. What angers me is that most of these ills result from our disorganised way of life: they are avoidable, if man has but his free use of common sense.

Denis Johnston has (I read) come back from New York to Dublin. He is reported as saying that "Happy as Larry" [2] failed because it was de-nationalised. He is at work on a new play about the Irish 1916 Rising, but not one in the O'Casey manner; nothing debunking in it. Once he said, too, that Producers are discussing possible productions of O'Casey's later play; but, so far, it is only talk. He doesn't like the later plays, sure that the faculty of playwrighting was lost when I left Dublin; though, oddly enough, he's been out of Ireland just as long himself, & was educated in St. Andrew's Dublin, Marchiston Castle, Edinburgh, Christ's College Cambridge, & Harvard. Dublin, Scotland, England, and Massachusetts teaching him a b c. He seems never to rest no where.

I think I told you I have sent in MS of another biographical vol.—"Rose & Crown." Macmillan's say it will displease a lot of people, though H. Latham, of the American Company says it's fine work. I'm at work now on what I hope may be the last one. Its title, I think, will be "Goodbye at the Door."

Still hoping for an American production. One thing to the good is that much more tribute is given to me there than is given here. It's interesting to watch the different attitude, there with you, & here, with me. Many Americans have come here connected with the theatre & literature; not one here. Odd.

Well, George a vic mo chree,[3] we'll keep going, whether they come or stay away. On guard!

Mind yourself, my dear friend.

With my love.
Sean

---

[1] Richard J. Madden, O'Casey's American agent, died on 8 May 1951, at the age of seventy-one. Some of his other clients were Eugene O'Neill, T. S. Eliot, W. Somerset Maugham, Paul Vincent Carroll, Cole Porter.

[2] Donagh MacDonagh's *Happy as Larry* opened in New York on 6 January 1950, and closed after three performances.

[3] Son of my heart.

To Mrs. Val Dora Frazer [1]

TC. O'CASEY

[TOTNES, DEVON]
11 JULY 1951

Dear Mrs Frazer,

Thank you very much for your letter and for the Bulletin of your College; and great thanks for your kind article about my work. It is a fine and intensely interesting article, and should make a very fine part of your Essay. Its Title—"Warrior for Justice"—sent a shiver of embarrassment through me; but it would be dishonest if I pretended that I didnt take pride out of the award. If not a "warrior," then, I hope, at least, a soldier.

I cant understand why the A and M College, the Research Committee, or the Editorial Board should refuse to associate themselves with the remarks about the Roman Catholic Church, for the remarks made in the article are those made by, held by, and promulgated by, the Roman Catholic Church Herself. Surely the Heads of your College do not deny that this Church claims Infallibility on the questions of faith and morals, which, according to Lord Acton, one of their most prominent members (he probably would have been excommunicated had he not been a prominent and important Peer of the Realm of Britain; and so one of the untouchables), a famous historian of their own ecclesiastical history, and a man of wide culture and deep scholarship, extended to almost everything connected with life and life's activities. Indeed, Card. Newman said that probably the only impartial recorder of ecclesiastical history was the agnostic, Gibbon, who wrote, as you know, "Decline and Fall of the Roman Empire." Card. Newman said this, not Mrs Val Dora Frazer or Sean O'Casey. Will the Roman Catholics not believe the words of their own master minds? And if anything met with opposition in the Roman C. Church, it was the claim of Infallibility. It had to be shelved for hundreds of years, the opposition against it was so great. Even the doctrine of The Immaculate Conception was opposed for centuries, even by a number of Roman Catholic Saints! Then there was the scandalous Cardinal Gasquet affair. This Card. was Prefect of the Vatican Archives, President of the Papal Commission for revision of the Vulgate, and Abbot President of the whole Benedictine Order—a big, brave nob. This prelate was convicted of deliberately and intentionally falsifying history to suit the ends of his own thesis. Hundreds of errors were pointed out to him again and again, but he published several issues of his work without even taking notice of the damaging accusations

---

[1] Mrs. Val Dora Frazer, Florida Agricultural and Mechanical College, Tallahassee, Florida. Mrs. Frazer had written a graduate thesis on O'Casey; the second chapter, "Warrior for Justice," was printed in the *Bulletin* of Florida A and M College. Some members of the editorial board had approached her privately and urged her to "tone down" the section on the Roman Catholic Church, but she had refused.

of historical fraud and falsification. No Roman Catholic now likes to mention the name of Gasquet. Think of Duchesne, put on the Index for honesty—one of Rome's finest historians; and Acton, and Dollinger, to name but a few. Roman Catholics refuse to hear their own! What Blanshard has said in his book are facts, and no R.C. can deny them, since they are taken from their own official announcements; but the Roman Catholic authorities dont want them mentioned, and so try to suppress even their own commitments. Well, they are a fine lot of "warriors." They dont want the laity to hear too much about them; for, as always, and forever, the laity form the biggest part of the church by far. They must be kept ignorant. Within the last few weeks turmoil over the conduct of the bishops has caused the defeat of the Government, and forced a new election. The Irish Parliament introduced a new Social Act giving free medical attention to all, with special attention to mothers and children. The Bishops maintained that such a Bill without a Means Test was contrary to faith and morals! And by a secret negotiation with the Ministers, they got what they wanted. The Minister responsible for the Bill resigned his ministry in protest, and all the secret letters of the bishops were published to their indignation. They expected that their part in the affair would remain a profound secret, and now the Minister responsible for publication is being denounced. But he was returned to Parliament by a tremendous vote, mostly, of course, from Catholic citizens. Even in Ireland, it seems the bishops are not going to be let have their own sweet way. They wont even permit free meals for schoolchildren on the plea that "community meals is the thin edge of the wedge of Communism"! But they dont mind community feeding in the richer Catholic boarding-schools. Not a word about Communism in this. It's only the poorer schools that are kept in their proper sphere of hunger and misery.

But controversy of this kind, unless made public in Press or on platform, is a vexatious thing and utterly useless. When it is public, those who read or who hear can judge for themselves; and that is exactly what the clerics dont like, and wont have, if they can help it. Sean O'Faolain has declared that one "cannot be a good Catholic without being an anticleric". Where are we at all! By the way, John Gassner of Columbia College, in an article appearing in this month's THEATRE ARTS,[2] seems to agree with you that in the fight for social justice, I am something of a warrior. I hope to God that both of you are right.

Under another cover, I am sending you a booklet written by a Jesuit who was for 25 years (I think) a Dr of Canon Law in the R.C. Seminary of St. Edmund's. It is another revelation of the Hierarchy's duplicity and deliberate deceit.

---

[2] John Gassner, "The Prodigality of Sean O'Casey," *Theatre Arts*, July 1951, the second part of a three-part article. The other two parts appeared in the June and August issues.

Thanks again for your letter, the Bulletin, and your good and generous article.

Yours sincerely,
Sean O'Casey

To Frank McCarthy

MS. McCarthy
Totnes, Devon
17 July 1951

Dear Frank,

What an odd place to be—Eton! Christ, I'd love to see you in jacket, collar, and tall-hat. What is, or who are, the "Mustians"? [1] I've heard of the Oppidians; [2] but don't know what species of fauna these are. Take care of yourself that you don't be talking Latin, soon.

O'Faolain's article [3] was, as you say, a frothy one. He is, I fear, a frothy, brothy, broth of a boy. The [Dr. Noel] Browne affair seems to be over now. They've done a quiet penance, I daresay; have taken their necks in, & are, once more, on the way to the kingdom of heaven. I wonder why do the Irish still keep sending boys to Eton—and to Harrow? [Wolfe] Tone, I suppose. One would think the Lords of Iveagh [4] would find a good enoughsky school in N. Ireland. I hope you get on well with the parson Housemaster. I haven't read Hone's Life of Moore. [5] Certainly, nothing inspiring or exciting in his Life of Yeats. [6] Moore wanted Morgan —a personal friend—of the Sunday Times, to do it; but Hone had bundles of letters which he wouldn't give to Morgan (Charles) even at Moore's request. So Morgan wrote a short Memoir, [7] published by Macmillan's. My own experiences—with the Volunteers—of Maurice [Moore], didn't show him off as a fine man. There was something of Edward Martyn in him. He hadn't the guts of George.

Well, all the best. As ever,
Sean

P.S. Windsor Castle anything like the Dublin wan?

[1] Mustians, a student house at Eton.
[2] Oppidians, paying students, as distinct from scholarship students.
[3] Sean O'Faolain, "The Dail and the Bishops," *The Bell,* June 1951.
[4] Iveagh, the title enjoyed by the Guinness family, owners of the famous brewery.
[5] Joseph Hone, *The Life of George Moore* (1936).
[6] Joseph Hone, *W. B. Yeats, 1865–1939* (1941).
[7] Charles Morgan, *Epitaph on George Moore* (1935).

From Eric Gorman

TS. O'CASEY

23 JULY 1951

Dear Sean O'Casey,

As one of the old brigade I knew you would be distressed by the news that the Abbey which you knew was no more.[1] I thank you for your kind telegram and your hopes for the future.

The actual stage is intact but the roof and grid are gone, the dressing rooms, paint room, wardrobe rooms and scene dock are gone and also the roof of the Green Room.

The seats in the floor of the auditorium are all right bar small damage by water but the seating in the balcony has been damaged by heat. The paint on the walls and ceiling of the auditorium has also suffered badly from heat.

The vestibule and rooms over it were not touched by fire but heat did some damage to the paint.

All our pictures were saved.

We have salvaged quite a lot of clothes but it will take some time to find out what has been lost.

In order to preserve the continuity of the theatre we opened in the Peacock on Wednesday night with THE PLOUGH AND THE STARS so we can say with justifiable pride that there was no break and that the show went on.[2]

The stage staff and actors worked like Trojans in order to get the play on, as scenery, clothes and props had to be gathered in a few hours. . . .[3]

[*Eric Gorman*]

[1] On the night of 18 July 1951 at 12:30 AM a fire broke out in the Abbey Theatre, just two and a half hours after a performance of *The Plough and the Stars*. The fire destroyed the backstage area, including many valuable manuscripts in the script press in the Green Room.

[2] On the night after the fire, 19 July, "the show went on" when *The Plough* was performed at the adjoining 102-seat Peacock Theatre, where the play continued to run until the end of the month.

[3] Page missing.

To Eric Gorman

TS. CHRISTINE GORMAN

TOTNES, DEVON

26 JULY 1951

Dear Eric,

Thanks for your letter and enclosure. I kept back the receipt for the previous cheque because I wasnt sure where to send it. I enclose it now with the latest one for cheque received.

It isnt the actual burning of the Abbey that is so bad; it is the disorganization that follows such a happening that breaks one's heart; the restoration, in a patchwork way of all that has gone in the fire. It must mean a swift and tiring time for players and for staff.

Of course, the Peacock wouldnt be of much use to you. It would hardly cover the postal bill.

The Rupert Guinness Hall seems to be a good one; [1] but the snag is that it [is] such a long distance from Dublin's centre. And Watling Street isnt well known in Dublin. The majority of Dublin's people have, probably, never passed through it. I know it well; and St. James's Street, where Guinness's had their Office. I used to collect a monthly cheque from them there for Hampton & Leedom's, where I got my first job. [2] What a rich smell of malt there was the moment you entered the door of the building.

Isnt it like things that a fully-equipped theatre should be built by those who dont know what to do with one? These monopolists who can build how and where they like, without any idea of how and when to use what they build. Better, if the Guinnesses had given the cost to an extension of the Abbey. But the rich dont always do the things they ought to do—even with their money.

I hope Watling Street will become one of the best-known streets in Dublin.

I hope you did well in Cong. [3] I'm sure Barry Fitsg. and the Boss [Arthur Shields] are in good form—they must be putting them up on their edges. Barry among the heather, watching the gulls! Now the labourer's task

[1] The Abbey Theatre arranged to set up temporary quarters at the Rupert Guinness Hall in James's Street, a short distance from the Watling Street bridge. *The Plough* was transferred from the Peacock, and opened at the Rupert Guinness Hall on 30 July for a two-week run.

[2] See "Comin' of Age," *Pictures in the Hallway* (1942), and the following six chapters, for O'Casey's account of his first job at "Hymdim and Leadem" (a religious jest at the firm's Protestant owners, Hampton and Leedom), the wholesale chandlers in Henry Street, Dublin.

[3] Many of the Abbey actors had been in Cong, Co. Mayo, working on location in the filming of *The Quiet Man*, directed by John Ford and starring John Wayne, Maureen O'Hara, and Victor McLaglen. Besides Barry Fitzgerald and his brother Arthur Shields, the other Irish actors in the cast were Gorman, Eileen Crowe, May Craig, and Jack McGowran.

is o'er. Odd, I mention Cong in the MS of the next biographical vol,[4] sent in to Macmillan's some time ago. Imagine doing a film "Round O'Connor's sepulcre in Cong"! Last of Gaelic monarchs of the Gael! These from Rolleston's lovely poem, *The Grave of Rury*. Well, Rury's another Quiet Man, now.

Warm regards and all good wishes,
Yours very sincerely,
Sean O'Casey

[4] See "Ship in Full Sail, *Rose and Crown* (1952). Rury O'Connor, the last of the Irish kings, was buried in Cong. O'Casey comments on this fact, and quotes two stanzas from T. W. Rolleston's poem "The Grave of Rury," *Sea Spray: Verses and Translations* (1909), pp. 19–20.

To Shaemas O'Sheel

TS. O'SHEEL

TOTNES, DEVON
27 JULY 1951

Dear Shaemas,

Yes, the number of readers have increased, but not vol by vol.[1] The sale of the first two were the same—well under 2000 copies; then the third ran into 3000, and interest in them began to grow. So long as the wife and children can live a decent life, I dont care a lot about interest; let it come, let it tarry, for it's all in the hands of the Man Above. I'm afraid more than Boland[2] degenerated. They are all—measured with Clarke, Larkin, Pearse, or Connolly, a sorry lot now. Dev went to Rome for the Jubilee,[3] and there wasn't a church within a radio Eireann of a hundred miles that he didn't visit, bend the knee, duck the head; and the last glimpse Eire got of him was marching in the procession at Aylesford Kent, folleying the pot-bellied bishops carrying the few bones left of St. Simon Stock, to their old home in the Carmelite (Calced) Convent, there. He's worn out practising his faith. He's an oddity in Ireland—one of them who never tells a lie, and never said a curse, or even a naughty word. The oddest thing about him, is that he never seems to bring his wife with him anywhere; a bonny lass, when she was young, clever, too, and full of zeal for the rights of women. Seems to have fallen by the wayside; for all she does now, seemingly, is to

[1] O'Casey's autobiography.
[2] Harry Boland, Irish Republican leader who was shot by Irish Free State soldiers on 2 August 1922 during the Civil War.
[3] The Pope's Golden Jubilee. In 1949 Pius XII, who was ordained a priest in 1899, marked the golden anniversary of his first Mass.

write little plays in Gaelic for production by convent childer. Perhaps I do labor the points about AE too laboriously; but he was the richest humbug I have known; an article by a son in IRISH WRITING [4] confirms what I said of him (unintentionally). For instance, we are told that AE, for relaxation, read ten mystery and detective yarns a week! That doesn't fit in with the beautiful poetry. 520 yarns a year! The mighty mind had to relax.

Michael McCarthy's book PRIESTS AND PEOPLE IN IRELAND [1902] is unobtainable. I wish I could get it myself. The writing was very poor, but the photographs were amazing—the pompous churches towering over the Irish hovels; and the Lists of money left to the clergy for Masses for dying and dead souls! There was a tremendous sale of this book, yet it has disappeared completely. Like others: Wells's An Crux Ersatz,[5] or some name like that; published in a Penguin vol. meaning tens of thousands; yet one cant get a copy of it now. Ask me another about the data compiled by Fr. O'Flanagan on the ways of the priests with the people. McCarthy wrote another book, before PRIESTS AND PEOPLE, called FIVE YEARS IN IRELAND [1901], which cant be got anywhere, though after years of searching, one might come across a copy in some second-hand bookshop. All gone with the wind. Thanks for the PROTESTANT. Long ago, a Fr. Duffy sent me a copy, asking me to write for it; but I have too many things to do; no time to write half of what I'd like to write. Our three children take up a lot of thought and time, for I'm very interested in the young, and chat about things with them—from biology to cricket—when I should be working. I'm afraid the CP [Communist Party] do often fail to see the usefulness of an ally who cant wholeheartedly agree with them. They seem to think Marxism cant be moved; created once for all; cant adapt itself to varying circumstances. A dangerous delusion. It must adapt itself, and use present conditions of action and thought to further its interests and power. For instance, here, at least, they are blind to the fact that the most powerful and unscrupulous enemy they have is the R.C. Church. And, of course, the Protestant Churches are nearly as bad. A lot of them are comfortable in the midst of a good, solid life, and call on the Father, Son, and Holy Ghost to keep them there. A meeting to meet S[hane]. Leslie was held, probably to try to win him over to the I.R.B. That was sometimes done. One—a Commemoration of Wolfe Tone, I think—was held, and Francis J. Biggar of Belfast was chief speaker. They wanted to get him to join. He looked like he would, but when definitely asked, shied off, and never spoke at another National gathering, bar the Pipers' Club, or, maybe, a Gaelic League Feis.

You are probably right about COCKADOODLE DANDY. If I could only rewrite a lot of what I've written, I'd be a happier man. But rarely can a mood come over a man twice. I seldom venture to re-read what I've

---

[4] Diarmuid Russell, "AE," *Irish Writing* No 15, June 1951.
[5] H. G. Wells, *Crux Ansata: An Indictment of the Roman Catholic Church* (1943).

done. A rehearsal of an old play is torment. I write all first in longhand, then type a rough copy, changing all the time; then do a fair copy, changing again; then the galley-proofs get more changes; and when the page-proofs come, I'd like to make more changes than I can. George Jean Nathan has been a good friend to me. So have Brooks Atkinson, Richard Watts, Junr, & John Gassner in way of publicity; but Purple Dust, Cocka-doodle & Red Roses still wait. The play, so far, has never been produced, except in a little amateur theatre in Newcastle-on-Tyne; [6] a theatre I have a great respect for; they do fine plays, and gave a fine performance of COCKADOODLE. But one cant live by the Little Theatres. Here, they bring me about £20 a year. The committal of the Eleven, and their help-ers is the attempt to check the inevitable. The same thing was done in Ireland to try to do away with national sentiment. It didn't work. This latest attempt to check the New Age wont work either. Checked here, it breaks out there. Sean MacBride is as good as they make them, which isn't saying much. He, to me, is but a careerist, and a narrow one at that. The ques-tion of the Mother and Child Bill flung his government out. The Hierarchy said that a bill without a Means Test would be contrary to Catholic morals, and ordered (secretly) the Government to drop it. Dr. Browne let the cat out of the bag by publishing the letters,[7] and all P. Ulster roared out, We Told You So. But this clerical order isn't any new thing. It was there in '67, '48, '98, 1916, it downed Parnell; and that is why half the world is putting them over the frontiers; or in jail. They wont allow meals for schoolchil-dren, even; say it is Communism; but dont mind community feeding in the tony R.C. boarding schools. They dont want the people to taste good things; might ask for more; as they said in 1913 when the children of the workers were offered temporary homes in England. They might get "discontented," when they returned to their slums. They are original, anyway; others say, give security and a good life to the people, and Comm. will be kept away; give these things to the people, say the clerics here, and Comm. will be brought in. Hannington's [8] case is a sad one; but we can't stop to linger over bodies of fallen soldiers. We must go on. All the best to Mrs O'Sheel and to you.

Ever,
Sean

[6] *Cock-a-Doodle Dandy* was first performed by the People's Theatre in New-castle upon Tyne on 10 December 1949.

[7] See O'Casey's letter to Robert M. Smyllie, 22 April 1951, note 3.

[8] D. F. Hannigan who, according to O'Sheel, emigrated to America, wrote a novel, *The Bankruptcy of Bryan Kane*, under the pseudonym of "Victor Vane," worked for a newspaper in Rochester, New York, was fired, and returned to Ireland, where he died in poverty.

To Frank McCarthy

MS. McCarthy
Totnes, Devon
⁑ 1 August 1951

Dear Frank,

Thanks ever so much for the gloves. Mrs. O'C. is in London on business for me—I'm too tired to go there, now—and I'll give them to her soon as she returns this week-end, or early next week. Should have liked to have been present while yous all sang "Mother Eton" and the "Boating Song." Were you drunk when you wept? Shaw says "Englishmen behave when they're sentimental as Irishmen behave when they're drunk." Wasn't it D'Israeli who said, "I never knew one who'd come out of Eton who hadn't been cowed." It's a pity to see a son of the Mac Angusa Clan there. It's ironical to think of him there, while a play by the proletariat, O'Casey, is running in the Rupert Guinness Memorial Hall, Watling St. Dooblin. God has a good laugh sometimes!

Boots for the Butts of Refugees. I've yet to meet the rich person, or their fellow-travellers, or the rich institution, who know a god-damn thing about the workers. It is only the workers who know the workers; the workers who can help the workers; the workers who can free the workers. Even Noel Coward, in his "Cavalcade" thinks a butler is a representative of the workers!

Ay, I've been in The Brazen Head, The Blue Lion, Red Lion, Hole in the Wall, Nancy Hand's, Royal Oak, Bleeding Horse, Cat 'n Cage, Jolly Topers—to mention a few. Yes, Watling Street is "up-town"; the Hall is in James's St. where the "offices" are. I used to go there every month (first job, 3/– weekly) for Hampton, Leedoms & Co. to collect their monthly cheque for goods sold to Guinness's.[1] The smell of malt is all around one there.

I've been very busy, writing draft for next biographical book, with the children, all home, all day, now, and for Peace Youth Festival, as enclosure will show.

Yours as ever,
Sean

[1] See O'Casey's letter to Eric Gorman, 26 July 1951, note 1.

To Eric Gorman

MS. CHRISTINE GORMAN

TOTNES, DEVON

2 AUGUST 1951

Dear Eric,

Thank you for your letter & the cheque. I'm glad you've come out of the fire safely, so far; not quite so unharmed as Meshach, Shradrach, & Abednego, but whole enough to go on bravely. A friend of mine, Frank McCarthy, born in Drumcondra, late Sargeant in the Royal Signalling Corps, has just written to ask where Watling St. is. He was torpedoed in the Pacific during the last war, was in the sea for 48 hours, & then picked up, possessing nothing but a shirt and an oil-skin bag round his neck which contained a photo of Bernard Shaw. An odd kind of a scapular! Now he works in "Mustians," one of the Houses of Eton College. His letter, before that mentioning the burning of the Abbey, oddly enough, told me he had had a chat with a young Guinness of 16 years who was a scholar there. What a strange Race we Irish are! "Ubique"—if that's the right Latin for "Everywhere." The world's our oyster, but the pearls in it are rare for us, Irish. Still we've left our Monomark on the world, & are still making the impression clearer & wider. Wider still & wider may our boundary be, without shame to ourselves or harm to a soul.

All good wishes to you & yours.
Yours sincerely,
Sean O'Casey

To R. Palme Dutt [1]

TC. O'CASEY

[TOTNES, DEVON]

8 AUGUST 1951

Dear Mr. Dutt,

Your return of the cutting from THE NEW YORK TIMES showing the general revulsion of American youth against conscription as informa-

[1] R. Palme Dutt, editor, *Labour Monthly* (London).

tion of no use to you is, to me, a very sorry indication of ignoring valuable propaganda.[2]

It was proof that the American young man doesnt want war, and is interested—as a sensible human being—only in the normal and wonderful activities of life. Your indifference explains why the agitation against the Z call-up was a lamentable failure. You shouldnt keep your nose buried in theory.

The enclosed cutting from the Soviet Literary Gazette seems to show that it is more interested in the feelings of American youth in relation to war than you are; and that these feelings are of some importance.

Yours sincerely,
Sean O'Casey

[2] See O'Casey's letter to M. Bassett, 6 June 1951.

To Eric Gorman

TS. GORMAN

TOTNES, DEVON
15 AUGUST 1951

Dear Eric,

Thank you for your letter and for the cheque, formal receipt for which is enclosed.

I am glad you are, so far, weathering the gale of change and inconvenience; but it must be a good deal of a nuisance, and, of course, there is still the gnaw of uncertainty about the future.

I've read about the idea of the Queens;[1] a very good one, if the rent isnt too much against the general average of the Theatre's income. Isnt it an odd irony that a fellow like Ranke (or is it Rank?),[2] an English Methodist, should own the theatre that the Abbey needs! You see how short and meagre a thing is political freedom. Every bit of property in Ireland should be Irish property. Still a long way from Mitchel's demand—The land, sea, and air, and all that on them is and all that in them is, belongs to—Rank. The last word hasnt been properly chosen yet.

All good wishes to the Abbey and all its needs, and to you and yours.

Yours sincerely,
Sean O'Casey

[1] The Abbey had begun negotiations to move from their temporary quarters at the Rupert Guinness Hall to the Queen's Theatre, an old music-hall theatre of 950 seats on Pearse Street. See O'Casey's letter to Gorman, 30 August 1951.
[2] J. Arthur Rank.

To John Gassner

MS. GASSNER
TOTNES, DEVON
21 AUGUST 1951

Dear John,

I am sending this to Theatre Arts, asking them to forward it to you. All letters I consider first-class, I put away in a safe place, & often find afterwards that the whereabouts of the safe place is forgotten. Your letter to me has been put into this kind of a limbo, and search how I may, I can't discover it. I know you live in Brooklyn where a tree grows, but can't remember street or number.

I have read your two articles, and await the third.[1] I naturally read them, and remember them, with great pleasure. I'm glad you have such a good opinion of me, & hope I deserve it. I'm afraid, I like the good opinion of those who know what they are talking about—pretty few, when you come to think it out. Nothing annoys me so much as praise from them who know damn all about the drama, giving prolific praise to almost everything on the stage that has one bright light in it. I sent you the books when I had read your articles, for publication commits a critic to an opinion, & so could send them, without any suggestion of wanting to win a good one. I've sent the MS of every play—since Within the Gates—to G. J. Nathan, who always replied by letter; but I never used any of his remarks till he put them in print; for one may say things in a letter that one wouldn't venture to say in the Press. So I use only what a Critic says to the public at large, & not what may be privately said to me. Years & years ago, I was caught this way myself, a kindly (not critical) remark of mine flaring in huge letters as an advertisement in the Press. I am delighted with what you have said, & so is Mrs. O'C. I won't thank you, for they are an expression of your critical art, & so, in your opinion, due to the work on which your colorful comments are made. They are none the less gratifying to me. I am working on the 6th Vol of biography—the 5th is with the printer—"Rose and Crown." I've just written a song for a chapter—"All round me hat, I wear a band of green ribbon O." I love songs.

Cordially yours
Sean

[1] John Gassner, "The Prodigality of Sean O'Casey," *Theatre Arts,* June, July, August, 1951, a three-part article.

To James K. Boylan [1]

TC. O'CASEY

TOTNES, DEVON
28 AUGUST 1951

Dear Mr. Boylan,

Thank you for your most interesting letter. I know Pembroke St. and Howth Road well, of course. What strange opinions your relatives must have about you. I am very sorry that I couldnt allow myself to think of doing what you propose, for I have no time other than that needed for the work I have to do already, and, indeed, too little of it for that same.

I am engaged at the moment in writing the 6th biographical volume, and have a play or two to do yet—if I can find time in which to do them; as well as a great volume of correspondence. So you see, it would be impossible for me to undertake any additional work.

I thoroughly agree with you that you shouldnt let the story of your experiences die with you. It is imperative, for the sake of future generations that your story should be known. I suggest at least, that you should record them yourself in plain simple language, and leave it with someone you can trust—Paul Blanshard, for instance, who wrote THE CATHOLIC CHURCH AND AMERICAN FREEDOM [1949].

A Dr. J. V. Simcox, Professor of Canon Law for 25 years in St. Edmund's Seminary here in England, has written a booklet about his differences with Cards. Hinsley and Griffin on the Question of Grants to the Schools, and of the way he was treated when he quoted Canon Law to the Cardinals. If you like, I'll mail you a copy. He has now left the Church, and is working as a clerk, and still carrying on the controversy.

Do write what you remember, especially your experiences as a priest before it is too late, and, of course, your reasons for giving the whole thing up.

Yours sincerely,
Sean O'Casey

[1] James K. Boylan, 125 Fifth Street, N.E., Washington, D.C.

To Eric Gorman

TS. GORMAN

TOTNES, DEVON

30 AUGUST 1951

Dear Eric,

Well, well, to think of a play of mine going on in my theatrical Alma Mater [1] (Is this the right term?). Here it was, many many years ago, I saw my first play—*The Shaughraun*. It was a wonderful revelation. Then, it seemed, the world was lit by footlights. God be with them old days.

Yes, of course, you have my permission to do the play, if you wish to do it; but I'd like it to be done according to the slightly-revised version appearing in vol II of the recent issue of COLLECTED PLAYS. I hope you do well in the Queen's while youre there; it's a bit big, but the best place I could think of during your exile from the Abbey, which, I hope, when it rises again, will be a finer place for you.

With warm regards and good wishes,
Yours sincerely,
Sean O'Casey

PS. Writing a song for last vol. of biography—"All Round Me Hat, I Wear a Band of Green Ribbon O." Now what d'ye think o' that!

[1] The Abbey directors had taken over the Queen's Theatre, the old music-hall theatre in Pearse Street, and decided to open with a revival of *The Silver Tassie* on 24 September 1951. The play was directed by Ria Mooney, and the leading role of Harry Heegan was played by Barry Keegan.

To Anthony Firth [1]

TC. O'CASEY

[TOTNES, DEVON]

31 AUGUST 1951

Dear Mr. Firth,

You have been badly mis-informed. I never said Mr. [Eddie] Byrne was "the greatest actor in the world." Nor do I consider him to be, either. How the hell could I venture to make such a stupid, impudent, nonsensical statement? Or even venture to hint it without knowing all the acting powers and achievements of all the actors in the world? It's like you Film peo-

[1] Anthony Firth, Group 3 Ltd., Southall Film Studios, Middlesex.

ple to think that others are prepared to make the wild claims so commonly made by yourselves.

Mr. Byrne knows what I think of him, judging by his acting of "Brennan" in RED ROSES FOR ME; [2] and that it was a disgrace to the English theatre and to the English drama-critics that he hasnt been continually employed on the stage. I said what I thought of him in letters to Mr. Byrne himself, and, if he wishes, he can quote any, or all, of these remarks. But I am not going to join in the commercial publicity of a film. I wouldnt do it with my own work. Indeed, only for Mr. Byrne's sake, I'd wish he would do badly in it so that he could be reserved for the Theatre. Instead of NOTHING TO LOSE, he will probably lose a lot as Barry Fitzgerald has, since he plunged into Hollywood; lost a lot of himself, and of art that is true. No gifted actor should take more than a sip of the films; for kinema art, if it be an art, isnt the art of an actor (that is for the living stage), but the art only of the camera, art of an artificial and mindless eye. The camera is the actor of the Kinema; that is why the films damns an actor. I have said this years and years ago to Sydney Carroll,[3] who, though, he said, had seen thousands and thousands of films, couldnt understand me. Films warp the minds even of the lookers-on.

Well, there you are, my friend, my opinion goes to you, and you may take it or leave it, as you will, and, also, my good wishes to you and to Mr [John] Grierson, who, years ago, showed me some interesting, and some less interesting films in his own little studio.

Yours sincerely,
Sean O'Casey

[2] Eddie Byrne played Brennan o' the Moor in Bronson Albery's production of *Red Roses For Me*, which opened in London on 26 February 1946. For details on the production, see O'Casey's letter to Mrs. Una Gwynn Albery, 6 March 1946, note 1.

[3] See O'Casey's letters to *Time and Tide,* 17 February and 3 March 1934, Vol. I, pp. 503–5, 507–8, for his controversy with Sidney Carroll on the cinema and his favorable comments on John Grierson. Grierson (1898–1972) is often called the founding father of the documentary film.

To George Jean Nathan

MS. CORNELL

TOTNES, DEVON
3 SEPTEMBER 1951

My very dear George:

Thank you very much for your article, & for the glittering reference to me in it. If I don't deserve it fully, I do against those who, somehow, bleat themselves into a dead eminence with poor work. But I can blame those who know me not, when those who do (too well, maybe) sing dumb, or positively try to freeze my work into a room without a view. In an article on Ireland's literary value, Bruce Williamson, Literary [Editor] of "The Irish Times," says "I have little space left to tie up loose ends with which, as Scott Fitzgerald's wife once said, men hang themselves. I've said nothing about the Drama. The truth of the matter is that, of all the literary arts, drama is in the worst health. The most original contribution to the Irish Theatre since the war was Donagh MacDonagh's 'Happy as Larry.' There are other young dramatists who may show promise in the course of time" & so on, without a single mention of O'Casey. Eire is in an amazing terror of displeasing the clerics in any way. The usual reason for silence is in the moan "If it wasn't for the wife & kids."

Well, old son, in spite of your illness, you haven't lost the old sparkle. It still shoots out of your article, &, if it touches, it burns. God give you many years of life for the sake of a theatre, unafraid of blow or kiss; sucking itself out firm on the earth, or arising among the stars. I enclose cutting. A prize of £150 was given to this play. Tis first given to Enid Bagnold (She wrote "National Velvet"), £500, for a play nearly as bad, which will hardly be seen again. Before, I could have shone with either prize. What will the third one be like! They can't blame the critics this time. We're still Pioneers, George, a vic!

My deep love.
Sean

To the Rev. Stanley Evans [1]

TC. O'CASEY

[TOTNES, DEVON]
10 SEPTEMBER 1951

Dear friend,

I amnt able to do it. I should like to write an article about the book for the worth that is in itself, and for the reason that the Reverend writer wears a green feather in his cap. But, my friend, one of my eyes is no more, and the other one bears but half a normal vision, so that I have to strictly limit the work I try to do. These things, these bad handicaps, are the results of starvation in my childish days; and these hardships were shared by

[1] The Rev. Stanley Evans, editor, *New Central European Observer*, 40 Great Russell Street, London WC.1.

thousands of other kids in Ireland and England, too, largely due to the fact that money was needed to pay for wars here, there, and everywhere, so as to show the world how mighty the British Empire was. Well, I'm out for one to try to prevent the perpetuation of this criminal stupidity; out against the maiming of any body—which Christians call the Temple of the Holy Ghost—either by stupidity in peace or by the bloody meanness and rapacity of war. I have three children myself, and I dont want any of them to be harmed. Our elder lad has already done his term in the Royal Artillery, but he is as much opposed to war as I am. He wants to get on with life, as all sensible, intelligent young men and women do.

I think the Rev. H. J. L. Armstrong's booklet about the Warsaw Peace Congress [2] a fine one, and wish to God every cleric, Anglican, Hibernian, and Roman Catholic, would spare time to read it. It is just stupid or malevolent egoism that says we cannot align ourselves with those who believe differently from us. Good God, we have to live day by day with persons who quietly or violently disagree with many things we regard as being bathed in the light of truth; and we do it well. Not only is it possible, but it is even easy to live in quietness or busyness with those who differ from us, because there is between us all the unbreakable bond of common humanity. How Christians, who believe in the double bond of union with the humanity and divinity of their Sacred Lord, can support expressions favouring war, or even a low whisper commending it, is beyond my comprehension. Well, The Rev. H. J. L. Armstrong has made a good start for the bond of brotherhood. One among the Irish Protestant Clergy is a small voice, but no one can tell how far a small voice may range. Farther, maybe, than an atom bomb. May it be carried everywhere with the four winds of Eireann. Old and young want to live (let us say) till God takes us. God, mind you, not man. He should give us a span of at least a hundred years of life. If we were sensible and sober and wise with all we know, we'd have had it long ago. He offers it; we must take it. We have many, many things to do first before we can reach the offering hand; and the first thing we must do is to do away with war, forever, and utterly. I return the booklet.

I send my warm regards to you and all you do.
Yours very sincerely,
Sean O'Casey

[2] Henry Joseph Livingstone Armstrong, *A Visit to the Warsaw Peace Congress as an Observer* (1951).

To Frank McCarthy

MS. McCarthy

Totnes, Devon

12 September 1951

Dear Frank,

Thanks so much for sending the cutting about Breon. I don't take in the Chronicle. Up to the time of the row over the Mother & Child Bill, I took in the *D. Worker* only; now I get the *Irish Times*. But the Mother & Child Bill has been put away into a secret drawer, & we'll hear little about it from now on.

Now Bishop Browne (of Galway) has proclaimed *The Bell* to be venomous and anti-Catholic; and Sean O'Faolain has had to defend himself.[1] No wonder they're hunting them out of China. What a crowd they are! And in holy Catholic Eire they daren't publish the Commission's report on Criminal conditions, taken 20 years ago, & never published. Recently, in the I.T. there was a dispute between R. Catholics & Protestants as to which body was the most immoral; what was the percentage of syphillis among their members. The Kerry dancing and the piper's tune.

I hope you like your new quarters. "Mustian" has nothing to do with ghosts. There's a Latin word meaning "muttering," "fear," etc. which, maybe explains it. Or does it, subconsciously, apply to the whole [Eton] College—The "Mustians"? I'll leave it to yer honor.

As ever,
Sean

[1] In an open letter, "The Bishop of Galway and *The Bell*," *The Bell*, September 1951, Sean O'Faolain replied to some remarks by the Rev. Michael Browne, Bishop of Galway, made "in a recent address to a Congress of University students in Galway." The bishop was reacting to the controversy over the defeat of Dr. Noel Browne's Mother and Child Health Plan by the Roman Catholic hierarchy (see the editorial policy of the *Irish Times* in the months leading up to Dr. Browne's resignation on 12 April 1951; see also O'Faolain's article, "The Dail and the Bishops," *The Bell*, June 1951). O'Faolain quoted the bishop as saying: "For all who have not faith the Church was a human institution merely, and all the gradations of bitter hostility, hatred, or mere indifference that she evoked from the fury of the Orangemen of Sandy Row, to the venom of the *Irish Times* and the rancour of *The Bell*, all derived from a refusal to see in her the divine." To which O'Faolain responded at some length that the bishop was denying to everyone the right of honest disagreement with the temporal Church over political questions in Ireland; and he concluded: "Could a Graham Greene live here? A Mauriac, Bernanos, a Péguy, a Mounier, a Pierre Emmanuel?" A Sean O'Casey? he might have added.

To George Jean Nathan

MS. CORNELL

TOTNES, DEVON
25 SEPTEMBER 1951

My very dear George:

Your Theatre Book came to me yesterday morning, bringing me well inside the American Theatre during 1950–1951.[1] A big flame, blessing the good & blasting the bad. I shall be in the Theatre now for a long time. Once a year, I go, listen, laugh, & clap hand vigorously—when your book comes. I am beginning to read it now—the Arena Theatre—,[2] & will tell you some thoughts in my next letter. I can't understand the Arena. I don't see how it can suit plays written for the stage of today. If the A. becomes the accepted platform, surely the technique of the drama must be changed to suit it? And a thousand thanks for the book.

I enclose clipping about the drama Prize Awards given by the Arts Theatre. The Drama Critics have had a deserved laugh this time. It is obvious that the selections have been very bad. I've been wondering if the whole affair hasn't been influenced by sissyism—the choices were so bad. Anyway, I don't think a playwright makes a good drama judge. I'm a fairly cute boyo myself, but, as I said before, I wouldn't attempt to give a first judgement to say "Cocktail Party" or "Lady's not for Burning." After other critics have spoken—yes; I'd comment on the comments all-right, for then I'd be on a path levelled out by others.

Know anything about a Carleton Smith, organising a "Roosevelt Foundation," for helping art & literature in all lands? He has been here—a charming man—, & wants me to give my name. Left a document for me to do so. I haven't yet. Don't know that I should. The venture is "National Arts Foundation," 60. Broadway. New York City.

I hope you are keeping well, & not trying to do too much.

My love to you, dear George.
As ever,
Sean

[1] *The Theatre Book of the Year, 1950–1951* (1951).
[2] *Ibid.,* pp. 12–16.

To Harold Macmillan

TC. O'CASEY

[TOTNES, DEVON]
29 SEPTEMBER 1951

Dear Harold,

Thank you very much for taking the trouble to send me the review from *The Times Literary Supplement.*[1] I had not seen it, and so it was very welcome. I have no comments to make on it. The writer evidently knows a lot about my work, and about me, too, and has, I think, set it down very cleverly; and very kindly, too. I am always grateful for sensible reviews. This writer (whoever he may be) loves the Theatre, and knows what he is writing about. I cannot expect, nor do I expect, that everyone should like, and agree with, my "judgement." [2] I dont think "judgement" to be the right word about what I state or seem to imply in play or biography. They are opinions only; honest ones, taken after thought and long and wide experience of men and things; but they are, for all that, far from being infallible. Only God or Time can vindicate or repudiate the judgement of man. To me one thing alone is certain—we are all one in the tremendous and glorious bond of humanity. Jew, Gentile, bond and free, Tory and Communist can never break away from this grand bond. We are born, we die, and we must do the best we can between the day of birth and the night of death. But this writer about the Theatre is one who deserves to be a writer about the Theatre, against so many who look upon this work as merely a job to be done and finished with so that they may be able to turn their thoughts to something else. Thank you again for sending it to

---

[1] "The Paradox of Mr. O'Casey," *Times Literary Supplement,* 21 September 1951, a review of the *Collected Plays* (1951), Vols. III, IV.

[2] The anonymous review summed up what he believed to be the O'Casey "paradox":   .

> When, forgetting James Joyce, he resists the lure that is purely verbal, when he is not merely letting a single word lead him where it will, "with his sleek, sliddery, sludery, sloppery gob going peek-a-boo," he can discover a superb Elizabethan energy. He uses then the language of the English Bible, the language of the Dublin streets and the language of the Irish literary tradition to comic or to tragic ends, compelling his audience to acceptance, now by sheer bewitchment of phrase, now by an onslaught of rhetoric. Yet for all these natural affinities with the theatrical trends of his day the fact remains that he has been out of fashion for the best part of two decades. If, seeking to explain the fact, we re-examine the plays in the light of his autobiography, it is unlikely that we shall deny his genius, which appears in even his worst plays, but studying the course it has taken we may well conclude that it has been ridden with lamentably false judgment. It is his judgment, not his genius, that has separated him from the intelligent playgoing public. As a serious artist and a man of enormous integrity, he has insisted on the right to go his own way, whether we liked it or not; and the public have exercised their equal right not to like it.

me. I have had a somewhat similar review written by Brooks Atkinson [3] (a great friend of mine), drama critic for *The New York Times,* deploring the fact that my plays arent being performed in New York. He gives, too, a fine send-off to the third and fourth vols of *COLLECTED PLAYS.* The odd thing about it is that no mention of the vols has been made by any Irish Journal; except a line in *The Irish Times,* saying they had been received. Actually, in *The Star Turns Red,* not only the words, but the judgement, too, is that of the Bible. When G. B. S. read it, he saw it at once, and wrote to me saying, "You have given them the Authorised Version." [4] We have grown afraid of the Bible.

I was delighted (so was Eileen) to hear of the complete recovery of your boy.[5] What a terrible experience it was for him! He certainly saved his little son from death. To walk from where it happened to his home, with his boy, was indeed a great feat, and a brave one. Give him my love. I went through the whole horrible experience in my imagination.

My love to you and to Lady Dorothy, and to all that are yours.

Very sincerely,
Sean O'Casey

[3] Brooks Atkinson, "Case of O'Casey," *New York Times,* 16 September 1951, a review of the *Collected Plays.*
[4] See O'Casey's letter to Bernard Shaw, 29 April 1940, note 2, Vol. I, p. 860.
[5] The boy was bitten by a snake in the New Forest.

To Brooks Atkinson

MS. ATKINSON

TOTNES, DEVON
2 OCTOBER 1951

My dear Brooks:

Thank you for your kind letter & your thoughtfulness in sending your article to me. I needn't say how welcome it was; for I am one who accepts praise from those who are qualified to give it. I like the sound of "well done, good and faithful servant" when it is spoken by another good & faithful one. It's no good from one who sees a cloud as a whale, &, a minute afterwards, sees it as a camel. Thanks again, old man.

I've had a recognition in *Times Literary Supplement,* which I enclose, thinking you might like to read it (I'd be glad of it back, as it is the only one I have). It was sent to me by Harold Macmillan. So England & the United States have spoken. I mention it this way, Brooks, because, so far, the *Collected Plays* haven't been mentioned in any Irish paper. If New York & London think them worth mentioning, then, surely, Dublin should think so too. But Drama Criticism doesn't exist in Eireann. The other day,

Ireland's No 1 critic,[1] reviewing a performance of *The Silver Tassie,* triumphantly pointed out that the Stretcher-bearers, chanting in the 2nd act, kept in step, whereas Stretcher-Bearers actually never did. I never did! That's the sort of comment we get there. The fool couldn't see that they had to march with the rhythm of the chant; or that the entire act—much more than the stretcher bearers' march—was removed far from actuality. Well, I'm rather glad you've no more to do in the House. I think you were just overdoing things. Your last word in previous letter was "pooped." You shouldn't let yourself get "pooped." It's time, Brooks for you to go easy. "Stand easy!" is this officer's order to you. Your concern is with the theatre, & not with ovens, Dutch or any other kind. I'm glad you put the Phoebe in its proper place. Let her do her fly-catching somewhere else. Pheasants seem to be friendly birds. Not to me, though. Once staying with Lady Londonderry in Co. Down, I saw her go out, for a second, & down comes a golden pheasant to eat corn from her hands. I tried it then, but the bugger stayed in the tree. Children often seem fearless with animals. Our girl will pet any horse or dog she meets; or cow. She tells me bulls are really gentle. And how!

Give my love (by proxy) to your little grandson. I get on famously with children. They, too, are like animals—if they're let alone. The trouble is, we're so damned anxious they should grow up to be like us. Like us, be God! And us slaughtering each other everywhere. Oh, no, dear God: not like us, we Pray Thee!

My love to O & to you.
As ever,
Sean

[1] "K" (Seamus Kelly), "The Silver Tassie," *Irish Times,* 25 September 1951, a review of the Abbey Theatre's revival of *The Silver Tassie,* which opened on 24 September 1951 and was the company's first production in their new quarters, the Queen's Theatre.

To Roger McHugh

TC. O'CASEY

[TOTNES, DEVON]
16 OCTOBER 1951

Dear Mr. McHugh,

I couldnt consent to the use of the Record made by the B.B.C. of the discussion between M. Brown and me on *The Playwright and the Box-office.*[1] The only sensible thing the B.B.C. can do with it is to bury it.

[1] "The Playwright and the Box Office," a discussion between Maurice Brown and Sean O'Casey, published in *The Listener,* 7 July 1938; reprinted in *Blasts and Benedictions* (1967).

It was to be a simple and impromptu discussion, an open-minded chat, and, as it was my first experience of Broadcasting, I believed it. Then it had to be put on paper; then it had to be rehearsed several times, so that it would time accurately to the tick tick of a clock. After it had been given, I never saw so many manuscripts of a work before. I think I got half a dozen of them; and none of them was worth a damn. Spake your mind! Once was enough for me.

Since then, I have been asked to Broadcast several times—even the undertaking was given that the apparatus would be carried to my own hall-door—but I have always refused. Indeed, your own F. McManus wrote asking me to speak some of my own biographical work from a record that the B.B.C. would make for Radio Eireann; but this I, too, refused to do. When I am let say what I want to say, and say it in my own way, then I shall think seriously of letting my voice be heard. I dont hold that what I might say would be right, or interesting, but it would be my own thought sounded out in my own voice; and I am interested in nothing less. And, mind you, I should have been damned glad of the fees. Anyway, I find it hard to believe that your students would be interested in hearing the sound of my voice.

With all good wishes,
Yours very sincerely,
Sean O'Casey

To Otto Brandstädter

TC. O'CASEY

[TOTNES, DEVON]
23 OCTOBER 1951

Dear Otto,
DRUMS UNDER THE WINDOWS is out of print, and no copy can be got, except, possibly, in some shop selling second-hand books; or on some bookstall. I have searched for the proof copy, and, after a long hunt, found it, with a few last pages missing. I havent time to hunt out these, for I am working on the proofs of the next biographical vol—ROSE AND CROWN—which is to be published next year. I am sending you the proof copy of the book, and trust you to let me have it back when you have finished with it. The books I have already sent, you can keep as a present.

PURPLE DUST appears in Vol III of COLLECTED PLAYS of Sean O'Casey. There are four vols in all. These have been published by Macmillan, St. Martin's Street, London, W.C.2. some time ago; and the two latest vols—III and IV—have been published by The Macmillan Co. of America, 60 Fifth Avenue, New York City. N.Y. U.S.A. You should be able to get them in your City Library.

Your dates are all right, as far as I know. I never bother much about dates, though, they are important things at times.

Sean O'Faolain doesnt like my work; that is why I sent you his review. The others are friends of mine. My works are appreciated in the U.S.A. much more than anywhere else. Recently there appeared in *Theatre Arts* an appreciation extending over three issues of the Magazine from Professor John Gassner of Columbia College. I have but one copy of this, so cant let you have it. They appeared in the June, July, and August numbers for this year, 1951. They give me a fine appreciation, and, naturally, I think a lot of them. Maybe you could get these. Surely, some one gets the Magazine where you are. But, anyway, give your own opinion. Bad or good, one's own opinion is the more important.

I havent the time to tell things about myself since I came to England in 1926 and got married to an Irish lass in 1927—the most important act of my life. We have been together now for almost 25 years, and are great companions. We have three children—Breon 22, Niall 16, and Shivaun, a girl, 12; so with these and with my work and with all the questions of life near me and afar off, I am kept going. You will read a lot about what happened to me and what I did and what I thought in the next vol of biography when it appears next year.

Now this is the best I can do for you; so farewell, and my blessing on you and all good wishes for success in your work.

Yours very sincerely
Sean O'Casey.

To Brooks Atkinson

MS. ATKINSON

TOTNES, DEVON
25 OCTOBER 1951

My dear Brooks:
Thanks for sending me the cutting back. Perhaps, it was C[harles] Morgan—I haven't an idea. Harold Macmillan sent it to me; it is the only one I have—another arrow to shoot at enemies. I enclose another cutting —a very different one. The writer is a clever lad (about 40 now) who

wrote a fine satirical book in Gaelic, called An Beal Bocht—"The Poor Mouth," &, I think a play called "Faustus Kelly"; so he is no fool.[1] I've often wondered why the Silver Tassie aroused so much dislike & animosity, more than any other play of mine by far. The hatred to "Within the Gates" died out; so did that to "The Plough," but the dislike of "The Silver Tassie" persisted, & is as strong as ever today—at least in Ireland; though Lawrence of Arabia went a little wild about it in letter to Lady Astor,[2] particularly the 2nd Scene. He told me himself, one day at Shaw's that "the war wasn't fought that way; but it was the way it should have been fought." But the rest of Ireland! Don't return this cutting—I've a pack of them.

I daresay the song-birds have all streamed over your house by now; & the final act of putting up the storm-door has been done; the kitchen is dark, but the house holds firm. May it hold firm for many & many a year to come.

Busy now with galley-proofs of Biography vol—"Rose & Crown."

God be with O & you.
As ever,
Sean

[1] Myles na gCopaleen, "Cruiskeen Lawn," *Irish Times,* 3 October 1951. In this column the unamused Myles (Brian O'Nolan-Flann O'Brien) wrote the following savage attack on O'Casey, Synge, and the Abbey Theatre on the occasion of the company's reopening at the Queen's Theatre on 24 September 1951 with a revival of *The Silver Tassie:*

A down-to-earth variety theatre has been closed and the premises handed over, almost with awe, to an outfit that makes its debut with as loathsome and offensive a "play" that has ever disgraced Dublin's boards. The second act of this affair is a perfectly plain, straightforward travesty of the Catholic Church ritual. The rest is bunkum and drool. And don't take my word for it. Let me quote from an excellent notice written by "J. J." in the Evening Herald: [he quotes from J. J. Finegan's unflattering review of 25 September 1951]. . . . I do not make any issue on poor O'Casey. Like Synge, his stuff is strictly for export. Paud and Paudeen drooling on the stages of the West End, with the "poetry" slobbering out of their unwashed mouths, will always be a winner. I hope the rest of us know the phoney when we see it.

See also his column of the day that *The Tassie* opened, *Irish Times,* 24 September 1951, for another attack on O'Casey.

[2] See T. E. Lawrence's letter to Lady Astor, 15 February 1934, Vol. I, pp. 498–99.

To John Gassner

TS. GASSNER

TOTNES, DEVON

29 OCTOBER 1951

Dear Mr. Gassner,

Thank you for your kind letter. Of course, from my point of view, your review of my work[1] was magnificent; and, naturally, I hope you are right in all the good things you say about it. Though I know nothing about music, it is odd that whenever I listen to its flow, I feel, emotionally, a tremendous desire to write something to correspond to what I think I hear. So there is certainly something in what you say about the music influence; and, indeed, I love listening to folk-song. The negro folk-song
"This train is bound for glory, this train,"
is haunting me at the moment, having heard it on the wireless recently, sung by an American singer of folk-song, and, oddly enough, it has just come, quoted in a book written by a Negro.

I'm sorry Brooks didn't think more of COCKADOODLE DANDY,[2] for I imagined it was one of my best, flowing more smoothly (the music again!) than any other play of mine. However, he may be right. I enclose a review from a prominent Dublin paper of *The Silver Tassie,* which gave me a minor shock; for I thought all hatred of this play had died. Curious that the dislike of this play has exceeded in denunciation any other play of mine, and has persisted to this very day. I have written a whole chapter about the first manifestation of abuse in my next biographical vol, which, I am told, is to appear next year. Don't bother to return this cutting, for I have a pack of them. I got a few myself, and friends sent me copies. Also one from The TIMES LITERARY SUPPLEMENT, which is kind, and to a large extent gratifying. You may be interested to read it. I shall look forward to the copy of MASTERS OF THE DRAMA,[3] and thank you for remembering me. I shall let you have a copy of ROSE AND CROWN when it comes out next year. Macmillans here say it will annoy a lot of people, but Mr. H. Latham of The Macmillan Co. of America, says he found it "fascinating." He read the MS. Robert Chapman[4] is a dear man,

_____

[1] John Gassner, "The Prodigality of Sean O'Casey," *Theatre Arts,* June, July, August, 1951, a three-part article.
[2] At one point in his generally favorable review of O'Casey's *Collected Plays,* Vols. III, IV, "Case of O'Casey," *New York Times,* 16 September 1951, Brooks Atkinson wrote: "But a re-reading of *Cock-a-doodle Dandy* confirms an earlier impression that the subject is generalized and elusive and the characters people of one dimension."
[3] John Gassner, *Masters of the Drama* (1940).
[4] Robert L. Chapman, University of Michigan, Ann Arbor, Michigan, "forty miles from Detroit," had written to Gassner praising him for his article on O'Casey.

and may he prosper and live a long life; though, at times, I almost wish I wasn't "out of step." But God be with the tribute from forty miles from Detroit. Good fortune to you in your work for a bigger vol. I'd rather you'd do it than I; but, then, it would be utterly beyond me. Like everything else, this is a gift given but to a few.

All good wishes to you.
Yours very sincerely,
Sean O'Casey

To George Jean Nathan

MS. CORNELL

TOTNES, DEVON
3 NOVEMBER 1951

My very dear George:

I hope you are keeping quite fit, & that you are trying to take things easier. I am getting extraordinary enjoyment out of your Book of the Theatre. You are a Cad, indeed; but a golden one. You are merciless, but what has a critic to do with mercy? And, indeed, you have always been kind to any Dramatist in whom you saw a spark of promise. I wish a long, long life to the Golden Cad.

There has been a row here over a competition organised by the Arts Theatre, London. Prizes were offered for the best plays sent in. Enid Bagnold (Lady Jones), who wrote "National Velvet," won first one— £500; & the play was unanimously condemned. So with the second one; & so with the third; but there has been division of opinion about this one— as enclosed cuttings will show. The Judges were P. Ustinov, Dramatist, C. Fry, Dramatist, Alex Clunes, Actor, &; I think another—a manager or something. Anyway the whole affair was a frosty failure. I wish they could have thought of "Cockadoodle Dandy" or "Purple Dust," or even "The Red Star" [*The Star Turns Red*]. However, I got a good review of "Collected Plays" in "Times Literary Supplement," who thinks I am neglected because of my "lamentable judgements." [1] I am busy now with proofs of "Rose & Crown," which is to come out next year. Busy, too, writing the last of the biographical volumes.

[1] See O'Casey's letter to Harold Macmillan, 29 September 1951, note 2.

Take care of yourself, George, for all our sakes: those who write bad plays, to keep them from writing worse ones; & those who write good ones, to clap them on to writing better.

God be with you
My deep love,
As ever,
Sean

To George Gilmore [1]

MS. GILMORE

TOTNES, DEVON
7 NOVEMBER 1951

My dear George.

Thanks, ever so many, for your kindness to Niall when he was over in Dublin. Over there! He talked a lot about your little grey home on Howth Hill. I know the Hill well; worked there when all telegraph-poles were down with a weight of snow, & coming down, in the tram, had to dig a way along through the snow-drifts. At the Station, making for the train, every second wave came tumbling over the wall, sending itself right over train & station buildings. A dash for the train as soon as a wave went over, or we would have been swallowed up be the salt sea. Is the Stella Maris Convent, up halfway, there still? Went to a Gaelic League outing there. Sisters made the tea, & laid it out: we supplied the stuff. A private beach, & an easy way down, with seats every 100 yards, & a big telescope sticking out of a convent window. Oh, boys, weren't they in [a] hurry to get us away as soon as dusk began to fall! I hope you are keeping fit. We are waiting here to see the houses go up like lightning; with Churchill as supernumerary bricklayer. Attlee's got the O.M. OM, as AE. used to say. And all the older boys will have to go again into the Home Guard. I am busy with proofs of new biographical vol—Rose and Crown, to be out next year, if there's no war. I'll send you a copy. I daresay, the old boat is put away for the winter. Remember me to Seumas Scully, if you see him. A grand, decent lad, but a great Is that So! My warm wishes, George, oul' son, & thanks again.

Eileen sends her love.
Sean

[1] George Gilmore, The Slads, Howth, Co. Dublin, an IRA leader and Socialist who performed great deeds of heroism during the Irish War of Independence, 1919–22, and was with Frank Ryan and Peadar O'Donnell among the left-wing faction of the IRA during the 1920s and 1930s.

To H. F. Rubinstein [1]

TC. O'CASEY

TOTNES, DEVON
25 NOVEMBER 1951

Dear Mr. Rubinstein,

ROSE AND CROWN
Galleys

Greeting. Youve knocked me out of my rhythm and put me off me stride. I was busy with the last biographical vol when your warning letter came. Well, as the constable says in Lady Gregory's play, RISIN' OF THE MOON, "It's in the regulations, an' it must be done."

I have modified almost all the matters mentioned by you. Galleys 2–4. Beverley Nichols: [2] I have taken away a number of the words and remarks emphasising effeminacy, which I never intended to do, aiming at his want of interest in masse mensh: his disregard for life. Odd as it may seem, I hadnt any notion then, and very little afterwards of this defect in him. Indeed, I wasnt certain till this very month; till I read in this month's THE BELL, an Irish magazine, where a reviewer of a book by Graham Greene says, "Beverley Nichols is fair game for the high-brow critic, but G. Greene's chastisement of him is impermissible. Nichols, the man, is as God made him, is taunted as unmasculine boys are taunted in grammar schools, while Nichols the writer, who has substituted for his real self, a best-selling one, is allowed to escape." [3] I tried to concentrate on his dandyism. Not that I dislike well-dressed men—Eden, Daniel and Harold Macmillan are well-dressed men, but the clothes are part of them—, but, to me, Nichols dressed explosively. In other words, with all his gay grandeur, he was vulgarly dressed. Last week, we had a New York drama critic here with us for a week-end—another well-dressed lad, but, again, the clothes were part of the man—and I let him read the galleys. Afterwards, he told me that, through Otto Kahn, Nichols had got an interview with the then American President, Calvin Coolidge. He went on to say that he put to the President the very same questions he put to me; but the President hadnt the remotest idea of what he was talking about! So, I think, B. N. is safe now. Evidently, Greene's remarks were far worse than mine.

[1] H. F. Rubinstein, of Rubinstein, Nash, and Co., London, solicitors acting for Macmillan to check O'Casey's book for possibly libelous statements.
[2] See "London Apprentice," *Rose and Crown* (1952).
[3] Hubert Butler's review of Graham Greene's *The Lost Childhood and Other Essays* (1951), *The Bell,* November 1951.

Galley 9. The backer of "Juno": [4] I have altered this to make him a business man, and have cut out the mention of "Juno," and it is allright now. Anyway, there would have been little chance of an action here.

Galley 10, 11, 13, 19. Lennox Robinson: [5] as you can see, I have taken out the direct and indirect remarks connecting him personally with the rejection of "The Silver Tassie." I remain certain that L. R. was the main cause of the play's first rejection, and Lady Gregory confirms this in her *Journals.* I have had to fight for this play longer than any of the others, and am fighting for it still. A few weeks ago, the Abbey put it on, and the first week played to full houses; then came a shower of the usual denunciations, and the play had to come off. I have added this attack now to the previous ones in the chapter dealing with this antagonism. A Miss Ria Mooney produced it, and she and L. R. dont speak to each other; ignore each other completely, so, I suppose, the play suffers from the row. Anyway, this is nothing to you. All you are concerned with is the nature of the writing, and, as I said, it is now, I believe, in no way, suggestive that L. R. was responsible for the rejection.

Galleys 17–18. Gaffney and Macnamara: [6] I have emended this too, and have removed Macnamara's name. As for exposing them to ridicule and contempt, what they thought of the play and of me was published, and, I daresay, I have a right, at least, to make a preliminary defence of the play, and give an answer to some of what they have said of the play, and, implicitly, about myself. In any action, they would have to declare themselves hypocrites and humbugs, if they mentioned they were moved to write in envy or malice (the two are playwrights, one mediocre, the other, terrible). They would have to say that their motive was to defend decency and the Christian faith. So their comments say. They were warning all Christians of the evil in the play, its loathsomeness and its blasphemy. If so, then the warning today is as valuable and as necessary as it was then. And the wider publication the warning got the better; the more Christians who were warned by these comments the better they would like it; and here was O'Casey, himself, helping them in this way by publishing their comments in his book! If the comments they made were true, as their consciences must have told them they were true, then this wider publicity must be good for

---

[4] See "The Silver Tassie," *Rose and Crown,* for a reference to Billy McElroy, best man at O'Casey's wedding in 1927 and the coal merchant who backed the first London production of *Juno* in 1925. It was McElroy's singing of the ballad "The Silver Tassie" which inspired O'Casey to write his play.
[5] See "The Friggin Frogs, *Rose and Crown.*
[6] See *ibid.,* for the comments of the Rev. Michael H. Gaffney, O.P. ("the reverend member of the Dominican Order") and Brinsley Macnamara (the "horrified" Abbey Theatre "Director"); see also O'Casey's letter to Gabriel Fallon, 11 September 1930, note 1, Vol. I, p. 418; Father Gaffney's letter to the *Irish Press,* 14 August 1935, Vol. I, pp. 576–77; Macnamara's statements to the *Irish Times,* 7 September and 7 October 1935, Vol. I, pp. 583–84, 588–89.

all Christians; and, if they were defending the faith and decency, then no ridicule from me could in any way weaken or shake the truth contained in the comments they made. In any case, most of what I say was already said in reply to the comments when they first appeared. And, anyway, the whole chapter has been modified following your valuable advice.

Galley 18. Cu Uladh.[7] This warrior is dead; but, even so, I have modified what I said about him, again, following your advice. He was malicious, but ignorantly so, and he is but brought in to show, generally, the woeful state of Ireland as regards any idea above those of a moron.

Galley 19. L. J. Walsh.[8] Dead, too. I may have the letter, but I am not sure, and an effort to make sure would take months of searching. It is as fresh in my memory now as when I received it 26 years ago. Ever after Walsh never lost a chance of attacking the Abbey (through me), because, the Abbey wouldnt think of doing any of his plays; for they were worse than the worst the Abbey sometimes did. Under suitable government by a suitable Board, Walsh's plays would do nicely; but the chance never came.

Galleys 25–26.[9] I have altered this running after your suggestions. ["The turn-over paragraph, with its references to 'calculated robbery' and 'the Holy Law of extortion' would also be dangerous, unless toned down, in case the unnamed owner of the property in question might be too easily identifiable."—Rubinstein]

Galley 26. Diamond Jim Brady.[10] Dead, too. Anyway, it is hardly likely, were he alive, that he would say a word; or maybe, read my book; or even hear about it.

Galley 48. I havent asked Barry Fitzgerald to give his consent.[11] The quotation given represents a far fainter one than what was actually written by B. F. There is a purpose in the quoting of this letter. Barry never thought much of [F. J.] McCormick; there was, possibly, some jealousy between them. A tremendous attempt is being made in Ireland to boost up Roman Catholic art and culture; and part of the effort was one to give McCormick a big place in the world's art of acting. When Mc C. died, everyone was expected to exclaim about him; and B. F. wrote a fulsome article that

[7] See "The Friggin Frogs," *Rose and Crown*, a reference to Cu Uladh (Hound of Ulster), pseudonym of P. T. McGinley, president of the Gaelic League.

[8] See *ibid.*, for a reference to Louis J. Walsh, author of religious plays and of an article in the *Irish Rosary*, October 1935, attacking the Abbey and O'Casey.

[9] See "Feathering His Nest," *Rose and Crown* for a reference to the house in which the O'Caseys lived at 19 Woronzow Road, St. Johns Wood, London NW.8, from 1928 to 1931.

[10] See *ibid.*

[11] See "A Long Ashwednesday," *Rose and Crown*.

couldnt have represented what he really thought. I was pestered by telegram, letter and telephone to do the same. I couldnt agree with what was
being said. He was a competent actor, at times, a fine one, in suitable parts,
and his acting experience was, almost, confined to the Abbey Theatre, and,
of course, Irish plays. I have seen him very bad, indeed, in one of Shaw's; [12]
and most of the others were unimportant parts in unimportant plays. There
was a lot of pretence in the whole thing. What maddens me is that when a
great man does rise from their communion, they, not only negatively, but
affirmatively, denounce him—James Joyce, for instance. His book is still
banned in Ireland, perhaps, the one country in which it is still banned. The
other week, a Joycean Exhibition was held in Paris to honor the dead man,
and the Irish Minister of External Affairs, John McBride, refused to open
it, and the Irish Representative at Paris refused to go. Afraid it might injure
their careers, through, of course, the generated antagonism of the clerics.
B. F. who is really a great Artist of comedy (or was till the films got a grip
of him), was one of the Hollywood boyos who flung himself into the
Rosary campaign, and what B. F. thinks of the Rosary is nobody's business. This hypocrisy and humbug is a danger to us all; to literature and to
art. I should like the quotation to stay, and am fully assured that B. F.
wont publicly budge. However, I have modified it a little.

Galley 53. N. MacDermott [13] isn't functioning, far as I know; and isn't
likely to. His production of WITHIN THE GATES was generally held to
be a bad one.

Galleys 55 and 58. *The Universe.*[14] The story is practically verbatim. It
took the priest 30 days and nights of prayer and fasting; the evil spirit in
the kid flung him from the mattress while he slept, and tilted him out of an
armchair; strong reactions from the boy while he was being exorcised, with
the Protestant cleric looking on. This, too, I have modified—that is, my
own additions. I have also modified galley 58.

Galleys 56–59. Holy Cross Convent.[15] It still exists, I'm sure; but the holy
nuns wouldnt be pleased with you for calling their work a "business,"
unless you meant (and said so) God's business. Instructing the ignorant is
"a work of spiritual charity," and these women have devoted themselves,
not to business, but to God. Theirs is a very sacred vocation, and has
nothing to do with business, beyond making it pay. Anyway, the whole
chapter has already been published in, of all places, IRISH WRITING
which is published and printed in Cork. It appeared in No. 13. I dont
think we may fear anything here.

---

[12] See O'Casey's letter to Michael J. Dolan, 13 August 1925, Vol. I, pp. 138–40.
[13] See "A Long Ashwednesday," *Rose and Crown.*
[14] See "A Gate Clangs Shut," *Rose and Crown.*
[15] See *ibid.*

Galleys 60–64. Friar Clematis.[16] I have turned the whole thing into some-thing of a fantasy; a drowsy dream; have taken out the name of the place, the name of the Order; and so made it to a great extent anonymous. Of course the whole thing is true as told to me by the Friar himself; and the last debacle was known to the whole district, till it finally died down when a new prior, Father John, was sent down, and those nearly concerned refused to discuss it or mention it again to anyone.

In the chapter written by me, there's nothing against Father Clematis, except that he told a story of the Community's beginning; that they got their residence cheaply because there was hesitation on the part of. others to live in the house of a suicide. He may have told "a tale out of school," but this isnt any reflection on him, except from the point of view of his fellow-friars. It was the evident lack of sympathy with the unfortunate man who destroyed himself, and the odd connection, the friar gave, or seemed to give, to the suicide as an act of providence enabling the kingdom of God to be extended. As for the criticisms, what have they done for art or literature, except to condemn it? There's Joyce, and also, the notorious case of Noyes, the catholic poet, whose fine book on Voltaire was con-demned, and the poet ordered to write something in reparation! These things could be multiplied, but I havent the time or the energy to do it now. They really dont know what to do about Graham Greene or Mauriac. These two men have written unintentionally, I suppose, more terribly about the practices of catholics than ever I could do.

Galley 69. White Star Line: [17] I have changed the name to that of The Blue Comet Line, so that it may have been any of the numerous liner-lines running from one end o' the world to the other. This attack was published, in the form of a letter, sixteen years ago in *Time and Tide*,[18] though I cant remember now whether or no I used the name of the White Star.

Galleys 86–89. The Yonkers' Lawyer: [19] I have changed the name from Yonkers to New Amsterdam, and modified the wording somewhat. The lawyer will hardly hear of it, except it be from Pat McCartan, who is now in Ireland. But he'd hardly tell his friend about it seeing that it was he who brought me there.

After the attack on the "Silver Tassie" the other week by a writer in *The Irish Times*,[20] the following is added: "We are entitled to demand that the gang in the Abbey (The Directors) should be sent about their business, even if some of them had some hesitation in stating what their business is.

[16] See "A Friar by the Fireside," *Rose and Crown.*
[17] See "Ship in Full Sail," *Rose and Crown.*
[18] See O'Casey's letter, "Red Flag or White," *Time and Tide,* 6 June 1936, Vol. I, pp. 631–32.
[19] See "Wild life in New Amsterdam," *Rose and Crown.*
[20] See Myles na gCopaleen, "Cruiskeen Lawn," *Irish Times,* 3 October 1951; see also O'Casey's letter to Brooks Atkinson, 25 October 1951, note 1.

It is insufferable that fine artists should be in the hands of this ludicrous Abbey Board, worse that they should be compelled to prostitute their talent to the playing of stuff (The Tassie, he means) grossly offensive to most ordinary Christian folk. The tripe at the Queen's is not only offensive, but incredibly boring and naive (how anything that is offensive could be incredibly boring, puzzles me). It might be better for all concerned to fold the Abbey up quietly. Certainly, if it is to go on, the present gang in control, with the exception of Mr. Robinson, will have to be sent packing." Doesnt all this sound libellous? It's worse surely than anything I've written; yet there is no action; not even a word of a letter in protest!

Whether this writer's antagonism is directed actually against the play or the Board, I dont know. Looks to me as if he took the chance of using the play to make an attack on the Board. From what he says, it is evident that there is a difference between most of the Directors who support Miss Ria Mooney, their Producer, and Mr. Robinson who dislikes her; and that Miles Na gCopaleen is taking the side of Mr. Robinson against the rest of the Board. Some time ago, he had a play done in the Abbey [21] which was a failure, unfortunately; and, maybe, this has annoyed him; or that others he may have sent in have been rejected. It is all very complicated, and the one thing I can do is to defend what I do myself, and oppose the pretence and humbug which is so much a part of Irish and Roman Catholic practice. It is a great pity about Miles, for he is a clever fellow, and has fine talents, though they maynt run in the way of playmaking; and a greater shame about Robinson who should have stepped into Yeats's place when Yeats went away. He too is a very talented man, but seems to have some kink of weakness in him that stood in the way of his following Yeats's government of the Abbey.

Well, all this must be boring you stiff, so I'll end my catechism, release my hold of you, and let you go in peace.

With many thanks for your cute and clever examination of the proofs, better acknowledged by the changes I have made in the scripts according to your good advice.

And with all good wishes, adding that it pleases me very well that you liked the work. May there be many like you!

Yours very sincerely,
Sean O'Casey

[21] Myles na gCopaleen's *Faustus Kelly* opened at the Abbey Theatre on 25 January 1943, received mixed reviews, and ran for two weeks.

To Irma Lustig

PC. COLBY L.Q.[1]

TOTNES, DEVON
29 NOVEMBER 1951

Dear Irma,

Well, my dear, you have seen something of your own country—even if you haven't sailed the Mississippi—, I you don't seem to be any the better for it. Travelling in the U.S.A. can be just as satisfying as travelling in Europe, if you keep your eyes & ears open, & broaden your heart. If I got the choice tomorrow of Europe or America, I'd choose America without hesitation, for Whitman's more to me than Virgil. New York is as unique as Rome, Prague, Paris, or Venice, & it is more alive, and more alert, and more a probe into the future. And Europe's history isn't such a glorious one. Take the wars away, & there's little left. The great castles didnt do much for the people; the magnificent Cathedrals did little more; & the grand houses even less. If America has less of a history than Europe, she has the chance of making a far finer one in the future. There's as much monotony in Europe for a European as there is for an American in America. The English towns, for instance, are very much alike—each has its High Street as yours has its Main Street. Even the dignity of our Cathedrals has a lonely woebegone look now: they are shrinking farther and farther into a forgotten past. The new wine of life can't be put into the old bottles.

I have been very busy with many things—correcting proofs of the V vol of biography, Rose & Crown, which, by the way, says a few things about America; helping in the house; and working at the last biographical book Vol VI.

Barrows [Dunham] was here with his wife & boy—a very charming family; & we enjoyed our time together. He wrote to me, but I hadn't a second to write to him. I will soon. I daresay, he's with you again. Tom Curtiss, the New York Drama Critic was here for a week-end this month; & we journeyed along the streets of Totnes—& New York—together.

I wonder do the friends you mention know anything about what goes on in Altoona? A priest there, Father Sheedy, sent me his blessings when I was in New York in 1934. He was a life-long friend of Dr. MacDonald of Maynooth. I was so busy with Rehearsals that I had time only to write and thank him. I mislaid the letter, & forgot the address. Then it came to me suddenly, when I saw the name of the Town in an American Journal. He was an old man then; &, I fear, must be dead now. He wrote to me several times while I was in N.Y., & I replied as well as I could in the

---

[1] See O'Casey's letter to Mort and Irma Lustig, 28 November 1950, note 1.

midst of the furore of a new production. How sorry I am now, I didn't go down to Altoona. Give my love to Barrows & his family. My love to you & Mort.

As ever,
Sean

PS. I am, naturally, very pleased that your two friends were interested in my biographical books. There is nothing in them that even insinuates an assault on the Catholic Faith. Of course, if one assumes that Bishops form a Hierarchy of Heaven, then there's a lot in them to bring a frown on a Catholic face; a Catholic face without a Catholic mind. Medievalism is gone forever; & a new adoption to life as it is, & will be, must be accepted—as Dr. McWalter [Walter McDonald] of Maynooth so constantly proclaimed.

S. OC

To John Gassner

MS. GASSNER

TOTNES, DEVON

7 DECEMBER 1951

Dear John,

We know of each other well enough now to forego the title of "Mister." This doesn't occur in the Gaelic, & so, I think it odd to use; & it seems to cling to an outmoded manner. Anyway, there are so many Misters in the world now, that it's a relief to have a few honest-to-God Johns, Seans, & Georges, to give us a little more variety. Thank you very much for your letters and the letters within them. They are all very pleasant and very encouraging. At least, I will be able to put up a few totem poles of praise outside our hall-door. It isn't all praise, though, as enclosed cutting from an Irish daily, THE IRISH TIMES,[1] shows. It is odd, the insistent hatred of, & opposition to, the play, "The Silver Tassie"; especially in Ireland. There's been more shouting it down than was given to the "Plough & the Stars." Miles na gCopaleen (Miles of the Ponies—a character in "The Colleen Bawn") is a very clever fellow. He wrote a fine satire in Gaelic called "The Poor-Mouth," & I was one of the few (if there were any at all) who praised it.[2] He tried his hand at a play him-

---

[1] Myles na gCopaleen, "Cruiskeen Lawn," *Irish Times,* 3 October 1951; see also O'Casey's letter to Brooks Atkinson, 25 October 1951, note 1.
[2] See O'Casey's letter to Brian O'Nolan (Myles na gCopaleen), 2 April 1942.

self, but it didn't do. I never said a word about his playwriting, in public or private; so it wasn't resentment that made him attack the "Tassie." I'm afraid that all Irish writers now—those who can't get away—are mortally afraid of the clergy, & make continual efforts to show that they are on the Lord's Side. Miles, for some reason or another, evidently hates the Abbey Board. There's always the envy, hatred, & malice going on there. Tom Curtiss, the American drama-critic was in Dublin a few weeks ago, & came down here for a week-end. He told me Miss Ria Mooney—the Abbey's official Director—and L. Robinson do not speak now; pass each other by as if they were invisible, the one to the other, each to both! Of course, there's no Yeats now with a power of making achievement indifferent to these things. Thy are definitely harmful now. Not a single word appeared in *The Irish Times* in defence of the "Tassie." There was no voice in the silence. I wonder what will they think & what will they say about the next biographical vol, *Rose & Crown,* when it comes out? I've just looked over the Galley-proofs, & it is mentioned for next year. I am working now on the last vol. I've signed a contract of *Cockadoodle Dandy* for a New York production. Bob Lewis is to direct. I'm not very enthusiastic about ANTA. G. J. Nathan doesn't seem to think a lot of what they've done. If Broadway be bad, London's worse. Arts Theatre gave 3 prizes £500 first, for the three best plays, unproduced. 1000 came in, & they chose three, which, all the critics said, as kindly as they could, were very bad indeed. None of them will ever likely be shown again. Judges were, Alec Clunes—actor; C. Fry, playwright; Ustinov, playwright & actor. So that'll give you an idea!

Thanks again, John, for your kind interest in my work.

All good wishes to you.

Yours very sincerely,
Sean

To *H. F. Rubinstein*

and TC. O'CASEY

[TOTNES, DEVON]
12 DECEMBER 1951

Dear Mr. Rubinstein,

Thank you for your very kind letter. I am naturally very glad that you like my work, and hope you may continue to do so. It is very pleasant to be able to set up another totem pole of good-will in front of our home.

I have just had a note from the Chairman of the philosophical Society of Trinity College, Dublin, and so up goes another totem pole, with the harp as its symbol.

I have knocked out the phrase of "he had never forgiven her for this"; [1] and, I think, the comments are innocent enough now. As a matter of fact Lady Gregory's Diaries records that when she, Yeats, and L. R. were going up the Abbey stairs during the dispute over the play, she said that they "might, in spite of all, produce it; Yeats was inclined towards it, but Robinson said No, it is a bad play." [2] It might [be], indeed, but the policy lost its genuineness when plays upon plays were done far, far worse than the SILVER TASSIE could have possibly been.

I think now that R. was annoyed at L. Gregory's liking for me. It was all a new world to me then, and such an idea never entered my head. He was never in Coole Park, whereas I was there a number of times, and this, I think, hurt him, naturally. Then L. R. was looking over Lady G's letters with a view of writing her LIFE—which, for some reason, he didnt do— he wrote to me for permission to print some of my letters to her. In this letter he said "I have been reading her letters, you come out of it with flying colours, I not so well." I wish L. R. had been a bigger man—it would have been such a godsend to the Abbey, and to the Irish Theatre generally. He was a very clever fellow, and had the vitality of the Theatre in him; but he couldn't see, or refused to see, his limitations; though there's no one who hasn't some limitation or another. There'd be no struggle if one was limitless in capacity and achievement. Adventure would disappear from life. And, when he wanted to, he could be a most delightful host. Now, I fear, as far as the Abbey is concerned, he just lives in a kind of sullen isolation. Something went wrong somewhere. He has just written the official History of the Theatre; [3] but he should be really producing the plays of others and writing his own. It is a great pity, but, I daresay, it cant be helped. The prase "Old Lady says Yes" is a play on a play called THE OLD LADY SAYS NO. [4] L. R. isnt what I would call "a hot-headed Irishman"—not anything like Yeats, who, in a "hero rage" was an amazing sight.

Well, I've given a lot of trouble, but, maybe it was worth it, for I hope THE ROSE AND CROWN will bear out your good opinion of it. And my good wishes to you from my heart out.

[Sean O'Casey]

[1] See "The Friggin Frogs," *Rose and Crown* (1952), the Ward Costello letter. The deleted phrase probably came at the end of the following sentence: "And 'Mr. Robinson had answered with a flat "no," adding that it was a bad play; even though Lady Gregory had changed her mind about it.'" See also O'Casey's letter to Ward Costello, 22 October 1948.

[2] *Lady Gregory's Journals, 1916–1930* (1946), ed. Lennox Robinson, p. 110.

[3] Lennox Robinson, *Ireland's Abbey Theatre: A History, 1899–1951* (1951).

[4] Denis Johnston's *The Old Lady Says "No!"* was first produced by the Dublin Gate Theatre Studio on 3 July 1929, after it had been previously rejected by the Abbey Theatre.

To Seumas Scully

MS. SCULLY

TOTNES, DEVON
15 DECEMBER 1951

Dear Seumas,

Thank you so much for your kindness to Niall when he was in Dublin. You helped a great deal to make his visit an enjoyable one, which he still remembers vividly. Thank you, very much.

I understand you had a good time in France; &, soon, you will be a much-travelled man.

I see that Miles na gCopaleen and Patrick Kavanagh are boxing each other in the *Irish Times;* [1] and, seemingly, proving that Mrs. Shaw was right. Did P. Kavanagh manage to get to the U.S.A.? It was rather lowsy for the Government Minister to cancel his name from the list of grants, without an explanation.[2] Probably, it was Tarry Flynn [3] did it to him. Politicians are still afraid of the poets. Hope you'll like "Reamonn agus Niamh Og." [4] I'm sure it will be a lot different from "An Tinceoir agus an tSidheog," by Hyde.[5] All song and dance show, I daresay.

> *All the best to you.*
> *Yours sincerely*
> *Sean*

Eileen, Niall, & Shivaun send their love.
I am busy with proofs of next biographical vol.

[1] See Patrick Kavanagh's letter, "Culture and Barbarism," *Irish Times,* 10 December 1951; and a reply by Myles na gCopaleen, "Cruiskeen Lawn," *Irish Times,* 12 December 1951.

[2] The Irish government's Cultural Relations Committee had recommended that Patrick Kavanagh should be sent to America to read and talk about his poetry, but the recommendation was turned down by Frank Aiken, the Minister for Cultural Relations. See Anthony Cronin, "The Cultural Relations Committee," *The Bell,* November 1951.

[3] Patrick Kavanagh, *Tarry Flynn* (1948), a richly comic and sometimes irreverent novel.

[4] *Réamonn agus Niamh Og* (*Raymond and Young Niamh*), the Abbey Theatre Christmas pantomime.

[5] Douglas Hyde's *An Tincéar agus án tSídheog* (*The Tinker and the Fairy*) opened at the Abbey Theatre on 15 February 1912. It was first performed at the Gaiety Theatre in 1903, under the general supervision of George Moore, with Douglas Hyde and Sinead Ni Fhlannagain (later Mrs. Eamon de Valera) in the two title roles.

To Shaemas O'Sheel

MS. O'SHEEL

TOTNES, DEVON
24 DECEMBER 1951

Dear Sheamas,

The first thing you have to aim at now is recovery from your injury.
You do wrong to try to keep out of the doctor's hands. A fractured rib,
neglected, may become a serious thing. It can't unite without treatment, &,
even if it did, it might do so crookedly. If you rightly expect commonsense
in others, see that you have some of it yourself. Go, for goodness sake, to
a doctor, & take all the trouble necessary to get well again. I'll write again
about the rest of the comments in your letter. Look after your injury—
nothing else matters for the time being.

As ever,
Sean

To Irish Times

28 DECEMBER 1951

THE RED TICKET [1]

Sir,—Little did I think, when I wrote "Hall of Healing," that the conditions of fifty years ago in the dispensaries for the poor would be the same
to-day. And Ireland devoted to the Sacred Heart!

One of your correspondents said recently that the present opposition
to the Red Ticket was the first to be made. This isn't so. Jim Larkin, Connolly, Bill Partridge, and others, condemned it with vigour, as they did all
the evils of the Poor Law system. So did many of the then Republicans—
for instance, Mathew Stafford, an old Fenian, himself a Poor Law Guardian, carried on the fight on the Board and off the Board. I myself know
too well what that god-damned Red Ticket is like, having spent many an
hour, and wasted many a visit, seeking one.

These dens, called dispensaries, exist still! And flourish rottenly, and
no hand strikes them out of the life of the poor. I have been in many dispensaries, where the ragged, the cold, and the sick poor gathered, hustled

---

[1] See O'Casey's letter to Robert M. Smyllie, 22 April 1951, note 4; and his
letter to the *Irish Times,* 24 January 1952.

in and hustled out again, as if they had no claim on life, and it was an impudent thing for them to be seeking the comfort of health.

In all my experiences, I have never seen any cleric waiting there, regular or secular, or Protestant divine either. Their bodies were far more important than the bodies of the poor. One would think that in the holy practice of mortification, they would flock to these places, and so sanctify their souls. If they only had carried out this practice for a little while, the dispensaries would be better than they are, and the Red Ticket would have faded away into something better to suit their needs. But none of them bothered then, and none of them bothers now, except to oppose any effort made to better the state of the workers. If Mr. de Valera, instead of going in and out of monasteries and convents of Rome, visiting the restoration of St. Simon Stock in Kent, and running over the honour St. Columbanus in Switzerland, visited the dispensaries of Ireland, he'd be doing better work for God, for Ireland, and for his people.

Only this morning, I have had a Christmas greeting from a lady living in a very comfortable quarter of Dublin. On the card, she writes to say that "Ireland is a very different country, now that a native Government is in power." So Ireland by her exception, proves that the more she changes, the more she remains the same.

Mauriac has published a book called "A Knot of Vipers." [2] Some Irishman should now write a book to be called "A Bunch of Christian Humbugs." Well, time and Communism will sweep all the humbugs out of life.—Yours, etc.,

Sean O'Casey

Tingrith, Station road,
Totnes, Devon,
21 December 1951

[2] François Mauriac, *The Knot of Vipers* (1951).

To David Krause

TS. KRAUSE

TOTNES, DEVON
30 DECEMBER 1951

Dear David:

Thanks for your kind letter. I am, as you imagine, full up with things to do; and damn little time in which to do them. Of course, in my life,

I've wasted lots of time—years of it—which I'd like to have now. But gone's gone; and I'm too lazy and too busy to say an act of contrition. I'm near 72 now, and the puff of vigor isn't what it used to be. But I'm still going along with an odd laugh and an odd song; and, as long as we can keep a major war away, we can afford, however difficult life may be, to sing a song first thing in the morning, when we're not feeling too bright. I'm glad you saw something in "The Gunman." I daresay "Cock-a-doodle" has something to do with experience passed through, and recorded, in the book "Inishfallen, Fare Thee Well"; but it has a vital and much more vivid connection with the Ireland of today. As for "Father Domineer" making you feel "uneasy," that isn't surprising, though you feel uneasy for the wrong reason. He is both a symbol and a realism. The two main incidents—the killing of the man and the attack and denunciation of "Lorleen" are as real as facts can make them; and even part of the priest's words, the bitterest of them, were actually spoken by the priest concerned. The clerics have a power now in Ireland that they never had before. The censorship in Ireland over body, mind, soul, and spirit is almost complete—is complete, as far as I can judge—.

1st Jan. Had to put writing aside to do things in the house, and associate with our children 3.

Can you make in a play any priest human; rounded and life-full? Did you ever have one with you for a long time—two days; even one day? If you had, you'd find them hard to reach. Once they don the stole, they artificially change appearance and emotions. The priest, not the poet, wears the mask. They look upon themselves as separate, and, I fear, superior beings; "Custodians of heavenly things" as one of them comically called himself. There isn't, and never was, a "Father O'Flynn" [1] in Eirinn. "Domineer" is a true symbol of priest-craft everywhere. There are, of course, excellent fellows among them, but these are powerless among the many others, as Newman discovered. They're worse now. Compare Card. Newman with Card. Spellman! The first, kept a Deacon, and made a Cardinal only when he was near his end; the other made an archbishop, with no intellectual claims to go with the job—witness his two books. But, all the same, you may be right; and, anyway, your own opinion is more important to you than any of mine can be.

I have just finished correcting proofs of 5th vol. of biography, *Rose and Crown,* to come out in 1952; and am half-way through the first draft of the 6th vol.; so, you see, I'm hard at it.

I hope you get your Ph.D. without having to do too much to get it. Tell Dr. [David H.] Greene that Card. Spellman still has an eye on St. Peter's Chair. And give him my love. As for the other Irish writers you mention, I fear they are harming themselves by envying and harrying each

[1] Father O'Flynn, the idealized and jovial Irish priest in the popular ballad of that name.

other. Censorship is so strong, and they are so frightened, that this seems to be the one outlet they have. None of them can bear to hear one another praised. You should see what some of them say of "The Tassie"! "As loathsome and vile a play as ever appeared on the boards"—opinion of one of Ireland's cleverest writers—"Miles na g Copaleen." [2]

Well, all the best to you, my young friend.

Yours very sincerely,
Sean

[2] See O'Casey's letter to Brooks Atkinson, 25 October 1951, note 1.

IX

OF SALVATION AND IMMORTALITY, 1952-53

O F course there is personal salvation as well as the salvation of the group; but a lot depends on the group: it is the group that influences rather than the Ivory Tower. Environment in which we live, static and living; the house we live in, the girl we court, the friends we have, the way we make our living—all contribute to form us, and powerfully, too, though in the last resort, it is our personal will that counts most of all. In my opinion, salvation can be won better and more bravely in a crowd than in a cloister.

It was indeed sad to hear of Gene [O'Neill]'s death. He certainly died too young. God help us when such as he go. They leave us lonely; especially when their touch is still warm on our hands. O'Neill and Shaw—their going rends a lot from the Theatre. One would want to be just only about to leave school not to miss them. I still can't imagine Shaw as having gone. Maybe, be God, he hasn't. When great ones go, a fellow begins to believe in immortality.

The Irish reviewers had rejected *Cock-a-Doodle Dandy* as a travesty of Irish life, but early in 1952 a militant Catholic association organized over a thousand Dubliners in a series of protests against liberal artists which, as a travesty of Irish hospitality and freedom, only seemed to confirm the point of O'Casey's play. Acting as if they had been roused to launch a witch hunt by a Father Domineer, the protesters picketed the Dublin theatre where Arthur Miller's *Death of a Salesman* was playing; and later, when Orson Welles was invited to visit the Gate Theatre, where years earlier he had made his start as a young actor, they paraded outside the theatre and demanded that he leave the city. Left-wing liberals were not welcome in holy Ireland, and Miller and Welles were automatically condemned as evil Communists. Similarly, O'Casey's continued objection to the use of the Red Ticket as an inhuman and un-Christian practice was treated scornfully in the letters column of the *Irish Times* and put down as a Communist maneuver. Some months later, in April and May letters to the *Irish Times,* O'Casey defended the memory of Frank Ryan, the now dead Irish Republican leader who had fought against the Fascists in the Spanish Civil War, when another aspect of McCarthyism emerged in Dublin and an attempt was made to discredit Ryan as a Catholic renegade and Communist. But O'Casey, who had known and admired him, and spent some days with him before he returned to Spain after recovering from battle wounds, insisted that whether or not Ryan had been a Communist, he had certainly remained a loyal and practicing Catholic all his life: Catholic and revolutionary, Irish and anti-Fascist. His remarks in a later letter might have been applied to those right-wing Catholic action groups in Ireland: "We continually prate of our Christian way of life—for Jesus' sake, then, let us show some useful sign of it."

But Ireland was not his only problem. In East Berlin the Deutsches Theater decided it could not produce *The Star Turns Red* for fear of "offending Roman Catholic clerics," a situation which the director felt might harm the ultimate attempt to unify Germany. O'Casey couldn't understand such expediency, and reminded the cautious Germans that Shaw had once said there was nothing in the play "that is not in the Authorised Version of the English Bible." Thus, a variety of fears were rapidly making him one of the least produced major playwrights of his time. He was aware of the alternative and pointed out to the German director that if he had chosen to write expedient and inoffensive plays, "I should have been very rich, instead of having to remain in a state of uncertainty as to what may happen in the future." Even when religious and political expediencies were apparently not an issue, he suffered from uncertainties beyond his control, as, for example, when his well-meaning friends in New York, who were planning to present the *Cock,* had a business disagreement and had to call off the production. Nevertheless, nothing could deter or discourage him—neither bad news nor those recurring attacks of influenza that confined him to his bed. He had written three new one-act comedies; the fifth volume of his autobiography was published in the summer of 1952; and he was already working on the sixth and final volume. "I am fairly free from the sin of idleness," he told Miss Sheila. When he was confronted by excessive demands, he often had to rely on his comic sense of word play to escape. For example, when he was asked in March to sign yet another protest message, this time against the alleged American use of bacteriological warfare in Korea, he refused because he claimed he had seen no verifying evidence, but his denial was written in the form of a comic affirmation of total peace: "Of course, I am against any kind of bacteriological warfare; but I am also against atomic warfare, against high-explosive warfare, against cannon-fire warfare, against rifle-fire warfare, against bow-and-arrow warfare—even against the warfare of one nation spitting at another."

The only warfare he condoned and practiced artfully was verbal combat. When Louis MacNeice wrote an unflattering review of *Rose and Crown* in July 1952, O'Casey sprang into action with an immediate reply, which the editor of *The Observer*—as he had done on two previous occasions involving reviews by Gogarty and Orwell—refused to publish, and MacNeice ignored, but which now appears here for the first time. In one instance MacNeice teasingly alluded to O'Casey's silence on the repression of the arts in an unnamed country, and O'Casey answered bluntly: "I judge he is making an oblique reference to thought and action in the Soviet Union. If he does, then, speaking plainer than he, I hold that Zadanov is no more infallible in things of literature than say, Professor Leavis." And he went on to mention his recent letter to Mikhail Apletin, in which he defended Eliot and Picasso, and exposed the folly of "Socialist realism."

Throughout 1952 and 1953 his letters contain his forthright opinions of many people. On the poet Patrick Kavanagh and the Irish: "What you attribute to Paddy—bluster, extreme sensitiveness, and deep pride—is really, as Shaw pointed out, only cowardice. We Irish all have a dose of it in us; it is the Irish original sin." On Francis Stuart and other Catholic writers: "Are you sure Stuart is a good novelist? I should like to think so, but cant. He seems to me to be an imitator—first of Hemingway, and now of Graham Greene and Mauriac; but as good as neither of them; Mauriac, of course, being the best, though afflicted with a terrible certainty that there is nothing good under the sun, especially among Catholics." On James Joyce: "Joyce's 'exile, silence, and cunning' wasn't a separation from the people, but from the tiny group of Irish writers who were jealous of his great genius." On George Jean Nathan: "He is a man after my own heart, who can play seriously on the harp, but is never ashamed, never daunted from playing a tune or two on the ole banjo." On R. M. Fox's book on Jim Larkin: "Fox has turned a flaming torch into a flickering taper." On homosexuals: ". . . the kink in them is probably resented by the kink in me, for today I am just as enamoured by the trim figure & pretty face of a lass as I was when I was twenty-one." On singing Canons, for a production of *Purple Dust:* "The Canon singing a song is out of the question. Canons dont sing in company—even Protestant Canons rarely—all my life, I heard one only sing at a Social at All Saints, Grangegorman, a district in Dublin that houses Ireland's most famous Lunatic Asylum—maybe that explains the Canon's singing." On the Jews: "On the whole, I think, the Jew has a quicker sense of art, & greater love of color than the Goy, or Gentile. Music, too; as well as painting." On the Irish: "What is called 'fear & love o' God' has ruined us. But there is greatness in the land that gave the world Tone, Emmet, Parnell, Betsy Gray, Larkin, Lady Gregory, Yeats, Shaw, & Joyce. So in all our snarling, we can shout Hallelujah in Gaelic."

In 1953 he had high hopes of at last seeing the first London production of *Purple Dust,* with the help of the imaginative Sam Wanamaker as director; but after going to Edinburgh for the tryout run, and then waiting for the tour of the English provinces, which unfortunately drew poor notices, he saw the play fold just outside "the gates of London" when one of the principal backers withdrew his support. O'Casey was "broken-hearted" when he wrote to Wanamaker, but with his typical resolution he added, "we just must face it, fight it, and overcome it." Once more he had tasted defeat as a dramatist, yet no one could say he was a defeated man.

To Brooks Atkinson

MS. ATKINSON
TOTNES, DEVON
6 JANUARY 1952

My dear Brooks:
Thanks ever so much for the meat. It stood up well on the table for Christmas, & the boys & girl dived into it. As you know, meat is doled out here to the tolling of the funeral bell. It matters little to me; for such conditions mean but a return to type—to the time when, for years, I was content to have a passing look at it in the shops. I always thought the English ate far too much meat—a la Broadbent; but now they carry on—have to—a perpetual Lenten Fast; unless, of course, one has ample funds to pay big prices for additionals or accessaries. The Roast Beef of old England's no more!

Well, Christmas is over, thank God. It's a difficult time now for a lot of people, & too old a custom to be given up. It's a difficult time, too, for many Americans. I've just had a letter from a friend who is a Professor [1] in an American University (I met him in Harvard as a student when I was

---

[1] Professor David H. Greene of New York University.

with you all in the Thirties. Then he was in the American Navy at Plymouth, & used to come here twice or more a week—what a pity you didn't come to Plymouth instead of going to Chung King!), saying "Mommy & Daddy are charging everything so there will be a terrible day of reckoning in January. But we'll enjoy Christmas (he has four children), & worry about January when it comes." And this friend lives on the shore of Lake Success!

I've had a letter from Murray Schumach, who is in Korea now. From Totnes to Korea! D'ye know, Brooks, I've come to the conclusion that there's a wild streak in you Americans. Something of Daniel Boone left in all of yous. Well, it's not a bad streak, anyway. I have heard you have had a poor season theatrically. Well, it's as bad here. The Arts Council chose 3 from a 1000 plays, giving them prizes and productions, saying "None of them showed any originality or any adventurous vein." Commonplace things. There's been a row in Dublin over Orson Welles [2] coming to see a play. Ordered by a Committee to keep out because he "was a Communist," or a fellow-traveller. We're getting worse—"Death of a Salesman" was picketed when it ran in a Dublin Theatre. Worse & worse, we're getting.

Thanks again Brooks & Oriana, for your great kindness. But you mustn't offend again. You have a family to mind, and, by all that's reasonable, these days one family is a little more than enough for one fella to care for.

My love to you & Oriana, & all.
As ever.
Sean

[2] The following report appeared in the *Irish Times,* 19 December 1951:

When Orson Welles, stage and screen actor, playwright and film director, arrived in Dublin last night from London to see the play, "Tolka Row," by Maura Laverty, at the Gate Theatre, he was greeted outside the theatre by about a dozen people carrying placards. The placards bore inscriptions: "Dublin rejects Communistic Front Star," "Not Wanted, Orson Welles, Stalin's Star," "Welles Spiritual home is Moscow, Stay out of Ireland." The protest was organised by the Catholic Cinema and Theatre Patrons' Association.

A crowd of about a thousand people was in front of the theatre when Welles, who had been invited to the Gate by Hilton Edwards, came out, and he commented:

I have never been a Communist or a Communist sympathiser. I was always against Communism. I didn't come to Dublin to apologise for anything. I came to see a play. I think you have a free country here and I am entitled to take a ticket on an airplane and a ticket to a theatre.

To Irish Times [1]

TC. O'CASEY

[TOTNES, DEVON]

15 JANUARY 1952

Dear Sir,

Some time ago, I sent a reply to odd and curious remarks (false, incidentally) sent in to you by the Rev. Edwin Owen, Rector of Birr,[2] which, he alleged, were made by a co-cleric of his concerning my attitude towards this clerical friend of his when he was killing himself to get a few houses built in the parish he cared for.

As the letter, or, indeed, any part of it, hasnt been printed, I should like to know if it has been received. If not, I shall be glad to send a copy to you. If, on the other hand, you received it, I should like to know if you intend to publish it; and, if not, respectfully ask the reason why.

The letter in question was posted to you on the Third of January. With all good wishes for the New Year.

Yours sincerely,
Sean O'Casey

[1] This letter was not published. The editor replied that he had not received the letter of 3 January, and O'Casey sent him another copy, which appeared on 24 January.

[2] The Rev. Edwin Owen, Rector of Birr, "The Red Ticket," *Irish Times,* 1 January 1952, a reply to O'Casey's letter of 28 December 1951.

To Irish Times

24 JANUARY 1952

THE RED TICKET [1]

Sirs,—Mr. Edwin Owen is a bit hasty in shoving O'Casey into the dock. He seems to do it with a little glee. Well, one's allowed to speak from the dock. The question I raised was that of the Red Ticket and the Poor Law dispensary system, but the rev. gentleman evades it by bringing in the housing question, lustrously illustrated by another rev. gentleman trying to solve the problem in the building of a few poor houses for a few poor people in his own poor particular parish.

[1] See O'Casey's letter to Robert M. Smyllie, 22 April 1951, note 4.

The Rev. Edwin Owen declares that Canon Hall [2] told him "how much O'Casey's co-operation would have meant to him in those days (while trying to provide houses for the poverty-stricken people of the united parishes of St. Thomas and St. Barnabas in the twenties); Canon Hall had asked for the co-operation because he was convinced that only the power of O'Casey's pen was needed to awaken the conscience of Dublin." Mr. Owen adds himself that "if O'Casey did co-operate in Canon Hall's plans for the betterment of his own fellow-parishioners, then his condemnation of the clergy is false; and if he didn't, then it is the dramatist, and not the cleric who is in the dock." Canon Hall must have had a good dream, for O'Casey had left the parish and the Church before even the twenties had begun, so he was then neither a fellow-parishioner nor a co-religionist of the residents of St. Barnabas' Parish.[3] His mind was then with work as secretary to the Committee to get Jim Larkin freed from an American jail; with the Bolsheviks fighting the Interventionists, and with the problems of play writing; so what Canon Hall may have been doing then didn't even exist in his world. I was then far away from Mr. Hall's parish, and he didn't know even where I was living. Even had he asked for the help of the O'Casey "pen," it wouldn't have been any use to him, for then there was no "power" in it. If any assumption of power came to the O'Casey pen, it came when O'Casey was far away in England; and even this "power," if it was there at all, was lured out of it again by the sudden and odd rejection of "The Silver Tassie" by the Abbey Theatre. So it seems that the worthy Canon Hall must have been fancying things when he told Mr. Owen that he had asked for "the help of O'Casey's powerful pen." But where, then, were the powerful voices of Dublin and Armagh? Years and years before this, there had been a Commission set up to inquire into the condition of the tens of thousands living in one-room tenements; a Commission provoked by the terrible denunciations of Jim Larkin helped by the sympathy of the then M.O.H., Sir Charles Cameron. The findings of the Commission were issued in the form of a Blue Book.[4] It was a book of black and most dismal splendour, but it didn't rouse the conscience of Dublin; neither did it rouse the conscience of the clergy. As far as I know, not one Protestant cleric commented upon it; and, if any did, they commented in a whisper few could hear; and, as far as I know again, only one Roman Catholic cleric shook a fist at those indifferent to poverty and want—Father O'Flanagan. And we, or some of us do, know what happened to him.

For fear the Rev. Edwin Owen might think I am stealing away from a responsibility of refusing to help Canon Hall, let me say that had he asked me to do so; had he even visited me personally, and appealed to me to do

---

[2] Canon David Henry Hall, Rector of the parishes of St. Thomas and St. Barnabas, Dublin, in the 1920s.

[3] O'Casey had left the parish of St. Barnabas toward the end of 1918 after his mother died.

[4] Sir Charles Cameron, *Report upon the State of Public Health and the Sanitary Work performed in Dublin during the Year 1909* (1909).

so, I should have refused; for his scheme, whatever it may have been, or any scheme of a like nature, is useless. There's no use of building houses for poverty-stricken people. What must be done is to do away with conditions that bring "poverty-stricken people" into existence. This is a job, not for one, but for all; and that is why Socialism or Communism alone can effectively deal with the problem. We have done with the Bosco businesses, the Protestant Orphan Society's pittances, the St. Vincent de Paul means-test gratuities, and with the pathetic efforts of someone helping the poor in an effort "to serve his Master." We are demanding these beginnings of a fuller life, not as doles from heaven, but as part of the Rights of Man.

Now the voice from the dock again asks if the clergy will deny that they have refused to strengthen their souls by enduring the inconveniences and hardships suffered by the workers in the Poor Law dispensaries; or that they have consistently shown themselves indifferent to the hardships suffered by the people in those wretched and humiliating places—Yours, etc.,

Sean O'Casey

Totnes, Devon, 3 January 1952
(Delayed in transit.)

To Wolfgang Langhoff [1]

TC. O'CASEY

[TOTNES, DEVON]
26 JANUARY 1952

Dear Herr Langhoff,

Very well, dont do the play. It doesnt matter to me, but the reasons for its abandonment do. I cannot agree that you should give up the idea of performing it because you are afraid of offending the Roman Catholic clerics. There isnt going to be any Socialist victory, if you continue to be afraid of these gentlemen. May I ask why do these clerics object (and prevent it when they can) to the production of such plays as THE STAR TURNS RED? If it had the effect you surmise it would have, then they'd welcome its production everywhere. It is because they fear the opposite effect that they oppose it, and have banned it in my own country, Ireland.

The Uniting of Germany on a democratic basis is a grand idea, but I fail to see how a production would harm it. The clerics have always been opposed to democratic, or even any kind of liberal thought; and, whether

[1] Wolfgang Langhoff, Deutsches Theater und Kammerspiele, Berlin.

the play be produced or not, they will continue to oppose the idea of democracy for Germany. The reason is obvious; for a democratic State cannot allow the clerics to dominate the State's way of life. If they are allowed to do so, then it is equally obvious that the State is not and cannot be democratic.

It strikes me that if your contention be right, and that expediency is so important, then we do wrong to condemn the writers who adopt this outlook on life. You are taking the line of least resistance; therefore you cannot blame others for doing the same thing. To do so would be inconsistent, if not downright hypocritical. If I had adopted the expedient attitude of mind I should never have written THE STAR TURNS RED. Or, indeed, other plays as well, not to speak of many things in my autobiographical books. I should have been very rich, instead of having to remain in a state of uncertainty as to what may happen in the future. Anyway, there is nothing in the play, as Bernard Shaw saw at once, and wrote to me to say so, that is not in the Authorised Version of the English Bible.[2]

Have it your own way, however. As for the PLOUGH AND THE STARS, that has been licensed to another for translation into the German and Austrian language, and so I cannot give you permission to do it. So too with JUNO AND THE PAYCOCK, and, I believe with other plays, too. So I'm afraid I can give you no other play to do. I should have replied sooner, but a severe attack of Influenza laid me low, and leaves me low still.

All good wishes,
Yours sincerely,
Sean O'Casey

[2] See O'Casey's letter to Bernard Shaw, 29 April 1940, note 2, Vol. I, p. 860.

To Richard B. Buckley [1]

TC. O'CASEY

[TOTNES, DEVON]

27 JANUARY 1952

Dear Mr. Buckley,

I am afraid you dont get the true sense of what a vocation should be. Every way of life ought to be a vocation—work done for which we are the best fitted and for which we have the best liking; so that we work at our best, and are in harmony with ourselves. That isnt so now, and is only in the process of achievement in the USSR. Whatever you may think, I'm afraid most of the professions are chosen, not to serve the community,

[1] Richard B. Buckley, 3 Windsor Villas, Cork.

but to make a good living, to get on in the world—the only true Christian materialism. Luckily, many professionals—say doctors—like their work, and are passing clever at it; but do they get the chance of doing what they want to do, or what they know they can do, for the elimination of sickness and disease? Will you tell me how much the Irish State allocates to research work in medicine, surgery, pathology? Less than England—in proportion to revenues—, and that is shamefully small. They are continually begging here for donations to carry on research work for the elimination and cure of cancer—Churchill today, Cardinal Griffin tomorrow. You say that many enter medicine "in the higher sense—they wish to administer to the sick." You are, my friend, behind the times here. The new outlook of doctoring is not the curing of disease, but its prevention. Surely you have heard of "preventive medicine"? To do away with sickness and disease is the new science, and it is a glorious one. Huge sums are devoted to all kinds of medical research in the USSR—more, far more than that of the U.S.A., Britain, and Ireland put together. There are no Merrion Squares or Harley Streets in the USSR. I wont argue with you about the Mother and Child Scheme; except to say that Dr. [Noel] Browne who introduced it, and fought for it, is a Roman Catholic, and, per se, as important as any bishop of the Communion. So you must fight that question out between you. To me it is just another indication of the growing determination of the Catholic (so apparent and powerful in other countries) laity to assert themselves against the tyranny of the Prelate. But one thing is certain—as long as the system allows some to provide medical aid for themselves "out of their own pockets," there will be the scandalous—and un-Christian—abuse of some getting medical aid utterly beyond the reach of others. They will be the favourites of the doctors, except for the few Doctors "Abernethys" in the medical profession. The present Dispensaries are a proof of this. The better-off never go near these kips, and, of course, neither do the clergy. The Right Rev. Mickey Monsignor Muldoon wouldnt be caught dead there, though it would do their souls (according to Christian teaching) good to mix with poverty and bear some of its hardships. You certainly have a high opinion of bishops. You should read what Dr. Walter McDonald, for forty years Professor of Theology in Maynooth College, said about them. You evidently think they should never be criticised; and, of course, to criticise a Cardinal is going beyond the beyonds. Well, read Card. Spellman's book THE FOUNDLING; [2] or the book, VICTORY [3] he wrote during the war years. Compare them with what has been written by Newman, and then tell me what you think of Spellman. As far as literature, or even theology, he is, indeed, a chancer. In last week's UNIVERSE we are told while he was in Korea, he visited Hong Kong, and there hauled out of a pocket £350 which he gave to one charity, and out of another, he hauled another £350, which he gave to a second charity—

2 Francis Cardinal Spellman, *The Foundling* (1951).
3 Francis Cardinal Spellman, *The Road to Victory* (1942).

all, the Catholic weekly says, out of HIS PRIVATE POCKET. You couldnt do that, and I wouldnt say you were a poor man. A nice thing to be able to dip into a pocket to take out £350 at a go! Certainly, from what we are told, St. Peter couldnt do it either. But Spellman has had his eye for a long time on the Chair of St. Peter, and he does all he can to keep himself, like a film star, before the public eye. Why do you say "You do not really believe what you say"? You are rather clumsily calling me a hypocrite, you know. I do believe what I say, my young Cork friend. And I have suffered a lot for saying them. You do set out statements for which you cant supply an iota of proof. How do you know that Stalin goes about in an armoured car? I didnt say Stalin was a "humble" man. As a matter of fact, he is a proud man, invested with the grace of Humility, which is very different from being "humble." Uriah Heep was humble, you know; and, say what you like, by his talk, his actions (one of which is quoted above) and by his attempt to enter the world of literature, Spellman has proved himself to be a conceited man.

As for your last paragraph, I dont wish to enter into a theological discussion, for that is a matter for your own (and mine) personal soul. But it isnt as easy as you make it out to be. Again I refer you to Dr. McDonald of Maynooth—to mention but one—, who found belief more difficult than you seem to have found it. It is interesting to read of his flinging book after book of accepted theology away, as useless, out-of-date, absurd. Read what the dying Catholic scientist (a genuine scientist) said of what was being taught in the Catholic seminaries and Catholic colleges. And what Acton said, and Lingard, and Langland, and even the easy-going Chaucer. Surely you have read Chaucer and what he said of the clergy of his time—all Catholics then; long before there was any breakaway. Now, of course, the Church is challenged by hundreds of millions, even from the theological point of view. And from the social point of view, I need only remark that there [are] eight million Communist votes in Italy; votes surging to the very doors of the Vatican. You might read, too, what Dante said about the clergy, while you are at it.

Well, that's all, except to ask that you dont call me "sir." I am just a man like yourself, seeking the truth according to my lights. O'Casey's my name, and it doesnt need a "sir" in front of it. I'd have written sooner, but Influenza laid me flat for a time, and even now remembers me with what Mitchel called "a whoreson cough." May you be a good doctor, and may you strive to be a great one, knowing to the last day that you could know more.

All good wishes
[Sean O'Casey]

To George Jean Nathan

MS. CORNELL

TOTNES, DEVON

18 FEBRUARY 1952

My very dear George:

I am wondering how you are keeping. I hope the Winter hasn't been too hard on you. Anyway, the Spring is near us now, and here, in Tingrith, the door is wide open for her to come in & sing a song to us. I've been some weeks in bed with Influenza & its affects, but feel better so far now & doing some work, as well as sitting for a painting by our elder boy.

I daresay, you've heard about Miss [Margaret] Webster doing "Purple Dust" for Kermit Bloomgarden; though this isn't altogether certain, for Miss Rubin [1] writes to say Miss Webster hasn't yet signed any contract for the job. I can't afford to worry one way or the other, for it would hinder me from "work in progress." Miss Rubin tells me that money is coming in well for "Cockadoodle"; so there is hope knocking about, any way. I got a copy of "Poetry," sent to me by Eric Bentley, who has in it an article on the Abbey: [2] a good article, but a little unfair. The Abbey at the moment is beset by snarlers. One can't expect it to be as it was with a Yeats & a Lady Gregory; and such persons don't come happening into the world every time the clock ticks. Recently, a revival of "The Tassie" was denounced.[3] I enclose a cutting. But how are you—that's the main thing? God keep you fit for a long time.

My love.

Sean

[1] See O'Casey's letter to Jane Rubin, 17 May 1952.
[2] Eric Bentley, "Irish Theatre: *Splendeurs et miseres,*" *Poetry*, January 1952.
[3] See O'Casey's letter to Brooks Atkinson, 25 October 1951, note 1.

To Richard B. Buckley

TC. O'CASEY

[TOTNES, DEVON]

22 FEBRUARY 1952

Dear Mr. Buckley,

Thanks for your letter, which was very interesting. I've been in bed with Influenza, and still feel sorry for myself. However, a last word, if I may. I shouldnt have used the word "humble." It was very stupid of me. No great man is humble. Stalin is a modest man: more, he has the grace of humility, which, as you probably know, forms the first three steps to heaven. Dont you believe what some Labour leaders or labour men say of Stalin going about in an armoured car. If you read the Soviet papers and magazines, you'd see him at meetings, and at the Anniversaries of the October Revolution. Standing among his comrades inconspicuous, interested in all that is happening. You know Churchill is followed about everywhere by C.I.D. men, and so, too, Truman is guarded everywhere he goes. Wasnt there an attempt on Truman's life recently? I seem to remember hearing of one. I dont know what you really mean by "enforced labour." We all of us have to work. Stalin didnt institute this necessity—it was God. See Genesis. "In the sweat of thy face shalt thou eat bread." Anyway, work is a fine thing for man, if it be for the need of the community, and not for profit. It is the robbery in rent, interest, and profits, only, that make work evil. I dont haggle at words when I put "prevention" before "cure." You must know the old proverb "Prevention is BETTER than cure." So it is, by God! Do you really mean to put Douglas [A.] Hyde before me as a worthy exponent of Roman Catholic theology? You arent serious, are you? Or even of Marxism? Why even recently when he went to Fatima, and gave his impressions of the event, he uttered what was nothing less than a heresy. Indeed, I'm afraid many of you Roman Catholics are woefully ignorant about your Faith. It is true that for a long time the custom has been to have Italians in the posts of Pope and Papal Secretary of State (the Red Pope, as he is called); but times have changed. Today the revenue from Italian laymen isnt what it was; there are eight million Communist votes in Italy, and two and a half million Communists—not counting the Socialists. Large parts of the Continent have gone Communistic, and, as well, there isnt now the wealthy boyos and lassies who poured so much into the Vatican Exchequer. The most of the contributions now come from the United States, and the Church there is well aware of it, and is beginning to say that he who pays the piper should call the tune. And so [Cardinal] Spellman has an eye on St. Peter's chair. The "custom, or unwritten law" can be changed, you know, or ignored. They darent make it an article of the Canon Law, much more an article of faith. Since the last one died, no Secretary of State has been appointed—His Holiness does the two jobs. It is said that S. had an expectation of this job as a big step to the Chair; and so no one was put in it. To Argue about The Mother and Child Scheme would mean a long, maybe an interminable, correspondence for which I have no time, and have more important work to do. And. . . .[1]

[1] Page missing.

To J. C. Trewin [1]

TS. TREWIN

TOTNES, DEVON
15 MARCH 1952

Dear Mr. Trewin,

On the 28th of October, 1945, Mr. Orwell, shaking a shillelagh, had an article (review) published in THE OBSERVER which he called "The Green Flag." [2] It was a review of my book, DRUMS UNDER THE WINDOWS.

I replied to that Review and sent the letter to *The Observer.*[3] You kindly wrote me a note to say that it had been received, and that you had sent my letter on to Mr. Orwell.

Searching the OBSERVER afterwards, I couldnt find ever either my letter or any reply to it by Mr. Orwell.

I should be glad to know if Mr. Orwell did send any reply to you which may have failed to be printed for any or for many reasons. I think myself that Mr. Orwell just ignored my letter,[4] leaving me behind him as one of the animals in his delectable ANIMAL FARM.

Oliver Gogarty did the same thing—this time in THE SUNDAY TIMES [5]—, ignoring a letter sent to the Paper by me [6] as a reply to a Review of my first book, I KNOCK AT THE DOOR; rebuking me for opening my heart in the book, and deploring my lack of reticence, pointing out the delicate manner of the Chinese in concealing their inner feelings; while at the time the Red Army of China was proclaiming the feelings of the people everywhere. Gogarty hiding in a Greek vase, couldnt see the way the world was going. It was very funny. He was a very shy man at retorting; so, evidently, was Mr. Orwell.

I enclose a stamped and addressed envelope for your convenience.

Yours sincerely,

Sean O'Casey

[1] J. C. Trewin (1900–   ), English writer and critic, *The Observer,* London.

[2] George Orwell's review is reprinted above in chronological order.

[3] See O'Casey's unpublished reply to *The Observer,* 29 October 1945.

[4] Orwell ignored the letter. O'Casey wanted to be sure because he was probably writing his chapter on Orwell at this time, "Rebel Orwell," *Sunset and Evening Star* (1954).

[5] Oliver St. John Gogarty, "The Unlocked Heart," *The Observer,* 12 March 1939, Vol. I, pp. 782–84. O'Casey was mistaken about the *Sunday Times.*

[6] See O'Casey's unpublished reply to *The Observer,* 13? March 1939, Vol. I, pp. 785–86. See also his letter to Charles Davy, 21 August 1952.

To David H. Greene [1]

TC. O'CASEY

[TOTNES, DEVON]
26 MARCH 1952

My dear Dave,

Just after Christmas, I fled into bed chased (and caught) by an attack of Influenza, and for a long time put away from me all the pomps and vanities of this wicked world (I dont believe it's such a wicked world as the Catechism (Protestant) says. For a long time I had the old chest troubling me with a whoreson cough, which lingers with me a little still; but the crocuses and the daffodils are out, and O'Casey's getting ready to cheer. I hope you got through Christmas allright—I left you in a bustle of C. shopping. I'm sorry P[atrick] Kavanagh didnt go to NYU; it would have done him good, and, I'm sure, opened his eyes a lot wider on the world. We Irish need this badly; we cling too much together, instead of spreading out among people. The Irish in London, in Birmingham, in Boston, in New York, all keep too close together. He should have made you aware of what was happening. I'm afraid his air of devil-may-care is a pose, far worse than any attributed to Yeats. I'm certain he was longing to go to New York but just wouldnt show to you (or the Americans) that he was; and so, lost the chance; for if you had had the chance of supporting him, the Cultural Committee would probably have planked down a grant. Like you, I got to know about it when I read about it in the Press. I would have helped him willingly as much as I could, as I did when I had to write three letters to him before he was persuaded to send his poem to you. He makes a cult of persuasion—like Byron's lass, who "swearing she would ne'er consent, consented." It was lousy of the Cultural Committee to refuse him a grant.[2] But, of course, for many reasons, Paddy wouldnt like me to join in the controversy. I get very few letters from Eirinn, bar anonymous ones calling me anything but a gentleman. However, I dont think we should blame either [Austin] Clarke or [Robert] Farren. They have, I believe, some kinds of jobs under the Government— Farren's a Director of Radio Eireann; but a chance to go to beautiful France, with all expenses paid (or Belgium, I forget which place it was), wasnt to be sniffed at, and one cant blame them for jumping at it. What you attribute to Paddy—bluster, extreme sensitiveness, and deep pride— is really, as Shaw pointed out, only cowardice. We Irish all have a dose of it in us; it is the Irish original sin. I dont know anything about [John] Ryan either. Never heard of him, till his name appeared in the papers. ENVOY'S

---

[1] David H. Greene, Professor of English, New York University, co-author with Edward S. Stephens of *J. M. Synge* (1959).
[2] See O'Casey's letter to Seumas Scully, 15 December 1951, note 2.

gone now.[3] It had good points, but was a bitter kind of a magazine, finding faults everywhere and with everything.

Are you sure [Francis] Stuart is a good novelist? I should like to think so, but cant. He seems to me to be an imitator—first of Hemingway, and now of Graham Greene and Mauriac; but as good as neither of them; Mauriac, of course, being the best, though afflicted with a terrible certainty that there is nothing good under the sun, especially among Catholics. He is, as you know, the great Catholic writer; but, to me, as with [Graham] Greene, it seems he is a Jansenist, if ever there was one, but powerful and biting and bitter. No sense of humour; neither has G. Greene; nor does Stuart show any either.

Robert Lewis is very much charmed with the COCKADOODLE DANDY, and is busily trying to get a production. I have a contract for a production next Fall. The husband [4] of Julie Harris, who has made a great hit in acting, has formed a group to do it. He and Julie were down here last summer with me, and so was Bob L. They were delightful friends. There is talk, too, of a production of PURPLE DUST, to be directed by Miss Margaret Webster. I hope that one of them, at least, may go on this Fall.

Meanwhile, to keep things going, I am working at the biographical books. It was these that managed to keep us out of the workhouse; so they are very important works, Dave. The 5th vol is advertised for May, but I havent had the page proofs yet, so it will hardly be out then; but more certainly during the summer or the Autumn. It is called ROSE AND CROWN. I have written a lot of what will be the last vol—the 6th—; so that will end the series.

How's David Krause? I hope he's getting on fine. Yes, I think COCKA-DOODLE DANDY as fine a thing as I have ever written. I hope Horace [Reynolds] is doing well. His two children are now married, and forming a world of their own. How odd it must be to father and mother when the children leave their world, and make a world of their own. Breon is doing this now, partly. He is in London trying to become a painter. Shivaun is now teaching me all about Shakespeare, and Niall telling me all about biology. I'm only beginning now to realise how damned little I know.

I hope my "reputation" will hold fast in the U.S.A. That is very important to me. I get quite a crowd of letters from the States—from Texas up to Illinois; from New York to California. Did you read, or hear of, a book called THE SIN OF THE PROPHET [1952]? It is a story of Boston in the 1850's, about the slave agitation, just before Lincoln became known. I think it finely written, in, I think, the style of Thoreau; so quiet and so exciting. The author is Truman Nelson, and publishers, Little Brown, of Boston. The best I've read from the U.S.A. for some time.

[3] *Envoy: A Review of Literature and Art,* edited by John Ryan, a monthly magazine in Dublin which started in December 1949 and ended in July 1951.

[4] Jay Julien, lawyer and theatrical producer, then husband of the actress Julie Harris.

I hope your book has appeared, and that it is doing well.[5]

My love to Catherine and to all the little ones, and to you, old friend.

Yours as ever,
[Sean]

[5] *1000 Years of Irish Prose: The Literary Revival* (1952), edited with an introduction by Vivian Mercier and David H. Greene.

To Vincent Duncan Jones

TC. O'CASEY

[TOTNES, DEVON]
28 MARCH 1952

Dear Mr. Jones,

I'm not sure about the germicidal conditions of the particular case of the alleged use of them in Korea, though, in war, anything may be done. Therefore, I cannot say anything definite or give any positive judgment on the matter.[1]

Of course, I am against any kind of bacteriological warfare; but I am also against atomic warfare, against high-explosive warfare, against cannon-fire warfare, against rifle-fire warfare, against bow-and-arrow warfare—even against the warfare of one nation spitting at another.

There you are; I have had enough of war experiences. There is no reason, in my opinion, for any more of it. We know each other well enough now to live together in peace, and work together in peace, too. I want the young to experience the excitement of peace in solving the problems of life. More light, more heat, more leisure, more food, more art and literature, music, and science all things of good report, all things lovely, all things necessary—that is what I want to work for and encourage; and, I believe, that is what the young long for, and that is what they want to busy themselves with from the cradle to the grave.

By the way, I havent money to spare on telegrams or phone-calls to London. I am not in any way as well-off as I'd like to be. I could have been, if I did what others wanted me to do, but I didnt, and that is my business.

With love to you, and all good wishes,
Yours sincerely,
Sean O'Casey

[1] The British Peace Committee asked O'Casey to condemn the use of germ warfare by the United States in the Korean War, and to let them know by "telegraph or telephone" if he agreed with their statement on it.

To Irish Times

5 APRIL 1952

FRANK RYAN [1]

SIR,—I knew Frank Ryan over in Dublin, and I knew him in London.[2] As far as I know, he wasn't technically a Communist. Bernard Shaw, in the preface to his novel, "Immaturity," says that one is born a Communist or one isn't a Communist at all. That's what Frank Ryan was—a born Communist, just as Sean O'Connolly was a born Nationalist, though never a member of the I.R.B.

Frank never needed, to my knowledge, to be "reconciled to the Church." He was almost a born Catholic, too—certainly one from the day of his baptism. One in theory as well as practice. He came to our place in London several times when he was home from Spain because of a bullet wound in his arm. When we saw him the wound was more than half healed, but it looked even then a very ugly wound. I used all my eloquence to persuade him to stay at home, feeling in some way that, if he went back to Spain, we should never see him again. He refused to stay, saying that he "couldn't think of leaving the boys by themselves." On one of the visits, he was with Jack Carney and the representative of a big Dominion Press Amalgamation, a stout and fine-looking Presbyterian from Belfast, well known to both of us. As usual when Presbyterian and Catholic get together, provided they be Irish, an argument arose about religion, and Frank defended very sincerely and very cleverly the faith that was in him. It was

[1] In a lecture on "Communist to Catholic" in Dublin on 9 March 1952, Hamish Fraser, a former officer in the International Brigade during the Spanish Civil War who became a convert to Roman Catholicism, started a controversy in the letters columns of the *Irish Times* by describing Frank Ryan (1902–44), the IRA leader and Socialist who also fought for the Loyalists in Spain, as "a typical Irishman who became a Communist but was reconciled to the Church before he died." Among the people who insisted that Ryan never lost his faith in Catholicism or Socialism was his friend Desmond Ryan, the noted historian (*Irish Times,* 7 April 1952). Frank Ryan had been captured by Franco's Fascists when he returned to Spain after his wounded arm had healed in 1937; he was in prison until after the outbreak of World War II when he was transferred to the Germans, who tried unsuccessfully to use him to stir up an Irish revolt against the British; he died in Germany, broken in body but not in his Catholic-Socialist principles, on 10 June 1944. See Francis Stuart's two-part article, "Frank Ryan in Germany," *The Bell,* November, December 1950.

[2] Ryan was one of the leaders of the protest against *The Plough and the Stars* in the Abbey Theatre on 11 February 1926; but later he and O'Casey became close friends. See Mrs. Hanna Sheehy-Skeffington's letter to the *Irish Independent,* 15 February 1926, note 2, Vol. I, p. 167; the news story, "The Plough and the Stars," *Irish Independent,* 2 March 1926, note 1, Vol. I, p. 177; O'Casey's letter to Horace Reynolds, 19 March 1937, Vol. I, p. 656, in which he talks about a visit from Ryan.

quite evident to me that the lad was a Catholic well versed in his faith, and very astute in putting forth points in its favour. I acted as moderator, keeping heat out of the discussion, though there were a few shouts now and again, particularly from the Presbyterian. It was all very amusing to me, who didn't care a damn one way or the other.

The trouble with those laddoes who swing from Communism into Catholicism is that they know as little about the Communism they abandon as they do about the Roman Catholic faith they embrace. Certainly the dogmatic Mr. Hamish Fraser knows damn all about Frank Ryan.—Yours, etc.,

Sean O'Casey

Devon, 2 April 1952.

To George Jean Nathan

MS. CORNELL

TOTNES, DEVON

8 APRIL 1952

My very dear George:

I'm glad that Birthday Festival [1] is over, and hope you have fully recovered from its affection. Sometimes people's love for us does more harm than their hatred, tho' I, for one, prefer the love. It's curious that the two of us should have been growing up at the same time, you in Indianapolis (I think), and I in Dublin; O'Casey beating Nathan in time by two years—I was 72 last March.

Of course what the Irish Drama critics say doesn't matter much, except from the financial point of view. There denunciation from the religious & moral point of view make people nervous about going to a play, & so the chance of royalties are harmed. Indeed, I imagine, this is what they aim at. I'm troubled about Ireland. The writers there seem to spend their time biting each other; & there is no courage left in the land. Yeats was a terrible loss; they speak, usually, well of him now; but they're glad he's gone. I enclose cutting of a criticism from the magazine, The Bell—it is typical of them all: wailing, wailing; but with no guts to even whisper a welcome to a play that might excite controversy, or the wagging of a clerical finger. They're arguing now about ceremonial dress—morning suits for occasions. They complain that morning suits were (& top hats) worn at the

---

[1] The celebration of Nathan's seventieth birthday.

late king's funeral; but soft hats when paying a visit to Christ the King! I'm working now at page-proofs of "Rose & Crown"—a hateful job; &, also, writing the next, & last, biographical vol. Miss Webster was to get into touch with me from London last February, but, so far, she hasn't. I hope your work for Theatre Arts isn't taking too much out of you. Eileen went down with Influenza, so I've been a busy man for weeks.

My love, George, as ever.
Sean

To Robert Lewis

MS. LEWIS

TOTNES, DEVON
25 APRIL 1952

My dear Bob,

I was very glad to hear that "The Grass Harp" [1] had arrived on the stage, & glad again, for your sake, first; & again glad, because the play, according to Brooks [Atkinson], was a good one, that it had got such a good notice. Nothing needed now, but a good run—hardest of all to get. I do hope it may do well.

We have had onslaughts of Influenza here; first myself; then, when I was back to a staggering, depressed normal, Eileen went down; & I had a busy time climbing up & running down stairs: in all journeys, reckoned together, I must have got to the top of Mount Everest.

Here I am, now, back at the old table, working at the page-proofs of "Rose & Crown," due out in May, but more certain to come out in September.

Thank you, Bob, agradh—Gaelic for "love"—for the parcel of tea, sugar, & tins of butter & beef. They were welcome—too welcome, in fact; for you shouldn't be putting yourself out to send these presents. Flying dollars have taken the place of flying saucers. It's funny, really, to look at so many nations gathered round America's door, calling backsheesh, backsheesh, sahib. Once the once so wealthy England, too, with a begging-bowl in her hand. Oh, monstrous! I'm afraid, Bob, quite a lot of the dollars go astray. I've seen it so with UNRA, plain calico before; rich taffeta & fur coats after.

---

[1] Truman Capote's *The Grass Harp,* directed by Robert Lewis and produced by Jay Julien, opened in New York on 27 March 1952, and closed after thirty-six performances.

Well, anyway, your parcel didn't go astray, & we thank you again.

All good wishes to "The Grass Harp," to Jay [Julien], & to you.

As ever,
Sean

To Brooks Atkinson

TS. ATKINSON

TOTNES, DEVON
1 MAY 1952

My dear Brooks:

Thanks—or as we say in Irish, Go raibh mile maith ogat—a thousand thanks; literally a thousand good, bright things be at you; for the parcel of good things. I don't really feel uncomfortable about it—not while I'm enjoying them, or watching Eileen & the children enjoying them. But isn't it a deplorable way for the once wealthy England to be in! The land of roast beef has become the land of fish & chips. I hope the U.S.A. won't go on acting too much, & get herself in the same condition: even her huge reservoir isn't inexhaustible. And, you know, Brooks, a lot of your dollars go to the wrong places and pockets. I've seen it several times myself with UNRRA: poor people getting a job on it, &, before another Sunrise, appearing in a car, almost filled with a mink coat. I daresay, these things are inevitable: the oxen treading out the corn!

Your trouble may look like only "filling out a blank form"; but there's more, a lot more to it than that: there's the thought, and there's the payment for what CARE sends along. They don't do it for the love of God or of man; they wouldn't be in the business long if they did. Well, thanks, again, to O and you for the great kindness.

Rose & Crown was catalogued for May, but there are many difficulties here in the printing trade, & I don't think it will appear now till Summer. I'll send you on one of the first copies. I've sent in the corrected page-proofs a fortnight ago, so there's nothing to do but wait. I'm working now at the last chapter of the last volume whose title I haven't yet chosen. I imagine it might be "Sunset and Evening Star." I did it all first in long-hand, then typed it roughly, changing, adding, taking out; then did it in better typing steps, changing, adding, & taking out again. I'll leave the last draft quiet for a few months, & then go over it all again, cautiously, getting a number of shocks from the scrutiny. The biographical books have kept me from singing in the streets, so, for that reason, I respect them a lot.

I wish I could have been with you at George's Birthday Party. He seems to have been highly gratified with it. I'm so glad he got such an affectionate tribute. You lads are far, far more humanly affectionate than your brother-critics of London. They are a cold crowd here. I mention this in Rose & Crown, & so make more enemies. A good time to you & O in the country. The lilac will soon bloom—I mention it in Rose & Crown, too! But don't poop yourself working. Remember your desk takes a lot out of you. Drama-critic is no easy job. My love to O, & to you, Brooks.

As ever,
Sean

To Harry Cowdell

MS. Texas

Totnes, Devon
7 May 1952

Dear Mr. Cowdell,
Yes; of course, you may send the photograph to The Macmillan Company [New York]. I have just made out your name on the jackets surrounding Osbert Sitwell's books of biography; the name nearly lost in the design. The Jackets are fine; I like them well, especially the one proclaiming the Great Morning.[1] They are worthy of the books, which says a lot, for O. Sitwell is, indeed, a writer. Just now, I'm reading again his description of The Tower.[2] I, myself, prefer the new to the old—the Echo—, but he makes the Tower live magnificently again, & in so very & curiously quiet a way.

When I was young, it was my hope to be a painter & designer, but circumstances said no; & I had to turn my thoughts to other things.

All good wishes to you.
Yours very sincerely,
Sean O'Casey

[1] Osbert Sitwell, Great Morning (1948), the third volume of the autobiographical sequence.
[2] In the first chapter of Great Morning, Sitwell describes the background of the Tower of London.

To Harry Cowdell

MS. TEXAS

TOTNES, DEVON

10 MAY 1952

Dear Mr. Cowdell,

I am returning the sample book-jacket of the "Rose & Crown" with this note.

Eileen (Mrs. O'C.) likes it, so do my two sons & one daughter; so do I; so, if you like it, we can pass it unanimously.

Indeed, I am very fond of painting—the art—, & would, if I could, spend most of my time looking at these, enjoying the world of painting from Cimabue to Matisse. Augustus John is a great friend of mine. We have little time to do what our hearts desire to do. Its brevity is the one fault I find with life. So many things to be done, too, to keep it going. There are few of us who haven't to earn a living, & this robs us all of many lovely hours. I have to do many things about the house—I just washed up the delft used by six for dinner. I've been washing up now for the last ten years —just one of many domestic chores. So you see, I, too, am "a spare time artist." Well, it's a grand way to use it, anyhow, but I wish we had more time to spare. When I was Secretary of a Pipers' Club, long years ago, I sent out over a hundred letters adorned with a picture of a piper, done in coloured inks; [1] & it was surprising how the picture enticed people to send us a subscription. And I did my own Christmas cards then, too.[2] Ah, well, I can now only look at work done by others, but this is very pleasant, too.

With warm regards,
Yours very sincerely,
Sean O'Casey

[1] See O'Casey's letter to Lord Castletown, 14 May 1911, Vol. I, pp. 5–9.
[2] See the Christmas card verses in O'Casey's letter to Fergus O'Connor, 9 March 1918, Vol. I, pp. 77–78.

To Irish Times

10 MAY 1952

FRANK RYAN

SIR,—It seems that Mr. Hamish Fraser hasn't replied to the questions asked by Dr. Owen Skeffington, probably because he has no answer to give.[1] He stays silent. It is the usual practice of these laddoes. When they meet with anything that tilts them into staggering back, they run home to hide. Chesterton had this cute habit, too, and there are many instances of it in his controversies with Dr. Coulton. Either he stayed mumb, or he replied in some clerical paper where he knew that his opponent's answer would never be permitted to appear. Let's give a parliamentary shout to Mr. Fraser: Answer, answer, sir!

As for his complaint that I am one who "foments disobedience to the Holy See," [2] I assure him I am but one among hundreds of millions. In fact, the disobedience seems to have begun in the first days of the Church, when Paul "withstood Peter to his face, because he was to be blamed." Since then we have had the Orthodox Church, the Waldenses, the Huguenots, the Anglicans, the Non-conformists in all lands, the Lutherans, and God wot what else. Even among his own flock; for instance, when Dr. McDonald and other Professors of Maynooth publicly subscribed to the Land League when it had been condemned by the Pope. Acton was another disobedient boy; so were Dante, Dollinger, Anatole France, Voltaire, Shaw, Joyce, and even Cardinal Newman said some sharp things about affairs in the Roman Catholic Church. Lately there was Dr. J. V. Simcox, for 25 years Professor of Canon Law in St. Edmund's here, who abandoned his position because of Hinsley's attempt to get him to agree to the Church saying one thing in private and another in public about the educational question of the right of parents to teach their children error. Mr. Fraser will find it all told in the booklet, written by Dr. Simcox, published by Watts and Co., Johnson's Court, London. The booklet is called "Is the Catholic Church a Secret Society?"

Mr. Fraser warns all that I am one who writes to Left journals—trying to tell *Irish Times* readers something they don't know! The odd thing is that I'd make a bet that Mr. Fraser knocks out more through his devotion to his faith than I do through my attachment to Communism.—Yours, etc.,

Sean O'Casey

Devon, 6 May, 1952.

[1] After an exchange of several letters, Dr. Owen Sheehy-Skeffington asked Fraser, *Irish Times,* 22 April 1952, how support of the Spanish Republican Government against Franco could be, in Fraser's words, "to act in defiance of the Holy See and to champion the cause of Anti-Christ," since such renowned Catholic writers as Mauriac, Maritain, and Bernanos had all condemned Franco.

[2] Fraser replied to O'Casey, *Irish Times,* 19 April 1952, and stated: "It is quite understandable that a contributor to the *Daily Worker* and the *Irish Democrat* should wish to justify, and thereby foment, rebellion against the Holy See—especially Mr. O'Casey, whose damn-bespattered letter shows that he cannot even condemn the Christian faith without profanity."

To George Jean Nathan

TS. CORNELL

TOTNES, DEVON

15 MAY 1952

My very dear George:

I got the book [1] and am reading in relays—with Breon, who is with us for a few weeks. It helps a lot to have so many apt quotations at one's elbow. I think it is a fine selection. It deserves a big sale. I hope you've fully recovered from the Influenza. Eileen got it when I recovered, so I have had a busy time. My new book, "Rose & Crown" was to be out in May; but things in the publishing trade are bad here, & so it has had to be delayed. They're working on the jacket now, designed by Breon; & it should be out before September—probably in the summer. I've just finished the last vol in a third draft. This I'll lay aside for a few months, & then examine & amend it finally. I expect to call it "Sunset and Evening Star." Well, so much done!

Got a letter from Brooks [Atkinson] saying how delightful the Birthday Party. Brooks has a real affection for you. He speaks very lovingly of you. Now, keep fit, or, at least, as fit as you can; and no minor birthday parties, either. You have work to do. I shall be writing to Tom [Quinn Curtiss] shortly. Give him my love, should you see him. How is Gene [O'Neill]?

My love to you, George.
As Ever,
Sean

Alfred A. Knopf, Esq.
Publisher, New York City

The *World of George Jean Nathan* is a fine world, and makes a grand book. It is like a long row of living, glittering stained-glass windows looking in at the Theatre, looking out at life. Nathan is a gay philosopher, and in him is a divinity that is elegant and gorgeously human. In other words, he's a genius; and, while belonging to America, belongs to the whole world, too. I have no hesitation in claiming him for Ireland. The book isn't the whole man, or the whole statue of the man; but it is an outstanding and delightful bust of the critic. People say he is a hedonist, concerned only with his own happiness (he says so himself), and one utterly indifferent to mankind. The fact is that he is devoted to mankind, and serves mankind through the Theatre with the heroic devotion of a Saint; and more,

---

[1] *The World of George Jean Nathan* (1952), edited by Charles Angoff. O'Casey enclosed the copy of his letter to the publisher, Alfred A. Knopf.

he is vitally interested in everything mankind thinks about, imagines, and does within the Theatre, and outside the world's stage. The interests catalogued in the book show that Nathan as soon as the curtain falls, keeps busy, sauntering here, there, and overseas probing into life. It is this interest in life that makes the fellow so enchanting. I felt this years before I ever met the man. He knows every good and gay human habit, and can write wittily about them all. Truth comes sparkling out of his laughter. He is a man after my own heart, who can play seriously on the harp, but is never ashamed, never daunted from playing a tune or two on the ole banjo. He is a great democrat, as the Editor tells us G[ordon]. Graig has said "He is an artist, and let us sleep all the better for the fact"; and wake up the better for it in the morning, too. In our hatred of him, or in our love for him, we show how great a critic he is. I am delighted to have this book. The Editor says "Nathan will be remembered and read for a long time." Ay, for a long, long time—as long as intelligence and coloured hilarity live in the Theatre and live in life.

I congratulate the Editor on his selections, and I hope everyone who has entered a theatre, or may be about to enter one, will get this book, and so get closer to a great American.

Yours very sincerely,
Sean O'Casey

To Jane Rubin [1]

TC. O'CASEY

[TOTNES, DEVON]
17 MAY 1952

Dear Miss Rubin—

Yours is a melancholy letter but there's no use in being melancholy about it. These things happen. It is very regrettable but we must try to bear it patiently.

I cant agree with the departure of Robert Lewis from the scheme. His partnership was, from the very first, an essential part of the bargain. To me, at the moment the departure of Bobby Lewis would mean the virtual departure of the play. He has been interested in the play since it was published, and has thought about it continually as letters to me prove, and

[1] Jane Rubin, Richard Madden Play Company, New York, O'Casey's agent in America. Since Richard Madden's death on 8 May 1951—see O'Casey's letter to George Jean Nathan, 7 July 1951, note 1—Miss Rubin had been in charge of the company.

has mapped out in his mind how he thinks the play should be done. He came down here to me, and we discussed it together; so how could I agree to the suggestion that he should have no more to do with it.

Jay Julien is a grand guy but the play is terribly important to me, though a difference with Jay is a thing I would do a lot to avoid. But, in this case, it is unavoidable for I cannot agree to the proposal of Jay's and must remain convinced that Bobby Lewis must be retained, unless someone equally good—and this would be a hard task—be got for the job. If that were done, and Bobby Lewis himself recommended him, I might think it over; but only if Bobby definitely okayed the new choice.

It is hard to have to write all this, but after all's said and done, I am the one who will suffer most; but, as I've said, there's no use of lying down about it. Sooner or later someone will do the play, so all we can do is to start to wait once more.

Sincerely,
Sean O'Casey

To Irish Times

21 MAY 1952

FRANK RYAN

SIR,—I should like one more word on the questions raised by Mr. Hamish Fraser.[1] Owen Sheehy-Skeffington has him cornered by placing Maritain, Mauriac and Bernanos side by side with Ryan. To add to this worry, the *Observer* announced last issue that both Mauriac and Maritain had refused to attend the forthcoming Eucharistic Congress in Barcelona because Franco was to be there in an official robe. So those two are keeping the thing up!

In regard to "Communist excesses," so beloved of these puppy apostles (without a word about excesses on the other side), one can only say that herein John's no worse than his master. The man learned from his master. Apart from the fact that there never has been a civil war without shooting, and never shooting without someone getting shot. But what about our own civil war, waged between Catholics to iron out the difference between a treaty and a Document No. 2; a difference no more than that between Tweedledee and Tweedledum? Perhaps, Mr Fraser means to refer to the churches, chapels and monasteries that the "Reds demolished" in

---

[1] Fraser replied to Sheehy-Skeffington, *Irish Times*, 7 May 1952.

their fight for Republican principles. Well, if they did this sort of thing, and we have Mr. Fraser's word for it, then they probably learned to do this from their master, too. It was done, and copiously, too, by Roman Catholics themselves in 1918. Where? In Ukrainian Galicia. Here's a quote from one who knows: "Worse was to come. After a period of incredible confusion, Poland in the autumn of 1918 assumed sovereign authority over Galicia. Civil war followed immediately. The war was pursued with detestable bitterness on both sides. When one reads the outrages perpetrated by Catholic Poles in the churches, monasteries, libraries, and so on, of their fellow Catholic Ukrainians, one can hardly be surprised if certain Ukrainian priests so far forgot their Christian duty as to 'preach in their sermons the extermination of the Poles'—as the Polish Government, truly or not, alleged."

Regarding Orthodoxy of the Eastern Rite, in union with the Roman See, we are told that the Polish State reproduced in miniature the position in Russia in Tsarist days (with the difference that the Polish Government was composed of Catholics). Further on we are told: "More recently the Government has gone further and sunk to allowing persecutions of the Orthodox by organisations which try to coerce them into the Catholic Church by destroying their churches. On this painful subject, it is sufficient to quote from a protest issued by the Catholic Ukrainian Archbishop of Lwow, Mgr. Szepticky, on July 20th, 1938: 'Nearly a hundred churches (around Kholm) have been pulled down and many others burnt. People have been forced to join the Catholic Church in her Latin Rite, and many harmless priests have been prevented from carrying out their pastoral duties by expulsion, fines, and imprisonment. They are forbidden to preach and to give religious instruction in their own language. This attack on the Catholic Church has tacit approval and sometimes wild applause from many Catholics.'"

Maria Duce on the warpath.[2] An ironic item is that the famous Lady of Czestochowa, beloved of Poles the world over, is an Orthodox eikon. Now that the Reds have taken Galicia over, peace reigns on the Ukrainian front. The above quotations appear in no Left journal, but in *Studies,* Vol 28. No. 112. December, 1939. There's a lot more in the article that should shock Mr. Fraser, but hardly those who peer into the windows of others, rather than spending a life looking out of their own. It is evident that the Roman Catholic can wield a billhook—even on the head of a fellow-Catholic—as well, if not better, than any Red. After all the talk, Frank Ryan still stands out in my memory as a fair mind, a brave fellow, and a Catholic gentleman.

By the way, sir, the claim that [William] Thompson of Cork (I think) caused the Russian Revolution isn't so fantastic as "Thersites"[3] thinks it

---

[2] Maria Duce, a right-wing Catholic Action group with neo-Fascist inclinations, active in Dublin in the 1950s.

[3] "Thersites" (Thomas Woods) in his column "Private Views," *Irish Times,* 10 May 1952.

to be. No one man caused it—not even Lenin. It was a spontaneous outburst of the war-weary soldier, worker, and peasant; but Lenin and his
comrades were ready to guide when it came. G. B. S. tells us of the great
influence Thompson had on Karl Marx, and of that philosopher's tribute
to what he gained by studying him; which Lenin must have read, too. The
smaller places of the world aren't so unimportant as some seem to think.
Their influences go far.

Yours, etc.,
Sean O'Casey

Devon, 16 MAY 1952.

To Shaemas O'Sheel

MS. O'SHEEL

TOTNES, DEVON
21 MAY 1952

Dear Shaemas,

Since you wrote, I went down with Influenza, & then, when I got up,
the wife went down; so I had a time of it, including correction of proofs &
some work for Peace & the International Welfare of Children. I am very
glad you have got over your accident, though I still think it unwise to
depend too much on nature. As the Irish say, Even God likes a little help
at times. I can't agree, either, with your idea of man. How could we live
without him? And, in spite of Influenza & a lot of other things, I'm still for
life, though I was 72 last birthday. As I write, the wife & our 3 children
are in the next room, singing & laughing gaily and loudly; & I like it, though
it often keeps me from meditation. Woe is the one thing I dislike in man.
But I don't believe man's disobedience brought death into the world & all
our woe. A lot of it is due to ourselves, & most of it due to the venomous
prank called profit. I'm afraid the "good news" about Cockadoodle Dandy
is dead. It has been called off; but I'm getting used to this now, and hardened to seeing a bright light going out to give way to darkness deeper than
the darkness before. I don't think Clifford Bax is right about Yeats' en-
cyclopaedium knowledge of Detective & Mystery yarns. Not altogether
right. Yeats read a lot when engaged in deep work. While he was doing
an Anthology of Poetry, I visited him,[1] & saw his mantel-shelf piled up with

---

[1] See O'Casey's account of his visit to Yeats in London early in 1935 after
O'Casey had returned from America, when Yeats was preparing his edition of the
Oxford Book of Modern Verse (1936), in a room filled with books of poems,
Western, and detective novels: "Black Oxen Passing By," *Rose and Crown* (1952).

them—probably borrowed from AE. AE could answer the challenge all-right. I knew this; but didn't think he was quite so bad till I read an article on him in "Irish Writing" by his son, Dermot; [2] who wrote that AE read from 8 to 10 of them a week! I don't like the name of Clifford Bax—he refused to give his name to a demand for the release of I.R.A. prisoners rotting away in Dartmoor Jail, most of whom had already done 10 years there. The French Revolution is simple enough. They've clouded it over in history & essay to suit themselves. Claude Bowers doesn't seem to have mentioned St. Just—the most selfless of them all; though that says nothing against Marat. The knife of C. Corday went thro' every French worker's heart as well as the heart of Marat. What we want, Seamas, is Socialism to develop towards "Communitarianism" not vice-versa: it couldn't work. What about [William] Thompson, the Cork millionaire, who had such an influence on Marx, & who gave him, thro' his views, many a tip for "Capital." So G. B. S. says Marx said himself. No one can explain Adam's murder—the reason, or the motive. So with Trotsky. It may have been because of a woman, even. As there is no trustworthy evidence, we can't say. It is unwise to worry about these things: they belong to humanity's past, like the Irish "Famine." It's futile, & that is worse than unwise. Remember, however we mingle with humanity, each has to mind himself. Even in battle, the brave, sensible soldier doesn't waste his life. As for Rajk,[3] I don't know. I do know of the lovers of Ireland, clever fellows, who betrayed Parnell. He had won, & had he become Leader, there would have been a few trials. Even Davitt intrigued against him to get his place. Only opinions these, Seumas; not judgements.

All good to you & Mrs. O'Sheel.

Yours
Sean

[2] Diarmuid Russell, "AE," *Irish Writing* No 15, June 1951.
[3] Laszlo Rajk, Foreign Minister of Hungary, was hanged for treason in 1949. In 1956 Matyas Rakosi, Hungarian Communist leader, stated that Rajk had been innocent.

To Eric Gorman

MS. GORMAN

TOTNES, DEVON

27 MAY 1952

Dear Eric,

Thank you for the cheque, receipt for which is enclosed with this note. I remember O'Riordan's play well.[1] I heard the reminder of Moore on the B.B.C., and thought it a little hard on the songwriter. They laughed at "Tulip Lips"—a lovely name—, but, anyway, Lalla Rooka is as good as, say Scott's "Marmion," or even "Lady of The Lake." A remarkable achievement for one who had never seen a lilac grow in Persia.

I hope you & all may have a good holiday. We have a heat-wave here, too, & all are glad, for, previously, it had been chill & wet—"winter lingering chilling the lap of May"—Goldsmith, I think. I hope you may have flocks and shoals of tourists. Isn't it asking for it to settle on March as the month for a Festival? [2] Maybe, though, the conditions may force the Festival seekers into the Abbey. It's an ill wind—

All good wishes to Mrs. Gorman & to you.

Yours sincerely,
Sean O'Casey

[1] Conal O'Riordan's *An Imaginary Conversation* opened at the Abbey Theatre on 13 May 1909. O'Riordan used the pseudonym of Norreys Connell for this one-act dialogue between the poet Tom Moore and the patriot Robert Emmet.

[2] An Bórd Failte (the Tourist Board) had announced that Dublin's first An Tóstal (Festival) to celebrate Irish culture and attract tourists would take place in April 1953. It should be noted that O'Casey's last full-length play, *The Drums of Father Ned* (1960), is centered on the celebration of a Tóstal. The controversy over that play is recorded in Vol. III.

To Irish Democrat

JUNE 1952

"Stop the Drift to War"
Irish Writers Call For Peace

The "Irish Democrat" is glad to publish the following declaration for Peace which has recently been signed by a large number of Irish writers:

We writers believe that our civilisation is unlikely to survive another world war. We believe that differing political and economic systems can exist side by side on the basis of peacefully negotiated settlements.

As writers we want peace, and through our work will try and get it; we pledge ourselves to encourage an international settlement through peaceful negotiation.

We condemn writing liable to sharpen existing dangers and hatred. As signatories we are associated with no political movement, party or religious creed, but are solely concerned with trying to stop the drift to war.

Sean O'Casey	*Ewart Milne*
L. A. G. Strong	*Michael P. O'Connor*
Austin Clarke	*Seumas O'Sullivan*
C. Day Lewis	*Helen Waddell*
B. Farrington	*J. De Courcy Ireland*
Robert Greacen	*Ethel Mannin*
Maurice Collis	*Liam O'Leary*
Seumas MacCall	*Rosamond Jacob*
Desmond Ryan	*Mary Lavin*

To David Bell [1]

TS. MEINEL [2]

TOTNES, DEVON
5 JUNE 1952

Sean O'Casey: It was a review of his first one-man show by Augustus John (a very dear friend of mine) that led Mrs. O'Casey and myself to go to see it. It was a charming exhibition, but unfortunately, we hadn't enough money to buy a picture. However, helped by Augustus John's praise of it, Evan did well, and sold quite a lot of his work. We met Evan there; invited him to come and see us, and we became great friends. We went to see him in his Hampstead studio, and found the studio to be a shocking and miserable hovel. Some time after the exhibition closed (Evan visited us for dinner two or three times a week), I learned that he couldn't get the money due to him—well over £300. I persuaded him to become an Associate of the Authors, Composers and Artists Union. This Union

---

[1] David Bell compiled a feature program on the life and work of the Welsh painter Evan Walters (1893–1951), "Portrait of an Artist," which was broadcast on the BBC Welsh Home Service on 5 June 1952. The first passage, O'Casey's contribution to the symposium, was recorded by Bell in Totnes. The second passage is part of a letter from O'Casey to Bell, which was also used on the program. See O'Casey's letter to Walters, 8 February 1939, Vol. I, pp. 776–77.

[2] From a copy made by Erna Meinel, executor of the Walters estate.

demanded the share of the money due to Evan, and after a correspondence, accompanied by a threat of legal action, Evan got most of what
was due to him—again well over £300. I wanted him to go on a trip to
the South of France (John had recommended this, for Evan was reared
up in the Coal Age, and most of his pictures were sombre and bleak; he
needed the revelation of light and colour, John thought; and I think this
great artist was right.) Evan didn't go, however. Though unable to buy
any of Evan's oil paintings, we got a number of Watercolours—a really
beautiful "Hydrangeas," one of his mother watering her garden and a picture of "Pip, Squeak and Wilfred" that we got him to do for the nursery;
also some charcoal drawings—one of our first boy in his nurse's arms; of
him when he was three or four; of myself, for the frontispiece of a book—
a drawing which wasn't good; and a fine drawing of Mrs. O'Casey.

In 1930 or thereabouts, we passed through a bad time and had to
leave London for a cottage in Buckinghamshire. Our own struggle was as
great as Evan's and we had to fend for ourselves. Then, in 1934, I went
to America, and afterwards came here. I saw no more of Evan. We had
too hard a time during the war to try to get into touch with him. I remember, he had an illness that seemed to leave a permanent mark on him.
Several times I intended to write but couldn't remember his address in
Wales. I am not competent to attempt an assessment of his work. He had
in him the makings of a first class artist. I thought he would develop into
one, blending John, Van Gogh, with Evan. Whether he did or not, I could
not say. My own opinion is that Evan suffered some set-back from his
illness. He never seemed to be able to care for himself wisely, having had
no experience of London. Welsh and Irish countrymen seem to have little
knowledge of the world and of city life, and are prone to be bewildered
when they begin to experience it.

Sean O'Casey: Evan, at his best, was in my opinion, a splendid artist
especially when he went simply for whatever he wanted to paint. Indeed,
he could be beautiful as he was in the "Hydrangeas" he did for us. This
double vision was, I think, due to an actual physical defect of his eyes;
the muscles had been pulled or had moved out of their proper place.
I have a friend in Dublin who is a surgeon-oculist, and who knew a man
with treble-vision—could see three moons in the sky at the same time. This
oculist-surgeon kept at him for years trying to induce him to agree to an
operation to put the muscles back in their place. Evan, I think, thought
this defect to be a new discovery in art.

To Robert Lewis

MS. LEWIS

TOTNES, DEVON

10 JUNE 1952

My dear Bob,

Well, we've all heard the sad news now, and once more the Cock has had to unstretch his neck, & keep from crowing.

> Stretch up the neck,
> And clap the wings,
> Red Cock, and crow! (Yeats) [1]

Well, not this time. I've had a sad letter from [Jay] Julien, which I haven't answered yet. It's so hard to know what to say; though the heaviest force of the blow has, I imagine, fallen on myself.

As for your suggestion—gallant enough—to do the play in your own Workshop, in a free performance, to show it off—a chanticleer mannequin parade—, I'll think it over, Bob. I don't quite know what to think of it yet. The reason for hesitating is that I hope for some money out of a production. One has to go on living, and, up to now, the plays haven't done so well this way as I had hoped. The biographical books have kept me going. Sometimes, I wonder if it be of any use writing a play. There's so many things between a play and production on the stage. Mrs [Margaret] Webster is to come here this month about a production of "Purple Dust." Shouldn't be alarmed, if that fell through, too.

I've just got out of Influenza—second visit of the whoreson thing in three months; And I feel, now, as if I needed a lot of tidying up.

I'll think over your suggestion, Bob; &, meanwhile, a thousand thanks for your great interest in my play.

"Rose & Crown" is to come out next month. When it does, I'll send you a copy. You look fine in the snapshot. Glad that "Brigadoon" is still on the boards. How is "The Grass Harp"?

My love & Eileen's to Jay & you.

Yours very sincerely,
Sean

[1] W. B. Yeats, *The Dreaming of the Bones* (1919).

To Miss Sheila ————

MS. PRIVATE

TOTNES, DEVON

11 JUNE 1952

Dear Sheila,

Just out of a bout of Influenza—second one in 3 months. And I've been busy with "Rose & Crown" which is to be published next month, to say nothing of new work, letters to be answered, and help to be given in home affairs. So I'm fairly free from the sin of idleness. I should be the last to advise anyone to have anything to do with "Writing." It was always precarious, & now is worse than ever. Besides it takes years of practice. Letters are allright; there's no risk there—one isn't hoping to make a living out of them.

I am so glad you are feeling better after your accident.

The change all have to bear, when one we know & love well dies, is the real inconvenience of death. The life left has to learn a new rhythm. It comes with Time—the most merciless & most merciful power we know. Age has made me quieter, of course, but not Conservative; tho' some Conservatives are far less so than some of our Labour Leaders. When you write letters, try not to say the same things too often; dont repeat yourself too much. This is the hardest thing writers have to fight. Write as simply as you can; & be certain of what you want to say; then say it with as few words as you can; but be sure your meaning is clear. I am still trying to do this. I enclose a pamphlet that may interest you. And forgive a busy man, Sheila, for ending now.

Yours very sincerely,
As ever, Sean

To Eric Gorman

MS. CHRISTINE GORMAN

TOTNES, DEVON

9 JULY 1952

Dear Eric,

Thank you for the cheque, formal receipt of which I enclose with this note. I've just been reading an article called "English Poetry set to

Music by Russian Composers," in a Soviet magazine. As well as the poetry of Shelley, Byron, Burns, Shakespeare's "Romeo & Juliet," Shaw's "Devil's Disciple," et al, mention is made of Rubenstein's—"one of his most important works"—the opera "Feramors," whose libretto was taken from Thomas Moore's "Lalla Rookh"; and Taneyev's "Origin of the Harp," based on the poem by Thomas Moore. Moore's "Lalla" seems to have had more honor in the USSR than in his own land. Mention of above is apropos of what I said in my last letter. The USSR is very interested in affairs of la belle Irlande.

All good wishes.
Yours sincerely
Sean O'Casey

To Gordon Rogoff [1]

MS. ROGOFF

TOTNES, DEVON
11 JULY 1952

Dear friend,
You shouldn't feel "disconnected"—no one is away from his "roots," wherever he may be; for a man's roots are in himself, like the Kingdom of heaven. I don't remember our previous association—though I do the name. I have so many things to do, family & my own work; so many letters to answer; & I· am getting very old now; so it is impossible to remember everything. However, the main point of your letter is your proposed visit to me. Now Gordon, I can't be certain as to what I may be doing or where I may be when your cycle carries you within sight of Totnes. If you do come that way, ring me up on the telephone, &, should I be here, I'll answer, & we may be able to arrange a meeting.
As for justifying the generous part your people have played—don't worry about this too much. You have your own life to live, your own way to take; & what you do, do it for its own Sake, & not for the sake of others. You belong to a new generation, & to that generation you owe your allegiance, & not to the one gone past (mine).
Well, we may talk further later on, if all be well.
All good wishes to you, with my love.

Sean O'Casey

[1] Gordon Rogoff (1931–   ), drama critic and teacher. In 1952–53 he was attending the Central School of Speech and Drama, London.

To Miss Sheila ———

MS. PRIVATE

TOTNES, DEVON

11 JULY 1952

Dear Sheila,

I shouldn't advise you to spend your last guinea—or any guinea—on buying my "Rose & Crown." Can't you get it from the Library?

However, if you do, & send it to me, I shall be glad to autograph it for you.

I do care what some say about my work, but Peter Quennell isn't among them. He should try to do better in his own work. A book of his "Years of Fame," on Byron,[1] the great Byron, whose words are in the dedication [2] of "Rose & Crown," a book that I, for one, could hardly read; indeed, I haven't finished it yet. I read a little now & again, & always with irritation, which is bad; &, usually with boredom, which is worse.

Well, all the best to you, & take care of the guineas, & the bobs will take care of themselves; & keep well, & sit safe on your bicycle.

As Ever,
Sean

[1] Peter Quennell, *Byron: The Years of Fame* (1935).
[2] *Rose and Crown* (1952) is dedicated: To the Young of All Lands, All Colours, All Creeds:

> Shadows of beauty,
> Shadows of power;
> Rise to your duty—
> This is the hour!
>
> (From Byron's play,
> *The Deformed Transformed*, 1822)

To The Observer [1]

TC. O'CASEY

TOTNES, DEVON

15 JULY 1952

Sir,

In his review of ROSE AND CROWN, Mr. Louis MacNeice says "O'Casey assumes that everything Latin or Roman is alien to England. Odd for an admirer of Milton . . . in refusing to hear any good at all of the Middle Ages, he is equally perverse. . . . As a playwright he might have remembered that there were once Miracle Plays and that some of these are very gay."

Gay, oh God! Now these Miracle Plays were moulded from episodes taken from the Scriptures, few of which were gay, none of them "very gay." The Fall, the Expulsion of Adam and Eve from the Garden, the Killing of Abel by Cain, Noah and the Flood, Abraham taking his son out to slit his throat and offer him as a sweet-smelling sacrifice to Jehovah, Israelites in Egypt, Plagues and Passage of the Red Sea; themes of battle, murder, and sudden death, and Mr. MacNeice calls them gay. The Scriptures certainly do not allow God to have a sense of humour. It remained for a Scot to give Him one. Even the episodes taken from the later Testament, and made into plays, weren't what could be called gay; such as Massacre of the Innocents, Flight into Egypt, Temptation of Christ, The Betrayal, the Denial, Trial before Herod, Remorse of Judah; to call such themes gay would seem to say that Mr. MacNeice, like God, had no sense of humour; or, maybe, one above all others. Even in the play about Noah, the one human feeling is that of Noah's wife, anxious that her friends should be saved; but she was forced away into the ark, and her friends left to perish—not very gay for Mrs. Noah, or for anyone feeling human with her. The plays are crude, clumsy, and dull, brighter only than the life lived around them, and, for that reason, suitable to the time, giving life a little colour and a little zest. Even these, though, were frowned on by the Church. "It is forbidden him by decree to make or witness miracle plays, because miracle plays, once they are begun, become gatherings and sights of sin." It was only when life started to pull itself out of the Middle Ages that we come to more human thought in the Morality Plays, a very different genre from the Miracle Plays; when life thought more of earth and less of heaven. Even these weren't what could be called "very gay," containing, as they did, more of satire than of merriment. By far the best of

---

[1] This letter was refused publication by the editor. It was a reply to Louis MacNeice's review of *Rose and Crown* in *The Observer*, 13 July 1952. For another comment on MacNeice's review, see "Sunset," *Sunset and Evening Star* (1954).

these is Lyndsay's *Ane Satyre of the Thrie Estaits,*[2] in which there is more of Mr. MacNeice's hate than there is of Mr. MacNeice's love. Here we find little gaiety in the Pauper's story of how when his old father and mother died, the landlord took his grey mare, the vicar took his best cow, the same boyo took his second cow, and got his Clerk to take away the Pauper's clothes when his wife died from grief, leaving him only with a groat, which, we are told, he intends to give a lawyer as a fee to win, through the law, justice from the Church; to which, when he hears it, Diligence replies: "Thou art the daftest fuill that ever I saw; do you expect to get remedy from the clergy by the means of the Law?" Diligence knew more about the gay custom of the Middle Ages than does Mr. MacNeice. A comic interlude, is not, necessarily, gay, either, but may even have deep pathos, as, for instance, when Mistress Quickly announces the death of Falstaff. I suggest that Mr. MacNeice should read Coulton's FIVE CENTURIES OF RELIGION and his other volumes of life in the Middle Ages. Of course, the people danced, the people sang, but these gaieties didn't free them from terrible poverty, ridiculous superstition, and pitiable ignorance. Even when the Bastille was falling, there were three quarters of a million ecclesiastical serfs in la belle France alone.

I admire Milton, not because of his Latin, but because of his English, in spite of the fact that he was Latin Secretary to the Protector, Cromwell; His Latin poems are forgotten, his English poems remembered; I admire Milton because he was a great Republican; I admire him because he was a man well in advance of his time. The introduction of the Roman mythology into his verse is but the tiny Latin buttons on an English suit of serge. Of course there were good things in the M.A., or thereabouts; there was Chaucer and Langland; there was inspiration, even, in the Rising of Wat Tyler with 100,000 people to assert the rights of man; but the M.A. weren't the merry medley Chesterton and others made them out to be.

In his last paragraph about "O'Casey ought perhaps to have explained in exactly what circumstances interference with the arts—or with science—is justified," he isn't quite clear; but I judge he is making an oblique reference to thought and action in this respect in the Soviet Union. If he does, then, speaking plainer than he, I hold that Zadanov is no more infallible in the things of literature than, say, Professor Leavis. More, I wrote to my Soviet friend of twenty-seven years standing, Mr. Apletin,[3] Chairman of the Soviet Union of Writers, Foreign Commission, to say so. This dif-

[2] Sir David Lindsay's *The Three Estates* (1540) was performed at the Edinburgh Festival on 25 August 1948, directed by Tyrone Guthrie, and was revived by Guthrie at Edinburgh on 21 August 1951. The following comment from a review of the 1948 production in *The Times*, 26 August 1948, might have been used to describe some of O'Casey's later satiric comedies, particularly *Cock-a-Doodle Dandy* (1949): "*The Three Estates* is half morality, half political satire and wholly a piece of angry, inspired knockabout. It preceded the Scottish Reformation by some 20 years and so angered the clergy that they ordered the manuscript to be burned by the public executioner."

[3] See O'Casey's letter to Mikhail Apletin, 10 February 1950.

ference of opinion has made no difference in my friendship for him or in his for me. There is poor literature and poor painting in the Soviet Union as there is poor literature and poor painting here. We are one there, anyway. I have no place, for instance, in my thought for the work of Sartre or the Sartre resartres who have, and are, imitated him. Finally, let us first look to our own faults. Let us remember the reception to the first appearance of the Impressionists, to the great sculpture, Epstein, to the Picasso Exhibition held recently here in London; and to the boycott of James Joyce's great work *Ulysses,* and even to the tremendous opposition to his *Dubliners* which can be read fully in the preface to the American edition of the first book. In his recent book, Augustus John [4] makes the noble suggestion that Picasso should be made an honorary Member of the Royal Academy. So far, no indication has been given that this will be done. Even the recent Festival of England met with a lot of open and overt opposition. Put out less flags was the cry in a lot of places. We are getting lob-sided with self-righteousness. It would be fitter if we first removed the beam from our English eye before we made any effort to take the mote from the eye of our Russian brother. We continually prate of our Christian way of life—for Jasus' sake, then, let us show some useful sign of it.

Yours sincerely,
Sean O'Casey

[4] Augustus John, *Chiaroscuro* (1952).

From Peter Newmark
To John O'London's Weekly

1 AUGUST 1952

In Defence of O'Casey

Peter Newmark, 22 Shepherds Lane, Guildford, Surrey, writes: I wish to make a protest against the despicable review of Sean O'Casey's *Rose and Crown* by Austin Clarke in the issue of July 18th.

Mr. Clarke's last two paragraphs, in plain English, mean this:

"After the success of *Juno* and the *Plough,* O'Casey made a big mistake in maintaining his integrity as an artist. He would have done far better if he had cashed in on his early popularity. What's the use of writing a fine play like *Cock-a-doodle Dandy* if it earns one no money at all?"

The rest of the review is negligible, containing instances of misunderstanding of the author's intention ("he can scarcely remember details") and unsupported criticism ("glow of self-esteem"). It seems a cavalier way of treating such a fine writer.

To Seumas Scully

MS. SCULLY

TOTNES, DEVON
10 AUGUST 1952

Dear Seumas. Thanks very much for the Papers. It was interesting to read R. M. Fox's account of Jim Larkin [1]—very prosy & flat; Fox has turned a flaming torch into a flickering taper.

I have been very busy these days & those days, including time spent in seeing friends from the U.S.A., so hadn't time to write to thank you before. Breon was over in Eirinn recently, & Niall has spent some weeks with a school-mate in France; the schoolmate's mother lives & works in Fernay Voltaire, a few miles from Geneva.

I daresay you have had your holiday—I hope it was a good one.

You have all been having a quiet time for the past few weeks—no papers; [2] time to think for yourselves. A lot must be pining for the Sunday Indep. & the Sunday Press. I wonder who was the learned lad who wrote in the S. Press the snappy review on "Rose & Crown"? [3] It's a wonder none of the Irish papers ask me to write something for them. But I suppose most of them pay according to length & breadth of an article. Is the "Standard" [4] still defending the Keys & fleas of the Kingdom of Heaven?

All good thanks & good wishes to you.

Yours sincerely,
Sean O'Casey

[1] R. M. Fox, "Jim Larkin," *The Bell,* January 1952.
[2] There was a newspaper strike in Dublin.
[3] " 'Hit me, naow!' cries O'Casey," *Sunday Press,* 6 July 1952, by "H. T."
[4] *The Standard,* the ultra-Catholic weekly newspaper in Dublin which consistently attacked O'Casey and his works.

To Dr. Frank Morrell [1]

MS. MORRELL

TOTNES, DEVON

11 AUGUST 1952

Dear Frank,

Hope you got back safe. I don't think you are wise to go rushing about so much, cramming so many distances into such a few hours. Look after your health—the only Capital you've got. I hope that cold—or tired cough—is better. And try to remember that your best Communism is your growth in the knowledge of neurology. Don't waste what you already know of this branch of physiological science. The Red Flag flies over this science as well as over anything else—even blathering from a platform: much more so, in fact.

Well, all the best to you.

Yours sincerely,
Sean

[1] Dr. Frank Morrell (1926–), neurophysiologist, Montefiore Hospital, New York; Professor and Chairman of the Neurology Department, Stanford University, 1961–69; since 1969, Professor of Neurology, New York Medical College. In the summer of 1952, when Dr. Morrell was an intern in a London hospital, he stayed with the O'Caseys in Totnes for a week.

To George Jean Nathan

MS. CORNELL

TOTNES, DEVON

15 AUGUST 1952

My very dear George:

Thanks for your very kind letter about "Rose & Crown." I'm very glad you liked it. I had a letter from R. Watts, Junr., praising it, too, with some very sensible criticisms, which, I fear, my nature won't allow me to follow. I feel he's right & I am wrong; but a fellow has to be wrong if he's ever to be right. However, I'll think over what he says, for he says them with obvious sincerity and affection. I hope the great heat has subsided, & that you are more comfortable now. Moving from the city to country isn't much good. The country can be an oven as well as a city, having learned this from experience. Extreme heat is very trying. I've often spent hours sitting still, unable to do anything but gasp during the hours of a hot week of a hot summer. The only chance of a modification is to sit by the margin of a sea; & then the journey to the sea & back again takes more than all the good out of the attempt to get cooler. In great heat, the one activity one can practice is to try to keep alive. Richard W. tells me you are looking better than you've looked for a long time, & he writes very affectionately of you.

I've signed another contract for Cockadoodle Dandy, & Bob Lewis hopes it may "go into production, this time, this time, this time." So do I. The fellow [Ronald Kerr] that gave a terrible production to "Oakleaves & Lavender," accused of an assault on a boy, & unable to face the charge, has left the world by way of a gas-oven. The Theatre here seems to be redolent with Cissies. [James] Agate, I'm told, when he suddenly collapsed, was at a party of them, dressed up as a Fairy Queen. It seems almost incredible to me; but then the kink in them is probably resented by the kink in me, for today I am just as enamoured by the trim figure & pretty face of a lass as I was when I was twenty-one.

We have had a number of your country-men & country-women visiting us this Summer in Totnes—mostly Americans who haven't dollars to throw away, which is hard on them; for here, & on the Continent it is thought that all Americans have their pillows full of dollars, & sleep on mattresses stuffed with them. They seem to believe Americans have no need ever to work for a living.

It is very sad about Gene, sadder because one can do nothing about it.[1] And such a fellow, too. I loved him before I said goodbye, that day when you & I visited him & Carlotta in the Madison Avenue hotel: an unforgettable lunch. When you write or phone to him, give him my earnest love & deep appreciation of his greatness. A great American. And my deep love to another great American, too—G. J. Nathan.

Yours ever & ever.
Sean

[1] Eugene O'Neill was suffering from a rare and incurable ailment similar to Parkinson's disease. See O'Casey's letter to Nathan, 26 June 1942, note 3.

To Charles Davy [1]

TC. O'CASEY

[TOTNES, DEVON]
21 AUGUST 1952

Dear Sir,

Thank you for replying to my letter, and telling me that Mr. Louis MacNeice had sent no reply to my comments.[2] I will not send a second

[1] Charles Davy, assistant editor, *The Observer,* London.
[2] See O'Casey's unpublished reply to Louis MacNeice, 15 July 1952.

letter to him, for I am in no way desirous of worrying him. He probably thought my comments either not worth answering, or he had no answer to give to them. I am used to this kind of conduct by now. This is the third time of asking for me. Once over I KNOCK AT THE DOOR when Oliver Gogarty writing in THE SUNDAY TIMES [3] protested against what he called "the unlocked heart," instancing China as an example to me the very time China was busy un-locking both heart and mind in a gigantic revolution, though Gogarty hadnt noticed it. I sent a few comments, but the Journal didnt publish them sending them to Gogarty, who remained silent; then Orwell made an onslaught on INISHFALLEN, FARE THEE WELL,[4] because it was Irish in spirit, instancing a few verses as a particular example of nationalistic bitterness, though, unknown to Orwell, those verses were by Tennyson, appearing in one of his most famous poems. I wrote to THE OBSERVER,[5] but the Journal didnt publish them sending on the comments to Orwell, who remained silent. Now there is the instance of THE OBSERVER refusing to publish my comments on the review given by MacNeice, sending the comments on to him, and again, the poet remaining silent. I cant help feeling that if my comments had been contemptible, these chaps would have been glad to show how contemptible they were, so I am forced to the belief that the comments were, in each case, too hard to answer. It's a pity you didnt see your way to publishing mine. They were good copy, more effective and interesting than some of the articles appearing from time to time in your Journal; and, more, being in the form of a letter, they would have cost you nothing. But there you are—more interested in China and Peru and the USSR than you are in the liveliness and literature of your own country.

Well, thanks again for your courtesy in replying to my letter, which, I feel sure, will be in print one day, with yours to me, assuming (as I do) that you have no objection to the publication of what you have written to me.

All good wishes to you.

Yours sincerely,
Sean O'Casey

[3] See O'Casey's letter to J. C. Trewin, 15 March 1952, note 5.
[4] *Ibid.,* note 2.
[5] *Ibid.,* notes 3 and 4.

To Barbara A. Cohen [1]

TS. COHEN

TOTNES, DEVON
2 SEPTEMBER 1952

Dear Miss Cohen,

Your letter about making a record, my own voice speaking parts of my own work, is a very interesting one.

I am inclined to make a shot at it, but there are difficulties. A record lasting 45 or 60 minutes would mean a lot of reading, and frightens me a little. My sight isnt good, and this may mean that I'd have to learn the parts off by heart, which would mean a lot of work and take away a lot of time.

I live down in Devon, distant from London comparatively as Texas is distant from New York. I rarely go to London, and, I'm afraid, if the record is to be taken, your Representative would have to come here: the mountain would have to come to Mahomet.

All my business, or almost all, in America is done by my Agent,

> Miss Jane Rubin,
> The Richard Madden Play Company,
> 522 Fifth Avenue,
> New York City 18
> Tel: MUrray Hill 2-9145.

to whom you should write or phone regarding the business end of the scheme.

If you consider the mentioned difficulties can be overcome, then I'll try to make a worthy record. I am forwarding your letter on to Miss Rubin.

Yours sincerely,
Sean O'Casey

[1] Barbara A. Cohen, Caedmon Publishers, New York.

To Peter Newmark

MS. NEWMARK

TOTNES, DEVON

3 SEPTEMBER 1952

My dear Peter,

Macmillan's sent me the cutting from "John O'London's," in which you came forward "in defence of O'Casey." [1] It was very kind of you to do so, and I thank you for it, heartily. A. Clarke is a well-known Irish Poet; he is regarded now as the Dean of Irish poetry, and fills in a Shadowy way the place once held by the redoubtable Yeats. I never spoke to him, never, to my knowledge, saw him. He has a curious dislike of me, even slating "Juno" & "The Plough," when they were first produced in the Abbey. However, it's not very important, really—that or this.

I hope you and Monica are doing well, & as contented as any can be with things as they are. We are all fairly well here; though Eileen & I are a bit tired. I don't seem to have a second now. The Summer was a busy time with American visitors, who think more of me, apparently, than does Austin. Am working now on last vol. of biography "Sunset & Evening Star."

Love to you both,
as ever
Sean

[1] See Newmark's letter, "In Defence of O'Casey," *John O'London's Weekly*, 1 August 1952, reprinted above, a reply to a review of *Rose and Crown* by Austin Clarke, "Exiled O'Casey," *John O'London's Weekly*, 18 July 1952.

To George Jean Nathan

TS. CORNELL

TOTNES, DEVON

6 SEPTEMBER 1952

My very dear George:

Don't read this if you don't feel up to the mark, for it is a questionaire; so shove it aside, if you're not feeling fit.

Miss Rubin has sent me a letter from a Group that wants to take over PURPLE DUST on a five month's option. The Group is called THE

THEATRE CIRCLE (no address given), and the following are listed as "an active producing organization," though they add that they have been in existence only for a few months, have read 400 plays, and have selected mine as the best of them. Mildred Dunnock, Uta Hagen, Paula Lawrence, Thelma Schnee, Mary Welch, Jane White, Eric Bentley, Herbert Berghof, Harry Horner, E. G. Marshall, George Matthews, Alexander Scourby, Hiram Sherman. Special adviser: David Haber. They say "We intend to invest our creative and financial resources, to free our artistic vision (I don't like that phrase), returning control to the maker and taking it from the salesman." All fine and large, but have they got the ability to do all this, as, say, Yeats and L. Gregory had?

Miss Rubin says the above are "among our leading actors and actresses, an intelligent group. I am beginning to lose faith in our so-called first-line producers. They have lost courage (had they ever any? S. O'C.), & lack imagination (How often have you said this!), and I, therefore, would like to go along with this group." Well, so would I, but will they give the production the play needs, and that it, in my opinion, deserves? I have had an experience lately with an enthusiastic Group who did my three new one-act plays, who, according to all accounts reaching me—and they were a good many—, made an awful bad business of it.

I wonder do you know anything about the Group? Miss Rubin warmly suggests I should agree to their taking up the option; but I am inclined to feel cold about it, due, of course, to my ignorance of what they may do, and due, too, to past experiences of best intentions. Of course, the dollars obtained from the option would be very welcome. Kermit Bloomgarden has, as you doubtlessly know, abandoned the idea of doing the play.

I have been asked by Caedmon Publishers, Fourth Avenue, to do a record of 45 to 60 minutes from parts of plays and biography, and have tentatively agreed to have a shot at it. Maybe, too, I will sing a little song I wrote some time ago, called "Green Bushes."

My love as ever to you.
Sean

Memory getting a little uncertain these days. But still fighting on.

To Barbara A. Cohen

MS. COHEN [1]

TOTNES, DEVON

11 SEPTEMBER 1952

My dear Miss Cohen,

After I got your letter, Mr. [W. R.] Rodgers of the B.B.C. London, came to see me. He had written before, but I had refused to participate in the Programme. However, he came to the district to make a Broadcast, rang me up, & I thought it was a good chance for an experiment, anyway. His apparatus was an oblong box, on the top of which were two spools— one filled with tape, the other empty. When the talk began, the tape moved from one spool to the other, recording what was said as it travelled. A tiny Recorder was held close to the speaker. The apparatus was carried on the back, quite easily, & the whole thing seemed simple. As you can read, he says the recording was very good; so, it would seem, there'll be no need for a photostatic enlargement. I'll select passages from plays & biographies for the recording—&, maybe, a song.[2] October will do. Your representative can ring me up, or write. If I'm well, & voice isn't gone, then he can come along. I daresay my voice will be the last thing to go.

All good wishes,
Yours sincerely,
Sean O'Casey

P.S. The record made by Mr. Rodgers was for a "Feature Programme" about G. Bernard Shaw, of which mine was to form a part.

---

[1] O'Casey wrote this letter at the bottom and on the reverse side of the letter he had received from W. R. Rodgers dated 10 September 1952, so that Miss Cohen could read Rodgers' remarks about the "very good quality" of the recording he had made in O'Casey's home in Totnes for the BBC radio program on Shaw. See O'Casey's letter to Frank McCarthy, 23 September 1954, note 1.

[2] The recording was made at O'Casey's home in Totnes on 12 November 1952, *Sean O'Casey Reading,* Volume One, Caedmon TC 1012, consisting of passages from *Juno and the Paycock, Pictures in the Hallway,* and *Inishfallen, Fare Thee Well.* For details about O'Casey's second reading for Caedmon, see his letter to Miss Cohen, 24 November 1953, note 1.

To Miss A. Munro-Kerr

MS. LEAGUE OF DRAMATISTS

TOTNES, DEVON

18 SEPTEMBER 1952

Dear Miss Munro-Kerr.

They probably mean "The Devil Came to Dublin," [1] to be performed there this or next week. It was done—Irish Times Pictorial says—in England under the name of "The Chuckeyhead Story," & in America as "The Border Be Damned." It is by PAUL VINCENT CARROLL author of SHADOW & SUBSTANCE. I dont know his address. The play is to go on—or is on at THE OLYMPIA THEATRE, DUBLIN. I daresay a letter there would find Carroll.

Of course, entre nous, the Devil has always been in Dublin. Remember R. Burns.

> As true as is the Deil's in hell,
>   And Dublin City

That's all the information I can give you about the play & oul' Nick, himsel.

Yours sincerely,
Sean O'Casey

[1] Paul Vincent Carroll's *The Chuckeyhead Story* (1950), revised and published as *The Devil Came from Dublin: A Satirical Extravaganza*, in *Irish Stories and Plays* (1958).

To Gordon Rogoff

MS. ROGOFF

TOTNES, DEVON

19 SEPTEMBER 1952

Dear Gordon,

A line or two to show I haven't forgotten you. I've been very busy— too much so to be comfortable—since I saw you; & am busier today than I was yesterday, & will be busier tomorrow than I am today. Of course, no-one can teach another: each must learn himself, out of himself & within himself. I have just read a book—"Sense of Shakespeare's Sonnets" [1952] written by an American scholar named Edward Hubler, published by the Princeton University Press. It has told me a lot about Shakespeare, quietly, sensibly, and with scholarly affection for the Poet. One can learn a lot in the hurly-burly of life & more than a little sitting calm under a sycamore tree, with a good companion or a good book. I know some of those sickly ascetics, & have as little use for them as life has. The greatest art in life is to live. Shakespeare lived, so does Picasso. Between times, the one wrote immortal verse, the other, I believe, paints eternal pictures. Pity you didnt touch against "The People's Festival" in Edinburgh. A friend of mine [Hugh MacDiarmid]—finest poet in Scotland since Lyndsay & Burns—was in the midst of it.

I haven't had time to read your Thesis yet; but I will do so soon. I'm doing a gramophone record for an American Publisher—45 to 60 minutes—, & when this is done, I'll take an hour off. Till then, Slán leat, which is the Irish Goodbye, meaning health & safety be with you.

Sean

To George Jean Nathan

MS. CORNELL

TOTNES, DEVON

10 OCTOBER 1952

My very dear George:

I have taken your advice regarding the proposed production of "Purple Dust" by the Theatre Circle. Anyway their desire to open their Season with it seemed to me to be a desire to carry it forward as a banner rather than a play: good for them but very little good for me. Today, two of your countrypeople, born in your own townland 100 miles from Indianapolis, have been here with us—Mr. & Mrs. Pollak. He is connected with the "Chicago Sun"—they are wandering around England, rather than touring; &, from here, go to Stratford-on-Avon, via the Devon moors. A young New Yorker—George Bellak, a very charming lad, has had a success with his play, "The Trouble-makers." I've just got an advanced copy of the American edition of "Rose & Crown," which looks fine in a simple but tasty format. The Irish Reviewers & Critics have gone wild about it, denouncing it vehemently, oblivious to rhyme or reason; striking their breasts, & shouting fie, fie, fie. One excuses the favour shown O'Casey by U.S.A. reviewers by saying that "the venality of American critics is notorious." So now you & comrade critics have been warned. A Dublin laddo as well as the Skibereen Eagle has his eye on you.[1] These are the boyos who glorify Lord Longford, who gives very good plays very bad productions, after, I'm told, he gives them a snack & a glass of wine behind the scenes after a first production.

There isn't any inspiration in the title of "Sunset & Evening Star"— it is from Tennyson's "Crossing the Bar." Bob Lewis has asked me to let him do Cockadoodle in his Workshop on a Sunday night, before an audience of rich patrons of the Theatre & Producers. I am thinking it over. I've hung back, for I prefer an option which brings in something; & his proposal is a gamble that might lose even this. So, so far, I've hung up the idea, looking at it only once in a while, and taking my glance away quick. But what about your own Book—"Theatre Book of the Year"? [2] Shouldn't there be one due now? I hope so. So do we all here.

And we all pray you may be keeping well. You have done a lot, my very dear George; but there is still a lot more to be done. May the Lord preserve you to do it.

All our love to you, and especially mine.

As ever,
Sean

[1] For the background on the *Skibereen Eagle,* see O'Casey's letter to Jack Carney, 26 August 1943, note 8.
[2] Nathan's *Theatre Book of the Year* series ended with the 1950–51 edition.

To New York Herald Tribune

12 OCTOBER 1952

"Sean O'Casey, Formerly of Dublin"

The first startling thing to be written is that I was born in Dublin more than seventy-two years ago. That's a very long time ago, a very long time ago; startling that I was born at all, and that it was in Dublin the odd event happened. Though these two things don't mean a lot, they mean something, for being born at all's a big thing, and being born in Dublin's a bigger thing still; sharing this exasperating honour with Shaw, Joyce and Yeats. I shouldn't like to be the one born in Dublin now; no sir. Dublin today is palled by the biretta, and this boy prefers even the bowler to the biretta. Another startling thing is that I am now two generations behind the one I mingle with today, so I have to pull myself along to get into line with younger thought and new ideas; a good thing to do, even though it makes one puff at times. Thanks be to God, I am a student still, learning, if not from babes and sucklings, from young women and young men.

Free from attending school when I was a kid, and having to learn to amuse myself on my lone, I early learned to open an ear and an eye to things heard and things seen; and so, unconsciously, I think, acquired a quick observing eye and a cocked ear for the sharp word and the quaint phrase. I have them so today. I set down in my mind any odd thing seen, and strange thing heard, snapping up material for any future biographical book or contemplated play. For instance, the wind from a softly whistled tune of Robbie Burns by a business man [1] in his prosaic office, carried into my mind the seed of the play called "The Silver Tassie." Whistle, and I will come to you!

All work is first written down in longhand, then a rough script is typed from this, changing, adding, and taking (making the script better, and sometimes making it worse), till the whole work is roughly done; a second draft is then done, changing, adding and removing again, and from this what is thought to be a final copy is typed, which as the days pass, and new thoughts come, proves to be unsatisfactory in many places, for a lot of changes are made in the galley proofs, and some, even, in the page proofs, before they are passed for printing. Work? Ay, man-alive, it is, and I don't like it, and never shall. I'd liefer sit listening to birds singing, watch flowers blooming, or hoist myself into a reverie of years that time has taken away; rushing again through quick-moving crimson, green, black or blue jerseys, after a ball in the glorious Irish game of hurling, or, dancing gayly in later hours, the jig, the reel. All over now; over forever; unless there be a heaven, and we dance again on its crystal flooring.

Haven't much time, though, for reverie. Things have to be done—giving a hand to the wife about the house; peeling potatoes, preparing string beans, shelling peas, getting the breakfast during the holidays to give Eileen a rest, and many other chores that help to make a home go. Washing up's the worst; but having done this for more than eleven years, am able to do it with my mind shut away from the task. I've often wondered if Yeats ever peeled a spud.

I dare say I have read unwisely and well; all sorts: from Frank Reade Jr., Old King Brady, Dion Boucicault's plays, up through the Elizabethans, works on theology, comparative religion, mythology, history, the American classics, Balzac, Tolstoy, Dickens and a lot of others. Among the more recent American works, Hawthorne, Emerson, Whitman and Moby Dick are still with me. Out of a dozen recent novels the best two, to my mind, are Truman Nelson's "Sin of the Prophet" [1952] and Peter Martin's "The Landsmen" [1952]. During the last few months I have

[1] William McElroy, coal merchant; backer of the first London production of *Juno and the Paycock* in 1925; best man at O'Casey's wedding on 23 September 1927. See O'Casey's letter to Timmie McElroy, 26 May 1928, note 1, Vol. I, p. 253.

read Hitti's "History of the Arabs" [2] and his "History of Syria," [3] Berg's "Natural Regions of the U.S.S.R.," [4] Carre's "History of Soviet Russia," [5] "The World of George Jean Nathan" [6]—a book that sets life dancing, keeping her thinking all the time; "Elizabeth's Irish Wars," [7] Hubler's "The Sense of Shakespeare's Sonnets" [8]—a grand book; one every mother's son shaking hands with Shakespeare should read; "Introduction to a Science of Mythology," [9] and Maisie Ward's Life of Oh Gee K. Chesterton.[10]

Well, here I am, aging still and singing away. Wrapped in many experiences which, with my self-education, to use a phrase from G. J. Nathan, have given me something of the mind of a gentleman with the emotions of a bum. A condition far from perfection, but it often has a lovely feeling.

"Rose and Crown" will be published in a couple of weeks.

[2] Phillip K. Hitti, *History of the Arabs* (1937).
[3] Phillip K. Hitti, *History of Syria* (1951).
[4] Lev S. Berg, *Natural Regions of the U.S.S.R.* (1950).
[5] E. H. Carr, *A History of Soviet Russia* (1950).
[6] See O'Casey's letter to George Jean Nathan, 15 May 1952.
[7] Cyril Falls, *Elizabeth's Irish Wars* (1950).
[8] See O'Casey's letter to Gordon Rogoff, 19 September 1952.
[9] C. G. Jung and C. Kerenyi, *Introduction to a Science of Mythology: The Myth of the Divine Child and the Mysteries of Eleusis* (1951).
[10] Maisie Ward, *Gilbert Keith Chesterton* (1944).

To John Gassner

MS. GASSNER

TOTNES, DEVON
14 OCTOBER 1952

Dear John,

Thanks for your very kind letter. I'm very glad you liked Rose & Crown a little. You should have read the Irish comments. I haven't tried to write a chronicle, nor have I set down judgements: all I've done is to picture (as I saw it) the world of life as it flooded around me, & as it welled up within myself. I've looked in and I've looked out, and I have seen things, weaving them with words into a tapestry, showing pictures of men & movements that life has given & that life has taken away.

Your suggestion of a volume, compounding together the best of all the volumes, is a fine idea. Oddly enough, it is just being done in Italy, by a Turin publisher. Odd that it should be done next door to the Vatican. Time brings strange changes. I doubt, though, a book-club would be interested. Besides, this way isn't so profitable as one might imagine. In all these ventures, half goes to the Publisher. And Authors, in general (not those accepted by a book-club, of course), stand by disliking book-clubs as a danger to new authors & newer thought. There is a great deal to be said for their suspicion & dislike. G. J. N. is a good choice for an Editor; but George is 70, &, like myself (73), easily tired, so I wouldn't think of putting him under such a burden; &, even if he wished to do it, wouldn't allow him even to start. A younger man, with more age-time left to him (yourself, for instance) would rather be my choice. Book-clubs, as a rule, are interested only in what will have a big sale; & I doubt that such a book as you recommend would have a big enough sale to satisfy them—bar the smaller ones. Indeed, in my opinion, no book-club should be permitted to tower over another. The sales of each should be limited so as to give all clubs & all authors a better chance. But that's a big question that would take a time to (as the politicians say) iron out. By the way, I'm skeduled to make a Record of near an hour's length for an American Publisher, next month, so that "the people will hear me forever." Breon is 23, & is just now, reading your "Treasury of the Theatre." Niall, our younger boy is 16, & Shivaun, our girl, is 13. Now, John, & you, Mrs. Gassner, you mustn't think of sending them anything for Christmas—bar a card. You & your good wife are not of those few Americans who can throw dollars out of windows. And your taxes are going up & the $, in America, isn't the $ it used to be. It is more bright here than ever; but duller with you: so forbear, please.

I enclose a sample of Irish Comment on *Rose & Crown*. One critic, explaining why some American critics liked O'Casey's work, said "The venality of American Critics is a byword." So you have been warned.

My love to you & Mrs. Gassner
& all good wishes.
Sean

To Roger McHugh

MS. McHugh

TOTNES, DEVON
14 OCTOBER 1952

Dear Dr. McHugh,

Thanks for your kind letter. I'm sure your Students are all as you say; but they won't be always with you. I amn't anxious to have my voice heard in Eirinn, and recent comments read by me convince me further that what I thought yesterday is confirmed today, & will be further confirmed tomorrow. However, that need not trouble you or trouble me—we know our own know.

Success to your candidature for the Senate. Had I a vote, you'd get it.

Yours very sincerely
Sean O'Casey

To Robert Lewis

MS. Lewis

Totnes, Devon
17 October 1952

My dear Bob,

First a sheaf of cordial thanks for the gracious & tasteful reminder to Eileen & me of our twenty-fifth year of companionship.[1] It was very welcome.

I've been thinking & thinking of your proposal in between a thousand things done & to do. Lordy, how chuckling time flies! The real reason, Bob, why I've hesitated is this—I fear that if no-one came forward after the performance; if no-one seemed interested, I'd lose the chance of a possible option on the play. I daresay, $100 or $150 a month seems to be no more than feed for pinkeens (smallest fish known to Dublin Kids); but it has meant, & still means, a lot to me, to us all. I've just declined an offer to do "Purple Dust" made by the Theatre Circle Group. I've had devastating experience of productions by Groups; & now am afraid of them all, all, all!

I know as well as man can know that "Cockadoodle Dandy" would get a production of all that was in you to give—& there's a lot there; so I'll let you know in about a week or so. If no option comes by then, or the present option lapses, then I put up the signal Go ahead, Bob Lewis, in the name o' God!

All fit here, Bob, bar Eileen having an abscess under a tooth, which has been removed, & she is chirping again; & myself who can't run about as he used to in a hurling field, & who hasn't as good a voice as he had 25 years ago chanting out a song.

---

[1] On 23 September 1927 O'Casey married Eileen Reynolds Carey in the Roman Catholic Church of All Souls and the Redeemer, Chelsea, London.

I send you my love, & all the same for Jay [Julien], hoping both of you are well.

Thanks again, grand lad, for the great encouragement of your interest in my work.

As ever.
Sean

To Brooks Atkinson

TS. ATKINSON

TOTNES, DEVON
23 OCTOBER 1952

My dear Brooks:
Thanks a lot for your very kind article.[1] A Labour friend sent it to me, & yesterday a copy came from the Macmillan Co. They didn't seem to be angry in any way; rather were they proud of having it to send on to me. I can't see how the Publishers would mince such a ringing of bells for an author they published. I could understand the Reviewer being annoyed at you taking the wind out of his sails; but, I'm sure, he'll soon sail into the wind again, and do his own talking in his own way. I wish we had something like your Book Review Magazines here. Anyway, Brooks, I gave it a welcome as one of your readers anxious to know something about the book before it was published. Richard Watts, Junr, too, wrote a column about it—in a very kindly way, too. You should see the Irish Reviews! I enclose a cutting of the best as an example. One bright chap [2] roar'd laughter & ridicule because I made the frogs say Brek Kek, Koax Koax, though this form is the one used by Aristophanes & by Joyce in his "Finnegans Wake." As we used to say in Dublin—"We're rearin' them yet!" I don't mind you calling me a mystic; I don't mind you calling me anything that comes into your mind to call me, for I know, however you may criticise, or complain even, you criticise as a friend, & as one who knows a few things; not only a friend of mine, but much more—a friend of man, even of birds & of all animals. There we are one, Brooks. I think I am a Rationalist, but I love a helluva lot of things. I can see wonder & beauty in

---

[1] Brooks Atkinson, "O'Casey in England," *New York Times,* 14 September 1952, a review of *Rose and Crown.* Commenting on the whole autobiography, Atkinson wrote: "It is an extraordinary piece of dramatic literature written in the most incandescent prose of our time."
[2] Niall Carroll, "O'Casey's Crown," *Irish Press,* 23 September 1952.

the holly-berry, the barberry blossoms, Radio Centre, & in a clanging trolley-car swinging round the corner of a New York street.

As for "Sunset & Evening Star," I don't know that it will be solider— I was aiming at making the end less upright, less vivacious, to trail along with my own physical condition; the lessor certainty of old age—trying to do too much. Alas! There's no inspiration, for it is taken from Tennyson's "Crossing the Bar."

> Sunset and evening star,
> And one clear call for me!

Thinking of "mystic" again, Brooks, I'm no scholar, nor am I an expert on any subject. I know very little about things, & so, must try to sing about them.

And now, friend, take care of yourself. It is really irrational to go and take half the life out of yourself building this & building that. If you must do a little, take it slow. One can near kill oneself doing the right thing the wrong way. Hammer steadily, take slow steps with a barrow. Pause after every journey, bend when you lift though—don't lift with a strain on the spine, use your knees to force a shovel forward—not your arms: These few precepts in your memory; &, when you feel tired, give up. Samuel Wanamaker & Mr. Sherreck—two Americans, I think—have asked about "Purple Dust" for London. They've just put on Odets' "Winter Journey." [3] Am to do a record for Caedmon Publishers. Heaven send they get it done before the frosts & the rains make me hoarse.

My love to Oriana & to you, dear friends.

As ever.
Sean

[3] Clifford Odets's *Winter Journey* opened in London on 3 April 1952, directed by Sam Wanamaker, with Wanamaker playing the lead role of Bernie Dodd, for his first appearance on the London stage. Under its original title of *The Country Girl,* the play opened in New York on 10 November 1950. Henry Sherek (1900–   ), English theatre manager and producer, produced the play in London with Wanamaker.

To P. J. Brady [1]

TC. O'CASEY

[TOTNES, DEVON]
24 OCTOBER 1952

Dear Mr. Brady,

You dont seem to realise what you do when you ask me to become
Vice-President of your Club. Any connection whatsoever by me with your
Club would, I fear, do you a lot of harm. Arent you aware that I am a
Communist, and dont you realise the opinions held in Ireland about Communism, and, indeed, about everything even remotely reminiscent of it.
If I were to become an Officer of your Committee, you would probably
find all Feiseanna [2] and Competition organisers unwilling to allow your
Club to participate; and, even if they did, the Judges wouldnt be inclined
to give (however excellent your Band might be) your Club any chance of
winning a prize. So, my friends, forget your request, and then forget all
about me.

I am not in the photograph mentioned by you. It was I who got the
lads together so that it might be taken. The band at that moment was
scattered, and all members couldn't be collected. Tom Clarke couldn't wait
too long, and so the photograph was taken while I was rounding up the
rest of the Band. It was taken, oddly enough, by a semi-conservative,
Protestant friend of Mr. Clarke's who was a Newsagent and Tobacconist
like himself—a Mr. Parsons, if I remember right. The only photograph I
know of in which I appear, is one taken of the actual Procession on its way
to Bodenstown. In this one, I am shown walking by the side of the St. Laurence O'Toole Pipers. [3] It appeared as a reprint in an issue of An Poblacht,
then edited by the late Frank Ryan, who, as you know fought against
Franco on the Republican side of Spain, and who died in Germany during
the recent war. There's no use of me asking to be remembered to any old
members—they would like it—, such as F. Cahill, L. Mackay, Jim Moore,
et al.

Well, there you are, and here I am, so I wish you all good fortune, and
many successes.

Yours sincerely,
Sean O'Casey

[1] P. J. Brady, Honorary Secretary, St. Laurence O'Toole Pipers' Band, Dublin.
O'Casey was a founder-member and first secretary of the band. See O'Casey's 1910
letter, the first in Vol. I, pp. 5–6; also his letter to Lord Castletown, 14 May 1911,
pp. 7–9.
[2] Festivals.
[3] This photograph is reproduced in Vol. I.

To Marguerite Buller [1]

MS. BULLER

TOTNES, DEVON

24 OCTOBER 1952

Dear lass,

I hope by now that you are yourself again; that you have left the bed, & that all illness has departed from you.

Fry is, as you say, a very fine poet, & his "Lady's Not For Burning" is delightful, though he doesn't know a lot of the facts of the Middle Ages. Their witch-hunting was by no means such a pleasant thing as he makes it out to be. It was a game with screams from the midst of flames at the end of it.

Naturally, I'm very glad you like my plays, & I thank you for telling me so.

So Devon was your father's home. Were his people anything to General Buller? My brother, Tom, served in the Army Gen. Redvers Buller commanded in the Boer War.

With renewed wishes that you are well & fit again.

Yours sincerely,
Sean O'Casey

[1] Marguerite Buller, 104 Banbury Road, Oxford.

To Shaemas O'Sheel

TS. O'SHEEL

TOTNES, DEVON

27 OCTOBER 1952

My dear Shaemas,

It is all very sad about Louis Adamic,[1] but the whole affair seems to be beyond full understanding. Strange and terrible things are still done by man. Stranger and more terrible things are done during a revolution, and the world's in revolt at the moment. We can but let the dead—comrades or enemies—rest in peace, and go on our way. No good is served

[1] Louis Adamic, a Marxist political writer and native Yugoslavian living in America, was mysteriously found in his home dead of a bullet wound in September 1951, at the age of fifty-two; it was never established whether the death was due to suicide or murder.

by going over and over again all that happened or didn't happen before
they died, or that happened to cause their death. We must wait for quiet
times before we can separate time out to see these things. It hasn't been
given unto us yet to see into the hearts of men. I am afraid that many are
using Tito to bite their thumbs and have at the USSR, so that they may
align themselves safely in the bread-line. I have a friend who was a C. and
who left the C.P. over Tito; a very clever chap and a very good fellow. He
has married a R.C., and his responsibilities have increased. Anyway, he's
fairly safe now; and materially he has succeeded better than before. He
sent me pages of argument for the conduct of Tito, pages and pages, which
I read, but which I put aside; for I wasn't going to spend my years in an
argument. I have still the same liking for the man, and I realise that he
had had a problem before him. You see, we all have to live, and we all
have to live in a certain system that comes down on us if we dont yield it
opinioned support; so we have to choose one way or another. There isn't
any writer here who would get encouragement to write for any big paper
unless he looked out of the same window as the owner, and saw the same
sights. I can't trust the one who is rewarded for (however slightly), or
benefited by, a change of political or literary outlook. You may say what
about the USSR? This fact is to be found there, I daresay, but there there
is the feeling of being hated and of being surrounded by potential attack
by all the wealth and power of a capitalistic world, and it is this feeling
that makes them afraid of anything they think isn't a spear-point thrust out
for defense. It will change as the USSR gets more powerful; it is even
changing now. They are getting very tired of the pictures that show only
black on one side, white on the other—like the Christians with their sheep
and their goats. Stalin's Pact with Hitler was a very different one from
Tito's Pact with the W. Powers. The first was done only when England and
the USA and France refused to make an alliance with the USSR. There
was no alternative but to make a gamble to set aside a space to prepare
to meet the attack Stalin knew full well wasn't far away. I myself in a
Christmas message to the Australian Papers (asked for) years before,
stressed that the finest Cmas gift to the world would be an alliance between these countries—E. F. USA. and USSR. Hitler the poor fool thought
the USSR could wait; E and F were the tougher ones; the USSR's destruction would be but the matter of a month's hurry, as, indeed, thought the
rest of the world. Bevin, himself, said that the USSR would be able to
withstand the Germans for one month, maybe two, possibly three; and that
would give E and F time to assemble and defeat the Nazis. The vitality
and invincibility of the Red Army was the most colossal surprise the world
got—they haven't got over the shocking surprise yet. Devil a much I can
say about Bella Dodd.[2] She need never have left the C. Faith. A good

2 Bella Dodd (1905–69), left-wing leader of the New York Teachers' Union;
joined the American Communist Party in 1943 and served as one of its officials until
June 1949, when she was expelled; became a militant anti-Communist, and was received back into the Roman Catholic Church in 1952.

Catholic should be a good Communist. But Catholics get conscience-stricken, go to the confessional, tell there their sin of being one, and are ordered to fly out of it. We just can't bother about those who take their hand from the plough. I daresay it is natural for the C.P. to sail in with attacks on her for her political "apostacy"; though, in my opinion, they are better without her. They do say tactless things at times; silly things, too; damnably silly things; and vicious things as well. But long ago, in the Sunday Worker, after writing the Irish Plays, I was therein called a "Judas" by a correspondent, and Mike Gold in the D.W. of America came down on me like a ton of bricks—time I was in the USA—but I take these things aswim, and go on, realising that Mick just didn't know what he was talking about. I just can't understand Bella's charges of "careerism" among Party leaders. What "careerism" could there be in the CPUSA? What high-toned jobs have they got to give? Can they even pay a living wage? Bella's wrong there. She may be right about the "beaureauocrats." Communism here and there has many god-damned ignorant fool-minds within it. That is why "culture" is such a big thing in the USSR. Read, read, and inwardly digest. Reading maketh a full man; with experience of life added, it maketh a whole man. Every Marxist, however ruthless, must be warm-hearted, and a broad culture only can give him a warm heart to go with the probing mind.

Thanks, Sheamus, for the cutting of Fallon's Review [3]—it was welcome. I dont know what he means by "eyeless in Gaza" or "slave at the mill." England, I suppose. He used the same title in an article in THEATRE ARTS,[4] New York. Story of Gabriel F. is a long one. He was an Abbey Player, and I met him there; we became friends. He was a clever young man, fine sense of humour; a civil servant; he still is. He began to hate the Abbey, Yeats, Lady G. and all. He was (as I thought) a freethinker; so he said, and so he acted. He was a weekly visitor to my room in the tenement in Dublin. He, B. Fitzgerald, and I were really great friends, but Barry was cuter than I. He never trusted G. Anyway, G. was in love with a c. service lass, and she with him—more so than he with her. I think she resented his freethinking; and, threatened to have no more to do with him. He broke to pieces, and even went so far as to ask me to bring him to my friend Dr. Cummins, an Eye-surgeon, to ask him about psycho-analyses, for he'd heard me say Cummins was deeply interested in it. I brought him there; Cummins gave us dinner, and laughed the idea to scorn—he knew nothing about it. Still, Gabriel stayed disconsolate, telling me that he was afraid of his freethinking, and that he didn't know what to do. Well, neither did I, but I ventured to suggest that since he felt so, he should go back to the Faith; that he could be just as clever, just as freethinking, with it as

[3] Gabriel Fallon, "Ashes of Exile," *Irish Monthly,* November 1952, a review of *Rose and Crown.*

[4] Gabriel Fallon, "Pathway of a Dramatist," *Theatre Arts Monthly,* January 1950.

without it. He did, and blessed me for the advice. Then he and Rose married, and she began to have children regularly year by year, till they had seven or eight, I think. He got a job (still remaining C. servant) as drama critic on an ultra-montane Catholic weekly—*The Standard*—the real McCoy! and began to be a devil of a good practising Catholic. He and I wrote regularly to each other; but I began to see that he was trying to get me where he was himself; and it became a strain to write, fencing him off, but always holding myself in for fear of hurting him. We, Eileen and I, visited him and his family in 1934, in Dublin. Afterwards, Eileen told me that the children were afraid of their life of him; and one little girl who was "brought down to see me" shook like an aspen while she talked, or rather, I talked to her. Eileen told me after that there was a terrible scene in the child's room before her mother could persuade her to come; the child weeping and begging not to be made to come to see Mr. O'Casey. That, I fear, made a deep impression on me. Eileen told me, too, that he had a prie-dieu in his bedroom before a crucifix—a kind of lay monk, like Chesterton. When the Tassie was refused by the Abbey, G. was vehement in his encouragement to "give it to them," saying what a wonderful play it was; and it was he who egged me on to let Yeats have it good and hard. Then, he urged me not to come back; now, of course, the Tassie is the worst, one of them, play I've ever written, and his constant chant is "Won't you come home, Bill Baily?" He has a hope! When the *Red Roses For Me* was done in Dublin, he said in his criticism that the play showed "a cold, calculated bigotry on the part of the dramatist." [5] I challenged him to point out where this showed itself in the play. He then challenged me to debate in Dublin, which was, not only to deal with the play, but with my life for years past. I insisted on my point, but, as far as I know, he never placed in his paper any indication of the bigotry he had stated was shown in the play. I wish to God he had, for I well knew the part he had thought of; but like all these "Catholics," he showed that discretion, etc. That ended our correspondence. He has made several tries to renew it, but I have done with him. He became President of the Catholic Stage Guild, and when some American came over to speak in Dublin, he pointed out that this lad had been connected with some you know what in the USA. Afterwards, some other lad came over who had offended, too, but G. didn't know, or didn't mind; and there was a row. Some time afterwards, he resigned from the C. S. Guild, and, presumably, his reference to a "red witch-hunt" had something to do with it. There were jealousies, too; many resenting him being in the limelight, wanting to be in it themselves. Well, there's a short history for you. In ROSE AND CROWN my reference to B. Crosby and the song, Holy Nickel is based on B's article in the Irish Stage Guild's Magazine. G. clanks along now in

[5] See Gabriel Fallon, "Roses with Thorns," *The Standard*, 28 June 1946; and "Calling Mr. O'Casey," *The Standard*, 9 August 1946; both reprinted above. See also O'Casey's reply, "And Sean O'Casey Wrote," *The Standard*, 9 August 1946.

his own way, though he seems to insist that I go his way too. He has followed all I do for years with odd rancour; but he's no worse than the rest; less ignorant; indeed, as I said, he is an educated man, and very clever, which makes it worse.

I had nothing to do with Easter Week, except to give sympathy; nor was I ever in the GHQ, though I knew all its members. I never cared for Zilliacus. The CP here, for a time beslavered him with praise. They do this too often. They did it with Priestley, leading the USSR astray in their estimate. Friends there receiving a defence of T. S. Eliot, the poet, were astonished too at being warned about Mr. P. Mr. P. never cared a damn for the USSR, nor for anything, in my opinion, bar Mr. P. himself. I'll read Shoaf's red outburst the minute I get a minute of quiet. Now my love to Mrs. O'Sheel and my love to you.

as ever,
Sean

P.S. I brought Fallon to see C. B. Cochran, for Fallon was thinking of risking a chance of becoming a Director here; but C. B. C. saw no sign in him, & a telegram from Rose, his wife, brought him back to Dublin; & so the vision faded. He forgets that C. B. didn't do Within the Gates, Red Roses, Purple Dust, Star Turns Red—only the "Tassie."

To Sam Wanamaker [1]

TS. WANAMAKER

TOTNES, DEVON

4 NOVEMBER 1952

Dear Mr. Wanamaker,
Thank you for your letter about PURPLE DUST. The play is free from any committment now; here, or in the U.S.A. A Group calling themselves THE CIRCLE THEATRE or THE THEATRE CIRCLE wanted a two months option on the play, but, after consideration, I decided upon a refusal. Mr. [Kermit] Bloomgarden found difficulties with the casting, especially the part of "Poges," and so relinquished his option.

Your suggestions seem very good. I mentioned Miles Malleson to Miss [Margaret] Webster, who came down here to see me on behalf of Mr. B. There are three names that come to my mind—Eddie Byrne, who

---

[1] Sam Wanamaker (1919–), American actor, director, producer. For details on his production of *Purple Dust,* see O'Casey's letter to him, 28 April 1953, note 1.

played "Brennan" in RED ROSES FOR ME, and gave an exquisite performance. He is a Dublinman, and would make a splendid 2nd Workman; Siobhain McKenna, who acted this season in Stratford-on-Avon, and is a very clever young woman; she, I think, would be fine either as Souhawn or as Avril. I send you a page of a letter from an American friend of mine, Lecturer of Eng. Literature in Harvard, who mentions a Milo O'Shea as a comedian. I know nothing about this lad—never heard of him before. His name appears in the main part of the play in a program sent to me by Eric Bentley. Incidentally, they used this play without my permission, and, of course, I got nothing out of it. Two times, twice before, friends told me of this company. However, maybe you have heard of Milo. Regarding B[ronson] Albery's conviction that the play isnt a "commercial" gem, I am in full agreement. But can B. Albery or any other Manager assuredly lay a hand on his heart and a hand on a play, and say "This is bound to be a money-maker"? He may do both, but will he be right? There isnt a soul in the Theatre World who can select a play bound to be a winner. That's where we non-commercial artists have the laugh on the bronson alberyies. The point about these cocks is that not only can they not certainly select a "winner," which is bad, but they dont even know a good play from a bad one, which is worse. C. B. Cochran was the one man here in London— business-man, that is—who knew; the one man I met who could. If you get Linnit and Dunfee to draft an option-contract, and they send it to me, I of course, shall be glad to consider it, and, if it pleases, sign it, too. The Glasgow idea seems a good one to me. If you came down here, you would have to stay at least one night. We could, I'm sure, put you up fairly comfortably—if you didnt mind getting into touch with the O'Casey family.

I'm sorry to hear "Winter Journey" is coming off—I understood it was in for a long run.

All good wishes,
Sean O'Casey

To George Jean Nathan

MS. CORNELL

TOTNES, DEVON
16 NOVEMBER 1952

My very dear George:

I hope you are keeping fit now that Winter's on us again. Such a long time since I used to run out hilarously when the snow fell; now I run in the minute a flake falls. I've had the usual attack of Influenza—came early this winter—, but am up and about again, though still wondering a little where I am. However, I managed to do the record last Wednesday for Caedmon [1]—an hour and a half of it, "Cat 'n Cage" from "Pictures in Hallway." Part of "Mrs. Casside's Death," "Song of a Shift" from "Drums Under the Window," the stars & moon chat between Joxer & Boyle, & the last drunken dialogue, from "Juno," and a song, "Green Bushes." It was a trying experience, & a tiring one, but interesting. While I spoke & sang above, the family listened below as it came through on a receiver to be checked & o.k'd.

Today, Sam Wanamaker came here to talk about his proposal to do "Purple Dust" in London. He is eager to do it, and suggests a good cast, though there's a long day & night between suggesting & acquiring.

It is very disappointing to hear that we won't have a Theatre Book from you this year; but what's the use of wasting God-given energy on trivialities, unless one has to do so to earn a living. We shall look forward to your Book on the Theatre, not as it is, but as it might be, if you had your way, a way of song, of colour, light, & sympathy.

Thank you, George, so much for sending me the cutting. "Rose & Crown" seems to have a fair start. The Irish Critics are still screaming. One laughed & laughed at the "ridiculous" use of Brek Kek Koax Koax to symbolise the croak of the frogs. And another, commenting on favourable reviews of Americans, bawled out that "the venality of American Critics was a byword!" So, you have been warned.

Now, that the Presidential Election is over, the Theatre may settle down to better things, if the things that belong to our peace are permitted to come among us again.

Take care of yourself, and don't go to the theatre too often, if you can manage to live without these journeys that so often stray from the golden road to Samarkand.

> *My love, George, to you*
> *as ever,*
> *Sean*

[1] See O'Casey's letter to Barbara A. Cohen, 11 September 1952, note 2.

To George Brett [1]

MS. MACMILLAN, N.Y.

TOTNES, DEVON
20 NOVEMBER 1952

My dear Mr. Brett:

Thank you so much for your kind letter. It was grand of you to think of affording me a chance to come to America again, and, heaven knows, I wish I could take it. It would be a great pleasure to me to visit a University or two, & to speak to the students; but, I fear, the pleasure would be mine alone; & hardly likely to overflow into the minds of the listeners. After speaking at Harvard in 1934,[2] several Professors told me they "wished they could lecture as I did"; a remark born out of American generosity; for the fact is, if they lectured as I did, they wouldn't hold their jobs for half a year.

But I am too old now to do anything but whistle an odd tune. The old bark is strained & creaking, & is no longer able to put out into deep waters, but must hug the coast, and be satisfied with a limited view of low hills, modest valleys, & near-by people.

I give you my warm thanks for your invitation.

I owe a lot to America. (I don't mean dollars, though these, too, were, & are, tremendously useful, & grandly welcome.) My arrival in England brought me a step forward in life-development, & my sojourn with you sent me flying forward in a wider & grander development still; and all without abandoning any of my Irish origin and characteristics.

My love to you and yours, & to New York City, where my Irish feet first landed on American soil.

Yours very sincerely,
Sean O'Casey

---

[1] George Brett, president, Macmillan Company, New York. See O'Casey's first letter to him, 20 September 1939, Vol. I, p. 816.
[2] See the letter from Richard C. Boys to O'Casey, 17 January 1935, note 1, Vol. I, p. 533.

To Seumas Scully

MS. SCULLY

TOTNES, DEVON

22 NOVEMBER 1952

Dear Seumas,

Thank you for the papers and for the very interesting program of the S. Literary Society. I'd like to be present at the Inaugural Meeting [1] certainly. I suppose, they all think the individual is dead in the USSR, and threatened with death almost everywhere, bar Ireland. But I ask you is there One soul in Ireland who would dare stand up on platform, street, or pulpit, & say all he, or she, had in his mind to say? As Dr. McDonald had the courage (he was a brave man, & said a lot while alive).[2] No. One cannot wonder at this when one reads the haste made to apologise, by the Men Who Struck O'Hara, to his Exaltation, the Papal Nuncio [3]—Paddy, or is it Mick? Were I younger, & had I been there, Mr. O'Brien wouldn't have closed down the meeting so quietly. One individual would have lived on for an hour longer. Looks like the "Standard" is coming out into the open platform. So much the better, for, sooner or later, the "Standard" will be told things, & the "Standard" will have to stand & Listen; & so will the bold O'Hara. Breon was in Ireland this Summer, & went from Dublin

---

[1] Dr. Owen Sheehy-Skeffington was scheduled to address the Technical Students' Literary and Debating Society in Dublin at its yearly inaugural meeting on 29 November 1952 on the topic, "Can the Individual Survive?" An ironic answer to the question came when the address was suppressed at the eleventh hour.

[2] Dr. Walter McDonald's *Reminiscences of a Maynooth Professor* (1925) was published five years after his death.

[3] The Most Rev. Dr. Gerald Patrick O'Hara, Papal Nuncio, was "insulted" and walked out of a meeting of the International Affairs Association in Dublin on 31 October 1952. At the meeting Peadar O'Curry, editor of *The Standard,* had read a paper on "The Pattern of Persecution in Yugoslavia," after which Dr. Owen Sheehy-Skeffington made a motion that the subject should be opened to questions from the floor. Hubert Butler asked about persecutions during the Nazi control of the country when "Archbishop Stepinac had allowed himself to be deceived by the Croatian Quisling, Pavelic, who claimed to have set up a Catholic government." At this point the Papal Nuncio, who was in the audience but not as an invited guest, felt "insulted" and walked out. After some confusion, the chairman, Mr. O'Brien, closed the meeting, over the protests of Dr. Sheehy-Skeffington, Mr. Butler, and many others. A heated controversy over the "insult" was waged in the letters columns of the *Irish Times* through November and December.

On 28 November, a day before he was to give his lecture on the survival of the individual, Dr. Sheehy-Skeffington, as one of the men who had "insulted" the Papal Nuncio, was informed by "higher authorities" that his lecture was prohibited. This information was disclosed by Christopher Gore-Grimes, Honorary Secretary of the Irish Association of Civil Liberties, a last-minute substitute lecturer, whose remarks to the Technical Students Literary and Debating Society were reported in the *Irish Times,* 1 December 1952. See Dr. Owen Sheehy-Skeffington's letter, "The Insult," *Irish Times,* 20 December 1952; Paul Blanshard, "The Papal Nuncio Incident," *The Irish and Catholic Power* (1953), pp. 186–91; and O'Casey, "Outside an Irish Window," *Sunset and Evening Star* (1954).

down to Cork & Kerry, but the only one of my friends he met was George Gilmore. He is shyer than Niall. France—the whole Continent—is an expensive place for a holiday now, unless one has friends living there. England is safer. All here send their love to you, & so do I.

All the best.
Sean

P.S. Things written 32 years ago, appearing in THE KERRY ANNUAL, just out, bring back strange memories.[4]

[4] Sean O'Casey, "The Sacrifice of Thomas Ashe" and "Lament For Thomas Ashe," the latter a poem, both published originally by Fergus O'Connor in 1918, were reprinted in *The Kerry Annual* (Tralee, 1953), edited and published by Michael Glazier.

To Miss I. M. Johnson [1]

MS. LEAGUE OF DRAMATISTS

TOTNES, DEVON
[? NOVEMBER 1952]

LORD CHAMBERLAIN'S OFFICE
ST. JAMES'S PALACE, S.W. 1
24TH NOVEMBER, 1952

Madam,

"Hall of Healing"

I am desired by the Lord Chamberlain to write to you regarding the above play, and to ask for an undertaking that the word "bugger" on page 7, will be either omitted or altered.

Any alternative word should be submitted for approval.

Yours faithfully,
(Signed) R. Mandeau.
p.p. Assistant Comptroller

Miss I. M. Johnson.

"Blighter," then. He should be used to this word. Hydrogen bombs, Atom Bombs, Napalm Bombs, and a new Gas, which, if a drop falls on the eye, suffocates, & kills in a few minutes; but it takes two or three drops on

[1] O'Casey's note, written probably at the end of the month, appears at the bottom of the letter of 24 November from the Lord Chamberlain's office, forwarded to him by Miss Johnson from the League of Dramatists.

the skin to do the trick—see "Atomic Scientists News" for November; & yet this Lord shys & shrinks from a word! What a gang of elegant hypocrites these are!

S. O'Casey

To Marguerite Buller

MS. BULLER

TOTNES, DEVON

12 DECEMBER 1952

Dear Miss Buller,

Thank you so much for the book, "The Wanderer," [1] which I have nearly finished reading. I read slow, having to rest my eyes frequently, and to use them mostly in writing for a living. I wrote slow, too, & so, I am myself something of a wanderer, though kept stepping out straight and strong by the claims of our three children.

I liked the book very much. It is, as you say, a tender story, wrapt up in a steady quietness, and yet moving with an unruffled passion. Life often goes through a quiet storm, without thunder or lightning, or fierce wind: just soft rain and a breeze that quivers rather than shakes the trees; but a storm that leaves us more sorrow than one which we have to fight.

It was most interesting to hear that your father was an oculist—Eye-surgeon, as we Irish call them; or Eye-doctor. God only knows how many Eye-doctors have peered into my eyes. I owe a lot to them—even though most of it was the easing of sharp, continuous, & bitter pain. Well, one eye is gone, the other still works well, & it is wonderful all it can see. I hope you are keeping fairly well, & minding yourself. No ego is "miserable," each is very important, bar that of an imbecile.

My cordial regards,
Sean O'Casey

[1] Alain Fournier, *The Wanderer* (1928).

To Dr. Frank Morrell

MS. MORRELL

TOTNES, DEVON

17 DECEMBER 1952

Dear Frank,

Glad to hear you're back safe in New York again. I am beset by many persons and things, but that isn't a bad thing—keeps one from feeling lonely, though it tires one at times. You were just as tired as I—running around too much & too quickly. Breon stays in London as long as we can let him have a few pounds a week; when we can't, he comes here to paint. He's just done one of Eileen—the best so far, I think. The house in which his flat is was damaged by a bomb, so the rent isn't so much as it would be, had the house escaped. We keep the flat for him by paying the rent. When Eileen goes to London, she uses it, & so saves some expense. But it is hard to live anywhere now.

I'm glad you liked my article—really just a note—in the "New World Review." [1] All that concerns our world now is Peace. If that goes, all goes with it—for our generation & yours anyhow. But I don't think there will be war—the last one frightened us too much. There is, of course, a spark of war in Korea; a big spark, & we should do all we can to quench it. Americans are still making graves for themselves there; young, lively Americans, too; and English lads, too, & some from Ireland. All so senseless & shameful.

How is that red-haired Irish lass you spoke to me about? Young Patricia Nolan. I did intend to send her a blessing, but she might have resented it. Give her my love, if she be in a humor to accept it.

> *All the best to you.*
> *Yours very sincerely,*
> *Sean*

---

[1] Sean O'Casey, "The Song of the Soviets," *New World Review* (New York), November 1952.

To Sam Wanamaker

MS. WANAMAKER

TOTNES, DEVON
18 DECEMBER 1952

Dear Sam,

Like yourself, I've been busy, working in a fog of a tired feeling; but alive allright. I'm not too knowledgeable or competent to deal with what you say about possible cast. I don't like the loss of Malleson in the part of Poges. I thought that Joan Greenwood wouldn't come for your cooing.

Since seeing you, I've written many letters, written an article "Artist's Place in Life" [1] for the N. York Times Book Review, & another "Irish Thro' the Tare & Ages" [2] for the N.Y. Times Magazine; & I've written a song which may suit Avril instead of the "Maid of Bunclody." It is called, tentatively, "The Blasted Rowan Tree," and is a better one than I first set out to do; indeed, I think, a damned good folksong.

As well, I am working at the 6th (and last) vol of Biography— "Sunset & Evening Star"; so you see, Sam, I've been as busy as yourself. All our children are with us, now, so we have a full house; & a lot to do with attending to them; so Eileen & I are on our feet for quite a time each day; & after on our toes, doing an impromptu ballet dance.

I pray your new play may have a good body & soul, a good introduction and a long run.

My cordial regards to you and to Mrs. Wanamaker.

Cheerio! about the only slogan we can safely use now, for "Cheerio" has in it a ray of resigned hope and a tinge of a threat about things to come.

Yours very sincerely,
Sean

---

[1] The title was changed by the editor to "With Love and Kisses from Mr. Shaw," *New York Times Book Review,* 9 November 1952, O'Casey's review of *Bernard Shaw and Mrs. Patrick Campbell: Their Correspondence* (1952), edited by Alan Dent.

[2] The editor asked O'Casey to change the title to "St. Pathrick's Day in the Morning," *New York Times Magazine,* 15 March 1953.

To Sylvia O'Brien [1]

MS. SYLVIA O'BRIEN

TOTNES, DEVON

19 DECEMBER 1952

Dear Mrs. O'Brien,

Thank you for your kind letter. I'm glad you liked "Inishfallen Fare Thee Well"; and that you rather liked the comments on Maynooth & all its ways; comments in no way as sharp as those made by Dr. McDonald, one of their own Theological Professors, so brave & searching that his name is never mentioned there. Yes, the Rosary beads are plentiful in Ireland, though they were originally a Syrian method of prayer, & came to the Roman Catholics through the Mohammedans. So Professor Hitti says in his "History of Syria." [2]

I wonder how you came across "Inishfallen Fare Thee Well." It is, I think, out of print; and you'd hardly find it in any Irish Public Library. Most of the other biographical books—"I Knock at the Door," "Pictures in the Hallway" & "Drums Under the Windows," have been banned; [3] and no wonder—look at how Dr. Skeffington has been treated. I'm afraid Eire has become a Clerically-controlled Republic. Not Wolfe Tone, but Matt Talbot! And the Protestants are largely to blame. They never merged with the Irish; &, even now, are timid touchers of everything Irish. Never a word of Irish spoken at their Synods, Diocesan or General. And they claiming Patrick, Brighid, Columba, Finnbarr, Aidan, & the rest of them! The British Government shot a lot of our best men after "Easter Week." We feel their loss now. I doubt if there is any left in Ireland to fight the clerics. Eire's one hope is for the North to join in.

Well, however it goes, good be with you. If you be a housewife, I'm a house husband, doing daily many things about the house. We have 3 children, & Eileen (Mrs. O'C.) has a busy, busy time.

My love to you.

Sean O'Casey

[1] Mrs. Sylvia O'Brien, 51 Belgrave Square, Dublin. A young housewife and actress, Mrs. O'Brien later emigrated to America, where she appeared in many Off-Broadway and Broadway plays, most recently in the successful production of Hugh Leonard's *Da* in 1978.

[2] Philip K. Hitti, *History of Syria* (1951).

[3] *Drums Under the Windows* was never banned officially, although it was difficult to obtain copies in Ireland. Many of O'Casey's works were unofficially banned, suppressed by some bookstores and libraries, but only the first two volumes of the autobiography were officially banned by the Censorship of Publications Board; see O'Casey's letter to Jack Carney, 20 May 1942, notes 1 and 3. *Windfalls* was officially banned in 1934; see O'Casey's letter to Gabriel Fallon, 29 August 1934, note 1, Vol. I, p. 519; and O'Casey's letter to George Jean Nathan, ? October 1935, note 2, Vol. I, p. 592. *The Green Crow* was seized by the Irish Customs Office in 1957 and unofficially banned.

To George Jean Nathan

MS. CORNELL

TOTNES, DEVON
22 DECEMBER 1952

My very dear George:

Greeting from the middle of Winter—I daresay, you are having it there as we are having it here. The first vision I have here now is the vision of Summer icomen in. God speed it.

Sam Wanamaker has sent me the usual contract—for a London production of "P. Dust," & seems to be trying his best to get a suitable cast. Yesterday, a cable came to Mrs. Elmhirst, of Dartington Hall, from her daughter, Beatrice Straight, saying City Center wanted to do the play, & requesting me to hold back any further effort for a London production. I've told Sam Wanamaker about the cable, &, of course, added that I couldn't do what was asked of me without his cordial consent. And I'm doubtful about "City Center." Maybe, it's one of them groups who thinks there must be a lot of heavies in a production nobody likes—or understands.

Dunsany said (to me) an extraordinary thing in the 21st Birthday Number of "Irish Writing," about "A.E.": "His voice is lost and there will remain only his poems when the memory of the man has faded with the last of the generation that knew him, but the beautiful melody of those poems, in which is enshrined so much of the twilight on Irish hills, should be enough for posterity to know him as the greatest poet that Ireland ever produced." [1] Oddly enough, though he quotes Ledwidge [2] & Yeats, briefly, he doesn't quote A.E. at all. I can't understand this great crowning. To me, A.E. has less of the poet in him even than Clarence Mangan. Certainly, he throws twilight over hill, dale, & valley of Ireland, but only by the use of the word. It is everywhere with the colours of purple & violet wrapping it in a robe. I hardly think anyone has read A.E.'s poems [more] often than I; and I've always thought very little of them. Perhaps, I am altogether wrong. But still, to me, A.E. can't come near even the shadow of Yeats.

The Guggenheim memorial has sent me two forms on behalf of two applicants, who put my name in. I've "reported" on these two, and also made an affidavit, sent to the Guggenheim Trustees, saying no more; never again. I am not competent to venture on such judgements.

[1] Lord Dunsany, "Some Irish Writers Whom I Have Known," *Irish Writing,* Double Number 20–21, November 1952.

[2] Francis Ledwidge (1891–1917), Irish poet, killed in action in World War I.

At the moment, I am going over "Sunset & Evening Star," trying to make it better; & trying to think out a couple of songs that Wanamaker wants for "Purple Dust" (He thinks that there should be some in 2nd & 3rd acts; pointing out that there are a lot in the 1st one). I have just thought out one for Avril, instead of the "Maid of Bunclody," called "The Ruined Rowan Tree"; and writing a lot of letters, as well as trying to fit myself into the Christmas stir promoted & admired by our three children— the hardier job of them all.

Well, God be with you; & take care of yourself, my very dear George.

My deep love.
Sean

To George Jean Nathan

MS. CORNELL

TOTNES, DEVON
23 DECEMBER 1952

My very dear George:

I posted a letter to you before I got yours telling us you had been ill. It is good to hear that you are recovering. It is a trying time before one feels fit again. I undertook to do a Recording for Caedmon Publishing Co., who were to send down the Recording-men in the middle of October last. I was then as fit as I ever could be, & ripe for the work. But the visit was postponed till middle of November. As this month commenced, I was assailed by a virus, & tumbled into bed. Got up five days later, moved about; got bad, and tumbled into bed again. Had recovered enough, however, to shove myself through the Recording, hoarsely and laboriously. Recording-men said it was good; but what else would they say? The Record has been held up by the customs, so I wait to hear how it goes. I daresay, you got the infection at the Theatre: crowded houses and heated atmosphere. But I don't often be in crowds, & yet the damned virus comes seeping in somewhere, somehow, & one is laid low. Looks like there's no escape, even were one to wrap oneself up in a plaster-cast of Sulphor.

Do take care of yourself till you are fully well; & don't bother about anything, however fiercely you feel you should. Eileen & Breon send their sympathy, though sympathy's damn little use.

My heartfelt wish that you may soon be well, & my love go to you.

As ever,
Sean

To David H. Greene

TC. O'CASEY

[TOTNES, DEVON]

1 JANUARY 1953

My dear Dave,

I got your Anthology [1] safely, and have read it through, finding that it is a fine and invaluable guide to the later Irish prose expressions. I think it an excellent selection. If the prose be not superb, that isnt the fault of the selectors: there is none better anywhere else, as far as I know. But one thing is very Unsatisfactory about it—you both got too little dough for your pains and hard work. The task must have been a terrible one. You must try to get more for the next one, and for the next two, too—the examples of earlier Irish prose, and the one you are to do for Random House. Perhaps, "The Gunman" [2] was a bit too long, and the other Irish writers felt aggrieved at O'Casey getting so much space. There is anyhow only a little "outpouring" from Davoren in the first act; in the 2nd, he's human, like the rest; and, anyway, the central character is, not Davoren, but Shields. But truly all writers (Irish) are determined to try to keep me in my place. But who's Hogan, who is Hogan? [3] Christine Longford [4] seems to be prominent in THE BELL for some time. I imagine she and his lordship have a hold on it now. It has been struggling for a long time, and they may have given something to keep it going, which invariably means ownership. Recently, most of those who used to write for it—Cronin, [5] for instance, who is now a teacher in London—seem to have quietly gone from its pages. I dont know what Salkeld [6] means by "the book has no reverence for its subject." What subject? and what is "reverence" in this respect? I imagine, on the other hand, that the book may have had too much reverence for its subject. Mary Colum seems to be a disappointed woman. Her book, "Life and the Dream" [7] seems to suggest it. Besides, women often

---

[1] *1000 Years of Irish Prose: The Literary Revival* (1952), edited with an introduction by Vivian Mercier and David H. Greene.

[2] *The Shadow of a Gunman* was included in the Mercier and Greene anthology.

[3] Thomas Hogan (1921–   ), a native of Galway, graduate of University College, Galway, and University College, Dublin, working in the Irish civil service, a regular contributor of articles and reviews to *The Bell, Irish Press,* and other papers.

[4] Christine Longford reviewed *1000 Years of Irish Prose* in *The Bell,* October 1952.

[5] Anthony Cronin, associate editor and a regular contributor to *The Bell* until 1952.

[6] Cecil Salkeld reviewed *1000 Years of Irish Prose* in *Irish Writing* No. 20–21, November 1952.

[7] Mary Column, *Life and the Dream* (1947).

get snarly when they've no children. They are physically disappointed. However gifted, a woman, if she can, should have a few children. This is her greatest satisfaction, and nearly so with a man, too. I dont know what she means by Anglo-Irish. The biggest sign of being A-I surely is the speaking of English, coupled with an ignorance of Irish. Well, then, four-fifths of us are A-I, along with Mary herself. What about Maxwell, a Protestant cleric, who did more for Irish when the tongue was nearly dead, than anyone else? And Dan O'Connell, who thought the speaking of Irish a sign of a slave! The truth is, Dave, that now the Irish have to depend on themselves and can no longer wail about English interference, they are finding the going hard. They have to take their place out in the wide world, and there are cold winds there, and snow on the high ground, with slippery frost under their feet; so that it's hard to stand up, harder to walk, hardest of all to run. And all are so amazed, so irritated, that they spend their time snarling at each other, and trying to bite away any little achievement accomplished by one of them. [Patrick] Kavanagh V [Austin] Clarke, Gogarty V Joyce,—all yelping at the other's work. And they all united in their hatred of Yeats. Now Miles na Copaleen is snarling at "Gabby" Gabriel Fallon,[8] drama-critic of *The Standard,* not in righteous indignation, but simply out of spleen. It is all really pitiable. Random House's MODERN LIBRARY is a fine issue.[9] I have the vol edited by G. Jean, and Sinclair [Lewis]'s "Babbit"; beautifully turned out, and delightful to handle. As for the inclusion of "The Raid" in it, that's as you think. I shouldnt mind. I am no judge fit for selecting, for I had no experience whatever of criticism, which, like all other professions, is a whole-time job. "The Raid" may be a bit too long, and give rise to grumbling again. There's no necessity, Dave, to include me—I wont mind in the least. You will have more room then for lesser-known Irish writers. I have just refused to do an article, or give a chapter of my new. biography, to IRISH WRITING. I reluctantly gave them one some time ago, saying it would be the last; but they've asked again. I hold it should be kept for the younger lads, but they say these younger ones wont sell the magazine. Well, I cant help that. By the way, Ned Sheehy wasnt the worst. I preferred his to Clarke's. Dunsany has said an odd thing in last edition of IRISH WRITING: "A.E. is the greatest poet that Ireland ever produced." I dont think he's as great as Tom Moore, or even Clarence Mangan. There must be many gems of Old Irish knocking about in many places, in many manuscripts Present-day Ireland's afraid of them; like Hyde in Raftery's poem translating the poet playing his fiddle "with his face to the wall," when it should be "with me arse to the

---

[8] Gabriel Fallon had politely scolded Micheál MacLiammóir in "No, Mr. MacLiammoir," *The Standard,* 21 November 1952; Myles na gCopaleen, defending MacLiammoir, wrote a parody of Fallon as a dramatic critic, "Cruiskeen Lawn," *Irish Times,* 16 December 1952.

[9] Greene's projected anthology for the Random House Modern Library series, *An Anthology of Irish Literature* (1954), edited with an introduction by David H. Greene. It included O'Casey's "The Raid," from *Inishfallen, Fare Thee Well* (1949).

wall." [10] How could, or would, anyone play a fiddle with his face to a wall? Like, too, the singing of "The Palatine's Daughter" in Gaelic circles, a jolly love song, lively rather than jolly, the last verse was never sung because it invited all to the christening of the baby. And, mind you, the couple had been married with consent of parents, and, presumably, with all the approval of the Church! It was years before I discovered the third verse. It was omitted in all song-books. No one ever knew how we Irish got our children.

Tell David [Krause] that he is wrong about Toller. Toller has had no influence whatever upon me. Old melodrama had—Boucicault's had, and such ones as THE HARBOUR LIGHTS, SAVED FROM THE SEA, THE UNKNOWN, PEEP O' DAY BOYS, and many others. So had Shakespeare and all Elizabethans, Strindberg, Wedekind, Shaw, Constable and Turner and Hogarth and Van Gogh; Beethoven, Mozart, and the Irish balled and folk-song; and the Irish dance—enough to go on with. I have never read a play by Toller twice, and admire only his MASSES AND MEN, though I find this too timid and too much of a wail. I got D's letter this morning, and I'd like you to tell him I'll try to answer it when I manage to fan myself out of some of the bewilderment it stirs up in my now wandering mind. I'm glad you have decided to have no more children. You are wise, I think, for Catherine's sake. Four children's as much as any woman can mind sensibly and well. You do be away most of the time, and dont know the trial and trouble it all is—a most wearing task. There are few men who have been among children as I have been; all my life I've been surrounded with them; and one has to have the patience of a god; for few saints, if any, ever had this job to do. You didn't mention the names of the twins. All the family were in the photo mentioned by you; all, save Shivaun and me, must have been cut out. There are few places where I go that Eileen isnt there, too. Well, Dave, achree, my love to the Twins, to Judie, to Caddie, to Catherine, and to you. Dont you overdo it with your own work and anthologies. Take care of yourself. You can do this; Catherine cant, for the children demand never-ending care. My love to you all again. All well here, with O'Casey busy as hell.

As ever,
[*Sean*]

[10] See O'Casey's letter to Roger Hayes, 24 November 1945, note 5.

To David Krause

TS. KRAUSE

TOTNES, DEVON
8 JANUARY 1953

Dear David:

I'm very glad you found something in ROSE AND CROWN. You fairly fence me in with questions—a chevaux-de-frise (I am acquainted with this word because one surrounded a Magazine in the Phoenix Park, Dublin, where we played hurley, and I often climbed the damned thing, at the risk of a limb, to salvage a lost ball. One of our lads going over it slipped, broke a leg and sent one of the rusty spikes right through his hand) sparkling with rusty points.

Your question about the individual and the group would take a volume to answer. When you say your query about "the problem of the individual identity in modern life" you imply that individualism is being swallowed up by the way we socially and politically live now. And may I ask you where was the identity of the individual held sacred in tribal, Feudal, or Capitalistic life? Were the unfree clans, even the clansmen of the free ones free? Did each live an individual life as implied by you? Did the serf? Did, does, the worker? Isn't this adoration of the individual identity something of a cod? I remember John Lehmann writing in the way of the "individual" gassing about the right of the "artist" to watch a cloud, a kingfisher, sun shining, rain falling, and his right to meditate upon them, and compose his thoughts in poem, or picture about them. Right, of course, for Lehmann, for he presumably had the time and the chance—as some few more have—to do these things. Can the miner when he wants to come up out of the mine to have a look at the sun or to watch the plunge of the brilliant kingfisher? Not damned likely: he has to do his stint first. He has to obey the law of the community that needs the coal, under conditions far, far better than those known to his elders years ago. I talked to a miner some time ago here in Totnes. He worked in the mines for fifty-two years. He had no pension, and for a hard week's work, he got twenty-three shillings a week. He was a man of seventy, eloquent and full of the poetry of Wales. Did the employers, the mineowners care a god-damn about the right of his individual identity? They organized into a community against the individual owners; first in groups—the Durham miners, S. Wales Miners, Miners of Scotland, Yorkshire miners, and, finally, into a solid block called the National Union of Miners which finally took the mines from the owners and made them Public Property. So with the Railwaymen, so with the Transport Workers. More, these three now form a great alliance, bound by rules and resolution. Once, in my days, the building industry consisted of craft unions, the Plumbers, the Bricklayers, the Carpenters, and so on; each out for his own particular Union—individual groups; and a snare and a nuisance they were to the workers as a whole. I myself was one who fought for Industrial Union in those days. Now it is so: the Building Industry here is a Union of all workers: individual groups have gone, and so much the better. The tendency is all this way, and is even now moving towards a world confederation of workers. It can't be stopped. It is all a development of what Fintan Lalor wrote about more than a hundred years ago, in 1848: "You are far less important (the owners) to the people than the people are to you. You cannot stand or act alone, but they can. You cannot act against them, you cannot act without them. A clear original right returns and reverts to the people—the right of establishing and entering into a new social arrangement. The right is in them because the power is in them." That is but one quotation from a book of Lalor's writings,[1] and he wrote more than a hundred years ago. "Individualism" can't stand in the way of this change. It must join up! It isn't a question of what David Krause or O'Casey likes, it is the inevitable development of democracy, of life itself. Oddly enough, each member of the workers' unions I mentioned has a greater economic certainty of providing for himself and family than our friend, Professor Greene has, or you have, or I have; and, more, each has a wider scope for expression of free thought than either you or David. Each could say things, fringed with blessing or cursing, that would fade on the lips of a Professor of Harvard or Yale, or Oxford or Cambridge. Bernard Shaw and I saw eye to eye on social questions. Read his "Intelligent Woman's Guide to Socialism," [2] witty and damnably clever, and when you come to his signature on its last page, you may set down an Amen before the Signature of O'Casey. "Individualism" as it is declared to be is hardly existent. It is a most difficult thing to be one in any of life's activities—art, science, or politics. Remember Harvey the Surgeon, Faraday the worker in Magnetism, the pioneers of Railways, when a man had to go before the train bearing a red flag; the same with motor-cars; remember Galileo, and a host of others. Look at the fight that had to be waged (I was in it myself) before votes were given to women. Think of the books on the Catholic Church Index; think of the suppression after suppression suffered by Dr. McDonald, forty years Professor of Theology in Maynooth College. Of Alfred Noyes's book "Voltaire" condemned by the Church (his own Church),[3] and the fact that he had to withdraw it for publication, and, as far as possible, make reparation for his "error" of writing it, though the book was written only to try to prove that Voltaire was not such an anti-Christian as he was generally made out to be.

[1] *James Fintan Lalor* (1918), edited by L. Fogarty, a collection of the articles Lalor contributed to *The Nation* and the *Irish Felon* in 1847–48.

[2] Bernard Shaw, *The Intelligent Woman's Guide to Socialism and Capitalism* (1928).

[3] See O'Casey's letter to Daniel Macmillan, 26 August 1948, note 5.

Read the Preface to the American edition of "Ulysses," [4] and see the abominable opposition given to the publication, not of that book by Joyce, but to his simple volume of stories, "Dubliners." Nothing much can be done by the "individual"; nothing at all without the help direct or indirect of the group. The very University where you work is the result of group activity. It didn't spring up like a mushroom, or come down, ready-made from heaven. All in the U.S.A. today is the result of hundreds of years of development, of millions of minds thinking, of millions of hands working. To me, the tendency is not towards suppression, but a world-wide and terrible desire to do things. Here, when an Exhibition of Picasso's works were given in the Tate Gallery, there was a shocking chorus of screams against it. Not from Communists, but from the respectable middle-class, and quite a number of the rich and powerful; and the sculptor, Epstein, suffered from persecution for years. A figure of The Mother and Child on a maternity hospital in the Strand, was chipped by someone firing a rifle at it from a window in a house opposite. Had I time, I'd give you hundreds of examples. Only the other day, Louis McNeice, the poet, reviewing ROSE AND CROWN, criticised my remarks on the Middle Ages (not mine, really, but the records of others who were scholars), told the world that I should have remembered that the "Miracle Plays" were gay things. He confused the "Miracle" ones with the "Morality Plays." I replied giving reasons why there weren't "Gay," pointing out that he had confused the M. plays with the other M plays—possibly he didn't like this. Anyway, my reply was [not] published by the *Observer*.[5] I wrote about it, and the Editor told me my letter had been sent on to L. McN. I waited three weeks, then wrote again, asking if McN. had said anything, and requesting if he hadn't, then my letter should be published. I was answered and told that L. McN. hadn't replied, and that my letter couldn't be published. I haven't heard a word from L. McN. since. One would imagine that he would have been delighted to show how much a fool I had been in my remarks about the M. Ages; but these "individualists," I find, when confronted with sharp and pointed protests or disagreements, run off, and climb away up the stairs of their winding towers. Wait till you read a chapter in my next Bio. book about Orwell's review of DRUMS UNDER THE WINDOWS.[6] Jasus, he did squeal! And implicitly, called for its suppression in England. He denounced it as roaringly as he could. The apostle of the free mind for all! And made a fool of himself over a quotation. My friend, the individual mind has often to defend itself against, not the group, or the crowd, but against other individual minds who are shouting out for intellectual free-

[4] See the "Foreword" to the 1934 Random House edition of James Joyce's *Ulysses* on Judge John M. Woolsey's decision lifting the ban on the book, and Joyce's letter to Bennett A. Cerf of Random House.

[5] See O'Casey's unpublished reply to Louis MacNeice, 15 July 1952.

[6] See "Rebel Orwell," *Sunset and Evening Star* (1954); see also Orwell's review, "The Green Flag," *The Observer*, 28 October 1945; and O'Casey's unpublished reply, 29 October 1945.

dom only when this freedom coincides nicely with their own. As for those who flee the crowd—the Existentialists and Ivory-Tower warriors, life doesn't care a damn about them; doesn't even know they exist. They influence only themselves; those who make life life have no time even to throw them a glance as they march by. Of course there is personal salvation as well as the salvation of the group; but a lot depends on the group: it is the group that influences rather than the Ivory Tower. Environment in which we live, static and living; the house we live in, the girl we court, the friends we have, the way we make our living—all contribute to form us, and powerfully, too, though, in the last resort, it is our personal will that counts most of all. In my opinion, salvation can be won better and more bravely in a crowd than in a cloister. Socialism is largely in practice already. Without it, as Shaw points out, we wouldn't be able to live for a fortnight. Just think of all the activities in the U.S.A. even that are carried on by the State today. Without them the State would totter, the State would fall. You should read William Morris's Songs for Socialists [7] and his NEWS FROM NOWHERE.[8] Joyce's "exile, silence, and cunning" wasn't a separation from the people, but from the tiny group of Irish writers who were jealous of his great genius. I don't think these opinions or "theories" were present in my mind when writing plays or even when writing biography. I looked at the life around me, saw it, heard it, felt it, and wrote about it all. Propaganda plays or books—other than those deliberately meant to be such—are not worth a damn as plays or books. They are too obvious and too damned wearisome. "Two things I can't read," said Shaw, "books about my work and books about Socialism." And on the whole he's right, except when the books are written by himself. Take this long letter: I'd rather be singing a song or writing one. I have written one during the past few days—"The Ruined Rowan Tree"; and felt gayer doing it than I do doing this. Well, I imagine the original artist will always meet opposition in any form of society, even the best. Mayakovsky met it, fierce opposition, not from the crowd, but again from the tiny bunch of lesser spirits who hated him for his genius. Look at the opposition the French impressionists met when they first showed their beautiful paintings. Even George Moore was among the scoffers, and worse than they, for he knew the worth of the paintings, knew that they were a new thing and wonderful. However, he was a man and redeemed his soul afterwards by the vigorous help he gave them towards recognition and honor. By the way, George Moore seems to be an under-rated writer. He is held up to scorn in Ireland, yet there isn't one writer there, in my opinion, who could hold a candle to him. His "Hail and Farewell" [3 vols., 1911, 1912, 1914], his "The Untilled Field," [1903] his "Esther Waters [1894]" are fine and large and delightful. Well, if some in the U.S.A. refuse to take my Communism at its face value, I hope they will take it at its Heart value anyhow. I think the Producers

---

[7] William Morris, *Chants for Socialists* (1885).
[8] William Morris, *News from Nowhere* (1896).

and those you spoke to are right about the reason for the non-production of my plays there. The Business Men are ignorant, and if less ignorant, then afraid to chance one. Bad business men for they lose as much, far more, on trivialities than they ever could on plays having a life and a soul in them.

All good wishes to you in your work for the Doctorate. Above all, be a student forever no matter how many hoods you may have the right to wear. My love to you and to our dear friend, David G[reene].

As ever,
·Sean

Never expect a letter as long as this again.

To Robert Lewis

MS. LEWIS

TOTNES, DEVON

[? JANUARY 1953]

My dear Bob,

I intended to write to you earlier, but I was busy, and an attack of Influenza laid me low, leaving a cough with an echo that is with me still. I decided to wait awhile longer for a chance of the play, "Cockadoodle" being done full out, without a single ahem, directed by you in the season to come. I contracted with Sam Wanamaker for a production of "Purple Dust" here, with an option on an American one; so this may help on more interest in "Cockadoodle." The City Center wanted to do "Purple Dust," but I couldn't let them, for I was already committed to Sam's proposal. I think there may be a good chance next season for us to have our way; so keep yourself steady & ready & heady for the great occasion.

I believe Eileen has written thanking you for your grand Christmas parcel, and I now send my thanks hot-foot after hers. It was very kind of you to think of us in this valuable way. I've been working at the next vol of biography; have written an article—"The Artists' Place in Life"— for the N. York Times Book Review, & one for the N.Y. Times Magazine, called "Irish Through the Tare & ages," [1] to go in—if the Editor thinks it suitable—Sunday before next Patrick's Day; I've made an hour and a half record a story, excerpts from "Juno," & a Song, for Caedmon Publishing Co. [2] The record's still in the Customs, & I don't know when it may be

---

1 See O'Casey's letter to Sam Wanamaker, 18 December 1952, notes 1 and 2.
2 See O'Casey's letter to George Jean Nathan, 16 November 1952, note 1.

released; & I've written a pile of letters, as well as taking part in all the children's interests—music, singing, painting, so that I have been hopping about like a grasshopper out for a mate. George Jean [Nathan] has told me that the season has been a wretched one for drama. "Dearth of new plays!" Bad there, it has been worse here, with never a critic to tell us so. If it weren't for American plays & musicals, the London stage would have been like a cob-webbed Christmas tree. I hope you have had your share of productions, & have been able to keep going. Too many business-men who can afford to lose money loose in the Theatre today. Jasus, help us! He will, one day.

Remember me cordially to Jay.

Thanks again, lad, & my love & love of the rest of us goes to you.

Yours
Sean

To Sam Wanamaker

MS. WANAMAKER

TOTNES, DEVON

14 JANUARY 1953

Dear Sam,

Here's a few names (possible) for you: [1]

Eithne Dunne—Souhaun or Avril

Siobhan (Shivaun) MacKenna. Souhaun. First choice to me.

John Stephenson: Barney or CANON CHREEHEWEL (1st choice) or third workman: a good singer.

Joe Tomelty—Postman—he'd do well with this, I think; near sure: yellow-bearded man.

Noel Purcell 1st Workman. He'd be very good; a fine cynical foil to Poges; or grand contrast to Miles Malleson.

Eddie Byrne (who you have already). 2nd Workman

Cyril Cusack. O'Killigain.

Norrie Duff. Might do for Avril; anyway she'd make a good understudy. Played in Red Roses: very charming & young.

Denis O'Dea. Don't know anything about him, bar that he acted with F. J. McCormick; must be 50 now

Maureen Pook. Good, intelligent; played lead in Red Roses: Nice voice; possibly Souhaun or Cloyne

[1] For the casting of *Purple Dust*.

With M. Malleson as Poges, Siobhan MacKenna as Souhawn, Purcell as 1st Workman, E. Byrne as 2nd Workman, Stephenson as the Canon, Tomelty as Postman, Cyril Cusack as O'Killigain, you'd have a fine framework of a workable Caste, with your choice for a Stoke.

I've heard the name of Wendy Hiller mentioned. No, no, no. She wouldn't know a thing about the spirit of the Play. All I've mentioned would; it is in their bones, as it is in mine. Also, these Big Names mean big money, though they'd play no better; in fact a lot worse, in my opinion.

All good fortune to "The Shrike." [2]

> *Most sincerely,*
> *Sean*

In the Abbey are also a W. Gorman & Brighid (Bridge) Ni (o') Loinsigh (Lynch), & others who continually play in Abbey Co. I've never seen them, but I've heard they can be good or very good. Shivaun MacKenna would know.

> *Sean*

[2] Wanamaker was directing and playing the lead in Joseph Kramm's *The Shrike*, scheduled to open in London on 13 February 1953.

To Sylvia O'Brien

MS. SYLVIA O'BRIEN

TOTNES, DEVON
21 JANUARY 1953

Dear Sylvia O'Brien,

Thank you for your letter. I hope you may like "Rose & Crown"—when you get it. I wonder it is allowed in an Irish Library at all. I wonder what would James Gleeson of the Vocational Council think of it; or Duce Maria [1]—who are, at any rate, far nearer to Canon Law than is the suave, liberal letter written by Kathleen Duignan in Tuesday's issue of the "Irish Times." [2]

I tried to get Radio Eireann this evening; [3] but it is always hard to get, and many interruptions & fadings always spoil any attempt to hear a special programme. Even the 3rd Programme, B.B.C. is spoiled in the

[1] See O'Casey's letter to the *Irish Times*, 21 May 1952, note 2.
[2] Kathleen Duignan, "Protestantism—Whither?" *Irish Times*, 20 January 1953.
[3] Mrs. O'Brien had written to tell O'Casey that she was to sing a selection of Irish songs on Radio Eireann on 21 January 1953.

same way. The S. West isn't good to hear, except our own West Regional, & Wales.

We have three children—Breon, 23; Niall, 18; Shivaun, 13, all with us here, making a full house.

My love to your little girl.

All good wishes to you all & to you.

Yours sincerely,
Sean O'Casey

To Barbara A. Cohen

MS. COHEN

TOTNES, DEVON

22 JANUARY 1953

Dear Miss Cohen,

Miss [Jane] Rubin tells me (some time ago) that you wrote explaining the holding up by the Customs of the Recording. I dont remember getting your letter—the posts here are, at times, erratic. Surely, the recording isn't held up for political reasons? Hardly that, because there's nothing in it that could be said to be political. Not hearing about it, led me to conjecture that the Recording was Bad, & that you didn't like to say so. I hope you may have good news by the time this note gets to you. Oh, these customs, passports, identity cards, and credentials! What a damn nuisance & a shame they all are! I work for the time when there'll be none of them, or of frontiers either; only men, women, & children of one family the world over.

With all good wishes. I've been very busy with all kinds of work, from washing up, peeling potatoes, to writing songs & another vol of biography.

All the best to you
Sean O'Casey

To Frank Hugh O'Donnell [1]

TC. O'CASEY

[TOTNES, DEVON]

23 JANUARY 1953

Dear Frank (again, presumably),

Thanks for your letter. I am not certain that I am writing to the proper man, for I couldnt make the name supplied out with certainty. Even after consultation with wife and son, they and I thought it appeared to be "O'Donovan." However, the business details associated my memory with you as well as the name of "Frank," and so I venture to rely on my judgement, and address the young man I knew when in Dublin, and who paid us a visit when we lived in St. John's Wood, in London. Also, the fact that you had become a Senator (I knew F. H. O'D. was standing); and that the one O'Donovan I ever knew was he who acted in the Abbey.

Youve got hold of the wrong end of the stick regarding McElroy. When I came to London, he hadnt a bean—to use his own words. He had spent all he got from "Juno," [2] much more than I did, in a trip to France and Italy with his wife and Herbert Hughes, the Musical critic and "composer," and HIS wife. Then the General Strike of 1926 took place, followed by the Miners' strike; and there was no coal to be got, though even if there were, there was little money to pay for it. Some friend of his discovered a Dump in the north, top layers that had been discarded, and on which the grass grew; but enough of B.T.U's in it to make it a possible seller. He asked McEl. to go in with him, but there wasnt a bean in the locker. He asked me, and I consented, to place all I had at his disposal, at the time, and signed a guarantee with his Banker, Tom Berry of the Hendon Branch of Lloyd's Bank, afterwards Baker St. It was terrible stuff, but it sold, for then, business firms would take anything, and it gave out some heat. It was bought cheap and sold dear. Fortunately for him (and for Me), it was a success, and he was able to give back the guarantee after a few months. I wonder did he tell you that? Actually, he made more out of me than I made out of him; and, if you read my biographical books, you could see as much; for why should I have to sell my amateur rights to French's, if he had done all you say he did? There are a good many more instances, but I havent time to set them down in this letter. Billy was a glorious companion while one was in a free and irresponsible position; but

---

[1] Frank Hugh O'Donnell, Abbey Theatre playwright, member of the Irish Senate (1943–44, 1951–57); died at his home in Killiney on 4 November 1976. For a reference to his play, *Anti-Christ*, see O'Casey's letter to Lady Gregory, 18 March 1925, note 2, Vol. I, p. 133.

[2] William McElroy, best man at O'Casey's wedding on 23 September 1927, was the backer of the London premiere of *Juno and the Paycock* on 16 November 1925. See O'Casey's letter to Timmie McElroy, 26 May 1928, note 1, Vol. I, p. 253.

when one got married and had children, one couldnt waste time with him, even though he was always a delightful, though irresponsible, talker. As for him not having "much longer to go," none of us have. I am 73 now, with a wife and three children—about enough to take up all, and more, of my time. You are surely safer in the Senate than you'd be in the I. Academy of Letters. Why do you think that "I am as cross-grained as ever"? Outside of the obvious fantasy in the books, it is a factual account of men and things, there with you, here with me. Macmillan's, St. Martin's Street, London, W.C.2 might be able to give or get you I KNOCK AT THE DOOR: I think it is still in print with their American House. Finally, are you Frank Hugh O'Donnell?

[*Sean*]

To R. F. Allen [1]

TC. O'CASEY

[TOTNES, DEVON]
7 FEBRUARY 1953

Dear Mr. Allen,

Enclosed is the letter you asked for. I still don't think the trouble you may have to take worth the time or the energy used to do it. However, if you think it may, then, I leave it to you, though I dont like the idea of you taking a lot of trouble for nothing, or next to nothing.

The authorities in East Germany were afraid (it was said) of offending the Catholic people outside of their Republic—in Bavaria, etc, thinking it might retard the plans for unity. I think they were sincere in their fear, but, to be, extremely foolish, for no one now can say a word without offending some prelate or Monsignor of the R. C. Church. The situation in Ireland now is as bad as it can be. The English neither know nor care, and small blame to them. The Hierarchy there are the sole custodians of the truth, the whole truth, and nothing but the truth.

Yours very sincerely, and dont bother too much.

[*Sean O'Casey*]

[1] R. F. Allen, Macmillan and Co., Ltd., London.

To George Jean Nathan

MS. CORNELL

TOTNES, DEVON

12 FEBRUARY 1953

My very dear George:

I hope you have fully got over your illness. I, too, have been invaded by a damned virus, and, though up and about again, am feeling very untidy within myself. These virus attacks are disheartening experiences. It has spread all over England, so with floods & snow, & the bitter cold piercing to the bone, few are chanting the old carol of "comfort & joy."

Sam Wanamaker is going ahead with "Purple Dust," though, in his enthusiasm, he is inclined to put too much into it in the way of music, & he wants more songs. I've written two, but no more, for I find it very hard to creep again into a mood of long ago. I am busy re-reading & re-writing (in parts) the next biographical vol, & hope to finish it before the sun gets strong enough to tempt me away from it. Irish critics & reviewers are still trying to convince all that O'Casey is no more. Yet they haven't got a new play worth a damn. Even "Time to Go" leaves them all at the tagline.

My deep love to you, George, & my fervent wish that you are allright again.

As ever,
Sean

To Frank Hugh O'Donnell

TS. O'DONNELL

TOTNES, DEVON

14 FEBRUARY 1953

Dear Frank H. O'Donnell,

You wrote to me while you were in London, and in the letter, asked me to write to you. I did so, but, so far, havent got a reply. Did you get my letter? In your letter, you said quite a lot about Mr. [William] McElroy; and I told you of one incident connected with our relationship. I'm afraid you didn't read my book, or you would have known another. This one: When leaving London Mac presented us with a cottage in Buckinghamshire in which his daughter and her husband had lived for quite a time. We thought he owned it, 1 Misbournes Cottages,[1] and that it would be suitable till things straightened out. You can read about it in "A Gate Clangs Shut" in ROSE AND CROWN. Well a fortnight or so later, in comes the Landlord's agent asking for twenty pounds owed in rent. We didnt pay it; but, of course, we had to pay from the date of our entry. Eileen had gone down before me, found the phone cut off, and a bill of £7 owing. Anxious to get in touch with me, she signed a document taking responsibility for the debt, and yours truly had to pay it; though postal authorities said when it was too late that I should never have done so. There are other things, too. But I'd like to hear from you first. I dont blame [McElroy]. That was the man's glorious irresponsibility; but it could be irritating at times.

As ever,
Sean

---

[1] O'Casey wrote a letter to Jack Carney from this address, 2 Misbourne Cottages, Chalfont St. Giles, Bucks, on 18 September 1931; see Vol. I, p. 234.

To Brooks Atkinson

MS. ATKINSON

TOTNES, DEVON

16 FEBRUARY 1953

My dear Brooks:

I got your charming article allright [1]—a dozen or more of them from good friends. Thank you so much. Irish critics & reviewers didn't like it. It irritated them that an American Critic should write about their antagonism to "poor little O'Casey." They laughed it off, but the laugh was neither loud nor deep, & had something of a snarl in it.

I am up & about again though still feeling something like some of "the ruins Cromwell knocked about a bit." I thought you'd be hearing my voice months ago. November 12 I did an hour & a half o' record for Caedmon Publishing Co. Fourth Ave—just after rising from another spell of Influenza—the record was 2 stories from biography, extracts from "Juno," & a song, "Kate Kindly Kissed Me." But ever since, it has been held up by the Customs, & Caedmon's say "God knows when they'll release it." By next Christmas I hope. I hoped it would be on the market for last Christmas.

Busy now with biography, & with Sam Wanamaker's prospective production of "Purple Dust."

[1] Brooks Atkinson, "O'Casey in England," *New York Times,* 14 September 1952, a review of *Rose and Crown.*

Eileen has written to you telling you how pleased we shall be to see you & Oriana. I hope you may have good weather. My thanks, again, dear lad.

> Love to Oriana & to you.
> As ever,
> Sean

To Sam Wanamaker

TS. WANAMAKER
TOTNES, DEVON
16 FEBRUARY 1953

Dear Sam,

I do hope THE SHRIKE [1] is doing well, after so much effort and work, it deserves a break; but to make a play go is always a hard job (or almost always).

Thank you for your letter. I hardly like to bother you now with anything about PURPLE DUST, for your mind must be full of the play that you are now doing. However, you can lay the letter aside till your mind has settled down somewhat.

I've read your scheme for the music, and, on the whole, it seems to be attractive, though we mustnt over-load it, or make it too fulsome. I dont think we should have any music for the "Bull" scene; I think it ought to go by itself. I dont know about music for the "entry of the Riders"; doubtlessly the rehearsals would show whether the suggestion would be good or not. I'm afraid the dialogue may be clouded over, and I want it to come forth clearly.

I enclose the words of two songs that I have written—one of them your famous "We're Ready For Anything Now!" God help me. The other, THE RUINED ROWAN TREE, makes, I think, a fair effort at a song. A teacher of music is to come here on Friday to set down the airs for me; but, if you are in touch with Liam Redmond, or any other Irish actor or actress, they should know the air of "Carrickdhoun." "On Carriagdhoun, the heath is brown on Carrigdhoun, the clouds are dark o'er Ardnalee" etc. They should know, too, the air of the other, "Says Herself to Meself." " 'twas down at Mulreddin, at Owen Doyle's Weddin' ", etc. However, I'll send the notation as soon as possible. Redmond is, I think, a very good

---

[1] Wanamaker's production of Joseph Kramm's *The Shrike* ran in London for five weeks, opening on 13 February and closing on 21 March 1952.

actor, but I thought he was engaged at other work. I hope you get S[iobhan] McKenna. What about Eddie Byrne?

I am up and about again, but shrinking from doing or thinking anything hilarious. I understand that you yourself had a tough time of with a bad cold. Colds are a curse in the theatre.

All the best to Mrs Wanamaker, the children, and to you.

Yours,
Sean

READY FOR ANYTHING NOW

Air: Says Herself to Meself

Oh, dont I look happy, and dont I feel merry,
Out here in the heart of the country, agra,
For we'll be as frisky and healthy as urchins
Who've spent all their time in a life-giving-spa.

I see it, I feel it, I know it, sweet neighbours,
We're ready for anything, anything: Ah!
Here in this old Tudor house by the river,
Life will be one, long, resounding hurrah!

Ready for anything, ready for anything,
Ready for anything, anything now;
With our eyes on the stars and our hand on the plough,
Sure, we're ready for anything, anything now!

Let frost lay a carpet of steel on each road
Let floods turn the magic fields into a moat;
We'll snap our brave fingers and laugh like a good one,
As we gayly go gadding about in a boat.

Let summer be winter, and winter be summer,
We'll live and we'll laugh in our Tudor abode,
Though cattle grow wild and the singing-birds mutter,
Though trees tumble down and the bushes explode.

We're ready for anything, etc.

THE RUINED ROWAN TREE

Air: Carrigdhoun

A sour-soul'd cleric, passing near,
Saw lovers by a rowan tree;

He curs'd its branches, berries, bloom,
Through time and through eternity.
Now evil things are waiting where
Fond lovers once found joy;
And dread of love now crowns the thoughts
Of frighten'd girl, of frighten'd boy.

The rowan tree's black as black can be
On Kilnageera's lonely hill,
And where love's whispers once were warm,
Now blows a wind both cold and shrill;
Oh, would I had a lover brave
To mock away its power,
I'd lie there firm within his arms,
And fill with love one glorious hour.

Then branches bare would leaf again,
The twisted ones grow straight and true;
And lovers locked within its ken
Would nothing fear and nothing rue;
Its bloom would form a bridal veil
Till summer days were sped;
Then autumn berries, red, would fall
Like rubies on each nestling head.

To Mikhail Apletin

TC. O'CASEY

TOTNES, DEVON
21 FEBRUARY 1953

My dear Friend,

Greetings. Yes, it's some time since you heard from me, or I heard from you; but, I'm sure we've been busy, each in his own Distant Point, doing work for the greater safety and glory of man. Last time, we had a little argument about the form and content of literature; about the Soviet attacks on such as Picasso and T. S. Eliot;[1] and, more important, I gave you a muffled warning about the turn and twist of a Mr. J. B. Priestley. Well, Mikhail, we know now the type of a man Priestley is. To me, he was always, at his beginning, in the middle of his career, and will be at the end of it, thinking of J. B. P. alone; caring only for his own interests. But

[1] See O'Casey's letter to Apletin, 10 February 1950.

suspicious and all as I was of him, I never thought he would end with such a shocking article as the one he sent from his bosom to *Collier's Magazine*.[2] On the whole, I dont think he served even his own interests by writing it. Well, let's put him forever behind us. I congratulate you on your amazing work in Canal Construction. Spiritually, I have sailed in your first Boat all along your waterway from Leningrad to Rostov. I am not sure about the "indomitable will" you mention. I have my hours of depression like most people, and often have to shake myself out of them. Then, again, I am never satisfied with what I do, and this dissatisfaction with work doing, and work done, keeps me tensely trying to do better, which is tiring, too. But we all get tired, and we all rest, and we all begin again. Again, letter-writing is a weariness of the flesh to me, but I write numerous letters all the same to people I know, and people I dont know in almost all countries in the world. I will withdraw from work and the world only when I am dead. I am, on the whole, doing well, in spite of physical handicaps; and our three children keep me on the go; besides, I have a splendid wife. So you see, I am very fortunate. Some time ago, joining the French Society of Authors, I had to provide them with my birth certificate. So for the first time I became certain about my age, according to the calendar. I never had a "birthday"; the struggle for life was too hard to allow us to bother about birthdays. The certificate tells me that I was born in 1880, so, next March, I shall be 73 years old. So old that I have flung calendar and clock out of the window so that I shall have nothing to remind me of the passing years or passing time.

As you ask for a copy of ROSE AND CROWN, I shall be very glad to write to my publishers, Macmillan & Co. of London, asking them to forward a copy on to you. At the moment I am working at another vol— "Sunset and Evening Star," as well as being busy about a projected production of a play of mine in London, next month. Oh, Mikhail, we have a lot to do! I've known you a long time now, so let me be Sean to you, and let you be Mikhail to me, in the bonds of peace, and in our love for all peoples. My deep love to the Soviet Peoples, to their Leader Joseph Stalin, and to all comrade Soviet Writers.

Yours affectionately,
Sean O'Casey

---

2 J. B. Priestley, "The Curtain Rises. . . ," *Collier's,* 27 October 1951; an article on the arts in a hypothetical Russia after the "defeat and occupation" of the country in World War III. It was part of a series of similar articles in this special issue of *Collier's,* written by well-known anti-Communists, including Arthur Koestler, on Stalinist repression.

To John Lonergan [1]

MS. JOY LONERGAN

TOTNES, DEVON

22 FEBRUARY 1953

Dear John,

Thank you for your kind and warm letter. I'm very glad you liked my biographical books. I'm at work on another now—having sent out a fifth, "Rose & Crown"—, to be called "Sunset & Evening Star." So you have Tipperary blood in you! Not bad blood to have in one's veins. You remember Thomas Davis's picture of the Tipperary man?

> Tall is his form, his heart is warm,
> His spirit light as any fairy!
> His wrath is fearful as the storm
> That shapes the hills of Tipperary! [2]

Well, he wasn't far out. Tipperary was a great stone-throwing County. Remember Mat, the Thrasher, the great hammer-thrower in Kickham's "The Homes of Tipperary"? [3] I competed myself once in our Club, throwing the weight against a lad from Tipp., but never could come near him, try as I might. So your father came from Clonmel, "the town with the cloud over it." It is in the Golden Valley, & Clonmel means "The Vale of Honey." Here in Totnes, during the war, a bomb's concussion blew our ceilings down, and a Tipperary plasterer put them back again. The one Postwoman in our town, during the war, came from Nenagh, Tipp.; so you see, I know something about your father's County. I can understand your father's dreaming memories. "These dreams, these scalding dreams!" G. B. Shaw makes Larry Doyle explain in his "John Bull's Other Island." [4] Tipperary is sadly depleted since your father left. Thousands have fled away, & they go still whenever they find half-a-chance to fly. So it is with Cork, Mayo, Galway, Sligo, Roscommon, Limerick, & other counties—the Irish

---

[1] John Lonergan (1857–1961), Irish-American painter, engraver, and lithographer.

[2] Thomas Davis, "Tipperary."

[3] Charles J. Kickham, *Knocknagow; or, The Homes of Tipperary* (1879). In his letter to O'Casey, Lonergan mentioned that his father had been a stone thrower in Clonmel.

[4] G. B. Shaw, *John Bull's Other Island* (1904), Larry Doyle's speech in Act I:

> Oh, the dreaming! the dreaming! the torturing, heartscalding, never satisfying dreaming, dreaming, dreaming! (Savagely.) No debauchery that ever coarsened and brutalized an Englishman can take the worth and usefulness out of him like that dreaming. An Irishman's imagination never lets him alone, never convinces him, never satisfies him; but it makes him that he cant face reality nor deal with it nor handle it nor conquer it. . . .

skies always have in them wild geese flying off to other lands. It is a melancholy story. But facing facts, for instance, what would you do in Clonmel (were you there), except get away from it, quick as you could. But, fortunately, you are an American, so don't you start "dreaming," which but scalds the Irish heart, & does no good. I'm glad you have a decent job in a Quaker School.[5] What can be more important to life than wood, metal, leather, and pottery—or to give it its grander name—ceramics? And to give shapeliness & grace of form to all raw materials is a blessed work indeed. If you can, read my article, "Always the Plow & the Stars" which appeared in the Book Review part of the New York Times, a week or two ago.[6] The first school my elder boy went to was run by a Quakeress. I'm glad the Jews give you a thought: on the whole, I think the Jew has a quicker sense of art, & greater love of color than the Goy, or Gentile.[7] Music, too; as well as painting. By all means send me the picture of part of Monhegan Island. I shall be glad to get it.

My love to your wife and to you.

> *Yours very sincerely,*
> *Sean O'Casey*

[5] Lonergan told O'Casey that he couldn't make a living as a painter, and had to teach arts and crafts in a Quaker school in Philadelphia.
[6] "Always the Plow and the Stars," *New York Times Book Review,* 25 January 1953; reprinted in *The Green Crow* (1956).
[7] Lonergan had told O'Casey: "Let me reveal a secret to you, dear Sean. I've rarely sold a painting to a Gentile. All the paintings I've ever sold have been to Jewish people. Riddle me this, Sean."

To Sam Wanamaker

MS. WANAMAKER

[TOTNES, DEVON]
[? MARCH 1953]

Below is a suggested verse for SOUHAUN. It is the same air as that attached to O'Killigain's verse sung just previously, "There are many fair things in this world as it goes" etc.

> How I grieve for the time when my heart was mine own,
> When I laugh'd at all lovers left sighing alone;
> Till a lusty lad, passing, glanc'd love from his eye,
> Then peace in my heart and mind whisper'd goodbye,
> And all th' world's gladness sank into a sigh.

For he turn'd not, but left me there standing, Ochone,
Like an empty nest left there when fledglings have flown;
Though I watch at my window and watch at my door,
My heart tells me I'll see this Laddie no more,
Or ever hear his voice say Kiss me, asthore!

There, be god, I've written another before I thought of it. In "Old Days" song, change "Old days are coming again," to "Old days are with us again," in all lines. In the second-last line of verse 2, change "Though never too near us, the people will cheer us" to "All those who live near us will come out to cheer us."

Siobhan McK[enna]. rang us last night on her way to the boat for Ireland, where, she says, she will be for 10 days; &, if she finds she cant join the Caste, she'll let us know. The delay is something of a nuisance.

I'm sure we have enough songs in the play now. The opening chorus is long enough—too long already, in my opinion. The Canon singing a song is out of the question. Canons dont sing in company—even Protestant Canons rarely—all my life, I heard one only sing at a Social at All Saints, Grangegorman, a district in Dublin that houses Ireland's most famous Lunatic Asylum—maybe that explains the Canon's singing. Don't like the idea of a duet sung by B[arney]. & Cloyne. Better leave it out. By the way, Sam, a "blonde" wouldn't do for "Avril." Blondes are very rare in Ireland. All other shades are plentiful, but blondes hardly exist. I only ever met one—golden-haired (rather than the white blonde) lad, chief piper of Lusk Band; afterwards murdered through forcible feeding in Mountjoy jail, by the British.[1] I wrote a few ballads about him. One written in 1919 has been reprinted in "The Kerry Annual" for 1953, & a booklet I wrote about him now exists only in the National Library [of Ireland].[2] They sent me a photostat copy of it. So perish the "blonde idea" for the play.

My love to Mrs. Wanamaker, your two little ones, & you.

Sean

[1] See O'Casey's tribute to Thomas Ashe on the occasion of his death as the result of forcible feeding, *Dublin Saturday Post,* 6 October 1917, Vol. I, pp. 64–65.
[2] See O'Casey's letter to Seumas Scully, 22 November 1952, note 4.

To Sam Wanamaker

MS. WANAMAKER

[TOTNES, DEVON]
[? MARCH 1953]

OLD DAYS ARE WITH US AGAIN

I

Oh, Ive got a wonderful tale to tell,
Tale to tell, tale to tell;
Old manners and customs are ringing a bell,
The old days are with us again.
Without further biding, bold horsemen are riding,
And ladies will wear all the old fashions well.
We'll foot it so nately in minuet stately,
That all who can see it will murmur, How swell!

Chorus

And welcome the old ways,
The silken-clad old days,
Old days are with us again!

2

Oh, we shall have wonderful suits to wear,
Suits to wear, suits to wear;
With ruffles and silver things shining there—
The old days are with us again.
The ladies well scented, will drive men demented
In flowing flounc'd dresses and petticoats fair,
All those who live near us, will come out to cheer us—
And life'll be one long, grand, gorgeous affair!

Chorus

The old ways, the bold ways,
The silken-clad old days,
The old days are coming again!

The air of the above is "BARNEY O'HEA" (O'Hay). It begins with "As I was going to Bandon Fair, to Bandon Fair, to Bandon Fair," the chorus, "Impudent Barney, none of your blarney, impudent Barney O'Hea!" It was written, I think, by Lever or Lover. It is a well-known ditty, and is probably well-known to Mr. M[alcolm] Arnold. Shivaun McKenna didnt ring up last night, probably the fog was to blame. I heard the play "God's

Gentry." Seemed to want form, and the songs seemed to upset it—verb sap.
Shivaun wasnt bad. She should be well able for Avril, but if she hesitates
longer, then it might be well to seek another.

Harry Hutchinson & Tony Quinn were good in "God's Gentry," [1] &
would do well in parts, I think—say Barney; or Quinn for 1st Workman, or
Yellow-Bearded W. man. One of them might even do the Canon.

S OC

[1] Donagh MacDonagh's *God's Gentry* was broadcast on the BBC radio Home
Service on 2 March 1953, with Siobhan McKenna, Harry Hutchinson, and Tony
Quinn in the leading roles.

To Sam Wanamaker

TS. WANAMAKER

TOTNES, DEVON

8 MARCH 1953

Dear Sam,

I hope Mr. [Malcolm] Arnold found, or already knew, the air of
BARNEY O'HEA, which I made to Go with THE OLD WAYS ARE
WITH US AGAIN. Regarding Souhaun's song, I GRIEVE FOR THE
TIME, in the first line, "Oh, I grieve, etc, change "Oh" to "How," so that
it goes "How I grieve for the time," etc. and in the last line of the first
verse, "And all th' world's gladness turn'd into a sigh," change the word
"Turn'd" into "Sank," making it go "Sank into a sigh."
In the second verse, first line change to *"For* he turn'd not, but left me
there standing. Ochone."
Second line to "Like an empty nest left there when *fledglings* have flown."
The third line change "the" to "my," so that it goes, "Though I watch at
my window and watch at *my* door." I dont like to leave such a song as this
one incomplete—or as I think it to be incomplete; so I have added another
verse as follows,

Though I circle my coming and going with pray'r,
Yet wherever I be, I see him laughing there;
And all that I read in a holy book's lore
But tells me I'll see my dear laddie no more,
Or hear his young voice whisper, Kiss me, asthore.

The air of this song, and the one sung by O'Killigan, is, of course,
Moore's well-known "There is not in this wide world a valley so sweet." If

you are busy, and all this bothers you, take no notice of it. Anyhow, I have two more songs now to my repertoire—last sylabble or syllable or sylable pronounced "twar." Now you know. I hope Mrs. Wanamaker and the two children, Abbe and Zoe, and you, are well.

Yours sincerely
Sean

To George Jean Nathan

MS. CORNELL

TOTNES, DEVON
11 MARCH 1953

My very dear George:

I've been a bit anxious about you since your last letter you were just recovering from a bad virus attack. I do hope you are allright, or nearly so, again. The damned thing they call Influenza is indeed a pestering menace, it has so many forms, & the doctors seem to know very little about it. We had a bad epidemic of it in England, and it is still going strong. The damned thing kept me miserable for weeks. When I was young, I used to fling it aside on my feet, but no longer, no. I hope you have some one to look after you, when you're down. That is the awkward thing of being alone. Do take care of yourself, & take things easier. It is bitterly cold here, so what must it be with you.

I've written 4 new songs for "Purple Dust," asked for by Sam Wanamaker; two said to be "amusing," & two I like myself, which can be printed; Kinda folk songs: "The Ruined Rowan Tree," & "How I Grieve for the Time When My Heart was mine own."

Take care of yourself.

My love.
As ever
Sean

To George McCalmon [1]

TC. O'CASEY

TOTNES, DEVON

11 MARCH 1953

Dear Mr. McCalmon,

Thanks ever so much for your kind letter telling me about the University performances of JUNO AND THE PAYCOCK. Very acceptable indeed. As well as bringing me to the presence of new friends, and showing my work to them, it means a few dollars into a purse, wide open and waiting. I dare say you know that your American dollar to a great many now has become the pearl of great price.

Thanks, too, for the chaste and charming program. I wish our Universities and Colleges here took as much interest in things of the theater as you do over there.

Thanks the third time for your suggestion that the University Drama Club may, in the future, do another of my plays. You know, I daresay, that I have to reserve "Purple Dust," "Red Roses For Me," and "Cockadoodle Dandy," for a possible production on Broadway. At the moment, there is a fine prospect of the first play being done in London soon—oddly enough, by an American. Perhaps, it isnt odd.

I am working now on a sixth volume of biography, "Sunset and Evening Star," and hope to make it presentable in a month or two; though it will hardly appear openly this year.

All the best to you and to your comrades in the University Theater, and all comrades in the University. I understand your University has over 5000 students—more than the population of our town of Totnes. If my good wishes isnt loud enough for all to hear, I hope those at a distance may hear the echo of them.

Yours very sincerely,

Sean O'Casey

[1] George McCalmon, director, University Theatre, Cornell University, Ithaca, New York.

To Horace Reynolds

MS. REYNOLDS

TOTNES, DEVON

21 MARCH 1953

My dear Horace,

Many thanks for sending me the note from L. Club.[1] I knew about the choice, for this is arranged by Macmillan's. It brings me a few hundred dollars, which are more welcome than flowers in May, these days. Fees are divided 50-50 with author & publisher. I hope you gave your consent to the use of the quotation—a very nice choice by L. Book Club. I've been doing a helluva lot of things—working at "Sunset & Evening Star"; biographical; fighting two attacks of Influenza; and writing additional songs for a production of "Purple Dust," four in all; two "funny" & short-lived, & two good ones. Something in the nature of folk-songs; that, I think, may be worthy of printing in a book. All our 3 children are with us here—Breon painting away, & hoping to strike lucky some fine day; Niall & Shivaun still at school, though in June, Niall goes off to the Army as a National Service unit. In intervals, I try to help the Cause of Peace, with other writers, but too old now to be what I once was with Jim Larkin. You didnt say anything in the note about Peggy & John; father and mother now! Holy God, how time fuges! And Kay as anxious as ever over the new lives coming. My love to her, to Peggy & John, & to you, me lad.

As ever.
Sean

[1] The Left Book Club in New York offered *Rose and Crown* as one of its choice selections.

To Robert Emmett Ginna [1]

TS. GINNA

TOTNES, DEVON

31 MARCH 1953

Dear Mr. Ginna,

Thanks and many of them for your kind letter. Both Miss Rubin and Mr. Lewis have written to me about the scheme you have in mind for setting my play, COCKADOODLE DANDY strutting through the pages of

[1] Robert Emmett Ginna, *Life,* Rockefeller Center, New York City.

your LIFE.[2] Well, all I can say is that it [is] a great scheme—to, and for, me. It seems a gorgeous idea to me. I have written to Miss Rubin and to Bob Lewis saying so. I shall be glad to help in any way I can, of course.

I imagine that the Irish Film Institute would be the best medium to approach, if you decide to take some of the scenes in Ireland. I'm sure the members of the Committee, or members of the Society, would readily help you, though one cant be sure about anything in my country. If not, there will be others willing to lend a hand.

I and Mrs O'Casey are in favour—if it be possible—to employ those who are not "famous" actors, or even professional ones, if they can be done without. We have few, if any, famous actors in Ireland now, or out of it either. We have quite a number of good ones, but these have yet to weave the cloak of fame for themselves. These, quite naturally, would be thinking only of their own appearance.

We know LIFE well. Mrs O'C. gets it regularly. I've just read O'Faolain's article about the conditions of courtship and marriage in Ireland,[3] and a clever article it is, too. I wish I had O'F's gift for writing articles. My own plays—PURPLE DUST, and, especially, COCKA-DOODLE DANDY, deal with this really dreadful state of things in Ireland. I've heard from an American friend—Irish and a Catholic—that the clergy and bachelors (Irish) condemn the article, but that the married Irish are cheering. He tells me that the College of Notre Dame sponsored it; and, if it be so, that is good news, and shows that we have some sense left which may prevent my country from committing racial suicide.

With all good wishes.
Yours very sincerely,
Sean O'Casey

[2] This illustrated article eventually became "The World of Sean O'Casey," *Life,* 26 July 1954, unsigned, with photographs by Gjon Mili.
[3] Sean O'Faolain, "Love Among the Irish," *Life,* 16 March 1953.

To Robert Lewis

MS. LEWIS

TOTNES, DEVON
31 MARCH 1953

My dear Bob,

The bells seem to be ringing an old year out & a new year in. I'm near certain I had a chat with Walter Chrysler when I was in New York.

I do hope the hope may be realised, & that "Cockadoodle Dandy" may cry loud on the New York Stage this year. I am busy with "Purple Dust" rehearsals, with Sam Wanamaker directing. He tells me he had his first lessons with you, & has, indeed, a very high opinion of you. The play seems to be shaping fine, & there is a distinct chance of success, at last. A letter came this morning from Robert Emmett Ginna of "Life," telling me all about his idea of a display in the Magazine. I am very much for it, & am writing Mr. R. Emmett Ginna to say so. Thanks, ever so much for valiantly getting me a fee for co-operation; &, whisper, I hope to God you havent forgotten yourself; & that your work will be paid for. You know, dear Bob, one's nearest neighbour is oneself. We must be kind to ourselves before we can be kind to others. I hope you are busy & doing well. Eileen sends her love, & do Breon & Niall & Shivaun; to you & Jay. And I, too, and I, too, warrior of the Theater.

As ever,
Sean

To Roger McHugh

MS. McHugh

Totnes, Devon

31 March 1953

Dear Roger,

I mislaid your letter, & couldn't recollect your address. I came across it this morning. You can have any recording you like of my plays for your students, provided you are sure they won't be bored by them. By the way, Bert Rodgers, of the B.B.C., the poet, down here, took a short bit of talk from me about G.B.S.; &, afterwards, took down a song I did my best to sing—"Kate Kindly Kissed Me." Have you heard them? I read about the result of the election. It was irritating to come so close, & miss. I am very sorry you didn't get in.[1] Time we had new thought in our Senate. An article on the low marriage rate in Ireland, by S. O'Faoláin, in LIFE, is causing something of a stir. I hear the clergy & the bachelors (Irish) condemn it; & the married Irish are cheering. I'm told the outstanding Catholic College of Notre Dame sponsored the idea, & so a lot of the menacing guns are spiked.

All good wishes to you.

Sean

[1] McHugh lost his bid for election to the Irish Senate by one vote.

To Seumas Scully

MS. SCULLY

TOTNES, DEVON

31 MARCH 1953

My dear Seumas,

Thanks ever so much for the Papers. I hope the Students Society won't break up; that a Committee will be elected brave enough to stand up to the Gleesons. I am busy, as you may have read, with a production of "Purple Dust," just now.

Do you know who form the Committee of the Film Institute? I don't know if this be the right name. I mean the Society in Eirinn who show films from time to time that are not usually shown in the ordinary Cinemas. If you know about the Society, I'd like you to let me have the names & addresses of its Executive members—President or Secretary. If you don't know, maybe you'd ask Dr. [Owen Sheehy-] Skeffington for them, or any member of the Society.

Eileen sends her love to you, & so do I.

All good wishes.
As ever,
Sean

To Sam Wanamaker

TS. WANAMAKER

TOTNES, DEVON

3 APRIL 1953

My dear Sam,

Thanks for your letter. Sorry the LIFE letter wouldnt be any good to you. I shouldnt have bothered you with it. I'm glad you sent your refusal to allow PURPLE DUST to be done in Cambridge, U.S.A. A letter from you has more authority in it; for, as you say, such a production might do harm to your own production there. I'm very glad to hear that the re-hearsals are going well. I was sure they would from what I saw during the week I was there. I note that you, [Bernard] Miles, and Walter [Hudd], have "fiddled" with the new stuff, "anglicising it," making it shorter, etc. That's allright by me, for the less "new stuff" there is, the more the play goes back to its original form. But dont forget that the Eng. language stands, not on the stumbling stones of the magazine or the newspaper, but on the rock of the Bible and Shakespeare. What is sometimes (often, often) taken for an Irish "twist," is really an Elizabethan turn of speech. I rather liked the new speech I gave to Poges, but, as you say, it may have been as well to change and shorten it. I hope you havent (page 48—book; p.2, typed) taken out Poges's imitation—"cuckoo cuckoo," and Stoke's "too whit too whoo." Regarding the new section between Poges and O'Killigain, just before Souhaun runs in about the roller, page 72 of the book, and the jointure given to it, it suits me allright.

Regarding the following doubt about the scene between Souhaun and O'Killigain, it is quite within the play, its positive spirit, and its subsequent change. It was, at the first, thought out and set down deliberately, and I could never agree to any alteration in it. It portrays, as it was intended to portray, a part of Autumn in Souhaun's life. It is quite within the sphere of O'Killigain's love for Avril that he should take an interest in a good-looking woman, other than his real choice. All intelligent Irishmen have an eye for a "comely-built lass" and O'Killigain is no exception. It is part of his readiness to admire all things that have within them the stimulus of admiration. He would do the same with Cloyne; and Avril would understand it, for tribute to a comely lass but adds to the value of his choice of her. So much of O'Killigain. As I said a moment ago, this is an autumn episode in Souhaun's life. It is not only natural, but inevitable that she should have been first attracted to O'Killigain, the young and the handsome. It is just as inevitable that, in her heart, she knew he wasnt for her. That is why I wrote the song, you asked me for, as it is written. Even Cloyne tries her hand at getting into touch with O'Killigain—the third chord in the attraction, Souhaun, the second, Avril the first. That is how I saw it, felt it, and set it down, and I cannot change it now. To do so would spoil the rhythm, and give discord to the orchestration. Besides, as I saw and heard it done, even at the rough rehearsal, it was a lovely and wistful scene. My dear Sam, think over it again.

3rd act scene between O'Killigain, 2nd Workman, Souhaun, and Avril—starting on Page 105 of the book:

Souhaun and 2nd Workman will have to remain still. There is nothing in that that isnt common in all plays worth more than a damn. You get these situations in the plays of Shaw, Strindberg, Ibsen, (in his best play, too—P. Gynt), Shakespeare, O'Neill, quite a lot of it in THE ICEMAN COMETH, and in crowds of other plays. Besides, in this connection, Avril and O'Killigain have had to stay still while S. and 2nd W. were talking together. The dialogue between O'Kill. and Avril lasts for but one page, and the attention of the audience will be transferred from S. and 2d W. over to them; just as in an orchestra many instruments go silent while a few play their piece that will soon be linked together again with the full assemble of instruments. The 'cello first (S. and 2nd Workman), then the violin (Avril and O'Kill.). This was the first difficulty that W. B. Yeats and Lady Gregory met in their first creation of the Abbey Theatre—the task of getting the actors to stay still. Yeats once thought (see his PLAYS AND CONTROVERSIES, I think) of putting the actors into barrels, and armed with a long pole, pushing them into any new position he wanted them to take.[1] He and the Old Lady overcame this difficulty, and sent into the world a number of the finest actors the world ever saw. Our newer "Abbey" actors seem to have gotten the old fear—those who never knew Yeats—, and so signs on it, The Abbey is a poor shadow of what it once was. If the dialogue be broken up, then it will be to the play's damage, bringing it closer to those plays of snappy dialogue which, when once withdrawn, are dead forever. I believe that this play will live for a long time, but only if it remains an O'Casey play, done in the O'Casey manner. So I cannot agree to the proposal of dividing the dialogue.

Your last point—"A need for a clearer statement", etc: I think that the points mentioned are implicit in the play; much more clearly, for instance, than points are in the plays of Jean Jaques Bernard, who very dimly and vaguely implies the reason and outcome of his plays. Actually, the play shows and says quite loudly, I think, that the two women arent being "asked to give up material security and comfort for the insecurity of living a clean, independent, and progressive life." The manner of their life, in the play, has no comfort, and at home with such men, it wouldnt have any comfort either. Such as they—the two girls—couldnt possibly have any security. They could be dispensed with at a moment's notice. And the life they fled away to to live isnt "progressive," in any social or political sense. It is Life, and that is enough. I confess I dont like the word "clean"—it sounds too much like the word used by the unco' guid—"clean plays, clean literature, clean pictures." Life is never wholly what we call clean, and, to be life, it must take in all that which is part of our humanity—the soiled with what is shining white; the curse with the blessing; the song with the sigh. To state explicitly and plainly all the incidents, impulses, manners, and actions, would be to turn it into the "well-made play." I shouldnt like this at all. I'm sure, as any mortal man can be sure, that the play, as it is now, including the changes already made, is more than sufficient to make a stirring event on the English stage—and the American stage too. To alter it any further would separate it from the O'Casey style.

[1] W. B. Yeats, "The Irish Dramatic Movement," *Plays and Controversies* (1923), p. 20:

> I had imagined such acting, though I had not seen it, and had once asked a dramatic company to let me rehearse them in barrels that they might forget gesture and have their minds free to think of speech for a while. The barrels, I thought, might be on castors, so that I could shove them about with a pole when the action required it.

I dont say this of myself. I have good warrant from others. I altered the play (as I shall show you when I see you again) when it went to the printers to go into COLLECTED PLAYS; I added some since, and took out some; I did the alterations we suggested together; and I am convinced that these changes have been enough. About the others: You know what B[rooks] Atkinson thought of it, what [George Jean] Nathan thought of it, I'm sure. I havent their tributes handy, but they were fine ones. I came across Richard Watts's tribute today, accidently, when I was looking for the only one of the original copies left. His opinion written in the HER-ALD TRIBUNE, Sunday, Feb. 2nd, 1941, is: "PURPLE DUST, which Eddie Dowling is planning to produce, *is a rich, beautiful, and humorous work*." The one thing that prevented it being done then was its references to England, and that because the war was on, and it might make American audiences uncomfortable that this beautiful play would provide comfort to the foes of democracy. "Despite its merits, I feel it would be a mistake to produce PURPLE DUST until the Nazis are defeated." Well, the Nazis are defeated, and the sting to England has been taken out of it; so with these voices proclaiming its merits, I feel, Sam, avic, I can not go farther in the way of alterations.

Dont be afraid of the technique (standing still). Here's a quotation from an Introduction to Odets's play, AWAKE AND SING, which I came across accidentally yesterday. It is written by Harold Clurman, who, I'm sure you know; he is opposing the idea that Odets is like Chekhov, and asserting that Odets is more like O'Casey: "They have a tendency to give to all the occurrences the same importance and sympathy. If we be disconcerted at first by such treatment, it is not only because we are used to more rigid patterns, but because these playwrights are saying something through their plays that demands their special technique." [2] Near enough to the truth this. The audiences are more used to it now. There is Eliot and there is Christopher Fry, though neither of these yet, in my opinion, have acquired the faculty of gambolling about the stage with ease.

Reverting to the expression "clean," it is odd that, theologically, the life of the women with the two boyos, P. and S. is cleaner than that to be lived with the 2nd W. and O'Kill. They did the former for a living, and found no pleasure in the sex connection. On the other hand, great pleasure is foreshown in the attachement to the 2nd W. and to O'Kill., so that this is by far the greater sin. There is the theological implication, Sam: the more pleasure derived from the attachement, the bigger the sin—unless, of course, they were united under the ceremonial and matrimonial blessing of the Church. So a priest would tell me and you that the latter state of Souhaun and Avril would be worse than the first; but dont say anything of this to the Caste. Mum's the word, here. To me, the one weak spot in the play is the Postmaster; he doesnt seem to come near the character; but maybe he is better now.

[2] Harold Clurman, Introduction to Clifford Odets's *Six Plays* (1939).

I feel that the play will be a success; I never felt about the others as I do about this one—I mean, of course, a material success, a commercial success. I am known much better than I was when the last one appeared; and it—RED ROSES FOR ME [3]—was a fine success, and would have been far better if Kieron O'Hanrahan (Moore) and others didnt leave it for a film. Besides, Brooks Atkinson is here now, and, I feel sure, will do a lot to arouse interest in the venture.

Who is Boorne? What paper does he write for? What a lout he must be, though he is undoubtedly Irish. I never said what he atributes to me; never even met the man to my knowledge. The fellow who wrote "Mr. O'Cathasaigh comes to town." Showing off his knowledge of Irish, though no one with any knowledge of it would stick a "Mr." in front of the name as he writes it. He should have written "Mac Ui Cathasaigh", etc.; or Seaghan O'Cath., etc. Where ignorance is bliss!

It is fine what you say about PICTURE POST. I am sure I'll get a lot of publicity which, at any rate, wont do any harm; though I hope most of it will be (and is sure to be) better than the pauperised writing of Bill Boorne.

Yis sir; me birthday was on the 31st of March.

My love to Charlotte, to Abby, to Zoe, and to you.

Yours very sincerely,
Sean

[3] See O'Casey's letter to Una Gwynn Albery, 6 March 1946, note 1.

To Sam Wanamaker

TS. WANAMAKER

TOTNES, DEVON

5 APRIL 1953

My dear Sam,

Charade, is it? Oh, Sam, Sam, Sam! I dont write charades. PURPLE DUST is a comedy, if ever there was one. Here's a quotation from THE SPECTATOR, Tory paper (24 Feb, 1950) "*The strength of O'Casey is the strength of the Elizabethans.* In an age nurtured on the slick telegraphese of the cinema and of Coward's dialogue, he gives memorable language. *It is the language that stabs straight to the heart of those who still have ears with which to hear.* He blends realism with expressionism, is ever fertile of ideas, and ever seems to have more material than can be squeezed into the pint-pot of a play. *Yet his plays are carefully constructed*

and not jerry-built." [1] My italics. Everyone who has read P. DUST calls
it a comedy—Nathan, R. Watts, Junr.; and here's a quote from Brooks—
"P. DUST has never been produced in Broadway, though it is a more prac-
ticable play than COCKADOODLE DANDY. It is closer to both people
and theater. Under the robustiousness of the satiric *comedy* and behind
the occasional scenes of phantasy, there is a tangible problem to deal with
and recognisable people to fool with." [2] As I said in my previous letter,
people are now more accustomed to this kind of playwriting—witness Fry
and Eliot there, and T. Wilder and Miller in your Country. It would seem
that they have been influenced by what I have written; or so, Brooks
seems to think. He says "Since the time when Mr. O'Casey wrote THE
SILVER TASSIE, something very crucial to the drama has been happening; theater-goers have acquired considerable agility of mind. The trend
of the drama has been away from naturalism toward flexibility of style,
conspicuously so in the works of Thornton Wilder, Tennessee Williams,
and most recently in Arthur Miller's DEATH OF A SALESMAN. The
form of THE SILVER TASSIE is accordingly more congenial than it was
when Mr. O'Casey broke with his previous work and composed this drama
in a more subjective manner." [3] If I had thought for a moment that the
songs I wrote would have moved the plays an inch towards the shape of a
"charade," I should never have written them. I give you one more quotation—from Nathan's THE THEATRE BOOK OF THE YEAR—1950–
1951; pages 89–92: "With the exception of the matchless O'Casey, there
is no one among living English-speaking dramatists who equals Fry's ability
to weave words together with more music, to weave into them at the same
time so wryly amusing a look at life, and to make the whole warble like
nightingales in a theater of sparrows. . . . This Fry is such a fellow. Like
O'Casey, though very far from being anywhere near his equal as a dramatist, delights in the beautiful sounds of words."

If I hate one thing more than another, it's talking of or writing about
my work, and only do so, Sam, when I think I must; so forgive this ego-
tism conjured up to do away with the thought that PURPLE DUST is
anything in the way of a charade. If we change it any more, it will cease
to be the play that has been praised by so many; and, in my opinion, would
then stand a far less chance of succeeding. Of course, what those above
have said may be wrong—they aren't infallible; but, naturally, I am inclined to go by them, to look to where they point.

By the time you get this, I dare say, and hope, you have seen Brooks.
If you see him after getting this, tell him I hope to see him when I go to
London. Eileen has already written to Charlotte and to you about our com-

[1] John Garrett, *The Spectator,* 24 February 1950, a review of the *Collected Plays,* Vols. I, II.
[2] Brooks Atkinson, "Case of O'Casey," *New York Times,* 16 September 1951, a review of the *Collected Plays,* Vols. III, IV.
[3] *Ibid.*

ing earlier than we had first thought of going. The children are on holiday, and this lets us go, bringing them along with us. They would like to get a glimpse of the rehearsals in progress, and, I'm sure, you will permit them to have a look at the way the theatre works without the lights.

My love to all.
As ever,
Sean

To Brooks Atkinson

MS. ATKINSON

TOTNES, DEVON
7 APRIL 1953

My dear Brooks:

Greetings, comrade! True comrade to a vagabond playwright, & wandering singer of songs. I look forward (we all do) to seeing you soon. I'll ring you up when we come to London this week; and, then, shake hands with Oriana & you. I'm just entering in "Sunset & Evening Star" a song-prayer to W. Whitman, written in 1950.

Till I see you, my love.

As Ever,
Sean

SAINTLY SINNER, SING FOR US [1]

Walt Whitman, one of the world's good wishes
Is the one that wishes you here today,

To sing, shake hands to the world's peoples
To listen, cock-ear'd, in a way of wonder,

To all the others have got to say;
Then with your own embracing message,

Lead all correctly, or lead us astray;
For either is goodness with God, and gay,

Like song of a thrush or screech of a jay;
They'll mingle miles on, from each other learning

That life's delightful at work or play.
So enter in spirit the sharp contentions

[1] Originally published in the *New Statesman and Nation,* 16 December 1950; reprinted in *Sunset and Evening Star* (1954).

> Of brothers belling each other at bay;
> And soften the snout of the menacing cannon
>
> With the scent and bloom of a lilac spray.
>
> S. O'Casey

Sunday 19 November 1950
Totnes, Devon

To Brooks Atkinson

MS. ATKINSON

LONDON

21 APRIL 1953

My dear Brooks:

Rehearsals are now held in the Princes' Theatre, Lower Shaftesbury Avenue—going in direction of Covent Garden—at 2 till 5 P.M. and then from 7-30 to God knows when.

I've been very busy, and am a little tired; but I've just made a vow to take dinner from this day forth, so help me God, only with those who have an abiding place in my old heart.

"Walt Whitman" [1] is a grand book, & I look forward to reading it under the Devon skies, when the fury has softened into a flowing production on the stage. I've taken

> Think not we give out yet,
> Forth from these snowy hairs
> We keep up yet the lilt.

as the motto for "Sunset & Evening Star." [2]

My deep love to Oriana & to you, a mhic mo chroidhe. [3]

As ever,
Sean

---

[1] *Poetry and Prose of Walt Whitman* (1949), edited by Louis Untermeyer.
[2] He changed his mind later, and used the following motto:

> You cannot prevent the birds of sadness from
> flying over your head, but you can prevent them
> building nests in your hair.
> Chinese Proverb

> I'm gonna wash 'em all outa ma hair.

[3] Dear friend of my heart.

To Roger McHugh

MS. McHUGH
[LONDON]
[24 APRIL 1953] [1]

Dear Roger,

Burn and blast the record you mentioned. It was the first & last time I did a broadcast.[2] It was to be an impromptu talk; but by the time it came on, I was tired rehearsing the time it took—pauses, a quick period, and scores of MS's.

Since then, last November, I did an hour & a half speaking chapters from biography, with a song thrown in for good measure, for a New York Firm, in the form of a gramaphone record. This was held up by American Customs, but, I understand, has now been released. I look forward to hearing my own voice prating.

I've read about Meldon's "Aisling," [3] and hope it may be a fine success. The difficulty is to go on writing plays, & keep on living. Experimenting playwrights get more stones than bread. More power to O'Faolain —he had a fine article, recently, in "LIFE." I've come across more than one instance of the effect of what, I think, [H. G.] Wells called "Irish ferocious chastity." If you ever come to Devon, I'll show you some curious letters written by an Irish lass "vowed" to chastity.[4]

I'm in the midst of rehearsals here in London, & haven't a bare minute to myself.

> *All the best,*
> *Yours very sincerely*
> *Sean*

---

[1] Postmarked date.

[2] "Playwright and Box Office," a discussion between Maurice Browne and Sean O'Casey, broadcast on BBC and printed in *The Listener,* 7 July 1938; reprinted in *Blasts and Benedictions* (1967).

[3] Maurice Meldon's *Aisling* opened in Dublin at the 37 Theatre Club on 4 April 1953, directed by Barry Cassin.

[4] See the letter from Miss Sheila ———— to O'Casey, 9 April 1945, note 1.

To Sam Wanamaker

TS. WANAMAKER

TOTNES, DEVON

28 APRIL 1953

Dear Sam,

Dont mind overmuch the Press reaction in Glasgow.[1]

You may remember that I mentioned doubts about reception in Glasgow while the rehearsals were proceeding. There, like Liverpool, there is a powerful section of the Roman Catholic Church which is organised to a man, and acts silently when it doesnt dare come into the open. Besides being as I say, the Press chaps there dont know much about drama. I imagine Edinburgh will be very different. As far as I know, there's no power of the R.C. Church there as in Glasgow, where the Irish are very numerous, and, I fear, pretty ignorant, and so under the thumb of the clerics, I'm sorry to say. In my opinion, Glasgow Press opinions dont count in any important way. Wherever R.C's are organised, one gets opposition, as was the case in Houston, Texas,[2] and Newcastle-on-Tyne,[3] in Durham. Wait till we see what Edinburgh thinks, though, of course, the real important place remains London. I should take out, however, the two repetitive songs which the 2nd W. and O'Kill. sing—you know the two I mean. So dont let Glasgow frighten us, Sam.

As ever,
Sean

[1] *Purple Dust* opened at the Theatre Royal, Glasgow, on 27 April 1953, presented by Sam Wanamaker and Thane Parker, directed by Wanamaker, music by Malcolm Arnold, dances by John Cranko. The cast: Liam Redmond as 1st Workman; Joseph O'Connor as 2nd Workman; John McDarby as 3rd Workman; Miles Malleson as Cyril Poges; Walter Hudd as Basil Stoke; Siobhan McKenna as Avril; Eithne Dunne as Souhan; Dermot Kelly as Barney; Doreen Keogh as Cloyne; Shamus Locke as O'Killigain; Peter Garstin as Yellow-Bearded Man; Harry Hutchinson as Canon Chreehewel; Bartlet Mullins as Postmaster.

The play was reviewed unfavorably in the *Glasgow Evening News,* 28 April, by "W. C. G.," who attacked the production more than the playwright.

[2] See O'Casey's letter to M. W. Bennit, 14 February 1950.

[3] See O'Casey's letter to George Jean Nathan, 26 May 1951, note 2.

To Christopher Murray Grieve [1]

MS. GRIEVE

TOTNES, DEVON

1 MAY 1953

My dear Chris,

I expect to be in Edinburgh on Sunday, the 3rd, but must come back here by Wednesday. I just want to have a look at the play to see how it goes on the stage now. I hear it didn't go too well in Glasgow. However, that's not new news to you or to me, for we have ever been fighting adversity. Your home in Lanarkshire seems to be far more than a mile from Edinburgh town; so don't put yourself to a lot of trouble or a long journey to see me. I hope you are managing to slow down a little, & able to enjoy more interludes of rest and reading.

My deep love to you & yours.

As ever,
Sean

[1] Christopher Murray Grieve (1892–1978), the Scottish poet, Communist, and nationalist who wrote under the pseudonym of Hugh MacDiarmid. The dedication to *Sunset and Evening Star* (1954) reads: "To my dear friend Hugh MacDiarmid, Alba's Poet and one of Alba's first men."

To George Jean Nathan

MS. CORNELL

TOTNES, DEVON

11 MAY 1953

My very dear George:

Here I am back again in Totnes after five weeks rehearsing "Purple Dust" in London, & a wild time in Edinburgh where the play went on a tour, before coming to London.[1] Here I am, still fairly full of Scotch whis-

[1] After its one-week run in Glasgow, *Purple Dust* went on tour, on its way to London, playing a series of one-week engagements at the King's Theatre in Edinburgh on 4 May, the Grand Theatre in Blackpool on 11 May, and the Theatre Royal in Brighton on 18 May. And as O'Casey explains in his 23 May letter to Peter Newmark, the play folded after the run in Brighton because of a lack of funds and poor reviews, and never got to London. For O'Casey's account of the tour, see his impressions of "The English Pilgrimage" in his letter to Brooks Atkinson, 20 September 1953.

key, in addition to a quantity of a special brand, called Drambuidie—pronounced Dram boo ee; and full, too, of the Gaelic songs—lovely & melodious—sung informally at gatherings in this home of that Scot, & that home of this Scot. I embraced Scotland's greatest poet, Hugh McDiarmuid, whom I've known for 23 years. The play itself is puzzling—doesn't seem so good on the stage as it seems to be in the book. A fine "Poges" during rehearsals, but not so good on the public stage. A bad "Postmaster" and "Yellow-bearded Man"; the rest very good. Reception divided—Half take it enthusiastically to their bosom; half reject it as "poor, illformed, & stale in its humour." I'm hoping it may go for awhile in London; long enough to bring in a little money. If it doesn't, we're going to have a difficult time. However, there's hope still. But I'm discovering how hard it is to get comedy played properly. There aren't a lot of B[arry]. Fitzgeralds or [Arthur] Sinclairs knocking about.

I do hope you are keeping fit. We had a most enjoyable time with Brooks & Oriana [Atkinson] in London. My deep love to you.

As ever,
Sean

To Roger McHugh

MS. MCHUGH

TOTNES, DEVON
18 MAY 1953

Dear Roger,
Thanks for kind wishes. There is a one-act play—"Hall of Healing," Poor Law Dispensary experience—in Vol III of "Collected Plays"; & two more—"Bedtime Story" and "Time to Go"—in Vol IV; one of which might do for your Dramatic Society.

I've had a whirl of a week in Edinburgh—first visit there: two Ceilidhte;[1] beautiful Gaelic songs; many clan kilts; scotch whiskey, including a few drams of Drambuidhe—a potent and tasty liqueur made from a "secret" recipe in the Isle of Skye. A charming City.

All good wishes.
Yours sincerely,
Sean

---

[1] *Céilidhithe,* plural of *céilidhe* (modern spelling, *céilí,* pronounced kay-lee,) a party of song and dance.

To Peter Newmark

MS. NEWMARK

TOTNES, DEVON

23 MAY 1953

My dear Peter,

Oh, Peter, Peter! This canard about Charlie and Sean has brought me congratulations and inquiries from the four quarters of the Globe; [1] from America & from Ireland—letters, telegrams, & phone-calls. There is nothing in it, as far as I know. I know absolutely nothing about it. Charlie came to see me while I was in London, and this, I imagine, caused the rumour—for damned publicity purposes—to be born & to float about like the downy seed of a noxious weed. During my chat with Charlie, he never once mentioned such a thing, even indirectly; & the idea never once crossed my mind. You can imagine how I felt when I read the first announcement in the Press, for, of course, I knew there wasn't the shadow of substance in it. Since then, friends have been sending me cuttings announcing it, & congratulating me. And, now, your letter comes along (Thanks, a lot, all the same, for your very kind and sincere good wishes.) As for the play—it has lost me a lot instead of giving me something. There wasn't enough money to carry it to London, & so it folded up, peering through the City gates, & longing for strength to go a little farther, but failing to win the strength to do so. I never worked so hard at a play in my life, attending all day five weeks rehearsals in London, & one week in Edinburgh; interviewed, photographed, & tortured.

Here I am again, the worse for wear, & convinced that my last play has been written—I've more important work to do.

---

[1] In her "Show Talk" column in the *Glasgow Evening News,* 27 April 1953, commenting on the opening of *Purple Dust,* Mamie Crichton wrote the following remarks about Wanamaker, O'Casey, and Charlie Chaplin:

CHAPLIN FILM

But last night before he took dress rehearsal of "Purple Dust" at the Theatre Royal, Sam Wanamaker hinted that Hollywood film-makers may be forestalled in acquiring the rights by their erstwhile colleague, Charles Chaplin, who has just announced that he will not return to the United States and will make films in Europe.

Wanamaker said that while Chaplin was in London last week he sent innumerable invitations to author Sean O'Casey to have a meal with him. Seventy-three-year-old O'Casey, sitting in on rehearsals, replied that he was too busy.

So last Wednesday night, about 11 o'clock Chaplin turned up at rehearsal, sat beside O'Casey and as the play proceeded indicated his interest in it as a possible basis for his next film to be made in England.

Just now, I'm writing an article, "The Arts Among The Multitude" for an American Arts Magazine; [2] & have been asked to do one on "Laughter" by a Canadian Magazine.[3] Well, there's quite a lot to laugh at, including myself.

I do hope you and Monica are doing well, & are as happy in Guilford as circumstances will allow. Anyway, I think Peace has won, & that's a lot for us mortals to begin with. My love, & Eileen's love to you both.

As ever,
Sean

[2] "The Arts Among the Multitude," *7 Arts*, No. 2 (1955), ed. Fernando Puma; reprinted in *The Green Crow* (1956).
[3] "Laughter," *Saturday Night* (Toronto), 3 October 1953; reprinted as "The Power of Laughter: Weapon Against Evil" in *The Green Crow* (1956).

To Sam Wanamaker

TS. WANAMAKER

TOTNES, DEVON

26 MAY 1953

Dear Sam,

A bad situation for both of us.[1] Here I am broken-hearted—nearly, and you, I'm sure feeling the same damned way. It cant be helped now; and we just must face it, fight it, and overcome it—God knows how; but overcome it, in some way, we must. Forget it all as soon as we can, and go on to other things. It was a grievous disappointment. Pity I didnt first take the American offer, for its acceptance would have saved you and me a hell-long time of trouble, anxiety, and hard work; and a fearful waste of time. But—as we thought—I chose the better way, which so often turns out to be the worst one. Still there was good hope and bright prospects in the beginning in play and Caste, and the decision, at least, was a reasonable one. It is a puzzle how the play failed to succeed, even on tour, though, of course, it did reasonably well in Blackpool. I thought the London Drama Critics would do something (say something at least) to provoke or persuade the play's advent into London; but they, as far as I saw and read, stayed dumb. One would imagine they would have done a lot to encourage the production of, at least, an unusual play among the so many pitiful ones seen so often on the London stage. Brooks Atkinson, Nathan, and R. Watts wouldnt have been so silently-indifferent had they occupied the places of the London critics.

[1] See O'Casey's letter to George Jean Nathan, 11 May 1953, note 1.

I am still being congratulated on the idea that C. Chaplin is to film the play—even VARIETY in the U.S.A. has carried the news to its readers. It is curious how this canard spread about everywhere. Makes one's feelings worse. It's just as well the play didnt go to the Arts Theatre; that wouldnt have been much good to you or to me. I certainly shouldnt have been enthusiastic about it. All our little plans have gone west now, and we are far worse than we were; for I was confident that PURPLE DUST would hunt uncertainty away for a year or so. It was a sore tumble, but all we can do is to work ourselves up to our feet again.

One thing I am positively sorry for—that you asked Mrs. [Dorothy] Elmhirst and Sydney Bernstein for financial help to get the play to London. Even had I been sure of their support, I shouldnt have asked them. It would be almost unbearable for me to be under an obligation to them. I have been always like that—rather to suffer than to ask for help; foolish pride, I daresay; but there it is, and, I'm afraid, there it stays. Well, Sam agradh,[2] there's nothing for it but to forget, and to work at other things. We did our best, and to do one's best is enough and as much as one can do. My love to Charlotte, to Abby, and to Zoe.

Yours very sincerely,
Sean

Thanks for cuttings—they are poor examples of drama criticism.

[2] My dear Sam.

To Dr. Frank Morrell

MS. MORRELL

TOTNES, DEVON
1 JUNE 1953

Dear Frank,

Thank you very much for your very welcome gift of ham as a May-Day Greeting: a very fine greeting indeed.[1] It came under the name of a Mr. Weiss, a name not mentioned in your note. I will write a note of thanks, too, to Paul and Nan, to Herbert and Edith soon as I can snatch another second from the many things crowding in on top of me, & flooding a way under my feet. I've been busy with a play which went for 4 weeks on tour, & was to come to London; but a friend who guaranteed some

[1] The gift was sent by Dr. Morrell, Paul and Nan Ross of New York, Herbert and Edith Kurz of Brooklyn.

money, failed to keep his promise, & the play had to halt outside the city. We have some hope of getting it to London in August or September. I hope so, for the play had much labour & time poured into it—5 weeks rehearsal in London; & one in Edinburgh, where I drank quite a lot of Scotch, roared out Gaelic songs, and made many friends among the poets, the bards, & the miners, who were having a May-day celebration there. Now I work on my biography, & have sent an article for the next number of "THE 7 ARTS," called "The Arts Among the Multitude." [2]

Thanks again, Frank, & all the best to you.

As ever,
Sean

[2] "The Arts Among the Multitude," *7 Arts*, No. 2 (1954), selected and edited by Fernando Puma; reprinted in *The Green Crow* (1956).

To Paul and Nan Ross [1]

MS. ROSS

TOTNES, DEVON
3 JUNE 1953

Dear Nan & Dear Paul:

Frank [Morrell] has written to say that you helped in sending us the ham that came as a very welcome assistance in providing a number of tasty meals for Eileen, meself, & our three children.

I give you both our hearty thanks for your kind thought and kind gift. I am very busy just now with a world of things—home affairs, affairs (Peace) abroad, biography, an article, "Art among the Multitude" for New York's Magazine "7 Arts" which I hope they may print, and, as well, trying to cope with letters daily coming to me from all parts known, & from God knows where.

Thank you both again.

Yours very sincerely,
Sean O'Casey

[1] Paul and Nan Ross, Brooklyn, New York. Paul L. Ross (1902–78), lawyer and social activist, made an unsuccessful race for mayor of New York City in 1950, and led a successful fight to integrate the Stuyvesant Town apartment complex. Active in his law practice, he frequently defended left-wing figures in civil rights cases. A native of the Ukraine, Mr. Ross was eight when his parents brought him to New York.

To Eric Gorman

TS. GORMAN

TOTNES, DEVON

8 JUNE 1953

Dear Eric Gorman,

Of course, you can have SHADOW OF A GUNMAN, if you wish to do it.[1] There wasnt any necessity to ask permission. Royalties from The Abbey are as welcome as the flowers in May. You can do in Dublin any play of mine—three-act, two-act, or one-act, when you like, on the usual terms, of course. I hope next year's Tostal will be a greater success than this Year's.[2] I imagine that Ireland should concentrate on literature, art, pottery, and the drama, and such things, rather than on decorations. These tend to be lavish, must be, according to present tastes, and are costly. We, if we're to shine, must invent, evolve, create newer ideas outside of competition with those lands richer than we. All the best to you. Hope your two new plays will be fine ones.

Yours sincerely,
Sean O'Casey

[1] A double bill of *The Shadow of a Gunman* and the first performance of M. J. Molloy's *The Paddy Pedlar* opened at the Abbey Theatre on 5 September 1953.
[2] See O'Casey's letter to Gorman, 27 May 1952, note 2.

To Eric Gorman

TC. O'CASEY

[TOTNES, DEVON]

14 JUNE 1953

Dear Eric Gorman,

In a recent letter I said that you could do any of my plays that the Theatre wished to do. The letter was written hastily in a very busy hour, and went too far in permission.

COCKADOODLE DANDY and PURPLE DUST are not available for performance (not that you would be likely to do either), for they are under contract.

I'm sure this correction will put you to no inconvenience.

With all good wishes,
Yours sincerely,
Sean O'Casey

To Raymond Marriott [1]

MS. TEXAS

TOTNES, DEVON

17 JUNE 1953

Dear Raymond,

Thank you for the programme of "Three in a Row," [2] which I was glad to get. I'm glad they did them well. Odd how anything like "Time to Go" hunts producers into hesitation. I suppose it is natural to be at home only with what is familiar. One must be patient. By the way "End of the Beginning" is a folktale, known in many parts of Europe. I found it in Gaelic in a Book, "An baile seo 'gainn"—"In Our Townland." [3] Of course, I've added a lot to it—an additional character & all the dialogue. The reviewer of the D.W. didn't know; & an Irish Reviewer mentioned it as one of O'Casey's usual slum plays. A great patriot, he'd never read the tale in his own Gaelic.

Thanks for all the very kind things said by you on the Programme.

All warm wishes to you.
Yours very sincerely,
Sean O'Casey

[1] Raymond Marriott (1911–   ), drama critic, assistant editor of *The Stage* (London).

[2] *Three in a Row*—three of O'Casey's one-act plays, *Time to Go, End of the Beginning,* and *Hall of Healing*—was produced at the Unity Theatre, London, on 22 May 1953.

[3] For O'Casey's explanation of the source of the theme of *End of the Beginning,* in *An Baile Seo 'Gainne-ne,* by An Seabhac (Padraig O Siochfhradha), see his letter to the *Irish Time,* 23 February 1937, Vol. I, pp. 651–52.

To Seumas Scully

MS. SCULLY

TOTNES, DEVON

17 JUNE 1953

My dear Seumas,

Thanks again for the papers, & many more thanks for the details about the Irish Film Institute—they may be useful to me later on. The "play" [*Purple Dust*] didn't come to London. The money backers put into it wasn't enough to cover cost of a London production, so one more disappointment is added to the cairn of them heaped together during a life-time. However, war isn't so near as it has been; the Red Flag with its Hammer and Sickle has appeared in Spithead (when's it going to fly at Dunleary?); &, so, there's cause for rejoicing. I hear that The Irish Press has mentioned Czechoslovakia in a praiseworthy way. Aha, Seumas, we're nearer, nearer to you! There's no chance of any of us showing up in Ireland this year—funds too low. Anyway, Ireland will have enough to do entertaining Bing C[rosby] when he alights there, with a sash of rosary beads around him.

Eithne Dunne is a very intelligent lass.[1] I met her for the first time during rehearsals. Indeed, I met all the newer Irish Players for the first time then. You see, Seumas, how time & age separates us from a younger generation. They were all fine lads & lasses, &, I think, I got on well with them; but it is irritating that they hadn't the fortune to get to London. Most of them were very good. I have almost finished my last biographical vol, & will soon be sending the MS to Macmillan's.

Eileen & Shivaun send their love, so does Niall; & so do I.

As ever,
Sean

[1] Eithne Dunne played the role of Souhan in Sam Wanamaker's production of *Purple Dust*. For details of the production, see O'Casey's letter to Wanamaker, 28 April 1953, note 1.

To Horace Reynolds

TS. REYNOLDS

TOTNES, DEVON
19 JUNE 1953

Dear Horace,

Thanks ever so much for your letter, cheque, value of $75.00. (royalty payment on performance of COCKADOODLE DANDY),[1] and Press-cutting. I didnt suggest any alternative, and would never have suggested the play done, for the "Cock" is one, the best, of my few hopes for an American production that would ease things a lot for me. All these one-sided productions of plays are dangerous insomuch as they often spoil a chance of what one hopes for; they are usually, in the nature of things,

[1] *Cock-a-Doodle Dandy* was performed by the students of Emerson College, Boston, on 4–6 June 1953, directed by Mrs. Gertrude Binley Kay, Professor of Drama.

not well done; people see them; are disappointed, and bang goes a chance of a more profitable production. Dont do it again, me son, without getting into touch with me. I dont suppose this performance did the chance of a New York performance any harm, however. Sam's vision of Purple Dust didnt come off; one of the backers having promised help, backed out of it when the play was on the move, and there wasnt enough to bring the play to London. "So there it ends," as Poges remarks in one of his scenes— a big disappointment to us all, and a big loss to me. I had refused a New York offer, before signing up with Sam, an offer that gave a 1500 dollar advance. I daresay it cant be helped. Sam did his best, and I never worked so hard over a play before, attending rehearsals, writing new songs, going up to Edinburgh—a grand city, where I made quite a lot of new friends at ceilidhithe, where many Gaelic songs were sung and stories told, and the barley brew went round to foster animation.

It's all over now, and, somehow, life will have to make up the loss some way some day, aha, me son. I've written an article "Art Among the Multitude" for the Magazine "7 Arts," and the Editor has written to say it's a fine one; and I've just written another for The Statesman (maybe they wont like it), funny, called "Jeeps Be Jeepers." [2] I'm glad you brought but two reviewers to see the Cock. My good wishes to Rod Nordell. Kay is, alas, right in her thought about the ecclesiastical spectre. In Ireland, not Communism, but the spectre of the Church is the menace. Kay's a wise lass. My love to Peggy and to John, and to all the two of them love.

Give my thanks to Mrs G. Binley Kay for all the trouble she took with the play, and for her interest in my work. How I wish I was as well off as to be able to allow any production I thought well of; but economic laws are mine enemy as well as yours, and of all of us.

As ever.
Sean

[2] Sean O'Casey, "Jeeps, Be Jeepers," *New Statesman and Nation,* 18 July 1953; for two other versions of this comic skit, see "Outside an Irish Window," *Sunset and Evening Star* (1954), and *The Bishop's Bonfire* (1955), Act 2.

To Gordon Rogoff

MS. ROGOFF

TOTNES, DEVON

27 JUNE 1953

Dear Gordon,

Glad to hear you are well and active. This must be a short letter, for I have a helluva lot to do. I read your thesis hastily, & liked it. I've lent it to a Plymouth Schoolmaster who is to give summer lectures on my work, who asked me a lot of questions I'm tired of answering. Told him it was a fine exposition from which to build ideas about my work. I don't mind what you said about "Star Turns Red"—you may be right. Nathan said it was "the feeblest play O'Casey has written"; so you are in grand company; except that he regarded it from the drama point of view; you, largely, from the political point of view. In fact, as Nathan observed—Preface to "5 Famous Irish Plays," Random House—it was a prophetic play. Written long before the war, what it implied has come to life in Czechoslovakia, Hungary, Bulgaria, Roumania, Poland, & China. The Red Star shines over them all. I couldn't advise you about things in the U.S.A. I don't think they can last, even there. The theatre profession is woefully overcrowded, & will be till saner controls grip it, & bring it to an expression of art rather than as a means of making money. Still one must fight on, for changes must be forced from present conditions. I think you do well to go home to join your family. My love to them all & to you.

Yours very sincerely.
Sean O'Casey

P.S. Your Thesis is relatively unimportant. What you continue to do is all-important.

P.P.S. Always put your address on your letter. I had to hunt out the envelope to get it. You might lose a job some day by neglecting to do this.

To Chancellor of the Exchequer

TC. O'CASEY

[TOTNES, DEVON]
28 JUNE 1953

The Right Honorable, the Chancellor of the
Exchequer, House of Commons, London

Dear Sir,

I hope you may kindly read what follows, and, if you have time, that you would give it a few moments' consideration:

I have been resident in England for the last 28 years, and during that time, each year, like everyone else, or almost everyone else, I have paid taxes levied yearly. They havent been paid "on the nail," but they have been paid off when circumstances allowed, and, at the moment, he who writes this letter has cleared off all that had been owing. Recently, for the past four years, however, things have been made difficult by the curious attitude of a local Head Inspector of Taxes, who, to my mind, acts in a way contrary to the spirit of the law calling on citizens to meet their dues. I give the following instances:

In June, 1952, I received a visit from a Collector, who had visited me on previous occasions, a civil and courteous man, accompanied by one who I found out later was a bailiff. The sum at the time owing was £150, from which was deducted £25 sent to the Collector by cheque the previous night. I suspected the man was a bailiff, but, not being sure, asked him if he were one. He replied only that "bailiffs in England were very different from bailiffs in Ireland" (a difference no one save himself saw). He nosed around the room, among the books, asking me "if I had any rare sets?" Finally, he offered a document to me, and I signed on being told it was all a mere formality. When these two had gone, I found, hours after, a distraining order on the table, demanding full payment within 5 days, or, as the back of the slip warned, "typewriters, original Mss, and sets of books" would be taken and sold. The amount wasnt paid in full within the time specified, but was paid off in sums of £50, 40, 20, etc. In the meantime, it was discovered I had overpaid the sum of £40 odd, and, in the end of the payment, £1.3.6 went to the amount due for 2nd period.

In April, 1953, a sum of £47 was due out of £174. Again came the two visitors, the bailiff nosing around my books—many of which had been bought for the price of a much-needed meal—till I stopped him with a few vehement phrases. I asked the Collector, a Mr. Mason, how much was owed. He said £49 odd, never telling me that part of this was a bailiff's fee. I took him to mean that that was the amount of the Tax owed, and gave him a cheque for it. This was on the 12 of June. On the 15 of June, I got a receipt for the amount paid; and with this was enclosed an Order of Restraint, dated the 13 of June, which said that, if the amount wasnt paid within five days, the following articles would be seized and sold: Typewriters, books, bookcase, two rugs (one of them 28 years old) filing-cabinets, table, chairs, carpet (there isnt a carpet—the floor is covered with linoleum) desk, anglepoise lamp—all, be God, that I owned!

It seems odd to me that since the amount was paid on the 12th, the receipt for the amount dated the 13th, that the Distraining Order shouldnt have reached me till the 15th; in other words, how could the Order be valid after the money had been paid three days previously? I wrote to Mr. Mason pointing out these things to him, and received the following from the Chief Collector:

Office of Collector of Taxes,
1st Floor, Castle Chambers, Hr. Union Street, Torquay, Devon.
S. O'Casey, Esq.,
Tingrith, Totnes, Devon

Dear Sir,

22nd June, 1953.

Schedule D 1st Instal. 1952/53

I have been handed your letter addressed to my Collector, Mr. John Mason, but would point out that when he called on you on the 12 of June, he had with him the Bailiff who had accompanied him to distrain, but as you paid the fees they did not actually seize any definite goods, but it would appear the distraint was in order and the fees charged thereof correct.

Yours faithfully,

J. S. Sampson. Chief Collector.

May I ask how definite goods could have been seized since no distraining order was received, but came only on the 15th, while the fees had been paid on the 12th? And, even had the order been handed to me on the 12th, since the order says goods will be seized if payment is not made within five days from date of order—the 12th—how could any definite goods be seized on that day? What does the man's letter mean? What does "It would appear" mean? Should he not be sure in a matter like this one?

Again, isnt it odd that in the instance of a distraint of a sum of £154 the goods marked for seizure should number only 4 items, while the seizure order for £47 enumerates 12 items? All, in fact, I own, except the bed housing me when I sleep. Doesnt this "appear" (to use the Chief Collector's phrase) to have something of malice in it? Again, isnt it damned stupid to make an order for the seizure of the "definite goods," the seizure of which would leave me utterly unable to work so as to pay off the very sum of money due to the Revenue?

It is ironical to note that, in the case of the £47 owed, I had, and have still, Tax Credit Notes, which should have been returned when reclaimed, or redeemed, but which I didnt bother to do, covering an amount which would offset the amount due in Tax.

I hope, sir, you do not stand for this sort of bullying persecution. I dont believe you do. A record on my part of 28 years as a taxpayer (one year a tax of £1200) is surely enough to show that there is no intention on my part to evade payment, though I like paying tax no more than most persons. On one occasion when the amount due was £250, I found myself interviewing Mr. Crusoe and Mr. Lowry of Victory House, Kingsway, London, who told me then that it was clear I had made every effort to pay what was due, and that they would bother me no more, but leave it to myself to pay when circumstances allowed it.

It may be that Sampson considers an Irishman something of an alien, and he may be right. He may, as some do, resent it, thinking that I, as some do, live on the English people. I dont, and owe nothing to this in this respect. More than eighty per cent of my income comes from the

U.S.A., and half of the remaining percentage from my own country; so that I pay in tax more than I get from the country in which I live.

I respectfully suggest that I shouldnt be subject to this bullying pressure on the part of one, who, to me, is an ignorant and unimaginative beaurocrat (spelling deliberate).

Certainly, if this Bailiff comes again, I shall not permit his paws to roam over the books so precious to me; and, if he carries away anything, he'll have to carry me away with them, a job that wont be quite so easy as he may think it to be.

> *Yours sincerely,*
> *Sean O'Casey*

To J. C. Trewin

TS. TREWIN

TOTNES, DEVON

13 JULY 1953

My dear John,

I am quite agreeable that you should use the quotations [1] mentioned in your letter to me. Sorry your typewriter is misbehaving—a lot of things are behaving badly these days. I hope Macmillans will agree to the quotations, too.

I am very sorry to hear of your departure from *The Observer.* Seems lousy to me that you should be shunted after sixteen years service. Perhaps it's for the better, anyway. My opinion is that The O. and I. V. [Ivor] Brown were having (and had) a bad influence on you. I seemed to see in your tiny notices some resemblance of style to that of I. V.'s. You have your own style, so use it, and save your soul. I knew The Hon. David Astor well some years ago—then a very intelligent, charming lad; though, to me, a little timid of his own opinions. Seems to me that he now screens his opinions behind those of I. V. It's a pity, if this be so; for he has enough intelligence to be himself in all things—making many mistakes, of course, like all of us. I'm busy just now with 6th vol of biography, "Sunset and Evening Star." I'm sorry myself about *Purple Dust,* but I'm so used to disappointments that one more doesnt take more than one feather outa me. No, I

---

[1] Passages from *Juno and the Paycock, Purple Dust,* and *Cock-a-Doodle Dandy,* to be used in Trewin's book, *Dramatists of Today* (1953).

wont be able to go to Bideford. Too many things to do—writing, washing up, peeling spuds; and too old.
My love.

Sean

Hope you havent lost (or wont lose) much of a salary when you go from O.—this is the serious side of it. After sixteen years! You see how badly writers need a Trades Union, a vigorous one, right in the centre of militant Labour. We have all kept ourselves to ourselves far too much, like the graduates of our Universities. Our "artistic" independence is a costly cod.

Sean

To Elizabeth Freundlich [1]

TS. FREUNDLICH

TOTNES, DEVON

16 JULY 1953

Dear friend,

Thank you very much for your letter of July 8th. It is very odd how the hatred of, or fear of, *The Silver Tassie* has persisted. It has lasted now for twenty-eight years, expressed in Dublin, and London, and now in Vienna and Berlin. But I am fain to believe that the opposition was nor Dublin, London, Vienna, or Berlin: it came from parties, interested, one way or another, in things that do not belong to the peace of God or to the peace of man. They lie and the truth is not in them who say that the play has nothing to tell after the second World War; it has more to say than it ever had, and that is why they cry out against it. Its need today is not less, but more since the second World War devastated and destroyed so much of what the first World War left standing. It tells too much, and that is why they hate it. If they think a newer play is needed to depict, or even to suggest, the greater devastation of the last war, then let one of the critics

---

[1] Elizabeth Freundlich, Hornbachstr. 54, Zurich 8, Switzerland, who, with Gunther Anders, had translated *The Silver Tassie* into German. In her 8 July letter, she gave a report of the production of the play, as *Der Preispokal,* at the Schiller Theater in West Berlin on 20 June 1953, directed by Fritz Kortner. There was considerable uproar and a near riot in the theatre on the stormy first night, partly as a protest against O'Casey and the theme of his play, partly as an objection by Catholic groups on grounds of blasphemy, and partly as an anti-Semitic attack against Kortner's return to the Berlin theatre.

write it. It is not only a Christian duty, it is a moral one to try to stop any further devastation. Even the last war has shown that the day of victory for one side or another is over forever. No one side can ever win again, so even that sombre satisfaction is lost—and a good job, too. Another war would almost, if not quite, annihilate both sides; indeed, it might well destroy the world utterly. Every speaker touching on war has stated that fact; it isnt said alone by those called Pacificists; it has been said by Churchill, by Eisenhower, by Bidault, by Stalin, by the man in the street of Berlin, New York, London, Moscow, Vienna, Paris, and even Dublin. My *The Silver Tassie* isnt an exposition; it has simply turned out (unanticipated by me) to be a terrible prophecy. The facts of war are in the play, reduced to the size of the insignificant stage, and if these finite symbols frighten, then what should we not do to prevent the terrible reality that would destroy us all. I am not, and never have been a pacificist. I have been a fighter all my life; but I am not fool enough, nor am I invested enough in Invested interests, not to see clearly what another war will bring to all peoples; and, insofar as I can, I am determined to do what in me lies to prevent one, and to fight for the union of all men in sensible brotherhood, and co-operative achievement for the greater glory of man and his destiny. Indeed, these critics will find something to cry out about in my next book, *Sunset and Evening Star* dealing with the war they evidently think so much about. We, too, have wide gaps remaining in many of our cities still, giving a good view of desolation. The critics of my play arent satisfied evedently with the extent of the view in Berlin; they want devastation that will give them an uninterrupted view from one end of the world to the other. Well, They wont get it. The attack on your Director because of his race is a meaner and more cowardly one still; so hypocritical, too, for Christians, for they owe their hope and their joy to the Jew; and the world owes a lot more to them; Moses for monotheism—a new heaven; Freud, for a revolution in psychology, and Einstein for a new universe—to mention only a few. Give my thanks and my love to FRITZ KORTNER for his devoted ruling of my play, and for making it so impressive in the midst of interested opposition. There must be a kick in the play and a kick in him to provoke venomous attacks, and, in that, he and I and you and your husband and all who took part in it, can put out their hands, and say, WE ARE ALIVE.

I am in as good health as seventy-four years will allow, and as full of fight as ever, and as animated as ever with love for a world of life, of brotherhood, and achievement. So are all our three children. Our younger boy who is 18 goes into the Air Force next week for "National Training"; our elder one has already done his in the Royal Artillery—such a waste of time, of energy, senseless dissipation of life. Our girl is hard at work in school; and Eileen is busy with household affairs with which I give her a good hand—washing up, making a bed, peeling potatoes, and getting a meal when it is simple and straightforward work.

I enclose Photograph of The Family, taken a few years ago.

My love to you, your husband, to Fritz Kortner, & all the Jews, and to the German People.

Sean O'Casey

To Mrs. Oriana Atkinson

TS. ATKINSON

TOTNES, DEVON

18 JULY 1953

My dear Oriana:

Greeting and a kiss. You are back in the U.S.A. again, and I am back in the old spot by the river Dart, in front, now, of a fire for it is bitter cold, though I amn't altogether sick at heart. As you doubtlessly know, PURPLE DUST failed to come to London. A party who had guaranteed a lot of dough, failed to keep his promise, and the play had to fold up just as it got within sight of the City; so hear I am, trying to make up for lost time, to re-habilitate myself into the habit of common work again for awhile till another chance comes along to make some money sitting still, and smoking. I have started with an article "Art Among the Multitude," asked for by the Editor of *7 Arts,* who responded by saying it was a lovely article. It is to be with all the others forming the 2nd issue of *7 Arts,* which the publishers are sending out in a hard cover—the first was in a paper one— all over the world. I hope it may be a success.

I am reading the precious book you gave me, and finding it swell; very remarkable; a moving tale of one man's brave and breezy life. Thank you, dear, very much for it. I am reading it as, I think, it should be read, slowly, and with great attachment. When I have read it through, I'll turn to the lovely book Brooks gave me, telling all about another great man's brave and breezy life. How one we are all after all! Gorki the Russian; Whitman the American. It is odd to me that man is taking such a long time to love the other man. Anyway, the two books, the American and the Russian, stand shoulder to shoulder on the bookshelf.

The other day, Shivaun had to write an article for a school test examination. She came to me, asking me to suggest a subject. I suggested "Totnes." Too long; she had to write an article of about 150 or 200 words, and Totnes and its history would take a thousand. "Some thing", she said, "like a tree, or something". I suggested the chestnut tree in the garden which had grown from a chestnut planted by herself 9 or 10 years ago. "Fine," she said; "that will do well." She wrote about neither. I found after that she had written about her visit to Brooks and Oriana. Not a bad one either. Being a girl, I daresay, led her to give most of her thought to you; but she put in a rather charming picture of Brooks, describing his tallness, his glasses, his greying hair, and his "kind and clever face." She told how well you looked, your infectious liveliness, and your humour. She certainly has linked herself with the Atkinsons. She didn't forget to mention Brooks' famous honey-dew tobacco.

You did look fine, Oriana; right handsome, and every intelligent Irishman has an eye for a handsome woman. It was, indeed, a delight to meet you again. Tell Brooks I will be writing to him in a few days, as soon as I get through another MS chapter of SUNSET AND EVENING STAR, which the publishers want next month; so I am going through it again for the last time, and have but three chapters to examine now.

My deep love to you, Oriana, and thanks again for the lovely book.

As ever,
Sean

To Raymond Marriott

MS. H. D. JONES

TOTNES, DEVON

26 JULY 1953

Dear Raymond,

Yes, I know. These unexpected sickening blows often stun us, even as we are laughing. We've just got to bear them, and forget them, quick as we can. A lot of our life is spent putting disappointment and sorrow behind us. This sort of separation of friends has often happened before: David & Jonathan, Hallam and Tennyson, and Shelley washed ashore from the sea to his friends, dead. Fred Higgins,[1] manager of the Abbey, given the post by Yeats, fell dead, just as he had set himself to do things, leaving a loved one [2] lonely; one who never married, & still lilts an Irish song, sung by a girl who had lost a lover, which says, "We will walk with each other now and then." She sang it, low & soft, here, where I am writing now; resigned, but still remembering. You are, I hope, enough of a philosopher to realise that all this is a part of life; & that we have to go a long way before we can

---

[1] Frederick Robert Higgins (1896–1941), Irish poet, playwright, and managing director of the Abbey Theatre after the death of Yeats, from 1939 to 1941. See O'Casey's first letter to him, 19 February 1939, Vol. I, p. 779.

[2] Ria Mooney, the Abbey Theatre actress.

free life from the sudden sorrows. Or, if a stoic, finding these griefs inevitable to our experiences; common to all, the life remaining having to push sorrow aside, and go on, till it, too, falls and leaves the glitter and the glow. "The one shall be taken and the other left" happens now as it did in the time of Jesus. If those separated had been friends, then there is nothing for the one left but to go forth from his sorrow, and go on in the way of life. There is nothing else to do; & so must you & your friend do; glad, at least, that you all had many good & pleasant hours together. What more can one ask for?

All good wishes to you.
Yours very sincerely,
Sean O'Casey

PS. If Macmillan's cant give you a photograph, I might be able to rake out one for you.

To Miss Sheila ———

MS. PRIVATE

TOTNES, DEVON
8 AUGUST 1953

Dear Sheila,
    Yes, of course, I'll sign the book for you. You should have just sent it along to me.
    I have been, & am, very busy. I've just now sent a "Message"—just a few fierce thoughts to "CLARTE," a magazine that goes to 10,000 Swedish Students. I am working on my biography, answering many letters, & meeting American friends over here on holidays. So you see!
    I've been through Salisbury Cathedral several times—I've mentioned it in "Rose & Crown." I wanted to write a lot about it, but hadn't room. I like Salisbury a lot, & Wilton, & Stonehenge. Shivaun is now fourteen, & growing into a fine young lass. She isn't "fat & chubby," but tall & strong, a fine runner & a splendid swimmer, clever at drawing, & good at the piano—going along well & usefully. Our younger boy, Niall, goes into the Air-Force in a week or two. The elder lad, Breon, of course, has already done his turn in the artillery. Sometime, later on, I may answer the lad who thinks the mind is entirely separate, or distinct, from the brain—that is, I suppose he means, the body. Ask him if the "soul" be part of the mind, or if the mind & the soul be one & the same; or, if different parts of the spiritual

nature, how are they united, or how do they mingle; or are they joined like Siamese twins.

All the best.

As ever,   Sean

I hope you are well over your accident.

To Robert Emmett Ginna

TS. GINNA

TOTNES, DEVON

17 AUGUST 1953

Dear Bob,

Very glad that you and Gjon [Mili] seem to be enjoying yourselves in the odd, odd land of Ireland. I hope you will continue to do so. Glad that you spent so much time in the West. Once the West was awake—when Yeats and Lady G. roamed round it; now it seems to have gone to sleep again. What a mournful thing that there are but a few dusty stones hidden in the grass where the main entrance of Coole Park once stood! In the Republican national museum in Dublin, I'm told they keep every little thing once touched by every little hand of every little fellow who had the remotest connection with the Easter Rising. I dont know about James Stephens. I never heard of him in Coole; never remember Lady G. mentioning him, or he mentioning Lady G., which is strange, now I come to think of it. Augustus John's [name] is away up among the higher branches. A fine thing that the tree's still standing. The smashing of the House was the worst thing that Dev's Government did.[1]

The *Battle Royal* [2] took place in Brady's Lane, near St. Barnabas's Church. I lived then in 4 Abercorn Road, afterwards changed to 18 Abercorn Road: It was three doors down from a Pub, owned by an ex-Fenian, a Mr. Nolan, who was at first our landlord. He went bankrupt, and the houses four or five of them, passed to a Mr. Crowe, of Church Rd, an ex-constabulary man. At the back of Abercorn Rd, is a street called Church st. Here there was another Pub—off license and general shop, selling Milk as well as beer—we bought our milk from them. They were named Brady's, and it was Mrs Brady—a woman who was "fond of the sup," but a very warm-hearted woman—who used to provide the [sheets] and the candlesticks for the Wake of anyone who died in the near vicinity.

[1] See 'O'Casey's letter to Quidnunc, *Irish Times,* 6 March 1942.
[2] See "Battle Royal," *I Knock at the Door* (1939).

It was this woman who provided the sheets and a candlestick for my own mother's wake; she provided also a crucifix for those who were Catholics; and, I think, my mother was the only Protestant who was served in this way, for she and Mrs Brady were great friends because my mother took her part when Mrs Brady's childer abused their mother for making "a show of them." The children were, in a sense, right; but they didn't mind because the drink injured Mrs. Brady, and hastened her end, but because when she was tight, it offended their growing bourgeois sense of respectability. Now Brady's Lane ran behind these houses of which Brady's was one, and it was from Brady's Pub that the muddy lane took its name. It was Barnabas's School I went to, smaller then than it is now. The Rev. E. M. Griffin, to whom I dedicated a book,[3] added a wing, to seperate classes, and also got a Verger's (sexton) house built beside it. When Ella (Bella) taught in Dominick St. School, I was too young to go to school, though I went several times—say a month, off and on, and was then only promoted to trousers, previously wearing a red and black plaid petticoat. It was here, after a year or maybe a little more (I cannot be certain, being so young) that Ella married her soldier boy, and, according to a rigid rule (I think it's in force still) had to leave; had to abandon her profession. We were in Dominick St only for a short time. Seumas (Scully) tells me he went to a school opposite, a much more swell affair.

No, I never went to school from Lr. Dorset Street.[4] It was there I was born, and, as far as I can remember my mother's talk, left it when a year old or so. We shifted from Dorset St to Inisfallen Parade, where my father died when I was six years old. The brother next to me was eight years older than I. It was in Inisfallen Parade that we all, except Tom, had scarlet fever, and my mother nursed us all by herself, me, Archie, Mick, and Ella, putting Tom in the same bed with Mick, who had the worst attack, so that Tom would get it, and let her be done with it; but Tom never contracted it —a curious problem for doctors to solve. There is a Bank in Lr. Dorset St, or I must be dreaming. It may be 80, or the numbers may have been changed, as they were in Abercorn Road. I remember looking for it, and, I think, pointing it out to Frank McManus (who you should see. He lives at 101 The Rise, Mount Merrion, Dublin, and is (or was) Programme Chief in Radio Eireann, The General Post Office, Henry St., Dublin, and has just returned from a trip to the USA, a friend of mine in New York University tells me—a grand chap) as he, Eileen, and I returned homewards from a visit to a friend's house, at 1 or two in the morning. It is, if I remember right, a red-brick building, half way from the corner of the North Circular Rd, to North Frederick St. On the right hand side going towards North Fred. St; on the Left going towards where 422 North Circular Rd. down Lr. Dorset St. I was in Mountjoy Square for about a year, maybe less. It was there that the Raid took place from which THE GUNMAN is

---

3 See the dedication to *Pictuers in the Hallway* (1942).
4 O'Casey was born at 85 Upper Dorset Street, on 30 March 1880.

written. I did nothing there beyond trying to live. From there I went to 422 N. Circular Road, and it was here the first 3 plays done by the Abbey were written. Mountjoy Sq. was in the time of the Black and Tan Terror; N. Circular Road, in the time of the Civil War; and here, too, raids took place; and it was here the Free State Troops and C.I.D. lads, searched for Capt. Hogan, the lad who was found dead on a lonely Finglas Road, as per Juno and the Paycock. He was captured just at the Dorset St end of the road, and hurried away in a lorry to his death. I was looking at his photo only yesterday, given to me by the lass he was courting in 422.

But I had made a start in Abercorn Road, writing there FROST IN THE FLOWER, HARVEST FESTIVAL, and CRIMSON IN THE TRI-COLOUR, all rejected by the Abbey, but, in each case, with a typed note suggesting that I should go on.[5] (I still think FROST IN THE FLOWER a far better play (from memory—I havent got the MS) than many done by them)

What about Maynooth? You should try to see Dr. Roger McHugh, of University College, Dublin. I wrote his address in my "Notes," but cant find it now. I'm sure it will be in the Dublin Telephone Directory. Also Peadar O'Donnell, who was Editor of THE BELL, 14 Lr. O'Connell St. There's Dr J. D. Cummins of 38 Merrion Square East. Dublin, to whom I dedicated *Red Roses For Me*. He attended me for my eyes, and I spent many evenings in his surgery chatting till the small hours of the mornings. Joe is a recluse, seeing no one, and mightnt see you; but you might try. A strange man, one I could never quite fathom, but we were great friends. My room in 422 was on ground floor, on the level of the hall. Jim Kavanagh whose mother rented it to me, lives there still, I believe, and would show it to you. But a picture of it appears in Inisfallen Fare Thee Well, as it was when I had it. It couldn't be the same room now, for none of my things—books, table, etc. would be there.

I'll send an official note asking Mt Jerome to allow you to take the burial plot; though I fear it must have disappeared by this. The last burial there was my mother in 1919, the summer during the great Influenza plague—probably July or August.[6]

All our love to Gjon & to
you, Bob.

As Ever
Sean

[5] See the Reader's Opinion from the Abbey Theatre, 26 January 1920; Lady Gregory's critique of *The Crimson in the Tricolour*, ? October 1921; Yeats's critique of *The Crimson in the Tricolour*, 19 June 1922; all in Vol. I, pp. 91–92, 95–96, 102–103.
[6] O'Casey's mother died on 12 November 1918. See his letter to Fergus O'Connor, 17 February 1918, note 1, Vol. I.

To the Secretary, Mount Jerome Cemetery

TC. GINNA

TOTNES, DEVON
17 AUGUST 1953

Dear Sir,

I shall be very much obliged if you would allow Mr. R. E. Ginna and Mr. Gjon Mili, of the American Magazine LIFE to take photographs of the O'Casey (Casey) burial plot in your Cemetery.[1] The last burial there was that of my mother, Susan Casey, who died in 1919, during the summer of that year, July or August, I think. The first burial was in 1886, I think, that of Michael Casey, my father. I'm sorry I cannot give you further details. The plot was registered for a number of years (5/- a year then, I believe), but we discontinued this when times became so hard that even this was beyond our means. I thank you for any help given to the two gentlemen named by me.

Yours sincerely,
Sean O'Casey

---

[1] The Casey family plot at Mount Jerome Cemetery, Lot A35-247, contains the bodies of O'Casey's father, mother, sister Isabella, and brothers Tom and Michael. Michael died on 11 January 1947, and was the last to be buried there. See O'Casey's letter to Fergus O'Connor, 17 February 1918, note 1, Vol. I, p. 71; and his letter to Mrs. Isabella Murphy, 20 January 1947, note 2.

To Joseph Jay Deiss

MS. DEISS

TOTNES, DEVON
25 AUGUST 1953

Dear Jay,

Think of me as Sean, by all means—there's no "Mr." in Irish. In the vocative, we say A mhic Ui Cathasaigh = Oh, son of O'Casey; or intimately, A Sheain = Sean. Yes, Devon's a long way from London. Here the big city's either Exeter or Plymouth. Sussex isn't far away on the S. Coast. I enclose, with this note, Macmillan's letter. I'm sorry they didn't do the book.[1] Glad it is being translated, though you won't get much dough out of translations—only a lot of trouble, & many letters to write. England has her

---

[1] Deiss's novel, *A Washington Story*. O'Casey sent it to Macmillan "with a strong and hearty recommendation." See O'Casey's letter to Deiss, 7 March 1950.

own way of walking. We do some boycotting in a quiet, silent way. However, England, by and large, is a very sensible, decent, & tolerant land. There seems to be a definite pull against McCarthy in America now; beginning to appear, anyway. I don't think McCarthy will become a secular Pope of the world. I think Macmillan's decided against your book simply because, & solely so, they thought there wouldn't be a sufficient sale for it. It is a most honest & broadminded Firm. They publish everything I write, &, in these days, that's no small sign of courage & tolerance. They don't agree with what I write, but they let whomsoever wants to hear it, hear it. And I know they don't agree at all with MaCarthyism. I have great respect, & indeed, affection, for Harold & Daniel Macmillan & Lovat Dickson, the Directors.

All good wishes & warm regards to your wife and you.

Yours very sincerely,
Sean O'Casey

To John H. Hutchinson [1]

TC. O'CASEY

[TOTNES, DEVON]
10 SEPTEMBER 1953

Dear Mr. Hutchinson,

The surviving member of the "Junior National Literary Circle," mentioned by you, is only vaguely right. The activities in the small slumroom, back of Ewing's house, in Seery's Lane—which is, I take it, the one in your mind—were many more than you think, or the "surviving member" remembers. It was for years the Headquarters of the Drumcondra Branch of the Gaelic League and of the Branch's Camoguidheacht [2] Club and of the Cumann Iomana na Laimhe dheirge—Red Hand Hurling Club. I was more than an "occasional visitor." I taught Irish classes there, every second night for some years, and, on Sundays, went to Moyvalley to teach there. I was an active member of the hurling club, and Secretary of the Gaelic League Branch [3] till I left it to form the St. Laurence O'Toole Pipers of that

---

[1] John H. Hutchinson, 55 Lansdowne Road, Dublin.

[2] Camogie.

[3] In an old record book which lists the branches and secretaries of the Gaelic League (National Library of Ireland, MS. 11572), the following entry appears: "June 10, 1918—Drumcondra Branch—S. Ó Cathasaigh—24 Abercorn Road, North Wall Dublin." The houses were later renumbered, and the number of the house in which the Casey family lived was changed from 24 to 18 Abercorn Road.

parish, whose Club Room was as big a slum hovel as the one in Seery's Lane. The O'Toole room was in a back shanty off of Strandville Avenue, North Strand, before they acquired present premises in 100 Seville Place. We were then, apparently, unconscious of the way in which we lived, and stayed so till Jim Larkin came to show us all how shocking were the conditions that surrounded us. There was a kind of a workers club (where they played house) next to the shanty in Seery's Lane, and these workers kindly lent us their rooms whenever we had an allnight Ceilidh in our own premises. We used to take our supper in the workers room, and the tea was brewed there. There were occasional visitors during the reading of our "Manuscript Journal." Ours was called, if I remember right, An Laimh Dhearg—the Red Hand. Donnach Doyle, for some time a Dublin Corporation Councillor, came there; so did Seumas Deakin, then a Chemist in Phibsboro, formerly Manager of Hoyte's in O'Connell St; so, once, did Sinead Ni Flannagain, now Mrs De Valera. I remember her challenging one speaker who held the opinion that the woman's place was the kitchen, she holding that the woman's place was an equal place in every movement, national, social, and political, with the men. She was right, of course, though her voice hasn't been heard now in any Movement for many years. We were almost all poor. None of the respectable Gaelic Leaguers of Drumcondra would come into such a place; and the only two who were fairly well off were a Mr. Liam Mac Giolla Phoil (W. Guilfoyle) Manager of the "Golden Key" in Capel Street, and one of the Keogh Bros. who have a photographic Firm in Dorset Street, near the N.C.R. There is more than one survivor. There's S. Kavanagh of 422 N.C.R. with whom I lived before coming to London—last St. Patrick's Day, he sent me shamrock; Leo Rush, a cabinet-maker, who married a girl of the Club, Kathleen Walsh; Fran Kelly (Francis), who is secretary of a Dublin Society for introducing classic music, by records, to the Dubliners interested in music; Paddy Callan, who carries on a builders Firm, with others. There was a Michael Murphy, who became Gaelic Literary Editor in the Daily *Independent,* the two brothers Brown, carpenters, who should still be alive, and a Sean O'Reilly, a Collector for the Dublin Gas Co, whose brother was killed in the Easter Rising. The S. Deakin mentioned above, was then a Member of the Supreme Council of the Irish Republican Brotherhood. Mr. Ewing who lent the room, was a "Protestant Home Ruler," and very old-fashioned in opinion and dress; he wore customarily the morning coat and shiny tall-hat; a handsome man, well-cut face, thick and handsome, short beard, then beginning to silver, well built, with a charming voice, a little show in intonation. He used to ask us how we ended our meetings, suggesting that we, he supposed, sang My Dark Rosaleen or Who Fear to Speak of Ninety-eight. A man who didnt understand the new spirit rising out of the Gaelic League and the other national movements. It was kind of him to give the shack, such as it was, for we all spent many a happy hour there, in song, story, and dance; though it must have been a great threat to the health of those whose work kept them indoors all day. I worked hard in the open air, so it had little effect on me.

I never lived within the border of Drumcondra. Then I lived in the North Wall, miles away, and many a night I ploughed through frost and snow (for I had to open up, sweep the floor, light the fire, and get the room ready for classes), or walked through heavy rain to help in keeping Ireland's language alive. The one experience of Drumcondra I had were the walks with my brothers to Cat and Cage, and, later on, with a girl, past Drumcondra, into Whitehall, and beyond; for then that part of Dublin was equal to any countryside. The hedges began where the tram stopped at Whitehall. What these old shacks in Seery Lane were originally, I dont know. They could hardly have been stables for the Houses in front of them. Probably they were cottages for workers when Drumcondra was more of a country place, like the old cottages beside the Tolka, where the Statue of the Blessed Virgin still stands.

Well, there you are—a few details of the life that then flourished in the old shack, at the back of Ewing's, in the squalid channel, called Seery's Lane.

With all good wishes,
Yours sincerely,
Sean O'Casey

To Brooks Atkinson

MS. ATKINSON

TOTNES, DEVON
20 SEPTEMBER 1953

My dear Brooks:

Thanks for your kind letter. I'm glad you didn't carry the hod or swing the sledge this time at Prink Hill. I'll allow you a paint-brush. It was really a delightful time we all spent with Oriana & you in London. It was a joyous coincidence that Brooks appeared, like a god, amid the dust of the rehearsals. The last night I saw you, we were in the Theatre till near two of the morning, doing all we could to damn the play. I had refused to go to supper with Charlie [Chaplin]; but he came to the theatre to watch the work, & I had a spasmodic chat with him.[1] Bar Trewin, second Critic of the *Observer*, & Marriott of the trade Journal *The Stage*, no Critic came to

---

[1] See O'Casey's letter to Peter Newmark, 23 May 1953, note 1.

say hello. It's odd that British Critics seem to be unable to relax away from the theatre, & to live life away from it; though it may be that they don't like me; *though* again, it seems foolish to dislike a person unknown; though again, it may be my politics they don't like; but surely a living man is more than a political opinion. However politics may differ, all have a multitude of things in common—laughter, tears. Personal problems, the quest for food & raiment, the finds and fumbling in family life, the desire to make life safer; and a host of other things.

I enclose a typed impress of news about "Purple Dust".* Many thanks, dear Brooks, for the really lovely Walt Whitman book.[2] Breon loves it, too. I've sent the MS of "Sunset & Evening Star" to the Publishers. Henry Hewes of the *Saturday Review of Literature* has been here with us, discussing many things—even politics. Gjon Mili, a photographer from LIFE, has been here, too, with Robert Emmet Ginna—two lovable lads—, & I've been photographed all ends up by them. They went to Ireland to take pictures there, & one of them shows the only property the O'Caseys ever possessed—the family grave in Mount Jerome.[3]

I don't wish to be rich as Shaw—it didn't matter a damn to him either—, but I'd like to be, or feel, a little more secure at the age of 74; but these things don't count a lot in the long run. My own fault; I could have had some silver in the house, had I done things for the Films people wanted me to do, but in which I had little interest.

Now my deep love to Oriana & to you, dear Brooks.

As ever,
Sean

The English Pilgrimage

* The English pilgrimage—for that is what it turned out to be—was a failure, or, more correctly, a miscarriage. I never put so much work into the rehearsals of a play before. The Producer, or Director, who had money sunk into it, was Sam Wanamaker, a most delightful man, with an equally delightful family. He was very able, but a little too restless. I predetermined, being so long away from a rehearsal of any kind, and sensitive of being thought interfering, not to interfere, and to agree with all suggestions as far as might be possible. I never saw a Director work so hard, or so enthusiastically, on a play. He worked, I fear, too hard, and tried to put too much into it. I wrote, at his appeal, four new songs for the play —"The Old Days are with Us Again," "The Ruined Rowan Tree"—rather a good song this—"We're Ready For Anything Now," and "How I Long for the Time When My Heart was Mine Own." These went into the play, but one actor couldn't sing, so "The Old Days" was said. The other songs were found to be long, and in the case of the Rowan Tree, the girl

---

[2] *Poetry and Prose of Walt Whitman,* ed. Louis Untermeyer (1949).
[3] Mount Jerome Cemetery, Dublin.

couldn't adapt herself to the Orchestra, so it had to be sung right through by her partner; and, then, one verse, afterwards, two, had to be taken from the others, till me heart was near broke. Had a busy time with Press photographers, reporters, for publicity purposes; and stuck it all like a man (or like a fool?). Followed up the Company to Edinburgh (a tour), and had more excitement with more photographers and more reporters, including the Drama Critics there, though the Critics of London gave me the frozen mit. Only one, [J. C.] Trewin, second Critic of *The Observer,* came to see me, took a cup of tea with me, and Raymond Marriott, a fine chap, of the commercial, trade stage Journal, *The Stage,* were interested; and only the latter mentioned the coming of the play.[4] I have since heard from Trewin that he has had notice to quit from the Ob., though I fancy his friendliness towards me had nothing to do with it. In Edinburgh I had a fine time with the Gaels, and Scotland's grand poet, Hugh McDiarmuid; meeting many at Ceilidhithe, hearing the old songs and even singing some myself. Had some whiskey, and a celebrated liquer brew called "Drambuaddhe" the recipe for which comes from the outer Hebrides. I was at home among the clans and the kilts. A Gael meself, sir. Half-way home to London, the Play heard that a person who had promised £1,500, failed to keep the promise, and there wasn't anything left in the sack to propel the play to the London stage. Sam Wanamaker lost a good deal, and got agitated, as he well might, with a wife and two children; and kept changing and rehearsing till we were all tired; but it was all no good, and we folded up right at the gates of London. One thing above all the rest struck me— barring Trewin and Marriott, not a single Critic came to have a word; or mutter God Speed to the play while I was in London for three weeks; and not a single one said a word about the play—bar Marriott—, or of its effort to come to London. For myself, I imagine the theme of the play frightened them; the laughter at the struggle to preserve old things, and the special Tudor scene of the House, and all its gone traditions, dead forever now, came rawly in on all the pseudo carnival attempt to bring the flavour of Tudorism back again, and make it at home in honour of the new Queen Elizabeth. I daresay it was natural, though I think the English who have money are afraid of any laugh going against themselves. Sam disturbed at the thought of loss by friends and himself, changed and altered, and, worst of all, pleaded the money needed from two persons I should have never asked, although I requested him not to do it. I don't blame him; he was desperate, and much more perturbed than I about the ill-success of the play. It is all old history now, but, while it lasted, it wasn't pleasant.

You all have travelled some! 500 miles is a long way here; you couldn't tell where it might land you. And to see Shakespeare's plays. By a coincidence, I and the family travelled to Stratford-on-Avon, they to see the plays specifically; I to meditate on the places that knew the Poet in

---

[4] *The Stage,* 27 April 1953, a preview comment on the opening of *Purple Dust* in Glasgow.

the body so many, many years ago. Certainly, the Trust are looking well after all the special places—though Shakespeare's House is there only in outline; one thinks one sees the boundary-walls of the different rooms; just as Gjon Mili told me that there is but a curb & a few scattered stones pointing out lazily where once lay the main entrance to the Coole Home. Even the outlines of the rooms are gone now, & all signs of the lady of the laurelled head are hidden by rough grass & spiky thistles.

Well Brooks, a lot of us are savages yet. Still, we're aware of it, and that is something.

My blessing on your grandchildren, on Oriana, & on you. Amen.

Sean

To George Jean Nathan

MS. CORNELL

TOTNES, DEVON
20 SEPTEMBER 1953

My most dear George:

Like yourself, I'd like to feel a bit fitter: 74 years running around life, however, is bound to have an effect of slowing down, wincing with many an ache, & forced to pull myself to do the things that were much easier to do some years ago. One has to lean on an elbow oftener now. You said you were going on a holiday, &, in my case, I shouldn't have bothered you till I thought you had come back.

I enclose a few notes, typed, about the recent attempt to bring *Purple Dust* to London.[1] Not a single London Critic said a word of regret about the play's non-arrival in London. Well, it can't be helped, & I amen't going to cry about it.

I've been very busy since getting "Sunset & Evening Star" ready; &, last week, the MS went to the Publishers. Also, we had two Americans here —Gjon Mili, who does photograph work for *Life,* and [Robert] Emmet Ginna, who organises articles—for 3 weeks photographing the family and me in all sorts of poses. Then the two went to Ireland for 2 weeks to take pictures there; Gjon came here again, & took more photographs. Both were fine lads, & I enjoyed the association thoroughly. I've never met such an original photographer before as Gjon. We had a good many Americans here this Summer, including the Critic for "Saturday Review."

---

[1] O'Casey enclosed a copy of only the long first paragraph of "The English Pilgrimage," which appears in the letter of 20 September to Brooks Atkinson.

E. Bentley sent me a book on Shaw,[2] curiously philosophical, which I find hard to read. I and Breon look forward to the coming of your Book about the Theatre in the Fifties. For the last week or so, I and the family have been in Stratford-on-Avon, where Shakespeare's worshipped with great pomp & much ritual. T. S. Eliot has another success here [3]—he seems to have replaced Fry. You try to rest as much as you can, George, & keep fit. God be with you & my love around you.

As ever,
Sean

[2] Eric Bentley, *Bernard Shaw* (1947).
[3] T. S. Eliot's *The Confidential Clerk* opened in London on 16 September 1953.

To John H. Hutchinson

MS. TEXAS

TOTNES, DEVON
21 SEPTEMBER 1953

Dear Mr. Hutchinson,

Thank you for the Press-cutting. No, I hadn't seen it, & was very glad to get it. Some time ago, I had a letter from "Dinny" Doyle,[1] denouncing me in red, round terms for my plays & biographical books, which, he said, were ruining the good name of Ireland. In his letter, he wistfully inquired if "I possibly remembered him"; & I returned such a detailed picture of him, as he then was, that it maddened him more than ever. Over 40 years ago, he gave me a confidence which I reminded him of in my reply to him, which brought back a fierce denunciation for "breaking a confidence," though the confidence, after near 50 years, had been mentioned only to the man who gave it! He is living nicely down in Glenealy, Co. Wicklow, full of years and, I hope, pleasant memories, aside from those I brought to his mind. He calls the "Avenue" "Seery's Lane," &, as he was a Drumcondra bird (his nest was near the lane), he should know; so I think, Seery's Lane must have been the original name. Deakin died in his daughter's house in (Drumcollogher?) Limerick some short time ago. A chemist wrote to me, enclosing a cutting about the funeral; & it showed to me that the James Deakin mentioned was the Seumas D. I knew so well so many years ago. I knew Matt Stafford intimately—a fine old skin, & a brave, honest man. I did not know Gerald Ewing, but often listened to him singing at Cuirm Ceoil.[2]

[1] See O'Casey's letter to D. M. Doyle, 15 May 1950.
[2] Musical parties or concerts.

Ah, many things happened to us all, & it's a wonder so little has been written around it all.

All our yesterdays are sinking into the dust.

All good wishes.
Yours sincerely
Sean O'Casey

To Barrows Dunham [1]

MS. DUNHAM

TOTNES, DEVON

22 SEPTEMBER 1953

My dear Barrows:

By this time, I hope you have heard the best of news; and that you are free again to speak to the young as you speak to all in your very fine "Giant in Chains." [2]

I kept no copy of the letter I sent to the President of your University.[3] I thought a type-written letter would be too formal, too much of a business appeal, & so I wrote in longhand, wrote as I felt towards you; respectfully, for it was no light matter for a foreigner & a stranger to write to the President of such an important Pennsylvanian University. I hope it may have done you some good, that it proved to be even a minor shield against the darts aimed at your reputation and your living. I am half-way through your book; & like it immensely. It is impregnated with a cold light of sense and a warm light of love for man plunging about the problems & puzzles of life

---

[1] Barrows Dunham (1905–   ), writer and teacher, until 1953 Professor and Chairman of the Philosophy Department at Temple University, Philadelphia, Pennsylvania. On 27 February 1953, Dunham was declared guilty of contempt of Congress by the House Un-American Activities Committee, which was investigating alleged Communist influences in American colleges, when he invoked the Fifth Amendment privilege against self-incrimination and refused to answer questions about his educational background and occupation. He was dismissed from his position at Temple after his appearance before the committee. For the account of his exoneration in the Federal Court two years later, see O'Casey's letter to Dunham, 11 November 1955, note 1, Vol. III.

[2] Barrows Dunham, *Giant in Chains* (1953), a philosophical study of the democratic traditions and values in American life, written before his appearance before the Congressional Committee, in which he says he has been influenced by philosophical Marxism, as well as the stronger link to men in the American tradition like Thoreau and William James. His thesis is that any American who is ignorant of the country's great democratic traditions is a "giant in chains."

[3] O'Casey wrote a letter in defense of Dunham to Robert Livingston Johnson, president of Temple University.

here & life or no life beyond him. You are a brave man, Barrows, and worthy of the real America.

I never doubted America; do not doubt her now: I have seen & conversed with too many of her men & women. Away from the greatness of the White House, I not only feel, I know I should be at home with President Eisenhower cooking his breakfast, or watching him fish in a stream: but never at home with [Senator Joseph] McCarthy. The scowl from the Vatican would make this gay old dog bark and bristle and bite. Your book is most readable, & I am very happy reading it. My fond love to Alice, to Clark, & to you.

As ever,
Sean

To Paul and Nan Ross

MS. ROSS

TOTNES, DEVON
1 OCTOBER 1953

Dear friends,

Your letter carries sorrowful, white-faced news. It is shocking to hear of the death of young people. Nan and you have Mrs. O'Casey's (Eileen) deep sympathy and mine. I daresay the strain of flying through the war years had an affect on him. These young lads who "came safe through" these experiences are rarely the same. War takes a toll of the living as well as the dead. I had a young friend here, son of our Doctor, who is a Dublin man. This young fellow had been a few months married when he went on a flight, and the under-wheels of his plane never rolled over England's land again: he just disappeared with his plane over the sea; and not a scrap of him was ever seen again. It is all very dreadful.

Your Gilbert (Gil, we called him) is a delightful lad. We, Eileen & I, liked him much. Pity I & she were so occupied, while he was with us, with Gjon Mili & R. Ginna, busy taking "shots" for an article in an American Magazine. However, I had time to embrace Gil, & so had Eileen, & his nature left with us a fine feeling of affection for him. By the way Paul and Nan, don't press responsibility down too much on Gil. He has his own life to live, & his studies will be hard; he must have room to laugh. I am sending you a "shot" which shows him in our wee garden, & me sitting on a doorstep. This is not to be published. I got Gjon Mili to give it me, thinking Gil might like to have it.

My love to Frank Morrell, to Nan, to Paul (yourself) & to Gil; & our deep sympathy, too. God be with you all.

Yours very sincerely,
Sean O'Casey

To Barbara A. Cohen

MS. COHEN

TOTNES, DEVON
10 OCTOBER 1953

Dear Miss Cohen,

Thank you for sending me your Catalog, which has a very fine collection of voices, excluding O'Casey's, for one of the 74 croaks rather than talks. I had the idea that Caedmon's was a big, big Firm, like "His Master's Voice" here; a Combine, a huge Emporium, printing Records by the tens of thousands. Last week, our elder lad read an article in "The New Yorker," telling the world you were two young girls from College who had ventured to rush into places where the big Firms feared to tread.[1] I wish I had known this before. You should have told me; I thought Miss Cohen was just one of the Staff of a big warehouse. Had I known, I should have felt far more friendly.

If you have time, I should like you to send me a record of the croaking; but I wish to pay for it; so take it from the first royalty due; or, if that be too long a wait, ask Miss Rubin of the Richard Madden Play Co., to pay for it out of the first royalty due to me.

All the best to you both; & may your venture be a great success.

My love,
Yours sincerely,
Sean O'Casey

---

[1] "The Talk of the Town" column of *The New Yorker,* 14 March 1953, featured an article on Barbara A. Cohen and Marianne Roney and their formation of Caedmon Publishers, a company devoted to making recordings of the voices of noted authors.

To Seumas Scully

MS. SCULLY

TOTNES, DEVON

11 OCTOBER 1953

My dear Seumas,

Thanks for the papers. Of course the Germans are kind people; the ordinary people, those whose life is a life of work. But there are still in Germany many who sigh for the time when Germany ala allah Hitler strode Europe like a huge Collossus. That is one reason why it is a good thing the USSR has the hydrogen bomb. I got your letter—and, indeed, answered it—mentioning Owen's adventure among the elect; & your suggestion to enter it (like an entry into a ledger) into my next biographical book.[1] It wouldn't be within my temperament to make a thesis of it; but I have referred to it in a fanciful way. My love to Mick O'Hara.

Thanks for showing Gjon [Mili] & Bob [Ginna] around Dublin. They are grand chaps; & are now back in New York. Bob works for LIFE, & Gjon is said to be one of the world's finest photographers. Bob seems to have seen and spoken to everyone—possibly because of his connection, thro' his family, long years ago, with Ireland, as his name proclaims. Emmett seems to be a popular name with Americans whose origins were Irish.

I'm very glad you had a fine time in Germany. We have had a wretched summer here, but I've had a week, with the family in Wilmcote & Shottery. Sat in a seat where—they say—S[hakespeare]. courted Anne. Niall leaves us on Thursday when he goes to Oswestry to become a gunner in the Royal Artillery. God, we are a scattered race, able to do all for others, damn all for ourselves.

Well, my love & our love to you; & thanks again.

As ever,
Sean

I hope you will have a good time in the North. Your Committee is a fine one, & will do more than guns to bring Orange & green together.

1 See O'Casey's letter to Scully, 22 November 1952, notes 1 and 3.

To Leo Keogh [1]

TC. O'CASEY

[TOTNES, DEVON]
12 OCTOBER 1953

Dear Leo,

Glad to hear from you. It's a long, long trail since we two met together under the rays from the Sword of Light.[2] The Malachy Branch, of course, was my first direct contact with the G. League. It assembled over Tyler's the bootshop in Talbot Street. I was there, after our failure to keep going, when, with Peadar O'Nuallain—of Summerhill and Amiens Street Station, the benches were carried away by Clann na hEireann, who had bought them; while Peadar saw them go with tears. Afterwards, the room was taken by a Cumann na nGaedhael Branch, and it was here that the composer [Patrick Heeney] got The Soldiers' Song taken down in tonicsolfa, a method you know something about, for you may remember trying to teach it to a group of dead wood in the Malachy Branch. Wasnt Mr. Eggleso a tenor? I remember Francis MacNamara well, captain of the Catholic Boys Brigade—what a limp, humorless, jellyfish the fellow was! Michael Mapother was much more brisk, and had a fine sense of humour— the two of them seemed to be always together. I'm glad to hear that P. Callan and his brother, Phil, are still under the moon. I remember the premises in Carlingford Road well, for it was I who spent every Saturday half-holiday giving the rooms a coat of wallpamur till they were finished, with Paddy Callan dropping in to see how the work was going. It was a shop front, ground floor, with a room up a small flight of stairs, unfinished, for the builder·(a Councillor Dermott?) was prevented from completing it because of a neighbour's action against the house cutting away the light from the windows of the house next to it. Same neighbour complained of us lowering the caste of the Road, and so we had to get back to the old house in Seery's or Boylan's Lane.

I cant comment whether the ideals of the early days are in course of realization, for it is twenty-eight years since I left the land, and many thousands more, apparently, have followed suit since then. All the young, too, and the fittest among the young. It is a dreadful drain on Ireland's virility and potential strength. But the young surely know something of Ireland's History—even though it be the romantic side of it? Dont they learn it in the schools? Certainly, Edmund Curtis's History [3] is a poor one, in my opinion. The best book I've read so far is "Elizabeth's Irish Wars," [4] written, not by a friend, but well-written, and realistic, and surely docu-

[1] Leo Keogh, 14 Rathdown Road, Dublin.
[2] The Sword of Light (*An Claidheamh Soluis*), emblem of the Gaelic League.
[3] Edmund Curtis, *A History of Ireland* (1936).
[4] Cyril Falls, *Elizabeth's Irish Wars* (1950).

mented. Ireland's Story has yet to be written. I remember having lunch with you once, you and Mrs. Keogh, in, I think, the house you are living in now. All the best to all whom I know, and who are still with us; and my best regards to Mrs Keogh, all who are yours, and to yourself. With us, new things have passed away, and all things have become old. Well, God be with the young.

Yours sincerely, remembering old days.
[Sean]

To Otto Brandstädter

TC. O'CASEY

[TOTNES, DEVON]
16 OCTOBER 1953

Dear Otto,
You ask a helluva lot of questions, my dear young friend! I like the effort to get into touch with countries outside our own, by visits (the best way), by reading what those who live in them write, and by looking at the pictures they paint. But dont forget that each country has its own slanting way of looking at things, of feeling life. And dont start to yell out when that slant doesn't agree with our own slant. Then there's the way of life, and, within life, the way of art—a curious way, beginning we know not how; not even Freud could tell its secret. Life doesn't produce art the way life produces nylon. So we shouldn't talk of Culture as if we could spread it about as one spreads manure over the land. It is like the kingdom of heaven, and quiet growth within, manifesting itself outwardly in the glow of what a people say, do, and sing. It isnt put on like paint on a woman's face. That is, I'm afraid, what some of us are doing today— forcing a false aspect on our appearance; trying to look nice rather than thinking of how we feel. For instance, young friend, I think you could be better and more enjoyably employed otherwise than in tracing out a bibliography of what I've written.[1] For instance reading Goldsmith. Well, well, here we go:

1. Yes; there must be lots—appeals, articles, and God knows what else, scattered over magazines and journals, here and in America. I have never kept a record of them, and never will. I enclose a comment on

[1] Brandstädter was working on his "Ein O'Casey-Bibliographie," *Zeitschrift für Anglistik und Amerikanistik* (1954).

an article about "Laughter" in the current number of Toronto's (Canada) SATURDAY NIGHT.[2] A week or so from now, and I wouldn't know when it had appeared, and wouldn't care. What matter about dates, and how do they concern what the human mind says out loud?

2. Macmillan's are my one publishers. There have been translations of course, in French, in German—recently, and as long ago as twenty-five years; in Italian, in Dutch, and in the Scandinavian languages; in Finland, recently, and in Hebrew—Tel Aviv. I dont bother to remember the particulars, for with a family totalling six, I've other things to think about.

3. I dont think there have been any studies of my work other than those you mention; certainly none in book-form that I know of. By the way, do you know anything about THE STAR TURNS RED, translated recently by a Mrs Jokl, rehearsed, and almost performed in Berlin, but suddenly abandoned because "its production might have offended the Roman Catholic Church"?[3]

My good and warm wishes to you.

Yours sincerely,
Sean O'Casey

By the way, some of the "progressive writers" are damnably poor ones.

[2] Sean O'Casey, "The Power of Laughter: Weapon against Evil," *Saturday Night,* 3 October 1953; reprinted in *The Green Crow* (1956).

[3] Anna Marie Jokl translated *The Star Turns Red* into German in 1951. See O'Casey's letter to her, 28 March 1962, Vol. III. I wrote to Mrs. Jokl in 1962 asking about the canceled production of *The Star Turns Red,* but she replied in a letter of 12 November 1962 saying she no longer had her papers concerning the situation. Although she had not kept her letters from O'Casey, she had copied out the following paragraph from one of his letters written in May 1951:

> I appreciate your difficulties with the Irish idiom, and the O'Casey idiom, too. It is nonsense to think that the language of "ordinary life and people" are not connected with big issues; they are connected with life and death—the biggest issues of all, either to ordinary or extraordinary people. Of course, the man who carries Goethe about with him, and kills babies, hasnt read Goethe at all. It can be nothing but a pose; the thoughts of great men are something bigger than poses. Great names are linked with Life, for they have enriched it. Here, too, they think humour cant go with tragedy: more nonsense.

To Robert Emmett Ginna

MS. GINNA

TOTNES, DEVON
18 OCTOBER 1953

My dear Bob,

I was very glad to hear that you had escaped from Ireland, and had landed safely in your own Townland of New York. Your American way of life, with all its hostilities, its uncertainties, & its hurrying restlessness, is a far and away preferable way to the ways of Ireland's chattering, pietistic, corruscating humbug: with its beer-stained pub-counter circling round, & joined to, the Holy Altar, and the reverberating Sweep Drum. I'm sure it must have been a mystifying experience for you, from the talk of Lennox Robinson, the Episcopalian Protestant, the talk of sacerdotal-minded Catholic, Gaby Fallon, to the muttering of a lady—lowering a pint of the best. Had you stayed there a couple of years, it would have been more bewildering. Yet we are really a brave people & generous, too—like you Americans; but what is called "Religion," north & south, has numbed our greater qualities, & sharpened all our snarling and meaner propensities. What is called "fear & love o' God" has ruined us. But there is greatness in the land that gave the world Tone, Emmet, Parnell, Betsy Gray, Larkin, Lady Gregory, Yeats, Shaw, & Joyce. So, in all our snarling, we can shout Hallelujah in Gaelic.

I hope your personal problems are moving towards straightness; & that you will have a good time in Germany, or wherever you may go. We, here, are all very fond of you. Gjon has told me that the Feature about O'Casey has been accepted by TIME-LIFE, which was pleasant to hear, & we all look forward to giving it an O'Casey welcome here.

All good wishes to you, & we all send our love.

Yours very sincerely,
Sean

To George Jean Nathan

MS. CORNELL

TOTNES, DEVON

25 OCTOBER 1953

My most dear George:

Your book, "The Theater in the Fifties" [1953], came safely, day before yesterday; and all the bells rang. It will be delightful to read it, when I get a chance—Breon has seized it, & has wrapped himself in it in his own room; & there it'll stay till he reads the last line. He loves your humor.

Thanks to you, dear George, for sending it to me, sending it to us, for the household welcomes it—Here's George's book! Breon is with us at the moment. We had to suspend paying for him in London, which is costly; but he is painting here, & has done a picture of me, which, I think, is good. He is acquiring a surer touch, but it is too early to say yet if there be magic in it. Our younger lad, Niall, is away doing his term in the Royal Artillery—a nuisance that shatters two valuable years from his life, & separates him from his real interests. Strange irony for the Irish Patriot to have had two sons in England's Imperial army.

I hope your holidays did you good, for you & I have now the winter to face: well, we'll face it. How is Gene? Dear Gene. When you see him, or write to him, give him my dear love.

My love to you, dear George, while I wait the delight of reading your book.

Ever,
Sean

To Robert Lewis

MS. LEWIS

TOTNES, DEVON

11 NOVEMBER 1953

My dear Bob,

Aha, you seem to have done it again, & are agoing to have a sunny time in the Teahouse of the August Moon.[1] I sincerely hope so. Brook's

[1] John Patrick's *Teahouse of the August Moon,* based on a novel by Vern Sneider, directed by Robert Lewis, opened in New York on 15 October 1953.

article gives you & all a glow of praise; and a review by Henry Hewes in "Saturday Review" does the same. Henry spent a night with us here some months ago. I hope the Teahouse will give you a chance to sit down for a while.

I daresay you know the scheme of "Cockadoodle Dandy" for LIFE is abandoned. They found it impracticable; & have substituted a Feature "The World of O'Casey" instead. It can't be helped. It means a loss of dollars to me (& to you, I suppose), but, still it can't be helped. I had a guess it would be impracticable. Well, I hope the Teahouse will make up for it, for you have obviously put a pile of work, & many imaginative thoughts into it. By the way I hear (or read) that you are a 'cellist. Well, for you, if you be one. Wish to God, I could play a tin whistle. Music takes weariness from one's walking. Niall, our younger lad, is now in the Royal Artillery; all the rest of us are here, & all send their love to you. And so do I, me bucko. Take a rest now. Congratulations.

As ever,
Sean

To Barbara A. Cohen

TS. COHEN

TOTNES, DEVON
24 NOVEMBER 1953

Dear Miss Barbara,

Thanks for your letter and for the most interesting account of your activities. Nonsense aside, it should be a good whistle drawing attention to what you and Marianne do. I hope it may bring many to your Firm. As for the sketches not being a bit like you both, that often happens, though none of us knows how we look—a good job for a lot of persons. Each of us can be seen only in the eye of another. We think we see when we look at a reflection, but we see but a shadowy indication. An outline of the body, whereas others see us in a three-fold way—body, soul, and spirit; and even they are often mistaken. The shadow of oneself the sun makes is the nearest one can get to his or her own personality. Shine out fair sun! Well, there's a little erudite lecture from a nix professor for you.

Regarding your new proposal,[1] I am game to have a shot at it right

[1] Miss Cohen had proposed that O'Casey do another reading for Caedmon; the recording was made at his home in Totnes on 26 December 1953. This record, *Sean O'Casey Reading*, Volume Two, Caedmon TC 1198, was not released until September 1969, and consists of readings from *I Knock at the Door, Rose and Crown*, and *Sunset and Evening Star*. For details about his first reading for Caedmon, see his letter to Miss Cohen, 11 September 1952, note 2.

enough, but there are others to consider. There are two lassies, Marianne and Barbara, and Peter Bela [Bartok], Eileen (Mrs. O'C.), and the 3 children, though all are grown up now—24, 18, and 13. Let me set down the gamble squarely:

I am in my 74th year; I have a tough time of it, and bear many scars; at this age, one can never be sure of feeling fit; I have but one eye, and that one only half the normal value of a normal eye; and almost always painful. So it might be that you, Peter, and Mrs. O'C. would have gone to a lot of trouble arranging all, and then, pop! the old boyo might be hors d'euvres just when everything was ready. If you are willing to take these risks, then I'm game to try. The last time, I had been just two days out of bed after a sharp attack of influenza; yet we got through it fairly well. Well, I've laid the facts before you and Marianne; so, if you like to risk it, well and good. If I'm anyway right with the world, I could struggle through an hour of reading, speaking, and singing; an hour or so. By the way, there's a lad here who takes down this work; an electrical engineer. Last summer he did a tape record for Gjon Mili who is connected with LIFE of me, to be attached to a short cinema of us all—Mrs. O'C., Breon, Niall, Shivaun, and myself: in the garden, on the Devon roads, washing up in the scullery, taking tea in the kitchen. He did this for his own personal use, and, I believe, is to show it to friends sometime in the future. At the same time, he and a friend from LIFE were over here for a feature article which entre news, I believe, is to appear in LIFE in the Spring. Gjon is a grand lad, and, I'm sure, would tell you about him who did the recording, if you are interested. I couldnt guarantee him, of course, for I've no technical knowledge of the work; but, if he were suitable, it might be cheaper to have him do it. He lives in Torquay, 7 miles from Totnes. Gjon Mili's address is—6 East 23 St. New York. Algonquin 4-7222. Dont tell anyone else—I think Gjon wants it to remain a secret till he shows the film. My love to you both.

Yours sincerely,
Sean O'Casey

What a pity Marianne hasn't another 'o' in her name—"Rooney"; it would have forced her to be born in Dublin, Cork, or Galway; or somewhere near.

To Harry Cowdell

MS. TEXAS

TOTNES, DEVON
25 NOVEMBER 1953

Dear Mr. Cowdell,

You have me bet! (beaten, in Dublin lingo) I can't, for the life of me, suggest anything in the way of an "eyecatcher" for "Sunset & Evening Star." I'll have to leave this difficulty for you to solve. By all means work on the idea conveyed by the title. It is odd how difficult little things can be sometimes. I've been busy, doing a long record for Caedmon Publishers—song, story, & play [1]—, and have been asked to do another next month; giving information & help to Plenipotentiaries from LIFE doing an article, "World of O'Casey," [2] which, I understand, is to appear in the Spring; & a short walkie-talkie film for an American friend,[3] who is to show it at a party in New York this Christmas.

I'm trying to keep fit, but don't like the winter & its fogs—here grey & thick, cold and damp, seeping into the marrow; but not so stifling as the black, satanic fogs of your London. I do hope you and your comrades manage to breathe a way safely through them.

> *My good wishes to you.*
> *Yours sincerely,*
> *Sean O'Casey*

[1] See O'Casey's letter to Barbara A. Cohen, 11 September 1952, note 2.

[2] See O'Casey's letter to Robert Emmett Ginna, 31 March 1953, note 2.

[3] "A Conversation with Sean O'Casey and Robert Emmett Ginna," presented on television on 22 January 1956 by the National Broadcasting Company in its Wisdom Series. The program was filmed at O'Casey's home in Totnes, produced and directed by Robert D. Graff, photographed by W. Suschitzky.

To George Jean Nathan

MS. CORNELL

TOTNES, DEVON
9 DECEMBER 1953

My most dear George:

It was indeed sad to hear of Gene's death.[1] He certainly died too young. God help us when such as he go. They leave us lonely; especially when their touch is still warm on our hands. O'Neill and Shaw—their

[1] Eugene O'Neill died on 27 November 1953 at the age of 65.

going rends a lot from the Theatre. One would want to be just only about to leave school not to miss them. I still can't imagine Shaw as having gone. Maybe, be God, he hasn't. When great ones go, a fellow begins to believe in immortality.

I enjoyed your book [2] intensely. The season, evidently was a poor one; & it is sad to think that the one Star in the sky of the Theatre is the criticism of itself. But you are hard at it still, making enemies—V. Leigh & L. Olivier this time [3]: enemies here; for these two artists are of a divine nature here. I've seen Olivier only twice—as Mercutio & as Romeo. He, to my mind, was better than Gielgud in either part. But one has to hush & shout hurrah at most things. The Theatre here's as bad as the Theatre there. We are better stocked with Cissies than you are. I doubt very much that Shakespeare was a homo; I don't see how he could create such virile characters—like Dickens—, & be one. But it is so common here, that if one man walks with another, he is a declared homo. But it is quite possible for the love of man for man to be above that given to a woman—like David & Jonathan; & David was no cissy.

It seems Saroyan is as naughty as ever. Isn't it a pity such a one won't take more pains; so few would send his plays dancing on the stage. And such as he, full of natural human warmth is needed there badly. Plays, mostly, are pure silliness or a dirge for the world's ineradicable sin. War play of long ago: I remember how thrilled I was with "Held by the Enemy." [4] You are wise & witty about the Directors. A lot of them are the Dramatists' executioners. Thanks a thousand from Breon for your grand book, & a thousand more from me.

My dear love to you.
Sean

[2] *The Theatre of the Fifties* (1953).
[3] *Ibid.*, Nathan's negative reviews of Laurence Olivier and Vivien Leigh in an alternating repertoire of Shakespeare's *Antony and Cleopatra* and Shaw's *Caesar and Cleopatra*, which opened in New York on 20 December 1951.
[4] William Gillette's *Held by the Enemy* (1887).

To New Statesman and Nation

26 DECEMBER 1953

SIR THOMAS MORE [1]

Sir,—Pointing an Aha finger at Mr. Trevor-Roper as being ill-informed about the Catholic Church, Mr. Waugh himself seems to be a

[1] In the "Books in General" column of the *New Statesman and Nation,* 5 December 1953, H. R. Trevor-Roper commented ironically on the four-century delay in the canonization of Sir Thomas More. Evelyn Waugh replied in a letter of 12 December.

worse example, according to what he says in his letter, and what he said in a recent broadcast. Mistaking by less than a month the date of More's and Fisher's execution can hardly be thought of as an "offensive and clumsy attack on the Catholic religion." Nor can the fact of forgetting (or ignoring) that at the time, Fisher had been made a Cardinal be any indication of one either. Fisher was a Bishop, and that position is more important than that of a Cardinal, for the Church could do without Cardinals, but cannot get on without her Bishops: The Apostolic Succession is of more importance to the Roman Catholic Church than the Cardinalate. And surely recusant has a stronger meaning than the one associating it with the refusal to attend Anglican Church Services: it has within it the tinge of the meaning of rebellion; of opposition, of disobedience; especially during the time in question, when all England was in the throes of a fight for her National entity; busy, consciously and unconsciously, forging a unity of independence, politics, and faith; as Joan of Arc before had battled for the nationhood and unity of the French People.

As for the Bishops being "chary of encouraging men of their faith to take University degrees," may the reason be, not that implied by Mr. Waugh, but the stronger one of fearing they may get to know too much, delivering them from a false loyalty, such as that which prompted the Roman Catholic Historian, Cardinal Gasquet, to deliberately and insistently falsify history to buttress up a thesis written to uphold and strengthen the historical position of the Church.

In his broadcast, Mr. Waugh, rather disdainfully, shoved aside the question of why he seemed to dislike humanity, by answering that to love humanity was God's prerogative. Since God is love, there is no prerogative; this prerogative is given to the Catholic Christians, and, indeed, to all calling themselves Christians. Mr. Waugh either despises it, or neglects it, at his peril. In the same way, he brushes children aside, saying in a reply to a question, I associate with them when they reach the years of coherent speech; I dont carry them on my shoulders, or play ball with them. Perhaps, it's just as well—it would appear he wouldnt be a very lovable companion.

Is this recusancy in affairs of the world's humanity and affairs of the life of children a new fashion among the members of the Roman Catholic Church? No; dates are of little importance: they form no part of the deposit of Faith once delivered to the apostles. Mr. Waugh is but playing at tiddley winks.

Sean O'Casey

[14 December 1953]

X

OF THE IRISH SOUL AND IRISH SUFFERING, 1954

I DON'T know what you say about the soul—the soul can be a nuisance at times. John Mitchel, the 1848 Irish patriot once said, "The Irish people would have been free long ago, if it weren't for their damned souls!"

Ireland's becoming an odd land. Last night I listened to a Father Polac, or some name like that, telling the Irish that Pain and Woe and Suffering were not only the Will of God, but must be looked upon as favors from Him. When I think of fever in swine, fluke in sheep, pip in poultry, foot and mouth disease in cattle, I wonder are those, too, to be thought of as favors from God?

Now in his seventy-fifth year, the exiled Dubliner in Devon sat listening to the Christmas music of his children, and, heigh ho, the wind and the rain outside, and meditated, perhaps prophetically, in a January letter to Brooks Atkinson: "Feel as if I were developing into a minor Prospero." The old wizard was counting his simple blessings in a mellow mood, but there were storms ahead and he was soon brandishing his wand of magic words again in many directions, pointing out the folly of mortal Christians and still looking for a Communist Eden on earth. His concern for the fate of Ireland made him extremely critical of the frailties of his country-men and women, and in another January letter he identified the excessive pieties of religion and nationalism as the twin hypocrisies of Irish life: "But then, Irishmen & women, when they exhibit particular falsehood & treach-ery, always do so behind noble causes—holy church or holy nation." When a Dublin woman wrote in February to scold him for his unfair attacks against Catholics, he was determined to convince her that he was free from religious bigotry and could never forget the suffering of all his Cath-olic friends: "You see, I've worked with Catholics—many of them great Union men, under Larkin—but what a man Larkin was!—, I've been on strike with them, went hungry with them, sat in Dispensaries with them, helped them to bury their dead—*lived* with them & loved them; but did not like their faults, their indifference to their own needs; their ignorance that the world was theirs." Behind that ignorance and indifference he saw the shadow of the clergy who urged the Irish people to accept their misery as a sign of divine grace—not only the will of God but a special favor from Him. For that reason he wanted more Christianity not less, and the closer Christianity came to the brotherly principles of Christ, the closer it came to displaying the glory of God in the practical needs of man. For O'Casey that was a common goal that should have linked Christianity with Communism, though most Christians and Communists were reluctant to accept such a general unity of faith and purpose.

In many of his letters he was consistently trying to broaden the base of what he called his Shelleyan Communism to include every faith practiced by people everywhere. If this hope was a sign of his quixotic idealism, he often tempered it with comedy and commonsense in everything he wrote. As if to make certain that no one would accuse him of becoming too theo-retical about his vision of the good life, he wrote the following warning in April to a friend who was probably so full of abstract Marxist dogma that he must have sounded like a pompous American Covey: "Live at your work; live with your sweetheart or your wife; with your children; live with music, art, literature; football, baseball, or table tennis. And remember all the Bourgeoise aren't villains; often a damn sight more charming & inter-esting than those who are no more than peripathetic Communist pamphlets." Dogmatic Communists distressed him as much as dogmatic Christians, and he was more partial to open-hearted people who were full of laughter and the life-spirit.

Although he was genuinely optimistic about man's potential for good, he recognized, from a lifetime of pain and disappointment, that if hardship was a common experience for most people, it also posed a daily challenge that had to be confronted. In June he told Francis MacManus, whose child was suffering from a serious illness, that people were united by the difficulties they had to endure and fight to overcome: "Trouble at least unites us into one family. Only by settling the problems of others can we settle our own. Improvement can only come through community. It isnt a question of communism, but one of commonsense; and, willy nilly, we have to come to each other's help." Later in the year he wrote to a woman in England: "It will be a fine world when we begin to bless each other with the things we do." Perhaps people who are put off by O'Casey's use of that taboo word, Communism, should bear in mind that, above all else, it represented his abiding faith in mutual good deeds.

He often complained that part of the problem of religion and politics was that Christians and Communists were ignorant of the doctrines they professed to follow. Furthermore, in making his plea for Communist virtue he was more likely to quote from the Bible than from Marx. In November he told Peter Newmark that it was not necessary to read Marx in order to be a good Communist, and in one of his characteristic surprises he proceeded to make a connection between Communism and St. Paul that goes to the heart of his eclectic vision: "There are many good Communists who never read a line of Marx. A man who sets out to be a doctor, & becomes a good one, becomes a Communist; a man who sets out to be a teacher & becomes a good one, becomes a Communist; doing good to his neighbours, & bringing the world onwards. 'Whatsoever thy hand findeth to do, do it with all they might'—good Communist doctrine, though it was said by St. Paul."

It must be said that he practiced what he preached, and used his writing hand to inspire his readers to help each other with all their might. Words were his weapons of enlightenment, and besides maintaining a constant flow of them in letters to his intimate audience all over the world, he continued with his formal writing. He finished the final volume of his autobiography; he went on writing articles and messages; and before the end of the year he completed a new play, *The Bishop's Bonfire,* and was making plans for its production by Cyril Cusack in Dublin. In the midst of all this work, he and his family had to cope with the upheaval of a move from Totnes to a flat in St. Marychurch, which involved the added burden of a doubled increase in rent, when after sixteen years the landlord forced them out of their house. Some American friends who heard of his problems wanted to try to get a Foundation grant for him, but he politely and proudly refused the offer saying: "The difficulties we are meeting are similar to those everyone has to meet some day, one way or another."

No special favors for O'Casey. Nothing could discourage or defeat him. "I am going on 75," he told MacManus, "and though one foot may be in the grave, the other is beating time in the future. I love children, and even the shyest, after ten minutes or so, become fast friends. . . . As a Communist should, I am interested in all things; always learning; always watching, listening, always full of curiosity; always ready for a laugh." He was always convinced that good would ultimately triumph over evil, and that the sinister Senator McCarthy "in the end, won't have any more prestige, even in Wisconsin, than a cold hot-hog." When his dear old friend George Jean Nathan suddenly married the young actress Julie Haydon, he included with his congratulations the following comment: "It may not be wise to marry, but I think it's sensible." His curiosity ranged from the plays of Claudel and Fry to the poetry of Rilke and Blok; from the death and vindication of Roger Casement to the original design of the Irish Citizen Army flag; and from skepticism about "the rattle of Father Peyton's blather of the Rosary," to a careful recitation of his simple eating habits—"there isnt a monk here or elsewhere that eats more chastely than I do."

He maintained his faith in the freedom of the individual and the good of the community: "nothing shall tame me to submit my mind to any bishop, pope, or politician who does not put the needs and rights of the People first." He defended victims of McCarthyism; he encouraged and wrote references for young writers; he inspired and amused friends and strangers everywhere with his magic words. In the boundless realm of his letters, he was something of a visionary comedian—a mad and merry Prospero.

To Brooks Atkinson

TS. ATKINSON

TOTNES, DEVON
[? JANUARY 1954]

My dear Brooks and Oriana,
Thank you deeply for your kind and valuable present. It came to us on Christmas morning, as the bells rung and our Christmas Tree bloomed into coloured light. We were all here—"Christmas Day in Killarney, and all the folks at home!" Niall, our younger lad, who has been a gunner in the artillery for some time, was with us too, on leave for the first time. My mind was a little distracted from the bright briskness & the bells by remembering that on the following day Peter Bartok, from Caedmon Publishing Co., was to arrive the next evening to set up a huge array of apparatus for a long-playing Record of O'Casey reading "a story," singing some songs, & reciting a discussion between two Irishmen as to the best way to defend Ireland from Invasion, if another war came tumbling on

top of us.[1] It was a tiring job, and I was glad when it was over; more tiring, coming in the middle of the masse-hustle of Christmas time—an extraordinary & bewildering exhibition of hectic, reckless mass-psychology, rushing hither & thitherwards, like the hasty, whirling waters of Livia Plurabelle in Finnegans Wake. And now the New Year has silently slid in before us, to give us a black band to wear on our arm, or a coloured plume to fix in our hat. May it be a ming-tien from beginning to end.

I have finished checking the galley-slips of "Sunset & Evening Star"; &, though the Page proofs have to come in, & be checked, too, I hope the book may appear before this year ends. Whether the work be good or bad, I don't know. I done me best, & so me conscience is quiet.

Your Journal, The New York Times, has reprinted two articles of mine in an Anthology,[2] which is very pleasant. It's odd, though, that this sign of approval (or anything else like it), instead of filling me with elation, gives me a slap of fright. I usually wonder if they be worthy of selection. A weak spot in me somewhere. Out damned spot! But it never goes. Niall was selected to train as an officer, but has refused to go on with it. I'm glad, for I've no wish he should develop a military mind; though I made no attempt to influence him. Better to let him shape his own destiny by thinking himself of, and acting upon, the life around him. He prefers the noise of a trombone to the bang of a gun, & I think, he's wise. Shivaun is learning the guitar, so with piano, trombone (when Niall comes home); & a guitar, there are many & various sounds in my ears as well as those from the sounds of the wind and the rain. Feel as if I were developing into a minor Prospero.

Here, from the first-floor window of the Devon house, I can see you glancing from yours at the scud in the wind without, &, maybe, at icicles hanging from the eaves of the house opposite. We may be leaving here before long—the landlady has sent us notice to quit, wanting, she says, the place for her own purposes. We had hoped to stay here for another two years, till Shivaun had finished her time in Dartington school, but it looks like we'll have to go before this happens: a problem I don't like facing. Oddly enough, if we could have stayed the two years, we had our eyes on Stratford-on-Avon; they had, at least, though I should have chosen Salisbury or Winchester.

Well, my sincere love to your pretty, charming, & lively Oriana, and, dear Brooks, to you; & to yours.

As ever,
Sean

---

[1] See O'Casey's letter to Barbara A. Cohen, 24 November 1953, note 1.
[2] *Highlights of Modern Literature: A Permanent Collection of Memorable Essays from the* New York Times Book Review, ed. Francis Brown (1954), includes the following O'Casey essays originally printed in the *New York Times Book Review:* "Always the Plough and the Stars," 25 January 1953; "Bernard Shaw: An Appreciation of a Fighting Idealist," 12 November 1950.

To New Statesman and Nation [1]

TC. O'CASEY

TOTNES, DEVON

2 JANUARY 1954

Dear Editor;

Allow me a few last words to fling from my window-sill at Mr. Waugh passing by on the other side of the street, with noble nose cocked. Like all Roman Catholic Apologists, he twists things to suit his argument. He covers Trevor-Roper's neglect in giving the title of Cardinal to Fisher by saying, "He (Trevor-Roper) excuses himself on the grounds that 'Cardinal' is not a legally recognised title in this country. Yet in the same essay he refers to 'Cardinals' Wiseman and Manning."

Now Trevor-Roper uses the word "Was," which Waugh changes to "Is." The title was not recognised in Fisher's time, for England was at war with the Papacy's power, and hot in revolution to secure its independence from all outside clerical interference. In the times of Wiseman and Manning, things had changed, for England then could let the R.C. Prelates call themselves anything they liked (much more so now), for the weakness of the Roman Catholic Church here today compels her to be damned cautious and very humble. She waits for worse days. That is how these Apologists twisted things in the days of H. Belloc and G. K. Chesterton, and how they twist them now. But, maybe, it's natural for Waugh to resent Mr. Trevor-Roper's neglect to give Fisher his grand title: the higher the rank, the greater the martyr—the snob-appeal again!

If Mr. Waugh consults his dictionary again, he will find that "Recusant" has additional meanings to the one he allows it. But Waugh evidently looks upon himself as an authority, since, in his broadcast, he conferred upon God the Father, Maker of heaven and earth, the prerogative of Loving all Humanity. It only remains now for the Pope to make God a Papal Count. As for tutors to "Christian undergraduates," I suggest to Waugh that he should read what Dr. McDonald, for forty years Professor of Theology in Maynooth College, says of these things, and that he should read, too, the opinions of ex-students from Roman Catholic Colleges about the education they got and the manner in which it was given. If he be interested, he'll find some quotations in my next biographi-

[1] This letter was refused publication by the editor. Evelyn Waugh had replied to O'Casey in a letter of 2 January 1954, and Trevor-Roper replied to Waugh in a letter of 9 January. Waugh and Trevor-Roper replied to each other in letters of 16 January.

cal volume. He might, too, ponder the reason why Dublin's R.C. Archbishop has ordered all Roman Catholics from entering Trinity College under ban of excommunication, except they bear a special, well-written permissu from Him. But the Bishops' chariness in letting their innocent young undergraduates mingle with the common colleges seems to be a failure, since we are told that near a thousand a week abandon the Faith in England alone. As for "intellectual emptiness," let him read Cardinal Spellman's novel, or his "The Road to Victory"; or, alternatively, the writings of Daniel Lord, S.J., in the popular Roman Catholic Press, and the Bishops' Pastorals. Here's richness for him!

Yours sincerely,
Sean O'Casey

To George Jean Nathan

MS. CORNELL

TOTNES, DEVON
4 JANUARY 1954

My very dear George:
Inclosed is an effort to review Odets' "Big Knife," [1] which may interest you. It puzzles me. Ivor Brownian reviews always do. He seems to me to be a clever juggler throwing up coloured balls, but failing to catch most of them. For instance, if a dramatist, because of his outlook, wants to have a bang at a Capitalist, why not? Or at the Proletarian, why not? So long as the play's a play. Fry's "Lady's Not for Burning" wasn't true to true medieval history of witch-hunting; but there's music in it, & a lot of loveliness, & what more can the Theatre want? Oh, God, I'm talking drama criticism now, about which I know damn all!

I do hope you are keeping fit & well. Have started a new play—but God knows if I'll ever finish it—"The Bishop's Bonfire."

My deep love to you.
Sean

[1] Ivor Brown, "Golden West," *The Observer*, 3 January 1954, a review of Clifford Odets's *The Big Knife*, which opened in London on 1 January 1954, directed by Sam Wanamaker.

To David Krause

TS. KRAUSE

TOTNES, DEVON
8 JANUARY 1954

My dear David:

Thanks a lot for the card and for your many rich wishes and words. I am passing through a very busy time of it. I've just finished correcting galley-slips of new biographical vol., "Sunset and Evening Star," and am waiting for the page-proofs to come in. Day after Christmas, Peter Bartok, son of the composer, came down with a load of electrical equipment, and I spent that night and the following day making a long-playing record for the New York Caedmon Co. Christmas was like "Christmas in Killarney with all the folks at Home"; there were six of us, and with practically no help other than our own efforts, you can see what a turbulent time we had. Then came Peter with his wires, flexes, and sounding boxes, and a Christmas went by unlike any other one experience up to now. I've started a new play, too, to add to the confusion; but facing it all bravely. I don't know what you say about the soul—the soul can be a nuisance at times. John Mitchel, the 1848 Irish patriot once said, "The Irish people would have been free long ago, if it weren't for their damned souls!"

I hope you are doing well in your University. Give my love to the other David [H. Greene], and tell him to give my love to Catherine and her children.

Take care of yourself.

Yours very sincerely,
Sean

To Shaemas O'Sheel

MS. O'SHEEL

TOTNES, DEVON
12 JANUARY 1954

Dear Shaemas,

Thanks for card showing your Big House, & for letter. I've been very busy, & get tired very quick now. I don't envy your job of re-reading biography. Rather you'd do it than I. I hoped I haven't judged Devalera, for

I couldn't. I never came close to him. Saw him in the young days in the Ard Craobh [1] of the Gael. League; &, of course, later on, marching with I[rish]. Volunteers—him, not me; & later still as the opposer of the Treaty, battering it with his Document No. 2.[2] The man has always been a puzzle to me—what is he at all? Yet a friend of mine in Ireland, one who fought with the Republican forces in Spain, tells me Dev. & Fianna Fail are the only remaining hope of Ireland; that they alone stand between Ireland & a link-up with the Brit-Amer-Fran-coalition for European attack on the USSR. Personally, I doubt it; but that's what he says.

Mrs. [Hanna] Sheehy-Skeffington is another I never came close to: I knew the husband intimately, as I knew Dev's wife, Sinead Ni Flanagain in the younger days of the Gael. League. But then, Irishmen & women, when they exhibit particular falsehood & treachery, always do so behind noble causes—holy church or holy nation. You seem to have had a busy time in hell and hot water for Ireland—the old sow that eats her farrow. I wonder was Joyce right? Ireland is still ashamed (and afraid) of him. Name never mentioned: the one land in the world far as I know that bans "Ullyses." And the young are still pouring out of the country—Catholics from the "South," Protestants from the North. All the smaller towns of Kerry, Mayo, Galway, Cork, Clare, et al, are now housing the old & a few children. The noble causes have ceased to breathe, & the dead remains are too small to be embalmed in anyone's memory. Yet Dev. goes along, head up; confident as ever. Is it blindness or vanity; or blindness brought on by vanity? The wonder of the world is no longer the Irish Exile: the wonder is the one who stays at home. I will remember what you say about "The Scalpel, the Sword."

My love to Mrs. O'Sheel & to yourself.

All the best,
As ever,
Sean

[1] Ard Craobh, the High or Central Branch, a well-known branch of the Gaelic League.

[2] Eamon de Valera presented his Document No. 2 on 4 January 1922, as a counterproposal to the Free State Treaty signed by Arthur Griffith and Michael Collins.

To George Jean Nathan

MS. CORNELL

TOTNES, DEVON
18 JANUARY 1954

My very dear George,

A letter from Brooks [Atkinson] tells me you haven't been well. It is sad news, but I'm hoping you may be better before this note gets to you, though, while Winter's here, it's hard to turn a corner. When one gets to seventy, the winds blow cold, & one has to cling a lot to the chimney corner. At least, I have to; & more, grow tired too damn quick. For some time, I haven't felt myself even to be half-way to the top of the world; nor do I ever expect to feel like that again. One has to get satisfied with less & less.

It's a comfort to hear that you are not altogether alone, & that Miss Julie Haydon stands near you often. That is grand, & must be a consolation.

Take it quietly, & wait for the Spring as I do; for then the summer's near to bring us, I hope, under the memorised shadow of younger days.

All my love to you.
As ever,
Sean

To Frank McCarthy

MS. McCARTHY

TOTNES, DEVON
24 JANUARY 1954

Dear Frank,

Thank you for your letter and for the Christmas enclosure of—was it Dublin Castle in the 18th Cen.? I've read some of Norah Hoult's novels, & I think she's a clever lass; much better than Kate O'Brien who shocks me a little with her pretensions. But then writers have to earn a living, & it's a hard job nowadays. Last Christmas was the busiest I ever had—like "Christmas in Killarney, with all the folks at home." Our younger lad, now a gunner in the Field Artillery, was home on leave; so we were all together. On Boxing Day, Peter Bartok, son of the Hungarian Composer, came here with a huge collection of Recording tackle, and I did a long-playing Record—near enough for two of them, indeed—for a New York firm. The old voicé streamed out in readings, songs, & discussions. Last November twelve-month, I did one, too, for the same Firm; so the Old Voice will be heard in many American places. Yes, indeed, Joyce's stories would' make good one-acters; & so would the scene of the Christmas Dinner, & the dispute about Parnell, in his "Portrait of an Artist as a Young Man." But, I'd rather do my own work. Wonder some of the boyos don't think of Joyce, instead of Anouilh, who isn't good enough even to lay a leaf on Joyce's grave. No, I was never in St. Bartholomew's of Smithfield; but often in St. Bartholomew's in Phibsboro', a district in a place called Dublin; & saw many odd things there. Dr. Soper [1] is a brave, good man, but lacks the revolutionary Spirit of an Apostle. He—like so many—is always looking down at his feet to see how far they are going.

I hope you'll keep the job you're in for some time. I've just corrected galley-slips of "Sunset and Evening Star," and am now trying to set down another play—a three-act one.

My love to you.
As ever,
Sean

[1] Dr. Donald O. Soper (1903–   ), Methodist minister and superintendent of the West London Mission at Kingsway Hall since 1936. McCarthy was now one of Soper's assistants.

To Seumas Scully

MS. SCULLY

TOTNES, DEVON
24 JANUARY 1954

Dear Seumas,
Thank you so much for the papers. They give a curious picture of Ireland; dealing with all problems in such a way that they deal with none. Thanks, too, for the Abbey Program. I never met Louis D'Alton,[1] though I had many letters from him. His picture shows him a fine handsome fel-low. I acted with his father & uncle on the old Abbey stage—the Me-chanics—years & years ago, when I was just sprouting out of kidship.[2] It

[1] Louis D'Alton, the well-known Abbey Theatre playwright and director, died suddenly in 1951 at the age of fifty-one.
[2] In 1895 at the age of fifteen, O'Casey had acted the role of Father Dolan, the patriotic priest, in Dion Boucicault's *The Shaughraun* at the Mechanic's Theatre in Abbey Street, which was rebuilt as the Abbey Theatre in 1904. The play was pro-

was rather sad that he died just as he was becoming really successful. What killed him? I'd never heard that he had had any kind of sickness. But it is good that his widow is benefiting by "This Other Eden." When Blanshard's book [3] comes here, I shall get it. Honor Tracy has sent out another blast—"Mind You, I Said Nothing!" [4]—which gives another shake to Ireland's shoulder. There won't be a screed left on Kathleen by the time they'd all done with her. The article for LIFE [5] has been set up, I'm told, & is to appear in the Spring. Articles for this Journal are made out months in advance. I've done—St Stephen's Day—a long-playing Record—the second one—for a New York Firm: a tiring job, taking all one day, & part of another. Niall is away from us now, a gunner in the Royal Artillery. We had him on leave with us for Christmas. I've just finished correcting galley-slips of last biographical volume.

All good wishes to you.

Remember me to Owen S. Skeffington when you see him.

All the best.
Sean

---

duced by the traveling company of Louis D'Alton's father, Charles D'Alton, the comedian and actor-manager. When the actor playing Father Dolan became ill, the young O'Casey, who knew all the Boucicault plays by heart and also knew the D'Alton family, was called in to play the role.

[3] Paul Blanshard, *The Irish and Catholic Power* (1953).

[4] Honor Tracy, *Mind You, I Said Nothing!: Forays in the Irish Republic* (1953).

[5] "The World of Sean O'Casey," *Life,* 26 July 1954.

To Mrs. Mary Frances Keating

TC. O'CASEY

[TOTNES, DEVON]
26 JANUARY 1954

Dear Mrs Keating,

First and foremost, banquets arent in my line.[1] During my whole life of 74 years, I attended one organised dinner—that of the Critics' Circle when I first came to London. They never asked me again; and a luncheon given by C. B. Cochran. I detest them, so you could hardly have selected a worse one to help you than I.

I eat to live, rather [than] live to eat, and there isnt a monk here or

[1] Mrs. Keating, who wrote a column for housewives in the *Irish Times,* had been asked by the Sons of St. Patrick, an Irish-American organization, to describe O'Casey's favorite meal, so that they could serve it at their St. Patrick's Day banquet.

elsewhere that eats more chastely than I do; and this with no intention to mortify myself, or to offer up anything to God. It is simply the rational and the sensible way to eat. I spent some years on my own in Dublin, where I cooked for myself; and then my menue or menu or meanu was made from boiled eggs, raw tomatoes, cooked prunes and figs or apple-rings, tea, bread and butter, and, once a week, a pound of roast pork which lasted for three meals. I've never been an enthusiastic meat-eater, disliking the usual greasy look of it whatever way it had been cooked. I'm very esthetic in my desire for clean food and for a chastely layed-out table. To this day, I like roast (very little of it) pork, but it must be of prime quality. So must anything I eat, for, naturally, I have a delicate palate, though if food placed before me be not to my liking, and I pass it by, I dont create a fuss, but take it philosophically, and wait for the time when food of a better quality may be set before me.

As for drink, I am with this as I am with meat, rarely touching it, though when the family is all together, I have no objection to a glass of good white wine—at birthdays, or at Christmas. For an occasional, very occasional, liqueur, I like one from a recipe of the Hebridean Isles, Scotland, called "Drambuaidhe," which I first sampled in Scotland—in Edinburgh, among a crowd of singing, talking, kilted Gaels. I like, too, on festive occasions, a meringue of Apricots, or apple, or peach. I dont care for snow-white napery, preferring delicately or boldly-coloured cloths. I like plain-patterned table-ware above those ringed with roses, or similar ornamentation. And I love glass-ware from which to drink, and glass-ware for cooking: it has a delicate and a chaste appearance, infinitely above the look of saucepans, pots, or tins.

That's all I can think of telling you, and I suggest (knowing more about these things than I) that you should put together a menu of your own choice, built, maybe, on some of the items mentioned above. I shant mind if you add something of your own preference; you can say it is a favourite O'Casey dish; but dont make it pompous.

I'm glad to hear you are back again in *The Irish Times,* earning a little to set aside for your stricken boy. It is a great trial for you and for your husband. Francis McManus, Radio Eireann, has a son in a similar way; and it is maddening to me to feel sure that if less attention was given to religion and to war and more to the glorious uses of man's body, there would be far less sorrow of this kind in the world today. Indeed, my next biographical book has in it a chapter on children, called "Childermess."

Cookery is very important; it is an art comparable with literature, painting, or sculpture; more important than Retreats or Novenas, or the rattle of Father Peyton's blather inducing people to neglect more important things for the babble of the Rosary.[2] Cookery is important because it is the

---

[2] Father Patrick Peyton (1909–   ), the Mayo-born priest who launched his Family Rosary Crusade in 1942 with the slogan: "The Family that prays together stays together."

more important way of nourishing the sacred body, making it healthy and useful, and a true glory to God. When I think of (during 74 years) what my feet have done, my hands, how my heart worked, and how all the other organs helped to give my whole body fire and function, I am amazed, and I extol the body electric over all the declarations of stupid Jansenist clerics.

I can no more than sympathise deeply with you in your trial, and with your lad. Perhaps, he may be able to enter into a good deal of life yet; for none of us can enter into it fully with things as they are around us.

I hope Miss McCann is still with the I.T.[3]

I hope this letter may be of some help to you.

My love to you, your husband, and your boy.

Yours very sincerely,
Sean O'Casey

[3] Miss McCann was the secretary of Robert Maire Smyllie, editor of the *Irish Times.*

To Mrs. Mary Frances Keating

MS. KEATING

TOTNES, DEVON

4 FEBRUARY 1954

Dear Mrs. Keating,

Fine! a charming menu, though one we could afford to have only on Christmas Day—with luck! Curious, you should have thought of scallops. I'm fond of them eaten on their shells, &, long ago, have enjoyed them (two as a full meal, with bread & tea); but they have become expensive, & so, far as I'm concerned, can swim in the sea safely. I like fish, too; but it must have in it the full flavour of the sea—nothing is so insipid as fish kept too long in the ice. Turbot is lovely—again only when it's fresh from the sea; & so is a grilled herring, with the delicious tang of the sea still vibrant in its flesh; But either of these—piece of turbot or herring—would make a full meal, with a spud or two, or a slice of bread & butter—if butter be there; if not, as is most often the case, then margarine.

This is a hasty note—the big tank under our roof burst, & flooded the house, so we are busy drying it out & making it presentable for our lad who comes home on leave this week-end—he's a gunner in the Field Artillery. It was a most unpleasant experience for me, though Eileen (Mrs. O'C.) bore the brunt of it in macintosh & sou'wester.

I hope Miss McCann is allright. She wrote to me several times, &

mentioned leaving her job, which I advised against. She seemed to be disillusioned about the Faith.

Should you see Frank McM. [MacManus] give him my love.

I think your Menu fine, and think part of it, at least, should be more usual on all our tables. I wonder why the Sons of St. Patrick chose me to suggest a menu—me with my terrible bad name.

My love to your husband, your boy, & to you.

Yours very sincerely
Sean

To the Director, Arts Council of Great Britain [1]

TC. O'CASEY

[TOTNES, DEVON]
6 FEBRUARY 1954

Dear Sir,

I am venturing to invite your attention to the work of Thurso Berwick, and to suggest, with respect, that he is a worthy worker in Drama and Literature to receive an Arts Council grant. I know Thurso Berwick only from his work, which, of course, can be the one thing to recommend him to your notice; which may be the means of providing him with a spell of time, free from general cares, and of allowing him to usefully concentrate on the difficult job of playmaking.

I have read the MS of his two plays, *Quackpot* and *Don Juan,* both built up on themes furnished by the plays of Moliere. *Don Juan* is written in the Lallans, and is very entertaining in its tartan dress. It is brisk, in many parts comic, and the dialogue, on the whole, is terse, bracing, and picturesque. The play isnt without defects (the ending is weak), and it isnt everything it could be—though this applies to many first-class plays, and to all I've written myself; but it is, in my opinion, a very fine effort, and, if produced in a first-class way, would be well worthy to take its place with the rest and best of Scotland's drama. The play is under consideration by Glasgow's Citizens Theatre, and I hope it may be produced there, for it is by production alone that potential playwrights can learn to get a good grip on the curious and manifold ways in which drama is given colour and line and form.

Quackpot is written in English, and retains to a large extent the mode and manner of Moliere's play. The dialogue is good, though not so pic-

[1] The Director, Arts Council of Great Britain, 29 Queen Street, Edinburgh.

turesque as the Lallans in the other play. It is written more in what I suppose would be called a classic way, but it is deeply tinted with the Thurso Berwick peculiar style and character of movement. It reminds me of Lady Gregory's adaptation of *Le Bourgeois Gentlehomme* which was a great comic success in the Abbey Theatre. Its central character would need a first-class actor—say Miles Malleson—, and given this, would prove, I think, a fine comic example of drama on Scotland's or any other country's stage.

Thurso Berwick is also a satirist as his verses around the incident of the Stane can show—witty and at times biting; but more important still, he is a serious poet and has written a lot of fine lines. He seems to prefer the Winds before the Sun, and has written forcibly and charmingly about them. There isnt a doubt that the man is a poet.

I enclose a number of biographical details, showing that he has had a very diversified life and many experiences; that he is a scholar, and a very fine linguist. It is evident that he is deeply interested in the drama, and would profit by any help given to him; though I think he should coop his thoughts more tightly up in Scotland, rather than let them flow too freely over Europe and Asia.

But a poet he is, and, I believe, a fine potential dramatist, and so I submit the name of Thurso Berwick for your kind and wise consideration, naturally hoping that he may receive the reward that, in my opinion, his work deserves.

Yours sincerely,
Sean O'Casey

To Nan Ross

MS. ROSS

TOTNES, DEVON
6 FEBRUARY 1954

Dear friends,
Thank you very much for the good things that came to us from you around Christmas, though you mustn't do the like again, reserving all you have for your boy. I've been very busy since writing a new play, correcting proofs of a new biographical vol. "Sunset & Evening Star," writing many letters, &, worst of all, looking for a new place to live in, though Eileen does most, or all, of this. After 16 years, our landlord has decided he wants

to have the house for himself, & has sent us Notice to Quit, with all the seals & symbols of our holy laws upon it.

It is difficult to find a place to rest—places for sale are plenty; but the O'Caseys, for some reason or another, are bad savers, & can't keep even a fifteen shilling certificate safe (guaranteed to become a pound in Ten Years). So tell Gil, I won't be looking any more at the Foxgloves, pendant with their purple or white bells, which interested him (though almost all the bells had gone) because the plant gave Digitalis, a stimulant for the heart. Had I had time, I'd have shown him Valerian, a good stimulant for a nervous stomach; & other herbs that give relief & help to man—atropine plant—deadly nightshade—which so often helped to heal ulcers on my own eyes years ago. The chestnut tree, too, planted by Shivaun from a "conker" when she was six, & now full twenty feet & more high. Good by to all that.

If we can, we shall take a flat in the locality within six or eight miles of the school our daughter, Shivaun, goes to, so that she can be with us from Friday evening to Monday morning. She comes home daily while we live here. England has been bound tight in a bitter frost for the past two weeks, & still is, bringing woe to the method & manner of British plumbing. The tank under our roof burst the other evening, & flooded the whole house. Eileen and I had a time of it clearing the flood away, working in "macs" & sou-westers, with the waters cascading down on us till the main was cut off from without the house, after a search for the place where the stop-cock was buried. All the inefficiency isn't in the USSR.

Well, I pray, and many more pray with me, that the Berlin Conference will bring a surer peace.

My love to you all. Thanks again for your great kindness. My affectionate remembrance to my young friend, your young boy.

Yours very sincerely,
Sean

To Thurso Berwick

TC. O'CASEY

TOTNES, DEVON
7 FEBRUARY 1954

Dear Thurso Berwick,

I have sent off to the Director of the Arts Council of Britain my appeal on your behalf—sent by registered post.

I sincerely hope you may be among the six called, and, further, be one of the chosen; though, when all's said and done, this way's a poor way of bringing Art to England, or Scotland, or Ireland, or Wales. Like picking a blade of grass from a meadow. Art to be of the people should be everywhere, and artists should be in all places giving gifts to their own localities.

Well, we must make the best of it, for, at least, it's a beginning.

By the way, if I were you, I shouldnt "study" drama, if you are trying to write plays. Read them, and enjoy them, just as audiences do, or should do, and not as the critics. If you "study" too much, what you write will be a study too, and will be cut off from spontaneous life.

And why Rilke? He was a poet, of course, but one who never entered into active life, never mixed with them who do, with them who live. He was cooped up within a world within his own poor finite mind.

Well, no more literary controversy—it, too, is very often a barren subject. I hope you have completely recovered from your illness. And I hope your singing will reach the sun as well as the four cold winds.

Warm regards to your wife and to you. I enclose your plays and your poems.

> *Yours very sincerely,*
> *Sean O'Casey*

To Elizabeth Freundlich

TS. FREUNDLICH

TOTNES, DEVON
8 FEBRUARY 1954

Dear friend,

I have been very busy—as well as being bound up by frost, with flooding from burst pipes, trying to write another play, and correcting the proofs of a new biographical book—"Sunset and Evening Star"; so couldnt reply to your kind letter sooner.

It is very good news to hear that THE SILVER TASSIE is to be shown in Vienna, and I hope that the production may be taken to Vienna's bosom; and that its passion may be seen to show what we may expect from war; and that war may come the way of man no more.

I am sorry that COCKADOODLE DANDY is thought to be "too dangerous." From the nettle danger, we pluck the flower to safety, said Shakespeare; and I've always believed this to be true. I've never let myself dwell on the danger of saying this or of saying that, once my conscience was certain that what I said was honest—however mistaken it might be. East Berlin wants to do SHADOW OF A GUNMAN—they some time ago, thought THE STAR TURNS RED too dangerous, after rehearsing it, and having it ready to go on the stage. I'm not interested in the proposal about THE GUNMAN. It would hold little interest for the German People; and I dont see how they could understand it.

We are all well here. Our younger boy is with us now, home on leave—he is a gunner in the Field Artillery—such a waste of time, though I'm glad that the time spent in the army sends him among many men of different kinds, showing him that there is a wide world outside his family.

I trust that you are well, and send you our love and my love.

Yours very sincerely,
Sean O'Casey

To Mrs. Kay O'Riordan [1]

MS. O'RIORDAN

TOTNES, DEVON

19 FEBRUARY 1954

Dear Mrs. O'Riordan,

Thank you for the Christmas Card. I don't think I shall ever see Ireland again.

You confuse "Red Roses For Me" with "The Silver Tassie." The latter play had no "Catholic women praying, as it were, to a statue." In the former play, there is a group singing before a statue of Virgo Potens, a gilded, colored symbol, indicative of their desire for a brighter & better life. I've seen & heard them singing before the statue that used to be—may be still there—below the Tolka Bridge in Drumcondra, not far from the Archbishop's Palace. I've heard Catholics singing—I was among them on both occasions—in front of a Statue of the Virgin in the Convent of Stella Maris on Howth Hill; singing "Pray for the wanderer, pray for me"; & I can see "nothing derogatory in that" (as Fluther might say). The weakness is, in my opinion, that most of them are content with singing their hopes, while doing little to bring them into effect. And, if you knew mem-

---

[1] Mrs. Kay O'Riordan, 37 Victoria Street, South Circular Road, Dublin, wife of Michael O'Riordan, the Dublin bus conductor who fought for the Loyalists during the Spanish Civil War. Mrs. O'Riordan is a Catholic, her husband, a Communist. See O'Casey's letter to Sean Nolan, 21 May 1951, and his letter to Michael O'Riordan, 5 April 1955, Vol. III.

bers of Confraternities as well as I did, you'd know what an "ineffective bunch" most of them were; but no more ineffective than the Protestants who do the same things—singing instead of doing. You see, I've worked with Catholics—many of them great Union men, under Larkin—but what a man Larkin was!—, I've been on strike with them, went hungry with them, sat in Dispensaries with them, helped them to bury their dead— *lived* with them & loved them; but did not like their faults, their indifference to their own needs; their ignorance that the world was theirs.

Well, my love to you & to your husband.

Yours sincerely,
Sean O'Casey

To Barrows Dunham

MS. DUNHAM

TOTNES, DEVON
25 FEBRUARY 1954

My dear Barrows:

Very glad to hear from you, but anything but glad to hear you have been exiled from your College.[1] What a stupid act that was, is, & will be. What more noble man could students have among them? You are a good husband, a good father, a good friend, a good American; a bright-mind, eager only for the sensible good of all men. Some time ago, I wrote you about a "Giant in Chains," & hope you got my few remarks. I found it a wise book and a valuable one. Really, the use of reason to make the crooked ways of life straight; &, in this way, you walked by the side of Jesus. It is written very simply; not so simply as one who runs can read; but simple if one sits down & takes a thought for today and another for tomorrow. Your book is part of the gospel story as it comes from the mind of a warm-hearted philosopher. And in it, & through it, is great love, sensible love and reasonable love, as well as warm love for America, & for all that America can do. I'm just writing this in haste, for I've little time at the moment. Eileen slipped, fell, and broke her right wrist badly, & will have but one hand for many weeks; so I have a lot more to do, including a helping hand when she's dressing. It was very painful, but not so painful now; so she can be still while I help her with bodice or jersey.

I had a worker here a few weeks ago, a member of the Teamsters' Union; & we talked about you. It was he told me of your father's death; &

[1] See O'Casey's letter to Dunham, 22 September 1953.

that you had been sent away from your University. It was odd to hear an Irish Teamster, working on the New York Dock, talking about Barrows Dunham. But why should it be odd to listen to one good man talking of, & telling about, another good man.

My deep love to your wife, to your boy, Clarke, & to you.

Yours very sincerely,
Sean

To the Rev. John A. O'Brien [1]

PC. COLBY L.Q. [2]

TOTNES, DEVON
8 MARCH 1954

Dear Dr. O'Brien,

I delayed answering your kind letter for two reasons—because I wanted to get a decko at the book [3] first; and because my wife slipped a week ago, fell, and broke her right wrist badly, so that whereas before I had fifty things to do, now I have a hundred of them waiting for me everywhere.

Well, the book has come, and it will, indeed, be a joy to every soul hating Ireland, and to every mind who hopes that one day soon (sooner the better) the Irishman will be as rare on the shore of the Shannon as the Red Indian is rare on the shore of Manhattan. Funnily enough, the book will give joy to every heart and mind that has any affection left for Ireland because it is the loudest and clearest and wisest call ever given to my knowledge to Ireland to wake up, and lie dying and dreaming no more. Its great slogan is Muscail do mhisneach, a Banba! [4] All the articles

---

[1] The Rev. Dr. John A. O'Brien, Research Professor of Theology, University of Notre Dame, South Bend, Indiana.

[2] Richard Cary printed this letter in his article, "Two O'Casey Letters," *Colby Library Quarterly,* June 1972. The original letter is in the Colby College Library, and there is also a carbon copy in O'Casey's private papers, without the final paragraph, which was added in longhand.

[3] *The Vanishing Irish: The Enigma of the Modern World* (1953), edited by Dr. John A. O'Brien, a collection of essays by Irish writers on the causes of the decrease in Ireland's population. The following quotation on the title page, by the Most Rev. Cornelius Lucey, D.D., Bishop of Cork, shows the relevance of O'Casey's remarks about his wife's family: "The rural population is vanishing and with it is vanishing the Irish race itself. Rural Ireland is stricken and dying and the will to marry on the land is almost gone." In his introductory essay, "The Irish Enigma," O'Brien uses the following quotation from O'Casey: "We've been polishing the silver to shine in everybody else's place and leaving our own to sink into the dullness of lead."

[4] Wake up your courage, Oh Ireland!

are, with one exception, fine ones, well written, cogent, sharp, and implicitly appealing for a change in the view towards life in Ireland, and wherever the Irish may be; that is the world over. The book should be read by every Irish soul, lay and clerical, for two generations backwards, and unto the third and fourth generation forward; if the white candle before the holy rood (as Yeats pictured Kathleen ni Houlihan) is not to gutter out. I have been trying to say something similar myself for a long time now; but only got reprobation and malice for my pains. Indeed, COCKADOODLE DANDY is a secular hymn to life so despised and mocked at by the Irish Catholic, and, by your leave, by the Protestant, too. Whether the book will be effective in banishing the stupidity it aims at is another question. If it doesnt, hardly anything will. I doubt it myself; but I do hope most fervently that it may.

I know many instances of this deadly love of sterility among the Irish. A farming family, ten miles from Athlone had two daughters and three sons. The farm was one of 40 acres or so. The eldest son when a young man left the farm, became an accountant by self-education, and, afterwards became the father of my wife. The youngest son by marriage got a smaller farm, and had two sons; the other son with the two girls worked the original farm. He toiled for years just making ends meet, unable, so he said, to improve the farm in any way. He died suddenly, and it was found he had left no Will; and discovered, too, that he had near 4000 pounds in the bank. Banked secretly, without a soul knowing, till it came out after his death. Now, as the daughter of the eldest son, Mrs O'Casey was entitled to almost all the money, including the farm when it was sold. She got a letter from an Athlone Solicitor telling her all this, and asking her to make a legal declaration renouncing her claim. The two daughters were then old women, one well over eighty, unmarried, of course, though the younger one, Kate, was considered a beauty in her day, and from the look of her (we went to see them when on a visit to Eire in 1935), she was certainly that in her young days. She was well over eighty, and her sister but a few years behind; but they both still worked in the house and on the farm. The two boys of the brother working the other farm were grand handsome lads. One has since left for the world outside, and the other stayed on the land. We havent heard for some years now about them. But afterwards, a few years or so, along comes another letter from the Solicitor asking Mrs O'C. to renounce all claim to the farm again, and to add that to her well-known knowledge the Farm was to go to the surviving brother (him with the two sons) when the old ladies died. It appeared that they had gone leaving no will behind them either. Mrs O'C. did what was asked of her, and I hope the young lad left on the land has married and has children; for if not, there's no scion of the family left there to keep the name going in the part of Westmeath. What lonely places are all the places where the river Shannon flows! And Wicklow! We went all over it with Barry Fitzgerald, and found it populated with sheep, but hardly a child to be seen: not one in fact did we see wherever we went. Loneliness everywhere. At Roundwood we saw a lonely priest standing in the road talking to a bus-driver about to continue his journey. We had expected to get lunch there, but the one little "hotel" had been burned down, and there the four walls stood bleak and dead. Father Lavelle asked us to his place, but we decided to go on to Glendalough, with Father Lavelle delighted to go with us, and to be able to deliver himself from loneliness for an hour or so. Oh, I hate to think of it.

The one false note in the book, in my opinion, is the article by P. V. Carroll,[5] with his "mystical Irish soul"! And his pampered American women, unaware of the millions of Amer. women who have to work as hard and as diligently as women anywhere else.

All the reasons given in the Book are sensible ones, and are all written lively; but, in my opinion again, the cause goes deeper; it goes down to the Faith Itself, the Renunciation of the world, the flesh, and the devil. The Devil we know now isnt such a bad laddo, and, at worst, is but an illusion; and the world and the flesh are beautiful things, fashioned by God himself; so it seems to be a curious thing to renounce the works of His Hand.

This is all written in a hurry, for I've many things to do—just going now to help Eileen (Mrs O'C.) with the supper. Curiously, I have been working on a play for some months which touches upon the question in front of us—THE BISHOP'S BONFIRE.

Well, God speed the Book of yours into every Irish hand. The Irish have out-lawed the lover and his lass, may the Book bring them back into the glory and vivacity of our Irish life. Amen.

With thanks for your kind letter, and many, many warm and good wishes to you.

It is grand to have the Protestant and clever Arland Ussher, standing with the Catholic and clever Sean O'Faolain on this question of our survival. The death of the Irish would be the death of many grand things.

Sean O'Casey

[5] Paul Vincent Carroll's contribution, "The Mystical Irish."

To Barbara A. Cohen

MS. COHEN

TOTNES, DEVON
10 MARCH 1954

My dear Barbara,

I haven't heard a word from you or from Peter [Bartok] about the Record made in December of last year.[1] Has Peter gone down in the Atlantic—records and all? Or is it that the Record was poor, useless, terrible? Certainly, Peter & I worked hard, & did our best; &, from what I heard of it, it sounded good—but then I was listening to myself.

I hope Peter has recovered from the chills of our house; though bleak as it is in winter—a furnace in summer—, we have to leave it soon, for the landlord wants it "for his own purposes." Sixteen years of residence is no claim, once a landlord says "Go." Peter came at a busy time—around Christmas, with our younger lad, in the Artillery, on leave; but we did the best we could for him.

I should like to hear how you think the Record sounded from the tape, & if you have abandoned it, or have made a disk of it.

All good wishes,
Yours very sincerely,
Sean O'Casey

[1] See O'Casey's letter to Miss Cohen, 24 November 1953, note 1.

To Anthony E. Harvey [1]

PC. RANDOLPH-MACON [2]

TOTNES, DEVON
12 MARCH 1954

Dear Mr. Harvey,

I don't think Oliver Gogarty, D. Johnston, or Sean O'Faolain know what I am doing now, or what I've been doing for some time past, for I never met S. O'F., & haven't seen or heard from Gog. or Johnston for years and years.

[1] Anthony E. Harvey, a student at Randolph-Macon College, Ashland, Virginia, was working on his senior project, "The Blending of the Tragic and the Comic in the Plays of Sean O'Casey," and wrote to O'Casey about it.

[2] This letter and seven others appeared in Harvey's article, "Letters from Sean O'Casey to a Randolph-Macon Senior," *Randolph-Macon Bulletin,* September 1954.

As for blending "Comedy with Tragedy," it's no new practice—hundreds have done it, including Shakespeare up to Dion Boucicault in, for instance, "Colleen Bawn" & "Conn, the Shaughraun." And, indeed, Life is always doing it, doing it, doing it. Even where one lies dead, laughter is often heard in the next room. There's no tragedy that isn't tinged with humour, no comedy that hasn't its share of tragedy—if one has eyes to see, ears to hear. Sorrow & Joy are sisters, though Joy isn't always Joy or Sorrow Sorrow; they change appearances often and rapidly.

In the matter of "Flying Wasp" and "Windfalls," I can't help you, for they are long out of print, & I've no copy of either. It's a pity you can't lay hands on "Flying W.", for, I think it is worth reading, even today. You haven't missed much in the other, bar one story, "The Star Jazzer." There are two others, the two one-act plays, "Pound on Demand" & "End of the Beginning," which are in "Collected Plays." All the rest in "Windfalls" is "poetry," which isn't worth reading. I believe that a book of articles, called, I think, "7 Arts," cloth-covered—not the magazine, (published some time ago) both edited by Fernando Puma, published by Doubleday & Co., Inc. Garden City, New York. This cloth-covered edition should have in it an article by me which might help you. And an article on "Laughter" appearing some time ago in the Canadian "Saturday Night."

I don't know how I can help you further. As for what I am doing now, well, mostly housework; for, recently my wife fell & broke her right wrist badly, & I have to give a bigger hand than ever. However, I'm used to it, having done a lot since the war when house helpers weren't to be had; & have been hard to get since—and expensive. As well, I'm working at proofs of a new book & have another 3-act play in some shape; &, at the moment, waiting for Bob Lewis, Director of "Tea House of the August Moon," who comes here on a visit tomorrow; &, as well, writing lots of letters, including this hasty one to you.

If you have any questions to ask, ask them, & I shall try to answer; though your own opinion is more important than mine; for you are of the coming world; "I a poor life on the ebb, you a full life on the flow."

All good wishes to you,
Sean O'Casey

To Anthony E. Harvey

PC. RANDOLPH-MACON

TOTNES, DEVON
26 MARCH 1954

My dear Anthony Harvey,

From what you say in your letter, it seems to me you know more about the Theatre & Drama than I do. Quite right, too; for you—like my own children—belong to a generation of bright eyes, brown or black hair, while I am lingering in on eyes that are dim, & hair that is grey. The set-up of your Project, as you describe it, seems fine to me; though, God help me, you put me (or seem to) with tremendous figures—Shakespeare, Euripides, Plautus, & Fletcher; though, Thank God, only to show that they did splendidly what I am aiming at trying to do now. Your questions are terrific! Would Amer. aud. react same as Irish? I hope not, in a lot of ways. You can read how many re-acted to "The Plough" and "The Tassie," just as Boston did to "Within the Gates"—never attempted professionally or by amateurs in Ireland. American audiences differ—I'd say they enter into the humor & sorrow if the audiences had a liking for drama, & weren't afraid to realise that Drama (as well as life) shouldn't be all cakes & ale. Whether the elements of the plays would be clearer & more colorful on the stage than in the book would depend on the production & the acting. If good, yes; if bad, no. And, after all, the humor & tragedy, in book or on stage, must also be in the imaginative mind of the on-looker or reader. Nothing can be done or said without the aid of another. That's why so many bother God so much—because they don't get enough (think they don't) attention from their neighbours. Man refuses to think of them as big fellows, so they try to be big fellows with God.

By the way, I never labor to mix grief with laughter: they just grow into the play, without any striving, just as I see them arm-in-arm in life. Which of the plays is the best example, I can't say. I think myself that, technically, (the form) "Cockadoodle Dandy" is the best example of workmanship; &, in humor & pathos, no less than any of the others.

My favorite play is always the one I happen to be working at. A weakness of mine is that I lose interest in what has been done, &, if the chance comes, I have to force myself to take an interest in rehearsals.

My new book, "Sunset & Evening Star" is the last of my biographical books. Yes, T. of the A. Moon seems fine. It is coming to London in April. The Director R. Lewis, was with us here last week.

I don't like to say anything about the Abbey Theatre. They have done no play of mine since "The Plough," except a production of "S. Tassie," which caused a terrible row, & the resignation of a Director, B. Macnamara:

all described in "Rose & Crown." They give odd performances of "Plough," "Juno," & "The Gunman"; & that is all.

Well, Anthony, there you are. All one can do is to keep "Leathering away with the Wattle O." So I will; so I do.

I'm sending by ordinary post the article "Laughter" as it appeared in the Xmas No. of the "Canadian Journal," who reproduced it from "Saturday Night." When you've read it, let me have it back, for it's the one copy of the article I have.

My good & warm wishes to you,
Yrs. very sincerely,
Sean O'Casey

To Mrs. Oriana Atkinson

TS. ATKINSON

TOTNES, DEVON

5 APRIL 1954

My dear Oriana:

A big bouquet of thanks for your valuable Easter Gift. It was generous of you to think of us. We all thank you—for some of it went to our boy in London.

You are probably right about the Gorki book. I'm afraid it has been badly translated. It seems to keep a common level from start to finish. But Gorki's Grandma is a great character, and the folk tales—the few recorded—she tells him are indeed jewels shining forth from dust & ashes; and the scenes in the shop where the Icons are made are very remarkable. A lot has been left out. Years ago, I read "Fragments from my Diary," in a Penguin edition—paper covered—, & my memory tells me it was much better, if not much brighter. I remember a wonderful description of a forest fire, watching which, Gorki indeed became a poet. His plays, too, are fine, though, usually, only "Lower Depths" is performed. There was a lovely piece in the Diary, too, of Gorki and Tolstoy on horseback, stopping to watch a cobbler making a pair of boots; a job Tolstoy worked hard at, and studied assiduously, but could never succeed in doing. The great Tolstoy could never mold a pair of boots properly.

I can't see anything wrong with your pink-orange notepaper. I have tried for years to get paper to satisfy my eye, but never could. I admire the American habit of typing things; & the variety of American notepaper is delightful. So many hues, so many ways of printing the address. We hang on here to the sober and demure manner; to "good taste," Oriana, which means always doing what has been done before.

I shall be delighted to welcome your new book,[1] & shall look forward to reading it. May the book be blessed. I have received a cordial letter from Dr. John O'Brien of Notre Dame University, Notre Dame, Indiana, praising my work! He has edited a book called "The Vanishing Irish," which trumpets forth what I've been trying to say for years.

I daresay, Shivaun told you of Eileen fracturing her right wrist, but it is getting on fine, & she can do some housework now.

I fear George Jean is seriously ill, by what he tells me. And, of course, no one can help him.

Tell Brooks, Oriana, that I've just finished a three-acter—"The Bishop's Bonfire."

My love, dear Oriana, to you & to Brooks.

> *God be with you both.*
> *Ever yours,*
> *Sean*

[1] Oriana Atkinson, *Manhattan and Me* (1954), with drawings by Al Hirschfeld.

To Raymond Marriott

MS. TEXAS

TOTNES, DEVON
5 APRIL 1954

Dear Raymond,

Thank you very much for your letter, & for the American Magazine. The old gob looks odd among the Spanish terms & pictures; & the letter of greeting odd, too; though it does give a shake of the hand to all S. Americans.

Sam [Wanamaker] has told me nothing about any idea of his to put "Purple Dust" on in the Westminster.[1] I hope he doesn't. He and I have had enough of it; and I, as well, don't look to London any more for production of my plays. As far as my plays go, my eyes seek—no, not Moscow—but New York. "The English playgoers have," as the Critic of Times Lit. Supplement said, when reviewing "Collected Plays," "English p. have

[1] For the background on that ill-fated production of *Purple Dust,* see O'Casey's letter to Sam Wanamaker, 28 April 1953, note 1; to George Jean Nathan, 11 May 1953, note 1; and see his comments on "The English Pilgrimage" in his letter to Brooks Atkinson, 20 September 1953.

decided to have nothing to do with O'Casey & his work because of his lamentable judgements"; and adds, "which, if they wish, they have a perfect right to do." [2] Of course, the one answer to that is to go on writing; which I do; &, indeed, have just ended a three-act play—"The Bishop's Bonfire."

I hope the Lindsay Theatre may be something of a success, even for Liam Redmond's sake; for he's a fine actor; though I'm a little inclined to favour plays written later. Robert Lewis, who's producing "Tea House of the August Moon," was down here with me a Sunday or two ago. He loves "Cockadoodle Dandy," & he is the lad to do it, if it ever be done: in New York, of course. The American Colleges do my plays at times, & that helps a lot. I see Mr. Ivor Brown says in last Sunday's "Observer," writing about Giraudoux's "The Enchanted," says that "Chesterton scored all the anti-science points 40 years ago in his play 'Magic,' as well as in his books." Did he, now? Hooray! Two things, among many, that Chesterton knew nothing about were Science and Theology. He was a dummy that Vanity carried about & made it speak for her. I.B. should read what was written about Science & Theology by Dr. McDonald, Professor of Theology in Maynooth for 40 years. Then he wouldn't rush rashly out to say such a thing. He should read what McDonald said about Motion & Divine Grace.[3] Or did he ever read Mivart? [4] Or even his last words?

You are right: there's no experiment here in either Theatre or play; neither is there a whisper of humanity—even in Eliot's. He's all God & no man. You're right, of course, about Unity. They run around seeking what they'll never find. They, & all they say about the Drama, worry me. They don't read enough. They hear little men in little groups speaking, & are deaf to what the world says.

We are pegging along. Eileen fractured her right wrist, but she is about allright again. We have to leave here soon: we're been under the Rent Restriction Act; but now the Landlord has hopes of a change, so he has declared he needs the place "for his own purposes," has sent us notice to quit; & so we've got to go. A bit of a nuisance after 16 years of residence; & he was damned glad to get us when we came. Our younger lad is now a gunner in the Field Artillery; so we serve Landlord & Queen.

All good wishes
Sean

[2] "The Paradox of Mr. O'Casey," *Times Literary Supplement*, 21 September 1951, a review of O'Casey's *Collected Plays*, Vols. III and IV (1951). See O'Casey's letter to Harold Macmillan, 29 September 1951, note 2.

[3] Dr. Walter McDonald, *Motion: Its Origin and Conservation* (1898).

[4] For O'Casey's attitude toward the placing of one of St. George Mivart's books on the Papal *Index*, see O'Casey's letter to David Marcus, 6 January 1951, note 3. St. George Jackson Mivart (1827–1900), the English biologist who tried to reconcile the conflict between religion and science, was excommunicated for his repudiation of ecclesiastical authority.

To Dr. Frank Morrell

MS. MORRELL
TOTNES, DEVON
6 APRIL 1954

Dear Frank,

Good to hear you've been so busy, and that you have had a fine time studying. Gil Ross is a grand lad, & Eileen & I liked him very much. Judy hasn't written to me so far, so I can't give you any news about her (Judith Auslander, that is). We shall be leaving here soon. Though the landlord was very glad to get us as tenants 16 years ago, now that there's a chance of a rent-rise thro the new Rents Act—though it wouldn't apply to us; but to the next tenant—, he has decided that he "wants the place for his own purposes," & and has sent us a notice to quit. So we have to go. We've taken, or almost so, a flat near Torquay, which will mean half our present space, & three times the rent. It's a nuisance, this change, but it can't be helped. I'll let you have the new address soon as things are fixed.

Well, well, Frank, what a sentence! "Tentative steps will be taken to express in practice what had previously been an abstract & purely theo-retical unity of my political & scientific philosophy." "Life and work" are better: you have to keep your political & scientific philosophy within your life & your work. If it doesn't grow out of these two things, it's no more than smoke. That's what annoys me with so many with their webs of words that can't mean anything, or express anything but sounds made by fools. They never live at all. Live at your work; live with your sweetheart or your wife; with your children; live with music, art, literature; football, baseball, or table tennis. And remember all the Bourgeoise aren't villains; often a damn sight more charming & interesting than those who are no more than peripathetic Communist pamphlets.

Eileen fractured her right wrist some weeks ago—giving me a lot more to do!—but she's almost allright again now. Niall's a gunner in the Field Artillery; Breon's in London; Shivaun's here. My love to Mr. & Mrs. Ross, to Gil, & to you.

As ever,
Sean

To Frank McCarthy

MS. McCarthy

Totnes, Devon

12 April 1954

My dear Frank,

Thanks for your letter & enclosures; even for that thunderful exclamation a mile long from Brother Lawrence.[1] What an egoist! Indeed, all these fellas are self-centred.

Me and God. How precious they think themselves to be; & yet there isn't a thought in the lay brother's gospel that's worth a devil's damn. [Dr. Donald A.] Soper is a different chap: he goes out from the centre of himself towards every beating heart that hasn't been corrupted with gain, or isn't afraid of losing a job. Of course, they're down on him. Whereas, they'd pat Brother Lawrence on the back, tickle him under the chin, they'd like to knock Soper out of this world. See the difference between dope and a stimulant. Don't be surprised about what the Methodist or Wesleyan Press may say—most of them, I'm told, are owned or controlled by Brother Rank, the Film Apostle. Billy Graham suits the big desk with its battery of telephones. We're all God's children—we are, like hell. We'll all work together, wha'? Yep. And all go to heaven together, wha'? Yep. An' all draw dividends together, wha'? Where's he? He's gone.

Very busy. Eileen broke her right wrist some weeks ago, making me busier. Nearly allright now. We're moving from here soon. New Rents Bill has caused our Landlord to decide he wants the place for himself (raise the rents on the next in—I hear B. Graham singing), and has served us with Notice to Quit; so we've got to go; which will be a big nuisance. And I've just got page proofs to correct of "Sunset and Evening Star," so, Frank, me boy, I'm busy.

My love to you,

As ever,
Sean

[1] Brother Lawrence, *The Practice of the Presence of God* (1943).

To George Jean Nathan

MS. CORNELL

TOTNES, DEVON
12 APRIL 1954

My very dear George:

I've heard rather good news about you from Tom Curtiss, writing from Paris. He tells me you were in good form at a gathering with Lillian [Gish], & that you entertained the Company wtih your reminiscences. Well, that's fine, & God grant it may continue. He tells me you intend to take a long holiday, which, if you can do it, is fine, too. He says you've worked too hard, which I often thought myself. May the long rest give you a new lease on life.

We have to leave here soon—June at the latest. The Landlord says he wants the place for himself, & has given us notice to quit. I'm sure he wants to sell it, which he can't do while we're here. After 16 years, it is a big pull-up, & means a big change & a lot of work settling into a new place. It can't be helped.

I've finished "The Bishop's Bonfire," & will send it away to a professional typist to have it done better than my typing can do. I'm working on the page-proofs of "Sunset & Evening Star," thinking over some excisions wanted by Macmillan here, including the exclamatory word "balls!" There's still a lot of frightened people in the world. Mrs. O'C. fractured her right wrist lately, which gave me more to do; but she's almost ok now.

Had a blessing for my fine plays from The Rev. J. O'Brien Ph.D. of Notre Dame University, Notre Dame, which is in your own State.[1] I shouldn't have given you these bits o' news had I not heard from Tom.

God be with you, my dear George.
With my love.
Sean

[1] Nathan was born in Fort Wayne, Indiana, in 1882.

To Anthony E. Harvey

PC. RANDOLPH-MACON

TOTNES, DEVON

14 APRIL 1954

Dear Anthony Harvey,

Well, I can't think of anything more to say about C. Dandy. Here with me, the other day, Robert Lewis, Director of "Teahouse of the August Moon" said the play reminded him of a symphonic poem in music; and spoke earnestly of how the play flourished with fun for so long, & then gradually merged into pathos & sorrow so curiously & so quietly, but so effectively, that those who have laughed began to wonder why they had done so; for cause for laughter had gone, and sorrow & pathos walked the stage. Bob Lewis has been my chosen Director for the play since it was written; he knows it by heart; he has done it thro' the students, helped by actors, in his New York Studio, to see how it would work out; & he says the result was amazing. That's his view of the play, &, I suppose, it is as good as any of mine. The play, first of all is a play, irrespective of the theme; & if it fails as a play, it falls altogether. Broadly, it stands against anything interfering with, or hindering, the natural joys of life, applicable to all men, but cast in a gay, Irish mold. It shows, or tries to show—regarded this way—that Ireland is the world; just as Ibsen made Norway a world, & Strindberg made a world of Sweden.

Of course, I'm familiar with O'Neill's work; but couldn't say for certain what all the various symbols in the play were meant to convey. I think it one of the finest works; one that tries to show by symbol & psychology the passage of a soul through life as O'Neill saw it go. It is, by & large, true of us all. The mask is always too ready there for the hand to seize. How often are the hands the hands of Esau, though the voice be the voice of Jacob! We are other than ourselves too damned often.

By the way, you'll find two articles of mine in a book, "Highlights of Modern Literature" a "Collection of Essays from The New York Times Book Review," [1] if you are interested. The other essays make the book worth buying by anyone. The Book is called "A Mentor Book," & is published by the New York American Library.

Thanks so much for sending me your picture. You are young and charming, & have a lovely smile; may it stay forever in your heart.

Well, I gotta go now. Remember, all I've said are but opinions; that is a world where all should be equal, & where the young should be heard more often.

My warm regards to you as ever,
Sean

[1] See O'Casey's letter to Brooks Atkinson, ? January 1954, note 2.

To Harry Cowdell

MS. MACMILLAN LONDON

TOTNES, DEVON
21 APRIL 1954

Dear Mr. Cowdell,

Thanks for showing me the design for "Sunset & Evening Star."
I imagine it looks effective & bold; but I have, of course, no experience
of Jackets other than my own.

I should like two minor changes:—

a. blot out the thin white line (or ray) leading from wine-glass to the star;
I've experienced "per ardua" allright, but am still a far way from "ad
astra."

b. bring the wine-glass to a more upright position, & a little closer to the
body.

At present, it seems to look as if the figure had tossed the star into
the sky. The symbol is allright, though it—the star—usually (the ray from
a star) enters a lady's ear, as Yeats mentioned in one of his poems.[1] Otherwise, I think the design fine; but you, of course, will know better.

All good wishes,
Yours sincerely,
Sean O'Casey

[1] W. B. Yeats, "A Nativity," in *Last Poems and Plays* (1940):

What woman hugs her infant there?
Another star has shot an ear.

The Virgin and the star are Tarot symbols.

To Paul Green [1]

MS. GREEN

TOTNES, DEVON
24 APRIL 1954

My dear Paul Green,

Thanks & thanks for your fine book, "Dramatic Heritage."[2] It is very
interesting, a most interesting book. You are a very hopeful man; more

[1] Paul Green (1894–   ), American playwright, novelist, teacher.
[2] Paul Green, *Dramatic Heritage* (1953), a collection of essays on drama.

. decidedly so than Claudel; [3] not Noah in the Ark on the wide waters; but a babe in an ark of bulrushes beside a meandering stream. What a loud voice the babe in the bulrushes has! What is really in the "Satin Slipper"? Not a brogue or a clog or a sabot, by the way; but a satin slipper. God looks after the satin slippers. What a medley he makes of the world and the church—church-world—in his play. And, by and large, only heretics and unbelievers read it; and no Catholic stage produces it. What a rum lot these Governors are—Camillo, Rodrigo, & the rest of them. Well, give me Gandhis before these curious guys. The very opening scene, meant to be so serious, is very comic: the Jesuit tied to the mast-stump, the great heap of nuns on the deck, & the ship going, going, but not quite gone. Claudel is so like so many of our religious leaders, Chesterton, Belloc, Eliot—no grip on life; no touch even to the hem of life's garment. Well, well, I don't like Claudel, as he didn't like Gandhi; so we're quits. You've written a lovely thing about Washington.[4] And your "Tragedy—Playwright to Professor" [5] is fine.

I was, naturally, interested (and truth to tell, delighted) by G. B. S.'s references to me.[6] But he was a dear friend of mine, and his liking for me may have coloured his good opinions.

[3] "Paul Claudel," *ibid*. He wrote *The Satin Slipper* in 1942.

[4] "A Figure For Drama," *ibid*.

[5] *Ibid.*, An essay on dramatic theory and practice.

[6] "The Mystical Bernard Shaw," *ibid*. In a little-known passage Green recorded the following comments by Shaw:

> I asked his opinion then about some of the contemporary dramatists writing for the English stage. He didn't seem to have a high opinion of any of them except Sean O'Casey. "He is a man of genius," he said heartily, "yes, of genius. It's a pity he started writing so late. But then he has time to accomplish a great deal yet if he is careful of his health."
>
> "I like him, too," I said. "He is a poet in the theatre, and poets are rare."
>
> "Yes, a poet," he affirmed with a nod of his head.
>
> "Sometimes though, I think," I added, "that he lets his poetry outrun his dramatic sense."
>
> "Do you really think so?"
>
> "Yes, his speeches get to be too long. They go beyond the story point and are piled on for the sake of the language itself."
>
> "And why shouldn't they be?" he snapped. "Let him talk, let the words pour out. Why be niggardly with speech? It's glorious. If he has something to say there's no reason why he shouldn't continue saying it page after page. Yes, it's all a question of whether he has something to say—something important, something interesting, something—yes, beautiful. I think he has. Shakespeare did it now and then and rather well at that, and look at Dickens, how rich, profuse, what a gorgeous spilling of language."
>
> "Yes, sir, but Dickens wasn't a playwright."
>
> "It makes no difference," he declared vehemently. "Speech is speech, whether it occurs in a play or a novel. That's the great trouble, one of the great troubles with modern playwrights. They cramp everything down. Every line must tell, every sentence must have some plot point, must hurry on toward the inevitable denouement, straight as an arrow in its flight. What's the result? Something dry and dead. There's an old saying about that. Consider the lilies of the field—that's it, that's what was meant. The flowers, the greenery, the luxuriant foliage of life. O'Casey has that. He's a man of genius, and I hope all good things for him." (pp. 127–28).

I hope you are well, & let me say I have enjoyed your novel & all the plays of yours that have come to my hand. Not the novel—I didn't enjoy that; it made me remember itself vividly for a long time; & I remember it vividly still.

All good wishes. Yours very sincerely,

Sean O'Casey

To Mrs. Annette K. O'Sheel [1]

MS. O'SHEEL

TOTNES, DEVON

28 APRIL 1954

My dear Annette,

You send me sad news indeed. Sudden sadness, too, for I never for a moment saw death close to my friend Shaemas.[2] His letters, including his last one, were vigorous and outspoken, giving an impression of hardihood & a far, far longer life. We became close friends through our correspondence, and it grieves me greatly that Death has taken away a friendship I valued so much.

I'm afraid our dear Shaemas entered too deeply into the troubles of others—a noble fault, but one that takes a dire toll of human vitality. His letters showed what an open heart he had; open wide to the troubles & sorrow of all sorts and conditions of men. He just didn't spare himself enough. He was a little rash in giving of himself to what others had to bear. And now he has gone himself, & those who knew him and loved him will miss him much. I am sorry I can't be with you & his friends on May the 4th. But let my name be mentioned there as one who had a real love & a deep respect for a noble soul.

My love & sympathy to you, & let the sympathy mingle with the loss suffered by his friends. Shaemas was a fine man, & such souls are none too plentiful among us today, nor shall they be too plentiful tomorrow; & so such men as Shaemas are a sad, deep loss to us all.

May God be near him & near you.

Yours very sincerely
Sean

[1] Mrs. Annette K. O'Sheel, 1 Riverside Drive, New York.
[2] Shaemas O'Sheel died in New York on 4 April 1954 at the age of sixty-eight.

To Cyril Cusack [1]

MS. CUSACK

TOTNES, DEVON

30 APRIL 1954

Dear Mr. Cusack,

Thank you for your letter asking me about me new play. I've just finished amending it today, & next week will send it to Professional typists to have some fair copies done. It is a three-act one, and it's called "The Bishop's Bonfire." There are no "crowds" in it, and the characters number eleven—two women & nine men. There is a little comical phantasy in it, but not near so much as in Cockadoodle. Your request to produce it in Dublin is another matter of course. What about some of the newer ones done recently by the Abbey? And again, I still, foolishly enough, hesitate to give permission for a new play in Dublin till the Abbey has had time to notice it, & has passed it by with eyes shut, or eyes open, but her nose in the air. I could let you have a gawk at it (when the good copies return) provided you give a guarantee for the return of the Typescript when you had read it. I'm by no means a well-off fella, & can't spare scripts, other than those sent to publishers & to America. I have been busy with book proofs, & now, in a week or so, will be one in the throes of a flit. The new Rent Bill has stirred our Landlord. He can only raise the rent on us by a certain percentage, but if we go, he can get whatever new tenants would be willing to pay. So we've got Notice to Quit, &, after 16 years, must pack up and go.

How did you know I had a new play? I hope you'll give your Vote to the right man in the coming Election—or is Dalkey a free town?

All good wishes to you.

Sean O'Casey

---

[1] Cyril Cusack (1910–   ), Irish actor and producer, began his acting career with the Abbey Theatre in the 1930s, distinguishing himself in the plays of Synge and O'Casey, and thereafter played in many notable productions in Dublin, London, and New York, as well as in many films.

To Harry Cowdell

MS. MACMILLAN LONDON

TOTNES, DEVON

7 MAY 1954

Dear Mr. Cowdell,

Thanks for copies of Frontispiece,[1] one of which I return with this note. I've written the caption on the bottom margin. It is a very clear reproduction. I'm glad you think the alteration to the Jacket is an improvement. The ray from the Star would have made me look too important altogether, and rather impudent, too. It's hard enough to be mortal without aiming at looking to be one of the immortals. I'm glad all like it; it should, as you say, look a striking Jacket. Pray God the book will prove as good.

All best wishes,
Sean O'Casey

[1] The frontispiece of *Sunset and Evening Star* is a photograph of the O'Casey family by Alfred Eris: Nially, Breon, Sean, Shivawn [sic], Eileen. For a comment on the spelling of "Shivawn," see O'Casey's letter to Cowdell, 7 July 1954.

To Gordon Rogoff

MS. ROGOFF

TOTNES, DEVON

9 MAY 1954

After June 7, 3 Villa Rosa Flats,
40 Trumlands Road, Marychurch, Torquay,
Devon

Dear Gordon,

Glad to know you are safe home again. I hope you managed to bring the lovely bicycle you had safe home, too. Oh, give up any thoughts of the Theater—it's the last place to be, the last thing to have anything to do with. Your order about the proposed "Juno" recording is a stiff one, agradh! You see I'm 74, & have no financial reserves, & so must try to keep going for there's five and a half of us—five of ourselves & Eileen's mother to whose keep we contribute. It's not easy going, & I have to conserve energy much as possible. At the moment, I couldn't even think it out, for we're leaving here, & I live in quasi-chaos. The Landlord decided he "wants the place for his own purpose"—that is in legal terms he wants to live in it himself; but he really wants to be either able to get the highest rent a new tenant might be willing to pay (our new "Rents Act" allows this now), which he couldn't do to us. So he sent us notice to Quit, & we have to go, after 16 years of residence here. It's a nuisance, but it can't be helped. It means half the space for us, & more of a rent, plus all the upset of moving. That's the reason for the new address above. I couldn't, cant, think of anything at the moment, bar the move; though I've finished correcting proofs of "Sunset & Evening Star" & designing the jacket, as well as writing a new three-act play, "The Bishop's Bonfire."

I am very glad to hear of Caedmon's expansion. It's a good sign, if it be done prudently, & overheads aren't allowed to become too heavy.

This winter was a brutal one. A huge tank under our roof burst with the frost, & flooded the house—shocking time of it. Some days later, Eileen fell and badly fractured her right wrist—another shocking time; but the house is dry now, and Eileen's wrist near as well as ever, so we can call hurrah!

My love to Marianne [Roney] & Barbara [Cohen], & to you. Niall (I'm not sure if you met him) is now a gunner in the Field Artillery, Breon & Shivaun are here & well. Eileen sends her best wishes.

Yours very sincerely,
Sean

To Joseph Prescott

MS. PRESCOTT [1]

TOTNES, DEVON
10 MAY 1954

Dear Joseph Prescott,

Thanks ever so much for the "Conversations with James Joyce." [2] Everything about Joyce is interesting. A curious, but a great mind that thought out of laughter. Deep laughter, but none the less comic. It is odd how anyone could hate Joyce, yet many do. I've often wondered why the poet, Alfred Noyes, hated him & all his work so venomously; for he even hated those who ventured to say that they admired Joyce.

---

[1] This letter was reprinted in the *Massachusetts Review,* Winter 1964.

[2] A translation, by Joseph Prescott, from the *Neue Zürcher Zeitung,* 3 May 1931, of Georges Borach's "Gespräche mit James Joyce," in *College English,* XV, March 1954. The translation was reprinted in *Meanjin,* XIII, Spring 1954, and *London Magazine,* I, November 1954.

We are in the midst of moving—an irritating transition. The landlord wants this place "for his own purposes"—a legal quibble; & has given us notice to quit. The New Rent Act will provide him with the opportunity of asking rent as high as anyone may like to give; or be prepared to give.

So we have to go.

A safe journey to you back to Wayne University.
I hope you have enjoyed your stay here.
Eileen & I give your our warm regards.
Yours very sincerely,
Sean O'Casey

To George Jean Nathan

MS. CORNELL

ST. MARYCHURCH, DEVON
11 MAY 1954

My very, very dear George:

I hope you are feeling fairly fit, & that you take things quietly, & not worrying because you can't do as much as you used to do. I'm going on 75 now—what a sobering thought—, and can't hum & haw as I did in earlier days; and, like Yeats, I don't like it.

I've sent my typing of the play—"The Bishop's Bonfire"—to a professional typist to be done properly, & when it comes back, I'll send a copy to Miss Rubin, asking her to let you have it when you are feeling better— I don't want to bother you while your feeling low. I think the work good— as, of course, I should, or not write it at all—but thinking and knowing are two mighty different things. I see C. Morgan's "Burning Glass" hasn't done well in New York.[1] I imagine that Morgan takes himself too seriously. A lot of playwrights seem to be leading God on his way; or trying to guide evolution in the way it should go.

I must be careful of myself. There was a bit of a row here over "Bedtime Story."[2] An Amateur group chose to do it for a festival, but the

---

[1] Charles Morgan's *The Burning Glass* opened in New York on 4 March 1954, and closed after twenty-eight performances.

[2] In February 1954 the Chingford Unity Theatre, an amateur group in suburban London, was forced to withdraw its production of O'Casey's *Bedtime Story* from the Essex Adult One-Act Play Festival when the adjudicator, Jack Carlton, M.B.E., called the play "blasphemous and unsavoury" before it was performed in the competition. A controversy arose and Mrs. Edith Miller, director of the play, sent a protest to the League of Dramatists on 11 February 1954, a copy of which was forwarded to O'Casey, stating that no adjudicator should have the right to prejudge a play that had been passed by the Lord Chamberlain.

Adjudicator wouldn't allow it, declaring it to be "blasphemous, salacious, & indecent." So I lost a guinea fee. The fellow, I'm told, was in charge of the swing-boats & punch & judy show in the Festival of Britain's Pleasure Garden. He was appointed Adjudicator by the Educational Committee of the Essex Co. Council.

Christopher Fry has a new play on here now.[3] I've read the various criticisms, but they all seem vague & non-committal, concentrating on the performance of Edith Evans. The play seems "obscure," but the reviews, to me, seem to be as obscure as the play. None of them will risk making a mistake; though misses are as much a sign of life as hits.

There's no first-class news yet from the Abbey, though they give a yearly prize of £250. Wish they'd give it to me. Prizes seem to make bad plays worse. Look at the plays the Arts Theatre gave prizes to a few years ago: £500 to me that will never see the stage here or hereafter, & chosen by poets & playwright, with ne'er a critic near. The critics would have done better; they couldn't conceivably have done worse.

I am busy burning papers prior to moving—like an Ambassador ordered to quit.[4]

I hope this finds you fairly well, my dear George.

My love as ever to you.
Sean

[3] Christopher Fry's *The Dark Is Light Enough* opened in London on 30 April 1954, starring Edith Evans.
[4] Although O'Casey put his new Torquay address on this letter, as well as on several others in late May, he was still at Totnes and did not move until 9 June.

To Thomas Mark

TS. MACMILLAN LONDON

TOTNES, DEVON
15 MAY 1954

Dear Mr. Mark,

Song "Red Roses For Me"

The air is semi-traditional, that is I took it from an air known as "Eamonn a' Cnuic," "Ned o' the Hill"; but altered it to suit the words, as I did with many others in various plays. The words are my own as they are in all songs except those obviously by others.

Miss Edwards comes here to take them down as I sing them, putting them into notations for me. She was here the other night putting down notes and times of airs appearing in the play "The Bishop's Bonfire." Even the airs in "Within the Gates" which Mr. [Herbert] Hughes attributed to himself are all mine.

So the copyright is mine, too, and I sign the Form accordingly, and return it to you.

With all good wishes,
Yours sincerely,
Sean O'Casey

To Gordon Rogoff

MS. ROGOFF

TOTNES, DEVON
18 MAY 1954

Dear Gordon,

A quick note to you crying halt! I mentioned all that had happened & was happening simply to show you and Marianne [Roney] that it wouldn't be possible for me to think of acting for a Record till we had departed from where we are, & had settled down (or up) in our new flat. It will mean a lot of reorganising for us, & that will take some time. My letter wasn't meant to be an S O S. So tell Marianne that she isn't to try any of the Foundations for help for me. The difficulties we are meeting are similar to those everyone has to meet some day, one way or another. If I happen to be ever in dire need, I'll ring the tocsin allright: a mile away, a woman with five sons has lived in a place for 13 years (a place bought by the R. Catholic church, & rented to her) in which she built up a business. Now the Church wants it for a Parish Priest, & the Court has just given her a month to get out of it. Perfectly legal, but wholly dishonest & unjust. Now, don't forget, & do it at once—stop Marianne from doing anything; and at the same time, give her my love for her kind & generous intention.

By the way, looking through papers in preparation for flight, I find that in 1951 The Decca Company wanted to record "Juno" with the Abbey Co. or a company of Abbey players & others, acting the parts. I find I refused the offer; & since then, had forgotten all about it. The find came as a surprise to me.

I do hope you will pass into Television; you've a better chance there than in the Theater. Of course the way is restricted, but so is the way of the Drama. An Amateur Group doing my "Bedtime Story" was stopped in the last lap by the Adjudicator, who declared it to be "dirty, blasphemous, & obscene." We're all restricted in one way or another. We've a long way to go before we shall be able to halloa out as we may like. You didn't mention your bicycle. As for "Bishop's Bonfire," of that anon. Barbara [Cohen] & Marianne will just have to record only what they think may sell. Eternal rest on a Record is no better than an eternal rest in a book.

So farewell for the present, except to remind you once again to warn Marianne to keep away from help for me at the moment. I can still whistle and sing.

All the best to you & all.

Sean

To Mrs. Oriana Atkinson

MS. ATKINSON

ST. MARYCHURCH, DEVON
AFTER JUNE 9
22 MAY 1954

My dear Oriana:

No mean city either. Your book, MANHATTAN AND ME came safely to us. I read a few pages before it was snatched from me by Breon. He has read it, and was delighted with it. Then it was snatched away by Eileen who is reading it now; & she tells me she is enjoying it immensely, saying it is very funny indeed; though there's a serious chord sounding through all the laughing. She is to write to you herself to tell you how she enjoyed it. She reads it when she has time, that is at night when in bed, just the time when I like to settle down (not in bed) to read too. I thought I could wait till I had read it before writing to you; but the others were so eager to get it that I decided to send the preliminary note to let you know that your book was now part of the O'Casey's properties; not a lot of properties to be sure, but all of value, & some of dear value, to us. So— when I've read it—I read slowly, if the book be good, pausing to think over & enjoy what has been written, page by page—, Oriana's book will be set beside the 2 books by Brooks; between them, rather, making three in one and one in three. I thank you, dear Oriana, for sending it to me, or to the O'Casey's really, sure of a good and pleasant time when the book comes my way; knowing by what Breon & Eileen say that MANHATTAN & ME is something to read—a rare thing these days to me. Breon is a fine judge, though very shy & inclined to silence; & he has a splendid sense of humour; & more, refuses to say he likes what he doesn't, even for my sake. A troublesome characteristic at times.

As soon as I have read it, I'll write again. The page or two I've already read shows you have a shining sense of humour; as, indeed, I know from being with you, watching you, & listening. You are a grand lass, & Brooks should be happy in having you.

Thanks again, dear Oriana, with Breon's, Shivaun's, & Eileen's love to you (Niall's away in the Artillery), and mine going along with theirs—and love to Brooks.

Sean

To Horace Reynolds

MS. REYNOLDS

ST. MARYCHURCH, DEVON
24 MAY 1954

Dear Horace,

More papers, books, MSS, etc! Who are you tellin'? I know it now as well as you do. I congratulate Kay & you on having your move behind you. We're beginning it. After 16 years here, the landlord suddenly decided he "wanted the place for his own purposes", & so we have to pack up & go. Eileen & Breon are busy taking up our bits of carpets to lay them down in the new flat; & they, too—like yous—have done a bit to the walls while they were bare & helpless. It means half the space for us & double the rent; but one has to put up with all, for no house here, big or small, can be had except by purchase. We haven't any means for such a venture; so have to put up with what we can get—at a price. All fit here. Breon is painting away—at the moment, I'm his model; Niall is away a gunner in the Field Artillery; & Shivaun is still at school. I've been busy with proofs, &, as well, have written another play—God forgive me—"The Bishop's Bonfire."

I am so glad to hear of the continuous life of your & Kay's Peggy & John. I still have a vivid vision of them coming in on the door that evening in 322 H. Street; a sharply-chill one, & they well-clad in brightly-coloured jerseys & woolen hats; & then they sitting at the table listening to what two great men were saying. Well, they're saying things now themselves, & more will depend on this than on that of long ago. Give my love to Peggy & to John, & to their little ones. John & Peggy with children, & they coming in on the door but a day or two ago! Begod, we must be gettin' old, or some-thing! A slower pace now for the two of us, Horace. I have written a song or two to lighten the road. Remember me to Oliver [St. John Gogarty] when you see him.

My love to Kay & to you

Aye, too.
Sean

To Francis MacManus

TS. MacManus

Totnes, Devon
26 May 1954

Dear Francis,

Enclosed is notice of change of address, in case your Firm [Radio Eireann] should have any possible occasion to write to me in future. I hope you are well, & doing fine, though you seem to be very quiet in writing, these days.

I've been listening to B[rinsley] Macnamara—coming on the broad-cast by accident—plaintively explaining the poet, T[homas] Moore; & how dignified the poet was, ay, and independent, too, among the ladies & the lords of his day. And he hadn't a brogue either. Had he even an Irish voice? He's buried away in Wiltshire, in Bromham Churchyard, not far from where O[liver] Cromwell had a great camp. We passed by it the time we were in Wiltshire. Silent, O Moyle! The plaintive voice of Macnamara speakin'.

All the best to you & yours.

As ever,
Sean

(Change of address to:
Flat 3, Villa Rosa,
40 Trumlands Road,
St. Marychurch,
Torquay, Devon.)

To T. L. Blau [1]

TC. O'CASEY

TOTNES, DEVON
[? JUNE 1954]

Dear Mr. Blau,

Thank you for asking me to think again. I have—a little—but have decided to abide with my first thought.

I prefer the rascals and toughs I know to the toughs and rascals I dont know.

High-toned chaps usually get a publicity they dont merit. They are always expendable; life can do without the best of them. It is the others that life needs. When they sit down, go on strike, refuse to do what they are told, life becomes impossible. When railway men stop, a lot of life stops, when the miners stop, a lot of life stops with them; when they and the others stop together (1926), England can only moan, and the higher-toned chaps are useless.

I'm sure Mr. [Yousuf] Karsh is a great picture-taker, and I'm sure there are many trying to be like him, for that is but natural; but that is beside the point of my disinclination to be photographed too often. I hope his book will be a great success, and I'm sure it won't need my gob staring out of it to make it one.

Yours sincerely,
Sean O'Casey

[1] T. L. Blau, Camera Press, London.

To Francis MacManus

TS. MacManus

TOTNES, DEVON
1 JUNE 1954

My dear Frank,

I was glad to get your letter showing, however many and heavy your troubles were, that you were still leathering away with the wattle O. Mrs [Mary Frances] Keating in a letter to me mentioned in passing that you had a lot of trouble lately, but that you had surmounted most of them, and were fairly settled in your condition now. Oh, these troubles! They smite all those who hope in God as deeply as those who dont. That is one reason why I have ever been fighting to unite all in rebellion against a stupidity and a carelessness that bring a lot of them into existence. Trouble at least unites us into one family. Only by settling the problems of others can we settle our own. Improvement can come only through the community. It isnt a question of communism, but one of commonsense; and, willy nilly, we have to come to each other's help. Prebendary Durling of Bideford, preaching at the annual Mayoral Sunday Service, a day or so ago, said from the *pulpit* (what an appropriate name!) said "Pain and sorrow in human relations today was the result of disobedience and rebellion against God. People tried to live with others not on the basis of God's Kingdom (basis!), but on the basis of selfishness. Nations had refused to take the rule of God as their collective aim and purpose. The kind of mess the world was in substantiated everything Christianity taught. The puzzling problem facing many people, however, was where was God in these difficult days, when suspicion and hatred was (sic) tearing the world in two (pull, boys, pull!) The answer was that they had to have faith and trust." Well, there you are—all solved. God Almighty, what clowns we have among us! Here is a quotation from a song in Blaitin agus an Mac Ri: [1]

> Bhi duine ann trath gur shloinne do Marx,
> Ni Groucho ach Karl ata 'gam a lua,
> Is b'e rud aduirt se go laidir is go garbh,
> "An te ata thios, is e a bheas thuas." [2]

The boob who wrote this didnt know that Irish poets have been saying this for centuries, long before Marx was born; that the Blessed Virgin said it in her exulting song after the Annunciation; that Lady Gregory said it in her "Rising of the Moon." But this ignorance would be forgivable were the song witty and gay; but it descends to a lower depth than the low one reached by the lowest English broadcasts trying to be funny. And "Creidim Fein"! [3] And "Ruagaire Reatha"! [4] and Clipiti-clop. Christ, who writes these songs? The English have some excuse, for what they do is a nightly and daily event, the Irish have a year to think it out. And all in the midst of horns blowing and drums beating for God, and hosts carrying banners reciting the Rosary trotting "Le clip agus clop tre shraideanna Atha Cliath." [5]

Ireland's becoming an odd land. Last night I listened to a Father

---

[1] *Blaitin agus an Mac Ri* (*Blaitin and the King's Son*), by Ernest Blythe, the 1953 Christmas pantomime performed at the Abbey Theatre.

[2] There once was a man named Marx,
It isn't Groucho I mean but Karl,
And this is what he said strongly and forcefully,
"The man who's down will rise."

[3] "I Myself Believe."

[4] "The Running Rogue."

[5] "With a clip and a clop through the streets of Dublin."

Polac, or some name like that, telling the Irish that Pain and Woe and Suffering were not only the Will of God, but must be looked upon as favors from Him. When I think of fever in swine, fluke in sheep, pip in poultry, foot and mouth disease in cattle, I wonder are those, too, to be thought of as favors from God?

Ay, indeed, B. M. [Brinsley Macnamara] has a strange plaintive voice, but the man is as plaintive as the voice. Indeed, plaintiveness seems to be the badge of every Irish speaker and thinker today. Do you read *The Bell?* Young Anthony Cronin [6] seems to be in a sorry way about the condition of Art in Ireland. No long ago, wasnt it Donagh McDonagh who wrote the *Diaries* [7] plaintively writing about this Irish writer and that Irish writer? Austin Clarke is plaintive too; and, recently Patrick Galvin shouted at me for lowering the prestige of Ireland in my writings.[8] There's a lot of talent running off into waste places in Ireland today; so many writers bent double in watching what other writers are setting down, instead of setting things down themselves. Everywhere I turn an ear, I hear their moaning. Idle moaning, idle tears, idle Irish tears.

Regarding the fortune in Moore's unknown songs, I think you are mistaken—he was too good a song-maker to forge a fortune out of them. One would have a better chance, apparently, with Creidim Fein. When B. M. was talking of the poet, he compared him with James Stephens, how each was a little man, both were gay, and both maintained their dignity and independence among the great and grand ladies of their times. I wonder how B. M. knows this? Was he there watching? I'm afraid he isnt quite right about J. S. James had no independence to defend; he had no clear opinions that ran counter to what the grand ladies thought. Moore, too, wasnt anything of a rebel. James looked very odd clad in his little evening dress suit; didnt suit him. He'd have looked far better in the cap and bells; diamonds flashing in the cap. He seemed to drift when the grand ladies

[6] Anthony Cronin, "A Province Once Again," *The Bell*, June 1954.

[7] He may have meant Padraic Fallon's *Journal*, which was serialized in *The Bell* in 1952.

[8] Patrick Galvin (1927–   ), Irish poet and Socialist, then living in England, felt that O'Casey had betrayed the Socialist cause after he saw a production of O'Casey's one-act plays, *Three in a Row*, a triple bill of *Time to Go, End of the Beginning*, and *Hall of Healing*, which opened at Unity Theatre, London, on 22 May 1953, directed by Ivor Pinkus and David Dawson. Distressed because "there was no real Socialist thought" in these satiric and knockabout comedies, Galvin wrote a strong attack against the playwright, "An Open Letter to Sean O'Casey," sent a copy to O'Casey, and then tried unsuccessfully to have it printed in *Tribune* and the *Irish Democrat*. The letter was never published. Thereafter O'Casey and Galvin exchanged a number of sharp letters on Socialism and comedy, which I have not been able to find; however, O'Casey quoted some passages from Galvin's letters in the last chapter of his final volume of autobiography, "And Evening Star," *Sunset and Evening Star* (1954). After the book was published in October 1954, Galvin threatened to initiate a libel action unless he received an apology. O'Casey refused, but Macmillan apologized and the action was dropped. Subsequently the men were reconciled. See O'Casey's letters to David Marcus, 28 July 1954, note 1; and to G. W. Head, 31 December 1954, note 2.

descended from their higher status; but then, he had a terrible domestic tragedy in his life. That, I think, was the real reason why he wrote no more. Harold Macmillan asked me several times to try to get him to work, and that is why I dedicated COCKADOODLE DANDY to him [9]—to try to encourage him to start again. It didnt work. Perhaps, he was too financially sound. I was surprised to find that he died leaving more than 9000 behind him. What happened to Mrs Stephens? Where is she? Never heard a word, never read a word about her for years before he died, or after he had gone. I think his American Tour, broadcasting on behalf of a commercial firm did him harm, too. All in all, he was a grand little man, though he allowed himself to send his unfortunate son to Oxford. It is odd how Moore (George) seems to be forgotten in Ireland, though he was, to my thinking, a far greater artist than either Stephens or Gogarty or AE (Aeolus, as Gogarty called him once in a letter to me), and more alive to life than Yeats.

The two Americans mentioned by you are alive and kicking—one an Albanian [Gjon Mili], the other of Irish descent [Robert Emmett Ginna]. The work they did for LIFE is set, pictures and all, but hasnt yet been printed. They all made a good thing out of it, and I got a few dollars, too; 500 in all. Whether it will ever appear, I dont know. I have a fine collection of photographs here, sent to me by Gjon Mili, but cant touch them till I get the word that none of them will be wanted by LIFE. Gjon did a film of the family, and uses it for the entertainment of friends. We all had a fine time together throughout the three weeks they were here with us.

Yes, the family is grown up now—Breon going on for 25, Niall (now a gunner in the Royal Field Artillery) going on for 20, and Shivaun going on for fifteen. But for all that, I live in their world, for I've grown up with them, and have shared in all they did and do (Just now, I have been discussing some points in economic outlook with Shivaun who is doing a paper for school), in things of their school, in sport, in reading, and in music. I get along splendidly with the young inside the family and without. Most of the Americans who come here are young, and all who write to me —many Irish, by the way—are young, too. I am going on 75, and though one foot may be in the grave, the other is beating time in the future. I love children, and, even the shyest, after ten minutes or so, become fast friends. Our own come in as they please while I work, and many and many a time I have to stop to answer questions, give paper, pen, or listen to news. I keep close to life, and so life is all one to me, neither old nor young, but simply living. As a Communist should, I am interested in all things; always learning; always watching, listening, always full of curiosity; always ready for a laugh. At the moment, I am sitting as a model for Breon who hopes to be a painter; have done it often before, and am now doing it again. And through it all, I've managed to write another play—God forgive me!—a 3

[9] *Cock-a-Doodle Dandy* (1949): "To James Stephens, the jesting poet with a radiant star in 's coxcomb."

act one, called THE BISHOP'S BONFIRE. So I havent time, Frank, to be plaintive. [W. R.] Rodgers, the poet, remarked recently, I believe, that a number of Irish writers were arrested in Grafton Street and charged with loitering with intent to work. Maybe, he's right, and maybe they do loiter too much.

Things are becoming muddled in my room now on account of the move, and I find it difficult to do anything definite, so I've been listening to Radio Eireann whenever I can get it, which isnt often, other voices and sounds breaking in, and banishing the voice of mother ireland; or is it mother riley? Last night I heard the critics reviewing the week's plays— [Gabriel] Fallon on Tomelty's THE PRIEST AT HOME,[10] and [Maurice] Meldon on ALL OUR SONS.[11] It's an odd hour to give criticism. Is it chosen in the hope that all listeners have gone to bed? I'm always hunting for the program that relays the singing of songs in Irish—I like that the best.

Are there two Benedict Kielys? Is there one for the CAPUCHIN ANNUAL and another for the USA? Some time ago, I saw an ad. for a book called, I think HONEY IS BITTER.[12] The ad. was in *The Herald-Tribune,* and ran A Story of Gentle Love and Savage Lust: of a Wedding Ring—and a Hangman's Noose. Oh, Benedict, Benedict! Dont mention this to anyone, for I have no desire to harm or hurt him. I am told he is a very clever writer, and, if he be one, then the Ad. doesnt matter much.

This is beginning to look like a Thesis, so it's time to halt for a prayer ala Father Peyton,[13] or ala Billy Graham—theyre both alike in thinking that God's a trifle deaf.

I dont like you saying that exhaustion has been troubling you. Sloth is alright if it's natural; but exhaustion may be due to physical causes, and you should look after it. Why not see a good doctor? I've been tired myself, and didnt bother about it, but the family doctor, a Dublin man, one of the Varians of Talbot St. Brush Factory, comes off and on in to have a chat, and takes the chance of looking me over. Last time he found blood pressure was very low, so now I take a glass of sherry a day (less than St. Benedict took when his stomach gave way), and a syrup of hypo phosites, I think, for a few weeks. Not feeling any younger from them, but just a little lighter in body, if not in heart. Dont you think you should have a chat with your doctor? We all need a stimulant at times, however brave the heart may be. Think over it, Frank; youre a very young man still.

Remember the Nun I mentioned some years ago; the one who was abandoned by her Order here after 34 years service; the one that you murmured about, saying "one would think a nun of her age would be past

---

[10] Joseph Tomelty's *Is the Priest at Home?* opened at the Abbey Theatre on 31 May 1954, produced by the Ulster Group Theatre.

[11] Arthur Miller's *All My Sons* opened at the Dublin Gate Theatre on 31 May 1954, produced by the Dublin Globe Theatre.

[12] Benedict Kiely, *Honey Seems Bitter* (1954).

[13] See O'Casey's letter to Mrs. Mary Frances Keating, 26 January, 1954, note 2.

that sort of thing." Well, it wasnt that "sort of thing" at all. She had out-lived her usefulness for one thing. In the older days she had been an embroiderer, making those truesos of lace and fal de lals for brides—a curious worship of fertility—; but this has died out now: these things are too dear, and young girls now dont wear these things. So she had become an economic burden; and, as well, she had fought with the mother superior over a lay sister who had dropped dead in the Kitchen, due, the abandoned nun said, to too much slave work. So they layed Madame de Portaigne off, giving her a five pound note, two pillow slips, two sheets, a small piece of scarlet felt, and their half blessing, after fitting her up in a purple skirt, a green jumper, a brown coat, and a large black hat, feathered gayly; and sent her out into the world. There's a lot more, but this letter would be a book if I told all. We had her working for us for over a month doing mend-ing, make do, and we still use a tea-cosy made from the scarlet felt, embroidered with cornflowers, pansies, etc. The poor lass some two months ago dropped dead herself in Totnes streets, from over work too. It was a shocking instance of Christian kindness; and it is odd how these things seem to come my way. The Totnes people were very kind to her all the time.

Be God, this letter's long enough! So my love to you and yours, with the reminder that you should try to see about getting rid of some of your physical exhaustion. Of course, Radio Eireann must be a wearing job. The Theatre nearly killed Shaw after 3 years; broadcasting, or anything to do with it, would have killed him in a week. I know something, for I've done hours of reading, singing, and blathering for two records published by an American Company; and it did me in—nearly.

My love again to you and to all Irish FRIENDS.

As ever,
Sean

To Christopher Murray Grieve

MS. GRIEVE

TOTNES, DEVON
[8 JUNE 1954]

My dear Chris,

Writing this in a dismantled house—we go to address on back to-morrow. After 17 years here, landlord suddenly said he "needed the place for his own purposes"—I think he wants to be able to raise rents on any incoming tenant, or to sell it; anyway, we have to go. Sorry T[hurso]. Berwick didn't get the Bursary, as enclosed note will show. I hope he's well. Haven't heard a word from [him]; he didn't say he got back the MS he sent me; but he must have, for I registered it. Hope you and Mrs. Grieve are well, & your boy. My deep love to the Three of you.

Sean

To Grellet Simpson [1]

PC. RANDOLPH-MACON

ST. MARYCHURCH, DEVON

11 JUNE 1954

My dear Dr. Simpson,

Your young Pupil, Anthony Harvey, tells me you would like to publish letters I sent to him in your College Bulletin.[2] The request frightens me a little, for I can't imagine they would be worthy of a place in the Bulletin. I'd like you to read them again, and, then, should you think them worth publishing, you will be very welcome to do so.

I have a good liking for the young who are about to face life, who are bound to have some troublesome hours, troublesome days, even troublesome years, maybe; & I long that they should have courage to meet these troublesome times bravely.

Anthony tells me you will be coming to Europe next March, that you will be in England then. Tho' the daffodils take the winds of March with beauty, that month is usually a harsh one here; very different, I fear from Virginia. Our place is a long way from London, very near to the Devon seacoast—we can catch a glimpse of it from a window; but, if you, for any reason, come to Torquay, we shall be glad to have a visit from Mrs. Simpson and you.

Our flat is but half the size of the house we have to leave—after 17 years here, the landlord has decided that he "needs the house for his own purposes," & so we had to go. One of those troublesome moments that must be faced bravely.

Anthony says you'd be willing to send the proposed printing for me to censor. Don't: I don't fear anything I've written, though I might laugh ruefully at a lot of it, for I'm not destitute of foolishness. However, the

---

[1] Grellet Simpson, Professor of English, Randolph-Macon College, Ashland, Virginia, was Anthony E. Harvey's advisor.

[2] See O'Casey's letter to Anthony E. Harvey, 12 March 1954, note 2.

foolish things I've done, said, or written, are part of the living man, and should not be concealed so as to suggest infallibility—which God forbid! or make a mask to cause a man to look more like an angel—which God has already forbidden.

I hope you don't mind me writing personally to you.

With all good wishes to Mrs. Simpson & to you.

> *Yours very sincerely,*
> *Sean O'Casey*

To Mrs. Oriana Atkinson

MS. ATKINSON

ST. MARYCHURCH, DEVON
14 JUNE 1954

My dear Oriana:

Your book![1] It is very exasperating to me. First Brooks,[2] now you, till I realise I knew nothing whatever about New York; almost persuaded that I have never been there. I must have had just a little dream about it. Lord God, it is very humiliating. An' I writing my little piece about New York,[3] a city I never saw. Ah, your book (and Brooks) shows what only a life can see. Still an' all, the two books linked up, one on either side of my frail experience, make me more of a New Yorker than I had been; & I thank you and Brooks for it.

Your book is really very funny, very witty indeed, & full of womanly sparkle. You certainly have an open ear and a quick and a roving eye. Your criticisms are many, very caustic, and very lovable. You skelp New York constantly, and keep many a kiss for its lovely ways & many a bow for its greatness. Your vision at the end of the first chapter is a lovely one; one that I myself had I some of your generosity, might see of Dublin. The twanging blue changed to a tender violet. The golden bubbles of the street lights, golden fruits hanging from their own trees; and the people hurrying home. You love New York; as does Brooks; and, indeed, so do I. Your picture of the old big church, your running hither & thither in your young days are all set down gayly & fine. And the penalties of having a hair-do! And Klein's.[4] What a pity I missed Klein's: going day after day to the

---

1 Oriana Atkinson, *Manhattan and Me* (1954).
2 Brooks Atkinson, *Once Around the Sun* (1951).
3 Sean O'Casey, "In New York Now," *Rose and Crown* (1952).
4 A cut-rate department store on 14th Street, New York.

Theatre to watch rehearsals of a play and closing my eyes to the tremendous and immortal drama of New York flooding and surging around me. It was all great foolishness. It is a strange book in a way: a critical & caustic report of a great City's mistakes, meanderings, & comic complacency, submitted to be read in a scroll of laughter. The laughter bites at times; and deep, too.

But in all & through all is the deep love and irritated understanding of a well-loved place.

I enjoyed your work, Oriana, immensely, and I thank you very much for letting me have it. You are a very clever lass, and your sense of humor is glorious.

I was sorry to read of "the late Gil Gabriel." [5] He couldn't have been very old. Brooks mentioned him in his book as having visited you in your country home, & no—I saw none—reference in an English paper mentioned his death.

We move tomorrow, & I'm surrounded now by bare walls & all sorts of packages. I shall be glad when it's all, all over.

My deep love to you both, to Brooks & to you, my clever, laughing lady of Manhattan.

Sean

[5] Gilbert Gabriel, New York drama critic, died on 3 September 1952 at the age of sixty-two.

To Otto Brandstädter

TC. O'CASEY

ST. MARYCHURCH, DEVON
16 JUNE 1954

My dear young friend,

Thanks for your kind letter. You will see by above address that we have moved to another home. After 17 years, the landlord suddenly decided that he wanted "Tingrith" "for his own purpose," meaning that he needed it to live in, which, legally, was the one way he could order us to leave. The New Rent Act provides a chance for him to raise the rent on any incoming tenant, a thing he couldnt legally do to a tenant already living there. Everyone is convinced that he either wants to let it at a higher rent, or to sell the place outright; so, anyway, on the plea of him wanting it "for his own use," we had to leave. It is a nuisance, but it cant be helped, and is one of those inconveniences that must be overcome.

Indeed, I did object to any production of the SHADOW OF A GUN-MAN, and got the League of British Dramatists to tell the producer so, backed with a personal letter from myself forbidding it.

I have no sympathy with your arguments against the production of THE STAR TURNS RED. There is nothing whatever in it against any Christian or Catholic DOGMA. It is, as Bernard Shaw saw at once, a great modern exposition of the Authorised Version of the Bible.[1]

The R.C. Church as represented by the Vatican is the enemy, not only of Ireland, but of the world, of every human endeavor, of every progressive act, of every enlightened and courageous thought; and must be opposed whether the feeling of some, or even many, R. Catholics are hurt or not hurt. It is the most powerful organization in the United States today, led by Cardinal Spellman, who is acting as a shield and a buckler to [Senator Joseph] McCarthy. It is not wise to say that this church is of no importance to your Republic—your very remarks about offending Catholic opinion shows how important it is; and powerful too. If I thought as you seem to recommend, I shouldnt write the way I do; and, indeed, if I had not, but wrote to please most, I shouldnt be as poor today as I am; but nothing shall tame me to submit my mind to any bishop, pope, or politician who does not put the needs and the rights of the People first; People of Germany as well as the People of my own country.

I have no time now to go on arguing, for we live in a dismantled place, and it will be some weeks before we can straighten things out and relax in some quietness and comfort.

Anyway, my dear young friend, you have to think of yourself more than of me, for the world is with your generation, and half-way lost to mine; with you and my three children who belong, too, to your generation, and who, I hope, will enter an era of peace so that they may give their thought and time to making the world what it ought to be and what it can become. So gather all the knowledge you can and keep into touch with Life, for it is from life we learn most things, and it is life that gives us experience, without which knowledge can hardly be active.

My love to you.
Yours very sincerely,
Sean O'Casey

---

1 See O'Casey's letter to Bernard Shaw, 29 April 1940, note 2, Vol. I, p. 860.

To Seumas Scully

MS. SCULLY

ST. MARYCHURCH, DEVON
23 JUNE 1954

My dear Seumas. Your news is bad, very bad, indeed. It is a shocking thing to be shown the door after such a long service. First of all, you'll have to husband whatever money you may have, and, if you invest it, you should sink it only in safe securities, war loan, or whatever investments may be within the category of gilt-edged bonds & shares. For you to venture into anything else would be stupid. Sure money, however small, coming regularly, is always a help.

I've read Bob's [Ginna] kind letters to you; but I should say that the U.S.A. is the last place you should turn your thoughts to: it is hard to get in for a start; hard to get a job; & the conditions, if you did get one, are such as to threaten your health. At your age, it would indeed be a difficult thing to start all over again; and since you couldn't be among the most fortunate, you'd have to brave the winter's cold—and winter is severe there—and the insufferable heat of the summer, which, I imagine, wouldn't be good for your health. If you did decide to go anywhere far, then Australia or New Zealand, from the health point of view, would be better. But they need craftsmen or tough lads for the sheep farms, & wouldn't show open arms to anyone armed only with a pen. England is nearby; but she, too, has no need for clerks, except those who would be specially efficient. Judging from what I know about you, I'd say Ireland still offered the best chance in life for you. Going far—Canada, U.S.A. or Australia—would need a lot of money; & if you failed in these places, your last state would be a damned sight worse than your first: Do try to get another job in Ireland. You see by Bob's letter how expensive it is to live in N. York. Few can afford it. Tens of thousands pour out of it every evening—the rush hour—for fields further away, mostly by underground.

Thanks so much for the press-cuttings. I'm glad you didn't try to send me a birthday congratulation. If I were each year getting a year younger, by all means send me a whoopee telegram; but considering next birthday, I'll be 75, I refuse to regard either calendar or clock.

Sorry to hear how bad the Theatre is doing. As for my plays, the theatres where they are are small—smaller much smaller than the Abbey—so financially, they aren't much good.

Lord Longford seems to be a valiant man.[1] Does he aim at creating a new Abbey as it was in the day of Yeats, Gregory, and Synge?

By the time you get this, I hope you may have seen another good chance within range of your reach.

[1] Lord Longford had taken over and remodeled the Dublin Gate Theatre.

I return the letters from Bob.

All good wishes to you from Eileen, Shivaun, & myself. Niall is a gunner in the Royal Field Artillery.

Don't know much about the article in Life. Not sure when it may appear—this year, next year, some time—

As ever,
Sean

I lived only a block away—West 44th St—from where Bob has his office.

To M. E. Barber

TS. LEAGUE OF DRAMATISTS

ST. MARYCHURCH, DEVON
26 JUNE 1954

Dear Miss Barber,
      Greetings and a few questions, and, very sorry to have to bother you. I daresay you know that Macmillans of London and the Macmillan Co. of America have separated; not only so, but London has established a rival Firm in New York, and New York a rival one in London. I fear it is going to be embarrassing for Macmillan's authors. 'Tis for me. Now the questions; with a brief reason as to why they are asked: A good while ago, Ian MacKenzie, head of the St. Martin's Press (Macmillan's), New York, wrote to say that The Book Find Club wished to publish nine of my plays in one vol (they did I KNOCK AT THE DOOR before), and MacKenzie mentioned general terms which seemed to have altered as time went on. You will see from enclosed letters that Royalties on the transaction amount to 2500 dollars from which, they say, 1500 are to go to pay for the printing plates, ten percent to each of the Macmillan Companies, and the remainder, $900 to me. It seems a big sum to deduct from royalties, and unpleasant to me that out of 2500, I should get only 900. I asked MacKenzie who were to own the plates, and he replied that they would be the property of the St. Martin's Press; curious that they should take what the royalties paid for. The plates, I daresay, wouldnt be of any use to me, or, maybe, of any use to St. Martin either; but the principle seems wrong. In a previous letter, MacKenzie said the amount that would probably come to me would be $750, an appreciable difference from $900. Also, you may see in Mac-Kenzie's letter that St. Martin's Press would be responsible for administer-

ing the subsidiary rights of the plays, a consession that I wouldnt or couldnt grant. The Richard Madden Play Company have been in charge of these rights now for 29 years, and it seems to me a rather sly insertion of a clause that would give to St. Martin's Press a right they arent entitled to, and one which the Macmillan Co. of America never asked for. I'm afraid, I dont altogether like this Mr. MacKenzie.

I should be grateful for your opinions on this matter before I reply to the letters I enclose—one from MacKenzie, the other from Mr. Lovat Dickson of Macmillan's of London. In a number of similar instances of reprinting my works, I KNOCK AT THE DOOR by the Book Find Club, and other vols by The Liberty Book Club, transacted by the American Company before the split, no mention was ever made of a charge for printing plates. I should add that I knew nothing about the split till an argument arose between the rival firms over a play of mine that was asked for to be reprinted in a collection of other works by a College; and, of course, the difference is no concern of mine outside of the way it may, and does, effect publication of my work in the U.S.A.

Yours sincerely,
Sean O'Casey

PS. Please note *new address* above.

To Frank McCarthy

MS. McCARTHY
28 JUNE 1954
3 VILLA ROSA FLATS,
40 TRUMLANDS ROAD,
MARYCHURCH
TORQUAY, DEVON.

My dear Frank,

What a long address (above) to have to write! I'll be glad to get the notepaper with its printing there, and leave the writing of it to others. We're waiting for a telephone & its number before getting it done. It's damned hard to get a telephone, even though we've agreed to share with another. After having one for 29 years, one finds it hard to be told to wait. Yet, Observer & Sunday Times are always pointing out inefficiency in the USSR. Last Friday the USSR's First Secretary, his wife, and the Editor-in-Chief of "Ogonëk" (the "little but steady flame") were here with us talking about many things.

I read Dr. [Donald] Soper's sermon, and, naturally, liked it a lot; but I'm afraid it won't bring a garland of roses to the Doctor. Too damned honest and too damned true. Oddly enough, I say some of the things he says (in my own way), by one of the characters in the new play "The Bishop's Bonfire"—for instance about bothering God with things we can damn well do ourselves. I'm glad you're one of the Editors; [1] a good work; & it will help you to write—tho' you aren't a bad hand at that already. I enclose a cutting showing Dr. Soper's Procession, taken from the United States weekly paper "The Guardian."

Busy here trying to sort out books, papers, and many other things— a hard job. Very hard to get one's mind down to writing, even an article, even a letter. By the way, an article called "World of Sean O'Casey" is to appear in LIFE, the American magazine, next month. It's to have 5 pages of pictures (I think) in color, & 7 or 10 pages of pictures in black & white, many of them of places and people in Ireland.

All good wishes to you, with my love.

As ever,
Sean

[1] McCarthy was one of the editors of Dr. Soper's Methodist magazine, the *Kingsway Messenger*.

To David Marcus

TC. O'CASEY

ST. MARYCHURCH, DEVON
[? JULY 1954]

Dear David Marcus,

No, cant do what you ask.[1] Have neither time nor energy. Besides, what I said before applies today. There is too much envy in the hearts and minds of the younger writers of Ireland for me to butt in on their limited space. Only the other day, I had a bitter article and letters from Patrick Galvin maintaining that my work injured the prestige of Ireland. I have had enough of this sort of thing; enough to last for a long time. If what he said be so, theyre in a better way of adding to Ireland's prestige than that of sending whining things to me. There's no one—I least of all—preventing him from showing the greatness of Ireland in his own writings, his poetry and his prose. I leave him, and the others, to do it.

[1] Marcus had asked O'Casey to write an article for *Irish Writing*, No. 28, September 1954, edited by David Marcus and Terence Smith. Beginning with issue No. 29, December 1954, the magazine was under the new editorship of Sean J. White.

This doesnt mean that I'm not sorry that IRISH WRITING has had to hand in its gun. It is a sad event; though I dont think the younger writers have done a lot to keep it alive and kicking. Indeed, there isnt any kick in the newer writers of today in Eirinn. Or so it seems to me. Theyre all suffocating under the ecclesiastical cassock. You have done your best anyway, and, I fear, lost some of your money in the venture. Unless, of course, you be very rich.

Take P. Kavanagh's IRISH STEW [2]—he hasnt made much of a fight for his little car, his wife, his little house, and all the necessaries that every normal man (poet as well) ought to have. And Norah Hoult doesnt face up to the facts of Stephens' life either.[3] Maybe she doesnt know them, but, if so, why should she write about him? You yourself romanticised him in that article showing him reciting his stories or poems to a spell-bound audience in a restaurant. He was really a most unhappy man for years and years, mainly brought about by the tragedy that befell his son. I saw him in New York with Mr. Howe.[4] Tailing after him and his friends—charming men and women, but not to be given the devotion of doulia. Mr. Howe wanted me to succeed James; to travel with him speaking over the wireless, or telling stories, incidentally, by an announcer, advertising his Book Company; but I'd have none of it. Stephens made a big mistake to do it. They brought Stephens about like an organ-grinder brings about a monkey —all that was wanted was a string. For years, James did no work. Mr. Harold Macmillan asked me several times to use my influence to persuade him to begin work again; but that wouldnt have worked. By dedicating COCKADOODLE DANDY to Stephens, I thought that might quietly influence him towards a renewal of himself; but, probably, he never even saw the book. Anyway, he never mentioned anything about it. I think he lived on his Civil List Pension, thinking this some kind of an expiation for the tragedy of his son. Anyway, he seemed to be in poor circumstances, but he left £9000 odd behind him. In all the references I've read of him, I never saw a word about his wife. What had happened to her? Even Miss Hoult says nothing about her; doesnt seem even to think of her. Why? . . .[5]

[2] Patrick Kavanagh, "Irish Stew," *The Bell,* July 1954, a poem.
[3] Norah Hoult, "James Stephens," *Irish Writing,* No. 27, June 1954.
[4] W. T. H. Howe, president of the American Book Company, Cincinnati, Ohio. O'Casey met him with Stephens in New York in 1934.
[5] Page missing.

To Harry Cowdell

MS. MACMILLAN LONDON

ST. MARYCHURCH, DEVON

7 JULY 1954

Dear Mr. Cowdell,

Regarding "Shivauwn" in under-description of photo: [1]

Both are wrong and both are right. Both are phonetic soundings of the Gaelic form of the name: so we'll let both stand as they are—the one under the picture, the other in the book. The name in Gaelic is "Siobháin," used as an alternative for "Susan," but in the Gaelic meaning "fair or white fairy." Sidhe-Shee=fairy; bán-bawn=white or fair. It is found in the title of the play, "The Colleen Bawn," meaning the fair-haired girl=Cailin= girl-bán=fair.

Well, Mr. Cowdell, there's a lesson in Gaelic for you!

What weather! Instead of i cumen in, the summer seems to be a goin' out.

All good wishes,
Sean O'Casey

[1] See O'Casey's letter to Cowdell, 7 May 1954, note 1.

To John McKerchar [1]

MS. H. D. JONES

[ST. MARYCHURCH, DEVON]

7 JULY 1954

Dear friend,

As you will see by the card enclosed, we have done a flit from TINGRITH. Had to: after 17 years there, the landlord suddenly decided he needed the place for his mother and her daughter; there was little use of contesting the need of 5 against the need of 2, when the 2 owned the property; so we had to go. It was very inconvenient & expensive; but we had to go. The joke is that we were no sooner gone than the notice For Sale went up. As well, the son of the mother had a house of 20 rooms; and they wonder why the masses are turning to Communism! Life is more than meat, but life is nothing compared with property.

[1] John McKerchar, 5 East Adam Street, Edinburgh.

Thanks very much for your very charming Adventian Triptych. It is very well written, well thought, and has a hidden warning. I believe that He is here again in Communism. Blok,[2] the Russian poet, saw Him marching thro' Leningrad at the head of the Red Guards. The "men of property," as Wolfe Tone scornfully called them, can hardly see anything [but] banks, and God's showers to them can only be showers of cheques. On Radio Eireann the Holy Angelus bell sounds its chimes at six of the clock; and, as the last chime falls, we hear a voice say "Here are the latest prices on the Stock Exchange."

I am very sorry I didn't meet you in Edinburgh. I understood that one of those with whom I spoke was the man who read my books & marked the proofs. I was surprised that the proofs of "Sunset & Evening Star" were examined by Mr. [Thomas] Mark of Macmillan's. I came to the conclusion that this was being done on the score of economy. That is very annoying. I don't know how they got to know you had written to me; unless, innocently, I mentioned it myself. Why should they resent you writing to me— or anyone else? Who the hell am I, anyway? All or any resentment I could show would be the ignoring of it thru lack of time & lack of energy. Indeed, I find it hard to reply to all the letters I get; but I do my best. It is galling to think I have been deprived of your co-operation because you wrote to me. Even if you wrote to tell me to go to hell, what would that be to anyone but to you & to me? I wish more would learn the Gaelic song of "What's that to anyone, whether or no?"

Since you wish it, my friend, I'll say nothing to a soul in Edinburgh about our friendship; tho' I claim the right to try to make a friend of anyone who interests me.

My warm wishes & love to you, good & worthy, most worthy, Craftsman in the Printing Industry.

Sean O'Casey

2 See O'Casey's letter to *Daily Worker,* 31 May 1948, note 6.

To Frank McCarthy

MS. McCARTHY
St. Marychurch, Devon
14 July 1954

My dear Frank,

Here's the book, signed as requested. I took it that your brother's name "Graham" was his first one, & so set it down accordingly. I hope I was right.

I hope the Conference in Evansville, Illinois,[1] will be a good one; & that it will sound a bugle-call for Peace. The old, halcyon days of the Church are over—& she will have to give a hand to the work of living; think more of Bread for all than she used to do; end arsing after the privileged & rich—baptism, marriage, & death—they were always there, and still are, among the baronets & the barons. I'm afraid, Dr. Soper will never have the soul-saving aids (money mostly) given to Billy Graham. No, sir. Billy's well in with the Lord's rich. First-class fare all the way here & all the way home. And England's problems are the same as ever. How many tons of coal we dig is more important than how many prayers we say.

Cockadoodle hasn't been done yet, though there's a chance of a production in New York this Fall. The producer [Robert Lewis] of "Brigadoon" & "Teahouse of the August Moon" has it in hands, & loves it. He was with us in Tingrith while producing the second play in London. You may be sure [Cardinal] Spellman won't be at the first-night performance. I hope you'll have a good time in the Church of the Young Women—Killiney. The Deverell Brothers [2] who owned Hampton & Leedoms where I first worked looked on Merrion Hall as the New Jerusalem; & many who worked for them went there to worship the Devilerells. They tried to get me to go, but the "bad language" I used frightened them off. I wonder does the Hall work still, or is it a closed shop?

All the best,

As ever,
Sean

P.S. I've written a new 3 act play—"The Bishop's Bonfire"—God forgive me!

[1] Conference of the World Council of Churches.
[2] Characterized as the "Dovergulls" in "Comin' of Age" and the following chapters, *Pictures in the Hallway* (1942).

To David Marcus

TC. O'CASEY

[ST. MARYCHURCH, DEVON]
28 JULY 1954

Dear David Marcus,
I hope Sean J. White will do well with the Magazine.
I'm afraid that Ireland is less than a forlorn hope, judging by the

look of the Sunday Press and the Sunday Independent. And the Royal STANDARD! What would Jesus do without it?

I wasnt a bit distressed over P. Galvin's attack;[1] but I was over the ignorance and pomposity expressed in it. I dont know why he wanted to send his article to me, though I guess that he thought to provoke me into a public retort, and thereby gain a little publicity for himself. For instance his main distress was, apparently, caused by the one-act play called HALL OF HEALING, for he maintained that I was trying to show that the dispensary system in Ireland was now what it had been fifty years ago. Yet but a short time before, a letter from me appeared in the IRISH TIMES[2] attesting that the period of the play was that of fifty years ago, adding that the vile Red Ticket of that period was in use when the letter was written, proved by an article in the same Paper, an article that lost the writer a job.[3] It just distresses me that the young writers deliberately keep their eyes shut and their ears closed; or that they are afraid to open them, except when they know a virtuous attack can be carried out without a wound.

Since I didnt shirk a dispute, a dangerous one, with the great Yeats, it's hardly likely I care a lot about Galvin. Indeed, if every Galvin were in six parts and every part a Galvin, and every Galvin shouted down with

[1] See O'Casey's letters to Francis MacManus, 1 June 1954, note 8; G. W. Head, 31 December 1954, note 2. When I wrote to Patrick Galvin in 1969 asking him about his "Open Letter" and O'Casey's response to it, he replied in a letter of 10 December 1969, stating that although O'Casey had misrepresented him, he now saw the whole controversy about Socialism and art and O'Casey in a different light. He has kindly given me permission to quote the following significant passages from his letter:

> Of course, the whole thing was much ado about very little. Writers of my generation (and background) have always demanded too much of O'Casey. We seemed to believe that in some mysterious way he owed us something—when in fact it had always been the other way round. We expected him to answer letters, deal with our complaints, come forward and explain himself. And we have always insisted that he give solid proof of his good Socialist intentions.
>
> Later, when we discovered that O'Casey was first and foremost himself (and like all true artists, continued to remain so) we felt betrayed. We raked through his work looking for all those faults and subtle deviations, and like all good social realists we found them in plenty. We found his language phoney, his characters unreal, and his politics naive and out of date. For many, it was like that devout Christian who had suddenly discovered that Christ was not, after all, the Son of God, but a brothel-keeper in the back streets of China.
>
> Needless to say, O'Casey had betrayed no one. If betrayal there was, we had betrayed ourselves. You took O'Casey as he was—warts and all—or you left him alone. The wonder of it is that he managed superbly well to survive the attentions of his friends and the wishes of his enemies.
>
> No Irish writer of my generation can repay the debt we owe to O'Casey. He kept the flag flying against Church and State for longer than most of us can remember. And though he was certainly not always right—by intention he was never wrong. May he rest well.

[2] See O'Casey's letters, "The Red Ticket," *Irish Times,* 28 December 1951, 24 January 1952; see also his letter to Robert M. Smyllie, editor, *Irish Times,* 22 April 1951, note 4.

[3] See O'Casey's letter to Mary Frances Keating Newman, 4 May 1951.

O'Casey, it wouldnt flutter me a bit. It's when he, as a poet, seems to echo the bawling of the STANDARD that I become afraid, not for myself, but for him.

You agree that the young Irish writers have nothing to say. Nothing to say! What condition could be worse than that condition? The fault of the times and the conditions? No, it isnt; the fault isnt in the stars, but in themselves that they are underlings. It is theirs to make the times and to change the conditions, if they are to become the power that Shelley claimed the poets to be. The rams' horns, blown bravely, can still knock down Jericho's walls; but the young Irish poets arent even a tin-whistle band.

All goodness to you.
[Sean O'Casey]

To Robert Emmett Ginna

MS. GINNA

ST. MARYCHURCH, DEVON

29 JULY 1954

My dear Bob,

It was fine to hear from you again, & to learn that you had seated yourself in another chair that you say is more suitable, if more severe.[1] If the new job gives you enough to live decently & a little gayly, you do well.

I'm sorry you didn't end the story of "O'Casey's World"[2] as you began it. I fear I agree with you about the writer doing a job like that, hating him he writes about, or liking him with a great liking. If there be anything of talent in either writer, the work is bound to be interesting. It has come here to me; it looks fine. There's one mistake of making me act the part of "Davoren" instead of that of Boyle.[3] Imagine, Michael Mullen still in the same room of 35 years ago.[4] It is odd how easy it is to satisfy so many of us Irish. The walk thro' the wood of Coole is the picture I

---

[1] Ginna had left his job at *Life* and gone to work for *Scientific American*.

[2] "The World of Sean O'Casey," *Life*, 26 July 1954, an unsigned article, apparently partly written by Ginna, with photographs by Gjon Mili.

[3] In one of the photographs O'Casey is acting out the role of Captain Boyle, but the caption says he is Donal Davoren.

[4] In 1920 O'Casey shared a room at 35 Mountjoy Square with Mullen, who lived there until his death in 1956. Pictures of Mullen and his room appeared in the article. See O'Casey's letter to Micheál Ó Maoláin (Michael Mullen), 17 December 1945, note 1.

like best; possibly because I knew so many who walked that way.[5] The main thought that came to me was the realization of how far I had gone from the most of what was behind me. As for the "wonderful O'Casey family," it is wonderful only when "wonderful" come into contact with it. When dull people come to us, the O'Caseys become as dull as the dullest. We loved Bob Ginna, and that's why we appeared to be so charming to him.

All here (which is all, bar Niall) Eileen, Breon, & Shivaun, send their love to you. Niall is coming home on the all-night train, & will be here tomorrow. He expects to be going East.

With the love of the others, I send mine.

Sean

[5] This was a picture of the tree-lined walk leading into Coole Park, Lady Gregory's home in Galway.

To Francis MacManus

TS. MacManus

St. Marychurch, Devon

30 July 1954

Dear Frank,

Tell Miss Moira Cranwell [1]—the lass photographed from a hundred angles—that her picture—a very pretty one—appears in the American edition of LIFE for July 26, 1954. Give her my love.

And my love to you.

Had a letter from a Doctor who was a student in Maynooth from 1908 to 1913; knew "Watty McDonald" [Dr. Walter McDonald]. God, he comes down on the episcopal & monsignorial boyos there!

All the best

Sean

[1] Miss Cranwell was MacManus's secretary at Radio Eireann.

To George Jean Nathan

MS. CORNELL

ST. MARYCHURCH, DEVON

1 AUGUST 1954

My very dear George:

The address was correct. Anyway the letter came to me, & that is all that matters. It is a very cumbersome address. I wish you had stopped longer in South America. I often wondered—and still do—why so many Americans hasten off to Europe, to see less than what they could see in the American Continent. To me, the Rockefeller Center Building is finer & more amazing than any leaning Tower of Pisa. That of course, is only a beginning; rivers in the U.S.A. not to mention the Amazon—are as good & mightier than any Blue Danube—tho' the Waltz be lovely. I'm glad you didn't do any work for some time, & for God's sake, do as little as you can till you find yourself fit for it.

Dick Watts & Tom Curtiss were here with us a few weeks ago, & I lent the copy of my play that I was going to send to Miss Rubin to them. I've heard nothing from them since one left for Paris & the other for Dublin. Probably they don't think much of it, & hesitate to say so. It isn't a sensational play in any way; but, maybe, has a few moments of pathos & comedy. It's hard for a playwright to judge his own work, or the work of other playwrights either. God help us, we can't do without the critics, grumble how we may. I'm getting two more copies typed, & when these come, I'll send one to Miss Rubin with a request to send it to you, provided you tell her you have time & energy to be bothered with it.

We had a very very pleasant time with Tom & Dick; they & the family—bar Niall, now in the Artillery—dining together in a local hotel, & chatting our heads off. We stood together on the cliffs of Babbacombe, but the rain fell & the wind blew, & I was damned glad to get back to an electric fire.

I do so hope that the Cruise has done you great good, & has loosened some of the harness of illness from you. But take it quietly during the busy season. Try to, anyway.

My deep love to you, lapped up in many fond memories of our days together in New York.

Sean

To Marguerite Buller

MS. BULLER

ST. MARYCHURCH, DEVON

2 AUGUST 1954

Miss M. Buller
My dear,

I'm so sorry to hear that you have had the Influenza upon you—twice, too. I had that experience a few years ago—got up too soon—, and it was a very unpleasant one. Rest as much as you can, and take life quietly. It takes a time to get rid of the effects the cursed thing leaves behind it.

Where we live here now is some distance from Torquay, but near the cliffs that frown out over the sea. It is indeed fresh, too much so at times. From our window we can see a field where Boy Scouts are holding a Jamboree; not a very jolly one, for the field is sodden, the tents soaked, & the camp-fires blown about by the wind. We are all pining after our lost summer; but the young can stand it steadily, & wait for the next one; but the older feel its loss very much indeed. Well, we have to stand it too, & we'll do our best in all this wind & all this rain.

And you just keep quiet, keep warm, and don't begin to do things too soon.

With all warm wishes to you, my dear.

Yours very sincerely,
Sean

To Cyril Cusack

MS. CUSACK

ST. MARYCHURCH, DEVON

12 AUGUST 1954

Dear Mr. Cusack,

Are you still desirous of reading "The Bishop's Bonfire"? If you are, I can send you a copy to be kept for a week, and read by yourself only, and a close adviser—Mrs. Cusack, probably.

I'd like to make it clear to you that I never send a play to the Abbey, or, directly or indirectly, ask them are they interested. They (I presume) know about them, & if they were interested, they'd ask me to let them read what they happened to be interested in. I wait awhile to see, out of an old sentimental loyalty: that is all. They haven't asked for "The Bishop's Bonfire"; so they can't be interested. I've never sent a play or asked them if they were interested in one since the Affair of the "Silver Tassie."

This writing staggers a little, not because I'm drunk, but because of a blood-poisoned hand got from the prod of a rose-tree thorn. The hand had to be opened under an anaesthetic, & I'm writing in a heavily-bandaged mit.

I've heard you had a good time in Paris.

All good wishes to you; though, of course, this note doesn't constitute a contract; just as well for you as me, for, most probably, you won't be attracted in any way to the play.

Yours sincerely,
Sean O'Casey

I stood on the stage once with Breffni O'Rourke [1]—the Queen's. G[erard]. Croft was giving a Song-play Scena there. Breffni did the Irish burglar in "Special Pleading." [2] I was with the O'Toole Pipers Band. Oh, years ago!

[1] Breffni O'Rourke (1889–1946), Irish actor, stepfather of Cusack.
[2] Bernard Duffy, *Special Pleading* (1916), a one-act play.

To G. W. Head [1]

MS. HEAD

ST. MARYCHURCH, DEVON
12 AUGUST 1954

Dear Mr. Head,

Thank you very much for your kind letter. Yes, LIFE sent me a copy of the magazine, but I could do with a second one for a friend who has asked me for it. The article doesnt appear in the International Edition.

Of course, I know of Captain Monteith, & of his adventures.[2] I was a friend of one of the I.R.B. men—Charles Monaghan—who went over the cliffs (taking a wrong road) into the sea, & who was one of the group sent down to meet Casement & Capt. Monteith. I read C. M's article recently in the "Kerry Annual." Should you see him, or write to him, give

[1] G. W. Head, manager, advertising and sales promotion, National Cash Register Company, Dayton, Ohio.
[2] Robert Monteith, *Casement's Last Adventure* (1932; revised and rewritten, 1953). See O'Casey's letters to Head and Monteith, 31 December 1954.

him my love & warm admiration. There were too few with his knowledge & experiences among the officers of the Irish Volunteers. I haven't seen or heard of his book. I'm afraid Ireland now wants to forget a lot of things she should remember.

I'd have written earlier, but got an injury to my right hand, my good right hand; it became septic, & I had to have an operation to have it opened. I'm writing this with a heavily bandaged mit.

All good wishes to you.

Yours very sincerely,
Sean O'Casey

To Francis J. Kelly [1]

TS. KELLY

ST. MARYCHURCH, DEVON
15 AUGUST 1954

Dear Frank,

Go ahead—I've no objections.[2] I could hardly have time to vet everything that is said about me. Anyhow, there isnt anything "derogatory" in anything youve set down. Authors usually complain and kick up a row when anything's said that would harm their livelihood.

There are two points, however, about which, I believe you are mistaken: 1. That I was a highly-regarded member of the Gaelic League. No, sir. I didnt belong to the class that ran it—the Civil Servants, Customs Officers, Teachers, and others of the budding Irish Gentry. I remember Peadar O'Nualain giving me a homily on the sin of wearing a muffler instead of a collar as we left a meeting held in the Ard Craobh [3]—ard in more ways than one. The Keating Branch was much more democratic, but it kept itself to itself: Is sinn fein Sinn Fein. And that my knowledge of Irish wasnt good. I imagine it was very good; and is very good; so good that it [couldnt] stick Hyde's "Irish" then, or [Sean T.] O'Kelly's or De Valera's "Irish" now. Not that it matters a damn now whether it was, or is, good or bad.

But say what you think to be right, a vic. It's all a long time ago,

---

[1] Francis J. Kelly, 20 Oakley Road, Ranelagh, Dublin. See O'Casey's letter to Mrs. Elizabeth Kelly, 20 July 1955, Vol. III, on the occasion of Kelly's death.
[2] Kelly had sent O'Casey his manuscript "Recollections of O'Casey," which he planned to submit to Radio Eireann.
[3] High branch.

the time I remember you scaling a cliff in the gardens of Stella Maris, with
Peadar MacPheadar Porter, son of Peter, and Francis Macnamara, a one
from the brain down to the toes paralysed without the paralysis, shep-
herding us all; and the flutter of the nuns when the twilight began to come
to get us away, for fear something might soil the holy ground on which
we tried to show what a gay lot we were; and the end coming by the
singing on chorus of Pray for the sinner, prayer for me—pray for the
wanderer, rather. The time when we went on an "excursion" to the Scealp,[4]
and the frantic anger of P. J. Kelly and P. O'Calahan when a Seonin [5]
group came into the hall as we were leaving, and began to play "foreign"
dance music that had so recently given us out such lovely Irish airs. And
Buggy, the Ingoldbys, and Mister Eggleso. Well, well; I remember your
articles on the stars given to the Evening Herald, tho' now you seemed to
have changed the music of the spheres for that of the dulcimer and the
sackbut. And MacGiolla Bridhe, and Old Thunder with his family of fifty-
two, one for every week of the year. All the labour we gave to Ireland in
those days! I dont regret it: it was a great experience and something of
an education. I dont think your review is vivid enough, but that's your
lookout. Anyway, I daresay R. Eireann doesnt pay too well.

Good luck and good broadcasting to you.

Yours sincerely,
Sean

I cant hold a pen; injured my right hand, and had to have an operation
to get it opened, so it is thickly swathed in bandages. I return the MS.

[4] The Scalp, a rocky pass in the Dublin mountains.
[5] *Seonin,* a West Briton or Irishman with British sympathies.

To Cyril Cusack

MS. Cusack

St. Marychurch, Devon
18 August [1954]

Dear Cyril Cusack,

I'll send the Typescript to Clonquin [1] towards the end of next week.
I'd rather send it there than to London; or do you think you'd rather
have it sent to London? I'd like Maureen & you to read it. The lad (God
bless him) is a little young yet. The theme of the play is a helluva long

[1] Cusack's home in Dalkey, Co. Dublin.

way from St. Patrick's Purgatory; [2] but quite close to John O'Brien's (Ph.D. LLD, of the big Catholic University of Notre Dame, Notre Dame, Indiana, U.S.A.) book, "The Power of Love," tho', alas, Love has little power in Eireann now. It would have been an experience indeed for you to go straight from Loc Deargh to Moscow, the great Turbine of Communism. I'll send the play to Clonquin say between the 28 & 30, so that you'll have it there when you return. It has a relatively small Caste (for me), &, I think, all characters have a good moment in it—a good acting moment. I like it myself, but that doesn't bring it very far.

All the best,
Sean O'Casey

Breffni [O'Rourke] was a good actor, I think. Saw him do Broadbent in Shaw's "J. Bull's Other Island." I thought him good, but a bit nervous. F.J. [McCormick] did Larry Doyle, &, if I remember right, G[abriel]. Fallon did Fader Keegan. Breffni was a big fella. The song you mention was written by Peadar Carney of the "Soldier's Song." Never saw it printed—too suggestive for the holy Gaels maybe.

[2] Cusack had just returned from a pilgrimage to the shrine of St. Patrick's Purgatory, Loc Deargh, Donegal, a holy isle where the barefooted pilgrims spend a night and a day, sleepless and fasting.

To Seumas Scully

MS. SCULLY

ST. MARYCHURCH, DEVON
18 AUGUST 1954

My dear Seumas,
Thanks very much for your kind letter and clippings. You were a great help to David [Krause] [1] a good shepherd, indeed, to a half-lost sheep. He is a very clever lad, gentle and kind, like a lot of Americans.

It is sad to hear that you haven't yet found a suitable job. You can't go on living on the few pounds you may have gathered together. Do you know Frank Hugh O'Donnell of Vartry Lodge, Killiney? He is, or was, a Senator, &, long ago, used to write plays for the Abbey. He is a member of the Business Men's or Employers Association. He is a damned good fellow & very kind. I have always been very fond of Frank. Why not ring

[1] I had made my first visit to O'Casey in St. Marychurch and to Dublin during the summer of 1954.

him up, or write, & try to see him? Tell him I suggested this, & that you are a friend of mine; & that I'd consider it a personal favor if he could do something for you. If you met him, you could tell him what you did in Shell-Mex, (clerical work, I daresay), and what kind of a job you're looking for. It wouldn't do any harm to try to get into touch with him. It's a pity Lord Moyne's play was bad [2]—he evidently could be a good friend to the Abbey. Didn't he write other things? Pity, too, about Robinson's play.[3] I'm sure, like most of us, he could have done with a little money. I don't see how [Hilton] Edwards got £50 a week for 5 weeks for producing a play—that would be good money here.

I wish Lord Longford did better with his money. However, £3000 in a year isn't a lot to lose in the Theater. Backers who wouldn't give a penny for a play of mine put on a Musical in New York & lost $270,000:00 on it—about 65 thousand pounds. The Musical died after the 3rd night: so £3000 is only chicken-feed.

Never met Edwards; often met [Micheál Mac] Liammoir—he used to be in & out of the Abbey & I there.

I have had a bad three weeks with my right hand. A little bush of red roses gave me a prod from its thorns, & I had to go under an operation to have the hand opened to get the poison out. Better now, but still bandaged.

My love to you. I hope you may soon be working again. If not already, do try to get an interview with Fr. Hugh O'Donnell.

> *Yours very sincerely,*
> *As ever,*
> *Sean*

[2] Bryan Guinness's (Lord Moyne) *A Riverside Charade* opened at the Abbey Theatre on 26 July 1954.
[3] Lennox Robinson's *Crabbed Youth and Age,* a one-act play, was the curtain raiser before John McCann's *Twenty Years A-Wooing,* both of which were revived at the Abbey Theatre on 2 August 1954.

To Miss Sheila ———

MS. PRIVATE

ST. MARYCHURCH, DEVON
29 AUGUST 1954

Dear Sheila,

You can see that we have left "Tingrith" for a new home. The Landlord said he wanted the house for himself to live in, & so we had to go.

He really wanted to sell it, & it is now advertised to be sold. I've been busy with the shifting; with the inconvenience of a poisoned hand, got from the stab of a thorn—had to go under a black-out to have the hand slit; from an infection of the left ear; & now from a congested chest; so, you see, I have had a lot to counter. Our younger lad, a gunner in the Field Artillery goes overseas on Wednesday, & we have had him here on Embarkation Leave, which kept us busy, too. My biographical book can't come out now till October. I've written a new 3 act play, called "The Bishop's Bonfire," which will be published in time. Did you see the article "The World of Sean O'Casey" which appeared in The International Edition of LIFE, the American magazine?

By the way, Sheila, you are, you know, inclined to be nervy, & should take things more calmly. Don't worry yourself about what Lord Dennings does or says; or how or where his son or his daughter marries; & there is more in life than the 10 Commandments; & Card. Griffin is, I'm sure, a jolly good fellow; but he isnt the last or the first word of wisdom or of truth. Lady C——— shouldn't worry if her laddo doesn't get the Red Hat. After all, there were damned few Cardinals like Newman; & he was as great a man without his red robe as he was within it.

Now go quietly, lass,
Yours as ever. Sean

To Gilbert Ross

MS. ROSS

ST. MARYCHURCH, DEVON
[? SEPTEMBER 1954]

My dear Gil,

Just a line or two of greeting, & the cordial wish & hope that you are doing well. During recent weeks, I haven't been too good, tho' I'm sailing along on an even keel now again. A thorn-stab from a rose-tree in the hand became infected, & I had to go under an anaesthetic to have the hand sliced. I mention this to say that when the hand had swelled & the pain was on me, I wasn't looking for one who was a Communist, but for a good surgeon. I found one—a young woman. I didn't know, dont know yet, what Church she went to (if any), or what political opinions she held; & I didn't care a damn. She gave my hand a clever cut, &, after a few weeks, it was as good as ever. You see? First things first. A doctor is a body who is good at healing, not just clever & zealous in his political opinions. As a Doctor, healing must come first, & always remain first with him or her. Well, there's a lesson for you!

Now, let me hope your father & mother are well, & you, too; advancing in your knowledge, & growing in confidence thro' that knowledge.

We are setting down here in our new place, though it isn't so commodious as where we were before.

For peace and unity among all men. My love, my dear Gil, to you & yours.

As ever,
Sean

To Cyril Cusack

MS. CUSACK

ST. MARYCHURCH, DEVON

1 SEPTEMBER 1954

Dear Mr. Cusack,

Here's the play [*The Bishop's Bonfire*]—for a week's duration. Heard "Doctor's Dilemma." [1] You were good, &, on the whole, so was the production; so different from the usual drama abominations preening themselves through the sound of voices into the ear of England. Shaw comes over well as a rule. T[ony]. Quinn seemed to drawl a little too much.

All the best
Sean O'Casey

[1] Bernard Shaw's *The Doctor's Dilemma* was broadcast on the BBC radio Home Service on 30 August 1954, with Cyril Cusack as Louis Dubedat and Tony Quinn as Sir Patrick Cullens.

To Richard Courtney [1]

PC. *Act*

[ST. MARYCHURCH, DEVON]
3 SEPTEMBER 1954

Dear Mr. Courtney,

Thanks for your kind letter and for the invitation to write something for your Magazine. You've got a bad way about getting articles, I'm afraid, by not paying anything for what is written. Authors get little enough, but if they get nothing, how are they going to live, to write? As for me, I'm not good at articles; to write one takes me as much time and as much labour as to write an act of a play. And I don't like the work either. I am very busy now in various ways, with my own work, and with things to do in the house, for I can't let my wife do everything. And I must use my eyes very cautiously, having but one, and that one not very good either; so I'm sorry that I won't be able to do as you ask.

Your remark that in England "there is a great interest in anything you produce" is a rosy libel. My income from England is a small one. I am better known in Israel, Iceland, the U.S.S.R., Germany, Denmark, etc., than in England. I get most of my income from the U.S.A. I wish the tale was different, but there it is. You may say, "Well, how the hell can you expect it to be otherwise when you refuse to write for our Magazine?" I don't refuse; I simply haven't the time nor the energy, nor the reserve of eyesight, to do so. I wish I had all these things so that I could come into closer contact with the young of the Universities. They will be the future leaders of life, and I pray that they be better and braver than we were, old now, and passing out of the world we did so little for.

My love to all your comrade students in Leeds. I'm glad that the Universities separate from Cambridge and Oxford are beginning to realise their importance to England; to speak out; and to take the place in England's life they should have taken years ago.

Yours very sincerely,
Sean O'Casey

[1] Richard Courtney, editor, *ACT,* the drama magazine, Leeds University. This letter and O'Casey's letter of 10 November 1954 were printed in *ACT,* January 1955, the first issue of the magazine, with the following comment by Mr. Courtney:

I wrote to Mr. O'Casey on 25th August, 1954, and asked if he could honour us with an article. I stressed that we could not afford to play him for it, as we had to keep the price of "ACT" as low as possible so that students would be able to buy it. It seemed unfair that people with a high I. Q. would not be able to read the magazine if the price were too high. But I assured him that we were non-profitmaking, and that any money we did make would go to improve our quality.

To Richard Watts, Jr.[1]

MS. WATTS, JR.

ST. MARYCHURCH, DEVON
5 SEPTEMBER 1954

My dear Dick:

Many thanks for your kind letter and for the Cuttings. Oh, Lord, Dick, would I were what you think me to be! All my American friends think well of me, and I often wonder why. I've asked Eileen about this, but she can't tell why either. I'm inclined to believe, nay, I do believe, that the qualities are rather in my American friends than in me. Even so, Dick, your good opinions & theses give me joy, and warm the Irish blood in my veins that again is making desperate efforts to cool. Thanks again for your kind words.

The Typescript of the play [*The Bishop's Bonfire*] came to me safely last Thursday from the Savoy.

I've had a pretty bad time of it since you & Tom [Quinn Curtiss] were here. It began in our patch of a garden. There, taking bindweed away from its tangling grip on a little red rosebush, the bush gave me a stab from a thorn between the fingers of my right hand. It grew septic, & I had to go under a blackout to have the hand slit. Then the infection seemed to go into the left ear, & that had to be probed & slit, too; then it got into my chest and throat, & it lingers there still. Hand and ear are well, & I hope the throat may clear up brightly soon. Six weeks so far that have been ornamented with pain, but it might easily have been worse. I sent the "B.'s Bonfire" to Cyril Cusack (Dublin), who asked me to let him read it. Cyril is just back from a week's pilgrimage in St. Patrick's Purgatory, in Loc Dearg, Donegal. The pilgrims do the Stations of the Cross in their bare feet over rough edged stones so many times a day, fortifying themselves on black tea & a cut of dry bread. Heaven knows what Cyril the Pilgrim will think of the play.

If you should think of mentioning that Cyril has the play, don't mention the Pilgrimage; for he told me of it by letter, he might be hurt if it were published. But it all confirms the theme of my play. The Irish are in the throes of self-mortification, objectively; but inwardly are close to the world, the flesh, & the Devil as ever. In the same letter, Cyril told me a Benedictine monk told him "there was very little love left in Ireland"; & Cyril agreed. Cut & bleeding feet, but no love. Oh, Eire, Eire, where in the name of God are you going.

· *My love to you, Dick.*
As ever,
Sean

---

[1] Richard Watts, Jr. (1898–   ), drama critic of the *New York Herald Tribune*, 1936–42; drama critic of the *New York Post,* 1946–74. Retired in 1974.

To Cyril Cusack

TS. CUSACK

ST. MARYCHURCH, DEVON
11 SEPTEMBER 1954

Dear Cyril,

Thanks for your letter and for returning the play which came back safely today. I'm glad, naturally, that you and Maureen think so well of the play. If it be three-quarter as good as you both seem to think it to be, I shall be well pleased. Regarding what you say about weaknesses here and there, and some remarks which you think might divert sympathy from and understanding of Father Boheroe, I amnt at the moment aware of them, but they may well be there, for I am far from perfection yet. It wouldn't be surprising if one of 74 nodded occasionally.

Regarding your wish to do the play in the Dublin Gaiety, I'd like you to think over the idea again—you and Maureen; so's not to pounce on it too impulsively. Of course, I'd like to have the play done in Dublin, now that the Abbey has no desire, evidently, to have even a squint at it; for they've never sent whisper of word about it to me.

I, too, regard the declining numbers of our race with sadness and some tremours, and for us Irish to lose our influence over the world would be, in my opinion, a great loss to humanity,—bad and irresponsible as we may sometimes be. "Oh, the Irishman so foolish in his cleverness!" as G. B. S. said sorrowfully.

I daresay, you've heard of Dr. [John] O'Brien—not Phelim—of University of Notre Dame, Indiana, Editor of "The Vanishing Irish"? He's something of a friend of mine; has written to me several times; and his last letter says "Keep pounding away at the Bishop's Bonfire!" Well, I'm still leathering away with the wattle O!

If you finally decide to do it, we'd have to set down things in a formal agreement so that things might be done—vide St. Paul—decently and in order.

About coming here—it's a long way, but I'd be glad to see you, if you gave us one or two days' notice. Had we stayed in Tingrith, we could have put you up, but our flat here wont allow it. However, there are a few reasonable places near by where you could stay comfortably, should you come down, and which we could get for you if you decide to travel. That's all, I think for the present, except, if you decide, and want it, I can let you have the script again.

I wonder will Smillie's death effect the I. Times? [1] Bound to, but how? All good wishes to Maureen, your little one, and to you.

Sean

[1] Robert Maire Smyllie, editor of the *Irish Times* since 1934, died on 11 September 1954, at the age of sixty.

To George Jean Nathan

MS. CORNELL

ST. MARYCHURCH, DEVON
18 SEPTEMBER 1954

My very dear George:

Thanks for your very dear letter. It was a joy to see your handwriting again. I entirely agree that the "Bishop's Bonfire" would have been a better play had "Cockadoodle Dandy" never been written. That play, possibly by accident, came out in a very colorful way, and it is damned hard to get up to its standard. However, I can safely say that the "Bishop's Bonfire" was the best I could do in the mood of the moment. It is gratifying, too, very gratifying to know you think it has some good writing & genuine humorous characterization. Hurrah! for these even aren't easy to do.

I have had a bad stretch of 6 or 7 weeks of it. It began with a jab of a thorn from a pretty little rosebush I was saving from the strangling of bindweed. The wound got septic, & I had to have an anaesthetic to get the hand slit. Then the infection seemed to wander into the left ear and throat, & I was laid up (tho' I wasn't laid down) for a long period of pain. Nearly allright again, & waiting to think of what I shall try to do next. I daresay you are right in what you say about the Hierarchy of the U.S.A.—all jolly laddoes, as they are here in England; tho' when off guard, showing themselves to be what they really are. [Cardinal] Spellman hopes to be Pope one day; and every new Curate carries a Red Hat in his breast pocket, ready for use. Father McGinley has got on, I see—he's a Monsignor now. He sent me a Breviary when I was in New York; [1] I have it still, and have often dipped into it, wondering how intelligent minds could bury thought in its outworn texts and testimonies. Purple Dust! It's flying, floating about everywhere—in the Cathedrals, the Vatican, House of Lords, chasubles, amices, birettas, orders of Garters & Baths—all turning to dust, with McCarthy's here & McCarthy's there hanging on to the hands of the clock to keep them from moving. The falling dust, tho' still clogs the wheels. I

[1] See O'Casey's letter to Gabriel Fallon, 11 September 1938, Vol. I, p. 740.

hope Cockadoodle Dandy may have a chance this Season, or one of the others, so that a few dollars may fall into the letter-box of Flat 3 in 40. Tr'n Road.

Tom Curtiss & Dick Watts were here; & David Krause, a student, now a College Teacher, who is writing a book on the O'Casey Plays.

I hope N.Y. may have a good Season this time. Here, the dust of past themes & past styles is still falling on the British stage; and no one dramatist seems to weave anything finer than thistle-down or tinsel.

You didn't say anything about yourself in your last letter: not a damn word.

I do hope you are keeping fairly fit, and that you are really taking care of yourself.

All warm wishes to you, my very dear George, & my deep love, too.

As Ever.

Sean

To Curtis Canfield [1]

MS. CANFIELD

St. Marychurch, Devon
20 September 1954

My dear Mr. Canfield,
I'm writing this immediately after getting your letter. How could I just cable "no" to the Drama Department of Yale? or cable just a terse "no" to F. Curtis Canfield? [2] I have to explain the difficulty of cabling or saying "yes." You see, I've pledged myself that no-one save Robert Lewis (Teahouse of the August Moon), R.R.2—Box 217, Pound Ridge, New York, that no one, save he, would be allowed to handle the Cockadoodle doo. He has made big efforts to get the money necessary, and he hopes to manage a production this Season sometime. I am writing to him now asking him what he thinks of your kind proposal; and also asking him to write to you.

Another thing, too: we have been looking forward—all the family—to a production which might solve many financial problems; for, between you and me, it is hard going to keep five of us in a way that prevents us from hanging heads and wistful eyes that see a vague and uncertain future.

[1] Prof. F. Curtis Canfield (1903–   ), Yale School of Drama, New Haven, Connecticut.
[2] The Yale School of Drama presented *Cock-a-Doodle Dandy* for a one-week run beginning 1 November 1955.

I am ending this so's to catch a post for this letter and the one to Robert; and will delay only to add my best wishes and warm regards; and many thanks, too.

Yours very sincerely,
Sean O'Casey

To R. L. De Wilton [1]

TS. DE WILTON

ST. MARYCHURCH, DEVON
20 SEPTEMBER 1954

Dear Mr. De Wilton:

Your letter under the reference of RLD/mh presents me with a poser. It's this way: I write the play in longhand first; then take a rough draft of typing, adding, rejecting as I work, going from act 1, and leaving each act lying till the whole play is roughly drafted; so that when I come back to the 1st act, after many months, my mind is fresh, and I can see some terrible things I've done. I then do a fairly straight edition of the play, again adding and rejecting; and, finally, a fair copy of the finished work, which, when read over, soon becomes a scattered mass of emendments. When this has been done, I get a professional typist to make some decent copies, which, when they come back, are again spattered with emendments. It was one of these I sent to you (if I remember right). I then got fresh copies from the professional t. which, with a few changes, I sent to Macmillans here, and to Miss [Jane] Rubin, Richard Madden Play Co., 522 Fifth Avenue, New York, 18. This is the copy that should be used in the setting, if the tally sheets can't be sent to me. If this doesn't do, then the only alternative is to ask the Macmillan Company here to send the proofs when corrected on to you. So when I hear from you, if the proofs can't be sent to me (tally proofs), or the copy held by Miss Rubin can't be got, then I'll ask Macmillans here to oblige me.

There you are now—you know the worst, as the old melodramas used to say, and, in my opinion, some of them said it well; better than some of the more enlightened playwrights are saying it now.

The poisoned hand seemed to infect an ear and the throat, so that I had an uncomfortable 7 weeks of it, but I kept going, and am allright again; in a more cheerful mood to face the Fall and the winter.

[1] R. L. De Wilton, Macmillan Company, New York.

That was a fine letter from Brooks Atkinson in The New York Times.
He is a very dear friend of mine, he and his wife, Oriana.

Take a blessing from me.
Yours very sincerely,
Sean O'Casey

P.S. I've written Miss Rubin asking her to send you the MS of my amended
"Bishop's Bonfire." I shall forward the music for songs in the play under
another cover.

To Frank McCarthy

MS. McCarthy

St. Marychurch, Devon
23 September 1954

My dear Frank,

Thank you for your letter and for the p. card giving me a decko of
Sandycove again. Ay, I listened in to the Broadcast about G. B. S.[1] I'm
not sorry I didn't say more; it was bad. You see, reading, I have to keep
my nose to the print, and sometimes guess at a word, so that my voice goes
down to the book or the script, & not towards the microphone. I did a bit
extempore, about Shaw's opinion of me to a landlord asking for a reference; but this wasn't included, which was a pity, because it would have
come out clear. [St. John] Ervine was indeed fine, in my opinion; and true,
too. I can't understand the snarling objections Denis Johnston had to
G. B. S. But then he seems to have the dignity and importance of Merrion
Sqr on the Brain. I agree, that there can hardly be an old codger left in
Dalkey who remembers him. You'd be surprised how many have written
me claiming they worked with me in jobs I was never in. Where G. B. S.
lunched or how, doesn't matter now: he repaid a hundred-fold all he got
from man. The book-stalls were there on the Quays & in the streets off the
Quay, right enough, for my own father patronised them every week, never
coming home without a volume. It was from these old volumes, left behind when he died, that gave me a big part of my first Education—Dr. Watts'
Dictionary, for instance; now forgotten.

Your idea of a Broadcast of Dublin Life, 50 years ago, is a good one;

---

[1] "George Bernard Shaw: An Irish Portrait," a radio broadcast on the BBC
Third Programme on 20 September 1954, produced by W. R. Rodgers. Among the
people who spoke about Shaw were O'Casey, St. John Ervine, and Denis Johnston.

but it would be a big job, & would mean the going over & over of old work. Besides, it would get only two Broadcasts—if it got any; & what one would get wouldn't pay for the work.

Curiously enough, there's a chance of "I Knock at the Door" being dramatically performed this year or early next year, in New York.[2] A group two years ago did "The Life of Sholom Aleicim," something similar in Jewish life. It was to be given 20 performances: instead it ran for months & months; then did as well in Chicago; then went on Tour; & there is to be a revival in New York now. After this, mine is to come, if all goes well. The same principals who did Sholom are doing mine. The Producer has dramatised it—a work that would weary me. I've signed the Contract, & am waiting. But the U.S.A. is very different from England to me. 90 & more percent of my income is from the U.S.A., and all States know me. As some critics say, "O'Casey is becoming an Institution in America." I'm afraid I'm but an imposition in England. Indeed, a Firm in Jerusalem wants to do "I Knock at the Door" in Hebrew. I hope they do. No fear of it ever being done in Gaelic.

The critics' tribute to John Bratby may mean little to him. He may not sell a single picture. I hope he sells them all.

I'm glad you had a good time in Ireland with Katrine. A grand-looking little kid. Is she your brother's child? Give my warm regards to her mother and her father. And my warm regards to Dr. Soper. He will find a lot against war in "Sunset & Evening Star." Our younger lad is now wasting his time as a gunner in the Royal Field Artillery. Oh, Jesus, Jesus, looks as if you were but a dream of the fanciful.

> *My love to you, my lad.*
> *As ever,*
> *Sean*

[2] Arnold Perl, writer and producer, who adapted and produced, with Howard da Silva, *The World of Sholom Aleichem,* at the Barbizon-Plaza, New York, on 1 May 1953, planned to adapt the first volume of O'Casey's autobiography in a similar production, *The World of Sean O'Casey.* It was eventually abandoned. Later, Paul Shyre made adaptations as concert readings in New York of *I Knock at the Door* (1956), *Pictures in the Hallway* (1956), *Drums Under the Windows* (1960). Patrick Funge and David Krause made adaptations as stage plays in Dublin of *Pictures in the Hallway* (1965), *Drums Under the Windows* (1970), *Inishfallen, Fare Thee Well* (1972). For details on these productions, see Vol. III.

To John Gassner

MS. GASSNER

ST. MARYCHURCH, DEVON
25 SEPTEMBER 1954

My dear John,

Thanks a hundred for your letter of the August moon. I, too, have been away from any business life for some weeks. A thorn did it! Got a stab from a little red rose tree I was protecting from the grip of a bindweed. The wound got bad, had to be slit; then sundry injections of penecillin didn't prevent (maybe caused) an infection from left ear, throat, & chest. Voice is a bit husky still, but nearly allright now. I think you would be the man for Galway regarding the getting together of a one-volume life of the O'Casey.[1] I daresay, you haven't yet mentioned the idea to Macmillans? Would you like me to tell them about it? Curiously, when in London recently, Eileen (Mrs. O'C.) went to see the London Firm—American & British Houses are now divided, & are business rivals—, and the Head of the London House put the same idea to Eileen; without knowing anything about our idea. As yet, I have made no comment on the proposal, waiting to see how our own idea grows into definite shape. Your suggestion that I should travel through the old territory again, & put up sign-posts of dates on the way, is a good and terrible idea! Recollection of dates is the one thing under God's heaven & in man's earth I can't remember. However, I've already dated—well as I can—the first vol, & have the 2nd one beside me so that I may be tempted at some moment to do that, too. E[ric]. Bentley has sent me his "In Search of Theater" [1953]. Very interesting: he has talent, this fellow; but is, or seems to be, too positive. He seems to have sailed every high sea, every low sea, climbed every hill, and forded every river in his search. He races along, never out of puff, and springs from one item to another—The Spring-heeled Jack of criticism; &, worse, there seems to sound a fanfare of trumpets before each of his chapters: for a critic, he knows too much; but he has talent. You'd think "The Bishop's Bonfire" a good play, if you hadn't come across "Cockadoodle Dandy." It is a similar effort at Drama music, but not so fanciful or so good. However, while the "Cockadoodle" stands no chance whatever of being done in Ireland, the Bonfire may be lighted there. It is on a matter greatly troubling the Irish now—see Dr. [John] O'Brien's "The Vanishing Irish." Dr. O'B. is professor in University of Notre Dame, Notre Dame, Indiana; & writes me very friendly letters. I think "The Bishop's Bonfire" would cause a stir in Ireland. It is far above the plays done there for the past number of years; tho' God Knows that's not saying much for

---

[1] A proposed single volume of selections from the six-volume autobiography.

it. Don't stay dispirited because a friend has died. Many of mine are gone—
Lady Gregory, Yeats, Shaw, & many minor souls but lovable & true. I
thought the world vanished when my mother left me; but I had to live on;
live on, and fight, & like Yeats's red cock, even lifted the head, clapped
the wings, and crew.[2]

My love to you, my friend.

Sean

[2] Up with the neck and clap the wing,
Red cock, and crow!
The first musician's song in Yeats's *Dreaming of the Bones* (1921).

To David Krause

MS. KRAUSE

ST. MARYCHURCH, DEVON
30 SEPTEMBER 1954

My dear Dave,

So glad to hear from you, & know you are again safe in the "terror
firma" of the U.S.A. I hope you had a good voyage, with a stilly sea under
you, and a warm sky over head. And thanks a thousand & one for the
generous parcel you sent to us. But if we are to remain friends, send no
more. If you could use dollar bills to paper your room, it would be another
matter; but you can't afford to throw one one-dollar away even by accident.

A Doctor of Literature doesn't wade to his rostrum thro' them; and
you won't always be young; so get a few—if you can—together for the
time when the step's unsteady, the hair grey, the voice husky.

Your account of O'Casey [1] is, I think, a fine one; but it would be
better for expansion in the way you mentioned to me. It is by far the
best "Thesis" I've read about myself. Atta-boy! I've sent notice of a few
mistakes on this sheet (other side), which you can easily correct.

After you left us, I had a bad five weeks with hand for infection
seemed to go with chest, throat, & ear; but all's gone now, bar a little huski-
ness still to remind me that even a charming little rose can be a deceiver.

Niall is in Germany with his artillery Troop; Breon's in London; &
Shivaun's boarding at school; so the two of us are here alone, till Saturdays,
when Shivaun returns to us till Monday morning.

[1] David Krause, "Prometheus of Dublin: A Study of the Plays of Sean O'Casey,"
doctoral dissertation, New York University, 1954.

Haven't managed to settle down quite yet, but hope to soon.
Eileen sends her love to you, & so do I.

As ever,
Sean

BOOK ON O'CASEY
David Krause

Mistakes

Page 15. I was never Secretary of the Transport and General Workers Union—Jim Larkin was its Secretary till he left for the U.S.A. I was Secretary of the Irish Citizen Army, official, but an honorary job. I did other work of course in Liberty Hall, all kinds, and during strike from early morning often till early morning again; but did it for the sake of The Trades Union Cause; never paid a penny; never asked for payment; never expected it. This statement (of being [me]) Secretary to the Transport Union is repeated on page 181.
This is a serious one, Dave, and must be corrected.

Had more than £40 a year, Dave, though some years that amount would represent royalties got from *England*. At times had only £15 in the bank; and once or twice had that amount in the Red; would have been a lot more, but the yearly receipts didn't encourage a bank to allow any bigger overdraft. When bound for America—as mentioned in ROSE AND CROWN—had but a few pounds in the world which I divided with Eileen down in Chalfont, preparing to come to the Battersea Flat in London, and myself on the voyage to New York. Nothing beyond the few quid bar resolution and faith in those behind the Statue of Liberty. Have rarely allowed myself to be free from the uncertainty of not having enough to pay a simple way forward for all.

Page 260. I suggest you change the word "murder" to "killing." [2] This incident, savage and all as it was, wasn't technically or theologically "murder." The priest didn't mean to kill him. It was an act of blind and Jansenistic fury.

[2] The incident at the end of Scene II in *Cock-a-Doodle Dandy* when Father Domineer accidentally kills a man.

To Cyril Cusack

MS. Cusack

St. Marychurch, Devon

15 October 1954

Dear Cyril,

Thanks for your letter. Connor would indeed be right for "Manus." That's my opinion, fallible, of course. I haven't his address, but I'll write to B.B.C. to ask them for it. He acted a number of times for them. If an act be bright, it won't be too long; a dull act, however short, is always too long. However, perhaps, we could cut some out of it—the showing of the watch by Rankin, & the chatter of Prodical about it, for instance; not very funny. About the sketch for the sets—oh, Lord! I'll think of it. Breon doesn't know much about Theatre designing. I'll ask Breon about it. There was a girl, Maureen Pook who acted in "Red Roses," but that's 13 years ago. I'll write to Macmillans for a copy of the music.

As for the business end: I suggest you send me your idea of a fair arrangement, suiting your circumstances, and I'll consider it kindly. However, take time to think of the whole scheme, before you decide. I'm sure it would go in Dublin, & this might arouse interest here in London.

All the best to Maureen, the three little ones, & to you.

Sean

To Mrs. Oriana Atkinson

MS. Atkinson

St. Marychurch, Devon

24 October 1954

My dear Oriana:

Thanks, dear lass for your kind letter. Indeed, I don't mind you laughing through my angrier hours, for without laughter, how could a lot of us live? So laugh away, &, God knows, I only wish I was there to laugh with you, with Brooks, maybe, laughing, too. I didn't mean to be angry; but all good people grow angry at times. In "Manhattan & Me," I seem to hear a growling through all the glittering laughter, & dear Oriana isn't quite satisfied with things as they are—thank God; & even the kindly

Brooks—kindlier than you or I, I'm afraid—has a few sighs in his "Once Round the Sun."

I don't believe what you say about what you think of children, even those who are a menace to life and limb. When I think of those who have mustaches, even beards, & remember what they have done, & are doing, children, to me, even the wildest of them, appear floating before my mind as Cherubim and Seraphim—the atom Bomb, Civil War in Ireland, denunciation of Parnell, Hollywood, the English Theatre, Lord Montgomery prating about the "hot war," frighten me, and I long for sleep. Of course, I'm glad you like "Sunset & Evening Star" on the whole; very glad, for you are a most intelligent woman, and have the gift I love so much in all, the ability to laugh, and the zest for life. I like and love the likes of you, Oriana. I was angry just a few minutes ago: slipping on Radio Eireann, I heard a priest appealing on behalf of a Charitable Institution: the voice said—"The world will never be a Utopia" (right, sir; no one wants it to be a utopia. Even Morris's world, in his "News From Nowhere," wants a utopia), "We will" went on the voice, "always have the poor and destitute with us." Christ's words weren't good enough for him—he had to add the one of "destitute." God, how they love destitution in Ireland! No, no utopia; but we can have sense, decency, and grace in the world, & we shall fight till they come to us, with laughter as they come, & laughter still when they are entered in as members of the family.

I'm sending this to 120, R. Drive, in the hope it may come to you. Away back in May—before we came here, I sent our change of address & a note to Brooks; but it came back after many days with notes on the envelope (enclosed) saying you weren't known there. I've looked & looked at the address I wrote, & I've looked & looked at the address you wrote, & both seem to be the same; so here's hoping.

I'm just emending the script, here & there, of "The Bishop's Bonfire"; phrases which, when re-read, seem stilted & unnatural; & I've sent an article to "Saturday Night,"[1] a Canadian weekly; so you see, I'm not idle. Niall is away now in Germany, but we hope to see him at Christmas. Shivaun is writing an essay for School; Breon's in London painting; & Eileen is busy shaping the ends of the whole of us. Like your watching over Brooks. How I get breathless when I read how you blazed a trail down the aisle for him after a first night—only a woman, & a brave one, could do that. I couldn't do it. Call me brave! Jasus, I couldn't do it. Well, lass, you are a brave one, & Brooks has a fine & lovely mate & friend.

My love to her & to Brooks, his dear companion, & my dear friend.

Sean

[1] Sean O'Casey, "The Flutter of Flags: A Healthy Pride," *Saturday Night* (Toronto), 24 July 1954; reprinted in *The Green Crow.*

To Cyril Cusack

MS. Cusack

St. Marychurch, Devon
26 October 1954

Dear Cyril,

The address of Joseph O'Connor is 18 Melville Road, Barnes, London. S.W.13., which may be out of date, for the B.B.C. book him from his Agent, AL PARKER, 50 MOUNT STREET, LONDON. W.1.; but I imagine you might think of some Actor in Dublin for Manus. A myth here in Eng. thinks every Irishman "a born actor"! There is a multitude who act the fool; but the gift goes no farther.

I've revised the stilted parts in the play, and have the one between Foorawn & Codger comic rather than solemnly unnatural. I've got copies of music from Macmillans, & will send it on when you have finally decided. If you have, I'll be glad for you to let me have the music-script back—if possible—when you've finished with them. They are the only copies I have, & it's a hard job singing & singing the airs while they're being taken down, paying, too, for the work done in setting down notation. If you send me your script of the play, I'll make the changes in it from the one I have here.

Good wishes to you & Maureen & the three children.

Sean

———

To G. A. Hayes-McCoy [1]

TS. National Museum of Ireland

St. Marychurch, Devon
31 October 1954

Dear Sir—G. A. Hayes-McCoy,

I hardly think that my memory was at fault, for reasons that shall be set down later on in this letter to you.

The Flag depicted in the Photograph is not the original Citizen Army Banner; not the one I knew and handled. But, on the other hand, I have no doubt that the Flag is a genuine one: That it was a Citizen Army flag, that it flew over the Imperial Hotel, and that the Sender, when he was a

---

[1] Dr. G. A. Hayes-McCoy, Department of Education, National Museum of Ireland, Kildare Street, Dublin.

British Officer, took it down, or picked it up, from the burning building, kept it safe, and has now kindly and generously returned it to Ireland. I hope you will let him know how grateful you (and I am) are for sending back such a dear Symbol of Ireland's battle for political freedom in 1916.

But it isn't the original flag. The one in the photograph is almost square; the original was oblong, much longer in its length than in its width. The Symbols on the field were more stylised, and much better displayed in form, the shafts of the Plough were wider apart, and formed a far more graceful design. The design was bordered by warm, red-brown tracing, not by black ones. The fringe wasn't gilt, but a long frill fringe of deep and dark yellow, probably meant to be orange. The flag-pole was topped, not by a point, but by a Red Hand Grasping a Green Dragon, and squeezing the lights out of it. The Red Hand was, as you know, the then Badge of Jim Larkin's Union, and the Dragon represented Capitalism. The field was blue.

Why do I think it was blue? Well, when I deal with facts, I like to try to make them as factual as I can. I went to see AE about this very flag (after the Rising—1921 or thereabouts). It was he who suggested the design to Capt. J. White and to Countess M[arkievicz]. But he didn't set the design down; he was too busy, he said, and suggested some other should be got to do it. As far as he could remember it was the Teacher of Art in Galway Technical School who drew the design for the C.A. Flag. My memory fails me here as to the name of this teacher; all I can recollect is that it began with an Mac or Mc—not much news in Ireland. But I wrote to this lad asking for a copy of the design, promising to pay him for it. He sent me a coloured sketch of the design, adding that payment wasn't necessary; but I paid him two or three guineas for the work. This design is somewhere among my papers, but I haven't time to go through them—it might take a week—but since I've made several sketches myself from it for American Groups who wanted it for a production. In this design the Field is Blue; though the Plough on the field—much more slender than the squat-looking bully on the photograph—was more realistic than the symbol which eventually appeared on the original flag. Another thing helped to fix these things in my memory. I knew, of course, the man who carried the flag. He was one of three brothers named Espell, I am nearly sure; three magnificent lads, six foot three or more; but withal, he found it hard to carry the banner when the wind was blowing moderately, and how he carried it at all, I don't know, just with his hands and arms, without any other aid. However, he complained of the job, and I persuaded the Army Committee to allow the expense of a harness, strapped over both shoulders, and having the socket in the middle of the body, facing the belly. This was made by a saddler from a sketch I had already done for a similar one for the O'Toole Pipers of which I had been Secretary a short time before. So you see, I had a lot to do with the flag.

My opinion is, for I remember, or seem to remember—how disappointed most of the C.A. Men were that the color wasn't green instead of blue; green to them being the one color known to poor oul' Ireland—that the green aspect of the flag rose from the almost sub-conscious idea that every Irish flag must be necessarily green.

Now for the flag of the Photo: The whole format seems, to me, to be rather crude, and the symbol is displayed very awkwardly and clumsily on the field—it seems to me to be a very amateur attempt to copy the original flag. My explanation is this: Connolly had a very sentimental attachment and reverence for "our own immortal green" witness his hoisting the green flag with the harp—a beautiful flag, by the way—over Liberty Hall; and, in my opinion he or someone else changed the original for the one pictured in the photo for two reasons, namely, that the Green field was much more national than a blue one; and that the size of it made it far easier to carry about in promenades or processions. I surmise that the original flag was left in Liberty Hall and destroyed in the bombardment of that building.

Well, there you have all the information I can give you; and there is nothing to add except that the photo-flag is a genuine one as being the flag of the C.A. that went out to fight, and so should be precious, and kept safely for display to the generations yet to come.

With all good wishes,
Yours sincerely,
Sean O'Casey

Please note	3 FLAT
new address	40 TRUMLANDS ROAD,
	ST. MARYCHURCH.
	TORQUAY,
	DEVON.
	ENGLAND

To Peter Newmark

MS. NEWMARK

ST. MARYCHURCH, DEVON
1 NOVEMBER 1954

Dear Peter,

Thanks a lot for your letter. Here is the book. I have signed my name in it, assured you won't mind for old time's sake.

I've made no mistake about my night's "lodging on the cowld, cowld floor" of St. John's.[1] St. Catherine's Shirley Society it was who invited me, & for whom I spoke. That College was full up; 40 or 50 were lodging in the Town because of the crowding—ex-mural or extra mural; or, in English, outside the walls of the College. After the discussion in a Student's room, I was led round the lawn to St. John's to spend the night in the room described in the book.

It was good for Nathan to get married,[2] even at the 11th hour. The mistake he made was not to have married long before. I several times in New York advised him to get a companion, & often hinted the same thing in letters to him. He has been intermittently ill for a year or so, & Julie Haydon, now his wife, cared for him, & nursed him, as only a woman can. I was very glad to hear that he had decided to induce her to enter into a good companionship with him.

All well here, tho' I had seven weeks of pain & illness of ear & throat due to the prod of a thorn from a little red rose in our patch of a garden; & had to go under gas to have a hand slit. Breon served his time in the Heavy Acks Acks, & now Niall is in Germany serving as a gunner in The Field Artillery. Shivaun is still at school.

Love to Monica & to you.
As ever,
Sean

Note new address.

We had to leave "Tingrith". Landlord wanted the house "for his own purposes," & so sent us Notice to Quit, so we had to git after 17 years. I sent you a card long ago with new address on it.

S. O'C

---

[1] O'Casey's account of his visit to Cambridge University in February 1936, "Cambridge," *Sunset and Evening Star* (1954). It was during this visit that he first met Newmark, then a student at Cambridge. See also O'Casey's letter to Alfred A. K. Arnold, 18 January 1936, note 1, Vol. I, p. 603.

[2] George Jean Nathan married the actress Julie Haydon on 19 June 1954. Apparently he had not yet mentioned it in his letters (see O'Casey to Nathan, 1 August and 18 September 1954), and it is referred to for the first time in O'Casey's 22 November 1954 letter to Nathan. But O'Casey must have heard about the marriage from someone else.

To David Krause

MS. KRAUSE

ST. MARYCHURCH, DEVON
2 NOVEMBER 1954

My dear Dave:

I'm not Mr. O'Casey to my buddies: I'm Sean. I'm a "Mr." to no one. There's no "Mr." in Irish: I'm either Sean or O'Casey, or, as we would say in Gaelic, if an acquaintance was addressing me, o son of O'Casey—a mhic Ui Cathasaigh. Let that be a lesson to you. Your letter isn't bladher—an Irish word, by the way. It is very wise and very well written; tho' Ernest Blythe doesn't know very much about me. During my stay in the Gaelic League, I worked harder at night than I did in the daytime—teaching Irish, sweeping floors, and lighting fires before classes began; an all for love! There's nothing whatever wrong with the white collar. I tried it out, & rejected it, not because it was "respectable," but simply because it was uncomfortable. I had to feel my neck free, as I had felt it at work for so many years.

James Plunkett Kelly [1] writes under the name of Plunkett in "The Bell," which, I fear, is now dead. All Trades Union Leaders in Ireland have gone soft; but there are a few among the rank and file who have some spirit left in them still. Any new branch premises opened in Ireland now is three-quarter filled with clerics, & no red flag is seen anywhere; tho' it was an Irishman who composed the song "The Red Flag." [2]

I'll be writing to the Macmillan Co. of New York in a day or so; & I strongly and urgently mention your proposed book to them. Of course, I am part of Judeo-Christian philosophy & facts; so are we all. It is part, a vital part, of the onward march of man. The Jew took from Babylon & Syria, the Christian from the Jew; & Communism takes from both. There is nothing that past man has done that hasn't gone into the making of our life today. I like the title of your Book "Prometheus of Dublin," but suggest you should think over a few more possible ones, & weigh them together, before deciding finally: such as, "Green Prometheus" Prometheus of Eblana—Pliny's name, I think, for Dublin. The hesitation in above title is the name "Prometheus." It is hard to say, & many won't know its mean-

---

[1] James Plunkett (1920–   ), Irish novelist and playwright. In 1954 he was a union representative for Jim Larkin's Workers' Union of Ireland, and had worked with Larkin until the time of the latter's death in 1947. Plunkett's play about Larkin and the 1913 General Strike, *The Risen People*, was produced at the Abbey Theatre in 1958. His short stories appeared in *The Bell* in the early 1950s, and he later wrote two notable novels, *Strumpet City* (1969) and *Farewell Companions* (1977).

[2] Jim Connell (1852–1929), born in Kilshire, Co. Meath, worked in Ireland and England as a docker, wrote two books on poaching, as well as the song, "The Red Flag," in 1887, to the air of "The White Cockade."

ing. I'll engage many who stare at New York's towering building have never heard the name. The title of a book is very important. However, it is a part that can be easily changed; & we've plenty of time to think about it. Perhaps, I'm wrong about Prometheus, tho', to me, a name like, say, "The Shouting Harp" would be easier to say, just as Irish, & have a readier meaning.

Thanks ever so much for Blanshard's book.[3] A clever, fair, & most sincere man; tho' I don't agree with a lot he says; & sometimes—not often, indeed—he seems to be illogical. But a well-written book, and a fearless one. I'll say more about it when I think over it awhile. Blanshard's a fella one can't answer off-hand. I hope it may have a big sail.

But one word—you mustn't, really, mustn't be spending your little heap of spare money on sending these things to me. Listen, now to what I've said. You have too many things to do with what you have above your essential needs to do these things David.

There is, of course, Nyadnanavery [4] in the USSR. It takes a long time for public consensus to become a common thing. We are not perfect; & we do not know all things yet; very little in fact; but we're trying to learn, & that's a good hold on God's hand.

Take care of yourself; rest well, & often; & don't just let the book take too much out of you.

Our love & my love to you.
Sean

I wrote to Dave [Greene], a few days ago.

Regarding your suggestion about making a book of my sketches, I'm afraid they would be insignificant things; & even, if they happened to be twice as good as they are, there wouldn't, I fear, be enough of them to make a book. The idea has great attractions, worth considering. What about some of the best, as a feature in your own book? That is if we finally decided that they were possibly good, & worth inclusion?

Sean

[3] Paul Blanshard, *The Irish and Catholic Power* (1953).
[4] *Cock-a-Doodle Dandy* (1949) is set in the Irish village of Nyadnanave, meaning in Irish a nest of saints, with O'Casey's pun of a nest of knaves. Nyadnanavery is thus a symbol of repression.

To Cyril Cusack

MS. Cusack

St. Marychurch, Devon
3 November 1954

Dear Cyril,

Eileen has received a letter from Oscar Lewenstein (OSCAR LEWEN-STEIN), Manager of the Court Theatre, asking for "Cockadoodle Dandy" as an opening in Glyndebourne, Sussex, which he can't have. Failing Cocka-doodle Dandy, he asks for the new play, "The Bishop's Bonfire," which he can't have either, if you do it in Dublin with the hope of bringing it to London.

He has also formed a Company of his own formed in partnership with Wolf Mankowitz. They are "to rent the Embassy Theatre for an in-definite period, commencing early in January with a production of "The World of Sholom Aleichem (a startling success in New York. S.O'C.) & we very much hope that in the course of 1955 we can arrange a series of O'Casey plays." I wonder what you think of this? I hope plays by other Irish playwrights might get a chance of production, too.

The Glyndebourne idea won't take place till May. I daresay you've heard of Glyndebourne. It holds a Festival of first-class music & opera yearly; & now, apparently it is now planning a drama festival as well.

Oscar Lewenstein's address (private) is
1 PARK VILLAGE WEST,
LONDON.N.W.1.
His phone No. EUSton: 6497.

All good wishes
Sean

To Frank McCarthy

MS. McCarthy

St. Marychurch, Devon
4 November 1954

My dear Frank,

Here's the book back to you. Thanks for your letter. I like your suggestion of "Juno" as a film—it was never done, tho' it was done before.

They put someone named Langley or Langsome in as Boyle, with Sinclair &
B. Fitzgerald among the audience! Hitchcock! [1] I hear Eileen, our girl, &
boys talking a lot about "On the Waterfront," [2] how fine it is. I'm cold
about films—they're such shams. Haven't seen one now for twenty years;
not since I saw the Russian ones in London—"Modern Babylon," [3]
"Chapoyev," [4] "Potemkin," [5] "Last Days of St. Petersburg," [6] "The
Mother," [7] et al. Well, I haven't been in a theatre for 26 years, so I'm not
in the way of speaking of either. I hope Dr. Soper goes to the USSR. A
few weeks ago, I had the 1st Secretary of the USSR Embassy, and the
Editor of "Egonyck" down here with us. Lively lads. Came in a Moskva
Car.

Yes, send me any cutting you come across you think I'd be unlikely
to see. Expect very venomous ones from Ireland.

All the best to you.

Sorry about Nora: how can we, these days, avoid politics or religion?
They're in the air & in our hair, and we can't wash 'em out of it.

My love to you.

As ever,
Sean

[1] In Alfred Hitchcock's film version of *Juno and the Paycock* (1930), Edward
Chapman played the role of Captain Boyle; Sara Allgood was Juno; Sidney Morgan
was Joxer Daly; while Barry Fitzgerald and Arthur Sinclair had such small parts that
they were not listed in the cast. For the credits and full cast, see O'Casey's letter to
Gabriel Fallon, 28 February 1929, note 4, Vol. I, p. 342.
[2] *On the Waterfront* (1954), a film based on a novel by Budd Schulberg, starred
Marlon Brando.
[3] *New Babylon* (1929), a Russian film directed and written by G. Kozintzev and
L. Trauberg.
[4] *Chapaev* (1935), a Russian film written and directed by the brothers G. and
S. Vassiliev.
[5] *The Battleship Potemkin* (1925) a Russian film directed by Sergei M. Eisenstein.
[6] *The End of St. Petersburg* (1927) a Russian film directed by Vsevolod
Pudovkin.
[7] *The Mother* (1926), a Russian film directed by Vsevolod Pudovkin.

To New Statesman and Nation

6 NOVEMBER 1954

"SEAN AND MR. WORSLEY"

Sir,—In his review of my *Sunset and Evening Star,* Mr. Worsley [1] makes some mis-statements. He says that this book is the concluding volume of four: It is the concluding volume of six.

He says that George Orwell reviewed the first biographical volume: He didn't; he reviewed the third one.

As for the rest, I can only declare before God and the whole livin' world that in writing the book I had no evil intention of rousin' Mr. Worsley out of his snooze, or of hurtin' his feelin's.

But there it is—the book is written, puns an' all, for betther or for Worsley.

Devon

Sean O'Casey

[1] T. C. Worsley, "Backgrounds and Foregrounds," *New Statesman and Nation,* 30 October 1954. Worsley wrote a negative review of the book, especially objecting to the "Cambridge" chapter, pointing out that since he was an undergraduate at the time of O'Casey's visit to Cambridge, he was in a position to question O'Casey's description of his experiences at the university. He also objected to O'Casey's penchant for puns.

To Peter Newmark

MS. NEWMARK

ST. MARYCHURCH, DEVON
10 NOVEMBER 1954

My dear Peter,

Many sincere thanks for your letter, and for rough draft of article—tho' I could make nothing out of it. "A damned piece of crabbed penmanship as ever I saw!" I do hope, tho', it may be seen in the S. & N. this week.[1] I need a friend or two there, I think. Interesting item about his year of graduation. Was he mistaken or was he lying? I know my "lecture" was

[1] Newmark wrote a reply to Worsley's review of *Sunset and Evening Star,* but it was refused publication by the editor of the *New Statesman and Nation.* Among other things, Newmark pointed out that since Worsley had graduated from Cambridge in 1929, seven years before O'Casey's visit in 1936, he had been less than honest and was hardly in a position to question O'Casey's facts.

sometime after my return from America, & I was there in 1934. What was the year of the lecture? I'm jotting down a few dates for an American friend who thinks of editing a one-vol book from the six books of biography. I didn't want to let Worsley off lightly. Just I had neither time nor energy for a long letter. I've been very busy looking over "Purple Dust," making some changes for a proposed production in New York; & working at a few changes in another play that may get a show in Dublin. As well, between ourselves—I've been looking up a few things in preparation for two threatened libel actions—one by T. C. Murray over a comment on a review written by him or a next-of-kin about "Drums Under the Windows," in "S. & E. Star"; [2] & another by a new young Irish writer named Patrick Galvin,[3] for comments on a letter & an article he sent to me some time ago. Then I have many letters to write to American friends; so, you see, I've no time to tackle Worsley. Besides, I get 9/10ths of whatever income I have from the U.S.A., & what English critics may say doesn't harm me there.

We had to leave "Tingrith." The landlord wanted it "for his own purposes," & so we had to quit. It's not bad here, tho' much smaller, and a much higher rent. However, we were fortunate to get it after Eileen had been searching for some months. Yep, the Professor was Mr. Peckthorn. I'm quite sure you're right about "The road to Wigan Pier" [4]—why didn't he write "The Way to Wigan Pier"? All I wanted to show was that he wasn't the God-impartial boyo he was set up to be; & his article "The Green Flag" [5] set me angry from an Irish point of view; for the "Green Flag" is, esthetically, the loveliest flag flying; & his denunciation of the "Irish National" ballad was annoying from one who was said to have known so much. I'm glad Monica & you are so busy, & hope you are economically sound.

I don't wonder you left the C.P. [Communist Party] God almighty, how stupid a lot of them can be! I gave up writing for the D.W. [Daily Worker] when I found conceited clowns taking chunks out of what I had written with great care & trouble; & altering the titles I had taken so much trouble to think out.

I sent P[alme]. Dutte a cutting from N.Y. Times once, giving great glimpses of the young G.I.'s resentment against Conscription. Sent back, & told it was useless. A few days after, long comes Moscow's "Literary Ga-

---

[2] See O'Casey's use of the quotation from the Dublin *Evening Mail* in the opening pages of "Rebel Orwell," *Sunset and Evening Star* (1954). The action was dropped.

[3] This action was also dropped. See O'Casey's letters to Francis MacManus, 1 June 1954, note 8; David Marcus, 28 July 1954, note 1; G. W. Head, 31 December 1954, note 2.

[4] George Orwell, *The Road to Wigan Pier* (1937).

[5] George Orwell, "The Green Flag," *The Observer*, 28 October 1945, a review of *Drums Under the Windows*, reprinted above. See also O'Casey's reply, 29 October 1954, refused publication; and "Rebel Orwell," *Sunset and Evening Star*.

zette" quoting the cutting, & writing a long article about the unrest. This was the time of the "Z" [Zilliacus] agitation.

I'm so glad you've got such confidence in yourself, my dear lad. You have many talents, & the responsibility of using them; so self-confidence is a splendid assistant, so long as one gets neither pompous nor conceited.

My love to Monica & to you.

As ever,
Sean

To G. A. Hayes-McCoy

MS. NATIONAL MUSEUM OF IRELAND

ST. MARYCHURCH, DEVON
11 NOVEMBER 1954

Dear Dr. Hayes-McCoy,

In going through some letters, I have come across the colored sketch of the "Plough & the Stars," mentioned by me in my letter to you; a sketch which was done by an Art Teacher in Galway (I think) Technical College or School—I shall send it to you, if you be interested, provided you return it to me; or, if you would wish to retain it as a Museum Exhibit, then that you send me a photograph of the sketch so that I may be able to provide a sketch of the flag for anyone needing it at a production of my play.

Yours sincerely,
Sean O'Casey

To Barrows Dunham

MS. DUNHAM

ST. MARYCHURCH, DEVON
12 NOVEMBER 1954

My dear Barrows:

It was fine to hear from you again, and to know that you still held the Sword of Light tight in your hand. It is, difficult, of course, for us here to follow the legal ramifications of all the curious repressive acts to thought about the clauses in your Constitution. They seem to be making barbed-wire entanglements of them. We should know more—for you are our Allies—but it is astonishing how little we know here about the way the U.S.A. sets out to govern herself. I myself have always believed that [Senator Joseph] McCarthy isn't the American Flag, tho' he seems to think he's the Flag's bright & particular star. I don't know much about America, but enough to know that McC., in the end, won't have any more prestige, even in Wisconsin, than a cold hot-dog. But to bring this about, many have suffered deeply, yourself included, & some more may have to suffer too: that is the hard part of it all. I pray God you may do well in any indictment that may be forced upon you. It is a big trial in every way, and hard on all the three Dunhams. Still the whisper from Jefferson, Whitman & all must be stealing still into many American ears. Those are not silenced, & these are not deaf.

I hope your plan for a trip to California goes well, & that nothing may stop it; you & Alice & Clarke among the orange groves; or are they only in the deep South? A letter from a friend told me of passing thro' them on a visit to Florida, orange trees in full fruit, in full blossom, & in faint leaf-bud at the one time.

My hand got bad thro a thorn-stab, & it seemed to go to throat & ear, so that I lost my voice, & had a bad seven weeks of it; tho' I imagine myself that throat & ear may have been caused not by the poor little thorn, but by doses of penicillin injected to make its stab harmless. Still, I'm singing once more, in spite of the penicillin.

Yip Harburg & his wife were here with us, & Eileen had many lunches & theaters with them when she went to London.

Now take care of yourself, & be as wise as the serpent while danger lasts.

My love to Alice, to Clarke, & to you.

Very sincerely,
Sean

To Carmen Capalbo [1]

TC. O'CASEY

[ST. MARYCHURCH, DEVON]
[15 NOVEMBER 1954]

Explanation of terms in PURPLE DUST

(1) Make Souhaun and Avril friends; it doesnt matter—they are two handsome women, one a little older than the other.

(2) Say, then, that Souhaun's age is 32 or 31—it doesnt matter.

(3) Pronounce the name of Souhaun "Soohaun."

(4) The reference to O'Killigan's skirmishing in Spain no longer arises, for it has been cut out, as you will see if you refer to the alterations already sent to you.

(5) Omadaun means, in Irish, a male fool, a stupid man—there is a distinct term "oinseach," for a fool of a woman.

Fergus

One of the great heroes of The Red Branch Knights of Ulster. It was he who gave his word to Naoise, Ainnle, and Ardan, the three sons of Usnach (in the story and play of "Deirdre") that they could safely return to Ireland when Naoise had fled away with the Girl to Scotland, in despite of her betrothal to Conor, King of Ulster, who, in spite of the word of Fergus, had the three young men slain on their return. Yeats and Synge wrote plays about this old, legendary story. So, I think, did AE, or George Russell, one time Editor of THE IRISH STATESMAN. Fergus was a mighty warrior, and rode in a thundering bronze chariot. He was the last King of Ulster. The headquarters of the Red Branch Knights was at Emain Macha, now called Armagh, archipiscopal Sees of the Roman Catholic and Protestant Primates of all Ireland.

Nuad of the Silver Hand

One could write a book about Nuad. He was a legendary King of Tara. No one could take on kingship of Tara who had any physical imperfection. Nuad had lost a hand in battle, but a great craftsman in precious metals is said to have made him a Silver Hand, so perfect that it grafted itself unto the wrist of flesh, so that the hand of silver functioned as neatly and as perfectly as any hand of flesh and blood could do. But Nuad is really a sun-god, and the silver hand is but an indication of the sun's brightness. He is said to have been the deity who led a great im-

---

[1] Carmen Capalbo, an American theatre director and producer who had taken an option to produce *Purple Dust* but later gave it up.

migration into Ireland, and to have been the progenitor of the Irish race, sons of Mile or Ebir. "O Nuadait atat sil Ebir uile—from Nuad comes all the seed of Ebir." Maynooth, the place where the great Roman Catholic Ecclesiastical College stands, is called after him—The Plain of Nuad.

Ormond the Duke

Why change the phrase from Avril to Souhaun? The whole thing's an elaborate joke, with Avril making herself ridiculous by trying to impress the men in claiming connection with Ireland's premier Duke in the age of the Tudors and Jacobeans. Leave it as it is. A "distant cousin" in Ireland is no connection at all.

Yes "Feis" means an organised festival. Feis Ceoil—Festival of music, held annually for competitions in music and singing. It is pronounced "Fesh" to rhyme with "flesh."

Spirit of the Grey of Macha

Spirit of Cuchullain's Grey, one of the Hero's two great chariot horses. Cucuchullan was the noblest and bravest of the Heroes of the Red Branch Knights; hero of the great saga—The Cattle Raid of Cooley.

A.R.P. This means "Air Raid Precautions". There were different Air-raid wardens for different jobs, each wearing a differently-colored steel helmet—black, white, brown.

"Score of fianna" and the Sword of Light." The Fianna were the armies of Ireland, half historical, half legendary. The Fianna were commanded by Finn McCool, and numbered among their warriors Oscar and Osheen so often mentioned by Yeats; who wrote a famous poem about Osheen's joruney to Tir na nOg—the Land of Youth; the Otherworld. Many stories are told of the Fianna's conquests the world over; and, of course, it is an historical fact that a great loosely-joined Keltic Nation ran from Ireland over to the coasts of the Black Sea. A great revival is taking place in the study of this people today, the living remains of which, speaking the Keltic tongue, are the Welsh, the Scots, the Irish, the Cornish people, the Bretons in France, and the manxmen of the Isle of Man. Mendes France is a Kelt; so was Lloyd George. The present Army of Ireland is called Fianna Fail, after the old one commanded by the great Finn McCool.

Sword of Light

The Hero's Sword, the lightning. When Nuad drew his sword, it was irresistible; none could escape from it. Sword of Mac Cecht gave out sparks that illumined the whole house. Fergus to cool a rage, smote off the tops of three hills in Meath with his lightning sword. An Otherworld Weapon which has survived in the name of the Sword of Light; a sword of a Hero, making him irresistible, with its light showing him the way onwards. Probably connected with the Flaming Sword that turned everyway, held by an angel keeping guard over the Tree of Life. Certainly with the Sword of King Arthur (of the Round Table), called Calibourne or Escalibur. The flash (badge) worn by the Headquarter Staff of General Eisenhower during the last World War was a Sword within a Shield—the Hero Sword and its symbol coming down to us from the times of historical mists and legends.

"Portion, *too, with them, who,* ruddy-faced," etc.

No, this cant be, and isnt to be, changed. The 2nd Workman is here linking the older warriors, Cuchullain, Conal Cearnach, Finn, Oscar, etc, with the most recent Irish warriors who went to scaffold, or were shot by the British in their mad desire to hold Ireland in perpetual subjection. He is one with the men who went to the gallows and one with the ancient warriors of the jewelled belts and the crimson cloaks.

It doesn't matter if a name or title here and there be unfamiliar—the spirit of the speech is obvious—a proud and defiant one. It will depend on the actor. I hope you may get a Director who has some affinity with Irish characteristics, sensible and foolish; one who, say, like Eddie Dowling, whom one would expect to respond generally to the way we Irish think and the way we Irish act—the warrior one minute, the fool the next. The Irishman, as Shaw said, so foolish in his cleverness, the Englishman so clever in his foolishness.

By the way, if you type a full copy of the play with the changes that I have sent to you, I should be greatly obliged if you could let me have a copy for inclusion to further published editions of the play.

Yours sincerely,
Sean O'Casey

To Cyril Cusack

MS. CUSACK

ST. MARYCHURCH, DEVON
17 NOVEMBER 1954

Dear Cyril,

Got your letter. Will reply more fully later. Don't quite get your "queries." I take it, the lines underlined are queried. Unexpectedly, the galley-proofs of the play are coming in (I didn't expect them for months), so I am correcting them. I've already changed "Mr. Reiligan would never ask you to do anything unseemly" etc, to "We're all laborers, Rankin. When you are working for Councillor Reiligan," etc.—quite orthodox Catholic Doctrine, by the way. "The coat's better without one" (a rose) to "you're too old Reiligan to go about with a rose in your coat." If you don't like, or feel unhappy, about "The B. Virgin is rose enough"; you can silence it, tho' I'll let it go in the printed version; because, Cyril, it's extraordinary what Irish Catholics say about their sacred beliefs in casual conversation—without really any irreverence whatever, tho' it often sounds highly comic. But then, are we going to deny a sense of humor to the Blessed Virgin?

What I want to say here is that Breon is trying his hand at a First-Act Set. He's sent me two, one of which I'd like, with a few structural alterations. I've sent it back to him to do this.

Maybe, you could, when you've time, get into touch with him & have a look at it. It is partly expressionistic, partly realistic; & I think would look fine. I laid out the rough sketch for him, & gave him a few hints of what I'd like. He is in London.

29 Abbey Gardens, St John's Wood, N.W.8.

Telephone: Maida Vale 8232.

All the best, & will write again. Good fortune to your job in the Film.

Sean

To Richard Courtney [1]

PC. *Act*

[ST. MARYCHURCH, DEVON]
19 NOVEMBER 1954

Dear Mr. Courtney,

Thanks. Oh, God, I'm not eager to have my hasty letters published! But go ahead if you think it worth printing. What is a high "I.Q."? And you are going to use (devote) any profits you make to "improve your quality." You can improve your quality by enlargement, or by using better paper; but the true quality can be improved only by thought, imagination, and courage; and not by profits.

These things, this Trinity, is what is needed in the English, and, at the moment, Irish drama. The English stage to-day is a disgrace to the English living and to the English dead. We need colour in the drama, too; the colours that to-day are the prerogative only of the Musical Show and the Ballet; a colourful banner over the Theatre instead of the Black Flag that flutters over it now. Even Eliot, even he, and all the others, are hanging on the lanyard of the Black Flag. Well, let's have a laugh or two beside the coffin.

In a hurry again,

All the best to all your students,
Sean O'Casey

P.S. You can print this, too, if you like.

[1] This letter was printed in *ACT*, January 1955. See O'Casey's letter to Courtney, 3 September 1954, note 1. Courtney had written to thank O'Casey for his interest, and asked if he could print the 3 September letter.

To G. A. Hayes-McCoy

TS. NATIONAL MUSEUM OF IRELAND

ST. MARYCHURCH, DEVON
19 NOVEMBER 1954

Dear Dr. Hayes-McCoy,

Here is the colored sketch of the PLOUGH AND THE STARS, the design from which the original Flag was made.[1] The Flag itself differed

[1] This sketch of the Irish Citizen Army flag is on display at the museum.

insofar as it was spread more evenly over the field, and the design of the Plough was more stylized; but in all essentials it was similar to the design appearing on the sketch. For instance, the shafts of the Plough were set more widely apart so as to occupy a greater space on the blue field; they were of a richer and warmer brown, picked out with a golden yellow. But it seems to be quite plain from this sketch that the Flag you have was not the original one; though History has made it just as precious.

The colour "Blue" was popular at the time, for we had such a wilderness of green around us for so long, that most of us welcomed a change. Indeed, the change from the idolatrous worship of green was first brought about by The Gaelic League. The colour of the Drumcondra Branch was for instance a deep yellow, with the name of the Branch embroidered in red, blue, and black on the field. It may interest you to know that before the Citizen Army, and indeed, after, by those who hadnt uniforms, the members wore an armlet of blue, the officers wearing one of red.

The sketch is a little crumpled after over thirty years, but quite plain to be seen. Keep it, by all means, but I should like to have a picture of it to remind me of old days, and the photograph of the "tall man" holding the furled flag—surely one of the brothers Espell? each of whom was about six foot two or more. One of them was with me the time I was in St. Vincent's Hospital, a fine figure before, now bending in two from an injured spine, and doomed to slowly die.

By the way, the original top of the staff was, as I mentioned before, a Red Hand strangling a Green Dragon; but this was a delicate structure, and easily broken, so the lone Red Hand was finally passed there.

I am very glad to have been of any help to you.

Yours Sincerely,
Sean O'Casey

To Micheál Ó hAodha [1]

TC. O'CASEY

[ST. MARYCHURCH, DEVON]
19 NOVEMBER 1954

My dear Mr. Ó hAodha,

Thank you very much for your recent letter suggesting an "O'Casey Festival" sometime next year.[2] The idea is a very kind and a very gen-

[1] Micheál Ó hAodha, Productions Director, Radio Eireann, Dublin.
[2] For the details on Radio Eireann's "O'Casey Festival," see O'Casey's letter to Philip Rooney, 29 April 1955, note 1, Vol. III.

erous one. It surprised me, but, frankly, I was very pleased to get the suggestion.

I have been thinking about it, and I am hesitant about agreeing for a few reasons, which I set down below.

1. Such an event would cause, I fear, a lot, at least some, envy among many writers and playwrights in Ireland, young ones and old ones; and I have experienced this envy so many times that I dont like to furnish myself with any more of it.

2. Younger ones would resent the time and opportunity given to me which would interfere with the broadcasting of their own work, which, naturally, they are anxious, at least eager, to put before the Irish People.

3. I dont wish in any way to get in the way of any younger writer who believes he has a gift that should be publicly acknowledged.

As for the recorded talks—that too is a question that I should have to think about before consenting. I might prove to be a bore. You see, my eyes make me look close to a paper when reading so that my voice is a little muffled by not being straight in front of the microphone. I should probably have to commit to memory almost all I wished to say; and, then, what in the name of God am I to talk about? Two years ago, I did a record of reading, talking, with a song, lasting an hour and a half, for Caedmon Publishers, New York City; and during the Christmas season last year, I did a 2nd one, longer, of readings from plays, biography, with a few songs slung in, for the same Company.[3] I didnt get much for the first, which is still selling, or for the second one, for they are anxious to get all they can from the first, before they send the 2nd on to the market. Five months ago, I got a request that they should get a company together, in which I was to act the part throughout of Capt—Boyle! I havent even answered this request yet; for I'm very busy, and havent time to think it over yet.

As for your "best fee being only £25 for each recording," do you think I'm a millionaire? £25 is still a fine sum to me. . . .[4]

[3] For the details on O'Casey's two recordings for Caedmon, see his letters to Barbara A. Cohen, 11 September 1952, note 2; and 24 November 1953, note 1.

[4] Page missing.

To Doris Leach [1]

MS. LEACH

ST. MARYCHURCH, DEVON

20 NOVEMBER 1954

Dear Doris,

Thanks & thanks for your kind letter. I have, indeed, been naughty, and have set a number of critics dancing, not so much with sorrow as with anger—here, in Ireland, and away in America. Oh, I can't help it. When I'm writing, I don't seem to be able to forehear the yells my words will provoke; and when I've written, what I've written, I have written. Oh, I can't help it. Especially about Orwell,[2] though they don't seem to realise that the worst things said about him in the book, come, not from me, but from his friends; nay, his lovers. It is, of course, a Literary Canon here that a critic should never be criticised; but, then, I've always been careless about things canonical.

Of course, send me the book, and I shall be very pleased to sign it.

Of course, they won't print my protests—when they are barbed. A critic in the Statesman & Nation, objecting to my review of my visit to Cambridge, said he was a graduate there at the time, and so could contest some of the things said.[3]

One of the then students, one who came to hear me talking, has written to say that an examination of Cambridge Register shows the critic to be lying, for it is shown (he says) that the Critic graduated from Cambridge years before I went down there.[4]

I'm so glad you found Windsor's "Juno" good. It isn't easy to play a number of characters in my plays. I wish I could write more quietly—good for my health and good for my purse. Everything I write seems to raise up wrath somewhere. You should see the Irish reviews.

We are settling down here fairly well. It is easier to run when our children are away in, as they are at the moment—Breon in London, Shivaun at school, coming home Sat. to Mon., & Niall an artillery gunner in Germany. The rent is double that of "Tingrith," but we save something in help, in fires, & in what we had to pay to keep a garden trim. But it all takes a toll of time. I like it very much, & the surroundings are charming, & we are but ten minutes slow walk from the cliffs. A lot of the houses look exactly like those Utrillo has put into so many pictures. The Parish Church is still largely a wreck—bombed in 1943, in which children, coming from a Service, suffered heavily in killed & injured.

1 Mrs. Doris Leach, 2 Chantry Road, Maidenhead, Berkshire.

2 "Rebel Orwell," *Sunset and Evening Star.*

3 See O'Casey's reply to T. C. Worsley, "Sean and Mr. Worsley," *New Statesman and Nation,* 6 November 1954.

4 See O'Casey's letter to Peter Newmark, 10 November 1954, note 1.

Well, there's a lot to do in a flat for two, or a house for two, if the residents are to live a decent life; so you & we have to keep going.

You're right about China; but England can easily keep her wheels going if those who govern be sensible. The world cant do without English skill and English science; they can give many a blessing, even to the USSR. It will be a fine world when we begin to bless each other with the things we do.

All good wishes to your husband, your mother, & to you.

As ever,
Sean

To Frank McCarthy

MS. MCCARTHY

ST. MARYCHURCH, DEVON
20 NOVEMBER 1954

My dear Frank,

Just you take care of yourself. You can't afford to be falling down exhausted: you're trying to do too much. Be careful of what you eat, for a helluva lot may come from the stomach. However, you do well to have an X ray examination. Don't hesitate to have one: an intelligent mind should have no fear of knowing what is wrong. To know is the only way of fighting a weakness. So go, and have it done. Thanks, a lot, for your kind letter in the paper. The trouble with most Christians is that they don't know what Christianity is, or even the doctrinal declaration of their own religion. What is religion? Ask them, & listen to what they say! Rosary beads, The Sacred Heart, the Bible. They know all about God! Truth is, we know little even about a mouse.

Austin Clarke is obsessed with what he calls "O'Casey's spectacular success," though O'Casey himself knows damn little about it, and, honestly, cares less. My one anxiety is to use whatever talent I may have to the full.

Tell me how the X ray went, &, however it may be, take more care of yourself. Your health is your one banker.

My love & warm wishes to you.

As ever,
Sean

To Peter Newmark

MS. NEWMARK

ST. MARYCHURCH, DEVON
21 NOVEMBER 1954

My dear Peter,

Thanks a hundred for your kind letter and the synopsis of your letter to the "New S. and Nation." Sorry, they didnt publish it; but I'm used to that by now. That is why there's so much yelling about things in "Sunset & Even. Star". Things which were hidden have been revealed, & the revelation isn't liked. I'm afraid you're right about the Literary cliques of the S. & N.; but, then, they are, or seem to be, on every paper, a group of Buz Fuzzers; tho' some are able & attractive writers—[V. S.] Pritchett, for instance. As you say, criticism is rare—criticism that has courage in it as well as punch and principle. It is very hard, though, to have courage; it's always risky; and men have to find bread. If Worsley wasn't at Cambridge when I spoke, then he's a liar, and a deliberate one, too. I can hardly believe that of him. As a matter of fact, the worst things said of Orwell were said by his friends—quoted by me in the book. His desire to rank with Joyce, & his effort to get my affirmation, were human traits at least. I imagine he was mad to be known, & got recognition thro' his "Animal Farm" [1945] and his "18–?" [*1984* (1949)] I never could understand why men should think man debased & mocked by changing them to animals. What's wrong with animals? We are animals. St. Francis called the ass his brother—and why not? And Keegan, in Shaw's play [*John Bull's Other Island*], called the pig—or Doyle said it—his brother—& why not? Animals are a sacred part of nature's or God's universe; and, anyway, man has no reason to crow very loudly over life, maybe, a little lowlier than himself.

I am not worrying about the threatened law actions. Slyly enough, the complaintants haven't whispered a word of it to me: they have written only to Macmillan's. They would be made very uncomfortable, if they brought their cases to court; for I can't see how they could keep me out of it then.

And don't you be too eager to get your opinions hugged by others. There are many good Communists who never read a line of Marx. A man who sets out to be a doctor, & becomes a good one, becomes a Communist; a man who sets out to be a teacher, & becomes a good one, becomes a Communist; doing good to his neighbours, & bringing the world onwards. "Whatsoever thy hand findeth to do, do it with all thy might"— good Communist doctrine, though it was said by St. Paul.

I have a lot to do with students myself. Leeds University students asked me to speak to them; but I wrote I couldn't. They're getting out a magazine on the Theatre, I think; & now, they want to print my letters. No; they didn't want me to come—they wanted an article, now that I think of it; & so, they have but two letters.

I hope you keep fit & well.

My sincere love to Monica & to you.

As ever,
Sean

To Oscar Lewenstein [1]

TS. Lewenstein

St. Marychurch, Devon
22 November 1954

Dear Oscar,

Thanks for your letter. I've been very busy looking over "The Bishop's Bonfire," sketching a rough design for Breon to do one for the Garden Scene, emending "Purple Dust," and correcting proofs of the first play for Macmillan's, so I hadnt time to reply to your letter.

Regarding the list of plays for the proposed assembly in the Embassy, first, PURPLE DUST will have to be set aside, for two weeks ago, I signed a contract for a New York production, and a possible option for a London production goes with it. If it be ever done here again, it should be done more simply; letting the play be dominant rather than any spectacular design. But, for the present, anyway, the play cant be thought of for production on account of the New York agreement.

So, as a substitute, I think we could have either "Juno" or "The Plough"—the Lindsay performance wouldnt have harmed, I think, any future production so far away as March or May of next year.

Or, instead, there might be a performance of three one-act plays as a bill—say "Time To Go," "Bedtime Story" and "Hall of Healing." For the one-acter to go with "Shadow of a Gunman," I suggest "End of Beginning"; but I think it would be better to have a talk with Cyril Cusack (that is, if he finally enters into the adventure) before deciding. I'd like to see "The Silver Tassie" done by Irish Players—in the London production—fine as it was—a number of the characters werent done well; the English actors were too timid of the language; and, of course, [Charles] Laughton was utterly miscast as "Harry Heegan."

---

[1] Oscar Lewenstein, theatre manager in London.

I'm glad you arent so progressive as to yell out denunciation at my "slam at Orwell." The boyo in the "N. Statesman and Nation," I'm told, was an ardent left-winger when he taught in the public school of Wellington. One who was a student when I spoke in Cambridge, and who came to hear me, got a friend to look over Cambridge Register, and found that Worsley graduated years before I went there—though he says in his review that he was a graduate there when I spoke. However, it doesnt matter much what Worsley says about me. He will go on burying himself under trivial plays till he's miles down, and other theatres are built and blooming on top of him.

Eileen's love and mine to Mrs Lewenstein and to you.

Sean O'Casey

To George Jean Nathan

MS. CORNELL

ST. MARYCHURCH, DEVON

22 NOVEMBER 1954

My very dear George:

Be God, that's good news! It may not be wise to marry, but I think it's sensible. You need someone soft and sensible beside you; and no one can be this but a woman. I'd be half lost without my Eileen (wholly lost, maybe). I think you have done well, and I'm sure you won't be sorry. I wish I knew Julie [Haydon], for I'm sure she will take care of you. To me a woman can be a curious quietening comfort. You stayed alone too long, as I have ventured to hint in some of my letters to you. Well, God be with Mr. & Mrs. Nathan.[1]

Thank you so much for saying you'd help Carmen Capalbo all you could with my "Purple Dust." I've amended it a good deal, cutting out two episodes that were dull & pointless; & though it isn't yet what it could be, I think it is better than it was.

I was sorry to read in "The Irish Times" that Macken's play "Home is the Hero" has ended its run.[2] He is a clever man, and Ireland needs a good playwright. He had a record run in the Abbey, but, then, New York isn't Dublin. I imagine Macken should give all his time to one or the other thing—acting or writing—He has written some lusty novels as well.

[1] See O'Casey's letter to Peter Newmark, 1 November 1954, note 1.
[2] Vivian Mercier, "From Galway to Broadway," *Irish Times,* 2 November 1954, an article on the failure of Walter Macken's *Home Is the Hero* in New York. See O'Casey's letter to Cyril Cusack, 11 December 1954, for a number of quotations from Mercier's article.

Between ourselves, there's a good chance of "The Bishop's Bonfire" going on in Dublin—not in the Abbey, unfortunately, but in the Gaiety Theatre, sponsored by a young actor named Cyril Cusack. There's never a chance of Cockadoodle Dandy being done in Ireland—bar by some little group who think themselves into running all they lay hands on; but "The B.'s Bonfire" can fare more safely, & so gives me a chance of getting before Dublin again. I hope you have the book [*Sunset and Evening Star*] by now. I sent it by ordinary post—which takes time now—for air mail for a book is a bit costly. Ireland has already sent out blasts against the book, but that was to be expected.

Take care of Julie—I hope I may call Mrs. Nathan Julie—and give my love to her.

My love to you, dear lad, as ever.

Sean

To Daniel Macmillan

MS. MACMILLAN LONDON

ST. MARYCHURCH, DEVON
26 NOVEMBER 1954

Dear Mr. Daniel,
I wonder would you send a copy of "Sunset & Evening Star" to

Barrows Dunham,
127 Bentley Avenue,
Cynwyd, Pennsylvania.

I enclose a letter I got from him recently. He was a Professor of Philosophy In Penn. University, but lost his job for the reasons he mentions in his letter. Now he is threatened with a jail-sentence if the renewed inquiry goes against him. Why it should, only [Senator Joseph] McCarthy knows, for God is puzzled about it all.

Barrows Dunham is simply an Emersonian in politics, or rather political opinion, for he has never had any connection with politics, other than any citizen there or here—thinking of, & then deciding, whom to vote for in an election. From my political view-point, he's away on the nadir of politics; but he is an honest and most upright man, with a fine intelligence, & a good sense of humour: a very worthy American, if I'm not mistaken.

I shall be grateful if you send him a book. He hasn't many dollars now, I fear, with which to buy one. Please charge it to my account.

Yours very sincerely,
Sean O'Casey

To Barbara A. Cohen

MS. COHEN

ST. MARYCHURCH, DEVON

28 NOVEMBER 1954

Dear Barbara,

I hope you & your Comrade are still going strong, for it's long since I heard from you, & long since you heard from me. I have been very busy in various ways, fighting age, writing a new play, and settling down in our new home, even helping our girl, Shivaun, with her essays.

I haven't had the energy to write to Gordon Rogoff, whose last letter was full of a fairy vision of coming over here and selling millions of records. Possible, of course, but a hard task. What you ask of me—to act the part of "Boyle" in "Juno" for a record—would be beyond me now. Radio Eireann has asked me to make 3 or 4 quarter of an hour talks on a record for a prologue of plays they think of doing. I haven't replied yet. I may try to do two; but I hesitate to do even this much.

I don't honour the idea of letting my voice loose to travel wherever others may wish it to be heard.

I hope you are doing well, and Gordon, too; tho' I daresay he is somewhere else now.

My love,
Sean O'Casey

To Miss Sheila ———

MS. PRIVATE

ST. MARYCHURCH, DEVON

3 DECEMBER 1954

My dear Sheila,

I have been very busy for weeks and am very busy now. I am correcting the proofs of a new play; sketching the design for the two scenes in it for Breon to do finally, & put grace and polish on them; answering a horde of letters, as well as a multitude of other minor things. I've parcelled up & autographed 22 books, till I'm tired of my own name; & have four letters here still asking me for the same favour. So you see—

Never mind what they say of me. At any rate, you can tell them all neither I nor Eileen married for money; for neither of us had much more than what we stood up in. And we haven't a lot today; for we are not of them who see God's face on a coin, or see any message from Him on a pound note. We earn what we get—me by my writing; Eileen by her work for home and children. You can tell them who talk of me that O'Casey said they can go to hell.

Now, you take things more quietly; keep calm, & try to occupy yourself with some hobby. Your quotation wasn't quite right: It was "Frailty, thy name is woman," & it was Hamlet who said it.

Well, I'm sure a trip to Wiltshire will do you good, if the weather be any better than it is. I hope you may see the sun shine there.

> *With all good wishes,*
> *Yours affectionately,*
> *as ever,*
> *Sean*

To Miss J. Sala [1]

TC. O'CASEY

ST. MARYCHURCH, DEVON
4 DECEMBER 1954

Dear Miss Sala,

Thank you for your quotation-letter which reached me this morning though the date at the top of your note is the 18 of November.

If you have any fondness for G. K. C[hesterton]., I should be the last to try to win you away from it. You havent read my book probably, for there you would see that a reply was sent to a criticism appearing in a well-known journal of another book of mine, but the comments made by me were never published; and another to another Journal; and a third to another journal, but none was published. Supposing I had sent a few comments on Ivor Brown's review [2] what do you think would have happened to it? Would it have been published? No, Miss; no. So, in all instances, I have to bide my time to answer these fellows who are so wise,

---

[1] Miss J. Sala, 6 Pidgeon Close, Blandford St. Mary, Dorset.
[2] Ivor Brown, "End of Series," *The Observer,* 14 November 1954, a review of *Sunset and Evening Star.*

so fair, so jaunty, but who shy off from allowing an answer to what they say. Just as Chesterton usually did with Dr. [G. G.] Coulton. Print an attack on him in a R.C. journal, but when Dr. Coulton replied, he was told that the journal didnt open its pages to controversial subjects, thus allowing its jubilant readers to believe that Dr. Coulton had no answer to make to G. K. C. the Great.

It is odd that while you implicitly challenge what I say, you never make any effort to challenge Brown. Did you not ask yourself Is Brown right? Or do you take all he says without an hesitating thought? Was G. K. C. such a fine poet as Brown implies? If I put this G. K. C. beside other poets, then, I must say he wasnt much of a one to blow about. I dont think "Chuck it, Smith" a poem at all. There are many far better appearing week by week in the New Statesman and Nation by Sagittarius. But Brown damns himself by this laus deo salutation for the gift of G. K. C. by never mentioning one word of a genuine poet; a poet stars above the mouthing Chesterton; a fellow-countryman of Brown's; and a poet to whom I dedicated the book that Brown was reviewing.[3] In my opinion, G. K. C. was as good as a poet as he was great as a theologian. I wonder who were the atheists who sat in the English Cabinet? I've never remembered any English Cabinet Minister declaring that he was an Atheist. Have you? If you have, I should be glad to hear what he said about the existence or non-existence of a God.

As for Shaw—well, Shaw was an inordinately kind man.

But these things dont interest you, maybe; so for fear of boring you, I'll say goodbye.

Yours sincerely,
Sean O'Casey

[3] *Sunset and Evening Star* was dedicated "To my dear friend Hugh MacDiarmid, Alba's Poet and one of Alba's first men."

To Mr. B——

TC. O'CASEY

ST. MARYCHURCH, DEVON
6 DECEMBER 1954

Dear Mr. B——

I couldnt arrange to see you, for a long time to come. I am very busy with many things, and have many to see.

Your story isnt an unusual one.[1] There have been many instances of the clergy benefiting in the way you mention. Old and young when the time comes to go get anxious about their souls, and, if they have any worldly wealth, engage to give it for a quota of treasure in heaven. Well, the clerics know it, and I daresay, cant be blamed for taking advantage of the fear in man's mind of invisible and unknown things.

As for Lawyers, if you intend to contest the Will, then you will have to employ them. But I cant agree with you that lawyers are in any way generally untrustworthy. All the men of the law whom I have known were not only as honest as lawyers should be, but excellent fellows as well. The law is an intricate thing; but let us not forget that it isnt the lawyers who make the laws, but we ourselves; or, at least, if we want to, then we can make the laws which govern our lives. Parliament makes the laws; the lawyers interpret them; and a hard job it often is to do so.

The best thing, in my opinion, that you can do is to try to come to an arrangement with the ecclesiastical beneficiaries by which you may receive part of the estate willed to them by Mrs. B———. If you dont do that, the clerics will fight you to the bitter end; and probably win, for it is hard to upset a witnessed Will.

Yours sincerely,
Sean O'Casey

[1] Mr. B———'s "story" was about his late mother, a woman from the Dublin tenements of "the O'Casey country" who had married a wealthy Ulsterman; and when she died at the age of eighty-six she ignored her children and left all her money to the Catholic Church, on the advice of her Catholic lawyer. Mr. B———, one of her sons, was trying unsuccessfully to contest the will, and he mentioned that the lawyer had in a number of similar cases directed other people to leave their money to the Church.

To Cyril Cusack

MS. Cusack

St. Marychurch, Devon
11 December 1954

Dear Cyril,

Thanks for your letter. You didn't mention the children, so I suppose (and hope) everything is allright with them—especially the little one who was down with Scarlet Fever. We must try to keep our children well, play & film, or no film or play. So I hope they're allright again. No hurry for the music-score back. I've been correcting the galley-proofs of the

THE LETTERS OF SEAN O'CASEY

play—it is to be announced in Macmillan's Spring Catalogue—, & have made a number of additions & some changes, tho' which of them may be, or may not be, in your script, I don't know. Perhaps, some time, before you type parts, I could have your script back, & then I could let you have mine which is the full & final copy—I hope; or, maybe, the page-proofs, tho' I don't think they will come in time.

As for Siobhan [McKenna], I think we shall have to do without her. Naturally, she'll be eager to renew as often as possible the success she won in the Arts Theatre [1] (I do hope she won't let it go to her head). It would be hardly fair to ask her now to do "Foorawn." St. Joan will be playing music in her mind for a long time to come—as "Juno" did in Sally [Allgood]'s mind. It is a sad indictment of Irish acting, that, with all the theatrical activities—The Abbey, the Gate, Longford's, etc, we find it so hard to get an actress to play Foorawn. Is there no-one in the B.B.C. groups you could think of? There was a girl, Maureen Pook, I think, who played in "Red Roses"; & another Norreys Duff, I think, tho' without experience, who did a charming "Finnoola." I think her mother owns Bushell's Hotel in Dawson, or Nassau, St. What about the later comers— Dórin Ni Maidin, Brid Ní Loinsigh, et al? Or Brian O'Higgins as "The Canon"? Is he any good?

I agree with Bill [2] & you about the Embassy—there's no comparison between this theatre & the Court; but "Airs on a Shoestring" (an intimate Revue) [3] has been on for 2 or 3 years, & looks as if it would go on for ever.

I'm not so sure about W[alter]. Macken for "Boheroe." An article in the *Irish Times* of November, the 2nd, tells us a lot about him & the play. It's written by Vivian Mercier, whom you may know, or have heard of. He takes an opposite view from you. "Mr. Macken should take heart, allot himself a minor part in his next play, concentrate his undeniable talents on writing, rather than acting, & turn his present defeat into a future victory." Again—"Mr. M. seems obsessed with strength in his plays & novels; it is also the one quality that his acting strives for at the expense of everything else, including, ultimately, strength itself." This would never do for Boheroe; there is none of the bully or shouter in Boheroe; tho' there is enthusiasm & fun in him, as in the scene between him, Dan, and Keelin. Again Mercier says—"The lines were all right; it was Mr. M's handling of them that were nearly all wrong." I fear, too, Mr. Macken will hold a grudge for me. Mercier says "He may yet prove a worthy successor to Sean O'C. with whom the N. York critics are prone to compare him to his disadvantage." I wish the critics wouldn't do this, for it doesn't add to my

---

[1] Siobhan McKenna played the title role in a revival of Bernard Shaw's *Saint Joan,* which opened in London at the Arts Theatre on 29 September 1954.

[2] William P. Ryan, Cusack's business manager.

[3] Laurier Lister's *Airs on a Shoestring* opened in London at the Royal Court Theatre on 22 April 1953.

friends. I do hope, he wont take the failure too much to heart. Carroll (P. V.) did, & it does no one any good. We all have to suffer defeat— maybe many times.

By the way, if you still think of Macken as Boheroe (What of the Canon? Might he not be better here; or would he indulge in that besetting sin of "strength" again in this part?) by all means get him, if you can— you know more about Casting than I do. But Boheroe power is a gentle power; none the less strong for that.

As for Program-Pamphlet, go ahead with it, if you like, tho' won't it greatly increase cost of programme; tho' I'd rather it did without me, for what I've said, I've said in the play. But it would be fine & interesting to read what you, Father Nolan, S.J. (I thought your Stage Guild was a Franciscan), and Dom Tom McCarron had in their minds about the play.[4] God and Joyce! Not a bad choice, for Joyce surely is the one who has heard God Almighty whispering to Himself about Ireland and Dublin.

I am sending under another cover to you, here in Chelsea, a design Breon did for 1st Scene of B.'s Bonfire. He likes it best, but I thought it, maybe, a bit too colorful. Your mention of combined fantasy & realism, however, put me into the mind of sending it to you. Breon thinks it much better than the others. The house, you'll see, is at the wrong angle, facing forwards, instead of sideways—to allow the Codger scope for destroying the Bishop's carpet.

I've just been thinking if it would be quite fair to ask Dom McCarron or Father Nolan to write in a programme about a play of mine? Could they do it without permission?

I've changed the incident of the hiding of the bottle, & made it, I think (and hope), much funnier.

Don't bother to brood over any of this if you and Maureen are still anxious about the little ones. I do hope they are well, or almost well, again.

My love to Maureen & to you.

Sean

---

[4] Cusack had intended to print some favorable comments by these two priests about O'Casey in the theatre program for *The Bishop's Bonfire*, but the idea was later abandoned. For details on the production, which opened in Dublin at the Gaiety Theatre on 28 February 1955, see O'Casey's letter to Cusack, 5 March 1955, Vol. III.

To J. D. Alexander [1]

TC. O'CASEY

[ST. MARYCHURCH, DEVON]
14 DECEMBER 1954

Dear Mr. Alexander,

No, my friend, I wont be either good enough or bad enough to address the Students on the subject of Ireland and England.

You say the talk would commence at 10 A.M., but you dont say when it is to end. Your kind invitation to lunch possibly just an adjournment, for a talk of Ireland's past, present, and future relationship with England would see the sun sink on the century. And which Ireland is meant? There are a hundred Irelands: the Ireland of the North and the Ireland of the South; the Ireland of the Seige of Limerick and the Ireland of the Siege of Derry; the Ireland of the Battle of the Yellow Ford and the Ireland of the Battle of Boyne; there is the Ireland of the church chant and the bawdy song; the Ireland of Katheleen ni Houlihan and the Ireland of Mick McGilligan's Daughter, Maryanne—to name a few. So you see, what a time it would take to speak about Ireland alone, much more to bring England into our Island Story. If I may advise, Oxford had better leave Ireland here and England there till George and Patrick are forgotten, and a newer generation lives.

I'd really love to go to Oxford to chat with the students, but I find 75 years leaves me too old and tired to go anywhere except to bed.

I wish your gatherings every success, and I'm sure you'll easily get someone better than I to speak unto the young men and women, and tell them to go forward.

Yours sincerely,
Sean O'Casey

[1] J. D. Alexander, Oxford International Committee, Christ Church, Oxford.

To Cyril Cusack

MS. CUSACK

ST. MARYCHURCH, DEVON
14 DECEMBER 1954

Dear Cyril,

This is the first design Breon did for the 2nd Scene in the "B.'s Bonfire," which he has sent to me. I like it well; better than the other one.

I don't think the doors as they are in it would hamper the action. Anyway, I thought it better you should have a look at it. The Clouds & the tree are blotted out in the Scene he sent to you, which I think is a pity. Anyhow, you can make a choice of one or none.

Sean

I've sent on the design to Thorncastle St. so as not to bother you in your lodgings.

To Micheál Ó hAodha

TC. O'CASEY

[ST. MARYCHURCH, DEVON]
14 DECEMBER 1954

Dear friend,

Thanks very much for your letter. I have been so busy that I couldnt reply to you sooner. So Seumas [O hAodha] of "The Watchword of Labor" is dead. I remember the first time he sang the song, in full evening dress, before a proletarian audience. A clever lad who didn't really know how to use the cleverness; or, maybe, never had a real chance to develop it. Like [Patrick] Heeney of the air for "The Soldier's Song"—a poor tune, but the lad had the makings of a composer in him, if he had got a chance. Hard work, poverty, and tuberculosis, killed him too soon.

For the talks [1]—I suggest that I do one as a test, for I amnt enamoured of my ability to talk to a tape, to a crowd; tho' I've done this well twice or three times here; and many times in my own townland of Dublin. Now, I feel at home only at home; a fine actor in front of a fire, but a mute on a stage. There is a Recorder, one
Donald W. Aldous; Sound Recording Consultant, F.R.S.A.
    M. Inst. E. M.B.K.S. Treforis, Bronshill Road,
        Torquay, Devon. Tel: Torquay: 88360.,
Who did recording of me for Gjon Mili, of New York. What about him doing the test? I know him well, and he knows me, so we would be at home together. If you should think well of this, then Radio Eireann would have to pay him. He is very reasonable, and wont put you into the poorhouse. I'd do it myself but I amnt safe enough financially to do it.

---

[1] O'Casey made a series of talks for the Radio Eireann "O'Casey Festival," as introductions to his plays. See his letter to Philip Rooney, 29 April 1955, note 1, Vol. III.

If you dont agree, let me know, at your convenience, whom you would send; and then I'll think it over again. The snag is, I dont know what to talk about it; so I'd have to choose a theme that wouldnt be a theme at all, but might be larded with a song or two; or any other fancy that would come into my mind. I certainly couldnt talk about my plays—not more, anyway, than a word or two.

All good wishes, my love to Frank McM[anus].
Yours sincerely,
Sean O'Casey

To Seumas Scully

MS. SCULLY

ST. MARYCHURCH, DEVON
22 DECEMBER 1954

My dear Seumas,

Thank you for your card and kind wishes. I have been very busy and a little confused trying to get papers and books into order, as well as correcting proofs & writing a play.

I haven't had papers from you for a long time; but don't bother, for I haven't time to read half of what I have.

I hope you may have had a fair Christmas—I daresay this won't reach you till it is all over; & that part of the fairness may be that you are at work again.

That is the most important point, for it is hard especially to get a new job as a Clerk; harder than that of laborer or tradesman.

We expect Niall to come tomorrow—he is in Germany—on leave, but fear he may be delayed by the gales. Heavy winds are out here as I write this.

What a lot is being said about "Partition" these days; & now a number of young men may be in prison for years. No sooner some come out than others go in.

All well here, save that I grow older. Marychurch is rather charming, though the winds are often fierce—we are but a few minutes walk from the sea; & can see it, between two hilly cliffs, from our doorway which is pretty high up.

I do hope you are settled in a job again. Breon, Eileen & Shivaun send their love; so do I.

Yours as ever,
Sean

To Joan McAlevey [1]

MS. MCALEVEY
ST. MARYCHURCH, DEVON
24 DECEMBER 1954

Dear Joan,

Enclosed is a synopsis of what the last play [*The Bishop's Bonfire*] is about, and you must make the most of it; for it is not easy for me to write and explain my work. So you see, it is hard for your Professor to tell you about it, since the playwright himself knows little more. The play will be listed in Macmillan's catalog for Spring, so it will hardly appear in bookform before the summer. I have been busy correcting the galley-proofs; page-proofs have to come yet; & many more things have to be done before the play does its dance in public. However, it may be done—performed—in Dublin in February or March; &, afterwards, will probably come to London. And don't be too anxious to set the Faculty on its Academic Ear. After all, they have studied hard and long, and know a good deal, even tho' they be mistaken at times, as, God knows, we all are.

I can't retire, even if I would, for a family has to be kept, and I am one of the family, so have to keep myself, too. I have no reserve (never had) on which to sit down—not even a simple 15/– savings certificate; so I have to go on, like it or no; and, all things considered, it is just as well. To be idle in action or thought is to be dead without dignity. I was never busier, & hope to be so when my eyes begin to close & my last few breaths mingle with the breath of the world's peoples.

It is still, then, au revoir and not goodbye. As I write this, the family is gathered together, and we but wait for our younger boy, Niall, a Lance-bombadier in the Artillery who comes home on leave from Germany, & will be with us in a few hours.

My greetings to you, Joan, and my love.

Yours very sincerely,
Sean O'Casey

[1] Joan McAlevey, 241a Windsor Place, Brooklyn 15, New York.

To Frank Hugh O'Donnell

MS. O'DONNELL

ST. MARYCHURCH, DEVON

28 DECEMBER 1954

My dear Frank,

Thank you for your kind Christmas Card, and for the generous promise that should we come to Ireland, there would be a lighted candle in
your window for us.

I didn't see the "flattery" in "The Times"; but which Times? Irish
Times, Times Pictorial, London Times, or New York Times?

I'm sorry you could do nothing for Seumas Scully. One would think
it would be easy for a man like Seumas to find a job. Maybe he has. If he
hasn't, do keep an eye open for him. He is an active, kind, and excellent
lad.

I couldn't go over for the Abbey Theatre jubilee festival.[1] I hope
it went off well, tho' it's a bad sign that no play of the 47 submitted was
worth a prize—£250's glitters a lot. Nothing like that knocking about
when you & I stood under the Abbey Awning.

I hope your young ones are well, & growing up "in grace & wisdom";
and Mrs. O'Donnell, & the fella called Frank.

All the best to you all.

As ever,
Sean

[1] The fiftieth anniversary of the founding of the Abbey Theatre, which had
opened on 27 December 1904 with a double bill of Yeats's *On Baile's Strand* and
Lady Gregory's *Spreading the News,* was celebrated with a revival of the same two
plays on 27 December 1954.

To G. W. Head

MS. HEAD

ST. MARYCHURCH, DEVON

31 DECEMBER 1954

Dear Mr. Head,

Could you send the enclosed to our friend, Robert M.? I haven't
his address. Thank you for sending me the book.[1] Never you mind our

[1] See O'Casey's letter to Head, 12 August 1954.

Irish publishers—we have a fine way of not doing things in Ireland. To one magazine, I sent my new address three times, but it still goes to the old one.

I am engaged at the moment with anticipating a law action by a young Irish poet, who alleges I committed an infringement of his copyright by publishing some scathing remarks of his about me as an Irish writer & as a Socialist.[2] If there be any infringement, it can but be an insignificant technical one; but the time lost, & energy wasted will be just as great as if it were a terrible example of infringement, To me, the fact is, the young poet couldn't, or wouldn't, stand up publicly to his written words; & saves face by calling me all sorts of names, "Unctuous timidity" again.

All good wishes for the New Year.

As I was, & am,
Sean O'Casey

2 The libel action by Patrick Galvin was dropped when Macmillan offered him an apology, which O'Casey refused to do. See O'Casey's letters to Francis MacManus, 1 June 1954, note 8; and to David Marcus, 28 July 1954, note 1.

To Robert Monteith [1]

MS. HEAD

ST. MARYCHURCH, DEVON
31 DECEMBER 1954

Dear Bob:

Thank you for your Book, and for the kind words written within it. It is a fine book, so simply and so vividly written. It is a curious tale of victorious defeat. I had to read it very very slowly, for every paragraph sent old visions into my mind, and I found myself living my life and Ireland's over again & again. All that was said & done then was not only a challenge to the British Empire, but to the Gods; and the gods didn't seem to like it; for they ranged themselves against everything done, everything said. Tho' maybe, it was we Irish whom the gods helped, for they acted & prepared as if everything depended on the gods. It must have been heartbreaking to you to realise how little they know, or wanted to know about the hard facts of battling. They surged on as if a romantic impulse was impervious to British ball & British bayonet. Your description of arrange-

1 Robert Monteith (1878–1956), a Captain in the First Battalion, Dublin Regiment, Irish Republican Army, accompanied Sir Roger Casement on the ill-fated landing in Ireland in 1916. Monteith wrote about his experiences in *Casement's Last Adventure* (1932; revised and rewritten, 1953).

ments in Tralee to conquer an army [is] astonishing even to me who knew
so much of our ignorant innocence, led by Bulmer Hobson who thought
the fight would ever be a battle of phrases; and Pearse—one of the noblest
of Irishmen with a Gaelic song. They never realised, any of the Volunteer
Leaders, that a brave man wasn't necessarily a soldier; indeed, bravery
alone was often a nuisance. I knew many who hadn't the slightest idea of
the way to take cover—scorned the idea in fact. But you met all this yourself as you describe so simply and effectively about the Lads of Tralee &
the nearby villages. There was too much of an Irish heaven in the preparation & too little of the Irish earth. I'm very glad you wrote this book—it
clears up more than one dark page in the account of events before, during,
& after 1916. It is part of Ireland's History. What a time you had! Your
account of your experiences on the run are very sad, but stimulating, for
they show what hardships a life can stand up to, for the sake of an ideal,
without hope of, or, indeed, any desire for, any reward, except that of a
good conscience.

You have nobly vindicated Casement.[2] Many regarded him as a spy.
I knew a priest, Father Breen (afterwards Canon, & P.P. of Arklow) of
St. Laurence O'Toole's Dublin, who persisted in regarding him as one,
till the British rope was around the indomitable man's neck.

I hope your fine book may have a wide reading wherever Irishmen
and Irishwomen are, at home, or away in teeming city or lonely wild.

God be good to you and yours.

Yours very sincerely,
Sean (O'Casey)

[2] Sir Roger Casement (1864–1916), Irish nationalist, had served with distinction in the British Colonial service in Africa, and had written significant reports on
the inhuman treatment of native laborers. He was knighted in 1911, retired in 1912,
and a year later joined the Irish Volunteers. Arrested by the British in 1916 after
landing on the west coast of Ireland from a German submarine that accompanied a
ship loaded with guns for the Easter Rising, he was tried, found guilty of high treason, and sentenced to be hanged. British authorities circulated "black diaries" alleged to be in his handwriting, in which homosexual practices were recorded, a maneuver that was intended to present him to the public as a tarnished traitor rather
than an Irish martyr. He was executed on 3 August 1916.

To Sean O'Rourke

MS. O'ROURKE

ST. MARYCHURCH, DEVON

31 DECEMBER 1954

My dear Sean,

I am very sorry to hear that my friend, Seumas O'Moore, has left the world and Dublin forever. Yes, indeed, when we lived in London he came to see us whenever he happened to come there on business; and when I was last in Dublin, I went from his office in Findlater's Place (I think) to his home in Fairview to chat together with his wife and children, till some of the O'Toole lads came to go over old times till it was past time for sleep. Death has caused a few vacancies among the old Larriers. 'Liam Hampson, S. Redmond—long, long ago; K. O'Loughlin, Tommy Lynch, Sean Fitzharris and, now, the bould Seumas is gone too. And all who are left are old. You didn't mention Macki Kirwan, Mick Lawless, him who carried the banner, Fay, was it? Him who beat the big drum, Paddy . . . . . ? who worked in T.C. Martin's, & had lost one or two fingers from a hand; Sean Fay, a side-drummer; and, of course, Mick Colgan, now, I believe, a Senator (or was), and a great warrior against us, poor Communists. Many more of the football club—Carey, Stephen Synnott & his brothers. Mat Carroll—only an occasional visitor to the old place on the Strand, or the Foresters Hall, in Oriel Street. And the kind household of the O'Cahills—the Old Lady, Josie, Kathleen, Mollser, Martha, Jack, Tom, & Mick, & Mrs. Pollard. How I remember chatting to the Old Lady about articles in the Catholic Bulletin, & Father Burke's Sermons! A great old woman. And the brothers Rooney. And Frank's sweetheart away in the wilds of Meath:

Brief chronicles of the time. We come, take a look or two around; and then we go.

> For in and out, above, about, below,
> 'Tis nothing but a Magic Shadow-show,
> Play'd in a box whose Candle is the Sun,
> Round which we Phantom Figures come and go.[1]

A lovely Magic Shadow-show all the same while it lasts.

I daresay Seumas's children are fully grown now, & able to take care of themselves; but it must be a big blow to Mrs. Moore.[2] Give her my sympathy.

[1] Edward Fitzgerald's translation of the *Rubaiyat of Omar Khayyam* (1st edition, 1859), stanza XLVI.

[2] Mrs. Mary Moore, one of O'Casey's neighbors at 422 North Circular Road, Dublin, who provided some of the background for the plot of *Juno and the Paycock*. See O'Casey's letter to Jim Kavanagh, ? April 1926, note 2, Vol. I, p. 188.

Give my love to Lar, Paddy & Sean McDonnell, Fred Lynch, & Frank.

My love to you, too.
As ever,
Sean

We left "Tingrith" 8 months ago after 17 years there. Landlord said he needed the place for his mother & her daughter. He didn't, but wanted to sell it; so we had to go. It's allright here; less room, but more picturesque with the cliffs & sea but a few minutes walk away.

A good New Year to you all.

INDEX OF LETTERS AND
DOCUMENTS BY O'CASEY

INDEX OF LETTERS AND
CRITIQUES ABOUT OR
TO O'CASEY

INDEX OF REPORTS AND
REVIEWS ABOUT OR
BY O'CASEY

GENERAL INDEX

Note: Footnote page entries in bold-
face indicate references with bio-
graphical or background information.

Abarbanel, Bernard, "Variations on J
for Bray," 214, 214n
Abbey Theatre, 20n, 21n, 27, 27n, 81,
134, 152, 156, 167, 168, 170, 172,
181-82, 190, 191, 194, 285, 286,
302, 333, 358n, 367, 390, 405, 412,
450, 452, 468, 514, 548, 552, 564,
618, 621, 669, 685, 747, 773, **812,**
813, 819, 833, 845, 864, 913, 936,
958, 1078-79, 1088, 1122, 1128,
1134, 1134n; *The Plough and the
Stars,* 10, **10n,** 11, 15, 291, 291n,
305, 480, 501, **501n,** 510, 785, 812;
The Passing, 32, 32n; *The Silver
Tassie,* 33, 286n, 445, 446, 468,
468n, 562, 562n, 645, 681, 822,
822n, 838; *The Frost in the Flower,*
33, 33n, 149, 149n; *The Harvest
Festival,* 33, 33n, 43, 43n, 149,
149n; *Juno and the Paycock,* 86,
86n, 776, 776n; *Talbot's Box,* 98n;
The Shadow of a Gunman, 353,
353n, 721, 721n, 972, 972n; *The
Righteous Are Bold,* 414, 414n,
514; *Rossa,* 597n; *Katie Roche,*
636n; *Design for a Headstone,* 706,
722; *Tristan agus Iseult,* 721; *Goldfish in the Sun,* 747; *The House
Under the Green Shadows,* 776,
776n. *See also* Gorman, Eric
Abyssinia, 265
Acheson, Dean, 719

Achilles, 90
Ackland, Richard, 484, **484n**
Act of Union (1800), 300
Acton, Lord (John Emerich Edward
Dalberg-Acton), 432, 542, 697,
809, 810, 863, 876
Adamic, Louis, 911, **911n**
Adler, Larry, 723, **723n**
AE. *See* Russell, George W.
Afinogenov, Alexander, *Distant Point,*
220, 220n
Agate, James, 4, 45-46, 48-49, **48n,**
49n, 50, 51, 53-54, 53n, 59, 117,
301, 306n, 310, 351, 351n, 352,
353, 355, 355n, 392, 418n, 445,
445n, 463n, 477, 502, 600, 617,
618, 895
Aiken, Frank, 313n, 847n
Aiseirghe, 129, 711
Alamein, 308
Albery, Bronson, 191, 192, 193, 193n,
195, 203, 213, 215, 216, 218, 220,
225, 261, 284, 284n, 289, 290, 291,
302-303, 323n, 324, 335, 350n, 355,
356, 360-61, 366, 372-73, 372n,
374, 375, 400-401, 411, 417-18,
421-22, 425, 440, 452-53, 458-59,
462n, 507, 620, 916
Albery, Una Gwynn, 284n, 323n,
335n, 348n, 350, 351, 355, 356,
404, 411, 620
Aldrich, 374

Cosgrave, William, 31, 156, **156n**, 300, 326n, 660
Costello, John A., 503n, 515, 699, 787n
Costello, Ward, 562, 562n
Costigan, Giovanni, 687
Coulton, George Gordon, 540, 651, 738, 876, 1126; *The Scandal of Cardinal Gasquet,* 431n, 445, 445n, 649; *Five Centuries of Religion,* 454, 454n, 593, 719, 757, 891; *The Medieval Village,* 593; *Two Saints: St. Bernard and St. Francis,* 593; *The Death Penalty for Heresy from 1184 to 1921 A. D.,* 806
Council for the Encouragement of Music and Arts (C. E. M. E.), 116, 154, 156, 156n, 184, 213, 221, 263
Counter Point, 184, 189, 212-13, 469
Courtaulds, 73
Courtney, Richard, 1086, 1086n, 1115
Coventry, 248
Coverdale, Miles, 84
Coward, Noel, 195, 345, 369, 504, 569, 600, 633, 654; *Blithe Spirit,* 18, 18n; *Cavalcade,* 120, 817; *Point Valaine,* 477, 477n; *In Which We Serve,* 504
Cowdell, Harry, 183, 516-17, 625, 874, 875, 1007, 1044, 1048, 1071
Cowles Jr., Gardiner, 129, 129n
Craig, Humbert, 171
Cranko, John, 965n
Crawford, Cheryl, 485
Crecy, Battle of, 523
Crichton, Mamie, "Show Talk," 968n
Cripps, Sir Stafford, 74, **74n**, 77
Critics Circle, London, 1022
Critics Circle, NY, 60
Croagh, Patrick, 310
Croce, Benedetto, 154
Croft, Lord, 16
Crome, John, 297
Crompton, Vincent, 488
Cromwell, Oliver, 100, 296, 635, 642, 685, 891, 941, 1055
Cronin, Anthony, 927; "A Province Once Again," 1058

Crosby, Bing, 396, 434, 653, 685, 914, 974
Cross, Eric, *The Tailor and the Ansty,* 85, 85n, 87, 91, 107
Crowe, Eileen, 10n, 11, 501n, 721n
Croydon Park, Dublin, 442, 580
Crumlin, 207
Crusades, 100, 137, 264
Cuba, 89
Cuchullain, 186, 258, 312, 315, 668, 674, 715, 1113
Cullen, Cardinal Paul, 431
Cullen, Cepta, 123n
Cumann na nGhaedheal, 156n
Cumming, Burt, 188
Cummins, Dr. Joseph, 4-5, 17, 17n, 96-99, **96n**, 123, 190, 190n, 333, 393n, 914, 987
Curley, Dan, 341
Curran, D. L. E., 455, 455n
Curran, Sarah, 258
Curry, William, 144, 165-66
Curtin, John, 147
Curtis Brown, 220, 221
Curtis, Edmund, *A History of Ireland,* 1000
Curtiss, Thomas Quinn, 186, 187, 188, 191, 219, 355, 355n, 599, 617, 684, 740, 745, 843, 845, 877, 1042, 1077, 1087, 1090
Curzon Line, 227, 228
Curzon, Lord George N., 228
Cusack, Cyril, 935, 1047-48, **1047n**, 1078-79, 1081-82, 1085, 1087, 1088-89, 1097, 1099, 1105, 1114, 1123, 1127-30, 1130-31
Cusack, Ralph, 123n, 378
Cyrano de Bergerac, 194
Czechoslovakia, 225, 547, 609, 631, 681, 974, 976

D. 83222, *I Did Penal Servitude,* 326n
Daiken, Leslie, 64, 114, 132, 133, 143-44, **143n**, 159, 161, 177n, 214; *They Go, The Irish: A Miscellany of War-Time Writing,* 77n, 152n, 177n, 178, 214n; *Shamrocks for Mayakovsky,* 150
Daiken, Senator, 687

Legion of Mary, 98

Legouis, Emile, *History of English Literature,* 216

Lehmann, Beatrix, 142, 184, **184n,** 188-89, 192-93, 195, 219-22, 282, 288-89, 291n, 302-303, 360, 405n

Lehmann, John, 451, 451n

Lehmann, Rosamond, 783n

Leigh, Vivian, 337n, 1008

Leinster House, Dublin, 158

Lemass, Sean, 10, 10n, 218

Lenin, V., 12, 29, 62, 67, 160, 184, 245, 253, 273, 362, 442, 521, 592, 661, 690, 703, 719, 792, 796

Leningrad, 81, 184, 208, 245, 308, 540

Leningrad Medal, 164

Leno, Dan, 640

Leo X, 536

Leo XIII, 535

Lermontov, Mikhail, 245

Leros, Cos, & Thomas, 150

Leslie, Shane, 800, 815

Letterkenny, 136

Levellers, 642

Lever, Charles, 800; *Charles O'Malley,* 86, 86n, 299; *A Day's Ride,* 86, 86n

Lewenstein, Oscar, 1105, 1121-22, 1121n

Lewis, C. S., *The Screwtape Letters,* 171

Lewis, Robert, 727-28, **727n,** 728-31, 786, 798, 845, 868, 872-73, 878-79, 886-87, 895, 903, 907-908, 934-35, 953-54, 954-55, 1004-1005, 1035, 1039, 1043, 1073, 1090; "Visiting Sean O'Casey in Devon," 798n

Lewis, Sinclair, 736; *Babbit,* 928

Lewisohn, Ludwig, 413n

Libel Act, Ireland, 229

Liberties, Dublin, 314

Liberty Book Club, 1068

Liberty Hall, Dublin, 7, 8, 9, 24, 36, 64, 133, 234, 438, 442, 623, 776, 1096, 1101

Libya, 9, 62, 70, 73, 83

Lichfield, Bishop of, 185

Liddel-Hart, Basil, 529; *The Other Side of the Hill,* 679

Life, "The World of Sean O'Casey," 1022, 1069, 1075, 1076, 1079. *See also* Ginna, Robert Emmett; and Mili, Gjon

"Life, Laughter and Tears," 39n

Liffey River, 65, 98n, 234

Lilburn, John, 658

Limerick, 283

Lindsay, Sir David, 902; *The Three Estates,* 890, 890n

Lindsay, Jack, 234-35, **234n,** 615, 707-708, 720-21, 783n; *Song of a Falling World: Culture during the Breakup of the Roman Empire, A.D. 350-600,* 708

Lingard, John, 863

Linnane, Joe, 10n

Lisbon, 217

Listener, 830n

Lister, Laurier, *Airs on a Shoestring,* 1128

Lithuania, 181

Littlewood, Joan, 630-31

Liverpool, 164, 284. *See also* O'Casey, Sean, *Purple Dust*

Llewellyn, Richard, 95n; *How Green Was My Valley,* 95

Locke, Harry, 288n

Locke, John, 242, 571

Locke, Shamus, 965n

Logue, Michael Cardinal, 228, 236, 300, 313n, 431, **431n**

Loinsigh, Brighid Ni, 501n, 936

London, 20, 28, 47, 51, 70, 81, 86 99, 114, 133, 134, 164, 181, 201, 224, 229, 232, 248, 261, 289, 320, 320n, 334, 342, 356, 358, 460, 462, 462n, 465, 466, 467, 474, 476, 952, 968, 969, 980. *See also* O'Casey, Sean, *Purple Dust*

London, Jack, 800

London School of Economics, 334

Londonderry, Lady (Edith Helen Vane-Tempest-Stewart), 67n, 507, **507n,** 830

Lonergan, John, 946-47, **946n**